JAMES W. CEASER
University of Virginia

LAURENCE J. O'TOOLE
Auburn University

JOSEPH M. BESSETTE

GLEN THUROW
University of Dallas

American GOVERNMENT

ORIGINS, INSTITUTIONS, & PUBLIC POLICY

McGraw-Hill Book Company

New York   St. Louis   San Francisco   Auckland   Bogotá   Hamburg
Johannesburg   London   Madrid   Mexico   Montreal   New Delhi
Panama   Paris   São Paulo   Singapore   Sydney   Tokyo   Toronto

AMERICAN GOVERNMENT: Origins, Institutions, and Public Policy

This book was set in Times Roman by University Graphics, Inc. (ECU).
The editors were Christina Mediate, Allan Forsyth, and Susan Gamer; the designer was Robin Hessel; the production supervisor was Charles Hess. The photo editor was Flavia Rando. The drawings were done by Danmark & Michaels, Inc. R. R. Donnelley & Sons Company was printer and binder.

Cover Photograph Credits

The top flag photograph was supplied by The New-York Historical Society; the bottom flag photograph was taken by Randy Matusow.

1234567890DOCDOC8987654

ISBN 0-07-010275-9

See Acknowledgments on pages 667–670.
Copyrights included on this page by reference.

Library of Congress Cataloging in Publication Data
Main entry under title:

American government, origins, institutions, and public policy.

Includes bibliographies and indexes.
1. United States—Politics and government.   I. Ceaser, James W.
JK274.A54786   1984   320.973   83-19975
ISBN 0-07-010275-9

Contents

Preface

This textbook combines the traditional and the modern approaches to the study of American politics. The traditional approach has emphasized constitutional law, the formal characteristics of political institutions, and American political thought; the modern approach has focused on political culture, the policy making process, and political behavior. Few teachers of American politics would hold that the distinction between these two approaches is absolute, and almost none would say that students should not receive extensive exposure to both. Yet all too often materials available for classroom use reflect the research interests of writers who (quite logically) have concentrated their work in one of these areas. Our aim in writing this textbook has been to integrate these two approaches so that students can understand the interconnections between political thought and the formal structures of politics on the one hand, and the policymaking process and political behavior on the other.

The theme employed to combine these two approaches begins by looking at politics from the perspective of the constitution maker—that is, one who consciously and rationally considers transforming (or maintaining) the basic structure of the political system. We use the term "constitution" in its general sense to refer to the constituent elements that define a political order. In the United States, these obviously include the written Constitution, but also fundamental political beliefs, important laws and precedents, and the evolutionary development of institutions. The book's focus is therefore as much cultural and behavioral as it is legal. The student reader is placed in the position of a founder or would-be reformer and is called on to analyze past constitutional changes and to apply the same mode of thinking to important contemporary questions. By this technique we have sought to go beyond a passive presentation of the facts, challenging the student to ask what these facts mean for the possibility and desirability of effecting constitutional change.

Of course, political development in the United States has never been solely the product of conscious and rational efforts. Accordingly, we present other factors, including those deriving from sociological, economic, and technological causes, that have shaped and are shaping the system's evolution. Where possible, however, we view these factors from the standpoint of one having responsibility for constitutional change. For example, in treating the increasing influence of the mass media on the electoral process, we not only describe the developments that have taken place but also ask the reader to consider what changes (if any) legislators can and should adopt in response. This approach, we believe, encourages students to think in terms of political alternatives and to assess the consequences of contemplated political changes.

Learning about politics is largely a matter of expanding one's capacity to distinguish momentary influences from those that shape the character of a constitution over the long term. Throughout the text, we make use of political theory, comparative politics, and especially historical development in an effort to escape viewing yesterday's political crisis as the sole basis for political analysis. Our goal is to train readers to perform the mental act of checking day-to-day events against larger forces influencing constitutional change. Thus, although we have made every effort to include the most up-to-date materials, we have deliberately avoided faddish attempts to "peg" the book to the latest political crisis or problem.

One final point about the theme of this text is in order. Some books with a traditional emphasis have glorified the founding generation and engaged in the stale exercise of measuring the present system against the standards of the original authors of the Constitution. Our emphasis on constitution making, we believe, avoids this pitfall. We have naturally assigned an important place to the founders of the republic, both because they laid the basic foundation of our system and because the founding period presents the clearest instance of a conscious and full-blown experiment in constitution making. Nonetheless, our theme of constitution making implies that a constitution must be adapted and changed to fit the challenges of every generation. Therefore, we have viewed the development of the American system as a process and a dialog, bounded substantially by the original principles but constantly facing new issues and dealing with others that the founders left unresolved. It is precisely because the task of modifying the political order falls in some measure to every generation, including the present one, that we believe it is essential for students to learn to think about politics from a constitutional perspective.

While the theme we have adopted may seem distinctive, it lends itself readily to a standard arrangement of the material. Part One presents the overall approach of the book, analyzes the origins of the republic, and traces the broad outlines of constitutional development from 1789 to the present. Part Two deals with public opinion and with the various links between the public and the formal institutions of government. Much of the material in this section falls into the area of political behavior, but readers will quickly see how political behavior and constitutional considerations affect each other. Part Three treats the institutions of the federal government and the relationship between the federal government and the states and localities. One innovation in this section is the addition of a chapter on the separation of powers between the legislative and executive branches. We made this addition because it seemed to us that this distinctive element of American politics cannot adequately be covered in chapters focusing on each branch. Part Four looks at the policymaking process and analyzes the major substantive areas of public policy. Basic choices in the realm of policy are dealt with in terms of their constitutional significance as outlined in Part One, and each chapter in this section considers not only what policy choices have been made but also how and by whom they are made. This section complements Parts Two and Three, in that the readers can now systematically consider the effect of the allocation of power on governmental decisions.

We have organized the parts and chapters of the book in a way that seemed both logical and familiar. Each chapter, however, contains the constitutional perspective for the particular subject under consideration, and instructors will therefore encounter no major problems in rearranging the order to fit their own method of teaching the course. The text is also supported by two supplements: a study guide for students and an instructor's manual.

This text was written by four teachers who share a common approach to the teaching of American politics. James W. Ceaser, who coordinated the project, had the chief responsibility for Chapters 1, 2, 4, 5, 6, and 7; Laurence J. O'Toole, Jr., wrote Chapters 13, 14, 15, and 16; Joseph M. Bessette wrote Chapters 9, 10, and 11; and Glen Thurow wrote Chapters 3 and 17. In coordination with the authors, Chapters 8, 12, and 18 were prepared respectively by William F. Connelly, Jr., Alan Tarr, and David Clinton. A number of people lent their assistance in research, and we would like in particular to thank John Young, Alan Pino, Randall Strahan, Mark Rozell, James Pontuso, Marc Sawyer, William F. Connelly, Jr., Irv Resnick, and Kathleen DeBettencourt. Many also took the time to read and comment on all or part of the manuscript, and we would like to acknowledge their valuable assistance; these reviewers are William G. Andrews, State University of New York, Brockport; Herbert B. Asher, Ohio State University; William Avery, University of Nebraska; Lawrence Baum, Ohio State University; John Bibby, University of Wisconsin; Paul Blanchard, Eastern Kentucky University; Vincent Bonventre, University of Virginia; Jill Clark, University of Texas at Arlington; George Cole, University of Connecticut; Rita Cooley, New York University; Lawrence Dodd, Indiana University; Kenneth Dolbeare, Evergreen State University; Morton Frisch, Northern Illinois University; George Gordon, Illinois State University; Donald Gross, University of Kentucky; Marjorie Randon Hershey, Indiana University; Donald

Kettl, University of Virginia; William Kristol, University of Pennsylvania; John Manley, Stanford University; David Mayhew, Yale University; Gary McDowell, Tulane University; Michael Nelson, Vanderbilt University; David Nichols, Catholic University; Bruce Oppenheimer, University of Houston; Raymond E. Owen, University of Pittsburgh; Thomas E. Patterson, Syracuse University; David Rohde, Michigan State University; Steven Schlesinger, Catholic University; and Leo M. Snowiss, University of California at Los Angeles. The enormous task of typing the manuscript was cheerfully handled by Shirley Kingsbury, Bunny Stinnett, Jolie Delzell, Barbara Jones, Cora Pitts, and Edna Mitchell. Finally, we would like to thank the editorial staff at McGraw-Hill, who gave so freely of their time and encouragement, in particular Allan Forsyth, Susan Gamer, Alison Meersschaert, and Eric Munson.

James W. Ceaser
Laurence J. O'Toole
Joseph M. Bessette
Glen Thurow

Part One

The Fundamental Principles

Chapter 1

The Study of American Politics

CHAPTER CONTENTS

The political tradition of the United States is woven from a blend of continuity and change. Since the founding of the republic two centuries ago Americans have looked back to their origins as a source of guidance, seeking in the Declaration of Independence (1776), the Constitution (1789), and the Bill of Rights (1791) the fundamentals of their political beliefs. On the occasion of almost every inauguration, presidents speak of the principles of the founding. The great struggles for equality in American history—the antislavery movement, the women's rights movement, and the civil rights movement—have all invoked the "self-evident truths" of the Declaration. In the many crises over the legitimate powers of government and the proper role of our institutions, from the struggle over states' rights in the nineteenth century to the impeachment proceedings brought against President Nixon in 1974, Americans have consulted the Constitution and the founders' intentions.

Yet in looking back to their origins, Americans do not always find the same answers. The very documents and principles that provide continuity with the past serve as grounds for controversy in the present. American history is filled with conflicts in which the contending parties have all claimed fidelity to the same original principles. New challenges and circumstances have produced new interpretations of the meaning of the founding. When Abraham Lincoln began the Gettysburg address in 1863 by looking back "four score and seven years ago" to the Declaration, he ended by calling for a "new birth of freedom." When Franklin Roosevelt opened his state of the union address in 1944 by speaking of the principles of the Declaration and the Bill of Rights, he concluded that America needed a "second Bill of Rights" and a "new basis of security" (Mason, 1965:825).

The adaptation of original principles has been a constant feature of American politics. As one political scientist recently observed: "Other nations often see constitutions come and go every generation, . . . [but] the United States has still had only one Constitution and one system of government based on one set of political ideas" (Huntington, 1981:29). Change has taken place through the reinterpretation of these original elements. The founding generation, amidst profound disputes of its own, struck a balance among the nation's fundamental principles of liberty, equality, and self-government. Each succeeding generation has faced the responsibility of adjusting that balance anew. It is a responsibility that cannot be escaped.

Today is no exception. Beneath the daily contests for influence among our politicians and the struggle for advantage by interest groups lie fundamental choices about the scope of governmental responsibilities in society, the meaning of liberty in important areas of social policy, and the role that the United States will play in the world. As these choices are made, the character of the nation's political system will be altered, profoundly shaping the future course of American politics.

The dual aspect of continuity and change that characterizes the American political tradition suggests the need to study American politics in terms of the development of the principles of the founding as interpreted and modified by successive generations. The main purpose of this book, however, is not to provide a history of American politics, but to offer an approach that will enable one to think comprehensively about the nature of our political system. This approach requires that one directly engage the basic problems posed by our political tradition, problems that each generation of Americans has had to confront. To do so, it will be necessary to ask the same fundamental questions as the founders asked, thereby learning to think in terms of how to make—and to modify—a political order.

THINKING AS A CONSTITUTION MAKER

Imagine that you were asked to create a new form of government for the United States. Where would you begin? What issues would you raise, and what standards would you apply?

These are not easy questions, and it may therefore be just as well that none of us actually faces the full responsibility of answering them. Our form of government is something that has been given to us, the product of two centuries of accumulated thought, law, and practice. It originated with certain conscious acts of constitution making that remain largely accessible to us. When the leaders of the American Revolution declared independence from Great Britain in 1776, they presented in an official document, the Declaration of Independence, the rationale for their actions and a statement of the principles of legitimate government. Eleven years later, in the face of the failures of the nation's first government (under the Articles of Confederation), a group of leaders met during a hot summer in Philadelphia to devise a new form of government. Although the meetings of the Constitutional Convention were closed to the public, we have an extensive record of the deliberations (the *Notes,* recorded by James Madison), as well as a famous commentary on the Constitution, *The Federalist,* written during the ratification debate to explain the principles and purposes of the proposed government.

The frame of mind in which many of the founders undertook their task is also known to us. The leading proponents of the new government, including George Washington, James Madison, and Alexander Hamilton, were fully aware of the importance of the new undertaking and of the unique opportunity that confronted the nation. They consciously saw themselves as constitution makers, applying a "science" of politics to the task of preparing a new government. Could a group of political leaders, taking into account both political theory and practical interests, agree among themselves on a government and then convince a large part of the public of its wisdom and merit? As Alexander Hamilton observed at the beginning of *The Federalist,* it was for Americans "to decide the important question whether societies of men are really capable or not of establishing good government from reflection and choice, or whether they are forever destined to depend for their political constitutions on accident and force" (*Federalist* 1).*

The document finally ratified in 1788, known officially as the "Constitution of the United States of America," continues to serve as the basis of our government today and is the world's oldest written constitution still in use. But in many respects, our form of government today differs from the one created in 1787. Through amendment, interpretation, and the accretion of practice and precedent, the original system has been modified. If the framers were miraculously to return today, they would certainly recognize the outline of their handiwork but they would no doubt be surprised at the form it has assumed.

The government of the United States has changed and will continue to change. The question is not whether we become constitution makers—we must—but whether we base our decisions on "reflection or choice" or allow change to occur by "accident," without the benefit of the kind of systematic thought that went into creating the government. The need to think like constitution makers thus remains almost as important today as it was at the time of the founding. Thinking in constitutional terms does not mean ignoring daily events, but it does mean looking into them—and beyond them—to discover the enduring issues that shape our system's development.

The main issues that the founders confronted, abstracted from the immediate problems of their day, are easily identified. The founders' deliberations centered on four general questions which form the core of basic concerns faced by any constitution maker:

1 What are the ends of society as a whole?
2 What role should government play within society?
3 How are the institutions of government to be organized and power distributed?
4 How can the nation's security be guaranteed and its interests and values protected in the world?

These questions can serve not only to guide the task of constitution making but also to analyze the character of any political system or constitution. By a *constitution* (with a small *c*), we mean the basic form of government of any state. The term "constitution" is synonymous with other terms such as "political order," "political system," and "regime," but we shall use "constitution" more frequently because of its broader connotations. As defined by the *Oxford English Dictionary,* a "constitution" in its political sense is the "mode in which a state is constituted or organized, . . . the arrangement of its parts or elements, as determining its nature and character." An analysis of the four questions stated above provides us with a key for determining the character of any given constitu-

---

*As there are numerous editions of *The Federalist* which students may consult, we shall cite the number of the *Federalist* paper from which the reference is taken. *The Federalist* was written in 1787 and 1788 by James Madison, Alexander Hamilton, and John Jay.

tion. Once we have set forth the ends of society, the role of government, the organization of its political institutions and the distribution of power, and the system's basic posture toward security and foreign affairs, we have defined the essentials of any political order.

The issues raised by these questions go beyond the matters addressed in the legal document by which we are formally governed, the Constitution of the United States of America. It is essential, therefore, to keep in mind the distinction between our constitution (with a small *c*) and our Constitution (with a capital *C*). Our constitution is made up of a set of dominant beliefs, key laws, and established practices that are more than our Constitution and that may even deviate from a literal interpretation of its words. Our constitution includes the driving force of certain ideas, the interpretation of these ideas in the context of changing circumstances, the basic traditions and mores that derive from our historical experience, and the development of new institutions. While many important changes in our constitution have taken place by formal amendments to the Constitution, such as the abolition of slavery by the Thirteenth Amendment in 1865 and the outlawing of sexual discrimination in voting by the Nineteenth Amendment in 1920, other changes have resulted from extra-Constitutional developments. To cite only one notable example, the Constitution says nothing about political parties or presidential nominating methods, yet it is clear these are essential aspects of our current political system.

By emphasizing the significance of such extra-Constitutional developments we in no way meant to suggest that the Constitution is unimportant. On the contrary, those who wrote the Constitution—and those who amended it—sought to influence decisively the character of the political order. And they succeeded. Because the Constitution does in fact establish the basic outline of our governmental structure—and because Americans believe that it should—the Constitution must be taken very seriously. (By contrast, the written constitutions of some countries, such as the Soviet Union, are routinely ignored, and attempting to understand these systems by reference to formal constitutional provisions serves only to obscure how these countries are governed.) Yet however important our written

Constitution may be, it does not fully contain or define our constitution in the broader sense. No written document ever could. Thinking constitutionally, therefore, does not mean looking only at the Constitution or addressing every question in legal terms; rather, it means understanding the real and vital forces that structure the basic elements of our political system.

In this chapter, we shall look briefly at the four questions a constitution maker must ask. Many of the themes and examples discussed here will appear again later in the book and will be examined in greater depth. The object for the moment is less to master a detailed body of facts than to gain a sense of what these four questions mean and how they have been addressed in American politics.

THE ENDS OF SOCIETY

A constitution maker must first consider the ends of society—that is, the broad purposes to which society is devoted and the kind of human being it seeks to develop. Politics is so important as a human activity because the type of constitution influences what people value and how they lead their lives. This aspect of politics can best be illustrated by looking at events in Iran during the last decade. At the beginning of 1979, Iran was governed by an authoritarian ruler, the shah, whose main goals for Iranian society included the modernization of the nation's economy and the introduction of many western customs and values. The shah ruled with the aid of a repressive secret police and placed clear limits on the range of permissible political activity. But outside of the political sphere (narrowly conceived), the daily life of an Iranian urban middle-class person had come very much to resemble that of someone similarly situated in the west. People could purchase what they wanted, dress as they pleased, and entertain themselves by going to a nightclub, the movies, or the theater.

Iranian society changed abruptly in 1979 after a full-scale social and political revolution brought to power a group of Islamic fundamentalists led by a religious figure, the Ayatollah Khomeini. Khomeini's views about the ends of Iranian society differed greatly from those of the previous regime, and once in power, the new government moved quickly to rid Iran of the influence of western culture and establish its version of an Islamic way of life. Through propaganda and repression, frequently with the support of the people, the government imposed some striking new laws on Iranian society. It banned western music, closed the movie theaters, prohibited all alcoholic drinks, and required women to appear in public with long dresses covering their entire body and much of the head and face.

Because of the publicity surrounding the Iranian revolution, increased by the seizure in 1979 of hostages in the American embassy, the American public became aware of the awesome power of politics to shape a way of life. What many Americans perhaps did not realize, however, is that such efforts to use political authority to "form" a people, even against its will, are not unusual. History is filled with attempts by constitution makers to mold a particular kind of human being. In ancient Greece, for example, one of the most renowned of all founders, Lycurgus, established in Sparta a constitution designed to create the perfect soldier. Sparta carefully regulated the training of youth, established rules of marriage and sexual relations designed to help produce more perfect human specimens, and controlled all contacts with foreigners to prevent corrupting the populace. In America, during the seventeenth and eighteenth centuries, some of the New England colonial settlements were virtually theocratic republics in which the power of government was used to promote Christian virtue and ideals. In Connecticut and Massachusetts attendance at church was required, a religious orthodoxy was imposed, and premarital sexual relations were forbidden. (Nathaniel Hawthorne's classic novel *The Scarlet Letter* provides a striking picture of the rigid code of behavior that these societies imposed on their citizens.) Finally, in this century, there are many examples of communist states, such as China under Mao Tse-tung, in which efforts to create a new kind of "socialist man" have led to extraordinary political measures of enforced communal life, mass spying, terror, and intensive propaganda.

Politics has been defined by one political scientist as "who gets what, when, how" (Laswell, 1936). Much of politics does in fact involve struggles over scarce goods, as when government must decide between business groups pressing for off-shore oil drilling rights and environmental groups seeking to protect the beaches. Such policy struggles over "who gets what," while they make up the substance of most ordinary political activity, can make us forget the higher possibilities of politics as a method of determining the character and quality of society. As part of the "what" of politics, it is necessary to include the striving to mold or influence a community's way of life. It is this aspect of politics with which a constitutional perspective begins.

Modern-day Americans no doubt find this "formative" dimension of politics unacceptable and difficult even to comprehend. The reason goes back to the roots of our own tradition and to our conception of the proper ends of society. These ends are set forth in the Declaration and the Constitution and include the fundamental goals of liberty, self-government, and equality. Together, these form what some have called the "core" or "creed" of the American regime—the beliefs that have served to unite Americans, in the Declaration's words, as "one people" despite the size and diversity of the population. It is to these ends that we now turn.

Liberty and the Doctrine of Liberalism

The Declaration establishes in clear, if general, terms the legitimate end of government: to secure for the people certain "unalienable rights," which include "life, liberty, and the pursuit of happiness." By making the protection of rights a central goal of government, the Declaration formally elaborated what was then a relatively new idea, that public authority should for the most part remove itself from imposing a specific end or way of life on its citizens. According to the Declaration, the definition of moral ends should be left chiefly to the private sphere—to the influence of the family, religious institutions, the "culture" as it develops, and ultimately to each person's individual choice.

Government may, of course, limit the behavior of individuals insofar as that behavior might conflict directly with the exercise of the rights of others. (No one, for example, has a religious right to practice human sacrifice.) And government may prevent certain kinds of behavior in order to protect basic community values. (All states, for example, now ban polygamy in order to defend the family.)

But government gets out of the business of imposing orthodoxies in the moral and philosophic realms. Public authority, whatever its other obligations, is supposed to protect the setting in which the private pursuit of happiness takes place, but not define the content of happiness.

This understanding of the role of government is the core of the general doctrine of *Liberalism.* (This doctrine must be distinguished from the contemporary use of the term "liberalism," with a small *l,* which refers to the active use of government to promote economic security and provide welfare benefits.) Liberalism was originally formulated in the seventeenth and eighteenth centuries by certain political thinkers, three of the most influential of whom were John Locke (1632–1704), the baron de Montesquieu (1689–1775), and Adam Smith (1723–1790). These thinkers held that government should desist from its previously recognized responsibilities of saving souls and managing the economy, tasks which it often pursued by arbitrary and tyrannical means. Instead, modern government should ensure a sphere of free action for the individual. This is what these philosophers meant by "liberty ." The concept was best-defined by a famous nineteenth-century historian of Liberalism, Lord Acton:

> By liberty, I mean the assurance that every man shall be protected in doing what he believes his duty against the influence of authority and majorities, custom and opinion. The state is competent to assign duties and draw the line between good and evil only in its immediate sphere. Beyond the limits of things necessary for its well-being, it can only give indirect help to fight the battle of life by promoting the influences which prevail against temptation—religion, education and the distribution of wealth (Acton, 1907:3–4).

As strange as it may seem to us today, when the basic principle of Liberalism is almost universally accepted by Americans, many in the founding period questioned whether government should relinquish its role in forming individuals into virtuous citizens. Among the Antifederalists, a diverse group of opponents to the Constitution, there were some who thought that if the ultimate source of power in governing was to be the people, it would be necessary to ensure that citizens would remain virtuous and not become selfish and corrupt. Otherwise, popular government would degenerate into a destructive struggle among groups seeking their own narrow ends. In the view of this segment of the Antifederalists, Liberalism inevitably fostered a spirit of unchecked materialism. Reflecting this concern, one delegate at the Constitutional Convention in 1787 proposed giving the federal government the power to ban certain kinds of commerce that could "corrupt our manners" and undermine "republican views" (Farrand, 1911:II, 344,606). (Today, this would be equivalent to giving government the power to prohibit the purchase of sports cars, yachts, and videotape recorders on the grounds that the desire for such items might encourage a spirit of materialism and weaken the nation's moral fabric.)

Although those directly opposed to Liberalism were defeated in the contest over the Constitution, many of their concerns have survived. And even the original defenders of Liberalism, who intended to confine the sphere of government, never proposed completely ending governmental support for certain values and community standards, especially at the state and local levels. Accordingly, debates over the government's role in shaping the nation's way of life did not end in 1787, although the terms of the debate shifted dramatically and the range of permissible forms of governmental intervention were greatly reduced.

But what areas are beyond the scope of public authority? Two classic controversies illustrate the problem. With respect to pornographic books and films, most states have laws prohibiting or restricting materials deemed to be obscene. Such laws have been bitterly opposed as violations of the right of free speech. The issue here deals with the limits, if any, of free expression versus the wishes of communities to protect certain values (see Box 1-1). An even more difficult issue in recent years is the debate over abortion. The claim that women have a right to an abortion was asserted and accepted by the Supreme Court in the decision of *Roe v. Wade* (1973). Previously, abortions had been illegal in most states. Since this decision, many opponents of abortion have denied that any such right exists in the Constitution and have attempted to force a reversal of the decision or to pass a Constitutional amendment to overrule it. These examples are but

THE DEBATE OVER LAWS BANNING OBSCENITY

The continuing differences over the meaning of Liberalism are illustrated in the following arguments (the first by Judge Jerome Frank, the second by Harry Clor) about the legality and wisdom of laws that would limit materials deemed to be obscene:

> Governmental control of ideas or personal preferences is alien to a democracy. . . . The only completely democratic way to control publications which arouse mere thoughts or feelings is through nongovernmental censorship by public opinion (Judge Jerome Frank, concurring in *U.S. v. Roth,* 1956).

> The ultimate evils include influences upon the cultural and moral environment of a people and, hence, upon mind and character. . . . By means of laws against the more extreme forms of obscenity, we are reminded, and we remind ourselves, that ''We, the People'' have an ethical order and moral limits (Clor, 1971:110).

How should the government respond when a demand for individual rights clashes with community values? This question was raised at the Constitutional Convention, and it is heard today when Americans argue about such issues as abortion rights. *(Leif Skoogfors / Woodfin Camp)*

two instances of the more general problem of deciding between proclaimed individual rights and society's interest in protecting certain community values. The term "liberty" is continually subject to interpretation, though few voice dissent from the view that liberty is one of the chief goals of society.

A second aspect of the debate over the "way of life" in the United States involves conflicts not directly over rights, but over policy decisions that establish the context in which rights are exercised. Government may lend its support or provide incentives for activities or behavior that indirectly affect or define the character of the community. When such policies are of sufficient importance, they become constitutional conflicts. For example, in the early nineteenth century, the debate over tariffs raised important constitutional issues. The implications of tariffs extended far beyond economics since, by encouraging the development of manufacturing, they would stimulate the growth of cities. For those who shared Thomas Jefferson's view that farmers were "God's chosen people," the tariff was seen as a measure that would change the character of the nation and undermine the virtues required for republican government. In the words of one congressman from Virginia, a nation of city dwellers would produce a population "distorted and decrepit as respects both bodily and mental endowments" (Forsythe, 1977:73).

With government today affecting so many aspects of people's lives, it has become even more difficult for political decision makers to avoid influencing society's mores. Three recent examples illustrate the point. In 1971, President Nixon vetoed a law that provided for substantial federal aid for day-care centers on the grounds that it would "commit the vast moral authority of the national government to the side of communal approaches to child rearing." President Carter's proposal in 1980 to require women as well as men to register for military service was rejected by Congress. One columnist, George Will, opposed the measure because the "almost instinctive and universal exemption of women from combat has been inseparably involved in the organic growth of societies committed to such things as the sanctity of the family and civilian supremacy" (Will, 1980:120). Finally, in 1982, President Reagan proposed tax credits for parents sending their children to private schools. This pol-

icy was designed, among other things, to encourage religious education and thereby to provide a more favorable climate for religion itself.

As important as such policies may be, however, they represent only *indirect* means of promoting or discouraging certain values. The nation's fundamental commitment to Liberalism limits what government can do. No serious proposal in the nineteenth century was made to prevent people from moving to cities, and none today, including even the controversial proposed amendment to permit organized prayer in public schools, would enforce a particular set of religious beliefs or require a belief in the Almighty. While there have been many instances in American history in which fundamental liberties have been ignored and violated, American culture has nonetheless developed in a fundamentally Liberal society.

Because Liberalism does not allow government to establish an orthodox way of life, it seems to be essentially a neutral doctrine. While this assessment may be partly correct, those who have defended (or attacked) Liberalism have generally claimed that, when compared with other constitutions, it produces certain consequences for the character of society. As one might expect, Liberalism promotes a wide diversity in lifestyles, from libertarian "swingers" to ascetic members of religious sects whose lives are devoted to otherworldly concerns. If one travels the length of any of America's large cities, one will see many different subcultures. This diversity is usually thought to be a strong point of Liberal constitutions, allowing them to produce many individuals devoted to the pursuit of excellence in the arts, philosophy, and pure science. Defenders of Liberalism are also confident that a free society will be a decent one. While government does not directly inculcate religious beliefs or dictate a particular kind of virtue, it protects freedom in the private sphere, and by so doing it indirectly encourages free inquiry and supports religion, leading to a respectable quality of life and to a society that is dynamic, innovative, and resourceful.

Yet if liberty produces diversity, it may also promote, at least in one respect, a certain kind of uniformity. By allowing people to pursue their own individual ends without restrictions, liberty has been said to encourage a large degree of self-interested-ness," expressed most frequently in materialistic terms. A heavy emphasis on commercialism and physical gratification is thus in some measure the natural result of a Liberal society. These tendencies were noted in the nineteenth century by a Frenchman, Alexis de Tocqueville, whose classic work *Democracy in America* is still widely considered one of the best books ever written on American politics and society. Tocqueville identified the "taste for well-being" as the "most striking and unalterable characteristic of democratic ages" (Tocqueville, 1968:448). Unchecked, this feature could encourage people to think only of their private, material well-being, with the consequences of a decline in the level of culture and a growing apathy on the part of the citizens toward political affairs. In fact, many recent commentators on American society have expressed a deep concern over an emerging crisis in American values. These critiques, coming from both the left and the right, have warned of the possibility of a moral and spiritual vacuum amidst an ever-growing abundance of material goods. Such criticisms have spilled over into political movements, such as the new left in the 1960s and the Moral Majority in the 1980s, that have sought in different ways to regenerate American culture.

The presence of self-interest that characterizes a society based on liberty is not necessarily detrimental. When people pursue their self-interest, they generate an immense amount of energy, which in the case of the economy has contributed to an impressive record of dynamism and growth. The founders of our nation were aware of the inevitable connection between liberty and self-interest and therefore sought to build a society and government that did not rely exclusively, in James Madison's words, on "moral and religious motives," but which sought to balance "rival interests" and allow "ambition . . . to counteract ambition" (*Federalist* 10 and 51). The doctrine of Liberalism was based on a realistic understanding of human nature that took into account people's passions and did not assume, in utopian fashion, that "men were angels" (*Federalist* 51). Yet at the same time, the founders were aware that a republican form of government depends in some measure on the existence of certain moral attributes within the populace. The acceptance of Liberalism was not, accordingly, meant to end all political and cultural debate about the "way of life" in society, and current controversies on this question represent an ongoing dialog within American politics.

Self-Government

The second fundamental end of American society is self-government. Legitimate government, according to the Declaration, must derive its power "from the consent of the governed." No power external to society, such as a monarch asserting "divine right" or an ordained class of clerics asserting a religious mission, has a claim to rule independent of the will of the governed. It is conceivable, of course, that the governed might choose a monarchy or aristocracy as the best form of government, but the doctrine of the "consent of the governed" in the United States led quite naturally to the representative democracy established by the Constitution. The spirit of the American people after the Revolutionary War was essentially a democratic one, with the clear qualification that certain groups— slaves, women, and indentured servants—did not count as part of the consenting citizenry.

Interestingly, Americans use the same word— "freedom"—to refer both to liberty and to self-government. A "free" people is one that possesses rights *and* one that governs itself. The fact that these two basic values are somewhat confusingly given the same name is indicative of their central place in the constellation of American political thought. The two values tend to reinforce each other because a government based on popular consent eliminates the most frequent source of despotic government—government by the few.

Liberty and self-government can, however, conflict, for majorities can sometimes suppress the rights of minorities. Before the Civil War, for example, proponents of slavery supported the establishment of territorial governments ruled by "popular sovereignty," which in some cases would have permitted the establishment of slavery where the majority of (white) people wanted it. In the late nineteenth century, many states adopted provisions limiting the participation of blacks and requiring segregation of the races in public facilities. Tensions between liberty and self-government have been evident in many other areas as well.

Self-government in the United States has usually been understood in a much broader sense than rule by national majorities. It also includes the idea of citizen participation in political decision making, especially at lower levels of government (McWilliams, 1979). In the United States, political authority is divided among different governments: the federal—that is, the national—government; the fifty states; and the thousands of counties, townships, and cities. This division of authority is supported by the constitutional doctrine of *federalism,* in which the role of the national government is supposedly limited to certain specific ends, while the balance of political power remains with the states. Today political power is more centralized than at the time of the founding. Nevertheless, it remains the case that the exercise of power claimed by the national government, even when it is subject to the influence of national majorities, has often been resisted in the name of giving citizens more control at the lower levels of government.

Many citizens do not take advantage of the opportunity to participate in local government, and in many large urban areas "local" governments can seem far away from home. Still, many more citizens can hold office and have access to officeholders as a result of the dispersion of political power to lower levels of government. It is estimated today that there are over half a million elected officials in the United States, only 536 of whom hold elective office at the national level (Smolka, 1973). Serving on a local school board, a town council, or a jury provides the chance for citizens not just to express an opinion through their vote but to make decisions that affect the character of their communities.

Equality

The third and most ambiguous of America's fundamental ends is equality. According to the Declaration of Independence, "all men are created equal." In the eighteenth century, political equality had the limited, though still revolutionary, meaning of a society without legal titles of nobility. Individuals were entitled to equal treatment before the civil and criminal laws and an equal right to liberty. Equality in this sense not only had profound consequences for legal and political arrangements but also influenced customs in everyday life.

The belief that no individual is intrinsically of a different order or kind, and hence that all individuals have a right to respect and equal treatment, creates a "spirit" of equality that filters into the manners and daily encounters of citizens (Lipset, 1963).

European observers of the United States have always been struck by the absence of patterns of deference in American society when compared with customs in Europe. Many Americans, for example, are in jobs where they must serve others, but they do not think of themselves—nor are they generally treated by others—as being of a "servant class" that must defer to a class of superiors.

Werner Sombart, a German sociologist, remarked on this difference during a visit to the United States at the beginning of this century.

> The whole of public life has a more democratic style. The worker is not being reminded at every step that he belongs to a "lower" class. . . . The bowing and scraping before the "upper classes," which produces such an unpleasant impression in Europe, is completely unknown (Sombart, 1976:110).

Yet equality, even in this limited respect, was not originally accorded to all Americans. Slavery directly violated this principle until the Civil War, and for long afterwards legal discrimination against blacks existed; social prejudice still persists. Other groups, including Asians and Indians, were denied equality for much of American history. Finally, women in the United States, though never excluded from the political community in the same way, lacked a legal guarantee of the right to vote until 1919 and have faced discriminatory legislation and social practices. Equality, therefore, has often been more of a standard than a reality, something for which various groups have had to struggle and for which they are still struggling today.

Political Equality The founders' conception of equality stressed the idea of equality in liberty, a condition that gave citizens the basic right to own property, to have access to the courts, and to enjoy the protection of their liberties. The founders' idea of equality did not, however, directly include a universal right to vote. Although suffrage in America was from the beginning fairly widespread among the white male population, there were limitations in most states based on property ownership or on some other method of demonstrating a stake in the community.

In the early nineteenth century, however, the idea of equality assumed a greater significance in the political realm. By the 1830s most states extended the suffrage to almost all free white males. The notion increasingly gained ground that in order for individuals to protect their liberties and defend their interests, they needed the right to vote. Citizenship in this sense was an outgrowth of the assertion of equality.

The subsequent expansion of the suffrage to almost all citizens has been a long and complex process. It has been accomplished by Constitutional amendments banning states from discriminating on the basis of race (1870), sex (1920), or payment of taxes (1964), by numerous Supreme Court decisions, and by state and especially federal legislation. Although there is no one provision in the Constitution that directly grants a right to vote to all citizens—this matter being technically in the province of the states—the many Constitutional limitations on the states, together with federal court decisions and legislation, have all but established a national right to vote for all adults.

Economic Equality Questions relating to economic equality and security have never yielded the same clear answers as those relating to political rights. Nothing was said in the Declaration about ensuring economic equality, and unlike the revolutions in the Soviet Union in 1917 or China in the 1940s, the American Revolution had little to do with the issue of distribution of wealth. The concept of equality before the law, however, had definite implications for economic affairs. By creating a society free of legal privileges and titles of nobility, the founders expected to promote economic mobility and establish, relative to the economic systems in Europe, a much greater degree of material equality among the various classes in society.

A concern for reducing economic inequalities—or at least for not permitting them to grow—has, however, become a constitutional objective for many Americans. Debates over unjust economic privileges were common in the nineteenth century, but the issue of economic security began to receive sustained attention only at the turn of this century in the aftermath of large-scale industrialization.

Attention centered not only on the great gaps in wealth between the owners of business and the workers, but on the implications of these differences for social and political equality. By the time of the great depression, President Franklin Roosevelt asserted that "political rights have proved inadequate to assure us equality in the pursuit of happiness." While Roosevelt never proposed anything like an equal distribution of wealth, he did work to establish the claim that "true, individual freedom cannot exist without economic security and independence." In Roosevelt's statement lies the origin of the modern welfare state—the understanding that government has certain obligations to provide citizens with minimal levels of welfare and economic security. Some have extended this concept of collective welfare to include a concern over the distribution of wealth. Thus whenever tax laws or social policies are discussed, many argue that their effect should be to narrow the existing economic differences between segments of the population. In this sense, economic equality has become a constitutional concern.

In European democracies with strong socialist traditions, such as Sweden and Norway, large parts of the population favor active government policies to promote a substantial degree of economic equality. According to this view, which is shared by only a relatively small number of Americans, the wealth of society is thought of as being owned in the first instance by the community as a whole, not by the individuals who make it up. The distribution of wealth should be determined by a political decision designed to maximize the degree of economic equality consistent with an agreed-upon rate of growth (Rawls, 1971; Okun, 1975). Opponents of this view argue that any such attempt to socialize wealth would dangerously extend the power of government and conflict with liberties in the economic sphere.

Enforcing Equality Apart from certain measures associated with the establishment of the welfare state, efforts to secure equality until the 1960s consisted largely of attempts to prevent government itself from engaging in or supporting discriminatory policies, and to make government, within the normal sphere of its authority, enforce the laws equally. These efforts were required because many

The modern welfare state grew out of Franklin Roosevelt's efforts to relieve the widespread poverty brought on by the great depression. This Civilian Conservation Corps reforestation project was one of many federally funded job programs launched in the 1930s. *(Bettmann Archive)*

government policies before the 1960s, especially at the state and local levels, directly supported racial and sexual discrimination. Beginning in the 1960s, not only was there a more concerted effort to remove all such government-supported barriers, but many began to call for a new approach to achieve equality (Beer, 1978). This new approach asked government to penetrate into previously private areas of society in an effort to change conditions which created inequalities. Under the policies generated by this approach, the federal government established many important new aid programs for the poor and became involved in entirely new programs, such as regulating university admission policies and business employment practices, in an effort to promote equality of treatment. Affirmative action programs were established for persons from certain groups—blacks, women, Indians, and hispanics—that had been subject to past government discrimination. These new policies, which many contend conflict with certain liberties and create a meddling bureaucracy, have produced major polit-

ical controversies over such issues as school busing to achieve racial balance and "targets" or quota requirements for employment in businesses and universities.

Whereas the founders saw little or no tension between the principles of equality and liberty, today these principles are often seen to be in conflict. As government assumes greater responsibilities for reducing social (or material) inequalities, public authority inevitably impinges on and limits liberties. The clash of these two principles remains one of the central constitutional questions of this decade.

THE ROLE OF GOVERNMENT IN SOCIETY

The second question any constitution maker must ask is what role government should play in society. In some nations, government extends into almost every important sphere, whether it be the economy, the arts, or the dissemination of information. In the Soviet Union, for example, the state owns all the major industries and controls the labor unions, it determines what is taught in the schools (there are no private schools), and it runs television, radio, and major newspapers. The aim of such systems is the total control of society by the state—hence the term "totalitarian" government. (An *authoritarian* government, distinguished by some analysts from a totalitarian government, limits by repressive measures many forms of political dissent, but stops short of attempting to remake the entire culture or way of life.)

The theory of Liberalism discussed earlier has important consequences for the scope of government. It suggests a limited government—although precisely how limited, as we shall soon see, is now greatly disputed. Under the dominant interpretation of Liberalism, government is viewed as only one part of a society that includes other semiautonomous parts or systems. The cultivation of the arts, the dissemination of information, and the direction of business (at least in some Liberal governments) are left primarily in private hands or are aided but not fully controlled by the state. A crucial distinction thus exists in such systems between "government" and "society." The reasons commonly advanced for limiting government are twofold: first, the ends of society—principally liberty, the fruits of diversity, and the economic growth that diversity encourages—are better-served if government does *not* control most activity within society; and, second, government itself, if it should grow too large, would threaten people's liberties by managing every detail of their lives and by overwhelming the capacity of any element of society to offer resistance.

Just how limited government should be, however, has been a question that Americans have debated from the very beginning. Discussing this problem is made more difficult because of the aforementioned doctrine of federalism, under which the power of the national government is theoretically limited to certain broad objectives, such as national defense and the conduct of foreign policy, while the remainder of governmental power is left to the states. Before the twentieth century, most government services that directly touched the lives of the people on a daily basis—education, police protection, road building, and the like—were supplied by state and local governments.

Proponents of limited government have always recognized the need for government to operate in certain spheres, such as coining money, providing for national defense, protecting public order, and performing other tasks that promote the general welfare. Limited government does not necessarily imply weak government. Identifying the functions that properly fall within government's jurisdiction, however, and especially within the jurisdiction of the federal government, has long been a matter of controversy. Before the Civil War, the major political parties divided over how much authority the Constitution granted to the federal government. The Democratic party contended that the power of the federal government should be limited to the major functions explicitly enumerated in the Constitution; the Whig party asserted that the federal government had certain implied powers that permitted it to assist economic development. With large-scale industrialization at the end of the nineteenth century came the recognition that a strictly limited role for the federal government, along the lines once advocated, was no longer possible or desirable. New tasks and responsibilities have since been added to the federal government in areas such as insurance for unemployment, social security, medical care and research, welfare, and education. The list, in fact, can go on and on (see Box 1-2).

One of the most important changes in our constitution over the past half century has been the tremendous growth in government at all levels—national, state, and local. The federal government in particular now operates under few of the restrictions that once limited its role in comparison with that of state and local governments. It does more things by itself (like owning and operating Amtrak); more in combination with state and local governments (such as providing funds for public education); more to aid other institutions (major private universities may receive up to 40 percent of their funds directly or indirectly from the government); and more to regulate and control what goes on in the economic sphere (auto companies must produce a fleet of cars that average a certain number of miles per gallon of gasoline). The growth of government since the depression can be expressed roughly by the amounts it spends. In 1880, federal expenditures represented about 2.6 percent of the gross national product. (The gross national prod-

---

BOX 1-2

THE EXPANSION OF THE ROLE OF THE FEDERAL GOVERNMENT

Today, you can hardly turn around without bumping into some federal restraint or requirement. It wasn't always so; there was a time you could embark on almost any venture without encountering a single federal constraint. Now, however, if you should take it into your head, say, to manufacture and market a new product, you would probably run into statutes and administrative regulations on labor relations, occupational safety, product safety, and air purity. Your advertising would probably fall within the jurisdiction of the Federal Trade Commission. The Department of Justice would be interested in your relations with your competitors. Should you want to raise capital by the sale of stock or bonds, you would fall under the Securities and Exchange Commission.

You would need export licenses from the Department of Commerce to sell your product in some areas of the world. Federal prohibitions against race, age, and sex discrimination in hiring and promotion would apply to you. If you were to extend credit to your customers, you might fall under truth-in-lending laws. You would have to file sundry reports for tax, social security, pension, and census purposes. In some fields— communication, transportation, energy, insurance, and banking, for instance—restrictions and oversight are especially stringent. But firms of all kinds, large and small, are subject to diverse federal requirements. You can't just start and run a business without reference to federal specifications and officials.

Source: Kaufman, 1977:5–6.

---

uct—abbreviated GNP—represents the total value of goods and services produced by a nation during a given year.) In 1980, federal expenditures accounted for 23 percent of the GNP. Add to this the amount spent by state and local government, and one finds that government now accounts for nearly 40 percent of the GNP.

While government in the United States still is limited in many respects—it does not, for example, own the major business firms or control the major television networks—it is not nearly so restricted as it once was. Except in the areas of regulating individual expression (speech, publication, and association), where government control has in some respects diminished, the trend, at least until the early 1980s, has been one of government expansion. Entire spheres of activity that were once private have come under government regulation or have become dependent on government funds. Few areas, it seems, lie entirely beyond the reach of government, although many people continue to raise constitutional objections to new government initiatives. If, for instance, a political party advocated that the federal government should, as a matter of normal policy, buy and operate the nation's major business corporations, the proposal would surely provoke a

major constitutional debate. Indications of such resistance were clear from the federal government's decision in 1980 to provide government loan guarantees to the Chrysler Corporation, then on the verge of bankruptcy. This decision was made only after long and intense debate in which, despite the immediate action taken, most members of Congress upheld the principle of private ownership. The "Chrysler bailout," as it was sometimes called, shows both how far government has grown (the loan was made, and its legality under the Constitution was not challenged) and how much resistance still remains to large new extensions of public authority.

**The Concept of Power
under a Limited Government**

The fact that government in the United States is still limited—though less so than in the past—has led many to ask where power is lodged in the political system. The word "power," which is so often used in political discussion, is not as precise a term as one might think. Usually, it is employed to refer to control that *government* exercises and to the ability that groups or individuals have to influence what government does. But there is a broader definition of power that allows one to consider the role of government itself as a source of control in society. Under this broader definition, "power" is the capacity to affect the lives of others and control their access to resources. Using this definition, it is clear that in a system of limited government, a great deal of power in society is left to private entities. In education, for example, many admission decisions to professional schools are made by private universities according to their own criteria; these universities thereby exercise an important kind of power over access to careers such as law and medicine. In economics, the effects of private decision making can be even more dramatic. When, for example, a large corporation decides to close a plant in a small town, causing unemployment and social disruption, it has obviously exercised a great deal of power in that community. Most decisions in the economic sphere, in fact, lie with private entities.

For defenders of limited government, the exercise of power in social and economic spheres is generally better left in private hands. They argue that although particular decisions may be unjust, it is far more important to avoid a concentration of power in the state. If ever most of the power in society were transferred to government, they reason, not only would government become too powerful, but all controversies in society would become political conflicts, burdening political institutions with more responsibility than they could effectively handle.

Critics of limited government attack the existence of "private" power in important spheres of society, especially in the economic system. They contend that the line separating public from private control has been unjustly drawn to exclude whole systems of power and authority. The power relations within these private systems favor the interests of the wealthy and privileged. Thus, say these critics, even if *political* power is subject to popular control, our constitution as a whole is highly undemocratic because so little power in society is political and because so much power rests with private decision makers (Dahl, 1979). The authority of government in this view needs to be extended into new areas to bring about a genuine democratization of society.

Perspectives on the Role of Modern Government

Government has grown in the United States for a number of different reasons. First, conditions in society have become increasingly more complex and interrelated, requiring more government activity today to accomplish objectives that were more easily managed in the past. National defense is a prime example. In 1789, defense required little more than the arming, training, and supplying of soldiers; today, it depends on sophisticated technology and continuing research in areas such as microbiology and physics. Similarly, in the area of business regulation, most of the economic goods were once produced by small, privately owned firms, having a limited social impact. Today, huge corporations employing thousands of individuals account for much of the national economic output. To control these corporations and retain power for the individual, whether as a worker, a consumer, or a neighbor, requires extensive government intervention. Second, people want and expect more from government than they once did. With the emergence of the welfare state, citizens look to government to provide security for medical treatment and retirement and to supply an increasing number of services, ranging from job training to research on the most effective way to breed and raise hogs. Finally, for some citizens, as suggested, the doctrine of limited government has come into question. They maintain that private enclaves of power have resulted in an unjust distribution of resources. These enclaves should be brought under public authority, where the people can control the power for the public good. As broader demands for equality are pressed upon government, its scope must necessarily increase.

The dispute over the size of government, which has been a key issue in American politics since the New Deal of the 1930s, serves to define the two major public philosophies or "ideologies" of modern American politics: *liberalism* and *conservatism*. Proponents of both of these public philosophies claim to be the true heirs of Liberalism, but each interprets the requirements of Liberalism for modern times in a different way. Generally speaking, modern-day liberals, who have worked mostly within the Democratic party, have favored an expansion of the role of the federal government, con-

---

BOX 1-3

MODERN LIBERALISM AND CONSERVATISM

The Republican party's conservative view of the role of government is set forth in the following passage from the 1980 Republican platform:

> For too many years, the political debate in America has been conducted in terms set by the Democrats. They believe that every time new problems arise beyond the power of men and women as individuals to solve, it becomes the duty of government to solve them, as if there were never any alternative. Republicans disagree and have always taken the side of the individual, whose freedoms are threatened by the big government that Democratic idea has spawned. Our case for the individual is stronger than ever. A defense of the individual against government was never more needed. And we will continue to mount it.

On the other hand, Samuel Beer describes the New Deal liberalism of Franklin Roosevelt and the Democratic party in the 1930s, which continues to represent the core ideas of many liberals today:

> Roosevelt called not only for a centralization of government, but also for a nationalization of politics. . . . He exhorted voters and citizens to turn to Washington as the center of power on which to exert their pressures and project their expectations. . . . A principle and reiterated theme . . . of his administration was to assure the people that the federal government could solve their problems (Beer, 1978:8).

---

tending that more government is needed to protect the individual, provide security, promote a greater degree of equality, and, more recently, regenerate economic growth. Modern liberals argue that this reliance on positive government, while perhaps conflicting with the *form* of earlier Liberalism, best realizes its *substance* (Beer, 1978).

Conservatives, who have been more closely associated with the Republican party, have generally opposed the rapid growth of government and in recent years have begun to argue for a reduction in the size of the federal government. While conservatives are not always clear about just how much they would like to reduce government (just as liberals are not clear about just how far they would like to extend it), they are convinced that government has now grown to such proportions that it threatens not only the economic well-being of the nation but basic liberties as well. Conservatives stress their links with classical Liberal ideals by claiming that they are seeking to maintain the goals of Liberalism through the same means employed in the past. Conservatives believe that the liberty of individuals today is endangered by a large government that increasingly seeks to regulate and direct the lives of the people.

The debate over the size of government emerged

as the central constitutional issue of the early 1980s. The Republican party, under the leadership of an avowed conservative, Ronald Reagan, took steps to reduce—or at least slow—the rate of growth of the federal government in the areas of social welfare and business regulation. Leaders of the Democratic party fought many of these measures, arguing that they undermined the protection of security for many citizens and increased the gap between the rich and the poor. Disputes over the responsibilities of the federal government represent another instance in which the great constitutional questions of earlier generations of Americans confront us in a slightly different form today.

THE ORGANIZATION OF INSTITUTIONS AND THE DISTRIBUTION OF POLITICAL POWER

The third question a constitution maker must ask is how political power will be distributed within the government. The task in this instance is to determine who (or what) will hold the reins of power and make authoritative decisions. Traditionally, this problem was approached by asking *who* should govern: a single person (in which case the constitution would be a monarchy or, in the absence of law, a tyranny); the most able (an aristocracy) or wealthy (an oligarchy); the citizens as a whole (a democracy); or a mixture of these regimes, exclusive of a tyranny (a "mixed" constitution). People today do not always use these same terms, but it is still common to distinguish between constitutions by discussing who rules. Thus in the case of the United States, some claim that it is a wealthy elite that rules, while others insist that the government is controlled by the people.

Although one must ultimately come to grips with the question of who governs, the attempt to answer this question cannot fully describe the way in which power is distributed in a complex governmental structure like that of the United States. Power in the United States is held not simply by a specific group or social class, but by laws and institutions. In other words, along with inquiring into *who* governs, one must ask *what* governs. The need to examine our constitution in these terms results from the founders' decision to make government complex and to institute such mechanisms as the written Constitution, government by representatives, and separation of powers.

A Written Constitution

Under a system based on a written constitution, power is given to government in the form of a trust or agreement. This arrangement immediately establishes two sources of authority: the "fundamental law," which sets the terms of the agreement under which government exercises its powers, and the government, which acts at its own discretion pursuant to the fundamental law. In the United States, the fundamental law is the Constitution. Ratified in 1787, it has since been amended twenty-six times under a process spelled out in Article V. The Constitution specifically denies certain powers to government (for example, government may not grant titles of nobility) and grants other powers (for example, government may coin money and regulate interstate commerce). Although some of the powers granted to the government are very broad and subject to diverse interpretations, the Constitution nevertheless serves to define the powers of government and limit its actions. In a real sense, therefore, one may say that the Constitution rules on many of the most important matters in the United States.

Insofar as the Constitution governs, the question of deciding who governs becomes one of determining how the Constitution was originally ratified and how it may be amended. In both instances, the methods differ from the usual processes of governing. The Constitution was ratified in the period from 1787 to 1789 by special conventions in the states, which were quite democratic bodies *by the standards of the time.* (Slaves and women, of course, did not vote on the delegates attending these conventions, and there were other restrictions on the suffrage.) Amendments, which may theoretically be passed in one of four different ways, have with one exception been adopted by the method of securing a two-thirds majority of both houses of Congress and then approval by the legislatures of three-fourths of the states. In both the original act of ratification and in the amending process, neither the president nor members of the judicial branch played or play any official part, only special representatives of the people or legislators are empowered to act.

The founders made the claim that the ratification and amending processes represent a more direct embodiment of the "consent of the governed" than the usual process of governing. The people, in Alexander Hamilton's words, are the "master," and the government is the "servant" (*Federalist* 78). The Constitution in this view is not only the fundamental law but a law that more directly embodies the solemn will of the public. Of course, this claim can be debated at length, as it requires one to accept the authority of an act of the American people in 1787 and of an amending process that requires an extraordinary majority. But whatever one's views on this question, it is essential to understand that the doctrine of Constitutionalism creates two separate processes of governing. In effect, the public, insofar as it participates in these processes, wears two hats. When acting as a Constitutional agent in the amending process, the public helps determine the powers and limits of the government. When acting in a more ordinary way in the governing process, the public elects the officials of government who in theory can do nothing that conflicts with the higher law of the Constitution.

In practice, of course, this simple distinction breaks down somewhat. The "servants"—that is, the governing officials—may act according to their own views, interpreting the meaning of the Constitution to fit their actions. But the Constitution, though sometimes bent and stretched, does nevertheless serve to limit what the president and Congress may do. Time and again, presidents set aside actions they might want to take and members of Congress avoid passing laws they might prefer because of a perceived conflict with the Constitution. Moreover, the doctrine of Constitutionalism, with its sharp theoretical division between the people as grantor of authority and the government as the servant of that authority, explains the mystery of the extraordinary power of the judiciary in American politics. The Supreme Court, although itself one of the institutions of government, has come to be recognized as the final interpreter of the meaning of the Constitution. If Americans did not believe in the principle of limited government under a written constitution, it is difficult to see how the people would willingly submit to so great a concentration of power in the hands of nine unelected officials.

Representative Government and Separation of Powers

The American political system is a *representative government,* meaning a government exercised by elected or appointed officials in designated offices. The principal institutions of the government, whose basic powers are outlined in the Constitution, are the Congress, the presidency, and the judiciary. It is the officials of these offices who hold the immediate power of the federal government. Recognizing the significance of this obvious and simple fact is crucial to understanding why it is necessary in the United States to speak not only of *who* governs but of *what* governs.

If the government of the United States were a pure democracy, its decisions would not be made by representatives, but by the people voting directly on laws and policies—by means, perhaps, of votes taken in referendum or (in the future) by the use of computer consoles in the home. By the same token, if our government were an oligarchy, political decisions would be made directly by business leaders and the rich—perhaps by the heads of *Fortune* magazine's list of the largest 500 corporations plus members of the most wealthy families in the United States.

The plain fact of the matter, however, is that the power to govern is given in the first instance to Constitutionally defined institutions. These institutions, while they reflect the preferences of various elements of society, possess a certain amount of autonomy and discretion of their own. They were formed not to serve the interests of a class of nobles or an elite, but rather those of the people. To this end they were constituted to promote certain beneficial qualities in governing. The presidency, for example, was designed to provide energy and statesmanship, the judiciary to protect the rule of law, and the legislature to represent and deliberate. The institutions and their operation must therefore be considered in part on their own terms without regarding them simply as substitutes for outside forces. Government, in other words, is in some measure an independent force in society.

Precisely because the institutions govern, much of the debate about political power in American politics revolves around *how* power should be distributed among and within the three branches of government. To be sure, such debates often reflect claims of *who* should govern. Thus, in the 1930s, when the Supreme Court declared unconstitutional much of President Roosevelt's New Deal program, many attacked the Court as an oligarchic institution and sought to undermine its power in order to make the government more responsive to the wishes of the majority. Yet even in this controversy, the question of who benefited was not the sole issue in dispute. Many rallied to the defense of the Court, including some who opposed its decisions, on the grounds that a strong and independent judiciary was essential to the preservation of the Constitution. In the early 1970s, the great debate over powers of the presidency had even less to do with competing claims of power among different classes of society. Many at that time charged that the Constitution was being threatened by the emergence of an "imperial" presidency. These charges had little to do with how responsible the president was to the will of the majority, but centered instead on the argument that the presidency had assumed powers that belonged to other institutions. (This view, along with President Nixon's actions in connection with the break-in at the Watergate Hotel, led ultimately to the congressional proceedings to impeach the president which forced his resignation in 1974.)

Because he knew that the tyranny of a majority could be as dangerous to liberty as the tyranny of a king, James Madison built the separation of powers into the Constitution. *(Gilbert Stuart / Bowdoin College Museum of Art)*

The government of the United States is based on the premise that power should be separated and divided among different institutions in order to guard against the possibility that government itself might become tyrannical. This premise, the doctrine of *separation of powers,* was built into the fabric of the Constitution. James Madison, the chief architect of the Constitution, justified this doctrine not on the grounds of who governs, but on how power should be distributed: "The accumulation of all powers, legislative, executive and judiciary, in the same hands, whether of one, a few, or many, and whether hereditary, self-appointed, or elective, may justly be pronounced the very definition of tyranny" (*Federalist* 47). Many famous critics of the founders, from Woodrow Wilson to President Carter's counsel, Lloyd Cutler, have attacked the Constitution on the grounds that the separation of powers leaves the government weak, divided, and therefore incapable of engaging in sustained and systematic policy innovation (Cutler, 1980). Whether justified or not, it is revealing that

this criticism is again based less on *who* governs than on *how* power is allotted. It is, in fact, a general characteristic of debates over power in the United States that they have been partly transformed from arguments over the allocation of sovereignty among different elements of society into controversies over the respective role of the different institutions. This debate continues today.

Who Governs?

In the final analysis, however, every constitution can be characterized in part according to who governs or, in the case of a representative government, according to who exercises the major influence on the governing institutions. The institutions of the United States government, though having in some measure a will of their own, are not and were never intended to be disembodied entities that function in isolation from society. Officials operate under certain expectations about whose interests and wishes they are supposed to take into account, they are chosen by certain prescribed rules, and they are continually influenced by a variety of forces and pressures that impinge on them, such as the activity of lobbyists and the scrutiny of the press. A constitution maker must make a rough calculation about how these factors determine in the end "who governs"—that is, which groups or segments of society have the greatest influence on the operation of these institutions. Among the many issues that bear on this question—and we mention here but a few—are who may vote, how candidates are nominated for office, how campaigns are funded, who has access or standing to sue before the courts, and who is in a position to obtain access to a legislator or member of the executive branch.

Examining these factors and how they influence who rules will be an important part of this text. But the search for precise answers should not obscure the widely accepted—and, we believe, essentially correct—view that our government is in the final analysis a popular one—a government in which the public at large has the decisive influence on our governing institutions. Often one hears this form of government referred to as a "democracy," although a *pure* democracy, as we have indicated, is a system in which the people rule directly without the intermediary of representative institutions. Given this fact, it would be more correct to characterize the United States government as a type of popular government known by the founders as a "republic" and more commonly today as a "representative democracy."

If this assertion is true and if our government is in some general sense popular or republican, does it then follow that our government is now—or was intended to be—as responsive as possible to the majority? The answer, quite clearly, is no. Forms of government differ not only in kind, such as the difference between a tyranny and a representative democracy, but also, within each type, by degree. Representative democracies can vary in the extent to which they are responsive to the will of the majority, and such differences are very significant.

As originally constituted, our government contained many qualifications on popular influence, besides the obvious fact that certain groups were excluded altogether from participation. The Constitution provided for indirect election of the president and the Senate, a nonelective judiciary, and long terms (six years) for those chosen for the Senate. These qualifications were justified by the founders on the grounds that they would improve the quality of governmental decisions and lessen the danger that a majority itself, under certain circumstances, might threaten the rights of a minority.

The subsequent history of American politics includes numerous constitutional debates and struggles over the degree of popular influence. Most important of all has been the long story of the extension of the suffrage from a significant portion of the free white male population in 1787 to virtually the entire adult population—a transformation that was not substantially completed in the case of black Americans until the decade of the 1960s. As regards the institutions, there has been an ongoing conflict between a democratic or reform tendency that has sought greater influence for popular desires and a representative tendency that has sought to maintain more distance and discretion for governing officials. Generally speaking, more popular influence has been engrafted onto the constitution, whether by formal amendments or by changes in laws and practices. For all intents and purposes, the selection of the president since the 1830s has been by the vote of the public; political parties developed early in the century to facilitate popular rule; and senators have been selected by direct vote since 1913. On the other hand, new qualifications on democratic rule have evolved, some perhaps inadvertently. Large bureaucracies and independent regulatory commissions now exercise considerable decision-making authority, removing certain issues, such as the control of the supply of money, from the sphere of direct popular influence. And over the past twenty years, the judicial system has greatly broadened the range of issues subject to its control, often assuming authority that once was exercised by state legislatures.

The constitutional question of the degree of popular influence of government remains very much a matter of dispute today. Throughout the 1970s, a powerful reform movement, the avowed intent of which was to increase popular control of the governing process, succeeded in making many institutional changes in Congress and in the nominating process for presidential candidates. A motto that reformers sometimes endorsed was "The cure for the ills of democracy is more democracy." But in the decade of the 1980s, many have begun to reexamine the changes of the last decade and have openly questioned whether there has been too much infatuation with the idea of popular rule and too little attention paid to the importance of certain restraints. This debate remains a major issue in contemporary American politics.

Four Models of Political Analysis

Up to this point, we have discussed the question of who governs, without using any technical vocabulary. Yet because of the significance of this question to the study of American politics, political analysts have developed four alternative models that seek to specify the different possible elements in society that exercise influence on our government. These models are elitism, bureaucratic rule, pluralism, and majoritarianism. The first two, at least in their extreme forms, conflict with our contention that the government of the United States is a representative democracy. Yet even if they are inaccurate descriptions of our political system—as we believe they are—they can nevertheless provide helpful insights into how politics works. A government that is in the main a representative democracy may nonetheless be influenced in certain respects by nondemocratic elements.

BOX 1-4

FOUR MODELS OF THE DOMINANT INFLUENCE OF WHO GOVERNS

I   An elitist interpretation of the American political system

. . . Our government represents the privileged few rather than the needy many. . . . Elections, political parties and the right to speak out are seldom effective measures against the influences of corporate wealth (Parenti, 1980:2).

II   A bureaucratic interpretation of the American political system

David Brinkley, a leading journalist at ABC, provided one of the best anecdotal statements of the bureaucratic model.

This town [Washington, D.C.] is sort of like a great big steamboat that keeps going its way regardless of which way the wind blows, or how elections go, or how the current goes; it keeps going, and it might move one degree in one direction, but it essentially keeps going the same direction. It goes on grinding out paper, spending money, hiring people, getting bigger and bigger and more troublesome all the time, and nothing seems to affect it. Presidents don't affect it. Every President I have known has complained about the fantastically cumbersome size of this establishment here. As far back as Harry Truman, I was covering the White House and Truman said, "I thought I was the President, but when it comes to these bureaucrats I can't make 'em do a damn thing."

III   A pluralist interpretation of the American political system

Pluralism is the least precise of the four models of American politics, and its definition often varies according to the author employing the term. A leading political scientist, Nelson Polsby, has sought to provide an illustrative list of pluralism's major characteristics:

. . . Dispersion of power among many rather than a few participants in decision-making; competition or conflict among political leaders; . . . bargaining rather than hierarchical decision-making; elections in which suffrage is relatively widespread as a major determinant of participation in key decisions; bases of influence over decisions relatively dispersed rather than closely held (Polsby, 1980:154).

IV   A majoritarian interpretation of the American political system

In America the people appoint both those who make the laws and those who execute them. . . . So direction really comes through the people, and though the form of government is representative, it is clear that the opinions, prejudices, interests, and even passions of the people can find no lasting obstacles preventing them from being manifest in the daily conduct of society. In the United States, as in all countries where the people reign, the majority rules in the name of the people (Tocqueville, 1968:173).

Elitism   This view, which has several different versions, holds that the decisive influence in the United States is exercised by a relatively small number of individuals. In one sense, of course, a representative government is by definition a government by an elite inasmuch as only the small number of officials in the government actually make authoritative decisions. If elitism is to have any real meaning, therefore, it must refer to the simple fact that power is exercised not merely by the few, but rather by some specific group within society.

A mild version of elitism refers to a strong influence by certain highly educated and well-positioned individuals who have the right credentials or know the right persons. A class of "experts" or an elite in this sense may be thought, even by the public, to have a claim to rule on the grounds of some special qualifications. Such a group might well conceive of its role as serving the interests of the people. (Many scholars, for example, described Great Britain's representative government earlier in this century in terms of the rule—by consent—of such an elite.) It is clear, however, that where a pattern develops in which a certain group is repeatedly elevated to power and where individuals in that group come to think of themselves as being in some sense certified to govern, there is every reason to speak of an elite influence.

More often, however, elitism is used to refer to the rule of a group having an interest distinct from that of the majority. The most frequent such charge is that the United States is run by an elite of the wealthy and the heads of big business. This elite, it is claimed, exercises its influence in two basic ways. First, it keeps government authority out of the domains in which the elite already holds power. Thus the business elite is said to propagate the idea of limited government in the economic sphere because the operation of the free market serves by and large to protect the interests of big business. This aspect of the claim of elitist rule is an extension of the analysis of private power discussed earlier. It is based on the claim that the entire notion of limited government "stacks the deck" in favor of the privileged by defining legitimate governmental authority in such a way as to exclude it from control over the distribution of important resources (Lindbloom, 1977). The public in effect is duped into accepting the theory of limited government, which in reality is a doctrine that provides a cover of ideological legitimacy for the power of big business.

Second, within the limited sphere in which government does operate, the business elite is said to exercise a disproportionate degree of influence over its decisions. Few claim that government is totally "bought," but some hold that politicians are more readily disposed to favor the interests of the wealthy. The wealthy succeed in influencing government officials by such techniques as well-financed lobbying efforts, campaign contributions, favors (legal and illegal), and a reliance on an established network of social contacts. This power is used to protect or promote the interests of business and the wealthy by such means as securing special subsidies or favorable tax laws. While the government appears from the outside to be a representative democracy, in reality this appearance is a facade: behind the scenes, power is largely controlled by the few and in the interests of the few.

Bureaucratic Rule   This view holds that the power of government is exercised by governmental bureaucracies which follow their own interests and run according to imperatives generated by the needs of large public organizations. Elected officials sit atop this vast structure, trying to control it but in reality being controlled by it. The tasks of governing today are so complex and require so much special expertise that the elected officials

have no choice but to turn much of the operating authority over to the bureaucracies. Once entrenched in the structure of governing, these organizations accumulate more and more power. Unlike presidents and cabinet members, who serve for relatively brief periods, the officials in the bureaucracy serve for an entire career. The political officials come and go, but the interests of the bureaucracy remain. As one assistant to two secretaries of defense remarked: "The bureaucracy knows deep in its heart that it can outlast almost any secretary of defense" (*Newsweek,* 1982).

Bureaucracies, of course, have different interests, and, where their control overlaps, they struggle among themselves for influence. They seek to dominate decision making by forging alliances with other bureaucratic agencies and by generating demands from clients in the public that depend on their goodwill. The conflict among bureaucracies creates a kind of politics of its own, having certain distinct characteristics (Allison, 1969). As described by Henry Kissinger: "In bureaucratic societies policy emerges from a compromise (among bureaucratic agencies) which often produces the least common denominator, and it is implemented by individuals whose reputation is made by administering the status quo" (Kissinger, 1966:524). Bureaucratic politics in this sense stands at odds not only with popular rule, but equally with any kind of statesmanship of the sort noted above.

Although the founders briefly discussed public administration, the model of bureaucratic influence is largely a phenomenon said to have emerged in modern regimes. According to the famous German sociologist Max Weber (1864–1920), who pioneered the modern study of bureaucracy, "The future belongs to bureaucratization. . . . Once the modern trained official rules, his power is virtually indestructible" (Bell, 1973:67). Bureaucratization according to Weber is the overwhelming fact of modern social organization, both public and private. Important social functions are performed less and less by people working as individuals and more and more by officials in complex hierarchic organizations. Interestingly, these organizations seem almost to have a life of their own. Even those working within bureaucracies cannot really control them since there often seem to be inevitable dynamics that result from the very characteristics of

The 1963 civil rights march on Washington was a classic example of a group mobilizing to promote its interests—in this case, the rights of black citizens to equality of treatment under the law.   *(Dan Budnik/Woodfin Camp)*

large organizations. Those at the top may tinker now and then with the organization, but in the final analysis power lies with the human cogs (the bureaucrats) enmeshed in an uncontrollable machine (the bureaucracy).

Pluralism   This view holds that the major influence on government derives from numerous organized groups representing a broad spectrum of different interests in American society. Included among these are business groups such as the chamber of commerce, labor groups such as the American Federation of Labor (AFL-CIO), civil rights groups such as the National Association for the Advancement of Colored People (NAACP), and so-called "public" interest groups such as Common Cause. These organizations seek to protect and promote what they see as the interests of their members.

Most groups of any significance in society, according to pluralist theory, can "make themselves heard at some crucial stage in the process of decision" (Dahl, 1956:137). The governing process involves the formation of coalitions between these groups in a bargaining process. Moreover, because of the peculiarities of our institutional arrangements—in which, because of a separation of powers, there are so many ways to block actions—important groups are often in a position to stop action that is disadvantageous to them, but may find it more difficult to enact decisive new programs. The public interest in the pluralist view is discovered in the complex accommodations among these groups rather than in the abstract discovery of a public will, which is difficult to discern and not easily calculated by a complex system of popular elections.

Pluralism sounds like—and is—a model of government that reflects the interests of broad segments of the public. Yet it may deviate significantly from the more democratic ideal of government in which the will of the majority always prevails. Under the pluralist model, the ability to influence government decisions is greatly enhanced by the capacity of an interest to create an actual interest group, with an organization and a staff that can mobilize constituents and apply political pressure. Those who become the leaders of powerful interest groups may not represent the wishes of their constituents, but may speak for the interests of the organization itself, which can deviate from those of its members. In any event, whether or not these leaders accurately represent their members' views, pluralism implies that decisions of government are controlled by a relatively small number of individuals.

Another difference between pluralism and the ideal of majority rule is that interests, like big labor or big business, are in a position to organize with relative ease, while other potential interests, lacking the same means, face tremendous obstacles in creating viable and effective organizations. Because power is related in part to organizational capacity and not directly to the number of persons represented, distortions may result to the democratic ideal of equal influence for each citizen. Such distortions may reflect not only economic advantages but differences in the intensity of belief and the skills of different groups.

The analysis of how pluralism deviates from majority rule very quickly shades into criticisms of it. For example, many comment that, to the extent that pluralism accurately portrays the influence on government, the American public is represented in a peculiar and partly distorted fashion—in terms of its narrow and specific interests rather than in terms of the general interest. What pluralist decision making emphasizes is the special interests of organized groups, often ignoring interests too diffuse to be organized and neglecting a broader interest that lies beyond people's membership in specific groups.

Critics of pluralism charge that when all these tendencies of pluralism are taken into account, pluralism loses any claim to being a "popular" model of government and looks more and more like a form of elitism. However, many of those who have outlined a pluralist description of American politics reject any such attempt to collapse pluralism into something else (Polsby, 1980). In their view, pluralism retains its distinctive feature of actually representing in a reasonable way the broad interests of the American public. To be sure, there are problems of distortion, but these are inevitable in any system that allows groups to form and press their claims. The charges that certain groups are excluded or possess no power, moreover, are often exaggerated or possess little empirical evidence. Finally, defenders of the normative claim for pluralism—that is, those who see it not just as descriptive of how politics works but as worthwhile and worthy of choice—hold that pluralism is a method by which the interests of a complex society can be represented and weighed in a reasonably efficient way. The process of governing, in this view, should in some degree take into account not just the wishes of majorities, but also the intensity of feeling of different groups. When a significant element of society wants or does not want something very badly, this should "count" in the face of possible majorities that may be largely indifferent. Pluralism is a mechanism, albeit an imperfect one, for registering these sentiments of intensity.

Majoritarianism This view holds that the decisive influence on our institutions derives from the public at large, and in particular from the majority of (voting) citizens. The majority exercises its power both through the instrument of popular elections, relying in particular on the assistance of political parties, and through the help of the widely held norm among governing officials that the public interest should be served and that people's will should be carefully considered when making decisions. Politicians, knowing that they must obtain the votes of the majority to win office, will do either what the majority wants or else what they believe a majority can be persuaded to accept. (Between these two conceptions of majoritarianism, obviously, there is a tremendous difference.) Under a majoritarian model, it need not be claimed that a majority exists on every issue or that the government always knows or follows exactly what the majority wants. A less stringent version of majoritarianism would hold merely that on the important issues on which public opinion focuses, the will of the majority is the most decisive influence.

These four models have been used by different analysts of American politics to explain who governs the United States. In many cases, analysts either ignore or discount the fact that there is a government that in some degree has a will of its own. Our view is that the most important *influence* on the government—remember that the government itself is representative with its own partly independent power—derives from the wishes of the people. Translated into the more technical terms of these models, we would say that the models that provide the best descriptions of American politics are pluralism and majoritarianism. These two models are frequently mixed in complex ways, although in some instances one is clearly predominant over the other. Both, as we shall see, possess a degree of legitimacy in that constitution makers from the time of the founding have given each of them a place in our political system. The other two models—elitism and bureaucratic rule—are used by some commentators as descriptions of how our system operates, but almost never as prescriptions for how it should operate. Elements of these models are helpful, however, in accounting for important influences on government in certain policy areas. Indeed, none of the four models represents an absolutely accurate picture of reality; real political processes are usually complex compounds of all these models operating with different relative weights from one political era to another and, within each era, from one policymaking area to another. Despite this complexity, however, subsequent examination of the government should show the predominance of the two popular models—pluralism and majoritarianism.

SECURITY AND THE PROMOTION OF VALUES IN THE WORLD

The final question for a constitution maker is how to provide the nation with the capacity to protect and promote its interests in a world consisting of other nations having different and often hostile interests. The constitutional question here refers not to the strategies and tactics of conducting defense

and foreign policies, but to the broader questions of governmental powers and to the nation's political and moral purposes in world affairs.

This question is essential for the understanding of constitution making because governments are formed in part on the basis of what *must* be done in order to protect the security and preservation of society. Security could, of course, be included as an end of society, but we have singled it out for special treatment both because of its importance and because it raises considerations of a very different kind from those we entertained earlier. When considering "domestic" ends of society such as liberty, self-government, and equality, a constitution maker may be thinking about what is desirable or fitting as a way of life. The manner in which such issues are discussed suggests the existence of *choice*. When considering questions of security, however, the entire frame of reference shifts from choice to compulsion or *necessity*. The question is not what we might like to do for ourselves, but what we may be required to do in order to protect the nation's existence and promote its vital interests.

"Necessity" in Constitution Making

Considerations of necessity were at the forefront for many of the founders in constructing our form of government. The most important question that divided the nation in 1787 was whether to remain essentially a confederation of independent states or become a genuine union under a strong national government. This question, in the view of many founders, was a matter to be decided as much on the basis of necessity as on desirability. Whatever might be said of the dangers of union, they argued, it was needed to provide an effective defense of the nation against the possibilities of internal war and conquest by European powers. Much the same way of thinking influenced other important elements of the Constitution. Certain Antifederalists complained that too much power was granted to the government because the Constitution placed no limit on the size of the armed forces and that too much power was vested in the hands of one individual (the president). In *The Federalist*, Alexander Hamilton met the objection about the armed forces by arguing that "it is impossible to foresee or to define the extent and variety of national emergencies"; no one could know in 1787 what might be necessary for the defense of the nation under future circumstances (*Federalist* 23). As for the presidency, Hamilton contended that the conduct of foreign and defense affairs required that the government be able to act with "secrecy and dispatch"— qualities associated with unitary command rather than group decision making (*Federalist* 70).

The achievement of union, along with a fortunate geographic position and certain accidents of history, left the United States free from European interference after 1814, and no nation in this hemisphere was a serious match for American power. In large measure because the founders took into account the necessity for union, Americans were able to "forget" about the constraints arising from foreign affairs until well into this century. One drawback to this favorable state of affairs, according to former Secretary of State Henry Kissinger, was that "America entered the twentieth century largely unprepared for the part it would be called on to play" (Kissinger, 1979:59). Since the outbreak of World War II, the United States has been faced, in a more dangerous world, with relearning the constraints of foreign affairs. Since the end of the war, the United States has come to play a new and different role in foreign affairs, as a major world power involved in far-flung alliances and committed to the defense of scores of nations all over the globe. Changes in military technology— missiles, long-range bombers, and nuclear weapons—have eliminated the security that our geographic position once provided, and the rise in power of the Soviet Union coupled with the relative decline in power of the western European nations has left the United States as the only nation able to carry the major burden of defense of the noncommunist world.

More by necessity than choice, the United States has had to add a new dimension to its government: a large military and intelligence establishment. The size of the armed forces, once relatively small, has grown enormously, and military expenditures in 1982 consumed 28 percent of the national budget and 7.2 percent the gross national product. New agencies for gathering intelligence and carrying out covert activities, such as the Central Intelligence Agency (CIA), have been created, leading to inevitable debates on the tensions between the usual requirement in representative democracies for openness and the necessity in such security matters for secrecy. The pressures created by the conduct of foreign policy have led to new questions about the power and relations among the institutions of government. With the growing importance of foreign affairs, there has been an inevitable increase since World War II in the responsibilities and power of the presidency. In the 1970s, however, Congress reacted to assert certain Constitutional prerogatives in foreign affairs and involved itself more deeply in the details of decision making. Many wondered in the aftermath whether the United States government possessed the requisite unity and energy to conduct an effective foreign policy (Kissinger, 1982). In short, in assuming a new and more active role in international affairs, the United States has faced a new set of challenges, some practical in nature, but others genuinely constitutional. It has had to learn—and is still learning—how to adjust public attitudes to the demands and constraints of ongoing foreign policy involvement, and it has had to modify—and is still modifying—its institutional structures to cope with the requirements of constant interaction with other nations of the world.

Values in Foreign Affairs

The realm of foreign affairs is not entirely one of necessity and response to the needs of security. Nations may also seek to promote certain values in the world and to play a major role in the unfolding of world history. Under Marxist-Leninist theory, for example, the Soviet government has explicitly committed itself to the goal of spreading communism over the entire globe, although some now question the extent to which this remains an operative goal for Soviet leadership. For its part, the United States has a long tradition, dating back to the founding, of being endowed with a special mission or responsibility to spread the "light" of republican government in the world. This mission has been a continuing theme in the rhetoric of American presidents, even at moments when its significance for concrete policy has been minimal. The source of this theme can be traced back in part to the Declaration, in which the principles of liberty and self-government are grounded not simply in a declared belief in their desirability, but in the assertion that they exist as "truths" established by the laws of nature (Huntington, 1981).

The commitment to fostering republican government in the world has assumed very different forms, from a careful realism, in which American policymakers have limited America's role to fit the constraints of its position and power, to a moralistic isolationism, in which policymakers have sought to avoid besmirching republican ideals by withdrawing from an immoral world of international politics, and finally to a crusading internationalism, a theme given its classic expression in Woodrow Wilson's call to fight a war to "make the world safe for democracy." The commitment to fostering representative democracy in the world has given rise to what is often a moral dimension to debates over the conduct of foreign policy. Some have charged that the United States has not done enough to aid the cause of democracy, others that it has tried too hard and by its idealism has occasionally threatened world security, and still others that it is guilty of hypocrisy by making accommodations with authoritarian regimes in order to pursue broader strategic goals. All these assessments and charges require careful evaluation; what is important is the significance of the felt commitment to promote liberty in the world. It operates as an important force in American politics and constitutes an unwritten component of our constitution.

CONCLUSION

Analysts of American politics are frequently asked to assess the condition of the political system today and how it is likely to develop in the future. In this chapter, we have not attempted to answer such questions but rather to provide a meaningful way in which they might be approached. By adopting the perspective of a constitution maker and asking the four major questions implicit in that role, one is forced to confront the basic issues that determine the character of any political order. Studying these questions in the context of American political de-

velopment should provide a sense of where we have come from and what issues face us in the future.

Yet if what we have said about the evolution of our constitution is correct, and if each generation must make its own choices, it follows that there is no way of predicting future development. Each generation, within the circle traced out for it by its predecessors, has the task of modifying and remaking the constitution. The importance of thinking of politics in constitutional terms, therefore, lies not in improving the capabilities of prediction, but in better enabling citizens to assess current possibilities and make more informed choices about the constitutional questions that confront them in their time.

The present generation faces some special circumstances and formidable challenges. During the past generation—from the end of World War II until the middle of the 1970s—two general developments stand out above all others. First, there was a great increase in the size of government and the responsibilities that it assumed on the domestic front. In one area after another, from maintaining economic security to promoting greater equality, government became more active and undertook ambitious programs to change American society. Second, the United States began to play a new role in international affairs as the proclaimed leader of the "free world" and as a major world power with responsibilities for maintaining world order. As challenging as both of these departures were, Americans faced them under relatively favorable circumstances. In the postwar period, economic growth was unprecedented, providing enormous resources from which to finance the new responsibilities of government. At the same time, the United States emerged from World War II as the foremost world power, challenged by other nations, but still vastly superior in wealth and military might.

Today, the nation must cope with the legacies of the last generation in circumstances that seem much less favorable. If the last generation lived through a period that suggested a great deal of freedom and a sense of unlimited possibilities, this generation, at least for the present, faces greater constraints and limits. On the domestic side, the tremendous growth of government leaves Americans with the painful job of attempting to make big government work and perhaps even with the responsibility of rethinking whether government can do all that was once expected of it. The era of unprecedented economic growth has come to an end, at least for the short term, and there is consequently a smaller margin and tolerance of error. The closer scrutiny of governmental performance in these circumstances places a constant burden on our institutions and magnifies whatever weaknesses they may have. On the international side, while the United States has retained many of its responsibilities in world affairs, its predominance is no longer ensured. In both the military and the economic sphere, the United States has moved into an era of growing international constraints in which its ability to control events is uncertain. The Soviet Union now possesses a military that is equal or perhaps superior, while American industries face stiffer foreign competition and must rely on potentially vulnerable foreign energy resources.

The task of this decade, it would appear, is not likely to consist of addressing one single problem—like civil rights—but rather will involve learning to cope with, without succumbing to, a continuing set of pressures and limits. Whatever else may be needed, we shall require a better understanding of the fundamentals of constitutional thinking.

SOURCES

Acton, John: *The History of Freedom and Other Essays,* Macmillan, London, 1907.

Allison, Graham: "Conceptual Models of the Cuban Missile Crisis," *American Political Science Review,* vol. 63, no. 3, 1969, pp. 689–718.

Beer, Samuel: "In Search of a New Public Philosophy," in Anthony King (ed.), *The New American Political System,* American Enterprise Institute, Washington, D.C., 1978.

Bell, Daniel: *The Coming of Post-industrial Society,* Basic Books, New York, 1973.

Clor, Harry: *Censorship and Freedom of Expression,* Public Affairs Conference Center, Kenyon College, 1971.

Cutler, Lloyd N.: "To Form a Government," *Foreign Affairs,* Fall, 1980, pp. 126–143.

Dahl, Robert: *Preface to Democratic Theory,* University of Chicago Press, Chicago, 1956.

———: "On Removing Certain Impediments to Democracy in the United States," in Robert Horwitz (ed.), *Moral Foundations of the American Republic,* University Press of Virginia, Charlottesville, Va., 1979.

Farrand, Max: *The Records of the Federal Convention of 1787,* vols. 1–4, Yale University Press, New Haven, Conn., 1911–1937.

Forsythe, Dall W.: *Taxation and Political Change in the Young Nation,* Columbia University Press, New York, 1977.

Huntington, Samuel P.: *American Politics: The Promise of Disharmony,* Harvard University Press, Cambridge, Mass., 1981.

Kaufman, Herbert: *Red Tape,* Brookings Institution, Washington, D.C., 1977.

Kissinger, Henry: "Domestic Structure and Foreign Policy," *Daedalus,* vol. 95, no. 2, 1966, pp. 503–529.

———: *White House Years,* Little, Brown, Boston, 1979.

———: *Years of Upheaval,* Little, Brown, Boston, 1982.

Laswell, Harold D.: *Politics: Who Gets What How,* McGraw-Hill, New York, 1936.

Lindbloom, Charles E.: *Politics and Markets: The World's Political Economic Systems,* Basic Books, New York, 1977.

Lipset, Seymour Martin: *The First New Nation,* Basic Books, New York, 1963.

Madison, James: *Notes of Debates in the Federal Convention of 1787,* Adrienne Koch (ed.), Norton, New York, 1969.

Mason, Alpheus Thomas: *Free Government in the Making,* 3d ed., Oxford University Press, New York, 1965.

McWilliams, Wilson Carey: "On Equality as the Moral Foundation for Community," in Robert Horwitz (ed.), *Moral Foundations of the American Republic,* University Press of Virginia, Charlottesville, Va., 1979.

Newsweek, Dec. 20, 1982.

Okun, Arthur: *Equality and Efficiency, the Big Trade-off,* Brookings Institution, Washington, D.C., 1975.

Parenti, Michael: *Democracy for the Few,* St. Martin's, New York, 1980.

Polsby, Nelson: *Community Power and Political Theory,* Yale University Press, New Haven, Conn., 1980.

Rawls, John: *A Theory of Justice,* Harvard University Press, Cambridge, Mass., 1971.

Smolka, Richard G.: *Hearings on Voter Registration,* U.S. Government Printing Office, Washington, D.C., 1973.

Sombart, Werner: *Why Is There No Socialism in the United States?* C. T. Husbands (ed.), Sharpe, White Plains, N.Y., 1976.

Tocqueville, Alexis de: *Democracy in America,* J. P. Mayer (ed.), Anchor, New York, 1968.

Will, George: "Armies Should Win Wars," *Newsweek,* February 18, 1980.

Court Cases

U.S. v. Roth, 237 F. (2d Cir. 1956).

RECOMMENDED READINGS

Horwitz, Robert (ed.): *Moral Foundations of the American Republic,* University Press of Virginia, Charlottesville, Va., 1979. A selection of essays by leading political scientists on the general character of the American political system.

Huntington, Samuel: *American Politics: The Politics of Disharmony,* Harvard University Press, Cambridge, Mass., 1981. An interpretation of the role of core values in shaping the development of the American political system.

Lipset, Seymour Martin: *The First New Nation,* Basic Books, New York, 1963. A broad discussion of historical, sociological, and economic factors that help account for the character and development of the United States.

Chapter 2
The Founding

CHAPTER CONTENTS

Do the Declaration of Independence and the Constitution hold any importance for Americans today? After all, these two pieces of eighteenth-century parchment were written in a very different age and under very different circumstances. Two centuries ago, the United States was a mostly rural nation of scarcely more than 3 million inhabitants strung along the eastern seaboard of North America; now it is a commercial and industrial nation with nearly a quarter of a billion citizens, straddling the continent and reaching to the middle of the Pacific Ocean. Then, the free population of the United States was descended largely from the stock of the British Isles, distinctions of family and class still carried weight (although the hereditary aristocracies of Europe had been left behind), and one-fourth of the inhabitants were black slaves; now, the United States is a country of great ethnic and social diversity, aristocratic distinctions and customs are all but unknown, and the descendants of the black slaves are free citizens (although racial tensions persist). Then, the world stood in the infancy of modern science; now, modern communications and machinery have remade the globe. Then, wars were fought with musket and cannon; now, we command missiles and nuclear weapons.

Clearly, a great gulf exists between the founding era and our own. Nevertheless, the Declaration and the Constitution remain the two main pillars on which our political system rests. They were written under different circumstances, but their authors intended them to embody certain enduring principles. These documents are essential sources—though by no means the only ones—for understanding American politics in the 1980s.

The study of the founding presents a rare opportunity to observe constitution makers grappling with the fundamental problems of forming a new government. In this chapter, we shall discuss the main principles of the Declaration and the Constitution, paying careful attention to the social and political context out of which these documents emerged. This discussion will provide the basis for understanding our political system and for analyzing constitutional development since the founding era.

THE DECLARATION OF INDEPENDENCE

The principles of the Declaration of Independence have occupied a central place in American politics from the beginning of the republic. This prominence resulted in some measure from the example of those who signed the document and from their willingness to make sacrifices for the principles it embodies. Among the signatories were John Adams, Thomas Jefferson, and Benjamin Franklin. Of the fifty-six men who signed, nine would die during the Revolutionary struggle, five would be captured by the enemy, and seventeen would lose their property (Fehrenbach, 1968). These sacrifices gave meaning to their pledge in the Declaration to be ready to risk their "lives," "fortunes," and "sacred honor." But the enduring quality of the Declaration has probably owed even more to its contents. The Declaration transcended the particular facts of the eighteenth-century struggle, justifying the war on the basis of certain underlying principles of political life derived from the "laws of nature and of nature's God." This standard, in the philosophy of the Declaration, remains constant and true, notwithstanding any changes of place or circumstance. The appeal to universal principles has helped the Declaration achieve its global influence but has also resulted in widely divergent interpretations of its meaning and implications.

In certain respects the Declaration has a traditional and "conservative" tone. It does not encourage acts of revolution on superficial grounds. It acknowledges, for instance, that "governments long established should not be changed for light and transient causes." Yet if the Declaration is almost conservative in its apology for revolt, in its appeal to "nature" as the ultimate justification for revolt it is truly revolutionary. The Congress of the new United States government was not obliged to raise the issue of independence to the level of universal principle stated in the Declaration. Legally speaking, Congress had already settled the matter on July 2, 1776, by adopting Richard Henry Lee's resolution declaring the colonies "independent States." But Congress chose to go further and endorse a broader justification for independence.

This new justification was the product of a gradual but profound shift in American thought in the decade before the Revolution. As the crown and Parliament had attempted to tighten their grip on the colonies through a series of unpopular laws and policies, such as the Stamp Act (1765), the ties of affection and goodwill that had existed between the colonies and Britain began to loosen. Americans began to base their understanding of liberty not on the "rights of Englishmen," but on *natural* rights. And here they drew inspiration from a rather surprising source: English political thinkers, most notably John Locke (1632–1704). In the *Second Treatise on Government* (1690), Locke argued that human beings in a "state of nature" possessed equal natural rights to life, liberty, and property. Government came into being when individuals contracted among themselves to provide greater security for these rights. When a government persistently threatens or denies a people's natural rights, Locke declared, it has lost its legitimacy and the people have a right to resist its tyranny. Locke's ideas, and even some of his key phrases (altered only slightly), reappeared almost a century later in the Declaration.

As the colonists lost their love of Britain and the British inheritance, they also began to see more clearly the inadequacy of the British system of government, with its undemocratic features of monarchy and nobility. In rejecting Britain, therefore, they began to search not only for a new foundation of rights, but for new principles on which to erect a government. All these changes in opinion had actually begun to take place *before* the Revolution, so much so that Jefferson would later claim, with perhaps too much modesty, that the doctrines of the Declaration merely represented the "sentiments of the day, whether expressed in conversation, in letters, printed essays, or the elementary books of public right" (Ford, 1904:XII, 409).

The Principles of Nature

We have repeatedly referred to the novel and revolutionary principles embodied in the colonists' appeal to "nature" and to "self-evident truths." These principles, discussed in Chapter 1, consisted of equality, the possession of certain "unalienable

rights" (such as "life, liberty, and the pursuit of happiness"), and self-government (at least in the sense that governments must be established with the "consent of the governed"). Clearly, however, most societies in the world were not—and are not today—established on such principles. What then could it mean to say that these principles are based on the "laws of nature" and represent "self-evident truths"? If the principles are natural and hence universal, why are they recognized and embodied in only a very few societies? Were those who believed in such doctrines merely naive or ill-informed?

Such a charge against men with the learning and intelligence of Thomas Jefferson or John Adams would itself seem rather naive. The view of these men was *not* that all people understood the laws of nature or perceived these self-evident truths. They realized that throughout history false doctrines had been propagated to keep people in a state of submission and that many cultures had not yet developed the capacity for abstract political thinking. But the founders were convinced that beyond false doctrines and temporary incapacity there were certain principles of nature that *could* be appealed to as people became more enlightened. As Jefferson wrote, "All eyes are opened, or opening, to the rights of man. The general spread of the light of science has already laid open to every view the palpable truth that the mass of mankind has not been born with saddles on their backs, nor a favored few booted and spurred, ready to ride them legitimately" (Ford, 1904:XII, 477).

Unless falsely captivated by propaganda—by doctrines such as the divine right of monarchs, racial inferiority or superiority, and historical determinism—a people can be awakened to see the palpable truths expressed in the Declaration. While Jefferson may have been too optimistic in expecting that other peoples would readily embrace those truths, it is by no means apparent that the standards of the Declaration are naive or have become outmoded. In the struggle of groups within the United States for their rights, in the assertions of freedom by many former colonial countries, and in the resistance of many too brutal tyrannies, an appeal to nature—or something like it—continues to be used.

The Meaning of Equality

Of the three cardinal principles established by the Declaration—liberty, equality, and self-government—the founders' conception of equality is clearly the most controversial and least understood. We have already seen in Chapter 1 that by "equality" the founders did not have in mind the idea of perfect economic equality, not even perhaps of full political equality (one person, one vote). Nor did they mean that people were equal in their mental endowments or physical capacities. What they meant by equality was an equality of rights, the equal right to liberty, property, and the pursuit of happiness. But did they mean that *all* had such a rightful claim? If so, why did Abigail Adams complain to her husband John, just weeks before the vote on independence, that "whilst you are proclaiming peace and good-will to men, emancipating all nations, you insist upon retaining an absolute power over wives" (Adams, 1840:I, 98)? And more troubling still, how can one explain the continuation of slavery after July 4, 1776, and the fact that many of those who signed the Declaration owned slaves?

We know for certain that some of the signatories of the Declaration, among them the slave owners Jefferson and Washington, thought slavery to be immoral and inconsistent with the Declaration. At the same time, however, the most they could do was hope that as time went on, and slavery proved economically unprofitable and morally untenable, some kind of solution might be found. Yet even among the most enlightened thinkers, no practical plan of abolition was developed. Few, if any, thought that a multiracial society, with blacks and whites living together as equals, was possible. As Jefferson wrote in his autobiography: "Nothing is more certainly written in the book of fate, than that these two people are to be free; nor is it less certain that the two races, equally free, cannot live in the same government" (Ford, 1904:I,77). Following this logic, some called for vague schemes of emancipation followed by colonization, somewhere either on this continent or in Africa. The Declaration may have meant the right of all to equality (at some unspecified time in the future), but not necessarily *within* the same community. Even this logic, however, may not have been shared by all who signed the Declaration. No colonial Barbara Walters or Dan Rather interviewed all the signers and persuaded them to reveal their deepest sentiments about the prickly matter of equality. In any case, as we shall see in later chapters, the responsibility for developing the founding principles has rested not just with the founders themselves but with subsequent generations of Americans.

THE ARTICLES OF CONFEDERATION

The Second Continental Congress that approved the Declaration could scarcely be called a formal government. It was a council of the different colonies formed by delegates selected by revolutionary "second" governments that sprang up in the colonies beside the legal colonial institutions. Americans had had practically no experience with any form of continental union. Britain had ruled the colonies as separate entities, and, with the exception of the New England Confederacy (1634–1684) and a conference at Albany (1754), united intercolonial activity had been almost nonexistent.

The pressures of the revolutionary situation made it necessary to establish some form of national government. Accordingly, soon after appointing the committee to draft the Declaration, the Second Continental Congress formed another committee to prepare a "form of confederation" as an official government. The contractual character of the Congress as a meeting of separate colonies shaped the understanding that the ratification of any new government would require the consent of all the colonies. The committee preparing the Articles of Confederation reported a draft after only one month of deliberation. The proposal proved controversial and was not ratified by all the states until 1781, near the end of the Revolutionary War. For most of the war, the Second Continental Congress simply acted as the government, informally implementing most aspects of the proposed new charter.

The Government of the Articles

The formal government of the Articles began under very difficult circumstances. The Revolutionary War had exhausted the nation, and many communities lay devastated. A national debt of very considerable size had been incurred. The paper money used to finance the war was all but worthless. Finally, the nation had already settled into a pattern in which the public and most political leaders looked to the individual states as the centers of political activity. During the same years that the proposed government of the Articles lay unratified, the former colonies wrote constitutions for themselves, each forming a separate republic which secured the primary allegiance of its citizenry. A union of all Americans existed in the minds and hearts of the people, but it seemed to be secondary to their attachment to their separate republics.

The government established under the Articles of Confederation vested all the powers of the national government in a Congress of the states. There was no regular national judiciary and only the merest shadow of an executive power. Each state had one vote within Congress, regardless of its size. Important measures required the votes of nine of the thirteen states to pass, while amendments to the Articles required the unanimous consent of all the states.

A look at the powers of Congress indicates that its objectives went far beyond a mere league for defense. The Articles gave Congress the authority to make war and peace, enter into treaties and alliances, manage trade with the Indians, and borrow money and regulate coinage. The states were forbidden to make treaties or exchange diplomatic representatives with foreign nations, and any alliances or treaties between the states themselves required Congress's consent. On paper these powers seem considerable; in practice they proved difficult to exercise.

Weaknesses of the Articles

Among the problems with the Articles, the gravest was that they had to exercise authority through the *states* and not directly on the individual citizen. Where the laws of a government apply to individuals, they can be enforced by the police and courts. But where they apply to an entire state, compliance can be secured only by making sure that a state carries out its commands. The government con-

stantly ran into the problem of noncompliance, for it lacked power to enforce its will on "sovereign" states. This weakness was especially evident in military affairs. Without superior force, no government can claim the obedience of citizens. But Congress under the Articles could raise an army only by requisitioning troops from the states, which frequently failed to comply. Therefore Congress could do little or nothing in the 1780s to protect the national interest against British- and Spanish-inspired Indian raids against settlers in the west.

Similarly, Congress could raise funds only by assessing the states rather than individual citizens. Again, noncompliance was frequent. For example, in 1786 Congress's total revenue was equal to less than one-third of that year's *interest* on the national debt (Rossiter, 1966:49). Efforts to secure a more adequate source of funding by a tax on imports required an amendment to the Articles. But under the unanimous-consent provision a single state could block such a change, and on two occasions one state—first Rhode Island and then New York—did so. The government thus lacked the essential tools of force and finance.

In addition to its inability to enforce the objectives for which it had been established, the government lacked one crucial power: the authority to regulate commerce between the states and with foreign nations. Without this authority, the states individually imposed tariffs and erected trade barriers, often directed against other states as well as foreign nations. This competition retarded the development of the American economy and threatened to fulfill the prophecy of a prominent English contemporary who predicted that Americans would remain a "disunited people till the end of time, suspicious and distrustful of each other" and fragmented into "little commonwealths or principalities" with "no centre of union and no common interest" (Hofstadter et al., 1970:I, 226).

At the root of all these problems was the guarantee in Article II that each state would retain "its sovereignty, freedom, and independence." This assertion of a pure confederacy conflicted directly with some of the stated objectives of the Articles, which sought the blessings of a national union. It also prevented the formation of anything resembling a strong executive force, something essential to such a union. It was true, of course, that the record under the Articles was not entirely one of failure. The nation had fought the Revolutionary War to a victorious finish, obtained a favorable peace settlement, and resolved the problem of the western territories with the passage of the Northwest Ordinance (1787). But the *form* of government itself, with its clash of contradictory and irreconcilable principles, left little confidence in Congress's ability to handle future problems. George Washington perhaps summed up the situation most accurately when he called the government of the Articles a "half-starved, limping government, always moving upon crutches and tottering at every step" (Hofstadter et al., 1970:I, 239).

The Crisis in the States

Failure of the Articles was not the only cause, however, behind the growing movement to establish a new national government. Of equal concern was the increasing unrest in many of the states, which undermined public confidence in these governments among some elements of society and which threatened the sanctity of property rights. These problems became evident in the inability or unwillingness of the states to adopt sound measures of public finance during the difficult economic times of the 1780s. Pressured by depressed segments of the population, many states pumped excessive amounts of paper money into their economies, thus deflating the value of the currency. Creditors were often forced to accept this currency as payment of their loans. In Rhode Island, the situation became so bad that creditors sought to hide from debtors in order to escape being paid back in the worthless money which the state had created.

In some states whose legislatures resisted popular demands for inflated currency, events took a more violent turn. In New Hampshire, the state militia had to repel an armed mob that converged on the legislative meeting house in Exeter. More violent still was Shays' Rebellion in Massachusetts in the summer and fall of 1786. There, crowds of disgruntled citizens descended on state courts to stop foreclosure proceedings initiated by creditors. Soon an outright rebellion erupted under the leadership of Captain Daniel Shays, an embittered

Revolutionary War veteran. When the governor asked Congress to send troops to put down the rebellion, it was unable to raise the necessary money. Since the state militia was nonexistent, private funds had to be raised to hire an army that marched on Springfield and dispersed the rebels—but not before news of the revolt in Massachusetts, the cradle of the Revolution, had shocked many sober-minded Americans into assessing carefully the state of affairs in the country (McLaughlin, 1905:154–167).

Although much variety existed among the state constitutions, in general they reflected the influence of highly democratic theories. Property restrictions were in force on voting, but the suffrage for white males was by all past standards very broad. More important, most of the states followed the democratic doctrine of the era which called for vesting most of the power in the legislative branch and jealously limiting the powers of the executive and judiciary. These structures of government were generally supported by public philosophies that emphasized the sovereign power of the people, acting through highly responsive representatives, to work their will. As a result, many saw the crisis of instability in the states as a crisis of republican government. The state governments, as Madison and Noah Webster complained, were too weak to protect basic liberties and all too ready to implement the unjust wishes of the majority. The nation, in their view, was threatened by the emergence of legislative despotisms, and the entire experiment with a republican form of government was in doubt (Wood, 1969).

The movement to form a new government, accordingly, had a twofold basis. On the one hand, it was an effort to correct the defects of the Articles and create a national government capable of effectively exercising new national powers. On the other hand, it was an attempt to build a government that could counteract the instability in the states. It would be incorrect, as we shall see, to characterize the movement as an antirepublican effort. Rather, it was a movement to make popular government work. But those who took the lead in forming the new government were frank in acknowledging that a stable and effective republican system required more restraints on popular rule than had existed in many of the states. Saving the cause of republican government necessitated a rethinking of its form and structures.

The Road to the Convention

The idea to change the Articles grew directly out of a meeting of a small group of men at George Washington's home at Mount Vernon in 1785. James Madison, who was one of the participants, arranged to have the Virginia General Assembly invite all the states to hold a commercial convention in Annapolis, Maryland, in September of 1786. Only five states sent delegates, but these delegates passed a resolution calling for a new convention to meet in Philadelphia in May of the following year. The new convention, it was hoped, would devise ways of making the national government "adequate to the exigencies of the Union" (Farrand, 1913:10).

Congress later endorsed the idea of a Philadelphia convention, but only "for the sole and express purpose of revising the Articles of Confederation." Thus the Philadelphia Convention had two possible mandates, an informal one that opened the possibility for creating an entirely new government and an official one that limited its task to a mere revision. In choosing the first and more radical alternative, as it quickly did, the Convention put itself on a potential collision course with Congress. It was a risk the constitution makers of 1787 thought they must make.

CURRENTS OF OPINION IN 1787

Most leaders in the United States at the beginning of 1787 believed that the government established by the Articles of Confederation needed to be revised in some way. But no firm consensus existed about how it should be changed, and by no means did everyone think that the nation required an entirely new form of government. Opinion was fragmented. Later in the year, after the Constitution had been formally proposed, opinion crystallized under two different labels: the Federalists, who supported the Constitution, and the Antifederalists, who opposed it. Because the Antifederalists were an opposition group, they never needed to achieve complete unity among themselves and ended by attacking the Constitution from a number of different and conflicting viewpoints.

At the risk of imposing slightly more order on the situation than may have actually existed, it will be helpful to identify two main poles of political thought in the nation at the time the Convention met. The first is the *small-republic* position, which became the main—though not the only—element of thought in the Antifederalist opposition. The other was the *nationalist* position. Both positions were represented at the Convention, although most of the delegates had nationalist leanings and the small-republic advocates soon felt isolated. (Some of them, like Robert Yates and John Lansing, Jr., of New York, left the Convention; others, like George Mason of Virginia, refused to endorse the plan.)

The Small-Republic Position

Advocates of the small-republic position favored, if not the exact government of the Articles, then something close to it. They proposed a modification, not an abandonment, of the existing government. The basis of their view was the belief that a true republican form of government could not exist in a large, unitary state. Republican government could only endure in smaller communities with a relatively homogeneous population. It followed that the only form of national government consistent with republicanism was a confederation, in which most of the governing power was kept close to home and in which only a limited amount of authority, necessary for security against external threats, was given over to the national government. A national government was at best a necessary evil, and the sole way in which to guarantee that it did not destroy republicanism was to limit strictly its authority and make it subject to the principles of confederation. Small-republic advocates believed that any strong national government, even if it was organized in a highly democratic form, would tend over time to become despotic. A large and powerful national government was simply incompatible with republicanism and freedom. "You might as well attempt," wrote one small-republican, "to rule Hell by prayer" (Rossiter, 1966:284).

The small-republic advocates offered three main arguments to support their view. First, a republic required that the obedience of the people to the laws be voluntary. This was possible only if the people had confidence in their government. But large states, in which the government is both literally and figuratively at a considerable distance from the people, could not secure their attachment. In the view of one small-republic advocate, people "will have no confidence in their legislature, suspect them of ambitious views, be jealous of every measure they adopt, and will not support the laws they pass" (Storing, 1981:16). In order to enforce laws that might not have the people's confidence, the national government would require a large standing army. Force, not persuasion, would be the method of governance, and a large national government would therefore inevitably become a despotic state.

Second, republican government required a strict responsibility of the government to the people. A scheme of elective representation by itself would *not* be sufficient to ensure this responsibility. True responsibility, claimed the advocates of the small-republic position, required that the representatives mirror the characteristics of their constituents. Representatives "should be a true picture of the people; possess the knowledge of their circumstances and their wants; sympathize in all their distresses, and be disposed to seek their true interests" (Storing, 1981:17). But this would not be possible in large states, where representatives would necessarily be chosen in large and diverse electoral districts. The representatives, most of whom would probably come from an educated elite, would quickly develop an interest of their own apart from those of the citizens they had been elected to serve. The form of government might on paper appear republican, but its spirit would soon become something very different.

Finally, because republican government means government by the people, the people must be of a certain kind or quality. They must love liberty and have the independence of mind and spirit to guard their own and others' rights. They must, in other words, possess a high degree of civic virtue. In addition, to avoid the problems of one part of the community exploiting another, it is preferable to have a populace that is not too diverse, that possesses a certain homogeneity in wealth, education, and even religious views. The promotion of this civic virtue as well as the chance for maintaining a relative degree of homogeneity was possible only within the scope of a small republic. The small republic was seen as a school of citizenship as much as a method for governing. A large state, with boundless possibilities of growth and movement, promised to introduce distinctions of wealth and position and temptations to desert the simple, sturdy life of the true citizen (conceived often as an independent farmer). Large states would cultivate a taste for luxury, expand passions, and throw together under one government people of vastly different manners and morals. Under a large government, claimed the small-republic advocates, "indolence will increase. . . . The springs of honesty will gradually grow lax, and chaste and severe manners be succeeded by those that are dissolute and vicious" (Storing, 1981:20).

The Nationalist Position

The nationalist position, advocated by such men as Hamilton, Madison, and Washington, was based on views that were diametrically opposed to those of the small-republic advocates. The nationalists contended not only that strong national government was needed to achieve the goal of national security, but also that it offered the best prospect of creating a safe and stable republican order. It was both necessary and desirable.

The main aspects of the nationalists' critique of the small-republic position have already been suggested in the discussion of the Articles. It consisted first of the claim that a *confederal* form of government lacked the energy and cohesiveness to provide for the nation's defense and to conduct a stable foreign policy. Second, small republics had in reality failed to protect the liberties of individuals. In spite of the defenders' claim that democracy and the protection of rights were fully compatible, the reality of the situation suggested something very different. The experience of the states, Madison argued, proved the "necessity of providing more effectually for the security of private rights" (Farrand, 1966:I,51). The nationalists repeatedly pointed out that any form of government, including an extremely democratic form, could endanger individual liberties and that small republics were in

Alexander Hamilton was a leading advocate of the nationalist position at the Constitutional Convention and a powerful voice in persuading the states to ratify the Constitution. *(John Trumbull/Museum of Fine Arts, Boston)*

fact highly inclined to do so. Finally, the nationalists pointed to certain grave contradictions in the small-republic position. The stress on civic virtue and homogeneity in the populace might conflict with the very idea of liberty. The social control required to shape a virtuous citizenry might be incompatible with the freedom of individuals to "pursue happiness" in their own way. And wasn't it the case that some of the "small" republics—like Pennsylvania and New York—were already far too large to offer the kind of advantages that their adherents claimed?

It is one thing, however, to point to the alleged defects in the position of someone else; it is quite another to show that one's own position is superior. The nationalists favored a strong central government (relative, at least, to that of the Articles) in which the authority of the states would be subordinate to the national government and in which certain powers formerly exercised by the states would be granted to the national government. But what of the small-republicans' claim that a powerful government in a large territory could not re-

main republican, but must in the end become despotic? The nationalists, surprisingly, did *not* dispute the small republicans' claim that certain supports previously thought indispensable for republicanism would be lost or diminished in a government covering a large territory. Specifically, the nationalists acknowledged that in a large territory representatives would be unable to mirror perfectly the populace and that the government could not serve in the same degree as a "school of citizenship" or a teacher of virtue. But in a strikingly innovative argument, the nationalists claimed that a republican form of government could be made to work, and work even more effectively, without all the characteristics that small-republican advocates had deemed essential.

The substance of the nationalists' response will be presented in more detail as we move through the decisions of the founders at the convention. But the outlines of their position can be briefly summarized here. *First,* the nationalists believed that a national government that proved its efficacy in administering the policies of the nation could, over time, obtain the respect and confidence of the populace. People might not feel quite as close to the government, but if it was run wisely—and the nationalists believed that it could be—the public would accept its legitimate claim to their obedience without the need of any more force than moderate government by its very nature requires.

Second, the nationalists argued that a government unable to mirror the wishes of the public could be a benefit rather than a defect. It was true, as the small-republican advocates maintained, that a national government would inevitably be less democratic and less disposed to follow the public's immediate wishes. Yet, it was precisely this freedom from popular constraint that could serve to promote better government—as long as the government was *ultimately* accountable to the people. Able representatives could make use of their own qualities and intelligence to serve the public interest.

Finally, the nationalists believed that republican government could be made to operate without an extraordinary degree of civic virtue and in the absence of a homogeneous populace. To be sure, the nationalists expected a large degree of virtue, and presupposed its existence. In fact, Madison contended that republican government called for qualities of citizenship "in a higher degree than any other form" (*Federalist* 55). They believed, nevertheless, that in a nation in which liberty was the cardinal principle, there were limits on the extent to which virtue could be promoted. Their solution to this problem was to build a society and governmental system that did not seek to stifle self-interested passions, but to deflect them from doing harm and channel them into serving the public good. The large republic would permit a large variety of different groups and interests to exist, so many in fact that no single interest could as a rule constitute a majority. Conflicting and contending with each other, these groups could normally form a majority only by moderating their positions and forming into coalitions with others. An exclusive reliance on moral or religious motives was not required. In keeping with the attempt to safeguard liberty, the nationalists conceived the role of the national government to be that of regulating conduct rather than molding character.

Looking back on the conflict between the small-republic advocates and the nationalists, Americans today are apt to think of the small-republic position as a bit odd or foreign. The American tradition, after all, has been shaped largely—though not entirely—by the principles of the nationalists. But to understand the founding, it is essential to put oneself into the frame of mind of a constitution maker in 1787. At that time, it was the nationalist position that appeared foreign or new. For many years Americans had thought chiefly in terms of a confederation, and one of the widely read books of the time, Montesquieu's *Spirit of the Laws,* seemed unequivocally to support the view that a large state and a republican form of government were incompatible. In all of history, in fact, no example existed of a republic that covered an extended territory. If there was one point on which small-republic advocates and the nationalists agreed, it was that the position taken by the nationalists represented a "novelty in the political world" (*Federalist* 14). The small-republic advocates deplored the "phrenzy of innovation" sweeping the nation and appealed to the "ancient and established usage of the commonwealth" (Storing, 1981:7). The nationalists, while emphasizing a "decent regard to the opinions of former times," urged Americans not to

"suffer a blind veneration for antiquity, for customs or for names" (*Federalist* 14).

THE CONSTITUTIONAL CONVENTION

Throughout history, most governments have been formed in times of revolution and violence, with their character finally being determined by whoever has the greatest force. The American experience was much more fortunate. The Convention met in peacetime, and while the problems created by the government of the Articles of Confederation were serious, the nation was by no means in the midst of an immediate crisis. The delegates were therefore in a position to make significant choices about the government they formed. They came to Philadelphia with a willingness to discuss alternative plans and to make compromises for the sake of reaching agreement. Even so, some of the differences that emerged in the course of their deliberations were so great that the Convention at one point nearly broke up, with delegates threatening that the unresolved issues might have to be decided by force among the states.

The work of the Convention was greatly facilitated by a set of procedural rules that allowed time for second thoughts and that discouraged attempts to force proposals through without a chance for reconsideration. The idea of recording votes of the delegates was unanimously rejected on the grounds that "changes of opinion would be frequent" (Farrand, 1966:I,10). An even more important decision was to keep the deliberations of the Convention secret. Again, the objective was to allow the delegates to consider various proposals and voice opinions without fear that these would be published and used against them by political opponents. Most of the delegates, in fact, did at one point or another change their minds on important issues before the Convention, and this probably could never have occurred if they had been compelled to hold to certain positions by a public record. Our knowledge of the Convention's proceedings comes chiefly from an account kept by James Madison and published posthumously in 1840. Madison's decision to keep a record was entirely his own. It represented a truly prodigious effort, all the more so because at the same time he was playing a leading role in the de-

BOX 2-1

A CONTEMPORARY LOOKS AT HIS FELLOW DELEGATES

William Pierce, a delegate to the Convention from Georgia, observed his fellow delegates with a keen eye and made sketches of their characters. The following are some of his observations:

Gouverneur Morris (of Pennsylvania)—"One of those Genius's in whom every species of talents combine to render him conspicuous and flourishing in public debate:—he winds through all the mazes of rhetoric, and throws around him such a glare that he charms, captivates, and leads away the senses of all who hear him. . . . But with all these powers he is fickle and inconstant,—never pursuing one train of thinking, nor ever regular. . . . This Gentleman is about 38 years old, he has been unfortunate in losing one of his Legs, and getting all the flesh taken off his right arm by a scald, when a youth."

James Madison (of Virginia)—"Every Person seems to acknowledge his greatness. He blends together the profound politician, with the Scholar. In the management of every great question he evidently took the lead in the Convention. From a spirit of industry and application which he possesses in a most eminent degree, he always comes forward the best informed Man of any point in debate. . . . Mr. Madison is about 37 years of age, a Gentleman of great modesty,—with a remarkable sweet temper."

James McClurg (of Virginia)—"He attempted once or twice to speak, but with no great success."

Alexander Hamilton (of New York) "Deservedly celebrated for his talents . . . Hamilton requires time to think,—he enquires into every part of his subject with

the searchings of phylosophy, and when he comes forward he comes highly charged with interesting matter, there is no skimming over the surface of a subject with him, he must sink to the bottom to see what foundation it rests on. . . . He is about 33 years old, of small stature, and lean. His manners are tintured with stiffness, and sometimes with a degree of vanity that is highly disagreeable."

James Wilson (of Pennsylvania)—"He has joined to a fine genius all that can set him off and show him to advantage. He is well acquainted with Man, and understands all the passions that influence him. Government seems to have been his peculiar Study, all the political institutions of the World he knows in detail, and can trace the causes and effects of every revolution from the earliest stages of the Grecian commonwealth down to the present time. No man is more clear, copious, and comprehensive than Mr. Wilson, yet he is no great Orator. He draws the attention not by the charm of his eloquence, but by the force of his reasoning. He is about 45 years old."

Roger Sherman (of Connecticut)—"He is awkward, un-meaning, and unaccountably strange in his manner. But in his train of thinking there is something regular, deep and comprehensive; yet the oddity of his address, the vulgarisms that accompany his public speaking, and that strange New England cant which runs through his public as well as his private speaking makes everything that is connected with him grotesque and laughable; and yet he deserves infinite praise,—no Man has a better Heart or a clearer Head."

Source: Farrand, 1966:III, 87–97.

liberations of the Convention. A friend recalled Madison saying that the "labor of writing out the debates, added to the confinement to which his attendance in Convention subjected him, almost killed him" (Farrand, 1913:60).

The Delegates

The fifty-five delegates who attended the Convention—only thirty of whom participated regularly in

the proceedings—constituted an unusually talented group. They came from all the states of the union except Rhode Island, which refused to send a delegation. Some were merely respectable members of their communities, but many were highly intelligent, well-read, thoughtful, and experienced. Several of them engaged in historical and philosophical studies in preparation for the problems the Convention would face; Madison, for example, prepared a history of confederacies. Nearly all the delegates could boast extensive political experience.

Twenty-one had fought in the Revolutionary War, six had signed the Declaration of Independence, forty-six had served in colonial or state legislatures, thirty-nine had served in Congress, and seven had been state governors. For all this experience, however, the delegates tended to be rather young. Although George Washington was then 55, Hamilton was only 30, Madison 36, and Gouverneur Morris 35. Benjamin Franklin, at 81, was the oldest member of the Convention by some 15 years.

A few famous leaders of the Revolution were conspicuously absent, and one wonders whether James Madison, who so dominated the proceedings, could have played as prominent a role if they had been at the Convention. The two leading intellectual figures of the Revolution—Thomas Jefferson and John Adams—were serving as ministers in Europe; the great patriot Samuel Adams was ill; and America's most renowned rhetorician, Patrick Henry, refused to attend, claiming that he "smelt a rat" (Farrand, 1913:15).

Besides their extensive experience in political life, most of the delegates at the Convention had substantial business and propertied interests. This fact, together with the founders' arguments about the need to protect property, led many at the time to wonder whether the delegates were not attempting to establish a government for a propertied elite. More than a century later, when the Constitution again came under attack for elitism by progressive reformers, a well-known historian, Charles Beard, developed this line of argument into a full-scale economic account of the founding (Beard, 1913). Beard contended that those who had designed the Constitution and fought for its ratification made up an urban and mercantile elite that was seeking to profit economically from the new government. The struggle over the Constitution, according to Beard, was an economic battle between the oligarchically minded founders and the mass of simple democrats. The founders managed to win the struggle and institute a nondemocratic system by their superior organization and by restrictions on the suffrage.

Beard's thesis, which projected an elitist interpretation back onto the origins of American politics, initially found a large and sympathetic audience. Yet subsequent research has done much to call it into question. By one account, more than one-fourth of the delegates "had important economic interests that were adversely affected, directly and immediately, by the Constitution" (McDonald, 1958:349). Morever, in the ratification debate, people of all classes could be found on *both* sides of the question, indicating that economic interests were perhaps not the only question or were viewed in very different ways.

There is little doubt that concrete issues were at stake in the struggle and that many consulted their interests; and there is even less doubt that the founders sought the backing of propertied segments of the population, for they openly proclaimed the importance of protecting property as an element of liberty and of preventing abuses against it. Yet, merely because the founders sought to protect property does not mean that they were motivated chiefly by the desire to promote their own economic interests. Some at the Convention were surely concerned about their economic well-being, but clearly some were more concerned with a different form of self-interest—their chance for the glory and fame of founding a successful republic. Moreover, it is unlikely that many of those who had jeopardized their interests in the Revolutionary War a decade earlier would turn into petty calculators of economic gain. Without denying the importance of economic interest as a motive, we shall proceed without further attempts to explain the founders' thought and allow their arguments to speak for themselves.

The Choices of the Convention

The delegates faced an enormous task. They had to decide whether merely to revise the Articles (as they had been authorized) or to devise an entirely new national government (as many of the delegates had all along intended). They had to decide on the form of government and the role that the people would play in it. And they had to decide on the ever-vexing question of what to do about slavery. On each of these matters there were important disputes requiring compromise. The necessity for compromise does not mean, however, that the Constitution is merely a bundle of compromises, a "patch-work sewn together . . . by a group of extremely talented democratic politicians" (Roche, 1961:815). Rather, beyond the give and take of deliberation and bargaining the framers adhered in common to certain fixed principles—liberty and self-government, for example, and even the structural principle of separation of powers—which set the boundaries of debate and the limits of compromise. Without underlying theoretical agreement, no workable compromises were possible (Diamond et al., 1970:57).

To complicate their task, the framers could look to no single political system, past or present, as the model for a new American government. England, with its monarchy and aristocratic traditions, could not be copied. The state governments, in spite of a few admirable features, mostly furnished examples of what to avoid rather than what to do. Nor did the past offer much positive guidance. "It is impossible to read the history of the petty republics of Greece and Italy," Hamilton would later observe in the ninth *Federalist,* "without feeling sensations of horror and disgust at the distractions with which they were continually agitated, and at the rapid succession of revolutions by which they were kept in a state of perpetual vibration between the extremes of tyranny and anarchy." In trying to remedy the defects of bygone republics and compensate for the inadequacies of experience, the framers would have to ground the American Constitution on new principles.

A National versus a Confederal System

Certainly the most important question facing the Convention—and the one first debated—was whether to abandon the Articles and form a national government. Realizing, perhaps, that the manner in which an issue is formulated will often determine the outcome, James Madison decided it was best to present at the outset an entirely new scheme of government based on national principles. Introduced by Governor Edmund Randolph on behalf of the Virginia delegation, but drafted primarily by Madison, the proposal became known as the "Virginia Plan." It called for a "strong consolidated union." The national government, divided into three branches, would have extensive powers on all questions on which the states were not competent to act, and the legislature would be able to veto any laws passed by the states. The legislature would consist of two houses, the first or "lower"

house chosen by the people and the second or "upper" house elected by the lower house. (Nothing was said about equality of representation for the states in the second branch.)

This striking plan caught the opponents of a strong union off guard. After fighting a rearguard action for two weeks, the opposition finally offered a counterproposal. Presented by William Paterson of New Jersey and known as the "New Jersey Plan," the scheme called for a series of amendments to the Articles of Confederation that would have strengthened the power of Congress to raise money, and added a federal judiciary and an executive council empowered to use force to compel compliance with the Confederation's laws. Clearly, the New Jersey Plan had moved in the direction of a national government, but in its essentials, it remained confederal in character. The Congress would be chosen by the state legislatures and represent the states, not the people directly; federal laws would apply only to states, not to individuals; and the powers of the general government would be severely limited. The plan had the backing of those who were philosophically opposed to a strong national government. In addition, it drew support on practical grounds from some of the small-state delegates who worried that a national government along the lines proposed in the Virginia Plan would enable the larger states to dominate the new government.

The New Jersey Plan, however, was far from what the predominantly nationally minded delegates were seeking. It was decisively defeated when the convention voted seven states to three in favor of the Virginia Plan. Now the convention had finally resolved against any purely confederal plan. But the question of the kind of representation for the states in the national government remained unresolved, and the battle lines were immediately redrawn for the fiercest struggle at the convention.

The nationally minded delegates, having won the vote on the Virginia Plan, pressed ahead on their plan for a bicameral legislature in which representation in *both* the House and the Senate would be apportioned on the basis of population. The opposition now dug in, arguing that each state should have the same number of votes in Congress. The Convention decided after extensive debate that representation in the House would be based on population. But they could not agree on the principle of representation for the Senate, and here the Convention deadlocked.

At this critical point, with both tempers and late June heat on the rise, the Connecticut delegates, Dr. William Johnson and Oliver Ellsworth, stepped in. Johnson proposed a combination of the principles of representing the nation as a whole and by states. Instead of the two ideas "being opposed to each other [they] ought to be combined; . . . in one branch, the people ought to be represented; in the other, the States." Ellsworth concurred: "We were partly national; partly federal . . . on this middle ground a compromise would take place" (Farrand, 1966:I, 461–62, 468). This plan, known as the "Great Compromise" or "Connecticut Compromise," was voted by a committee appointed over the Fourth of July holiday. When the committee submitted its plan, it was narrowly adopted. The compromise created a House, apportioned roughly on the basis of population, whose members would be elected by the voting public. The Senate would consist of two senators from each state, chosen by the state legislatures. The plan also called for a single, independent executive and a judicial branch. Many important choices about the institutions still had to be made, and there remained many points on which the delegates continued to disagree. But with the single greatest hurdle cleared, the Convention was able to resolve other problems without the looming threat that all might end in bitter disagreement.

The Sectional Problem and Slavery

In addition to the great problem over the character of the union, which divided small and large states, there was the problem of conflicting interests between *sections* of the nation, particularly the north and the south. The south was primarily agricultural, while the north had developed a commercial component to its economy. This difference led to jockeying between the sections on several Convention economic issues. The south wanted a guarantee against export duties since much of its agricultural production was sent abroad. The Convention complied (Article I, section 9). The south also wanted a requirement that all internal commercial

regulations be decided by a two-thirds majority in Congress, thus giving the southern states a veto over laws that might, for example, require all goods to be shipped in American-built vessels. The Convention refused to require any extraordinary majority in this instance, but the south's interest played some part in the decision to require that all treaties be ratified by two-thirds of the Senate.

By far the most important sectional questions, however, had to do with slavery. This issue was dealt with in a series of compromises illustrating the Convention's skill at averting deadlock and resolving major disagreements between the sections. The most important of these compromises came after the Convention had agreed that the "direct taxes" Congress was empowered to levy be apportioned among the states according to population. The problem lay in defining "population." If the definition included slaves, the southern states would have to bear a larger tax burden. Consequently, southern delegates demanded that slaves be given less weight than free citizens for purposes of taxation. On the other hand, if slaves were counted as full members of the population for purposes of deciding on representation in the population-based House of Representatives, the south would possibly control half the seats. Accordingly, the north wanted slaves to have less weight than free citizens for the purpose of determining representation. From these conflicting sectional views emerged the "Three-Fifths Compromise." This formula, already in use under the Articles, stated that for purposes of both taxation and representation, five blacks would be counted the equivalent of three whites.

A second slavery-related compromise is reflected in Article IV, section 2, of the Constitution (now repealed). This required the extradition of fugitive slaves from one state to another. The third compromise dealt with the slave trade. Southern delegates worried that Congress, having been empowered to regulate commerce, might interfere with the importation of slaves from Africa. The result was a provision in the Constitution forbidding Congress to outlaw the trade for twenty years.

Some critics, most notably the nineteenth-century abolitionists, have attacked the founders for making "immoral" compromises. Many of the fra-

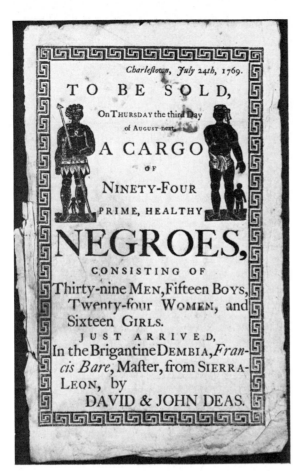

Charleſtown, *July* 24*th*, 1769.

TO BE SOLD,

On THURSDAY the third Day
of AUGUST next

A CARGO

OF

NINETY-FOUR

PRIME, HEALTHY

NEGROES,

CONSISTING OF

Thirty-nine MEN, Fifteen BOYS,
Twenty-four WOMEN, and
Sixteen GIRLS.

JUST ARRIVED,

In the Brigantine DEMBIA, *Francis Bare*, Maſter, from SIERRA-
LEON, by

DAVID & JOHN DEAS.

To preserve the union, the delegates to the Constitutional Convention accepted the continuation of slavery even though many of them knew that slavery could not be reconciled with the principles of the Declaration of Independence. *(Plimpton Slavery Collection)*

THE BASIC PRINCIPLES OF THE CONSTITUTION

As we noted in Chapter 1, the constitution of any society refers to how that society is organized, meaning its basic ends or goals, the scope of governmental authority, the distribution of power, the arrangement of institutions, and the basic provisions for defending the society's interests and values. As a *legal* document, the better part of the United States Constitution deals with the scope of governmental authority, the distribution of power, and the arrangement of institutions. The questions of ends and defense are noted in the Preamble to the Constitution and implied in the decisions made by the framers on the other three questions. In analyzing the basic principles of the Constitution, we shall accordingly treat the ends of society and the provision for defense within a discussion of the structure of the government.

The Scope of Government:
A Strong but Limited Government

Americans of the founding generation were highly suspicious of strong government, especially government far away from home. For many, this suspicion had been the central lesson learned from the colonial experience. After all, had not the government of Great Britain used its extensive powers to subvert basic liberties? And could not a strong American government do the same? This, at any rate, seemed to be the dominant frame of mind among many Americans in the 1780s.

The authors of the Constitution shared this suspicion of strong government, but only up to a point. Whereas opponents of the Constitution spoke constantly of guarding people's liberties against a new and powerful government, the founders spoke of the need for energy, stability, and order. Without an effective government, they argued, liberties could not be protected. "Vigor of government," Hamilton wrote, "is essential to the security of liberty" (*Federalist* 1).

Neither the opponents of the Constitution nor the founders wanted an unlimited government. But in drawing the limits of governmental power, the opponents would have been much more stingy. They wanted to keep more powers under the con-

mers were not insensible to the evil of slavery. Even southern delegates like George Mason, himself the owner of 200 slaves, lamented its continued existence. But clearly the southern states would not have consented to abolition. Therefore the delegates faced the choice of forcing the slavery issue with the risk of destroying the union and leaving slavery intact, or compromising and preserving the union, with the possibility that in time the whole slavery question could be resolved fairly and peacefully and without shattering the union.

BOX 2-2

CONSTITUTIONAL DISTRIBUTION OF POWERS

"The proposed Constitution," James Madison wrote in the thirty-ninth *Federalist,* "is, in strictness, neither a national nor a federal [i.e., confederal] constitution, but a composition of both." As might be expected from Madison's description, the Constitution divides power between the national and state governments. Listed below are some of the powers denied or delegated to each.

Some powers denied by the Constitution

To the national government

    To tax articles exported from one state to another
    To deprive a state of equal representation in the Senate

To the state governments

    To lay duties on imports and exports
    To coin money
    To enter into treaties, alliances, and confederations

To the national and state governments

    To grant titles of nobility

Some powers granted by the Constitution

To the national government

    To levy taxes, duties, and imposts
    To regulate commerce with foreign nations and among the states
    To coin money
    To declare war
    To create and provide for an army and navy
    To make all laws necessary and proper for exercising its constitutional powers

To the state governments

    To establish local governments
    To hold elections
    To regulate intrastate commerce

To the national and state governments

    To levy taxes
    To borrow money
    To establish courts
    To make and execute laws

trol of the states, deny further specific powers to the federal government, and tie more strings to those powers that were granted to it. The Constitution contains limitations of all kinds (see Box 2-2), but the founders also *transferred* authority from the states to the central government in certain areas. The power to coin money and print paper currency, for example, was shifted to the national government, not only because of the need for uniform currency, but because the states had exercised this power unwisely. In most cases the founders also fought the idea of hampering too much the exercise of important governmental power. For instance, the Constitution grants Congress the powers to "raise and support armies" and to "provide and maintain a navy." It does not limit how large

such forces may be or how much money may be spent on them. "Every power," declared Hamilton, "ought to be in proportion to its object" (*Federalist* 30). Since the amount of power needed to defend against enemies cannot be specified in advance, why limit the authority needed to provide for the common defense?

Government, then, was to be at once limited and strong. The Constitution would grant as well as withhold power. By twentieth-century standards, of course, the powers originally granted the national government seem rather meager. The Constitution has been amended and stretched through interpretation to encompass aims not originally specified—for example, the power to aid education and provide welfare and social security. These and other new powers of government have developed largely in the era since the 1930s, as the public has embraced the belief that more government power is needed to promote a basic level of welfare services. For Americans today, therefore, the Constitution, if interpreted literally, implies a government that most would judge far too limited. But to understand the conditions out of which the Constitution emerged, it is necessary to recall that the founders were claiming *more* power for the government than most Americans at the time were initially disposed to grant.

Given that government would be so strong—at least by the standards of Americans of that time—how could it be controlled? What could stop it from seizing powers that were not granted to it, or from exercising legitimate powers in a way that might threaten people's liberties? These were among the most important questions raised against the Constitution during the struggle over ratification. Part of the founders' answer were provisions in the written Constitution which specified the powers government would be granted and implied that the Supreme Court would be able to enforce Constitutional limitations. But this answer was not sufficient, for, as the founders realized, the power of the Court alone would be insufficient to prevent those in power from ignoring the Constitution or turning the use of its broad powers against the people. The founders' main answer was found in the doctrines of separation of powers and checks and balances. While the power of the government *as a whole* would be formidable, there would be a division of power among the institutions *within* the government that would erect a powerful barrier against tyranny. We shall return to this point, but first we must look at the basic distribution of power in the American political system.

The Distribution of Power: Who Rules?

Did the Constitution establish a democratic system? At the Constitutional Convention and in *The Federalist,* the founders constantly drew a distinction between a *democracy* and a *republic.* By a "democracy," they meant what we would call a "direct" or "pure" democracy—a form of government in which the people vote directly on the poli-

cies and the actions to be pursued. (Not even the small republics in the states realized this objective.) By a "republic," they meant a system in which the people do not govern directly, but turn power over to representatives who are chosen directly or indirectly by the public. Madison defined a republic very carefully as a "government which derives all its powers directly or indirectly from the great body of the people, and is administered by persons holding their offices during pleasure for a limited period, or during good behavior" (*Federalist* 39).

Democracies and republics are both species of popular government since the ultimate power in each system lies with the broad mass of the public and not with one particular class or element of society. But the distinction between a democracy and a republic (especially a large republic) is crucial. A pure democracy, the founders argued, was not only limited in its size—and therefore incapable of defending itself—but also could not be relied upon to protect freedom. Pure democracies as they had existed before (chiefly in ancient Greece) tended to degenerate into rule by mobs, in which the passions of the people (not their better judgment) posed a constant threat to the rights of others and even to themselves. A republic or representative democracy, on the other hand, offered the possibility of a government in which the sense of the majority would ultimately rule, but in which the rights of minorities and the requirements of effective government would also be protected.

In contrast to some of the opponents of the Constitution, who saw no tension between popular government and the protection of rights and property, the founders frankly warned of the dangers posed by what they called a "majority faction." A "faction," in the eighteenth-century sense of the word, is a group of people who advance their private interests at the expense of other citizens or the permanent interests of the nation. In a popular form of government, whether a democracy or a republic, a majority faction could seize control of the government and threaten the rights and interests of others. A republic, however, offered two ways of reducing the danger of majority faction: (1) government decisions might be made by representatives with broader sympathies and greater experience than the average citizen, and (2) a republic, unlike

---

BOX 2-3

THE FEDERALIST PAPERS

In the fall of 1787 Alexander Hamilton enlisted the aid of James Madison and John Jay to write a series of articles for New York newspapers explaining and defending the proposed Constitution. Together, these politically seasoned and reflective republicans wrote eighty-five articles, which collectively became known as *The Federalist.* Although written in haste to aid in the ratification fight in New York, *The Federalist* constitutes the best explanation and defense of the Constitution ever written, as well as the most profound examination of republican government ever produced in the United States.

The authors originally kept their identities secret, publishing the papers under the pen name of

"Publius." The original Publius, a statesman of ancient Rome, had been instrumental in establishing the Roman republic and in alerting its citizenry to dangers to freedom that lurked within it. The authors of *The Federalist* apparently saw themselves as playing a similar role as both founders and educators of the American republic. Today we know that Hamilton wrote fifty-one of the papers, Madison twenty-six, and Jay five, and Hamilton and Madison wrote three jointly.

The two most famous of the papers, *Federalist* 10 and 51 (both written by Madison), address the problems of "majority faction" and abuse of power by government officials.

---

a pure democracy in which the people had to be able to meet together, could be large. And a large republic was more conducive to liberty, the founders thought, than a pure democracy or a small republic. Let us consider further these two points.

Representation A representative is someone authorized to speak for someone else. The Constitution established a government in which all power was held by representatives or persons appointed by representatives and in which the people had no direct power in their collective capacity. Under the Constitution, the people directly chose the members of the House and indirectly selected the president and the members of the Senate. Supreme Court justices were appointed by the president and confirmed by the Senate, as were certain civil and military officers.

To the framers, representation offered a way to improve the decisions of government. The founders did not expect voters to elect people to office who were simply carbon copies of the electorate, but rather people who were generally more knowledgeable and experienced. Even more so would this be the case, they believed, with representatives chosen indirectly by other representatives. Furthermore, representatives would operate in an environment of established institutions that would foster collective

reasoning about common concerns. The average citizen, on the other hand, would usually lack the time, inclination, and means to engage in a similar enterprise.

Representation, then, is a way of refining and enlarging the judgment of the people. It requires, however, a certain balance. If the representatives are at too great a distance from the people, they will no longer reflect the sense of the community. The representative system would then be insufficiently democratic. Yet if representatives become too much like the people, they may no longer be able to perform the special tasks for which the people chose them. The fulfillment of the framers' hopes, therefore, depends on a number of other factors which we shall look at more closely later in this book: the availability and willingness of capable people to run for office, the intelligence of the voters and the information they are supplied, and the kind of candidates produced by the way in which elections are organized.

A Large Republic Representation offered only a partial solution to the threat of majority faction, for representatives, too, could be captured by the spirit of such a faction and made to serve its interests. In fact, it was exactly this, the founders argued, which had occurred in some of the small republics—that is, the American states—during the period of the Articles.

A large state had always been thought to offer the advantage of being better able to provide for the defense of its citizens than a small one. The founders now added a new doctrine to western political thought. A large *republic,* they argued, could better secure a people against the threat of majority faction than either a pure democracy or a small republic. The founders' reasoning on this point is crucial for understanding the Constitution and the operation of the American political system today.

The founders began with the premise that wherever liberty existed, factions would inevitably follow: "Liberty is to faction what air is to fire" (*Federalist* 10). Liberty creates factions because it enables individuals to pursue their own happiness and develop their talents in various ways. Differences of opinion and differences in the amount and type of property inevitably result. Individuals then naturally form into different groups or factions, seeking to protect and promote their interests.

The founders conceded that it might be possible to eliminate the cause of faction by creating a state that enforced the same opinions and divided property equally. This was the solution that some small republics had attempted in earlier eras, though with only limited success. The problem with this cure was that it was infinitely worse than the disease: in eliminating factions, it would also eliminate liberty. As long as liberty was accepted as the aim of political life, factions would have to be tolerated. The grave political error of the small-republic theorists in the United States, the founders contended, was that they were unwilling to face up to this reality. They wanted *both* liberty and the kind of civic virtue that would suppress factions. Unfortunately, they could not have both.

Given that liberty was the aim of political life and that factions would inevitably result, the problem of the constitution maker became how best to control the *effects* of faction. Here the superiority of the large republic over the small one became apparent. In a small republic, with a relatively simple economy and with people constantly in contact with one another, a strong probability existed that a faction would constitute a majority and seize control of the government. If, for example, the majority were made up of farmers and those farmers fell

into debt, they could quickly organize and press their advantage at the expense of their creditors. The same thing could occur in the case of conflict between two religious sects or two racial groups.

A large republic offered a much better chance of controlling the mischiefs of faction. A large republic, and especially one with a large commercial component, would encourage a multiplicity of economic interests, religious groups, and local attachments and loyalties. The very number and diversity of these different interests would make it unlikely that any one of them would constitute a majority, and even where a potential majority might exist, it would take much longer for a group to realize its situation and organize effectively. Majorities would form either by representatives looking beyond the stalemate of contending factions to a more general principle of "justice and the general good" (*Federalist* 51) or else by groups coming together to form coalitions. These broad coalitions would exact moderation as the price any faction would have to pay to become part of a majority.

Two important implications of this large-republic solution should be noted. The first is that such a political system includes as part of its normal course of operation the interplay of interest groups. *Pluralism,* or the competition of various groups to protect and promote their interests, is not only tolerated, but welcomed. As a result, much of American politics is devoid of great principle. It is—and was intended to be—in some degree a continuous process of adjustment and bargaining among interest groups. The constantly shifting alliances of groups would generally cut across the great divide of rich and poor, enabling competition among interest groups to replace the class struggle. The solution was designed to create a politics that was not so much elevated as it was effective in avoiding tyranny.

Second, the large-republic solution is based on a highly "realistic" view of human nature. It does not seek to solve the problem of factions by suppressing them and relying entirely on the public's love of the general good. Rather, it allows people to pursue their self-interest, but in a setting in which no great harm will usually result. The solution relies not on civic virtue but on an arrangement of the circumstances of society. It envisions compromise and bargaining as the order of the day. The quintessential American politician to perform these tasks is the one skilled at brokering various interests and discovering workable alliances.

However ingenious this solution may be, there are clear limits to its effectiveness. It is not, nor was it intended to be, descriptive of the entire political process. It can work tolerably well to avoid majority tyranny in most situations in normal times, but it cannot provide—and has not provided—answers for many of the great moral and political crises of American politics, like the battles over slavery and civil rights. These have required citizens whose actions transcend mere interest and leaders who are able to raise political debate to a higher level of principle. The founders certainly did not foreclose the possibility for this kind of politics, although they have sometimes been criticized for not sufficiently foreseeing the need for it. Their task, in any case, was to establish a government that could provide a solid grounding for a stable political order.

They could not reasonably have been expected to foresee every problem of American politics.

The Arrangement of Institutions: Complex Government

The founders were involved in a delicate balancing act. They were seeking simultaneously to prevent tyranny—tyranny of the many as well as of the few—and to promote sound governance. Their solution called for a complex government of separation of powers, checks and balances, and federalism. It is no wonder, then, that the American system of government is so difficult to understand when compared with simpler systems in most other nations. Nor is it any surprise that over the course of our history, the Constitution has been attacked from opposite sides, one claiming that the government is too energetic and powerful, the other that it is weak and ineffective.

TABLE 2-1
MAJOR CONSTITUTIONAL OFFICES

	House of Representatives	Senate	President	Supreme Court
Membership	Number determined by Congress (currently 435), apportioned by population with at least one for each state	Two from each state	One	Number to be determined by Congress (currently nine)
Method of selection	By the people	Originally by the state legislatures; after the Seventeenth Amendment (1913), by the people	Electoral college; if no majority there, House of Representatives chooses from among top three	Nominated by the president; confirmed by the Senate
Minimum age	25 years old	30 years old	35 years old	None
Other qualifications	Must have been a citizen for seven years and an inhabitant of the state from which elected	Must have been a citizen for nine years and an inhabitant of the state from which elected	Must be a natural-born citizen and a resident of the United States for fourteen years	None
Term of office	Two years	Six years, with one-third of Senate elected every second year	Four years; originally indefinitely reeligible, but as a result of Twenty-Second Amendment (1951) restricted to two terms	During good behavior

Executive power was dramatically demonstrated in 1957 when President Eisenhower sent Army paratroops to Little Rock to enforce a federal court's order to integrate the high school. *(Burt Glinn/Magnum)*

Separation of Powers The framers created a structure of government characterized by a division of power into three separate branches. Each of the three chief functions of government—making laws, enforcing laws and administering the government, and interpreting laws—is assigned primarily, but by no means exclusively, to one branch. The legislative function is given to Congress, the executive function to the president, and the judicial function to the court system.

Separating powers is one way of avoiding tyranny since no institution possesses by itself the full authority of the government. It is also a way, however, of providing for certain qualities in governing. The assignment of each distinct function of government principally to a different branch of government causes a branch particularly suited to perform that function to be shaped. Thus the principal task of Congress, to make laws, is best performed by a relatively large group of people who can bring to the task an awareness of the different views and interests that characterize the country as a whole.

Speed of decision making is sacrificed to the need for broad representation and deliberation.

Executive power, by contrast, is concentrated in the hands of a single individual because of the distinctive requirement for energy, secrecy, and speed in the execution of certain policies. Members of a council frequently must compromise with each other, making delay or deadlock more likely. But a single individual can act decisively. For example, when the governor of Arkansas resisted federal court-ordered integration in Little Rock in 1957, President Eisenhower was able to dispatch troops quickly to maintain order and carry out the court's directives. If the matter had been debated in Congress, there would have been heated and prolonged exchanges, a decision might have been postponed, and disorder might have increased. The founders also looked to the president as the head of the government, able to represent the public interest as a whole and exercise broad initiative, especially in the area of foreign affairs.

Finally, in the Supreme Court, the founders

tried to establish an institution that would protect the law and the Constitution. Confirmation of judges by the Senate after nomination by the president was the least democratic of all the methods of filling federal offices. It was designed to help ensure the selection of individuals possessing the special qualification of legal competence. In addition, the founders established a life tenure for the judges, believing that this would free the courts from the usual pressures of democratic representation.

Checks and Balances   Having decided on the wisdom of separating powers, the founders next pondered the practical question of how to maintain that separation in practice. The obvious difficulty was that one of the branches of government might overwhelm the others and eventually pull all the power of government into its own hands. Merely writing limits into a Constitution would be insufficient, for a piece of paper cannot by itself restrain the drive for power by headstrong individuals. Of course, free elections would provide one restraint. But the founders deemed it prudent to rely as well on the "auxiliary precaution" of checks among the institutions of the government. They reasoned that each institution must be given the means and the will to protect its prerogatives against possible assaults by the other institutions. In protecting its own powers, each institution would also serve the general public interest of preventing the other institutions from exercising tyrannical measures against the people.

But how to establish these checks? One way, paradoxically, was to mix or blend some of the essential powers of the government. Above, we said that the founders had assigned largely separate functions to the legislative, executive, and judicial branches. But to maintain the independence of each branch, the founders "violated" the maxim of *pure* separation by giving each branch some share of the power of the others. For example, the president was given a share of the legislative power through the provision of a qualified veto of all bills passed by the legislature; the legislature, in turn, was given part of the executive function through its ability to confirm executive appointments. Of course, as one begins to analyze the various powers of government, it often becomes impossible to spec-

ify exactly what is a pure legislative, executive, or judicial function. But the main point to stress here is that the founders deliberately sought to blend some of the functions of government. To some extent, then, we have a government of separate institutions *sharing* the same powers.

Another means of enhancing the ability of each institution to check the others was to assure each an essential independence. Thus the founders decided not to have the president elected by the legislature, as had originally been proposed in the Virginia Plan. One reason was that if the legislature selected the president, the president might soon become dependent on Congress. In the case of the Supreme Court, although its members would be nominated by the president and confirmed by the Senate, a life tenure would guarantee the judges' subsequent independence. The founders added one further practical measure. Congress, which had the initial power of the purse, was barred from ever reducing the salaries of the president or the Supreme Court justices while the same persons held office.

Of all the branches of government, the founders were clearly worried most about the power of the legislature. From observing the state governments, they had concluded that the legislature was the institution most likely to absorb all the power of government into its hands. (This was probably because the legislatures at the time were the most popular of all the institutions and therefore most likely to be able to claim the right to speak for the public.) In order to check the power of the legislature, therefore, the framers decided to create an internal balance by establishing two separate assemblies. In this system of *bicameralism,* both the Senate and the House of Representatives must concur in the passage of any piece of legislation. The Senate, whose members were elected indirectly (until 1913) and served a six-year term, was designed especially to serve as a kind of "upper house" that would frequently check the instability and populist demands of the House of Representatives. The Senate was yet another hedge against the possibility of majority faction seizing control of the government.

Underlying the effective operation of the system of checks and balances is the same "realistic" understanding of human nature that was evident in the solution to the problem of factions. The motives on which the founders relied to maintain the separation of powers included not only a concern for the public good but also the self-interested desire of officials to protect the power of their own institution. The founders believed that because politicians normally want to exercise more power, this motive, if properly channeled, could be used to fortify their resolve. As Madison wrote: "Ambition must be made to counteract ambition" (*Federalist* 51).

Federalism   The predominant spirit of the convention was nationalist, but this did not mean that the founders were opposed to the existence of strong and vigorous state governments operating within their proper sphere. The national government was intended to be strong but limited; beyond its limited authority, power would reside with the states. Moreover, the states, as we have seen, were partly represented as states—or at any rate their equality was acknowledged—within the national government in the Senate.

The existence of the states serves the twin purposes of making government more effective and providing yet another protection for liberty. The decentralization of authority to the states enables each particular area to develop policies according to the standards of local majorities, thus relieving the national government of a whole range of concerns on which it could not safely impose a uniform principle. At the same time, should the national government threaten to become tyrannical, the states could serve as a rallying point to help check it.

The division of power between the national government and the states was one of the most delicate of the tasks the founders confronted. Moreover, the argument over "states' rights," at the heart of the whole debate between nationalists and small-republic advocates, reemerged in the ratification process and again in the early struggles between the nation's first political parties. The use of states as "rallying points" to protect liberty lay behind the Virginia and Kentucky resolutions written in 1798 to protest the unconstitutionality of the Alien and Sedition Acts. These resolutions introduced the idea that states could nullify federal laws they believed unconstitutional. The states again became "rallying points" in the nullification crisis of 1832–1833, when South Carolina, drawing on the earlier

example, claimed the power to declare national laws invalid. This doctrine eventually formed the legal question that led to the Civil War, when the southern states claimed a right to secede from a union they deemed tyrannical. Even with the resolution of that crisis, the claim of "states' rights" remained as a justification for resistance until the 1960s. Today, the question of the proper division of power between the national government and the states remains a fundamental issue, but the notion of using a state as an agent of open resistance to the national government has been repudiated.

RATIFICATION

According to some of the great political thinkers of classical antiquity, one of the central problems in political life is that of reconciling wisdom with consent. Many previous constitution makers, as Madison observed, had been able to engineer consent for their governments by "mixing a portion of violence with the authority of superstition" (*Federalist* 38). Neither of these means, however, was sought by the framers or available to them. Instead, they had to win the free consent of the public. As much as the Constitution itself, the method by which it was ratified helped secure a firm foundation for the new republic. As Alexis de Tocqueville remarked about the two-year-long ratification process:

> That which is new in the history of societies is to see a great people, warned by its lawgivers that the wheels of government are stopping, turn its attention on itself without haste or fear, sound the depth of the ill, and then wait for two years to find the remedy at leisure, and then finally, when the remedy has been indicated, submit to it voluntarily without its costing humanity a single tear or drop of blood (Tocqueville, 1968:113).

The framers, of course, were not blinded to the practical problems of securing consent. They defined their own method for ratification, boldly ignoring the process of amendment outlined in the Articles. They went outside existing channels by stipulating in Article VII that the Constitution would go into effect after being ratified by *conventions* in *nine* of the states. The Congress of the Articles silently acquiesced to this plan by forwarding

BOX 2-4

ON THE ORIGIN OF THE TERM "FEDERALISM"

The choice of terminology during the ratification debate amounted to an important victory for the Federalists. Before 1787, the terms "federal" and "confederal" were synonymous. Strictly speaking, a federal system was a decentralized, confederate government like that of the Articles. In adopting the name of *Federalists* and forcing their rivals to accept the name of *Antifederalists,* proponents of the Constitution appropriated a term already in wide use, but gave it their own novel meaning: the modern sense of "federal," which refers to a government that is neither entirely unitary nor entirely confederal, but a mixture of the two. The Antifederalists were forced to accept a label which made them appear opposed to the very form of government they advocated. The term "federal government" today means the national government, but "federalism" refers to the division of power between the national government and the states.

the Constitution to the states for their consideration, though without ever approving it. No more, perhaps, could have been asked of a government that was placing its own existence in jeopardy.

This idea of using conventions, and thereby bypassing the state governments, was appealing on several counts. Conventions represented the most democratic method known at the time for expressing the public's will and therefore seemed the best way of instituting a government by the "consent of the governed." But this theoretical argument was probably less important than were pragmatic considerations. Because the new government would reduce the power and authority of the state governments, giving the decision to state officials would have been an almost certain prescription for failure. Going through the state legislatures would also have implied that the new government was a mere compact of the several states, rather than a national government formed by "we the people" acting through popularly elected convention delegates. Finally, by ignoring the method of amendment spelled out in the Articles, the framers were able to avoid its provision for unanimous consent, which had proved so unworkable in earlier attempts to change the Articles.

The Debate on Ratification

The process of ratifying the Constitution produced a sober and exhaustive discussion of the nation's political principles. Both sides could boast of some very formidable political leaders. Besides most of the delegates to the Convention, friends of the Constitution—who by now were calling themselves "Federalists"—included John Adams, John Marshall, and, with some reservations, Thomas Jefferson. Their opponents, who came to be known as "Antifederalists" (see Box 2-4), included such figures as the powerful George Clinton and Richard Henry Lee of New York and Patrick Henry of Virginia. Joining them were George Mason, Elbridge Gerry, and Edmund Randolph, all of whom had attended the Convention but refused to sign the Constitution. (Under Washington's influence, Randolph switched sides near the end of debate in Virginia.)

During the ratification proceedings of the various conventions, and in numerous newspaper articles and pamphlets published throughout the country, opponents of the Constitution—who by no means spoke with one voice—barraged it with criticisms, some petty and some to the point. It was argued, among other things, that under the new government the president might become a monarch; that the states would forfeit their sovereignty; that the people could ill afford to pay taxes to both state and national governments; that a standing army created by Congress would oppress the citizenry; that the Constitution gave too much protection to the institution of slavery (in part a Quaker criticism), or too little (the criticism of some southern planters); and that it contained too few safeguards for religious freedom (a Baptist concern). And, as already observed, many Antifederalists attacked the Constitution from the small-republic point of view, agreeing with Patrick Henry that it was hostile to the "spirit of republicanism" and would create "one great, consolidated, national government" that would crush the states (Rossiter, 1966:283–284).

The framers were able to answer most of these objections as well as to press home their major argument that the new government, even though not entirely satisfactory to everyone, represented the best possible scheme to which all might consent. Even so, the going was extremely difficult, and a successful outcome was by no means a certainty. In Pennsylvania, the legislature could only call a convention after a mob forced the attendance of Antifederalists who had been boycotting the session in order to prevent a quorum. In New York, ratification came about through the brilliant maneuvering of Alexander Hamilton, but by only three votes, and only after New York City threat-

ened to secede if ratification failed. The story in several other states was similar. Finally, however, on June 21, 1788, New Hampshire became the ninth state to ratify, and the Constitution became law. By 1790, even contrary-minded Rhode Island had joined the union.

The Bill of Rights

The difficult campaign for ratification would almost certainly have been lost if the Federalists had not agreed to one more implicit compromise: the addition of a bill of rights. The Constitution, of course, contained a provision for amendment (see Figure 2-1), but the framers certainly did not expect that a major series of amendments would be voted in the near future. However, as the ratification debate proceeded, support for a bill of rights gained ground, and several conventions agreed to ratify the Constitution only after they had recommended adding a set of amendments.

FIGURE 2-1
Methods of amending the Constitution. Article V of the Constitution specifies two methods of *proposing* amendments: a two-thirds vote of both houses of Congress or a national convention called by Congress "on the application of" two-thirds of the state legislatures. It further specifies two methods of *ratifying* amendments: approval by three-fourths of the state legislatures or by ratifying conventions in three-fourths of the states; in either case Congress chooses the methods of ratifying. To date, all amendments have been proposed by Congress, and all except the Twenty-First, which repealed the Eighteenth (Prohibition) Amendment, have been ratified by the state legislatures.

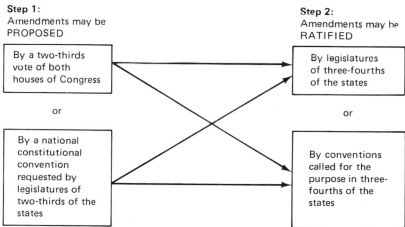

Step 1:
Amendments may be
PROPOSED

By a two-thirds vote of both houses of Congress

or

By a national constitutional convention requested by legislatures of two-thirds of the states

Step 2:
Amendments may be
RATIFIED

By legislatures of three-fourths of the states

or

By conventions called for the purpose in three-fourths of the states

---

BOX 2-5

CIVIL LIBERTIES GUARANTEED IN THE CONSTITUTION
BEFORE THE ADDITION OF A BILL OF RIGHTS

Opponents of the proposed Constitution complained that it lacked a bill of rights. Yet, as the Federalists pointed out, the new plan of government did include some provisions for the protection of personal liberties. These provisions are listed below in the order of their appearance in the Constitution:

1 Writs of habeas corpus may not be suspended unless, during rebellion or invasion, the "public safety may require it."

2 No bill of attainder may be passed by Congress or the states.

3 No one may hold a title of nobility.

4 No ex post facto law may be passed by Congress or the states.

5 Laws "impairing the obligation of contracts" may not be passed by the states.

6 Citizens accused of crimes are to be tried by jury "except in cases of impeachment."

7 Citizens of each state must possess "all privileges and immunities of citizens in the several states."

8 No one may be compelled to pass a religious test as a condition for holding federal office.

The Constitution provided the protection of certain rights (see Box 2-5), but it lacked an explicit statement protecting such basic liberties as freedom of speech and freedom of the press. The Federalists' explanation of this omission was based on the rather curious argument that because the government was one of enumerated powers, it lacked legitimate authority to pass any laws that would abridge these rights. Yet the Antifederalists pointed out the inconsistency of this position in light of the Constitution's guarantee of certain other liberties. In the end, the Antifederalists' argument prevailed, and the decision to add the Bill of Rights (see Box 2-6) was a victory for them and a sure sign that the open and free method of ratification had produced benefits of its own.

All the same, much of the credit for the Bill of Rights belongs to the Federalists, especially James Madison. Under the influence of his friend Jefferson, Madison had become convinced of the need for supplemental safeguards to liberty. In the first session of Congress, accordingly, Madison and his allies proposed twelve amendments, ten of which were approved and later became known as the Bill of Rights. Oddly, this action rekindled the whole Federalist-Antifederalist debate. States' rights advocates hoped to use the amending process to chip away at the powers of the national government. For instance, in what is now the Tenth Amendment,

they attempted to have the word "expressly" inserted after "delegated" in the clause that guaranteed to the states the "powers not delegated to the United States by the Constitution, nor prohibited by it to the States." Madison objected to the addition of this single word on the grounds that governments must necessarily possess *implied* as well as expressed powers; otherwise, the Constitution would have to "recount every minutia." He and the Federalist majority in Congress favored, and successfully pushed through the House and Senate, amendments which they felt would enhance individual liberty without depriving the central government of vigor.

It should be noted that originally the Bill of Rights gave citizens protection from the *federal* government, not from state government. The First Amendment, for example, requires that "*Congress* shall make no law respecting an establishment of religion"; nothing is said about the state legislatures, many of which had enacted, and would continue to enact, Sabbath laws and other religiously discriminatory legislation. Beginning with its decision in *Gitlow v. New York* (1925), however, the Supreme Court has increasingly used the "due process" section of the Fourteenth Amendment (1868) to incorporate most of the guarantees enumerated in the Bill of Rights. Now these rights are protected against actions by all levels of government (see Chapter 17).

BOX 2-6

THE BILL OF RIGHTS (AMENDMENTS I–X, RATIFIED 1791)

Positive rights

Amendment I   Freedom of religion, speech, press, and assembly; right to petition government for redress of grievances.

Amendment II   Right to bear arms.

Amendment III   No quartering of troops in private homes in peacetime.

Amendment IX   Rights not enumerated in Constitution are not necessarily denied the states.

Amendment X   Powers not delegated to the United States or denied to the states are reserved to the states or to the people.

Procedural rights

Amendment IV   No unreasonable searches or seizures.

Amendment V   Grand jury indictment required in serious criminal cases; no double jeopardy (standing trial twice for the same offense); no compelling of persons to testify against themselves; no taking of life, liberty, or property without due process of law.

Amendment VI   Right to a speedy and public trial by jury in criminal cases; right to legal counsel in criminal cases.

Amendment VII   Right to trial by jury in civil suits exceeding $20 in value.

Amendment VIII   No excessive bail or fines; no cruel and unusual punishment.

The Bill of Rights provides positive and procedural rights. *Positive* rights define the domain of individual or state freedom. *Procedural* rights protect citizens from illegal or arbitrary action by government. Speaking for the Supreme Court in *Barron v. Baltimore* (1833), Chief Justice John Marshall ruled that the Bill of Rights limits only the powers of the federal government, not the states; relying on the Fourteenth Amendment, the Court has applied most of these limits to state governments as well.

CONCLUSION

The two basic documents of the American founding are the Declaration and the Constitution. Many have charged that the two documents are inconsistent with one another, the Declaration speaking in a hopeful and democratic voice, the Constitution in a harsh and reactionary one (Beard, 1913). While there are clear differences in tone between the two documents, the authors of the Constitution believed it was basically consistent with the aims of the Declaration. The two documents, of course, had different purposes. The Declaration set forth the fundamental principles of legitimate government, but it did not specify a particular structure of government. The Constitution represented a choice about how these principles could be embodied in concrete institutional arrangements. Other choices, like the Articles, were possible and would have been equally consistent with the Declaration. (And all practical choices would have been equally inconsistent on certain great issues like slavery.)

Among the choices posed, the framers were convinced that they had established the best possible government under the circumstances. Its form was popular or republican, the only kind of government, in Madison's words, consistent with the "fundamental principles of the Revolution" (*Federalist* 39). And the system was further designed to fulfill the Declaration's basic goals of ensuring equality and protecting liberty, with the noted exceptions of those groups still excluded from a full place in the community. The consistency between the Declaration and the Constitution on these basic principles was probably what John Quincy Adams had in mind when he proclaimed both to be "parts of one consistent whole, founded upon one and the same theory of government" (Adler and Moquin, 1976:315).

The Convention of 1787 continued the work of 1776 and laid down the structure of the government and its basic principles. But not all questions about the American form of government were decided or definitively resolved by the founding generation, either in 1776 or in 1787. The modification and adaptation of our Constitution has been the product of subsequent acts of constitution making.

Studying the founders is the best place to begin to understand the nature of constitution making, but the development of our system requires that we look at the constitutional decisions of Americans after the founding generation.

SOURCES

Adams, Abigail: *Letters of Abigail Adams,* vol. 1, 2d ed., Little, Brown, Boston, 1840.

Adler, Mortimer J., and Wayne Moquin (eds.): *The Revolutionary Years,* Encyclopaedia Britannica, Chicago, 1976.

Bailyn, Bernard: *The Ideological Origins of the American Revolution,* Macmillan, New York, 1967.

Beard, Charles A.: *An Economic Interpretation of the Constitution,* Macmillan, New York, 1913.

Diamond, Martin, Winston Mills Fisk, and Herbert Garfinkel: *The Democratic Republic,* 2d ed., Rand McNally, Chicago, 1970.

Farrand, Max: *The Framing of the Constitution of the United States,* Yale University Press, New Haven, Conn., 1913.

—— (ed.): *The Records of the Federal Convention of 1787,* vols. 1–4, rev. ed., Yale University Press, New Haven, Conn., 1966.

Fehrenbach, T. R.: *Greatness to Spare,* Van Nostrand, Princeton, N.J., 1968.

Ford, Paul Leicester (ed.): *The Works of Thomas Jefferson,* vols. 1–12, Putnam, New York, 1904.

Hofstadter, Richard, William Miller, and David Aaron: *The American Republic,* vol. 1, 2d ed., Prentice-Hall, Englewood Cliffs, N.J., 1970.

Jensen, Merrill: *The New Nation,* Vintage, New York, 1950.

Koch, Adrienne, and Pedem Williams (eds.): *The Life and Selected Writings of Thomas Jefferson,* Modern Library, New York, 1944.

McDonald, Forrest: *We the People: The Economic Origins of the Constitution,* University of Chicago Press, Chicago, 1958.

McLaughlin, Andrew Cunningham: *The Confederation and the Constitution,* Harper, New York, 1905.

Roche, John P.: "The Founding Fathers: A Reform Caucus in Action," *American Political Science Review,* vol. 55, 1961, pp. 799–816.

Rossiter, Clinton: *1787: The Grand Convention,* Macmillan, New York, 1966.

Storing, Herbert J.: *What the Anti-Federalists Were For,* University of Chicago Press, Chicago, 1981.

Tocqueville, Alexis de: *Democracy in America,* J. P. Mayer (ed.), George Lawrence (trans.), Doubleday (Anchor), Garden City, N.Y., 1968.

Wilson, James Q.: *American Government: Institutions and Policies,* Heath, Lexington, Mass., 1980.

Wood, Gordon S.: *The Creation of the American Republic: 1776–1787,* University of North Carolina Press, Chapel Hill, N.C., 1969.

RECOMMENDED READINGS

Beard, Charles A.: *An Economic Interpretation of the Constitution,* Macmillan, New York, 1913. Argues that the Constitution originated in the economic motivations of the framers.

Becker, Carl L.: *The Declaration of Independence,* Random House (Vintage), New York, 1958. A lucid analysis of the principles and presuppositions of the Declaration.

Diamond, Martin: *The Founding of the Democratic Republic,* Peacock, Itasca, Ill., 1981. Thoughtful restatement of the founders' position.

Goldwin, Robert A. (ed.): *How Democratic Is the Constitution?* American Enterprise Institute, Washington, D.C., 1980. A collection of illuminating essays on the Constitution.

Hamilton, Alexander, James Madison, and John Jay: *The Federalist Papers,* many editions, 1787–1788. A classic of political theory, the definitive defense and analysis of the Constitution.

Jensen, Merrill: *The New Nation,* Random House (Vintage), New York, 1950. Sympathetic treatment of the Confederation period.

Padover, Saul K. (ed.): *To Secure These Blessings,* Washington Square Press and Ridge Press, New York, 1962. Records of the debates in the federal convention, topically arranged.

Rossiter, Clinton: *The Political Thought of the American Revolution,* Harcourt, Brace and World (Harvest Books), New York, 1963. Lively survey of Revolutionary political theory.

Storing, Herbert: *What the Anti-Federalists Were For,* University of Chicago Press, Chicago, 1981. A recent interpretation of and introduction to Antifederalist thought.

Wood, Gordon S.: *The Creation of the American Republic: 1776–1787,* University of North Carolina Press, Chapel Hill, N.C., 1969. A comprehensive survey of American political thought in the decade preceding the convention.

Chapter 3

Constitutional Development

CHAPTER CONTENTS

Although the Constitution written in 1787 continues powerfully to shape our political life, many significant changes have occurred in the basic elements of our political system since that time. Sometimes these changes have come through Constitutional amendment (slavery was abolished by the Thirteenth Amendment, women were guaranteed the right to vote by the Nineteenth). Sometimes they have come through new interpretations of the Constitution (legal segregation of the races was abolished in 1954 through a new interpretation of the Fourteenth Amendment). At other times fundamental change has come about through the development or decay of institutions, practices, or laws that are outside the Constitution (such as the rise of political parties). Important changes have also taken place in the respective roles of major political institutions.

Just as John Adams noted that the real American revolution had been the change in people's opinions rather than the outbreak of war, so, too, subsequent changes in the Constitution, laws, and practices of the country have rested upon shifts in people's attitudes and beliefs.

In each of the great controversies that have punctuated American political life, there has been a tendency for one or both parties to draw upon the sources of the founding, interpreting the Constitution and the Declaration of Independence to support their position. Jefferson, the author of the Declaration, was himself the leader of one of the parties in the first great controversy under the Constitution, that between the Federalist and the Republican parties in the 1790s and early 1800s. He believed that his opponents, the Federalists, had betrayed the principles of the Revolution and had sought to undermine the Constitution's separation of powers. Later, the Jacksonians saw themselves as the heirs of Jefferson, and Lincoln appealed over and over to the Declaration in resisting the spread of slavery. Progressives in the late nineteenth and early twentieth centuries sought to reform the Constitution. In the 1930s Franklin Roosevelt understood the New Deal as a renewal of Jefferson's struggle against a privileged elite.

This symbolic struggle reflects the fact that American politics has always involved disputes over principles as well as immediate struggles for advantage and power. The Declaration has been central to America's great political controversies because it is the most eloquent and authoritative statement of the purposes of government and of the standard of justice upon which the United States was founded. The Constitution contains the fundamental law governing its institutions. Those who would change the government have usually found it necessary either to show how the change is consistent with the common understanding of the Declaration and the Constitution or to bring about a new understanding of their meaning.

In this chapter we shall examine some of the fundamental changes in the opinions and sentiments of Americans since the founding. We shall see how these shifts in belief have resulted in changes in the Constitution and its interpretation and have brought about political and other changes which have had important effects on our constitutional system. We shall focus our discussion on the differing answers given to three of the fundamental questions of politics: (1) What changes have occurred in the ends and purposes of society? In answering this question we shall concentrate on changes in the understanding of the nation's commitment to liberty, equality and self-government, and in its conception of who is a citizen with the right to vote and to participate fully in its political life. (2) What changes have been brought about in the scope of government, in the tasks it is expected to perform, and in the relationship between the state and national governments? (3) Finally, what changes have occurred in the organization of the institutions of government and the distribution of power? (Matters relating to national security and America's role in the world will be discussed in Chapter 18.) In examining these questions we will see how citizens have continually been called upon to adopt the perspective of a constitution maker.

FEDERALISTS VERSUS REPUBLICANS

The first great controversy under the Constitution resulted in the formation of the first American political party, that founded by Jefferson and Madison in the 1790s and known as the "Republican party" (later the "Democratic-Republican party"). The party of their opponents, led by Hamilton and

Adams, became known as the "Federalist party." The quarrel between these parties developed during the 1790s over a great variety of issues, both domestic and foreign. It began with opposition to the financial policies Hamilton developed as secretary of the treasury under Washington. The partisan quarrel was heated by varying reactions to events surrounding the French Revolution and the subsequent war between France and England. Federalists and Republicans denounced each other as "Anglomen" and "Gallomen" or "monarchists" and "Jacobins" (a revolutionary French society favoring a radical form of democracy). The passage of the Alien and Sedition Acts in 1798 (acts which limited the right to criticize the government) brought the dispute to a head and led to the subsequent victory of Jefferson in the presidential election of 1800. Although the quarrel continued, the Federalists, defeated in congressional elections as well, never again won a national election and, as a party, soon faded forever from American politics.

The Ends of Society—
The Character of a Free People

Both Republicans and Federalists believed in the doctrine of Liberalism, movingly expressed by Jefferson in his first inaugural address:

> All, too, will bear in mind this sacred principle, that though the will of the majority is in all cases to prevail, that will to be rightful must be reasonable; that the minority possess their equal rights, which equal law must protect, and to violate would be oppression (Jefferson, 1904:III, 318).

The two parties disagreed, however, on the kind of country which should be fostered to fulfill this doctrine. Hamilton used his position as secretary of the treasury under Washington to formulate policies that would encourage the development of commerce and industry and create economic interests that would tie people to the national government. His policies were designed to create a diversity of economic interests which would check each other, provide an outlet for the ambitious, and leave scope for governmental discretion and leadership. "Fame," said Hamilton, is "the ruling passion of the noblest minds" (*Federalist* 72), and he envi-

sioned a commercial and political empire giving great scope for individual ambition (Adair, 1974).

The Republicans, on the other hand, did not believe that the way to protect minority rights was by creating a diversity of economic interests through commercial development. Rather, they thought that the key to successful republican government was to be found in a majority so educated and informed as not to desire to oppress minorities. Some Republicans, for example, believed that the country should be based on an agricultural, not a diversified, commercial economy. Cities and commerce, they thought, bred citizens with selfish habits and produced people more interested in manipulating others than in cooperating with them. Hamilton's policies fostered inequality and encouraged the kinds of people—speculators, stockjobbers, people out for a fast buck—who would corrupt government and undermine republicanism. Independent farming, on the other hand, taught personal self-reliance and self-discipline, as well as encouraged a "quiet life, and orderly conduct, both public and private." These were the qualities needed for good citizenship. Instead of relying upon the diversity of interest groups in a commercial society to check each other, the Republicans sought to foster one interest, the agricultural, as the source of sound republican opinion that could guide and check the government. "When we get piled upon one another in large cities, as in Europe," Jefferson said, "we shall become corrupt as in Europe, and go to eating one another as they do there" (Jefferson, 1904:VI, 392–393).

If under today's circumstances a nation composed mainly of independent farmers is impossible, the Jeffersonian view may nevertheless remind us of the importance of the qualities and opinions of the majority in a country in which the majority rules. Can the majority be so educated as not to wish to infringe upon minority rights, as the Jeffersonians thought they must be? Does the encouragement of private economic interest create beneficial diversity and increased scope for honorable ambition as the Federalists thought, or does it create undesirable inequalities and give scope to undesirable types of people as the Jeffersonians feared? These questions remain with us in the 1980s.

The Scope of Government

Because they thought effective government required freedom from the pressures of popular opinion, the Federalists sought to strengthen those institutions of government which were relatively remote from the voters. They favored liberal construction of the Constitution in interpreting the authority of the national government (giving its grants of power a broad rather than a narrow meaning). Not only was the national government more remote from the voters and hence less susceptible to majority tyranny, but a broad understanding of its powers enabled it to be used to foster the commercial development desired by the Federalists. In *McCullough v. Maryland* (1819) the Supreme Court under Chief Justice John Marshall (a Federalist) upheld the constitutionality of a national bank while striking down a state law which levied taxes on the bank. While acknowledging that the Constitution did not explicitly give Congress the power to establish a bank, the Court's decision, written by Marshall, found this to be an acceptable means of carrying out the financial responsibilities assigned to Congress by the Constitution.

The Republicans, on the other hand, thought the Constitution ought to be interpreted narrowly in order to restrict the powers of the national government and strengthen those of the states. Not only were the state governments closer to the people, but a less active national government would better serve the cause of protecting the agricultural interests. In response to the Alien and Sedition Acts, Madison and Jefferson wrote resolutions passed by the legislatures of Virginia and Kentucky which put forth the view that the states had a right not to obey a national law they thought unconstitutional.

As in many cases in American politics, the Republican-Federalist quarrel over the proper scope of the national government also reflected differing opinions about substantive policy. A strong national government for the Federalists was not only good in itself but also beneficial as a means to the end of commercial development, just as a weaker national government to the Republicans was not only good in itself but also conducive to the end of protecting agriculture. The context of politics sel-

dom provides an opportunity for considering questions concerning the power and structure of government apart from the policies that will be advanced or hindered.

Organization and Distribution of Power

The many disputes between the Republicans and Federalists reflected a fundamental disagreement about the organization of governmental power, both in the relationship between voters and their representatives and in the distribution of power between the branches of government.

Representation Jefferson said that the difference between his party and Hamilton's was that the Republicans trusted the people while the Federalists feared them. While this statement was a partisan exaggeration, it contained a germ of truth. The Republicans wanted a government much more directly responsive to people's opinions than the Federalists did. The Federalists thought that good government required decisions that were not immediately popular and desired representatives to be relatively free from the pressure of popular opinion. Sound financial policies required a government that could make and carry out unpopular decisions. Similarly, in foreign affairs unpopular decisions might also be required. The Federalists supported neutrality in the war between France and England in the late 1790s in spite of the fact that England had recently been the country's enemy and the sympathy and gratitude of the people were naturally attached to the country's former ally France.

In order to make it possible for representatives to support such unpopular decisions, the Federalists thought that the voters should select representatives on the basis of their reputation and accomplishments and judge them on the results of their policies, but not bind the representatives to their own opinions of what should be done. By fostering the growth of commerce and industry they hoped to create such a diversity of interests that the opinions of no one group would predominate, giving greater discretion to the deliberation of elected officials.

The Republicans, on the other hand, thought

BOX 3-1

JEFFERSON AND HAMILTON ON NATIONAL CHARACTER

What kind of people Americans were to become was one of the issues which divided Hamilton and Jefferson. Each recognized that the way people lived and made their living would affect their habits of mind and qualities of character. Jefferson favored encouraging agriculture; Hamilton, manufacturing. The effect each thought his policy would have on Americans is shown in the following quotations:

Jefferson

> . . . Those who labour in the earth are the chosen people of God, if ever he had a chosen people, whose breast he has made his peculiar deposit for substantial and genuine virtue. . . . Corruption of morals in the mass of cultivators is a phenomenon of which no age nor nation has furnished an example. It is the mark set on those, who, not looking up to heaven, to their own toil and industry, as does the husbandman, for their subsistence, depend for it on the casualties and caprice of customers. Dependence begets subservience and venality, suffocates the germ of virtue, and

prepares fit tools for the designs of ambition. . . . Let our workshops remain in Europe.

Hamilton

> It is a just observation, that minds of the strongest and most active powers for their proper objects fall below mediocrity and labour without effect, if confined to uncongenial pursuits. And it is thence to be inferred, that the results of human exertion may be immensely increased by diversifying its objects. When all the different kinds of industry obtain in a community, each individual can find his proper element, and can call into activity the whole vigour of his nature. And the community is benefitted by the services of its respective members, in the manner, in which each can serve it with most effect. . . . The spirit of enterprise, useful and prolific as it is, . . . must be less in a nation of mere cultivators, than in a nation of cultivators and merchants; less in a nation of cultivators and merchants, than in a nation of cultivators, artificers and merchants.

Source: Jefferson, 1904:II, 229–230; Hamilton, 1966:X, 255–256.

---

that representatives should be tied more closely to popular opinion. As Jefferson put it:

> The further the departure from direct and constant control by the citizens, the less has the government of the ingredient of republicanism; . . . it must be agreed that our governments have much less of republicanism than ought to be expected; in other words, that the people have less regular control over their agents, than their rights and their interests require (Jefferson, 1904:XV, 20, 22).

Jefferson thought that Hamilton's policies as secretary of the treasury created a corrupt union of bankers, bondholders, and governmental officials which threatened to make a mockery of republican government. Only the American people at the ballot box could prevent representatives from developing into a self-interested class that would advance its own welfare at the expense of the public.

Jefferson and others created the Republican party in order to bring public opinion to bear on the government. They saw the party as a means by which the majority could be mobilized to resist the dangers of self-interested minorities and be given a greater hand in shaping the direction of the government. Jefferson thought his victory in 1800 was a revolution as great as that of 1776 because it showed that the people could check their representatives when they threatened to undermine republicanism and could peacefully decide a great national dispute.

The Balance of Power   The Federalists supported a broad interpretation of the Constitution that would strengthen the powers of the president and the Supreme Court, as the branches of government most capable of resisting oppressive majorities. Although the Constitution had not explicitly granted the Supreme Court the right to declare laws of Congress unconstitutional, the Federalists

During his thirty-five years as chief justice, John Marshall made the Supreme Court a powerful force in American politics by establishing the Court's right to declare laws of Congress unconstitutional. *(James Lambdin / National Portrait Gallery)*

panding agriculture and greater security for trade in agricultural produce down the Mississippi River. Congressional predominance within a restrained national government was meant to serve a certain end; when that end could be served by strong presidential action, Jefferson was willing.

The result of the Republican triumph of 1800 was not a complete victory for the Republican view of the proper balance among governmental institutions. John Marshall, a leading Federalist, had been appointed chief justice by the outgoing President Adams. By the time of his death thirty-five years later, he had been able to forge the Supreme Court into a powerful political force, with the nearly undisputed right to declare laws of Congress unconstitutional. (The case in which Marshall established this right—*Marbury v. Madison,* 1803—is one of the great cases in American law.) Moreover, although Jefferson had advocated a deferential executive, and put forward this view as president, some of his conduct in the office provided precedents for a stronger presidency. Through his role as head of the Republican party, he actively led the legislature and was willing to go beyond his Constitutional authority (as he saw it) to secure the Louisiana Purchase for the United States. The strong presidency implied by such actions was gradually to find a Jeffersonian justification. The turning of presidential elections into party conflicts led the way toward seeing the presidency not as an undemocratic check upon democratic legislatures, but as a fully democratic office which could reflect the most significant political judgments of the voters.

In opposing the restrictions on speech and press of the Alien and Sedition Acts on the grounds that they usurped powers rightfully found in the states, the Republicans raised an issue that was to beset American politics through the Civil War and beyond. As sectionalism and the issue of slavery hardened, the question of the power of the states to resist acts of the national government became a question of life or death for the American union.

Although it proved difficult to maintain the United States as an agricultural country, and many Republicans, including Jefferson himself, came to modify their views, the issue raised by the Republican-Federalist conflict over the ends of society continues to this day. To what degree does repub-

favored this power of "judicial review" as a means of checking the more democratic Congress. The Republicans, on the other hand, opposed it. Jefferson argued that each branch of government had the right to decide for itself whether its actions were constitutional or not, and thought that "judicial review" undermined democratic control. Supreme power, according to the Republicans, ought to reside in Congress as the branch most representative of the people.

These opinions concerning the distribution of power were bound up with the opinions of the Federalists and the Republicans concerning the ends of society, a point vividly illustrated by Jefferson's actions as president. When Jefferson had the possibility of securing the Louisiana Purchase for the United States, he was willing to go beyond the constitutional authority of the government (as he understood it) in order to acquire new land for an ex-

lican government rest upon the public-spirited qualities of its citizens, and what can be done consistent with the principles of Liberalism to foster those qualities? To what degree can it rest on what *The Federalist* calls "auxiliary precautions"—pluralism fostered by a diverse economic life and institutions capable of resisting popular passions?

JACKSONIAN DEMOCRACY

After the War of 1812, politics settled into an "era of good feelings" in which the old quarrel between Federalists and Republicans seemed laid to rest. Within the overwhelmingly predominant Republican party a politics of personal rivalry developed, largely divorced from the stirring issues of the recent past. However, new and even more momentous issues soon arose. In 1824 the presidential election was thrown into the House of Representatives. John Quincy Adams emerged as the victor despite the fact that Andrew Jackson had received more popular and electoral votes. The supporters of Jackson charged that the election had been "stolen" by the maneuverings of Adams in the House. Beginning with this charge, a political movement developed behind Jackson that swept him into the presidency in 1828.

The Ends of Society— Equality and Democratic Voting

Andrew Jackson's name has come to symbolize the growing sway of equality, both social and political, in the United States at that time. With him the west, without the more aristocratic habits and traditions of the east, came to power. Jackson was from Tennessee (all previous presidents had come from either Massachusetts or Virginia). But what did this growing equality mean for the character of political and social life? Did it mean the "reign of King Mob," as Justice Story of the Supreme Court thought it meant? Would the country, like a mob, be governed by the passions and impulses of the majority, unguided by thoughtfulness and reason, perhaps resulting in the destruction of minority rights and constitutional government?

To the Jacksonians their movement was a rekindling of the cause championed first by Jefferson. The great issue was the "war against the Monster Bank"—the Bank of the United States. The Jacksonians characterized the fight over the bank as a great struggle between the "people" and "aristocratic privilege and plutocratic corruption" (Meyers, 1957:7). The bank fostered trades "which seek wealth without labor, employing the stratagems of speculative maneuver, privilege grabbing, and monetary manipulation" which nurtured "defective morals, habits, and character." In contrast, republican simplicity and responsibility were to be found in planters, farmers, mechanics, and laborers who performed some "immediate, responsible function in the production of goods" (Meyers, 1957:15). It was to give these people and their way of life political power that Jackson fought the election of 1828 and forged a powerful political coalition through the Democratic party. These ends also fostered a rapid extension of the suffrage in the states. Universal adult suffrage is a relatively recent development in America. However, this observation should not obscure the fact that, with the exception of women and blacks, the United States led the modern world in extending the right of suffrage to the broad mass of the people. The Constitution, although it did not require a democratic electorate by present-day standards, nonetheless allowed for the rapid extension of suffrage that took place after Jackson's election.

At the time of the founding, all the states had restrictions of some kind on voting. In addition to the limitation to white males over 21 years of age, the states restricted voting to those holding property or showing some evidence of being stable members of the community. These qualifications were based on the idea that citizens should have at least some stake in the community before being entitled to vote. While property and acreage qualifications in some states greatly limited the franchise, in others the requirement for voting was merely to be a "taxpaying citizen," which embraced most free and permanent members of the community. Even with these restrictions, however, the state legislatures of the time were considered by both friends and foes of the Constitution to be highly democratic bodies, a fact which calls into question the claims of some that the founders had wanted to establish a propertied oligarchy. Indeed, the federal Constitution, unlike the constitutions of most of the states, required no property qualification for

---

BOX 3-2

EDUCATION AND SELF-GOVERNMENT

With the spread of democratic voting, the movement for free public education grew. The connection between voting and education is expressed by one of the leaders in the fight for public education, Horace Mann:

> But, in the possession of this attribute of intelligence, elective legislators will never far surpass their electors. . . . It is not more certain that a wise and enlightened constituency will refuse to invest a reckless and profligate man with office, or discard him if accidentally chosen, than it is that a foolish or immoral constituency will discard or eject a wise man. This law of assimilation between the choosers and the chosen results, not only from the fact that the voter originally selects his representative according to the affinities of good or of ill, of wisdom or of folly, which exist between them, but if the legislator enacts or favors a law which is too wise for the constituent to understand, or too just for him to approve, the next election will set him aside as certainly as if he had made open merchandise of the dearest interests of the people by perjury and for a bribe. . . . The establishment of a republican government, without well-appointed and efficient means for the universal education of the people, is the most rash and foolhardy experiment ever tried by man (Mann, 1867:688).

---

holding office (Beard, 1913; McDonald, 1958; Brown, 1956).

After the ratification of the Constitution, the movement within the states quickly grew for the expansion of the suffrage. New states joining the union adopted either the taxpaying qualification or else the even more liberal residency requirement. (These new states, free of the established classes and traditions of most of the older ones, became an important source of pressures to democratize the regime.) The older states, stimulated by the national currents of democratic opinion that swept across the nation with Jefferson's election in 1800 and Andrew Jackson's election in 1828, began to reduce or remove their restrictions. By 1840, only two states—Virginia and Louisiana—still had property qualifications, and those restrictions were abolished by the 1850s. Just as important, after 1832, only one state (South Carolina) chose its presidential electors by means other than popular election. Thus by the 1830s, universal white manhood suffrage was in existence throughout nearly all the nation for both congressional and presidential elections.

The Scope of Government—States' Rights

For many of the same reasons that moved the Jeffersonian Republicans, the Jacksonians favored interpreting narrowly the powers of the national government. In the fight over rechartering the Bank of the United States, Jackson upheld "strict construction" of the Constitution (the view that the powers granted the government ought to be interpreted "strictly" or narrowly). Despite the contrary ruling of the Supreme Court in *McCulloch v. Maryland* (1819), Jackson believed creation of the bank to be an unconstitutional exercise of Congress's powers.

Yet Jackson also opposed the growing belief that the states were superior in authority to the national government. A tariff law passed in 1828 had placed higher duties on imported raw materials than on manufactured goods, to the disadvantage of the south, which was less industrialized than the north. In opposing this tariff South Carolina set forth the doctrine of "nullification." This doctrine held that the states, not the American people, had created the union and were still sovereign. Each state, acting through convention, had the right to judge the constitutionality of the actions of the federal government. If it found the national government acting unconstitutionally, it had the right to prevent the enforcement of the federal law in its territory. When a new tariff was passed in 1832 with many of the objectionable features of the tariff of 1828, South Carolina held a convention, declared the tariff unconstitutional, prohibited federal officers from collecting customs duties within the state, and threatened secession if force were used against it.

Andrew Jackson, although he strongly believed in the power of the states, was adamantly opposed to disunion. He denied that a state had the right to secede and took strong actions to enforce the federal law. However, before the issue reached a military showdown, Congress passed a compromise tariff and South Carolina repealed its nullification ordinance. The union had been upheld, but South Carolina's position had been maintained by a determined stand. Jackson saw what lay ahead. The "next pretext [for disunion]," he predicted, "will be the Negro, or slavery, question."

The Organization and Distribution of Power— Parties and the President as Popular Leader

The election of 1824 has proved to be the last time that a presidential election has been thrown into the House of Representatives. This is largely because of the development of the two-party system under Jackson, which has worked to ensure that one of the candidates would receive a majority of the electoral votes. This strengthened the presidency by diminishing the possibility that the election would be disputed or perceived as illegitimate. At the same time, the development of parties created a new role for the president as party leader. The Democratic party, which could trace its origins back to the Jeffersonian Republican party, changed its name to reflect the democratic spirit of the movement it represented. Its opponent, shortly to be known as the "Whig party," challenged the Democratic party for the next generation, establishing the basic pattern of conflict between two major parties, with occasional entries of significant third parties, that has persisted to the 1980s.

The Jackson administration also saw the development of the "spoils system." Under this system most national employees were dismissed when a new president was elected. The president would then fill the offices with personal friends. The system threw open federal employment to large numbers of new people, democratizing the executive branch and bringing in fresh blood. But these people were also frequently chosen for their political loyalties rather than their competence in their official duties.

The Jacksonian era shows that powerful forces of democracy could find scope under and give shape to the Constitution. By extending the suffrage, developing political parties, and providing a focus for change in the presidency, the country's basic political institutions remained intact while serving new goals and concerns.

SLAVERY AND THE CIVIL WAR

The events and debates that led to the election of Lincoln to the presidency and brought on the Civil War more sharply reveal the character of the constitution (with a small *c*) formed from 1776–1789 and its inner tensions than any other episode in American politics. The existence of slavery within a republic which proclaimed the equal rights of all was a great injustice in itself and opened free government to the charge of hypocrisy. A nation which proclaimed the equality of all people, but tolerated—and verged on endorsing—slavery was a nation at war in its soul. The attempt to extend slavery led Americans to examine more profoundly than ever before or since the fundamental meaning of the nation's dedication to liberty, self-government, and equality. In this section we will restrict ourselves to examining this great debate about the broad purposes of society and the meaning of American citizenship. After a short description of American slavery and the circumstances leading to the Civil War, we will look at the three disputed principles of liberty, self-government, and equality, ending with a discussion of the meaning of American citizenship which emerged from the war.

The Character of American Slavery

In treating people as property, slavery denies human beings the freedom to decide for themselves and to exercise those rights which characterize them as human beings. There was an additional feature of slavery as found in the United States that compounded the evil. Slavery was based on race: only blacks were slaves. In the ancient world where slavery flourished, individual slaves might be freed, and they and their descendants could soon disappear into the general free population. But in the United States, racial prejudice supported slavery, and slavery supported racial prejudice. To justify slavery on the basis of race, many contended that the black race itself was inferior to other races. Freed slaves could therefore never simply disappear into the general population; the badge of servitude could be seen in the color of their skin. The prejudice against slaves combined with racial prejudice made the life of the freed scarcely more hopeful, and often harder, than that of the enslaved. But even this dim avenue of escape from slavery, the granting of freedom, was largely cut off by the time of the Civil War. In the decades before the war, the laws of the slave states were gradually toughened to make it difficult or impossible to free a slave. The principle of slavery in the United States by the time of the Civil War was that people who belonged to a particular class (i.e., the black race), irrespective of individual merit, were permanently to be slaves.

Yet finding a solution to the problem of American slavery was incredibly difficult for the statesmen of the time, given the complications of the racial issue. Hundreds of thousands of people had an economic interest in slavery. Racial prejudice, fears, and loyalty to one's state swelled the ranks of those opposed to its abolition. In addition, most blacks were uneducated and unpracticed in the exercise of freedom and self-government. If blacks became free and voting citizens, the opponents of emancipation argued, would they not be prey to the manipulations of unscrupulous politicians or turn on the whites who had enslaved them? Many who sympathized with the plight of the slaves nevertheless believed that large-scale emancipation might have tragic and disastrous consequences for both black and white. Speaking of the problem of slavery, Jefferson wrote that he trembled for his country when he reflected that God is just and that "his justice cannot sleep forever." However, recognizing the absence of an easy solution to the problem, he also observed, "We have the wolf by the ears and we cannot let him go" (Jefferson, 1904:II, 227).

The Extension of Slavery

By the 1850s the situation was worse than in Jefferson's day because of the increase in the number of slaves. Forty percent of the population of the southern states was black, and in large areas blacks were in the majority. Not only did they constitute a great share of the wealth of the dominant class in the south, but the advocates of slavery viewed the numbers of slaves and their condition as a threat requiring that slavery be extended into the lands to the west. It was this issue which brought on the Civil War.

The admission of new states carved from the territories in the west offered the possibility (or the threat) that either the slave states or the free states might be able to assume a commanding position in the federal union and then use the power of the national government to attack the institutions of the minority states.

Self-Government and Popular Sovereignty

The smoldering dispute over the western territories had been temporarily dampened by two famous compromises during the first half of the century. The Missouri Compromise of 1820 divided the territory of the Louisiana Purchase into slave and free by prohibiting slavery north of the present state of Missouri, and the Compromise of 1850 settled the disposition of the territories of the southwest acquired from Mexico. But the moral questions at the base of the conflict failed to be resolved by the normal art of compromise, or "bargaining." After 1850 Stephen Douglas, a senator from Illinois, took the lead in trying to find a program and principles that would settle the slavery issue. The formula that Senator Douglas advanced was "popular sovereignty." According to this doctrine, the most fundamental principle of American republican government is that the majority in each state should be able to do whatever it wants. Congress should not attempt to legislate with respect to slavery in the territories; the people of each territory should decide for themselves whether they want slavery or not and, when they come to apply for admission to the union, decide whether the new state should be slave or free. In this way Douglas hoped to remove the slavery issue from national politics. He would gain the north's consent because economic and geographic factors would probably keep slavery out of the new territories by making it unprofitable. The south's consent would be gained because it would at least have the chance to extend slavery and would be reassured by the principle that slavery was a question of states' rights (Jaffa, 1959).

In this 1858 painting, Lincoln stands to denounce the extension of slavery to the Nebraska Territory while Douglas, to his right, prepares to defend his doctrine of popular sovereignty. *(Robert Marshall Root/Illinois State Historical Society)*

In 1854 Douglas secured the application of his doctrine to the Nebraska Territory (the present states of Kansas and Nebraska), thereby repealing the Missouri Compromise, which had forbidden slavery north of the present state of Missouri. The country was sharply split during the debate and the passage of the Kansas-Nebraska Act. Party lines adjusted themselves upon the single issue of extention of slavery. The Democratic party became the party of extension, losing some supporters and picking up others. The Whig party disappeared altogether, its northern members joining with "anti-Nebraska" Democrats to form the new Republican party.

Abraham Lincoln rose to national prominence and the presidency as a leader in the fight against the repeal of the Missouri Compromise and the idea of "popular sovereignty." Through the Lincoln-Douglas debates, held as Lincoln and Douglas challenged each other for the Senate seat from Illinois in 1858, Lincoln became the chief spokesman of the Republicans. Although Douglas won the seat, Lincoln went on to win the Republican nomination for president in 1860. Lincoln and his Republican followers maintained that the repeal of the Missouri Compromise and the doctrine of popular sovereignty threatened a revolution of such disastrous proportions for the United States that it was better to risk war than to let that revolution come to pass. What was that revolution, and on what grounds did Lincoln resist it?

The Principle of Equality

As president, Lincoln denied the right of the south to secede from the union and led the nation in war in order to preserve the union. But Lincoln believed the union to be more than the simple attachment of the various states to each other. He prized the Constitution, but did not believe the union to have been formed by the Constitution. In the Gettysburg address, as elsewhere, he identified the nation as having been born in 1776, the date of the Declaration of Independence. The union in its deepest sense, as Lincoln saw it, was a union of people "dedicated to the proposition that all men are created equal." Lincoln interpreted this to mean all Americans, regardless of race. But in the 1850s, Lincoln worried that a new idea, in favor of inequality and slavery, might replace the old one as the central sentiment of public opinion. It was to save the old opinion, as he believed it had been formed by the Declaration, that conflict must be risked.

Americans, of course, had never lived up to their creed; slavery was still in existence in the 1860s. But now there was a worse possibility: that Americans would resolve the tension between their declared beliefs and the existence of slavery by changing their declared beliefs. There were a few who simply maintained that the equality of humans, whether white or black, was a "self-evident lie." But it was difficult to attack the Declaration of Independence so directly. The subtler attack was to interpret the Declaration in such a way as to deny the manifest implication of its words. Douglas, who never explicitly endorsed slavery, nevertheless maintained that the majority had the right to have slaves if it wished. He argued that the famous phrase of the Declaration meant "all men of English descent" or "all white men." The evidence for this was the argument that the great founders would have been hypocrites if they had meant "all humans" by the phrase "all men," for they did not free their slaves. Lincoln's reply was that they did not make all white people or people of English descent immediately equal either. Douglas's view was later endorsed by the Supreme Court and by Chief Justice Taney in the case of *Dred Scott v. Sanford* (1857). By this argument one could uphold slavery without having to attack the Declaration and the prestige of its authors. Contrary to Lincoln's view that all human beings possessed certain natural rights, including the right of self-government, the Court, along with Douglas, said that white men could rightly subject blacks to slavery.

Liberty and Self-Government

In advancing the doctrine of popular sovereignty, Douglas espoused an interpretation of American principles that can recur and has continually recurred in politics down to today. Liberty, he argued, meant the right of the majority to do whatever it likes. Unrestrained majority rule thus seems to be the first principle of a free society. Lincoln

argued that it was not, that liberty must be subordinated to equality. Lincoln posed the problem in this way.

> The shepherd drives the wolf from the sheep's throat, for which the sheep thanks the shepherd as a *liberator,* while the wolf denounces him for the same act as the destroyer of liberty, especially as the sheep was a black one (Lincoln, 1953:VII, 302).

Whose definition is correct? It is the sheep's definition that Lincoln takes to be the true definition. That this is the right definition becomes evident when people see that equality is the ground of liberty. The majority can rightfully rule because among equals the decision is rightfully made by the majority. If individuals or majorities deny the equality of others, they undermine the basis for their own rights. No one person or no number of people has the right to undermine the principle of human equality.

To uphold the equal rights of all was the duty of Americans, Lincoln thought. They owed it not only to themselves because it was the very foundation of their own politics, but also to the rest of humanity. Lincoln's speeches are suffused with the sense that the world is observing and depending upon the fate of the American experiment in self-government. As he said at Gettysburg, only the resolve of the American people could determine that "government of the people, by the people, and for the people shall not perish from the earth."

Yet this politics of uncompromising principle seems distant from the pluralistic style of politics contemplated by *Federalist* 10 (see Chapter 2). Pluralism suggests that different groups must compromise in order to form a majority coalition, and majorities, once formed, may have to compromise with determined minorities in order to maintain peace and a general consent to the government. Pluralism can sometimes lead to a sordid and petty politics: "You scratch my back, and I'll scratch yours, and we'll both advance our selfish interests." On the other hand a politics of high principle can easily become fanatical and, indeed, terrifying: "We know the right course, and we will force society to follow it, even if we must destroy everyone's liberty and many people's lives to get them in line."

It seemed to be Lincoln's conviction that the politics of pluralism is proper only within the con-

---

BOX 3-3

SLAVERY AND FREE GOVERNMENT

The depth of the dispute which led to the Civil War can be seen in these quotations from John C. Calhoun and Abraham Lincoln. Calhoun argues that it is possible to have freedom only by making some people slaves. Lincoln claims the freedom of one requires the freedom of all.

Calhoun

> I fearlessly assert that the existing relation between the two races in the South, against which these blind fanatics are waging war, forms the most solid and durable foundation on which to rear free and stable political institutions. . . . There is and always has been in an advanced stage of wealth and civilization, a conflict between labor and capital. The condition of society in the South exempts us

from the disorders and dangers resulting from this conflict; and which explains why it is that the political condition of the slaveholding States has been so much more stable and quiet than that of the North.

Lincoln

> I can not but hate it [the view that regarded slavery as a matter of indifference]. I hate it because of the monstrous injustice of slavery itself. I hate it because it deprives our republican example of its just influence in the world . . . and especially because it forces so many really good men amongst ourselves into an open war with the very fundamental principles of civil liberty—criticizing the Declaration of Independence, and insisting there is no right principle of action but *self-interest.*

Source: Calhoun, 1968, II:632; Lincoln, 1953, II:255.

---

text of a fundamental commitment to the principle of human equality. Otherwise compromises might be made at the expense of the rights of others. Lincoln was willing to make certain compromises with slavery in practice as long as it did not erode the conviction in people's minds that slavery was an evil. Lincoln thought that if people believed that slavery was *wrong,* however much they might compromise with it out of *necessity,* the day would come when there would be an opportunity for abolishing it.

Politics is the art of compromise, but it is also the art of knowing when it is proper to compromise. The basic principles of free government ought never to be compromised, Lincoln thought, but as long as those principles were not threatened, compromises might be made with existing prejudices and evils without giving up the end one seeks. Indeed, such compromises might even be required if government by consent is to be maintained.

Results of the Civil War—Citizenship and Voting

The Civil War resulted in the abolition of slavery and the establishment of the principle that blacks and former slaves, as well as whites, could be citizens of the United States. These two great out-

comes were enshrined in the Thirteenth and Fourteenth Amendments to the Constitution. The war also established that individual states did not have the right to withdraw from the union—it was not the states but the people who stood as the foundation of the union. Yet ridding the country of slavery did not rid the country of racial prejudice. Not only did differences between the races and racial prejudice result in difficult social relations between blacks and whites, but new laws arose on the ruins of slavery to grant to blacks only a second-class citizenship. "Jim Crow" laws segregating the races were developed and justified under the banner of "separate but equal." But "separate" was in fact seldom, if ever, "equal." How different races ought to live together remains to this day a central question of our political life.

The third Constitutional amendment arising from the Civil War, the Fifteenth, ratified in 1870, prohibited the federal government or the states from denying the vote to anyone "on account of race, color, or previous condition of servitude." The Amendment, it should be stressed, did not remove from the states their discretion to establish qualifications for voting, but simply barred them from enforcing restrictions on racial grounds. The intent, nevertheless, was clearly to enfranchise black citizens. However, that intent was soon subverted in many southern states by a number of techniques including the use of allegedly "neutral" qualifications which in fact were designed to exclude black voters. (Similar techniques were employed in other localities to exclude either blacks or orientals.) The adoption of these legal ploys, accepted after the 1870s by a nation weary of conflict, meant that for almost a century the "right" of blacks to vote in many southern states was a mere promise on paper, honored more in the breach than in the observance.

The crudest method used to deter blacks from voting in the south was intimidation. As the white population regained control of the state governments in the south following Reconstruction, criminal acts committed against blacks who attempted to vote often went unpunished. In effect, local police authorities were in complicity with "private" vigilante groups, like the Ku Klux Klan, that systematically sought to prevent black voting through threats and violence. Although the federal government passed legislation in the 1870s to protect citizens in the act of voting, the Supreme Court disallowed federal prosecution of these criminal acts on the grounds that they were the activity not of the "state" but of private individuals, notwithstanding the fact that the states sometimes did little to protect their citizens. Thereafter, blacks who attempted to vote in some areas were subject for many years to every manner of harassment, physical intimidation, and, in some instances, lynchings.

By the end of the 1870s the nation and the Republican party had lost their fervor on the issue of race and black equality. This change of political climate gave southern states the latitude to adopt a series of laws which had the effect of excluding most blacks from voting by "legal" methods. Beginning in the 1890s, most southern states passed laws requiring the payment of a poll tax and the passage of literacy tests in order to vote. Since most former slaves were poor and uneducated, these laws effectively deprived most blacks of the franchise, which they had generally enjoyed, despite recent obstacles from the era of Reconstruction. For blacks who could pay the poll tax and who were literate, local registrars frequently applied literacy tests in blatantly discriminatory ways, demanding impossible "tests" of black citizens wishing to vote. Led by Mississippi, some states also employed

"character tests" that again were subject to biased enforcement by registration officials. To ensure that poor and illiterate whites were not similarly excluded, a number of states passed so-called "grandfather laws" that exempted from the poll taxes and the literacy tests all those whose ancestors had voted before the end of the Civil War when blacks, of course, had been unable to vote. (In some states, however, poor whites were effectively disenfranchised along with blacks—in part, it appears, in order that the wealthier whites could maintain control of the state government and prevent any alliance from developing between poor whites and blacks.) Finally, in many southern states, the Democratic party, using its status as a private association, excluded all participation by black citizens in its activities; and most states soon passed "reform" primary laws which enforced the party's "private" restriction of the votes to white citizens. Since nearly everyone elected to office in the south was a Democrat, the device of the "white primary" excluded blacks from any real influence, even where they were permitted to vote in the general election.

The result of all these restrictions was nothing less than the disenfranchisement of blacks throughout most of the south. Furthermore, because the great majority of blacks in the nation then lived in the south—the great migration of blacks to the north and west did not begin on a large scale until the 1940s—the black population in America was virtually without influence within the American electorate. By the simplest standards of representative democracy, the American regime was clearly defective. Although some improvements were made in small steps over a long period of time, it was not until the 1960s that a major transformation of this situation took place.

THE PROGRESSIVES

The Civil War set off a booming industrial development. Government sought to aid this development, and the Supreme Court found support for many of the principles of laissez-faire capitalism in its interpretation of the Constitution. The unrestrained development of large corporations raised the question whether the inequality of private wealth threatened to undermine the republican character of the United States. The "populism" of the late nineteenth century was the last attempt to meet this threat by means of an agrarian-based solution. The "progressive" movement, while sharing many of the ideas of the populists, accepted the industrial development of the United States and tried to find a response within the framework of industrial society. As finally shaped by the presidencies of Theodore Roosevelt and Woodrow Wilson, this movement sought to bring about major changes in the American constitutional system.

The Ends of Society— Democratic Equality and National Unity

The immigration of the nineteenth century had created a vast, heterogeneous population increasingly crowded into cities, and the growth of corporate wealth had created new centers of power. The progressives thought that it was necessary to create unity out of this new diversity, to remedy the scandalous working conditions in the burgeoning factories, and to restore democratic equality in the face of concentrated private wealth and power. While the emphasis upon equality in the ideas of

the progressives was by no means new to American politics as we have seen, the thought that this required the reshaping of economic and social life within the context of industrialism was.

The Scope of Government— Increased Power and Representation

In the eyes of the reformers, these goals required an expansion of the scope and power of the national government to control private power and a better way to make that government express the unity and will of the people. As Theodore Roosevelt put the new ideal, "The people . . . have but one instrument which they can effectively use against the colossal combinations of business—and that instrument is the government of the United States" (Schambra, 1982:42). Increased governmental power was used to break up trusts (supercorporations controlling a single industry in order to eliminate competition and set prices), to reform banking (the Federal Reserve system was established in 1913), to guarantee the right to organize unions (in the Clayton Antitrust Act of 1914), and to bring about many other social and economic reforms.

FIGURE 3-1
Absorption of immigrants into the United States. (*Source: Historical Statistics of the United States, Colonial Times to 1970*, 1975:105–106; *Statistical Abstract of the United States: 1981.*)

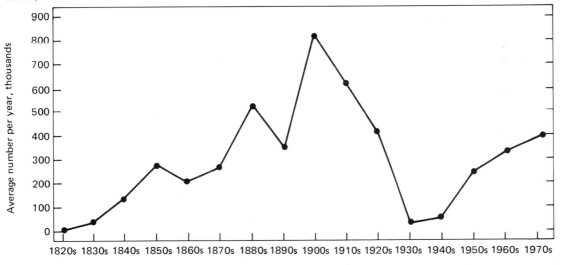

The Organization and Distribution of Power— The President as Popular Leader

In order to increase the power of government and use it in the proper way, the progressives as finally led by Woodrow Wilson thought that governmental power should be more unified in the hands of the president. The Constitutional separation of powers, according to Wilson, did not provide an effective government for the twentieth century. Instead of creating a government capable of representing the people and promoting the energetic leadership necessary to meet the danger of concentrated corporate power and special interests, it merely made for stalemate. Each branch could stand in the way of the others, preventing progressive legislation from being formed and implemented:

> As at present constituted, the federal government lacks strength because its powers are divided, lacks promptness because its authorities are multiplied, lacks wieldiness because its responsibility is indistinct and its action without competent direction (Wilson, 1956:206).

This political stalemate allowed the special interests to thrive. Political parties only compounded the difficulties. They were largely controlled by political bosses who, operating out of the public limelight, created unholy alliances and corrupt deals with the special interests, to the detriment of the public good. The government of the Constitution was a rudderless government that allowed the selfish sharks of commerce to rule society.

Wilson originally favored the creation of a "cabinet" form of government like that of Great Britain. Under the cabinet form, legislative and executive power are united and concentrated in a prime minister chosen by the legislature. But later Wilson came to believe that the defects of the Constitution could be overcome without major changes to it by reinterpreting the political system. In particular, the president's connection to the people could be exploited to bring about a stronger presidency and a greater concentration of political power. The president provided the key both for increasing the power of the government and for making it represent the general interest rather than special interests.

In place of the traditional system of checks and balances with a weak president, Wilson favored a government that would above all encourage strong political leadership. Leadership was the ability to marshall public opinion behind progressive policies. It required two things lacking in the Constitutional scheme: power and unitary direction. Power in modern democracies, Wilson felt, is to be found in the ability to move the people. Public opinion must provide the driving force for government.

The older view had not denied great importance to public opinion. We have seen that both Jefferson and Lincoln believed that behind the laws and the Constitution stood a set of public beliefs that made the right kind of laws possible. At critical junctures, both believed, public opinion might have to be marshalled to keep the laws and the Constitution on the proper track. Wilson radicalized this view. Public opinion could not only be a check on the government, it could be the regular authorizing and moving force. Officials could be directly empowered by the people to the extent that they could tap deep public sentiment in their policies.

Wilson viewed the power of the people as immense, but also diffuse. To give unity and direction to their power, he argued, it must be concentrated in one person. The only office in the American system capable of concentrating this power was that of the president. The chief quality necessary for the sort of president that Wilson desired was that of popular leadership. The president must be capable of articulating the unconscious aspirations of the people, thus attracting and concentrating their power. The president must become, as Franklin Roosevelt was later to say, the "moral trumpet" of the nation. Such a president, empowered by the backing of the people, could lead Congress and even force it in the desired direction if it resisted.

Wilson did not believe that to enhance the power of the people and concentrate it in one person was dangerous to liberty. Outstanding leaders would be attracted to the power and opportunities the new presidency offered. The dangers of demagogues, leaders who would serve selfish interests under the cover of flattery of the people, were much exaggerated. As Wilson put it:

> There is no permanent place in democratic leadership except for him who "hath clean hands and a pure heart." If other men come temporarily to power

among us, it is because we cut our leadership up into so many little parts and do not subject any one man to the purifying influences of centered responsibility (Wilson, 1973:284).

Checks and balances could be partly overcome by the ability of a leader to move mass opinion.

Wilson, and the progressives generally, favored Constitutional and political reforms that would help to bring about this new power for public opinion and the presidency. They favored changes that would increase the direct power of the people and that would concentrate power within the government in the hands of the president. The Seventeenth Amendment to the Constitution, providing for direct election of senators, was supported by the progressives and was ratified in 1913. By this means the Senate was brought under greater popular control and made more subject to a president backed by public opinion. On the state level the power of the people was enhanced by such measures as the *initiative* (the procedure by which citizens can propose a law by petition and ensure its submission to the electorate), the *referendum* (the submission of a proposed measure to direct popular vote), and the *recall* (the power of the people to remove an incumbent from office by means of popular vote). To destroy the power of party bosses, the progressives advocated primaries as the proper mode of nominating candidates. Presidential primaries, Wilson thought, would both free presidents from the control of bosses and also enable the executive to claim a popular mandate for a general direction of public policy. The president would become able to dictate to the party and would no longer have to court party bosses. When the Senate threatened not to ratify the treaty for the League of Nations after World War I, Wilson toured the country in order to arouse public opinion to force the Senate to acquiesce. Although he failed, he introduced a mode of dealing with Congress that presidents have used ever since.

Wilson did not completely succeed in achieving the aims of his reforms. Separation of powers continues to be a major feature of American constitutionalism and determinant of policy. But his new view of the presidency also remains, sometimes in uneasy tension with the separation of powers. Wilson's partial victory altered the shape of twentieth-century American politics.

The Extension of the Vote to Women

Another important constitutional change which occurred during the presidency of Woodrow Wilson was the extension of the vote to women. The movement for women's suffrage had much support from the progressives as a democratic reform. But the movement predated the progressives and had other roots, which is why we single it out for special attention. It had begun in the 1830s and was linked indirectly to the abolitionist movement. Both appealed to the same principle: citizenship implied the right of equal treatment before the law for every group. After the Civil War, suffragists under the leadership of Susan B. Anthony advocated the right of women to vote under the Fourteenth Amendment, which granted citizenship to all born and naturalized Americans and called for equal protection of the laws. Citizenship, however, was not understood by the authors of the Amendment, nor Americans generally, to include the right to vote. Susan Anthony, after trying to vote, was arrested in 1872 in Rochester, New York, and convicted of the crime of "voting without a lawful right to vote."

Suffragists thereafter pursued a dual strategy of pushing for acknowledgment of their right to vote from the states and attempting to amend the Constitution to guarantee a federal right of suffrage. The women's movement made some progress at the state level in the late nineteenth century, when four western states granted women the full right to vote in all elections: Wyoming (1870), Idaho (1870), Utah (1876), and Colorado (1888). Elsewhere, however, the movement met stiff resistance. During the progressive era, additional gains were made in several states, but the main effort by the movement was now directed at obtaining a Constitutional amendment forbidding denial of the right to vote on the grounds of sex. At first, many Democrats in Congress, following President Wilson's lead, refused to vote approval. But suffragists, using Wilson's own World War I rhetoric of "making the world safe for democracy," eventually won his endorsement in 1918. Congressional approval followed shortly thereafter. In 1920, the Nineteenth Amendment was ratified, denying any state the authority to abridge the right to vote on account of sex.

In the elections immediately following the passage of the Nineteenth Amendment, turnout of

President Woodrow Wilson resisted the movement for women's suffrage at first, but in 1918 he endorsed the idea, as this sign in a suffrage parade shows; two years later the right of women to vote was ensured when the Nineteenth Amendment was ratified. *(Bettman Archive)*

women was low (about one-third of all those eligible). Over time, however, beliefs and practices changed, and today women and men turn out to vote at approximately the same rates.

Supporters of women's suffrage originally included not only those favoring in principle the right of women to vote but also many who believed that adding women to the electorate would increase support for certain programs and policies such as prohibition, increased expenditures on education, and world disarmament. Some utopians went so far as to think that granting women the vote would "abolish poverty, protect family life, and raise educational and cultural standards." In fact, no dramatic changes resulted immediately from extending suffrage to women. Men and women differ marginally in their opinions in some areas—for example, men have shown a greater willingness to

favor the use of force in the solution of certain international and domestic problems—and these differences have had some impact on voting behavior. It appears that this impact has been greater since 1980 (see Chapter 7). In general, however, women and men vote in much the same ways, and the major factors that influence their votes are related not to gender but to other determinants that affect both sexes in the same fashion.

THE NEW DEAL

Franklin Roosevelt became president in 1932 in the midst of an economic crisis unparalleled in the nation's history. The great depression not only ruined businesses and put millions out of work but also threatened to arouse class antagonisms to such a point that fascism or communism might find fertile ground. Roosevelt tried simultaneously to meet both the economic and the political threats. His solution to these simultaneous crises has become known as the "welfare state." There have been two main thrusts toward the welfare state, the first under Roosevelt's "New Deal," the second under President Lyndon Johnson's "Great Society." While the two movements viewed the ends of society in the same way, the Great Society involved an even larger role for government and provided for a somewhat different distribution of power within the national government. We shall examine these two movements separately.

The Ends of Society—
The New Deal Critique of Free Enterprise

The pursuit of private wealth free from governmental control was justified by the defenders of free enterprise by means of the idea of the "invisible hand." If people were left free to pursue their private profit, the argument ran, the public good would also be served (quite unintentionally and hence invisibly). In developing a business that produced wealth for the owner, other people would be given jobs, new goods would be produced for consumers, and the wealth of society as a whole would be increased. Grocers, the defenders reasoned, provide us with food, not because they love us but because they desire to make money.

Supporters of the New Deal denied that this invisible hand worked. The frantic pursuit of wealth had resulted not in general prosperity but in the great depression. Private interest was not automatically converted into public benefit. It might be true, Roosevelt conceded, that the development of modern industrial society would have been impossible without unleashing private entrepreneurs. Creating an economic order capable of raising the standard of living for everyone required, in Roosevelt's words,

> the use of the talents of men of tremendous will and ambition, since by no other force could the problems of financing and engineering and new developments be brought to a consummation. . . . The financiers who pushed the railroads to the Pacific were always ruthless, often wasteful, and frequently corrupt; but they did build railroads, and we have them today (Roosevelt, 1949:452).

By the 1930s, however, the industrial plant was built. The task now, Roosevelt argued, was not "producing more goods. It is the soberer, less dramatic business of administering resources and plants already in hand, . . . of distributing wealth and products more equitably" (Roosevelt, 1949:454–455).

Roosevelt taught a new understanding of the ends of society. Government must protect the rights of the Declaration, but those rights were not what the advocates of laissez-faire thought them to be. The right to life must be understood to include the "right to make a comfortable living," and it must be understood that the paramount property right is the right to be secured against the burdens of sickness and unemployment and the disabilities of childhood and old age. Instead of the spirit of private competition and advantage, Roosevelt sought to cultivate the spirit of reciprocal self-denial for the common good among businesspeople as well as others. If business should lack that spirit, the "government must be swift to enter and protect the public welfare" (Roosevelt, 1949:456).

The Scope of Government—
Economic Security and the Welfare State

The New Deal did not seek to destroy the free enterprise system. It did not favor socialism: it did not seek to have business owned by the government, except in unusual circumstances. Nor were the advocates of the New Deal much attracted to the "trust-busting" approach earlier favored by the progressives. The progressives sought to break up large corporations in order to restore economic competition in the face of monopoly power. New Dealers wanted, not to preserve the competitive spirit of traditional capitalism, but to transform that spirit into one of cooperation between business, labor, and government in the service of public goals.

The public goal to be served was that of the "welfare state." The welfare state is a state in which the government assumes responsibility for guaranteeing the economic security of its citizens. Before the New Deal, it had not been regarded as the government's business to provide for economic security. At most, it was thought the government's business to keep open the opportunities whereby in-

---

BOX 3-4

THE FOUNDATIONS OF THE WELFARE STATE

The issues involved in the extension of governmental regulation of the economy and provision of economic security were not restricted solely to economic issues. Part of the debate concerned the issue of the effects of a welfare state upon individual character. Consider these opinions of presidents Herbert Hoover and Franklin Roosevelt:

Hoover

> This is not an issue as to whether people shall go hungry or cold in the United States. It is solely a question of the best method by which hunger and cold shall be prevented. It is a question as to whether the American people on one hand will maintain the spirit of charity and mutual self help through voluntary giving and the responsibility of local government. . . . If we break down this sense of responsibility of individual generosity to individual and mutual self help in the country in times of national difficulty . . . we have not only impaired something infinitely valuable in the life of the American people but have struck at the roots of self-government.

Roosevelt

> Those words "freedom" and "opportunity" do not mean a license to climb upwards by pushing other people down. Any paternalistic system which tries to provide for security for everyone from above only calls for an impossible task and a regimentation utterly uncongenial to the spirit of our people. But Government cooperation to help make the system of free enterprise work, to provide that minimum security without which the competitive system cannot function, to restrain the kind of individual action which in the past has been harmful to the community—that kind of governmental cooperation is entirely consistent with the best tradition of America.

Source: Hoover, 1934, II:424; Frisch and Stevens, 1973:307–308.

dividuals might provide for their own security. But now, as Roosevelt put it, it would become the aim of government to move toward "greater security for the average man than he has ever known before in the history of America." This greater security was to be achieved essentially by three means: governmental regulation of economic enterprise, social security, and income redistribution.

The Regulation of Economic Enterprise Because the New Deal sought to transform the spirit of private economic enterprise, the essential aim of the vastly expanded governmental regulation of business and labor that came out of the New Deal was to infuse private enterprise with public goals. This was possible, the New Dealers thought, if economic life were organized. While the private interests of individuals might frequently be in conflict with the public good, the interests of groups (such as labor unions and trade associations) were much closer to the public interest. When management and labor sat down together at the bargaining table, they would come to realize that they essentially shared the same interests. The general prosperity of the industry would mean general prosper-

ity for the workers as well. Early in his administration, Roosevelt seemed to have the hope that the transformation of the spirit of economic enterprise could come about without much permanent governmental regulation of business, but later he came to believe that it required the imposition of public goals by government. Government, labor, and business would cooperate, but government would set the basic public goals to be reached.

A good recent example of governmental regulation made in the New Deal spirit is the laws and regulations specifying that only automobiles getting a certain number of miles per gallon can be built. This does not make the government the owner of the automobile companies, but it imposes an explicit purpose—energy saving—upon a private economic activity by means of governmental regulation.

Social Security The New Deal saw that the goal of economic security for all could not be reached simply by the government's taking responsibility for a prosperous economy and by its infusing private enterprise with public purposes. There were many people who could not participate in the active life of the economy and who would not share in its fruits. Parentless children, old people, victims of accidents, the physically or mentally disabled—all could be guaranteed economic security only by some other means. Before the 1930s, these people were considered the concern of the states and private charity, not of the national government. But Congress in 1935 enacted a series of measures providing pensions for the aged; unemployment insurance; benefits to the blind, to dependent mothers, and to crippled children; and appropriations for public health work.

Redistribution of Wealth In seeking security for the average American, the New Deal necessarily also sought a greater equality of wealth and power. Although its primary goal was not to distribute wealth more equally, programs such as the social security system worked to bring about some amelioration of extreme inequalities. Roosevelt extolled the average person who sought "good health, good food, good education, good working conditions and the opportunity for normal recreation and occasional travel." By means of greater economic equality, the New Deal sought to bring about a stronger national unity.

FIGURE 3-2
Income distribution, 1929–1964. This graph shows the percentage of family personal income received by the top 5 percent of families and unattached individuals from 1929 (before the New Deal) to 1964. The changes reflect alterations in economic conditions as well as effects of governmental policies. (*Source: Historical Statistics of the United States, Colonial Times to 1970,* 1975:301)

Percent of total income

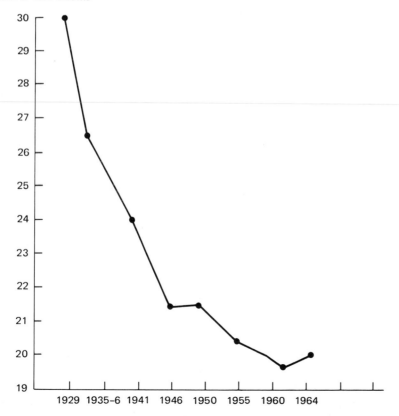

The impulse of the New Deal has been the primary source of movement in our politics from the 1930s into the 1970s. Only in the last decade has the New Deal agenda no longer simply dominated. The persistence of the issues of the New Deal is due in part to the fact that its aims could not be achieved once and for all. What constitutes economic security depends on the level of economic development. There is no definite quantity of economic well-being one can achieve and then have security. Hence the goal of economic security is constantly moving ahead even as people move to achieve it. It has often been said that today's liberal is tomorrow's conservative. Conservatives were originally simply opponents of the New Deal, but later conservatives became opponents of new manifestations of the New Deal, having accepted its earlier stages.

The friends of the New Deal have been called "liberals" because the New Deal saw economic security as essential to liberty. If people did not have good jobs and were not protected against the potential disasters of life, how could they be free? Liberty means something only to those who are able to make use of it. Economic security establishes the condition under which liberty will be useful to everyone. Without this condition, people may become willing to give up liberty for the sake of the satisfaction of their wants. "Freedom from want" is the condition of all other freedoms.

The opponents of the New Deal responded that if one makes economic security and equality the principal aim of government, the human personality may become submerged in the interest of a better-regulated economic life with its emphasis on health, welfare, and freedom from want. People may become willing to turn all the difficult choices of their lives over to a government that cares for their every want. Such people may be economically secure, but they will not be free human beings.

To reach the aim of economic security for all, the New Deal broke down the previous line between private economic activity and government. Government, business, and labor were to become partners in creating and equalizing wealth. This new view was resisted not only by the Republican party but initially also by the Supreme Court, which declared major aspects of the New Deal unconstitutional. President Roosevelt tried but failed to "pack" the Court with new appointees who

would support his program. However, the Court reversed its position in *West Coast Hotel v. Parrish* (1937), upholding for the first time a statute imposing major regulations on business activity (here a minimum wage law for women and children). The decision in *Wickard v. Filburn* (1942), which held that production of grain even for a farmer's own use could be regulated by Congress as interstate commerce, finally acknowledged a virtually unlimited power in the national government to regulate economic life.

The Organization and Distribution of Power— A Strengthened Presidency

At the same time that the scope of government was increasing, the shift of power within the national government toward the presidency (as originally desired by the progressives) was receiving new impetus. Representation, too, was understood by the New Dealers in essentially the same terms as it had been by the progressives. The government, and particularly the presidency, increasingly found its practical authority in its ability to portray itself as the leader of a great popular movement and national community. The increased role of the government in regulating economic life also led to an increase in both the size and the power of the bureaucracy.

THE GREAT SOCIETY

The 1960s witnessed a continuation and development of the ideas of the New Deal, with a new focus. In particular the Great Society programs of President Lyndon Johnson and the views of the Supreme Court under Chief Justice Earl Warren led to a new and expanded view of the importance of achieving equality of opportunity.

The Scope of Government— Protecting Civil Rights and Promoting Equality

The Great Society continued the effort of the New Deal to use governmental power to regulate the economy. At the same time it saw new scope for the government in protecting civil rights and promoting equality of opportunity for all Americans. We shall illustrate this concern of the Great Society here through a discussion of voting rights; a dis-

In the 1960s, the civil rights movement made the disenfranchisement of southern blacks dramatically clear to the nation, and the federal government intervened to guarantee voting rights that had been denied for decades.   *(Danny Lyon/Magnum)*

cussion of the increased protection for other rights brought about in the Great Society years can be found in Chapter 17.

As we have noted, there were some small steps taken to extend the vote to blacks during the first half of the twentieth century. The Supreme Court struck down the "grandfather clause" in 1915, the white primary in 1944, and some of the most discriminatory applications of the literacy tests in 1949. Some states also took certain remedial steps on their own, especially after 1940. So the situation for black voters was by no means equally bleak in all the southern states. But the major transformation in southern politics had to await the 1960s and was accomplished by means of national intervention into the states' traditional role in defining qualifications for voting. With pressure from the civil rights movement in the 1960s, the federal government finally began to move in earnest to topple the entire legal structure that supported discriminatory voting laws and practices. In 1963, the Twenty-Fourth Amendment, which banned the use of poll taxes for federal elections, was ratified. Two years later, the Supreme Court extended this ban to state

elections. In 1965, the federal government passed the landmark Voting Rights Act that barred the use of literacy tests and permitted federal authorities, at the attorney general's discretion, to order registration in states and counties where less than half of the voting-age population was registered or had voted in the last election.

These measures, in combination with the changing attitudes resulting from the civil rights movement, had very impressive results. Immediately, the level of black voting rose dramatically in the south. In 1940, only 5 percent of voting-age blacks were registered; by 1966, that figure had risen to 45 percent and by 1976 to 63 percent, nearly the same as the figure for white voters. For the first time since Reconstruction, black politicians were elected to many state and local offices, and black voters played a pivotal role in determining election results. Many white politicians who previously had spurned black support now began to court it. The Voting Rights Act of 1965 itself was passed partly because Democrats saw that black voters had held the balance of power in the Kennedy-Nixon presidential contest of 1960 and wished to consolidate this vote for their party. Although acquisition of the right to vote by no means proved a panacea for civil rights problems, it at least enabled blacks to assert their interests within the normal coalition-building processes of a representative system.

Suffrage was further extended by the Twenty-Third Amendment, which in 1961 gave electoral vote representation to Washington, D.C.; and by the Twenty-Sixth Amendment, which in 1971 gave the right to vote to all persons over 18 years of age. (Most states before this Amendment set the voting age at 21.) The Twenty-Sixth Amendment was ratified during the Vietnamese war, when 18-year-olds were being drafted for military service and were fighting and dying in southeast Asia. The chief argument put forward by proponents of the Amendment rested on this simple theme: "If you're old enough to fight, you're old enough to vote." Although some analysts expected the inclusion of younger voters to move the nation dramatically to the left, no such result has occurred. Young people do not vote exactly like the rest of the electorate, but the differences are variable and are likely to shift as each new group passes through this age bracket. Moreover, younger people turn out to vote at a significantly lower rate than the rest of the electorate, which dilutes the strength of whatever peculiar attributes they possess as a group. Their lower turnout rate is attributable mostly to the fact that many young people have not yet settled into a community and developed the habit of participation in citizenship.

Today, then, citizenship is understood to include the right to vote for almost all adults; and no distinction, such as was made in the past, now exists between citizenship that guarantees an individual equal protection under existing civil law and a fuller notion of citizenship that entitles one to the privilege of voting. Indeed, in an important Supreme Court decision of the 1960s, *Wesberry v. Sanders* (1964), the Court argued the position that the exercise of the franchise is necessary for the full enjoyment of other rights.

No right is more precious in a free country than that of having a voice in the election of those who make the laws under which . . . we must live. Other rights are illusionary if the right to vote is undermined.

Given this understanding of the franchise, it is not surprising that the federal government has now undertaken much of the task of protecting it. Although one can find a few persons who still advocate limiting the franchise by a minimum literacy criterion, Americans on the whole have now rejected this view and have adopted the simpler and more democratic concept of universal adult suffrage. Implicit in this extension of the franchise is the idea that whatever else the vote may be—such as a method for expression of policy—it is at least an instrument of self-protection through which individuals and groups can assert their interests in the electoral process.

Simultaneously the national government came to be used to protect other civil rights of Americans. Beginning in 1925, but proceeding most rapidly under Chief Justice Warren in the 1960s, the Supreme Court came to regard most of the protections of the Bill of Rights as applying to state as well as national governments. The result was a great extension of the use of federal power to achieve the protection of civil rights (see Chapter 17).

The Organization and Distribution of Powers— The Role of the Courts

The Great Society continued the New Deal emphasis upon the presidency, with Lyndon Johnson taking a vigorous lead in advancing its programs. The bureaucracy also expanded its role, more and more affecting major issues of policy as government supervision of social and economic life became more complex and detailed. At the same time, the Supreme Court achieved new power within the system, deciding many issues previously thought to be legislative or executive in character. Beginning with *Brown v. Board of Education* in 1954, the Court began to adopt a broader view of its role within the government. It saw itself as a body with the ability and the right to step into matters previously thought to belong to the legislative branch, especially when Congress did not take the steps the Court thought the good of the country required (such as desegregating the schools). It moved to regulate the electoral process, to desegregate the country and promote equality, to reform the criminal justice system, and to change the laws regulating families and the relations between the sexes. (See Chapters 16 and 17.) The Court has taken an active hand in most of the major political and social transformations in the United States in the past quarter century.

THE PRESENT AND FUTURE

Today we find ourselves in a time of uncertainty and potentially great constitutional change. Since the late 1970s it has been apparent that the ability of the ideas of the New Deal and the Great Society to determine the agenda for American politics has greatly weakened. Since the 1930s these ideas had dominated American politics, with Republicans arguing for going slower than the Democrats wished, but not disputing the general direction. In the election of 1980, however, it was the Republicans who proposed a new course for the nation and the Democrats who found themselves in the position of objecting to what someone else had proposed. New circumstances and new issues had brought about this change. Yet the direction of permanent change remains unclear. This is *our* opportunity and *our* challenge. In dispute are matters affecting the ends of society, the scope of government, and the organization and distribution of power.

The Ends of Society

Restricting ourselves to domestic issues, two great disputes of the early 1980s particularly involved our understanding of the proper ends of society. One is that over economic policy; the other, that over treatment of minorities.

The economic policies of the New Deal and the Great Society rested on the supposition that there would be continued economic growth in the United States. It was thought that the problem facing government was to control swings in the economy and to provide security for all through the proper distribution of the national wealth. The American economy grew steadily in the years following World War II. However, in the 1970s the economy's growth gradually slowed and then came to a halt. The issue of the *production* of wealth assumed a new priority over the issue of the *distribution* of wealth.

Faced with a stagnant economy and high infla-

tion, Ronald Reagan and his party suggested a new economic program, "Reaganomics," to deal with this situation. Its principal elements included lower marginal tax rates, a slowed rate of growth in domestic federal spending, and reduced governmental regulation of private business. In the Republicans' view, these policies would give a new dignity, greater scope, and higher rewards to those who work and produce, which would in turn stimulate the economy. The Democrats, in resisting this program, argued that it would merely give more wealth to the greedy and those already rich and that it would foster a selfish, uncaring society.

Although legal segregation of the races had been ended by the 1970s, inequalities between the races persist, and the question of how to deal with these inequalities has created new disputes and divisions. Inequalities involving other groups—women, hispanics, and others—have also received new attention. "Affirmative action"—the position that minorities should be given special attention in order to overcome the effects of discrimination they have suffered in the past—has gained increased support as a response to this situation, creating a potentially deep split over the meaning of justice in the United States. Is a just society to be defined by the equality in status of various groups within it, or by the degree to which it treats persons as individuals entitled to the same benefits or burdens regardless of the group to which they belong? While the Reagan administration did not oppose the principle of affirmative action, it moved to reduce the scope of affirmative action programs.

Both of these issues reveal that we, too, must reflect on the proper ends of society and consider the kind of people and the kind of society we wish to be.

The Scope of Government

Will the country continue to expand the scope of government into more aspects of life, or will it move toward reducing the scope of government? Ronald Reagan came into office believing that the government was trying to do too many things and that greater scope should be given to private initiative. Under Reagan the number of government regulations was reduced substantially. On the other hand, substantial opposition to this trend exists, particularly with regard to environmental regulations. Attempts on the part of the Reagan administration to reduce the scope of the welfare state created even fiercer opposition. Despite some successes in cutting certain federal programs, President Reagan fell far short of obtaining from Congress all the cuts he wanted. After the midterm elections of 1982, resulting in substantial Democratic gains in the House of Representatives, the chances for any substantial cuts in domestic welfare programs became even less. Yet, although large government is surely here to stay, how large it will be and what kind of concern it will show for economic and social problems remain undetermined.

The Organization and Distribution of Power

Two decades ago many political scientists would have confidently predicted that power would continue to gravitate to the presidency as it had done since the advent of the New Deal. However, political events have a way of upsetting confident predictions, and today the future strength of the branches seems much less certain. As a result of the Vietnamese war and Watergate, as well as changes in American political parties which we will discuss later in the book, much power returned to Congress in the 1970s. Congress asserted new control not only over domestic issues but even over foreign policy issues traditionally thought to be the particular province of the president. The 1980s opened with a show of presidential strength. During the first two years of his administration, Ronald Reagan was able to get much of what he wanted from Congress, even though it was partly controlled by the opposition party. After the elections of 1982, and partly as a result of Democratic victories in that election, Congress again asserted its power. Whether the balance of power will shift in the remainder of the decade toward president or Congress may well depend upon the outcome of political struggles currently being waged.

The power of the courts, enormous in recent decades, has also been challenged. Will objections to the use of judicial power by the federal courts lead to a lesser role for the judiciary? The Reagan administration made more conservative appointments to the courts, but this does not necessarily mean a weaker judiciary vis-à-vis the other branches. There can be conservative as well as liberal activists in the courts.

Finally, President Reagan, in his 1982 state of the union message, proposed shifting many federal welfare programs to state control. Strong opposition, however, has so far prevented any substantial moves in this direction. Despite such efforts to slow government growth, one cannot rule out some resurgence of our federal structure. Would a greater role for states result in more local diversity and greater awareness of regional problems, as some argue, or would it simply allow scope for local prejudice and incompetence, as others maintain?

CONCLUSION

American politics today seems fluid and undetermined in many ways—as it has often been in the past. Today, as in former times, Americans are faced with choices concerning the ends we believe society should serve, the scope that government should have, and the way power is to be organized and distributed. In looking at the alternatives Americans have faced in the past and at the choices they have made, we can see that each generation faces anew the challenge of constitution making—shaping, accepting, or overthrowing the understandings and choices it has inherited.

SOURCES

Adair, Douglass: *Fame and the Founding Fathers: Essays,* Norton, New York, 1974.

Beard, Charles A.: *An Economic Interpretation of the Constitution of the United States,* Macmillan, New York, 1913.

Brown, Robert E.: *Charles Beard and the Constitution,* University of Chicago Press, Chicago, 1956.

Calhoun, John C.: *The Works of John C. Calhoun,* Richard K. Crallé (ed.), Russell and Russell, New York, 1968.

Freehling, William W.: *Prelude to Civil War: The Nullification Controversy in South Carolina, 1816–1836,* Harper and Row, New York, 1966.

Frisch, Morton J., and Richard G. Stevens (eds.): *The Political Thought of American Statesmen,* Peacock, Itasca, Ill. 1973.

Hamilton, Alexander: *The Papers of Alexander Hamilton,* Harold C. Syrett (ed.), Columbia University Press, New York and London, 1966.

Historical Statistics of the United States: Colonial Times to 1970, U. S. Bureau of the Census, Washington, D.C., 1975.

Hoover, Herbert: *The State Papers and Other Public Writings of Herbert Hoover,* William Starr Myers (ed.), Doubleday, Doran, New York, 1934.

Jaffa, Harry V.: *Crisis of the House Divided,* Doubleday, Garden City, N.Y., 1959.

Jefferson, Thomas: *The Writings of Thomas Jefferson,* Andrew A. Lipscomb (ed.), Thomas Jefferson Memorial Association, Washington, D.C., 1904.

Lincoln, Abraham: *The Collected Works of Abraham Lincoln,* Roy P. Basler (ed.), Rutgers University Press, New Brunswick, N.J., 1953.

Mann, Horace: "The Importance of Universal, Free Public Education," in *Lectures and Annual Reports on Education,* Mary Mann (ed.), Harvard University Press, Cambridge, Mass., 1867.

McDonald, Forest: *We The People: The Economic Origins of the Constitution,* University of Chicago Press, Chicago, 1958.

Meyers, Marvin: *The Jacksonian Persuasion,* Stanford University Press, Stanford, Calif., 1957.

Roosevelt, Franklin: "Commonwealth Club Address, 1932," in *The People Shall Judge,* University of Chicago Press, Chicago and London, 1949.

Schambra, William A: "The Roots of the American Public Philosophy," *The Public Interest,* 67, spring, 1982, pp. 36–48.

Statistical Abstract of the United States: 1977, U. S. Bureau of the Census, Washington, D.C., 1977; and *Statistical Abstract of the United States: 1981.*

Wilson, Woodrow: *Congressional Government,* Meridian, Cleveland and New York, 1956.

————: "The Nature of Democracy in the United States," in Morton J. Frisch and Richard G. Stevens (eds.), *Political Thought of American Statesmen,* Peacock, Itasca, Ill., 1973, pp. 270–285.

Court Cases

Brown v. Board of Education of Topeka, 347 U.S. 483 (1954).

Dred Scott v. Sanford, 19 How. 393 (1857).

Marbury v. Madison, 1 Cranch 137 (1803)

McCulloch v. Maryland, 17 U.S. 316 (1819)

Wesberry v. Sanders, 376 U.S. 1 (1964).

Wickard et al. v. Filburn, 317 U.S. 111 (1942).

RECOMMENDED READINGS

Frisch, Morton J., and Richard G. Stevens (eds.): *American Political Thought: The Philosophic Dimensions of American Statesmanship,* Scribner's, New York, 1971. Essays on the political thought of pivotal leaders in the development of the United States.

Hartz, Louis: *The Liberal Tradition in America,* Harcourt, Brace, Jovanovich, New York, 1955. Explores the absence of class-based politics in the United States.

Hofstadter, Richard: *The American Political Tradition,* Knopf, New York, 1951. Critically examines various strands of political thought and practice in the United States.

Huntington, Samuel: *Political Order in Changing Societies,* Yale University Press, New Haven and London, 1968. Compares the development of political order in the United States with that in both European and third world countries.

Lipset, Seymour Martin: *The First New Nation,* rev. ed., Norton, New York, 1979. Examines how the process of nation building took place in the United States.

Lowi, Theodore: *The End of Liberalism,* 2d ed., Norton, New York, 1979. A critique of the liberal tradition.

Tocqueville, Alexis de: *Democracy in America,* vols. 1 and 2, Phillips Bradley (ed.), Knopf, New York, 1951. The classic study of the effects of democracy upon the United States.

Part Two

The Public and the Government: Intermediary Institutions and Electoral Politics

Chapter 4

Public Opinion

CHAPTER CONTENTS

"When public opinion decides that something has to change, it changes." This was the explanation given by Congressman Jim Jones in 1981 for the unexpected transformation that took place in the federal budget during the first few months of Ronald Reagan's presidency. Along with other members of Congress, Jones had witnessed a rapid growth in the federal budget throughout the 1970s, and, like most officials in Washington, he may have thought that significant budget cuts could not be achieved. Politicians might like to talk about holding down federal spending while running for office, but once in Washington and faced with the unrelenting pressure of well-entrenched interest groups, they give up the effort. Yet when Ronald Reagan took office in January of 1981, he decided to press immediately for deep cuts from the budget that President Carter had proposed. With the support of nearly all Republicans and some Democrats, the president managed to put through Congress most of his cuts. For better or worse, the "impossible" was accomplished.

But did these events prove Congressman Jones correct when he claimed that public opinion "decided" public policy in the United States? Clearly, Ronald Reagan's election in 1980 had signaled that the American public was prepared to accept some important changes. And just as clearly, it had become apparent to most politicians that the public was growing more and more dissatisfied with "big" government. And yet, it is certainly too simple to suggest that shifts in public opinion always initiate policy changes or that public opinion always has its way. Indeed, at the very same time that President Reagan was pushing for his budget reductions, he was also calling for a controversial tax-cut program that most Americans, as indicated in many public opinion polls at the time, did not then support (see Figure 4-1). No one, however, believed that it was inappropriate for the president to attempt to persuade the American people that his program was needed, and few questioned the right or legitimacy of the president and Congress to enact this legislation, even without the backing of a firm majority as registered in public opinion polls.

Quite clearly, then, the relationship between government and public opinion is a complex one, and if part of the genius of the American system includes the government's ability to respond to public opinion, another part consists of its ability to lead it and sometimes even defy it, at least for a reasonable period of time. As a form of popular government, a republican or representative system is supposed to be responsive in some sense to the will of the people. Elections and frequent contacts between the public and its representatives are designed to guarantee that responsiveness. But representative government is also based on the premise that elected officials are entitled not only to attempt to persuade public opinion to their point of view but also to exercise their own discretion on matters of public policy, if necessary by acting on specific occasions contrary to public demands. A president who failed to lead and who always followed the shifting sentiments of public opinion

FIGURE 4-1
Public opinion and public policy. Ronald Reagan's two most important policy initiatives during his first year in office were a cut in the projected budget growth of the federal government and a reduction of federal tax rates. The budget cuts had strong and widespread support but the public—at least initially—was wary of any tax plan that would leave the budget unbalanced. President Reagan eventually succeeded in persuading Congress to enact both programs. (*Source: a. Public Opinion*, 1980. *b. Public Opinion*, February-March 1981.)

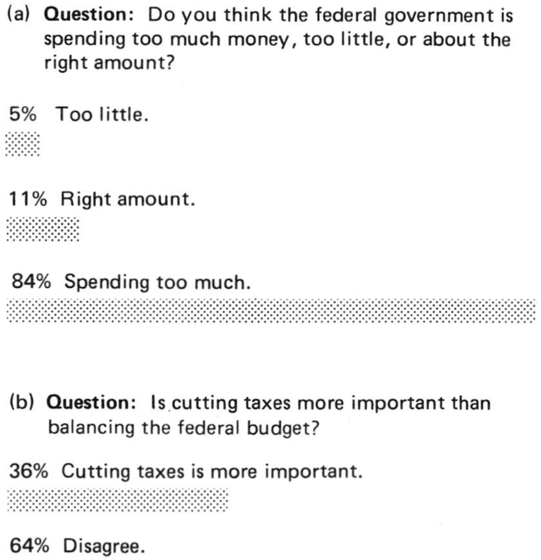

(a) **Question:** Do you think the federal government is spending too much money, too little, or about the right amount?

5% Too little.

11% Right amount.

84% Spending too much.

(b) **Question:** Is cutting taxes more important than balancing the federal budget?

36% Cutting taxes is more important.

64% Disagree.

would quickly win the contempt of the American people. Moreover, republican government also implies a guarantee of the sanctity of certain fundamental rights, which government is obliged to protect, regardless of public opinion.

There is, then, as we saw in Chapter 3, a partial tension that exists between the "representative" principle and the "democratic" principle. The representative principle stresses discretion for elected officials and a degree of insulation from the pressures of public opinion. The democratic principle emphasizes a more rapid transfer of the public will into public policy. Neither of these principles is absolute—that is, no one has seriously advocated representation without democratic elections or the rule of public opinion without representation. But the two principles nevertheless identify two basic tendencies in the American tradition that have pushed and pulled on the development of our political institutions. The Constitutional system established by the founders placed a heavy emphasis on the representative principle. Over the course of American history, we have witnessed many changes that have promoted greater democracy, such as the direct election of senators, the popular selection of presidential electors, and the nomination of most candidates by primaries. Nonetheless, the system remains representative in character in that all political power is vested in either elected or appointed officials and no governmental decision is made directly by the public.

The proper role for public opinion in our system raises issues that take us to the very heart of what characterizes our form of government. But before we can discuss these issues directly, it is necessary to have a clearer idea of just what is meant by "public opinion," for the term is often used in imprecise ways. In fact, for our purposes in this chapter, it will be helpful to begin by dismissing any idea of public opinion as just *one* thing having a uniform set of properties and characteristics. Instead, we shall speak of different types of public opinion as they exist in relation to the attitudes that people hold on three levels of politically relevant beliefs: (1) fundamental constitutional questions, (2) the general direction of governmental policy, and (3) specific policy issues of the day and opinions about politicians in office or running for office. In this chapter, after looking briefly at how opinion

is measured, we will analyze public attitudes on these three levels. We will then turn to the issue of how opinions are formed and conclude with the constitution maker's question of the role that public opinion plays—and should play—in a representative system of government.

MEASURING PUBLIC OPINION

Today, with the pervasiveness of public opinion polls, many probably equate public opinion with the reported results of polls. Americans, it is safe to say, are the most polled population in the world. Few campaigns for important offices operate without private polling data: there are several scholarly journals whose main focus is the analysis of polls; and newspapers, magazines, and television news often devote considerable space or time to reporting and discussing poll information. An entire business exists to tell Americans just what they are thinking.

Yet polling as we know it today is a relatively recent development that began in the 1930s and achieved validity in sampling techniques only in the late 1940s. To say, therefore, that public opinion is only what is measured by polls would lead to the obviously false conclusion that public opinion did not exist until the middle of this century. In fact, public opinion in its different forms was studied from at least the time of the founding, and some of the classic accounts of public opinion—by Tocqueville, Bryce, and Walter Lippmann—were written before polling was employed. Moreover, public opinion was known to people active in politics—and still is known to them today—by means of contacts with citizens, organizational activities of groups, and, of course, the interpretation of election results. It was also known by the politician's sense of what the community either demanded or would not tolerate. In certain respects, these methods of assessing public opinion, though less accurate than polls, remain more useful, for they focus on opinion as an actual or potential force that can come into play in political life on behalf of or against a certain course of action. Polls, by contrast, often measure highly abstract opinion.

Polling represents one way of discovering public opinion. It has brought new range and much greater accuracy to the study of the topic, but unless polls are interpreted with a great deal of care, they can be misleading. And whatever assistance they bring to the understanding of opinion, there remain certain dimensions that can be known only by other techniques, such as in-depth interviews or observations of political behavior. What these lack in "science," they sometimes make up for in richness. To talk with citizens on the street corner or to see them, angry or enthusiastic, at a rally or a convention may give one a "feel" for the nuances and intensity of opinion that no poll can provide. We cannot go into all the elements of polling here, but it is important to highlight at least a few of the problems connected with the use and abuse of polls. Polling, one should remember, is not a science but a human activity based on certain scientific techniques.

"How can pollsters claim to know what the public thinks when they have never asked me or anyone I know?" This is a question that probably has occurred to many citizens, for, despite all the reports of what the public thinks, few people are ever polled to determine any given opinion. Polls are based on the statistical principle of sampling, according to which the characteristics of an entire population can be known by surveying a relatively small number of randomly selected cases. Take a sack filled with thousands of marbles, 60 percent of them black and 40 percent white; shake the sack and pull out a sample of 500 marbles. In 95 out of 100 such drawings, the percentage of black balls and white balls in the sample drawn should be within 3 percent of the total in the sack, that is, between 57 and 63 percent black marbles and 37 and 43 percent white marbles. Increase the sample of marbles drawn, and your chances of error and range of error will diminish somewhat. With a few technical adjustments, the same basic principle is employed in opinion polls. Most national polls contact no more than (and usually less than) 1,500 people.

The first problem with opinion polling derives from the fact that people are not marbles. Those conducting the interviews may make mistakes in recording or reporting, while those who are interviewed may conceal their opinions or give false responses, deliberately or unconsciously. We know, for example, that more people claim in polls to vote than the number who actually vote. Many no doubt feel embarrassed to admit their failure to be model citizens. For other reasons, such as mistrust, suspicion, or uneasiness at holding an unpopular opinion, people may hide or distort their views. This distortion occurs more among some groups than others, and more in certain countries than others. The activity of polling, in other words, is affected by the culture or subculture in which the polls are conducted.

In the case of most polls taken in politics, there is no objective way to confirm their validity. A poll, for example, on the public's view on nuclear disarmament measures an opinion on which there will be no vote. It is only, in fact, in those few instances on which matters are directly settled by elections that we have a genuine "test" of poll results. From these tests, it can be said that in the United States the major polling firms have a fairly impressive record of accurately stating the *range* of the vote in presidential elections, though they frequently miss the mark in more volatile primaries and congressional elections. And one should always keep in mind that a poll is *not* a prediction, but a measurement of the state of public sentiment at a given time. On matters on which people are frequently changing their minds, which has increasingly been the case in recent presidential primaries and elections, the polls—if they are accurate—are reflecting popular sentiment only at the moment they are taken. The adage that a poll is good only for the day on which it is taken contains a good deal of truth.

A second set of problems in dealing with polling relates to the way questions are worded. To cite one fairly typical occurrence, two leading polling firms in 1977 sought to determine the public's view on one of the major issues of that year—the Panama Canal Treaty. In asking their question, the two polls summarized the substance of the treaty in different terms. In one poll, it was found that only 8 percent approved of the treaty, while in the other, 39 percent approved (*Public Opinion,* 1978:33). Clearly, the "opinion" on the treaty, as it was reported, was in part a function of how the question was posed. Carefully worded questions and the corroborating evidence of a number of polls can eventually provide one with the confidence to speak of a valid opinion. It is wise, however, to remain slightly skeptical of reports of "opinions" without knowing exactly what questions were asked.

A final set of problems deals not with how accurate the polls are or how accurately they are reported, but with the meaning of what they measure. Are all the opinions measured by polls "real" opinions in any meaningful sense? Polls frequently pose questions on matters that for the citizens at the time are completely hypothetical. A citizen giving an opinion on a proposed Constitutional amendment to increase the length of the president's term might respond very differently if this amendment were beyond the realm of speculation and on the agenda of serious debate. Polls frequently seek out opinions on issues that are not at the time, or that never become, matters of serious concern. In such cases, there is a question about whether what is measured is an existing opinion in any meaningful sense or merely a response created by the polls. Along a slightly different line, polls pose questions on separate problems, whereas policies must be made under circumstances where various factors interrelate and impinge on each other. For example, when asked if they would like lower taxes and less government, most Americans reply in the affirmative. When asked whether they would like various services cut, they reply in the negative. Such contradictions are not surprising, since only in the real-life situation of making concrete decisions are people forced to resolve their preference. Public opinion may in fact contradict itself, which lessens its claim to be taken seriously, but it is also true that the method of polling may exaggerate contradictory aspects of opinion by taking separate questions out of context.

All these cautionary notes do not negate the importance of polls. Polls have added something new both to our understanding of public opinion and to the role of public opinion in politics. With widespread polling, it is now possible to know with a reasonable degree of accuracy what the public thinks. This fact has its advantages, for now politicians can, where they wish, take into consideration public feeling without the danger of completely misperceiving it or speaking only for those who clamor the loudest. Moreover, polling has created a new resource for public opinion and has undoubtedly strengthened, at least marginally, its influence on the governing process. Both presidents

Carter and Reagan, for example, regularly consulted with their campaign pollsters while in office in order to keep informed about trends in the public's thinking. There are, however, certain dangers that may accompany an increased reliance on polls. Politicians can employ this information to follow public opinion rather than exercise an independent judgment, and in election campaigns, polling can be used to help "manufacture" a candidate who fits the model of what a pollster finds that the people want.

CONSTITUTIONAL OPINION

Public opinion, we said, exists on three basic levels. The first is what we call "constitutional opinion," meaning the public's attitudes on the fundamental questions about the nature of the political order that were discussed in the first part of this book—questions such as what people consider to be the ends of society and the best form of government. In addition, constitutional opinion includes the public's "world view" on such general matters as religion and authority, for these continually impinge on politics and help shape the character of the political order. Some scholars refer to the dimensions of constitutional opinion by the term "political culture," which suggests a stratum of belief that is deeper and more fundamental than the shifting opinions on issues of the day (Almond and Verba, 1963).

The founders were well aware of the significance of constitutional opinion as they fashioned the new government. They felt its constraints—for example, on the issues of slavery and the power of the states—and they realized its force. Popular government, they knew, rested on opinion, and it was essential in establishing government to put opinion on the side of the regime by including a respect and veneration for its principles and formal arrangements (*Federalist* 49). Stability in constitutional opinion was one of their chief goals, and it has by and large been realized, except at rare moments of crisis.

Still, constitutional opinions have changed, although usually much more gradually than opinions on general government policies and issues. The truly distinctive feature about constitutional opinion, however, is that when it does change, its impact is not limited to a single issue but instead radiates from a general principle and influences a whole range of policies. Transformations in constitutional opinion are thus of fundamental importance in understanding American politics, a point that has never been better expressed than in the following classic statement by Abraham Lincoln:

> In this and like communities, public sentiment is everything. With public sentiment, nothing can fail; without it nothing can succeed. Consequently, he who molds public sentiment goes deeper than he who enacts statutes or pronounces decisions. He makes statutes and decisions possible or impossible to be executed (Johannsen, 1965:64–65).

By "public sentiment" Lincoln of course was referring here not to ordinary opinions of policy, but rather to the public's view on one of the core ideas animating the constitution. His understanding was based on the idea that in a popular form of government, public officials find it difficult if not impossible to enact or sustain policies that diverge from a firmly held belief based on a central constitutional principle.

Because the beliefs that make up a nation's political culture are so ingrained, they often escape notice or are taken for granted. Acceptance of the rule of law is a case in point. When a presidential election is held in the United States, no one gives a thought to the possibility that an incumbent who lost might refuse to cede office or that military leaders might intervene. Yet in some nations, like Argentina, such extralegal maneuvers occur frequently, and the informed public is aware that the popular verdict might not decide the outcome. Often it is only by comparing our experience with that of other nations that we can distinguish some of the most important aspects of our political culture.

Consensus and Conflict

Perhaps the most striking general characteristic of constitutional opinion in the United States is the high degree of consensus—or uniformity of belief—that exists on the most basic political questions (Devine, 1972). Since the founding in 1787, Americans have shared a commitment to such gen-

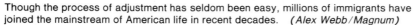

Though the process of adjustment has seldom been easy, millions of immigrants have joined the mainstream of American life in recent decades. *(Alex Webb/Magnum)*

eral principles as liberty, equality, the rule of law, and a republican form of government. For famous European observers who have studied the United States, such as Alexis de Tocqueville and James Bryce, the existence of this consensus has been one of the most significant features in understanding our Constitution. Europeans have been so impressed with this fact because agreement on fundamental principles has not been characteristic of the continental European tradition.

In the nineteenth century, while the United States was steadily developing democratic traditions, many European nations remained bitterly divided between supporters of monarchism and republicanism. In this century, European nations that have developed democratic regimes have experienced the challenges of fascism on the right and communism on the left, both of which openly reject republican principles. Even today in mature western European democracies like Italy and France, there are large and powerful communist parties competing in every election. For many in these nations, elections have a different meaning from elections in the United States because the question posed is not simply who should govern but rather what kind of society should exist. By contrast, the two major parties in the United States, while they often differ on important matters of policy, agree on the basic nature of the political order. The choice presented in American elections is one of how best to promote widely shared political values.

The existence of consensus on constitutional issues is all the more striking when one considers that the population of the United States is made up of citizens of very different ethnic, religious, and racial backgrounds. Originally sparsely inhabited by various Indian nations, the United States was settled predominantly by people of Anglo-Saxon stock, to which was soon added a large black slave population. The growth of the nation in the nineteenth century and early twentieth century came in large part from the influx of massive numbers of people from Asia and Europe. The United States became commonly known as the "land of the immigrants," symbolized by the Statue of Liberty in New York City harbor with its poetic verse, "Give me your tired, your poor, your huddled masses yearning to breathe free." In this century, the United States has absorbed large numbers of political refugees from Germany (chiefly Jews escaping the Nazi terrors), from Hungary (after the Soviet Union crushed a rebellion in 1956), from Cuba (after the Cuban revolution in 1959), and from South Vietnam (after the fall of South Vietnam to the North Vietnamese in 1975). Millions from Puerto Rico, Haiti, and Mexico have also entered the country in the past twenty years, adding yet further cultural dimensions to the American mosaic.

Contrary to the impressions given by many superficial historical treatments of the American experience, these differences in race, religion, and ethnicity led historically to terrible acts of brutality, tensions, and social prejudice. Yet they have not resulted in demands for separate communities, as one finds, for example, in Canada (with the tensions between the French and English-speaking populations) or Northern Ireland (with the tensions between Catholics and Protestants). The agreement on political beliefs, it appears, has been the one bond of unity that has gone deeper and proved more enduring than the other differences. While certain common cultural elements, such as the use of the same language, are often important in unifying a nation, the most significant factor seems to be the existence of a common set of political beliefs and aspirations.

Many have speculated on the causes for this relatively high degree of political consensus. Our unique historical experience undoubtedly holds one of the keys. As a new nation settled mostly by Europeans from the middle ranks of society, Americans never faced the great problems of dealing with an established class of nobles whose titles and prerogatives stretched back to the feudal era. Geographical and economic factors have also been important. The abundance of land on the continent contributed to a sense of independence among early settlers, an independence which meant that workers employed in menial jobs in the cities could eventually leave and purchase land of their own. Throughout the nineteenth century, the "frontier tradition" added constantly to the democratization of the nation by providing new opportunities for people in new communities. Finally, as a consequence of the nation's political stability, abundant resources, and economic system, the United States experienced a level of economic growth in the nineteenth and early twentieth centuries unsurpassed by that of any other nation. This wealth helped to moderate the conflict among economic classes that plagued most European nations during the era of industrial development. No single factor alone, therefore, can account for the relatively high degree of consensus in American politics; its development has been the result of accidents of history and geography and the capacity of a people to take advantage of its good fortune.

While consensus has been the norm in American politics, there have nonetheless been instances of fundamental conflict on constitutional questions. Opinion in America has been widely supportive of the general principles of liberty, equality, and self-government; but over the course of our political development Americans have either interpreted these concepts in very different ways or simply failed in practice to live up to their own principles. It is in these respects—and seldom in the outright rejection of fundamental principles—that the American consensus has been threatened and at certain points broken. Such moments of conflict, discussed at length in Chapter 3, are uncharacteristic of American politics in the sense of being infrequent, but highly characteristic in the sense that they have defined the basic parameters of constitutional opinion. These earlier conflicts should be kept in mind as we turn now to a survey of the opinions of contemporary Americans on the consensual values of liberty, equality, and republican government under the Constitution.

Liberty

Liberty includes as its core the protection of certain basic rights, such as freedom of speech and association and the free exercise of religion. Americans support such rights—in the abstract—by overwhelming margins (Devine, 1972). Yet certain students have produced evidence indicating that many seem unwilling to grant the full exercise of these rights to persons or groups whom they fear or dislike, such as homosexuals, communists, and racists. Although there has been a significant decline in such attitudes of "intolerance" over the last generation, there nevertheless remains a surprisingly large percentage of citizens expressing opposition

to the spirit and letter of certain rights (see Figure 4-2). On these issues, political leaders and more highly educated members of society are far more likely to support the application of general rights in particular instances (McCloskey et al., 1960; Lawrence, 1976). In findings in all of these areas, surveys point to the importance of safeguards in the Constitution and restraints by representative institutions to provide protection for fundamental liberties beyond that which majorities might normally provide.

Liberty for Americans includes not only civil liberties such as free speech but also certain economic rights, most noticeably the right to hold and dispense property. Economic rights, unlike those pertaining to speech or association, inevitably require more detailed definition and regulation by law, but this constant involvement of law does not mean that property cannot be regarded as a fundamental right, free of *unreasonable* governmental controls. The right to hold property carries with it, by direct implication, the existence of inequalities in the economic sphere. Inequalities flow from such factors as family background, inheritance, and luck, but also from different skills at managing property and differing inclinations toward making money. As James Madison wrote in *Federalist* 10: "From the protection of different and unequal faculties of acquiring property, the possession of different degrees and kinds of property immediately results." Thus some people may work at two jobs and carefully save and invest, while others prefer more leisure time or choose to spend most of their income, even when they make enough to save a considerable amount.

There is a distinction, however, that must be made between the right of individuals to hold and dispense property and that of legally created entities such as business corporations. Americans recognize and accept the private status of business corporations, but they also believe that the public impact of their activities is such that they must often be treated differently from individuals and regulated more closely. While Americans support a free enterprise system, there has been a long and powerful tradition of mistrust of large corporations dating back at least as far as Andrew Jackson's attack on the "monster" Bank of the United States as a symbol of undemocratic corporate power. Sim-

Question: Suppose an admitted atheist or communist wants to make a speech in your community. Should he be allowed to speak, or not? Suppose he is teaching in a college. Should he be fired or not?

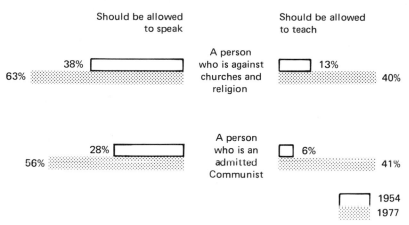

FIGURE 4-2
Tolerance of civil liberties. (*Source:* Stouffer, 1955; National Opinion Research Center, general surveys, 1977; *Public Opinion*, 1980.)

ilar attacks against corporate power surfaced during the Populist era in the 1890s, during the great depression, and in the 1970s, especially against the large oil companies during the energy crisis.

The right to property is connected directly to the general character of the economic system in the United States, which is roughly a *free enterprise* or *capitalist* system. Under such a system ownership of most of the means of production is in the hands of private entities (individuals, partnerships, and corporations), and inequalities in wealth and income are viewed as inevitable and necessary, at least up to a certain point. Socialism, by contrast, is an economic system in which the government owns the major corporations and means of production; individual private property and income differences may be permitted, but socialist ideology places a premium on government policies that strongly promote greater equality in income and property.

The nature of the economic system is a matter of constitutional significance, not just because of the importance of economics but also because of the connections posited between political values and the arrangement of the economic system. A free enterprise system, in the view of many theories, supports, though it does not guarantee, the maintenance of liberty. This view is based on two major premises: first, that the right to acquire property is itself an important liberty, and second, that private ownership of the means of production limits the power of the government over the economic system, thereby both providing an important check on political power and defending liberty (Friedman, 1962). Americans seem to accept these premises and to oppose any steps toward socialism and the nationalization of key industries (see Figure 4-3).

Americans' views about our political economy cannot be left, however, with this rather simplistic division between a free enterprise system and socialism. As we have seen, Americans, while favoring free enterprise, also accept the need for government regulation and control of business. Moreover, the public fully endorses the idea that government has an obligation to provide certain benefits, such

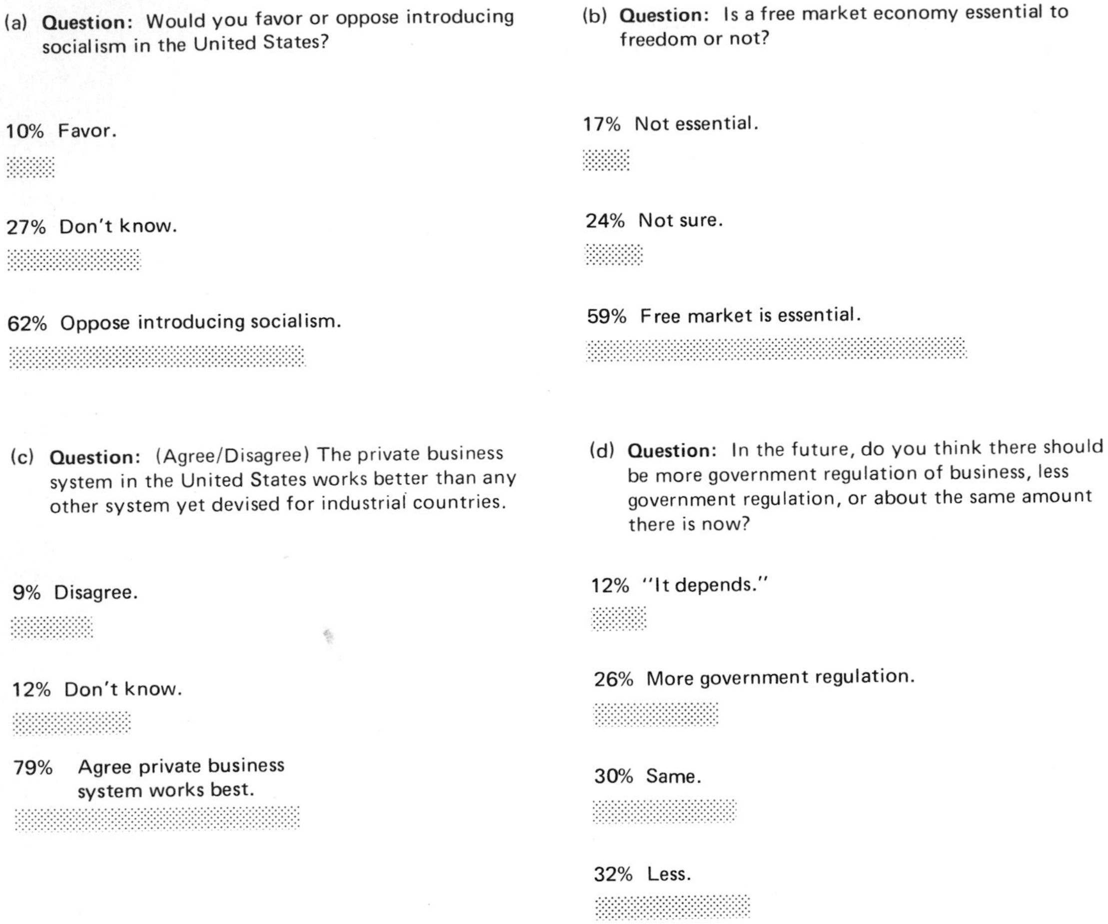

(a) **Question:** Would you favor or oppose introducing socialism in the United States?

10% Favor.

27% Don't know.

62% Oppose introducing socialism.

(b) **Question:** Is a free market economy essential to freedom or not?

17% Not essential.

24% Not sure.

59% Free market is essential.

(c) **Question:** (Agree/Disagree) The private business system in the United States works better than any other system yet devised for industrial countries.

9% Disagree.

12% Don't know.

79% Agree private business system works best.

(d) **Question:** In the future, do you think there should be more government regulation of business, less government regulation, or about the same amount there is now?

12% "It depends."

26% More government regulation.

30% Same.

32% Less.

FIGURE 4-3
Attitudes on political economy. Americans strongly support the free enterprise system but are not opposed to the regulation of business. (*Source: a. Cambridge Reports,* 1976. *b. Cambridge Reports,* 1979. *c.* Civic Service, Inc., 1981. *d.* Lou Harris and Associates, 1979.)

as universal education and medical care for the indigent and the aged. Public opinion accordingly does not support—and we do not have—a "pure" free enterprise system in which the government's role is limited to supervising an unbridled economic competition among private parties. The political-economic system in the United States today is a modified free enterprise system with a substantial degree of government regulation and intervention. It is sometimes referred to by such terms as "mixed economy," "positive state," and "welfare state"—

all of which are meant to suggest the hybrid character of the system. Public opinion supports this mixture, though the degree of government intervention within this broad consensus remains one of the chief points of dispute between the major political parties.

Equality

Given that most Americans favor a free enterprise system, it is clear that by equality they do not mean a guarantee of equal economic outcomes. Many people, of course, favor general governmental policies that tend to curb economic inequalities. In this sense, the concept of economic equality carries some weight; but, in contrast to socialist-minded nations, the idea of attempting to achieve full economic equality remains foreign to most Americans.

In what sense, then, do Americans subscribe to the concept of equality? In the first place, as we have seen in the earlier discussion of the Declaration of Independence, equality entails an absence of special legal prerogatives for any groups and an accompanying belief in the equal dignity of each individual. Although this last notion is elusive, it is essential for understanding American political culture and distinguishing it from other societies where feelings of superiority and inferiority among classes still prevail. Robert Lane, a well-known scholar of public opinion, explored some of the subtler meanings of equality by the technique of in-depth interviews with American workers. One of his conclusions illustrates the point being made here about equality:

> Woodside, a Protestant policeman, . . . says that men are equal "not financially, not in influence, but equal to one another as to being a person." Being a person, then, is enough to qualify for equal claim of some undefined kind. . . . And when Sokolsky, a machine operator and part-time janitor, says in an interview, "the rich guy—because he's got money he's no better than I am. I mean that's the way I feel," . . . he's saying, in effect, to his prosperous older brother and snobbish wife, "Don't look down on me," and to the world at large, "I may be small, but I will protect my self-esteem" (Lane, 1959:41).

Along with equal dignity, the concept of equality implies the existence of the same rights and privileges before the law for each person and—more broadly and elusively—the absence of the kind of prejudice within society that can bar an individual's advancement on the basis of qualities unrelated to competence or merit, such as an individual's race, religion, or ethnic background. This last notion, sometimes called "equality of opportunity," refers to one's chances in life and is dependent not only on laws but on attitudes. Individuals may have a legal right to run for office, but if most people will not vote for them because they are black or female,

the legal right can be meaningless. In this respect at least, the question of equality rests on community norms accepting the equal dignity of individuals who differ in race, religion, or ethnicity. The civil rights movement of the 1960s, which accomplished so many changes in the legal framework of society, has had a significant impact on attitudes about equality. Although no one can doubt the existence of strong prejudices in American society, the changes in attitudes respecting equality since the 1960s have constituted a genuine revolution in constitutional opinion (see Figure 4-4).

As an end embodied in law and supported by governmental action, equality of opportunity presents immense difficulties, for it involves more than the elimination of legally imposed barriers that support inequalities. Government may have to act positively to prevent private institutions, such as business corporations, from discriminating in the hiring and promotion of employees. And government must also supply certain general benefits to all citizens, especially in their formative years, to ensure them a reasonable, if not absolutely equal, chance to make their way in society. (Here, we are dealing not only with impediments to getting ahead that stem from social prejudices but also with the disadvantages of poverty.) Educational opportunity is a prime case in point. Without good schooling and a chance for a college education, persons may find in the claim of equality of opportunity little more than an empty slogan.

At a certain point, it is clear that governmental policies designed to secure equality of opportunity can conflict with liberty. In recent years, many such policies involving efforts by government to deal with past and present effects of racial and sexual discrimination have been controversial. Generally speaking, after 1965 the public either supported or did not oppose programs that were presented as self-help measures designed to provide people with the means of taking advantage of opportunities. Included in this category were programs of federal aid to school districts in poorer areas and job training programs. On the other hand, more direct efforts to ensure equality in areas of access to the opportunity structure—for example, guarantees of equal financing among school districts and busing of school children to ensure equality in the educational setting—have been

(a) **Question:** Do you think white students and Negro students should go to the same schools or to separate schools?

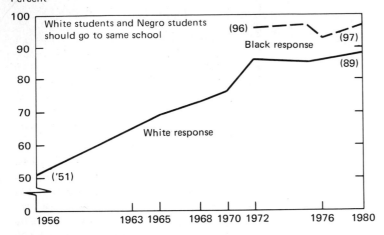

(b) **Question:** If your party nominated a generally well-qualified Negro or woman for president, would you vote for him or her?

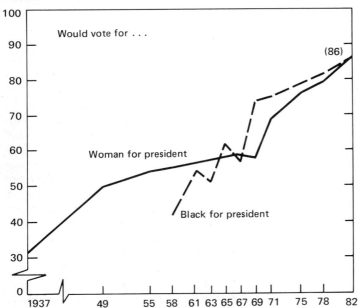

FIGURE 4-4
Attitudes on equality of races. Indications of changing public attitudes toward blacks and other minorities are provided by the public's response to questions asked in public opinion surveys. Wording of questions varies somewhat over the years. (*Source: a.* National Opinion Research Center, general surveys, 1956–1980. *b.* Surveys by Gallup Organization.)

widely opposed. Even more controversial have been policies that have singled out categories of people (women and minority groups) in order to compensate for past discrimination—for example, by requiring businesses or colleges and universities to hire a specified percentage of persons from each such category. Americans to date have generally been quite suspicious of programs that they view as being aimed at producing equality of results as distinct from equality of opportunity.

The Constitution and Republican Government

Another element of constitutional opinion in the United States is respect for the written Constitution as the source of legitimate authority. This support implies that on any given issue of public policy there may potentially be two kinds of opinion: an "ordinary" opinion that reflects what people may initially prefer and an opinion based on support for the Constitution that reflects an interpretation of what people think is permissible under the federal law. Support for the Constitution may be invoked to limit or direct ordinary opinion, as when Congress sets aside a public demand for action on the grounds that it would be unconstitutional or when the courts act to strike down a law or require certain action on the ground that the Constitution must be upheld.

Interpretation of the Constitution by the courts—known as "judicial review"—provides the most striking example of the ultimate importance of opinion in support for the Constitution. In effect what the courts tell the people is: "You may think you want to have such and such a law, but in reality you don't, because this law is contrary to the Constitution which you support and uphold above all other laws." The people may not always be convinced that the courts have interpreted the Constitution correctly, but support for the Constitution as a whole and for the courts' role as its interpreter will generally enable court decisions to prevail. Support for the Constitution will also help protect the courts against attacks on their legitimacy. During the 1930s, the Supreme Court declared unconstitutional some of the key programs that President Roosevelt had proposed to stimulate economic recovery from the depression; after the 1936 election President Roosevelt offered a plan to enlarge the

Court with the aim of changing its membership. Although Americans agreed by a margin of 59 to 41 percent that the Court "should be more liberal in reviewing New Deal measures," they rejected decisively (62 to 38 percent) Roosevelt's court-packing plan, which was seen as an attack on judicial independence (*Public Opinion,* June 1981).

Public support for the Constitution, then, constitutes a restraint on government. But it also serves to enhance the power of the judicial system, which has placed itself in the position of being the chief interpreter of the Constitution. As one scholar of the judicial process, Martin Shapiro, has written:

> When all is said and done, the Supreme Court's power stems . . . from the fact that its pronouncements are perceived as "the law" in a nation that believes in obeying the law—and not only "the law" but "the constitutional law" in a nation that believes that the Constitution is a higher and better law (Shapiro, 1978:195).

Americans strongly support their basic form of government as outlined in the Constitution and as it has evolved over the past 200 years. Although some polls show majority support for specific changes (such as a six-year presidential term), the general picture to emerge from almost all analyses is one of a public that believes in its system of government and shows highly positive attitudes toward the basic norms of democratic politics. These features of American public opinion were first documented in a famous study done in the early 1960s by two political scientists, Gabriel Almond and Sidney Verba. They compared fundamental political beliefs among the population of five democratic nations and found that Americans possessed more pride in their institutions and a greater sense of their ability to influence events than the other four nations did (Almond and Verba, 1963). The positive feelings about the system remain (*Public Opinion,* Februrary-March 1979:35).

Since the publication of Almond and Verba's study, however, students of American public opinion have detected a rather sharp increase in various measurements of dissatisfaction toward government. Over the past two decades, opinion polls have shown that more Americans have come to have doubts about the performance of our institutions,

(a) Aspects of nation in which respondents report pride, by nation, 1959–1960

Percent who say they are proud of:	United States	Great Britain	Germany	Italy	Mexico
Governmental, political institutions	85%	46%	7%	3%	30%
Social legislation	13	18	6	1	2
Position in international affairs	5	11	5	2	3
Economic system	23	10	33	3	24
Characteristics of people	7	18	36	11	15
Spiritual virtues and religion	3	1	3	6	8
Contributions to the arts	1	6	11	16	9
Contributions to science	3	7	12	3	1
Physical attributes of country	5	10	17	25	22
Nothing or don't know	4	10	15	27	16
Other	9	11	3	21	14
Total % of responses	158%	148%	148%	118%	144%
Total % of respondents	100%	100%	148%	100%	100%
Total number of cases	970	963	955	995	1,007

(b) Percentage of the public agreeing that the government in Washington can be trusted to do the right thing most of the time or always.

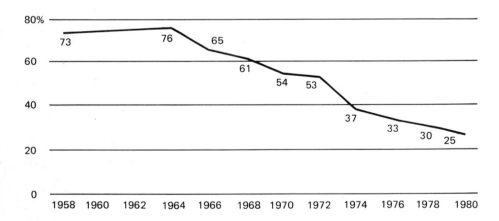

(c) Which of these descriptions do you feel best applies to our political system?

28% Not too sound; needs fundamental overhauling

72% Political system is essentially good; needs some improvement

feel less in control of events, and express more doubts about governmental policies. To some extent, during the decade of the 1970s, Americans began to regard the national government as something beyond their control—as *the* government rather than *our* government. Public opinion analysts variously labeled this phenomenon as "alienation," "cynicism," or "dissatisfaction" (see Figure 4-5). At bottom, it seemed to resemble the great disease of democratic opinion that worried James Bryce: the "Fatalism of the Multitude," which he defined as the "sense of the insignificance of individual effort, the belief that the affairs of men are swayed by large forces whose movement may be studied but cannot be turned" (Bryce, 1889:II, 32).

It is important, however, to separate this recent trend in alienation from the public's view about the basic political system which has remained very positive. Strictly speaking, the recent trends show a loss of confidence in the *performance* of institutions and political leaders rather than in the system itself. While this loss of confidence may be temporary, and its effects exaggerated, it is not unreasonable to suppose that persistent feelings of dissatisfaction could spill over into negative assessments of the political system itself.

Part of the explanation for this dissatisfaction can clearly be found in particular events that occurred between 1964 and 1974: a tumultuous period marked by the civil rights struggle, the Vietnamese war, and the scandals associated with President Nixon's tenure in office. The civil rights struggle left a positive legacy for many Americans, but the Vietnamese war and Watergate both had overwhelmingly negative effects. The Vietnamese war, the constitutionality of which was challenged, led many to regard the presidency as an imperial institution and to doubt either the government's competence (the war was lost) or its morality

(some considered the war entirely unjustified). The Watergate crisis compounded these feelings and added to the growing cynicism about the motives of politicians. Government came increasingly to be seen by many as a sordid business, manipulated by financial interests and run by people seeking personal gain.

Yet, if part of the feelings of dissatisfaction resulted from these specific events, another part may have had roots in more permanent changes in our institutions and in the environment in which government operates. Three factors seem especially important.

First, the vast extension of social and economic functions brought under the direction or command of the national government since the 1960s increased the number of issues and problems for which government is held accountable. Many of the responsibilities that the federal government has undertaken, such as improving education, reducing crime, and managing the economy, are by their nature difficult to handle with great success, even when government makes sound decisions. At the same time, the position of the United States in relation to the rest of the world has changed, as the relative decline in our economic and military power has made us less able than we were twenty years ago to project our will upon the rest of the world. With the increased burden on government and the greater constraints of the international environment, it is perhaps understandable that many people have lost confidence in government at the same time as they complain about its size.

Second, the method of debating national issues in political campaigns does little to quell the public's expectations about what government can supposedly accomplish. When politicians run for office, especially in the highly visible races for the presidency, which now last up to two years, they

---

FIGURE 4-5

Opposite page: Attitudes on support for the political system and on political culture. In 1960, Gabriel Almond and Sydney Verba recorded overwhelming support among Americans for their political institutions. Since that time, public trust in elected officials has eroded dramatically, but the fundamental support for our political system remains high. Note that in *a,* percentages exceed 100 because of multiple responses. (*Source: a.* Almond and Verba, 1963:102. *b.* Center for Political Studies, 1958–1980. *c.* Roper Organization, 1977; *Public Opinion,* January–February 1979.)

invariably promise that, if elected, they will be able to provide solutions to the major problems that the nation faces. Sobriety and realism are seldom the grounds on which popular constituencies are mobilized. As a consequence, public expectations tend to be elevated during campaigns, only to be upset by the subsequent realities of governmental performance. The resulting gap between raised expectations and performance naturally contributes to the feelings of dissatisfaction and cynicism.

Third, the growth of people's reliance on television as the major source of news has brought the problems of governing into the homes of Americans in a more direct form than in the past. The peculiar character of television news, which conveys intense impressions and emphasizes drama and conflict, has led to a widespread American perception of a world filled with difficulties and problems. However, television news does not apparently provide a compensating perception of broad trends or an overall context in which these problems take place. The consequence, as some studies have suggested, is that television news as a source of information tends to increase the viewer's feeling that matters are in a state of crisis and are not being adequately handled, creating a phenomenon that one scholar has termed "videomalaise" (Robinson, 1977). Whether Americans can learn to adjust to the greater difficulties encountered by big government and to the sources of information that report on them without further increases in feelings of dissatisfaction remains very much an open question.

Values and World Views

Constitutional opinion refers not only to what are clearly political opinions about the fundamental questions of politics but also to elements of the public's basic value system that shape the environment in which political action takes place. The people of any society tend to have certain values that make them, in some degree, different from the people of other societies. These values are shaped by political ideals, historical experience, and geographical and economic factors. The differences enable one to speak broadly of a French, a German, and an American "culture" or national character. Like the strictly political components of constitutional opinion, these cultural elements change in response to

developments in society and can occasionally undergo profound adjustments at certain moments. But the notion of culture suggests a set of deep-seated attitudes that resists quick or easy change. When one speaks of cultural transformation, it is usually something that takes place gradually over decades, not within one or two years.

Religion

The United States was settled in large part by religious groups like the Pilgrims and Quakers who came to the new world to practice their religion free from the persecution that they had known in Europe. America was seen by these religious refugees as the "New Jerusalem" or, as the famous colonial clergyman Cotton Mather called it, the "Heavenly City." Religion has therefore been taken very seriously in American culture. One American sociologist, in reviewing the commentaries of European observers of American politics, noted that they "have been unanimous in remarking on the exceptional religiosity of [American] society" (Lipset, 1967:160). Recent surveys on religion confirm this finding for the present era as well, although in the United States, along with most western nations, there have been signs of increasing secularization in society.

While the American religious tradition is strong, the relationship between religious values and political opinions is often difficult to discern. Unlike many other nations, such as West Germany and Italy, the United States has no avowedly religious parties such as the Christian Democrats. (These parties, while largely accepting the idea of religious liberty, were formed with the express purpose of fostering Christian values in political life.) The First Amendment, which protects the free exercise of religion and bans the establishment of a state religion, has also had the effect of promoting the idea of separation of church and state and a more general belief that it is unwise for religious institutions to intervene directly in political affairs. Thus most Americans believe that the position of the clergy and churches on purely partisan issues should not influence their votes, and most churches urge their clergy not to run for public office.

However, there is a distinction to be made between purely political issues on the one hand and political issues which involve moral or religious questions on the other. When members of the clergy identify issues which they judge to have profound religious import, such as civil rights, nuclear disarmament, or obscenity, they may take a stand even where such matters embroil them deeply in political controversies.

Although most Americans claim to judge political matters independently of church authority, taking their clergy's opinions only as matters for consideration, there is little doubt that religious beliefs have a significant influence on politics. A majority of citizens attest to the importance of religion on many of their concrete decisions, including those that fall into the political arena. The American political climate, as many have observed, is to a considerable degree suffused by values related to religious beliefs, a fact that gives a moral impulse to politics found in few other societies. Even the tradition of political and moral reform, so powerful in American society, has been traced to a secularized version of certain strains of Protestantism and Judaism (Banfield, 1974).

Yet—and this qualification is essential—religious beliefs and values have not led to unanimity in ideology or on particular issues, because of the tremendous number of religious sects and the diversity in religious traditions. People often bring a religious dimension to politics, but their values, deriving from different religions and denominations, often lead them to different conclusions. While the highly publicized growth in recent years of the Christian Evangelical right has brought a growing conservative influence to bear on certain social and national security issues, other denominations and religious associations have been espousing liberal causes. This pluralism in religious beliefs was not only foreseen by the founders but encouraged as a way of avoiding one of the most dangerous potential sources of majority faction. "In a free government," Madison wrote, "the security for civil rights must be the same as that for religious rights. It consists in the one case in the multiplicity of interests, and in the other in the multiplicity of sects" (*Federalist* 51).

Beneath this diversity in religious views, however, there is a sense in which the beliefs of the dominant religious groups in America have become mixed with and support the basic American political values of liberty, equality, and a republican form of government, creating what Robert Bellah has called an American "civil religion." The tenets of this civil religion, according to Bellah, have played a crucial role in the development of American institutions and still provide a religious dimension for the whole fabric of American life (Bellah, 1975).

The Culture of Capitalism

Part of Americans' understanding of liberty involves a respect for property and a belief in economic competition in a free market system. More fundamentally, a capitalist or free enterprise system is based explicitly on the freeing and encouraging of people's acquisitive instincts. As people seek to improve their economic lot, wealth is generated in society and both the nation and its populace become more prosperous and powerful. Obviously, this system of economic arrangements has a profound impact on the general tone or culture of society. Everywhere in a capitalist society the passion for moneymaking is strong, and capitalist economies by their nature encourage innovation, mobility, and change. By contrast with traditional agricultural societies, where patterns of life remain relatively static and the population immobile, advanced free enterprise systems are constantly in a state of flux and change as people and resources are moved about in order to adapt to new and more efficient ways of producing goods and services.

The culture of capitalism has, however, undergone a significant transformation in the past half century (Bell, 1976). For much of the nineteenth century, the commercial spirit, influenced by the pervasiveness of traditional Puritan religious values and by a lower standard of living, tended to emphasize the virtues of hard work, personal self-control, savings, and the deferring of personal gratification. Capitalism in the main was therefore compatible with, and even reinforced, a rather stern and moralistic tone in society. This tone, called by Max Weber the "protestant ethic," was reflected in the image of the stern Yankee entrepreneur who was interested in moneymaking but at the same time committed to thrift, order, and traditional values.

In this century, with the decline of religious values in some sectors of the population, with greater affluence in society, and with the advent of mass commercial advertising, the character of capitalistic societies has changed. Although hard work and personal discipline remain important, much more emphasis today is placed on consumption, immediate gratification, and self-expression. The notion of "grabbing for all the gusto you can," as one beer commercial so aptly puts it, has powerfully affected the character of modern commercial society, making it much less stern and moralistic. These tendencies have led to conflicts in society, with some on the left searching for ways to go "beyond" commercial values to some new, anticommerical humanist ethic and with others looking for ways to protect certain traditional, moral, and religious views.

Science and Pragmatism

"Americans," Tocqueville once wrote, "treat tradition as valuable for information only" and "seek by themselves and in themselves for the only reason for things, looking for results without getting entangled in the means towards them" (Tocqueville, 1968:429). In this statement, Tocqueville identified one of the most important features in American culture—a marked strain of antitraditionalism and pragmatism. With the exception of their commitment to basic constitutional values discussed above, Americans tend to be an open and experimental people, trusting less in schools of philosophy and tradition than in practical science and in what works. Accordingly, Americans readily adapt to innovations in business and culture—whether to computer technology or to eating at fast-food restaurants. Indeed, the entire idea of fast-food restaurants, like McDonald's, was an American innovation, which for better or worse was adopted with little resistance by Americans in the 1960s.

The emphasis on the practical and scientific pervades our entire policymaking process and even our national civil service. This tradition can be seen by contrasting the civil service in Great Britain with that in the United States. In Great Britain, the upper echelons of the bureaucracy are dominated by generalists trained in a liberal arts tradition with an emphasis on philosophy and the classics. Higher civil servants frequently move from one ministry of the government to another. Respect for

hierarchic authority and a tradition of serving the government as a whole result from this training and pattern of career development. In the United States, by contrast, the civil service at the upper echelons is dominated by "experts" who have shown a capacity to perform specific problem-solving tasks within a given field. Allegiance is often given first to the agency or to the values of one's profession rather than to the government as a whole. The same spirit of expertise and pragmatism pervades many other institutions in American society, including our colleges and universities, which have become "service stations" pragmatically instructing individuals in all areas, from hotel science to the great tradition of liberal arts.

Directly connected with these notions of pragmatism and antitraditionalism is another American characteristic: a suspicion of pomp and of deference toward those in authority. This attitude, which flows also from democratic precepts, is best captured by minor incidents. In 1787, the vice president, John Adams, pressed for a formal title for the president other than the simple "Mr. President." His choice: "His Highness the President of the United States and Protector of the Rights of the Same." Many in Congress found the title offensive, not to say ridiculous, and some opponents of Adams, in jest, privately played with the idea of giving the vice president the title of "His Superfluous Excellency" or "His Rotund Highness." More recently, when President Nixon took a trip to Europe and came back with a plan for dressing the White House guards in fancy costumes with decorated caps, the idea was greeted in Washington with a mixture of amazement and derision. As trivial as these examples may seem, they nonetheless point up an important aspect of American political culture: Americans, while respectful of high public offices and public ceremonies, expect their leaders to show a healthy dose of the common touch. Signs of snobbery and elitism by elected officials have been sore points for the American public. Similarly, Americans are suspicious of official prerogatives and seem to favor a governmental system that is open and gives the appearance of serving the public. Deference for officialdom is at a minimum in the United States, a fact that makes it much easier for politicians to criticize publicly the performance of the civil service and to attack big government.

GENERAL OPINIONS ON GOVERNMENT POLICY

The second level of opinion on general governmental policy refers to beliefs and attitudes with respect to the basic direction that government should follow—for example, whether the federal government should expand or reduce its activities, whether more or less power should be held by the states, and whether the United States should adopt a more active or passive role in international affairs. Opinion at this level is of a lower level of generality (and usually less stable) than constitutional opinion, but of a higher level of generality (and generally more stable) than opinions on particular policies or attitudes toward politicians.

There are, obviously, potential links that can be drawn between these three levels of opinion; for example, interpretations about what one means by equality (a constitutional opinion) can have an impact on what one thinks the government should do (a general opinion on governmental policy), which in turn can have an influence on what one thinks about a specific measure being considered (opinion on a particular issue). Yet, people do not always perceive the links between these levels of opinion. Nor is it the case that one and only one logical link exists. For example, people favoring greater equality may or may not support measures to increase the minimum wage, depending on whether they think this policy actually promotes greater equality. (Experts differ on this question.)

Unlike constitutional opinion, wherein consensus is the rule, opinion about government policy is usually divided. Yet, except during periods of constitutional conflict, these divisions are limited in character and do not threaten the basis of the political order itself. The most important divisions of opinion on this level can be studied by looking at the positions of our political parties and by analyzing the two major ideological tendencies in the United States, known as "liberalism" and "conservativism."

Political Parties and Partisanship

Important divisions on governmental policies have traditionally been expressed through political parties, which are the largest and most inclusive of all political groups in the nation. Our two major parties have served historically as the main vehicles for organizing policy differences and in so doing have served to stake out the boundaries of ordinary political conflict. Yet, as we shall see in Chapter 5, the major parties, because they usually encompass groups with different and partially conflicting policy views, tend frequently to moderate and blur certain divisions of opinion. The major parties serve, therefore, not simply to reflect, but sometimes to deflect, political divisions. Citizens who find this inadequate or unsatisfactory employ other means, such as interest groups, mass movements, and occasionally third parties, to express their policy views. By no means, therefore, have parties had a monopoly on the function of articulating policy positions.

Parties not only express opinions but also help to form them. They galvanize people behind certain positions. Moreover, once citizens identify with a party, they tend to develop emotional or affective ties to it, with the result that they are more apt to adopt the positions of "their" leaders. It is clear, however, that political parties over the past generation have lost a good deal of influence in structuring opinion to other agencies and currents in society, such as interest groups, campaigns of individual candidates, and especially the mass media. There have, in fact, been some very profound changes in society's system of "intermediary" agencies—that is, those entities that influence the structuring and formation of public opinion on the levels of general government policies and particular issues. In general, the more stable institutions (like parties) have lost ground to agencies that have less continuity and ballast. The result has apparently been much greater volatility in public attitudes (Polsby, 1983).

Ideology: Liberalism and Conservatism

It is common in political discussions today to use the terms "liberalism" and "conservatism" to identify general opinions about the role of government. So frequent, in fact, is this practice that it may come as a surprise to learn that these terms are relatively new as common political labels, developing only since the 1930s. One reason, no doubt, for their development at that time was that the party labels—especially that of the Democratic party—failed to convey any clear view about the role of government. President Roosevelt began to use the term "liberalism" to refer to *his* understanding of the proper role of government and to distinguish it from the understanding of others, including many within his own party, who held different views. Since the 1930s, we have thus had four labels—the two party labels (Democratic and Republican) and the two labels of ideology (liberal and conservative). These labels overlap somewhat, Republicans tending to be conservative and Democrats liberal, but the fit is far from perfect; this is why commentators sometimes use both sets of labels together, referring, for example, to "conservative Democrats" or "liberal Republicans."

For political scientists, liberalism and conservatism are *ideologies*. The use of the word "ideology" in this context is surely permissible, but one should be aware that it also has a more general meaning which refers to a total system of belief, like communism or Nazism. As defined by one analyst, "ideology" is an "all-inclusive representation of the history of the world, of the past, the present and the future, of what is and what must be" (Aron, 1965:53). An ideology in this sense provides its adherents with answers not only about the direction of government policy but also to more fundamental questions about philosophy, morality, history, and religion. The terms "conservatism" and "liberalism" as used in an American context are clearly not ideologies in this sense, since they refer to the much more modest idea of general views about the role of government and the kinds of policies government should pursue.

Conservatism and liberalism have been roughly defined in previous chapters according to differing views on the role of the federal government in the areas of economic and welfare policy. Here we need to add two other dimensions of division that are frequently used by commentators to distinguish the two ideologies: views of the role of government on social and cultural issues and views on issues of national security and foreign affairs. What needs to be emphasized is that these three dimensions of division are largely the creation of analysts who talk about politics and seek to bring a certain degree of order to a great diversity in opinion. In fact, there is no universal agreement on the meaning of these terms, and many not only define them differently but dismiss their validity altogether. Nor is it the case, as we shall see, that people who are conser-

vative or liberal on one dimension are conservative or liberal on the other two.

Economic and Welfare Issues Differences in this domain have constituted the most important line of division between the two ideologies since the 1930s. President Roosevelt used the term "liberalism" to refer to an active use of national power to intervene in the economy, create welfare and security programs, and help certain groups, especially labor unions, to achieve greater power. During the 1960s and 1970s, liberalism was associated with a further extension of the use of federal power to push for civil rights, for programs to help the poor and the disadvantaged, and for regulations on business for the protection of the environment (Beer, 1978). Currently, many of the so-called "neoliberals" are placing somewhat less emphasis on the use of government for the ends of security or redistribution and much more emphasis on the use of government programs to rebuild the American economy through aid for retraining of workers and high-technology research.

"Conservatism" was the term that political commentators in the 1930s used to refer to the ideology of those who opposed Roosevelt's New Deal policies. Initially, opposition Republican leaders like former President Hoover shunned the label, preferring to describe themselves as "true liberals," that is, in the older sense of the term, opponents of big government. But in the next generation, some Republican leaders accepted the term, and just as Franklin Roosevelt had sought to make liberalism the dominant public philosophy of the Democratic party, so Barry Goldwater (in 1964) and Ronald Reagan have sought to make conservatism the focal point of the Republican party. Conservatism is based on the view that a large central government active in the areas of domestic and welfare policies threatens personal liberty and endangers the right to property. Conservatives place a greater value than liberals do on the free market system and have been much more wary of programs for government economic planning and regulation. Liberals tend to emphasize what government can do and have confidence in its ability to solve problems; conservatives tend to emphasize what government cannot do and are dubious of the value of many government programs. Liberals tend to see

Ronald Reagan's call for greater military strength and more self-reliant individualism won him many supporters among organized labor during the 1980 election campaign.   *(Andy Levin/Black Star)*

the economic system in somewhat more collective terms, while conservatives stress much more the notion of individualism.

⌐ **Social and Cultural Issues** ⌐ This dimension of the division between liberalism and conservatism today refers to attitudes about government's role— often the role of state and local governments—in the protection of order and certain moral values and community standards. Although this division was clearly subordinate to economic questions in the aftermath of the New Deal, it gained much more attention in the 1960s with civil rights issues

and concern over increases in crime, and again in more recent times with such issues as obscenity, abortion, prayer in the schools, and the Equal Rights Amendment. No single label can characterize most people's position on all these issues, but one can speak of certain basic attitudes. "Liberalism" here refers to a set of beliefs that favors the extension of free expression and of each individual's right to experiment in matters of lifestyle, free of any attempts on the part of government to promote certain moral values. Liberals, at least in the 1960s, were also more apt to explain the origin of crime in terms of social causes like poverty rather than place the burden on the individual. "Conservatism" here encompasses a greater willingness to use the power of government, usually on the state and local level, to protect certain community values and to maintain a stricter attitude toward crime and punishment, including support for the death penalty.

Many of the issues in the social and cultural area have come to the forefront of national politics in the past twenty years because of Supreme Court decisions that extended the protections of the Bill of Rights (and the interpretations thereon) to all individuals. Conservatives opposed many of these decisions, arguing that they reflected liberal ideology more than valid Constitutional interpretation. Conservatives have sought to reverse many of these decisions, whether by Constitutional amendment, congressional legislation, or the appointment of more conservative judges. The controversies on such issues as abortion and pornography illustrate some of the differences between the two sides. On abortion, liberalism has been associated with those who endorse the right of a woman to have control over her own body, including the freedom to choose to have an abortion. Conservatism sees a community value on this issue and has been associated with supporting the prerogative of governments to enforce restriction and limitations. (The right-to-life position would simply decide this question unilaterally by a nationwide ban on abortions.) On the issue of obscenity, liberals place a great emphasis on the right of free expression and fear possible government intrusions into the artistic realm, while conservatives are more willing to allow communities to impose restrictions on the dissemination of materials they view as obscene.

On one level, it is possible to see tensions in the thought of both conservatives and liberals. Conservatives like to speak of limited government, but they mean primarily limitations in the economic sphere. On social issues, although many conservatives are highly ambivalent, they often favor the use of government to support what they see as basic community values. Liberals, on the other hand, speak of a guiding role for government in economic and welfare issues but generally oppose any state intervention on social and cultural issues. These internal tensions create problems, especially on the conservative side, where many take the limitation of government to be a fundamental principle of politics. Splits and debates among conservatives on these issues are frequent.

Issues of National Security and Foreign Policy
The ideological division on these issues is perhaps the most complicated of all three dimensions. From the onset of World War II until the escalation of the Vietnamese war in 1965, liberals advocated an active, "interventionist" role for the United States in world affairs. This policy was to be implemented not only in the cooperative rebuilding of Europe after the war and in aid for economic development in the third world but also in a steadfast determination to resist the spread of communism. Largely as a result of the Vietnamese war, however, many liberals changed position, and liberalism since that time has been associated with the view that the United States has spent too much on national defense, that it has been preoccupied with an inordinate fear of communism, and that these attitudes have led to disastrous military interventions such as the Vietnamese war.

Conservatives were associated between the two world wars with a more isolationist position; and while they were extremely anticommunist, many of them, for reasons of nationalism, sought to avoid foreign commitments after World War II. Slowly, however, conservatives changed to a more activist posture, although one based more on nationalism than that of the liberals. Conservatism today is associated with the position that the United States and its allies are threatened by the communist system in the Soviet Union, that a higher level of spending on national defense is necessary, and that the intentions of the Soviet Union should be regarded with the utmost suspicion. When consider-

ing the third world, conservatives are more likely than liberals to support authoritarian governments friendly to the United States since conservatives see the security problem as being foremost. On issues relating to national security conservatives have been more disposed than liberals, again for security reasons, to allow the government to classify state secrets and to give wider discretion to security organs such as the Central Intelligence Agency.

These, then, are the three major dimensions—economic-welfare, social-cultural, and defense-security—that constitute the lines of division between liberalism and conservatism. On each dimension, the views defined serve at best to point out general lines of belief from which specific policy stands may be deduced. Moreover, as observed, there is no absolute thematic connection from one area to another. Some have argued that the liberal positions are grounded in a more hopeful or optimistic view of human nature, based ultimately on a belief in progress and human community; but even if this is true, the links between the three areas are still far too vague and tenuous to let us assert the existence of a logically unified theory for each ideology.

Generally speaking, the Republican party is more conservative than the Democratic party today on all three of these dimensions. But within each party, among both leaders and voters, there are important differences of opinion. Republicans vary in their degree of conservatism, and many Democrats are conservative on one or more of these dimensions. (See Table 4-1, which charts roughly the ideological tendencies of different groups in society.) These conflicts provide an important clue for voting behavior. Republican candidates appeal to conservatives throughout the electorate, attempting in particular to lure Democrats and independents who are conservative on social-cultural and national security issues into their camp. Democratic candidates attempt to do the opposite.

Finally, in thinking about the meaning of liberalism and conservatism, one should bear in mind that both terms are partly *relative*. Conservatives in the 1930s and 1940s rejected many instances of federal intervention—as in social security and unemployment compensation—which today they accept. Liberals in the 1980s are, as a rule, much more cautious or wary of large government expen-

TABLE 4-1
ATTITUDES OF SELECTED GROUPS ON THE THREE DIMENSIONS OF LIBERALISM AND CONSERVATISM

	Economic attitudes	Social attitudes	Foreign policy attitudes
Blacks	Very liberal.	More conservative than most people think. Very religious, which fosters conservative social attitudes. Economic self-interest almost always overrides social conservatism.	Not particularly sympathetic to military spending or to foreign involvement. However, generally patriotic and somewhat hawkish at the general level. Not especially concerned about foreign policy.
Hispanics	Liberal, except for Cubans.	Like blacks, rather conservative and religious. May vote slightly more on social issues.	Chicanos and Puerto Ricans similar to blacks; Cubans intensely anticommunist, pro-military spending, and sympathetic to interventionism.
Blue-collar whites, including low-level clerical and sales workers	Traditionally liberal but skeptical of liberal performance on economy. Torn between desire for some social programs and desire for tax cuts.	More conservative than upper-status voters, but not uniformly conservative. Divided by age, religiosity, and religion.	Strongly anticommunist, increasingly pro-military spending, but skeptical of foreign involvement. Sensitive to decline in American prestige. Generally, relatively unconcerned about foreign policy, but can be key swing group.
Union members	More liberal than nonunionized workers, but share their ambivalence	Same as blue-collar workers.	Same as blue-collar workers. Protectionist in trade.
Nonbusiness professionals (the "new class")	Often rather conservative on economic issues. Torn between 1960s social consciousness and current economic self-interest. Some professions depend heavily on government spending.	Generally very liberal. Social issues very important to this group.	Generally dovish, skeptical of military spending except for a significant minority who work in defense-related industries. Generally opposed to American intervention abroad.
Catholics	Divided entirely by class. Lower-status voters more liberal.	Divided by class and religiosity. Segments of intense social conservatism.	Similar to blue-collar worker. On the whole, even more anticommunist. Substantial upper-status dovish minority.
Jews	Traditionally very liberal; segments increasingly sensitive to conservative economic self-interest.	Very liberal, except for small pockets of more conservative lower-status Jews.	Dovish in past, although deeply divided since Vietnam. Intense doves and hawks. Generally anti-Soviet. Deep worries about any weakening of American commitment to Israel, which have led many Jews to more hawkish foreign policy views in general.
Women	Divided by class; lower-status more liberal.	More divided on these issues than any other group. Lower-status women often intensely conservative. Upper-status women usually intensely liberal. Religiosity important here also.	As a rule, substantially more worried about war than men are.

Source: Orren and Dionne, 1981:32–33.

ditures and deficits than they were in the 1970s. Stated differently, liberalism and conservatism are in some measure tendencies in opinion that are defined not absolutely, but in relationship to the status quo. To some extent, moreover, the positions change and evolve, and what is conservative or liberal depends on the views adopted by leaders who have been traditionally identified with a particular ideology. Thus, to cite a recent example, traditional conservative economic doctrine before 1980 stressed a balanced federal budget as one of its most important goals. During the 1980 presidential campaign, however, Ronald Reagan adopted a different, "supply-side," theory of economics which placed greater emphasis on stimulating economic growth through tax cuts than on balancing the budget. This new view quickly became "conservative" doctrine, at least as it was being temporarily defined by many journalists and political analysts.

"Conservatism" and "liberalism" are complex and imprecise terms, so much so that many question whether they are even helpful. Perhaps the most that can be said is that while they are imprecise, no other set of terms that refers to general opinion about the direction of government policy has yet been developed that is any more helpful. As long as the terms are employed carefully, they can assist in organizing a discussion of public policy and indicating, in a loose way, the policy inclinations of various elements in society.

Levels of Ideological Thinking and Recent Trends

Thus far we have defined liberalism and conservatism and have shown where certain groups can be placed (roughly) on the different dimensions of these ideologies. But do most people actually think in these terms? That is, do they organize their responses to particular issues on the basis of those categories, or for that matter in terms of any other general ideological categories? Researchers have been greatly interested in these questions, not just for the practical reason of knowing how Americans think about politics, but also because the answers seem to have an important bearing on any judgment of a people's capacity for self-government.

Because ideological labels are used so often in political discussions today, most people easily respond to questions asking them to classify themselves as liberals, moderates, or conservatives. Yet it does not follow that these conceptions actually serve to organize the respondents' approach to specific issues. Recall that these terms were developed and defined mostly by political analysts and activists, and only to a limited extent have they become labels that citizens themselves use to describe their own way of viewing government policy. In fact, a number of studies have indicated that for many people, their self-categorization as a liberal or conservative (in response to pollsters' questions) does not help very much in describing their positions on various policies.

Determining who thinks in ideological terms and to what extent people think in such terms has proved a very complicated task and one on which scholars differ significantly (Converse, 1964; Nie and Anderson, 1974; Stimson, 1975). The most frequently cited figures indicate that the number of Americans who could reasonably be said to view politics in ideological terms in the 1950s was only around 15 percent. This figure had nearly doubled by the 1970s, a result that analysts attributed to the growth in the number of college-educated citizens, who are more likely to think in ideological terms, and to the greater ideological distance between presidential candidates in some of the elections after 1960. The second of these factors was more important, indicating that it is the degree of choice offered by politicians that most affects the level of ideological thinking within the mass public. Even so, the figures still showed only a modest number of citizens—30 percent—for whom ideology was important (Verba et al., 1976).

How one should evaluate this low level of ideological thinking—if this in fact is what we have—depends in large measure on what one expects of a democratic populace. Early researchers tended to be greatly dismayed by their findings of low levels of ideological thinking, arguing that this discovery called into question fundamental elements of democratic theory (Campbell et al., 1960). If the public, they reasoned, could not or did not judge the political world in general categories, then it followed that elections could not constitute the kind of fundamental policymaking choice that they were supposed to involve. For some practitioners who read these studies too quickly, the conclusion was apparently drawn that the public was ignorant and could be easily manipulated by campaigns run on images and symbols rather than on any serious discussion of public issues. Some political scientists began to worry that this picture of the American public, if it became implanted in the minds of political leaders, would prove to be self-confirming, since leaders would base their campaigns on increasingly trivial issues and end by producing the very ignorance that everyone so decried (Key, 1966).

There is, however, a very different way of evaluating mass opinion and the role of elections. If one begins with the idea that the "intelligence" of the electorate is not properly measured by levels of ideological thought, but rather by the capacity to make general judgments on the performance of candidates and to vote on basic notions of justice reflected in important questions of public policy, then the American public passes the test. It is clear from many voting studies that when the public thinks that a presidential incumbent has done a poor job or when people believe that a certain issue of importance to them is likely to be handled better by one candidate than another, they vote in a rational way (Key, 1966; Pomper, 1975). The picture of the political world held by most Americans is not that of a comprehensive ideological scheme even though political analysts can discern the ideological tendencies of certain groups according to where they stand on certain issues. Most Americans view the political world in more concrete terms—in terms of parties, personalities, and subjective measures of performance and in terms of certain specific issues that impinge on them and occupy their attention, such as inflation, a war, or social security benefits.

Still, the importance of ideological thinking should not be underestimated. While most citizens may not take ideological labels very seriously, a growing segment of the population apparently does, including those who tend to participate extensively in politics. Studies of political elites—those, for example, who hold positions as elected officials, interest-group leaders, and party officials—indicate that a high percentage uses ideological categories in thinking about politics, even though many take different stands on the three dimensions noted above. Moreover, activists in the Republican party are considerably more conservative, and activists in the Democratic party considerably more liberal, than their respective followers in the electorate (McCloskey et al., 1960; Mitofsky, 1980). Because elites and activists have such a significant impact on political life, American politics is more influenced by ideological considerations than an analysis of mass opinion would suggest.

Given both the imprecision of ideological labels and their relative character, it is difficult to say whether Americans have become more liberal or conservative over the past decade. Survey results vary according to the particular poll and the way the questions have been posed (see Figure 4-6). What seems clear, however, is that more people have moved away from calling themselves liberal, and more Democratic party leaders have grown uncomfortable with describing themselves by this label. Certainly, in choosing Ronald Reagan as president in 1980, a majority of voters demonstrated willingness to choose a conservative—a fact which marks a dramatic change from the 1964 election, when the conservative candidate, Barry Goldwater, was not only soundly defeated but widely viewed as an "extreme" candidate. The longer-term prospects of conservation probably will depend on how the public eventually judges Reagan's performance.

OPINIONS ON SPECIFIC ISSUES AND PERSONALITIES

When most people think of public opinion today, they probably have in mind the figures on specific issues and personalities cited by the various polling firms like Gallup and Harris and by the major networks and news magazines. These surveys cover an extremely broad range of issues. Polls are conducted to find out what people believe to be the important issues of the day, to determine how they stand on those issues, to see what they think of the performance of their president, and, naturally, to chart public attitudes on the candidates during a presidential campaign.

Characteristics of Public Opinion

Opinions on specific issues and personalities can have very different properties and characteristics.

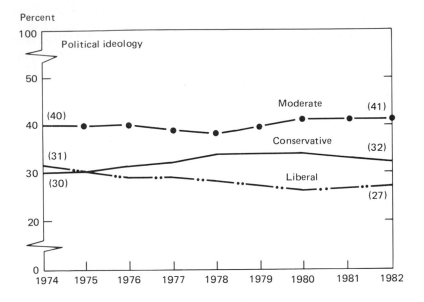

Percent

FIGURE 4-6

Ideological orientation of the American populace. Over the past decade, the percentage of citizens identifying themselves as liberals has declined slightly, while the percentage identifying themselves as conservatives has risen slightly. Overall, however, the changes have been small, and the differences fall within the margin of error for a national poll. The largest percentage of Americans, as the figure shows, continue to think of themselves as moderate or middle-of-the-road. (*Source:* National Opinion Research Center, general social surveys; and *Public Opinion*, 1982.)

Key: Liberal = extremely liberal, liberal, and slightly liberal. Moderate = moderate, middle-of-the-road. Conservative = slightly conservative, conservative, and extremely conservative.

Unlike constitutional and ideological opinions, which tend to be relatively stable, opinions on specific issues and personalities are frequently highly volatile, shifting with major changes in the political environment (see Figure 4-7) and sometimes even with daily events. During presidential campaigns, for example, a mistake committed by a candidate or an especially strong or weak showing in a primary can quickly lead to significant changes in opinion. For presidents, a well-handled crisis can boost support and reverse a declining trend of popularity. (In fact, almost any foreign policy crisis, whether well or poorly handled, boosts a president's popularity temporarily, as people "rally around the flag" and support their president.) Finally, the importance of certain issues for the public is a function not only of an objective problem in the real world—such as inflation or a shortage of energy—but also of the extent to which a problem is covered by the media. Public opinion in this sense has a way of "feeding" on itself: the reporting of a concern for a certain issue may lead people to think more about

it, which in turn may make reporters want to cover the issue at greater length.

In thinking about public opinion on this level, it is important to attempt to distinguish, at least intuitively, between different kinds of opinions. As noted earlier, not all opinions measured in polls are equally meaningful. The founders, for example, spoke of the difference between "sudden breezes of passion" and the "deliberate sense of the community," meaning the difference between opinion that forms momentarily and opinion that represents a more settled conviction (*Federalist* 71). Today, when people are asked in a poll about matters on which they have no firm beliefs or which are relatively unimportant to them, they may well express an opinion, but that opinion is of an entirely different order from one on a matter on which they have reached a firm decision and regard as important. In the first instance, the opinion is passive; in the second, it is potentially active and might well serve as a basis on which people would vote or organize for political action.

Question: What do you think is the most important problem facing the country today?

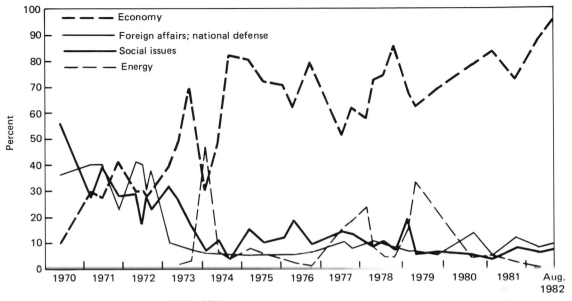

Most important problem, 1935–1982:

1982 Unemployment, high cost of living
1981 High cost of living, unemployment
1980 High cost of living, unemployment
1979 High cost of living, energy problems
1978 High cost of living, energy problems
1977 High cost of living, unemployment
1976 High cost of living, unemployment
1975 High cost of living unemployment
1974 High cost of living, Watergate, energy crisis
1973 High cost of living, Watergate
1972 Vietnam
1971 Vietnam, high cost of living
1970 Vietnam
1969 Vietnam
1968 Vietnam
1967 Vietnam, high cost of living
1966 Vietnam
1965 Vietnam, race relations
1964 Vietnam, race relations
1963 Keeping peace, race relations
1962 Keeping peace
1961 Keeping peace
1960 Keeping peace
1959 Keeping peace

1958 Unemployment, keeping peace
1957 Race relations, keeping peace
1956 Keeping peace
1955 Keeping peace
1954 Keeping peace
1953 Keeping peace
1952 Korean war
1951 Korean war
1950 Labor unrest
1949 Labor unrest
1948 Keeping peace
1947 High cost of living, labor unrest
1946 High cost of living
1945 Winning war
1944 Winning war
1943 Winning war
1942 Winning war
1941 Keeping out of war, winning war
1940 Keeping out of war
1939 Keeping out of war
1938 Keeping out of war
1937 Unemployment
1936 Unemployment
1935 Unemployment

FIGURE 4-7
Shifting concerns of the American public. (*Source: Public Opinion,* 1980; Gallup Organization, *Gallup Report,* 1982.)

Public opinion on different issues and personalities, accordingly, has very different attributes from one issue to another. Anyone studying public opinion will therefore want to know not only the overall *distribution* of opinion on an issue—that is, people's position about what should or should not be done—but also (1) the *intensity* of feeling within the population or within different subgroups and (2) the *stability* of opinion—that is, the degree to which people have made up their minds and are no longer changing from one position to another. Opinion, finally, can also be *latent,* meaning that it pertains to matters which are not currently objects of active concern, but which very quickly could become so in the event that certain actions are taken or certain developments occur.

Opinions about various issues may be classified according to the properties just discussed. Thus a few issues, such as the Vietnamese war, are of intense concern to many people and evoke after a time a stable distribution of opinion (Mueller, 1973). Divisions of opinion on such issues are potential national voting issues that can lead large numbers of people to decide their votes on the basis of the position that the candidates stake out on this question. In other cases, political leaders see certain issues as evoking latent opinion which could be intense, stable, and perhaps unfavorable. In 1981, for example, President Reagan quickly backed off from any suggestion of sending American troops into El Salvador for fear in part of the hostile response that such a position would evoke. There are other issues on which there is much intensity of feeling, but no clear distribution of opinion or stability. Included here are opinions on many economic issues, such as inflation and unemployment. The public in such cases may demand that "something be done" to handle the problem, but the notions people have about what should be done are often vague or inconsistent. People seem in such instances to wait and see how leaders act to resolve these problems and then judge by the general criterion of "whether it worked." Finally, there are other issues—and this is often the case—which are of relatively little concern to most citizens but which are highly important to specific subgroups of the population. These matters give rise to what are sometimes called "issue publics." Citizens respond with a great deal of intensity on a particular issue,

such as on the question of abortion or a nuclear arms freeze.

Effects of Public Opinion

From the viewpoint of those attempting to govern, public opinion can be seen as a resource and a constraint. It is a resource in that it can be called on by political leaders attempting to pursue certain policies. This is what presidents do, for example, when they appear on television and attempt to mobilize opinion on behalf of a given policy. Along with the possible effects of opinion on elections, an active and intense majority opinion is something that is recognized in popular regimes as having a

Polling can summarize public opinion accurately, but it cannot always measure the intensity or the persistence of feelings about specific issues, and these feelings often influence voting behavior. *(Andy Levin/Black Star)*

claim on government. (In fact, the idea that the public wants something and that this want demands consideration is part of what is meant by the abstract notion of the "force" of public opinion.) On the other hand, opinion may also act as a constraint on leaders who have a policy they might like to pursue but know they cannot (or cannot afford to). Numerous decisions of presidents are constrained in this way, as, for example, President Nixon's inability in 1973 to enforce the Paris Peace Accords for the Vietnamese war through further bombings (Kissinger, 1982:326). Of course, the leeway given to presidents is in part subject to their capacity to impress and ultimately persuade the public. In his characteristically blunt way, Theodore Roosevelt once remarked, "I did not divine what the people were going to think. I simply made up my mind what they ought to think and then did my best to get them to think it" (Kegley and Wittkopf, 1982:288). When presidents can succeed in persuading the public to their position, they can often get their way. Yet with all the sources of opposition to presidents, their attempts to win over public opinion, as we shall see in Chapter 10, often fail.

OPINION FORMATION AND CHANGE

How do opinions come into being and change? It is fair to say that if social scientists knew the answer to this question, they would hold the key to understanding not only the behavior of contemporary societies but also the movement of history over the past few centuries. For the most part, however, social scientists have only a rudimentary understanding of the processes of opinion formation and change. This should come as no great surprise, as the complexity of these processes is such as to confound all efforts to devise a single theory. To know how opinions form and change would require nothing less than a full understanding of individual psychology, the relationship of social groups to political culture, and the role played by every opinion-influencing agency in society. A great deal of research and speculation have been devoted to these questions, and some progress has been made, but social scientists have not reached and probably never will reach the point where these questions can be answered with scientific precision. The most

we can do here is to cite and briefly discuss some of the major influences affecting opinion formation.

Opinion Formation in Free Societies

First, however, mention must be made of the general character of opinion formation in free societies. Political scientists sometimes begin classifying governments by distinguishing between those that rule by force, holding the public down against its will, and those that have the active consent of the governed. This distinction is useful as a first step in thinking about different political systems. But it is essential to point out that modern totalitarian regimes, while not forsaking the use of terror and force, seek to engineer consent by total social control that includes staging rallies, dictating what is taught in the schools, and filling the media with government propaganda. It is testimony, however, to the resilience of the human spirit that such massive efforts at brainwashing meet resistance and that governments employing these techniques, despite all their efforts, must also have recourse to terror.

By contrast, free societies possess a plurality of opinion-forming agencies. Indeed, the absence of anything approaching a governmental monopoly over the formation of opinion is one of the single most important characteristics of a free society. Free societies differ, of course, in their relative degree of control over the communications system. In France, for example, the government owns the television channels and exercises a considerable degree of control over entertainment and news coverage, while in the United States, the three major television networks are privately owned. In all free societies, however, the written press is independent of the government and often critical of it, and there is a tradition of vigorous intellectual criticism.

Governments of free regimes do, of course, attempt to instill favorable opinions about their systems. To take only the most obvious example, public schools in the United States generally accept as part of their mission the teaching of the American political tradition, and few school boards would tolerate, let alone encourage, a fundamentally hostile presentation of basic American values. Civic education, as long as it allows questioning and inquiry, is to be expected in any system whose people believe in it and want to see it perpetuated. Still, civic education is a far cry from rigid indoctrination. And when all qualifications are considered, it remains the case that in free societies there are numerous opinion-forming agencies that are free of government control and that are often highly critical of the government. One need only mention, for example, the variety of opinions advocated in newspapers and periodicals by political groups of all persuasions, ranging from communists and Maoists on the left to Nazis and members of the Ku Klux Klan on the right. From the perspective of the social scientist attempting to study the formation and change of public opinion, this plurality in opinion-forming agencies adds to the difficulties of formulating a single, comprehensive theory. Liberty breeds diversity. As Madison observed in *Federalist* 10: "As long as the reason of man continues fallible, and he is at liberty to exercise it, different opinions will be formed."

Opinion-Forming Agencies

Family The learning of political opinions and the transfer of opinions from adults to children occur through a process of *political socialization*. The most important institution in this process has traditionally been the family; and while the family has probably lost some ground as a socializing agency over the past half century because of competition from television and the increase in the number of divorces, it is still the first place to look in understanding the development of opinions. The family's authority (and influence) is undoubtedly much greater in the realms of cultural and religious matters than in areas of more narrowly conceived political opinions. Partisan leanings (Democratic and Republican) are often transmitted from one generation to the next, at least temporarily; but one study found that the transmission of opinion on specific issues such as war and communism is very weak (Connell, 1972). Whatever the influence of the family, it remains the case that individuals may "unlearn" what they have imbibed as they come into contact with other views and experience events in their own lives. Thus while childhood socialization in the family is an important influence on opinions, it is far from being decisive.

Primary and Secondary Education Education is another major socializing institution, and one that sometimes operates in conflict with the family. Education, as we have seen, plays an important role in teaching children about certain basic constitutional values and, generally speaking, in inculcating a positive view of the American political system (Hess and Torney, 1967). Most public schools as such do not play a direct role in influencing ideological opinion or opinion on specific policy issues, but they may indirectly affect these views through the teaching of social studies and history. An important fact to keep in mind when discussing American public education is that the curricula of the schools are set by state and by local authorities, rather than by the federal government. As a result, the values promoted by the schools tend to reflect the values of different communities, although professional educators—teachers and administrators—have a great deal of influence. Frequently the politics of local school boards is the most intensely contested of all local issues, as groups in the community attempt to influence the content of education especially on issues that touch directly or indirectly on morality and religion.

Parents in the United States may also choose to send their children to private schools, the greater part of which have a religious application. (Currently, nearly 12 percent of the nation's primary school children attend private schools.) Most religious schools offer a more structured moral training, which can have a profound indirect bearing on children's subsequent political views. The training in such cases is frequently in accord with the parents' own values and represents an extension of family influence. Because of the importance of education as a socializing agency, the question of private education raises one of the most important issues of public policy. In nations such as France and Mexico, the great conflicts between church and state have been fought out in large part over private education, and important measures have been enacted to limit and regulate private education to reduce church influence. In the United States, from the 1880s until the 1920s, some states sought to discourage or ban private religious education and compel attendance at secular public schools. Such policies, designed to give children a common educational experience, were clearly at odds with the wishes of certain religious groups, especially Catholics. The Supreme Court, in the landmark case *Pierce v. Society of Sisters* (1925), declared

Oregon's law against private religious education unconstitutional.

While the major Constitutional issue relating to private education has been settled, policy questions remain very much in dispute. President Reagan called for tuition tax credits for parents sending their children to private schools, which if put into effect would almost certainly increase the number of children attending private schools. Opponents of this measure, including the major public school teachers' union, stress the benefits of the secular public schools and the opportunities they afford for children to be exposed to what they hold to be a more diverse education. They have also raised Constitutional objections to any tuition tax credit, claiming that it would violate the First Amendment.

Higher Education Higher education seems to have a more profound impact than primary and secondary education on ideological opinion and opinions on specific issues. In attending college, many students encounter a new environment away from home. They come into contact with the culture of the college campus and are introduced to new influences from the ideas that circulate in college communities. These ideas often conflict with earlier opinions, and important changes can result. Colleges and universities differ, of course, in their orientation. A religious, fundamentalist-supported university, such as Oral Roberts University, will have an atmosphere quite different from a secular state campus such as the University of California at Berkeley. Overall, however, there seems to be a general tendency for the ideas that dominate in the national intellectual community to permeate college campuses. After the 1950s, the intellectual community had a predominantly liberal cast of mind—a trend that may now be changing—and one result was that university education exercised a liberalizing influence on students (Ladd and Lipset, 1973). This influence probably reached its high point during the late 1960s and early 1970s when college campuses were seething with political activity, much of it directed against the Vietnamese war. In addition, universities often became the centers of the so-called "counterculture," in which many of the basic values and goals of American society were either held up to ridicule (such as individual economic achievement) or else alleged to

be empty or false (such as claims for racial justice and for protecting the free world). Beyond its influence on the content of opinion, higher education seems to promote a more attentive or engaged public, in the sense that college-educated persons more often express decided opinions on matters outside their immediate experience, such as views on international relations (Hennessy, 1982).

Reference Groups Another important influence on opinion is the reference group—that is, either a group to which individuals or families belong because of some shared characteristic (race, religion, or ethnicity) or a group they decide to join, such as a labor union. Reference groups are important in influencing opinions because members may have certain shared experiences that cause them to see the world in similar ways and because many within each group look to group leaders for cues about political matters. Opinion is therefore in some degree mediated by these groups and their leaders. Because of the importance of groups for understanding voting behavior, we shall withhold a discussion of their influence until Chapter 7.

Class Economic classes are sometimes considered as reference groups, but we single them out for special treatment because of the central role that many theorists assign to them in explaining opinion formation. Clearly the best known of these theorists was Karl Marx (1818–1883), the originator of the modern ideology of communism. In the view of Marx and many of his followers, political opinions derive chiefly from where people are situated in the economic system in relation to the means of production within society. Following this line of analysis, social scientists look to class and occupation to discover the most powerful determinants of political behavior. Beyond emphasizing the importance of economics, Marx went on to develop a theory of modern industrial society that predicted the eventual division of society into two classes—the bourgeoisie, or capitalist, class (consisting of those owning the means of production) and the proletariat (consisting of those toiling in the factories). This division, Marx argued, would spawn class-based parties characterized by the antagonistic economic views of each class. Capitalists would espouse some variant of Liberalism which would serve to protect their property rights and advantaged position, while the proletariat would eventually form into a revolutionary party that would call for the abolition of all private property and the formation of an entirely new mode of social organization, communism.

One remarkable aspect of American politics has been the absence of any major class-based party divisions. Party struggles have, of course, involved elements of conflict between rich and poor and owners and workers. In the nineteenth century, the Democratic party, especially under Jackson and Bryan, invoked class-related themes; and Franklin Roosevelt's 1936 presidential campaign stressed class divisions to an extent unprecedented in American history, an emphasis which reflected and helped to stimulate the tensions between labor and capital that reached a high point in the period during and just after the depression. Yet even in the midst of the depression and rather quickly thereafter, class-based divisions were to an extent obscured by differences based on interest groups, subcultures, and responses to events in international affairs (Ladd, 1978). For the most part in American history, divisions relating to class have been less important than those deriving from these other sources (Jensen, 1978). Today class-based responses are evident on certain issues, but voting patterns as seen in the 1980 election reveal the relative unimportance of class divisions (see Chapter 7). Those at the lower end of the income scale supported the Democratic candidate in larger proportions, and those at the upper end the Republican candidate, but the differences were not very great. Of course, if political conditions were to change and the division between rich and poor to become the major focus of political debate, this situation could be transformed. Under the Reagan administration, there were indications that cuts in some federal programs had begun to create more class-based responses, and leading Democratic politicians raised this issue in public debates.

Why has class played only a relatively modest role in American history, and why has the American working class failed to develop a distinct working-class consciousness comparable to that found in many European nations? One reason was outlined in the founders' discussion of social and economic pluralism, which in certain respects anticipated and refuted Marx's forecasts. According to Madison's argument in *Federalist* 10, the dangerous political division between rich and poor could be avoided in a large nation having a variety of economic groups—farmers, manufacturers, and different commercial interests. The effect of this diversity would be to induce people to be concerned about their particular interest rather than anything like the interest of a class as a whole. As a result, both the rich and the poor from one sector would form into temporary coalitions against the rich and the poor from another. Historical examples of this process can be found by analyzing coalitions in congressional voting, and today we continue to see frequent instances in which manufacturers and workers in particular sectors—for example, the automobile industry—join together to promote their common interests.

As the class basis of voting patterns during the depression suggests, however, a constant impoverishment of the American worker would eventually have brought some form of class-based party division. This result was avoided by the tremendous economic success that American workers enjoyed after the depression and especially after World War II. Because of this success, the concept of class as originally conceived by Marx has lost much of its meaning in the United States. In Marx's view, the proletariat was not only the working class but also an exploited class that owned nothing. Many of today's blue-collar workers, by contrast, earn relatively good wages, often wages far better than many white-collar workers. Plumbers, electricians, automobile workers, truck drivers—and one can add more and more occupations to the list—are not in any sense poor, either absolutely or relatively as compared with other Americans. By virtue of owning their own houses and property, many of these workers think of themselves not solely as workers, but as middle-class property owners having a stake in protecting the system.

Finally, a strict Marxist understanding of class has become partially obsolete as modern economies have advanced beyond the stage of traditional industrial capitalism. The growing sectors of modern economies like that of the United States are no longer in areas of heavy industry such as steel or automobile manufacturing, but in service sectors (the professions, government work) and high-technology fields. Moreover, the character of the wealthier classes in America has changed. Previously, wealth was based chiefly on the ownership of property and businesses. This connection remains true up to a point, but high-salaried personnel now are found among managers, technicians, experts, high-level government administrators, and professionals, many of whom do not identify with the interests of big business (Bell, 1976).

Interestingly, the well-educated members of the growing professional and service sector, called by some the "new class," do not act as a Marxist "class" analysis would predict. Though relatively well-off, they do not think of themselves as entrepreneurs or as owners of capital, which for the most part they are not. Nor do they form their opinions on the basis of class economic antagonisms. Members of the new class, to the extent that this segment can be spoken of as a group, are strongly influenced in opinion formation by the intellectual opinions to which they have been exposed, for example, through higher education and the journals and books that they read. Their economic position seems much less important than the ideas that they happen to espouse, and today one finds that a large portion of the activists on both the liberal and the conservative sides of the political spectrum are drawn from the very same strata of the educated upper middle class.

Ideas Thus far, we have looked at opinions as they are influenced by one's upbringing or one's position in the economic and social structure. But one may well wonder where families and reference groups obtain the opinions that they pass on to their members. In part, as we have seen, these opinions may come from their common experience and heritage or their "objective" situation in relationship to the economy. In part, however, their opinions are influenced by general ideas that group leaders find compelling and then pass on to their membership. Leaders mediate between the evolving structure of principles within a group and "new" ideas that they find outside of it or within different elements of its tradition.

Moreover, although individuals are influenced by the various groups to which they belong (and sometimes are pulled in different directions by conflicting identifications), they also respond *as individuals* to the arguments made by politicians and the ideas presented on television, in newspapers, and in journals and books. Citizens' views, in other words, are not fully determined by upbringing, group membership, or class, but—to some extent—are continually being tested and evaluated in light of experience and the various arguments that are offered in an effort to persuade. In modern society, moreover, the multiple contacts of individuals and the character of the communications system have left the individual less dependent than ever before on opinion mediated by traditional groups. Citizens are therefore members of a reference group that is larger than any group we have thus far discussed. They are all part of the political community known as the "United States of America" and as such are subject to the conflicting opinions argued and debated on the national level. Through books and exchanges of ideas, many in turn are also aware of the general concepts of political and economic life being discussed throughout the world. Ideas and arguments, then, powerfully affect public opinion, both as they are received and mediated through groups and as they are evaluated directly by individuals. But where, one may ask, do these ideas come from? John Maynard Keynes, the famous British economist of the last generation, once wrote:

> The ideas of economists and political philosophers, both when they are right and when they are wrong, are more powerful than is commonly understood. Indeed the world is ruled by little else. Practical men, who believe themselves to be quite exempt from any intellectual influences, are usually the slaves of some defunct economist. Madmen in authority, who hear voices in the air, are distilling their frenzy from some academic scribbler of a few years back. I am sure that the power of vested interests is vastly exaggerated compared with the gradual encroachment of ideas (Keynes, 1936:383).

This assertion may appear startling at first, for one seldom thinks of scholars and professors as being among the great power brokers of society. Only infrequently do they hold elective office, although more and more have been given appointive offices. Their greatest influence, however, derives not from holding power directly but from influencing those who do hold power. Politicians and journalists seldom initiate broad new theories of their own, but more often than not receive them once or twice removed from scholars and intellectuals. Ideas thus constitute one of the chief sources of opinion formation and one of the most important means of change in political life.

The influence of ideas on opinion became very evident to observers of American politics during the middle of the 1970s. The public philosophy of liberalism that had dominated American national politics since the New Deal came under increasing attack by a group of thinkers labeled "neoconservatives," writing in such influential journals as *Commentary, The Public Interest,* and the *Wall Street Journal,* These thinkers helped to alter the climate of intellectual opinion on both domestic and foreign affairs and prepared the way indirectly for the acceptance of some of Ronald Reagan's ideas among groups which, some twenty years earlier, would have regarded them as extreme. Our general point here, however, is not to assess the soundness of any particular theory but to illustrate an important factor in the process of opinion formation. And the conclusion is inescapable: ideas have power. In area after area, it is possible to trace back elite opinions and mass opinions to intellectual currents of thought. It is in no way surprising, therefore, that partisan leaders and advocates of certain ways of thought spend a great deal of effort and money sponsoring scholarly research and institutes and supporting the publication of various intellectual journals of opinion.

Of course, the ideas of intellectuals must be mediated through other opinion-influencing structures, and it is an unresolved matter as to why some ideas take hold at certain times while others do not. But setting aside all such qualifications, it is clear that ideas have immense force and influence. It is precisely because of this fact that this book places so much emphasis on ideas in understanding both institutional development and past constitutional and policy changes; and it is for this reason also that students of politics, as serious citizens, need to think through basic ideas about our constitutional system, for the ideas that are accepted by today's students and thinkers may well become the public opinion of the next generation.

THE MEDIA

Opinion formation and change are powerfully influenced by the prevailing communications system in society, so much so that some scholars have recently theorized that the nature of the communications system may well be the most important of all influences on the character of society (McLuhan, 1966). Like Marx's theory of economic determinism, these new theories of communication determinism have probably overstated their case. But there is little doubt that until very recently, many studies of public opinion had neglected the profound influence of the communication system on opinion formation.

Intuitively, the importance of the communication system should be obvious. Before the advent of the printing press in the fifteenth century, only a limited number of people had access to written material, and public opinion, to the extent that it existed at all, was more easily influenced by established authorities and institutions, such as the church. Even in the eighteenth century, before the advent of the mass newspaper, opinion was much more influenced than it is today by reference groups and established authorities. The successive revolutions in popular dissemination of opinion that occurred first around the time of the founding, when newspapers first became widely available, and then near the end of the nineteenth century, with the advent of the mass "penny press," increasingly freed the formation of opinion from groups and opened the process to general appeals that reached broader and broader segments of the public.

Scholars today have probably become more aware of the impact of communications because the last generation lived through a profound communications revolution—the advent of radio in the 1920s and television in the 1950s—akin in scope and importance to the advent of the printing press. The electronic media revolution has made it possible for the entire nation to be tied together in the same communications network, a union which has tended to nationalize the opinion-formation process. More pressure in the name of opinion is brought to bear on government, and leaders are in a position to address the public directly in an effort to counteract pressure or build constituencies. This revolution in communication has clearly affected the representative tone of the government by bringing leaders and the public into more "direct"—although perhaps less genuine—contact. Indeed, the founders had relied on a large nation with a slow

During the 1960 presidential campaign, Kennedy and Nixon introduced a new era in American politics by carrying on a live, face-to-face debate while the whole nation watched on television. *(Philip Drell / Black Star)*

communication system as one way of avoiding frequent mass pressure on government and giving officials greater discretion (*Federalist* 10). Today, radio and especially television each constitute, in almost the literal meaning of the word, a medium—something which stands in between the mass public on the one hand and those attempting to shape and influence public opinion on the other. Television has influenced and changed the way that groups and individuals attempt to persuade the public and has altered profoundly the relationship among various elements of the body politic in ways that are still only dimly perceived.

The effect of the media on opinion is complex and multifaceted. In analyzing television, the most influential of the modern media, it is necessary to separate the effects that derive from television entertainment and commercial advertising on the one hand from news and the coverage of public events on the other.

The Impact of Entertainment on Public Opinion

Surveys of viewers have shown that most people watch television chiefly for the purpose of being entertained. An adult in the United States, in fact, watches an average of twenty-one hours of television a week. Such exposure, many believe, is bound to have an impact on cultural and moral opinions, such as people's attitudes about violence, sexual morality, and material consumption. This impact may be especially strong in the case of children, who are now socialized to some extent by television. Although no one can really determine the precise impact of television in these areas, the belief that it must be substantial has led various groups in the United States to be concerned and to attempt to influence the content of television programming and commercials.

A leading scholar of television programming, Michael Robinson, surveyed the content of television entertainment and concluded that in the 1950s and early 1960s program entertainment tended to emphasize traditional values in the moral and cultural realms, whereas after the mid-1960s much more attention was given to liberal and experimental lifestyles, and more emphasis was placed on sex and violence (Robinson, 1977). By the beginning of the 1980s, a coalition of fundamentalist religious groups and certain groups on the left had joined together in an effort to pressure the television networks to reduce the amount of explicit violence and sex on television, with some instances of success. Others have voiced concerns about the character of commercial advertising, especially for programs watched by children.

Political Information and News

Television coverage of the news and politics has now become the major source of political information for most Americans. This is not reason to minimize the importance of the nation's principal newspapers and weekly magazines. Papers like the *New York Times, Washington Post,* and *Los Angeles Times* and magazines like *Newsweek* and *Time* are widely read by many of those active in politics, and those influential sources in the print media are closely followed by those in the electronic media and often help to focus their news stories. In addition, television is not quite as dominant in conveying news on state and local events. Nonetheless, the evidence clearly points to the conclusion that television is today the chief mechanism for mass communications in political life.

The change from a public influenced by the print media to one influenced primarily by the electronic media has many implications. One of the interesting differences concerns the legal status of the two media. The print media were—and remain— entirely private, beyond the regulation of the government. Private ownership of the print media once had—and to some extent still has—an important influence on the positions they supported, although today newspaper journalists have professional norms they follow which limit the impact of owners' interference with news. Still, newspapers can take whatever stand they wish, print the kind of stories they want, and refuse any kind of advertising.

Television stations and networks, while privately owned, are regulated in important ways by the government on the grounds that they occupy a limited space on "public" air waves. Stations must be granted licenses by the Federal Communications Commission, a process which some have asserted is a means by which government can control the media. Actually, though, the major impact of the federal regulatory process is to minimize overt political bias in political communications. Television stations can take editorial stands, but they are obliged to follow certain rules that include: the *fairness doctrine,* which requires that broadcast time be given to people to present opposing views on controversial issues; the *equal-time rule,* which gives a candidate the right to the same time as an opponent (both free time and the right to buy the same time for advertisements); the *personal-attack rule,* which gives individuals or groups a right to reply if they are attacked on the air; and the *political editorial rule,* which gives candidates a right to reply to an endorsement of another candidate.

Television communication of political information is presented to the American public through at least four different channels: (1) political advertising and editorials, (2) direct coverage of speeches and political events, (3) interview and discussion programs, and (4) news coverage. Each of these channels has unique properties.

Political Advertising Advertising is used mostly by groups and individuals during election campaigns to persuade the public to vote for or against a candidate, party, or issue on the ballot. Television stations have no say whatsoever on the content of these advertisements. Political advertising is often criticized for its alleged effect of trivializing politics and bringing it down to the same level as selling deodorant or soda pop. As we shall see in Chapter 6, however, political advertisements often contain important information, and there is no evidence to suggest that the American public is so "programmed" that it cannot understand the difference between soap brands and presidential candidates.

Direct Coverage Direct coverage of events, such as presidential addresses, news conferences, and campaign debates, allows political leaders to have direct contact with the American public and to present their views in an extended fashion. Of all the institutions that can profit from this new tool, clearly the presidency is in the best position, since the president is a single individual whose personality and policies are of deep interest to the American public. Although it is difficult even to conceive of a president without access, it is well to recall that most citizens never heard their presidents speak until Calvin Coolidge nor saw them "live" until Dwight Eisenhower. Yet the advantages a president gains by the use of television are offset by certain costs. Presidents are led into the temptation of thinking they can easily move public opinion by television addresses, and it has virtually become expected that presidents will address the nation when things are going poorly—even when they may have little or nothing to say.

Access to television is governed by laws and by a number of precedents worked out over the years by the networks and government. Although the networks retain the option of refusing the president time for an address, they seldom do so. To balance the time given to the president, the networks now generally offer the opposition party time to respond to presidential addresses. In general, the question of access has been resolved to the satisfaction of almost everyone, with the notable exception of third-party candidates in presidential campaign debates. John Anderson, for example, was excluded from the 1980 presidential debates and complained bitterly that this destroyed any chance he had of winning the election. (The event was covered as "news" and thus escaped the requirements of the equal-time provision.)

Interview and Discussion Programs Direct coverage in a slightly different form is found in programs like *Face the Nation* and *Meet the Press* in which leaders of government and public figures present their views in response to reporters' questions. The shows *Nightline* and the *McNeil-Lehrer Report* have added the dimension of give and take between advocates of different viewpoints, leading to extensive dialog and often heated debates. Such programs allow viewpoints to be expressed vigorously, but they also supply the "discipline" of forcing individuals to confront directly objections and different arguments. Many consider these shows to be television at its very best.

News Television news coverage is the most important source of political information for Ameri-

cans and also the most controversial channel of communication. Television journalists and editors must themselves decide what is newsworthy and how the news should be presented. As they do this, their judgments are affected by the practices of their profession, the pressures of competition, and perhaps to some extent their own political views.

The practices of reporting over the last generation, in both the print and the electronic media, have undergone a tremendous change. While reporters still hold to the value of objectivity, in the 1970s more and more journalists self-consciously adopted an investigative and adversary relationship to their subjects, attempting to uncover a lie or scandal hidden beneath official sources and comments. This attitude was fueled by the Vietnamese war, when official government sources continually sought to present the news in a favorable light by distorting the truth, and by Watergate, when President Nixon consistently lied about his relationship to the cover-up of the break-in at the Democratic campaign headquarters. Journalists certainly had reason for their suspicions, and there is no doubt that the government frequently attempts to "manage" the news in a way that, at a minimum, presents matters in the least unfavorable light and, at a maximum, involves outright distortion.

On the other hand, many in official positions of power complain that journalism today all too frequently neglects their explanation and rushes too quickly into commentary or hearsay evidence which casts doubt on the statements or interpretations of official sources. In seeking to uncover the "real" story, critics complain, journalists frequently exaggerate, distort, and preoccupy themselves with the trivial and the irrelevant. The feeling on the part of government officials that they are getting a "bad" press is common. All recent presidents at one time or another have complained bitterly about the press coverage of their administrations, and frequently with some justification.

Competition and the desire to make the news interesting can also lead to distortions. The news, especially television news, is a highly competitive business, and the networks and sponsors inevitably want to gain large audiences. As a result, there is pressure exerted to cover stories in a dramatic way and to focus on "interesting" items, often those involving conflict. (It is more interesting to show a cut from a rally or to show a demonstration than to cover a candidate's speech or to give the statistical background on a problem.) The character of what is selected for news naturally influences the behavior of those seeking access to the news. Thus groups may stage demonstrations for news coverage, and political campaigns today normally seek to provide an interesting "visual" for the evening news. News reporting also may tend to focus on the drama of events, rather than on the substance. In the coverage of presidential races, as we shall see, television journalism has had the tendency to play up fictitious upsets in primaries and concentrate more on the "horse race" among the candidates than on what they are actually saying (Graber, 1980).

Whether or not one chooses to call it a distortion, it is clear that the pervasiveness of television news with its dramatic visual impact has profoundly affected the entire political process. Groups that had little access to the American system have been able, with relatively modest resources, to gain public attention by staging dramatic events that can capture the eye of television journalists. It is perhaps no surprise, therefore, that demonstrations and terrorist acts have become more frequent in a media age, as they are obvious ways of gaining attention and creating interesting news. Television may also have contributed to certain institutional changes, such as the weakening of the power of party organizations, for television enables the candidates to appeal directly to the public and increases the importance of primaries as a mechanism for securing presidential nominations. In general, those activities or institutions that can be portrayed in and through television have tended to gain power at the expense of those which cannot (Robinson, 1977). At the same time, however, the negative and critical attention focused on these institutions may have made people more cynical about them. At the very least, the sheer amount of coverage, presented in a way that seems to impose demands on government and to magnify errors, makes governing more difficult. As the political scientist Austin Ranney has observed, "The media accelerate political consciousness and feed on impatience for quick results, no matter how complex the problems; they want things solved in 60 minutes" (Broder, 1982).

Finally, there is the problem of journalistic bias.

Like other people, journalists have their own political viewpoints, and these inevitably color, at least to some extent, the way in which they present the news. In television journalism—where so many people watch and where there are only three major networks—a concentration of bias toward a particular viewpoint can pose serious problems of objectivity in political communication. In the late 1960s and early 1970s, conservatives in the nation complained that the media were dominated by a "liberal establishment" which slanted the news against conservative positions and candidates. Spiro Agnew, the vice president between 1968 and 1973, launched a famous campaign against the media in 1970, paradoxically gaining media notoriety by his blistering attacks against the major networks and newspapers. There remains a great deal of controversy over the extent to which this attack was justified, and some reporters and scholars were prepared to admit that Agnew had at least raised a valid issue for discussion. Perhaps because of a greater consciousness of possible ideological bias and a greater emphasis on an adversarial relation whatever the viewpoint of those in power, criticisms on this point have become much less frequent.

Given the character of the American system of government and the great protections afforded to the news profession under the First Amendment, it is inevitable that there will be tensions between politicians and the press and equally inevitable that there will be occasional journalistic excesses. Politicians and governing officials prefer a favorable press, or at any rate a press that takes into account the difficulties and uncertainties that go into making any decision. Journalists, often suspicious of official explanations, have their own incentives to cover events in a more dramatic fashion and also to concentrate on failures more than successes. Within bounds, the tension between the two is healthy for democratic politics.

PUBLIC OPINION AND PUBLIC POLICY

Having examined the concept of public opinion in its various dimensions, we should now realize that the simple question with which this chapter began—does public opinion govern?—cannot be given a simple answer. Public opinion, we have seen, exists on at least three different levels, and on each level its nature and influence differ. For understanding the process of governing, it is necessary to appreciate both the constraints and the possibilities that people active in politics face.

The Role of Public Opinion

On the level of constitutional issues, public opinion has an influence that is pervasive, yet often invisible. Opinion on this level sets the broad boundaries of acceptable public discourse. Dominant opinions about liberty or equality may be challenged by radical groups like the Communist party or the Ku Klux Klan, but these views are for the most part simply ignored. Fundamental constitutional principles are, of course, frequently discussed by mainstream politicians to explain or justify their approach to a given problem, but these for the most part involve marginally different interpretations of these principles. Only on rare occasions have these constitutional issues been the subject of major, sustained controversy. At such moments, such as the period before the Civil War or (to a much lesser degree) the period of the civil rights struggle, political leaders may for a time raise issues of constitutional principle and place themselves "ahead" of current standards in an attempt to lead public opinion in new directions. Politicians at other times may adopt a long-term "educative" strategy in an attempt to change constitutional opinion, but their ability to force policies at odds with dominant opinion is necessarily limited. Statesmen and stateswomen must act within the realm of the possible. Lincoln, for example, thought that it was possible in the 1850s to reawaken support for the concept of equality in the form of a refutation of the assertion that there was a moral right for the institution of slavery, but he would not support the idea of full political or social equality of the races. As he explained, "A universal feeling, whether well or ill-founded, cannot be safely disregarded" (Johannsen, 1965:51). Constrained by such "universal feelings," the role of the statesman or stateswoman is necessarily different from that of the activist.

On the level of general opinion toward government policy, we observed that while most Americans may not think systematically in ideological terms, citizens nevertheless can be placed roughly on a spectrum of general policy opinion. There are certainly positions which, if broached by leaders, would evoke powerful opposition. New departures of general policy by political leaders, it seems, may not have the immediate support of a majority, but there probably has to be at least a general willingness to try something new. Thus in 1932, when Roosevelt was elected president, it was unlikely that a majority would have backed the new liberal principles on which he began to act. But it is clear that support for the principle of limited government had weakened as a result of the depression and that the public was willing to embark on a new experiment. By the same token, in 1980 it was questionable whether a majority in the public was in favor of President Reagan's conservative principles. Again, however, it was clear that by the late 1970s there had been a significant loss of confidence in "big government" and a willingness among a much greater number than before to try new approaches. An election victory, for whatever reasons, coupled with a significant movement of ideological opinion, can provide a strong-willed president with the necessary leeway to attempt a new departure. If the policies prove to be successful, a president can change the basic policy or ideological disposition of the majority.

Opinions on specific policies and issues are sometimes taken seriously and sometimes ignored. On certain issues, such as the Vietnamese war, opinion is intensely felt and pushes itself into the policymaking process by way of electoral pressures. Political leaders may be forced to change or accommodate their positions under the threat of being replaced. The reverse situation is found where leaders might like to act differently but are aware that the level of opinion needed to support their policies would not be forthcoming. President Roosevelt, for example, wanted to involve the nation more actively in the fight against Nazi Germany in the 1930s but was unable to buck the strong isolationist sentiment at the time. He therefore had to bide his time and wait for an event that would change public opinion, which came dramatically with the Japanese surprise attack on Pearl Harbor in 1941.

Potential national voting issues such as the Vietnamese war are more the exception than the rule. The public frequently wants to see an issue addressed (like slowing inflation or increasing employment), but it has no one particular means specifically in mind. It is true, of course, that in many instances the policies of government are at odds with what the majority wants (as measured in opinion polls). These may be matters on which people do not feel very intensely or have not had time to organize. Politicians in these instances have the leeway to act at their discretion. Moreover, in many instances majority opinion may be much less important to politicians than intense and well-organized minority opinions. The majority may be largely indifferent, whereas for various minorities the policies may well constitute a voting issue.

Limitations on the Influence of Public Opinion

Why is it that on many particular issues of public policy majority opinion does not have its way? The most important reason is the most obvious one: public opinion is not legally or Constitutionally empowered to govern. Under our representative scheme, power is given under specified conditions to certain officials, none of whom is required to follow popular opinion. In fact, many elements of the system are designed precisely to guard against a quick transfer of public sentiment to official policy. Thus, the courts, though not necessarily unmindful of public opinion, can act without its support. And Constitutional amendments, because they require the support of two-thirds of the members of Congress and three-fourths of the states to be ratified, can be prevented, notwithstanding the majority's preference.

These qualifications do not negate the essentially popular character of the system. The selection of most officers by election provides a vehicle by which public opinion can be translated into public policy. People can elect politicians who are in sympathy with their views and turn out of office those who are not (with the exception of federal judges). Popular elections stand at the base of power of the government, and it follows that a *strong and persistent* majority must, over time, have its way. In fact, we seldom see conflicts between this kind of majority and governmental policy, because the government already tends to reflect such opinions. Where, however, something less than a strong and persistent majority exists,

the mechanism of popular election does not produce—and was never designed to produce—a strict correspondence between majority opinion and policy. Consider the following three points about the nature of elections.

First, when voters cast their ballots for a candidate, they do not—indeed cannot—express their views on every issue. Voting decisions boil down to a choice among candidates offering a "package" of policy views, and voters can choose only the entire package. In the absence of a single dominating issue, elections cannot ensure that a candidate supports what the majority of the voters want on any particular issue. As noted, in fact, candidates often win support by taking stands on a series of issues favored by minorities, but supported very intensely.

Second, when people vote, they ordinarily consider not just the candidates' position on the immediate issue, but their party affiliation, the performance of incumbents, and especially the character of the candidates. Winning the trust of the public on character is normally as important for the candidate as being in accord with the public on many policy issues. Elections are not simply mechanisms for registering policy preferences, but devices by which people select those whose judgment and character they respect.

Third, the preference of the public as registered by polls can differ from that which counts in the electoral process. Polls provide an abstract measure of the views of the *entire* adult public. But this is not precisely the same public with which politicians are concerned. Turnout in federal elections since 1952 has ranged between 63 and 52 percent of the potential eligible electorate in presidential contests and between 59 and 35 percent in congressional elections. With a turnout in the range of 35 to 40 percent, the candidates are already aware that the voting public, consisting of the more politically active segment of the population, may differ in certain ways from the electorate at large. Furthermore, most candidates are nominated in primary elections, where the turnout is usually lower still and where the electorate may be even more specialized. Finally, an election itself is the last act of the electoral process, and in order to compete effectively, a candidate must raise funds and secure the help of volunteers. Once again, the calculations a candidate must make about whose support is

Despite many efforts to simplify the process of registration and voting, the percentage of eligible Americans who actually vote in elections has been declining for the last two decades.   *(Charles Gatewood/Magnum)*

needed for election differ from the information in general opinion polls.

These are the major reasons why public opinion as registered in polls is not always the prime consideration for politicians, even if we assume that politicians are interested only in reelection. But more important then any of these reasons is the fact that most politicians do *not* always think only in terms of being reelected. They often deliberate about what *they* think will work best, apart from what the public may want, and occasionally they do this at some risk to their electoral chances. In fact, in the case of presidents it is often in their interest not to follow public opinion. In the end, even when seeking reelection, presidents will be judged mostly by how well their policies work, not by how popular the policies are at the time. Moreover, most presidents are competing not just for popularity but for a place in history. This concern for fame

can lead them to take risks for policies they believe will ultimately prove their worth.

CONCLUSION: SHOULD OPINION GOVERN?

We have spent so much time indicating how public opinion influences policy in particular issues that it might seem that the question of the role it should play is uninteresting. But this is not the case. Institutions and laws can be arranged in different ways that give more (or less) weight to public opinion in the governing process. Constitution makers have realized this fact and have sought to adjust institutional arrangements to reflect their views about the role of public opinion on the governing process. The founders, although recognizing the legitimacy of public opinion as it would be expressed (indirectly) through elections, sought to place impediments on it as a *direct* force in the governing process by such means as indirect elections, separation of powers, and a teaching about the role of elected officials. They relied, too, on a different and less-developed communication system. Subsequent developments, as we shall see in the chapters that follow, have provided greater weight for public opinion. Not only have theorists accorded it more legitimacy, but changes in the electoral process have increased its influence, although not nearly as much, perhaps, as some had hoped. The question of the role of public opinion on government policy and issues lies at the center of current debates to "reform" and democratize parties and the electoral process.

As a general matter, most people probably have an initial preference for the majoritarian view that supports a greater role for public opinion. But further reflection would probably bring some appreciation of the need for qualification. Most would probably see some claim for taking into account, up to a point, the intensity of minority sentiments, which is a pluralist rather than a strict majoritarian concern; and most would also see the need for the "representative" values of statesmanship, deliberation, and protection of fundamental law. All these qualities require a certain degree of freedom on the part of governing officials from the immediate dictates of public opinion. Determining a workable balance can be done only in terms of establishing the concrete character of political institutions.

One way to think about the possible limits of public opinion is to consider two proposals that would increase its weight beyond anything known before in our representative system. The first, which was backed by a number of senators in the 1970s, is to pass a Constitutional amendment that would institute a national initiative and referendum, thereby enabling the voting public in certain cases to make final policy. (Many states currently have such a provision in their constitutions, and in some states, such as California and Oregon, it is frequently employed.) The second, not yet quite feasible, would be an amendment that would allow for regularly scheduled referendums on national issues to be conducted, not through regular elections, but through voting in the homes through two-way television hookups and computers. The public could listen to the debates of their "representa-

tives," after which they could then register their preferences. The votes would then become law.

Although this last suggestion may sound a bit ridiculous, it represents a logical extension of the principle that public opinion should govern. Given the state of communications technology today, representative government is no longer, as it was in the past, a necessity imposed by the fact that the public as a whole could not assemble and vote. If Americans are to continue to choose a representative system, it must follow from a recognition that, while majority opinion on particular issues has a legitimate role to play as it is expressed through elections and as it acts through other channels on the governing process, it is not finally equipped to govern directly. In part, this recognition could still be based on certain physical constraints: the people "assembled" through television hookups would not be able to carry on the kinds of adjustments and compromise that can take place only in a setting in which people can meet each other on a direct face-to-face basis. For the most part, however, this recognition would have to be based on the appreciation of other values besides majoritarian ones and on an acceptance of the notion that elected officials, who are chosen because of their expected or proven ability to perform and for whom politics is a full-time job, are better-equipped than the public to make day-to-day political decisions. To make such a claim is neither to denigrate the public's ability nor to put elected officials on an exalted pedestal. It is merely to assert that in a representative system the public and officials have different roles to play.

SOURCES

Almond, Gabriel, and Sydney Verba: *The Civic Culture,* Princeton University Press, Princeton, N.J., 1963.

Aron, Raymond: *Democratie et Totalitarisme,* Gallimard, Saint-Amand, France, 1965.

Banfield, Edward: *The Unheavenly City Revisited,* Little, Brown, Boston, 1974.

Beer, Samuel: "In Search of a New Public Philosophy," in Anthony King (ed.), *The New American Political System,* American Enterprise Institute, Washington, D.C., 1978.

Bell, Daniel: *The Cultural Contradictions of Capitalism,* Basic Books. New York, 1976.

Bellah, Robert: *The Broken Covenant: American Civil Religion in Time of Trial,* Seabury, New York, 1975.

Broder, David: "Second-Year Slump," *Washington Post,* Apr. 4, 1982, p. 1.

Bryce, James: *The American Commonwealth,* vols. 1 and 2, Macmillan, New York, 1889.

Cambridge Reports, March 12–22, 1976; and May 21–June 13, 1979.

Campbell, Angus: *The American Voter,* Wiley, New York, 1960.

Center for Political Studies: National election studies, 1958–1980.

Civic Service, Inc.: Poll, March 15–18, 1981.

Connell, R.W.: "Political Socialization in the American Family: The Evidence Re-examined," *Public Opinion Quarterly,* vol. 36, no. 3, Fall 1972, pp. 323–333.

Converse, Philip E.: "The Nature of Belief Systems in Mass Publics," in David E. Apter (ed.), *Ideology and Discontent,* Free Press, New York, 1964.

Devine, Donald: *The Political Culture of the United States,* Little, Brown, Boston, 1972.

Friedman, Milton: *Capitalism and Freedom,* University of Chicago Press, Chicago, 1962.

Gallup Organization: *Gallup Report,* March 1982, September 1982; and various surveys, 1937–1983.

Graber, Doris: *Mass Media and American Politics,* Congressional Quarterly Press, Washington, D.C.. 1980.

Harris, Lou, and Associates: Poll, August 2–11, 1979.

Hennessy, Bernard: *Public Opinion,* 4th ed., Brooks-Cole, Monterey, Calif., 1982.

Hess, Robert D., and Judith V. Torney: *The Development of Political Attitudes in Children,* Aldine, Chicago, 1967.

Jensen, Richard J.: *The Winning of the Midwest: Social and Political Conflict, 1888-1986,* University of Chicago, Chicago, 1971.

Johannsen, Robert W.: *The Lincoln-Douglas Debates,* Oxford, New York, 1965

Kegley, Charles W. Jr. and Eugene R. Wittkopf: *American Foreign Policy: Pattern and Process,* St. Martins, New York, 1982.

Key, V. O.: *The Responsible Electorate.* Harvard University Press, Cambridge, Mass., 1966.

Keynes, John Maynard: *The General Theory of Employment and Money,* Harcourt, Brace, Jovanovich, New York, 1936.

Kissinger, Henry: *Years of Upheaval,* Little, Brown, Boston, 1982.

Ladd, Everett, Jr.: *Transformation of the American Party System,* 2d ed., Norton, New York, 1978.

——— and Seymour Martin Lipset: *The Divided Academy: Professors and Politics,* McGraw-Hill, New York, 1965.

——— and ———: *Academics, Politics and the 1972 Election,* American Enterprise Institute, Washington, D.C., 1973.

Lane, Robert: *Political Life,* Free Press, Glencoe, Ill., 1959.

Lawrence, David G.: "Procedural Norms and Tolerance: A Reassessment," *American Political Science Review,* vol. 70, no.1, 1976, pp. 80–100.

Lipset, Seymour Martin: *The First New Nation,* Anchor, New York, 1967.

McCloskey, Robert J., et al.: "Issue Conflict and Consensus among Party Leaders and Followers," *American Political Science Review,* vol. 54, no. 2, June 1960, pp. 406–427.

McLuhan, Marshall: *Understanding Media: The Extensions of Man,* McGraw-Hill, New York, 1966.

Mitofsky, Warren J., and Martin Plissner: "A Reporter's Guide to Published Polls," *Public Opinion,* vol. 3, no. 3, June–July 1980.

Mueller, John: *War, Presidents and Public Opinion,* Wiley, New York, 1973.

National Opinion Research Center: General surveys, 1956–1980; and general social surveys, various dates.

Nie, Norman H., with Kristi Andersen: "Mass Belief Systems Revisited: Political Change and Attitude Structure," *Journal of Politics* vol. 36, no. 3, 1974, pp. 540–591.

Orren, Gary, and E.J. Dionne: "The Next New Deal," *Working Papers,* May–June, 1981, pp. 25–35.

Polsby, Nelson: *The Consequences of Party Reform,* Oxford University Press, Oxford, 1983.

Pomper, Gerald: *Voter's Choice,* Dodd, Mead, New York, 1975.

Public Opinion, January-February 1979; February-March 1979; December-January 1980; February-March 1981; June 1981; October-November 1982.

Robinson, Michael: "Television and American Politics, 1952-1976," *Public Interest,* Summer 1977, pp. 3–39.

Roper Organization: *Roper Reports,* vol. 77, no. 3, February 12–26, 1977.

Shapiro, Martin: "The Supreme Court: From Warren to Burger," in Anthony King (ed), *The New American Political System,* American Enterprise Institute, Washington, D.C., 1978.

Stimson, James A.: "Belief Systems: Constraint, Complexity, and the 1972 Election," *American Journal of Political Science,* vol. 19, no. 3, Aug. 1975, pp. 393–417.

Stouffer, Samuel A.: *Communism, Conformity, and Civil Liberties,* Doubleday, Garden City, N.Y., 1955.

Tocqueville, Alexis de: *Democracy in America,* J.P. Mayer (ed.), George Lawrence (trans.), Anchor, Garden City, N.Y., 1969.

Verba, Sydney, et al.: *The Changing American Voter,* Harvard University Press, Cambridge, Mass., 1976.

RECOMMENDED READINGS

Almond, Gabriel, and Sydney Verba: *The Civic Culture,* Princeton University Press, Princeton, N.J., 1963. A pioneering study of attitudes on political culture in five democratic nations.

Bennett, W. Lance: *Public Opinion in American Politics,* Harcourt, Brace, Jovanovich, New York, 1980. An analytic discussion of the nature of public opinion.

Devine, Donald: *The Political Culture of the United States,* Little, Brown, Boston, 1972. An overview of opinions of Americans on basic questions of political culture.

Graber, Doris: *Mass Media and American Politics,* Congressional Quarterly Press, Washington, D.C., 1980. A survey of the role of the mass media in contemporary American politics.

Hennessy, Bernard: *Public Opinion,* 4th ed., Brooks-Cole, Monterey, Calif., 1982. An introductory text to the study of public opinion.

Lane, Robert: *Political Life,* Free Press, New York, 1959. An exploration of the fundamental beliefs of American workers as revealed by the method of in-depth interviews.

Lippmann, Walter: *Public Opinion,* Free Press, New York, 1965. A thoughtful account of the role of public opinion and the character of news in modern democratic states.

Chapter 5

Political Parties

CHAPTER CONTENTS

In 1844, the telegraph wire that stretched between Baltimore and Washington carried the first message ever conveyed by that medium. It slowly ticked out the news from Baltimore that James K. Polk had been nominated by the Democratic party as its candidate for the presidency. Democrats in Washington, who had anxiously been awaiting the news, ran jubilantly through the streets shouting, "Hurrah for Polk," only pausing now and then to inquire of each other, "Who is James Polk?" Today, by contrast, when a presidential candidate is nominated, everyone will recognize the individual and few will find cause for celebration merely because their *party* has chosen a nominee. Americans today are much more likely to take interest in the *individuals* who are running for office. The party label is important, but no longer decisive.

This change is one aspect of a general development that political analysts have recently begun to study: the decline of political parties. This decline is evident in a number of different areas. A century ago, the press routinely branded the few voters who considered themselves independents as "oddballs"; today, more than 30 percent of the voters call themselves "independents" without feeling the least sense of inferiority. A century ago, the party organizations, working through a system of conventions, chose the party's nominees for all elective offices. Today, party organizations have lost much of their influence in determining which candidates run under their own label. Most candidates are now nominated in primary elections in which the individual candidates present themselves directly to the voters. (In presidential nominating contests, party conventions still make the final choice, but most of the delegates are chosen in primaries.) A century ago, the major media source in the nation was the newspaper; and most newspapers, being associated with one or another of the parties, presented highly partisan accounts of events. Voters, moreover, received much of their information from local party workers who walked a "beat" for their political parties. Today, the candidates for federal offices contact the voters largely through the newspapers and television, which provide news on a nonpartisan basis and which feature paid advertisements that focus more on the candidates' individual qualities than on their party identification. The list of the contrasts between the role of parties today and that of a century, or even a generation ago, could go on and on (Burnham, 1970; Crotty and Jacobson, 1980).

The perception of the decline of parties by the end of the 1970s had reached the point where many—perhaps too quickly—began to fear a possible collapse of our traditional party system. Political scientists referred frequently to the "end" of our parties, and one journalist wrote a widely read book entitled *The Party's Over* (Broder, 1971). Politicians, sensing the same development, began to act on their perceptions. In 1980, a congressman from Illinois, John Anderson, ran for president, not as a third-party candidate, but as an independent. His view, shared by many others at the time, was that America might be on the verge of entering a nonpartisan era in which candidates could "nominate" themselves, and, by means of the attention gained through the mass media, present their candidacies to the public at the general election without the need of party support.

Nothing, of course, approaching any such collapse of parties materialized in 1980. Indeed, in the early part of the 1980s there were signs not only of a rejuvenation of the parties but also of an increase in support for their position in the political system. The organizations of the major parties grew stronger at the national level and in many states, enhancing the parties' capacity to help in the campaigns of their nominees; and a growing number of political leaders, worried about the influence of parties, began to search for changes that would strengthen the parties' role in deciding presidential nominees. The current situation, accordingly, cannot be summed up by a single slogan. On the one hand, it is clear that American parties have declined in strength relative to the position they held a generation ago. Our politics are more fragmented, and electoral competition often focuses on the individual candidates, not the parties. On the other hand, it is highly doubtful that our parties will collapse, and it is even possible that we could see a reversal of some recent trends.

Does it matter if parties decline? Some think it a positive development, arguing that simpler and more democratic methods have replaced unresponsive and oligarchic party organizations (Bode and Casey, 1981). Others, however, see in the decline a great loss for our system that has made effective

---

BOX 5-1

AN ELECTORAL SYSTEM WITHOUT PARTIES

In launching an independent candidacy for the presidency in 1980, John Anderson, previously a lifelong Republican, declared in one of his speeches:

> They say it is mission impossible. They go back to 1912 and they go back to 1924. They say Teddy Roosevelt and Fighting Bob LaFollette couldn't do it and neither can you. They say the two-party system has a lock on this country. I say no. I say that 1980 is not 1912 or 1924.

An indication of the difficulty of Anderson's bid as an independent could be gauged from the reaction of one member of his audience: "I just can't get used to the idea of voting for an independent. It sounds almost un-American to me."

Anderson received 7 percent of the vote but failed to carry any states and received no electoral votes.

Source: Washington Post, 1980.

---

governance all the more difficult to achieve (Ladd, 1982). One point, however, seems clear: Important choices must be made in this decade about the future of parties, and these choices must require a constitution maker to decide what role parties should play and what changes, if any, should be instituted to promote that role. To help with this task, we shall begin by attempting to define what a party is and then analyze the roles that constitution makers have assigned to parties throughout our history. We shall then turn to the more empirical questions of how parties have been influenced and regulated by law, how they have been organized, what issues they have struggled over, and, finally, what impact they have had on the relations of Congress and the presidency. This is a long list of topics, but parties—as will quickly become evident—are complex institutions that affect our political system at almost every point.

WHAT ARE POLITICAL PARTIES?

Parties have changed greatly from one generation to the next, and therefore any definition tailored to fit them all would have to adopt the lowest common denominator. Perhaps the most that can be said of all parties in the United States is that they are organizations that compete for political power under a specific label. But this definition, while technically correct, tells us very little about the life and spirit of a party. A much better way to proceed is to analyze a party in the process of formation and then look at the parties as we find them today as established institutions. We can then combine elements of the two conceptions to arrive at a more satisfactory definition.

Imagine, then, that you wished to establish a new political party. Most likely, this would occur under circumstances in which you were convinced that important policies being followed by elected officials were wrong and that no existing party adequately reflected your views. Finding others in sympathy with your position, including perhaps a few elected officials, you would join together and form an association. The association would adopt a name, agree on rules by which to conduct its internal business, and proceed to nominate candidates for various offices and support them in their election campaigns. The final objective would be to win power and enact the party's program.

Notice certain points that emerge from considering a party in the process of formation. In the first place, a party is not an "official" public institution. It is, on the contrary, a semiprivate association of citizens and leaders who come together on their own to win political power. Parties accordingly stand between the people and the official institutions of government, serving, so to speak, as intermediary bodies that link citizens and their opinions to the government. Second, parties are highly "democratic" in the sense that they give many citizens an influence on the government that goes beyond merely voting for or writing to elected officials. The party cuts across electoral districts and potentially organizes a nationwide, self-governing association. Finally, parties form to accomplish a given purpose. True, they are organizations that compete for power under a specific label, but they compete for power in order to accomplish a larger political goal.

Taking all these characteristics into account, we can define a party tentatively as an association of citizens with a shared political purpose that recruits and supports candidates for office under a common label with the expectation that these persons, if elected, will work to promote the association's goals. This definition accurately describes many new parties. But it would not quite fit our two major political parties—the Democrats and the Republicans. These parties are much more than temporary private associations, and they have been sustained over their long history by motivations other than the agreed-upon political goals. The Democratic party, which was organized in the 1820s and can perhaps trace its origins to the 1790s, today is the world's oldest political party; the Republican party, formed in the 1850s, has existed for nearly 130 years. As long-standing bodies, these (once) private associations have become virtually accepted elements of the political system. Congress is organized along party lines, party channels are part of the folkways in Washington, party mechanisms are the accepted means of nominating candidates for federal offices, and the laws of the states and the federal government implicitly recognize and regulate the conduct of these two parties.

Because of their longevity, widespread acceptance, and legal status, our two major parties can be considered semiofficial institutions of our political system. It is not surprising that parties, as the accepted gatekeepers for acquiring political power, have over the years attracted candidates and supporters for reasons other than promoting a larger political purpose. People have joined parties to win power or obtain government jobs, so that at certain times, when these motives have predominated, parties have lost all but the slightest connection with achieving political principles.

We have, then, two conceptions of a political party, one deriving from the party in the process of

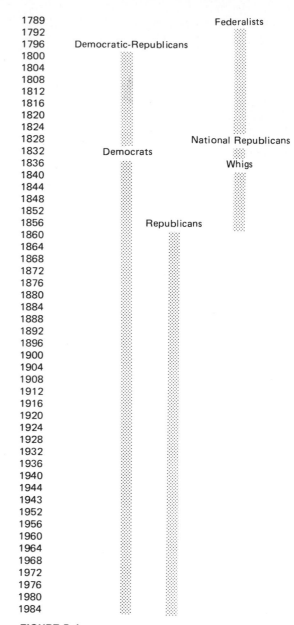

FIGURE 5-1
Major parties. (*Source: Congressional Quarterly's Guide to U.S. Elections,* 1975:176.)

formation as an association of like-minded citizens and the other deriving from the specific characteristics of our two major parties, which have become semiofficial institutions. Both conceptions, however, are needed to understand parties, for our major parties still bear the imprint of and partake partly of the character of purposive associations. Our major parties began as associations of (relatively) like-minded individuals; and, while from time to time they have lost a sense of purpose or have been paralyzed by internal disagreement, they have nonetheless been periodically renewed as bodies of common purpose, as succeeding generations of citizens have reestablished new agreements on general goals and programs.

The party, as an association and institution in the sense just defined, includes many different elements. At the core of the party are the officials of the party organization (national party chairs, state party chairs, and local precinct leaders) and its elected officials (presidents, members of Congress, governors, and mayors). Next one can speak of the party workers, whether paid or volunteer, who perform the work of the party, ranging from sophisticated polling to calling and reminding people to vote on election day. Further removed are the party members, official or unofficial, who attend meetings and lend occasional support. Finally, at the periphery, there are the voters who identify with the party and vote regularly in its primaries, or at least support most of its nominees in the general election. In this chapter we shall be concerned chiefly with the organization and structure of the parties, saving the treatment of the behavior of voters for Chapter 7.

In discussing parties, the political analyst is interested not only in their internal organization but in how they affect the political system as a whole. In striving to fulfill their own goals, the parties also perform certain important political functions. At the electoral level, parties participate in recruiting candidates for office, mobilize support for those candidates, and influence the policy choices presented to the voters in elections. At the governing level, parties build coalitions out of diverse interests in the nation and influence how relations among leaders are coordinated under a system of separation of powers and federalism. By observing how parties affect the performance of these functions

and how these functions are altered by changes in the character of the parties, a constitution maker can begin to make some of the judgments necessary for deciding the proper role and structure of the party system.

THE DEVELOPMENT OF POLITICAL PARTIES

What accounts for the role and strength of an institution in any given historical period? Besides the Constitution and legal powers, one of the most important factors is the prevailing doctrine or theory of what a given institution's role should be. Doctrines about the role of our institutions are the products of experience and of ideas. In the case of the "formal" institutions—the presidency, the Congress, and the Supreme Court—the ideas have been strongly influenced by the thought of the founders, the language of the Constitution, and precedents of Constitutional law. Ideas from other sources, of course, have also been important, but the fact that these institutions all have a source of power written or implied in the Constitution has greatly limited the character of doctrinal debate.

Political parties present a very different case. They are never mentioned in the Constitution and therefore lack a permanent foundation in fundamental law. Their initial justification came well after the founding period, mostly in the Jacksonian era. Lacking the weight of authority of Constitutional sanction or endorsement in the founders' thought, doctrines about political parties have been more malleable and have undergone more profound changes than those of the other institutions. Originally, parties were considered dangerous and nearly illegitimate. By the mid-nineteenth century, parties were, if not highly respected, at least universally accepted and recognized as vital to the effective operation of our government. In this century, the parties have been scorned and attacked in their existing form, though often idealized in some possible forms which they *might* assume (Ranney, 1975). In large measure our parties have been what we have wanted them to be, and their current status of relative weakness reflects a low estimate of— or perhaps a confusion about—the role they should play. An understanding of the different historical conceptions of the role of parties, accordingly, is essential for considering their position today.

The Founders and the
Case for a Nonpartisan System

The founders opposed national political parties, preferring instead a nonpartisan system in which candidates would compete for office on the basis of their individual qualifications and political beliefs. The founders wanted no formal associational links between candidates for the presidency, the House, and the Senate; no permanent national political organization of citizens for nominating candidates; and no labels dividing the population into opposing camps.

Nominating candidates is one of the most important functions performed by political parties; and the founders—at least in the case of the presidency—established a formal Constitutional alternative to party nominations. The original plan for the electoral college was to select the president in a nonpartisan fashion by elevating individuals of outstanding national reputation. No initial choice by parties was envisioned to limit the field of candidates. The nonpartisan character of the founders' intentions becomes even more strikingly evident when one considers that the vice president was selected not as a candidate on a ticket with the president but as the runner-up in the total of electoral votes. This arrangement, perhaps defensible in a system without parties, is unworkable in a system with parties. In 1980, for example, it would have produced Ronald Reagan as president with Jimmy Carter as vice president! In part, a result no less strange occurred in 1796 when John Adams, a Federalist, was elected president and Thomas Jefferson, the opposition leader, became vice president. By 1804, the Twelfth Amendment was adopted, which implicitly acknowledged the existence of political parties and provided for separate balloting by the electors for president and vice president.*

Why did the founders oppose party competition? Their hostility to parties was based in the first place on their fear that parties were usually subversive organizations committed to overthrowing the existing form of government, as had been the experience with parties in England a century earlier. And even if parties should stop short of such revolutionary challenges, the founders thought that they would stir up unnecessary and dangerous divisions, "agitating the community," as George Washington argues, "with ill-founded jealousies and false alarms" (Boorstin, 1966:213–227). The proper way to express conflict was through elections of individual officers and not through party organizations. In fact, something of the same mistrust of parties exists today, as indicated by the appeals of leaders, often in moments of crisis, to put "petty" partisan concerns aside and consider the true national interest.

Second, the founders worried that permanent national parties would conflict with the intended roles of the presidency and the Congress. A president elected as the head of a party might have to defer to partisan demands rather than exercise personal judgment and might lose the intangible claim of being "president of all the people." It is an indication of the importance of these concerns that many candidates, after being elected president, downplay their party role. As President Taft once explained, "It seems to me impossible to be a strict party man and serve the whole country impartially" (Kallenbach, 1966:286). In the case of the Congress, the founders feared that parties would prevent genuine deliberation. Representatives would meet in party caucus, decide together on a party position, and then vote automatically as a bloc in formal congressional missions. Congress would cease to be a forum in which serious debate

---

*The original system for the electoral college was extremely complex. Each elector had *two* votes for president. The candidate receiving the most votes, providing that the number was greater than the majority of all the electors, would be president; the runner-up would be vice president. In the event that no candidate received more than a majority, the House would select the president from among the top five electoral vote recipients. (In the event of a tie for first place among candidates receiving more than a majority, as occurred in 1800, the House would also make the decision by choosing among those tied.)

When the House voted, each state delegation—not each member—would have one vote, and a majority of the votes of all the states was required for election.

The Twelfth Amendment (1804), which still governs the Constitutional rules, provides for separate elections for president and vice president, with each elector having *one* vote for each office. In the event that no candidate for president receives more than a majority of the number of electors, as occurred in 1824, the House decides among the top *three* recipients of electoral votes by the same state voting system described above.

BOX 5-2

A FOUNDER'S VIEW OF POLITICAL PARTIES

Let me warn you in the most solemn manner against the baneful effects of the spirit of party generally. This spirit . . . exists under different shapes in all governments, more or less stifled, controlled, or repressed; but in those of the popular form it is seen in its greatest rankness and is truly their worst enemy.   —George Washington, 1796

A mistrust of parties has long been part of the American tradition. As one political scientist, William J.

Keefe, has remarked, "American political culture contains a strong suspicion of the political process and the agencies that try to dominate it, the political parties" (Keefe, 1980:10).

A study conducted by Jack Dennis in 1966 found 63 percent of the American people agreeing with the statement "The political parties more often than not create conflicts where none really exist" (Dennis, 1966:605).

---

took place and would instead merely register predetermined party positions. Again, it is an indication of the enduring relevance of the founders' concerns that whenever parties in the Congress have sought to bind the votes of their members, many representatives have resisted and worked to "save" Congress from the "tyranny" of parties.

Finally, some of the founders feared that powerful parties would introduce too popular an influence on the political system, undermining its representative character. Parties, as we have indicated, are instruments for bringing representative institutions closer to the people by linking elements of the public with the elected officials. The founders saw dangers in this link, especially if it resulted in elections that would bind both the president and Congress to a party program backed by a national majority. Elections, as founders understood them, should not closely tie down the decisions of the government, but should instead indicate in a general way whether the public approved or disapproved of past governing decisions.

Even though the founders opposed political parties, they never considered introducing a Constitutional ban against them. Under a system that guaranteed political liberty, government could not prevent people from combining into peaceful associations to influence the selection of public officials. What the founders hoped was that national parties could be avoided because the government could function without them and because most people would believe that parties were dangerous associations.

Plainly, the founders' expectation that the United States would be a nonpartisan regime proved incorrect. Yet we should not conclude that the emergence of parties totally transformed the political system. Parties have clearly modified the original Constitutional design, but they have just as clearly been shaped by it. They never, as we shall see, assumed the rigid form that founders feared; and, paradoxically, many scholars believe that the way in which they eventually developed served to promote many of the founders' most important goals (Banfield, 1961).

The Formation of Parties and the Case for Party Competition

The transformation from the founders' nonpartisan system to a system of party competition occurred in two phases: during the Jeffersonian era, when parties formed temporarily but were not widely regarded as permanent institutions; and during the Jacksonian era, when parties were reestablished and eventually accepted as legitimate and normal components of the political system. In the first phase, political leaders made use of political parties but never really embraced the concept of permanent party competition. As we saw in Chapter 3, after the crucial election of 1800, in which Jefferson's party won control of the presidency and both houses of Congress, the Federalist party went into a rapid decline. By 1816, the Federalists had dwindled to a tiny regional party and ceased to offer candidates for the presidency. Thereafter, in the

Martin Van Buren argued that political parties could limit the length of presidential campaigns, reduce extremism and regional factionalisms, improve coordination between the president and Congress, and keep the House from deciding elections.   *(Library of Congress)*

period known as the "era of good feelings" (1817–1824), the political system had effectively returned to a nonpartisan—though Jeffersonian—footing, and most of the leading politicians of the period were as firm in their denunciation of the evils of party competition as the founders had been in the early 1790s.

The task of reestablishing parties and transforming public opinion toward them began in the 1820s and was led by Martin Van Buren, a senator from New York who later would become president (Hofstadter, 1969). Van Buren tried to view parties in a way different from the founders—"in a sincerer and wiser spirit [that] recognizes their necessity and gives them the credit they deserve" (Van Buren, 1867:3–4). As a focal point for his analysis of parties, Van Buren took the presidential election of 1824, a nonpartisan contest between four major candidates, none of whom could win an electoral majority. The outcome was eventually decided in the House of Representatives, with John Quincy Adams defeating Andrew Jackson and William Crawford.

According to Van Buren, the experience of 1824 pointed to three significant problems with the existing nonpartisan system. First, without party nominations to mark the beginning of the race, the activity of governing was distracted and agitated by an open campaign begun some two years in advance of the election. Second, with nothing to restrain or moderate the positions of the candidates, the campaign itself featured dangerous appeals stimulating sectional animosities and popular appetites for charismatic leaders. Finally, with so many contenders allowed to enter the race, the possibility that any candidate would capture a national majority was small, and the incentives for the candidates were therefore to establish a firm base of support in a particular region or with a particular constituency. As suggested by the controversial selection of John Quincy Adams in the House of Representatives in 1824, which Jackson claimed had robbed him of the presidency, no one was satisfied with a system that allowed the House to decide the presidential contest.

Beyond the specific events of 1824, Van Buren thought that during the era of nonpartisan politics the necessary level of coordination between the presidency and the Congress had broken down. Without parties, there was no common program or coordination between the two institutions and no mechanism for helping to push through a legislative agenda. The policymaking process, therefore, tended to lose focus, and the government lacked the necessary energy to follow a coherent line.

The Theory of Party Competition   All these problems led Van Buren to the conclusion that if parties were not reestablished, the stability of the political system itself would be threatened. Along with a group of pro-party politicians, Van Buren set forth the basic case for party competition that remains today the core of a defense of reasonably strong political parties.

It consisted of four points:

First, party competition would prevent the election from being decided by the House because the nominees of a majority party would have the broad support of a large segment of the people, enabling them to win a majority in the electoral college. (In fact, with minor parties, it is possible for the election to go to the House, but since 1824 this has never happened.)

Second, party competition would limit the appeals of candidates to the safer issues backed by the broad parties and their general principles. Narrow demagogic appeals or sectional pleas would be avoided. The parties in effect would be placed "above" the individual candidacies, forcing presidential aspirants to adopt a general set of party principles rather than appeal to momentary issues of the candidate's own devising. (The parties have, in fact, tended to avoid such appeals, with the notable exceptions of the period before the civil war, when the parties disintegrated, and after the war, when memories of the conflict were constantly invoked.)

Third, under party competition, voters would more easily be able to understand what elections were all about, for the parties, more than the individuals, would have a long history and set of principles that most voters would come to know and understand. Nonpartisan competition, by contrast, would give an advantage to narrow interest groups able to push a particular candidate in the short term without the great body of people knowing what that candidate's sympathies were.

Fourth, party competition would provide a greater degree of coordination between the president and Congress than that provided in a nonpartisan system. Van Buren's intention was not that parties would override the Constitutional separation of powers, but that they would help smooth the relationship between the executive and the legislative branches, at least when both were controlled by the same party.

Of course, these benefits of party competition were dependent upon the existence of a certain kind of party. If the parties formed on the basis of radically different ideas about the first principles of government—for example, one favoring commu-

nism and the other monarchy—the solution would not work. Van Buren's entire plan for party competition rested on the precondition that parties would *not* disagree on first principles, but rather would be limited in their conflict to secondary issues about how to achieve certain commonly accepted goals. This fundamental agreement was itself to be the basis for a new attitude on the part of party leaders about party conflict. While believing in the principles of their own party, party leaders would no longer attempt to eliminate the opposition; they would instead respect its right to exist and learn to accept and tolerate the doctrine of permanent competition between political parties faithful to the principles of the Constitution.

Van Buren's entire theory of party competition was based on the view that parties would not simply reflect political divisions but also to a certain extent manage and moderate them, screening out those of the most dangerous kind. Yet this posed a problem: What would happen if the two major parties ignored or closed out a substantial body of opinion? Van Buren addressed this problem when considering the question of third or minor parties. Originally Van Buren assumed that the norm of American politics would be competition between *two* parties. And, in fact, many of the benefits he outlined would be threatened if competition among three or four parties became the usual practice. Nevertheless, as Van Buren realized later—in 1848, when he headed a third-party ticket for the Free-Soil party—there are also dangers if the norm of two-party competition ever became so rigid as to exclude minor parties. The result would be that groups advocating new ideas might be denied access to the political process. Van Buren therefore accepted the need for the party system to be open to change, either by replacing one of the major parties (as it can be argued the Republicans did to the Whigs after 1852) or by forcing a majority party to change its position for fear of being replaced (as the Populist party did to the Democratic party in 1896). Under this solution, the electoral process is dominated by two parties but is still open to challenge by minor parties. Uncontrolled political change through electoral politics is not encouraged—since starting a new party is difficult—but neither is it completely foreclosed.

The Establishment of Permanent Party Competition Articulating this body of theory about the need for party competition was one thing; getting it accepted in the 1820s, when most leaders regarded parties as undesirable, was something very different. Van Buren had to persuade politicians that submitting to party regularity and tolerating a permanent opposition were legitimate codes of political conduct, and he had to convince the American people that joining and identifying with parties were not violations of the principle of good citizenship.

Van Buren managed to accomplish this feat by using a most unexpected method. He persuaded Andrew Jackson, who previously had opposed party competition, to associate himself with the new Democratic party in return for its support in the election of 1828. Jackson was such a controversial figure at the time that his presence by itself helped to draw a partisan division with a new opposition party, which would soon adopt the name "Whigs." This partisan division was solidified in the great struggle over the chartering of the National Bank in 1832, and by 1840 both sides had accepted the idea of permanent party competition (Hofstadter, 1969).

The Consequences of Party Competition The advent of party competition altered the character of American politics. Parties assumed control of the conduct of political campaigns. They recruited and nominated candidates, created strong partisan feelings in the electorate, and exercised control over the dissemination of news by the creation of party-run newspapers. Party competition also stimulated political interest within the electorate and contributed to the extension of the suffrage, as the parties vied to mobilize new segments of the public. Finally, the governing process was altered. Parties provided a new, extra-Constitutional institution that helped to bridge the separation of powers and to tie national politics to the politics of the states.

While these changes were significant, they were by no means revolutionary. They took their place within the basic Constitutional structure, modifying it, but not overturning it. In fact, as different as the "form" of partisan competition was from the founders' goal of nonpartisanship, the effects of partisan competition frequently paralleled objectives sought by the founders. Van Buren, like the founders, sought stable competition in an electoral process that regulated the ambitions of politicians and promoted moderate majorities; and while Van Buren clearly favored a democratic system of choosing the president, democracy was not the only objective he valued. Like the founders, he thought that the electoral system should operate to prevent dangerous divisions and promote candidates having the support of broad coalitions. While the electoral process, in Van Buren's view, was responsible for expressing divisions, electoral choice should be structured to express them in a responsible way. One of Van Buren's main arguments, in fact, was that the nonpartisan electoral system that had emerged in the 1820s did not promote the founders' own goal of political stability.

Because of the many similarities between the goals of the founders and those of Martin Van Buren, many later analysts of American politics have tended to see the party system as virtually a part of the basic Constitutional design (Burns, 1963). There were, of course, differences, but the main feature of the model of parties that Van Buren established—governing with the aid of broad and moderate majorities—effectively promoted the Madisonian goal of safe majority coalitions. Yet parties on occasions, as in the cases of 1800, 1856–1860, and 1932–1936, have also been the vehicles for the coalition of national majorities that have reinterpreted the American constitutional order in principled terms that their opponents have viewed as dangerous and extreme. Parties, in other words, have performed the dual function—at different moments—of maintaining continuity and promoting change. As agents of change that emerge in part from the mass public, parties have added a distinctly new element to the original political system.

The Attack on Parties: The Nineteenth-Century Reformers

All in all, Van Buren had accomplished a remarkable feat of supplementary constitution making. But the results were not without defects that critics seized on, sometimes forgetting what Van Buren had accomplished and attacking the entire system of partisan competition. The substance of these attacks, which received greater support after the Civil War, consisted of two interrelated criticisms. The first was that the major parties no longer stood for any important principles; the second was that they existed only for the corrupt purpose of securing public service jobs for their members. These two criticisms were summarized by a German political analyst, Werner Sombart, as he looked back over party development during the nineteenth century.

> When in 1824, Van Buren organized the opposition to the just-elected John Quincy Adams, he was in a dilemma as to the reason for a fight. As is well known, he chose Jackson as a leader and understood perfectly how to raise enthusiasm for the new man out of nothing. . . . The raison d'etre of the political party (as a body of persons with a purpose) had disappeared. . . . However, they did not disband, thanks to their own staying power and out of consideration for the other purpose that a political organization can serve in a democratic commonwealth—the hunting for office (Sombart, 1976:47).

Sombart probably exaggerated the total absence of the party principles during the nineteenth century, even allowing (as he did) for the exception of the highly principled struggles on the slavery issue before the Civil War. But there can be no disputing the significance that he attached to the "hunting for office" of nineteenth-century parties. Patronage was—and in some places still is—crucial to the operation of the parties. *Party patronage,* simply defined, is a system in which the victorious party distributes jobs in the public service to faithful party workers, with personal qualifications frequently playing a secondary role and with continuity in administrative service taking a backseat to responsiveness to the party majority.

The acceptance of patronage as a principle of government employment was closely connected with the rise of parties. Before the 1820s, government employment at the national level had been, except at the top political levels, mostly a career occupation. Andrew Jackson began to change this practice after 1828, when he proclaimed the principle of rotation in government service and began to fire and hire employees at his own discretion. For Jackson, the objective of party patronage was secondary to the goals of opening up government em-

ployment to newcomers, making the public service more democratic, and ensuring its responsiveness to those in power. But this change soon opened the doors to mass party patronage. When an administration of a new party came to power, it dismissed the existing employees and hired new workers faithful to the party. All this was done under a motto coined by Senator Marcy in 1832: "To the victor belong the spoils." Hence another name for the mass use of patronage—the "spoils system."

The system of patronage became so widespread after the Civil War that a group of intellectuals, journalists, and working politicians—known as "reformers"—began to argue that our parties had lost their rightful character. Instead of being organizations devoted to principle which incidentally awarded jobs to their adherents, parties at all levels had become organizations of office seekers that incidentally proclaimed a concern with principles. The spoils system, according to reformers, undermined the efficiency of the public service by driving away anyone who wanted a serious career, and it degraded the entire system of politics by giving effective control of the nomination of candidates to political organizations that were unconcerned with matters of policy and principle. As a cure, reformers proposed that government jobs be placed beyond the reach of political hiring or firing and made subject to merit standards. Then, according to one reformer, "the nation might see the correction of corruption in politics and the restoration of political parties to their true function, which is the maintenance and enforcement of national policies" (Curtis, 1887:813). Known as "civil service reform," this proposal made great headway for federal employees after President Garfield was assassinated by an unsuccessful government office seeker in 1881. The Pendleton Act of 1883 began a long process of federal civil service reforms that gradually reduced party influence by establishing a bipartisan Civil Service Commission that based federal employment on competitive examinations. Later, in 1939, Congress passed the Hatch Act, which forbade most forms of partisan activity by federal employees, thus further separating government employment from partisan politics. At the state and local levels, the success of reformers during the nineteenth century was much more limited. Some states and localities preferred not to adopt civil service reforms, while others passed weak laws and did little to enforce them. Thus, while parties lost most of their source of national patronage, they retained for a time much patronage at the state and local levels. In some areas of the country, the parties still exercise great patronage power, although for the most part their control has been severely limited by state and local laws passed in this century and by recent federal court decisions.

The Progressive Attack on Parties

The attack on parties assumed more far-reaching proportions during the "progressive era" (1908–1916). The progressives rejected the reformers' view that parties could be saved merely by changing the rules for employment in the public service. The abuses and deficiencies of the parties, the progressives believed, were too deep-seated to be cured by such mild reform. The parties were corrupt, wedded to old and outmoded ideas, concerned primarily with politics in the states and localities, and unable to offer new ideas to solve the problems of a rapidly industrializing national economy. There was no way to proceed other than by attacking and destroying the existing party organizations.

In addition to this objective, the progressives had the positive goal of instituting a more popular or democratic method of selecting candidates. The existing system of nominations by the party organizations, they argued, took from the people their right to a free choice of public officials. The progressives had in mind a new idea of a rational and public-spirited electorate that would select candidates without the interference of party bosses and without any old-fashioned attachment to party labels. Exactly how this would work in practice, however, was a matter of dispute between two strains of progressive thought.

One group favored the gradual elimination of parties and the establishment of a democratic, nonpartisan system. Adherents of this group led the movement for a legal ban on party activity from local elections. For higher offices they favored primaries open to all voters. This group extended its attack upon parties to an attack on representative institutions, advocating in the name of democracy the referendum, the recall, and direct popular election of judges. This "populist" understanding of

nonpartisanship was obviously very different from the nonpartisan system of representative government that the founders had advocated.

A second strain in progressive thought took a different view of the role of parties, though the difference has turned out to be much greater in theory than in practice. Like the other progressives, this group advocated primaries as a way of destroying traditional parties. But instead of establishing a nonpartisan system, this group favored rebuilding new and more powerful parties. These parties would be democratic, focus on national issues in federal elections, and hold together as cohesive units at the governing level. Some progressives went so far as to claim that the founders' doctrine of separation of powers was outmoded. Instead, the nation needed strong national parties that would allow the majority party to govern without the impediments of checks and balances. The check on power should come from democratic elections, not free separate institutions contending with each other. Advocates of this doctrine of "pure" party government, modeled after the British parliamentary system, never succeeded in winning much popular support for their views or in articulating a practical method for changing the American political system.

Both strains of progressivism agreed on the need for a more democratic electoral process. The nineteenth-century system had favored nominations made by party leaders, after which the voters would choose from among the party nominees at the general election. The standard of legitimacy for electoral politics had been that of *interparty* democracy. The progressives considered this insufficient and, where they still tolerated parties, called for the additional criterion of *intraparty* democracy—democracy within the parties—enforced through state-run primaries.

The progressives believed that the country needed the stimulus of new programs and new ideas and that this stimulus could be best attained by allowing individual leaders to compete for nominations in primary elections. Instead of putting the party "above" the presidential aspirant as a means of limiting the appeals of candidates to safe principles, as Van Buren had wanted, the progressives favored placing the individual candidate "above" the party and having the party take shape around

---

BOX 5-3

A PROGRESSIVE'S VIEWS ON PARTY NOMINATIONS

"Put aside the caucus and convention. They have been and will continue to be prostituted to the service of corrupt organization. . . . Substitute for both the caucus and the convention a primary election . . . where the citizen may cast his vote directly to nominate the candidate of the party with which he affiliates. . . . The nomination of the party will not be the result of compromise or impulse, or evil design . . . but the candidates of the majority, honestly and fairly nominated." —Senator Robert La Follette

Source: La Follette, 1913:197–198.

---

the principles of the nominees. Woodrow Wilson best encapsulated this formula: "No leaders, no principles; no principles, no parties" (Wilson, 1925:I, 37). The progressives went a long way toward establishing the idea of presidents as popular leaders who commanded their parties and the nation through their ability to shape public opinion.

Progressive thought on political parties left a confused legacy. By all accounts the progressives succeeded in giving traditional parties a bad name, though they never managed to destroy them. The progressives criticized parties—and not without justification—for being closed, selfish, boss-ridden, and obsolete in their principles. They went on to deplore what many considered to be the virtues of traditional partisanship—the spirit of compromise within party counsels, the warm enthusiasm of voters for party traditions, and the willingness of elected officials to accept some party discipline from traditional organizations. But having attacked parties for all their supposed faults, the progressives were divided on what should take their place. Where they favored strong parties—as many did—they failed to establish any method for securing them, leaving the nation instead with a set of norms and laws that in fact have weakened the parties.

Modern Reformers (1968–1980)

The progressives had a great impact, as we shall see in more detail later, on the legal status of parties. As Table 5-1 shows, they succeeded in transforming the method of nominations for senators and House members, though they did not com-

pletely undermine the influence of the party organizations on these nominations. In the case of the nomination of the president, the progressives had less success. They tried but failed in 1913 to pass legislation establishing national presidential primaries. They then turned their attention to the states and persuaded many of them to adopt primary elections either to select delegates to the national conventions or to register the voters' presidential preferences. Yet these changes, though significant, failed to pass the critical point at which a majority of the delegates were chosen in primaries. Most delegates continued to be selected in party-run caucuses in which the organizational regulars tended to dominate. Thus, as late as 1968, aspirants for the presidency did not necessarily have to enter primaries or build large personal organizations years in advance of their party's convention, although participation in some primaries was the usual practice.

The modern reformers arose in reaction to this one remaining vestige of "traditional" organizational control. The immediate impetus for the movement came in 1968, when Hubert Humphrey was nominated at the riot-torn Democratic convention in Chicago. Humphrey had not entered any primaries, and the prospect of his being nominated in 1968 was likened by many in Chicago to the very kind of corruption and back-room management that the progressives had deplored. Large public protests followed, fueled by the strong feeling of those who had favored the candidates opposing the war in Vietnam, one of whom had been Senator Robert Kennedy who had recently been assassinated at a victory party following the California presidential primary. The disappointed followers of

TABLE 5-1
DEVELOPMENT OF METHODS OF NOMINATION AND ELECTION FOR FEDERAL OFFICES

Office	Original practice	Nineteenth-century practice	Twentieth-century practice
House			
Nomination	Nonpartisan; no regular nominating agency	Party nominations, by local party conventions	Nominations by primaries in most states
Final election	By voters, in districts or by state general tickets	Requirement of single-member districts by federal law of 1842	Requirements of equal population of congressional districts in states, Supreme Court ruling, 1966
Senate			
Nomination	Nonpartisan; no regular nominating agency	Party nominations, mostly by state party conventions	Nomination by primaries in most states
Final election	By state legislatures	By state legislatures	Direct, popular election of senators, Seventeenth Amendment, 1913
President			
Nomination	Nonpartisan	Party nomination, by caucus of members of Congress, 1800–1816; party nomination by convention, beginning 1832	Selection of some convention delegates by primaries (1912–1964); selection of most convention delegates by primaries, 1976
Final election	By electors, acting at their own discretion, chosen in manner determined by states; some chosen by legislatures, others by the people	Separate election of president and vice president, Twelfth Amendment; by 1840s, electors bound to candidates and chosen by popular election within states, mostly by winner-take-all	No new developments

those candidates insisted on the need for wholesale changes in the presidential nominating process that would eliminate the influence of party organizations and increase the power of the rank and file voter. To accomplish the latter goal, reformers alternatively proposed national primaries, more state primaries, and "open" caucus procedures in those states still using party-run selection processes.

Like the progressives, these new reformers had a highly ambivalent view about parties (Ranney, 1975). Some of them opposed partisanship altogether, preferring a democratic form of nonpartisan politics that focused on competition between individual leaders. Others wanted to strengthen the parties and place them on a new footing, although their attacks on the prerogatives of party organi-

zations had the effect of eliminating much of the influence of party leaders and party organizations in the nominating process. Clearly, the most important structural change of the reform era has been the decline in the number of party-run selection procedures in favor of primaries. In 1980, thirty-five states held presidential primaries and selected over 70 percent of the delegates. In presidential nominations, parties have tended to become merely labels under which individual aspirants compete for public support, often from independents and members of the other party. Nevertheless, because the electorate voting in each party's primaries is different, the parties still retain very different characters. It is the power of the state party organizations that has diminished, and this

Vice President Hubert Humphrey's selection as the Democratic presidential candidate in 1968, with the support of Chicago's powerful "boss," Richard Daley, inspired immediate rioting and long-term reform. *(Hiroji Kubota/Magnum)*

decline has reduced the capacity of the parties to function as cohesive associations (Kirkpatrick, 1978; Polsby, 1982).

Postreform?

The modern reformers—or at least one strain of the movement—raised expectations about creating stronger parties while at the same time making institutional changes that have made it more difficult for parties to exercise genuine responsibility. Beginning in 1980, many party leaders began to recognize this paradox; and a new movement, still relatively small, has gotten under way to change the situation and restore some prerogatives to the party organizations. Many people within the parties are now calling for a renewed look at the role of the party organizations and for a greater say for party officials in the selection of the presidential candidates. Along with this has come an effort by some to change the prevailing antiparty doctrine in American culture.

The thesis of the postreform group, which is reminiscent of Van Buren's position, is that our political system does not work very well with weak parties. Without strong parties, there is no way of tying together all the individuals running for office, nor of effectively coordinating policymaking between the president and Congress (Ladd, 1982). Typical of the new postreform ideas are the views expressed in the report of the *President's Commission for a National Agenda for the Eighties:*

> In light of the trend of weaker political parties, the Panel views processes to strengthen the parties as important steps in encouraging the coalition-building approach to decision-making. Strong parties and party leadership can provide incentives for cooperation in policy-making (1980:26).

So far, the postreform movement has had a limited, but by no means negligible, impact on the party system. More attention, as we shall see, has been paid in recent years to upgrading the technical capacities of both national political parties. And in 1982 the national Democratic party adopted a change in its delegate selection rules that has added 561 new delegates to be drawn from among party leaders and elected officials (members of Congress, chairs of state parties, and mayors of large cities). These delegates are chosen outside of the primary process and are not officially bound to any candidate. Although this contingent makes up only 14 percent of all the delegates to the Democratic party's convention, it marks a first step in an effort to "reform the reforms" and return more power to party organizations and elected officials. Whether the postreform movement will have a more lasting and profound impact remains to be seen.

AMERICAN PARTIES AND THE LAW

The doctrines about parties that we have just discussed refer to general ideas about the role and function they should play. One of the ways in which these doctrines can be embodied in practice is through legislation by the states and by the federal government. Of course, not all the laws passed concerning parties reflect these general doctrines, because the motives of lawmakers are diverse and because laws, once passed, have effects that were never intended or foreseen by those who wrote them. Nevertheless, the general development of the body of law respecting parties follows roughly from the basic doctrines discussed above.

Given the fact that parties were never intended by the founders, it is not surprising that when they developed they were entirely private associations, unregulated by federal or state law. From a legal standpoint, they had no official status. They were simply groups of citizens coming together voluntarily to accomplish a certain purpose. As one political scientist remarked about their early legal status: "It was no more illegal to commit fraud in a party caucus than it would be to do so in the election of officers of a drinking club" (Key, 1964:375). Yet, although they were private associations in a legal sense, parties performed crucial public functions, such as nominating candidates, organizing and funding election campaigns, and even staffing most government jobs. After the Civil War, when reformers' objections grew about the way parties performed these functions, states began to take steps to regulate parties and control their operations. This process of legal "incorporation" and regulation gathered momentum at the turn of the

century and created a dynamic of its very own: each step in the legal regulation of parties led to new problems that many believed could be resolved only by further regulation.

Today the movement for greater legal regulation of parties seems to have slowed, probably because most major regulatory steps have already been enacted. In any event, our parties today are best described from a legal standpoint as semiofficial bodies, in part private associations and in part public institutions. They retain some control over their internal structure and procedures, but important aspects of their organization and jurisdiction, especially at the state and local levels, are fixed by laws and court decisions. Because most of the laws that govern or influence party procedures are made at the state level, parties vary greatly in their legal aspect from one state to another. As a result, the national arms of the parties, which rely for their own organization on the various state organizations, are very complex bodies.

The Parties as Private Associations (1790s–1860s)

In the early nineteenth century, most of the states limited their role in the electoral process to supplying the ballot boxes and counting the ballots. From the standpoint of the law, what happened before the election, insofar as nominating and campaigning were concerned, was entirely a private matter. The activity of nominating candidates was carried out in the nineteenth century primarily in party meetings called "conventions," for which delegates were selected in party-run procedures. The process usually began with open meetings for party members in local districts and precincts, where delegates to attend city or county conventions were chosen. The methods of selection at this initial stage varied from area to area in the degree of their procedural fairness, ranging from the corrupt to the perfectly democratic. In general, however, in areas where party organizations were strong, they dominated this stage of the process and the meetings tended to endorse decisions already made by party leaders in advance. The local meetings chose the delegates to attend city or county conventions, where local candidates were nominated and delegates chosen for the state conventions. The state conventions, in turn, nominated statewide candidates (governors and senators) and selected delegates to the national conventions. The state and national conventions were dominated by blocs of delegates managed by powerful party leaders who negotiated and bargained among each other (Bryce, 1889; Ostrogorski, 1964).

In the conduct of elections, the state stepped in to provide the voting places, where balloting was done openly before election officials, and to count the votes. In theory, it was up to the citizens to make up their own ballots, writing on a piece of paper their preferred candidates and thereby both nominating and electing in the same act. In practice, however, the parties had already nominated a slate of candidates in advance of the election and were able to carry the elections for their candidates by publicizing their nominees and by providing the voters with colorful "tickets" on which the names of the candidates were already printed. These tickets were distributed to the party faithful, usually just outside the voting area, and most voters simply deposited them in the ballot box. For all practical purposes, the parties printed the ballots.

The Regulation of State Parties
(1860s–1980s)

The pervasive role played by parties in American politics led increasingly to demands for some kind of legal control, both on their effects, as in the case of civil service reform, and on the handling of their own internal affairs. Soon after the Civil War, statutes in several states were written requiring the parties to ensure against fraud, intimidation, and coercion in their internal proceedings. While these laws did little in practice to interfere with legitimate party activities, they ended certain gross abuses and established the important principle that parties, because of their important political consequences, could be regulated by state law.

In this century, state laws regulating the internal procedures of party organizations have in some instances grown very complex. Although some states continue to leave the internal organizational framework entirely to the determination of the party, other states regulate in detail almost every

provision of the parties' operation. In Massachusetts, for example, the state law regulating parties fills a book of almost 500 pages. In some states these regulations have become so burdensome that the real organizations of local parties convene "unofficially" in order to escape the detailed rules imposed on them.

The legal situation of state parties in the south presented a special case. From the end of the Civil War up until the 1950s, the Democratic party was in most areas the only party capable of winning office. (The Republican party for southern whites was the despised party that had begun the Civil War and freed the slaves.) Many Democratic parties in the southern states relied on their "private" status to ban participation by black citizens, which effectively eliminated whatever influence the few black voters could exercise. The Democratic party, it was often said, was a "white man's club." State primaries in many southern states enabled the parties to continue this discrimination under the fiction that the parties were private associations (Key, 1950). The Supreme Court declared such primaries unconstitutional in 1944 (*Smith v. Allwright*), and since the 1960s both national parties have taken steps to ensure that parties in their internal dealings do not discriminate on racial grounds.

In contrast to the state parties, the national party organizations have never been directly regulated by any comparable legislation by the federal government. It is important to emphasize, however, that some of the functions that the national parties once performed, such as campaign financing for presidential contests, have now been preempted and regulated by federal law. Nevertheless, the freedom from direct legislation that national parties have enjoyed has been important, and the courts have resisted limiting the discretion of the national parties (Ranney, 1978). In recent years, the national parties have used this freedom to great effect in enacting party rules to change the process of selecting delegates. These rules have on occasion conflicted with the methods of delegate selection prescribed in certain state laws, but the Supreme Court upheld the parties' general right to set their own qualifications for seating delegates (*Cousins v. Wigoda,* 1975). Because the states want their delegations to be accredited to vote at the conventions, they have usually complied thus far with national party rules.

The Australian Ballot (1888–1900)

A second change in the legal status of parties resulted from the passage of the Australian ballot laws, a reform enacted in most states between 1888 and 1900. The Australian ballot, which took its name from the changes mandated by the Ballot Law of 1856 in Australia, had an immense impact. The laws provided for secret voting on ballots printed by the states. Secrecy was designed, among other things, to put an end to the practice of vote buying, which had become widespread in many areas in the latter half of the nineteenth century. The logic of this regulation was simple: if those buying votes could no longer observe citizens at the ballot box, they would be unable to guarantee their investment.

The elimination of this form of corruption, however, was by no means the only consequence of the Australian ballot. Now that the states printed the ballots, they had a new power to determine how candidates would qualify for access on the ballots. The exercise of this new power immediately became controversial, especially as it related to minor parties. In nearly all states, access was automatically given to the candidates of parties that had received a specified minimum of votes in the last elections. For new parties, however, another method of qualification was obviously necessary, and most states adopted laws requiring candidates of new parties to submit petitions by a certain date bearing the signatures of a certain number of citizens. These requirements, though clearly justifiable for practical administrative reasons, could also be used to block access for new parties. By the 1920s, the leaders of the major parties in some states had managed to use these qualifying devices to limit competition and to keep certain "undesirable" parties, like the Socialists, off the ballot. The laws required large numbers of signatures (in some cases 10 percent of the electorate) and very early filing deadlines (in some cases five months in advance of the election). The presidential campaigns of Robert La Follette for the Progressive party and George Wallace in 1968 for the American Independent party were both hampered by these obstacles (Mazmanian, 1974). Wallace challenged the constitutionality of some of these laws in federal court and succeeded in having the petition requirements lowered in a number of states. The legal battle was not over, however; and in 1980 John Anderson's campaign managed through court action to ease still further the restrictions on ballot access for new parties. Although legal obstacles for new parties still remain, especially for elections on the state and local levels, the intervention of the federal courts in this area has brought a much greater degree of equity.

The issue of ballot access for new parties bears directly on some of the theoretical questions raised earlier about the role of parties. Martin Van Buren, we may recall, stressed the advantages of the *norm* of two-party competition, but he also saw the need for keeping the electoral system open to minor-party challenges as a check on the major parties. Before the states printed the ballots, the major parties had no legal advantages over minor parties, although they clearly had many informal advantages. When the states assumed the function of printing the ballots, new questions arose: Could the public's interest in maintaining the norm of two-party competition extend to the point of allowing the states to create legal advantages for the existing major parties at the expense of minor-party challenges? And if so, how extensive could these advantages be? These questions, relevant not only to ballot access but to campaign financing as well, remain highly controversial today and will undoubtedly continue to be fought out in the courts and the legislature.

The states' assumption of the function of printing ballots created another set of controversies over the format of the ballot. Almost all states print the candidates' party affiliations on the ballot—Virginia being one exception—but the ways in which the states display the party labels differ. There are two basic ballot forms: the *party-column*, or "Indiana," ballot; and the *office-bloc*, or "Massachusetts," ballot. The party-column ballot lists the candidates down a series of columns or rows, each column containing candidates from the same party. This arrangement, favorable to parties and particularly to the largest party, enables the voter to go quickly down the column and vote for all the candidates of that party (a "straight-ticket" vote). In

Recent court decisions have made it easier for third-party presidential candidates like George Wallace to get on the ballot, but most state and local elections remain two-party contests.   *(Ed Caram, Black Star)*

addition, many party-column ballots allow the voter to mark a box or pull a lever at the top of the ballot to cast automatically a vote for all candidates of that party.

The office-bloc ballot lists the candidates office by office, requiring the voter to go through each office to identify the party's candidates. No single mark will cast a ballot for the slate of the entire party. Obviously this system is more favorable to "split-ticket" voting (voting for candidates from different parties). Not surprisingly, progressives favored the office-bloc over the party-column ballot in order to discourage "blind" partisan voting.

In the nineteenth century, split-ticket voting was rare. Partisan feelings were strong, and the parties, which printed most of the ballots, naturally listed only their own nominees. When the states began printing the ballots, split-ticket voting became much easier and the practice increased greatly. The growth in ticket splitting leveled off by the 1920s, only to begin to rise again after the 1950s. The recent increase in ticket splitting obviously cannot be explained by legal factors alone, because

the ballot changes had already been adopted over a half century earlier. The explanation for the recent trend accordingly must be sought in nonlegal factors, such as the decline in the percentage of partisan identifiers in the electorate, the greater willingness of voters to disregard party labels, and the increased focus on individual candidates rather than party affiliations.

Primaries and Party Membership

As legally private associations, parties in the nineteenth century performed the critical function of nominating candidates through their own internally established processes of selecting delegates and holding conventions. The adoption of primary laws, first urged by the progressives, took this function away from the private control of parties and gave it to the states. A primary is an election run by the state or under its auspices that determines the official nominees of the party. Primaries are now used in nearly all the states to nominate candidates for the House, the Senate, and most state and local offices. For the presidency, as noted, there is no national primary; but in some thirty-five states the delegates to the national conventions are chosen in state-run primaries and are normally bound by state laws for a specified number of ballots at the convention. (The national parties, however, will not enforce these state laws and currently permit the delegates to vote as they wish.)

Of all the legal regulations affecting political parties, the primary laws have without question been the most significant. The reason is easily stated: "He who can make the nominations is the owner of the party" (Schattschneider, 1942:64). Before the passage of primary laws, the party organizations and "regulars" in the party dominated the nominating process. The passage of primary laws did not immediately undercut the ability of all organizations to control the nominations, because some of them were powerful enough to control the outcome of the primary contests. In a few places, party organizations still retain this capacity. Over time, however, the primary laws, together with the weakening of the party organizations and the rise of mass media campaigns, have removed control of nominations from the party organizations.

Primaries have helped to create a situation in which no limited and specifiable group "owns" the party. The party label belongs to whichever candidate can win the primary election. The power situation is one in which various individuals build their own personal organizations, bargain with special interest groups, and devise programs and media strategies in an effort to capture the party label. The regular party organizations often have little or no influence in this process, and therefore fewer potential activists may find it worth their while to become party members. Instead, political activists today are often attracted to the personal campaign organizations of individual candidates or to organized groups promoting certain general policies, such as the National Right to Life Committee, the Moral Majority, and the National Organization for Women. The legal change from party-run nomination procedures to primaries has clearly encouraged these developments, although other factors to be noted have played a role.

Once states adopted primaries, a new legal question immediately arose: Which voters would be allowed to participate in them? Previously, the parties as private associations had the power to decide who could take part in the nominating process—a situation that still holds in some states not using primaries. In most states, however, and in all states using primaries, the state law determines who may participate. In some states, like Wisconsin, where the tradition of progressivism is strong, no barrier whatsoever is placed in the way of primary participation. Voters can take part in whichever party's primary they prefer, without regard to their party registration or affiliation. Such primaries, held in eight states for all offices except the presidency, are *open primaries*. (Open primaries today, however, have been banned from presidential nominating contests in the Democratic party by a national party rule.) Two states—Alaska and Washington—go a step further and give citizens a combined ballot, allowing them to vote for the candidates of either party for any particular office. This is a *blanket primary*. In thirty-nine states, the law requires voters to indicate or establish a party preference in order to vote in a given primary. These elections are considered *closed primaries*, although many of them are closed more in name than in fact; thus, in some states holding "closed" primaries—as in Virginia, where there is no official registration by party—there is no way of determining who is a "valid" member. In other states—such as Indiana and Illinois—there is party registration, but voters can declare their party preference at the primary election itself, making the restriction of party membership very weak. Only in those states which require a person to be registered in the party *before* the primary election is there a significant restriction on party membership. Formerly, states could be very strict on the length of time required to be eligible to participate in a primary. New York, for example, once required a two-year period. The federal courts, however, have placed a limit of ninety days on the length of the preregistration requirements. Thus, the concept of party membership, even in closed primaries, is not very restrictive as judged by historical standards.

Primaries have had an immense impact on American politics and have been one of the most important factors in undermining the strength of political parties. They are consistent with the antiparty strain in American political culture, and they seem to realize Americans' desire for a democratic electoral process. Yet, as we shall see in Chapter 6, they seem to have produced many questionable effects, including long and drawn-out campaigns, divisiveness within the parties, and a weakening of party discipline. Even their theoretical claim to being exercises in pure democracy can be questioned, given the low turnout rates in most primary elections. In any institutional change of this magnitude, however, it is difficult to be certain of the precise effects, given the large number of other factors involved in the electoral process. For this reason, the debate on the merits of primaries is likely to continue, although most Americans seem wedded to the primary system, at least for most offices.

Campaign Finance Legislation

The reform era of the 1970s led also to the enactment of a goal once championed by the progressives: stringent regulation of campaign financing for all federal election campaigns, including public financing for presidential elections and contribution limitations not only for individuals and groups but for parties as well.* The details of the complex legislation are discussed in Chapter 6. Here, it is necessary only to point out its general effect on the role of the parties. In the case of presidential campaigns, the public funds go directly to the candidates, encouraging the trend of "autonomous candidacies" (Ladd, 1982:70). For congressional offices, the national and state parties may continue to provide limited, but significant, funding for their candidates; and this assistance has recently been growing in importance. But one of the major effects of the legislation, largely unforeseen, has been the stimulation of new organizations, known as "political action committees" (PACs). These committees, which in some measure now are partly competitors of parties, have been formed to contribute money to campaigns and to spend on behalf of certain candidacies. As of 1982, there were 3,479 such

---

*Each level of the party (federal and state) can contribute $5,000 per election (primary and general) for congressional campaigns. There are, however, certain coordinated expenditures, like polling, that can be added, and the total sum that the parties can contribute is much larger than an initial reading of the law would suggest.

committees, growing from 1,146 in 1976. They consist of organizations from labor unions (389), business corporations (1,542), trade associations (655), cooperatives (49), and independent organizations (794) that promote ideological or special interest concerns. Among them are the well-funded National Conservative Political Action Committee (NCPAC), the National Organization for Women (NOWPAC), and some amusing ones: BeefPAC, EggPAC, and the beer distributors' group named "SixPAC" (Sabato, 1983). The committees, often formed on the basis of ideological positions or as support for single-interest groups, now wield important control over the financing of congressional campaigns and tend to pressure candidates to support their positions. They have thus complicated the moderating and consensus-forming functions once performed by political parties, and the best one can hope for is a *Federalist* 10–type solution in which so many competing interests flourish that none becomes too significant.

Legislation is one of the tools that can be used in an effort to enforce a given doctrine of the proper role for an institution. The laws regulating parties, though they have had many different objectives and have been derived from many different sources, have by and large reflected the dominant view of hostility toward parties that emerged early in this century. Thus, for the most part, the increase in regulation of parties cannot be equated with a strengthening of their role. On the contrary, it has more often served to limit their power by removing from their control important functions which they once performed. Whether certain laws should be altered to create a more favorable environment toward parties is a matter that will require much more attention.

PARTY ORGANIZATION

Doctrines about parties help form people's expectations of their proper role, while legal rules codify certain aspects of party behavior and create part of the environment in which they operate. In the final analysis, however, the character of our parties is shaped by their organizations—by how parties arrange their own affairs and by the activities of those who work on their behalf.

Any discussion of party organization must take

TABLE 5-2
PARTY ORGANIZATION IN AMERICA

Party levels	Party components	Major elected officials backed by party
National parties	National convention National committee National party chair National party headquarters and staff Congressional party campaign organizations	President Party leadership in Congress
State parties	State convention State committee State party chair State professional staff	Governor Party leadership in state legislatures
Local parties	Local conventions (county, city, ward) Local committees Local chairpersons Ward or district leaders Precinct captains Regular participants and workers	Mayors Members of Congress Local politicians

great care to distinguish between their "textbook" organization and the real power relations within the organization. In a textbook chart (which the parties themselves, incidentally, never publish or proclaim), American parties are organized on a hierarchic basis, with the power flowing down from the national level through the state party organizations to the local level and finally to the neighborhood precinct captains. In practice, however, the various levels of organization—national, state, and local—operate with a great deal of autonomy, and only rarely is the national organization in a position to command or direct the activities of state or local organizations. For the most part, the organizational strength of American parties is found at the state and local levels, and the national parties are in many respects confederations of state and local parties. As we look in this section at the form and power of these party organizations, however, it is important to keep in mind that the party organization as a whole now plays a different and somewhat more limited role than it did in the past. Functions have been stripped from the organizations, and certain new technological developments in communications (especially television) have made mass organizations less important in reaching voters and winning elections.

The National Parties

When parties first formed in the 1790s, the impetus derived from a division on *national* issues and party organizations tended to be built from the top to the bottom. This pattern was partially reversed when parties were reestablished in the period between 1824 and 1840. Although the struggle over the presidency and certain national issues served to galvanize the new parties, the national organizations in many states were created by linking up with existing party organizations that had operated during the era of nonpartisan politics. Although it would be an exaggeration to say that the parties were built from the bottom to the top, it would be accurate to say that much of the organizational strength of our parties originally existed—and has since remained—at the state and local levels.

For much of their history, the national parties existed as functioning bodies only during the presidential election campaign, from the national convention through the election and until the debts were paid. In between, the national organizations existed on paper only. Today, both national parties maintain permanent staffs, remain continuously in operation, and raise and distribute some funds for their candidates. But the basic relationship between the national organizations and their state and local affiliates has not fundamentally changed, with the important exception (discussed later) of the entrance of the national parties into the area of creating rules for the selection of delegates to the national conventions.

The formal structure of the national party has changed very little since the middle of the nineteenth century. Then, as now, each party had a national committee, a national party chair, and the national party convention, which is the supreme rule-making body for the party as a whole. Both parties added campaign committees for House elections after the Civil War and for Senate elections after the ratification of the direct-election amendment for senators in 1913. All the aforementioned party organs constitute the official parts of the party's formal organization. Yet in discussing the national party power structure, it is necessary also to include the party's major elected officials—the congressional party leaders and the president. While not official party officers, they often wield the most power.

National Committees The national committees of the Democratic and Republican parties are made up of members selected by the parties in each of the fifty states, the District of Columbia, Puerto Rico, and certain territories. The national committees have certain functions to perform related to calling conventions and carrying out business assigned to them by the national conventions. For the Democrats in recent years this has included overseeing and revising the work of party commissions that have had important rule-making powers for the selection of delegates.

Generally speaking, however, the committees are not very powerful bodies, and the evaluation of a newspaper writer in 1949 is only slightly exaggerated: "A national committee never nominated anybody, never elected anybody, [and] never established party policy" (Bone, 1965:202). Indeed, one of the most important formal powers of the national committee—choosing the party chair—is

often accorded in practice to the president or to the presidential nominee, with the national committee serving merely to ratify the choice. Only when the chair of the party out of power resigns or where there is division in the out party after a presidential defeat will the national committee actually make the choice.

The National Chair and National Staff The national chairmen and chairwomen have the job of running the national headquarters, helping to raise funds and to decide how they are spent, and occasionally "representing" the party when the opposition controls the presidency. In general, however, the national chair runs the organization more often than he or she deals with party policy. Indeed, for the out party, no one really speaks authoritatively for the party's policies. The "titular" leader—that is, the party's last nominee—will be influential only insofar as that person has a prospect of recapturing the nomination. The role of spokesperson is played by various party figures, including on occasion the chair, but more often congressional leaders and aspirants for the next presidential nomination. In the United States, in contrast to Great Britain and Canada, there is no designated opposition leader or shadow cabinet.

The national party staff, which is responsible to the party chair, performs such functions as data collection, training of candidates and party members in modern campaign techniques, and preparation of numerous publications related to party affairs. The national party chair is also sometimes designated as the official head of the nominee's presidential campaign, though this title is now usually a fiction. Formerly, the national chair sometimes performed this role, but with the development of extensive preconvention campaigns, the candidates have already put together their own personal organizations whose leaders enjoy their full confidence. This change leaves the national chair with the secondary role of being an important adviser in the campaign and of integrating the regular permanent organization with that of the candidate's own personal organization.

The national party chair, when working under an incumbent president, serves very much at the president's pleasure; increasingly presidents have tended to keep the chair on a short leash. When the national Republican chairman Robert Dole attempted to put some distance between the national party and the president during the Watergate crisis, he was summoned by the president to Camp David and dismissed. As Dole later quipped, "I had a nice chat with the president, while the other fellows went out to get the rope" (*Washington Post,* 1973).

The chair of the out party has much more room in which to operate, not having an immediate boss to accommodate in the person of the president of the United States. While Jimmy Carter was president (1977–1981), the national Republican party chairman, William Brock from Tennessee, exercised about as strong a leadership as his position allowed. In fact, Brock began what has amounted to a quiet transformation of the role of the national party, adopting modern techniques of fund raising and campaign training that have strengthened the national party despite other tendencies operating in the opposite direction. The national Republican party since the mid-1970s has been far more active than ever before in funneling money to candidates at the grass roots level, providing polling information, and helping candidates and local organizations to learn new campaign techniques. The Democratic party has openly acknowledged the Republicans' superiority and has been trying to catch up. It has made improvements, but the Republicans have moved ahead even more quickly, far outspending the Democrats. In 1981 to 1982, the three national organizations of the Republican party (the national committee and the House and Senate campaign committees) raised about seven times as much money as their Democratic counterparts, and they have raised this money by relying more than the Democrats on smaller donors (Sabato, 1983). Although the functions of both national committees are limited, the cumulative impact of their efforts can be very important. Elections are frequently won at the margins.

Congressional Campaign Committees Both parties have their own congressional campaign committees in each house of the Congress, which consist of members of Congress and have small, permanent staffs. These committees are independent of the national committees, though they sometimes work informally with them. Their role is to help their party in Congress, especially the incumbents. The committees raise and distribute funds, conduct research, help to devise campaign strategies, and provide other services such as writing speeches and preparing position papers.

National Conventions and Party Commissions
The supreme authority of each national party is vested ultimately in its national convention, which meets every fourth year to select the party's platform. Since 1974, the Democrats have also held "mini-conventions" in the midterm year between the regular conventions to discuss party policy. The national conventions are made up of delegates from the states and territories, selected in accordance with rules and formulas devised by the national parties and in accordance with the laws of the states and the rules of the state parties.

The conventions today are huge bodies, in 1984 comprising 3,923 votes for the Democratic party and 2,235 votes for the Republican party. These figures actually understate the number of delegates in attendance, since both parties have alternative delegates. With the number of observers and journalists in attendance, the national conventions are indeed huge and sometimes confusing (or confused) assemblies. The size of the conventions has increased dramatically since even the early 1950s, when the convention vote total for the Democratic party in 1952 was 1,230 and that of the Republican party 1,206. The increase in size of the conventions may be workable largely because the nominating decisions have in recent times been made before the convention met.

The conventions, in addition to nominating the candidates and approving the party platforms, make the final determination of the party's rules, some of which have great political significance. One of the most important party rules in American history was the Democratic party's requirement from 1832 until 1936 that presidential nominees be chosen by a two-thirds vote of the convention delegates. This rule gave the south a virtual veto over the party's nominee. After the rule was abolished, the center of gravity of the national party moved to the urban areas of the nation and the party's presidential nominees represented for a time its liberal constituency. The Republicans have always chosen their nominee by a simple majority.

The most significant development in the history of rule making by national parties occurred in the Democratic party after 1968. Between 1964 and 1984, the convention established a series of commissions that for the first time wrote detailed national rules regulating the selection of delegates to the national conventions. Previously, the national parties had generally been content to accept the methods of delegate selection provided for by the state law or by the rules of the state parties. Challenges to the seating of state delegations were commonplace, but the convention decisions usually dealt only with the question of which of the contending delegations claiming to represent a state should be seated. These decisions were usually made by the political forces contending for immediate advantage in the presidential nominating contest.

The Democratic party commissions established after the conventions of 1968, 1972, 1976, and 1980 were different in character and approach. The rules devised by these commissions took effect well in advance of the selection process and set down in detail how the delegates would be chosen. It was through the vehicle of the first three commissions that the modern reformers were able to "legislate" rules that undermined much of the power of traditional party organization in certain states. Included in these rules were provisions that required open and highly publicized caucus meetings, that banned the automatic selection of delegates by virtue of their position (for example, governors or state party chairs), and that mandated the selection of delegates in proportion to the preferences of the voters or caucus participants. The Republican party did not engage in a similar process of national rule making, in part because the party had already eliminated some of the abuses that Democratic reformers were struggling against in 1968. Nevertheless, many of the states that enacted new primary laws between 1968 and 1980 applied provisions mandated by Democratic national party rules to Republican presidential primaries. As a result, the primary process of the Republican party has in large measure been swept along by the reforms of the Democratic party.

The intention of the Democratic reformers, as observed, was to diminish or eliminate the power of party organization leaders at the national conventions and to give the rank and file a greater say in the choice of the party's nominee. The evolution of the party system since 1968 has gone even further in the direction of intraparty democracy than the reformers expected, for many state parties, faced with the prospect of tightly regulated caucus proceedings, lent their support to adopting primaries for the selection of national delegates. With over thirty-five states now having presidential primaries, presidential nominations are in effect made by popular vote before the convention ever meets. The convention merely ratifies the determined choice and does not, as it ordinarily did in the past, serve as a decision-making body having discretion over which candidate to select as the party's nominee. Only in the event that none of the candidates should emerge from the primaries with a majority of the delegates would a convention today actually deliberate and choose the nominee. Clearly, then, the party organizations have lost a great deal of power in the presidential nominating process.

The reform commissions present an interesting paradox in the history of American political parties. They represent one of the few instances in which the national party has dictated structure and procedures to state and local parties, and in this sense a claim can be made that they have significantly strengthened the national parties. This new authority was used between 1968 and 1980 to remove control from the state party organizations and turn the nomination decision into an electoral contest between the various presidential aspirants. After 1980, however, many party officials began to use this same rule-making authority to restore certain prerogatives to the party organizations. In 1982, as noted, the Democratic national party enacted a new rule to include as delegates certain categories of elected officials and party officers.

The President   Although not a part of the official hierarchy of the party, the president inevitably becomes the head of the party during tenure. Some presidents relish this role and have attempted to build up their party, both as a source of support for their own programs and as a legacy for the future. Franklin Delano Roosevelt played this role as much as any president in this century. Other presidents, however, have largely ignored party affairs and have sought to present themselves as chiefly nonpartisan figures. President Carter, for example,

---

BOX 5-4

THE PRESIDENT AND THE POLITICAL PARTY

One of the most powerful national party chairmen in history, James A. Farley, advised his chief, President Roosevelt, not to undertake his effort to "purge" thirteen anti-New Deal Democrats in the 1938 primaries. Roosevelt's effort was largely unsuccessful, and Farley later wrote about the incident:

> I knew from the beginning that the purge could lead to nothing but misfortune, because in pursuing his

course of vengeance Roosevelt violated a cardinal political creed which demanded that he keep out of local matters. Sound doctrine is sound politics. When Roosevelt began neglecting the rules of the game, I lost faith in him. I trace all the woes of the Democratic party, directly or indirectly, to this interference in purely local affairs. In any political entity voters naturally and rightfully resent the unwarranted invasion of outsiders (Farley, 1948:146–147).

---

did little to build the Democratic party, and President Eisenhower largely preferred to take a stance above partisan conflicts. President Reagan, by contrast, showed much more interest in party building. It has been the case that, to the extent that a president has needed support from his party in Congress—which is the usual situation—he has felt virtually compelled to campaign for his congressional delegation in midterm elections. Presidents may avoid building the party apparatus, but they cannot fully escape being associates with the electoral fate of their parties' elected officials. A president's power has been typically gauged in part by the perception of the strength of his party; and as others in the party have depended in part on the president for their electoral fate, so he has depended on them for his own capacity to govern. It is in ways like this that the American party takes on a reality not evident from observing the legal forms of our government.

An issue of great significance is the extent to which national party organs can directly control local party decisions on nominations. It is by means of such control that many European parties are able to solidify national party discipline. In the United States, the national chairs and staff have seldom attempted to exercise such powers openly. At least two presidents have made such an attempt—Woodrow Wilson in 1918 and Franklin Roosevelt in 1938. Both intervened in the primary campaigns of certain members of Congress in an effort to defeat candidates who did not support the

"national" party program as determined by the president (see Box 5-4). These efforts have never met with much success, largely because the voters and the state parties do not accept the propriety of a national party figure dictating local decisions. In this sense, federalism has become a "norm"; and it is generally accepted that the national party organization and the president should help out only "after" the local nomination decision has been made, not before. Because of primary laws and other developments, no party organization—national or local—is in a position to control most nomination races. Ultimately, then, parties that are hierarchic in their command structure do not exist in the United States, because they are in tension with the constitutional principle that the states and localities should determine the character of their own representation.

The Role of the National Party Organizations
When all is said and done, the most noteworthy observation to make about the national parties is that they are not all-powerful bodies that run and direct the activities of the state and local party organizations. In the first place, the national party itself is fragmented into different power centers. Second, the supreme rule-making body—the convention—meets only once every four years, and its chief purposes are to select (or ratify) a presidential nominee and write the platform, not to manage the affairs of the party. While the national party, along with the state parties and state governments, de-

termines the basic mechanism for choosing presidential nominees, the process is dominated both before and after the convention by the candidates' personal organizations. Finally, while the national parties can be very helpful in assisting local parties and candidates by providing funds, expertise, and information, they do not have the power to compel local parties or voters to support certain views or candidates. To the extent that coordination exists, it comes, as we shall see, from methods other than organizational command.

State and Local Party Organizations

The strength of party organizations exists generally at the state and local levels. By a "party organization" we mean a group of persons, whether consisting of employees or volunteers, who can be called on to perform activities on a regular basis on behalf of the *party*—that is, on behalf of all or most of its candidates and the organization itself. Among the activities performed by party organizations are recruiting candidates, identifying potential voters, distributing campaign materials, raising money, organizing local party activities, and engaging in a wide range of detailed work needed to keep an organization operating.

The strength and character of American political parties vary greatly from state to state. In some states, the state chair and party staff run highly efficient organizations with computerized mailing lists, telephone banks, and training resources for the candidates. In other states, the organization is run virtually out of the trunk of the party chair's automobile. In recent years, many state parties have made efforts to upgrade their procedures by attempting to adopt the new techniques of campaign management (Huckshorn, 1976). At the local level, where the final and crucial activities of talking to voters and getting them to the polls take place, the strength of the parties varies even more. In some localities, the parties have hundreds of people who can be relied on to do at least some work; in other locations, party organizations hardly function or exist only on paper.

What is it that induces people to join political parties as organizations? In the actual world, motives are seldom unmixed, and organizations never fit perfectly into any one model. Nevertheless, to get a rough handle on how party organizations operate, we can distinguish three major types of party organizations: the machine, the "social" organization, and the ideological or policy-oriented organization (Wilson, 1973). Here, we are excluding officially paid party staffs and focusing on the motivations of citizens who participate.

The Machine A political machine is a form of organization which sustains itself by offering tangible benefits, usually jobs, to its members and which is frequently controlled at the local level by a single leader, or "boss," who may or may not be an elected official. Machines were the predominant organizational form in many large urban areas from the middle of the nineteenth century until the middle of this century. Machines have declined in most cities and can be found today in anything resembling their classic form only in relatively few places such as Chicago. Many organizations still rely heavily on jobs to reward some party workers; but much patronage has dried up, and what re-

Tammany Hall, New York's Democratic political machine in the late 1800s, became notoriously corrupt and powerful under the leadership of "Boss" Tweed. *(Thomas Nast/Bettmann Archive)*

THE "BRAINS"

THAT ACHIEVED THE TAMMANY VICTORY AT THE ROCHESTER DEMOCRATIC CONVENTION.

mains is frequently used today not by parties but by individual mayors and local officeholders for the purpose of strengthening their personal organizations.

The "classic" machine operated by giving government jobs to the party's faithful; in return, the party faithful were expected to work for the party's ticket and to donate money—often deducted from pay envelopes as a "tax"—to pay for the organization's activities. Jobs came from the federal government, from the state government, and from the local government, and it was for this reason that the machine sought to win at all levels. After the Civil War, in the 1870s, for example, about one in eight voters in New York City held government jobs of some sort, of which a significant number came from federal employment in customhouses and the postal system. Federal employees were appointed to help the party keep power. In Indiana, a state well known in the nineteenth century for its rough-and-tumble politics, it was said that the postmaster general was "appointed not to see that the mails were carried, but that Indiana was carried" (Keller, 1977:256).

The machines, of course, could not offer a job to everyone and therefore had to devise ways of appealing to a majority of the voters. To accomplish this, they relied in particular on the work of their local precinct captains, who either were on the government payroll in jobs that took no time or else were paid directly from the party's coffers. The precinct captains "hung around" their neighborhoods, befriending voters and offering them small favors. Precinct captains often served their local constituents as welfare agents, helping people to get settled and coming to their aid in time of need (see Box 5-5).

Machines are remembered today as a part of American folklore; they are feared but admired, somewhat like the outlaws of the wild west. Some analysts celebrate the role that machines played in stimulating voters' participation, in serving as welfare agencies in an era before the welfare state, and in providing an avenue for poorer ethnic politicians to work their way up in American politics. Though based largely on self-interest, machines (according to their defenders) promoted the public interest. As George Washington Plunkitt wrote: "The politi-

---

BOX 5-5

THE VIEWS OF A MACHINE POLITICIAN

A famous little book, *Plunkitt of Tammany Hall,* written by the ward boss and later United States senator from New York George Washington Plunkitt, captures the flavor of party work by a precinct captain in New York City at the turn of the century:

> If a family is burned out I don't ask whether they are Republicans or Democrats, and I don't refer them to the Charity Organization Society, which would investigate their case in a month or two and decide they were worthy of help about the time they are dead from starvation. I just get quarters for them, buy them clothes, if their clothes were burned up, and fix them up till they get runnin' again. It's philanthropy, but it's politics, too—mighty good politics. Who can tell how many votes one of these fires bring me? The poor are the most grateful people in the world, and, let me tell you, they have more friends in their neighborhoods than the rich have in theirs. . . .

> There's only one way to hold a district: you must study human nature and act accordin'. You can't study human nature in a book. . . . If you have been to college, so much the worse for you (Riordan, 1963:28, 25).

Today, machines are much less in evidence; still, in many states and localities party patronage remains a very important source of maintaining party organizational strength. In suburban Nassau County, for example, the *New York Times* reported that the Republican organization was the "most effective political machine east of Chicago," employing some 17,000 public employees who (allegedly) pay 1 percent of their annual salary (*New York Times,* 1974).

cian looks after his own interests, the organization's interest, and the city's interest all at the same time" (Riordan, 1963:29). Finally, for national politics, the machines brought an element of non-ideological pragmatism to bear on the choice of presidential nominees, as the bosses were interested in candidates likely to be elected. Reformers, of course, have always stressed the negative aspects of the machines, such as the corruption and the trading of jobs and favors for votes. These were said to degrade the political process. Reformers have never denied that machines are democratic in the sense that they stimulate popular participation in politics. (Voter turnout in areas where machines exist has typically been much higher than one would expect, controlling for all other factors.) But reformers argue that the *quality* of participation must also be considered, and by this standard machines are undesirable. Voting and other forms of political participation, according to the reformers, should follow not from self-interested motives but from an expression of peoples' views on public policy.

Machines, as observed, have declined in strength and importance in American politics. The reasons are not difficult to identify. Civil service reform has taken away much of the available political patronage, and recently the courts too have intervened to deny political authorities the discretion of dismissing many government workers for "political" reasons (*Elrod v. Burns,* 1975). The immigrant groups on which machines depended for so much of their support in the northern and midwestern cities have declined as a percentage of these cities' population. The welfare state, which provides citizens with services by legal entitlement, has ended any role for the party as a welfare agency. Finally, the political culture is now dominated by reform ideas, which are inhospitable to machines. Even where they still exist, machines attempt to hide their true character and present themselves in a reformist light.

"Social" Organizations   Some people will join and work for party organizations because they enjoy the opportunity to be with and to work with other people. Although these party members normally have a general commitment to their party's purposes, questions of public policy are less impor-

tant to them then the social and human contact afforded by the opportunity to be part of an organization. Studies of party organizations in many areas indicate that this social motivation is currently one of the most important sources of party activism and has helped at least partly to fill the ranks depleted by the loss of patronage. Social organizations, like machines, are apt to be flexible and pragmatic in their choice of candidates because members are not highly ideological. On the other hand, the social organization may be less effective in its political work because its volunteers may shy away from certain tasks like door-to-door canvassing that do not allow for sustained social interaction (Wilson, 1973).

Ideological and Policy-Oriented Organizations
People will join party organizations because they want to further a cause or a set of policies in which they believe. Most third parties, which have never controlled very much patronage, have relied on members devoted to their cause. The antislavery parties before the Civil War, the agrarian and prohibition parties in the late nineteenth century, and the Socialist and Libertarian parties in this century have all relied on a core of "true believers" to run and maintain the organizations. The major parties also have always had members who have been motivated chiefly by policy concerns, and this proportion has increased in periods when the parties have adopted clear positions on the issues, as one or both parties have done in 1860, 1896, 1936, and 1980.

In recent years, some party organizations have drawn increasingly from policy-oriented activists as patronage resources have dried up. These activists—sometimes called "amateurs" by political analysts—look to political activity not for material rewards or as a social outlet, but rather, in the progressive vein, as an opportunity for promoting policy ends. Generally speaking, amateurs have tended to be much less willing to compromise on "electable" candidates than party members drawn in by other motives have. They tend to be not only ideologues, whether liberal or conservative, but ideologues who adopt a particular style in politics. Purity of commitment rather than flexibility is considered the supreme political virtue. Yet as some of these people become involved in party activities and assume positions of responsibility, they moderate their "purity" somewhat and adopt more flexible positions.

It is important to bear in mind that the three organizational types discussed above are abstract models. No organization consists entirely of persons animated by the same motives, and few individuals are moved by only one consideration. Real-life organizations are always mixtures of some kind. Thus, while machine politicians may have been primarily concerned with jobs and winning elections, they were by no means completely unmindful of policy positions. Likewise, modern policy activists, though always speaking in terms of policy commitments, frequently have their eye on government jobs or preferments of some kind.

Personal Followings, Ideological Groups, and Single-Interest Groups

Today, much of the organizational activity in political campaigns is carried on not by the regular party organizations but, as we have repeatedly stressed, by personal organizations attached to the candidates and by political associations and interest groups that agree to support a particular candidate. With nominations now made in primaries that the party organizations do not control, each candidate must build his or her own organization in an effort to capture the party label. After succeeding, the candidate will then usually maintain this organization for the general election campaign, accepting as much help from the regular organization as it can provide. This individualistic style of politics has also been facilitated by the modern mass media. Candidates in large constituencies can now be seen directly on television by millions of voters and do not require large organizations to contact the voters. Candidates can rely initially on a small group of pollsters and media consultants, hoping that as their appeal grows they will be able to obtain more and more organizational support.

From the presidential level down to the congressional and local races, it is the personal campaign organizations that dominate the political scene today—as far, that is, as organization itself counts in political campaigns. This situation is different from anything we have seen in the past. There exist a large number of potentially active organizational participants in America, often of a rather strong policy or ideological cast of mind; and as educational levels rise and leisure time increases, the number of self-motivated and politically active individuals grows larger and larger. People of this description today often join policy-oriented groups like Common Cause or the American Conservative Union, agreeing to work on a selective basis for particular candidates rather than for the party ticket as a whole.

The system of primaries and individual organizations seems in one respect to be the very embodiment of democratic fairness. Yet critics point to difficulties that it creates for candidates and elected officials. First, the candidates of the same party have no common responsibility to any core organization. As fellow party members they may share many of the same views, but no supplementary bonds deriving from reliance on an organization hold them together. Second, in the absence of party organizations, the candidates are left in an exposed position before the voters. They must devise their own electoral strategies, which in a competitive situation can encourage empty image appeals or demagogic issue campaigns. Third, and somewhat paradoxically, without parties standing as a buffer between individual candidates and the electorate, the candidates may be more indebted to the groups with which they must frequently deal in order to obtain money, receive organizational support, and win votes.

Perhaps the most alarming aspect of this system of organization relates to its impact not on the candidates but on the citizenry. Party organizations traditionally taught local leaders the values of compromise and conciliation necessary for establishing enduring party coalitions. By contrast, the individual campaign organizations and the separate policy interest groups encourage participants to assert only what is in the interest of their candidate or their own particular cause. Ultimately, the kind of majorities envisioned by Madison and Van Buren depend in part on the ability of people to practice the arts of coalition building, and it is precisely this value that would be threatened by a further decline of the power of party organizations relative to personal organizations (McWilliams, 1981).

PARTY COMPETITION AND PARTY COALITIONS

Even without centralized and hierarchic national party organizations, American parties have managed to acquire a semblance of unity in their ideas and programs. The reason is that, in the final analysis, the parties become identified with a general public philosophy articulated at the national level in presidential elections (by the party platform and by the presidential candidates) and in the process of governing (by congressional leaders and especially by the president). These public philosophies, such as welfare state liberalism for Democrats since 1932 or the "new" conservatism for Republicans since 1980, create national party "images" which permeate the nation and penetrate into the states and localities, where the voters and local organizations tend to adopt them. As one leading student of American parties has written:

> The fact that our parties have been organized mainly in state and local units should not lead us to forget that the electoral alignments producing their support, initially and to a large extent subsequently too, have been national and specifically presidential. The state and local party organizations may themselves have become more interested in winning state and local offices, but the party labels under which they would win such offices derive much of their electoral value from their national association (Epstein, 1980:17).

It is essential to note, however, that this process of national penetration represents a *tendency* and not an iron law. To begin with, the national principles are often articulated in broad enough terms to allow most party members to believe that there is a rough consistency between their position and that of the president. In certain instances, however, clear and essential differences exist that cannot be papered over. Accidents of geography or strategy can lead to the inclusion within the party of candidates or groups that do not fit with the national party image. These differences are made possible by the decentralized character of American party structure, which enables states and local parties and voters to nominate the kinds of candidates whom they prefer for Congress and for all state and local offices. The results can play havoc with

European notions of party discipline. From the 1930s through the present era, the national Democratic party has been characterized by its support of welfare state liberalism; but in some districts, especially in the south, the Democratic party has for many years sent members to Congress who are conservative and who vote regularly with the majority of the Republicans.

It should be observed that these geographical centers of support for alternative views do not always serve to protect "old" ideas that have no chance of gaining a national majority. On the contrary, geographical centers often become bases of support that generate new conceptions of the party's national position. Thus, over the last generation it was Republicans in the far west who generated much of the initial support for the new conservatism of Ronald Reagan, which in the end won control of the party from a more traditional form of conservatism that prevailed in the midwest and east. At times, in fact, the geographical and ideological struggles of a party's factions may be so intense and evenly balanced that the party cannot be said to stand for any one point of view; the party is in a state of confusion or turmoil in which the content of its public philosophy is the chief point at issue.

Critical Realignments

The two major parties in the United States, in their quest for political power, must seek the support of a majority of the electorate. This process usually leads them to cast a broad net that appeals to a variety of different constituencies. By the standards of political parties of most other democratic nations, our parties tend to be much more nonideological, although as other nations have developed two-party systems, their parties have become somewhat more "American" in style. Nevertheless, American political parties do have different centers of gravity, and at certain moments, far from offering no choice, they embody very different public philosophies about how the nation should be governed. However much parties may be seeking to hold power, they have always been influenced, at least in some degree, by persons who have sought power for certain ends and who at times have been willing to risk defeat for the sake of promoting certain principles.

New public philosophies emerge, not in every electoral campaign, but only infrequently. In fact, there seems almost to be an informal law at work that governs the surge and decline of powerful public philosophies influencing public policy. Only in a few elections is the nation presented a new or fundamental choice; in many elections the differences between the parties are relatively minor. Ironically, one of the reasons for this similarity between the parties is the decisiveness of the outcome of elections in which a fundamental choice has been offered. As it has happened, a party's victory in a decisive election establishes the fact that a majority in the nation favors its public philosophy. The defeated party then faces the choice of adhering to a public philosophy that has been rejected (and facing continual defeat) or else moving in the direction of the majority party (and thus having some prospect for success). Not surprisingly, it often chooses the latter alternative, thus minimizing ideological conflict.

Political scientists consider these decisive elections *critical realignments* (Burnham, 1970; Sundquist, 1973). A critical realignment, more precisely, is an election or a sequence of two or three elections in which a large number of habitual voters change their party preference in response to new issues and partisan choices, or in which new voters enter the electorate in significant numbers and identify with one of the parties to a much greater extent than the rest of the electorate does (Andersen, 1979). Usually this process of change results in a net shift in the underlying strength between the two parties. (By "party preference" here political scientists are referring not to a formal legal designation, but to a voter's feeling of identity for a particular party.) Critical realignments are periods in which major changes in public opinion take place and in which the people adopt a new governing public philosophy that has been articulated by one of the major parties. It is at these moments that the parties take on the aforementioned images they have in the minds of most voters. These images may last for up to a generation, until a new set of issues arises and another realignment occurs.

Realigning periods usually leave one of the parties in a dominant position, although after a period of time, changes in the population and marginal shifts in voters' sentiments can erode its advantage. Of course, the fact that one of the parties has more adherents than another does not mean that it will win every election. Elections that are won by the smaller party are sometimes called "deviating elections," whereas those that are won by the larger party are called "maintaining elections." Deviations occur because party adherents do not always vote for the party with which they identify. While maintaining their basic partisan identification, certain voters will nevertheless cast their ballot for candidates of the other party because of temporary or short-term factors. They may, for example, disapprove of the recent performance of their party or find a particular candidate from the other party to be especially qualified; or, in some cases, they may find the position of the opposition party on a pressing short-term issue to be especially attractive. Moreover, deviations occur because the electorate has a certain percentage of independents who in particular elections vote decisively for one party, thus tilting the balance in its favor. Accordingly, to say that a party is the dominant or majority party in a particular historical era means, not that it will always win, but only that it enjoys an advantage if "all other things are equal," which of course they never are in politics. Each election has its own features, and critical realignments merely set the broad contours within which the particular struggle of each campaign is waged.

Over the course of American history, we have had five clear realignments associated with the "critical" periods of change discussed in Chapter 3: 1796–1800, 1828–1832, 1856–1860, 1896, and 1932–1936. In the first period (1796–1800), the Jefferson Democratic-Republicans displaced the Federalists as the majority party and established the dominant public philosophy of limited government in the name of agrarian virtues. The election sequence of 1828–1832 saw the Democratic party, usually considered the heir of the Jeffersonians, again hold out against using federal power for developing the nation, arguing that federal programs, like the creation of the National Bank, established monopoly privileges and advantages for the wealthy classes. The opposition party, at first

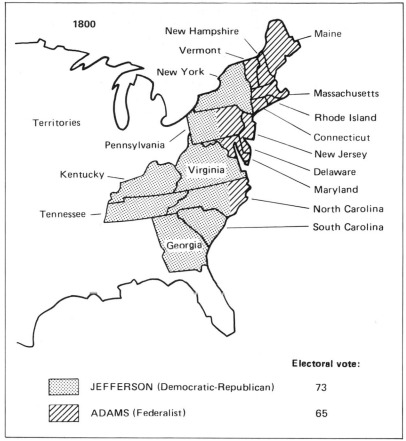

1800

New Hampshire
Vermont
New York
Maine
Massachusetts
Rhode Island
Connecticut
New Jersey
Delaware
Maryland
North Carolina
South Carolina

Territories
Pennsylvania
Kentucky
Virginia
Tennessee
Georgia

Electoral vote:

JEFFERSON (Democratic-Republican) 73

ADAMS (Federalist) 65

FIGURE 5-2
The election of 1800. From 1800 to 1826, the Republican Democrats won every presidential election and controlled both houses of Congress in every session. So complete was their dominance that after 1816, during the so-called "era of good feelings," the Federalist party ceased to offer opposition in the presidential contest and collapsed as a national party. (*Source: Congressional Quarterly's Guide to U.S. Elections*, 1975:222.)

named the National-Republicans and later the Whigs, countered with the contention that a broad-based program of federally sponsored aid would promote economic development. The party disintegrated after 1852, however, in the great struggle over slavery. The Republican party arose as a new party in the mid-1850s to stop the spread of slavery into the territories and to reclaim the principles of the Declaration of Independence. In the election of 1860, the Republican Abraham Lincoln received

only 38 percent of the popular vote but nonetheless won a clear majority of the electoral vote. After the Civil War, the Republican party, relying on its support for the cause of the union and on the Democrats' betrayal of that cause, dominated the national political arena for the next two decades. The realigning election of 1896 solidified, rather than reversed, the Republicans' advantage. The election focused on both economic and cultural issues. The Republicans under William McKinley favored

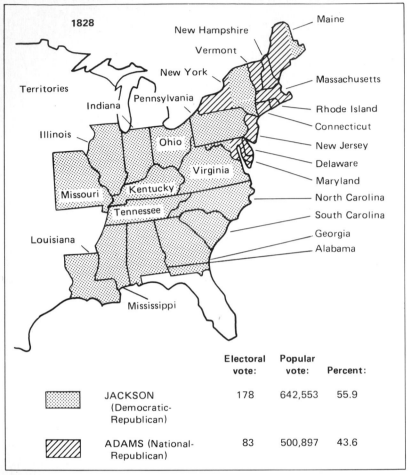

		Electoral vote:	Popular vote:	Percent:
	JACKSON (Democratic-Republican)	178	642,553	55.9
	ADAMS (National-Republican)	83	500,897	43.6

FIGURE 5-3
The election of 1828. During the 32-year period from 1828 to 1860, the division of popular support between the parties was very close, but the Democrats had a slight edge. The Democrats won six of eight presidential contests and controlled the House for all but six years and the Senate for all but four years. (*Source: Congressional Quarterly's Guide to U.S. Elections*, 1975:226.)

sound money and steady industrial development. The Democrats, under William Jennings Bryan, adopted a populist line of agrarian discontent, favored free silver (cheaper money), and called for extensive government regulation of industrial development. The Republicans remained firmly in control of the government until the depression, with the exception of two terms during which Woodrow Wilson was president (1913–1921).

The last decisive realignment took place in 1932–1936, as Franklin Roosevelt led the Democratic party to two sweeping victories and articulated the new Democratic public philosophy of welfare state liberalism. The Democrats favored more federal government intervention in the economy, reversing their old hostility to a strong central government. The Republicans now became wary of federal solutions to social and economic problems

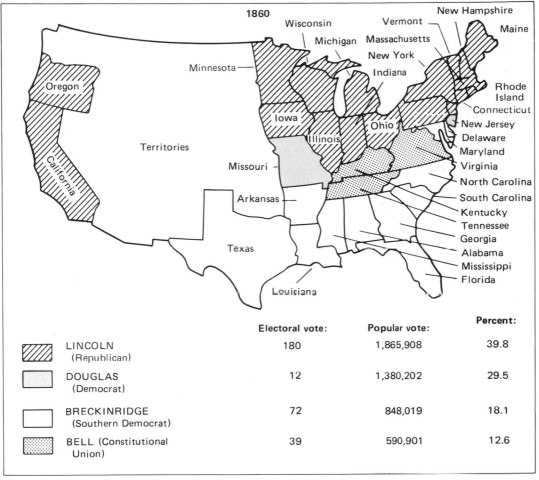

1860

	Electoral vote:	Popular vote:	Percent:
LINCOLN (Republican)	180	1,865,908	39.8
DOUGLAS (Democrat)	12	1,380,202	29.5
BRECKINRIDGE (Southern Democrat)	72	848,019	18.1
BELL (Constitutional Union)	39	590,901	12.6

FIGURE 5-4
The election of 1860. During the 36-year period from 1860 to 1896, the Republicans won seven of the nine presidential contests and controlled the Senate for all but four years. Republicans had a majority in the House for 20 years, but the Democrats were regularly in command after 1880. (*Source: Congressional Quarterly's Guide to U.S. Elections,* 1975:232.)

and feared the growth of a large federal bureaucracy. In the elections of 1932 and 1936, Roosevelt helped forge the New Deal coalition of union members, workers, and minority groups that moved the electoral center of gravity of the party from the south to the urban areas—though the south voted intermittently for the party in some presidential elections and continued to send a majority of Democrats to the Congress.

The New Deal coalition dominated American politics from 1932 until the late 1960s. Throughout this period, the Democratic party held a substantial margin over the Republican party in terms of the percentage of self-identified adherents, and the perception was that the party could normally count on the backing of its supporters. The Democrats were stronger among workers, minorities, and southerners (at least in presidential elections). Re-

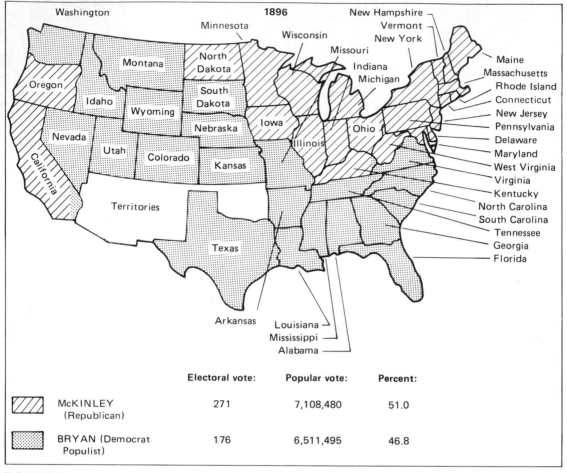

FIGURE 5-5
The election of 1896. During the 36-year period from 1896 until 1932, the Republicans won six
of eight presidential contests and controlled the House for all but 10 years and the Senate for all
but six years. (*Source: Congressional Quarterly's Guide to U.S. Elections,* 1975:242.)

publicans were stronger among professionals and
business groups and, to a lesser extent, farmers
(further details will be presented in Chapter 7).
Both parties had a broad spectrum of opinion
within their ranks, but of the two, the Democratic
party was substantially more diverse (and disunited). The center of gravity of the Democratic
party was liberal and that of the Republican party
conservative, but Democrats had a substantially
larger share of voters outside of the party's own
mainstream. As a result, in Congress the effective

majority on many issues was often a coalition of
Republicans and conservative Democrats.

A Modern Realignment?

By the beginning of the 1970s, the Democrats
began to lose their grip on the electorate. This did
not immediately take the form of a Republican resurgence, and indeed for a time Democrats even
seemed to gain relative to Republicans. But clearly
the belief of Democrats in the public philosophy of

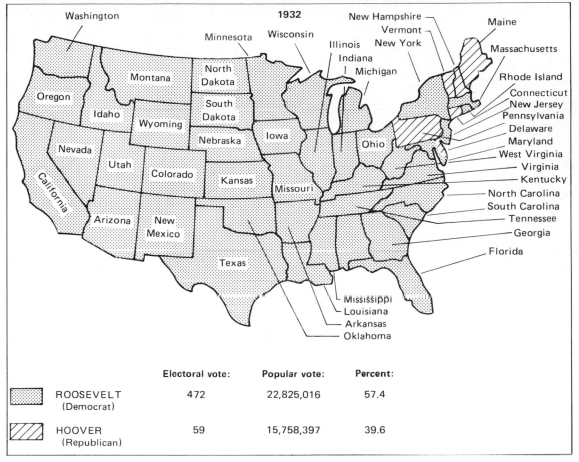

		Electoral vote:	Popular vote:	Percent:
	ROOSEVELT (Democrat)	472	22,825,016	57.4
	HOOVER (Republican)	59	15,758,397	39.6

FIGURE 5-6
The election of 1932. During the 36-year period from 1932 to 1968, the Democrats controlled the presidency for six of eight terms, the House for all but four years, and the Senate for all but two years. (*Source: Congressional Quarterly's Guide to U.S. Elections, 1975:250.*)

liberalism had begun to weaken. More voters began to identify their preference as independent, and more partisan voters—especially Democrats—began to forsake their party and vote for candidates of the opposition. While the Democrats controlled the Congress during the 1970s, they lost the presidency in 1968 and again in 1972 by a landslide. In 1980, they lost both the presidency and the Senate. The group basis of electoral behavior became less important, except for blacks. Most groups tended to split on ideological lines, and Democrats began to lose supporters from among

blue-collar workers and especially from among southern whites. Republicans lost support from among businesspeople and professionals, especially in the northeast (Schneider, 1981). The Republican party in 1980 presented a reasonably coherent political program based on conservative principles, while the Democrats still admitted to being in the midst of attempting to redefine their public philosophy.

Throughout the 1970s, accordingly, the electorate was clearly in an unsettled condition. The Democrats lost their firm majority, but the Republicans

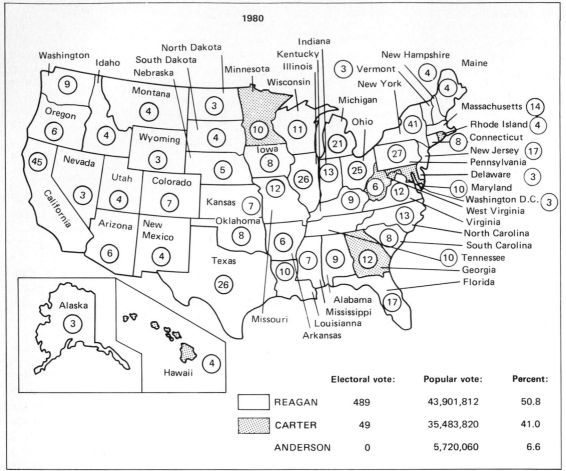

FIGURE 5-7
The election of 1980. (*Source:* Scammon and McGillivray, 1981:19–20.)

did not replace them as the dominant party. Analysts have disagreed on what this unsettled condition implies for the future. One school of thought holds that it is likely to be a permanent feature of our politics, while another holds that we have only been experiencing the natural disarray that occurs before a realigning election. According to the first view, party alignments as we have known them are a thing of the past. Voters have ceased to take parties seriously. The current "open" selection process for the presidency turns each election into a discrete event, with individual candidates riding temporary waves of voters' sentiments—whether of

mood, image, or recent issues—about their party's nomination and about the presidency itself. The electoral process has no continuity, and each election is dominated by personalities and individual programs. What we have is a condition of permanent *dealignment* (Ladd, 1982). At most, in this view, the electorate has become somewhat less liberal, but the Democratic party has shifted sufficiently to avoid facing minority status.

The alternative view is that the unsettled condition of the electorate in the 1970s was a signal that it was ripe for another realignment and that voters were only "waiting" for the parties to discover the issues that could clearly galvanize them into two distinct camps. Although we have no precise data on party identification before earlier realignments (scientific polling did not take place until the 1940s), it seems fairly clear from the other evidence that partisan attachments underwent severe stress before a realigning period. As some analysts read it, the election of 1980 provided some evidence for the view that this long-awaited realignment might finally have begun and that the party may have started its climb to being the dominant party of the next era. Not only did Ronald Reagan win an impressive victory, but the Republicans captured the Senate for the first time since 1954 and made significant gains in the House. In this view, many people who call themselves "independents" may well be ready to shift into the Republican party (Schneider, 1982). Yet the polls of party identification still have the Republicans trailing, and it is doubtful that Republicans can emerge as the majority party unless a Republican administration is perceived to have solved the nation's economic problems.

The two alternative views discussed above—permanent unsettlement (or dealignment) and continuing realignments—are clearly in conflict, but it is possible to combine them into a third, or middle, position. Under this view, we might continue to have realignments; but because of the weaker hold of political parties, these realignments might be neither as strong nor as enduring as in the past. Voters could shift somewhat in their ideological position without adhering firmly to a political party (Schneider, 1981).

Critical Realignments Assessed

In the introduction to this book we asserted the general proposition that the American system is a popular form of government. By this we did not mean that the public makes every major decision before elected officials take action or that it determines every turn or adjustment of public policy. Rather, we meant that the voting public, whether by signaling its intentions in advance or by retrospective approval, can set the *major* outlines of policy. Such choices are made to some extent in every presidential election. In many elections, the lines drawn between the parties are unclear, and the issues are not yet ripe for decision; in certain elec-

tions, however, the public is presented with distinct choices that may set the policymaking agenda for an entire era. The choice, as seen by the voters, may be as clear-cut as being for or against slavery or for or against the development of a welfare state. In these elections, the public emerges as a decisive influence on the governing institutions.

No doubt the wishes of the public could be registered without political parties. But parties, with all their imperfections, have facilitated popular influence on the government. They have provided a degree of continuity from one election to another, and they have connected, to a limited extent, basic public philosophies with a common party label and with an organizational structure that exists throughout most of the nation. Realignments in particular have offered powerful "majoritarian" mechanisms for ensuring popular control of the government and for facilitating presidential leadership. No president having in mind a dramatic shift in the nation's politics can hope to accomplish every goal in the course of one or even two terms. To fix an imprint indelibly on public policy, a president must ordinarily find a way to keep power, so to speak, after leaving office. Realignment offers the means. It allows a president to articulate a new majority public philosophy that sets the boundaries for future policymaking; and it bequeaths to the president's successors the political support in the form of a majority party status that can accomplish the long process of passing the many laws that transform a set of ideas into a working framework of public policy.

MINOR PARTIES

The American electoral process has sometimes been referred to as a "two and one-half party system." The "half" is what we have referred to alternatively as the "minor" or "third" party. Minor or third parties in American history have come in a variety of sizes and forms. Paradoxically, those that have endured for a long time, like the Communist party, have exercised little influence, whereas some that have been short-lived, like the Populist party of the 1890s, have had a significant impact on the direction of American politics. With the exception of the Republican party at its inception, however, no third party has ever won the pres-

TABLE 5-3
NEW AND MINOR PARTIES IN AMERICAN PRESIDENTIAL ELECTIONS SINCE 1828*

Year	Party	Candidate	Percentage of popular vote	Number of electoral votes	Description
1832	Anti-Mason	William Wirt	8.0	7	A party that opposed the influence of the Society of the Masons.
1848	Free-Soil	Martin Van Buren	10.1	0	A party that opposed the extension of slavery into the southwest territories; a part of the antislavery movement.
1856	American or Know-Nothing	Millard Fillmore	21.4	8	A strongly nativist party that opposed the immigration of foreigners and that favored limiting public offices to native-born Americans only.
1856	Republican	John C. Fremont	33.1	114	A party that opposed slavery and its expansion to the territories; replaced Whigs as the second major party.
1892	Populist	James Weaver	8.5	22	An agrarian protest party that sought to regulate railroads and banks.
1912	Progressive or "Bull Moose"	Teddy Roosevelt	27.4	88	A section of the Republican party that favored progressive measures including reforms such as expanded suffrage and antimonopoly laws. Received more votes in 1912 than the Republicans.
1912	Socialist	Eugene Debs	6.0	0	A workers' party with the goal of ending economic classes. Sought public ownership of utilities and transportation, income tax, election of judges.
1924	Progressive	Robert La Follette	16.6	13	A party that continued the earlier progressive label and favored strong action to control or break up corporate monopolies.
1948	States' Rights or Dixiecrat	Strom Thurmond	2.4	39	A conservative faction of the Democratic party from the south that opposed Truman's civil rights program. The party sought to protect segregation.
1968	American Independent	George Wallace	13.5	46	A protest party against Democratic Great Society programs that fed on frustrations with civil rights activism, urban riots, and antiwar demonstrations.
1980	Independent	John Anderson	7.0	0	A challenge to the adequacy of both parties; it stressed the qualifications of its candidate more than it did any program

*New or minor parties that either carried one state or more in the electoral vote or received more than 5 percent of the popular vote. The election of 1860, where the parties were split, is excluded.

idency or come even close to controlling either house of the Congress.

Many have wondered why the United States has never developed sustained competition among more than two major parties. Part of the explanation lies with the acceptance of the doctrine of the norm of two-party competition. But there are important institutional factors that also support two-party competition. American elections are conducted in single-member districts in which the victor is decided by a plurality vote. If congressional seats were chosen in multimember districts with proportional representation (which is the system used in some democratic regimes), a third party receiving 15 or 20 percent of the vote would win a substantial number of seats and would have an easier time and a greater incentive to maintain its separate identity and avoid accommodation with a major party. A single-member-district, plurality-based system is usually the electoral arrangement considered most helpful to a two-party system (Sorauf, 1980). Similarly, the presidential race, which itself is a "winner take all" contest, serves as a focal point that brings a *national* identity to the parties. The effort to capture the presidency leads many potential third-party groups to attempt to form coalitions with one of the major parties in order to have leverage on an incoming president.

In the final analysis, however, these structural explanations depend on the willingness of major political forces in America to enter into workable coalitions that can appeal to the majority of the citizens. This willingness in turn reflects the fundamental fact that almost all Americans share a general commitment to the basic values of the political system and that such differences as we have can usually be accommodated within one of two parties. Where political forces disagree fundamentally on the basic issues, coalitions among them are rare and unstable. Accordingly, because Americans have not supported in significant numbers such divergent political tendencies as fascism or communism, the major political constituencies have usually been able to find a home within one of the major parties.

If two-party competition has been the norm, however, this has not prevented minor parties from offering strong competition in certain cases. Nor is victory necessary in order for third parties to exert influence. Their greatest influence, in fact, has come not from winning elections but from pressuring the major parties to make changes in response to the threat that they might lose votes or be replaced. The role of minor parties, therefore, cannot be assessed by looking simply at their electoral performance. Especially in periods preceding realignments, third parties have been influential in bringing into the electoral arena the new issues over which the major parties subsequently divided. Thus, the antislavery parties in 1840 and 1848 served as forerunners of the Republican party, and the parties of agrarian discontent between 1880 and 1892 embodied positions that were adopted by the Democratic party in 1896 and later included in the policy proposals of the progressives. More recently, George Wallace's American Independent party of 1968 pressured the Republican party under Richard Nixon to move to the right, at least in its rhetoric, in an effort to co-opt Wallace's support.

Minor parties have also served in the past as a way for a faction within a major party to test its political influence in the party. A faction which feels that it has been shut out or denied its rightful place may attempt (or threaten) a third-party challenge. Its objective may be not to win but to prevent its own party from winning by draining away critically needed votes. If that attempt is successful, the major party will then have to accommodate the faction in the next election on more favorable terms. The Progressives in 1912 succeeded partly by this strategy, while the States' Rights party in 1948—a disgruntled southern offshoot from the Democratic party—tried but failed.

In recent years—1976 and 1980—a new type of minor party, the independent candidacy, has emerged. In 1980, John Anderson offered himself not as the head of a new-issue constituency, like the Free-Soilers or the Populists, or as the leader of a bolting faction, like the States' Rights party, but rather as an alternative candidate, one better qualified than the major parties' nominees to hold the presidential office. A candidacy of this sort would probably have been inconceivable before the decline of the parties and the increased influence of the media. But with organization today counting for less and with voters' ties to their political parties being weaker, independent candidacies are now possible.

Do minor parties play a constructive role? The

answer is not easy. On the one hand, a system of regular multiparty competition could result in the same evils as a nonpartisan system—narrow factional candidacies that are potentially demagogic and that prevent the formation of broad, majority coalitions. Two examples of minor parties in American history bear out this concern: the American, or Know-Nothing, party of 1856 appealed blatantly to prejudice against Catholics; and the American Independent party of 1968 had clear racist overtones. On the other hand, as we have seen, minor parties can serve as potential checks on the major parties in the event that these parties lose contact with the voters or refuse to offer alternatives on significant issues. Entering the presidential race periodically, minor parties can help to keep the major parties responsive and ensure that the electoral process remains open to new ideas. The history of electoral competition has clearly demonstrated that on occasion minor parties have performed this role very well.

The lesson to draw from this historical record appears to be that the electoral system should remain open to third parties, but not encourage them. Legislation that directly discriminates against third parties, such as unreasonably long filing periods, probably goes further than desirable in foreclosing the opportunity for third parties to compete. On the other hand, changes in the political system that weaken the major parties and provide encouragement for third parties need to be closely scrutinized. If the case for a two-and-one-half-party system is sound, legislators must keep a careful watch on all proposals that affect the delicate balance between encouraging minor parties and maintaining the major ones.

PARTIES IN GOVERNMENT

Parties are not merely electoral organizations. Once elected, governing officials continue to wear their party hats, and there is at least some expectation that fellow party members will work together in some fashion to promote their goals. Yet parties in the American system are only one influence at work on elected officials, and the degree of party unity in American politics has almost always been a disapointment to those who measure our parties by the standards of parliamentary systems.

Elected officials have pressures and duties that invariably conflict with their party loyalty. A president is not merely a Democrat or a Republican, but the president in some sense of all the people. A member of Congress is not merely a partisan, but the representative of a particular district or state. Moreover, both the president and the members of Congress have their own institutions to defend, and our system was established with the expectation that some measure of conflict would be the norm in the relationship between these two institutions. The most telling point of all, however, is that the public does not expect that party loyalty should be supreme. Fully 63 percent of the population disagrees with the proposition that a "representative should follow his party leaders, even if he doesn't want to" (Dennis, 1966:620).

The alternatives for party involvement in the functioning of government range from complete dominance by parties ("pure" party government) to no involvement by parties whatsoever (nonpartisan government).

"Pure" Party Government

Under this model, favored by many progressives and at one time by many political scientists, the political party would act as a cohesive unit, with both the president and the members of Congress from the same party adhering strictly to a common program. In effect, separation of powers would give way to pure party government; and voters, in deciding on their representatives, would be choosing a national party program. According to its proponents, this model would give more energy to government, enabling presidents to put their programs into law without running into the opposition of a fully independent legislative branch.

Setting aside such obvious problems as how to change local control of party nominations, this system could produce the desired form of majority government only if the presidency and Congress were controlled by the same party. Often this is not the case, especially in recent times, when Republicans captured the presidency for five of eight terms between 1952 and 1984 but never had control of both houses of Congress. In addition, party government would require the parties in Congress to enforce by disciplinary measures a party line on all

TABLE 5-4
PARTISAN UNITY AND DIVISION IN THE PRESIDENCY AND CONGRESS

Years	Years president's party has a majority, % of range		
	In *both* houses of Congress	In *one* house of Congress	In *neither* house of Congress
1801–1828	93	0	7
1829–1860	63	25	13
1861–1896	61	28	11
1897–1932	83	11	5
1933–1968	78	0	22
1969–1984	25	25	50

members of Congress, something which they have been reluctant to do. Adherents of party government argue, however, that if their scheme were somehow to become the accepted norm, split government would become a rarity. As examples of moments when government "works" on a model resembling party government, adherents point to the first administrations of Jefferson, Wilson, and Franklin Roosevelt. But whether such temporary instances of cooperation can serve as a model for the normal process of governing, without radically changing the Constitution, seems very doubtful.

Nonpartisan Government

Under this model, which was favored by the founders, neither Congress nor the president would be "party" bodies. Congressional majorities would form on each issue, with the coalitions varying according to the type of issue in question. The president would be identified with no preexisting organization and could accordingly make accommodations with Congress on a case-by-case basis. No doubt temporary blocs and working alliances in Congress would emerge, but without the sustaining force of a party label they would probably change with its shifting membership. This model existed in practice only during the First Congress in 1789 and during the period from roughly 1818 to 1824. In the latter period, Martin Van Buren, at least, believed that cooperation between the president and Congress had become especially difficult.

American Constitutional Government

American parties have operated in practice somewhere between these two models, being closer at some periods to party government and at others, despite the existence of party labels, to nonpartisan government. Given our system of government, this in-between status hardly comes as a surprise. By permitting parties, the system allows for such coordination as parties on their own can develop. Yet the system does not, like a parliamentary regime, encourage party cohesiveness. The government does not fall, as in a parliamentary regime, when legislative members of the executive's party break ranks; and each institution, as we have seen, has its own interests to protect. Within Congress, one finds that because of the penetration of national party ideas into the localities, party members *tend* to share certain views in common. But the federal structure of representation and the separation of powers allows for disagreements within the parties.

Obviously, in this model there is a great deal of room between stronger and weaker parties—between parties that move closer to the pole of party government and parties that, while maintaining their names, scarcely serve to guide or discipline their members. Whether parties move closer to the one pole or the other makes a great deal of difference for the operation of our government, and it is on the issue of more or less party-related behavior that much institutional debate has taken place. Over American history, the cohesiveness of parties has varied greatly. Since the 1920s, there is evidence based on analysis of congressional roll-call votes that party unity has markedly declined, although there have been notable periods of unity for the Democrats after the elections of 1932 and 1964 and for the Republicans after the election of 1980 (Davidson and Oleszek, 1981). The reasons for this decline are various: within Congress, power has become more dispersed, and party leaders have less leverage over their members; in the nomination of presidential candidates, fewer institutional connections exist between congressional leaders and presidential nominees, and presidential election results have had a diminishing impact on the outcome of congressional races. As in the case of the weakening of parties in the electorate, many today have begun to ask whether the parties ought not to look for mechanisms within the government that would facilitate greater party cohesiveness.

CONCLUSION

In this chapter we have presented two aspects of political parties: as vehicles for promoting a general set of principles and policies, and as structures and organizations influenced by various legal arrangements and incentives for participation. On the second count, our treatment has pointed to a steady decline or weakening of most structural and organizational aspects of the parties. On the first count, as vehicles for promoting principles, parties throughout American history have regularly alternated between strength and weakness—between bodies that vigorously present rather clear goals and bodies that flounder about as loose coalitions in search of a purpose. The "decline" of parties on this count that was evident in the decade of the 1970s may well have been temporary, as indicated by the Republican party's relative coherence in the election of 1980.

A clear sense of purpose can hold a party together as a cohesive and powerful instrument even with a weak organizational structure. But, as just observed, American parties tend to possess this firmness of purpose for only relatively brief periods. If a strong commitment to a common goal is the only thing American parties rely on to hold themselves together, it is unlikely that they will be able to operate most of the time. To play an effective

role as bodies that can accommodate fairly broad coalitions with a general sense of direction, they need a structure strong enough to carry them through "normal" times.

In considering the place of parties in our scheme of government, the constitution maker must look well beyond the founding. The founders opposed political parties, although they largely had in mind different kinds of parties from those which subsequently developed. The case for political parties was made by thinkers and political leaders after the founding, in part to realize certain of the founders' goals and in part to correct or "amend" the original constitutional scheme. In particular, the addition of parties to the political system was seen as a means of providing for more democratic influence on the government and for supplying some kind of common glue among elected officials in a system of separation of powers and federalism.

In the past, the strength of the parties rested on some foundations, like mass patronage, that Americans today are unwilling to tolerate. Other factors that have contributed to the decline of traditional parties stem from technological changes, like the advent of television, and from major political developments, like the rise of the welfare state and the civil service, that are beyond the control of those seeking to strengthen the role of parties. There is, then, no possibility of returning to the style of party politics of a previous era. The practical question facing Americans today is whether certain steps could be taken, consistent with modern conditions, that could restore some of the functions to political parties—supposing, of course, that this objective is desirable. Whether this can be done should become clearer after we analyze how campaigns and elections are conducted in American politics—the subject of Chapter 6.

SOURCES

Andersen, Kristi: *The Creation of a Democratic Majority,* University of Chicago Press, Chicago, 1979.

Banfield, Edward: "In Defense of the American Party System," in Robert Goldwin (ed.), *Political Parties, U.S.A.,* Rand McNally, Chicago, 1961.

Bode, Ken, and Carol Casey: "Party Reform: Revisionism Revised," in Robert A. Goldwin (ed.), *Political*

Parties in the Eighties, American Enterprise Institute, Washington, D.C., 1981.

Bone, Hugh A.: *American Politics and the Party System,* 3d ed., McGraw-Hill, New York, 1965.

Boorstin, Daniel J. (ed.): *An American Primer,* University of Chicago Press, Chicago, 1966.

Broder, David S.: *The Party's Over: The Failure of Politics in America,* Harper and Row, New York, 1971.

Bryce, James: *The American Commonwealth,* 2 vols., Macmillan, New York, 1889.

Burnham, Walter Dean: *Critical Elections and the Mainsprings of American Politics,* Norton, New York, 1970.

Burns, James MacGregor: *The Deadlock of Democracy,* Prentice-Hall, Englewood Cliffs, N.J., 1963.

Congressional Quarterly's Guide to U.S. Elections, Congressional Quarterly, Washington, D.C., 1975.

Crotty, William J., and Gary C. Jacobson: *American Parties in Decline,* Little, Brown, Boston, 1980.

Curtis, George William: *Harper's Weekly,* Nov. 12, 1887.

Davidson, Roger, and Walter Oleszek: *Congress and Its Members,* Congressional Quarterly Press, Washington, D.C., 1981.

Dennis, Jack: "Support for the Party System by the Mass Public," *American Political Science Review,* vol. 60, no. 3, 1966, pp. 600–615.

Epstein, Leon D.: "Presidential Parties and the Nominating Process," a paper prepared for a Wilson Center Colloquium, May 13, 1980.

Farley, James A.: *Jim Farley's Story: The Roosevelt Years,* McGraw-Hill, New York, 1948.

Hofstadter, Richard: *The Idea of a Party System,* University of California Press, Berkeley, Calif., 1970.

Huckshorn, Robert J.: *Party Leadership in the States,* University of Massachusetts Press, Amherst, Mass., 1976.

Jacobson, Gary C.: *The Politics of Congressional Elections,* Yale University Press, New Haven, Conn., 1983.

Kallenbach, Joseph E.: *The American Chief Executive,* Harper and Row, New York, 1966.

Keefe, William J.: *Parties, Politics, and Public Policy in America,* 3d ed., Holt, New York, 1980.

Keller, Morton: *Affairs of State,* Harvard University Press, Cambridge, Mass., 1977.

Key, V. O., Jr.: *Southern Politics,* Knopf, New York, 1950.

————: *Parties, Politics and Pressure Groups,* 5th ed., Crowell, New York, 1964.

Kirkpatrick, Jeane J.: *Dismantling the Parties,* American Enterprise Institute, Washington, D.C., 1978.

Ladd, Everett: *Where Have All the Voters Gone?* Norton, New York, 1982.

La Follette, Robert: *Autobiography,* R. M. La Follette, Madison, Wis., 1913.

Mazmanian, Daniel L.: *Third Parties in Presidential Elections,* Brookings Institution, Washington, D.C., 1974.

McWilliams, Wilson Carey: "Parties as Civic Associations," in Gerald Pomper (ed.), *Party Renewal in America,* Praeger, New York, 1980.

————: "The Meaning of the Election," in Gerald Pomper (ed.), *The Election of 1980,* Chatham House, Chatham, N.J., 1981.

New York Times, July 7, 1974.

Ostrogorski, M.: *Democracy and the Organization of Political Parties,* abridged by Seymour Martin Lipset (ed.), Anchor, New York, 1964.

Polsby, Nelson: "Reform of the Party System and the Conduct of the Presidency," in James Sterling Young (ed.), *Problems and Prospects of Presidential Leadership in the Nineteen-Eighties,* vol. 1, University Press of America, Washington, D.C., 1982.

President's Commission for a National Agenda for the Eighties: The Electoral and Democratic Process in the Eighties, Government Printing Office, Washington, D.C., 1980.

Ranney, Austin: "The Representativeness of Primary Electorates," *Midwest Journal of Political Science,* vol. 12, May 1968, pp. 224–238.

————: *Curing the Mischiefs of Faction: Party Reform in America,* University of California Press, Berkeley, Calif., 1975.

————: *The Federalization of Presidential Primaries,* American Enterprise Institute, Washington, D.C., 1978.

Richardson, James D. (ed.): *The Messages and Papers of the Presidents, 1789–1897,* vols. 1–16, Government Printing Office, Washington, D.C., 1896–1899.

Riordan, William L.: *Plunkitt of Tammany Hall,* Dutton, New York, 1963.

Sabato, Larry: "PACs, Parties and Independent Groups," in Thomas Mann and Norman Ornstein (eds.), *The American Elections of 1982,* American Enterprise Institute, Washington, D.C., 1983.

Scammon, Richard, and Alice McGillivray (eds.): *America Votes,* Congressional Quarterly, Washington, D.C., 1981.

Schattschneider, E. E.: *Party Government,* Rinehart, New York, 1942.

Schneider, William: "The November 4 Vote for President: What Did It Mean?" in Austin Ranney (ed.), *The American Elections of 1980,* American Enterprise Institute, Washington, D.C., 1981.

———: "Realignment: The Eternal Question," *PS,* no. 15, pp. 449–457, Summer 1982.

Sombart, Werner: *Why There Is No Socialism in the United States,* International Arts and Sciences Press, White Plains, N.Y., 1976. Originally published in 1906.

Sorauf, Frank: *Party Politics in America,* 4th ed., Little, Brown, Boston, 1980.

Sundquist, James: *Dynamics of the Party System,* Brookings Institution, Washington, D.C., 1973.

Van Buren, Martin: *Inquiry into the Origin and Course of Political Parties in the United States,* Hurd and Houghton, New York, 1867.

Washington Post, Jan. 20, 1973; and May 8, 1980.

Wilson, James Q.: *Political Organization,* Basic Books, New York, 1973.

Wilson, Woodrow: *Colleges and States,* Ray Stannard Baker and William E. Dodd (eds.), vols. 1–2, Harper, New York, 1925.

RECOMMENDED READINGS

Eldersveld, Samuel: *Political Parties in American Society,* Basic Books, New York, 1983. A comprehensive text of American parties.

Epstein, Leon D.: *Political Parties in Western Democracies,* Praeger, New York, 1967. A comparative study of the functions and organization of parties in the United States and European democracies.

Goldwin, Robert (ed.): *Political Parties in the Eighties,* American Enterprise Institute, Washington, D.C., 1980. Descriptive and theoretical essays on the possibilities of party revival.

Polsby, Nelson: *Consequences of Party Reform,* Oxford University Press, New York, 1983. An account of the causes and effects of the party reforms of the 1960s and 1970s.

Pomper, Gerald (ed.): *Party Renewal in America,* Praeger, New York, 1980. Descriptive and theoretical essays on the possibilities of party revival.

Riordan, William L.: *Plunkitt of Tammany Hall,* Knopf, New York, 1948. The party machine at the turn of the century as described by an old-style party boss.

Sundquist, James: *Dynamics of the Party System,* Brookings Institution, Washington, D.C., 1973. A history of parties and voting alignments from the Civil War era to the 1970s.

Chapter 6

Campaigns and Elections

For most Americans, elections—especially presidential elections—are the most interesting of all political events. They contain all the elements of the human drama, ranging from the tragic to the ridiculous and from the pathetic to the heartwarming. In presidential campaigns over the past two decades, Americans have witnessed the assassination of one candidate (Senator Robert Kennedy in 1968) and the shooting and paralysis of another (Governor George Wallace in 1972). They have seen a leading contender, Senator Edmund Muskie, break into tears before the 1972 New Hampshire primary and fade quickly from the presidential race. And they have watched as candidates have delivered moving speeches on one day, only to commit inexplicable blunders on the next.

The unfolding of electoral campaigns brings to mind the kind of contest that everyone readily understands: a race in which there can be only one winner. Given the drama of the process, it is tempting to focus on the most exciting aspects of campaigns, emphasizing, as the media often do, the "horse race" quality of the contests. But this is a temptation that students of politics must resist. Without neglecting the day-to-day developments of a campaign, we must also look at the underlying factors that help explain how campaigns operate. As any lover of sports knows, games are played according to certain rules and norms, a change in any one of which can affect how the game is played and who wins. By the same token, the political analyst needs to understand the basic rules and norms of the electoral game, including how and why they have developed and in what direction they may be evolving. But unlike sporting contests, winning an election is only a small part of the story. We sometimes become so involved in following the events of the campaign that we forget that elections are meant to prepare for the real business of politics, which is governing. Accordingly, the electoral process must be considered not only from the point of view of how it affects who wins and loses but also from the perspective of its impact on the operation of our institutions and the behavior of elected officials.

In this chapter, we shall look at the major structural and behavioral aspects of elections for the presidency and Congress. This will include a study of the laws and norms that govern electoral contests, the factors that influence the choice of the candidates, and the way in which candidates plan and execute their campaigns. We shall also assess some of the major proposals for change in our electoral institutions, evaluating the current system and the proposed changes in terms of their impact on campaigns and on prospects for governing effectively.

PRESIDENTIAL SELECTION: GENERAL CONSIDERATIONS

No aspect of our political system has been the subject of more controversy and change lately than our method of selecting a president. Since the 1960s, the nominating process has been completely transformed, financing for campaigns has been changed from a private to a chiefly public function, and numerous Constitutional amendments have been proposed to alter the electoral college system. Many of the issues remain controversial, and additional changes in the years ahead can be expected. Our task in this section, as we move through the selection process from the start of the campaign to its conclusion, will be to consider the important influences upon presidential campaigns, paying particular attention to those areas where changes are likely to be proposed.

Eligibility: Legal Qualifications and Working Norms

Age and Residence Who runs for president of the United States? The field of potential candidates is limited in the first instance by certain Constitutional standards of eligibility, which by now have become so widely accepted that they are seldom discussed. They continue, however, to influence the careers of our leading politicians and the character of the presidency. Article II of the Constitution requires that the president be at least 35 years old and a natural-born citizen. The age requirement hardly seems restrictive, as few voters today would probably even consider someone younger than 35. The youngest person ever elected president was John Kennedy at 43, and the average age of an incoming president has been 54. At 69 years old, Ronald Reagan in 1980 was the oldest person ever to be elected president. Perhaps this

At 43, John F. Kennedy was the youngest person ever elected president, yet he was eight years older than the minimum age limit set by the Constitution.   *(Charles Bonney/Black Star)*

preference for older people represents a natural inclination on the part of voters, although it may also result in part from the legal "conditioning" of the Constitution, which establishes age qualifications for all federal elective offices. It is clear, in any case, that the founders' intention in establishing an age qualification was to limit the consideration of presidential candidates to persons of maturity and, ordinarily at least, some experience in public affairs.

Requiring the president to be a natural-born citizen (and a resident for fourteen years before election) might conceivably be considered unfair to aspirants who are excluded. Such requirements, however, illustrate the founders' concern with structuring electoral rules with a view to the object of *governing*. The nation's highest office, the founders reasoned, had to be above even the slightest suspicion that the deepest loyalty of a president might be to another nation; this concern took precedence over any theoretical right of an individual to become president. Henry Kissinger, a German-born citizen who served as secretary of state under presidents Nixon and Ford, represents the most recent example of a person whose political career may potentially have been limited by this provision.

The Constitution, it should be observed, imposes no religious, racial, sexual, or economic qualifications for holding office. Legal qualifications, of course, set only the outside limits for consideration. Until recently, the party politicians who controlled the nominating process employed certain "unwritten laws" or norms in making practical judgments about electability. For example, at the turn of the century, it was generally held that only white, Protestant males—preferably of English stock—were electable. The Democrats challenged the religious barrier in 1928 when they nominated a Catholic candidate, Al Smith. Smith lost the election to Herbert Hoover, with the religious question playing an important role in the decision of many voters. In 1960, the Democrats again nominated a Catholic candidate, John F. Kennedy, who won a narrow victory over Richard Nixon. Although the religious issue again influenced the votes of many citizens, one remarkable result of Kennedy's election has been that since 1960 Catholicism has never been considered a disqualifying factor. Today, no doubt there would still be resistance in some quarters to the nomination of certain people on the basis of their race, religion, or sex. But poll surveys have indicated that such resistance is weakening, and presidential candidates today frequently mention blacks, Jews, and women as potential running mates, an important sign that people from these groups are no longer barred as a matter of course from being considered for high office. The informal norms that restrict the choice of presidential candidates, while they have not yet achieved the pure nondiscriminatory standard of the Constitution, seem nevertheless to be gradually approaching it.

Term Limitation A second Constitutional qualification on eligibility was not adopted until 1951, when the Twenty-Second Amendment was passed, limiting any president to no more than two elected terms (or ten years, in the event of a vice presidential accession). This amendment was passed largely in reaction to the four consecutive elections of Franklin Roosevelt from 1932 through 1944. Before Roosevelt, and dating all the way back to George Washington, who stepped down after his second term, a tradition had developed that a president would not serve more than twice. This tradition, however, was not considered completely binding; and a number of presidents in the past either genuinely contemplated a third term or, perhaps to protect their power, refused to remove themselves from consideration until the last moment.

The question of limiting the number of presidential terms was debated at length during the Convention in 1787. Ultimately, the founders rejected any limitation, on the grounds that it would be unwise for the nation to deny itself the services of an especially talented individual during a period of crisis. Precisely this argument was used by the supporters of Franklin Roosevelt in 1940 and 1944, when he ran for his third and fourth terms amidst the international crisis of World War II. The argument in favor of a term limitation is based on a view that a republican system should not have to rely on the abilities of any one individual. Allowing someone to serve for more than two terms could change the spirit, if not the letter, of the political system, transforming it from a republic to a kind of elective monarchy. The public, according to this argument, would come to identify the government not with its laws and institutions but with the character and personality of a particular individual.

Whatever the merits of the term limitation imposed by the Twenty-Second Amendment—and this clearly is an issue on which both sides have strong arguments—its adoption has had important consequences for American politics. Calculations of who will hold power in the future influence the willingness of officials in Washington to follow a president. As one scholar, Fred Greenstein, has observed: "Modern presidents, at least since the Twenty-Second Amendment, have generally been recognized by political observers as short-run participants in Washington policymaking. . . ." This fact disposes some in Congress and the bureaucracy to resist presidents and "wait them out," while it may lead presidents to adopt a "hurried approach to the making of policy," attempting to make their mark before their effective powers begin to dwindle (Greenstein, 1978:64–65).

Screening and Selecting Candidates

Within the broad boundaries of eligibility marked out by laws and norms, a mechanism must be established to survey the possible candidates and limit them to a manageable number for making a final choice. The founders thought this process could normally be handled entirely by the electors, who would decide among the nation's leading figures without any popular campaigning. Since the advent of political parties in the early nineteenth century, however, the process has been carried out under a two-step arrangement: first, a nominating stage, in which the major parties narrow down the number of candidates to two (with an occasional serious third-party contender); and, second, a general election, in which the public, voting within the fifty states, selects electors bound to the candidates, who in turn officially choose the president.

The number of people actually considered in this process is rather limited. No one would—or perhaps should—expect the parties to conduct a talent hunt at election time to discover some unknown leader. Electoral institutions are ideally designed to select candidates with the combination of skills, experience, and political support needed to meet the burdens of one of the world's most demanding political offices. Both political considerations and common sense suggest, therefore, that the field of candidates must be confined to prominent persons who are knowledgeable about politics and who generally practice the art themselves. It is hardly surprising, therefore, to find that our majority-party nominees have mostly been politicians of some kind—vice presidents, governors, and senators.

Nevertheless, compared with Great Britain, where the prime minister is almost always drawn from existing leaders of the parliamentary party, the pool of potential candidates in the United States is much broader. Over the course of American history, our parties have on occasion gone outside the usual sphere of politicians—to generals like Grant or Eisenhower, to Supreme Court justices like Charles Evans Hughes (the Republican nominee in 1916), and to business figures like Wendell Wilkie (the Republican nominee in 1940). Nor does a candidate need to be a leading member of Congress or highly experienced in national politics. For example, a rather obscure ex-governor of Georgia, Jimmy Carter, was able to win the presidency in 1976, and neither President Carter nor President Reagan had any service in national political office before being elected. Openness of this sort, which seems more likely under the current system of choosing nominees largely through primary elections, has prompted a great deal of concern among observers in foreign nations, who worry in particular about the danger of "amateur" presidents in international affairs (King, 1981).

THE NOMINATING STAGE

Candidates today frequently enter the nomination race for reasons other than that of winning their party's nomination: to publicize a cause, to gain recognition for a future race, and to strengthen their chances of being considered as a vice presidential nominee. The truly serious aspirants for the presidency, however, enter the nominating phase with two basic objectives: to obtain enough delegates to win the nomination and to do so in a way that will not disrupt party unity and thereby diminish their chances of victory in the general election. Unfortunately these two objectives are not always compatible. Candidates must put first things first, worrying initially about winning delegates and then, only if they have the luxury of certain victory, concerning themselves with building party unity. This was illustrated in the case of Ronald Reagan's 1980 campaign, in which Reagan began as the strong front-runner and sought to avoid creating divisions in his party. Yet after suffering attacks from the other candidates and losing the first contest for the selection of delegates in Iowa to George Bush, he felt obliged to take the offensive, saying: "I can't be the only one concerned with unity. . . . I'm going to have to think of self-survival" (Jones, 1981:81).

The way in which nominating races are conducted today makes the task of securing party unity all the more difficult. Since most delegates are chosen in popular contests, candidates must create large personal organizations and develop mass campaign appeals. The nature of this process, consisting as it does of a long, open campaign against other contenders, places severe burdens on the eventual nominee's ability to unite the party. Elections frequently draw lines of division, and attacks made publicly on opponents during primary campaigns can make the subsequent process of healing party rifts very difficult. President Ford in 1976 and President Carter in 1980 both blamed their loss in the general election in large part on the difficult nomination campaigns they had to wage, Ford against Ronald Reagan and Carter against Senator Edward Kennedy.

Nominating Systems: A Historical Glance

Earlier methods of nomination posed fewer problems for party unity, though they raised difficulties of other kinds. The first method of nominating candidates (1800–1816) was by vote of the party's membership in Congress (the congressional caucus). Although this system was never fully recognized or respected by all candidates, it nonetheless became a focal point of controversy. Critics charged that it was undemocratic and that it diminished the president's independence from Congress, thereby threatening the doctrine of separation of powers. In 1812, for example, James Madison was pressured by his party members in Congress to agree to declare war against Great Britain as a condition for his renomination for a second term.

The Pure Convention System (1832–1908) Following the reestablishment of party competition after 1828, the parties had to devise a new method of nomination. The solution arrived at was the national party convention made up of delegates selected by the state party organizations. This method appeared to satisfy (for a time) the desire for a democratic system and at the same time avoid any threat to presidential independence. With the power to choose the nominees now in the hands of the party leaders at the convention, candidates campaigned by attempting to win their favor and by positioning themselves to be acceptable to a widespread following within the party. Actually, "campaigning" is probably the wrong term to use. Following the norms implied in the Constitution, standard practice in the nineteenth century was for the party to seek out the candidate, and not the candidate the party. Candidates—in theory—were supposed to appear reluctant to seek office. (Whether genuinely or for mere display, the Democratic nominee in 1868, Horatio Seymour, was heard to exclaim to a friend upon learning of his nomination, "Pity me, Harvey, pity me"; Seymour was subsequently spared a greater burden of pity by losing the election to General Grant.)

The "courtship" between the candidates and the party was conducted according to customs that today seem very odd. Candidates known to be genuine possibilities for nomination did not attend the conventions, but stayed home and put up a pretense of indifference. (In point of fact, however, after the invention of the telegraph, candidates were often in frequent contact with their lieutenants at the convention.) After the convention made its choice, it would send out a delegation to inform the candidate of his nomination. In a forerunner of the modern "media event," the candidate would receive the delegation at his home, listen to its request, and then agree to accept the proffered honor. Interestingly, delegations are still sent by the convention to "inform" the nominated candidate. In 1980, Ronald Reagan was driving to the convention hall to announce his preference for a running mate while the delegation that was to inform him of his nomination was still being selected by the chairman of the convention.

The Mixed System (1912–1968) After the advent of presidential primaries in 1912, some candidates began to campaign openly for the nomination, much as they do today. Yet because the majority of the delegates were not yet selected and bound in primary contests, it was not necessary for candidates to win in primaries in order to receive their party's nomination. Candidates could still follow the old "inside" method of making their appeals to the uncommitted delegations chosen by party-run caucuses. In 1916, Charles Evans Hughes, who never campaigned, was nominated while still sitting as a Supreme Court judge; and neither Adlai Stevenson in 1952 nor Hubert Humphrey in 1968 entered any primaries, yet both received the Democratic party's nomination. Most of the nominees during this period did in fact enter at least some of the primaries. Their nominations, however, were the result of a combination of support from primary states and from the backing of party leaders. The method of nominating candidates during this period can therefore best be described as a "mixed system" in which a balance of sorts existed between the previous method of discretion by party leaders and the "new" method of selection by the voters.

The Primary System (1972 to the Present) Since 1968, the balance has been tipped decisively in favor of primary contests (see Table 6-1). We have today what nearly amounts to a nominating system by direct election in which the candidates do not wait for the party to "give" them the nomination, but instead vie to capture it by winning enough popular support to obtain a majority of delegates. Delegates are chosen by three basic processes: primaries, caucuses, and (only in the Democratic party) meetings of the congressional caucus. Of these, primaries constitute by far the predominant method, choosing or mandating some 70 percent of the delegates. (In some primary states, though the delegates are actually chosen completely or in part by party caucuses, they are often mandated by state law to vote according to the results determined by the popular vote.) The caucus states, because they now choose so small a portion of the entire number of delegates, behave quite differently from before. Instead of selecting unbound delegates to the conventions, they, too, tend to choose delegates committed to particular candidates because all participants know that the winner is likely to be determined before the convention ever meets.

The predominance of primaries also helps account for the differences between contemporary

TABLE 6-1
PRESIDENTIAL PRIMARIES, 1912–1980*

	Democratic		Republican	
	Number of primaries	**Percent of total delegates chosen in primaries**	**Number of primaries**	**Percent of total delegates chosen in primaries**
1912	12	32.9	13	41.7
1916	20	53.5	20	58.9
1932	16	40.0	14	37.7
1960	16	38.3	15	38.6
1972	22	65.3	21	56.8
1980	29	71.4	33	76.0

*Because of legal complexity, these figures are approximate.
Source: Adapted from Arterton, 1978:7

campaigns and those that took place under the mixed system. Consider, for example, the characterization of the races under the two systems provided by David Broder, one of the nation's leading journalists:

> John Kennedy [in 1960] ran in four contested primaries. Contrast that with the thirty-five that await anyone who wants the nomination in 1980. After Kennedy won in West Virginia, he still had to persuade the leaders of his party . . . that they could stake their reputation on his qualities as the best man to be the standard bearer of the party. Contrast that with Jimmy Carter, who never had to meet, and, in fact, in many cases did not meet, those similar officials until after he achieved the Democratic nomination (Broder, 1979:7).

Candidates today press their courtship with the voters with an openness and aggressiveness that would have shocked nineteenth-century political sensibilities. With the first real contest for delegates coming now in the winter of the election year, and with a long time needed to organize a campaign and raise funds, candidates usually make an official declaration of their candidacy in the year preceding the general election. "Outsiders"—that is, candidates who are not initially considered to have much chance—may begin even earlier, as many as two years before the general election. No wonder some analysts have begun to speak of the "continuous campaign."

The Campaign Organization in the Nomination Race

In launching a campaign, a candidate must first assemble the professional core of a personal national organization. It normally will consist of a campaign manager, fund raiser, press secretary, pollster, and media consultant. Pollsters and media consultants now generally run firms of their own and are hired by the candidates. The fact that many of the vital functions of the modern campaign are performed by such specialists, rather than by traditional party leaders, speaks volumes about the nature of modern nomination campaigns; they are no longer efforts at coalition building among party leaders, but instead exercises in mass communication and persuasion.

The main advisers, along with the candidate, devise the basic plan for the campaign. The plan, which may evolve as circumstances change, outlines at any point the themes and issues the candidate will stress, the priorities for the candidates' time, and the allocation of campaign resources. Consider, for example, President Carter's 1980 campaign plan, written early in 1979 by his manager, Hamilton Jordan. It involved not only a strategy of where to spend time and money but also a plan to induce certain states to schedule their caucuses and primaries at favorable moments:

> It is absolutely essential that we win the early contests and establish momentum. . . . The easiest way

... is to win southern delegates by encouraging southern states to hold early caucuses and primaries.... It is in our interest to have states that we are likely to win scheduled on the same day with states that we might do poorly in (*Washington Post*, 1980).

Each of the advisers also has a basic role to perform, though the exact specifications vary with each campaign. The campaign manager, in addition to overall management responsibility, builds the rest of the personal organization. Beyond the basic core, viable campaigns will normally have a series of paid regional or state coordinators, plus a volunteer staff within every state. The campaign manager is generally responsible for developing and coordinating the activities of the organization. In certain respects, the use of the term "manager" is revealing. Like the baseball manager, the campaign manager often receives much of the credit for the candidate's success and much of the blame for failure. Hamilton Jordan, who masterminded Jimmy Carter's campaign in 1976, quickly became regarded as a political whiz kid and was later appointed by President Carter as his White House chief of staff. Ronald Reagan, whose nomination bid in 1980 started slowly with a loss in the Iowa caucus, dismissed his manager, John Sears. The candidates' supporters are usually unwilling to criticize the candidate personally and therefore tend to vent their frustrations on the campaign manager.

Pollsters in a campaign perform a quite different function from pollsters syndicated in newspapers, like George Gallup or Lou Harris. The latter mostly inform the public where, at a given time, the candidates stand in relation to each other. The campaign pollster is more interested in discovering what a candidate can do to improve his or her standing. For a relatively unknown candidate at the outset of the campaign, measurements of voters' preferences are of little significance: candidates like Jimmy Carter in 1976 and George Bush in 1980 began with little national recognition. The pollster attempts to learn from the polls what the electorate is thinking and what themes the candidate might be able to use. A pollster will also look for weaknesses in the support of opponents, with a view to helping the candidate develop effective lines of criticisms for the campaign. As the campaign gets under way, polls assist the staff in deciding whether its strategy is working and how the candidate might best expend additional resources. In a sea of uncertainty, which is the usual condition of political campaigns, the pollsters at least possess some "hard" evidence and therefore tend to be relied on very heavily as general advisers. Jimmy Carter's pollster, Patrick Caddell, helped him develop his successful campaign theme in 1976 of stressing "basic values" of honesty, compassion, and a return to fundamentals. Ronald Reagan's pollster, Richard Wirthlin, tested a variety of campaign issues and themes in the early primaries and found that Reagan had "a very unique appeal to blue collar workers.... We determined [that] the emphasis on the family and the neighborhood and values generally and an appeal for hope were very,

---

BOX 6-1

CAMPAIGN POLLSTERS

Polls are of obvious value to candidates devising their strategy and tactics, but Robert M. Teeter, President Ford's pollster in 1976, warned that opinion surveys should be kept in perspective.

Too many people have the idea that our job is to find the hidden lever to move all the voters. There's an incorrect public perception that they (polls) can measure everything to a precise degree. Polls should provide some guidance on what candidates ought to talk about or how they should frame their presentations—but I don't think polls should ever override good judgment or replace people's brains.

Source: National Journal, 1976:574–579.

BOX 6-2

MEDIA CONSULTANTS

Campaigning for federal office is now done mainly through television. The reliance on television means an increased role for the media consultant, whose job it is to make the candidate seem more attractive to the public than his or her opponent is. Because of costs and restrictions imposed by the broadcasting industry, consultants normally attempt to get their message across in a thirty- to sixty-second ad. This, combined with the fact that, as one top consultant put it, "TV is basically a visual, entertainment medium," means consultants must emphasize a "look," a "quality," a quick overall impression (*Washington Post,* 1982).

The consultant Robert Goodman claims that he managed to get Malcolm Wallop of Wyoming elected to the Senate in 1976 because he "put a white hat on the Republican candidate and, to the beat of sweeping music, had him lead a horse caravan to Washington. . . ." Ray Strother, a consultant who

handles only Democratic candidates, says he tries for the "soft look"; and Roy Pfautch, president of the American Association of Political Consultants, claims that the key is to get across a "subliminal message" (*Washington Post,* 1982).

While some consultants are concerned by the extent of their influence, the costliness of their product, and the shallowness of their message, many openly relish their assumed power and talk in terms of creating or controlling a candidate. Whether consultants are actually as influential as they sometimes claim, however, is very questionable. First, opposing consultants probably neutralize one another in many campaigns; second, the cause and effect relationship between seeing an ad and voting for a candidate is uncertain; and, finally, every campaign is a sea of uncertainty in which events, personalities, and ideas affect people in unpredictable ways.

---

very strong thematic elements that had good impact not only in solidifying that early support, but also in building a base for a strong run for the presidency in November" (Moore, 1981:40). Both Caddell and Wirthlin went on to become important advisers to their candidates after they had won the presidency.

Media and advertising consultants produce and help to plan the candidate's advertising campaign. In modern campaigns huge sums of money are spent on television and radio advertising, and a great deal of effort goes into attempting to find the right kind of advertising strategy—the best way to show the candidate's personality, to convey the campaign's themes and issues, and to raise questions about the opponents. Though widely attacked for being empty and degrading—for "selling" the candidates like brands of soap—media ads frequently do provide valuable information about the candidates' positions (Patterson and McClure, 1976). Ads attacking opponents can also be effective, though they are risky. Early in the 1980 Democratic race between President Carter and Senator

Kennedy, Gerald Rafshoon, President Carter's media consultant, released an ad showing the president with his daughter, Amy, while a voice at one point said, "Husband, father, president: he's done all three jobs with distinction." The "Amy ad," as it was known among consultants, was a not so subtle attempt to call attention, by way of contrast, to Senator Kennedy's marital problems and rumors about his personal life. Kennedy resented the ad, and his anger was one factor that kept him in the race and prevented the harmony that Carter was seeking.

Candidates today invest well over half their campaign expenditures in media advertising. Yet, for all the money spent, paid advertising is not nearly as important as the "free" time that candidates receive from the media in the form of interviews, debates, and news coverage. Several studies conducted during the 1980 campaign suggested that the ads had very little effect—either during the primaries or during the general election campaign (Robinson, 1981). Of course, no candidate is likely to run the risk of not advertising, for effective ads can be important if they are not neutralized. But media consultants today, realizing the possible limits of ads, have made it their business to advise the candidate on the themes and images to project during the campaign as a whole (Sabato, 1981).

If a campaign is to have any prospect of success, the professional campaign staff must be supplemented by organizations of unpaid volunteers in each of the states. The professional staff makes the key strategic decisions such as where to allocate the candidate's time and resources; the volunteer organization is left with the more mundane tasks of telephoning voters, setting up meetings, and getting supporters to the polls. Volunteers participate, generally speaking, not because they expect a job in Washington, but rather because they believe in the candidate and the cause. (Motives, of course, are frequently mixed, and volunteers may enjoy the "fun" of politics or may be seeking to work their way up in local political circles in preparation for running for office.) Volunteer organizations are particularly important in smaller states, where a large percentage of voters can be contacted personally, and in caucus states, where public participation is generally very low. In these instances, a strong volunteer organization often provides the margin between victory and defeat.

Candidates seeking to build an effective volunteer organization must be especially solicitous of those segments of the population most likely to participate. In recent years, there has been a pronounced tendency for such participants to be committed strongly to a particular cause or ideological viewpoint, a fact that can create problems for the candidate. Early in the campaign, the candidate may need the support of committed activists to get the campaign off the ground; but as the campaign proceeds and achieves success, the candidate may seek a broader base of support by making more moderate appeals to the general public. Early organizational volunteers are then likely to resist this "pragmatism" and put pressure on the candidate not to betray earlier commitments. This can prove highly embarrassing and damaging to the candidate, as in 1972, when George McGovern tried to moderate some of his views on the Vietnamese war only to find his early volunteers threatening to "revolt" and turn on him at the convention.

The "Invisible Primary"

Campaigns have become so drawn out that the phase before the first delegates are actually chosen has been given a distinct name of its own—the "invisible primary" (Hadley, 1976). During this period, roughly from November of the year preceding the election until the first contest for the selection of delegates late in the winter, the candidates vie for media exposure and attempt to control the emerging issues of the campaign. The invisible primary is the period in which news columnists and leading journalists begin to form "pictures" of the candidates that can help or hinder them in their efforts to attract campaign contributions and organizational volunteers; this period is very important for candidates with little national recognition. In this phase of the campaign, journalists play an important role as "power brokers" influencing public perceptions of the candidates (Arterton, 1978).

Yet the influence of the media during this phase can easily be exaggerated. Of equal significance is the groundwork that the candidates lay for the early delegate contests, for if a candidate can do well in these contests, media attention and money will follow. Winning an early contest will not, of course, assure a candidate of the nomination, but it will immediately draw attention to the campaign and can quickly raise a candidate's status from that of an also-ran, lost in the pack, to that of a genuine contender. Indeed, one of the best barometers in predicting primary contests is how the candidate did in the previous contests. To win, it helps to have won.

The early phase of the campaign consists of two very different activities. The invisible primary finds the candidate seeking coverage in the national media, especially among influential newspaper columnists, who, in turn, can influence the television media. At the same time, however, candidates are engaging in intensive one-on-one campaigning in the living rooms of voters in states like Iowa and New Hampshire. The political campaign is thus at this stage a combination of mass politics and "village" politics. Following the first phase of the campaign, which ends, roughly speaking, after the first two or three primaries and caucuses, the focus shifts almost exclusively to mass politics; the can-

Ronald Reagan speaks during the 1980 Republican primary in New Hampshire while John Anderson, Howard Baker, and Robert Dole impatiently await their chances for national television coverage.   *(Wyman/Sygma)*

didates now spend less time in any one state and contact most voters either through advertising or through news coverage of their campaign appearances.

The Calendar of Contests
for the Selection of Delegates

The selection of delegates takes place over a lengthy period that begins in the winter of the election year and extends until early June. Since 1980, Democratic national party rules have set an opening date for the selection of delegates and have been shortening the season for delegate selection. In 1984 more of the large states moved their selection process up to the first three weeks of the primary season. The early contests, as noted, are highly important, not because of the number of del-

egates they select but because they strongly influence the voters' perceptions of which candidates are viable, which in turn has a strong impact on how voters react in subsequent primaries. The first two contests in 1980, Iowa and New Hampshire, chose less than 4 percent of the total delegates, yet received sustained media attention. A poor performance early on can quickly finish a campaign. Thus on the Republican side in 1980, two major Republican candidates, Howard Baker and John Connally, had quit the race by mid-April. By the time the final eight primaries were held on June 3, Reagan's nomination—and President Carter's—were already ensured. Voters in the later contests, at least in 1980, had a vote but no real influence. (In other campaigns, however, the later primaries have been very important in deciding close races.)

The current arrangement of delegate contests

does help to narrow the field, as candidates who fare poorly either drop out or are forgotten. But it also introduces certain biases. The earliest contests take place in states having a voting population that, in demographic and political terms, is not representative of the American population as a whole. More important, the "village-style" politics of these first contests, though offering an opportunity for lesser-known candidates to get started, also gives a relative advantage to candidates who are in a position to invest a great deal of time campaigning in these states. This circumstance, some contend, gives a boost to the "politically unemployed," that is, those holding no office at the time of their campaign. In this group have been Jimmy Carter (1976), Ronald Reagan and George Bush (1980), and Walter Mondale (1984).

Campaign Financing

Campaigns are expensive enterprises. Candidates must have enough money to pay a staff, move themselves and others about the country, produce advertisements, and buy the media time to air them. Without financing, a campaign can come to a virtual standstill. Before the 1972 election, presidential campaigns were financed by private funds and were largely unregulated, except for a ban on loans or direct contributions by business corporations and labor unions. Money for campaigns was raised by the parties (for the general election campaign) and by the candidates' personal organizations (for primary and general election campaigns). The importance of the personal organizations as fund raisers grew in the 1950s and 1960s, as the candidates became more active in the preconvention period and developed capacities to raise funds on their own. They had little choice but to continue their efforts, for the costs of conducting campaigns increased dramatically with an increased reliance on television advertising.

Funds for presidential campaigns were raised from a variety of sources—from small contributions of under $500 (often solicited by direct-mail contacts), from dinners and benefits by celebrity performers, and from large contributions by so-called "fat cats," like W. Clement Stone, who donated $2.8 million to Richard Nixon's campaign in 1968. The sources of funding have varied from one campaign to another. George Wallace in 1968 and George McGovern in 1972 received well over half of their funds for their campaign from relatively small contributions, while President Nixon's campaign in 1972 relied much more heavily on large contributors.

The pressure on candidates to raise funds, the potential inequities introduced by differences in campaign spending, and the fear that large donations could buy influence over elected officials brought increasing demands for legislation. These demands reached a crescendo following the 1972 election, in which President Nixon's campaign engaged in numerous illegal activities, including the receipt of millions of dollars of illegal campaign contributions from business corporations and the funding of the infamous break-in at Democratic headquarters in Washington's Watergate hotel. "Watergate" became a symbol of corruption that not only toppled Nixon's presidency but served as the impetus for extensive reforms in campaign financing.

During the 1970s, Congress passed a series of laws regulating campaign financing that changed the earlier system. The most important piece of legislation was the Campaign Finance Law of 1974, which was challenged in 1976 before the Supreme Court in one of the most celebrated Court cases of the decade, *Buckley v. Valeo*. Parts of the law, including the provision to limit the private expenditures of groups and individuals, were struck down as unconstitutional, though most sections of the law were left standing. The legal framework in place today, therefore, represents a patched-up system that is a product of congressional legislation and administrative rulings as modified by various decisions of the federal courts.

The rules for financing (1) limit the campaign contributions of individuals and groups (including parties), (2) require that all contributions over a minimum amount be recorded or publicly disclosed, and (3) in the case of presidential elections provide for federal funding of elections (see Table 6-2). The expenditures of individuals and groups *not* coordinated with the candidates' campaigns remain uncontrolled. It is difficult to generalize about the effects of the legislation as a whole, for in reality it consists of three separate "laws"—one governing presidential primaries, another the final

TABLE 6-2
RULES GOVERNING FINANCING OF FEDERAL CAMPAIGNS

Basic Rules Governing Contributions and Expenditures

Reporting	Limits on individual contributions	Limits on contributions by political action committees	Limits on expenditures by candidates
All contributions over $100 and all expenditures must be filed with the Federal Election Commission, which is responsible for ensuring compliance.	$1,000 per candidate per election with an annual ceiling of $25,000 to all candidates. $5,000 on contributions to PACs (subtracted from $25,000 ceiling). $20,000 on contributions to national party committees (subtracted from $25,000 ceiling).	$5,000 per candidate per election; no annual spending ceiling. $15,000 to a national party committee.	Candidates may spend an unlimited amount on their own behalf unless they accept public financing.

Rules Governing Individual Federal Campaigns
(Note: There are no limits on independent expenditures in any federal election, i.e., on expenditures by individuals or PACs having no connection with the official campaign.)

Presidential primaries	Presidential elections	House and Senate elections
Public financing optional. Federal government will match all contributions of $250 or less up to $7.5 million, provided at least $5,000 is raised in each of 20 states. If candidate accepts public financing, he or she must observe a ceiling on campaign expenditures ($15 million in 1980).	Public financing is optional for major candidates—all have accepted it thus far. $29.4 million was given to each candidate in 1980. If candidate accepts public financing, he or she must observe a spending ceiling. Minor-party candidates can receive public financing after the election in an amount proportionate to their percentage of the vote, provided they receive at least 5 percent. The same amount is automatically awarded before the next presidential election if the candidate chooses to run.	No public financing, but federal limitations on contributions and expenditures still apply. There is no ceiling on overall campaign expenditures.

presidential campaign, and another the campaigns for the House and Senate. The legislation, however, has achieved, at least in part, two of its main objectives: reducing the campaign contributions of "fat cats" and opening up the entire process of campaign spending and contributions to much closer public scrutiny. But it has also produced certain unintended consequences, the most important of which has been the growth in the number and significance of special fund-raising agencies, the *political action committees* (PACs). These have been especially active in congressional campaigns, though they have begun to play a larger role now in presidential nominating campaigns. As highly professional organizations, certain of the PACs have been in the best position to take advantage of the opportunity to spend without limits for campaign activities uncoordinated with the candidates' campaigns.

In campaigns for the presidential nomination, candidates have the choice of accepting public funding on a matching basis (and accepting the spending limits that accompany it) or rejecting public funds and raising and spending as much as they can. Only one important candidate thus far— John Connally, an aspirant for the Republican nomination in 1980—has rejected public funds. Connally raised $13 million early in the 1980 campaign and easily outspent his opponents in the early stages. The effort netted him only one delegate— called facetiously by some the "$13 million delegate." If ever a case disproves the contention that money alone decides elections, Connally's 1980 campaign stands out as the prime example.

The full effects of the finance legislation on presidential nomination campaigns are still subject to dispute. Analysts generally agree, however, that it has (1) encouraged candidates to begin their campaigns very early in order to meet the requirements for matching public funds, (2) helped lesser-known candidates get started by nearly doubling the amount of money that they would have been able to raise on their own, and (3) limited the amount of money that the prominent and successful candidates can raise and spend by capping official expenditures when public funding is accepted. The last consequence may be the most important. By limiting the amount of official expenditures at rather low levels, the door has been open to a greater role by PACs spending independently of the campaigns. Moreover, these limitations affect the way in which campaign resources are allocated. To ensure the most cost-effective way to reach voters, campaigns may spend less on organizational activities and more on television. In the words of James Baker, campaign manager for George Bush in 1980, "The first things you cut are the grassroots items—pamphlets, buttons, bumper stickers.... You save for the tube" (Orren, 1981:57). The result may be less participation by the average citizen and more power in campaigns for the professional campaign managers and media consultants.

Spending limitations and public financing have helped to reduce, though not eliminate, the differences in the amount of money available to the major aspirants. Candidates must still raise more than half of their money privately, and it remains the case that money tends to flow to the candidates who have shown that they can win. Losers quickly find that their funds dry up, and candidates must maintain some momentum to induce people to contribute.

Candidates' Strategies

Despite the sophisticated technology used in modern campaigns, it is impossible to be entirely scientific in planning or analyzing campaign strategies. Each campaign is new and different, involving its own unique issues, strategic setting, and cast of characters. As in the "science" of warfare, knowledge of previous battles is essential for intelligent planning. Yet any general who tries to duplicate actions that were successful in the last war is in danger of being upset by an opponent who has developed a new strategy. Candidates in presidential campaigns must be aware of the same dangers, especially because recent campaigns have seen constant alterations in the rules and important changes in campaign technologies.

Nomination campaigns can be divided into two basic categories: (1) those in which the president is not a candidate, and (2) those in which the president is seeking renomination. In the first case, the candidates—and there will usually be more than two—attempt to capture the nomination by presenting, in some combination, appeals based on their ideological stance and positions on major issues, a general campaign theme (such as "Get America Going Again"), and their personal qualifications to be president. At the beginning of the campaign, there is often a front-runner, whose previous reputation and initial standing in the polls put the candidate ahead of the others. (This was the position of Muskie in 1972, Reagan in 1980, and Mondale in 1984.) The front-runner position has many obvious advantages, but also certain disadvantages. It makes a candidate the object of close scrutiny by the media and leaves the candidate prey to the desire of many to see an established figure toppled by an underdog. George McGovern managed to capitalize on this desire against Edmund Muskie in 1972, and George Bush sought to do the same against Ronald Reagan in 1980. The fascination of the "new" candidate unexpectedly "coming on" is powerful, a fact that has not gone unnoticed by media consultants such as Charles Guggenhelm:

> There's a phenomenon in American politics (in primaries) which television has emphasized: men who have no record are often more appealing than men who have a record; . . . TV dramatizes this political virginity. Before there was television an unknown couldn't run at all because he couldn't get the exposure. With television, he can become known in a very short time (Wolfson, 1972:15).

A quite different situation exists when an incumbent is running. In this case, the challenger (and there is usually only one serious opponent) must focus attention on the incumbent's record. Owing perhaps to the difficulties of governing today and to the method of nominating candidates, many recent incumbents have faced strong opposition: President Johnson from Senator Eugene McCarthy in 1968, which led Johnson to drop out of the race; President Ford from Ronald Reagan in 1976; and President Carter from Edward Kennedy in 1980. In all these races, the challengers sought to justify opposing the president (and temporarily dividing their party) by attacking the performance of the incumbent.

Challengers have the advantage of being able to criticize the incumbent's record without having to take responsibility for running the country. Most other strategic advantages, however, seem to lie with the incumbent. A sitting president who has managed to grab the lead enjoys the option of ignoring the challenger and "tending to the business of running the country"—the so-called "rose garden" strategy. The incumbent can appear "above the battle," making an opponent seem opportunistic. President Carter used this strategy very effectively against Senator Kennedy in 1980. Trailing Kennedy in the summer polls in 1979, President Carter experienced a surge in popularity in the winter following the seizure of American hostages by the government of Iran. He then canceled a scheduled debate in Iowa with Senator Kennedy and avoided campaigning for most of the primary season, arguing that he could not concern himself with "politics" while such important matters of state were pending. Although there were sound reasons for this decision, it turned out to be excellent politics in the short run. Incumbents are also able to command the media's attention in a way that no challenger can. A press conference, an announcement, or a speech will be covered as a regular presidential activity, even though its purpose and effect may well be political. Finally, incumbents can act, while challengers can only talk. A bold stroke, a new policy, or merely the giving or withholding of project grants to a state or locality is an action only a president can take.

Generalizing about nomination campaigns, we can say that candidates base their campaign appeals on one or more of the following four elements: (1) the record of the incumbent (when running), (2) positions on issues and ideological stances, (3) themes or moods, (4) personal qualifications and character. These elements are woven into campaign strategies, and their relative emphasis helps to define the character of each campaign. A campaign in which the leading contenders emphasize—and differ fundamentally on—important issues gives a greater ideological component to the campaign. In 1972, for example, Democrats faced a fundamental ideological choice between George McGovern on the left and George Wallace on the right. In many cases, however, major ideological differences are absent, as in the case of the Republican nomination campaign of 1980, when all the candidates (except John Anderson) adopted varying shades of conservatism. In such instances voters are unable to distinguish easily between the positions of the candidates, and the choice turns on

Presidential primary campaigns are relentless, physically exhausting public performances, and the camera and microphones are always ready to record even such minor lapses as Edward Kennedy's gesture of weariness. *(Alex Webb/Magnum)*

general themes and on the candidates' qualifications and character.

Candidates communicate their appeals through a number of different channels—speeches, television advertisements, interviews, position papers, and articles (often provided to groups interested in a candidate's stance on some particular issue). As the campaign progresses, the candidates may shift their emphasis from a greater to a lesser reliance on issues (or vice versa). Campaigns, therefore, "develop" and take on a dynamic character of their own. But anyone who expects campaigns to be high-minded seminars in which the candidates continually offer new positions on every subject is likely to be disappointed. Candidates during a campaign are pushed to the limits of physical endurance. Moving from one city to another with little rest or time for reflection, they cannot be concerned chiefly with educating the populace. Their effort is usually directed at delivering a basic political message which contains their theme and positions on a few key issues. Most candidates, in fact, tend to repeat the same basic presentation to every

audience, an address which is called "the speech" by reporters, who hear it until they grow weary with boredom. The reporters, accordingly, often begin to look for news in developments unrelated to the candidate's basic message, even though most people hearing the speech for the first time may find it new and fresh.

Finally, political campaigns—and especially primary campaigns—are affected not just by the candidates' deliberate strategies but by unplanned actions and responses. Over the course of a long campaign, the candidates are barraged by thousands of questions, give scores of interviews, and are asked to comment on news events, often with little or no time to prepare their responses. Not everything can be programmed or planned. A blunder can cripple a campaign, especially in the primaries where candidates are attempting to establish their personal credibility and where other candidates can be turned to as alternatives. Thus when Senator Muskie broke into tears in 1972, his prospects were damaged; and when George Bush in 1980 insisted on a head-to-head debate with Ronald Reagan that would exclude the other Republican candidates, he lost ground for appearing as selfish and unfair. The danger of a "fatal" slip is much greater nowadays because reporters following the candidates tend to look for the exceptional story that can make or break a campaign. It is perhaps only a slight exaggeration to say that the blunder—which cannot always be easily distinguished from a genuine mistake in strategy—has been as decisive in determining the outcome of nominating campaigns as the effectiveness of the overall strategy has.

To speak, as we have spoken, of candidates developing strategies in conjunction with pollsters and advertising consultants may convey the impression that candidates are people without principles who change like chameleons with shifting popular moods. Such a conclusion, however, is unduly cynical. Politicians running for the presidency usually have long records of public service and have been identified with certain causes or principles, and they frequently have strong convictions. Within the framework of these constraints, they may, in the interest of winning, tailor their demands or appeals to "fit" the best strategy, but this is quite a different matter from being putty in the hands of media advisers who "package" them for public consumption.

Instances, of course, can be cited of campaigns that have very nearly fit the advertising model of candidates running only to pander to images of what the people want at the moment. Such campaigns are justly deplored. But it is important to avoid falling into the opposite trap of identifying the healthy campaign as one that is run indiscriminately on issues of any kind. Issue campaigns can also be dangerous when they are conducted on demagogic grounds that appeal, whether cynically or sincerely, to people's hatreds, fears, or unfounded hopes; and they can split a party when the candidate's position represents only one of its factions, as occurred in 1964 when the Republicans chose Barry Goldwater and in 1972 when the Democrats chose George McGovern.

In the end, one should be neither too generous nor too cynical in evaluating the behavior of politicians. As in all political activities, people can be expected to display a range of skills, seriousness, and commitment to the public good. The main question in judging the campaign process is therefore not whether one can find specific examples of empty or demagogic campaigns, for these may exist under any system. Rather, the important issue is an institutional one: whether the system tends on balance to encourage or discourage a campaign process that leads the candidates to avoid trivializing politics, and that adequately takes into account the candidates' qualifications for the presidency and their potential for winning a broad base of support. This is the perspective from which the constitution maker judges electoral institutions.

Media Influence

It is impossible to talk about the modern campaign without taking into account the role of the media. In large measure, the entire campaign is conducted in and through the media, as candidates vie for media attention, arrange their schedules to conform to media deadlines, and seek to fashion a positive media image. At the heart of the "media problem," however, lies the question of whether somehow the media manage unduly to structure the entire choice, making popular control more an illusion than a reality.

The key to media influence during the primaries lies in the fact that the decision of voters in primary elections is strongly influenced by what they perceive to be the candidates' chances of winning the nomination. This perception is based in part on the objective performance of candidates in primary contests. A series of extremely poor showings is enough to convince voters that a candidate is finished, while a series of strong showings will indicate a winner. But in between these extremes, people's perceptions can be affected by how well the candidates do in the primaries in relation to the vague standard of how they are expected to do. A candidate who does better than expected conveys the impression of coming on, which gives that candidate an added boost. By contrast, a candidate who does not do as well as expected is suddenly a fading star whose prospects are diminished. Obviously, the criterion of "what is expected" is in some degree a judgment made by reporters in the media, not a fact in any objective sense. When journalists depict the rise of a candidate on the basis of performance against expectations, they become part of the nominating process rather than merely recorders of that process. It is in the news interpretation of primary results that journalists exercise their greatest influence on the nominating campaign.

One scholar of the media, Michael Robinson, has coined the term "medialities" to refer to "developments or situations to which the media have given importance by emphasizing, expanding or featuring them in such a way that their real significance has been modified, distorted, or obscured" (Robinson, 1981:191). Robinson cites two specific examples from the 1976 campaign: (1) emphasis on a Carter "victory" in the Iowa caucus, in which Carter received 28 percent of the vote, which was more than any other candidate but considerably less than the 37 percent who voted uncommitted; (2) Reagan's "unexpected" loss—that is, unexpected by the media—to President Ford in New Hampshire by a mere 1,100 votes, a margin so small that the result might have been interpreted as a dead heat. In 1980, one could cite the example of John Anderson's showings in Vermont and Massachusetts. Anderson narrowly lost both primaries, but did so much better than expected that he received a tremendous amount of media attention, which provided part of the impetus for his subsequent independent candidacy.

No doubt, many such examples of media interpretation could be cited in the coverage of presidential nominating campaigns. To some extent, however, criticisms of the media miss the larger point. In focusing on what is interesting and newsworthy, journalists emphasize aspects of the campaign that frequently differ from those which politicians in a more deliberative process might take into account. The criteria of news are different, ultimately, from those normally employed by politicians (Polsby, 1981). The fact is that even with "perfect" reporting—which no one can quite define anyhow—the media would still exert an enormous influence on the nominating process. Because the nominating process is arranged as a series of public contests in which the results of one round of contests affect those in the next, the reporting of these inevitably takes on a great deal of significance. Blind criticism of the media is often a cover for a failure to consider the logical consequences of a system in which the media are permitted to play so important a role.

The Conventions

Depending on one's taste, the national party convention may be judged the most absurd or the most ingenious of all political institutions. From their inception, conventions have been the largest of formal political gatherings and certainly the most boisterous. Where else can adults get together and yell, shout, march around, and blow balloons and horns and have all this behavior judged acceptable? And where else can so many people from the same party come together, build personal contacts, forge alliances, and come to understand the complexity and diversity of American politics? H. L. Mencken, the famous humorist and essayist, perhaps described it best: "... There is something about a national convention that makes it as fascinating as a revival or a hanging. It is vulgar, it is ugly, it is stupid, it is tedious, it's hard upon the cerebral centers, ... and yet it is somehow charming."

Conventions, however, have lost much of their influence in recent years, if not their charm. Thirty years ago a textbook treatment of presidential nominations would have had relatively little to say about primaries, but a great deal to say about conventions. Today, the emphasis must be just the reverse. The reason is obvious: nomination decisions were once made at the conventions, whereas recent conventions have merely ratified a decision that is made and known in advance. An entire vocabulary that once used to describe convention politics has now virtually vanished; and a new one, derived from the preconvention contests during which delegates are selected, has taken its place. Words such as "stampede" (the sudden transfer of delegates to one of the candidates) and "dark horse" (a candidate with little initial support or prominence who is nonetheless a possible choice as a compromise on a later ballot) have been replaced by terms such as "momentum" (the enthusiasm engendered by a strong primary showing that will carry over to the next set of primaries) and "outsider" (a candidate with little national prominence and few party con-

Modern national party conventions often lack drama because the nominees are known in advance, and so the cameras of the media tend to focus on the more lighthearted moments—and costumes. *(Diego Goldberg/Sygma)*

nections who nonetheless hopes to win public favor). Although a "postreform" movement now exists and has been trying to restore some of the previous prerogatives to the convention, it seems likely that until some of the current laws are changed, nomination decisions made by the convention will remain a rarity.

The transformation of the role of the convention can be seen in the role of the delegate. Formerly, delegates were selected as discretionary agents, able to move from one candidate to another as they chose—or, more likely, at the direction of key power brokers who exercised important influence over blocs of delegates. Sometimes, the decisions were made by the delegates *before* the convention met, but the choice still remained with the delegates. (Since 1952, every nomination has been made on the first ballot.) Today's delegates are usually bound by the results of the selection process to a specific candidate. As long as one of the can-

didates manages to win a majority of the delegates, which has been the pattern in recent years, the conventions will merely record the results of the primaries and caucuses.

It is no small irony that conventions began to lose their effective power at just about the same time they became widely observed by the American public through television. Advance knowledge of the nominee makes for poor television, and the news coverage of conventions has become, at times, a rather tiresome show. "News" frequently consists of reporters dredging up rumors, spreading them, and then asking various people for their reactions. In the reporters' defense, it must be acknowledged that it is difficult to make an interesting program of a four-day event in which little of genuine interest may be taking place.

Representation Almost everyone who studies conventions nowadays has puzzled over the question of how representative they are of the party rank and file. Curiously, political reformers became highly preoccupied with this issue at just about the same time that the delegates were losing their most important power—the discretion to make an independent choice in selecting the nominee. The Democratic party reforms in 1968 were sparked in part by the claim that the delegates did not accurately reflect the party's constituencies—in particular, certain minority and disadvantaged groups. Accordingly, the McGovern-Fraser reform commission (1968–1972) took the extraordinary step of requiring quotas for certain groups—blacks, women, young people—in proportion to their population within each state. This action, based on the theory which equated representation with a precise mirroring of specified groups, met with a good deal of resistance and was subsequently removed as a formal requirement except in the case of women, who are now guaranteed half of the delegate seats at Democratic conventions. (Strong affirmative action programs for including the other groups are still in effect.) For many—but not all—groups in society, today's conventions are more representative of their parties' constituencies than conventions of the prereform era.

Proportionate correspondence between the number of delegates from a group and that group's size in society is not, however, the only aspect of representation. Political analysts also ask whether the delegates reflect the ideological views of their rank and file and whether the delegates are well-suited to deliberate and act on behalf of the interests of the party. As long as extensive surveys have been made of convention delegates (since 1952), it has been found that Democratic delegates have been more liberal than the average rank and file Democrat and Republican delegates more conservative. Yet a finding about the delegates' ideological position, while interesting, may tell us little about how they *behave* at the conventions. In the past, many delegates were regulars of their state and local party organizations; and although they themselves may have been more liberal or conservative than their constituents, they defined their role at the convention in terms of promoting their party's overall interest. Quite often, this conception of their role led them to moderate their personal ideological views and adopt more flexible and pragmatic positions.

Thus the question of representation turns to a large extent not on criteria of the race, sex, or ideological disposition of the delegates but on the particular delegate role that they adopt. A "professional" orientation refers to a delegate's willingness to put the party's overall interest over personal positions. An "amateur" or "purist" orientation, by contrast, refers to a delegate's insistence on promoting a particular cause or viewpoint regardless of its effect on the party's chances of success (Polsby and Wildavsky, 1980). Analyses of conventions after 1968 have found not only that delegates tend to be even more ideologically differentiated from the parties' followings than in the past, but also that more delegates define their role in platform issues as "amateurs," advocating the particular demands of their ideological or special interest group (Malbin, 1981). The postreform movement in progress will probably change this somewhat.

The Platform While recent conventions have not made an independent choice about the nominee, they have played an important role in writing party rules and in determining the platform. The platform is the party's statement of principles and pledges, written in part with a view to informing the people of where the party stands, in part with a view to attracting votes. Once a rather brief document, today the platform has grown into a book-length statement that addresses in great detail the party's positions on most areas of public policy. The prospective nominees will generally have the greatest influence in determining what goes into the platform; but there are frequent instances today in which, because of the character of the convention delegates, the nominees lose control of certain issues to defeated opponents or special interest groups. One delegate at the 1980 Democratic convention, serving as an organizational whip for President Carter, described the problem as follows:

Last night they were Carter delegates pure and simple. Today they are Carter delegates who are labor delegates, . . . who are women delegates, . . . who are teacher delegates. It's just not possible for a Carter whip to walk up and down the aisle and say "thumbs up," "thumbs down" (Malbin, 1981:134).

Platforms today, therefore, often contain some provisions that can prove difficult or embarrassing for the candidate attempting to appeal broadly to the American people. It is not uncommon, therefore, for candidates not to endorse each and every one of the platform's provisions. And even when they do accept all its promises, they will not always follow through on them once in office. Cynicism is not the only explanation. Circumstances change rapidly in politics, and judgments made by a candidate during a campaign—tinged, as they are likely to be, by the desire to win votes—may have to give way to the realities of governing the nation. The many instances in which presidents ignore or disregard their party's platform have led some to assert that platforms are meaningless: "The platform is generally regarded as a document that says little, binds no one, and is forgotten by politicians as quickly as possible after it is adopted" (Truman, 1951:282). Yet researchers who have analyzed the relationship between platform pledges and party performance have generally concluded that the platforms present fairly accurate and serious statements of intention; and in elections when the parties have been opposed to each other on fundamental issues, these differences have been clearly reflected in the language of the platforms (Pomper, 1980; Kessel, 1977).

As documents that influence voting behavior, however, platforms have almost certainly diminished in importance. Before 1912, when candidates did not ordinarily give campaign speeches, the platform was the single best statement of the candidate's (and the party's) position, even if it wasn't always adhered to. Today, the platforms are too long and detailed for most voters to bother reading or studying them, although voters may become aware of certain key planks or of positions that affect their own special concerns. Candidates today also have other means—advertisements, debates, and speeches—by which to communicate their own positions. Indeed, the nominee's acceptance speech, which is now one of the highlights of the convention, usually provides a better statement than the platform of the basic themes of the campaign.

(Franklin Roosevelt in 1932 was the first candidate to deliver in person an acceptance speech at the convention, breaking with the tradition of waiting to be informed of the convention's decision.) Overall, then, voters today focus more on the candidates' own rhetoric than on that of the platforms to learn about the candidates' intentions, and candidates probably feel bound more by their own words than by their party's statements.

Vice Presidential Nominations One matter of genuine suspense in most modern conventions is the choice of the vice presidential candidate. Actually, conventions today only go through the motions of choosing the vice presidential nominee; the real decision is now made by the presidential candidate and ratified by the convention. The last time a convention decided the vice presidential nominee was in 1956, when Adlai Stevenson left the choice to the convention. Since that time, some delegates have occasionally resisted—or talked about resisting—the presidential candidate's decision, but to no avail. The prerogative of the presidential nominee to pick a running mate is now generally recognized.

With the exception of incumbents, presidential candidates generally wait until the convention to make known their choice of a running mate so as not to appear presumptuous (after all, they have yet to be officially nominated) and to maintain at least some element of drama in the proceedings. Presidential candidates generally select their vice presidential nominees with an eye to balancing the ticket and finding a candidate who can be helpful in the upcoming campaign. Balancing the ticket means choosing a candidate with a different base of strength and support within the party; for example, a southerner (like Jimmy Carter) may look for a northerner (like Walter Mondale), or a conservative (like Ronald Reagan) may look for a moderate (like George Bush). Balance, however, must itself be balanced with compatibility: presidential candidates would appear simply opportunistic and lose credibility if they chose candidates who differed significantly on major issues. Finding a "strong" running mate is also important, for today vice presidential candidates receive a great deal of public scrutiny during the campaign, in part because people are aware that, with the number of assassination attempts in recent years, the vice presidential candidate might well have to accede to the presidency. Moreover, with nominations for president now made by the people and not party leaders, everyone is aware that a vice president will acquire the "name recognition" and reputation that can help launch a presidential campaign. It might be too strong to say that vice presidents today are heirs apparent for the presidency, but it is well known that the selection of an attractive and relatively young vice presidential nominee marks the beginning of the presidential selection process of four or eight years hence.

The Current Nominating System: Evaluation and Proposed Changes

The nomination process is in one respect a key phase of the entire presidential selection process, for it is at this stage that the field of potential candidates is narrowed to the two major contenders. The nomination process is, therefore, clearly an important constitutional issue, even though its major elements are fixed not by Constitutional provisions or by federal law, but mainly by state laws and party rules. Although never "legislated" in a single, comprehensive act of constitution making, the nominating process by the 1960s had nevertheless evolved piecemeal (and with numerous changes along the way) into a process that operated with a reasonable degree of consistency and that enjoyed the confidence of the American people. By 1968, however, this "mixed system" crumbled under reform pressures for a more open and democratic system. But the new system that resulted from the reforms has itself generated a great deal of criticism, and many proposals for change are currently being discussed.

Pros and Cons of the Current System Defenders of the current system point first to its greater "openness" when compared with previous systems. Voters now play a much larger role than in the past, and the nominations are determined largely by popular choice. Second, defenders argue that the selection process now makes it possible for outsiders to raise new issues and, if successful in their appeals, to win the nomination. As a result, it is

said, the people enjoy the opportunity to choose among a wider variety of candidates and are not limited to the compromise choices that party leaders allegedly favor.

Critics of the current system contend that because of the low participation in primaries, the unrepresentativeness of the electorate, and the degree of media influence, the actual degree of popular control has been greatly exaggerated. Just as important, critics argue that too much emphasis has been placed on the value of democratic participation to the exclusion of other important values, such as ensuring the experience and high quality of the nominees, creating and maintaining broad coalitions within the parties, and avoiding some of the dangers posed by a selection process that is too long and open.

The quality of nominees is of course a very difficult matter to assess objectively. Many argue, however, that there is danger in a choice made by the voters alone that avoids the check of "peer review" by politicians who may know the candidates firsthand and who may have had to deal with them on a regular basis. The current system, critics maintain, presents the electorate with a choice that is in one respect too wide and in another not wide enough. It is too wide because it opens the field to outsiders who, though capable of capturing the people's affections temporarily, may lack the experience to govern effectively. Indeed, it may be precisely the quality of being an "insurgent" that endears a candidate temporarily to the primary electorate, even though this very quality may make it more difficult for the candidate to win the support of other politicians. On the other hand, the choice is not wide enough, because it limits the field to those willing to declare an active candidacy and campaign in the primaries. For a former president (like Gerald Ford in 1980) or for a senior leader in the party it may seem inappropriate. Yet the failure to campaign today excludes one from consideration, in contrast to the previous system in which the convention could draft reluctant or inactive candidates.

Critics have also argued that the current system does little to ensure that the electoral coalition of the victorious candidate can be transformed into a governing coalition. Nominees today capture the party label on their own without necessarily having to build close relations with members of Congress and local elected officials, whose political support is so important once the president has been elected. The backing of the people, though an important element of strength, is no substitute for the support of governing officials, since their power base may help even a president whose standing at the polls has declined. Nor is it the case that the nominee under the current system is always the choice most satisfactory to the party as a whole. The nominee may be the favorite of the largest faction of those voting within the party but may not have the support of the majority. Voting cannot perform the act of weighing degrees of preference, nor can it reflect the voters' second or third choices.

Finally, critics argue that the current system creates problems for the conduct of government. The selection system, they contend, should be viewed not as an end in itself, but as a means to ensuring sound governance. Apart from the difficulties of coalition building just noted, the length of the current nominating process places incumbents, when challenged, in the position of acting— or seeming to act—throughout the final year of their first term for short-run political advantage. Moreover, when elections are uppermost in the people's minds, there is a tendency for everyone to look ahead; and this state of mind can drain the presidency of its constituted authority and some of its prestige and respect.

Proposals for Change   What should be done with the present system? Advocates of a predominantly democratic system would be content to leave it as it is, or else to "rationalize" the process by developing a series of four or five regional primaries. Some would even prefer to make it more democratic by doing away with the "fiction" of convention choice and having the nominees chosen in a national primary, with provision for a runoff in the event that no candidate received a majority (or in some proposals, 40 percent) in the first round. All these alternatives are based on the premise that the most important value in the system, and the only one that can ensure its legitimacy, is democracy in the choice of the nominees.

Some critics favor mechanisms for reintroducing an element of discretionary authority for party leaders in the selection of the nominees. The nominating decision, at least in part, should be the product of a representative process of decision making, rather than a product of direct democracy. This objective could be accomplished in a number of different ways. One would be to reduce (somehow) the number of primaries and to shorten the primary season to a period of approximately five weeks. Under such a system, a rough idea of the popular preference would become known, but the convention would still have the prerogative of assessing the results of the primary process and making its own decision. Another idea, already implemented in a modest way by the Democratic party in 1982, allows for the selection of unbound delegates outside of the usual primary or caucus systems. In a similar vein, some have advocated limiting the number of delegates formally bound to candidates to a certain percentage—say 50 percent—of each state's delegation. These and similar proposals all share the view that the nominating process would be improved if the delegates, either before or during the convention, had a degree of independent discretion in choosing the parties' nominees. This would strengthen the parties, help ensure a less chaotic selection process, and increase the likelihood of finding candidates who could hold together the diverse element of their coalitions.

THE GENERAL ELECTION CAMPAIGN

Imagine that you have campaigned for over a year, participated in over thirty primaries, delivered hundreds of speeches, and shaken thousands of hands—and then you wake up one morning only to say, "Now the *real* campaign begins." This is the enviable—or perhaps unenviable—position of the successful candidates in the nomination contests: all they have earned for their labor is the right to wage another campaign.

Victory in the general election is achieved by winning a majority of the electoral votes. From the moment of the nomination until the eve of the final election on the first Tuesday after the first Monday in November, the candidates expend every effort to obtain the magic number of 270 electoral votes. Because electoral votes are awarded on a state-by-state basis, with the candidate winning a statewide plurality receiving all the state's electoral votes, candidates gear their campaigns to fifty separate

TABLE 6-3
TIME OF PRESIDENTIAL VOTE CHOICE, 1952–1980
Percentages of Those Voting

Decision time	Year							
	1952	**1956**	**1960**	**1964**	**1968**	**1972**	**1976**	**1980**
By the end of the conventions	68	78	62	66	59	63	54	59
After the conventions	21	12	25	21	19	23	22	15
Within two weeks of the election	9	8	10	9	15	8	17	16
On Election Day	2	2	3	4	7	6	7	10
Total	100	100	100	100	100	100	100	100

Sources: SRC / CPS election studies; and Asher, 1980:316.

races. Although it is unlikely for a candidate to win the presidency while losing the popular vote, the strategies of the campaign nonetheless are based first on winning electoral votes and not on gaining a national plurality.

The Primaries versus the General Election

General election campaigns differ in many crucial respects from nomination campaigns. Recall that in primary campaigns a candidate, while seeking to defeat all opponents, also has to keep in mind (if possible) how to mollify them and bring them back into the fold to support the ticket. Normally, this imperative operates to impose a degree of restraint. In final election campaigns, by contrast, all the chips are on the table, and fewer political advantages are gained by holding back or pulling any punches. As a consequence, presidential elections often have undertones of fairly nasty campaigning, though one check on overtly bad behavior is the possibility that it will backfire in the eyes of the public.

The general election campaign also differs from nomination campaigns in that the contest is now between the parties, not within each party. To some extent, voters are selecting not just an individual but a "representative" of a party having a long history and record of its own; and, despite a decline in partisan identification over the past two decades, most voters still retain a standing preference for one of the major parties. The "party" element, absent from the nomination races, becomes an important factor influencing voting behavior in the general election. Candidates campaign not only on the basis of the four elements noted in relation to primary campaigns—the incumbent's record (when running), stands on issues and ideology, general political themes, and qualifications—but also on the basis of the records, reputations, and public philosophies of the political parties.

Last, the choice in the general election is narrowed to two, or at most three, significant candidates. The qualities of these candidates are much better known to the voters than are those of the candidates in primary contests, where there are sometimes several aspirants and some "new" faces. With fewer candidates, and with the "stabilizing" effect of party identification, final election campaigns tend to be somewhat less volatile than primary campaigns. More voters have already all but made up their minds before the campaign begins, barring, of course, a wholly unexpected development. Still, there are many voters who do not make their choice until the campaign is under way; and as partisan attachment in recent years has grown weaker, the number of voters able to be influenced by the campaign has increased. In this sense at least, general election campaigns have taken on more of the characteristics of nominating campaigns, in that more voters are now open to persuasion during the campaign itself.

Financing

Before the campaign finance legislation of 1974, the funding for general elections, as noted, was raised privately by the parties and the candidates' organizations. Raising money was an important part of any campaign, and it became all the more so as campaign costs began to skyrocket in the 1950s. But while money has always been an important campaign resource, it has by no means been decisive. This has especially been the case in presidential elections where both parties were generally able to raise at least enough money to run a credible campaign, and where so much of the information and publicity of presidential contests has come "free" as news coverage. Thus, between 1932 and 1972, which was a period of "private" campaign funding, Republican presidential candidates regularly outspent Democrats, but lost more races than they won; and when Republicans were elected, their advantage in money spent was, if anything, only a small factor in explaining their success.

The campaign finance legislation of the 1970s has greatly reduced the differences in funds expended by or on behalf of the two major-party candidates. Both candidates receive the same amount in public funds—$29 million in 1980—and public funds constitute the greater part of the total expenditures of the campaign. Differences in spending on behalf of the candidates result today from two sources: (1) independent expenditures by groups and individuals on behalf of a candidate and (2) expenditures by state and local parties, which are now permitted to spend without limit on certain campaign activities like voter registration and getting voters to the polls. The growth in spending in these categories in the future could effectively undermine the law's intention to equalize campaign spending. In 1980, political action committees became more active than before in the campaign, and the Republican state and local parties spent $14 million while their Democratic counterparts spent only $4 million.

Minor parties occupy a complicated status under the law. Any party that has not received more than 5 percent in the last election is ineligible for public funding *before* the elections. Since the minor parties must still raise funds privately under the contribution limitations imposed by the law, many have argued that the system places them at a double disadvantage: the minor party receives no public funds and can raise money only in tiny amounts. If, however, a minor party receives more than 5 percent of the national popular vote, it is entitled to receive a share of public funding after the election, based on its proportion of the vote, and is automatically given the same share for the *next* election, if it competes. The general effect of the law might be said to make it difficult for a minor party to get started but, once it has started and has received more than 5 percent of the vote, to encourage it to remain in existence. This effect would seem to run counter to one of the constructive roles played by minor parties in the past, which was to enter the competition temporarily, force a readjustment of the positions of the major parties, and then go out of existence.

The Character of the Campaign

The presidential campaign is an extra-Constitutional development that has evolved into its current, loose form as a result of changes in norms, traditions, and technology. The founders' plan to avoid anything like a popular campaign gave way quickly to the party-run campaigns, with their mass rallies, slogans, and torchlight parades. The campaigns provided the electorate with theater, spectacle, and the thrill of involvement in a major national event (Rubin, 1981). Yet, in a bow to the founders' norms, candidates in the nineteenth century seldom went out to campaign or make speeches. Their positions were made known in letters of acceptance of their party's nomination and through occasional communications to citizens or to newspapers. The first candidate to campaign in earnest for the presidency was Stephen Douglas in 1860, and his experiment was not repeated in any extensive way until William Jennings Bryan went on the campaign trail in 1896. And Bryan, despite logging thousands of miles and delivering hundreds of speeches—all without the benefit of electronic amplifiers—lost the race to William McKinley, who conducted a "front-porch campaign," in which he stayed at home and received citizens, from time to time stepping out on the front porch to deliver a speech. Woodrow Wilson in 1912 was the first victorious presidential candidate to have campaigned extensively. In general, then, campaigns before 1916 were run *for* the candidate *by* the party. The candidate's positions were the positions enunciated in the platforms, voters were contacted by the party organizations, funding was handled by the parties, and debates about the candidate's merits were conducted through party-run newspapers.

Today, in contrast, candidates crisscross the country at a dizzying pace, making one speech after another and issuing various statements on the issues of the day. Funding is provided by the federal government; and the voters are contacted largely through television by means of campaign advertisements, news coverage, or direct candidate access in speeches, debates, and interviews. The organization of the campaign relies in part on the regular apparatus of the national and state parties, but the campaigns are actually headed up by the candidate's personal organization formed during the nominating campaign.

The campaign is all the candidates have; whether far behind or far ahead, they know the stakes are too great to leave anything undone. Candidates who know they are likely to lose—like Barry Goldwater in 1964 or George McGovern in 1972—still live in hope of a sudden turn of events; and candidates aware that they are likely to win— like Lyndon Johnson in 1964 and Richard Nixon in 1972—will begin to think of winning by as much as possible. It is not just victory, but the margin of victory that counts: a landslide will give a president a much stronger claim to possessing a broad mandate, thereby increasing the chances of getting more programs enacted.

One remarkable aspect of American politics is that the outcome of so many races remains in doubt up to the last moment. The elections of 1960, 1968, 1976, and 1980 were all considered by pollsters to be too close to call, even though Reagan's victory in 1980 turned out to be substantial. The closeness of campaigns adds to their excitement and provides confirmation of what the candidates already know: the campaign counts.

Each campaign is a story unto itself with its own special characteristics and decisive events. About the only influencing factor that can be said to be a constant in campaigns is whether or not an incumbent is running. If an incumbent is running, no matter what the positions of the candidates may be, and no matter what strategies they may adopt, the election is bound to turn in large measure on the public's judgment of the president's performance and on whether things are "going well." When an incumbent is not running—as in 1968—the candidates stand a bit more on their own. But even here, an indirect incumbency factor still exists because the candidate of the party holding the presidency is held partly accountable for the performance of the incumbent. Thus, in almost every presidential election, voters are taking the measure not only of the issues, themes, and qualifications of the candidates but also of whether a change is needed from the policies of the incumbent or the incumbent's party. Campaigns look backward as well as forward.

Campaigns have now developed a certain tempo and center on a few key events. The first is the nominating convention itself. Millions of people watch the convention proceedings, and a bitterly divided convention can harm a candidate by revealing deep tensions within the party. The convention also provides a forum for what is probably the most important address a candidate will make: the acceptance speech. It is here—and virtually here alone—that the candidates are provided with a national television audience for a long speech in which they can communicate their ideas without the intermediation of journalists. In 1980, it was Reagan's widely acclaimed speech that helped get his campaign off to so strong a start.

The next (possible) key event in the campaign is the face-to-face television debate. No firmly established tradition exists for debates—they have been held only in 1960, 1976, and 1980—but the pressure to hold them now seems to be growing. The idea of a direct showdown or "shoot-out" generates a tremendous amount of attention, so much so that some analysts feel that too much emphasis has been placed on debate performance. In general, the debates have tended to be rather tepid affairs, with the candidates attempting to guard against making blunders such as President Ford's statement in 1976 that Poland was *not* in the Soviet sphere of influence. The media, naturally disposed to play up the competitive aspect of a contest, look to establish a winner, and that fact itself can turn out to be more important than the content of the debates. The extent of the impact of the debates on the voters has been a matter of dispute among pollsters, although it is clear that in a close campaign debates can be decisive. If there is any one generalization that can be made about the debates thus far, it is that they have helped the candidate initially perceived as having less experience—that is, the challengers Jimmy Carter (in 1976) and Ronald Reagan (in 1980) and the young Senator John Kennedy (in 1960). The debates provide a forum where the two candidates are placed on an equal footing. The less experienced candidates who have held their own have been in an excellent position to counter any charges that they could not measure up to their opponents.

Campaign strategies involve hundreds of different decisions based on geographical considerations and the targeting of various groups. For example, in the 1980 campaign, Reagan's strategists sought initially to boost their candidate's standing in Carter's home base in the south, not necessarily to win these states but to force President Carter to spend valuable campaign time ensuring his support. (In the end, and somewhat unexpectedly, Reagan carried every southern state except Carter's home state of Georgia.) In regard to the targeting of groups, President Carter's strategists found that women voters were especially sensitive to the threat of war, and the Carter campaign made special efforts to depict Reagan's stands as bellicose and likely to endanger peace.

Underlying all the strategies, however, is a rather simple idea: to make the issues and factors on which the candidate is strongest—and the opponent weakest—the focal points of the campaign. Thus a candidate whose personal experience and qualifications seem well regarded in comparison with the opponent's may attempt to make them the focal point of the campaign. The opponent, sensing the possibility of convincing the electorate on certain key issues, may seek to make issues the focal point. Each candidate, in other words, attempts to set the terms of the campaign debate and force the other candidate to fight on that ground. The opposing candidate may at some point have to meet the challenge, if only to blunt the criticisms. But often one finds the candidates talking not *at* each other but *past* each other, with each candidate attempting to fix the terrain on which the campaign debate takes place.

In the 1980 campaign, for example, President

Carter's strategists revealed afterwards that they sought to keep the discussion away from Carter's record or his own leadership qualities. In the words of his pollster, Patrick Caddell:

> His [Carter's] approval rating was negative. . . . In terms of his competence and vision, we found that the feelings about the president's competence had a very high negative [rating]. . . . In addition to that, the events that we were looking at [inflation and the Iranian situation] were not particularly good (Moore, 1981:188).

With all these disadvantages, the decision was made to fight the campaign on party loyalty and especially on the doubts that the public was felt to have about Ronald Reagan's leadership ability— the fact that "his solutions were too simplistic," that he had the tendency of "shooting from the hip," and that he was perceived to be more of a risk on "keeping us out of war." For Reagan, on the other hand, the key was to focus the campaign debate on Jimmy Carter and his record. To be sure, he had to present his own positive message and prove his own capacity, but the central issue, in his pollster's words, was to make the "election a referendum on the performance of the incumbent president, Jimmy Carter" (Moore, 1981:195). Reagan's success in the television debate in Cleveland was generally credited to his closing statements in which he posed the simple questions, "Are you better off than you were four years ago?" and "Is America as respected throughout the world?"

The Current Electoral System: Evaluation and Proposed Reforms

The Electoral College   The most controversial structural feature of the presidential election is the electoral college system. The electoral college as it operates today is based on a combination of Constitutional provision, state law, and practice. The Constitution assigns to each state a number of electoral votes equal to the sum of its senators and representatives. When voters cast their ballots in the general election, they are in reality voting not directly for the candidates but for a slate of electors within each state that is pledged to vote for a par-

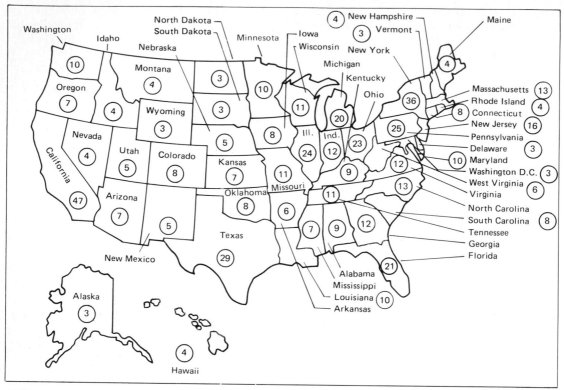

FIGURE 6-1
Electoral votes by states. Total electoral votes: 538. The winner must receive at least
270 electoral votes.

ticular candidate. By *state* law, all the states except Maine stipulate that the candidate winning a plurality of the statewide votes—that is, more than any other candidate—will receive *all* that state's electoral votes. Within each state, accordingly, the race for the electors is conducted under a "winner take all" system.

Critics attack the current system on two grounds. First, they point out that it allows the electors to vote as they please despite state laws to the contrary. (By Constitutional provision, state laws may not bind the electors.) Known as the problem of the "faithless elector," this aspect of the system is theoretically troublesome, but in practice faithlessness has been rare and has never affected the outcome of an election. The difficulty could be

eliminated by an amendment that would assign electoral votes automatically without using electors themselves.

A second and clearly more substantial objection centers on the fact that it is possible for a candidate receiving a nationwide plurality in the popular vote to lose the electoral vote and not be chosen president. This result can occur when a candidate wins some states by a large margin while losing others narrowly. It has occurred unambiguously in only one instance, 1888, when Grover Cleveland, the Democratic candidate, received 90,000 votes more than his Republican opponent, Benjamin Harrison, but lost decisively in the electoral vote, 233 to 168. In three other cases—1824, 1876, and 1960—an argument can be made that the plurality winner of the popular vote did not become president, but the cases are far from being clear-cut.

The most frequently suggested plan for reform is to replace the electoral college with a direct national election in which the winner of the national popular vote would become president. In order to prevent the possibility of electing a president with a narrow plurality, advocates of this plan generally add the further provision that in the event that no candidate receives more than 40 percent of the vote in the election, a second, runoff election would be held between the two candidates who received the most votes in the first round.

Defenders of the current system concede that the choice of a "minority" president could pose problems. They point out, however, that the nation has survived such a result (or results) in the past and would do so again in the future. On the other hand, defenders see certain merits to the current system. First, it provides an important support for federalism because it makes candidates and strategists think in terms of separate states and increases the importance of working through existing state party organizations. Second, the current arrangement minimizes the danger of having a long-drawn-out dispute in a close election like that of 1960, when Kennedy and Nixon were separated by less than two-tenths of a percentage point (if that). Under a direct-election plan, a recount would require that every ballot in the nation be recounted while all waited in suspense, and in any recount there is always a certain percentage of error. Under the present system, on the other hand, recounts are limited to those states that are closely contested, making the problem much more manageable. Finally, defenders of the current system argue that the direct-action plan is fraught with serious difficulties. Because of the necessity of a runoff provision under the direct-election plan, there would appear to be an increased incentive for third parties to compete because they would be able to demonstrate their strength in the first round and then hope to bargain their support in between the two elections. Indeed, it is the unpredictability of this aspect of the direct-election plan that has led many people to favor the present system, even with its possible flaws. The dangers of the present system are at least known and manageable; those that

might result from a new system are unknown and largely incalculable.

The Single, Six-Year Term   Another reform that has attracted wide support in recent years is the proposal to limit the president to a single, six-year term. Advocates of this amendment argue that it would give the president more time to develop programs and govern without the threat of being quickly replaced. More important, it would eliminate the unsavory aspects of incumbent politics during election years. Proponents argue that elections tend too often to make incumbents act irresponsibly. In order to improve their chances for the upcoming election, incumbents play politics with the issues, withholding or bestowing federal grants in order to win support, exploiting various foreign policy ventures, and stimulating the economy to make it look healthy in the short run, whatever the injurious consequences over the long run. By removing the temptation to engage in such politics, and by putting presidents above any suspicion that their policies are merely election-year devices, the six-year term would greatly improve the prospects for sound presidential governance.

Critics of this proposal counter that it would deprive the country of the sanction of an electoral contest to restrain presidents; that six years is too long to give someone power without a chance to take it away, but too short to provide ample opportunity for a person of great distinction to make a mark on public life; that it might weaken presidential power by making the president a "lame duck" (that is, an officeholder who everyone knows must leave by a certain date); and that, given the unpredictable consequences of change, no change of such importance should be undertaken unless the evils of the current system are so clear and unmistakable that almost any alternative would be preferable.

CONGRESSIONAL ELECTIONS

Moving from presidential to congressional contests is a bit like changing accommodations from a first-class hotel to a slightly run-down roadside inn. It is not just that presidential candidates, unlike those running for Congress, have someone else to carry their luggage; it is also that presidential campaigns seem to offer much more glamour. In presidential contests, the candidates are followed by a retinue of aides, besought by the media to offer interviews, and cheered (or jeered) by large audiences. In congressional contests, and especially those for the House, the candidates often move around obscurely within their districts, seeking out media coverage and looking for gatherings of people willing to tolerate an intrusion and listen briefly to a political appeal.

Contests for the presidency and Congress could hardly be more different. These differences are woven into the fabric of the Constitution and flow from the nature of the offices in question. In the case of the presidency, we are dealing with a constituency that spans a vast and heterogeneous nation and an office whose occupant is an executive responsible for foreign as well as domestic affairs. In the case of Congress, we are speaking about very different constituencies—some, as in the case of a Senate seat from California, almost as diversified as the nation itself and others, as in a rural district in Kansas, relatively homogeneous. The officers being chosen are not executives, but representatives, and they are selected often on the basis of how well they can bring to bear the concerns of a particular district or region on national policymaking, with domestic considerations usually being of paramount concern.

But even with these vast differences, it was common practice until quite recently to treat many elements of presidential and congressional campaigns together. A combined analysis was possible because many of the general aspects of the campaigns were similar to one another: financing was governed by roughly the same rules, party organizations played an important role in both cases in determining the nominees, and voting behavior in both instances was strongly influenced by partisan identification and by tides of national opinion related to the performance of the incumbent party.

Over the course of this century, however, many of these similarities have diminished; and while some new ones have grown up—such as a common reliance on new technologies of campaigning—the overall result has been an increasing degree of differentiation between the two electoral processes. Congressional campaigns now operate under very different rules for financing. Party strength and

party identification, which have weakened in both processes, have led to quite different results in each, favoring incumbents in congressional elections while having little effect on incumbents in presidential contests.

General Features and Constitutional Provisions

The system of separation of powers in the United States is closely tied to the nation's electoral process. The outcome of the elections for the legislature is independent of that of the chief executive, a fact that allows Congress to register its own expression of the national will. In fact, every second congressional election takes place in the midterm of the president's four-year tenure, an arrangement that provides Congress with a "mandate" entirely independent of the presidential campaign. Most important, the American theory of representation for members of Congress* regards their role in large part as representatives of their states and localities and as agents chosen to exercise their personal discretion.

To be sure, the addition of political parties has modified the original system by providing a common label across presidential and congressional elections that allows, to some extent, for an expression of opinion on national party programs. But the key words are "to some extent." Because of the basic Constitutional provisions and the practices and traditions linked to them, the influence of common national party programs on presidential and congressional elections is limited. Voters can—and do—vote for a presidential candidate from one party and congressional candidates from another. Voters can—and do—modify presidential interpretations of the public will by changes in the midterm elections. And voters within each district and state can—and do—define the nature of their local parties in often strikingly different ways.

Terms Whereas presidents are limited by the Constitution to two terms, members of Congress face no such restriction. They may serve without limit, and increasingly since the last century more

*The term "member of Congress" will be used here to refer to both senators and members of the House. Members of the House are also called "representatives."

TABLE 6-4
THE ADVANTAGE OF INCUMBENCY IN THE HOUSE AND SENATE, 1946–1982

	House				Senate			
		Defeated				Defeated		
Year	Seeking reelection*	Primary	General	Percent reelected	Seeking reelection*	Primary	General	Percent reelected
1946	398	18	52	82.4	30	6	7	56.7
1948	400	15	68	79.2	25	2	8	60.0
1950	400	6	32	90.5	32	5	5	68.8
1952	389	9	26	91.0	31	2	9	64.5
1954	407	6	22	93.1	32	2	6	75.0
1956	411	6	16	94.6	29	0	4	86.2
1958	396	3	37	89.9	28	0	10	64.3
1960	405	5	25	92.6	29	0	1	96.6
1962	402	12	22	91.5	35	1	5	82.9
1964	397	8	45	86.6	33	1	4	84.8
1966	411	8	41	88.1	32	3	1	87.5
1968	409	4	9	96.8	28	4	4	71.4
1970	401	10	12	94.5	31	1	6	77.4
1972	000	12	13	93.6	27	2	5	74.1
1974	391	8	40	87.7	27	2	2	85.2
1976	384	3	13	95.8	25	0	9	64.0
1978	382	5	19	93.7	25	3	7	60.0
1980	398	6	31	90.7	29	4	9	55.2
1982	381	2	29	91.9	30	0	2	93.3

*Counting both primary and general election bids.
Source: Congressional Quarterly Weekly Report, Apr. 5, 1980:908, and Nov. 8, 1980:3302, 3320–3321.

members seek reelection, and more have been re-elected. Although there have recently been more retirements in the House, some no doubt less than voluntary, the general point stands. Incumbency is one of the major facts about the modern Congress. As compared with the period before the Civil War, representatives now serve on an average nearly five terms as opposed to about two terms, and senators serve nearly two terms as opposed to one. Incumbent representatives since 1950 have generally won over 90 percent of their races; the record of incumbent senators has been more erratic, but nonetheless still fairly impressive (see Table 6-4).

Nothing in the Constitution itself can account for this trend of longer congressional tenures in office. In fact, the founders would be greatly surprised by the average length of service in the House. The founders' original idea of unlimited reeligibility for the *president* was designed in part to provide stability in the government as a counter-weight to the expected turbulence of the House. Of course, the properties that promote stability in an institution involve more than the number of years served, and in many respects the presidency with its four-year term remains more stable than the House; but the shifts in average tenure, up for the House and down for the presidency, have changed the character of executive-legislative relations. The House is no longer a body made up mostly of amateur legislators who serve in Washington only for brief stints. For many representatives today, serving in Congress has become a career, a fact that has important consequences that will be discussed in Chapter 9.

The Senate, with its six-year term and system of staggered elections in which only one-third comes up for reelection at any time, was designed by the founders to be the more stable body. Thus, even with the lower rates of incumbent victories for the Senate, the percentage of the change of membership in the body as a whole is lower in the Senate than in the House. Members of the House serve only a two-year term, and all stand for reelection at the same time. This allows for the possibility of truly dramatic shifts in membership. To take two examples from realigning periods, the Democrats in 1894 lost 113 seats, and the Republicans in 1930 lost 97 seats. Today, however, with the increased importance of incumbency as a factor in determining election outcomes, there is much less likelihood of changes on the magnitude of 100 seats, even in realigning periods. The strong Republican trend in 1980, for example, brought the GOP a net gain of 33 seats, an impressive but far from dramatic shift.

Size of Congress The Constitutional provisions for the size and districting of the Senate are clear and practically self-executing: each state, no matter what its population, has two senators, who, since the Seventeenth Amendment (1913), are chosen by popular election. In the case of the House, the provisions for size and districting are not automatic, and the result has been a long history of controversy.

The Constitution provides for the apportionment of representatives among the states on the basis of population, with each state having at least one representative. The number of representatives, however, was left to Congress to determine by law. Originally, in 1789, the House had only 65 members. The number increased quickly to accommodate an expanding population, rising to 240 members in 1833 and to 433 members by 1911. At this point House leaders, realizing that the House was on the verge of becoming unmanageable as a deliberative body, put a stop to the growth of membership. The House has since retained a limit of 435 members, which works out to districts of approximately a half-million people. With this agreed-upon limit, a gain in representation for one state must now be made up by a loss in another. Each census accordingly brings the agony for some states and members of seeing their districts abolished.

Apportionment of House Districts Although the founders may have intended that House seats be apportioned into single-member districts of roughly equal population, this requirement and other laws concerning apportionment of House districts were not included in the Constitution. Instead, the power to decide these questions was assigned to Congress, if it chose to exercise it; otherwise, the states would determine how seats were apportioned. Congress originally left the issue to the states, and a number of them decided to elect their representatives on a statewide basis, which generally enabled the majority party within the state to win all the seats. After much debate, Congress finally ended this practice in 1842 by a law requiring states to select representatives in single-member districts.

Congress did not act, however, to guarantee equal population among the districts. (For a time a law to that effect was on the books, but it was not enforced.) Some state legislatures proceeded to draw district lines (or not redraw them) so as to create (or allow) differences in population among the districts. This problem of malapportionment became especially acute in this century, with the dramatic population shifts from rural to urban areas. Members from rural districts, who dominated many of the state legislatures—again because of malapportionment—often refused to relinquish their advantage and grant equal representation to urban areas. For example, during the 1960s in Georgia, one rural district had 272,000 people, while a district made up of part of Atlanta and its suburbs had more than three times as many (823,000). Representatives in the House, many of whom were the beneficiaries of this malapportionment, were reluctant to pass national legislation to correct the problem.

It was finally the Supreme Court that entered into the thicket of legislative districting and imposed a judicial remedy that sought to ensure the equal weight of each vote. In the decision of *Baker v. Carr* (1962), the Court established the principle of districts of equal population for state legislatures, arguing that the "debasement" of the vote for citizens in larger districts violated the Fourteenth Amendment's equal protection clause. Two years later, in the case of *Wesbury v. Sanders,* the Court extended this principle to congressional districts, holding that the Constitutional provision in Article I that apportions representatives among the states "according to their respective numbers" means that "one man's vote in a congressional election is to be worth as much as another's." Under cases that followed from this decision, the states after each census must reconsider their district lines to ensure equality in population.

The Court's action, however, has certainly not put an end to the political maneuvering involved in drawing district boundaries, for equal districts can still be drawn to protect the seats of incumbents or to help one of the political parties. Politics is inseparable from the process of apportionment. The drawing of district lines with political purposes in mind is *gerrymandering,* a name taken from a particularly ingenious district supposedly drawn up by Elbridge Gerry in Massachusetts in 1812. Paradoxically, the Court's apportionment decisions, while banning the most flagrant kind of gerrymandering, have increased the occasions to practice it, since the states now *must* reconsider their district lines every decade. (Formerly, many states avoided such battles by leaving district lines in place for several decades.) States use various methods to draw up district plans; but in the end there is little question that the parties, where they can, usually attempt to advantage their own candidates. It is for this reason, among others, that the national parties have begun to pay more attention to state legislative and gubernatorial contests, realizing that control of the House may be determined by the decisions of state governments.

Financing in Congressional Elections

"Money," a pragmatic politician once declared, "is the mother's milk of politics." Candidates for Congress cannot help imbibing, for without money an effective campaign in the face of serious opposition is all but impossible. Although the importance of money is often exaggerated relative to other factors like organization and strategy, there is no question that money counts. And it counts overall more in congressional than in presidential campaigns because of differences in the laws and the nature of the races.

Current legislation limits what individuals and groups (including national and state parties) may contribute. There is, however, no provision for public funding in congressional campaigns. Candidates must raise all their funds privately, and there are no overall expenditure limitations for the cam-

paigns as a whole. As a result, the amounts spent on various congressional campaigns vary greatly, and these relative differences can have an important bearing on the results. In addition, money seems to be able to buy something of greater value in congressional races. Primary elections for the House and Senate, as well as many general elections for the House, are frequently low-visibility races in which the voters may not know much about the candidates or even recognize their names. Money can buy exposure and recognition. (Senate races in the general election generally receive a great deal of media coverage and free exposure, which makes them a bit more like presidential contests and perhaps gives more equality to challengers of incumbents than is the case in the House.)

There are two types of candidates for whom buying name recognition is unnecessary: incumbents (people cannot always name their members of Congress, but they can usually recognize their names on the ballot) and persons with public reputations, derived from holding other offices or from activities outside of politics, like sports or entertainment. Because reputation is so valuable, people who attain public stature are often tempted to enter politics. In the 1982 Senate were John Glenn, a Democrat from Ohio who was the first American to circle the earth in space; and Bill Bradley, a Democrat from New Jersey, who was a former basketball star from Princeton and the New York Knicks. Formerly, California was represented by an entertainer, George Murphy, a situation which led one satirical songwriter to note that "at last we have a senator who can really sing and dance." And of course President Reagan, formerly a movie actor, launched his political career in California with the benefit of his reputation as an actor.

With so many incumbents running for office, the question of financing in these races deserves special comment. Incumbents usually find it much easier to raise funds than challengers do, largely because they are likely to win, which is an important consideration for groups and individuals wishing to have access in Washington. Campaign spending by incumbents, however, is not nearly as "valuable" as it is for challengers. The challenger is the one who needs to spend to overcome all the advantages the incumbent already possesses. In general, the chal-

Many Americans have built political careers on the basis of their public reputations; Senator John Glenn, a former astronaut, gestures like a fighter pilot as he describes his plans to some constituents. *(David Burnett/Contact)*

lenger will have to spend a great deal of money— and often outspend the incumbent—in order to have a serious chance of winning. The level of spending in a race therefore tends to be set by the challenger. When a challenger is capable of mounting a serious campaign, the incumbent will be forced into a major fund-raising effort; usually, incumbents can raise what they need, but their best strategy is to attempt to discourage a serious challenge altogether by convincing everyone in the district that they are invulnerable (Jacobson, 1983).

Sources of Funds Before the campaign finance legislation of the 1970s candidates for Congress funded their campaigns from a variety of sources, including personal resources (if available) and contributions from groups and the local and national parties, and especially from fairly substantial con-

tributions from a limited number of friends and sponsors. (Earlier in the century, when parties were stronger, the local parties often provided most of the financing for the campaigns.)

The picture today has been substantially altered by the current finance legislation. Individual contributors remain the largest single source of campaign funding, and party contributions are not inconsequential (see Table 6-5). Spending by the Republican national and state parties has been especially important, for the GOP has raised more funds and is in a position to help many of its candidates to the maximum allowable under the law. As before, individual candidates can also spend on their own behalf without limit; this has given wealthy candidates an even greater advantage than they had before because opponents cannot rely on wealthy friends to counterbalance these expendi-

TABLE 6-5

SOURCES OF CAMPAIGN CONTRIBUTIONS TO HOUSE AND SENATE CANDIDATES, 1972–1980

Elections	1972*	1974	1976	1978	1980
House					
Average contributions	$51,752	$61,084	$79,421	$111,232	$148,268
Percentage of contributions from:					
Individuals	60†	73	59	61	67†
Parties	17	4	8	5	4
Nonparty committees	14	17	23	25	29
Candidates‡		6	9	9	
Unknown	9				
Senate					
Average contributions	$353,933	$455,515	$624,094	$951,390	$1,079,346
Percentage of contributions from:					
Individuals	67	76	69	70	78†
Parties	14	6	4	6	2
Nonparty committees	12	11	15	13	21
Candidates‡	0.4	1	12	8	
Unknown	8	6			

*Some contributions before April 7, 1972, may have gone unreported.
†Includes candidates' contributions to their own campaigns.
‡Includes candidates' loans unpaid at time of filing.
Source: Jacobson, 1983:53.

tures. Wealthy individuals have especially been attracted to the Senate. The major change, however, has been in the increased role played by the political action committees. Although PAC money given *directly* to the campaigns is still less than 30 percent of all campaign expenditures, it has been growing tremendously. In addition, PACs spend a significant amount of money outside of the official campaigns.

The growth in the number and importance of PACs has importantly altered the character of congressional races. In the past, nearly all the funding went through the official campaigns of the candidates, and much of it came from individual contributors who gave money out of friendship, without putting much direct pressure on candidates to back positions. (The size and secrecy of money contributions, however, made this system very questionable.) The PACs tend to be more "rational" in their contributions than individuals, targeting money to candidates who they expect will deliver on key issues. And because so many of these committees are either highly ideological or centered on one particular interest, candidates may

feel more pressure than in the past to accommodate the viewpoint of their contributors, although the limited amount PACs can contribute lessens their influence. Finally, independent spending by certain PACs producing their own television and radio ads has sometimes resulted in more negative advertising and extreme attacks than the candidates themselves would have condoned. In sum, it is clear that the larger role played by political action committees has provided new incentives for fragmented and ideological politics (Davidson and Oleszek, 1981).

Proposals for Change Nearly everyone who has studied the current financing legislation for congressional elections has come away dissatisfied. The agreement that something is wrong with the present method, however, has not translated into any agreement about what alternative—if any— would mark an improvement. Some favor a system of much higher (or unlimited) private and party contributions, with public disclosure of the amounts and sources of donations; others favor a system of public financing. Proponents of higher private contributions argue that it would enable candidates without personal wealth to match wealthy candidates by relying on wealthy contributors and would permit a greater role for individual contributors and political parties relative to interest and ideological groups. Although there might be a greater possibility under this system for abuse in the form of influence buying, proponents argue that monetary contributions are a legitimate form of participation by citizens and that disclosure provisions would enable candidates to make an issue of any unseemly or excessive gifts.

The alternative of public financing, favored by reform groups like Common Cause and Public Citizen, seems like a simple solution but has many problems. It would, of course, eliminate differentials in campaign spending and advantages of wealth. Yet, apart from the issues of how to deal with third parties and how to distribute funds during primaries, this system would not necessarily be fair, if in "fair" one includes the concept of a good chance for challengers to unseat incumbents. The problem, we may recall, is that while incumbents usually can raise more funds than challengers, challengers may have to spend a great deal of money in order to win. If public financing were limited to a modest amount—as it might be, given that incumbents would write the laws—the result would probably help incumbents. Where incumbents and challengers spend equal but modest amounts, incumbents have the advantage of greater visibility and recognition.

Congressional Races

Nominations Congressional candidates are generally chosen in a two-step process of nomination by a major party and then a general election. Third-party activity at the congressional level, once an important factor in American politics, is now rare. Party nominations in the nineteenth century were made by district and state conventions, a practice which had the modest effect of promoting a degree of party discipline in Congress, although the highest level of control came from the state parties. Today, in all but a few states, the nominations for members of Congress are made in primaries, not conventions. As a general rule, this system weakens the role of political parties and turns congressional candidates more into individual entrepreneurs, dependent on their own reputations, organizations, and bids for support from interest groups and highly motivated issue constituencies. Parties play some role in helping to recruit candidates to run, but just as often the recruiting function is now played by individuals themselves or by groups within the constituencies. House members and senators generally prefer to build personal campaign organizations rather than to rely on the regular party organizations (Kayden, 1978).

Voter turnout in congressional primaries is generally rather low, especially in House races. In many districts, as few as 25,000 votes can secure a primary victory. Under these circumstances, it is clear why incumbents, when they run, enjoy such an advantage. In addition to their recognition and greater ability to raise funds, they have all the privileges of being in office: a record of constituency service for many voters; a large staff that contacts citizens and (indirectly) helps the incumbents with the campaign; free mailing in between elections; and "credit-taking" methods in which incumbents announce to their constituents many grants received for government projects, making it appear—rightly or wrongly—that they had a role in securing the favors (Mayhew, 1974; Fiorina, 1977). Through such resources and techniques, members of Congress attempt to build a network of personal supporters who can serve as a crucial "core" constituency (Fenno, 1978).

All these methods, however, are helpful in explaining congressional nominating races only where incumbents are running; and even for incumbents, such personal followings are often not sufficient. Candidates must therefore build support on other grounds and with the help of others. In most districts, the party organization's role in the nominating campaign is limited, and candidates must appeal to and rely on the support of portions of the highly motivated segment of the electorate that turns out in primary elections. The key is often to rely on various issue constituencies. One congressman explained how this method worked for him in the mid-1960s:

Everybody needs some group which is strongly for

him—especially in a primary. You can win a primary with 25,000 zealots. The most exquisite case I can give you was in the very early [Vietnamese] war years. I had very strong support from the anti-war people. They were my strongest supporters and they made up about 5 percent of the district (Fenno, 1978:18–19).

More recently, these constituencies have centered not on one single national issue, but on a variety of questions, whether it be the economy, abortion, environmentalism, or nuclear disarmament. Such voters are often organized and activated in modern campaigns by interest groups and political action committees, many of which are from Washington, D.C. No wonder, therefore, that more and more politicians have begun to lament the decline of the nominating role of the party organizations, which once stood as a buffer in the electoral process between the candidates and the pressure of particular groups.

General Elections Congressional elections have long confounded analysts of American politics, and they will probably continue to do so. The reason is as simple as it is complex: when citizens vote for members of Congress, they are not simply casting a vote on some national idea or party program; they are also deciding which individual—with which reputation, qualities, and positions on issues—should serve as their senator or representative. Only to a limited extent can one speak generally about congressional elections; rather, there are separate congressional elections, each with its own cast of characters and particular issues. National trends play an important role, but they are only one factor among others and must be reflected through the particular forces working in each race. No general theory of electoral behavior, accordingly, can come close to explaining the outcome of these elections.

Analysts have identified three broad categories of influence in congressional races: (1) judgments made on the particular candidates, including their personal qualities, their record of service, and their stance on issues; (2) the party of the candidates (which usually tells one something about their positions on issues but does not define these entirely); and (3) perceptions of national political trends—judgments, in presidential election years, about the presidential campaign and, in midterm elections, about how well the incumbent president is doing, particularly regarding the performance of the economy (Tufte, 1978).

The first of these three categories—the candidates' personal qualities, records, and positions on issues—is relatively more important today than it was in the past, probably because of the weakening of strict partisan voting patterns and the increased advantages of incumbents. Whatever the precise cause, however, the result is that congressional races tend to be fought out increasingly in different ways in each state and district. Congressional races today are *not* more isolated than in the past from the issues of national politics—the very opposite may be true—but the way these issues are developed and exploited in each campaign is less easily accounted for by general statements about swings in national partisan support.

The increased importance of voters' judgments on the qualities and stands on issues of the particular candidates, as distinct from partisanship and national trends, has produced a relative gain in influence for incumbents and for ideological and single-interest groups. Both fill the "vacuum" left by the decline of partisanship. In many districts, of course, the incumbent is from the party already having the greater following in the district, which makes it difficult to determine whether the incumbent's success is due to incumbency rather than party. Both clearly play a role and reinforce each other. Recent studies, however, suggest that the incumbency factor is the more important of the two; this finding is supported by the numerous cases in which a representative manages to win in a district having a normal majority for the opposition party, after which he or she is repeatedly reelected.

A typical general election campaign, then, will find a challenger criticizing aspects of the incumbent's voting record and position, and charging the incumbent with having lost touch with the feelings of the state or district. Incumbents may respond by explaining their positions in light of general national concerns, by indicating their influence in Congress, and by reminding voters of their clout with the bureaucracy. One particularly amusing example of an exchange came in the 1980 senatorial election in the state of Washington. Slade Gorton was challenging Warren Magnuson, who was 75 years old and a six-term incumbent. Gorton showed television ads in which he was seen jogging and riding a bicycle. Magnuson, chairman of the powerful Senate Appropriations Committee, responded with the statement, "I may be a little slower than I used to be, but the meeting can't start until I get there anyway."

While it is striking that incumbents win so often, and generally by larger margins than before the 1960s, it does not follow that they think of themselves as "safe" or beyond accountability to their constituents. Members of Congress, Richard Fenno has observed, operate with "a terrific sense of *uncertainty* . . . and perceive troubles where the most imaginative outside observer could not possibly perceive, conjur or hallucinate them" (Mayhew, 1974:35). Nor are they being paranoid. Without the relatively solid support of partisan voters who tend to stick with their party's candidate, incumbents, even when they win by wide margins, may reasonably conclude that their support could very easily desert them. In fact, incumbents may be reelected in large part *because* they know so well what their constituents want—at least on major issues—and make every effort to stay in tune with them. Thus, during the period of the early 1980s, when national sentiment for cutting the budget was running very strong, many liberals in Congress took up this theme. Far from indicating a great deal of independence from constituents, then, the high reelection rate for incumbents could just as easily indicate a growing *dependence* on public opinion.

To some extent, the services that House members perform for their constituents make them appear to many as nonpartisan representatives who help their districts rather than as political decision makers who form national policies. Indeed, while people have a quite negative view today of Congress as an institution, representatives are frequently able to persuade their constituents that the problem is with the institution as a whole and not with their own representative (who naturally is working to clean things up). To some extent, representatives run for Congress by running against it

(Fenno, 1978). Senators, being more visible, find this little trick a bit more difficult than House members, which may be one reason why they have been somewhat more vulnerable.

Although voters' attention to the candidates' personal qualities and stands on issues is more important *relative* to partisan factors or national trends, the latter two are far from being inconsequential. The pronounced and systematic role these two categories once played—and still play to some extent—is best appreciated by stating the traditional "coattail" effect that was once so pronounced in influencing congressional voting patterns. Under the coattail effect, voters favoring a certain candidate for president would also tend to vote for members of Congress from the same party. This meant that a strong presidential candidate would bring in ("on his coattails") a gain for his party in Congress (and almost always a majority in the House). In so doing, an important link was created between the president and members of Congress from his own party. Members of Congress would, so to speak, live or die by the results of the presidential election.

In midterm elections, the swing in the number of seats between the parties could be read in part as a popular judgment on the performance of the president. As a rough benchmark, it was—and still is—regarded as "normal" for the president's party to lose seats in the midterm election, as frustrations accumulate and as the voters who were swept along by the presidential campaign either stay home or return to their own party. (Obviously, the more seats the president brought in, the greater is the number of seats to protect, increasing the number of likely losses.) In any event, if the president's party loses only a small number of seats—again, what is "expected" becomes critical—the results are generally discounted. If, however, the president's party loses a large number of seats, it is a definite sign of trouble for the administration and a sign that the public has lost confidence in the president. And finally, if—as happens only rarely—the president's party gains support, the midterm election results can be read as an endorsement of the president's tenure.

From 1960 until 1980, when the Democrats consistently controlled both houses of the Congress, the coattail effect in presidential election years was greatly diminished. Although Democrats still preferred to have a strong presidential candidate at the head of their ticket, the effect of presidential campaigns on congressional elections seemed to become less and less significant. To take the most striking example, when President Nixon won his landslide victory in 1972, the Democrats still captured a solid majority in Congress. With the weakening of coattails, many members of Congress in this era proceeded on the assumption that their own electoral chances were essentially isolated from presidential politics. Without question, this attitude contributed to the declining cohesiveness of the Democratic party as a policymaking instrument during President Carter's tenure. Members in Congress felt less of a need to cooperate either with each other or with a president from their own party.

In 1980, however, this "nonpartisan" trend seemed to abate, as Ronald Reagan's election brought a net increase of thirty-three seats for Republicans in the House and an unexpected twelve-seat gain in the Senate. Moreover, as noted, the Republicans made a concerted effort through national advertising and through their strategies in most campaigns to try to make voters think of the *partisan* consequences of their votes in congressional elections. Whether the 1980 election began a resurgence of the coattail effect and a reversal of the increasing isolation of presidential and congressional elections remains to be seen.

CONCLUSION

The electoral process is an intricate maze resting on Constitutional provisions, federal and state laws, party rules, traditions, and norms. Together, these make up a central "institution" of our political system that helps determine who governs and how power is distributed. The electoral process affects the type of people who are elevated to public office, the nature of the campaigns, the kinds of choice offered to the public, and the way in which the formal institutions of government operate. Although the Constitution structures many of the features of this complex system, much of what constitutes the electoral process today goes well beyond what the founders ever contemplated. The rule of constitution making in this area, therefore, requires a great

deal of attention to developments after the founding.

The most striking fact about the electoral process in this century has been the weakening of political parties. The nomination process is more open to outsiders who have less support from party leaders; campaigns are more idiosyncratic, relying less on traditional party positions and more on the particular programs and appeals of the candidates; and the choices Americans are provided with are less predictable and stable. The electoral process also affects the relationship between governing officials in a separation-of-powers and federal system. On this point, the decline of parties has left the various governing officials and institutions with somewhat weaker ties to each other. While the founders' system of separation of powers was clearly intended to provide separate bases of authority for each institution, parties traditionally provided what most analysts considered to be a helpful mechanism for forging a degree of harmony and cooperation among them without undermining their independent authority. With weaker party structures, the institutions operate in greater isolation from each other, producing further fragmentation in the governing process.

Some see in this new electoral process important gains for our political system. The transfer of power from party leaders to the people makes the constitution more democratic and majoritarian, taking power away from structures said to be insufficiently responsive to popular wishes. Others deny that the various reforms of recent years have in fact had this majoritarian impact. Moreover, they assert that our system works better with parties of modest strength—as judged by criteria of governing effectiveness and a due consideration for valid pluralist concerns.

If this last position has merit, the question becomes one of how parties can be sustained and perhaps strengthened. The general approach in any such strategy is contained by implication in V. O. Key's remark that "institutional decay follows from a deprivation of function" (Key, 1964:375). Reversing this statement, it follows that restoring functions to parties might lead to institutional revival. The steps taken might include returning more control of the nominating process to the parties and allowing the parties to play a greater role in funding political campaigns. In contrast to the period of reform of the last decade, more leaders now appear ready to explore proposals that would accomplish these objectives.

Whatever steps are contemplated, however, it is clear that success must hinge on the willingness of Americans to accept some discretionary role for representative institutions such as the conventions that nominate candidates. As long as people deplore an intermediary role for parties and insist on "direct democracy" in the recruitment and selection of candidates, the chances of party revival seem very slim. Whether Americans can be led to accept the price of stronger parties is the major issue in party reform in the years ahead.

SOURCES

Arterton, Chris: "The Media Politics of Presidential Campaigns," in James David Barber, *Race for the Presidency*, Prentice-Hall, Englewood Cliffs, N.J., 1978.

Asher, Herbert: *Presidential Elections and American Politics*, rev. ed., Dorsey, Homewood, Ill., 1982.

Broder, David: "Choosing Presidential Candidates: How Good Is the New Way?" *American Enterprise Institute Forums*, American Enterprise Institute, Washington, D.C., 1979.

Congressional Quarterly Weekly Report, Congressional Quarterly Press, Apr. 5, 1980; and Nov. 8, 1980.

Davidson, Roger, and Walter J. Oleszek: *Congress and Its Members*, Congressional Quarterly Press, Washington, D.C., 1981.

Fenno, Richard: *Home Style*, Little, Brown, Boston, 1978.

Fiorina, Morris: *Congress: Keystone of the Washington Establishment*, Yale University Press, New Haven, Conn., 1977.

Greenstein, Fred: "Change and Continuity in the Modern Presidency," in Anthony King (ed.), *The New American Political System*, American Enterprise Institute, Washington, D.C., 1978.

Hadley, Arthur: *The Invisible Primary*, Prentice-Hall, Englewood Cliffs, N.J., 1976.

Jacobson, Gary C.: *The Politics of Congressional Elections*, Yale University Press, New Haven, Conn., 1983.

Jones, Charles: "Nominating 'Carter's Favorite Opponent': The Republicans in 1980," in Austin Ranney (ed.), *The American Elections of 1980*, American Enterprise Institute, Washington, D.C., 1981.

Kayden, Xandra: *Campaign Organization*, Heath, Lexington, Mass., 1978.

Kessel, John H.: "The Seasons of Presidential Politics," *Social Science Quarterly*, vol. 58, December, 1977.

Key, V. O., Jr.: *Politics, Parties, and Pressure Groups*, 5th ed., Thomas Y. Crowell, New York, 1964.

King, Anthony: "How Not to Select Presidential Candidates: A View from Europe," in Austin Ranney (ed.), *The American Elections of 1980*, American Enterprise Institute, Washington, D.C., 1981.

Malbin, Michael J.: "The Conventions, Platforms and Issues," in Austin Ranney (ed.), *The American Elections of 1980*, American Enterprise Institute, Washington, D.C., 1981.

Mayhew, David R.: *The Electoral Connection*, Yale University Press, New Haven, Conn., 1974.

Moore, Jonathan (ed.): *The Campaign for President: 1980 in Retrospect*, Ballinger, Cambridge, Mass., 1981.

National Journal, May 1, 1976, pp. 574–579.

Orren, Gary: "Presidential Campaign Finance: Its Impact and Future," *Commonsense*, vol. 4, no. 2, 1981.

Patterson, Thomas, and Robert McClure: *The Unseeing Eye: The Myth of Television Power in National Elections*, Putnam, New York, 1976.

Polsby, Nelson W.: "The News Media as an Alternative to Party in the Presidential Selection Process," in Robert Goldwin (ed.), *Political Parties in the Eighties*, American Enterprise Institute, Washington, D.C., 1980.

———— and Aaron Wildavsky: *Presidential Elections*, 5th ed., Scribner, New York, 1980.

Pomper, Gerald, with Susan Lederman: *Elections in America: Control and Influence in Democratic Politics*, 2d ed., Longmans, New York, 1980.

Robinson, Michael J.: "The Media in 1980: Was the Message the Message?" in Austin Ranney (ed.), *The American Elections of 1980*, American Enterprise Institute, Washington, D.C., 1981.

Rubin, Richard: *Press, Party and Presidency*, Norton, New York, 1981.

Sabato, Larry: *The Rise of Political Consultants*, Basic Books, New York, 1981.

SRC/CPS (Survey Research Center/Center for Political Studies): Election studies, 1980.

Truman, David B.: *The Governmental Process*, Knopf, New York, 1951.

Tufte, Edward: *Political Control of the Economy,* Princeton University Press, Princeton, N.J., 1978.

Washington Post, June 8, 1980; and June 5, 1982.

Wolfson, Lewis W.: "The Media Masters," *Washington Post,* Feb. 20, 1972, Potomac supplement.

RECOMMENDED READINGS

Jacobson, Gary C.: *The Politics of Congressional Elections,* Yale University Press, New Haven, Conn., 1983. An excellent overview of the legal, institutional, and behavioral factors that influence congressional elections.

Keech, William R., and Donald Matthews: *The Party's Choice,* Brookings Institution, Washington, D.C., 1977. A careful analysis of presidential nominating politics from 1940 through 1976.

Lengle, James I., and Byron Shafer: *Presidential Politics: Readings on Nominations and Elections,* 2d ed., St. Martin's, New York, 1983. A collection of contemporary readings on the presidential election process.

Polsby, Nelson W., and Aaron Wildavsky: *Presidential Elections: Strategies of American Electoral Politics,* 5th ed., Scribner, New York, 1980. An analysis of the entire presidential selection process by two of the nation's leading political scientists.

Rubin, Richard: *Press, Party and Presidency,* Norton, New York, 1981. A survey of the development of the modern presidential campaign and the role of the media.

Sabato, Larry: *The Rise of Political Consultants,* Basic Books, New York, 1981. A comprehensive study of the role of the professional media advisers and pollsters in modern American politics.

White, Theodore: *The Making of the President, 1960,* Atheneum, New York, 1961. A widely acclaimed full-length story of the 1960 presidential campaign; White wrote similar volumes for the elections from 1964 through 1972.

Chapter 7

Voting Behavior and Political Participation

CHAPTER CONTENTS

A republic, as James Madison once defined it, is a "government which derives all of its powers directly or indirectly from the great body of the people, and is administered by persons holding their offices . . . for a limited period or during good behavior" (*Federalist* 39). In this simple definition, Madison captured the core of the founders' principle of representative government: a government which relies for its foundation on the public will, but which operates at enough distance from it that it can act independently for the public good.

The chief instrument of the people's influence on government is the vote. Originally accorded directly only for elections for the House, it has since been extended to the Senate and, in practice, to the presidency. The relative importance of deriving powers "directly" versus "indirectly" has thus been reversed since the time of the founding, with the result that the electorate has a much greater influence on the operation of the government. It is not by the vote alone, however, that citizens influence governing officials. They do so as well through other kinds of participation—some linked to the electoral process, such as campaigning or giving money to candidates; and others taking place outside the electoral process, such as contacting officials or demonstrating on behalf of some position.

In this chapter we shall look at the American citizen as a (possible) voter and participant. We shall ask who votes, what considerations weigh in voting decisions, and who participates beyond the act of voting. The discussion of these questions will take us into areas in which political scientists have recently done a great deal of work in an effort both to provide precise information on political behavior and to offer theoretical explanations of that behavior. This knowledge should serve also to help one evaluate the claims and counterclaims about American democracy and to assess further some of the institutional changes in the electoral process discussed in previous chapters.

VOTER TURNOUT

Americans, with the exception of certain minority groups, have enjoyed the right to vote longer than the citizens of any other nation. Yet, many now contend, Americans exercise that right less than the people of almost all democracies (see Figure 7-1). This observation has given rise to a great deal of controversy and concern. Some question the health and even the legitimacy of democratic decision making in the United States. If so few people vote, they ask, doesn't this indicate mass indifference and call into question the claim that our government truly reflects the popular will? And how, they ask, can one speak of our president as being the choice of the American people when less than 30 percent of the adult citizens ordinarily ever vote for the person who is elected?

Nor are these the only complaints. Americans, it appears, not only vote less than citizens in other countries but vote less than they did in the past (see Figure 7-2). Although the numbers cited in Figure 7-2 require further discussion and analysis, the conclusion seems inescapable: of the potentially eligible voters, a smaller percentage today actually vote than did in the nineteenth century. Some see in this decline clear evidence of a deterioration of support for the political system. Others go even further and argue that the nonvoters represent an "alienated" segment of the population that could possibly be mobilized on behalf of a radical alternative not currently represented by the two major parties (Burnham, 1979).

These are, of course, very serious charges that call into question claims that our government is influenced by majoritarian considerations. No one looking at Figures 7-1 and 7-2 will find much reason for celebration. But whether they should lead to the dire conclusions noted above or to a more modest degree of concern depends upon a much more sustained analysis of the reasons for nonvoting and the character of those who do not vote. It is on issues such as these that the careful work of political scientists in recent years can help us reach a balanced view of the problem. The task of constitution making must begin with consulting the facts and looking at experience, "the oracle of truth" (*Federalist* 20).

General Factors Affecting Turnout

Turnout rates among the adult population depend in the first instance on the legal right of the franchise and protection from intimidation, harassment, and undue hardship. Voting is impossible if one is denied the right or threatened with violence

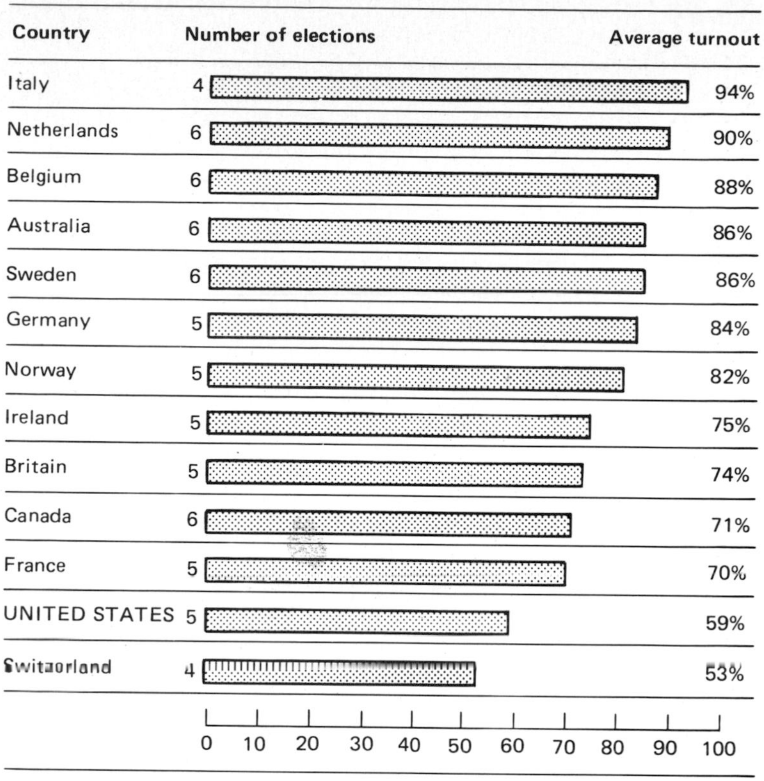

Country
Number of elections
Average turnout
Italy 4 94%
Netherlands 6 90%
Belgium 6 88%
Australia 6 86%
Sweden 6 86%
Germany 5 84%
Norway 5 82%
Ireland 5 75%
Britain 5 74%
Canada 6 71%
France 5 70%
UNITED STATES 5 59%
Switzerland 4 53%
0 10 20 30 40 50 60 70 80 90 100

FIGURE 7-1
Voter turnout in major national elections in western nations, 1960–1978. Turnout is calculated as a percentage of voting-age population. (*Source:* Powell, 1980:6.)

Percent of voting-age population participating
80
75
70
65
60
55
50
45
40
35
30
Presidential elections
House elections
1860 1868 1876 1884 1892 1900 1908 1916 1924 1932 1940 1948 1956 1964 1972 1980

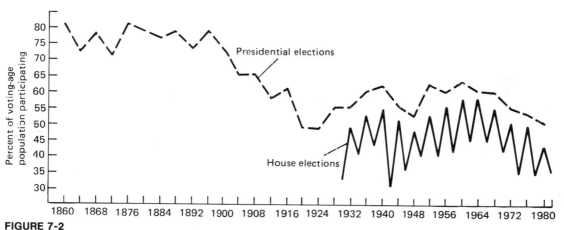

FIGURE 7-2
Participation in presidential elections (1860–1980) and House elections (1930–1982). Percentages are based on estimates of potential eligible voters. Women are excluded in years before state laws or the Nineteenth Amendment accorded them the right to vote. Eighteen-year-olds are excluded before state laws or the Twenty-Sixth Amendment accorded them the right to vote. Other adjustments have also been made. (*Source: Historical Statistics of the United States, Colonial Times to 1970,* 1975:1071–1072; *Statistical Abstract of the United States—1980,* 1980:517; Ornstein et al., 1982:37; *Congressional Quarterly Weekly Report,* 1982:2850.)

BOX 7-1

FEDERAL DEFINITION AND PROTECTION OF VOTING RIGHTS

Determining qualifications for voting was originally a state function, the sole exception being the Constitutional provision in Article I, Section 2 giving the right to vote in federal elections for the House to the same people eligible to vote for the most numerous branch of the state legislature. Over the course of American history, Constitutional amendments, court cases, and federal laws have established what amounts to a national right to vote. Some of the major developments have been:

The Fifteenth Amendment (1870), providing that race shall not be a condition for denying suffrage
The Nineteenth Amendment (1920), providing that sex shall not be a condition for denying suffrage

The Twenty-Fourth Amendment (1964), prohibiting the use of the poll tax or any other tax as a means of denying anyone the right to vote
The Voting Rights Act of 1965, outlawing the use of tests for denying anyone the right to vote in certain areas of the country
The Voting Rights Act of 1970, banning literacy tests nationally
The Twenty-Sixth Amendment (1971), guaranteeing 18-year-olds the right to vote
Dunn v. Blumstein (1972), a Supreme Court ruling declaring long residency requirements unconstitutional
The Voting Rights Act of 1975, requiring states to provide bilingual voting information.

---

in its exercise; and voting is difficult if one is required, when in great poverty, to pay a special poll tax. Yet precisely these kinds of exclusions were common in some states before the 1960s. The control over the suffrage in the United States still rests nominally with the states, subject to the requirements of Constitutional and federal law. But, as noted earlier and summarized in Box 7-1, the scope of federal protections has now grown to the point where, in all but name, one can speak of a national right to vote for all adults.

As a result, turnout rates in the United States today are no longer limited by the denial of the right of suffrage. The explanation of turnout, therefore, lies with other factors that we can group under three broad headings: (1) legal and administrative regulation of voting, such as registration requirements and practices; (2) general institutional factors, such as the strength of parties or other organizations to stimulate the vote and the amount of money spent to mobilize the electorate; and (3) citizens' attitudes about voting, such as the extent to which they consider voting a duty and the extent to which they feel that voting and elections can make a difference. It is with reference to these factors that voting turnout rates must be discussed.

The United States and Other Nations

Comparing turnout rates in the United States with those of other democratic nations is not as easy as one might think. National elections in most other democratic countries—usually for parliament, which in turn chooses a prime minister—decide where almost all political power in those nations will be vested for the ensuing years. In the United States, by contrast, power is more fragmented and decentralized; and while the presidential election is clearly the most important single election, state and local elections often decide matters that are of greatest immediate interest to large numbers of citizens. Not everything, therefore, is at stake in an American presidential election in quite the same way that it is in elections in other countries. Moreover, because of the fragmentation of power and the method of nominating candidates in the United States, there are many more elections than in other democratic countries. Typically, important elections in the United States are held in three out of every four years, often with primaries in advance of the general election. Not only does this make any one election seem less important and create a degree of fatigue in voters, but it raises the question of whether one should actually be comparing not the turnout rates in national elections, as in Figure 7-1, but the turnout rates for elections over a four-year period. If the latter comparison (which has never been calculated) were used, American turnout would no doubt compare more favorably, since many in the United States who do not vote in the presidential election vote at least once in a four-year cycle in a primary, congressional, or state or local election.

Granting, however, that American rates would still be lower than those for many other countries, it is important to consider the possible causes. Different legal regulations on voting clearly explain part of the difference. In a few nations having turnout rates higher than the United States—Australia, Italy, and Belgium—voting is compulsory, whereas in the United States it is voluntary. (The penalties imposed in these countries are minimal, but the requirements nevertheless seem to have a significant effect.) In some countries, elections are on a weekend or a holiday, whereas in the United States they are on a working day. Perhaps most important, the burden of registering voters in many other nations is often assumed by the state, whereas in the United States it falls on the individual citizen. The degree of that burden varies with the state and locality. In some cases, one may register when one votes (Minnesota and Wisconsin) or by mail; in other cases, registration must be done in advance, sometimes in inconvenient places. Two political scientists have estimated that if all states adopted one of the easier forms of registration, turnout might increase in the range of 8 to 10 percent (Wolfinger and Rosenstone, 1980). The registration issue becomes especially important in the United States because people move more frequently than in other nations, and each move requires that the citizen reregister.

These legal factors account for part of the difference in turnout between the United States and other nations. They leave one, however, with more questions than answers. What legal changes, if any, do Americans wish to adopt to increase voter turnout? Do Americans prefer to live with much of the "problem" rather than adopt some of the possible solutions?

The right to vote, as Americans see it, includes the right not to vote. As for changes in registration laws, there has already been a very marked trend in the last decade toward easing the burdens on registration which has resulted from the *separate* actions of different states and localities. Many, however, would like to see even stronger measures toward making registration easier; in the late 1970s President Carter supported legislation for a *national* registration system that would rely on postcards. The legislation failed, in part because many feared that it would lead to increased voting fraud and in part because many resisted any steps toward a national takeover of the process of election administration. While it is clear, therefore, that there are some legal steps which could be taken to increase voting turnout, it is debatable whether these steps are desirable.

After the legal considerations are taken into account, the two remaining factors that could explain lower turnout in the United States are institutional factors and citizens' attitudes. Institutional factors would seem to play some role. Parties in the United States are generally weaker than those in most western democracies. In particular, most other nations have strong labor or socialist parties, and these probably do a better job of mobilizing the working-class segments of the population than either American party does. Finally, citizens' attitudes may or may not account for any remaining differences. Americans, we noted, seem to cherish their liberty *not* to vote if they do not wish. Nevertheless, even with the recent loss of "trust" in government's capacity to solve problems, Americans remain *more* confident than the citizens of other nations of their ability to affect events by their political actions.

Historical Trends in Voting

Declining turnouts in relation to the past raise a different set of issues. Actually, the evidence here suggests two separate problems. First, there has been a sharp decline reported in turnout rates from the nineteenth to the twentieth century; second, there has been a gradual decline in turnout from 1960 to the present.

Turnout in the Nineteenth Century The discovery of the decline of voting in comparison with the last century came as something of a shock to many students of voting behavior. High voting rates were thought somehow to be the property of advanced democracies; and within advanced democracies, it was well known that the higher the level of formal education, the more likely it is that a person will vote. On the basis of these suppositions and current relationships, it could hardly be expected that the citizens of former times, when the level of formal education was so much lower, would be much *more* likely to vote. Yet this is exactly what the numbers showed.

To be sure, there are problems with the reliability of the figures. Election statistics in many areas of the country in the nineteenth century were doctored in accord with the corrupt practices of the time. (Such practices, of course, are not unknown today.) There are numerous instances in the nineteenth century where counties reported the turnout rates in excess of the number of eligible voters in their area! (This "trick" resulted from merely fixing the figures or from having people in one town travel across to another and vote two or three times.) Yet even allowing for a considerable degree of corruption, it is still almost certain that in the nineteenth century, turnout among those eligible to vote was much higher than it has been in this century. The explanation for the change must be sought in looking at the three general factors identified earlier.

First, there have been changes in legal regulations. Attempts to eliminate corruption, which lay behind such reforms as the Australian ballot and voter registration laws, have made voting less "profitable" to some citizens and more "costly" to others. Once the state began printing ballots, parties had more difficulty buying votes; and with the adoption of registration laws, potential voters had to go to the additional trouble of registering before the election.

Second, among the institutional factors that have a bearing on turnout, the greater strength of political party organizations in the nineteenth century certainly is one reason accounting for the higher levels of participation. Where the parties in the nineteenth century were not buying votes or inflating the figures, they were busy organizing the voters and making sure they made it to the polls. By contrast, with much weaker party organizations today, it is up to the individual citizen to *decide* to vote. Given the extent to which parties drilled citizens and mobilized voters in the nineteenth cen-

tury, some have questioned the quality of much of the voting. Although people voted, they often did so without knowing why they were voting. In this view the decline in voting turnout was not necessarily an unhealthy development, for it left as participants in the electorate a higher percentage of citizens who truly wanted to vote and who saw their vote as an instrument for policymaking (Rusk, 1974).

Finally, in regard to citizens' attitudes toward the vote, the impression one gets from the evidence is that, despite the corruption, the act of voting was more highly valued in the nineteenth century. Politics tended to be followed more closely because there were fewer alternative forms of entertainment, such as movies or television. Politics, in effect, was the only "game" in town (Burnham, 1970; Jensen, 1971). More important, some have suggested that the substance of political controversy, which revolved around what were highly emotional social issues, made citizens feel involved with issues they thought they could understand. Today, by contrast, many campaigns focus on economic matters that may seem more confusing to the citizens. Some have even suggested that the transfer of much political power away from the parties and legislature into the courts and bureaucracy has left many with the view that the vote doesn't "count" for many things that matter (Jensen, 1978).

Turnout Since the 1960s Concern over voter turnout has focused not only on the differences between participation in the nineteenth and twentieth centuries but also on the decline in turnout since 1960. Actually, to view the matter in historical perspective, turnout today is no less than it was in 1928 and 1932, which at least provides the comforting thought that the current situation is not unprecedented. Nevertheless, there are certain factors, such as the easing of registration laws and the increase in the level of education, which would make one think that participation should be increasing, not diminishing. Analysts of the issue are not of one mind in explaining the recent decline; but the principal factors, besides some "temporary" trends resulting from the age distribution of the electorate, are, first, the decline in the strength of party organizations and strong affiliations to parties and, second, an increase in feelings of inef-

THE VOTING-PLACE, NO. 488 PEARL STREET, IN THE SIXTH WARD, NEW YORK CITY.

This scene of a polling place in New York in the 1800s, complete with free drinks and party posters, gives some idea of how the political machines of the day accomplished high voter turnout.   *(Culver Pictures)*

ficacy—that is, the belief in such sentiments as "People like me don't have any say about what the government does" (Abramson et al., 1982). No one knows for certain whether the trend in declining turnout will continue; but if, as observed in Chapter 4, the feelings of inefficacy or disaffection were partly the result of particular events like the Vietnamese war and Watergate, then a leveling off of the turnout rate and perhaps an increase would be likely.

Nonvoters: Who Are They?

If one says that nearly half of the electorate does not vote in a presidential election, the problem sounds very grave. It calls up the specter of millions of disaffected citizens, waiting perhaps to be mo-bilized by a radical party to oppose the political system. Yet this way of depicting the matter creates a serious distortion. Nearly half of the citizens do not vote in any *particular* election, but they are not the *same* citizens from one election to the next. In examining the reasons for nonvoting, it turns out that *most* nonvoters have not removed themselves permanently as participating citizens. One group of nonvoters consists of those who recently moved and didn't manage to register; another of those who were ill, couldn't find transportation, or faced some sort of conflict; another of those who deliberately sat out an election because of dissatisfaction with the particular candidates running. In most of these instances of nonvoting, nonvoters will come back into the electorate in another election, just as many of those who voted will for one reason or another *not* vote in some future election. In short, the non-voter frequently turns out to be an *average* citizen—one's neighbor, one's teacher, or perhaps one's own self.

Much nonvoting is explained by or related to the life cycle. At the very top of the age bracket, voting declines among the oldest voters, probably for reasons of health or loss of interest. At the other end, young voters (18 to 24 years of age) turn out at a very low rate, probably because many are not yet settled in communities or habituated to the duties of citizenship. Being young, however, is not a permanent affliction. Young people eventually grow older and then, surprisingly, behave like older people.

Insofar as there is a potential problem of mass disaffection, it centers on that portion of the non-voting citizenry that is permanently outside of the active electorate and that never intends to vote. Although the number of such persons is not insignificant, it is considerably smaller than the "nearly half" who don't vote in presidential elections, and probably much closer to 10 or 15 percent of the electorate. Many of these people are simply indifferent to politics, while some small percentage constitutes the genuinely disaffected element that many all too readily associate with the nonvoter.

Of course, it is important in assessing the representative character of elections to consider the overall rates of nonvoting and not just the "permanent" nonvoters. If in every election the voting population were somehow dramatically different from the nonvoting populace, then one might begin to speak of nonvoting as making an important difference for the outcome of elections. What one finds, however, is that while there are some differences between the composite picture of voters and nonvoters, they are not very dramatic. Nonvoters, as one would expect, register a somewhat greater dissatisfaction or "alienation" than voters. And nonvoters include somewhat higher percentages of poorer, less well educated, and nonwhite persons than are included among voters (see Table 7-1). Of all the factors shown in Table 7-1, education seems to be the one most strongly associated with rates of participation.

Whether these modest demographic differences between voters and nonvoters make an important political difference, however, depends in the final

TABLE 7-1

PARTICIPATION IN NATIONAL ELECTIONS, BY POPULATION CHARACTERISTICS, 1972–1980

Characteristics	Percent reporting they voted		
	1972	1976	1980
Male	64.1	59.6	59.1
Female	62.0	58.8	59.4
White	64.5	60.9	60.9
Black	52.1	48.7	50.5
Age*			
18–20 years old	48.3	38.0	35.7
21–24 years old	50.7	45.6	43.1
25–34 years old	59.7	55.4	54.6
35–44 years old	66.3	63.3	64.4
45–64 years old	70.8	68.7	69.3
65 and over	63.5	62.2	65.1
Residence			
Metropolitan	64.3	59.2	58.8
Nonmetropolitan	59.4	59.1	60.2
North and west	66.4	61.2	61.0
South	55.4	54.9	55.6
Education			
8 years or less	47.4	44.1	42.6
9–11 years	52.0	47.2	45.6
12 years	65.4	59.4	58.9
More than 12 years	78.8	73.5	73.2
Employment			
Employed	66.0	62.0	61.8
Unemployed	49.0	43.7	41.2
Not in labor force	59.3	56.5	57.0

*Covers civilian noninstitutional population, 18 years old and over; also includes aliens.

Note: These are the percentages of people who say to an interviewer that they voted. People tend to overreport their participation, and thus these percentages are higher than the percentage actually voting.

Source: Statistical Abstract of the United States, 1980:500.

analysis on the *political* views of voters and nonvoters. On this point, polls of voters and nonvoters suggest no great differences between the two groups. What seems clear, first, is that the nonvoters as a whole are *not* outside the political mainstream, ready to join a radical party on either the right or the left. Their policy views contain no *radical* differences from the voters (Wolfinger and Rosenstone, 1980). Second, within this pattern of general similarity, nonvoters include a slightly higher percentage of potential Democratic voters. This confirms the conventional wisdom that a higher turnout generally helps the Democratic party, although not by very much.

The Problem of Voter Turnout

No one needs to be reminded that voting is an important form of participation. How power is allotted in our system and, in particular, who governs are matters determined in large measure by who can and who does vote. Voting is the chief majoritarian mechanism in the system designed to ensure the responsiveness of officials to the community. For citizens, voting presents an opportunity to protect certain interests and promote certain goals. It is an important tool, though not the only one, through which citizens express their sense of what direction the governing officials should (or should not) be taking. Finally, the act of voting tends to create a feeling of connection between the individual and the political system and to confirm for the individual that the government is not some alien mechanism. By involving people in this fashion, voting helps promote the overall level of support and legitimacy of the system.

For all these reasons, low levels of voting participation cannot be lightly dismissed. The analysis of nonvoting presented above was intended, not to answer all questions relating to the issue, but to provide some perspective on the problem. Much nonvoting, as we have seen, can be explained in terms that give no great cause for alarm. Nonetheless, the overall extent of nonvoting, along with certain recent trends, indicates a problem that merits close attention and great concern.

VOTING BEHAVIOR

Few areas of political science have received more attention in the last twenty years than the attempt to explain why citizens vote as they do. More is known today about voting behavior than a generation ago, but the hopes some may have had for a theory that could predict voting patterns have foundered on the same grounds as the theories that have sought to predict political opinions. The com-

plexities of human behavior are too great and the array of political stimuli too various to build a foolproof predictive system. What a generation of scholarship has taught is the difficulty of fully explaining the "simple" act of voting.

If, however, a predictive model is now impossible, we can list the general factors that influence voting behavior and indicate what is known about their relative weight and how that weight varies under certain circumstances. The purpose of such models is not to predict elections far in advance but to assist one in understanding elections as they unfold and to help one analyze long-term trends in the electorate. Ultimately, of course, the knowledge of how and why voters behave as they do has very important implications for a constitution maker's judgment about the role of elections and about issues of electoral reform.

The factors that weigh on the voter's decisions can be grouped under five general headings.* A voter may be influenced by or make assessments of:

1 Partisan identification
2 The performance of the incumbent
3 The characters and qualifications of the candidates
4 Issues and ideological stances
5 The moods, themes, and character of the times

These five categories serve to identify the types of appeals that candidates make during their campaigns. This should come as no surprise, for campaigns and voting behavior are intimately related. Voters are responding in part to what is "offered" by the candidates, and the candidates base their appeals in part in terms of what they know may influence the voters' decisions. Thus, when candidates emphasize the issues, it is more likely that the issues will weigh more heavily in the voters' mind.

The correspondence between the campaign appeals of the candidates and the behavior of the voters is, however, far from complete. The electoral system is an echo chamber, but only partly so. Information comes to voters from many sources that are not under the control of the candidates, such as

*These categories are fairly standard in the literature on voting behavior, but they are adapted here specifically from Page, 1978, and Abramson et al., 1982.

the media. More important, voting behavior is governed by dynamics of its own that are set well before the election and that candidates can affect only marginally, if at all. Candidates may seek to build their case on issues, but voters may judge them in terms of character; candidates may seek to talk about character, but voters may judge them in terms of their partisan attachment. A campaign is a momentary event, whereas some of the factors that influence voting behavior derive from ingrained habits and long-standing attitudes.

The five categories noted above are not entirely exclusive, and each tends to influence the others. One's view of the character of the candidates, for example, inevitably affects one's assessments of their positions on issues and vice versa. And one's party identification, which generally exists before the specific campaign gets under way, importantly influences one's assessment of the other factors. Because of the overlap and interaction among these categories, it is difficult to build a model that can specify precisely which factor is most important and by how much. What we can say, however, is that the relative weighting among the factors *varies*. It depends in the first place on the type of election in question. Voters behave differently in presidential elections and congressional elections, and differently from both of these in primary elections. Not only is the choice structured differently in these elections and the flow of information different, but the object of the vote is different. In one respect, of course, this is obvious: in primary elections, the factor of partisan identification plays no role, because all candidates are from the same party. But more than this is involved in the variation in voting behavior between elections. People weigh the various factors differently according to the *office* for which they are voting. For example, voters apparently rely somewhat more on party labels in congressional elections than they do in presidential elections, probably because the question of the character attributes of the individual seems more important in the case of the presidency than for Congress.

Second, the weighting among the five factors may vary over time as institutional arrangements and norms change. These "baseline" changes are especially important to consider, for they give us some indication of general trends in political behavior that operate in the face of short-term variations. The most important of these trends is the loosening hold of partisanship already mentioned in previous chapters.

Finally, the weight of the five factors varies with the immediate conditions in any election—that is, with the particular candidates involved, the issues they raise, and the immediate problems facing the nation. Each campaign, as observed, is partly a story unto itself.

In the sections that follow we shall look at voting behavior in presidential primaries and in presidential elections. We shall say a word in each case about turnout, viewing it here not from the earlier perspective of democratic theory but rather from the perspective of its impact on election outcomes. When analyzing presidential elections, we shall discuss the key questions that have concerned so many political scientists over the past two decades: What is partisan identification, how does it operate, and how has it changed in recent years as a general influence on voting behavior?

Presidential Primaries

Turnout Who votes in primaries is often as important as how people vote. Turnout is generally quite low, on the average of about one-quarter of the electorate in states holding primaries, or about half the number voting in the final election. These averages, however, mask significant state-by-state variations, which ranged in 1980, for example, all the way from 6.3 percent in Rhode Island to 44.6 percent in Wisconsin. A number of factors affect the rate of turnout in a state, including the level of competitiveness (a close race that is still undecided will stimulate high turnout), the amount of attention focused by the candidates and the media on a given state, the history and political culture of the state (states with a longer history of running primaries tend to attract a greater turnout), and the other matters being decided in the primary election (states holding primaries for other offices or presenting referendums to the voters tend to attract a higher turnout).

With turnout for primary elections being so low in comparison with that for general elections, one naturally wonders whether the primary electorate is representative of the general voting electorate and the voting electorate of the party. Much research is still being done on this issue, but there is little question now that there are significant differences between the two sets of voters. The primary electorate—as one might expect—includes a significantly higher percentage of well-educated and wealthy voters when compared with the electorate as a whole (or the electorate of each of the parties). These sociological differences do not necessarily mean that the primary electorates are unrepresentative ideologically of the voters in the general election, and on this point the evidence is not entirely clear. Most professional campaign analysts believe, however, that the primary voters, consisting of the more "activist" elements of the population, "overrepresent" the highly ideologically minded voters at the expense of the more moderate elements of the population (Shafer, 1982).

Voters in primary states must decide not only whether to turn out, but also, in some cases, which party's primary they wish to participate in. As we have seen, primary laws vary from state to state with respect to how easily voters can cross over and vote for candidates from the opposite party. In many states, the process is not very difficult, and the candidates compete actively for votes from independents and supporters from the other party. In 1976, for example, Jimmy Carter did well in many small-town and rural areas among voters who frequently voted Republican; and in 1980, Ronald Reagan made important inroads in some states among ethnic blue-collar workers who traditionally had voted Democratic. Candidates receiving support from independents or members of the other party will normally make use of it in their campaign statements as evidence of their broad appeal. Candidates who are defeated in primaries, on the other hand, will sometimes seek to minimize their loss on the grounds that their opponent received votes from members of the other party, making the contest not truly representative of the sentiments of their own party.

The Voting Decision On what basis do voters make their choice in primaries? Any one who has followed the fate of candidates in the primaries is aware of the tremendous swings in popular sentiment that can take place during the primary season. A candidate leading by a wide margin in the polls at one moment can plummet and be trailing in the next. Thus in 1980, in national polls of Republicans and independents, Ronald Reagan led George Bush in early January by a margin of 32 percent to 6 percent, fell behind Bush after the Iowa caucus (29 percent for Reagan, 32 percent for Bush), and then pulled comfortably ahead again by early March, 39 percent to 23 percent.

Rapid shifts in voters' sentiments are sometimes taken as an indication of ignorance or irrationality, but this conclusion seems unwarranted. While it is true that the knowledge voters have about the candidates' positions in the primary races is often vague or incorrect, it should also be kept in mind that, with the number of candidates and the amount of new information, a great deal is being asked of the voters—more, perhaps, than one should reasonably expect. More important, volatility and shifts in public opinion are understandable and even logical consequences of the situation in primary contests. Voters are deciding among a number of candidates *within* the same party, which makes the election in effect a nonpartisan race. The tie of party loyalty, which in the general election tends to hold many voters to their party's candidate, does not apply in primaries, and voters are often choosing among candidates who do not vary greatly in their ideological positions. From the voters' viewpoint, therefore, the candidates may be seen as essentially interchangeable. Unable to choose on ideological grounds, voters may then make up their minds on the basis of their assessment of the candidates' personal qualities or their perception of which candidates are potential winners. Both of these opinions are subject to rapid changes, as voters get to see the candidates for the first time, and as they evaluate the candidates' performances (with the help of the media) in the preceding round of primaries.

General Election for the Presidency

The general election for the presidency has been the object of most of the studies on voting behavior, and it is from these elections that the most elaborate models of voters' motivation have been constructed. The voter's decision in the general elections, as noted, is a complex weighting of partisan identification, the performance of the incumbent, the characters of the candidates, issues and ideology, and the mood of the time. Partisan identification has received the greatest attention, in part because of its importance but also because it is the one factor that can be discussed in depth without considering the particular issues or candidates running in any given election. Using the terminology of voting analysts, partisanship is a "long-term factor," whereas the others are "short-term factors." We shall save the discussion of partisanship for last.

Turnout   The rate of turnout for general elections, treated earlier as a consideration of political participation, is also marginally affected by the very same factors that motivate voter behavior. A certain percentage of voters in any particular election are making a rational decision about whether or not to vote, as determined by their evaluation of the choices. For some voters, the decision is not between the two candidates, but between voting for a particular candidate and "going fishing" or "staying home." In 1980, for example, only a small percentage of black citizens were considering a vote for the Republican, Ronald Reagan; for many black citizens, the real question was whether to turn out for President Carter (as most blacks had done in 1976) or not vote at all. (In the end, the turnout rate was slightly lower in 1980 than in 1976.) Such rational decisions of whether to vote will depend on how voters evaluate the choices before them. Although we have no poll data to confirm the point, it appears that in the latter half of the nineteenth century, when the electorate was strongly attached to political parties, elections were often decided less by people switching to vote for a candidate from the opposite party than by voters, unenthusiastic about their own party's candidate, deciding to go fishing.

Assessing Incumbency   When an incumbent runs, it is clear that most voters are making an assessment of how that candidate has already performed. What a candidate promises to do in this case may be less important than what has already been done. Of course, voters may also take into account the alternative; but where that alternative is acceptable, the voting decision will be largely backward-looking, or retrospective. The voter in this re-

spect stands, in V. O. Key's words, as a "rational god of vengeance and of reward," deciding whether to reward the president or "throw the rascal out" (Key, 1964:568).

Retrospective voting, while it is strongly affected by one's partisan identification and by one's assessment of the other factors of voting behavior, is nonetheless partly an independent judgment based on the voters' initial perception of "how well the president has performed." To the extent that voting is based on this standard, one can see how certain democratic expectations about policymaking through elections are unfounded. Voters frequently do not have specific policy positions in mind when they vote, but instead are judging how well a person has done in the job. This standard is especially compatible with a representative model of government that emphasizes leeway for elected officials in making policy decisions, with the vote being used more as an instrument to decide who should govern rather than to tie those governing to specific policies. It is therefore not surprising that the founders, in their brief discussion of standards of voting behavior, emphasized the retrospective element as the preferable standard of judgment (*Federalist* 72).

Retrospective voting is not limited only to campaigns in which an incumbent is running. When vice presidents run as successors to presidents, they inevitably assume in the voters' minds much of the responsibility for the incumbent administration. It is almost impossible for a vice president to break completely with a president, although a vice president has sometimes tried to put *some* distance between himself and the incumbent's policies. Adding up the elections in this century in which either an incumbent president or vice president has run, one has most of the elections—17 of the last 21. Even where an incumbent president or vice president is not running, however, a *partial* retrospective element can be present through the vehicle of the party. The nominee of the incumbent party may assume some of the responsibility for the past administration. Because the nominee and past administration share the same party, voters probably reason, they would govern in much the same way.

Issues and Ideology   Some voting is specifically based on voters' assessments of the candidates' po-

Presidents like to claim that their programs reflect the voters' mandate for change, but many of Reagan's supporters were startled by the effects of his administration's cuts in domestic spending.   *(Don Rypka/UPI)*

sitions on issues and their ideological stances. To the extent that this consideration is involved, the voting choice emphasizes what candidates will do rather than what they may already have done. For this type of voting to operate, voters must be concerned about some particular issue or issues, must see that the candidates actually have stands on these issues that are different, and then must consider basing their decision on this difference. Making these kinds of judgments may require more information than many voters normally possess; however, much recent research on voting behavior has indicated that the prospects for issue voting depend greatly on the situation. It will increase where there are important issues that are of concern to large numbers of voters and where they perceive that there are in fact differences between the candidates (Fiorina, 1981). In some elections, where the candidates were strongly differentiated (1964, 1972, and 1980), issue voting was an important factor; whereas in other elections, where the candidates were perceived to be much the same (1960, 1968, and 1976), it was less important.

Some voters consider the candidates' basic ideological position and, depending on their preferences, vote for the more conservative or the more liberal candidate. For the most part, however, ide-

ology is important not in and of itself but as it operates through voters' responses to different issues. By knowing something about the ideological disposition of voters in various areas, therefore, we can predict their likely responses to the issues that emerge in campaigns.

Journalists and politicians often speak of an electoral "mandate" for a president to act in a particular way on some policy issue raised during the campaign. Much of this talk, however, is poetic (or political) license. To provide a clear mandate, voters would have to vote on the issues (which they frequently do not do) and would have to consider the *same* set of issues as being of greatest concern (which is often not the case). These criteria, technically speaking, are seldom met. Nevertheless, presidential elections do indicate, in a general way, relative swings in sentiment on major issues; and victors, even if they stretch the point somewhat, will never cease to speak of their mandates. Such talk is a (partial) fiction in which almost everyone collectively indulges.

Character   Never quite separable from all the other factors influencing voters' behavior is the voters' assessment of the candidates' qualifications and character. The presidency is a highly personalized office in which the individual attributes of the president, including qualities of personality and style, decisively influence how the nation is governed. Voters realize this, and they also realize that many of the critical decisions a president may face are not known at the time of an election, but will emerge in response to events. For all these reasons, voters want someone in the presidency whom they feel they can trust to do the job. This judgment, though affected by the candidate's party and stands on the issues, is partly beyond partisanship and ideology. It is a consideration very much compatible with a representative model of governing, although in practice certain kinds of character appeal are based on qualities irrelevant or even dangerous to a healthy political order (Page, 1978; *Federalist* 68).

Trying to inform voters about character—or to "sell" an image—constitutes a major part of any campaign and is also a major factor in the voter's decision. All the qualities people esteem or dislike are not easily catalogued. But it is clear from poll data, to take a few examples, that most voters had an immense amount of respect and admiration for Eisenhower, who had been a World War II hero; that many viewed both McGovern in 1972 and Carter in 1980 as weak and ineffective leaders; and, finally, that many saw Goldwater in 1964 and McGovern in 1972 as extreme in their views and not especially competent (Asher, 1980).

Moods, Themes, and the Character of the Times Elections, somehow, deal with more than records, specific issues, and character; they tap and register in different ways general moods and assessments of where the nation is going and what it stands for. Candidates may appeal to such diverse themes as the need to get the nation moving again (Kennedy's appeal in 1960), the need to restore its moral purity (Carter's appeal in 1976), and the need to restore its self-confidence (Reagan's appeal in 1980). Voters make their decisions, in some measure, on their "feel" of the times and on which candidate embodies the right direction for the United States.

Because this aspect of voting behavior is rather vague, it has often been viewed with suspicion or dismissed as merely symbolic. Yet these considerations, even when they do not translate into iden-

tifiable policies, can, like character considerations, be legitimate clues to how candidates will respond to issues in the future. Moreover, there is a sense in which elections are legitimately symbolic. Voters use them not just to determine who will hold office, but to establish which view of American culture is in the ascendancy or the decline. For example, in the symbolic appeals of Nixon supporters in the election of 1972, a vote "against acid, amnesty, and abortion" was an effort to express, however vaguely, that "the people" stood more firmly for order and traditional values.

Partisan Identification

Partisan identification is a voter's perception of the party to which he or she feels attached. It is *not* a legal concept, but rather a political reality which politicians have long been aware of and which pollsters now can measure. Partisan identification is discovered in polls by simply asking the citizen which partisan position—Democratic, Republican, or independent—best describes his or her outlook. (The precise questions differ with different polling organizations, and some polls attempt to probe the *degree* of partisan strength by asking whether people consider themselves to be strong or weak Democrats or Republicans, or independents that lean toward the Democratic or Republican party.)

Partisan attachment is important because it serves as a partial anchor for many voters. The significance that voters attach to parties means that each election is *not* viewed as an entirely new event conducted on a clean slate. Rather, the partisan begins the campaign with a certain disposition or tendency to support his or her party. Each of the parties has a long history that evokes certain reactions which influence the voter's behavior. For the partisan, therefore, the presidential campaign is a race, not simply between two particular candidates, but rather between two parties. In 1980 Ronald Reagan was not just an individual candidate by the name of "Ronald Reagan." He was the *Republican* party's nominee, and that fact weighed heavily for many voters. In some cases, it was almost enough by itself to determine the vote, while in other cases it was a factor that influenced how other matters, such as issues and the candidates, were judged.

Evidence of the importance of partisanship is

TABLE 7-2
VOTING PATTERNS OF PARTISAN IDENTIFIERS, 1952–1980

Group	1952 Dem.	1952 Rep.	1956 Dem.	1956 Rep.	1960 Dem.	1960 Rep.	1964 Dem.	1964 Rep.	1968 Dem.	1968 Rep.	1968 Wallace	1972 Dem.	1972 Rep.	1976 Dem.	1976 Rep.	1976 M†	1980 Dem.	1980 Rep.	1980 A†
Republicans	8	92	4	96	5	95	20	80	9	86	5	5	95	9	91	1	11	84	4
Democrats	77	23	85	15	84	16	87	13	74	12	14	67	33	82	18	*	66	26	6
Independents	35	65	30	70	43	57	56	44	31	44	25	31	69	38	57	*	30	54	12

*Less than 1 percent.
†M = McCarthy; A = Anderson.
Note: The numbers represent the percent of the total persons voting in each party in a given year.
Source: Gallup poll, published November 1968, December 1968, December 1972, and December 1976. 1980 data, CBS News/ *New York Times* poll.

easily provided by comparing partisan identification and voting decisions (see Table 7-2). No one, perhaps, will be surprised to learn that in election after election, most Democrats vote for the Democratic candidate and most Republicans for the Republican candidate. As obvious as this may seem, however, it is nonetheless very important. The underlying ratio of partisan strength affects the probability of the outcome (the larger party has the advantage); and it influences the strategies adopted during the campaign (the majority-party candidate will normally remind the voters of the importance of parties, whereas the minority-party candidate may often seek to emphasize other factors). Moreover, basic historical changes in the character of the American electorate are best described by looking at the respective role of partisanship from one era to another. As we have already observed, modern campaigns differ in important respects from those of a century or even a generation ago because of the fewer number of partisans and their weaker ties to their party.

How Partisanship Operates   It is clearly not sufficient to cite statistics on the degree of partisan support for a party's candidates. One must also consider how and why partisan attachments actually work to influence a voter's decision. Without understanding this connection, it is impossible to determine when or why voters will defect from their party.

Studies on this question have uncovered a variety of ways in which voters form partisan attachments and allow these attachments to influence their vote. For some partisans, it appears, the attachment is chiefly a matter of habit and emotion, formed over a long period and perhaps even inherited from their parents. Barring a major change in the fundamental issues of the political environment, they will vote for the party with which they identify. For these voters partisan identification is not entirely different from the loyalties people demonstrate for the social groups to which they belong or for their favorite team. An interview with a voter in the 1950s is typical of this kind of partisan attachment: "My father is a Democrat and I'm one by inheritance sort of. I know nothing about politics but I like the Democratic Party . . ." (Campbell et al., 1960:238).

For other partisans, the attachment is based on their commitment to certain positions or values which they see their selected party as embodying over the long run. In this case, the partisan attachment is less emotional and more rational; it is based on a stand of the voter. But the attachment is still long-term. The voter's partisan identification represents a tally of past experience and an expression of political memory (Fiorina, 1981; Abramson et al., 1982). This running tally is then applied to the specific election and used, consciously or unconsciously, to evaluate the other factors and to save time gathering information. In the words of another voter, "Democrats helped the farmers . . . and are more for the working class people. . . . I think the Republicans favor the richer folks" (Campbell et al., 1960:136). In a "typical" situation—that is, one without an especially important new issue or without especially compelling or repulsive candidates—the partisan attachment will usually determine the voting decision.*

While partisanship is clearly important in influencing the vote, it is far from determinative. In every election millions of partisans deviate and vote for the candidate of the other party. (Thus, in 1980, Ronald Reagan won the votes of more than a quarter of all Democrats.) And those who do vote for the candidate of their own party must still be won over in each campaign. Partisans—or at any rate most of them—weigh the short-term factors of the campaign, and only a relatively small number of them are so committed to their party that they will vote "automatically" for their party's nominee. Indeed, even for the most committed partisans, a radical deviation by the party from its own traditional positions can lead to defections. For example, if George Wallace, a former proponent of segregation, had been nominated by the Democratic party in 1972, most black voters almost certainly would have voted against him, despite their partisan identification. The frequent references that some analysts make about "habitual" voting, therefore, should not be taken to mean that voters are mere robots. The habit many citizens have of supporting their party (and frequently ignoring the immediate issues of the campaign) rests on the background assumption that the parties maintain a degree of continuity and that they support roughly the same positions as they did before.

When and Why Voters Change Partisan Identification   Once voters adopt or come to hold a partisan identification, they tend to keep it for a long time. In each election, of course, some voters change their party identification, and the overall strength of party following is also continually being affected by demographic changes, as new voters enter the electorate and others die. During certain periods there is an unusually high amount of shift-

*All scholars of voting behavior agree that some partisanship is primarily of the first sort described (habitual and affective) and some primarily of the second (a rational shorthand of past experience). Yet certain scholars have placed more emphasis on one or the other as the *major* explanation of partisan behavior. The authors of *The American Voter* (Campbell et al., 1960), an early landmark study of voting behavior, stressed the first explanation, while V. O. Key (1966) and Morris Fiorina (1981) have emphasized the second.

ing of partisan attachment, resulting ordinarily in a net gain for one party or the other. These are the realigning periods referred to earlier. During these periods, large numbers of voters decide not only to vote for a candidate from the opposite party, but to leave their former party and become either independents or supporters of the other party. Such a step is generally not made very easily. Voters will have to see a political issue as being extremely important and come to believe that the ideas and programs of their party are out of date or ineffectual. Young voters who have "inherited" a partisan identification are more likely to make such a change, since their attachment to their party is generally not as strong as that of older voters who may once have made a conscious commitment to one of the parties. A large portion of the shift in partisan support in any realigning period therefore tends to come from young voters and voters entering the electorate for the first time (Anderson, 1979).

The figures for partisan change in the 1970s show some weakening of the strength of the Democratic party toward the end of the decade and a slight gain for the Republicans after 1980. These figures, however, mask much of the movement in partisan identification over the last decade, since there has been a great deal of shifting among different voters from one party to another that has tended to balance itself off in absolute numbers (Nie et al., 1976). Many southern whites, for example, have been moving away from the Democratic party, while many young New England Protestants have left the Republican party. Although we have no figures for partisan attachment before the 1930s, it is possible that the amount of partisan shifting in the decade of the 1970s equaled that of many realigning periods, even though there has been no clear reversal in party dominance. Whether this shifting and sorting out will eventually lead to a large change in the overall strength between the two parties remains to be seen.

The Partisan Balance: Republicans and Democrats   The difference in strength between the two major parties, with Democrats having had so many more adherents in the post-New Deal period than Republicans, makes one wonder how Republicans have managed to do so well in presiden-

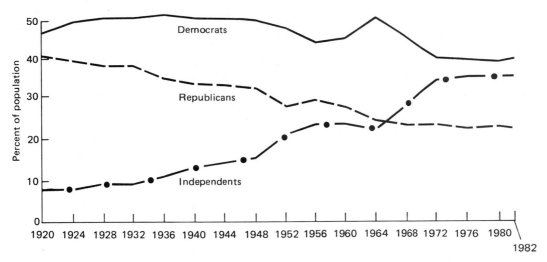

FIGURE 7-3
Party identification of the American electorate. (*Source:* Anderson, 1979:71; other data from
Center for Political Studies and National Opinion Research Center.)

tial elections, winning five of eight elections from 1952 through 1980. Accidental short-term factors may have favored Republicans more than Democrats; but this explanation, except perhaps in the case of the great personal popularity of Eisenhower and unpopularity of George McGovern (1972), is not the whole story. Several other factors are more important.

First, Republicans turn out to vote at a higher rate than Democrats, which narrows the voting strength between the two parties. Second, a certain number of self-proclaimed Democrats—found mostly among white voters in the south—actually vote fairly regularly for Republicans at the presidential level. Their identification with the Democratic party has grown out of politics at levels other than the presidency, and over the past twenty years they have shown an increasing willingness to desert their party in presidential contests. For national politics, it is false to consider them as Democrats. Finally, Democrats are much more likely to defect from their party than Republicans are. As a more diverse and heterogeneous coalition, the Democratic party ordinarily finds that its presidential nominee cannot satisfy all the constituent groups within the party. Many more Democrats are conservative on some dimensions of policy than Re-

publicans are liberal. These factors taken together should give one pause in claiming that the Democratic party is clearly ahead of the Republican party. The lead that Democrats enjoy in polls of party identification is partly fictitious and in any case not easily transferred into a national majority on presidential elections.

Long-Term Changes in the Nature of Partisanship Partisan attachment as a factor influencing electoral behavior has itself undergone two important changes.

First, as we have observed already, there are fewer partisans (and fewer strong partisans) in the electorate today than thirty years ago, when scientific polling on this question first began. The growth in the number of independents over the past thirty years, especially among younger voters, has been slow but steady and has left the electorate much less partisan than in the past. Research has shown that many independents tend to vote fairly regularly for one party or another; but, even so, these independents cannot be counted on to follow their "party" in the same way as a partisan voter can (Keith, 1977).

Second, partisan attachment is not as important in influencing the actual vote as in the past. Today,

Dwight Eisenhower's wartime leadership, his unpretentious charm, his honesty, and his nonpolitical background combined to make him the best-liked president since World War II.   *(UPI)*

voters who identify with one party are less hesitant to vote for a candidate from the other party. Partisan attachments simply do not mean as much to voters as they once did, and more and more voters behave like independents even when they declare a partisan preference.

The decline in partisan attachment is a result of both political and institutional factors. The political reason centers on the fact that the old issues of the New Dealers, which gave the parties their distinctive characteristics in the period from 1936 to 1968, have become less important, and new issues have taken their place. The institutional reasons center on the changes in the nominating process, which have focused more attention on the individual candidates; the decline in strength of local party organizations; and the increasing reliance on

the mass media as a source of campaign information. Whatever the precise causes, however, it is clear today that partisan identification structures the vote much less than in the past.

General Characteristics of the Modern Electorate   At the same time that partisan attachment has declined, there has been an increase in the last two decades in the number of voters who apply their ideological stance to their voting decision. Many of these voters classify themselves as independents, even though they normally vote Democratic if they are liberal and Republican if they are conservative. These voters represent a new breed of independents, committed firmly in their political views yet unwilling to cast their lot with either of the parties.

BOX 7-2

A SURVEY OF PRESIDENTIAL ELECTIONS, 1952–1980

1952 In their effort to recapture the presidency after twenty years of Democratic rule, the Republicans nominated former General Dwight Eisenhower, whose personal popularity was such that many Democrats had earlier sought Eisenhower out to be the candidate of their party. Eisenhower and the Republicans ran against the record of the incumbent party, blasting it alternately for mistakes made in the Korean war, the infiltration of communists into the government, and the corruption of certain high officials. These issues, and the general theme of an incompetent administration which they evoked, were summed up by the slogan ''Korea, Communism, and Corruption.'' These attacks on the Truman administration were as important as Eisenhower's great personal popularity, which exceeded that of any politician of his day. Adlai Stevenson, the well-spoken governor of Illinois, became the Democratic nominee and sought to rally Democrats to their traditional party loyalty on the themes of the New Deal and Fair Deal. Partisan considerations were important, but a sufficient number of Democrats and independents went for Eisenhower to give him a comfortable measure of victory. The Republican campaign buttons in effect summed up what was most important: I LIKE IKE.

1956 The 1956 election was a repeat of the 1952 election, with Stevenson challenging Eisenhower as the incumbent. This campaign was one of the most uninspiring of recent times. Stevenson attempted to find fault with Eisenhower's record, with little success, and sought again to rally the traditional Democratic majority. Nearly all his votes came from Democrats and were based on partisan attachment, but this was not enough to overcome the great personal popularity that Eisenhower enjoyed. Although the president's record was not viewed as great or inspiring, it was nevertheless sufficiently creditable to allow independents and some Democrats to vote their personal preference for Eisenhower as a candidate.

1960 The Democrats chose Senator John F. Kennedy, the first Catholic to be nominated since Al Smith in 1928. The Republicans went with their vice president, Richard Nixon. Few major issues divided the candidates during the election, though the basic principles of the two men reflected the positions of their parties, with Kennedy more sympathetic to federal solutions to problems like health and education, and Nixon more reluctant to endorse federal programs. Kennedy, while not attacking Eisenhower directly, nonetheless ran against the record of the Republican administration and appealed very strongly to the theme of ''getting the country moving again.'' His rhetoric emphasized the vague idea of a ''new frontier,'' which was a general appeal to a more active and progressive federal government. Nixon emphasized his personal experience (and Kennedy's inexperience), in addition to defending the Republican record. Nixon benefited from this appeal, but Kennedy, with the help of his running mate, Lyndon Johnson of Texas, was able to hold the support of enough traditional Democrats to win the election. The religious issue, though not debated by the candidates, played a significant role in voters' decisions. Kennedy did better than might otherwise have been expected among Catholic voters, and Nixon received somewhat more support from Protestants. The election was extremely close, with Kennedy winning by the narrowest of margins.

1964 The Democrats nominated the incumbent, Lyndon Johnson, who assumed the presidency after the assassination of President Kennedy in 1963. The Republican nominee was Senator Barry Goldwater, who was one of the most outspoken conservatives in the party. The ideological choice presented to the American people was more sharply focused than at any time since 1936, and it is not surprising that the role played by issues in the voting decisions of Americans was greater than that in any election since 1952. Goldwater argued that the American people had become disillusioned with the policies of Democratic liberalism and that the electorate was prepared to realign in support of the principles of conservatism. The election, however, proved differently. Not only did Goldwater fail to attract the support of Democrats and independents, but he actually lost the backing of many Republicans. Indeed, there is evidence to suggest that a substantial number of Republicans began to reconsider their allegiance to the party, and certainly Goldwater hastened the exit of the small but still significant percentage of blacks who had been Republican adherents. Goldwater did, however, manage to convert some Democrats to the Republican side in the deep south, which was the only area of the country where he did better than Nixon had done in 1960. Johnson ran on his record and on the Kennedy legacy, which he claimed to be carrying through. With the nation enjoying unprecedented prosperity, and with the passage of much new legislation, Johnson received a ringing endorsement, defeating Goldwater in a major landslide.

Continued on next page.

BOX 7-2

CONTINUED

1968 The 1968 election came in the midst of the Vietnamese war and after a series of racial riots that rocked the country. Divisions in the nation were much greater than usual, and political tensions ran high. In addition to the major party nominees, Nixon for the Republicans and Vice President Humphrey for the Democrats, there was a strong third-party challenge headed by George Wallace from Alabama. Wallace attacked the intrusion of the federal government into state and local affairs and decried the growing lawlessness of American society. His campaign fed on a reaction to the new social programs of the "Great Society"—Lyndon Johnson's extension of Democratic liberal policies—and on the frustrations of the Vietnamese war. Voters for Wallace were obviously not motivated by party attachment, as his party was a new one, but were activated by their response to the issues and themes of his campaign.

Humphrey led a divided Democratic party, trying in vain to defend Johnson's policies while putting enough distance between himself and Johnson to offer some kind of alternative. Nixon ran as the experienced statesman against the "failures" of the Johnson years and on the premise that new approaches to our foreign and domestic challenges were required. Nixon benefited in the race from the public's disenchantment with the Johnson record on the Vietnamese war, and from a growing reaction among Americans to aspects of the new phase of liberalism of the Democratic years.

The election raised a set of issues different from the standard economic issues of the New Deal era. These issues cut against the Democratic nominee, causing defections to Wallace and Nixon, but they did not provoke a permanent realignment in favor of the Republicans. Indeed, this election was nearly as close as the 1960 contest between Kennedy and Nixon.

1972 Repeating the Republicans' mistake of 1964, the Democrats nominated a candidate from the extreme of their party, the very liberal Senator George McGovern. McGovern based his campaign on opposition to the Vietnamese war, which he promised to conclude by a unilateral American withdrawal, and on a new plan for income redistribution. McGovern quickly became associated with elements who had supported his candidacy from the beginning of the primary season and who were viewed by many voters as radical. For those who have an interest in slogans, opponents of McGovern invented the "three A's"— "Acid, Amnesty, and Abortion"—which were depicted to be his campaign stand. An obvious exaggeration,

this slogan nonetheless captured the picture many carried of McGovern as an extremist. His political positions were only part of the problem, however. Coupled with this were the doubts people had about McGovern's capacity as a leader. These were reenforced by his ill-fated choice of Senator Thomas Eagleton as his vice presidential nominee, which had to be reversed after Eagleton's medical record became known. McGovern's personal credibility suffered immensely, and voters generally came to doubt his competence to be president.

President Nixon ran on his record, on his attempt to project statesmanlike qualities (especially in foreign affairs), and on his pledge to end quickly American involvement in the war on "honorable" terms. The race ended in a landslide victory for President Nixon, and talk again surfaced about a new realignment in American politics. Such talk proved premature, however. Masses of Democratic voters turned against their own nominee and were no doubt also expressing concern against the "big government" programs bequeathed by the Democratic party. They were not, however, willing to switch parties, and any sentiments they may have had along these lines quickly changed with the revelations of Watergate, which totally discredited Nixon as a leader and forced his resignation.

1976 The Democratic nominee, Jimmy Carter, faced the Republican incumbent, Gerald Ford, who had assumed the presidency after Nixon's resignation in 1974. Carter ran a campaign quite different from that of any of his Democratic predecessors. While professing to be a liberal, he nonetheless ran against the "big government" that liberalism had created. He promised to create a more efficient national government and directed much of his rhetoric against the waste and mismanagement of federal programs. Carter also ran against the economic record of the Ford years, blasting the administration for creating high unemployment and inflation. Perhaps the central element of the Carter appeal, however, was thematic. Carter promised truthfulness in government and proclaimed constantly his own honesty and integrity. This combined thematic and character appeal fell upon very sympathetic ears after the many revelations of corruption and wrongdoing in the Nixon administration. President Ford himself was not implicated in any of these activities, but inevitably he had to take some of the responsibility for his party. Moreover, by pardoning former President Nixon, Ford opened himself to charges of having engaged in a deal for the presidency

BOX 7-2

CONTINUED

and of protecting someone who deserved criminal punishment.

Carter did manage to attract enough support among Democratic identifiers to gain a narrow victory, but by no means was the edifice of the old Democratic coalition solidly reconstructed. Indeed, Carter's appeal, which, as noted, was based on the theme of honesty more than on a support for liberalism, indicated part of the problem that existed for the Democratic party. Democrats remained nominally the majority party, but a good many of their adherents were no longer attracted by traditional Democratic programs or by the traditional Democratic concept of using the power of the federal government to solve major social ills. Republicans, starting in 1968, had been able to capitalize in part on this disenchantment with liberalism, but they were unable as of 1976 to convert voters permanently to their side. Indeed, many analysts questioned whether any kind of "permanent" realignment was still possible, given the decline of parties and the increased tendency of voters to be independents.

1980 The 1980 election was a great victory for the Republicans, though it is still too soon to say whether it constituted the start of a full-scale realignment. The Democratic nominee, President Jimmy Carter, survived a strong challenge for the nomination from Senator Edward Kennedy. The party managed to unite behind the president, but the enthusiasm for his candidacy was at best lukewarm. Lacking a clear belief in the liberal philosophy of government and tentative about his own record, Carter adopted a twofold campaign strategy of attempting to rekindle partisan sentiments among Democrats and attacking his opponent as extreme and unreliable. At one point, Carter implied that Reagan was a racist and at several other points suggested that he was a warmonger. This negative campaign did succeed for a time in raising doubts about Reagan, but in the end it backfired. In the one televised debate between the candidates, Reagan successfully deflected the president's charges, and the president suffered badly as a result of his own attacks.

For his part, Reagan won his party's nomination more easily than most expected, surviving the challenges of a number of credible opponents, including his eventual vice presidential choice, George Bush. Reagan, who came from the conservative wing of the Republican party, articulated a "new" conservative program of progress and economic growth. He promised to cut the size of the federal government, while pledging also to increase defense expenditures and to take a much tougher stance toward the Soviet Union. While Reagan emphasized the positive aspects of his brand of conservatism, he also hammered away at Jimmy Carter's record, especially on the economy and on foreign affairs. His overall strategy, which proved successful, was to make people doubt Jimmy Carter's ability to govern while presenting a positive and credible alternative, both in regard to his personal qualifications and his governing philosophy.

John Anderson ran as an independent, appealing largely to voters who thought Carter incompetent and Reagan too extreme. Drawing mostly from independents, and about equally from Democrats and Republicans, Anderson managed 7 percent of the vote, which qualified him retroactively for a share of public funds in 1980 and assured him of funding for 1984.

Ideological voters still constitute a minority of the voting public, but their increasing numbers give them a larger influence than before. This influence may be greatest, as we have observed, in elections having low turnout rates, such as presidential primaries and off-term congressional races.

The modern electorate, in sum, is less tied to partisan voting patterns than a generation ago—although partisanship still remains a very important factor. An increased number of voters, among them many independents, are strongly committed to an ideological position, and their votes are cast in a relatively predictable way to support either the more liberal or more conservative candidate. For the most part, however, the decline in the percentage and binding strength of partisanship has left more voters somewhere in the middle, capable of being won over by the candidate of either party and highly subject to the short-term factor. The modern electorate is thus much more volatile in the sense of being able to swing dramatically from one party to another in succeeding elections. Formerly, because of the strength of partisanship, each party's candidate could anticipate a solid base of support within the electorate, and campaigns were directed at the relatively small portion of potential swing voters who could determine the outcome. In recent elections, more and more voters are open to persuasion in each campaign, and the base support that each party can firmly expect has diminished. This change makes the campaigns themselves more important in the sense that more voters are making up their minds about the candidates during the campaign. (We include here the preconvention period, in which voters are also taking the measure of the candidates.) More so than in the past, voters respond to the variable factors of each campaign—to the incumbent's record, the immediate issues, the character of the candidates, and moods and themes.

THE GROUP BASIS OF PARTISANSHIP AND VOTING

The five factors, including partisanship, that influence voters' decisions should help to explain why citizens vote as they do. But this sort of explanation also raises questions, for one immediately wants to know what leads citizens to adopt a certain partisan position or to judge issues from a liberal or conservative perspective. This kind of inquiry leads directly back to the kind of question posed in Chapter 4: What are the sources of political opinions?

Without our repeating the earlier discussion, it may be recalled that we traced opinion formation to such causes as the family, education, and reference groups. Reference groups, traditionally at least, have played an extremely important role in influencing partisanship and voting. People who share certain social characteristics tend to view the world in similar terms and therefore to vote in the same way. In addition, people in certain groups may consciously see themselves as having an interest of their own that should be represented by collective voting behavior. Politicians, of course, respond by thinking in terms of mobilizing certain groups or categories of voters, and they often do this by actively seeking the endorsements of group leaders and making appeals to the voters in terms of group interests.

The group basis of opinion and voting behavior is what enables one to pose the question "Who are Democrats and Republicans?" without responding with the unhelpful answer: Those who are Democrats or Republicans. One can say, for example, that Republicans are more likely to be businesspeople and farmers, and that Democrats are more likely to be union members and nonwhites (see Table 7-3).

What is noteworthy today, however, is the extent to which the group basis of voting has grown *weaker*. In the past, it was possible to give a fairly accurate portrait of party followings in terms of the groups that supported each party. Of course, it was never the case that everyone in any group voted exactly the same way. Still, one could characterize the Democratic coalition of the 1940s as consisting of labor union workers, southerners (whites), Catholics, and Jews. Today, by contrast, very few identifiable groups can be considered safe members of a party. More than two-thirds of the black and Jewish voters regularly vote for Democratic candidates, and more than two-thirds of wealthy businesspeople regularly vote for Republicans. Other

TABLE 7-3

WHO LIKES THE DEMOCRATS?

Percentage of Various Groups Saying They Voted for the Democratic Presidential Candidate, 1952–1980

Group	1952	1956	1960	1964	1968*	1972	1976	1980†
Sex								
Male	47	45	52	60	41	37	53	37
Female	42	39	49	62	45	38	48	45
Race								
White	43	41	49	59	38	32	46	36
Nonwhite	79	61	68	94	85	87	85	82
Education								
College	34	31	39	52	37	37	42	35
Grade school	52	50	55	66	52	49	58	43
Occupation								
Professional and business	36	32	42	54	34	31	42	33
Blue-collar	55	50	60	71	50	43	58	46
Age								
Under 30	51	43	54	64	47	48	53	43
50 and over	39	39	46	59	41	36	52	na
Religion								
Protestant	37	37	38	55	35	30	46	na
Catholic	56	51	78	76	59	48	57	40
Jewish‡	71	77	89	89	85	66	68	45
Southerners	51	49	51	52	31	29	54	47

*1968 election had three major candidates (Humphrey, Nixon, and Wallace).

†1980 election had three major candidates (Carter, Reagan, and Anderson).

‡Jewish vote estimated from various sources; since the number of Jewish persons interviewed is often less than 100, the error in this figure, as well as that for nonwhites, may be large.

Note: na = not available.

Source: Kirkpatrick, 1978:264–265; 1980 data from CBS News/*New York Times* survey.

groups display certain tendencies, but none that are entirely fixed. The general tendency—as shown in Table 7-4, where higher numbers indicate greater differentiation—is for less group differentiation in voting habits, not more. We have not yet reached the point of complete individuality in voting behavior wherein no social characteristics distinguish Democrats and Republicans (or liberals and conservatives). But the electorate today definitely is made up of more and more individuals who do *not* take cues from recognizable reference groups. Candidates when they run for president must accord-

ingly think somewhat less of the fixed attributes of voters and more of how unrecognized voters respond to the issues of the campaign.

The evolution of voting patterns of reference groups provides an interesting insight into the character of the electorate today. In the following sections we shall look briefly at the effects of race, religion, region, and sex on ideology and norms. Curiously, while group-related behavior has generally been declining, we have recently seen the emergence of slight, but nevertheless quite distinct, differences of opinion and voting based on gender.

TABLE 7-4

RELATIONSHIP OF SOCIAL CHARACTERISTICS TO PRESIDENTIAL VOTING, 1944–1980[a]

	Election year									
	1944	**1948**	**1952**	**1956**	**1960**	**1964**	**1968**	**1972**	**1976**	**1980**
Racial voting[b]	27	12	40	25	23	36	56	57	48	56
Regional voting[c]										
Among whites			12	17	6	−11	−4	−13	1	1
Among entire electorate			9	15	4	−5	6	−3	7	3
Union voting[d]										
Among whites	20	37	18	15	21	23	13	11	18	15
Among entire electorate	20	37	20	17	19	22	13	10	17	16
Class voting[e]										
Among whites	19	44	20	8	12	19	10	2	17	9
Among entire electorate	20	44	22	11	13	20	15	4	21	15
Religious voting[f]										
Among whites	25	21	18	10	48	21	30	13	15	10
Among entire electorate	24	19	15	10	46	16	21	8	11	3

[a]All calculations based upon major-party voters.
[b]Percentage of blacks who voted for Democrats minus the percentage of whites who voted for Democrats.
[c]Percentage of southerners who voted for Democrats minus the percentage of voters outside the south who voted for Democrats.
[d]Percentage of members of union households who voted for Democrats minus the percentage of members of households with no union members who voted for Democrats.
[e]Percentage of working class that voted for Democrats minus the percentage of middle class that voted for Democrats.
[f]Percentage of Catholics who voted for Democrats minus the percentage of Protestants who voted for Democrats.
Source: Abramson et al., 1982.

Race

Race is a very important trait for reference groups in American politics for blacks, Indians, and some whites. Blacks and Indians have had a distinct historical experience, and this has led members of each group to share certain common views. For blacks, the issues on which the most distinct viewpoint is found naturally relate to civil rights. Beyond this, blacks show strongly unified views on economic and social welfare issues that many black leaders have linked to civil rights themes. On these issues, blacks tend to be much more liberal than whites (see Table 7-5).

Up until the New Deal, blacks were overwhelmingly Republican in their partisan affiliation because of the historic commitment of the Republican party to greater racial equality. After the New Deal, blacks began to move into the Democratic party because of the party's position on economic and social welfare issues and because of its strong embrace, in the 1960s, of the cause of civil rights.

Not surprisingly, blacks today are the most solid supporters of the Democratic party of any identifiable group in the population, and their dissatisfaction with particular Democratic candidates is more often expressed by not voting than by voting for a Republican. Despite their overwhelming liberal position on economic and social welfare issues, however, blacks are rather conservative on social and cultural issues. On such issues, blacks and whites show little difference, a fact that may come as a surprise to those who fail to take notice of the different dimensions of liberal and conservative opinion.

Religion

Religious affiliation constitutes the basis of another important reference group in American society, the influence of which varies with the strength of attachment of its members and especially with the group's relationship at any given moment to the

TABLE 7-5

THE INFLUENCE OF GROUP MEMBERSHIP ON OPINIONS

Opinions	Sex		Race		Religion						
	Male	Female	White	Black	Baptist	Methodist	Lutheran	Presbyterian	Episcopalian	Catholic	Jewish
Favor reinstatement of military draft	52	39	63	53							
Favor increase in social security spending	43	56									
Favor more forceful dealings with Soviet Union, even if it risks war	65	47*									
Favor busing children to achieve racial balance in schools	16	18	18	67							
Favor affirmative action			27	46							
Favor amending the Constitution to require a balanced budget			87	89							
Believe that premarital sex is always wrong or almost always wrong					61	51	45	37	31	43	20
Favor permitting a married woman to obtain an abortion under any circumstances					36	50	47	62	69	35	83
Favor the death penalty					71	75	71	72	71	71	68
Favor allowing a person to speak out against churches and religion					50	60	65	73	86	70	83

*CBS News/*New York Times* poll; Frankovic, 1982:445.
Note: Numbers represent the percent of people in the respective subgroups agreeing with opinion cited.
Source: Public Opinion, 1981 and 1982.

rest of society. Religion, as we have seen, provides a general support for basic American values. But religion also gives rise to differences in opinions among groups that occasionally become important in determining political attitudes and voting patterns.

In the nineteenth century, for example, there were severe strains between native Protestants and Catholics over such issues as parochial education, immigration policy, and Prohibition. Because of the hostility directed against them, Catholics came to think of themselves as a distinct political group and bound together on many political questions. In addition, the Catholic population in the nineteenth century tended to be concentrated in the great urban centers of the east and midwest, where they

were recruited in large numbers into the Democratic party. Throughout the nineteenth century and, in fact, well into this century, religion was a strong "predictor" of party affiliation. The great majority of Catholics were Democrats, while the larger part of northern Protestants were Republicans.

With the decline of religious conflict between Catholics and Protestants in this century and with the changing economic status of Catholics (from predominantly blue-collar to white-collar), differences between the groups on ideology and on most specific issues have greatly diminished. So too has the traditional division in party voting; in both 1972 and 1980, a majority of Catholics voted for the Republican candidate for the presidency, a result that would have been inconceivable a half century earlier. On certain issues, such as abortion, the views of the Catholic church exert a distinct influence on the laity, but the great division between the two major religious groups has lost almost all the bitterness of the last century. Indeed, today the chief divisions within the Christian community on social and cultural issues are found less between Catholics and Protestants in general than between religious fundamentalists on the one hand, who tend to be conservative, and more secularly minded elements of the Christian community on the other.

American Jews, powerfully affected by their history of discrimination and persecution in Europe and to some extent in America, have had a long tradition in America of identification with liberalism and with issues relating to First Amendment freedoms. Like Catholics and blacks, Jews strongly supported the Democratic party after the New Deal, but there were signs at the beginning of the 1980s that this support was growing weaker. The liberalism of Jews, which stretches across economic lines, has been attributed to their own consciousness as a minority, their high education level, and their tendency to take the side of the underdog (Hennessy, 1981).

Regionalism

Just as a nation as a whole may have a particular political culture formed by its history, institutions, economy, and environment, so can regions, although to a lesser extent. These *subcultures* are more or less in harmony with the main values of American political culture as a whole. As a large continental nation, the United States has had a long history of sectional differences, based in part on the different economic activities of each section and in part on the different traditions, lifestyles, and attitudes. Foremost, of course, has been the regional conflict between the north and south. Following the Civil War, southern whites, rejecting the hated Republican party, made common cause with the Democratic party, and the region became virtually a one-party area until the 1950s. For most of this period, the Democratic party was more supportive of southern whites on the key issue of retaining segregation and white supremacy in the south. As the northern wing of the Democratic

party became more liberal on the race question, in the 1950s southern whites began to question their Democratic allegiance. Moreover, apart from racial attitudes, which have lost much of their significance as a national political issue since the 1970s, white southerners found themselves increasingly at odds with the white Democrats in the rest of the nation over social welfare and economic views. Southern whites tend to be more conservative and "individualistic" in their political beliefs and have therefore been much less supportive of regulation of business and extensive state welfare services.

The conservatism of southern whites has led to important changes in their voting behavior. Though many continue to call themselves Democrats and to vote for Democrats in local and congressional elections, they have regularly deserted the Democratic party in national presidential elections. Moreover, since the mid-1960s, Republicans have made important inroads in congressional elections. In 1960, there were no Republican senators from the eleven former Confederate states, and only 7 percent of the House members from that region were Republicans. In 1983, half of the senators and 28 percent of the House members were Republicans.

Despite nationalizing tendencies in recent years created by television communication and population movements, regionalism in the United States is hardly dead. Indeed, certain new developments have led to accentuated regional perspectives. The older northeast and midwestern communities— sometimes dubbed the "frost belt"—have recently experienced a decline, while the south and southwest, known as the "sun belt," have been growing. As a consequence of population shifts in the 1970s, the northern states lost seventeen House seats to states in the south and west, one of the greatest redistributions of regional power in the last century. This change may affect the balance of forces in the nation on welfare issues and perhaps on feelings of confidence in America's economic future. For the moment at least, inhabitants of the sun belt areas seem to have a greater faith in the free market and in the capacity of the United States to conquer new frontiers. It was precisely this optimism that Ronald Reagan managed to tap in the 1980 presidential campaign, when he shifted the emphasis on conservatism from that of "tightening one's belt" to growth, progress, and new possibilities.

Houston's new office towers typify the dynamic growth of the "sun belt," which has attracted millions of Americans from the declining industrial centers of the "frost belt."   *(Don Connolly / Liaison)*

Sex

At the turn of the century, when it seemed likely that women would win the right to vote, politicians and analysts began to wonder *how* women would vote. One school of thought foresaw no major differences between male and female voters; another predicted very significant differences. According to the latter view, women would change the character of the political system. For some, this tendency was construed as dangerous to the nation's capacity to defend itself. For others, there was the optimistic belief that women's voting would improve protection for the family, bring a greater political concern for poverty, and diminish any political pressures to go to war (Pomper, 1975).

Initially, women voted at a much lower rate than men, almost certainly because cultural norms in many areas still frowned on female participation in politics. As values changed and as new generations of women attained voting age, the differences began to close and today are not very great. (Men still vote at a slightly higher rate than women, but younger women and men—below 45—vote at about the same rate.) As to the voting behavior of men and women, there appeared—until recently—to be very little difference. Some attributed this initially to the dependence of wives on the opinions of

their husbands, others to the view that gender leads to no political differences (Campbell et al., 1960; Pomper, 1975). However, since 1976 analysts have noted a growing divergence between men and women in voting and on opinions on key issues. Women were more likely than men to vote for George McGovern in 1972 and less likely than men to vote for Ronald Reagan in 1980 (see Table 7-3).

What accounts for these differences? Specific issues related to women, such as abortion and support for the Equal Rights Amendment, while they are important to some voters, do not seem to explain very much of the difference in voting behavior between the sexes. Much more important is a nexus of issues relating to the threat of war and threats to life sustenance (nuclear power and environmental concerns). On all these issues women have a distinctly more "protective" view: they are more likely than men to fear a nuclear war, less likely to desire an aggressive posture by the government in world affairs, and more opposed to the construction of nuclear power plants and offshore oil drilling (Frankovic, 1982). Gender, then, does have a marginal influence on political behavior; whether this influence is the result of nature, nurture (environment), or ideology is a matter that is currently under study.

POLITICAL PARTICIPATION

Voting is the most frequent means of participation by citizens and, from the point of view of the operation of the system, probably the most important. But the act of voting itself might have much less significance to everyone if citizens did not participate in other ways, such as forming parties and interest groups. It is these free associations of citizens that help inform the electorate and mobilize the community on behalf of or against certain points of view.

Political participation, however, should be considered not only in terms of its immediate impact on the conduct of national politics, but also in terms of its long-term effect on the character or "virtue" of the citizenry. Participating in politics is an activity that influences and changes citizens; it gives them certain qualities important for the well-being of a free society. Viewed in these terms, voting as an act of participation is less important than other forms of participation that involve citizens in a much more sustained way, interacting with each other. When citizens serve on juries, take part in a local party caucus, or organize to change local school policies, they are engaging in an activity that may give them a new perspective on politics and new skills as citizens. Voting, by contrast, is a solitary act that takes place quickly (if the voting machines are operating) behind a closed curtain.

Constitutional Perspectives on Participation

The framers of the Constitution spoke only infrequently at the Convention of political participation, and it is a relatively minor theme in *The Federalist*. In part, this neglect was the result of the task at hand. The framers were creating the institutions of a *national* government that, especially given the communications system of the time, would be far away from home. Citizens' participation in such a government, apart from voting, was not considered practical or important. Nor, it seems, were the framers anxious to encourage organized popular constraints on the institutions.

A concern for participation was much more of an Antifederalist theme. Some Antifederalists, as we saw in Chapter 2, had rejected a large national government as inherently incompatible with the cause of popular government. Republics, they argued, could survive only if the character of the citizens was public-spirited, and this required direct participation with other citizens within the setting of a small country. Although this perspective never prevailed in its pure form, it was partly incorporated into the system through the doctrine of federalism and the insistence on a strong role for state and local governments.

Tocqueville   It was a Frenchman, Alexis de Tocqueville, who gave what most now consider to be the classic defense of the importance of political participation. Tocqueville combined the Federalist and Antifederalist positions by defending the framers' ideas of representation and discretion for national institutions yet also emphasizing the necessity for extensive political participation, beginning at the local level. Most of this participation, he held, would involve issues of local concern; but citizens in various communities might also form into national associations, such as parties and interest groups, thereby creating new participatory links between citizens and the national government.

At the center of Tocqueville's analysis of participation was a very simple insight: participation in politics requires certain skills, habits, and dispositions that are not automatically forthcoming and that are therefore easily lost. Citizens must *practice* participation in order to be able to participate effectively. Tocqueville stressed any number of mechanisms to encourage participation—decentralization of decision making (even at the expense of administrative efficiency), freedom of association, and an emphasis on the performance of citizens' duties, such as serving on juries. Citizens would learn to participate mostly in civic associations and local governments: "Local institutions are to liberty what primary schools are to science; they put it within the people's reach; they teach people to appreciate its peaceful enjoyment and accustom them to make use of it" (Tocqueville, 1969:63).

Participation, Tocqueville believed, would be helpful to citizens, first, because it would integrate them into the community and overcome what today is sometimes called "alienation" and, second, because it would give citizens the skill of knowing how to join together to promote their interests and ultimately to defend their liberties. Although Tocqueville never denied the importance of voting in national elections for maintaining a free regime, he placed an equal emphasis on the capacity of citizens to organize as a bulwark in defense of liberty.

Twentieth-Century Views   Outside of the struggles for basic political rights such as the right to vote, constitution makers have given limited attention to the broader themes of participation. A defense of participatory elements of local politics has long been a part of the defense for states' rights and federalism; yet, this defense, while often sincere, has been tainted historically by its use as a justification for denying civil rights to various minorities at the local levels. Frequently, moreover, the degree of participation in local communities has in reality been limited to certain groups. As a result, some who might otherwise have supported participatory elements in local politics have turned instead to the federal government as a way of reforming the localities and ensuring greater equality. While federal intervention has often been necessary, and in many cases has increased the opportunities for participation, it is also the case that in many areas incentives for participation by local citizens have diminished as a result.

Two movements in this century—progressivism and the reform movement of the 1970s—have made participation one of their central themes (see Chapter 5). Yet scholars are divided over whether these movements actually served to increase or diminish important kinds of participation. Progressivism took the power to nominate most elected officials from party organizations and vested it in the primary elections. In so doing, it allowed more citizens to take part in the nominating decision by the act of voting, but it severely weakened political parties and therefore diminished the power of an important intermediary organization. It is in such intermediary organizations, and not in the politics of primary campaigns, many would contend, that meaningful and ongoing participation takes place. In the case of the party reforms in the 1980s, again the reformers had as their avowed goal an increase in participation. And while it is clear that some of the changes that focused on state and local parties had this effect, others served again to diminish the

role of party organizations and to substitute the minimal function of expressing a preference for a national candidate for the much more meaningful function of interacting in local party organizations. According to one analyst, "When these reforms are reexamined for their impact on intermediary organizations, the logical outcome of each appears to be not a strengthening of the bonds between citizens and their government, but a weakening of those bonds" (Shafer, 1983).

Determining the impact of institutional changes on political participation is clearly a very difficult matter. What the arguments above suggest is that people are often not clear about what they mean when they speak of participation. Participation can refer to voting or to much more active forms of involvement in intermediary organizations. Usually no tension exists between these different forms of participation. Yet it is possible to weaken the institutional arrangements that tend to support viable intermediary organizations in the name of greater mass participation. In this instance, mass democracy might become the substitute for a richer and more complex form of participatory politics.

Often, too, the substitution of voting for control by intermediary organizations can result in decisions which are less representative of what the general public wants. As we have seen from the study of primary elections, turnout in some cases may be unrepresentative of the entire electorate, resulting in unrepresentative decisions. Of course, the decisions of party organizations can also be unrepresentative, but it is worth bearing in mind that forms of mass participation in certain areas do not necessarily mean greater democracy. This determination can only be made on a case-by-case basis.

Current Levels of Participation

Americans in comparison with the peoples in other democratic nations are more frequent joiners of various civic associations; while voting less, Americans participate more, if not always directly in politics then in community organizations of some sort (see Chapter 8). Much participation in the United States is in and through civic associations such as labor unions or farm organizations, which are not political but which from time to time may become active in political affairs. Most participation that is directly connected with politics comes at the state and local levels, not just in choosing the more than 500,000 elected officials for these governments, but in attempting to influence decisions at the local level, whether they involve something as ordinary as complaining about garbage pickups or as important as organizing to oppose or support local school plans for desegregation.

Throughout American history, a good deal of participation, at both the local and the national level, has been outside "usual" channels. There have been large-scale mass movements that have operated, initially at least, beyond national parties, such as the Grange movement of farmers after the Civil War, the Townsend movement in the 1930s for old-age pensions, and the civil rights movement in the 1960s. These movements may look to a central organized unit for some direction, but their strength derives mostly from spontaneous mass followings that initially are not fully organized. As methods of influencing politics, such movements may rely on mass demonstrations, public protests, and rallies. The civil rights movement employed the technique of nonviolent sit-ins that were often designed to challenge the constitutionality of state and local segregation laws. These sit-ins focused the attention of the rest of the nation on the problem, often by publicizing the brutality used against the protesters.

Violence, too, has been a technique employed by some groups. Sometimes it has been merely the unplanned reactions born of frustration, or the planned actions of deluded revolutionaries. But violence and the threat of violence are also used strategically to intimidate (as in attempts to enforce strikes) and to gain a political objective (as in the use of violence by the Ku Klux Klan to prevent blacks from voting in the south for much of the last century and as in the threat of violence by some civil rights and peace groups in the 1960s to stimulate negotiations with local officials or university authorities).

The types of political participation that have received the most systematic study—participation in electoral activity and contacting officials—constitute only a part of all the civic and political participation in the United States (Table 7-6). The fig-

TABLE 7-6
POLITICAL PARTICIPATION

Type of political participation	Percent
1 Report regularly voting in presidential elections*	72
2 Report always voting in local elections	47
3 Active in at least one organization involved in community problems	32
4 Have worked with others in trying to solve some community problems	30
5 Have attempted to persuade others to vote as they were	28
6 Have ever actively worked for a party or candidates during an election	26
7 Have contacted a local government official about some issue or problem	20
8 Have attended at least one political meeting or rally in last three years	19
9 Have ever contacted a state or national government official about some issue or problem	18
10 Have ever formed a group or organization to attempt to solve some local community problem	14
11 Have ever given money to a party or candidate during an election campaign	13
12 Currently a member of a political club or organization	8

*Composite variable created from reports of voting in 1960 and 1964 presidential elections. Percentage is equal to those who report they have voted in both elections.
Source: Verba and Nie, 1972:31, table 2.1.

ures show a substantial percentage of the public participating in politics, with over one-quarter of the respondents claiming that they have worked at one time or another for a party or campaign. Those who have not worked for a campaign may do so in the future.

As might be expected from what we have seen in studying voting, these more "difficult" forms of participation involve participants who are not completely representative, either sociologically or politically, of the populace as a whole. If one defines the politically active here as those who have helped somehow to get a candidate elected (beyond voting), it turns out that the activists are, from the point of view of sociological attributes, older,

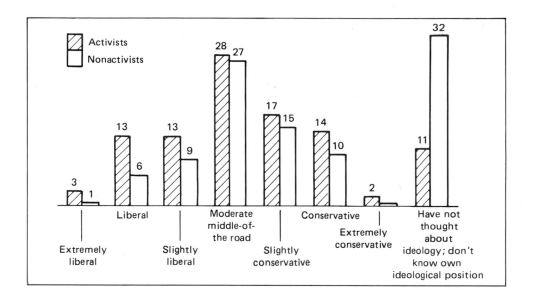

	All Democrats (%)	Democratic activists (%)	All Republicans (%)	Republican activists (%)
Make over $15,000 per year	18	35	28	47
Attended college	27	52	36	55
Have business or professional jobs	23	40	37	58

FIGURE 7-4
Characteristics of political activists. Political activists in both parties tend to be wealthier and better-educated than the average party identifier and tend to be more ideological in their views than the rest of the electorate. Activists are defined as those who help get a candidate elected by participation beyond merely voting. (*Source:* Wolfinger et al., 1976:206–207.)

wealthier, and better-educated than the rest of the population, with education being the best predictor, and, from the point of view of political criteria, considerably more likely to be strongly ideological, whether liberal or conservative (Figure 7-4).

CONCLUSION

Those who participate in politics, first by voting and then by more extensive activities, clearly have more influence on the political system. The voter has more say than the nonvoter; and the active participants, whose assistance candidates need in all sorts of ways, inevitably will count more than the "average" voter. It follows that the effect of participation is to skew the policy process in certain directions from what it would be under the hypothetical situation wherein everyone participates equally. The precise direction the policy process takes as a result of this effect is difficult to determine, as one cannot predict how people will act merely by knowing their income or profession or even by knowing their ideological disposition. (An activist, for example, might hold liberal opinions but act in party affairs as a broker among different viewpoints.) Probably, however, we can say that the effect of the greater influence by activists is to make politics somewhat more ideological and to provide somewhat greater protection for upper-middle-class values and programs.

Noting and objecting to such advantages, however, is often not very helpful. Although possible institutional changes can affect the type of participation involved (as in the case of nominations by primary elections instead of party organizations) or can regulate the character of permissible participation (as in the case of limitations on campaign contributions), by and large the "biases" of participation are a product of a free society. To do away with such biases would require some means either to make all people participate in certain ways or to prevent some from participating as much as they like. Enacting such measures in any extreme form seems unlikely.

In the final analysis, then, there is an inevitable tension between the freedom to participate and the goal of equality understood as each person's preferences counting exactly as much as another's. It is undeniable, of course, that some begin with more resources to participate, whether of time, money, or skill; in addition, some want to participate more than others. Yet without remaking society or imposing severe restraints, participation will lead to certain biases favoring some groups and tendencies within the population.

These biases pose a severe problem, however, only where they are significant and where no prospects of remedy seem possible. In fact, this hardly appears to be the case in American national politics today. Rates of voting and participation do skew the system somewhat, but not enough to negate the powerful majoritarian influence of national elections. Finally, an excessive concern with the tension between equality of influence and the freedom to participate may obscure the common benefit of participation. Participation, even when all do not participate equally, serves to protect the liberty of the citizenry.

SOURCES

Abramson, Paul R., John Aldrich, and David Rhode: *Change and Continuity in the 1980 Elections,* Congressional Quarterly Press, Washington, D.C., 1982.

Anderson, Kristi: *The Creation of a Democratic Majority, 1928–1936,* University of Chicago Press, Chicago, 1979.

Asher, Herbert: *Presidential Elections and American Politics,* rev. ed., Dorsey, Homewood, Ill., 1980.

Burnham, Walter Dean: *Critical Elections and the Mainsprings of American Politics,* Norton, New York, 1970.

———: Review of *Choices and Echoes in Presidential Elections* by Benjamin Page, *The New Republic,* Mar. 3, 1979, pp. 33–34.

Campbell, Angus, Philip E. Converse, Warren E. Miller, and Donald E. Stokes: *The American Voter,* Wiley, New York, 1960.

CBS News/*New York Times:* Poll, 1980.

Center for Political Studies: Polls, 1979–1982.

Congressional Quarterly Weekly Report, November 13, 1982.

Fiorina, Morris P.: *Retrospective Voting in American National Elections,* Yale University Press, New Haven, Conn., 1981.

Frankovic, Kathleen: "Sex and Politics: New Alignments, Old Issues," *PS,* vol. 15, no. 3, 1982.

Gallup Organization: Polls, various dates.

Hadley, Arthur: *The Empty Polling Booth,* Prentice-Hall, Englewood Cliffs, N.J., 1978.

Hennessy, Bernard: *Public Opinion,* 4th ed., Brooks/Cole, Monterey, Calif., 1981.

Historical Statistics of the United States: Colonial Times to 1970, U.S. Bureau of the Census, Washington, D.C., 1975.

Jensen, Richard: *The Winning of the Midwest: Social and Political Conflict, 1888–1896,* University of Chicago Press, Chicago, 1971.

———: In Seymour Martin Lipset (ed.), *Party Coalitions in the 1980s,* Institute for Contemporary Studies, San Francisco, 1978.

Key, V. O., Jr.: *Politics, Parties, and Pressure Groups,* 5th ed., Thomas Y. Crowell, New York, 1964.

———: *The Responsible Electorate,* Harvard University Press, Cambridge, Mass., 1966.

Kieth, Bruce E., David B. Magleby, Candice F. Nelson, Elizabeth Orr, Mark Westley, and Raymond E.

Wolfinger: "The Myth of the Independent Voter," paper presented at the annual meeting of the American Political Science Association, 1977.

Kirkpatrick, Jeane J.: "Changing Patterns of Electoral Competition," in Anthony King (ed.), *The New American Political System,* American Enterprise Institute, Washington, D.C., 1978.

National Opinion Research Center: Polls, 1979–1982.

Nie, Norman, Sydney Verba, and John Petrocik: *The Changing American Voter,* Harvard University Press, Cambridge, Mass., 1976.

Ornstein, Norman, Thomas E. Mann, Michael J. Malbin, and John F. Bibby: *Vital Statistics on Congress: 1982,* American Enterprise Institute, Washington, D.C., 1982.

Page, Benjamin I.: *Choices and Echoes in Presidential Elections,* University of Chicago Press, Chicago, 1978.

Pomper, Gerald: *Voters' Choice,* Dodd-Mead, New York, 1975.

Powell, G. Bingham, Jr.: "Voting Turnout in Thirty Democracies," in Richard Rose (ed.), *Electoral Participation: A Comparative Analysis,* Sage, Beverly Hills, Calif., 1980.

Public Opinion, April-May 1981; April-May 1982.

Rusk, Jerrold: "Comment," *American Political Science Review,* vol. 68, no. 3, 1974, pp. 1028–1049.

Shafer, Byron E.: "Reform and Alienation: The Decline of Intermediation in the Politics of Presidential Selection," *Journal of Law and Politics,* vol. 1, no. 1, 1983.

Statistical Abstract of the United States: 1980, U.S. Bureau of the Census, Washington, D.C., 1980.

Tocqueville, Alexis de: *Democracy in America,* J. P. Mayer (ed.), Doubleday, Garden City, N.Y., 1969.

Verba, Sidney, and Norman H. Nie: *Participation in America,* Harper and Row, New York, 1972.

Wolfinger, Raymond, and Steven Rosenstone: *Who Votes?* Yale University Press, New Haven, Conn., 1980.

———, Marvin Shapiro, and Fred I. Greenstein: *Dynamics of American Politics,* Prentice-Hall, Englewood Cliffs, N.J., 1976.

RECOMMENDED READINGS

Abramson, Paul R., John Aldrich, and David Rhode: *Change and Continuity in the 1980 Elections,* Congressional Quarterly Press, Washington, D.C., 1982. A discussion of the 1980 election which also covers the essentials of modern research on voter behavior.

Asher, Herbert: *Presidential Elections and American Politics,* rev. ed., Dorsey, Homewood, Ill., 1980. A survey of recent presidential campaigns and of how Americans have voted.

Burnham, Walter Dean: *Critical Elections and the Mainsprings of American Politics,* Norton, New York, 1970. An exploration of the meaning of realignments and of voter participation since the election of 1896.

Key, V. O., Jr.: *The Responsible Electorate,* Harvard University Press, Cambridge, Mass., 1966. Argues for the essential rationality of American voters and seeks to correct impressions of earlier studies of voter behavior.

Nie, Norman H., Sidney Verba, and John R. Petrocik: *The Changing American Voter,* Harvard University Press, Cambridge, Mass., 1976. Analyzes the shifts in voting behavior and political coalitions from the 1950s through the 1970s.

Petrocik, John R.: *Party Coalitions,* University of Chicago Press, Chicago, 1981. A discussion of the concept of realignments and an exploration of voting patterns since the New Deal.

Page, Benjamin I.: *Choices and Echoes in Presidential Elections,* University of Chicago Press, Chicago, 1978. Discusses candidate appeals and voter behavior, analyzing the interaction between them.

Verba, Sydney, and Norman H. Nie: *Participation in America,* Harper and Row, New York, 1972. Analyzes the factors that correlate with and help explain political participation.

Wolfinger, Raymond, and Steven Rosenstone: *Who Votes?* Yale University Press, New Haven, Conn., 1980. A thorough discussion of voter participation and of the potential impact of legal and institutional changes in electoral procedures.

Chapter 8

Interest Groups

CHAPTER CONTENTS

In his farewell address President Carter said:

> Today as people have become ever more doubtful of the ability of the government to deal with our problems, we are increasingly drawn to single-issue groups and special interest organizations to ensure that, whatever else happens, our personal views and our private interests are protected.
>
> This is a disturbing factor in American political life. It tends to distort our purposes because the national interest is not always the sum of all our single or special interests. We are all Americans together—and we must not forget that the common good is our common interest and our individual responsibilities.

Three days later, President Reagan noted in his inaugural address:

> We hear much of special interest groups, but our concern must be for a special interest group that has been too long neglected. It knows no sectional boundaries, crosses ethnic and racial divisions and political party lines. It is made up of men and women who raise our food, patrol our streets, man our mines and factories, teach our children, keep our homes, and heal us when we're sick—professors, industrialists, shopkeepers, clerks, cabbies, and truck drivers. They are, in short, "we the people," this breed called Americans.

In these speeches presidents Carter and Reagan were voicing the widespread feeling among the American people that a politics of "special interests" would not promote the national interest. Democrat or Republican, liberal, moderate, or conservative, Americans love to hate special interests. In 1975, for example, a Harris poll found that three-quarters of all Americans thought that Congress was too much under the influence of special interest lobbies.

Yet this does not mean that most Americans would like to banish interest groups from the political scene. Indeed, it is scarcely possible to imagine American politics without labor unions, veterans' groups, or farm organizations. Such groups are a natural outgrowth of a system that protects personal freedom. Contrast this with the regime in Poland, where workers tried in 1980 and 1981 to form unions independent of the Communist party, only to see their efforts crushed in 1982 by the Polish government. Preventing free associations is a characteristic of totalitarian systems, for associations independent of government represent a formidable source of power beyond the reach of political authorities. By contrast, in liberal democratic regimes groups are an integral element in the governing process. In the United States, the First Amendment to the Constitution expressly guarantees the "right of the people peaceably to assemble, and to petition the government for a redress of grievances." Direct contact between interest-group representatives and government officials—*lobbying*—therefore has Constitutional protection.

Despite the openness of the American political system to interest groups, past constitution makers have seen certain dangers in excessive interest-group influence. Interests, as James Madison made clear in *Federalist* 10, must be regulated by the same government in which they exercise some degree of influence. Speaking of the variety of interests that grow up in modern commercial societies, Madison commented that the "regulation of these various and interfering interests forms the principal task of modern legislation and involves the spirit of party and faction in the necessary and ordinary operations of government" (*Federalist* 10). While interests must be represented in government, they also must be channeled and controlled, for each interest, left to itself, might impose its own view and, in the extreme cases of factions, enact measures "adverse to the rights of other citizens." Government, therefore, must stand above the interests in order to moderate the conflict among groups with opposing views and to ensure that powerful groups do not dominate weaker groups or unorganized interests. In this manner government promotes the public interest.

From the time of the founding, constitution makers and political scientists have argued over whether the clash of interest groups can alone represent the national interest. At one extreme, a well-known political scientist of an earlier generation, Arthur Bentley, argued that *all* politics could be understood as the struggle between interest groups. For Bentley, the concept of the public interest was meaningless (Bentley, 1908). This view, however, has been widely criticized. Most have realized, for example, that if the government simply accedes to the demands of various interests for more and more benefits, the total of these demands can far outstrip the resources of government and massive deficits may result, leading to dangerously high rates of inflation. At the other extreme, some progressives came very close to identifying the public interest as something that almost always was in tension with the demands of particular interests. According to this view, which we discussed in earlier chapters, the government should be reformed to reduce the power of those institutions that are open to interest-group influence (such as the Congress) and to expand the power of those institutions that supposedly have a national perspective (such as the presidency and a "professional" bureaucracy).

The original framework of the government stood somewhere between these two roles. The founders clearly recognized a public interest independent of the sum of particular interests. Their challenge, however, was not to theorize about such matters but to construct the institutional arrangements that would best promote the public interest in practice. The outline of those arrangements reveals that the public interest was most likely to be known by a process that both summed up interests and sought to ascertain the public interest independently of them. No institution in the government could be entirely representative of one approach; but it was clear that the founders expected that the House, with short terms and small districts, would be the most open to the pressures of groups, while the presidency, with a longer term and a larger constituency, would be much more likely to consider the general interest. The separation of powers was originally understood not simply as a partial division among the functions of government, but also as a system for combining different methods of determining the public interest.

As long as we maintain the basic structure of our government, the issue we must confront is not whether interest groups should exist and influence public policy (they will), but how *much* influence they should exercise, under what conditions, and through what means. If their power has become excessive, why has this happened and what can be done about it? It is no exaggeration to say that of all the links between the citizenry and the formal institutions of government, interest groups have caused the most profound controversies for democratic theory and practice.

THE GROWTH AND DEVELOPMENT OF INTEREST GROUPS

An "interest group," as we define it, is an association of individuals sharing a common interest and *formally organized* to promote certain ends in the policy process. An "interest," by contrast, is an actual or potential set of ends that some number of citizens may hold. Not all interests have interest groups, nor are all interests necessarily represented best by interest groups. For example, a consumer interest existed long before there were organized consumer interest groups, and many besides labor unions make some claim to represent the interest of labor.

American history has witnessed a continuous, though not steady, growth in the number of interest groups. According to one political scientist, the "formation of associations tends to occur in waves" (Truman, 1971:59). In the initial years of the republic the number of interest groups was small, and there were virtually no *national* associations. The impact of interest groups was limited at the national level, in part because government itself has a limited role (Ornstein and Elder, 1978). What interest-group activity existed was found mostly at the state and local level. Still, the perception of different interests—urban, commercial, agrarian, and the like—was very strong at the national level, and many senators and representatives quite openly assumed the roles of "representing" these interests.

By the 1830s Tocqueville was celebrating the great number of associations in America, as well as their local and nonideological character. "In no country in the world has the principle of association been more successfully used or applied to a greater multitude of objects than in America" (Tocqueville, 1969:189). The associations Tocqueville described were not always groups that exercised pressure on government; they were often groups that sought to influence opinions in society or to perform certain functions, like distributing books, building hospitals, or caring for the poor. Such groups were often a substitute for or supplement to government activity, for they performed desirable social functions. The performance of such functions by groups is known today as "voluntarism." For Tocqueville, the proliferation of voluntary associations was a means of preventing the excessive growth of government. Different circumstances, of course, necessitate different responsibilities for government, but in general there has been greater resistance in the United States than in most other democratic countries to the politicization of all social functions. Tocqueville's description of voluntarism is still partly valid today: "At the head of any new undertaking, where in France you find government or in England some territorial magnate, in the United States you are sure to find an association" (Tocqueville, 1969:513).

The Civil War accelerated the nationalization and industrialization of American life. Following the Civil War the "government expanded and groups, including broad-based mass movements, began to multiply as well" (Ornstein and Elder, 1978:224). The articulation of interests by formal groups began to occur on a truly national scale for the first time. Farm organizations, social and fraternal groups, and business associations all formed by the turn of the century. Also, labor interests organized in response to the growth of large corporations.

The progressive era witnessed the greatest wave of organization and counterorganization in American history. There was a surge in the formation of both economic and noneconomic interests, especially those of national scope (Wilson, 1973). The National Association of Manufacturers, the American Medical Association, chambers of commerce, the American Farm Bureau, and other economic interests were organized in part because of the economic insecurity of this period. Public interest counterorganizations such as the Consumers League, the Child Labor Committee, the National Civic Federation, and the Pure Food Association formed partly in opposition to the growing strength of economic interests. Groups such as the National Civil Service Reform and the Non-Partisan League grew in direct opposition to political party machines. The NAACP, the Urban League, and various religious groups originated during this same period. Many existing associations underwent tremendous growth during these first two decades of the twentieth century.

What is today called the "progressive movement" was a reaction to the ill effects of commercial industrialism and the growth of private power. Progressivism sought the expansion of government and public power to balance the increasing power of special interests. The progressive view was essentially majoritarian, holding up "the people" or public opinion in opposition to the special interests. Progressive reforms opposed interest-group pluralism.

The New Deal as a response to the great depression represented a major shift from limited to positive government. The initiation of the welfare state was accompanied by the growth of numerous economic interest groups. The central role of the federal government meant that many of these new organizations were, of necessity, national organizations. Examples included the cozy relationship between the National Labor Relations Board and labor, between the National Rural Electrification Administration and the National Rural Electrification Cooperative Association. Farm groups dependent on agricultural subsidies and elderly citizens supported by social security are two more examples.

The 1960s and 1970s constitute the second great wave of interest-group formation. There was a sudden increase in the formation and development of public interest and single-issue citizen groups beginning in the sixties (Walker, 1981). Unlike the progressive era, the period of the 1960s and 1970s was overwhelmingly a social welfare, rather than an economic, reformation.

Lyndon Johnson's Great Society program and its aftermath were the social welfare equivalent of the economic intervention of the New Deal. In the sixties and seventies the growth of activist government was no longer limited to economic regulation; the "legitimacy barrier" to social welfare intervention—to public responsibility for private social welfare—was cast down. This led to a marked expansion of the political agenda, causing one commentator to observe, "Once politics was about only a few things; today it is about nearly everything" (Wilson, 1979:41). Noneconomic interest groups concerning social and cultural issues like abortion, gun control, civil liberties, women's rights, the environment, consumerism, and "good government" reform sprang into being or expanded in size. The "electronics revolution"—TV, WATS lines, computerized polling, and direct-mail solicitations—enabled individuals and groups to further their political aims. Racial tension, Vietnam, Watergate, the Santa Barbara oil spill, and other

Many of today's citizen groups seek to draw media attention to their cause through a series of marches and confrontations; these protesters are picketing to halt construction of a nuclear power plant. *(Martin Levick / Black Star)*

events gave them the needed impetus to reform existing political institutions.

The sharp rise in the number and influence of interest groups in the 1960s and 1970s has led to the widespread complaint that American politics suffers from an excess of pluralism. Some political observers suggest that this is, in part, a result of the expansion of government and the political agenda, as well as of the decentralizing and democratizing institutional reforms following Vietnam and Watergate. "The decade of the 1970s has seen a genuine explosion in group numbers and activity that has corresponded to reforms in Congress and changes in the presidency. . . . Political decentralization brought on by congressional reforms created more points of access for the groups" (Ornstein and Elder, 1978:227–228). Other scholars point to the weakening of the political parties as also contributing to this fragmentation of the political process.

The political scientist Theodore Lowi calls this excess of pluralism "interest-group liberalism"

(Lowi, 1969). Lowi argues that increased government intervention for purposes of economic stability, national security, and social welfare has led Congress to delegate greater authority to executive agencies. Increased government regulation has naturally resulted in greater concern with, and participation in, the regulatory process by the affected interest groups. The consequence has been the virtual domination of policymaking in certain areas by what many refer to as "subgovernments" or "iron triangles." Iron triangles are the close relationships that develop among executive agencies, the corresponding congressional committee or subcommittee, and their respective client interest groups. An example would be the Veterans Administration, the House and Senate Veterans Affairs committees, and such groups as the American Legion and VFW; together they control most policymaking directly concerning veterans' interests.

The advent of interest-group liberalism has led some to decry this domination of public policy by private interests. Morris Fiorina, another political scientist, says that the groups are too powerful and that our politics is nothing more than a mass log roll. "Public policy emerges from the system almost as an afterthought; . . . the typical public law is simply the outcome of enough individual bargains to build a majority" (Fiorina, 1977:73). Concern with justice and the common good, many insist, is given short shrift. Some of these critics propose majoritarian solutions to the problems posed by an excess of pluralism. However, we need to ask whether majoritarian reforms, such as the party and congressional reforms of the 1970s, have backfired and whether these reforms have weakened precisely those institutions established to regulate a pluralist system.

Even with the trend toward the nationalization of American politics, the interest-group system in the United States remains much less centralized than that in most other democratic nations. The system of interest groups in each country reflects in part the particular political structure. The American system of interest groups mirrors the decentralized federal political structure; this differs significantly, for example, from the British centralized, nationalized structure of politics and interest groups. In the United States, power is dispersed, and access points to the policy process abound because of the constitutional principles of separation of powers and federalism and because of the loose, coalition character of our parties. While there are a growing number of interest groups with headquarters in Washington, many interest groups continue to operate on the state and local level where the most important decisions of government are often made. On each level of government, interest groups continue to seek influence with executive, legislative, and judicial officials. Because American political parties are not like the disciplined, centralized British parties, interest groups seek to influence both party leaders and rank and file members (Beer, 1969).

TYPES OF INTEREST GROUPS

The number and variety of interest groups in America are enormous. The *Encyclopedia of American Associations* catalogs over 15,000 orga-

nizations, though even this listing is not exhaustive. As for the number of organized groups active in national politics, an estimated 1,600 entries under "associations" in the Washington, D.C., telephone directory can serve only as an approximation.

What accounts for such a large number of associations or groups? Foremost are the sheer size of our country and the variety of people, regions, religions, occupations, levels of wealth and education, and ethnic origins that a country of this size encompasses. Also important is the decentralized nature of our political institutions. The principles of federalism, separation of powers, checks and balances, and bicameralism all multiply the opportunities for the exercise of political influence and, therefore, the incentives for interests to organize.

Consider an example: a man who is a German-American, Protestant dairy farmer in Minnesota. His farm interests are affected by a number of agencies at the state, local, and federal levels. Let us suppose that the federal government is contemplating lowering dairy price supports and raising milk quality standards. Our farmer's interests are represented through his membership in the National Farmers Union. The state legislature wants to raise his taxes, so he contributes to a taxpayers' association to fight the increase. Because new highway construction is claiming part of his land, he may choose to join or even to form a neighborhood association in resistance. As a veteran of World War II, he may be a member of the American Legion or the VFW, supporting efforts to increase veterans' benefits. He attends the nearby Lutheran church and is a member of its governing board. Like his parents before him, he is a staunch Democrat and rarely votes for a Republican for any office. On top of all this, his son plays little league baseball; his daughter is a Girl Scout; his wife belongs to the League of Women Voters; and his elderly father, who lives with him and his family, is a member of the town's senior citizens' club (they're asking Congress to increase social security benefits).

This portrait may be somewhat exaggerated, but not by much. According to one study, 74 percent of all adult Americans belong to some association, and 57 percent claim to participate actively in at least one. How, then, do we compare with other countries? Americans join labor unions less

TABLE 8-1

ORGANIZATIONAL MEMBERSHIP IN DIFFERENT NATIONS

Figures Represent Percent of National Population

Organization	United States	Great Britain	Germany	Italy	Mexico
Trade unions	14	22	15	6	11
Business	4	4	2	5	2
Professional	4	3	6	3	5
Farm	3	0	4	2	0
Social	13	14	10	3	4
Charitable	3	3	2	9	6
Religious*	19	4	3	6	5
Civic-political	11	3	3	8	3
Cooperative	6	3	2	2	0
Veterans'	6	5	1	4	0
Fraternal†	13				
Other	6	3	9	6	0
Percentage who are members of any organization	57	47	44	30	24

*This refers to church-related organizations, not to church affiliation itself.
†United States only.
Source: Almond and Verba, 1963:302.

frequently than the British and Germans do; business, professional, and charitable organizations at roughly the same rate; and religious, civic, and political associations in much higher percentages (Almond and Verba, 1963).

The large number of organizational affiliations that are maintained by Americans clearly suggests the enormous variety of purposes and objectives pursued by the groups in which they participate. For the sake of simplicity we can classify interest groups into three basic types: economic, ideological, and social.

Economic Groups

In 1787, James Madison said, "The most common and durable source of factions has been the various and unequal distribution of property. . . . A landed interest, a manufacturing interest, a mercantile interest, a moneyed interest, with many lesser interests, grow up of necessity in civilized nations, and divide them into different classes, actuated by different sentiments and views" (*Federalist* 10). Few would deny the importance of Madison's observa-

tions, even for contemporary American politics. Organizations that promote discrete economic (or property) interests are among the most powerful and enduring forces in the political arena. These fall into four general categories: business, labor, agriculture, and professional associations.

Business In their relations with government, businesspeople are primarily concerned with regulations, subsidies, contracts, tax advantages, and international trade policy (quotas and tariffs). Business can be unified or fragmented, depending on the issue. For example, businesses are frequently united on issues like corporate taxes, consumer policies, and labor legislation, yet they are often divided on matters of international trade. Businesses are organized into a few umbrella organizations, the most prominent being the Chamber of Commerce, the National Association of Manufacturers (NAM), the Business Roundtable, and the National Federation of Independent Businesses (NFIB).

The Chamber of Commerce, with over 70,000 firms and individuals as members, is the largest

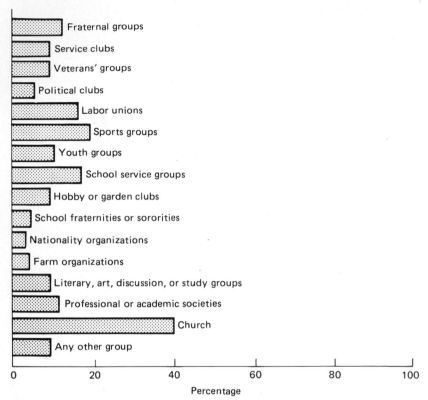

FIGURE 8-1
Membership in various organizations: percentage of the population belonging to selected organizations. (*Source: Social Indicators*, 1977:585.)

and best known of these. Although most Americans know it as a local organization, an annual budget of approximately $20 million and a Washington staff of roughly 400 make the Chamber of Commerce the closest thing to an all-inclusive business lobby in the United States.

In order to avoid alienating any part of its far-flung membership, the Chamber of Commerce must maintain a high level of generality in its appeals, as a vigilant defender of the private enterprise system and an opponent of high taxes. It takes positions only on issues of broad concern and refrains from addressing matters that solely affect a particular constituent industry.

More so than the Chamber of Commerce, the NAM represents "big business" interests. Although it comprises only 6 to 8 percent of all man-

ufacturers in America, among these are many of the largest in the country. NAM's diminishing membership in recent years has been partially offset by an increasing political aggressiveness. Even more representative of big business, and potentially more influential, is the newest umbrella organization, the Business Roundtable, founded in 1972. The Roundtable is made up of almost 200 chief executive officers of some of the nation's largest corporations, including AT&T, GM, and IBM. This organization refuses to rely merely on lobbyists, choosing instead to take advantage of its members' direct access to representatives, senators, and presidents. Finally, the NFIB, with a Washington staff of 14, is one of many organizations representing small businesses.

Along with these umbrella organizations, business is represented in Washington by thousands of *trade associations*. These organizations predate the formation of the umbrella groups and include everything from the National Cricket Growers Association and the Paper Bag Institute to the American Petroleum Institute (with an annual budget almost twice that of the chamber of commerce). Most trade associations exist to provide a wide variety of services to members, only one of which is political representation. Although less visible than the NAM or the chamber, trade associations have great influence over tax and tariff legislation. At the same time these groups frequently oppose one another. When the Beet Sugar Association seeks higher sugar prices, it is vehemently opposed by the Chocolate Manufacturers Association of America.

In addition to the trade associations and umbrella organizations, many individual companies have their own lobbyists in Washington. Among these companies are Sears, Du Pont, and GM.

Labor Labor is the largest group in terms of membership and, though hardly monolithic, is considerably more centralized than business. Unlike most other interest groups, unions are not, strictly speaking, voluntary organizations. This is because of "union shop" or "closed shop" agreements by which nonunion members can be prohibited from employment in a given factory, office, or other location.

Also unlike most interest groups, labor unions take positions and lobby intensively on an assortment of issues that often only remotely concern their memberships. Although unions focus first on concerns such as higher wages, better working conditions, and a boost in the minimum wage, they also work to promote interests that are not simply their own, as they have done in social issues, civil rights, and foreign and defense policy. Traditionally, labor has been affiliated with liberal causes and the Democratic party. However, as many Democrats were moving further to the left in the 1970s, labor acquired a reputation for having, at best, tainted liberal credentials. To many, its abiding concern for the economic interests of the worker no longer appeared sufficiently progressive. In 1972, many labor unions did not endorse the Democratic nominee for president, George McGovern; and the Teamsters went so far as to en-

dorse his opponent, Richard Nixon. In 1980, Ronald Reagan, the conservative Republican nominee, actively courted the blue-collar vote and also received the endorsement of the Teamsters.

The largest union organization is the American Federation of Labor–Congress of Industrial Organizations (AFL-CIO). The AFL-CIO has 14 million members constituting 107 "internationals," which include, among others, laborers, teachers, and white-collar workers. The AFL-CIO, a product of the merger of two formerly distinct organizations, clearly sets the tone for American labor. This is largely because of the influence, and now the legacy, of the tough-minded, outspoken, irascible, cigar-chomping George Meany, its president and the symbol of "big labor" for 25 years (1955–1980). Meany ruled the AFL-CIO with an iron hand and consequently had considerable personal political influence. The union's political department, the Committee on Political Education (COPE), augmented this influence. COPE conducts fund-raising and voter registration drives, provides political party support, and, with its large pool of campaign workers, is involved in considerable electioneering.

Other unions include the Teamsters, with 2 million members, mostly truck drivers; the United Mine Workers (UMW), with 220,000 members; the United Auto Workers (UAW), with 1.5 million members, mostly in the automobile and aerospace industries; the United Steel Workers (USW); and the National Education Association (NEA), consisting of 1.8 million teachers. None of these has made a bigger splash in national politics in recent years than the NEA, which now has an annual budget of around $50 million and a Washington staff of 500.

Agriculture Although the farmers of the American Revolution, working small plots of land to provide themselves with the basic necessities of life, have given way to large-scale "agribusiness" enterprises specializing in one or a few crops, the farming life still retains a nostalgic appeal for Americans, and thus its public image as an interest group remains largely positive. Yet farm groups, like business and labor, have never presented a united front.

There are three major organizations, represent-

When thousands of angry farmers blocked Washington traffic with their tractors, they received nationwide television coverage but could not win higher prices for their crops. *(Martin Levick / Black Star)*

ing 4 million farmers. The American Farm Bureau Federation, founded in 1920 and representing 3 million farmers, is the largest, most active, and most conservative of the three. The Farm Bureau originated with the U.S. Department of Agriculture's (USDA) Agriculture Extension Service, established to provide technical aid on a local level. It represents larger, more successful farm businesses, rather than the traditional family farm, and thus supports free market policies and opposes government regulation and price supports.

The National Farmers Union, on the other hand, represents 250,000 smaller, less profitable farms and is in favor of high price supports. The Farmers Union is heir to the agrarian populism of the 1880s and 1890s and is the most liberal of the traditional farmers' organizations. The National Grange is the oldest (1867) and least political of the three (600,000 members). Its history is primarily that of a social or fraternal organization.

Agriculture too has its equivalent of trade associations, called "commodity associations," which represent dairy, tobacco, and other distinct commodity interests. These associations exercise considerable influence within both the U.S. Department of Agriculture and the congressional agriculture committees, thereby benefiting from price supports and subsidy policies. In recent years, however, some farmers have rejected conventional means of influencing national policy in favor of more militant tactics. In December of 1977 and again in February of 1979 several thousand angry farmers, organized into a new group called the "American Agriculture Movement," rode their tractors to Washington, D.C., to draw attention to their plight and to lobby for increased price supports. They were remarkably successful at generating attention, but less successful in achieving their policy goals.

Professional Associations There are hundreds of professional associations in the United States, ranging from the American Medical Association (AMA) and American Bar Association (ABA) to the American Society of Golf Course Architects. Most professional associations exist not so much to influence public policy as to provide services to members. The American Political Science Association, for example, sponsors conferences, an employment service, and numerous publications of interest to political scientists. Among those associations that are involved in politics, the AMA and ABA are perhaps the most active and powerful, exerting considerable influence in local, state, and national politics. Like some other professional associations, the AMA and ABA maintain licensing and training standards in their respective professions and, not surprisingly, can usually count on the generous support of their memberships. On the national level, the AMA lobbies against policies such as compulsory national health insurance (as it did against Medicare); and the ABA rates all candidates for the federal judiciary and is, according to at least one authority on the subject, a "powerful factor in the selection process" (Abraham, 1980:29).

Ideological or Policy-Oriented Groups

Madison may have believed that economic interests were the most powerful, but he also realized that factions could form around "opinions," that is, deeply held beliefs or convictions about public policy. The political scientist James Q. Wilson defines such a group as one that "works explicitly for the benefit of some larger public or society as a whole and not one that works chiefly for the benefit of members" (Wilson, 1973:46).

Ideological groups can have broad or narrow interests. They may take stands on a variety of different public policy disputes or focus their attention on one or a few issues. Examples of the former type of group, which are sometimes called "public interest" groups, are Common Cause, the League of Women Voters, Americans for Democratic Action, Americans for Constitutional Action, and the Moral Majority. The so-called "single-issue" groups, on the other hand, include the Sierra Club (environment), the National Right to Life Committee (antiabortion), the National Rifleman's Association (anti–gun control), and Zero Population Growth.

Ideological groups are based on commitments strong enough to induce active participation by members, and for this reason they are often less flexible than economic groups. Members frequently bring zeal and militance to their work. Rather than promoting a politics of bargaining or compromising interests, they give rise to a politics of principle or ideology; it is more difficult to bargain or compromise principles than interests. It is not unfair to say that given the ideological fervor of many of these groups, they would rather lose with their principles intact than win at the cost of compromising firmly held beliefs.

Ideological groups are both old and new, large and small, little known and widely recognized. The Sierra Club was founded in 1892; the League of Women Voters, with its suffragist origins, in 1920; the Fund for Animals in 1967; and the Consumer Federation of America in 1968. Some ideological groups must make do with shoestring budgets and a few dedicated volunteers, while others, like the National Wildlife Federation, enjoy ample resources, professional staff, and a vast membership. Finally, while most Americans have never even heard of the Institute for Public Interest Representation, many people have an opinion, positive or negative, about Common Cause and the Ralph Nader groups.

Many of the more recent groups can trace their roots to specific events or controversies and the activities of particular individuals. Some environmental organizations formed after a huge oil spill near Santa Barbara, California, and often point to Earth Day, 1970, as their birthday. The New England Clamshell Alliance is a direct response to the attempt to build the Seabrook, New Hampshire, nuclear power reactor. And, of course, Vietnam and Watergate spawned a host of groups, the best known being Common Cause.

Although the genesis of Common Cause owes much to political events, equally important were the personal efforts of its founder, John Gardner, former secretary of the Department of Health, Education, and Welfare (HEW) under Lyndon Johnson. Similarly, the Fund for Animals was the work of the author Cleveland Amory. But the most famous of the political entrepreneurs of the past two decades is the charismatic Ralph Nader. Nader used his talents for writing, speaking, organizing, and attracting publicity to turn a one-man show into a public interest conglomerate.

The members of ideological groups tend to be

better-educated, wealthier, younger, and more politically aware than the average citizen. This is also true of the staffs of these organizations (sometimes the only members are the staff), which have considerable freedom of action. Although most public interest activists are ostensibly nonpartisan, they have tended to support Democratic programs and initiatives and to embrace a liberal political ideology, generally because they believe that greater governmental action is necessary to solve problems (like environmental pollution or automobile safety) that have too long been ignored. The conservative principles of limited government and a free market economy do not have much appeal to these groups.

In recent years, however, an increasing number of conservative groups have sprung up, also claiming to speak for the public interest. Most of these have focused their attention on the so-called "social issues" such as abortion, pornography, and school prayer. Such groups maintain that the traditional American values of family, decency, and religion are under attack in contemporary American society, often by the government itself. They point, for example, to Supreme Court decisions banning prayer in public schools and legalizing abortions. Such groups came into their own during the 1980 national election, when they helped to elect numerous conservatives to Congress and one to the White House.

Social Groups

Although economic and ideological groups are the most important politically, there are also thousands of organizations which, though not entirely oblivious to political life, exist primarily to promote friendship or camaraderie among their members. Social groups are of many different types: ethnic, religious, racial, and veterans' groups, as well as lodges and fraternal orders. The most common impetus for the creation and maintenance of groups of this type is the feeling of shared identity and the sense of kinship or belonging. Members join primarily out of loyalty or pride, a desire for sociability and prestige, or a need for reinforcing some self-identification. Specific examples of social organizations include ethnic groups such as the National Association of Polish-Americans and the Loyal Order of Hibernians, religious groups like B'nai

B'rith and the Knights of Columbus, veterans' organizations such as the VFW and the American Legion, and lodges and fraternal orders like the Elks, Rotary, and Kiwanis.

Many of these organizations have a special interest in noncontroversial community service activities such as sponsoring cultural and social events, fund raising for charitable causes (through paper drives, tag days, etc.), promoting youth activities like little league or summer camps, and providing college scholarships. Through these and similar activities such groups seek to promote a sense of civic duty or responsibility at the local level. This is one way in which such avowedly nonpolitical groups contribute to the political health of the community.

Another way in which social groups can be important politically is by serving as a conduit for political leaders or aspiring politicians to communicate, substantively or symbolically, with influential segments of a broader constituency. This is why politicians frequently speak before such groups; eat pizza, blintzes, and sausage on the campaign trail; and march in St. Patrick's Day parades.

Civil Rights Groups

We have described three basic types of interest groups, but these are not rigid categories. Many groups have purposes or functions that do not fit neatly into one specific category. The type of interest organization which is probably the most difficult to classify according to our scheme, but which has left an indelible imprint on American politics, is the civil rights organizations, specifically those groups formed to promote the well-being of black Americans. The best known are the National Association for the Advancement of Colored People (NAACP), the Southern Christian Leadership Conference (SCLC), the Urban League, and Operation PUSH of Chicago (People United to Save Humanity).

In one respect these are economic groups, for they seek to promote the material well-being of a segment of the population that has traditionally lagged far behind white Americans in income and wealth. In another respect they are ideological groups because they see their cause as more than merely self-interested, rather, as part of a larger effort to fulfill the promise of America and bring about a truly just society. Finally, they serve the ends of social groups by enhancing group identity and feelings of solidarity among the members.

Black Americans are not the only segment of the population that has given rise to organizations charged to promote the economic and political well-being of a specific group of Americans. In recent decades similar groups have been formed to aid women, chicanos, the elderly, and gays.

Governments as Interest Groups

A final type of interest group that again does not fit neatly into any traditional category consists of associations of state and local governments. In the extraordinarily complex web of intergovernmental relations that has developed in recent years, state and local governments have become increasingly dependent on the federal government for resources. As a consequence, the various associations of state and local governments, such as the National Governor's Association, the National Conference of State Legislatures, and the National Association of Counties, now lobby with the federal government to protect their benefits and promote their interests. (These groups will be discussed in Chapter 14.)

HOW ORGANIZATIONS FORM

The "Free-Rider" Problem

From the preceding discussion it may seem that there are such a great number and variety of groups that maintaining substantial membership is the least of the problems facing group leaders. Yet this is far from the truth. Many groups are in fact quite small, even though they may claim to speak for millions. It is remarkable how many organizations in Washington, especially ideological groups, use the word "national" in their title but have a membership of no more than a few thousand. Many such groups derive the funding necessary to support a Washington staff not from membership dues but from donations by foundations or corporations. Although other groups, such as labor and farm organizations, have millions of members, we should not lose sight of the fact that people need reasons to join groups and invest their time or money.

Consider, for example, a woman who works in an automobile factory. While she may believe that she and her fellow workers benefit from the efforts of the United Auto Workers, this does not mean that she would voluntarily join the union, since she may also figure that in a factory employing thousands her membership is hardly crucial. Thus, she may hope to reap the benefits of a strong union (higher wages) without paying the cost (union dues, attendance at union meetings, participation in strikes, etc.). This is the so-called "free-rider" problem. It is especially acute for those groups which cannot restrict their benefits only to their members. There is no way, for example, for environmental groups to limit the enjoyment of cleaner air to those who actively work to promote clean air. If membership is not necessary to enjoy the results of group activity, why join? Of course, if everyone tried to be a free rider, then organizations would find it impossible to recruit members.

Organizations attempt to solve this problem by giving people good reasons for joining. In the case of a labor union like the United Auto Workers the reason is one of the strongest of all: membership in the union is a necessary condition of employment in a "closed shop." (Some states with "right-to-work" laws—mostly in the south and southwest—prohibit closed shops.) Other groups provide reasons such as attractive monthly magazines, access to special services, and the personal satisfaction of working toward worthwhile goals. Although it may sound self-evident, it is worth noting that the largest interest groups are those that offer the most compelling reasons for joining to the largest number of individuals.

Who Governs?

When we want to know where the major interest groups stand on pressing national issues, we look quite naturally to the pronouncements of the group leaders. When George Meany dominated the AFL-CIO, his public statements were taken to reflect the opinions of the AFL-CIO membership, or even of organized labor generally. Similarly, Martin Luther King, who served as president of the Southern Christian Leadership Conference in the 1960s, was widely regarded as a spokesman for black Americans. It is probably safe to assume that in these

When the AFL-CIO called for a protest march against President Reagan's economic policies in 1981, more than 200 other interest groups joined the massive demonstration. *(Diego Goldberg/Sygma)*

cases, as well as in many others, leaders of interest groups do a rather good job of articulating the strongly held views, and deeply felt interests, of the members. But what if leaders venture opinions or views on issues *not* closely connected with the central purposes of the groups they lead?

This actually happens much more frequently than we might expect. The AFL-CIO, for example, has been one of the strongest and most persistent advocates of social welfare legislation that has had minimal impact on the well-being of unionized workers, who usually have incomes too high to qualify for programs directed to the poor. Similarly, the National Council of Churches regularly takes very liberal positions on foreign policy, even though foreign policy is not an issue of great concern for the millions of Protestants who belong to the churches represented by the National Council. What must be kept in mind in cases of this sort is that there is no necessary reason why the views of leaders and members must conform. Indeed, in many cases they simply do not.

Problems of this sort are less frequent in small

groups, which, because they are more homogeneous, are able to operate through consensus. In large organizations, however, decision-making authority tends to be concentrated among activist leaders. One student of organizational behavior has gone so far as to speak of an "iron law of oligarchy" inherent in all organizations (Michels, 1962). "Oligarchy" here refers to the rule of the few; the larger the organization, the smaller is the proportion of those who wield real power. This tendency is facilitated by the relative apathy of the rank and file on matters not directly related to their reasons for joining the organization. As long as the leaders are perceived to be doing a good job on the truly important issues, the general membership can be quite tolerant regarding the positions, statements, or actions of leaders on a range of other issues.

HOW INTEREST GROUPS INFLUENCE POLITICS

The late V. O. Key once observed that "where power rests, there influence will be brought to bear" (Key, 1958:154). Political interest groups employ a variety of different means for gaining access to and influencing the policymaking process. The choice of tactics used in any particular case will depend on the nature of the political process, the character of the organization and its resources, and the issue at hand. Five basic tactics are available to groups: direct lobbying, grass-roots lobbying, electioneering, public protest, and litigation.

Direct Lobbying

Mark Twain once observed that Americans have the best Congress money can buy. The point of Twain's comment was, of course, the supposed nefarious nexus between interest groups and Congress. The notorious image of lobbyists wining, dining, and bribing public officials was in part deserved. The motto of Sam Ward, "king of the lobby" in the 1870s, was "The way to a man's 'aye' is through his stomach." And that isn't the only appetite to which appeal has been made. In 1873, writing about women "lobbyesses" in *Behind the Scenes in Washington,* Edmund W. Martin observed that the "lever of lust is used to pry up more legislators to the sticking point than money itself avails to seduce" (Ornstein and Elder, 1978:97).

The question is whether in the contemporary Congress such behavior is the exception or the rule. The scandals of recent years have amply demonstrated that Congress is *not* free of corruption. The 1980 Abscam investigation as well as others has documented cases of outright bribery of members of Congress, leading to several criminal convictions. What must be kept in mind, however, is that it is the nature of the modern news media, especially television, to focus publicity on the handful of representatives and senators involved in scandal. The behavior of hundreds of others may be totally beyond reproach, but there is little that is newsworthy in the *absence* of scandal. Suffice it to say that there is no evidence of widespread corruption involving the members of Congress and the lobbyists who seek to influence them.

The traditional bad reputation of the lobbying profession is in part self-induced. In opposing one another, lobbyists tend to exaggerate their own virtues and effectiveness, while disparaging their opponents as rich, unscrupulous, and conniving. Lobbyists may be their own worst enemy, cultivating

an ill-deserved image. One detailed study concluded that the "image of lobbyists wallowing in ill-gotten and ill-spent lucre is one of the great myths of our time" (Bauer et al., 1972:341).

But this may not be the only sense in which the lobbyists' reputation is undeserved, or at least exaggerated, for they may not be generally as powerful as many believe. The same study concluded that a "close look at the pressure groups revealed them as something far short of the omnipotent, well-oiled machines that are protrayed in the political literature" (Bauer et al., 1972:349). Another study went further, arguing that there is "relatively little influence or power in lobbying per se" (Milbraith, 1976:354).

If this is so, then why lobby? And if lobbying is not primarily wining, dining, or bribing, then what is it? Consider the conclusion of the political journalist Bernard Asbell, who spent one year following the daily activities of former Senator Edmund Muskie:

> To the outsider who sees Capitol Hill only as a movie set, it may come as a surprise that more than ninety-nine percent of lobbying effort is spent not on parties, weekend hosting, and passing plain white envelopes, but trying to persuade minds through facts and reason (Asbell, 1978:370–1).

The fact is that most lobbyists spend most of their time providing friendly, or at least persuadable, representatives and senators with facts and arguments to back up their legislative positions. In effect, lobbyists help their friends in Congress to persuade other members of the soundness of their positions.

Another kind of information that lobbyists provide is "political" information. The reaction of lobbyists to various legislative proposals, the intensity of their views, and their willingness to work to promote or defeat a measure all give legislators political cues as to how constituents feel, or will feel, about the positions they may take in Congress. Interest-group representatives also help by communicating politicians' views to group members. The lobbying relationship is, in short, a two-way street.

There is a kind of built-in quality control on the information lobbyists provide. It is in the lobbyist's long-term self-interest to be honest and straightforward in order to maintain the trust of the official and ensure future access. As one member of Congress put it:

> It doesn't take very long to figure out which lobbyists are straightforward, and which ones are trying to snow you. The good ones will give you the weak points as well as the strong points of their case. If anyone ever gives me false or misleading information, that's it—I'll never see him again (Ornstein and Elder, 1978:77).

One set of researchers concluded that a "Congressman determines—consciously or unconsciously—what he hears. He hears most, for instance, from interest groups with which he is congenial" (Bauer et al., 1972:419). A lobbyist talks to and aids friends and allies, becoming in effect a "service bureau for those Congressmen already agreeing with him rather than an agent of direct persuasion" (Bauer et al., 1972:353). In other words, only rarely do groups directly pressure politicians. The image of interest groups co-opting members of Congress, committees, and executive agencies is largely overdrawn.

Grass-Roots Lobbying

Common Cause routinely includes an "alert" in its bimonthly membership magazine urging members to contact their representatives on a given issue. The National Rifleman's Association is famous for its ability to rouse its members to notify their elected officials of their opposition to pending gun-control legislation. And companies such as Mobil Oil regularly conduct national media compaigns to influence the course of public debate in order to influence public policy decisions.

Grass-roots lobbying includes both specific efforts directed at a legislator's home district and general efforts to influence the public agenda. The sharp rise in recent years of this form of lobbying is in part due to the growing importance of mass communications, the weakening of our political institutions, and the perfecting of Madison Avenue–style public relations techniques. The increase in grass-roots lobbying is also a response to the success with which it has been used. One researcher maintains that the most effective form of lobbying is that which affects the public official's image or reelection prospects (Greenwald, 1977).

Perhaps the most common type of grass-roots lobbying is the letter-writing campaign. Curiously, however, this tactic can produce virtually no effect, or it can produce great effect. Legislators are quick to identify and discount prepackaged, manufactured letter-writing campaigns, especially those in which they receive thousands of identical postcards. After all, how much effort or commitment does it take to sign a postcard? Such "commitment" by even thousands of constituents may not be a real threat. For this reason, organizations like Common Cause, which make regular effective use of grass-roots lobbying, refrain from providing members with specific wording or form letters. When representatives receive hundreds or thousands of independently drafted letters voicing similar views on a pending legislative issue, they are quick to take notice.

The power of grass-roots lobbying can be seen in the concern of elected officials with the "ratings" published by ideological, labor, and consumer groups, and especially in their sensitivity to such mediagenic tactics as Environmental Action's annual "dirty dozen" list of nonsupportive members of Congress. If misused, however, such tactics can backfire. In 1981, the National Pro-Life Political Action Committee (NPLPAC) issued a "hit list" of five representatives and four senators and planned to spend $400,000 trying to defeat them for reelection. This came as a surprise to the members of Congress on NPLPAC's advisory board. Some of them promptly resigned in anger. One said: "I'm not in any way going to participate in anything that is set up to defeat sitting members" (*Washington Post,* 1981:A1).

Most groups, however, do not overtly work to defeat incumbents, for this would risk antagonizing those whose support they may need. Moreover, if they are truly successful at grass-roots lobbying, then defeating incumbents is not necessary.

Electioneering

Interest groups are not political parties. They neither nominate candidates for office nor seek to win elections, and they are (generally) not as broad-based as political parties. It is unlikely that an AT&T candidate, or a Bow Tie Manufacturers Association nominee, or even a Moral Majority candidate could win an election. Groups such as the National Conservative Political Action Committee (NCPAC), following the 1980 elections, claimed credit for defeating a number of United States senators. It would be an interesting test of their true strength if they tried to nominate and run their own candidate against either of the two major political parties.

Although interest groups do not nominate candidates for national office, they do form alliances with political parties, usually of an informal nature. These alliances enable interest groups to influence platforms and nominations, and thereby affect the nation's political agenda. In recent years, as the parties have weakened, groups such as the AFL-CIO, the National Education Association, women's groups, and prolife groups have actively sought to get their members elected as delegates to the major-party conventions and to write their own planks into party platforms. But such groups are not so much seeking alliance with the parties as trying to win them over. And healthy parties as intermediary institutions should avoid the narrow-based appeal of special interest groups.

As elections have become more expensive and parties weaker, interest groups have come to play a greater role in the election process. Organizations such as the AFL-CIO's COPE provide money, workers, and expertise to candidates. Few groups can match the ability of unions to field workers for registration and "get out the vote" drives. The National Women's Political Caucus (NWPC) provides technical expertise and campaign consultant services to women candidates.

Probably the most important contributions interest groups make to candidates are financial contributions. It is through political action committees that interest groups solicit funds from members and contribute money to candidates or parties. There has been an enormous growth in the number of PACs and a tremendous increase in the sum total of their contributions since the close legal regulation of their activities resulting from the campaign finance legislation of 1974 (see Figure 8-2). From 608 in 1974, PACs have grown in number to 3,479 in 1982, with most of the recent increase coming from PACs formed by corporation employees.

FIGURE 8-2
Growth of nonparty political action committees, 1974–1980. (*Source:* Ornstein et al., 1982:75; *Federal Election Commission Record,* 1981.)

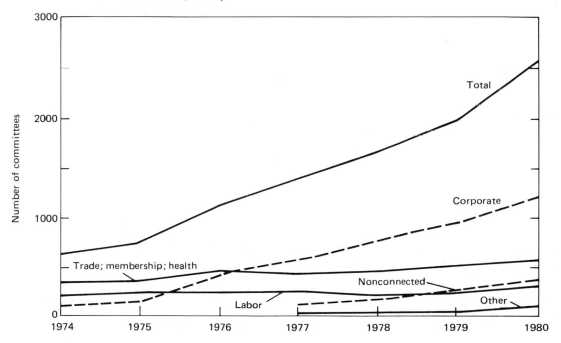

It is in congressional races, as noted in Chapter 6, that PACs exert their greatest influence. In 1972, it is estimated, PACs contributed $8.5 million, or 14 percent of the total raised by all congressional candidates; in 1980 the figure was $55.2 million, or 20 percent of the total. Certain predictable biases appear in the PACs' pattern of contributions. Corporate PACs tend to favor Republicans; labor PACs favor Democrats. Liberal and labor PACs were outspent by conservative and corporate PACs by an estimated 3 to 1 ratio in 1982 (Sabato, 1983). As reflected in their contributions, PACs overwhelmingly favor incumbents, reminding us that everyone loves a winner. And in congressional races, PACs disproportionately favor legislators on committees of interest to the organization.

Public Protest

Most interest groups most of the time do not engage in direct public protest when they are dissatisfied with the direction of public policy. Occasionally, however, an organization will stage a protest demonstration, boycott, march, or strike to call attention to its grievance in a particularly dramatic way. With the exception of violence, these tactics are protected by laws and court decisions; the Supreme Court has declared many to be free expression protected by the First Amendment.

The Boston Tea Party constitutes one of the earliest uses of protest tactics in American politics. In recent decades, civil rights and antiwar groups have resorted to active protest. Today, "propaganda of the deed" is a strategy of the right and the left, although such tactics seem to go in and out of fashion periodically (most recently, reaching a height in the late 1960s and early 1970s and a low in the late 1970s and early 1980s).

Direct-action tactics usually reflect intense emotional commitment to an issue and are frequently attempts to pressure policymakers by public opinion. The strategy depends for its success on drama and media attention. It can backfire if the attentive public perceives neither the cause nor the chosen

After a lull in the late 1970s, new causes brought new demonstrations to America's streets; this 1982 march in favor of a nuclear freeze was one of the largest demonstrations ever held in New York City. *(Rick Reinhard / Black Star)*

tactics as legitimate. For example, the Symbionese Liberation Army's kidnapping of Patty Hearst in 1974 attracted a lot of publicity, but won little sympathy for its cause. On the other side, however, many have argued that the large public demonstrations against the Vietnamese war were instrumental in ending our involvement, although there is no way to demonstrate whether these protests influenced or simply reflected public opinion. As a general rule, politicians respond more readily to their traditional publics than to protest groups.

Litigating

Most of the tactics of interest groups we have discussed are as old as interest groups themselves. There is one strategy, however, which is only a few decades old yet in this short time has become one of the most effective ways for groups to influence public policy. This is the increasing practice of resorting to the judiciary, especially the federal courts, when the desired results are not achieved through the regular political process.

The great landmark case that really inaugurated the use of litigation by an interest group to achieve substantive policy changes was the now-famous 1954 school desegregation case *Brown v. Board of Education.* The *Brown* case was the climax of a carefully planned legal strategy devised by the NAACP. The judicial route was pursued because the NAACP had virtually no chance of success in the political arena. The white-dominated southern state legislatures would not dismantle the dual school system voluntarily; and civil rights advocates in Congress could not muster sufficient strength to overcome a southern filibuster in the Senate (at least not until the 1960s), thus foreclosing a remedy through national legislation.

In recent decades the Supreme Court has made it easier to influence policy through litigation by liberalizing the rules on who has "standing," or the right, to sue in court and by allowing more class-action suits in behalf of a class of individuals in similar circumstances. The result has been an explosion in the use of the courts by interest groups, especially by ideological groups. None has been more successful in court than the environmental groups, who have frequently relied on the broad language of landmark environmental legislation to oppose actions which they believe harmful. The classic case is the Supreme Court decision in 1978

that protected the tiny snail darter from the destructive effects of the Tellico Dam in Tennessee. In this suit the Court ruled that the Endangered Species Act, passed by Congress in 1973, protected the snail darter (*Tennessee Valley Authority v. Hill,* 437 U.S. 153, 1978). Shortly thereafter, however, and to the chagrin of many environmental groups, Congress expressly authorized the completion of the dam, making it clear that the Endangered Species Act should not stand in the way.

This example (and others could be cited) illustrates how fragile a victory can be when the regular political process is avoided, particularly when judicial decisions rest upon statutory interpretation rather than on constitutional language. George Will, the noted political columnist, in reflecting upon the use of litigation by conservatives in the 1930s as well as liberals in the 1970s, observed that the "surest sign that political persuasion has become anemic is a dependence on litigation rather than legislation in pursuing policy goals." He notes that from time to time the courts "have become the principal weapon of persons impatient with democratic decisionmaking. But that is a weapon that will cripple any cause that depends on it" (Will, 1978:204). This recalls Justice Black's admonition: "To people who have such faith in our nine justices, I say that I have known a different court from the one today" (Black, 1968:11). In Chapter 12, on the judiciary, we will examine more fully the issues raised by the increasing role of the courts in formulating policy.

All the tactics discussed above represent means by which interest groups seek to influence the political process for objectives they deem important. The capacity of groups to employ these tactics effectively depends on the resources of the particular group in question. Resources, however, must be understood in a sense much broader than merely cash in the bank. While economic assets are very important, other resources that can be equally, if not more, important include the "size, distribution and degree of mobilization of the membership" as well as the appeal of the group's cause and the skill of the group's leadership (Ippolito and Walker, 1982:319). For example, the success of the civil rights movement in the 1960s owed a great deal to the extraordinary political and rhetorical skills of Martin Luther King, while the influence of the group Public Citizen has been heavily dependent on a single individual, Ralph Nader.

REGULATING INTEREST GROUPS

From what we have seen so far, it may seem that interest groups are as American as apple pie. They are an intrinsic and vital element of the American political system, and their actions, whether we approve of them or not, have a degree of constitutional protection. This does not mean, however, that interest groups must go unregulated. On the contrary, as we saw at the beginning of the chapter, James Madison, for one, believed that the regulation of interests was the "principle task of modern legislation."

The first significant effort by the national government to regulate the behavior of interest groups took place during the late nineteenth and early twentieth centuries in the progressive era. Through the creation of independent regulatory commissions, especially the Interstate Commerce Commission (ICC) and the Federal Trade Commission (FTC), the federal government sought to restrict the abuses and injustices of price-fixing, deceptive practices, and restraint of trade, perpetrated by large commercial enterprises engaged in interstate commerce. The purpose of these efforts was to regulate the behavior of powerful interests within the economic sphere. It was not until some years later that the lobbying activity itself—those practices by which interests sought to influence governmental policy—was first brought under regulation by the national government. There have been three distinct attempts to regulate legally the lobbying activities of interest groups: the Revenue Act of 1939, the Lobbying Act of 1946, and the campaign financing legislation of the 1970s.

Regulating Interests through Law

The Revenue Act of 1939 This law stipulates that nonprofit organizations—which include many, though not all, interest groups—whose activities are substantially directed toward "attempting to influence legislation" must pay income tax (U.S. Code 26, Section 501, c, 3). Tax-exempt status is vitally important to many organizations not only because they save money that would otherwise have to be paid out in taxes, but also because private individuals who donate money to tax-exempt organizations are not required to pay taxes on income used for such donations. Without this tax-exempt status, it would be much harder to generate private donations.

The 1939 act has had the effect of discouraging some organizations from devoting a substantial effort to direct lobbying of state legislatures or Congress. Occasionally, as happened to the Sierra Club in 1966, an interest group does lose its tax-exempt status for excessive overt lobbying. Some groups, however, sidestep the law by setting up separate organizations to collect tax-exempt money to be used for purposes other than direct lobbying. The Sierra Club, for example, revived its affiliated Sierra Club Foundation, which is a tax-exempt organization to which donations are tax-deductible.

The Lobbying Act of 1946 Acting in the belief that public disclosure of lobbying groups and activities would help legislators and the public to identify self-interested appeals without restricting or prohibiting legitimate lobbying activities, in 1946 Congress passed the Federal Regulation of Lobbying Act. This law required lobbyists to register with the clerk of the House and the secretary of the Senate indicating who they represented and what their general legislative goals were. It also required quarterly reports both by individual lobbyists and by organizations, detailing how much was being spent to influence the passage of legislation. By the terms of the act it applied to individuals or organizations who solicited funds "to be used principally to ... influence, directly or indirectly, the passage or defeat of any legislation."

The propriety of the new law was soon challenged by organizations arguing that it unconstitutionally abridged the right of free speech and petition. In a 1954 ruling in the case *United States v. Harriss* the Supreme Court upheld the validity of the act, but construed it rather narrowly to apply only to *direct* contacts between lobbyists and members of Congress, thereby excluding both contact with a legislator's staff and grass-roots lobbying. Further weaknesses of the legislation were its failure to provide an enforcement mechanism and to include in its coverage organizations that do a significant amount of lobbying but are able to argue that their "principal" purpose is not influencing legislation. Many politically powerful groups have refused to register for just this reason.

In the late 1970s, several attempts were initiated to pass a new lobby registration bill that would close some of the loopholes of the 1946 law, but these have not yet been successful.

Campaign Finance Reform   The 1971, 1974, and 1976 campaign financing laws, discussed in detail in Chapter 6, placed new restrictions and regulations on the financing of election campaigns for federal office. Some of these provisions were overturned in the Supreme Court case *Buckley v. Valeo;* others were upheld. One of the major purposes of these campaign finance restrictions was to limit the role of special interest money in the electoral process. Before the new limits, individuals or organizations could legitimately give hundreds of thousands, or even millions, of dollars to a single candidate. One doesn't have to be particularly cynical about human nature to realize that a legislator who receives large campaign contributions from an interest group might later seek to repay the favor. Now, no matter how wealthy the individual or group, the most that can be given to any one candidate is several thousand dollars.

One of the unintended consequences of the new campaign finance laws was the growth in the number and contributions of political action committees (PACs). It is through these organizations that large sums of money can be dispersed to numerous separate candidates for political office. Money that in the past went to the general presidential campaign is now being channeled into congressional races. Many congressional candidates, in turn, who might previously have relied on a few large contributions, are now the recipients of donations of several thousand dollars from dozens of separate PACs. Ironically, the campaign finance reforms may simply have converted one kind of interest-group dependence (heavy reliance on a few groups) to another kind (somewhat smaller reliance on many more groups).

Miscellaneous Actions   In addition to these three distinct efforts to regulate interest groups through law, there have been a variety of actions with a similar purpose directed not at the groups themselves but at the members of Congress and employees of the executive branch. These include provisions requiring financial disclosure by high

governmental officials, prohibitions on any outside work that might create a conflict of interest, strict limitations on how much representatives and senators may earn in outside income, and "revolving-door" legislation forbidding executive agency personnel who leave government service from representing any private interest in dealings with their former agency for at least one year. These kinds of measures make it less likely that improper relationships will result between those who make policy and those who are most directly affected by government.

Alternatives to Legal Regulation

The legal regulation of interest-group activity and of lobbying in particular is in part a problem of definition. What is or is not lobbying? Who is or is not a lobbyist? When is an organization's principal purpose lobbying, and when is a "substantial" part of its funds devoted to influencing legislation? Is it possible to make a clear distinction between campaign contributions and bribes? When a lobbyist buys lunch for a member of Congress, is it a subtle bribe or an effort to gain a sympathetic hearing? The attempt to define lobbying sharply is reminiscent of the effort by George Washington Plunkett, the Tamanny Hall political boss at the turn of the century, to differentiate between honest graft and dishonest graft.

In addition to this difficulty of legal definition, the attempt to limit interest-group activity through legal regulation poses a First Amendment problem: individual liberty must be weighed against the common good. Free speech and the right to petition government must be balanced with the public's interest in maintaining corruption-free politics. The political scientist E. E. Schattschneider recognized the difficulty of regulating interest groups precisely because their activities are based on First Amendment rights: "to regulate pressure politics by suppressing these great liberties is to cure the disease by killing the patient." Rather, he suggested, "at all points the problem of the management of pressures is a problem of the political parties" (Schattschneider, 1960:42). He was suggesting that the most effective regulation of interest groups will come not from laws but from sound political institutions.

The growth of government and the increased scope of its activities are in part responsible for the greater number of special interests concerned with politics. The weakening of the political parties has eliminated a buffer between interest groups and the policymaking process, making accommodation between contending interests less easy and less likely. The decentralization of Congress (to be discussed in Chapter 9) has augmented the opportunities for specific interests to initiate, and also to stall, legislation. And, finally, rulings by the courts have provided the basis for increased interest-group litigation.

If interest groups today are inadequately regulated, it may be because our national institutions have been weakened in their ability to mediate. In some cases "reforms" of recent decades seem to have exaggerated the problem. For example, when members of the House and Senate were made more accountable for their actions by opening up committee mark-up sessions, this also gave interest groups access into a decision-making stage previously closed to them. Moreover, when the Freedom of Information Act was passed to give the public access to government information, it also benefited interest groups who wanted to know what their competitors or the governmental regulatory agencies were doing. This is not to say that reforms of this sort have not had a variety of beneficial effects, but only that they may also have made it more difficult for the institutions of government to regulate interest groups.

Political interest groups employ a variety of different means for influencing the policymaking process. Which tactics are used in any particular case will depend on the nature of the political process, the character of the organization and its resources, and the issue at hand. As we have seen, the five basic tactics are direct lobbying, grass-roots lobbying, electioneering, public protest, and litigation. With respect to direct lobbying, a variety of studies have shown that the common public image of lobbying as a sneaky business of wining, dining, and bribing public officials is exaggerated. Most direct lobbying is a straightforward matter of trying to persuade policymakers with facts and arguments.

Although most interest groups do not engage in unethical or illegal means for influencing public policy, this does not mean that their actions should go unregulated; even if their tactics are strictly legal, they may influence decision makers in ways that do not promote the broad public interest. There are essentially two distinct approaches for regulating the ways in which interests influence government. One is the legal approach. Examples include restrictions on lobbying by nonprofit groups, registration and reporting requirements for lobbyists, strict limits on campaign contributions, and financial disclosure by government officials. The other approach, which is more like the framers' original plan but which has not appealed to modern reformers, is the institutional approach. Its goal is the fostering and strengthening of the ability of our national political institutions to withstand interest-group demands and to reach independent judgments about the public interest. There is reason for believing that in recent years our national institutions have more and more lost this ability.

CONCLUSION

Of all the links between the citizenry and the formal institutions of government, interest groups have caused the most profound controversies for democratic theory and practice. This is a result of the fact that while interest groups play a vital role in communicating public attitudes to government, they can also make the achievement of the public interest more difficult by distorting governmental policy in favor of politically powerful organizations. A political system designed to promote personal liberty will necessarily foster dynamic interest-group politics. Nonetheless, this same political system will be required to moderate and regulate the clash of interests.

The openness of the American political system to interest groups reflects a clear recognition of the legitimacy of pluralist elements in the decision-making process and the need to take into account, however imperfectly, the *intensity* of the views of certain groups and not just their numerical strength. Yet the desire to control and regulate group interests reflects an attempt to ensure that majoritarian concerns are not overwhelmed by the power of entrenched groups and that representative institutions are not incapacitated from acting on behalf of their perception of the public interest. It is incorrect, of course, to depict group interests as always in tension with majoritarian concerns or the public interest, for interest groups, as observed in Chapter 7, are a vital component of majoritarian politics and an essential component in discovering the public interest. Yet the potential conflict between the sum of organized interest groups and the wishes of the majority is of sufficient importance to merit the many constitutional debates about the role of laws and institutions in structuring the access of groups to the political process.

SOURCES

Abraham, Henry J.: *The Judicial Process,* Oxford University Press, New York, 1980.

Almond, Gabriel A., and Sidney Verba: *The Civic Culture: Political Attitudes and Democracy in Five Nations,* Princeton University Press, Princeton, N.J., 1963.

Asbell, Bernard: *The Senate Nobody Knows,* Doubleday, Garden City, N.Y., 1978.

Bauer, Raymond A., Ithiel de Sola Pool, and Lewis Anthony Dexter, II: *American Business and Public Policy: The Politics of Foreign Trade,* Aldine, Chicago, 1972.

Beer, Samuel H.: *British Politics in the Collectivist Age,* Vintage, New York, 1969.

Bentley, Arthur: *The Process of Government,* University of Chicago Press, Chicago, 1908.

Black, Hugo L.: *A Constitutional Faith,* Knopf, New York, 1968.

Calhoun, John C.: *A Disquisition on Government and Selections from the Discourses,* Bobbs-Merrill, Indianapolis and New York, 1953.

Federal Election Commission Record, March 1981.

Fiorina, Morris P.: *Congress: Keystone of the Washington Establishment,* Yale University Press, New Haven, Conn., and London, 1977.

Greenwald, Carol S.: *Group Power: Lobbying and Public Policy,* Praeger, New York, 1977.

Ippolito, Dennis S., and Thomas G. Walker: *Political Parties, Interest Groups and Public Policy,* Prentice-Hall, Englewood Cliffs N.J., 1980.

Key, V. O.: *Politics, Parties, and Pressure Groups,* Thomas Y. Crowell, New York, 1958.

Lowi, Theodore J.: *The End of Liberalism,* Norton, New York, 1969.

Michels, Robert: *Political Parties,* Macmillan, New York, 1962.

Milbraith, Lester W.: *The Washington Lobbyists,* Greenwood, Westport, Conn., 1976.

Ornstein, Norman J., and Shirley Elder: *Interest Groups, Lobbying and Policymaking,* Congressional Quarterly Press, Washington, D.C., 1978.

———, Thomas E. Mann, Michael J. Malbin, and John F. Biddy: *Vital Statistics on Congress: 1982,* American Enterprise Institute, Washington, D.C., 1982.

Sabato, Larry: "Parties, PACs, and Independent Groups," in Mann and Ornstein (eds.), *The American Elections of 1982,* American Enterprise Institute, Washington, D.C., 1983.

Schattschneider, E. E.: *The Semi-Sovereign People,* Holt, New York, 1960.

Social Indicators: 1976, U.S. Department of Commerce, U.S. Government Printing Office, Washington, D.C., 1977.

Tocqueville, Alexis de: *Democracy in America,* J. P. Mayer (ed.), Doubleday, Garden City, N.Y., 1969.

Truman, David B.: *The Governmental Process,* 2d ed., Knopf, New York, 1971.

Walker, Jack: *The Origins and Maintenance of Interest Groups in America,* American Political Science Association, Washington, D.C., 1981.

Washington Post, June 4, 1981, p. A1.

Will, George F.: *The Pursuit of Happiness and Other Sobering Thoughts,* Harper and Row, New York, 1978.

Wilson, James Q.: *Political Organizations,* Basic Books, New York, 1973.

———: "American Politics Then and Now," *Commentary,* February 1979, pp. 39–46.

RECOMMENDED READINGS

Bauer, Raymond A., Ithiel de Sola Pool, and Lewis Anthony Dexter II: *American Business and Public Policy: The Politics of Foreign Trade,* Aldine, Chicago, 1972. An examination of how business organizations have attempted to influence American foreign trade policy, based on a general analysis of how interest groups lobby Congress.

Greenwald, Carol S.: *Group Power: Lobbying and Public Policy,* Praeger, New York, 1977. A thorough study of interest groups at work in the policy process.

Lowi, Theodore J.: *The End of Liberalism,* Norton, New York, 1969. A critical look at the expanded role of pressure groups in American politics.

Milbraith, Lester, W.: *The Washington Lobbyists,* Greenwood, Westport, Conn., 1976. A description of lobbyists at work.

Olson, Mancur: *The Logic of Collective Action: Public Goods and the Theory of Groups,* Schocken Books, New York, 1971. Challenges the basic premise of group theory by arguing that lobbying is a by-product of group activity rather than the central purpose for group existence.

Ornstein, Norman J., and Shirley Elder: *Interest Groups, Lobbying and Policymaking,* Congressional Quarterly Press, Washington, D.C., 1978. A general study of groups in the American political process, describing their operation and evaluating their effectiveness, with three case studies.

Truman, David B.: *The Governmental Process,* 2d ed., Knopf, New York, 1971. A classic interpretation of the central role of groups and group conflict in American politics.

Wilson, James Q.: *Political Organizations,* Basic Books, New York, 1973. A theory of the internal processes of interest groups and political parties that focuses on the incentives these organizations use to attract members.

Part Three

The Institutions of Government

Chapter 9

The Congress

None of our governing institutions presents as many different faces or is subject to as many conflicting interpretations as the Congress. At times its long-established procedures and complex institutional structures seem to render it incapable of formulating coherent national policy; occasionally, however, it acts with great speed and determination in translating a new idea into a legislative mandate. It has been criticized as being out of touch with the nation it is supposed to lead, yet its members devote an enormous amount of time and energy toward remaining on good terms with their constituents. On some issues it appears to favor special interests over the broader national interest, while on others it passes legislation that imposes substantial economic burdens on powerful corporations. For over a decade Congress has been urged to reassert its rightful authority against an overly powerful executive branch, especially in the area of foreign relations; but after trying to do so, it has been attacked for meddling in areas where it is not competent to act or for interfering with the proper executive functions of the president.

What are we to make of these divergent char-acteristics and views of Congress? Does it function too slowly or too fast? Is it unrepresentative of the American people or perhaps too representative? Is it the captive of the special interests, or does it too frequently seek idealistic ends without regard for the actual costs that must be borne by the interests that make up American society? Can it be an equal partner with the president, or is it destined to play a subordinate role in the American separation-of-powers scheme?

These are not new questions. They have been asked of Congress throughout history. There is rarely anything like a consensus among journalists, academics, political leaders, and the people themselves about the nature of Congress and its proper role in the American political system. No matter how much the institution and its political environment change over time, each new generation seems vaguely dissatisfied with the American national legislature but uncertain about what could be done to improve it or even what an improved institution would look like. One reason for this perennial dissatisfaction is that we expect so many different things from Congress and from those who serve in it.

THE FUNCTIONS OF CONGRESS: ORIGINAL INTENTION AND HISTORICAL DEVELOPMENTS

When the founding fathers created Congress, they had two key tasks in mind: the passage of sound *legislation* and the faithful *representation* of what they called the "deliberate sense of the community." Over the years, in response to changes in the political system, Congress has taken on three other important functions: *oversight* of the bureaucracy, *investigations* to inform the public, and *constituency service*. A brief examination of these five functions will serve to illustrate the many different burdens placed on Congress.

Legislation

Article I of the Constitution of the United States begins with the words "All legislative Powers herein granted shall be vested in a Congress of the United States." It goes on to enumerate seventeen separate powers, some of which are among the highest powers exercised by any government: taxation, regulation of commerce, and declaration of war. Others of these are less significant: establishing of post offices and exercising of jurisdiction over the seat of government. The list of powers is followed by a special clause giving Congress the authority to "make all Laws which shall be necessary and proper for carrying into Execution the foregoing Powers." This clause makes it clear that the enumeration was not intended as a strict limitation on Congress. Although the president possesses a qualified veto over statutes passed by Congress and the Supreme Court retains the power to rule acts of Congress unconstitutional, Congress was designed to be the premier lawmaking institution of American national government.

For most of the nineteenth century Congress was, in fact, the chief policymaking instrument of the national government. This was especially true in the decades after the Civil War, a time when relatively weak presidents were no match for a determined House and Senate. In the twentieth century, however, the position of Congress as the nation's chief policymaking institution was eroded by three broad developments. First, the president became increasingly important as an agenda setter for Congress, especially on complex issues that cut across traditional policy areas. Second, with the growth of a large federal bureaucracy to regulate various sectors of the American economy, more and more "policy" decisions were being made by career civil servants or presidential appointees. Many of these decisions have the full force of law even though they are not made directly by Congress. Finally, the growing importance of foreign policy since World War II has enhanced the importance of the presidency at the expense of Congress, especially since much foreign policy is made through the day-to-day decisions of the executive branch, not through formal legislation.

In response to these developments, Congress has in the past decade tried to recapture its position as the nation's chief lawmaking institution. It is increasingly reluctant to take its direction from the president, even a president of the same party as the majority in Congress (as President Carter learned); and it has developed new institutions, such as the Congressional Budget Office and special ad hoc committees, to help it set its own agenda. It has also become more skeptical of policymaking within the bureaucracy, overturning administrative decisions through statutes and placing new restrictions on the power it delegates to the bureaucracy. And in the field of foreign policy Congress has passed new legislative restrictions on the president, including the landmark War Powers Act of 1973, which was designed to make Congress a full partner in decisions to undertake long-term military actions.

Representation

Before the modern era, the task of lawmaking was carried out by individuals (monarchs, tyrants), by small bodies of powerful leaders (hereditary nobles, the wealthy), or by the people directly (the Athenian democracy). In contrast to these schemes, modern liberal democracies place the official lawmaking responsibility in a representative body. Whether called a "congress," "parliament," "national assembly," or "diet," the lawmaking body is an assembly of individuals elected by the people who are expected to give voice to—to *re*-present—the attitudes and interests of the people themselves. The joining of the two tasks of lawmaking and representation into one body creates a strong likelihood that the laws promulgated by the government will broadly conform to popular desires.

The representative principle takes two different forms in modern democracies. In most western European nations, the individual elected to the legislature represents primarily the views of a political party. The personal characteristics and background of the candidates are less important than their party affiliation. On election day, the voters in effect choose one of the contesting parties and its particular program to govern the nation. In the United States, on the other hand, where political party is less important, individuals elected to Congress represent primarily those who reside within their legislative district.

This latter principle of *geographic representation* has several important effects. It virtually guarantees that interests and groups powerful at the local level will make themselves felt within Congress. Diffuse interests or values, however, such as a desire for a clean environment or a balanced budget, may not be well represented, especially if they conflict with powerful local interests.

Generally, members of Congress analyze legislative proposals in terms of the impact on their districts and tend to favor legislation that will benefit their constituents, sometimes at the expense of broader national considerations. When resources are scarce, this tendency may lead to serious geographic divisions and conflicts within Congress, as has happened in recent years in the struggle between representatives of the "sun belt" (the south and southwest) and the "frost belt" (the northeast and the midwest) over the distribution of federal funds, projects, and grants. Finally, geographic representation weakens party leadership within Congress by making the congressional district or state, and not the party, the first loyalty of representatives and senators.

Oversight

In the two centuries since the Constitution was written, the federal government has dramatically expanded its role in promoting the social and economic well-being of the American people. As it has done so, a huge bureaucracy, numbering some 2 million people, has grown up to administer hundreds of programs. Formally, this bureaucracy serves under the direction of the president: it is part of the executive branch of government. In this respect, the structure of the executive branch is, on paper at least, much like the structure of any large corporation: a pyramidlike, hierarchical arrangement with clear chains of command that bind even the lowest-level employee to the ultimate direction of the chief officers. Under this model the bureaucracy should carry out the laws as the president directs, and the president should be the one mainly responsible for determining that bureaucrats faithfully discharge their public trust.

Congress, however, has never been satisfied with this view of bureaucratic accountability. It has adhered, instead, to a very different notion: that the officers of the government are principally responsible to the law, and therefore to Congress, the lawmaking institution. Congress formulated this concept in 1946 when, in the Legislative Reorganization Act, it required that "each standing committee of the Senate and the House of Representatives exercise continuous watchfulness of the execution [of laws] by the administrative agencies." This "continuous watchfulness" is carried out (1) through the review by committees of Congress of requests by executive branch officials for new legislative authority to continue ongoing programs, (2) through the annual budget process when the appropriations committees set specific funding levels for these programs, and (3) by the two government operations committees (one in each branch of Congress), which have special responsibility for investigating and promoting the "overall economy and efficiency of government." More recently many committees in Congress have created special oversight subcommittees to consolidate the oversight responsibility within the committee. The bureaucracy in the American system, as we shall see in Chapter 13, in effect serves two masters.

Investigations and Public Education

If the members of Congress are suspicious about how faithfully or effectively the executive branch is carrying out its mandates, they may initiate a formal investigation by a congressional committee. Some congressional investigations, however, have a

The Senate's investigation of the Watergate scandals, like several other congressional inquiries in recent decades, became an absorbing national drama on all the television networks. *(Dennis Brack / Black Star)*

much broader purpose and importance. In the past several decades, congressional investigations of organized crime, of hunger in America, of the Watergate scandal, of the assassinations of John F. Kennedy and Martin Luther King, and of the Central Intelligence Agency all uncovered and publicized information of an important public nature. Investigations of this type can profoundly affect public opinion.

A century ago Woodrow Wilson called this the "informing function of Congress," and he argued that it "should be preferred even to its legislative function."

> The inquisitiveness of such bodies as Congress is the best conceivable source of information. Congress is the only body which has the proper motive for inquiry, and it is the only body which has the power to act effectively upon the knowledge which its inquiries secure. The Press is merely curious or merely partisan. The people are scattered and unorganized. But Congress is, as it were, the corporate people, the mouthpiece of its will (Wilson, 1969:197–198).

Certainly the modern media are a more important source of public information than the press about which Wilson wrote in 1885. Nevertheless, even today the direct examination of a public issue by the broadcast or print media rarely can match the public impact of a highly publicized congressional investigation. One reason for this is the public authority that Congress embodies, something that even the most prestigious newspapers, magazines, and television networks lack.

Constituency Service

The growth in the programs and size of the national government over two centuries has put greater demands on the members of Congress to assist their constituents in their dealings with federal agencies. As a former Virginia congressman announced to his constituents in a newsletter he mailed during his 1980 reelection campaign:

> Thousands of your neighbors have asked Herb Harris for help in cutting through red tape to get information or action. Some need replacement of a lost Social Security check. Others need help in getting veterans benefits they deserve. Others are trying to get a straight answer from the SBA [Small Business Administration]. What they all have in common is that they want the system to work the way it's supposed to work: fairly.

When Congress first began operating, years before the programs referred to here were even conceived of, there was much less contact between individual citizens and the federal government and therefore less need for members of Congress to play this kind of service role. Now, however, constituency service consumes a large fraction of the resources of every congressional office, especially the time of personal staff. Both representatives and senators assign this function a very high priority, for it can generate votes within the district or state from those who may pay little attention to legislative matters. And, unlike taking stands on controversial issues, constituency service rarely creates enemies, just friends. Some political analysts, disturbed by all the attention that members of Congress give to this nonlegislative function, argue that we are witnessing a "gradual transformation [of representatives and senators] from national legislators to errand-boy ombudsmen" (Fiorina, 1977:47). If this is true, then it raises serious questions about whether the contemporary Congress is fulfilling its proper constitutional responsibility to function as a sound lawmaking institution. We shall return to this issue later in the chapter.

The variety and importance of the five functions we have outlined give some idea of the vitality of Congress in the American political system. However it may rank against the presidency, bureaucracy, or courts in relative importance, Congress is, without doubt, the most powerful and dynamic national legislature among the world's major liberal democracies. In the parliamentary systems of countries like Britain, Germany, and Japan, the executive branch—prime minister, cabinet, and bureaucracy—is on a day-to-day basis the dominant in-

stitution. Although the parliament retains complete formal authority over public policy, in practice the majority party in the legislature nearly always supports the proposals of the party leaders, who head the executive branch. In the United States, the national legislature is, as it was designed to be, vigorously independent of the executive branch. Consequently, it has greater independent impact on public policy than do the legislative bodies in other liberal democracies.

In this chapter we will concentrate on the two original congressional functions: legislation and representation—not because these were the two the framers had in mind, but because they are the most important and inclusive. In many respects the three other functions help to fulfill the tasks of legislation and representation. Our focus here will be on how Congress rates as a lawmaking and representative institution, on what forces affect congressional performance in these areas, and on what Congress can do and has done to improve its effectiveness. Simply put, is Congress meeting its high constitutional responsibilities? It is impossible, however, to answer questions like these until we understand the distinctive characteristics of the two branches that together constitute the Congress.

A BICAMERAL LEGISLATURE

Although we commonly refer to Congress as if it were a single institution, it is more accurate to think of it as the combination of two distinct legislative bodies: the House and the Senate. Each body is a world of its own, and there is surprisingly little interaction between the two houses. They have separate members, staff, chambers for debate, and office buildings. Each body selects its own leaders, creates its own committee system, and determines its own rules and procedures. This formal institutional division extends even to the architecture of the Capitol and surrounding buildings. If a line were drawn east-west through the rotunda in the center of the Capitol, it would divide the offices, chambers, and support buildings of the Senate (north of the line) from those of the House (south of the line). The fact is that a member of the House or Senate can work a full day "on the Hill" without even seeing a member of the other body. The main exception to this pattern of separation is service on one of the several *joint committees* of Congress or on a *conference committee* (described below). These are two of the few ways in which an effort is made to bridge the gap between the two branches.

But why have two branches at all? Why have a *bicameral* legislature? What purposes are served by requiring two distinct institutions to agree on legislation? Why did the framers create both a House and Senate, and is their design still relevant today?

The Original Plan for the House and Senate

Bicameralism The creation of a bicameral legislature for the national government, as we saw in Chapter 2, was related to the conflict between the small and large states within the Constitutional Convention. Many delegates from the larger states wanted a legislative branch in which membership was based on a state's population, while delegates from the smaller states feared that this system would result in a union dominated by the larger states. A compromise was finally reached whereby representation in the House was based on population and representation in the Senate on the equality of the states.

The attention paid to this "great compromise" has tended to obscure the fact that well before the conflict over representation even arose at the convention, the delegates had decided that a bicameral legislature was necessary. Bicameralism, they argued, would improve the quality of legislation by requiring the concurrence of two distinct bodies, each possessing attributes beneficial to the legislative process.

In constructing the new legislature, the framers believed that one branch had to be especially close to the people. This, as its name implies, would be the House of Representatives. One delegate, George Mason, described the House as the "grand depository of the democratic principle of the Govt. . . . It ought to know and sympathise with every part of the community" (Farrand, 1937:I, 48). To ensure the democratic character of the House, the framers fashioned two key provisions: election directly by the people and short terms of office. Election by the people would make it likely that newly elected representatives would share the

basic values and political dispositions of their constituents. Short terms of office (together with no restrictions on reeligibility) would encourage incumbents to act in ways broadly consistent with the desires of those they represented.

Although the framers were firmly committed to a democratic assembly in the legislative branch, they also feared that it would be subject to some of the defects that had characterized many of the state legislatures during the revolutionary period. In particular, they were concerned that (1) a relatively large, popularly elected assembly would be a tumultuous and disorderly body easily manipulated by "factious leaders"; (2) because the members of the House would serve only a few months each year (after which they would return to their primary occupations as farmers, merchants, etc.), they would not acquire sufficient knowledge about national issues; (3) a rapid turnover of membership every two years would translate into frequent changes in the laws; and (4) the members of the House would too often judge legislative proposals on the basis of their immediate popularity rather than their long-term impact on the nation.

For these reasons the framers created a Senate which was considerably smaller than the House (only 26 members until new states were added), and whose members served six years instead of two, were not elected directly by the people, and had to be at least 30 years old (five years older than the minimum for the House). To ensure a basic continuity of membership, only one-third of the Senate would come up for reelection every two years. The framers hoped that this new institution would be less subject to passion and disorder than the House, more knowledgeable about national affairs, more stable and consistent in formulating national policy, and more capable of resisting short-term popular pressures for unwise legislation. As Madison explained at the Convention, the Senate would function "with more coolness, with more system, and with more wisdom, than the popular branch" (Farrand, 1937:I, 151).

It is important not to misinterpret the framers' desire to remove senators somewhat from the pressures of public opinion. After all, senators interested in reelection would have to be sensitive to the political views predominant in the state legislatures, which were very democratic bodies and usually accurate barometers of public opinion within the states. In giving senators some insulation from direct popular control, the framers sought to create an institution that had the capacity *temporarily* to resist unsound popular desires at those "critical moments" when the people might be "stimulated by some irregular passion, or some illicit advantage, or misled by the artful misrepresentations of interested men" (*Federalist* 63). Such temporary resistance would give the people time to reconsider their actions and thus reach a more deliberative opinion. The Senate was not intended, however, to thwart the long-term judgments of the American people.

Constitutional Powers   For the most part the House and Senate were intended to be equal partners in the legislative process. No bill could become a law unless both branches agreed to precisely the same language. There were, however, a few exceptions to this essential equality. The House, for example, was given exclusive authority to originate revenue bills, reflecting the framers' belief that the particularly sensitive power of taxation should be tied to the branch of government closest to the people. The Senate, nonetheless, retained full authority to amend House-passed tax measures as it saw fit.

On the other hand, the framers gave the Senate preeminence over the House in two other areas: the ratification of treaties and the confirmation of appointments to high executive offices and to the federal judiciary. The conduct of foreign policy in particular seemed to demand the qualities peculiar to the Senate: stability of membership, substantial expertise about national affairs, and a long-range view of the public good. Foreign policy, according to John Jay, was both too sensitive and too risky to be entrusted to a "popular assembly composed of members constantly coming and going in quick succession" (*Federalist* 64).

The House and Senate Today

The House and Senate are now very different institutions from those created nearly 200 years ago. The Senate has increased in size from 26 to 100, the House from 65 to 435. Where once only a handful of aides assisted the functioning of the institutions, there are now many thousands of such persons. The average size of a congressional district

has increased from about 40,000 to more than ten times that amount; and the senators from many states now represent more people than lived in the entire country in 1789. Moreover, since the passage of the Seventeenth Amendment to the Constitution in 1913 all senators have been elected directly by the people, rather than by the state legislature. Some things, of course, have not changed. The term of office within each branch is the same, the Senate is still considerably smaller than the House, the House remains more important on revenue matters, and the Senate continues to play a larger role in foreign policy and appointments.

Membership Turnover   As we saw above, the framers expected—though they did not mandate—a rapid turnover of membership in the House. And since the early Congress met only a few months each year, there was concern that a body of short-term, part-time legislators would not gain sufficient expertise about national issues. For a century the framers' expectation regarding turnover proved accurate. It was not uncommon in the nineteenth century for half the membership of the House to change at each election, and turnover was nearly always at least one-third (Price, 1971:14–27).

Although part of this turnover was the result of incumbents being defeated for reelection, much of it was also due to voluntary decisions not to run again. The simple fact is that service in Congress was not nearly as attractive in the past century as it later became. Washington at the time was a relatively small and unexciting city and could not compete with the social and cultural attractions of Boston, New York, and Philadelphia. Moreover, those who sought to exercise great political power were not necessarily drawn to service in Congress; during a time when the national government played a rather limited role in domestic affairs, the decisions of state legislatures were often viewed as more important. Finally, since service in Congress was only a part-time job (three to four months each year), it took time and attention away from the members' principal occupations and sources of livelihood.

The Rise of the Career Legislator   This frequent turnover began to change around the turn of the century. As the national government began to exercise greater influence in both domestic and foreign policy, more members sought to remain in the House and establish careers there. In the second decade of the twentieth century, institutional changes were made which ensured that members who served a long time (that is, accumulated seniority) would accrue power or influence within the House (discussed below). This, in turn, influenced the voters to reelect incumbents. As a result, by the middle of the twentieth century, the House had been transformed into a body of full-time, professional legislators. Few incumbents voluntarily retired, and the vast majority who sought reelection were successful. Since 1950, the success rate for incumbents seeking reelection has averaged 92 percent. During the same period an average of thirty-two representatives (7 percent of the membership) have voluntarily retired each two-year period, many to seek higher office. It is not uncommon now for many members of the House to spend most of their adult lives serving in Congress. Sam Rayburn, for example, who was Speaker of the House for seventeen years between 1940 and 1961, was first elected to the House in 1912 at the age of 30 and served forty-eight years continuously in that body.

The Modern House of Representatives We can see, then, that the contemporary House of Representatives is not subject to several of the defects anticipated by its architects. Because the members are full-time legislators and tend to serve for long periods, they are able to build up substantial knowledge about national issues. Moreover, the absence of the rapid turnover expected by the framers has led to greater consistency in policy: the contemporary House is not given to dramatic shifts in policy every few years. And as service in the House has become more professional, the rules, procedures, and internal structure of the institution have become more regularized and formalized. Rather than a loose, informal, factious assembly of legislative amateurs, the House has become a highly structured institution where business is conducted by career legislators according to regularized rules and procedures.

Continuing Differences between the House and Senate If these changes mean that the dissimilarity between the House and Senate is not as great as the framers expected, it does not mean that important differences do not now exist. The difference in size alone has important consequences for the structure and functioning of the two institutions. Because the Senate is less than one-fourth the size of the House, it is able to function much more informally. The rules are less rigid and can be more easily dispensed with. For example, procedural decisions like scheduling legislation in the Senate are usually made through informal discussion among the interested parties. Floor debate in the two chambers also reflects the effects of the difference in size. The House is so large that if it is to function efficiently, severe restraints must be placed on a member's opportunity to speak on the floor. In the Senate, on the other hand, any member may insist on debating a bill for a prolonged period (subject only, as we shall see, to a rare vote of "cloture" to end debate).

Another difference between the House and Senate, at least partly the result of the contrast in size, is that the Senate is a more prestigious institution. Consequently, membership in the Senate is generally more highly valued than membership in the House. One simple sign of this difference is that no senator in memory has voluntarily resigned to run for the House, whereas many members of the House regularly resign to run for the Senate.

The Senate and Presidential Ambitions Because the Senate is smaller and more prestigious than the House, a larger fraction of its members are able to develop visibility and reputations in the broader national community. Senators like Lyndon Johnson, John Kennedy, Barry Goldwater, Hubert Humphrey, George McGovern, Howard Baker, Edmund Muskie, Jesse Helms, and Ted Kennedy all established national reputations and national constituencies while serving in the Senate. Often senators consciously promote national visibility in order to foster presidential ambitions.

It is not unusual in the United States for prominent politicians to aspire to the presidency. Senators, in particular, have benefited from two twentieth-century developments: (1) the increased importance of foreign policy, over which the Senate has special responsibilities (ratifying treaties and confirming ambassadorial appointments) and (2) the growing dominance of television as the chief communicator of national news to the American populace. Before these developments, the gover-

---

BOX 9-1

SENATORS WHO CAMPAIGNED FOR PRESIDENT, 1960–1980

Year	Democrat	Republican
1960	Hubert H. Humphrey (Minnesota)	Barry Goldwater (Arizona)
	John F. Kennedy (Massachusetts)	
	Lyndon B. Johnson (Texas)	
	Stuart Symington (Missouri)	
1964		Barry Goldwater (Arizona)
		Margaret Chase Smith (Maine)
1968	Robert Kennedy (New York)	
	Eugene McCarthy (Minnesota)	
1972	Hubert H. Humphrey (Minnesota)	
	Edmund S. Muskie (Maine)	
	Vance Hartke (Indiana)	
	Henry M. Jackson (Washington)	
	Fred R. Harris (Oklahoma)	
	George McGovern (South Dakota)	
1976	Frank S. Church (Idaho)	
	Birch Bayh (Indiana)	
	Lloyd Bentsen (Texas)	
	Henry M. Jackson (Washington)	
1980	Edward M. Kennedy (Massachusetts)	Robert Dole (Kansas)
		Howard H. Baker, Jr. (Tennessee)

Source: Presidential Elections since 1789; Elections, 1980.

---

nor's office, especially in the larger states, was a more likely route to the presidency.

The Senate and the Legislative Process One way senators seek to develop reputations outside the institution itself is by investigating and publicizing national problems and actively promoting new policy initiatives. As a result, the Senate has become an "incubator" for national policy development.

The political scientist Nelson Polsby has described the modern Senate as:

a great forum, an echo chamber, a theater, where dramas—comedies and tragedies, soap operas and horse operas—are staged to enhance the careers of its members and to influence public policy by means of debate and public investigation. . . . It articulates, formulates, shapes, and publicizes demands and can serve as a hothouse for significant policy innovation, especially in opposition to the President (Polsby, 1976:98–99).

The danger is that if senators are mainly interested in fostering higher political ambitions, they may give more attention to their public image than to the substance of the legislation they promote. According to one student of Congress, this may lead to "statutes that are long on goals but short on means to achieve them," laws with "ambitious 'public interest' aims" that cannot be realized (Mayhew, 1974:134–135). Indeed, it is not uncommon for members of the House to regard the Senate as an irresponsible, publicity-seeking body rather than a serious lawmaking institution. As a member of the House Ways and Means Committee once commented on the way the Senate writes tax legislation:

With all due respect to the Senate, they don't know

what the hell they're doing over there. They're so damn irresponsible you can get unanimous consent to an amendment that costs a *billion* dollars! And the Senate is supposed to be a safety check on the House. We really act as the stabilizing influence, the balance (Manley, 1970:251).

In the mind of at least this one member of Congress, the framers' original plan for a bicameral legislature has been turned on its head.

The lesson to draw from this brief comparison is that the House and Senate remain quite different institutions. Each makes a distinct contribution to the legislative and representative functions of Congress. This must be kept in mind as we examine in more detail the members of Congress, the organizational structure of the two branches, the procedures used to pass legislation, and how Congress represents public opinion.

MEMBERS OF CONGRESS: WHO THEY ARE, WHAT THEY WANT, AND WHAT THEY DO

Personal Characteristics

The members of the House and Senate are not a cross section of the American populace. If they were, then half of them would be women, over 10 percent would be black, the average age would be 30, a majority would not have college degrees, a sizable fraction would come from blue-collar occupations, and less than 1 percent would be lawyers. In fact, in the present Congress 96 percent of the members are male, 97 percent are white, the average age is 49, over 90 percent have some college-level education, almost all come from white-collar occupations, and half are lawyers. Later in this chapter we will address the issue of how these disparities affect the representative character of Congress.

In terms of race and sex Congress has become more reflective of the population during the past several decades: since 1947 the number of blacks in Congress has increased from two to twenty-one, and the number of women from eight to twenty-three (see Table 9-1).

Moreover, Congress has become somewhat younger during the past three decades. The average age of members is now four years less than it was in 1949. Members of the House on the average are about four years younger than members of the Senate.

Religion Like the majority of Americans, most members of Congress claim an affiliation with an organized religion. In recent years the breakdown has been: Protestant, 68 percent; Roman Catholic, 24 percent; Jewish, 6 percent; other or unaffiliated, 2 percent. The Protestant sects with the most members in Congress are, in decreasing order, Methodists, Episcopalians, Presbyterians, and Baptists. The figures for both Roman Catholics and Jews have increased significantly during the past several decades, and both are now somewhat higher than the corresponding proportions for the general population. Interestingly, many new Catholic and Jewish members of Congress represent districts or states that are overwhelmingly Protestant (*Congressional Quarterly Weekly Report,* 1979:80). The specific religious affiliation of candidates for Congress does not seem to matter as much as it once did.

Party and Region Perhaps no characteristic of those who serve in Congress is more politically significant than party identification. With the exception of a few independents, nearly all representatives and senators identify with either the Democratic or the Republican party. The majority party in each chamber chooses the leader of the institution, organizes the committee system, and is largely responsible for determining whether a pattern of cooperation or conflict is established with the executive branch. Since Franklin Roosevelt's election as president in 1932 the Democrats have dominated in Congress. From 1932 to 1980 they were the majority party in both branches every year but four: 1947–1948 and 1953–1954. Until the 1980 election, when they lost control of the Senate to the Republicans, the Democrats controlled both branches for a continuous span of twenty-six years (1955–1980).

As we have seen in earlier chapters, however, our national political parties are not cohesive units of like-minded individuals. Voting within Congress is ample testimony of this fact. It is quite common, for example, for conservative southern Democrats and liberal northern Democrats to vote on opposite

TABLE 9-1
BLACKS AND WOMEN IN CONGRESS, 1947–1982

Congress	Senate		House	
	Blacks	Women	Blacks	Women
98th (1983–1984)	0	2	21	21
97th	0	2	16	19
96th	0	1	16	16
95th	1	2	16	18
94th	1	0	15	19
93d	1	0	15	14
92d	1	2	12	13
91st	1	1	9	10
90th	1	1	5	11
89th	0	2	6	10
88th	0	2	5	11
87th	0	2	4	17
86th	0	1	4	16
85th	0	1	4	15
84th	0	1	3	16
83d	0	3	2	12
82d	0	1	2	10
81st	0	1	2	9
80th (1947–1948)	0	1	2	7

Source: *Guide to Congress*, 1976:526–528; *Congressional Almanac*, 1977–1983.

sides of an issue. If the southern Democrats are joined by most Republicans, this constitutes the *conservative coalition* in Congress. Even when the Democrats have been officially in control of the House or Senate, proposals supported by a majority of them have often been defeated by a cross-party coalition. Sometimes this coalition results from direct discussion and negotiation between Republican leaders in the House or Senate and southern Democrats. At other times it is simply the result of policy agreement on the issues that come to the floor. In the past decade the conservative coalition has formed on about one-quarter of the roll-call votes in the House and Senate, and it has won about two-thirds of those votes.

The fact that southern Democrats often vote differently from their northern colleagues suggests that where the members of Congress come from has some relationship to how they behave within the institution. This is especially true when public policies have different impacts on different regions of the country. Water projects, for example, most directly benefit western states; regional development projects usually aid the northeast and midwest; and farm legislation is particularly helpful to those who live in the midwest, the plains, and the south.

The Constitution requires that every ten years the apportionment of seats in the House of Representatives among the states be adjusted to reflect population changes as reported in the national census. Throughout this century this has meant that the northeast and midwest have lost representatives while the south and west have gained. From 1910 to 1980 New England lost one-quarter of its seats in the House; the mid-Atlantic states of Delaware, New Jersey, New York, and Pennsylvania lost 21 percent; and the midwest lost 6 percent. On the other side, the south gained 10 percent more seats, and the west increased its representation by fully 155 percent, from thirty-three to eighty-four members. Not surprisingly, Congress has become increasingly responsive to the needs, desires, and attitudes of those who live in the south and west.

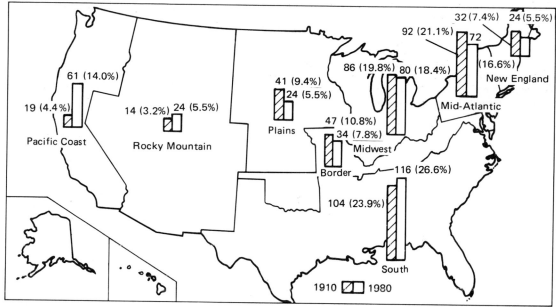

FIGURE 9-1
Apportionment of congressional seats by region, 1910 and 1984. Since the turn of the century, there has been an important shift in the strength of representation in the House of Representatives toward the south and the west. This map shows the number of congressional seats in each region in both years and the percentage of seats as total of the House membership. (*Source:* Ornstein et al., 1982:52; updated by present authors.)

An Influx of New Members   While it is true that incumbents in the twentieth century have been more likely to seek and achieve reelection than their predecessors in the nineteenth century, there has also been a much higher turnover of members in Congress in the 1970s than in the preceding decades. One reason for higher turnover is voluntary retirements in both the House and Senate (summarized in Table 9-2).

TABLE 9-2
VOLUNTARY RETIREMENTS FROM CONGRESS

	Average number of retirements per two-year session of Congress	
	1950–1968	1970–1980
House	27.7	40.3
Senate	4.6	6.7

Source: Bibby et al., 1980:14–15.

In the House voluntary retirements actually increased every year from 1966, when there were twenty-two, to 1978, when they reached forty-nine. Retirements were particularly high in the Senate between 1974 and 1978, when twenty-five senators, fully one-fourth of the whole body, voluntarily decided not to seek reelection.

There is no single explanation for the increase in retirements from Congress. Members of Congress usually retire because of age, health, likelihood of defeat in the next election, or desire to seek higher office (in 1980, for example, eight members of the House "retired" to run for the Senate). But there is also evidence that more members are now voluntarily leaving Congress because the pressures and demands of the job make it a less attractive place to be than it once was, as the discussion by Congressman William Brodhead in Box 9-2 illustrates.

In the Senate, turnover has also increased in recent years because more and more incumbents are

---

BOX 9-2

ONE WHO DIDN'T RUN AGAIN

Despite the long-term tendency for members to make Congress their career, a newer trend of early retirements may eventually alter the pattern. Consider the case of Congressman William Brodhead (Democrat, Michigan) in 1982.

Brodhead was assured of winning easily, yet he decided against running, unexpectedly announcing his retirement from Congress at age 40. Although he was initially enthusiastic about his job, Brodhead soured on life in the House: "It's a question of saving my health, my sense of perspective and my integrity. . . . How can you work 70, 80, 90 hours a week? . . . How can you be under this constant, growing pressure from lobbyists and special-interest groups? I had no friends, no interests, no energy; I had nothing but my job. . . . I think it's a nut house." Brodhead explained that work had not been rewarding because "As the years went by, I began to see that most of the people I was dealing with didn't want me to work for the good of the country. Most of the people were trying to work for some selfish good" (*Newsweek*, 1982).

Despite his opinion of the system, Brodhead still has faith in individual members of Congress, most of whom he considers hardworking. One wonders what sort of people will represent us in Congress if more members follow Brodhead's example.

---

losing their reelection contests. Since 1950, an average of 75 percent of Senate incumbents who sought reelection were successful (significantly less than the figure of 92 percent for House incumbents). However, in the three elections from 1976 to 1980 only 59 percent of incumbents were successful, slightly better than half. In fact, the worst year for Senate incumbents in three decades was 1980. Not only were thirteen of the twenty-seven incumbents who sought reelection defeated (48 percent), but this group included some of the best-known and most senior members of the Senate, including George McGovern of South Dakota (the Democratic presidential nominee of 1972) and Frank Church of Idaho (chairman of the Foreign Relations Committee). (On the House side, by contrast, fewer than 10 percent of the incumbents who sought reelection in 1980 were defeated.)

Not only are there more new members in Congress, but, most observers agree, they are more aggressive, more ambitious, and more interested in having an impact on public policy than their predecessors were. They are not inclined to defer to the judgment of more senior colleagues or to sit back and wait patiently for their influence to grow. This "new breed" is an outgrowth of the political turbulence of the 1960s, when a variety of new issues and movements came to dominate the political landscape (antiwar activism, consumerism, civil rights, environmentalism) and legions of "activists," dissatisfied with conventional political wisdom, sought to move government in new directions. Many of the new members of Congress cut their political teeth during this period. Consequently, they have brought with them into Congress some of the same skepticism about "politics as usual." Some years ago the powerful Speaker of the House Sam Rayburn advised new members that "to get along, you must go along." Few in Congress any longer observe this injunction.

Goals

The members of the House and Senate have different backgrounds, interests, and ambitions. Nonetheless, it is possible to generalize and to say that there are four basic goals that influence their behavior within Congress: reelection, power and prestige within the House or Senate, good public policy, and election to higher office (Fenno, 1973:1).

Reelection Although voluntary retirements are up for the past decade or so, it is still true that the vast majority of representatives and senators work hard to get reelected. Members of the House in particular seem to be running for reelection all the time, as evidenced by the dozens of trips they take home each year and the close attention they pay to

Like most of his predecessors, Speaker of the House "Tip" O'Neill earned his job through decades of service to his fellow members of the House and to his party.
(*Charles Steiner / Sygma*)

constituency service. Reelection, of course, is only an intermediary goal; it is not an end in itself but rather a means to other ends.

Power and Prestige within Congress Both the House and the Senate have been described as "little worlds all their own," in which members' reputations and standing have no necessary relation to how well they are known outside the body. Representatives like "Tip" O'Neill (Speaker), Jim Wright (majority leader), and Robert Michel (minority leader) have all achieved their high positions as a result of the respect of their colleagues generated by years of service to the House and the party. Members who expect to spend many years in the House or Senate often develop an interest in gaining prestige and influence within the body. Among the ways of doing this are treating colleagues courteously, carrying out legislative duties responsibly, speaking on the floor only when one has something important to say, and avoiding any actions that might bring the body into disrepute.

Good Public Policy Some members of Congress, however, are much more interested in influencing public policy than they are in achieving a prominent position within the House or Senate. They have strong opinions about what the national government should be doing, and they work hard to bring about new policies. They do this by introducing legislation, informing the public through committee hearings and floor speeches, and taking their case directly to outside audiences. Not surprisingly, these are the representatives and senators (more of the latter than the former) who become well known outside Congress itself.

Election to Higher Office Building a reputation outside of Washington, D.C., can also serve a fourth distinct goal sought by many in the House and Senate: election to higher office. Members of the House often have their eyes on one of the two Senate seats from their state or on statewide office back home (especially the governorship). Many senators, in turn, focus their ambitions on the presidency. Not all members of the House and Senate aspire to higher office, but those who do are especially inclined to find ways to use their legislative position to become better known in the home state or in the nation at large.

Personal Resources

Newly elected members of the House and Senate quickly discover that Congress provides them with ample resources to pursue their goals, whatever they may be. In addition to a personal salary of just over $60,000, each member is given a suite of offices in one of the buildings across from the Capitol as well as a substantial sum of money to hire personal staff aides. Members of the House are given $280,000 each year to hire up to eighteen assistants; senators get between $500,000 and $1 million dollars each year (depending on the size of the state) to hire as many assistants as they wish. (Some Senate staffs are as large as sixty members.) In addition, each member of Congress is allotted between $50,000 and $140,000 for official expenses for things such as postage, stationery, telephones, rental of space for district or state offices, and thirty or more trips home each year. Not all these resources are applied to the legislator's service in

Washington. Approximately one-third of all personal staff members work in district or state offices engaged in constituency service. Many members of Congress maintain two or even three such offices throughout the district or state in order to maximize their visibility back home.

The Job of Serving as a Member of Congress

No single word better describes the task of serving as a representative or senator than "demanding." Consider the following comments made by an exasperated member of the House to a group of his colleagues one evening while waiting for a vote in the House chamber:

> I came here to make laws, and what do I do? I send baby books to young mothers, listen to every maladjusted kid who wants out of the service, write sweet replies to pompous idiots who think a public servant is a public footstool, and give tours of the Capitol to visitors who are just as worn out as I am. . . .
>
> Take today, I wanted to hear this debate, because I'm not real sure on this bill. Since noon I've had five long-distance calls, and seven different groups of tourists have called me off the House floor to show them the Capitol. Two of them insisted on seeing the President. Today! They couldn't understand why I didn't just pick up the phone and tell him they were coming over. I'm just about fed up! (Tacheron and Udall, 1970:1–2)

Although this member of Congress may have been more upset than most, the problem he describes is one that confronts every one who serves in the House and Senate. They are sent to Washington to make the laws of the land; but they soon find out that they must devote a sizable amount of their time and effort (as well as that of their staff) to answering an enormous volume of mail, resolving constituents' problems with the bureaucracy, personally meeting with tourists or representatives of interest groups, and frequently returning home to mend fences or otherwise maintain good relations with the district or state. Demands of these sorts obviously make it difficult to focus attention on lawmaking.

The problem is compounded by the many conflicting demands that the legislative process itself places on representatives and senators. Although the rules of the two bodies seek to impose order by reserving the mornings for committee and subcommittee meetings and the afternoons for floor debate, exceptions to this rule are quite common. Not only must legislators often choose between a committee meeting and floor debate, but even in the mornings there may be simultaneous meetings of the committees or subcommittees on which they serve. This is particularly a problem in the Senate where in recent years members have served on an average of ten committees or subcommittees. Before a reform of the Senate committee system in 1977 the problem was even worse: an average of seventeen committee or subcommittee assignments per member. In the House a similar problem exists, but it is not as great. On the average representatives serve on about six committees or subcommittees.

It is hardly surprising, then, that most members of Congress spend much of their time hustling back and forth from one meeting to another. Since they have so many conflicting demands, they often arrive late, leave early, or miss meetings altogether. Consequently, committee and subcommittee meetings, as well as floor debates in both chambers, are often poorly attended. It can even be difficult, especially in the Senate, to get together the number of members necessary to do business (called a "quorum"). As former Senator Bill Brock once complained, "Many times I will have two, three, four or even five hearings going on at the same time. This type of scheduling conflict makes it impossible for me to perform my duties and obligations as a U.S. Senator in a legislative sense" (*Hearings,* 1976:4).

Brock's remark suggests that Congress falls somewhat short of the standard of an ideal legislative body. To assess the capacities of Congress as a lawmaking institution, we must examine its structure and functioning more closely.

THE STRUCTURE OF CONGRESS

The Importance of Committees

"It is evident," Woodrow Wilson once wrote about Congress, "that there is one principle which runs through every stage of procedure, and which is never disallowed or abrogated—the principle that the Committees shall rule without let or hindrance" (Wilson, 1969:66). Much about the congressional committee system has changed since Wilson's time. The number of committees has been reduced from over eighty to under forty (a result of the Legislative Reform Act of 1946); committees now deal with issues that in Wilson's time were not matters of national concern (like energy, health care, and housing); and large professional staffs have grown up to assist committees in their work. But one thing has not changed: the central importance of committees to the legislative process.

There are three basic types of committees: joint committees, select committees, and standing committees.

The *joint committees* draw their membership equally from both the House and the Senate. They are created to examine or oversee some matter of concern to Congress as a whole. There is, for example, a joint committee that reviews the operation of the Library of Congress. Perhaps the most important is the Joint Economic Committee, which studies the president's economic proposals and makes recommendations to Congress.

Select committees are created within each body for a specific purpose, often an investigation of some type, and usually go out of existence when their work is complete (although a handful of select committees in both branches have become more or less permanent—see Box 9-3). One of the most famous select committees was the Senate Watergate Committee, chaired by Sam Ervin of North Carolina, which was responsible for uncovering many of the misdeeds of the Nixon administration, thereby leading to formal impeachment proceedings in the House of Representatives.

By far the most important of the three types are the *standing committees,* of which there are now twenty-two in the House and fourteen in the Senate. Each of these has jurisdiction over a specific subject area as set forth in the rules of the House and Senate. These committees are responsible for considering and reporting legislation to the full bodies. In the vast majority of cases, approval by the standing committee is necessary for a bill to pass in the House or Senate. Although standing committees differ in their success rates, on the average the full House and Senate accept committee recommendations without revisions 65 to 70 percent of the time; and 15 to 20 percent of committee recommendations are passed with amendments. As

successful as these committees are, they do sometimes lose: 10 to 20 percent of their recommendations are defeated.

Ideally, any committee should be a microcosm of the full body. If it is, then the results of its deliberations will approximate what the full body would have decided if it had devoted the same time and effort to the issue before the committee. In fact, however, some committees are more liberal or conservative than the full House or Senate, while others draw a disproportionate number of members from certain regions of the country (for example, committees that handle water projects generally have large numbers of westerners). It is not surprising, then, that committees are not neutral or impartial actors in the legislative process. Committees dominated by liberals, for example, are not likely to support conservative policies. Committees dominated by legislators of one region of the country are not likely to support policies harmful to that region.

One way in which most committees do accurately reflect the parent bodies is the division of membership among the two parties. On most committees, seats are distributed between Democrats and Republicans according to the party split in the full bodies. Thus, if 60 percent of the members of the House are Democrats, then approximately 60 percent of the members of most House committees will be Democrats. There are, nonetheless, several important exceptions to this rule. Since the ethics committees in both chambers are supposed to operate in a nonpartisan way, membership is equally divided between the two parties. In addition, House Democrats have reserved for themselves one or two more seats on several important committees (including Budget, Rules, and Ways and Means) than their proportion of the full House membership would justify.

The Growth of Subcommittees

One of the most important developments in recent years in Congress is the increased number and power of subcommittees. Formally, they are agents of the full committees, made necessary because the full committees simply do not have sufficient time to consider carefully all the proposals referred to them. As a result, most bills are first analyzed in a subcommittee. If the subcommittee favors the leg-

BOX 9-3

COMMITTEES IN THE NINETY-SEVENTH CONGRESS, 1981–1982

Standing committees

House	Senate
Agriculture	Agriculture, Nutrition, and Forestry
Appropriations	Appropriations
Armed Services	Armed Services
Banking, Finance, and Urban Affairs	Banking, Finance, and Urban Affairs
Budget	Budget
District of Columbia	Commerce, Science, and Transportation
Education and Labor	Energy and Natural Resources
Energy and Commerce	Environment and Public Works
Foreign Affairs	Finance
Governmental Operations	Foreign Relations
House Administration	Governmental Affairs
Interior and Insular Affairs	Judiciary
Judiciary	Labor and Human Resources
Merchant Marine and Fisheries	Rules and Administration
Post Office and Civil Service	
Public Works and Transportation	
Rules	
Science and Technology	
Small Business	
Standards of Official Conduct	
Veteran Affairs	
Ways and Means	

Select committees (relatively permanent)

House	Senate
Aging	Aging
Intelligence	Ethics
Narcotics Abuse and Control	Indian Affairs
	Intelligence
	Small Business
	Veteran Affairs

Joint committees

Economic
Library
Printing
Taxation

TABLE 9-3
GROWTH OF SUBCOMMITTEES, 1945–1979

	Number of subcommittees of standing committees		
	House	Senate	Total
1945	106	68	174
1955	83	88	171
1967	133	99	232
1975	151	140	291
1979	149	91	240

Source: Patterson, 1978:160; Bibby et al., 1980:58–59.

islation, it is then taken up by the full committee. Although the full committees are not obligated to accept the recommendations of the subcommittees, they usually do.

Since 1946, when Congress reformed its committee system, the number of standing committees in the House and Senate has remained fairly constant, while the number of subcommittees grew by two-thirds through 1975, at which time they totaled 291 (see Table 9-3). (Recently, however, the number of subcommittees has declined somewhat.)

Not only are there many more subcommittees now than there were in 1946, but they are also more powerful, especially in the House. Until new rules were adopted in the 1970s, committee chairs exercised extensive control over subcommittees: they appointed the members and chairs of the subcommittees, determined their jurisdiction, and controlled their staff and monetary resources. Now all these powers rest in the hands of the majority-party members on the full committee. In practice, this dilution of power has meant that the subcommittees have become virtually autonomous units within the committee. Where once the term "committee government" seemed to describe the workings of Congress, now "subcommittee government" might be a more accurate label.

The Declining Importance of Committee Chairs

Two decades ago, most members and observers of Congress would have agreed with the following observation by a member of the House:

There are all sorts of ways to get things done in Con-

gress. The best way is to live long enough to get to be a committee chairman, and resilient enough to be a good one. Chairmen complain to me that they are frustrated too, but this is really beside the point. If things can be done, they can do them; we are very sure of that (Miller, 1962:39).

Now that subcommittees are more independent and powerful, however, full committee chairs have much less influence within their committees. Not only can they do little to influence how the subcommittees deal with the bills under their consideration, but they are also unable to hold out the reward of chairs of subcommittees to induce committee members to support them in their leadership of the full committee.

At the same time that House committee chairs were losing influence within their committees, they were also being brought more under the control of the majority party in the full House. This was the result of the landmark decision by the House Democratic caucus (the group of all Democrats serving in the House) in 1975 to refuse to reappoint as chairs of their committees three of the most senior members of the House, who most House Democrats felt had grown out of touch with mainstream Democratic opinion in the House or had run their committees unfairly. For the half century preceding this decision, appointments to committee chairs had been made in almost every case simply on the basis of *seniority:* the chair was given to the majority-party member who had the longest continuous service on the committee. The seniority principle was not a written rule of the House or Senate, but it was followed with such consistency that it had the force of a formal rule.

Because the seniority principle made the selection of committee chairs virtually automatic, it reduced any incentive the chair might have to follow the policy desires of the party leadership in the House or of the majority of party members in the body. Liberals, in particular, criticized the seniority system for benefiting conservative southern Democrats, who had little trouble getting reelected to Congress in the absence of a strong opposition party in much of the south, over northern liberals, who generally represented competitive districts or states and were less likely to be continuously reelected. (It is no longer the case, however, that seniority particularly benefits southern Democrats, since in the past decade or so two-party competition has decreased in many urban areas of the north—now reliably Democratic—and increased in many parts of the south.) The seniority system was also criticized for its tendency to give the most political power to the older members of Congress, those who were most likely to be out of touch with the changing needs and desires of the American people.

By the early 1970s, opposition to seniority was so widespread that the liberal Democrats in the House were able to change the rules so that chairs would be decided by a secret vote of the Democratic caucus, thereby making it easier to vote out someone who was unpopular. The decision to depose three committee chairs in 1975 was a signal to all present and future chairpersons that they were not beyond control of their party in the House. Although seniority has generally been followed for choosing chairs since 1975, it is no longer the absolute standard it once was. Committee chairpersons who wish to remain in power are less likely now to treat other committee members unfairly or to undercut the legislative desires of most of their party colleagues.

Committee Assignments

Because committees are so important to the legislative process in Congress, members of the House and Senate have a keen interest in serving on those committees that will best promote their legislative or electoral goals (Fenno, 1973). The Public Works and Agriculture committees in the House and Senate, for example, are especially valuable for reelection-oriented legislators, since service on them is likely to result in projects or legislation directly beneficial to constituents (for example, harbor improvements, dams, high price supports for crops). The Rules and Appropriations committees in the House, on the other hand, are sought by representatives interested in power or prestige within Congress. And some committees, like Education and Labor in the House or Foreign Relations in the Senate, are especially sought by those who wish to play an important role influencing public policy.

Because the committees are so diverse and so important to the goals of individual representatives and senators, the committee appointment process is an intense struggle among both new members seeking the choice committees and some veteran legislators seeking to upgrade their committee assignments. The decisions are made at the beginning of each new Congress by each party's "committee on committees" in the House and Senate. The selection process is governed by a set of formal procedures, and heavily influenced by personal lobbying by the interested parties, including the leadership of each body.

Strengths and Weaknesses of the Committee System

The greatest contribution which the committee system makes to Congress is the development of expertise on the issues that come before the national government. Most members of the House serve on one or two standing committees; most senators serve on three. Representatives and senators are not expected to become experts on all the issues that come before Congress—an impossible task—instead, they are expected to focus their time and energies on just a fraction of these. By staying on the same committee for many years, a member may eventually develop an expertise in a specific area that will rival that of anyone else in the national government. This expertise makes Congress a more competent institution for dealing with complex contemporary issues and, by freeing Congress from dependence on experts in the executive branch, enables it to reach truly independent judgments on national policy. Without some kind of committee system the Congress could hardly aspire to be the president's equal in guiding national policy.

There are, however, several weaknesses or disadvantages of the committee system. One results from the problem of representativeness. As noted above, there is no guarantee that the committees of the House and Senate will truly reflect the characteristics or political views of the full membership. Regional or ideological variations are quite common from committee to committee. This may result in policies that are biased in one direction or another, depending on the particular makeup of the committees involved.

A related problem is that most committees and subcommittees tend to become advocates of the programs under their jurisdiction. The terms "subgovernment" and "iron triangle" are used to describe the cozy relationship that is often built up between committees (or subcommittees), the bureaucracy, and the affected interest groups. Each participant has a stake in the preservation or expansion of existing programs, even if these are difficult to justify in terms of the broader national interest. This tends to create a bias in Congress in favor of past policies.

Of course, the full body is always free to reject the recommendations of biased or unrepresentative committees. Yet the simple fact that only the committee members have thoroughly digested an issue usually gives the committee's proposals substantial weight in the decision process. After all, the very existence of the committee system presumes that nonmembers will tend to defer to committee requests.

Another problem of the committee system is that it decentralizes the decision-making process in a way that makes collective action difficult and contributes to a lack of coherence in national policy. When the decision-making authority in an institution is centralized in the hands of a single person or a small number of individuals, the institution can react more quickly and decisively to changing events and can pursue a consistent series of measures designed to achieve its ends. When, however, the decision-making power is distributed among relatively autonomous groups within the institution, conflicting views and jurisdictional jealousies will often make it more difficult to reach collective decisions and to pursue a consistent policy on complex issues.

No issue in recent years has illustrated this problem more dramatically than the energy crisis. Any coherent national energy policy requires decisions in a variety of distinct areas: tax credits for energy conservation, decontrol of prices of oil and natural gas, production of synthetic fuels, allocation of gasoline during shortages, incentives to encourage use of coal, the role of nuclear power, etc. In Congress these issues cut across the jurisdictions of dozens of committees and subcommittees. In the Ninety-Fifth Congress (1977–1978), for example, eighteen different committees exercised some jurisdiction over the energy problem (Patterson, 1978:162).

As a result, each issue tends to be handled as a distinct problem, according to the views of a particular group of representatives or senators. The result has been, at best, a piecemeal approach to the energy problem.

In response, some within Congress have worked to make the structure of the institution more capable of dealing with the complex energy issue. In the Senate, most energy-related matters have been consolidated under the old Interior Committee, renamed the Energy and Natural Resources Committee. A similar effort failed in the House in 1980 largely because many members were reluctant to give up the jurisdiction their committees and subcommittees already had over the energy issues. One innovation which the House has used to improve decision making on the energy issue is a special Ad Hoc Committee on Energy, which was created by Speaker O'Neill in 1977 to examine the recommendations of several standing committees and propose amendments that would make for a more coherent approach to the energy issue.

Although structural alterations of these types can improve Congress's legislative capacity, they cannot eliminate the basic effects of decentralized decision making. Committee jurisdictions may be juggled in response to one particular issue, but they cannot be redrawn to address every subject that cuts across traditional jurisdictions. Ad hoc committees may help; but as long as the regular committee system remains intact, they will have only limited effects. The problem of decentralization cannot be resolved by tinkering with the committee system. Instead we must look elsewhere for centralizing influences. The strongest of these is political party.

Political Parties in Congress

Institutionally, the Democratic and Republican parties operate in Congress through three principal mechanisms: party caucuses, party committees, and party leadership systems.

Party Caucuses A party caucus (also called a "conference") is the collection of all the members of one party in one of the branches. Thus, there are four caucuses altogether. For most of this century party caucuses have served mainly to select party leaders and to confirm committee appointments. Earlier in our history the caucuses were more powerful, meeting frequently to debate policy issues and often instructing party members how to vote. In the 1970s Democrats in the House and Republicans in the Senate tried to recapture the potential of the caucus as a forum to debate and coordinate policy positions.

Party Committees Because the party caucuses are so large and unwieldy (the House Democratic caucus had 243 members in 1981–1982, while the Republican conference had 192), certain tasks are assigned to smaller party committees. Serving only as agents of the party, these committees perform three principal tasks: consideration of policy issues, nomination of committee members and committee leaders, and assistance for congressional campaigns of party members. In most cases, the party committees do not act independently, but make recommendations to the full caucus to accept or reject.

Party Leadership More important than either the caucuses or the party committees is the party leadership system. This is a hierarchical structure designed to connect each party member to a few officials elected to serve the broad interests and views of the party. It is essentially a communications device that sends information both up and down the party ladder. It gives the leaders the means for assessing the views of party members on issues before the House or Senate, and it provides a channel for the leaders to communicate their positions down to the full membership.

There are four distinct leadership systems, one for each party in each branch. (See Box 9-4.) In the House the leader of the majority party is elected the *Speaker of the House.* Under the Speaker are the *majority leader,* who serves as a kind of floor leader for the majority party; and the *majority whip,* who is in charge of communications with the members of the majority party. Under the majority whip are a *deputy whip* and a group of *assistant whips* who represent the different regions of the country. The minority party in the House has essentially the same structure with the exception that there is no equivalent to the Speaker: the highest-ranking minority member is simply the *minority leader.*

In the Senate, the highest-ranking officer is, according to the Constitution, the vice president, who serves as president of the Senate. This gives the vice president two powers: (1) to preside over the Senate and (2) to break tie votes. As a rule, however, the vice president does not preside, reserving appearances for possible tie-breaking votes on important issues. When the vice president is absent, these powers devolve to the constitutionally designated *president pro tempore* of the Senate. In practice, this is merely an honorific post which is given to the most senior member of the majority party in the Senate. The actual leaders of the majority party in the Senate are the majority leader and majority whip. The minority party has equivalent positions. As in the House, the principal task of the majority and minority leaders is to oversee floor debate for their parties, and the job of the whips is to communicate with the other party members.

The greatest contribution that party leadership can make in Congress is to offset some of the defects of the decentralized decision making of the committee system. To the extent that party leaders can guide or influence the actions of individual members, they can add a degree of unity or coherence to the legislative process that might otherwise be lacking. Their success depends both on the resources they have available and on the political skill they possess to get others to follow their lead. Their capacity for influence is limited, however, because they exercise almost no control over the electoral fate of their party colleagues. This is quite different from a parliamentary system in which party leaders are often able to deny party endorsement to those who fail to support party positions in the parliament. Since party labels are quite important in parliamentary elections, denial of official party endorsement can lead directly to defeat at the polls. In the American system, on the other hand, congressional party leaders exercise no such influence over the reelection prospects of the members of Congress.

This does not mean that congressional leaders are powerless. Some, like Speaker of the House Sam Rayburn and Senate Majority Leader Lyndon Johnson, had a great impact on their institutions. Part of what makes a leader effective is the skillful exercise of formal authority: the Speaker's power to preside over floor debate; the Senate majority leader's right to be recognized first in proceedings on the floor; and the power to make appointments to special committees or commissions and to select members of Congress to serve on of-

---

BOX 9-4

CONGRESSIONAL LEADERSHIP IN THE NINETY-SEVENTH CONGRESS, 1981–1982

House

Democrats	Republicans
Speaker	
Thomas P. O'Neill, Jr. (Massachusetts)	
Majority leader	Minority leader
Jim Wright (Texas)	Robert H. Michel (Illinois)
Majority whip	Minority whip
Thomas S. Foley (Washington)	Trent Lott (Mississippi)

Senate

Democrats	Republicans
Minority leader	President pro tempore
Robert C. Byrd (West Virginia)	Strom Thurmond (South Carolina)
Minority whip	Minority leader
Alan Cranston (California)	Howard H. Baker (Tennessee)
	Majority whip
	Ted Stevens (Alaska)

---

ficial delegations visiting foreign countries. More important, however, is whether the leaders take full advantage of their strategic positions in the legislative process. Lyndon Johnson, in particular, "made himself the leader by putting himself at the center of an enormous number of bargains in the Senate. . . . He was in a position to know more about the relative intensities of senators' positions on a variety of issues; in this way, he could create coalitions of senators who would never have thought to get together on their own . . ." (Polsby, 1976:97).

In recent years both Speaker of the House "Tip" O'Neill and Senate Majority Leader Howard Baker have received high marks for effectively guiding their party colleagues and fashioning party positions on salient national issues.

Other Groups within Congress

In addition to the party organizations themselves there are several other groups in Congress that make an important contribution to the legislative process.

State and Regional Delegations In the House, many state delegations seek to increase their influence by meeting together frequently to discuss local or national issues. Democrats and Republicans in the delegation will often join forces to take a united stand on a pending issue that has a direct impact on the state. Some delegations work quite hard to promote the interests of their state.

In recent years this concept has been extended to encompass an entire region of the country. Over 200 members of the House from 16 northeastern and midwestern states have joined together to form the Northeast-Midwest Economic Advancement Coalition to assert the economic interests of the frost belt against the sun belt in competition for federal funds.

Ideological Groups In the late 1950s, liberal Democrats in the House decided that they needed to organize themselves more effectively to combat the influence of the "conservative coalition." Thus they created the Democratic Study Group (DSG) as a loose coalition of northern and western Democrats to pool informational resources, digest issues coming to the floor, and maximize attendance of liberals on key votes. In the early 1970s, southern Democrats responded with the Democratic Research Organization, now called the Democratic Forum, to perform similar services for those with more conservative leanings. Conservative Republicans also have an organization, labeled the Republican Study Committee. There is also a variety of other issue-oriented groups that promote causes like international peace and environmental protection.

Economic Groups Few forces in Congress are stronger than the desire of legislators to promote the economic well-being of their constituents. Representatives from the Detroit area have led congressional efforts to soften the economic impact of pollution restrictions on the automobile industry. Those from Texas and Louisiana have fought to lift price controls on natural gas and crude oil. Others from districts with military bases have used their influence to try to prevent closings of those bases. Broader ideological dispositions rarely outweigh the desire to protect jobs or promote economic growth within the districts. Liberals and conservatives alike work just as hard to keep a military base open regardless of their positions on the overall defense budget.

When specific economic interests cut across many congressional districts or states, the legislators from those areas often work together to share information, develop legislative strategy, and generally coordinate their efforts. Until recently, this kind of coordination was usually handled through the relevant lobbying organizations. In recent years, however, representatives and senators have established numerous semiofficial coalitions, or caucuses, among themselves to promote common economic interests. Tourism, steel production, textiles, gasohol, and solar energy all have their own caucuses. There is even a mushroom caucus with over sixty members. Because these groups cut across the traditional committee, subcommittee, and party organizations in Congress, they can con-

tribute to the fragmentation of decision making. Nonetheless, the proponents of these congressional caucuses maintain that they make for more effective representation of important economic interests.

Ethnic Groups One of the most highly publicized groups within Congress is the Congressional Black Caucus. It includes the twenty-one black members of the House and the nonvoting delegate from the District of Columbia. It takes stands on a variety of issues of importance to blacks, and its leaders have come to be recognized as major national voices for the black community. Less prominent and influential is the Congressional Hispanic Caucus, which includes the few members of Congress with Spanish surnames.

Conflicting Forces

The structure of Congress can be viewed as a contest between centralizing and decentralizing forces within the institution. The committee and subcommittee system determines that important decisions will be made by hundreds of small groups of legislators acting more or less independently of one another. This is good for promoting expertise and competence within Congress, but bad for fostering a coherent approach to complex public issues. On the other hand, the party system and some of the other groups in Congress seek to fashion common approaches to public policy issues among large numbers of like-minded legislators.

In an almost paradoxical way, the changes in Congress of the past decade or so have simultaneously centralized and decentralized power within the institution. In the House in particular, the majority party has become more influential by making committee chairs more responsible to majority opinion. In both branches, however, power has also been decentralized by the increase in the number and power of subcommittees in Congress. Since there are so many subcommittees, any changes that make them more influential have the effect of distributing power widely throughout Congress. Because the Senate has more subcommittees than members of the majority party, nearly all Republicans in the Senate hold at least one subcommittee chair, and some hold two. In the House, about half of the Democrats are subcommittee chairs.

It is obvious, however, that these two recent trends are themselves in conflict. Rule by a strong and cohesive majority party is possible only when individual members defer to the views of the majority of the party or its leaders, even if they disagree. A more democratized distribution of power, on the other hand, encourages individual members to act according to their own beliefs. It seems reasonable to conclude that in the decades ahead democratization will prove the more powerful force.

One reason is that the members of Congress, especially those with less seniority, will be reluctant to give up their newfound influence. Another, more fundamental, reason is that there still remain very few incentives for an individual member of Congress to follow the views of the party leaders or the party majority when he or she disagrees with them. Why should conservative Democrats or liberal Republicans defer to majority sentiment within their party on matters they feel strongly about? Lacking the power to deny party members their seats in Congress, the party majority or party leadership is left with few means to discipline dissidents. And if the party should, for example, start denying choice committee assignments to those who deviate from majority opinion, it might force the dissidents into the hands of the opposing party.

In January of 1983, when the new Ninety-Eighth Congress was being organized, the Democrats actually did discipline one of their colleagues, Phil Gramm of Texas, by removing him from the House Budget Committee. Although several dozen other conservative southern Democrats had split with the majority of their party to endorse President Reagan's economic policies in the Ninety-Seventh Congress (1981–1982), Gramm was singled out because he had participated directly with administration forces in moving Reagan's bills through Congress. In reaction to the disciplinary action Gramm switched allegiance to the Republican party.

What happened to Gramm is quite rare. It is rare because no party wants to reduce its share of congressional seats (and therefore committee seats) by forcing its dissidents into the hands of the opposition, especially if such a coalition would constitute a majority of the House or Senate.

How power is distributed within Congress also affects the role of Congress within the broader political system. If Congress is ruled by a strong and cohesive party, as it was in the late nineteenth and early twentieth centuries, then it can assert itself as a forceful independent actor in American national government, an equal partner with the president. But if power is widely distributed within Congress, if congressional leaders exercise little real control over their colleagues, then it becomes quite difficult for Congress to function as a unified body and in a consistent fashion. While the individual members of Congress benefit from a wide distribution of power, the institution as a whole is more powerful if power is more centralized.

However, before we can reach any settled conclusions about the structure of Congress, we must examine the procedures that regulate how the various structural units influence the passage of legislation.

HOW (AND WHY) A BILL BECOMES A LAW

As Table 9-4 shows, Congress passes only a tiny fraction of the bills and resolutions which are introduced during each two-year session. In the Ninety-Sixth Congress, for example, only about 3 percent of the measures introduced survived the legislative process. Before we examine the details of lawmaking in Congress, it will be useful first to consider some of the broader forces that contribute to legislative success or failure. We can gain insight into this matter by looking at the passage of one particular bill which seemed to have everything against it when it was first introduced, but which eventually overcame the many obstacles of the legislative process in the House and Senate.

The Waterway User Charge Act

For nearly two centuries the federal government has established and maintained an inland waterway system to facilitate the transportation of agricultural products, raw materials, and manufactured goods within the United States. Through government support, rivers have been dredged and widened, and dams and locks have been constructed. All this has been done with general revenues and therefore at no direct cost to the barge lines, which benefit directly from the federal effort. In 1977, Pete Domenici, a first-term Republican

TABLE 9-4
CONGRESSIONAL WORK LOAD 1947–1980

Congress		Measures introduced	Reported from committee	Public laws enacted
80th	1947–1948	12,090	4,272	906
81st	1949–1950	16,670	5,880	921
82d	1951–1952	14,164	4,601	594
83d	1953–1954	16,385	3,411	781
84th	1955–1956	19,039	5,753	1,028
85th	1957–1958	20,706	5,252	936
86th	1959–1960	20,164	4,233	800
87th	1961–1962	20,316	4,853	885
88th	1963–1964	19,236	3,555	666
89th	1965–1966	26,566	4,200	810
90th	1967–1968	29,133	3,657	640
91st	1969–1970	29,041	3,250	695
92d	1971–1972	25,354	2,703	607
93d	1973–1974	26,222	2,787	649
94th	1975–1976	24,283	2,870	588
95th	1977–1978	22,313	2,968	634
96th	1979–1980	14,595	2,494	535

Source: "Final Daily Digest" of the *Congressional Record* for the various years. Includes all public bills and resolutions introduced in each Congress.

senator from New Mexico, sought to change all this by introducing legislation to require the barge lines to contribute to the cost of maintaining the inland waterway system, just as trucking companies, for example, must pay taxes to maintain the interstate highway system (Reid, 1980).

For Domenici this was an idea whose time had come, although he was not confident of success. "It's so frustrating," he complained. "This is an important issue—we're talking big money here. And anybody with common sense can see that this user charge is way overdue. But nobody around here takes it seriously" (Reid, 1980:12). Prospects of success were slim for several reasons: (1) similar legislation had been introduced many times in the past to no avail, (2) the waterway user charge involved a fundamental redirection in long-standing national policy, (3) the new legislation was adamantly opposed by powerful interests, and (4) it lacked the sponsorship of influential members of Congress. Yet a year and a half after its introduction a compromise version of the original bill passed the House and Senate and was signed into law by President Carter. The result was less than

Senator Domenici had wanted, but much more than anyone had seriously expected the year before.

Why, then, did Congress pass a waterway user charge, and what does this case tell us about the forces that affect the legislative process more generally? T. R. Reid, a reporter for the *Washington Post* who studied the progress of the bill closely for two years, concluded that four factors played a key role: policy, personality, parliamentary procedure, and politics (Reid, 1980:129–132).

Policy The structure and procedures of Congress are designed to help representatives and senators determine which public policy initiatives will be good for the nation and which will not. Serious efforts are made to accumulate and assess relevant information, to consider opposing arguments, and to reach intelligent judgments about the merits of legislative proposals. Congress is, at least in part, a deliberative institution. This does not mean, however, that every good idea is guaranteed success, or that every bad one will fail. But it does mean, according to Reid, that the "force of a good idea is a

Senator Pete Domenici's artful campaign for his waterway bill employed such traditional congressional lawmaking techniques as politicking, lobbying, logrolling, and parliamentary maneuvering. *(Rich Lipski / UPI)*

powerful influence. From the beginning of his up-hill fight to pass the waterway bill, Pete Domenici benefited from the general perception . . . that it was a good idea to end the barge lines' free ride" (Reid, 1980:129).

Personality Like the citizens they represent, the members of Congress are not purely rational beings. Each is influenced by a variety of personal characteristics that have a lot to do with how they interact in the legislative process. Reid notes in particular Domenici's "tenacious determination" to follow the issue through and President Jimmy Carter's "stubborn insistence" on threatening to veto an unacceptably weak bill. Personal friendships also proved important. At least one senator voted with Domenici on a crucial vote largely be-

cause of his close personal relationship with him. Moreover, Domenici's friendship with Secretary of Transportation Brock Adams "was one of the factors that prompted the Democratic Administration to undertake an intense effort to pass a Republican's bill" (Reid, 1980:131).

Parliamentary Procedure The procedures of Congress are not neutral to the passage of legislative proposals. They throw up numerous obstacles in the path of new policy initiatives. Moreover, relatively simple decisions like referring bills to committee can be absolutely decisive to the success of a bill. Domenici knew, for example, that if his bill were sent to the Finance Committee, which has jurisdiction over all tax measures, it would be doomed, since the committee's chairman, Russell Long, was one of the Senate's chief opponents of the waterway user charge. Through some subtle maneuvering and lobbying Domenici was able to get the bill referred jointly to two other committees, on one of which he served. Later in the legislative process, Long and Domenici became allies in an effort to get a compromise bill through Congress. With time running out at the end of the session, Long was able to use his finely honed parliamentary skills to circumvent several procedural obstacles that could easily have led to defeat at the last minute.

Politics Finally, the waterway user bill was subject to a complex interplay of political forces, not unlike those that affect the passage of any important bill: particularly, the political motives and ambitions of the major actors, pressures from powerful interest groups, and the bargaining and compromising necessary to build winning coalitions. Domenici, for example, worked so hard for the waterway user bill not only because he thought it was good public policy, as he certainly did, but also because it would be a legislative achievement he could point to in his reelection contest: "I knew I was going to run again, . . . and it would help if I could go back and say to the Alburquerque paper, or the Sante Fe paper, 'I had enough clout to get a tough bill passed'" (Reid, 1980:12). He also hoped that he could impress his fellow senators that he was a serious, hardworking legislator. Other senators, of course, were also influenced by political

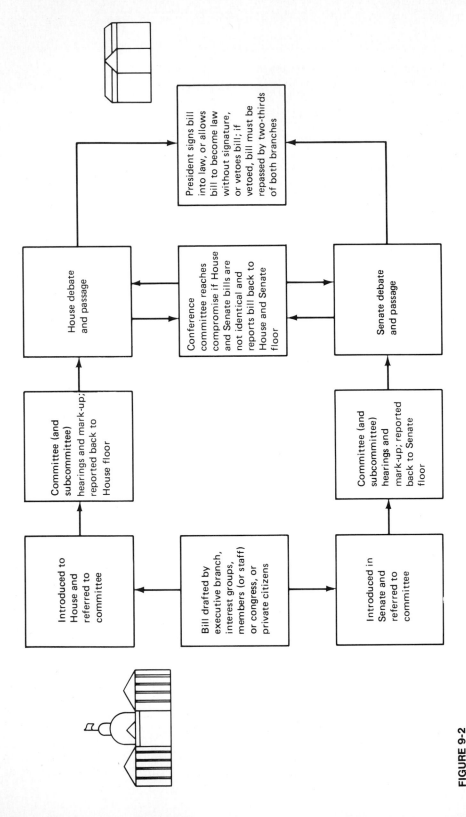

FIGURE 9-2
How a bill becomes a law.

considerations. Senator Jennings Randolph (Democrat, West Virginia) apparently promised his vote for the administration's position in exchange for President Carter's promise that he would campaign personally for Randolph's reelection in 1978—a time when Carter's popularity was still fairly high (Reid, 1980:61–62). And the first-term Democrat Daniel Patrick Moynihan, an early supporter of the user charge principle, apparently changed sides to earn the favor of Senator Long, on whose Finance Committee Moynihan served.

In Chapter 8 we examined the tactics and influence of interest groups in the legislative process. In this case, passage of Domenici's bill was made easier by the fact that the powerful groups opposed to the bill, the barge lines, were effectively balanced off by powerful groups in favor of the bill, the railroads who competed with the barges for the same freight. A few small "public interest groups" entered the struggle on the side of the Domenici bill. Some of these were secretly supported by funds from the railroads. After the battle was won, railroad companies across the nation contributed $30,000 to Domenici's 1978 reelection campaign. This illustrates the way in which interest groups try to help those who have previously shown by their actions in Congress that they are supportive of positions promoted by the groups. There is no evidence in this case that the *anticipation* of a campaign contribution directly affected Domenici's actions in the Senate.

Bargaining and compromise are rarely absent in any political institution which is entrusted with making important decisions. Both Domenici, who wanted a relatively high user charge, and Long, who wanted none, came to realize that they couldn't get exactly what they wanted. Compromise proved the only effective way of resolving the impasse in the Senate. And, as usually happens with a compromise, neither side was really happy with the outcome. Other forms of bargaining also played a role in the process. In several cases the votes of senators were influenced by "logrolling," or favor trading, with other senators. According to Reid, three conservative Republicans who were personally inclined to vote with Domenici—Paul Laxalt of Nevada and Jake Garn and Orrin Hatch of Utah—all joined the opposition when they discovered that the way they voted on the user charge would have repercussions in another area.

What had happened . . . was that Hatch had been talking to [John] Stennis, the Mississippian who chaired the Senate subcommittee on Public Works Appropriations, about the prospects for funding for the Central Utah Project, a giant irrigation plan that was of utmost importance to farmers in Utah and Nevada. Stennis laid things right on the line: if Hatch, Garn, or Laxalt were to vote for this waterway toll idea, he said, they could kiss their irrigation project goodbye for the 95th Congress (Reid, 1980:61).

As the history of the Waterway User Charge Act so well illustrates, Congress is a dynamic and complex collection of 535 distinct individuals in which ambition, interest, personal relationships, bargaining, and the exercise of power all make a contribution to the final product. With this in mind, we can turn to the actual procedures according to which a bill becomes a law.

Introduction of Bills

Only the members of each branch have the authority to formally introduce legislative proposals into Congress. Even presidents, with all their stature and power, cannot personally introduce bills. When presidents present their legislative programs to Congress, they seek influential members of the House and Senate to sponsor their bills. Thus, many bills introduced in Congress are written not by the legislators who sponsor them but by executive branch officials, interest groups, or even private citizens.

Although we commonly assume that representatives and senators introduce bills because they want them to become law, this is not always the case. Many bills are introduced even though they have no chance for passage. Sometimes bills are introduced for their symbolic significance, to mollify powerful interest groups, or to air novel proposals in the hope of generating new ideas and approaches to old problems. This partly explains why so many bills are introduced—an average of over 20,000 bills during each two-year legislative session over the past two decades (refer back to Table 9-4). Actually these are not all different proposals. Some differ only by the number assigned to them when several legislators introduce identical measures. This allows many members to claim credit for proposing a popular measure.

In the House, a bill is introduced by placing it in the "hopper," a box at the front of the chamber. In the Senate, a bill is given to one of the clerks and is usually accompanied by a statement on the floor by the sponsoring senator. In each chamber, bills are numbered consecutively, following the initials "H.R." for the House and "S." for the Senate. Usually the number has no particular significance. The exception is the designation "H.R. 1" or "S. 1," which is given by the leadership to a high priority item.

Committee Stage

As we have seen, the most important stage in the movement of a bill through Congress is its consideration by the standing committee to which it is referred. Most bills, once they reach the committee, will then be sent to the subcommittee of the full committee with jurisdiction over its subject matter. Subcommittee consideration takes two forms: hearings and mark-up.

Hearings The important decision to be made within the subcommittee is whether to hold hearings on a bill at all. Time limitations allow only a fraction of bills to reach the hearing stage; consequently, most bills die in subcommittee. The decision to hold hearings on a bill is no guarantee of eventual subcommittee approval, but it is a necessary first step.

The hearings are designed to elicit the relevant information on the matter at hand and the major arguments on both sides of the issue. Most hearings are open to the media and the public. The format is quite simple. Witnessess for and against the bill appear before the subcommittee, present brief oral statements, submit longer formal statements for the record, and respond to questions from subcommittee members. On important bills, witnesses will include the sponsors of the legislation from the House and Senate; high-ranking members of the administration (often department heads or their deputies); representatives of interest groups (including leaders of public interest groups); and experts from academia, think tanks, or private foundations.

The formal purpose of the hearing process is to foster the subcommittee's deliberation on the matter before it. As former Senator Edmund Muskie described it: "Committee hearings are supposed to make a contribution. . . . You try to shape the hearings so that there is dialogue, debate. Questions are raised so the committee understands the underlying complexities" (Asbell, 1978:42). Committee hearings, however, have other purposes as well, such as generating public support for bills, embarrassing the administration, and promoting the visibility of the members of the House or Senate.

Mark-Up When the hearings are completed, the subcommittee will meet to determine whether there is sufficient support to "mark up" the bill. The mark-up is a line-by-line reading and often redrafting of the original proposal. Although occasionally the subcommittee may bring in an outside expert to help, especially one from the executive branch, most of the work at this stage is done by the members themselves and the subcommittee staff. After the mark-up is completed, there is a vote on the final proposal. If a majority support the bill, then it is referred back to the full committee with a recommendation that the committee report the bill to the full House or Senate.

Full Committee Consideration At this point the committee has three options: (1) it may do as the subcommittee requested, (2) it may refuse to report any bill at all, or (3) it may amend the subcommittee proposal and then report it to the full body. Although the full committee is in no way bound to accept the subcommittee's recommendation, it is definitely influenced by it, since the subcommittee members can reasonably argue that they know more about the issues involved than others on the committee. If the committee decides in favor of the original or an amended bill, a written report is prepared (usually by the staff) explaining and defending the main features of the bill. Committee members who oppose the bill have the option of preparing a dissenting opinion which is included with the report. The presence of a written dissent is often a good measure of the intensity of feeling of those against the bill.

Scheduling Floor Debate

The Senate Once a bill has been reported back favorably to the full body, it must be scheduled for floor debate. This is one area where the procedures for the House and Senate are quite different. In the Senate, the decision is made through informal consultation among the leaders of both parties, the sponsors of the bill, and other interested senators. When agreement has been reached as to when the debate should take place, how long it should last, and who should control the apportionment of time during debate, then a *unanimous-consent agreement* is presented to the full Senate. It is usually accepted, since the arrangements have been cleared ahead of time with all the interested parties. If agreement on the rules for debate cannot be reached, this is usually a sign that opponents of the measure are planning to use obstructionist tactics, including the filibuster (discussed below), to prevent passage of the bill.

The House: Importance of the Rules Committee   In the House, the procedure for scheduling debate is much more formalized. With few exceptions, bills can get to the floor only through the Rules Committee. Rules is one of the standing committees of the House and has a relatively small membership of sixteen. Its main job is to determine the rules according to which bills previously reported by other committees will be debated on the floor of the House. Its rules serve the same function as the unanimous-consent agreement in the Senate, particularly setting the time for debate and determining which members shall control the apportionment of time. A rule will also stipulate whether and what kinds of amendments may be offered on the floor. On some complex matters, like tax legislation, amendments may be prohibited if they are not supported by the reporting committee (a so-called "closed rule"). On other matters only certain kinds of amendments may be allowed (a "modified closed rule"). Often, however, there are no restrictions at all on amendments (an "open rule"). The argument for debating bills under a closed or modified closed rule is that the complexity and political sensitivity of some issues make it impossible for the full body to do a responsible job of writing legislation on the floor.

The recommendation of the Rules Committee is not absolute. Formally, it is merely a proposal that must be passed upon by the full House. In fact, it is rarely overturned. This is evidence that the Rules Committee now does a fairly good job of reflecting the basic sentiment of the larger body it serves.

Just over two decades ago, however, the Rules Committee was more assertive in acting upon its independent judgment of the merits of a bill even when this appeared to run counter to prevailing attitudes in the House. In the late 1950s, a coalition of Republicans and conservative Democrats on the committee, including its chairman Howard W. Smith (Democrat, Virginia), was able to prevent the committee from reporting to the House a variety of bills desired by liberal Democrats. In reaction, the House voted in 1961 to expand the size of the committee from twelve to fifteen. This allowed the appointment of two more liberal Democrats (and one Republican) to create an eight-to-seven liberal majority on the committee. Since then, the committee has increasingly served as an ally of the majority leadership in the House.

Floor Debate

One of the frequent disappointments of tourists to the nation's capital is to sit in the gallery of the House or Senate chamber and observe a handful of representatives or senators reading speeches in a nearly empty room. In the Senate it is not uncommon for important bills to be "debated" with as few as three or four senators present. "We get in here working hot and heavy in debate," Senator Ernest Hollings (Democrat, South Carolina) complained, "but there is no one here to listen" (Oleszek, 1978:156). In the larger House, attendance is usually higher, but most of those present often seem more interested in private conversations, reading the paper, or even napping than in the discussion on the floor.

There are two basic reasons for the low level of interest displayed by members of Congress in floor debate. One is that the demands on their time are so great that they find it difficult to justify spending several hours on the floor to hear a bill discussed which they may know little about or have little interest in. The other is that by the time a bill reaches the floor, most of the serious deliberation on the measure has already been completed. Dozens of committee members and staff members may have spent months accumulating information, listening to arguments, fashioning compromises, and working out the details of a complex measure before it goes to the floor to be debated for a few short hours. In most cases, it is simply more efficient for a representative or senator to take guidance from the committee as a whole or some member of it whose views and judgment he or she respects than to try to learn enough in the debate to make an informed decision.

This is not to say that debate never affects votes. "Some votes are always changed by debate," House Majority Leader Jim Wright has argued (Oleszek, 1978:111). Debate may be especially important on controversial and closely divided issues when attendance is likely to be higher and some of the listeners may be undecided until the last moment.

Procedurally, formal debate begins in both chambers with a statement by the bill's leading proponents (usually subcommittee or committee chairs and other senior committee members) explaining and justifying their proposal. In the course of making their case for the bill, the proponents may be interrupted with questions from the floor. Some of these will come from the opposition, probing for weaknesses in the argument. Other questions, arranged in advance, will lead to a "colloquy" between two supporters of the bill as they seek to clarify some ambiguous point or to get a particular interpretation of the bill "in the record" (for possible later use by the courts or administrative agencies). The opponents of the bill are given equal time to deliver their speeches against the measure, subject again to interruption from the floor. Although any member of the House or Senate may seek recognition to speak on the bill before the chamber, in practice debate is dominated by the members of the reporting committee.

The Filibuster   In the Senate, opponents of a bill have available to them a parliamentary strategy that cannot be used in the House: they may refuse to agree to any limits on debate and engage in extensive speechmaking, or a *filibuster,* to prevent a bill from coming to a vote. Until 1917 there was no rule at all in the Senate limiting the amount of time that an individual senator could speak on the floor. This reflected the traditional respect which the Senate accorded the views of each member and therefore its reluctance to force a senator to stop speaking. Until the twentieth century, this privilege was not often used as a parliamentary device to prevent the full body from voting on a bill.

In 1917, however, a group of isolationist senators (labeled by President Wilson a "small group of willful men") filibustered to prevent the passage of legislation authorizing the arming of American merchant ships. In response to this action, the Senate enacted its first *cloture* rule, providing those present and voting with the authority to cut off debate and force a vote if two-thirds of them so desired. With only minor changes this rule remained in effect until 1975, when the Senate reduced the number needed for cloture to a constitutional three-fifths, meaning three-fifths of the membership of the Senate regardless of the number who actually show up to vote. At its current size, this means that sixty senators must vote to cut off debate.

On several occasions since 1975, senators have sought to get around the cloture rule by introducing hundreds of amendments to a bill after cloture was voted. Since it takes the Senate a minimum of about a half hour to read and vote on a single amendment, this strategy can effectively paralyze the Senate. In early 1979 the Senate adopted a new rule to prevent postcloture filibusters by stipulating that after cloture is voted, a final vote must be taken after no more than 100 more hours of debate. All time spent on parliamentary procedures is counted against this limit.

Although the Senate has placed restrictions on filibusters, it has not demonstrated a desire to allow a simple majority to cut off debate and bring an issue to a vote. The tradition remains strong that majority rule must be tempered by the minority's right to have its say. In reality, many so-called filibusters begin as serious efforts by the opposition to explore the relevant issues at length, hoping that, given enough time, other senators will change their minds. Some senators might be influenced by the arguments themselves; others by increasing opposition in the broader political community. The filibuster must be judged not merely as a parliamentary device but also for the opportunity it gives for extended deliberation on complex contemporary issues.

Voting   Each chamber has its own rules governing the voting procedures on amendments and final passage. In the House, there are actually five different ways of voting. The *voice vote* requires members to call out "aye" or "nay" at the appropriate time. In the *division vote,* the legislators stand to demonstrate approval or disapproval. During a *teller vote,* the members walk down the aisle in one of two lines and are counted as voting aye or nay. The *recorded teller vote,* instituted in 1970, is similar to the teller vote with the addition that members turn in cards with their names so that individual votes can be recorded and subsequently listed in the *Congressional Record.* The *roll-call vote* has been carried out electronically since 1973: members insert a special personalized electronic card into one of several devices on the floor and press a button for aye, nay, or present. In the electronic roll call individual votes as well as a running total are displayed on the wall at the front of the chamber. This makes it particularly easy for those voting near the end of the fifteen-minute period set aside for the roll call to seek voting "cues" from committee members or other representatives to whom they look for guidance.

Final passage on important bills is nearly always determined by a roll-call vote. Important amendments are often decided by a recorded teller vote. Since recorded teller and electronic roll-call voting were introduced in the early 1970s, there has been a marked expansion in the number of recorded votes that are taken in the House—from 266 in 1970 to 706 in 1977. This has had at least two consequences. First, more and more time on the floor has been devoted to the act of voting itself. Second, there is evidence that some members of Congress have not voted the same as they would otherwise have voted, because their votes were recorded. Defenders of recorded voting argue that this makes members of Congress more accountable for their legislative actions and thus enhances the democratic character of the system. Others maintain, however, that this simply makes it more difficult for legislators to resist politically popular but unwise measures.

In the Senate, which as a smaller body is able to operate more informally than the House, all voting is done through voice, division, or roll call. Moreover, the roll call is carried out in the traditional manner by the parliamentarian reading down the list of names alphabetically. In both chambers, bells are rung throughout the congressional offices whenever a roll call is about to take place. Senators who missed their names being called the first time through may still enter their vote if they arrive within fifteen minutes. Like the House, the Senate has had a substantial increase in recorded voting during the past decade, from 422 in 1970 to 636 in 1977.

Resolving House-Senate Differences: The Conference Committee

In order for a bill to become law it must be passed in identical language by both the House and the Senate. Each chamber is free to accept the language of the bill as passed by the other body. Often, however, the two branches disagree on a variety of points, ranging from the trivial to the fundamental. When differences exist between the House and Senate versions of a bill, a *conference committee* is appointed to resolve disagreements. A conference committee works on only one bill; and when its work is completed, it disbands. The members of the committee are chosen by the leadership in each branch and usually include the senior members of the reporting committee, including some who may be opposed to the bill. Settlement is reached within the committee whenever a majority of both delegations agrees to a final version of the bill.

The committee then reports the new version back to the House and Senate, and each branch votes on the compromise proposal. The full bodies nearly always accept the conference committee's recommendation. Nonetheless, they are free to reject the bill entirely or to send it back to conference for another try at a more acceptable version.

Presidential Action

The Constitution requires that any bill passed by Congress must be presented to the president before it becomes law. At this stage, there are three options. (1) The president may formally sign the bill, thereby making it the law of the land. (2) The president may formally veto the bill and return it to the house in which it originated with a statement listing various objections to the bill. A two-thirds majority in each branch is necessary to override the president's veto. (3) Finally, if the president does nothing for ten days and Congress is in session, the bill becomes law. If Congress has adjourned, the bill does not become law. This is a *pocket veto*. The vast majority of vetoes are not overridden, even when the White House and Congress are controlled by different parties. Since the presidency of Harry Truman, fewer than 18 percent of the nonpocket vetoes of public bills have been overridden by Congress.

The existence of the veto power obviously gives the president a substantial influence in the legislative process. Not only can presidents turn back laws they disapprove of, but they can seek to modify the content of laws earlier on by threatening to veto them if changes are not made.

Assessing the Legislative Process: A Bias against New Laws?

As the above description illustrates, lawmaking in Congress is a complex process. Not only are two separate institutions involved, but within each there are numerous distinct decision points: subcommittee, committee, and full body. Those advocating a new law must achieve success at each stage. Those in opposition have a variety of targets for blocking a proposal. This fact has led many commentators to conclude that the procedures of Congress are biased against new laws, that it is much easier to stop a law than to pass one. To some extent this is undoubtedly true. Indeed, this was one of the explicit reasons why the framers created a bicameral legislature. The experience within the states during the "critical period" (1776–1787) had demonstrated the dangers of numerous and constantly changing laws. The Senate in particular was intended to slow down the legislative process, to make it more orderly and responsible. Although this might mean that some good laws would not be passed as quickly as they would in a unicameral legislature, in the framers' view this was a price worth paying to guard against the passage of hastily drafted, ill-considered, and unwise measures.

Having noted this, however, it is important not to exaggerate the degree to which the structure and procedures of Congress inhibit the passage of new proposals. In fact, the modern Congress regularly passes more than 500 public laws during each two-year session. Although some of these are relatively uncontroversial and unimportant, many others deal with the most important matters facing the nation.

Moreover, since the early 1960s Congress has demonstrated a willingness and ability to undertake new legislative initiatives in a variety of areas. Many of these were part of President Lyndon Johnson's Great Society programs: Medicare and Medicaid, civil rights laws, and federal support of elementary education. Subsequent events have shown that this was not an isolated spurt of legislative creativity, for there followed in the late 1960s and 1970s new laws controlling environmental pollution, regulating safety in the workplace, reforming the nation's private pension systems, altering mandatory retirement policy, outlawing various kinds of discrimination based on sex or physical disability, deregulating the airline and trucking industries, and establishing a massive national program to develop synthetic fuels. More recently (1981), Congress adopted far-reaching reforms in the nation's tax system at the urging of President Reagan. Some of these laws required many years to move from idea to national policy; others, however, were enacted with surprising speed. In either case they demonstrate that the complex procedures of Congress are not a barrier to the enactment of novel proposals.

Having examined the structure and procedures that govern lawmaking within Congress, we have one last question to consider: whether the product is broadly consistent with the desires of the American people. Simply put, is Congress a truly representative institution?

CONGRESS AND THE PUBLIC: THE TASK OF REPRESENTATION

How Important Are Personal Characteristics?

We saw earlier in this chapter that the membership of Congress is not a mirror image of the American people. Proportionally, there are considerably fewer women, blacks, and other minorities than there are in the general population. Must a legislator, however, be a member of a specific demographic group in order to represent that group's interests in Congress? Because members of Congress are subject to reelection, they have an incentive to be responsive to the strongly held views of their constituents, whether or not they share the same race, religion, or sex.

Throughout the 1960s and 1970s, when blacks

and minorities organized to press for change, Congress—despite the demographic profile of its membership—passed landmark civil rights statutes, the Equal Rights Amendment to the Constitution, and a variety of laws to prohibit unfair discrimination against women in pay, employment, and credit. One can certainly question whether enough has been done in these areas, but it would be hard to demonstrate a systematic bias against the interests of these groups in the legislation passed by Congress.

When the framers drafted the Constitution, they had in mind a concept of representation different from merely mirroring the population. If Congress was to be an effective and responsible lawmaking body, then it should be filled with the nation's most knowledgeable and experienced citizens. Throughout our history women and minorities have not had full opportunity to participate and distinguish themselves in public affairs. As this has changed in recent decades, so too has the makeup of Congress (see Table 9-1, shown earlier).

Representation and Elections

The framers believed that frequent elections would ensure the democratic character of the House of Representatives. They believed that citizens would elect to the House those who shared their basic views, that the prospect of reelection would stimulate representatives to remain faithful to their constituents' interests and views, and that voters would refuse to reelect those who deviated substantially from their desires.

Research by political scientists during the 1950s appeared to shatter this assumption. A survey conducted during the 1958 election showed that more than half of the electorate knew virtually nothing about the candidates and that a large fraction of those who could identify the candidates had no knowledge of their stands on policy (Stokes and Miller, 1962:531–546). The authors of the study concluded that congressional elections did not turn on a comparison of the candidates' policy positions. Thus, once elected, members of Congress were largely free to do as they wished: "The Congressman . . . knows the constituency isn't looking." It seemed to follow that frequent elections did not have the democratic effect that the framers had intended.

The conclusions of this study have since been questioned and refined. It now seems clear that the electoral mechanism is more effective in promoting a democratic legislative body than previously thought. There are several reasons for this conclusion. First, the recruitment mechanisms within congressional districts are such that those who become major-party candidates tend to share the basic beliefs of their constituents (Kingdon, 1973:44–46). Second, in both the recruitment of candidates and the assessment of the records of incumbents, local elites such as newspaper editors, labor and business leaders, interest groups, and local public officials communicate information about congressional candidates to the voters. (For example, if a Democrat from a blue-collar district began to vote against prolabor legislation, union leaders in the district would waste little time in voicing their displeasure to a wider audience.) Third, prospective challengers keep a sharp eye on the actions of incumbents in order to exploit any divergence between their records and the interests or views of their constituents. Finally, members of the House *believe* that what they do in Congress will make a difference to their reelection, that they are running for reelection virtually all the time, and that they must work very hard, both personally and through their staff, to promote good relations with the voters back home.

This does not mean that a representative makes all legislative decisions with an eye on the next election. Each year a member of the House casts over 500 recorded votes on the floor, participates in hundreds more unrecorded votes, and makes innumerable important decisions within committees and subcommittees. In a large number of cases representatives are called upon to take action on matters that constituents know or care little about. This frees the legislators to follow their own judgment. The important thing for members of Congress is to establish an overall record on the major issues that will not put them on the defensive in the next election.

Delegates and Trustees

While virtually all the members of the House and Senate seek to fashion a voting record that will contribute to their reelection, not all of them understand the representative function in the same way.

Members of Congress often receive so many conflicting messages from the people back home that they must decide for themselves how to represent the best interests of their constituents. *(Erich Hartmann / Magnum)*

Some see themselves as essentially *delegates* or agents of those who send them to Congress. As one commented, "I'm not here to vote my own convictions. I'm here to represent my people" (Fenno, 1978:160). But others look with disdain on this theory of representation.

All some House members are interested in is "the folks." They think "the folks" are the second coming. They would no longer do anything to displease "the folks" than they would fly. They spend all their time trying to find out what "the folks" want. I imagine if they get five letters on one side and five on the other side, they die (Fenno, 1978:160).

Instead, these members insist that it is an intrinsic part of their job to exercise their own best judgment on the issues that come before them. When asked what he would do if a majority of his constituents signed a petition requesting that he vote in a particular way, one member of the House responded:

If that did happen, then no, I would not vote for it. I would still have to use my own judgment. . . . You

can express opinions. I have to make the decision. If you disagree with my decisions, you have the power every two years to vote me out of office. I listen to you, believe me. But, in the end, I have to use my judgment as to what is in your best interests (Fenno, 1978:161).

This is the *trustee* role of representation.

Although the delegate and trustee roles of representation are easily distinguished in theory, the distinction in practice is much fuzzier. Members of Congress who think of themselves as trustees realize that if they want to be reelected, they must vote in ways broadly consistent with the strongly held views of their constituents. On the other hand, those who subscribe to the delegate theory face hundreds of decisions each year on matters on which a clear constituency opinion does not exist or cannot be ascertained quickly enough to help. Delegates are forced to exercise their own judgment, while trustees are invariably led to take account of their constituents' opinions. This overlap of the delegate and trustee aspects of representation corresponds well with what most Americans probably expect from their legislators: effective representation of their basic interests and desires, but not blind obedience on every single point.

Representation, Reelection, and Nonlegislative Activities

The reelection incentive not only encourages the members of Congress to represent faithfully the dominant interests and views of their constituents, it also leads to a variety of nonlegislative activities useful for fostering electoral support. These include (1) advertising the legislator's name extensively back home by sending newsletters or questionnaires to constituents; (2) claiming credit for federal grants or projects that benefit the district (even if the legislator was not primarily responsible); (3) taking public positions that please constituents on issues of concern to them; and (4) generally assisting the citizens of the district or state in their dealings with the federal bureaucracy—the "constituency service" function described at the beginning of this chapter (Mayhew, 1974; and Fiorina, 1977).

Some political scientists argue that in the past decade or so members of Congress have become increasingly skilled at getting reelected by focusing their energies on these kinds of activities at the expense of traditional legislative duties like drafting proposals, contributing to committee sessions, reading committee reports, and attending floor debate. This is because there are greater political benefits to be had from maintaining a sophisticated public relations operation than from devoting hours to the often tedious process of formulating complex legislation for a complex society. As the members of Congress become better at getting reelected, Congress becomes less and less a deliberative institution, or so it seems.

There is, however, another way of viewing these nonlegislative activities. This is to see them as an essential and appropriate element of the representative function itself. They are some of the ways in which the member of Congress campaigns for reelection, and, as Professor Richard Fenno has argued, the legislator "cannot represent any people unless he knows, or makes an effort to know, who they are, what they think, and what they want; and it is by campaigning for electoral support among them that he finds out such things" (Fenno,

1978:233). To be a representative means more than simply voting as the constituents want. It also means engaging in a real communications process with them. Indeed, according to Fenno, "members of Congress believe . . . that two-way communication is more valued by their constituents than policy congruence" (Fenno, 1978:241).

As representatives, the members of Congress are not simply the receptor of opinions or demands from the citizens back home; they are also a source of information and instruction about national problems and Congress's attempts to deal with them. Members who are successful at explaining their particular contributions to the policy process may generate considerable respect and trust from their constituents. As a result, constituents grant these members a greater degree of freedom or flexibility in legislative actions. Representation and legislation are two sides of the same coin.

Representation and the Growth of Congressional Staff

No development in Congress in recent decades has raised more questions about its representative function than the enormous growth in congressional staff. As recently as 1947 the committees of the House and Senate had a total support staff of 399. By 1979 this had grown to 3,057. Similarly, between the same years the personal staffs of representatives and senators increased from 2,030 to 10,679. The 535 members of the House and Senate are now far outnumbered by personal and committee staffs of over 13,000 (Malbin, 1980:253, 257).

What do all these staff people do? While some perform strictly clerical and secretarial functions, others take a direct and active role in the legislative process: drafting legislation, scheduling witnesses for committee hearings, negotiating with other staff personnel and representatives of interest groups over the details of pending legislation, and briefing their bosses. It is not unusual for the total amount of staff time devoted to drafting a bill and navigating it through Congress to far exceed the time devoted by the members of Congress themselves.

If the thousands of staff members who work for Congress have a real impact on lawmaking in Congress, then how can we be sure that national policy will represent the desires of the people. After all, these 13,000 people are not elected by or accountable to the citizens directly. What does it matter if legislators are accountable, if their staffs, who often do most of the work, are not?

One simple fact which makes the growth of congressional staffs less of a threat to the representative character of Congress is that most high-level staff members do a rather good job of reflecting the interests and desires of those for whom they work. Representatives and senators tend to recruit as aides people who share their basic policy dispositions. Moreover, most staff professionals are intelligent enough to realize that they could lose their jobs if their actions deviate from the views of the legislators.

What, then, are the significant consequences which the growth of staff size has had for the functioning of Congress? At least four can be identified. (1) The independence of Congress from the executive branch is enhanced when Congress has thousands of its own experts to advise it on the myriad of distinct policy issues which come before it. (2) Individual members of Congress are able to make more informed judgments when advised by personal aides who research and analyze legislative issues. (3) The work load of Congress has increased in part because many staff members, anxious to impress their bosses or to shape public policy, have a strong interest in developing new legislative proposals. (4) With large staffs to manage increasing legislative work loads, there is less and less direct deliberation between the members of Congress. One student of Congress judges this last consequence to be the most serious implication of the growth of congressional staffs: "The members . . . need to talk to each other about the factual, political, and moral implications of the policies they are considering" (Malbin, 1980:242). In this scholar's view Congress has become a less deliberative institution as staff personnel have become more numerous and important.

CONCLUSION

Who Rules?

The United States Congress is hardly a passive medium through which the American people shape and direct public policy. It is a unique institution with its own history, tradition, norms of behavior, organizational structure, and complex rules and procedures. How it is organized and operates influences both the role it plays in the political system and the kinds of policies it enacts. As we saw in Chapter 1, it is necessary in the United States to speak of not only *who* governs but also *what* governs. Congress is not merely a collection of elected officials and their staffs, but an independent deliberative institution that contributes to the governing of the United States.

This does not mean, of course, that Congress is isolated from the broader political community, that its actions bear no relation to the needs or desires of the American populace. On the contrary, public opinion works *through* Congress, but in so doing it has other consequences than if it acted directly to fashion national policy.

There are two distinct ways in which public opinion influences Congress, following the *pluralist* and *majoritarian* models described in Chapter 1. Insofar as organized interest groups influence Congress, the pluralist model holds. Millions of Americans belong to organizations which seek to influence public policy in a way that will benefit the members of the organizations. This is why interest groups donate to political candidates, testify before congressional committees, and orchestrate letter-writing campaigns to members of Congress. Public officials, journalists, and social scientists debate how much influence interest groups have in Congress, but nearly all agree that interest groups make some difference.

For reasons described earlier, however, interest groups do not necessarily represent the will of the public at large. Public policy dictated by the demands of interest groups could deviate substantially from what the majority desires. Yet there *is* a mechanism through which the majority influences Congress. The process of periodic elections tends both to bring into Congress individuals who share the electorate's basic policy goals and to ensure the fidelity of incumbents to the essential interests and desires of the voters. This corresponds to the majoritarian model of policymaking.

Congress in Its Third Century

It is not possible to predict with any certainty how well Congress will meet its twin constitutional responsibilities of representation and legislation in the third century of its existence. Nevertheless, several conclusions seem warranted from what we have learned about the functions, procedures, and structure of Congress; the relationship of Congress to the broader political community; and the trend of recent changes in the institution.

Representation Congress shows every sign of remaining a vital and dynamic representative institution. The democratization of power in the House and Senate, the creation of informal groups within Congress devoted to specific economic or ideological ends, and the increased sophistication of members of Congress in serving their constituents will all ensure that interested individuals and groups will make their influence felt within the institution. In particular, the large number of relatively independent subcommittees will continue to provide numerous points of access for interested parties.

The danger in these trends, however, is that as Congress becomes more open and accessible to outside interests and opinions, it may be less able to make decisions in the broad national interest—decisions that, in the short run at least, work hardship on many individuals and groups.

Legislation As a lawmaking institution Congress will preserve several newfound strengths into the third century. The committee and subcommittee systems will continue to promote specialized expertise and technical competence. And since this expertise is coupled with a growing democratization of power, we can expect that Congress will abound with novel ideas and proposals for meeting the problems of the future. There will be no lack of policy initiatives to deal with issues still on the horizon.

This does not mean, however, that Congress will possess all the qualities necessary for passing sound and effective legislation. We can be sure that the issues of the future will be highly complex, cutting across traditional subject areas and requiring coordinated action in a variety of fields. Changes within Congress that have distributed power widely among the membership have made it more difficult for the institution as a whole to formulate, pass, and persevere in a coherent approach to complex issues. Congress is more than the sum of its members. In some ways the institution may not have

benefited from changes that have given more real power to individual members. It remains to be seen whether Congress can meet the challenges of this next century.

SOURCES

Asbell, Bernard: *The Senate Nobody Knows,* Doubleday, Garden City, N.Y., 1978.

Bibby, John F., Thomas E. Mann, Norman J. Ornstein: *Vital Statistics on Congress:1980* American Enterprise Institute, Washington, D.C., 1980.

Congressional Almanac, Congressional Quarterly Press, Washington, D.C., 1977–1983.

Congressional Quarterly Weekly Report, vol. 37, no. 3, Congressional Quarterly Press, Jan. 20, 1979.

Congressional Record, 1947–1980.

Elections, 1980, Congressional Quarterly Press, Washington, D.C.,.

Farrand, Max (ed.): *The Records of the Federal Convention of 1787,* vols. 1–4, Yale University Press, New Haven, Conn., 1937.

Fenno, Richard: *Congressmen in Committees,* Little, Brown, Boston, 1973.

————: *Home Style: House Members in Their Districts,* Little, Brown, Boston, 1978.

Fiorina, Morris: *Congress: Keystone of the Washington Establishment,* Yale University Press, New Haven, Conn., 1977.

Guide to Congress, 2d ed., Congressional Quarterly Press, Washington, D.C., 1976.

Hamilton, Alexander, James Madison, and John Jay: *Federalist Papers,* Clinton Rossiter (ed.), New American Library, New York, 1961.

Hearings before the Temporary Select Committee to Study the Senate Committee System, July 20, 21, and 22, 1976, U.S. Government Printing Office, Washington, D.C., 1976.

Kingdon, John W.: *Congressmen's Voting Decisions,* Harper and Row, New York, 1973.

Malbin, Michael J.: *Unelected Representatives,* Basic Books, New York, 1980.

Manley, John F.: *The Politics of Finance,* Little, Brown, Boston, 1970.

Mayhew, David R.: *Congress: The Electoral Connection,* Yale University Press, New Haven, Conn., 1974.

Miller, Clem: *Member of the House: Letters of a Congressman,* John W. Baker (ed.), Scribner, New York, 1962.

Newsweek, May 31, 1982.

Oleszek, Walter J.: *Congressional Procedures and the Policy Process,* Congressional Quarterly Press, Washington, D.C., 1978.

Ornstein, Norman J., Thomas E. Mann, Michael J. Malbin, and John F. Bibby: *Vital Statistics on Congress: 1982,* American Enterprise Institute, Washington, D.C., 1982.

Patterson, Samuel C.: "The Semi-Sovereign Congress," in Anthony King (ed.), *The New American Political System,* American Enterprise Institute, Washington, D.C., 1978.

Polsby, Nelson W.: *Congress and the Presidency,* 3d ed., Prentice-Hall, Englewood Cliffs, N.J., 1976.

Presidential Elections since 1789, Congressional Quarterly, Washington, D.C., 1975, pp. 529–643.

Price, H. Douglas: "The Congressional Career: Then and Now," in Nelson Polsby (ed.), *Congressional Behavior,* Random House, New York, 1971.

Reid, T. R.: *Congressional Odyssey: The Saga of a Senate Bill,* Freeman, San Francisco, 1980.

Stokes, Donald E., and Warren E. Miller: "Party Government and the Saliency of Congress," *Public Opinion Quarterly,* Winter, 1962.

Tacheron, Donald G., and Morris K. Udall: *The Job of the Congressman,* 2d ed., Bobbs-Merrill, Indianapolis, 1970.

Wilson, Woodrow: *Congressional Government,* Meridian Books, Cleveland, 1969.

RECOMMENDED READINGS

Asbell, Bernard: *The Senate Nobody Knows,* Doubleday, Garden City, N.Y., 1978. Excellent account of the inner workings of the Senate and of the legislative life of former Maine Democratic Senator Edmund Muskie.

Fenno, Richard: *Home Style: House Members in Their Districts,* Little, Brown, Boston, 1978. Detailed analysis of how members of Congress relate to their constituents.

Fiorina, Morris: *Congress: Keystone of the Washington Establishment,* Yale University Press, New Haven, Conn., 1977. Interestingly written discussion of how the reelection incentive of members of Congress leads to the growth of government and a large federal bureaucracy.

Kingdon, John W.: *Congressmen's Voting Decisions,* Harper and Row, New York, 1973. One of the best studies of how congressional representatives decide how to vote.

Malbin, Michael J.: *Unelected Representatives,* Basic Books, New York, 1980. Thoughtful analysis of how congressional staff members influence the legislative process.

Mayhew, David R.: *Congress: The Electoral Connection,* Yale University Press, New Haven, Conn., 1974. Short essay detailing the kinds of actions undertaken in Congress by legislators intent on reelection.

Miller, Clem: *Member of the House: Letters of a Congressman,* John W. Baker (ed.), Scribner, New York, 1962. Fascinating collection of letters written by a former California congressman to educate his constituents on the House of Representatives.

Oleszek, Walter J.: *Congressional Procedures and the Policy Process,* Congressional Quarterly Press, Washington, D.C., 1978. Most up-to-date and readable description of congressional procedures.

Reid, T. R., *Congressional Odyssey: The Saga of a Senate Bill,* Freeman, San Francisco, 1980. Short, interesting account of how and why Congress passed the Waterway User Charge Act in 1978.

Chapter 10

The Presidency

In the early 1960s, a leading scholar of American politics concluded a major work on the presidency with the following reflections:

> [The presidency] is a priceless symbol of our continuity and destiny as a people.... It is ... a standing reproach to those petty doctrinaires who insist that executive power is inherently undemocratic; for, to the exact contrary, it has been more responsive to the needs and dreams of a giant democracy than any other office or institution in the whole mosaic of American life (Rossiter, 1960:249–252).

Although not every observer of American politics at the time was quite as effusive in praise of the presidency, this view was broadly representative of most scholars and journalists. Whatever their criticisms of particular presidents, most in this community defended the presidency and insisted on the need for it to have more authority.

Two events shattered this consensus: the Vietnamese war and Watergate. The long and unsuccessful conflict in Vietnam, conducted without an official declaration of war, led many to view the presidency as an "imperial" institution exercising a virtual dictatorship over foreign and military policy (Schlesinger, 1973). The Watergate scandal exposed a presidency that many saw as corrupt and unmindful of Constitutional processes. The impeachment proceedings brought against President Nixon in 1974 were seen by many not just as an indictment of the president but as a trial of the inflated powers of the modern presidency.

One result of these events was a wide-ranging reexamination of the nature of the executive power in the American system of government. Many who had once praised the presidency now began to wonder if it had not become too powerful. Throughout this period (1965–1975) proposals flowed from many different quarters suggesting different ways of reducing the power of the presidency and increasing the authority and leadership role of Congress. A new mood developed for a somewhat more modest presidency, a mood conformed to by the administrations of Gerald Ford and Jimmy Carter.

By the middle of President Carter's term, however, public sentiment seemed to shift dramatically, and the "low-key" presidency lost much of its attractiveness. Critics of President Carter claimed that he was too reluctant to assert himself in contests with the bureaucracy and Congress, that he was unable to mobilize public sentiment to meet the challenges facing the nation, and consequently that he failed to exercise true political leadership. By the summer of 1979, the president himself became keenly aware of the growing public disenchantment with his handling of the office and undertook a campaign consciously geared to refurbishing the nature of his presidency, changing its role from "head of government" to "leader of the people." Although this campaign was not a great success, it did seem to signal a realization by the president and the public that, whatever the exact powers of the presidency, Americans want a president who exercises leadership.

As long as people discuss politics, they will argue about the exact meaning of the term "leadership." As used in relation to the presidency it refers to a president who, in Woodrow Wilson's words, is the "vital place of action in the system," who takes the initiative in identifying problems and formulating coherent programs to meet them, and who attempts to inform and persuade the public to adopt these programs (Wilson, 1961:73). Presidents in this view do not limit their efforts to the administration of the government, leaving to others the responsibility of charting the nation's course; rather, at least much of the time, they take the initiative and attempt to set and control the political agenda.

It is not entirely clear whether the founders intended the presidency to be the seat of leadership in the American system, and it is certain that for much of the nineteenth century the presidency did not have this role. For the past half century, however, Americans have generally come to regard this function as central to the presidential office, and they have maintained that view even after a decade of perceived abuses of presidential power. Many of the distinguishing characteristics of the modern presidency, as well as many of its problems, evolve from its role as the "vital place of action in the system."

THE TASKS OF PRESIDENTIAL LEADERSHIP

One way to gain insight into the varied tasks of presidential leadership is to examine the daily ac-

---

BOX 10-1

RONALD REAGAN'S SCHEDULE, JUNE 23, 1981

4:30 A.M. The President, having trouble sleeping, gets up and does some paper work. Goes back to bed about 6.

8:00 A.M. Reagan receives wake-up call from White House switchboard.

8:41 A.M. Senior aides James Baker, Edwin Meese and Michael Deaver join the President in the family quarters to discuss the day's schedule.

9:08 A.M. Reagan walks from second-floor residence down to the State Dining Room for breakfast with 38 Democratic lawmakers who backed his budget cuts.

10:15 A.M. The President goes to the Oval Office for daily national security briefing. Among those attending are Vice President Bush and National Security Adviser Richard Allen. Meeting concludes at 10:34.

10:37 A.M. At his desk, Reagan is briefed on the day's developments by aides Baker, Meese, Deaver, Max Friedersdorf, David Gergen and Larry Speakes. At 10:46, the meeting ends.

10:50 A.M. *U.S. News & World Report* editors interview the President.

11:09 A.M. White House advisers Melvin Bradley and Thaddeus Garrett enter Oval Office to prepare Reagan for meeting with NAACP officials Benjamin Hooks and Margaret Bush Wilson.

11:13 A.M. Hooks and Wilson begin discussions with the President. Also present are Vice President Bush and White House aide Elizabeth Dole. Meeting ends at 11:59.

12:01 P.M. Reagan poses for photographs in Oval Office with new U.S. Ambassadors Arthur Burns, Maxwell Rabb and Ernest Preeg and their families.

12:15 P.M. Ocean explorer Jacques Cousteau enters

for lunch with Reagan, Deaver and White House aide Richard Darman on patio outside the Oval Office.

1:31 P.M. Treasury Secretary Donald Regan briefs the President in the Oval Office on tax developments in Congress.

1:39 P.M. Reagan walks across the hall to the Roosevelt Room to meet with 11 Republican members of the Senate Finance Committee. Meeting ends at 2:01.

2:08 P.M. The President enters the Cabinet Room for meeting with the cabinet council on commerce and trade. Session ends at 2:27.

2:34 P.M. The Chief Executive convenes a meeting of the entire cabinet. It concludes at 3:38.

3:46 P.M. The President goes to the State Dining Room for meeting with the Presidential Advisory Committee on Federalism. Session ends at 4:24 and Reagan returns to the Oval Office.

4:33 P.M. Personnel Adviser E. Pendleton James enters Oval Office to discuss presidential appointments.

4:48 P.M. CIA Director William Casey enters for meeting with the President.

5:09 P.M. Reagan goes to Rose Garden reception for 175 teen-age Republicans.

5:16 P.M. The President returns to the Oval Office to do some paper work.

5:51 P.M. Reagan enters the East Room for a reception in honor of 190 House Republicans.

6:12 P.M. The President goes back to the family quarters, has dinner alone, telephones Mrs. Reagan in California, catches up on some reading and retires at 11:15 P.M.

Source: U.S. News & World Report, 1981:16–17.

---

tivities of a chief executive (Box 10-1). On June 23, 1981, the White House allowed reporters from the weekly magazine *U.S. News & World Report* to attend President Reagan's meetings and functions, public as well as private, throughout the course of an especially busy day. In one sense this was not a typical day for Ronald Reagan, for the schedule was made particularly active in order to demon-

strate the president's work capacity. With respect, however, to the *kinds* of activities the president engaged in, it was not exceptional.

The Activities of a President

Reagan attended a total of seventeen meetings on June 23. Some of these, like the picture-taking session with the new ambassadors, the lunch with Jacques Cousteau, and the reception for the teenage Republicans, illustrate the symbolic and formal importance of the office of the presidency. The president is the formal head of state in this country; there are few higher public honors than to meet personally with the president. The rest of President Reagan's meetings, however, had less to do with symbolism and formality than with the direct business of governing.

To govern effectively, presidents need information and advice, much of which they now receive from their personal staff. Three of President Reagan's meetings with staff members on June 23 were integral parts of his normal daily schedule: the early morning session with his three most senior advisers, the later meeting with the larger group that included his chief of congressional liaison and his press spokesman, and his daily briefing on international events with his national security adviser. While all presidents are to some degree dependent upon their staff, they have great latitude in how they structure and interact with the staff organization.

Presidents get their advice not only from personal aides but also from those they appoint to head the various departments and agencies of the executive branch. Interestingly, on the day in question Reagan sought the advice of department heads in three different forums: individual meetings (with Treasury Secretary Donald Regan and CIA Director William Casey), a session with a specific group of department heads (the Cabinet council on commerce and trade), and a meeting with the entire Cabinet (all the department heads and selected other high-level officials who are given Cabinet ranking). Usually, meetings with executive branch staff and officials are supplemented by briefing books on the various issues that the president faces. On this day alone President Reagan received a staff summary on the day's news, an inch-thick briefing book on the events for the day, a written report on national security matters, and a staff memo on the issue under consideration by the Cabinet council on commerce and trade.

Those outside the executive branch who are most important to the success or failure of a president's program are the members of Congress. This is well illustrated by the fact that on June 23 Rea-gan met with 239 members of Congress. As a general rule, the larger the number of representatives and senators who meet with the president, the less likely it is that the meeting will involve a serious discussion of political business. Still, sessions like the reception for the 190 House Republicans can serve the purpose of building personal relations between a president and members of Congress, which can translate over the long run into a greater willingness on their part to see things the president's way. What one must never forget is that beneath the institutional forms of government, there is a *community* of officials at work in Washington for whom personal relations have an important bearing on how they act.

Although Reagan's activities on June 23 provide a good glimpse of how the tasks of modern presidential leadership convert into the day-to-day business of governing, there are at least four things the president did not do that day that are important elements of presidential leadership. First, he did not give a *televised address* to the nation, which is something Reagan did quite effectively during his first year. Second, Reagan did not hold a *press conference*. This nationally televised freewheeling session with the White House press corps has become a virtual institution in American politics. How well presidents relate to the press can be very important to how well they get their message across to the American public. Third, the president did not meet any *foreign heads of state*. Although the Constitution created three separate branches of government, it designated the president as the one official representative of the United States in meeting with foreign ambassadors and, by implication, with foreign leaders generally.

Making an address to the nation, holding a press conference, and meeting a foreign head of state are fairly common, although not daily, activities of a president. Even less common, but of crucial importance when it occurs, is—fourth—*crisis management*. As commander in chief of the armed forces and director of foreign relations, the president is responsible for the initial reaction to any military or international crisis that threatens the interests or well-being of the United States. The normal daily schedule may be abruptly canceled in favor of hurried meetings with military and foreign policy advisers, briefings on rapidly changing events, and confidential communications with world leaders. Congress may eventually contribute to the final resolution of a dispute with a foreign nation, but in the first few hours or days the crucial decisions are up to the president. As Robert Kennedy related in his account of the Cuban missile crisis that confronted his brother, President John Kennedy, in 1962: "Saturday morning at 10:00 I called the President at the Blackstone Hotel in Chicago and told him we [a group of the president's most trusted advisers] were ready to meet with him. It was now up to one single man. No committee was going to make this decision. He canceled his trip and returned to Washington" (Kennedy, 1969:47).

Governing Style and Personality

The kinds of activities which President Reagan engaged in on June 23 are not much different from those of other recent presidents. Indeed, if one looked at typical presidential schedules for several recent administrations, it would be difficult to determine which president went with which schedule. This surface similarity, however, tends to obscure fundamental personal differences in how the occupants of the Oval Office actually go about the business of governing, for each president has an individual style of governing (see Box 10-2).

Some presidents are intensely energetic and delve into the fine details of administration and governing (Johnson and Carter); others delegate matters of detail to the White House staff and reserve their own time and energy for broader issues (Eisenhower and Reagan). Some prefer a highly structured and smoothly functioning staff organization (Eisenhower and Nixon); others see advantage in a looser and less settled division of staff functions and chain of command (Kennedy, Johnson, and Carter). Some treat their personal aides with consideration and respect (Reagan and Carter); others harass, intimidate, and embarass (Johnson). Some are guided by deep-seated beliefs in a few fundamental principles about society and government (Reagan); others have a more problem-solving, or engineering, type of approach to the task of formulating public policy (Carter).

The list could go on and on. Some like meetings; others don't. Some are effective one-on-one per-

suaders; others do better communicating to millions through television. Some prefer the challenges of foreign policy; others focus on domestic affairs. The point that needs to be emphasized is that the governing styles of presidents reflect their personal attributes and qualities—their views of executive leadership derived from long experience, their known strengths and weaknesses, their goals and public philosophy, and, finally, their character and personality.

The presidency cannot be understood apart from studying particular presidents. The presidency is clearly the most personalized of the national governing institutions. By its very nature as a "unitary" institution headed by—indeed, embodied in—one person, the presidency is and was intended to be an office that provides wide discretion to its occupant. Statesmanship, the framers realized, was not an attribute of collective bodies.

Descriptions of individual presidents have been traditionally found in biographies, memoirs, and historical accounts of different administrations. In recent decades, the field of political biography has been supplemented by the insights of modern psychology, which has led to such brilliant studies of presidential character as Alexander and Juliette George's work *Woodrow Wilson and Colonel House* (1964). Attempts have also been made to classify presidential character into different personalities (Barber, 1977; Hargrove, 1974; Nelson, 1982). What strikes one in reading the many accounts of the presidents, no matter what form they take, is the tremendous diversity in characteristics and talents of those who have served. There are some whose dignity and sobriety amaze (like Washington), and others who seem vain and undistinguished (like Harding). Some were clearly "in control" of themselves—here one thinks of the calm and well-integrated personality of Gerald Ford—while others seem to have been "driven" by unconscious needs and desires which they may never have fully understood or mastered, like Woodrow Wilson and Richard Nixon. Each person, no doubt, will have a favorite list of sketches; but the three selected in Box 10-3—of Lincoln, Wilson, and Nixon—serve well to illustrate the different personalities of presidents and approaches to the subject.

As important as personality is to the study of the

BOX 10-2

THE GOVERNING STYLES OF THREE MODERN PRESIDENTS

Ronald Reagan (1981–   )

Reagan keeps a tight schedule, but spurns long hours in the office. He spends most of his day with people, not papers. He insists on hearing an issue debated before making a decision. He sets broad policy and allows aides to work out the details.

As an administrator, Reagan is detached and sometimes formal. He never removes his suit coat in the Oval Office, even when he's working there alone with his feet propped up. Although he spends most of the day in meetings, he seldom joins in the debate and rarely asks questions.

At the same time, the Chief Executive makes strangers feel comfortable in his presence. . . . A good storyteller, he often rewards visitors to the Oval Office with a joke. . . .

Reagan occasionally yawns during long meetings. He doodles with paper and pencil, chews on his right index finger or plays with his glasses. . . .

Unlike most Presidents, Reagan is not usually an early riser. His day began at 8:00 A.M. and ended at 11:15 P.M. (*U.S. News & World Report*, 1981:13–15).

Jimmy Carter (1977–1981)

He grasps issues quickly. . . . He would resolve technical questions lucidly, without distortions imposed by cant or imperfect comprehension.

He is a stable, personally confident man, whose quirks are few. . . .

Carter is usually patient, less vindictive than the political norm, blessed with a sense of perspective about the chanciness of life and the transience of its glories and pursuits. . . .

He would leave for a weekend at Camp David laden with thick briefing books, would pore over budget tables to check the arithmetic, and during his first six months in office, would personally review all requests to use the White House tennis court. . . .

Carter thinks in lists, not arguments; as long as the items are there, their order does not matter, nor does the hierarchy among them. Whenever he gave us an outline for a speech, it would consist of six or seven subjects ("inflation," "need to fight waste") rather than a theme or tone. . . .

For certain aspects of his job—the analyst and manager parts—Carter's methods serve him well. He makes decisions about solar power installations and the B-1 on the basis of output, payload, facts, not abstract considerations. But for the part of his job that involves leadership, Carter's style of thought cripples him. He thinks he "leads" by choosing the correct policy; but he fails to project a vision larger than the problem he is tackling at the moment.

. . . While Carter accepts challenges to his ideas and is pleased to improve his mind, he stubbornly, complacently resists attempts to challenge his natural style (Fallows, 1981:141–157).

Lyndon B. Johnson (1963–1969)

With his own men, Johnson commanded, forbade, insisted, swaggered and swore. Verbal tirades and fits of temper became an integral part of his image. On occasion, it seemed as if Johnson *needed* to make his staff look ridiculous, that he was strengthened by his exposure of inadequacies in others. . . .

His energy [when he succeeded to the presidency] seemed redoubled. He talked with chiefs of state; sent messages to the Congress; issued orders to the executive branch; met with businessmen, labor leaders, and civil servants. The hours between 2 and 6 A.M. were all that Johnson grudgingly gave to sleep. Endowed with an encyclopedic memory, he had a command of the details of matters significant to his power and its exercise that was prodigious. In one sitting, he would deal in turn with issues of education, finance, poverty, and housing. His mind remained resilient even when his body was fatigued. He tended to rest from one kind of activity by engaging in another. . . .

His hierarchy was an orderly structure with many fixed relationships, but he alone was at the top with direct lines of communication and authority to the several men who occupied the level below. . . . The President was his own chief of staff: he made the staff assignments; he received the product of his staff's work and reconciled or decided between the competing reports; he set the pace of action and the tone of discussion. . . . And he extended that control down to the least significant levels of activity, handling such details as approving the guest list for social functions, checking the equipment for the White House cars, determining the correct temperature for the rooms in the Mansion. . . .

In the end no organizational chart could define Johnson's system of White House control (Kearns, 1976:176, 178, 239–240).

BOX 10-3

PERSONALITY SKETCHES OF LINCOLN, WILSON, AND NIXON

Lincoln

Lincoln must have been taxed near to the limit of what men have endured without loss of judgment, or loss of courage or loss of ordinary human feeling. There is no sign that any of these things happened to him; the study of his record rather shows a steady ripening of mind and character to the end. . . . He had within his own mind two resources. . . . In his most intimate circle he would draw upon his stores of poetry, particularly of tragedy; often, for instance, he would recite such speeches as Richard II's: "For God's sake let us sit upon the ground and tell sad stories of the death of kings. All murdered." Another element in his thoughts . . . [was the] play of humour in which he found relief . . . to the end (Charnwood, 1917).

Wilson

Men require ways of expressing their aggressions and of protecting their self-esteem. Wilson's ways of doing both, unhappily, involved demanding his way to the letter and hurling himself against his opponents no matter what the odds, no matter what the cost. . . . He *must* fight to have his way. But in doing so he must prove his devotion to the Treaty [of Versailles]. He must demonstrate that he had no personal motive for taking the position he took, that matters of great principle were involved. He must demonstrate his moral superiority and his opponents' "selfishness." He must be ready to die for his cause (George and George, 1964).

Nixon

Most men mature around a central core; Nixon had several. This is why he was never at peace with himself. Any attempt to sum up his complex character in one attribute is bound to be misleading. The detractors' view that Nixon was the incarnation of evil is as wrong as the adulation of his more fervent admirers. On closer acquaintance one realized that what gave Nixon his driven quality was the titanic struggle that never ended; there was never a permanent victor between the dark and the sensitive sides of his nature. Now one, now another personality predominated, creating an overall impression of menace, of torment, of unpredictability, and, in the final analysis, of enormous vulnerability (Kissinger, 1982).

---

presidency, the personal factor acts within the context of an institution which possesses certain powers, has certain expectations placed on it, and—increasingly—has a defined organizational structure that surrounds it. Whatever the particular personalities of presidents, we can speak of certain properties of the institution as a whole. And much of what needs to be said about the modern presidency is the product of a long history of evolution and of deliberate attempts by certain constitution makers to adapt and modify the office.

THE DEVELOPMENT OF THE OFFICE: THE ORIGINAL DESIGN

Today, the presidency is generally regarded as the seat of political leadership in the nation. But exactly what justifies this special role for the occupant of the White House? Why do we even call the presidency the "highest office"? Somewhat surprisingly, neither the Constitution nor our early history provides much direct support for ascribing to the presidency a premier position among the triad of national institutions. The Constitution itself places the presidency second after Congress and then vests the office with powers that by no means dictate a leadership role in national government. Moreover, for most of our history, Congress—*not* the presidency—has been the more influential branch. It is only since the New Deal administration of Franklin Roosevelt that the presidency has achieved and maintained a decisive leadership role in the political system. Before FDR there occasionally were strong presidents, but the norm for most of our first century and a half was congressional dominance over national policymaking. The roots of the modern presidency can, however, be traced to the Constitution and to the broad *potential* grants of power that the founders gave the executive. As Richard Pious has noted, the friends of the strong presidency at the Convention "gained a version [in the Constitution] that provided the opportunity for the exercise of a residuum of unenumerated power. . . . Much of the subsequent history of the presidency would involve the incumbent's claim that he had the power to act, and his critics' counterclaim that his exercise of authority was unconstitutional" (Pious, 1979:38).

The Experience of the Articles

The Constitution of 1787 was written in the aftermath of eleven years of political experience following the country's declaration of independence in 1776, and the form given to the presidency by the founders owed much to what they had learned about the need for effective executive power during those years. At the beginning of the revolutionary period, Americans shared a deep distrust of executive power. This opinion resulted from the perceived abuse of executive power by King George III, whom the Declaration of Independence attacked for being guilty of "every act which may define a tyrant" and therefore "unfit to be the ruler of a free people." Moreover, the actions of the king had followed a long history of conflict in the colonies between popularly elected assemblies and the royal governors appointed by the monarch.

The mistrust of a strong executive as a threat to liberty was reflected both in the Articles of Confederation and in the new state constitutions written in the early years after the Revolution. As noted in Chapter 2, the Articles established no independent executive authority. All the power vested in the national government resided with Congress. Important executive tasks nevertheless had to be performed, such as directing the war effort and negotiating with foreign nations. Congress at first assigned executive functions to committees of the legislature, later to semi-independent boards with both members of Congress and private citizens, and finally to distinct departments that were separate from the legislature but answerable to it (Fisher, 1972).

These experiments in developing an effective administrative apparatus were failures. Fearful of the growth of a powerful independent bureaucracy, Congress refused to divest itself of the details of administration. Both legislation and administration suffered. Jefferson complained that the "smallest trifle of [administration] occupies as long as the most important act of legislation, and takes place of every thing else." Hamilton echoed the same sentiment, contending that "Congress is properly a deliberative corps and it forgets itself when it attempts to play the executive" (Fisher, 1972:254–264). By 1787, many had come to the view that effective conduct of the national business required a separate administrative branch energized and supervised by a single head having a clear chain of command and protections from irregular legislative intrusions into the details of administration.

During the same eleven-year period (1776–1787), events in the states taught a similar lesson, but for somewhat different reasons. In the eleven states that drew up new constitutions after independence, provisions were made for a separate executive branch headed by a governor. But in almost every instance, these constitutions were designed to make the executive branch decidedly subordinate to the legislature. Terms of office for governors were short (usually one year), and many states prohibited reeligibility. The most common mode of election was by a vote of the legislature. The gubernatorial office was further weakened by the existence of executive councils that could overrule the governor on many important matters. Finally, most governors received their powers not from the state constitution but directly from the legislature.

Although these provisions were successful in preventing executive tyranny, they had the unexpected effect of fostering a form of *legislative* tyranny in the new state governments. In the absence of effective political checks, the state legislatures regularly overstepped their proper constitutional authority and encroached upon the executive and judicial spheres, undermining their independence (Thach, 1969). As Thomas Jefferson complained, "173 despots would surely be as oppressive as one. . . . An *elective despotism* was not the government we fought for" (Peterson, 1975:164). In addition, unchecked legislative power resulted in excessive and constantly changing legislation. A regular characteristic of these governments, according to the founders, was their instability (*Federalist* 62).

The conspicuous exception to this pattern of legislative usurpations and irresponsible lawmaking was the state of New York. There, the constitution established a relatively powerful and independent executive branch that was more than a match for the legislature. The governor was elected directly by the people for a three-year term with no limits on reeligibility; and gubernatorial powers were granted by the state constitution, not by the legislature. With the exceptions of appointments and vetoes, the governor was unchecked by an executive council. As a result, George Clinton, who occupied the governor's office for eighteen years, became the dominant force in the state, employing the executive powers to maintain public order and to guide measures in the legislature. Under Clinton's firm leadership, New York probably enjoyed a more stable and competent administration than that of any other state. Consequently, the New York governorship became something like a model for the framers when they constructed the American presidency.

The Constitution of 1787

By the time the Constitutional Convention met in 1787, most delegates already agreed that the executive office should be sufficiently strong and independent to serve two distinct purposes: to provide for a sound and effective administration of national law and to counteract and balance the legislative branch in order to prevent legislative tyranny and instability. Notice that these two purposes may be in some tension with one another. The first suggests an executive office that is basically ministerial, an agent of the legislature's will. But the second implies a *political* executive, one who plays an active role in the policy process and may occasionally thwart the legislature's will.

Whatever the difficulties of working out these two purposes in practice, it is clear that the framers rejected the notion that the executive should be simply the agent of the legislature. An examination of the Convention debates shows that they fought to fashion an office that would have a will of its own and the Constitutional means to resist legislative

encroachments on the executive sphere. In four different ways the Constitution of 1787 went beyond the practices in the states to establish a strong and independent executive branch.

Constitutional Grant of Power Most states allowed the legislature to define the powers of the executive branch. In contrast, Article II of the Constitution begins, "The executive Power shall be vested in a President of the United States of America." This cryptic declaration, as we shall see, has served as a focal point of debate between those who think the president has certain implied or inherent powers which by nature are part of the "executive power" and those who insist that the phrase adds nothing to the president's authority beyond what the Constitution otherwise expressly grants. The Constitution then goes on to spell out a variety of specific powers, including the power to command the armed forces, to issue pardons, to recommend measures to Congress, to veto legislative enactments, and to receive ambassadors. These powers are the president's alone. Two others are shared with the Senate: to appoint ambassadors, judges of the Supreme Court, and other high-level federal officers; and to make treaties with foreign nations. Formally, then, the source of the president's power is not Congress, but the Constitution.

Structural Independence from Congress The founders sought to ensure an institutionally independent executive by limiting Congress's control over a president's salary and by providing the president an independent electoral base. Both of these provisions differed from the prevailing practices in most states. In regard to salaries, Congress may raise or lower the presidential salary for future terms, but it cannot alter the salary of a sitting president during the current term. The question of salaries, incidentally, was discussed at some length at the Convention. Benjamin Franklin had proposed having the president serve without pay. Although his intent was to limit the office to the generous and disinterested, the delegates rejected the proposal because it would exclude all but the wealthiest prospects (or else subject poorer incumbents to the temptation of corruption). The founders' view was that popular constitutions, to avoid an elitist spirit, *require* reasonable salaries for elected officials.

As for the method of election, the founders removed the choice of the president from the legislature, except where no candidate received the requisite number of electoral votes. Because the founders were skeptical of the practicality and perhaps the wisdom of a direct election by the people, the Convention initially considered election by the legislature. Some delegates objected to this plan, however, on the grounds that it might render the president subservient to Congress. Consequently, the founders devised the mechanism of the electoral college, which established temporary bodies of special representatives to make the decision, with members of Congress being prohibited from serving as electors.

Substantial Term of Office and Indefinite Reeligibility The Constitution originally established a four-year term for the president and placed no restrictions on reeligibility. These provisions were designed to guarantee a degree of continuity and stability in the administration of the government and to give the president a real interest and desire to protect the executive domain from legislative encroachments. The framers were keenly sensitive to the force of personal ambition in the political arena, and they recognized that aspirants of high ambition would be attracted to the presidency. Consequently, they tried to construct the office in such a way that as presidents pursued their own interest, they would also promote the interest of the nation. Because good performance in office might be rewarded with reelection, presidents would come to see that personal goals—whether in the form of perquisites of the office, the prestige of the position, the power to affect national life, or the glory resulting from great accomplishments—could best be achieved by a responsible exercise of the powers of the presidency.

Early opponents of indefinite reeligibility worried that popular presidents might serve for life, thereby becoming dangerously powerful. This concern was quickly laid to rest when George Washington set a two-term precedent, and not until Franklin Roosevelt did a president serve more than eight years. In 1951, six years after Roosevelt's death, the states ratified the Twenty-Second Amendment, limiting all future presidents to two terms.

Lately there has been an effort under way to do away with reeligibility entirely, coupled with an extension of the presidential term to six years. Proponents of this plan, including several recent presidents, maintain that it would free presidents from concern over the narrow political consequences of their actions so that they could concentrate on the broad national interest. Opponents answer that presidential leadership depends crucially on the "political" nature of the office, that a prohibition on reelection would undermine the executive's influence with Congress, that the nation is well-served when presidents are forced to defend their policies in a reelection campaign, and that an inflexible six years is too long for an ineffective president and probably not long enough for an especially able chief executive.

Unity Perhaps the most important characteristic of the presidency, in the view of the framers, was the unity of the office: "That unity is conducive to energy will not be disputed. Decision, activity, secrecy, and dispatch will generally characterize the proceedings of one man in a much more eminent degree than the proceedings of any greater number; and in proportion as the number is increased, these qualities will be diminished" (*Federalist* 70). An effective executive must be able to make decisions quickly, to carry them out forcefully, and at times to do so secretly. A single individual is more likely to function in this way than a group is. Thus, the framers rejected one proposal that would have created a committee of three or more, perhaps selected from different parts of the country, to function as chief executive; and another that would have established an executive council, like those in the states, to share the authority vested in the presidency.

Those opposed to executive unity maintained, however, that the loss of some energy was a small price to pay for the safety of dividing the executive power among several hands. To this, Hamilton responded that to have more than one executive actually would make the office less accountable to the public and therefore more dangerous, for "plurality in the executive . . . tends to conceal faults and destroy responsibility" (*Federalist* 70). With one person in charge, the people know whom to reward for distinguished service and whom to punish (that is, refuse to reelect). It is an indication of the growth of the president's role in American politics that this principle of accountability is now so complete that the American people tend to credit presidents for whatever goes well in the nation and blame them for whatever goes wrong; many seem to forget that Congress is still the lawmaking body and on many matters has greater powers for good or ill than the president.

Although the framers sought to construct an independent and energetic executive, it is not clear whether they intended the president to be the focal point of governmental leadership. Certainly, the bare grants of power in the Constitution do not—and probably could not—establish any such role. In the discussions of the office at the Convention, many different views and interpretations were offered, some of which clearly suggest the leadership role, some of which do not. Often these discussions seemed vague and inconclusive, a situation which probably played into the hands of those wishing to lay a potential foundation for the president as the principal national leader. The capacity of the office to assume the role soon became evident.

THE PRESIDENCY IN THE FIRST CENTURY

As anyone knows who has tried to memorize the names of the presidents of the United States, many are rather minor figures. Although the first seven are quite well known—George Washington, John Adams, Thomas Jefferson, James Madison, James Monroe, John Quincy Adams, and Andrew Jackson—many of the next sixteen are rather obscure. Among this group are William Harrison, John Tyler, Zachary Taylor, Millard Fillmore, Franklin Pierce, Rutherford B. Hayes, James Garfield, Chester Arthur, and Benjamin Harrison. Only Abraham Lincoln and, to a much lesser extent, James Polk stand out as truly dominant figures of their time.

With few exceptions, the presidency was not an office of political leadership during the nation's first century. There were many reasons for this, including the modest role of the federal government, the nation's limited responsibilities in foreign affairs, and the continuance of powerful doctrinal opposition to a strong presidency, first by some in the Democratic-Republican party and later by many in the Whig party. Nevertheless, the presidents who did offer strong leadership are instructive for illustrating some of the leadership capacities of the executive office that were not fully developed on a permanent institutional basis until the twentieth century. Although the "strong" early presidents did not create a powerful presidency by contemporary standards, it is fair to say that without the views and precedents they established, the American presidency could easily have withered and become merely a ceremonial office. Four administrations were especially significant in setting the stage for later development: those of Washington, Jefferson, Jackson, and Lincoln.

George Washington (1789–1797)

As the first occupant of the executive office, George Washington was keenly aware of the precedent his actions would hold for the future. The Constitution charted the bare outlines of the office; it was up to Washington to bring the office to life. For Washington that meant making clear from the beginning that the presidency was Constitutionally and politically independent from Congress, especially in the area of foreign affairs. An early episode served to emphasize this independence. In 1793, while France and England were at war, Washington issued a Proclamation of Neutrality, asserting that the existing treaty between France and the United States—the same treaty that had brought France to the aid of the Americans during the Revolutionary War—did not require American intervention on the side of France. In the absence of any subsequent declaration of war by Congress, Washington held, the United States would remain officially neutral. Such a policy declaration, which today seems fully within the president's power, was strongly assailed by many in Congress as an unconstitutional usurpation of Congress's authority to decide matters of war and peace. None of the specific grants of power in Article II, they contended, allowed the president to make foreign policy in this sense. Indeed, the Constitution does not contain a "power to conduct foreign relations" (Henkin, 1972:16). For Hamilton, however, who defended Washington's view, the "executive power" encompassed the power to conduct diplomacy; and authority over foreign policy therefore belonged to the president, "subject only to the exceptions and qualifications which are expressed" in the Constitution (Pious, 1979:51–52).

In the domestic sphere, where the presidency possesses less formal authority, Washington could have limited himself mainly to the faithful execution of congressional policy. Instead, through the vigorous leadership of Secretary of the Treasury Alexander Hamilton, and through frequent implementation of the Constitutional injunction to "recommend to [Congress] ... such measures as he shall judge necessary and expedient," Washington's administration took an active part in determining the nation's early economic and commercial policies. The success of the new government in establishing sound national credit and in fostering the nation's economic well-being demonstrated some of the virtues of presidential policy formulation. In the area of law enforcement, Washington was equally forceful when in 1794 he called for 12,000 members of the state militia to quell the so-called "Whiskey Rebellion" in western Pennsylvania, a resistance movement by farmers against a recently passed federal excise tax on whiskey. Washington actually accompanied the troops on part of their march, and the resistance dissolved.

Thomas Jefferson (1801–1809)

The growing strength and assertiveness of the executive office through Washington's two terms led to fears by some that the national government was moving toward a kind of monarchy. As a result, John Adams, Washington's successor, faced an increasingly assertive Congress. In 1800 Adams lost his bid for reelection to the man who led the "antimonarchist" forces: Thomas Jefferson.

To the surprise of many of his political opponents, Jefferson did not reduce the presidential office to a position of subordination to Congress. On the contrary, he exercised considerable leadership over Congress on most of the important issues of

When the Whiskey Rebellion threatened the federal government's ability to raise taxes, President George Washington put on his old general's uniform and joined the troops he had called up to disperse the protesters. *(James Peale / Culver Pictures)*

the time. But he did this not so much by the vigorous exercise of presidential power as through his leadership of the Democratic-Republican party, which controlled both houses of Congress. Trusted allies of Jefferson served in key positions in the House and Senate, and they were willing to follow his lead. Where Washington had given shape to the Constitutional dimensions of the office, Jefferson was the first to use the political party, an extra-Constitutional institution, to enhance the influence of the presidency.

Andrew Jackson (1829–1837)

Jefferson's close friend James Madison followed him into the presidency in 1809. Neither Madison nor his immediate successors, James Monroe and John Quincy Adams, were able to give the presidency the influence it had under Jefferson. None of these men had the stature of Jefferson within his party. Moreover, as the opposition Federalist party died out, the method of nominating Republican candidates by a caucus of party members in Congress added to Congress's strength; although there were other factors besides the congressional caucus that influenced the nominating decision, the logic of the congressional method of selection in a one-party era pointed directly to a situation in which Congress effectively chose the president, thereby invalidating one of the founders' main guarantees of presidential independence. Those who sought their party's nomination had to curry favor with members of Congress. In 1818, Judge Joseph Story of the Supreme Court wrote in a letter to a friend, "The Executive has no longer a commanding influence. The House of Representatives has absorbed all the popular feeling and all the effective power of the country" (Story, 1851:I, 311).

The election of Andrew Jackson to the presidency in 1828 reversed this decline of presidential power. A military hero of the War of 1812, Jackson was at the time of his election the most popular political figure in the country, especially in the fast-developing regions west of the Appalachians. By 1828 the extension of white manhood suffrage and the introduction of the popular election of presidential electors had effectively vested the selection of presidents in the hands of the people. And Jackson was the people's choice, as he often reminded his opponents.

Extending Jefferson's example, Jackson asserted a new basis of authority for the president. He was the first president to claim to be the special representative of the American people. Under the original design, the mode of presidential election was not by direct popular vote; and the presidency was not generally conceived in popular or democratic terms. The role of the president as spelled out in *The Federalist* was frequently that of restraining popular majorities and steadying the national administration. The president's authority rested on the powers of the office as granted or implied by the Constitution. Jackson saw a much more immediate connection between the people and the presidency. The president was elected by all the people and had a claim to being their representative equal to that of Congress. (Indeed, Jackson

proposed eliminating the electoral college mechanism and instituting a direct popular election.) Although Jackson began as a nonpartisan hero, he later joined with Martin Van Buren and connected the idea of the popularly elected president to the notion of the president as head of the majority party. By adding to the presidency the claim of being the public's truest representative, Jackson expanded on Jefferson's extra-Constitutional basis of presidential authority, freeing the presidency from some of the shackles of his predecessors and altering the character of the institution.

No power exercised by Jackson had greater consequences, or generated greater controversy, than the veto. The six presidents who preceded Jackson vetoed a total of nine bills. The prevailing understanding was that the veto was intended only for extraordinary circumstances, especially to guard against legislative encroachments, not to give the president a regular check on the policymaking process. Jackson rejected this view and legitimized the use of the veto on policy grounds, maintaining that he had a responsibility as the direct representative of the people to oppose legislative measures that were not in the public's interest. During his eight-year administration he vetoed eleven bills.

Under Jackson, more than under any president until Lincoln, the presidency became the focus of public attitudes and desires. Jackson's reinvigoration of the executive office was due to his high standing with the public and the political influence it generated. Unlike more recent presidents, however, Jackson did not use his power to promote new federal programs and thereby to expand the scope of the national authority. On the contrary, Jackson, as an heir of the Jeffersonian tradition, was fearful of an energetic national government and frequently used his power in a "negative" way, as with the vetoes, to limit the reach of the federal government. Yet, while favoring the concentration of power in the states, Jackson was *not* prepared to see the union itself endangered. In the nullification crisis in 1832, when South Carolina threatened to withdraw from the union if a tariff law was enforced, Jackson declared his willingness to use force to protect the union, thus demonstrating the power of the presidency to act on behalf of the nation against movements of internal dissolution.

The strong Jacksonian presidency, even if used

largely for denying the government power, pro-voked a great deal of opposition. The Whig party that emerged to challenge Jackson and the Democrats had as one of its central themes the limitation of presidential powers, especially as exercised by a popularly elected figure. Various Whigs sought legislation or amendments to limit the president's veto power, to establish a single term for the presidency, and to eliminate the president's discretion in dismissing executive officials. Above all, the Whigs subscribed to the view that the president was not the leader or initiator, but merely an executor carrying out duties explicitly assigned by the Constitution or the laws. Although no major Whig measures restricting the president's powers were enacted while the party lasted, the existence of such "antiexecutive" views throughout the period itself probably served as a check on presidential power. This check would continue in one form or another throughout the nineteenth century.

Abraham Lincoln (1861–1865)

When Abraham Lincoln assumed the presidency in March of 1861, he faced precisely the political crisis foreshadowed by the nullification controversy: the formal secession of southern states from the union. Between Lincoln's election in November of 1860 and his inauguration in March of 1861, seven southern states formally "seceded" from the union and established the Confederate States of America. When Lincoln assumed office, armed hostilities had not yet begun between the north and south. In his inaugural address, Lincoln tried to assure the southern states that he had no intention of interfering with slavery where it already existed, and he sought to persuade them that secession was both Constitutionally improper and politically unwise. In contrast, however, to his predecessor James Buchanan, who stated that "it is beyond the power of any President, no matter what may be his own political proclivities, to restore peace and harmony among the States," Lincoln declared his determination to defend the authority of the federal government (Hirschfield, 1973:66–67). He firmly stated, "I shall take care, as the Constitution itself expressly enjoins upon me, that the laws of the Union be faithfully executed in all the States." One month later Fort Sumter fell to Confederate forces,

four more states seceded, and full-scale hostilities began.

Congress during this time was not in session and was not due back until December. Lincoln issued a call for Congress to reconvene for a special session. But before Congress met, Lincoln initiated a variety of military measures. He called out 75,000 members of the militia, asked for volunteers to increase the size of the regular Army and Navy, instituted a blockade of southern ports, and authorized the selective suspension of the writ of habeas corpus, thereby allowing the arrest and detention of suspicious persons without having to show cause. Constitutional historians have long debated whether Lincoln possessed the authority to undertake these and other actions during the Civil War, including the issuance of the famous Emancipation Proclamation, "freeing" all the slaves living in areas still under Confederate control. (Slavery in the areas under union control was not formally ended until the passage of the Thirteenth Amendment in 1865.) Some Constitutional experts have gone so far as to label Lincoln's actions the equivalent of a military or "Constitutional dictatorship" (Pious, 1979:57).

Lincoln, who himself had once been a Whig, saw in this emergency situation a clear justification for unusual powers. He defended his vigorous exercise of the "war powers" on several grounds. First, he maintained that some of the powers were logical implications of the explicit language of the Constitution. Second, he argued that it was often necessary in the first instance for the president to act for the national government as a whole until Congress could examine the matter and prescribe future actions. Third, he referred to both the "take care" clause ("he shall take Care that the Laws be faithfully executed") and the presidential oath ("I do solemnly swear . . . that I . . . will to the best of my Ability, preserve, protect and defend the Constitution of the United States") as an indication that the president bears a special responsibility for the preservation of the nation. Finally, he held that occasional violations of specific laws or Constitutional provisions may be justified if necessary to preserve the Constitutional order as a whole: "Are all the laws *but one* to go unexecuted, and the Government itself go to pieces lest that one be violated?" (Richardson, 1896:VI, 25). Or, as he put it in a letter to a newspaper editor, "Often a limb must be amputated to save a life; but a life is never wisely given to save a limb. I felt that measures, otherwise unconstitutional, might become lawful by becoming indispensable to the preservation of the Constitution, through the preservation of the nation" (Hirschfield, 1973:80).

Lincoln's argument defending technically illegal actions under extraordinary circumstances is the doctrine of *executive prerogative*. Actually, the doctrine was first propounded nearly two centuries earlier by the political philosopher John Locke in his famous *Second Treatise*. Because the legislature is not always in session and cannot through its general laws foresee all future contingencies, "the good of the Society requires, that several things should be left to the discretion of him that has the Executive Power." Locke went on to argue that prerogative might enable the executive to act "for the public good, without the prescription of law, and sometimes even against it" (Locke, 1965:421–422). The people in such cases must make a judgment as to whether or not the assumption of such powers was justifiable and "for the public good." (President Nixon sought to justify on the same grounds certain illegal activities undertaken by a special unit established by the White House, but the public in this case was entirely unimpressed.) Lincoln showed that the language of the Constitution, while not explicitly granting a general prerogative power, could be used to infer such a power during a national crisis. This "power," as we shall see, has rested in a gray Constitutional area ever since.

Lincoln's assumption of extraordinary powers, though almost certainly justifiable, was an emergency measure. It established certain precedents for presidential power in time of war or emergency; but it did not add to the powers of the office in "normal" times, and it may even have helped provoke a reaction against the presidency. For some thirty years after the assassination of Lincoln, the presidency dropped to its historical nadir in power and prestige. Fearful that Andrew Johnson, Lincoln's successor, would establish his own Reconstruction policy, Congress passed laws over Johnson's veto to undermine the president's authority over the Cabinet and the Army. When, in violation of one of these laws, Johnson fired his secretary of

the Army, the House of Representatives impeached him and the Senate came within one vote of convicting and removing him from office. Although Johnson survived this attack on his authority, most members of the House and Senate continued to believe that the "authority of Congress is paramount" and acted accordingly. For most of the rest of the century Congress remained the supreme branch of the national government, reducing the presidency to little more than a mere administrative office.

THE RISE OF THE MODERN PRESIDENCY

Signs of revival of the presidential office could be glimpsed in the first administration of Grover Cleveland (1885–1889) and in the administration of William McKinley (1897–1901). McKinley, chosen in the realigning election of 1896 over his Democratic-Populist rival, William Jennings Bryan, came to power with solid majorities for the Republicans in both the Senate and the House. Through close cooperation with powerful members of Congress, McKinley, as leader of the governing party, was able to restore some of the effectiveness and influence to the executive office that had been lost during the post-Civil War period. Ironically, however, it was the assassination of McKinley in 1901 that marked the beginning of the modern presidency, for it ushered into the office a man of exceptional vigor and force of personality, Theodore Roosevelt.

Theodore Roosevelt (1901–1909)

By character and disposition, Roosevelt would never have been satisfied to serve as a "mere" administrator. He was one who loved—or needed—to take the initiative and to lead, whether it was in charging up hills in Cuba as a Rough Rider in the Spanish-American War or in sending the Navy around the world while president. Roosevelt was able to project an image of dynamism at just the time that more Americans were looking to the national government for the solution of problems and just the time that much of the press began systematic news coverage of Washington politics (Cornwell, 1965). Roosevelt touched the imagination of the American public and brought the presidency

Teddy Roosevelt, heroic colonel of the Rough Riders at San Juan Hill, brought the same hard-charging leadership and initiative to the White House as president. *(Culver Pictures)*

into the headlines of the daily news; and he did so quite consciously, realizing that a strong public image and the capacity to reach the public directly, something that all the late-nineteenth-century presidents lacked, could be powerful resources on behalf of the presidency.

The personal factor was one element in Roosevelt's strengthening of the presidency. He also acted, however, with a conscious view of the possibilities of the presidency as an institution. According to this view, the president should assume the role of a prime mover in the political system, not waiting to be told what to do, but initiating action when that seemed to be required by the public interest. Roosevelt completely rejected all Whig-like notions of a modest presidency. Instead of a president who would do only what the Constitution demanded and the laws required, Roosevelt em-

braced the concept of a president who was at liberty to act in the public interest, limited only by what the Constitution prevented or the laws forbade. He later expressed this theory in his autobiography.

> My view was that every executive officer . . . was a steward of the people bound actively and affirmatively to do all he could for the people, and not to content himself with the negative merit of keeping his talents undamaged in a napkin. . . . My belief was that it was not only [the president's] right but his duty to do anything that the needs of the nation demanded, unless such action was forbidden by the Constitution or by the laws. . . . I did not usurp power, but I did greatly broaden the use of executive power (Roosevelt, 1958:198–199).

Woodrow Wilson (1913–1921)

The strongest and most elaborate theoretical case for the modern, activist presidency was made by Woodrow Wilson well before he became president. Unlike any other president since the Civil War, Wilson was not only a political actor but also an accomplished scholar and theorist of the American political system. Wilson's views about the presidency are important not only because they influenced his subsequent behavior, but also because they constitute a theory about the role the office should play in American politics that has been largely accepted by later generations of Americans.

Wilson developed his theory from two simple propositions: (1) leadership is necessary in every successful political system, and (2) in the American system only the president is really capable of leading. Because the individual member of Congress is elected by only a small portion of the nation, no single representative or senator can truly claim to speak for the American people as a whole. But this is not true for the president.

> The nation as a whole has chosen him, and is conscious that it has no other political spokesman. His is the only national voice in affairs. Let him once win the admiration and confidence of the country, and no other single force can withstand him, no combination of forces will easily overpower him. His position takes the imagination of the country. He is the representative of no constituency, but of the whole peo-

ple. When he speaks in his true character, he speaks for no special interest. If he rightly interpret the national thought and boldly insist upon it, he is irresistible; and the country never feels the zest of action so much as when its President is of such insight and calibre. Its instinct is for unified action, and it craves a single leader (Wilson, 1961:68).

Although Wilson recognized that the presidency is a Constitutional office with powers and limitations set forth in writing, he argued that the Constitution must not be interpreted in a narrow, legalistic way. The Constitution did not actually intend presidential leadership, but it has allowed such leadership to evolve: "The President is at liberty, both in law and conscience, to be as big a man as he can." In the end it is not so much the document written in 1787 that determines the president's power and authority as it is the special relationship that the president can develop with the American people. If the people are on the president's side, then Congress will allow the president to set the direction and tempo of national politics.

During his eight years in office Wilson worked to make his theory of presidential leadership a reality. Breaking a 100-year-old precedent, he became the first president since John Adams to deliver his state of the union message in person before a joint session of Congress. Moreover, he took the lead in promoting important new legislation. Among his major achievements were the passage of the Federal Reserve Act, the Federal Trade Commission Act, and the Clayton Antitrust Act. At the beginning of American involvement in World War I he received vast delegations of authority from Congress to mobilize the nation's economy for the war effort. During the conflict he proved himself a forceful wartime leader.

It was after the war that Wilson met with his greatest failure. He proposed, as part of the peace treaty he negotiated, the establishment of a new League of Nations, an international body that would provide a forum for the peaceful resolution of international disputes. The Senate refused to ratify the treaty without certain amendments and reservations which Wilson judged unacceptable. In perfect conformity with his theory of presidential leadership, Wilson took his case directly to the people to stimulate public pressure on the Senate. In a three-week period, he delivered thirty-seven speeches in twenty-nine cities. A physical collapse cut short his tour and incapacitated him for the balance of his term. Wilson had written that the president "has no means of compelling Congress except through public opinion" (1961:71). His failure to turn the country around on the League of Nations demonstrated the practical limits to popular leadership.

Franklin D. Roosevelt (1933–1945)

Theodore Roosevelt and Woodrow Wilson had laid the foundations for the modern presidency; but the three presidents who followed Wilson—Warren G. Harding, Calvin Coolidge, and Herbert Hoover—declined to make it the focal point of leadership in quite the way that Roosevelt and Wilson had envisaged. Just as there had been a reaction to the concentration of "emergency" power in the presidency after the Lincoln administration, so too was there a swing away from the presidency following Wilson's wartime administration.

It was Theodore Roosevelt's fifth cousin, Franklin D. Roosevelt, who finally established the modern presidency as a permanent feature of American politics. He did so less by theorizing about it than by acting—and by so doing created a permanent change in public expectations. Elected to the office four times, by large majorities, Roosevelt maintained the confidence and support of the people for twelve years, guiding the nation through two of its greatest crises: the depression and the Second World War. During Roosevelt's tenure, several major changes were also made in the institutional arrangements of the office, with the creation of the White House staff and the expansion of some of the support agencies in the executive office (these are discussed later). When Roosevelt died in office in 1945, he left a presidency very different from the one he entered in his first inauguration in 1933. After Roosevelt, people expected "leadership" from the office, and the office was institutionally equipped to supply it.

Like Theodore Roosevelt and Woodrow Wilson, Franklin Roosevelt brought into office an activist view of the responsibilities of the presidency, especially when domestic crisis threatened public order. "I assume unhesitatingly," he announced in his inaugural address of March 4, 1933, "the leadership of this great army of the people, dedicated to a disciplined attack upon our common problems." He expressed the hope that the "normal balance of executive and legislative authority" could be preserved, but frankly admitted that in his view an "unprecedented demand and need for undelayed action may call for temporary departure from that normal balance." It was the presidency that the people looked to for leadership, and it was only the presidency that could provide it: "In their need [the people] have registered a mandate that they want direct, vigorous action. They have asked for discipline and direction under leadership. They have made me the present instrument of their wishes. In the spirit of the gift I take it" (Hirschfield, 1973:165).

Roosevelt wasted no time in making good on his promise. The day after he took office he called Congress into special session starting March 9. The famous "hundred days" session of Congress deferred to Roosevelt's leadership on virtually every important point. Between March 9 and June 16 Congress passed laws delegating the president broad discretionary authority over commercial transactions and creating the Civilian Conservation Corps, the Agricultural Adjustment Administration, the U.S. Employment Service, and the National Recovery Administration. Some of these laws were passed within a few short days after their introduction. Others took only a few weeks or months to move from presidential recommendation to law of the land. Through these and other enactments the national government assumed direct responsibility for alleviating the human suffering caused by the depression and for fostering economic recovery. At no other time in our history has Congress passed so much novel legislation so quickly, and the record remains impressive even though many key elements of the program were soon declared unconstitutional by the Supreme Court.

With the approach of war in Europe during his second term, Roosevelt's attention and energies shifted to international relations. Isolationist sentiment was so strong during the 1930s that Congress passed several laws prohibiting the selling of arms to belligerent nations. Roosevelt attempted to persuade the public, initially with only some success, that the interest and security of the United States were bound up with the interest and security

of France and Great Britain. After war broke out in Europe in 1939, Roosevelt continued with his efforts to help the Allies, though Congress rebuffed some of his proposals for direct assistance. In September of 1940, Roosevelt acted without legislative authorization to transfer to Great Britain, which was by then standing alone against the Axis powers, fifty old American destroyers in exchange for long-term leases of British naval bases in the Atlantic. The action seemed to violate both statute and Constitutional law, demonstrating again the willingness of "strong" presidents in extraordinary circumstances to "act for the . . . public good, without the prescription of law, and sometimes even against it." After the United States entered the war in 1941, Roosevelt exercised tremendous powers; in nearly all instances, however, he did so with clear delegation of authority from Congress. Roosevelt's determination and vigor in the Allied cause more than matched that of Wilson a generation before and demonstrated once again the indisputable necessity of presidential leadership during wartime.

Truman to Reagan: The Activist Presidency Accepted

Throughout American history, strong, activist presidents have usually provoked congressional efforts to reassert the authority of the legislative branch in American government. Congress has often been supported in these efforts by a public uncomfortable with prolonged presidential dominance. Many historians have likened this movement to that of a pendulum: the center of gravity within the governmental system swings from periods of presidential preeminence to those of weak presidents and a dominant Congress. For the most part, in fact, the pendulum has rested more often nearer to the Congress than to the president.

After Roosevelt's death in 1945, the same historical pattern reemerged. Congress acted in several ways to reduce the power of the presidency. Shortly after the Second World War ended, Congress created two new advisory groups in the executive branch, the National Security Council and the Council of Economic Advisers. The hope of many in Congress was that these groups would reduce presidential discretion in national security and economic affairs by formalizing the decision-making process. No law, however, can force the president to take advice from any individual or group; and in practice, as we shall see, presidents have either ignored these councils or transformed them into resources *for* the presidency. In the 1950s, Congress also made several unsuccessful attempts to initiate Constitutional amendments restricting the president's power to enter into executive agreements with foreign nations. Finally, in the most significant attack on the Roosevelt legacy, Congress initiated action on the Twenty-Second Amendment, which limited the president to two terms.

In retrospect, however, these actions by Congress pale in comparison with those taken in earlier episodes of congressional reassertion. Nothing done by the post-World War II Congress, for example, comes close to matching the blatant encroachments of the post-Civil War Congress on the Constitutional powers of the president. Not only was Congress's reaction to the Rooseveltian presidency relatively mild by historical standards, but the broader American public demonstrated little desire to shackle the presidency. On the contrary, Roosevelt's twelve years at the "vital center of action" of the governmental system had a lasting effect in raising public expectations about the presidency and in fostering the belief that presidential leadership was an essentially beneficent force in American politics.

Under Roosevelt's immediate successors, Harry Truman and Dwight Eisenhower, the presidency retained its central importance in the American political system. Although neither of these men exercised the dynamic leadership of FDR, they presided over a growing presidential establishment that supervised a huge federal bureaucracy, fashioned and promoted wide-ranging legislative programs, and directed the increasingly complex foreign relations of the United States. Eisenhower's presidency was especially important, since under Franklin Roosevelt the expanding power of the presidency had become a partisan issue. Liberal Democrats tended to defend a powerful presidency for its contribution to governmental efficiency, policy coherence, and social justice. Conservative Republicans, on the other hand, saw it as the engine of a growing governmental machine and ultimately

as a threat to liberty. Eisenhower, departing from these partisan predispositions, preserved the enhanced stature and importance of the executive office and refused to defer to Congress on important national policy issues, thereby solidifying the power of the office across partisan lines. Although somewhat less of an activist than the Democratic presidents who preceded and followed him, Eisenhower played a much larger role than the three Republican presidents who served between Wilson and Roosevelt.

The "partisan" dispute over the modern presidency was ended, if not by Eisenhower, then certainly by Richard Nixon. Following the two self-proclaimed activist presidencies of the Democrats John Kennedy and Lyndon Johnson, President Nixon left no doubt that he as a Republican embraced the Wilsonian idea: "The days of a passive Presidency belong to a simpler past. . . . The next President must take an activist view of his office. He must articulate the nation's values, define its goals, and marshall its will" (Hirschfield, 1973:165).

In the aftermath of Vietnam, Watergate, and President Nixon's resignation in 1974 under the threat of an almost certain impeachment and conviction, the pendulum again swung against the presidency. Congress passed legislation in the 1970s of nearly Constitutional status defining and delimiting the president's role in the conduct of war and in the impoundment of public monies. In addition, Congress became far more assertive of its role in foreign policymaking and in the formulation of the budget. These changes, discussed in Chapter 11, were more significant in curbing the president's power than the measures enacted after World War II were. Yet, while partially redefining the presidency, they did not remove it from the role of leadership. Presidents Ford and Carter each asserted a strong presidency, although in more subdued terms than their predecessors. By the time of President Reagan's inauguration in 1981, the presidency again was at the "vital center of action." Some were comparing Reagan's activism in his first year to that of President Roosevelt. Though such comparisons are of little value, it is at least worth remarking that both an avowed liberal president (Franklin Roosevelt) and an avowed conservative president (Ronald Reagan) were perceived to be acting according to the same theory of the presidency.

Explaining the Rise of the Modern Presidency

The reactions to the modern presidency in the 1970s demonstrate that the pendulum continues to sweep back and forth between our two national political institutions. Nonetheless, the short-term variations have occurred within the context of a historical movement toward a more powerful presidency. The oscillations continue, but the entire pendulum has shifted toward the executive branch. What explains this historical dynamic? Why is presidential leadership now the rule rather than the exception? Along with the changing doctrines about the presidency, three historical developments have been particularly significant in accounting for the growth of presidential power: the increasing importance of international relations to the nation's well-being, the growth of the social welfare state, and the development of mass communications technologies.

The Importance of International Relations For most of the nineteenth century, American foreign policy embraced the principles of neutrality. Americans looked upon the 3,000 miles that separated the new world from the old as a natural buffer against attacks or interference from powerful foreign nations. Events in the twentieth century, especially the Second World War, completely changed America's relationship to the rest of the world. The United States emerged from the war as a world power, virtually compelled by circumstances to assume an active and ongoing role in world affairs with alliances around the globe.

As foreign policy has become more important to the overall task of governing the nation, the presidency has inevitably become more influential. The executive branch is the driving force in foreign affairs by Constitutional design, by tradition, and by the nature of the duties to be performed. Although power here has also ebbed and flowed, the presidency began with—and has always maintained—a much greater share of power in foreign affairs. Only the president can act with the speed, decisiveness, and secrecy often needed in conducting foreign affairs; and only the president has complete access on a regular basis to the varied sources of pertinent and often highly sensitive information conveyed by the foreign service, the armed forces, and the intelligence agencies.

The Growth of the Social Welfare State One of the distinguishing features of national policy in the twentieth century is the growing responsibility of the federal government for guaranteeing a minimum level of social welfare for all its citizens. Examples include laws setting a minimum wage; protecting the right of workers to bargain collectively; providing various kinds of assistance to the unemployed, the poor, the disabled, and the elderly; regulating safety in the workplace; and controlling environmental pollution. Although laws of this sort are a sign of the expanded reach of congressionally passed legislation, they have also increased presidential power in two distinct ways.

One is through the enhanced importance of presidential policy formulation. The growing reach of national policy has been matched by its growing complexity, which has increased the planning burden of the government. Because of its hierarchical structure, ready access to a mass of information, and responsibility for the well-being of the whole nation, the executive branch has become the chief policy planner, or "agenda setter," in the national government. Although the president has always had the Constitutional responsibility to recommend measures to Congress, it is only in the twentieth century that Congress has positively encouraged the president—sometimes through legislative mandate—to set the agenda for congressional deliberations. For example, in the Budget and Accounting Act of 1921, Congress imposed on the president the responsibility of preparing and sending to Congress each year a comprehensive national budget proposal. In 1946, Congress passed the Employment Act, which mandated that the president regularly formulate proposals designed to foster a healthy economy. Subsequent laws have imposed similar responsibilities on the president in other policy areas. In none of these cases was Congress forced to act as it did. Its delegation of the planning function to the president reflected its recognition that on many of the matters with which it deals the presidency is better-suited for analyzing complex issues and fashioning appropriate responses.

The other way in which the growth of the welfare state has increased presidential power relates to the execution of laws after they are passed. The same complexity that makes the president the "agenda setter" also leads Congress to vest in the executive branch substantial flexibility and discretion in determining precisely how to carry out the laws. This often takes the form of a departmental secretary issuing rules or regulations specifying grant levels, contract requirements, eligibility criteria, and the like. Usually these executive branch decisions have the full force of law. For all practical purposes, they constitute the policy of the federal government as much as the original congressional statutes. In addition to these formal rules and regulations, the executive branch also effectively makes policy whenever it interprets an ambiguous phrase or expression in a law one way rather than another. Congress delegates discretionary decisions to the administration both because Congress cannot foresee all the subtle issues that will arise in carrying out a program and because Congress may wish to avoid the political difficulties that come from making final decisions on some controversial issues.

Not all power shifted from Congress to the bureaucracy, however, is given to the president. The reality of American politics is that many matters within the executive branch are not fully (or easily) at the disposal of the president. One of the illusions of a superficial study of the modern presidency, fostered by simplistic analysis of organizational charts, is that the president "runs" the entire executive branch. Given the nature of large bureaucratic agencies, such presidential control would be impossible even if the president were the acting head of the government in the same sense as presidents of large business corporations are the heads of their firms; in fact, as we shall see, the entire structure of American government militates against any such control by the president.

The Development of Mass Communication
The growth in the importance of foreign affairs and the rise of the welfare state have increased the president's power within the governmental system. It is the development of radio and television communications, however, that has brought the presidency to the center of attention of the broader national community. Theodore Roosevelt, as we have seen, first made the president the center of attention by the press, while Franklin Roosevelt first made extensive use of the radio in his famous "fireside chats" to communicate directly with the American people. The perfection of television technology has given subsequent presidents even greater opportunities to reach the people through formal addresses on subjects of immediate national concern and through live, televised press conferences, which began during the Kennedy administration. Moreover, the network news programs cover the day-to-day activities of presidents, including speeches delivered to special audiences.

Radio and television have given the presidency a clear public relations advantage over the Congress. Because Congress is a large institution with a highly decentralized power structure and decision-making process, it is difficult for the broadcast media to cover its actions. And it is difficult for Congress with its many voices to use radio and television to communicate with the American people. In any struggle between the presidency and Congress conducted in the public arena, the legislative branch is at a decided disadvantage. This is not to say that the president always wins a struggle for the support of the people—our recent history frequently proves the opposite—but only to point out that the president will speak in a clearer voice than the members of Congress. The modern presidency is above all a visible presidency.

The modern media, however, are far from always being a help to the president. Although their technical capacities allow the president to address the people through televised speeches and press conferences, the primary way in which presidents reach the American people—and are perceived by them—is through the news. The press covers the president's every move, emphasizing information that presidents would rather see ignored, such as the presence of conflicts within the administration. In addition, presidential actions and decisions are interpreted by the press according to its own standards of what is newsworthy; these standards, of course, are quite different from those of the president's liking—and for that matter quite different from standards by which such information is processed among knowledgeable politicians. The relationship between presidents and the press tends

Franklin Roosevelt made masterful use of the newly developed electronic medium, appealing directly to the voters in their living rooms with his "fireside chats" on network radio. *(Brown Brothers)*

therefore to be one characterized by tension on both sides, mitigated usually by the common understanding that each in some sense needs the other.

THE POWERS AND POWER OF THE PRESIDENCY

The president's formal powers derive in the first instance from the Constitution. These powers, as they are understood today, depend not only on the plain meaning of the words of the Constitution but also on precedents on how these words have been interpreted by former presidents and by the Supreme Court. A second source of presidential pow-

ers derives from statutory law, in which Congress grants discretion to the president to make certain decisions, such as the power to impose wage and price controls or to set levels of farm price supports. Because such powers are based on statutes, they may be revoked by law or, if they are granted temporarily, simply allowed to expire. Congress may also pass laws designed to clarify a Constitutional power, as in the case of the War Powers Act of 1973.

The president's Constitutional powers, contained mostly in Article II, read initially like an odd mixture of the (seemingly) insignificant, the meaningful, and the general or vague. In the first group might be placed the power to require the opinion of executive officers, the power (or obligation) to give Congress state of the union information and make recommendations, and the power to receive ambassadors; in the second group would be the veto power, the role as commander in chief, the nomination and appointment power, the power to negotiate treaties, and the pardoning power; and in the final (general) group might be placed the "executive power clause" and the "take care" clause.

The Lesser Powers

The (seemingly) insignificant powers, on further reflection, turn out to be not quite as unimportant as they appear. The Constitution in these instances seems to be sketching in law a picture of the *position* of the president in the political system and giving that position Constitutional sanction. The powers to make recommendations to Congress and to give information on the state of the union, for example, suggest a president who has every right to be an active participant and initiator in the legislative process. The power to require opinions of executive officers leaves no doubt that the president is the head of the executive branch, free of any possible constraints from a council or Cabinet. And finally, the power to receive ambassadors, while not without significance in its own right, clearly establishes the president as the "head of state" in international affairs. Together with the treaty power and the "executive power" clause, this last provision makes the president the chief diplomat of the United States and, now with the backing of federal law, the only one able to carry out or authorize diplomatic negotiations.

The Major Specific Grants of Power

Of the president's important specific grants of power, two of the most significant (the role of commander in chief and the power to negotiate treaties) fall mainly into the areas of foreign affairs and national security, as does the president's more controversial implied power to commit the nation to war. These powers will be discussed in later chapters. Of the remaining powers, one is at least partly legislative: the veto. As we have seen, before Andrew Jackson, many considered the use of the veto illegitimate for anything other than a president's

view of what the Constitution required. Subsequently, the veto has been used as a policy instrument, giving the president a formidable weapon to stop any legislative initiative (unless the veto is overridden by two-thirds of the members of both Houses). Some presidents have not been shy about using this weapon. In his first term (1885–1889) Grover Cleveland vetoed (including pocket vetoes) 414 bills, the record for any single term. Only two were overridden. Franklin Roosevelt collected 631 vetoes during his tenure to lead the list of most vetoes by any president. In recent times the veto has not been used all that frequently. From 1961 to 1980, presidents vetoed about 2 percent of all bills presented to them, although many of these involved some of the most important issues facing the nation. Less than 12 percent were overridden.

The appointment power gives the president the authority to name, subject to the approval of the Senate, all Supreme Court justices, ambassadors, federal judges, Cabinet members, and, by law, non-civil service officials.* In the last group now are some 2,700 persons who serve in sub-Cabinet-level positions and on various agencies and boards. These people, along with the Cabinet members, help supervise the nearly 3 million federal civil servants. Presidents use their power to appoint executive branch officials not only to help manage the government by placing their own people at high levels in the bureaucracy, but also to fulfill the demands of patronage and to reward those who have given faithful party service.

Curiously, the Constitution does not say whether presidents may remove those whom they have appointed to positions in the executive branch. (Congress, of course, may impeach any executive official.) By extension of the appointment power, presidents have claimed the power to dismiss officials, and this power was finally recognized by the Supreme Court in the case of *Meyers v. United States* (1927). This power is limited only in the instance of appointments to independent regulatory commissions, a restriction decided by the Court in the case of *Humphrey's Executor v. United States* (1935).

The power to pardon comes closest to being a

*The process of judicial appointments will be discussed in Chapter 12.

prerogative-type power explicitly endorsed in the Constitution. It gives the president the authority to set aside, at discretion, the "normal" process of the law. Mercy may be one reason, but *The Federalist* makes clear that the primary justification for this power is to enable presidents to act for reasons of state—that is, to serve some general political good or security objective. The most famous recent use of the pardoning power was by President Ford in 1974, when he pardoned former President Nixon from any possible crimes relating to his conduct while president. President Ford contended that pardoning Nixon was essential in order to end the continuing trauma of Watergate and allow the nation to move on to consideration of important new issues.

The General Grants of Power

The Constitution, as already noted, vests the "executive power" in the president, and it further gives the president the power or obligation to "take care that the Laws be faithfully executed." Read in very broad terms, these words may give the president truly formidable power. The "take care" clause enables the president to employ the means necessary, including the use of armed force, to ensure compliance, as presidents have done on numerous occasions. The executive power clause may give the president the powers to do all that one may consider to be an inherently executive task, including assuming a broad prerogative in time of emergency.

Presidents, as we have seen, have either claimed the power they feel they need to meet a situation or else threatened Congress that they would claim such power if Congress did not delegate it. Although the Court on several occasions has given very broad interpretations of the president's power, it has never gone so far as to recognize any inherent power of prerogative. Sometimes it has issued presidents legal rebukes, but generally well *after* the president has taken his action and achieved his purpose. In one important case, however, the Court clearly rejected any broad grant of authority. In the steel seizure case, the Court directly rebuffed President Truman's claim to seize and operate the nation's steel mills to avert a strike during the Korean war (*Youngstown Sheet and Tube v. Sawyer*,

1951). Truman had cited as the basis of his power the "authority vested in me by the Constitution and laws of the United States." Truman in this instance backed down. In the final analysis, however, the limits of presidential authority in such matters may be determined less by legal reasoning than by the character of the particular circumstances that the nation faces.

The Power of the President

Having considered all the specific powers of the presidency, we may fairly say that while they are significant, they do not seem to add up to the formidable role of the president in our political system. It seems, in other words, that the power of the president is *more* than the sum of these powers. The president's power derives in part from the position as one individual able to command all the separate powers; as one individual elected by the entire nation; and nowadays, as one individual looked to as and expected to be the nation's political leader.

If, however, the power of the presidency somehow is greater than the sum of its formal powers, it falls far short of what is needed to meet the expectations that most have for the office. Here, in fact, we arrive at the central paradox of the modern presidency: it has clearly become a more powerful office, but relative to the expectations it has set for itself, it is woefully lacking in formal authority. Today, presidents are judged poorly if their legislative programs are not enacted; yet under the Constitution it is Congress and not the president that possesses the decisive legislative powers. Similarly, many hold a president responsible for the performance of the economy; again, however, much of the power to manage the economy (insofar as government can do so), lies with Congress, with the partially independent Federal Reserve System, and with the (partly) independent regulatory agencies. Even in foreign affairs, the president cannot conclude a treaty without the concurrence of the Senate or commit any funds without the passage of a law.

The existence of a gap between what is expected of presidents and what they are formally empowered to do is central to understanding the modern presidency. For many of the things presidents are expected to accomplish, they cannot rely on automatic powers of command. Consequently, we find that presidents are frequently in the situation of having to use their unique position in the American system (backed of course by their formal powers) to *persuade* (Neustadt, 1980). They must persuade rather than command because they need the assistance of others who are partly independent and who are capable of resisting them. Because a president's success in accomplishing many important tasks rests on the capacity to persuade rather than the right to command, we find that any president's effective power in Washington mysteriously changes from year to year and even from month to month. The capacity of presidents to persuade *varies* with certain factors not completely under their control, such as their standing with the public or with Congress. As perceptions of presidents' future political strength vary, so does their effective power to accomplish what they want. At one moment a president may seem invincible; at another, vulnerable.

The paradoxical character of the modern presidency has created two very different perceptions of its powers. Viewed from the inside, the powers usually seem inadequate; the president lacks the authority to do all that is expected of the presidency. Viewed from the outside, the concentration of power in the presidency appears formidable, perhaps even dangerous. From the inside view, it might seem that the problem should be resolved by giving the president more power, but this approach might solve the president's difficulties only at the cost of creating a much more dangerous problem for the entire political system. The alternative is to leave the office as it is: perilously close to being too strong for the system as a whole, but not strong enough to accomplish all its own missions. This might seem to put all presidents in an essentially tragic position, yet this has not deterred very many major politicians from seeking the office.

THE INSTITUTION OF THE PRESIDENCY

The modern presidency is more than just the president. The institutionalized presidency includes thousands of individuals who serve under the presidents and act in their name. Scholars divide the executive branch into four categories according to

their proximity to the president and their function in the operation of the government. As shown in Figure 13-3 (see Chapter 13), these categories are the White House staff, the Executive Office of the President, the Cabinet, and the departments and agencies of the government.

The large growth of the White House staff and Executive Office of the President in recent decades has brought to light serious questions about the operation of the presidency: Are the presidents truly capable of overseeing and controlling the actions of those who act on their behalf? Is too much political power being wielded by presidential appointees who are unaccountable to Congress and the American people? Are the authority and morale of the departments and agencies of the executive branch being undermined by the centralization of decision making in the White House? Does the presidential staff apparatus do a good job of communicating different ideas to the presidents, or does it insulate them from discordant views? To address these concerns we first have to know what kinds of people serve in the institutionalized presidency and what these people do.

The White House Staff

As recently as the beginning of this century only a handful of people served as personal aides to the president. The executive branch consisted mainly of the president, the Cabinet members, and the employees who served under the Cabinet officers in the agencies of the government. During Franklin Roosevelt's administration, it became clear—in the words of the Brownlow Committee, which studied the organization of the presidency—that the "President needs help" (Kallenbach, 1966:441). This heralded the formation of the modern White House staff, which numbers today (depending on whom one counts) over 500 people. As originally conceived, the major staff members would provide the president with advice from a presidential perspective—that is, advice not bound by the particular interests of the departments—and help to see that the president's decisions were carried out. The staff would serve as the president's "eyes and ears," being directly responsible to the president and appointed without the need of Senate confirmation.

Today, a few high-level advisers, known usually

as the "senior staff," meet with the president regularly to help in planning strategy and making decisions. President Reagan was assisted by the "troika" of James Baker, Edwin Meese, and Michael Deaver. Usually such highly placed individuals are longtime associates of the president in whose loyalty and discretion the president can have complete confidence. It is this trust the president places in them, along with their direct access to the Oval Office, that makes these officials among the most powerful figures in government.

Below this small group are another 150 or so professional aides, usually anonymous to the public, who assist the top advisers or otherwise serve the daily needs of the president. Their tasks include arranging appointments, drafting speeches, handling relations with the press and Congress, and maintaining contacts with outside groups. The balance of the White House staff are clerical and lower-level administrators who serve under the professional staff and perform such additional functions as answering the enormous volume of mail that the White House receives.

In recent years many have expressed the concern that the growth of the White House staff has been detrimental to the presidency. Attention has focused particularly on the power of the president's senior aides, who, it is charged, often make decisions that should properly be made in the regular departments and agencies of the government. Critics maintain that this practice both undermines morale in the departments and raises serious issues of political accountability since presidential aides, unlike department heads, are not answerable to Congress. During President Nixon's first term, for example, the president's chief aide in formulating and implementing policy was the national security adviser, Henry Kissinger, and not the secretary of state, William Rogers. The effect of this arrangement was to leave officials in the State Department unaware of some of the president's policies and to prevent Congress from being able to obtain information from the president's main foreign policy-making adviser. In both the Johnson and the Nixon administrations, many argue, the presidents were trying to run the government from the White House, ignoring or avoiding the permanent executive establishment (Greenstein, 1978).

Another important criticism leveled against the presidential staff organization is that it creates a "palace guard" around presidents, drastically limiting access to them and denying them the benefit of diverse opinions. Some argue that because high-level staff members have usually shared the president's basic policy views, they have tended to reinforce his original dispositions; and that because they have wished to retain the president's high regard, they have tended to tell him what he *wants* to hear. The staff members, in the view of a former aide to President Johnson, are "courtiers," who build a powerful barrier to "presidential access to reality" (Reedy, 1970:99).

Most "insider" accounts of the White House, however, describe a decision-making process that is

---

BOX 10-4

THE WHITE HOUSE STAFF

Henry Kissinger, national security adviser to President Richard Nixon from 1969 to 1973, describes the mentality of the Nixon White House staff:

> I had a better sense than almost anyone of the environment out of which—nearly imperceptibly—had grown the cancer of Watergate. The White House is both a goldfish bowl and an isolation ward; the fish swim in a vessel whose walls are opaque one way. They can be observed if not necessarily understood; they themselves see nothing. Cut off from the outside world, the inhabitants of the White House live by the rules of their internal coexistence or by imagining what the outside world is like. This in the Nixon White House became increasingly at variance with reality until suddenly the incommensurability between the two worlds grew intolerable; the bowl burst and its inhabitants found themselves gasping in a hostile atmosphere (Kissinger, 1982:98).

much more open to opposing opinions. Harry McPherson, another aide to Johnson, maintained that while the "danger of bias" was always present, Johnson's advisers generally "tried to give him both sides" (1972:292). Former Nixon aide William Safire relates that "Nixon told Haldeman, and Kissinger as well, that he wanted to see all the alternatives and the likely consequences of each" (1977:356). Although one may imagine that presidents, like most individuals, enjoy having their opinions confirmed by others, they also have an interest in being made aware of all the consequences of their decisions. They are the ones who will suffer the political consequences of unwise actions. Advisers may bias their recommendations one way or another, but, as McPherson notes, "Presidents are not helpless in such matters; any man who attains the office may be presumed to be familiar . . . with the tendency of staff men to shape what they tell him in accordance with their opinions" (1972:292).

A half century after its inception, the White House staff has become a permanent institutional appendage of the modern presidency. Although it has helped the president in many ways, its operation has resulted in certain unintended consequences. Paradoxically, a staff that came into being to help coordinate the bureaucracy has in some measure itself become bureaucratic and unmanageable, and the tensions it has created by interfering with Cabinet officials have sometimes added to the difficulties of governing. In addition, the White House staff, while it provides the president with personal advice to help unify the administration, also becomes a source of competing tensions within the White House. These conflicts often leak to the press and give an appearance of division and disarray. Like so many institutions, the White House staff has become in reality a mixed blessing; it may be absolutely necessary, but it is not always helpful.

The Executive Office of the President

President Roosevelt formally created the Executive Office of the President in 1939 under the authority that Congress granted him. Not including the White House staff, it now consists of approximately 1,700 people divided among several dozen distinct agencies, the most important of which are discussed below.

Office of Management and Budget   The Office of Management and Budget (OMB) began as the Bureau of the Budget in 1921. Congress created it as a staff agency to assist presidents in carrying out their new responsibility to formulate and present to Congress each year a coherent national budget proposal. Originally located in the Department of the Treasury, it was moved to the new Executive Office of the President in 1939. In 1970, Richard Nixon renamed it to reflect its broadened responsibilities for the general management of the executive branch. With over 500 employees it is now the largest single agency in the Executive Office.

In the preparation of the administration's budget proposal, the OMB serves as the voice of the president in dealing with the departments and agencies of the executive branch. Its purpose is to translate the priorities of the president into the hundreds of detailed requests that constitute the national budget. Its power derives from its ability to say no to the departments, to refuse to approve new spending plans when they are inconsistent with broader budget realities. This power extends not only to the preparation of the budget but also to the submission of substantive legislative proposals to Congress. Through the process of *central legislative clearance* the OMB examines any legislative proposal requested by an executive department or agency before it is submitted to Congress. Only if the proposal receives some kind of endorsement from the OMB may it be officially sent up to Capitol Hill (although some bureaucrats may take the risk of going around the OMB through informal contacts with members of Congress).

Council of Economic Advisers   In the Employment Act of 1946 Congress for the first time officially recognized the responsibility of the national government to foster and maintain a healthy economy. The act required the president in particular to oversee the nation's economy and to make proposals to Congress that would "promote employment, production, and purchasing power." To assist the president in devising economic programs, Congress created an advisory group of professional economists and staff aides. The purpose of the Council of Economic Advisers (CEA) was to translate its expertise on economic matters into practical advice in an area where the president may have little or no specialized training.

Economics is not, however, an exact science. Economists often disagree among themselves about the kinds of policies that will best promote a healthy economy. Presidents tend to select as members of the CEA those whose recommendations are likely to fit well with their own political and economic perspectives. The council, however, is no mere rubber stamp, but plays an active role in advising presidents and charting their economic programs. This is not to say that presidents always follow the advice of the CEA. The president has other economic advisers in the secretary of the treasury and the director of the OMB. Whether the CEA is the center of economic planning in the national government (as it was in the Kennedy administration) or just another advisory agency (as with the Carter and Reagan administrations) depends on the wishes of the president.

National Security Council Like the CEA, the National Security Council (NSC) was created by Congress in the aftermath of the Second World War (1947). It includes among its members, as defined by statute, some of the highest-level executive branch officials with responsibility for national security issues, including the president, the secretaries of state and defense, the director of the CIA, and the chair of the Joint Chiefs of Staff. It is headed by a national security adviser and has a staff of its own, sometimes called the "little State Department in the White House."

The NSC's functions include giving presidents advice in this important policy area and enhancing coordination among the many actors who play a role in national security decision making. Interestingly, when the council was created, many in Congress, dubious of President Truman's abilities, supported it in order to *reduce* presidential flexibility and discretion in this highly sensitive area. It was thought that by formalizing the decision-making process through a new institutional structure, the president's discretion would be reduced.

In fact, the NSC has had no such effect, indicating that the discretion of presidents cannot be limited by attempts to control the decision-making apparatus under their own Constitutional power. President Truman, who opposed the NCS's creation in the first place, virtually ignored it. President Eisenhower met with the council regularly to seek advice, yet never let it constrain him, often using the NSC to legitimize his own decisions. Since the Kennedy administration, presidents have relied only intermittently on the NSC, preferring to establish senior advisory groups of their own choosing. At the same time, presidents have used the national security adviser and staff as a source of information independent of the bureaucracy and in some instances have relied on them to formulate and implement foreign policy. This system of decision making was most fully utilized by President Nixon (with NSC adviser Henry Kissinger) and President Carter (with NSC adviser Zbigniew Brzezinski).

Domestic Policy Staff Following the original model for the NSC, Richard Nixon created the Domestic Council in 1970 to "formulate and coordinate domestic policy recommendations to the President." Officially, it included the secretaries of the ten executive departments that deal with domestic policy matters—a kind of domestic Cabinet. In fact, this group rarely met. Instead, the Domestic Council functioned as a staff organization under the direction of the presidential adviser John Erlichman (much as the NSC did under Kissinger).

When Jimmy Carter became president, he disbanded the formal organization of the Domestic Council and replaced it with a Domestic Policy Staff, headed by his assistant for domestic affairs, Stuart Eizenstat. Although the Carter administration had only modest success in getting its proposals through Congress, the Domestic Policy Staff was praised by many observers for its thoroughness and its ability to resolve conflicts between the White House and some of the agencies. Under the Reagan administration, which has placed its emphasis on cutting domestic programs, much less power has been given to the Domestic Policy Staff.

The Cabinet

The history of the president's Cabinet is largely one of disuse. The Constitution does not provide specif-

Cabinet meetings give a reassuring picture of the president consulting with top advisors, but most modern presidents have found the image more useful than the meetings.
(David Burnett / *Contact*)

ically for a Cabinet, and while the term was probably used as early as 1793, it was never mentioned in an official statute until 1907 (Cronin, 1980:254). As a formal institution, the Cabinet includes the head of each of the executive departments and several other officers of the government, such as the ambassador to the United Nations, who are given Cabinet rank by the president. Since the Cabinet as an organization has no Constitutional status—the framers expressly rejected the idea of an executive council—its role within the executive branch depends on the president. Most recent presidents have begun their terms by expressing high hopes for regenerating the influence of the Cabinet in executive branch decision making; but with the possible exception of Eisenhower, they have concluded that Cabinet meetings are not a useful forum for conducting the business of government.

There are several reasons why this is the case. First, because each department secretary is highly jealous of his or her jurisdiction, an implicit understanding is usually reached between them to refrain from trying to influence administrative policy in each other's areas. As a result, useful proposals or ideas often remain unexpressed. Second, the departments deal with such a variety of issues and policies that it is a waste of time for experts in one field (transportation, for example) to sit through a long discussion on a completely unrelated subject (foreign policy, for example). As President Kennedy once remarked, "Cabinet meetings are simply useless: why should the Postmaster [formerly a member of the Cabinet] sit there and listen to the problem of Laos?" (Pious, 1979:241). Finally, presidents have discovered that the advice they receive in Cabinet meetings is very much colored by each secretary's desire to promote the programs and interests served by his or her department. Cabinet members often "go native," making them, in the words of one presidential adviser, "natural enemies of the president" (Cornwell, 1965:180–181).

An interesting innovation in the use of the Cabinet has been President Reagan's creation of several Cabinet councils, forming, in effect, subcommittees of the Cabinet. By addressing particular areas of public policy rather than the entire range of issues that face modern governments, each council brings together the half dozen or so department heads and other high-ranking executive branch officials who have the most direct responsibility for the issue involved. Cabinet council meetings are therefore smaller and more focused than the sessions of the full Cabinet, although the new structure does not solve the perennial problem of parochialism.

It might be wondered, then, why presidents call full Cabinet meetings at all. The answer probably has much to do with public relations. Americans like to think of the Cabinet as a group of experienced and dedicated public servants whose collective wisdom will be an invaluable asset to the single individual who shoulders the immense burdens of the modern presidency. Regular Cabinet meetings foster the notion that the president is running a truly "open" administration, seeking the best possible advice from a variety of sources before acting.

The Executive Branch

Beyond the White House staff and the Executive Office of the President lies the executive branch, tied to the president by the Cabinet heads and the limited number of upper-echelon department and agency officials whom the president appoints. The executive branch consists of thirteen departments and some sixty other agencies.

One of the most difficult distinctions for those outside Washington to appreciate is that between the president (along with staff and support systems) and the executive branch. In "official" administrative theory proclaimed by various commissions that have studied the presidency, the president is the "head" of the executive branch. But the day-to-day politics of Washington makes this title in some cases more nominal than real. It is true that when presidents choose to, they can usually exert their authority. But resources of time, energy, and political will are limited. All recent presidents have expressed a frustration at moving the government similar to that voiced by Harry

Truman: "I thought I was the President, but when it comes to the bureaucracies, I can't make them do a damn thing" (MacKenzie, 1980).

The executive agencies, though "beneath" the president, must also consider the wishes of Congress, which writes the laws that create the bureaus and which decides the budget. And the government workers in the agencies are civil servants, not appointed by the president. The complex relations between the agencies, the president, and Congress will be discussed in Chapter 13.

In the final analysis, the presidency remains highly personalized. Although presidents rely on the advice and require the services of the institutional presidency, they are hardly its captives. Neither the White House staff, the Executive Office of the President, nor the Cabinet has, in any significant way, restricted presidential discretion.

If the personalized nature of the presidential office means that the nation may suffer the consequences of one person's shortsightedness, miscalculations, errors of judgment, rashness, pettiness, or even criminality, it also means that the office retains the capacity for speed, decisiveness, energy, and accountability intended for it by its creators—capacities for which there may be an even greater need now than there was two centuries ago. An equally important consequence of unity, if less central to the original design, is the capacity of the office for popular leadership.

THE VICE PRESIDENT

Besides the president, the vice president is the only other nationally elected official in the American political system. Until quite recently, this has perhaps been the greatest distinction of vice presidents—unless, of course, they have managed to succeed to the presidency. The list of former vice presidents includes many names that almost no one would recognize: Richard Johnson, William King, Thomas Hendricks, Charles Curtis. It is primarily only those who have succeeded as president, or managed later to become president on their own, who have achieved any renown. This list includes Theodore Roosevelt, Calvin Coolidge, Lyndon Johnson, and Richard Nixon.

The Constitution seems to embrace an ambivalent attitude toward the vice presidency. By awarding the office (originally) to the person who finished second in the presidential election, the framers apparently sought to ensure that the vice president would be like the president, a person of national stature and long political experience. Yet the Constitution gives vice presidents almost nothing to do. What little power they have is legislative, not executive. The vice president is officially the president of the Senate; and thus vice presidents may preside over Senate proceedings whenever they want (which they rarely do now), and they may vote to break a tie in the Senate. It is little wonder then that John Adams, the first vice president, considered it the "most insignificant office that ever the invention of man contrived or his imagination conceived."

The rise of political parties, with their combined slating of candidates for the presidency and the vice presidency, and the Twelfth Amendment's single-vote system for the two offices, overturned the founders' original mode of selection. As a result, vice presidents became party allies of the president, selected in large part for political reasons of "balance" discussed in Chapter 6. Only in recent years, with the rash of assassination attempts, has more pressure been exerted on parties and presidential candidates to consider more carefully the vice president's standing as a potential president.

The safest generalization about vice presidents today is that they are as important (or unimportant) as the presidents want them to be. Presidents may treat vice presidents as an extension of the presidency or may virtually ignore them. A president may assign important political responsibilities to the vice president or seek to keep the vice president preoccupied with unimportant tasks. In modern times, President Roosevelt did little to involve Vice President Truman in the administration, even though Roosevelt surely knew of his own failing health. Truman was forced to assume office with little direct knowledge of many administration plans. President Kennedy generally thought rather poorly of Vice President Johnson, and the bitter feelings between Johnson and many of Kennedy's personal staff members were well known. Still, Kennedy used Johnson extensively to relieve some of his ceremonial burdens, and Johnson, like Vice President Nixon before him, traveled extensively.

President Nixon used Vice President Agnew as a spokesman to say some of the "tough" things he wanted said but which would have seemed "unpresidential" coming from the president himself.

A truly dramatic change in the vice president's role occurred under President Carter, who integrated Vice President Mondale into his staff hierarchy and relied on him extensively for advice and assistance. Vice President Bush retained some of this authority, and it may well be that vice presidents are now becoming as a matter of precedent and expectation much more important figures in the institutional presidency. This larger role would seem to fit with their enhanced political standing under the current nominating system as likely future front-runners.

The real importance of the vice presidency lies in the possibility of succession to the presidency in the case of the president's death, resignation, disability, or impeachment and removal from office by Congress. The original Constitution is not clear whether in these circumstances the vice president should *become* president or simply take over the duties of president until the next election. Vice President John Tyler settled the question in 1841 when he assumed the office as well as the duties of the president upon the death of William Henry Harrison, who served just one month in office. Since then seven vice presidents have succeeded to the presidency after the incumbent's death, and one, Gerald Ford, became president upon the resignation of his predecessor (Richard Nixon). Thus, of the forty different men who as of 1984 had served in the nation's highest office, nine (23 percent) succeeded to the presidency from the vice presidency. In this century the ratio is five of fifteen, or 33 percent.

THE IMPORTANCE OF POPULAR LEADERSHIP

When Ronald Reagan became president in January of 1981, even his longtime political opponents conceded that he brought with him into office one indispensable skill: the ability to communicate effectively with the public. Even before he became governor of California (1966), his natural talents as a communicator had been honed through a lifetime of speaking in public: he had been a sportscaster, professional movie actor, and stump speaker

BOX 10-5

PRESIDENTIAL SUCCESSION AND THE TWENTY-FIFTH AMENDMENT

Although the Constitution originally recognized the possibility of a president's "inability to discharge the Powers and Duties" of the office, it did not define "inability" or establish any procedures for determining when a disability existed. Yet on several occasions throughout our history, presidents have been physically incapacitated. After being shot in July of 1881, President Garfield lingered for eighty days before he died. Eighteen months before the end of his second term, in September of 1919, President Wilson suffered a stroke from which he never fully recovered. And between 1955 and 1957, President Eisenhower suffered a heart attack, an ileitis attack, and a mild stroke. In all these cases the vice presidents were reluctant to press the case for assuming the powers of the presidency, and the presidents' aides were ready to oppose any such move. The few individuals closest to the president, including in Wilson's case his wife, managed in these instances to maintain at least the appearance of a functioning chief executive.

With the ratification of the Twenty-Fifth Amendment in 1967, formal procedures were established for handling situations in which presidents may be unable to carry out their duties. The amendment sets out three possible courses of action. First, the president may formally declare a state of disability in a letter to the president pro tempore of the Senate and the Speaker of the House. The vice president would then take over as acting president until the president gave notification that the disability was over. Second, since the president may be unable or unwilling to declare a disability, the vice president may move to notify congressional leaders, with the support of a majority of the Cabinet-level officers or some other body determined by Congress, such as a group of physicians. As soon as such notification is given, the vice president becomes acting president and continues to serve until the president informs Congress that the disability has ended. Finally, if there is a disagreement between the president and the vice president as to whether a true disability exists, Congress decides the issue, with a two-thirds vote of both branches needed to replace the president with the vice president.

One other important feature of the Twenty-Fifth Amendment is its provision governing the filling of vacancies in the vice presidency. Whenever the office becomes vacant (through death, resignation, or the succession of a vice president to the presidency), the president may appoint a new vice president with the concurrence of a majority of both houses of Congress. Gerald Ford was the first vice president appointed in this way, when his predecessor, Spiro Agnew, resigned in 1973 after pleading "no contest" to criminal charges. Ford later succeeded to the presidency when Nixon resigned in 1974.

---

for conservative causes. Communicating with the public is clearly an important part of being president and gives a good communicator, like FDR or Reagan, a decided advantage. But how does public communication translate into political effectiveness? What makes this skill so important for the contemporary American presidency?

Under the system of separation of powers, the presidents' institutional means for influencing Congress's response to their legislative proposals are limited. Presidents can try to persuade legislators of the merits of their recommendations; they can bargain with legislators, using the resources the office makes available (for example, the allocation of federal projects); or they can generate a public sentiment so strong that members of Congress inter-

ested in reelection would be foolish to ignore it. Recent presidents have frequently employed this last technique, confirming Woodrow Wilson's slightly exaggerated dictum that the president "has no means of compelling Congress except through public opinion" (Wilson, 1961:71).

Methods of Influencing Public Opinion

Perhaps the most direct way of trying to influence opinion is the nationally televised presidential address. It is rare that the three major networks will balk at giving the president up to an hour of air time during peak viewing hours to address the American people on some matter of national importance. Since a single speech by itself may not have any dramatic impact on the people, it is often followed by a carefully orchestrated campaign extending over many weeks to get the president's message out in a persuasive way. This may include news conferences, informal meetings with prominent reporters or editors, presidential addresses in various parts of the country, and a series of speeches before influential audiences by surrogates for the president. At worst, such public relations efforts take on the look of a propaganda campaign designed to manipulate public attitudes; at best, they contribute immeasurably to public awareness and understanding of pressing social problems.

Although the president, more than anyone else, has both access to the public and opportunity for influencing it, this is no guarantee of success. President Carter discovered this early on when he failed to mobilize public opinion on the energy issue. As hard as Carter tried in the first months of his new administration—a televised fireside chat, an appearance before a joint session of Congress, press conferences, and speeches before specific groups— he was largely unable to create a sense of urgency about the energy crisis (Edwards, 1983). While he likened this public issue to the "moral equivalent of war," others thought that the acronym "MEOW" was more indicative of the public response. Later in his term, he was more successful in selling an administration proposal when he managed to get the Senate to ratify his Panama Canal treaties turning the American-built canal gradually over to the authority of the Panamanian government. Carter had realized that there was little likelihood of getting two-thirds of the Senate to support the treaties if public opinion was adamantly opposed.

Consequently, he launched a two-pronged campaign involving both his direct appeal to the people and the use of hundreds of surrogate speakers traveling about the country with the administration's message. Although there is little evidence that these efforts dramatically shifted public sentiment, they did seem to moderate both the vehemence and the extent of the opposition, thereby making it easier for at least some senators from conservative states to support the treaties.

The importance of public support for a presidential program was demonstrated even more recently when Ronald Reagan, after only a few weeks in of-

fice, presented to Congress a plan to reduce expected growth in federal expenditures and taxes. Reducing outlays is guaranteed to upset many well-organized and highly vocal groups that benefit from government programs. From the beginning, Reagan believed that his only chance of success in turning around "business as usual" in Washington was to generate broad-based public support for his package of reductions. Consequently, he initiated an extensive public relations campaign highlighted by several nationally televised addresses over the course of the next few months. By the end of the summer of 1981 Reagan had succeeded in getting nearly all of his tax and spending package through Congress. Most commentators agreed that his effective appeal to public opinion was decisive in generating congressional support for his policies.

The success of presidential appeals to the public through televised addresses has been mixed. Studies comparing public opinion before and after presidents have spoken on an issue indicate some increase of support for the president's position. This increase has ranged from the negligible (a 4 percent gain for a tax cut following an address by President Kennedy on April 18, 1963) to the dramatic (a 43 percent increase in support for sending troops into Cambodia following President Nixon's address of April 30, 1970). One should keep in mind, however, that the president frequently makes the first effort at influencing opinions; subsequent challenges from other leaders and the confrontation of predictions with reality can quickly erode any temporary gains (Edwards, 1983:43–45).

One form, then, that popular leadership takes is public instruction about the substance of national issues. But it may also go beyond this to include what is sometimes called "moral leadership" of the American people. The president can exercise such leadership in at least three ways.

Standing as a Moral Example The president occupies the most prestigious position in American society. Presidents and their families are the focus of unremitting public attention. Many presidents have recognized, as a result, that their own personal conduct—not only what they say but also what they do—can influence public morality. If they set a high standard of personal behavior, then this might foster norms of good conduct throughout society. Eisenhower perhaps put it best when he wrote that the "President of the United States should stand, visible and uncompromising, for what is right and decent—in government, in the business community, in the private lives of the citizens. For decency is one of the main pillars of a sound civilization. An immoral nation invites its own ruin" (Hirschfield, 1973:123). It was no sign of hypocrisy but rather the realization of the importance of his moral example that led President Eisenhower to begin regular church attendance after he was elected president. Certainly one of the tragedies of the Watergate scandal was the extent to which the public disclosures of President Nixon's actions undermined respect for the office and reduced the public's trust in the institutions of government. Sensing the depth of public sentiment on this matter, Jimmy Carter made a special effort to portray himself as a man of high moral character when he ran for the office in 1976 and while he served as president.

Generating Confidence and Inspiring Public Opinion When Franklin Roosevelt came to power in 1933, the American nation was in the depths of a severe economic depression. Roosevelt realized that the public's basic confidence in the nation's economic and political institutions had been shaken. His responsibility, as he saw it, was not simply to promote legislation that would mitigate the human suffering caused by the depression, but also to reinstill confidence in the nation and its institutions. In his first inaugural address, he said that the "only thing we have to fear is fear itself—nameless, unreasoning, unjustified terror which paralyzes needed efforts to convert retreat into advance." He asked for a return to the "old and permanently important manifestation of the American spirit of the pioneer," and for the American people to "move as a trained and loyal army willing to sacrifice for the good of a common discipline" (Hirschfield, 1973:104–108). The president would stand at the head of this army.

Recent American presidents have not faced crises as severe as the great depression or World War II, but most have believed that inspirational leadership is an essential responsibility of the modern presidency. For Harry Truman, "one of the

great responsibilities and opportunities of the president is to lead and inspire public opinion." When running for the presidency, John Kennedy maintained that the country "will need a president . . . who is willing and able to summon his national constituency to its finest hour—to alert the people to our dangers and our opportunities—to demand of them the sacrifices that will be necessary" (Hirschfield, 1973:117, 133).

Perhaps the most remarkable example in recent years of a presidential effort to inspire the American people was Jimmy Carter's "malaise" speech of July 15, 1979. After holding a "domestic summit" at Camp David, where he met with well over 100 persons representing most segments of American society, Carter addressed the American people to discuss a national "crisis of confidence" that threatened to "destroy the social and the political fabric of America." He warned that the United States stood at a crossroads and that it would choose a path either of "fragmentation and self-interest" or of "common purpose and the restoration of American values." A united effort to solve the nation's energy problem could become the first step on the path of common purpose (*Congressional Quarterly Weekly Report,* 1979:1470–1472).

In these instances, some presidents have met with more success than others in their attempts at moral leadership. The president remains, however, the focal point for efforts to inspire and rally public confidence in the political system.

Articulating Principles and Ideals Occasionally a president will go beyond confidence building to try to instruct the citizenry in the principles and ideals of the nation. Carter attempted this in his malaise speech when he argued that self-indulgence was inconsistent with proper American values. Franklin Roosevelt did something similar in his first inaugural address when he castigated the greed of the "money changers" and called for making "social values more noble than mere monetary profit." Theodore Roosevelt caught the spirit of this presidential function when he called the executive office a "bully pulpit." From this pulpit presidents have combined the moral instruction of the preacher with the political education of the civics teacher. At certain crucial periods in our national existence high presidential leadership of this type may be essential for the preservation of fundamental American values.

Assessing Popular Leadership

Popular leadership of the sort we have discussed is clearly among the most important responsibilities of the modern presidency. However, it is possible to overestimate its effectiveness, necessity, and advantage.

Consider, for example, presidential efforts to move Congress by generating public pressures on the institution. Although most presidents come into office with rather confident views on how much can be accomplished in this way, they are often disappointed at the results. The fact is that only rarely can presidents so move the public that they get Congress to do something to which it was strongly opposed at the outset. And in the process of trying, they can sour relations with Congress. President Carter probably won few friends when he complained in 1979 of a Congress "twisted and pulled in every direction by hundreds of well-financed and powerful special interests."

The emphasis on popular leadership raises another problem—the tendency for presidents to promise much more than they or the political system can possibly deliver and to overestimate the willingness of the American people to make sacrifices in order to achieve collective ends. Consider in this respect the following remarks by President Lyndon Johnson in his state of the union message of January 8, 1964:

> Let this session of Congress be known as the session which did more for civil rights than the last 100 sessions combined; as the session which enacted the most far-reaching tax cut of our times; as the session which declared all-out war on human poverty and unemployment in these United States; as the session which finally recognized the health needs of all of our older citizens; as the session which reformed our tangled transportation and transit policies; as the session which achieved the most effective, efficient foreign aid program ever, and as the session which helped to build more homes and more schools and more libraries and more hospitals than any single

session of Congress in the history of our republic. All this and more can and must be done. It can be done by this summer. And it can be done without any increase in spending (Filler, 1964:409).

Johnson may have been more utopian than other presidents, but the tendency to overpromise is not untypical of recent chief executives. Nixon told the nation he had achieved "peace with honor" in Vietnam, although it soon became clear that he managed only to disengage American forces from a conflict that continued after American troops left and that ended in defeat. Similarly, he probably oversold the benefits of détente with the Soviet Union, thereby obscuring with his rhetoric some of the fundamental differences of principle and interest that still separated the two superpowers. President Reagan also exaggerated by overstating the immediate economic benefits of a reduction in federal income taxes.

The harmful effects of overpromising may not be obvious, but repeated instances of unfulfilled presidential pledges can lead to public disenchantment with our leaders and our institutions. At the same time, the claims of presidents to be able to solve problems, many of which may be insolvable, have undoubtedly inflated the expectations of the public for presidential leadership. As President Carter observed, "When things go bad you [the president] get entirely too much blame. And I have to admit that when things go good, you get entirely too much credit" (Edwards, 1983:189). It is surely ironic that the rhetorical tools that have served as such a powerful resource for the president have also created expectations for the office that probably no president can meet. Recent presidents have all followed the same pattern in their public opinion rankings—high marks from the public at the outset followed by plunges after their first year (see Figure 10-1). Part of this phenomenon might be explained by the personal qualities of the presidents, but the persistence of the pattern suggests a more fundamental problem in the public's basic perception of the office.

One final problem must be mentioned. The popular leadership role of the presidency emerges out of the fact that the president is the only leader elected by all the people. As such, the president is

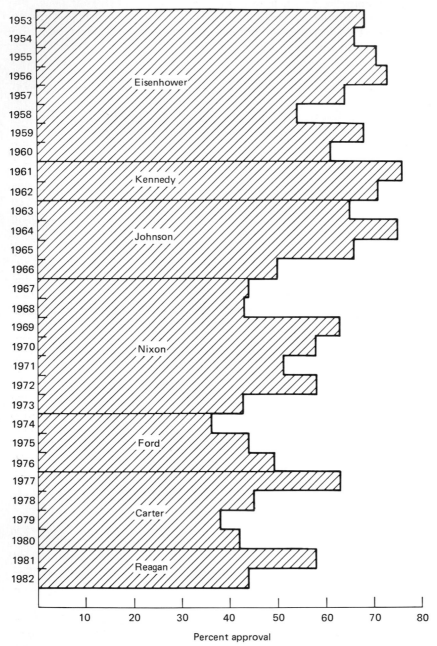

FIGURE 10-1
Average yearly presidential approval rating, 1953–1982. Since Eisenhower's presidency, the approval rating of each president has fallen after the first year of his term. (*Source:* Gallup polls.)

often portrayed as speaking for the nation. True political leadership, however, requires officeholders who are not merely a mouthpiece for the public but have confidence in their own judgments, even if these vary from the opinions of the majority. Otherwise, presidents become merely followers, not leaders. Additionally, true political leadership requires a citizenry that recognizes its own limitations and accords a degree of discretion to its representative institutions. The more the public comes to think of the president as essentially the voice, or "tribune," of the people, the more the task of effective political leadership is placed in jeopardy.

CONCLUSION

Those who created the American presidency wanted it to be strong and independent enough both to provide for effective administration of national laws and to play a creative role in the policymaking process. They did not, however, expressly establish the office as a principal source of leadership in the political system; and for over a century, it was Congress, not the presidency, that was the dominant direction-setting institution in the national government. A handful of presidents did not fit this pattern and thereby demonstrated that the office had capacities that under certain circumstances could place it at the forefront of national affairs. These capacities include the ability to formulate coherent domestic and foreign policies, to guide the legislative process through the leadership of the dominant political party, to act forcefully to meet military threats from both within and without, to serve as a focus for popular expectations, and to guide and instruct the citizenry.

Although these capacities were only occasionally important in the nineteenth century, by the twentieth century changes in our relations with the rest of the world, the rise of a more activist national government, and the development of new communications technologies had made the leadership capacities of the executive office essential to the effective functioning of the political system. With the growth of the president's new responsibilities came the growth of a new presidential bureaucracy that includes several thousand people whose main duty

it is to assist presidents in carrying out their job. The office, however, remains highly personalized, and presidential discretion has not been restricted in a significant way.

The Constitutional unity of the office, along with the selection of its occupant by what is in effect a direct popular national election, has made the presidency the focus of popular leadership in the American political system. In a way that neither Congress nor the Supreme Court can match, the presidency is the foremost communicator with the American people. While this makes for a formidable majoritarian office, there are dangers to popular leadership, including the tendency for presidents to raise expectations unrealistically and the possibility that an irresponsible president might inflame popular passions or prejudices. Moreover, the emphasis on the president's role as the people's "voice" can obscure the very real distinction between guiding public opinion and merely following it.

The solution to these problems of popular leadership is not to return to the dominant nineteenth-century model of the president as mere administrator. Historical events and the capacities of the office have thrust the presidency into the "vital place of action in the system." Contemporary presidents are not free to ignore the responsibilities which the times have placed on the office. Their task rather is to carry out these responsibilities in a way which both recognizes the opportunities and dangers that come with the exercise of great power and respects the Constitutional role of the other branches.

SOURCES

Barber, James David: *The Presidential Character,* 2d ed., Prentice-Hall, Englewood Cliffs, N.J., 1977.

Burns, James MacGregor: *Presidential Government: The Crucible of Leadership,* Avon, New York, 1965.

Charnwood, Lord: *Abraham Lincoln,* 3d ed., Henry Holt, New York, 1917.

Congressional Quarterly Weekly Report, vol. 37, no. 29, Congressional Quarterly Press, Washington, D.C., July 21, 1979.

Cornwell, Elmer, Jr.: *Presidential Leadership of Public Opinion,* University of Indiana Press, Bloomington, 1965.

Corwin, Edward S.: *The President: Office and Powers,* New York University Press, New York, 1957.

Cronin, Thomas, E.: *The State of the Presidency,* Little, Brown, Boston, 1980.

Edwards, George, III: *The Public Presidency,* Saint Martin's, New York, 1983.

Fallows, James: "The Passionless Presidency," in Peter Woll (ed.), *Behind the Scenes in American Government,* 3d ed., Little, Brown, Boston, 1981.

Filler, Louis (ed.): *The President Speaks,* Capricorn, New York, 1964.

Fisher, Louis: *President and Congress: Power and Policy,* Free Press, New York, 1972.

Gallup polls, 1953–1982.

George, Alexander, and Juliette George: *Woodrow Wilson and Colonel House,* Dover, New York, 1964.

Greenstein, Fred I.: "Change and Continuity in the Modern Presidency," in Anthony King (ed.), *The New American Political System,* American Enterprise Institute, Washington, D.C., 1978.

Hamilton, Alexander, James Madison, and John Jay: *The Federalist Papers,* Clinton Rossiter (ed.), New American Library, New York, 1961.

Hargrove, Erwin: *The Power of the Modern Presidency,* Knopf, New York, 1974.

Henkin, Louis: *Foreign Affairs and the Constitution,* Foundation Press, Mineola, N.Y., 1972.

Hirschfield, Robert S. (ed.): *The Power of the Presidency,* 2d ed., Aldine, Chicago, 1973.

Kallenbach, Joseph E.: *The American Chief Executive,* Harper and Row, New York, 1966.

Kearns, Doris: *Lyndon Johnson and the American Dream,* Harper and Row, New York, 1976.

Kennedy, Robert F.: *Thirteen Days,* New American Library, New York, 1969.

Kissinger, Henry: *Years of Upheaval,* Little, Brown, Boston, 1982.

Locke, John: *Two Treatises on Civil Government,* Peter Laslett (ed.), Mentor, New York, 1965.

MacKenzie, Calvin: "Personal Appointment Strategies in Post-War Presidential Administrations," a paper delivered at the Midwest Political Science Association, Chicago, April 24, 1980.

McPherson, Harry: *A Political Education,* Little, Brown, Boston, 1972.

Nelson, Michael: "James David Barber and the Psychological Presidency," in Thomas E. Cronin (ed.), *Rethinking the Presidency,* Little, Brown, Boston, 1982.

Neustadt, Richard: *Presidential Power: The Politics of Leadership from FDR to Carter,* Wiley, New York, 1980.

Peterson, Merrill D. (ed.): *The Portable Thomas Jefferson,* Viking, New York, 1975.

Pious, Richard M.: *The American Presidency,* Basic Books, New York, 1979.

Reedy, George: *The Twilight of the Presidency,* New American Library (Mentor Books), New York, 1970.

Richardson, James D. (ed.): *The Messages and Papers of the Presidents, 1789–1897,* vols. 1–10, U.S. Government Printing Office, Washington, D.C., 1896–1899.

Roosevelt, Theodore: *The Autobiography of Theodore Roosevelt,* Wayne Andrews (ed.), Scribner, New York, 1958.

Rossiter, Clinton: *The American Presidency,* rev. ed., New American Library (Mentor Books), New York, 1960.

Safire, William: *Before the Fall,* Ballantine, New York, 1977.

Schlesinger, Arthur, Jr.: *The Imperial Presidency,* Houghton Mifflin, New York, 1973.

Story, William W. (ed.): *Life and Letters of Joseph Story,* vols. 1, 2, Little, Brown, Boston, 1851.

Thach, Charles C., Jr.: *The Creation of the Presidency, 1775–1789,* Johns Hopkins Press, Baltimore, 1969.

U.S. News & World Report, vol. XCI, no. 1, July 6, 1981.

Wilson, Woodrow: *Constitutional Government in the United States,* Columbia paperback ed., New York, 1961; originally published in 1908.

RECOMMENDED READINGS

Barber, James David: *The Presidential Character* 2d ed., Prentice-Hall, Englewood Cliffs, N.J., 1977. An original attempt to categorize presidents into four distinct character types.

Cornwell, Elmer, Jr.: *Presidential Leadership of Public Opinion,* University of Indiana Press, Bloomington, 1965. An analysis of the development of the president as a popular leader from Theodore Roosevelt through Lyndon Johnson.

Cronin, Thomas F.: *The State of the Presidency,* Little, Brown, Boston, 1980. A survey of the characteristics of the modern presidency by one of the nation's leading presidential scholars.

George, Alexander, and Juliette George: *Woodrow Wilson and Colonel House,* Dover, New York, 1964. A fascinating psychological study of one of America's most interesting presidents and of his top advisers.

Greenstein, Fred: *The Hidden Hand Presidency: Eisenhower as Leader,* Basic Books, New York, 1982. An examination of Eisenhower's style of leadership that throws light on the general question of presidential leadership.

Neustadt, Richard E.: *Presidential Power: The Politics of Presidential Leadership from FDR to Carter,* Wiley, New York, 1980. A classic discussion of the nature of presidential leadership in the modern era.

Pious, Richard M.: *The American Presidency,* Basic Books, New York, 1979. A comprehensive survey of the presidency that emphasizes the historical evolution of the office and its powers.

Chapter 11

Congress and the Presidency: Conflict and Cooperation

In the fall of 1980 Lloyd N. Cutler, counsel to President Jimmy Carter, wrote a controversial article for the widely read and highly respected journal *Foreign Affairs.* "The separation of powers between the legislative and executive branches," Cutler maintained, "whatever its merits in 1793, has become a structure that almost guarantees stalemate today." The American system of government had a "structural inability . . . to propose, legislate and administer a balanced program for governing." Voicing his evident frustration with the failure of Congress to pass many of President Carter's key domestic and foreign policy initiatives, Cutler criticized a system in which a president can be elected to carry out certain expressly articulated policy goals but is then denied the means to translate those goals into public policy. At bottom the problem is structural and Constitutional, since the fundamental charter of our national government, the Constitution of 1787, gives the president so little power to influence Congress. Even worse, the Constitution created a *bicameral* legislature, with the result that three separate and distinct bodies— the House of Representatives, the Senate, and the presidency—have to agree before much public policy can be formulated, approved, and executed. The result, according to Cutler, is a "stalemate" (Cutler, 1980:126–143).

For Cutler, the governmental system that is superior to separation of powers is the one employed by most major western nations: a parliamentary form of government. In a parliamentary system the leaders of the executive branch—the prime minister, cabinet, and subcabinet (simply called the "government")—are chosen by the majority party in the legislature (or by a coalition of parties that constitute a majority party of the legislative body). These party leaders retain their seats in the legislature while also serving as high executive officials. In the United States it would be the equivalent of having only congressional elections and then allowing the winning party to install its leaders as president, vice president, department heads, and subcabinet officials. In the meantime these officials would still be members of Congress, debating and voting on the very bills they were introducing in their capacity as officials in the executive branch.

Obviously, the selection of the leaders of the executive branch by the legislature makes for much more cohesion between the branches of government than exists in the American system, where the Constitution expressly prohibits any person from serving in both branches simultaneously (with the partial exception of the vice president, who is also the president of the Senate). The cohesion produced by the parliamentary system is reinforced by the practice which dictates that if the legislature rejects a key part of the "government's" program or votes a resolution of "no confidence," then the government must resign and a new one must be formed out of the legislature, or new legislative elections must take place. Thus political leaders in parliamentary governments rarely lose votes in the legislature on important issues. In Cutler's view parliamentary governments display the merits of coherent policy formulation and implementation, prompt and consistent responses to external events, and clear accountability to the voting public.

Cutler's critique of separation of powers as inferior to parliamentary forms of government is not a new one. As long ago as the late nineteenth century Woodrow Wilson made essentially the same argument. More recently, this kind of critique was often found in the writings of American political scientists in the decades following World War II, especially during the administrations of presidents Eisenhower and Kennedy, neither of whom had great success moving his legislative program through Congress.

In this chapter we will examine in more detail the ways in which Congress and the presidency interact and how this interaction affects the ability of our governing institutions to achieve the purposes for which they were created. Specifically, we will analyze (1) the ways in which one especially effective president tried to influence Congress, (2) the underlying sources of conflict between Congress and the presidency, (3) the resources available to each branch when it does battle with the other, and, not least important, (4) the forces that make for cooperation between the two branches. In the conclusion we will return to the comparison of the separation of powers and the parliamentary form of government.

BOX 11-1

ON SEPARATION OF POWERS—CON

Any part of the president's legislative program may be defeated, or amended into an entirely different measure, so that the legislative record of any presidency may bear little resemblance to the overall program the president wanted to carry out. . . . This difficulty is of course compounded when the president's party does not even hold the majority of the seats in both Houses. . . . The former ability of the president to sit down with ten or fifteen leaders in each House, and to agree on a program which those leaders could carry through Congress, has virtually disappeared. The Committee chairmen and the leaders no longer have the instruments of power that once enabled them to lead. . . .

In this century the system has succeeded only on the rare occasions when there is an unusual event that brings us together, and creates substantial consensus throughout the country on the need for a whole new program. . . . Except on the rare issues where there is . . . a consensus, the structural problems usually prove too difficult to overcome. In each administration, it becomes progressively more difficult to make the present system work effectively on the range of issues, both domestic and foreign, that the United States must now manage even though there is no large consensus. . . .

We are not about to revise our own Constitution so as to incorporate a true parliamentary system. But we do need to find a way of coming closer to the parliamentary concept of "forming a Government," under which the elected majority is able to carry out an overall program, and is held accountable for its success or failure. . . . The most one can hope for is a set of modest changes . . . , with somewhat less separation between the executive and the legislature than now exists.

Source: Cutler, 1980:126–143.

BOX 11-2

ON SEPARATION OF POWERS—PRO

Mr. Cutler has a philosophy of governance that is at odds with what the framers of the Constitution embodied in that document. To Mr. Cutler good policy or good government is the product or the act of a single will. It is an act of management, of allocation, of balance. The framers, by contrast, thought that good policy could be recognized when it appeared, but to achieve it in the real world required a process of ambition counteracting ambition, leading thereby to the formation of coalitions—coalitions of partial, self-interested groups. They hoped the Constitution would lead these coalitions to emerge only on the principle of the common good. . . .

[Separation of powers] facilitates scrutiny, sometimes at the expense of action; it protects the particular and the individual, sometimes at the expense of the general. But it has brought about the capacity to engage in great national commitments when important national emergencies arise, and above all it has permitted a union to be created out of great diversity by providing separate constitutional places on which individuals could focus their loyalties. . . .

If we compare American policy with that of most parliamentary democracies, its leading characteristic is its moderation. There are many policies I do not approve of and regularly call immoderate. Taken as a whole, however, we tend to temper the enthusiasm of temporary majorities by the need constantly to reformulate that majority.

. . . If reforms are to be sought, we should seek them from within the American experience on the basis of those institutional arrangements to which the American people have become accustomed. We should not reach overseas for an approximation of the parliamentary system; we should look at state and city governments in this country and ask what modifications in federal arrangements already tested at the city and state levels might commend themselves.

Source: Wilson, 1982:179–182.

THE PRESIDENT AS CHIEF LEGISLATOR: THE CASE OF LYNDON JOHNSON

While it is undoubtedly true that an American president has a harder time getting programs through the national legislature than a British prime minister does, it is also true that some presidents are much more successful than others. In the period since Franklin Roosevelt, no president has been more successful with Congress than Lyndon Johnson. An examination of Johnson's techniques for influencing Congress will illustrate just how much energy and effort are needed, in Johnson's words, to "crack the wall of separation" that divides the executive and legislative branches.

Lyndon Johnson served as president from November of 1963 (when John Kennedy was assassinated) to January of 1969. His period of greatest legislative success came in 1965–1966 following his landslide election victory over Barry Goldwater in November of 1964. Not only did Johnson win 61 percent of the popular vote in the presidential race, but Democrats won 295 of the 435 House seats (61 percent) and maintained a lopsided majority in the Senate of 68 of the 100 seats. Given this dominance of the Democrats in the Eighty-Ninth Congress, it is hardly surprising that Johnson had some success with his legislative program. Nevertheless, most commentators agree that Johnson exhibited a skill and intensity in his dealings with Congress unmatched by any president since FDR.

> "There is but one way for a President to deal with Congress," Johnson maintained, "and that is continuously, incessantly, and without interruption. If it's really going to work, the relationship between the President and Congress has got to be almost incestuous. He's got to know them even better than they know themselves. And then, on the basis of this knowledge, he's got to build a system that stretches from the cradle to the grave, from the moment a bill is introduced to the moment it is officially enrolled as the law of the land" (Kearns, 1976:226).

There were, then, two key ingredients in Johnson's approach to Congress: intimate knowledge of the structure, procedures, and personalities that constituted the House and Senate and a "cradle to grave" system for involving the executive branch in the legislative plans and actions of the Congress.

For the first of these Johnson came into the presidency well-equipped. He had served in Congress for a total of twenty-two years, ten in the House and twelve in the Senate. Moreover, for six of his years in the Senate he was majority leader, and by all accounts an unusually energetic and effective one. While president, however, he did not rely simply on past knowledge.

> ... In the Eighty-Ninth Congress (1965–66), his favorite reading was the *Congressional Record*. A White House messenger picked up the newest issue at the Government Printing Office every morning, and an aide then read it before dawn, clipping each page on which a member of Congress praised or criticized Johnson and summarizing and marking up other important parts for Johnson's breakfast reading. ...
>
> Before retiring at night, Johnson read detailed memos from his staff on their legislative contacts of the day, specific problems that arose, and noteworthy conversations, all of which he absorbed rapidly and thoroughly. When Congress was in session, he received continuous status reports. ... Congress was for Johnson "a twenty-four-hour-a-day obsession" (Edwards, 1980:117–118).

The second ingredient of Johnson's success—his "cradle to grave" system of maintaining intimate contact with Congress—included the following: (1) congressional membership on confidential task forces established by Johnson to study and define major issues, (2) regular consultations with key committee chairs while a bill was being debated, (3) special White House briefings with congressional leaders conducted the night before a legislative message was sent to Capitol Hill, (4) regular Tuesday morning breakfast meetings with the congressional leadership to review the legislative schedule, and, when Johnson judged appropriate, (5) direct contact (on the telephone or personally) with undecided legislators to persuade them of the substantive merits or electoral benefits of supporting the president's proposals.

More detailed descriptions of the third and fourth of these activities give a vivid indication of the extent of Johnson's efforts to consult with Congress at each crucial stage. The special evening briefings "generally took the form of dinner meetings in the White House mess, to which Johnson

Whenever Lyndon Johnson signed a bill, he invited the House and Senate sponsors to share the publicity with him—and he used dozens of pens, so that each sponsor could have a reminder of the event.   *(UPI)*

invited the chairmen of the appropriate committee and subcommittee, the party leadership, and other legislators who were likely to be influential on this particular issue. At such meetings, Cabinet members, together with the White House staff, would review the contents of the message, provide background information, clarify language, and answer questions." Johnson likened this to the "question period" in the British system—"an opportunity for the members of Congress to get an advance look at my documents and then to confront my Cabinet members with all sorts of questions. . . . It gave the chosen ones—between the charts and the tables and the answers to their questions—a knowledgeable understanding of what often turned out to be complex legislation" (Kearns, 1976:223–224).

Johnson's Tuesday breakfast meetings were equally substantive and useful:

At these meetings Johnson stood beside an immense chart that rested on an easel in the corner of the room. There he went over the diagrams of the chart, which showed the course of each of his bills: which

were still in subcommittee, which were ready for the mark-up, and which were ready for consideration on the floor. The chart, which seemed to accompany Johnson everywhere, was also used to prod the members of his Cabinet, allowing him to request or demand explanations from the Secretaries whose departmental legislation was shown to be lagging (Kearns, 1976:223).

The result of all this effort was impressive: a range of new social welfare legislation, the so-called "Great Society" programs, in areas like education, health care, civil rights, and economic opportunity. In the midterm election of 1966, however, the Democrats lost forty-eight seats in the House and four in the Senate. Throughout Johnson's term the Vietnamese conflict continued to escalate, robbing the president of much of the goodwill previously felt for his administration by liberal elements of the Democratic party. Moreover, fiscal conservatives increasingly attacked his attempts to provide both "guns and butter." Federal deficits soared, taxes were increased, and Johnson's effectiveness with Congress dropped along with his public popularity.

Johnson himself well understood the cyclical nature of presidential influence with Congress.

> You've got to give it all you can that first year. Doesn't matter what kind of majority you come in with. You've got just one year when they treat you right, and before they start worrying about themselves. The third year, you lose votes.... The fourth year's all politics. You can't put anything through when half of the Congress is thinking how to beat you. So you've got one year. That's why I tried. Well, we gave it a hell of a lick, didn't we? (McPherson, 1972:268)

What lessons, then, about the American system of separation of powers can we draw from Lyndon Johnson's administration? One thing is clear: the gap between Congress and the presidency is not unbridgeable. In some circumstances the president can truly become the chief legislator. But what is also clear is that these circumstances are not present in the normal course of presidential-congressional relations. Most new presidents are not as experienced and knowledgeable as Johnson was in the ways of Congress. Most do not devote the same degree of personal attention and energy to congressional consultations. Most do not have the advantage of overwhelming majorities of the same party in control of the House and Senate. And, finally, most do not come into office with the electoral landslide that Johnson experienced in November of 1964.

Legislative success of the degree that Lyndon Johnson enjoyed in 1965 and 1966 is rare in American politics. In more normal circumstances the forces that generate conflict between the branches seem to predominate. It is to these that we now turn.

SOURCES OF CONFLICT

That there is conflict between Congress and the presidency is hardly suprising, for as we saw in earlier chapters, the framers actually designed their system of government to foster a certain amount of conflict and competition between the various branches of government. They hoped that each institution would oppose the excesses of the other, thereby preventing a dangerous consolidation of all power in a single set of hands. As Jefferson once put it, "The concentrating [of all powers of government] in the same hands is precisely the definition of despotic government" (Jefferson, 1975:164). In itself, then, conflict is not necessarily a bad thing (a point to which we shall return at the end of this chapter). The sources of this conflict are essentially three: institutional jealousy, structural differences between the branches, and differences in the way the branches represent the attitudes and goals of the American citizenry.

Institutional Jealousy

During the Carter administration, an episode occurred that illustrates one of the fundamental causes of conflict between the presidency and Congress. In 1978 an agreement was reached between the leaders of the Soviet Union and President Carter on the limitation of strategic (nuclear) arms (the Strategic Arms Limitation Agreement, or simply SALT II). It had generally been expected that President Carter would submit this agreement to the Senate for ratification as a treaty. Increasingly fearful, however, that he could not get the necessary two-thirds of the Senate to support SALT, Carter indicated publicly in August of 1978 that he was considering submitting the proposal in the form of a joint resolution, which would need only a simple majority vote in both branches. Reaction in the Senate was immediately negative. Senator Charles Mathias (Republican, Maryland) warned that this "would be viewed as an effort to circumvent" the Constitutional role of the Senate. Even the president's natural allies in the Senate, the Democratic leaders, opposed the move. Majority Whip Alan Cranston of California maintained that the maneuver to seek a joint resolution would virtually guarantee the defeat of SALT. And Majority Leader Robert Byrd of West Virginia chided the administration for trying to "end-run ... the Senate." "A pact as important as this," Byrd argued on the Senate floor, "must be sound in every respect and be able to withstand the constitutional test of advice and consent." Given the strength of Senate criticism, Carter dropped the idea of a joint resolution and submitted the agreement in the form of a treaty (Schmitt, 1980).

What is interesting about this episode is that even those senators who were inclined to support SALT did not want to see it passed in a way which violated their view of the Senate's proper role in the ratification process. Obviously, these senators were thinking not simply about the policy implications of their actions but also about the Constitutional authority of the institution in which they served.

This kind of effort by the members of a national political institution to resist actions that seem to encroach on the institution's constitutional prerogatives is not at all uncommon in American history. The House of Representatives, for example, has frequently opposed efforts by the Senate to weaken the Constitutional preeminence of the House on tax matters. And presidents throughout history have resisted congressional actions designed to weaken the executive branch. Andrew Johnson, for example, was impeached by the House and nearly convicted by the Senate for refusing to comply with a law passed over his veto designed to undermine his control over executive Cabinet officers.

Historical experience has demonstrated, then, that those who serve in the legislative and executive branches develop a personal attachment to the institution in which they serve. As Madison wrote in a famous passage of *Federalist 51*:

> . . . The great security against a gradual concentration of the several powers in the same department consists in giving to those who administer each department the necessary constitutional means and personal motives to resist encroachments of the others. The provision for defense must in this, as in all other cases, be made commensurate to the danger of attack. Ambition must be made to counteract ambition. The interest of the man must be connected with the constitutional rights of the place.

In a properly constructed government, individual officeholders will have a personal interest in preserving the "constitutional rights" of their office. Their ambition to play an important role in national policymaking will incline them to protect the institution which is the source of their influence. In the case of the SALT agreement, for example, individual senators would have lost influence in the ratification process if the mechanism of a joint resolution had been employed. Thus, the members of each institution develop "opposite and rival interests" which prevent any one branch from consolidating all power. As Madison argued, the "private interest of every individual [officeholder becomes] a sentinel over the public rights."

Structural Differences

Another source of conflict between the presidency and Congress lies in the fundamental structural differences between the two institutions. The presidency, as we have seen, is more unified and hierarchical; Congress is more pluralistic and collegial. The institutions were designed in this way in order to give them the qualities most suited to their particular function in the governmental system. According to Hamilton, plurality in the legislative branch would promote "deliberation and wisdom," while unity in the executive would contribute to "decision, activity, secrecy, and dispatch"—the essential ingredients of "energy" in the executive branch.

The framers believed that a legislative body should encompass a great variety of interests and opinions. It should make decisions only after listening to arguments on every side of an issue and carefully weighing these against one another. A relatively large body in which the members have roughly equal authority is more likely to function in this way than a small hierarchically structured institution. On the other hand, a large, collegial institution would make a very poor executive branch. The difficulty of reaching majority agreement among a numerous and diverse membership would render it almost impossible to make decisions swiftly, an essential quality of an effective executive. Moreover, in a large, collegial body the executive duties would be so divided up that it would never be entirely clear who was responsible for carrying out the various administrative tasks. Finally, it would make secrecy virtually impossible if hundreds of individuals had to be consulted on every important decision. If an effective executive must make decisions quickly, see that they are consistently and responsibly carried out, and at times maintain the secrecy of certain confidential or sensitive information, then the executive branch must be headed by a single individual.

That does not mean that a chief executive should act without taking account of varied viewpoints or that the legislature is never faced with the need to act quickly. On balance, however, the structure of the legislative branch should foster the kind of deliberation that results from the interaction of a multiplicity of interests and opinions, and the structure of the executive branch should promote the kind of energy and forcefulness that comes from vesting power in a single person.

Although these structural differences and corresponding institutional capacities may be essential for effective government, they also pose dangers for the governmental system and create conditions that may lead to conflict between the branches. One of these dangers is hasty or precipitous action by the president—action that is taken on the basis of incomplete information, without sufficient attention to a variety of viewpoints, or perhaps without broad-based public support. On the other hand, the slower and more deliberative legislative process may result in unwarranted delays or even failure to make decisions on pressing national problems—a failure made more likely in recent years by internal reforms that have further decentralized the decision-making process in Congress. Conflict arises because presidents tend to grow impatient with a legislative body that often seems incapable of acting decisively, while Congress becomes resentful of an executive branch that so often takes the initiative.

Representational Differences

The final source of conflict between Congress and the presidency derives from how these institutions relate to the American people. Members of Congress think of themselves principally as representatives of their own districts or states. Congress as a whole represents the entire nation because its members are drawn from all parts of the country. The presidency, on the other hand, represents the nation in a very different way. Its head is chosen in a single national election in which all registered voters may participate. No single member of the House or Senate can match the president's claim to speak for the entire American people.

A second important representational difference between the two branches lies in the length of tenure of presidents and members of Congress. Presidents serve a four-year term, renewable only once.

House members serve a two-year term, senators a six-year one, both renewable indefinitely.

What is the practical significance of these differences in how Congress and the presidency represent the American people?

Responding to Shifting Majorities One consequence of these representational differences is that Congress may respond to shifting majorities among the American people more rapidly than the presidency does. Such was the case following the congressional elections of 1982. Having strengthened their hold on the House as a result of public discontent with President Reagan's economic policies, Democrats were more disposed than before to challenge Reagan's policies in Congress. By contrast, the president seemed determined, as he put it, to "stay the course," resisting pressure to trim increases in defense spending and to raise taxes. One of the most important sources of congressional power is the fact that Congress in the midterm election possesses a partial mandate of its own which congressional leaders can use to justify opposition to the presidency.

Different issues divide the nation in different ways. While some issues pit the "frost belt" against the "sun belt," others divide urban areas from rural areas, or perhaps energy-producing areas from energy-consuming areas. One of the strengths of Congress as an institution is that different majority coalitions can form within it to reflect these divisions in the nation at large. We can expect somewhat less responsiveness to shifting majorities on the part of the executive branch, since the ultimate decision maker is a single individual who may possess a rather stable set of political beliefs or attitudes. The other side of this difference, however, is that Congress is less likely than the president to be consistent from one decision to the next.

Exaggeration of the Presidential Mandate Another consequence of the representational difference is a tendency for successful presidential candidates to exaggerate their popular mandate. The winner in a presidential election often interprets that victory as a mandate from the people to carry forth the policies advocated during the campaign. Yet because presidential candidates enunciate positions on so many issues, we cannot simply assume that a majority of the people agree with the president on each one, or even that issues themselves were decisive to the outcome. Other, nonissue factors like youthfulness (John Kennedy), integrity (Jimmy Carter), or geniality (Ronald Reagan) may have been more important. Because the entire nation elects a single individual to our highest office, there is a tendency to assume (often wrongly) that on each issue the president truly speaks with the voice of the people.

Staying Close to the People Important political effects follow from the simple fact that congressional constituencies are much smaller than a presidential constituency. The president represents over 200 million persons; each member of the House represents approximately a half million, and Senate constituencies vary from 400,000 to over 23 million. Because of this difference in size, members of Congress can maintain closer contact with their constituents than presidents can with theirs. Frequent (often weekly) trips home, numerous meetings with constituency groups visiting Washington, and the devotion of a large amount of staff time to constituency service are all ways in which those who serve Congress keep their fingers on the pulse of their district or state. Presidents, of course, have their own means of gauging the sense of the citizenry, but these are necessarily much less direct: reading the results of opinion polls, closely following the national news, and keeping abreast of trends in opinions expressed in the White House mail. Although Jimmy Carter, for one, supplemented these indirect means with trips to the homes of "average" Americans and participation in local "town meetings," such efforts exposed him directly to only a tiny fraction of the American people.

Both before and after his election, Jimmy Carter tried to get a sense of the public mood by talking to people in his hometown of Plains, Georgia. *(Ken Hawkins/ Sygma)*

Susceptibility to Special Interests There *is* something, then, to the claim that Congress as an institution is closer to the people than the presidency is and that the decisions of Congress often reflect public sentiment more accurately. The other side of this, however, is that the members of the House and the Senate may be more susceptible than the president to the force of special or narrow interests. The smaller the constituency, the more leverage any particular special interest can exercise. In the nation as a whole, however, the influence of any one group is diluted by the sheer size of the electorate. Moreover, there are so many different groups throughout the country, often with conflicting aims, that they have a tendency to balance each other off. This puts presidents somewhat "above the battle." It gives them more freedom to pursue the long-range national interest (as they understand it), whereas the members of Congress often look first to the short-range interests of their districts or states.

An excellent illustration of this difference of approach is the controversy that broke out during the Carter administration over federal water projects (dams, irrigation projects, river and harbor improvements, etc.). Traditionally, Congress has insisted on playing the preeminent role in determining national water policy. President Carter believed, however, that congressional decisions in this area had generally been based not on genuine assessments of national needs but instead on the desire of individual members to get all they could for their constituents. This led, in Carter's view, to wasteful overspending on a system lacking any coherent national purpose or direction. When Carter tried to change prevailing practices, he met with intense opposition and had only minimal success.

When Congress and the presidency do battle over issues like this, it is useful to ask which institution accurately reflects public opinion. The answer here is probably both, but in two quite different ways. Congress effectively gave voice to the millions of individual citizens or groups who wanted better flood control, cheap hydroelectric power, improved irrigation of farmlands, more efficient water transportation, and expanded outdoor recreational facilities. The presidency, on the other hand, articulated the general public sentiment for economy in government and for rational and co-

herent national policies, a sentiment shared even by those who favored the water projects.

Representing Diffuse Values As the previous example illustrates, the presidency often does a better job than Congress of reflecting the more generalized or diffuse values or goals of the American people, goals like a balanced budget, reduced inflation, and a clean environment. Individual members of Congress often share these same goals; but if achievement of these goals imposes substantial short-term costs on their constituents—for example, closing a military base, terminating or reducing federal programs, or shutting down a polluting factory—they tend to vote to forestall the costs. Members of the House in particular can hardly be faulted for behaving in this way, since the system was designed precisely to foster their close attachment to the strongly held views of the people.

Differences in Time Perspective No one makes a career of being president. Modern chief executives enter the White House with four years, or at most eight, to make their mark on history. Especially if they are "activists," they will be in a hurry to demonstrate their ability to lead, to shape events, and in general to "get things done." They will try to push their legislative program, or at least its major proposals, through Congress quickly. They may, and often do, express impatience and frustration with the snail-like pace and sometimes less than efficient procedures of the House and Senate. On the other hand, many politicians make careers as members of Congress. Career-minded legislators tend to be jealous of the prerogatives and practices of Congress, not to mention their own power and opportunities for advancement within the institution. Any of these things may concern them more than the president's program does, even if they belong to the same party as the president. In that case, of course, conflict may occur (Polsby, 1976:180–181).

WEAPONS OF INSTITUTIONAL CONFLICT

As we have seen, conflict between the executive and legislative branches is a deep-seated characteristic of American national government. We now turn to the legal, constitutional, and political weapons available to each branch when it does battle with the other.

The Resources of the Presidency

Presidents can draw on a variety of valuable resources when engaged in conflict with the legislative branch. The most important of these are taking the initiative, influencing public opinion, using the power of persuasion, cutting deals, and exercising the veto.

Taking the Initiative There is no single factor that benefits presidents more in trying to get their own way than their ability to take the initiative, or to act before Congress does. The classic case of this was President Washington's proclamation in 1793 that the United States would remain neutral in the war between Great Britain and France. Many in Congress believed that the United States was obligated to come to the aid of France under the terms of the treaty of 1778, which had brought France in on the side of the Americans during the Revolutionary War. Washington's contrary interpretation presented Congress with a *fait accompli*. Constitutionally, Congress retained the authority to declare war against Great Britain; but in practice this would have meant opposing the settled judgment and decision of the highly respected chief executive. The mere fact that the president was able to act first made it more likely that his preferences would hold sway.

More recently, critics of presidential initiative have complained not that it keeps us out of war, but that it gets us into it. Once the president has actually sent troops into combat, whether with proper authority or not, it is particularly difficult for Congress, if it is opposed to the president's actions, to undo them (especially given the public's tendency to "rally around the flag" in the midst of a crisis). As we shall see in Chapter 18, Congress's response to this problem was to pass the War Powers Act of 1973, requiring the president to consult with Congress before sending troops into combat. Yet even this act does not stipulate that the president must receive formal authorization from Congress before exercising the war powers. The authors of the law believed it wise not to restrict the president to the

point where the ability to meet emergencies would be impaired.

While presidents since Washington have found it relatively easy to take initiatives in foreign policy, the same cannot be said of domestic policy. Through most of the nineteenth century it was Congress that usually decided what domestic problems needed solving and what legislative solutions were required. It was Congress, in other words, that set the domestic policy agenda. In our century, however, and especially since the early days of the New Deal, presidents have increasingly set the agenda themselves. Consider, for instance, the president's annual legislative program. It has figured as a regular and accepted feature of American politics since 1948; indeed, when Dwight Eisenhower declined to submit a program to Congress in 1954, he was widely criticized, even by members of Congress. The legislative program permits the president to determine in large measure what proposals, problems, and issues will be debated in Congress as well as in the media and by the attentive public. For President Johnson in 1965, it was the Great Society that most merited consideration by Congress. For Jimmy Carter in 1977, it was the energy crisis and Carter's solution to it. For Ronald Reagan in 1981, it was budget and tax cuts. All three presidents succeeded in focusing Congress's attention where they wanted it.

As if the legislative program were not enough for this purpose, the White House also prepares three major messages to Congress every year: the state of the union message and the budget and economic reports. (The first is required by the Constitution, the last two by acts of Congress.) These messages, not to mention innumerable less important ones, give presidents another medium for defining and highlighting issues and policies of importance to them. Congress may reject a president's recommendations, but—given the intense media coverage the president receives—it can hardly ignore them. And a president who skillfully uses resources such as popularity, patronage, party support in Congress, and a recent electoral "mandate" stands a good chance of getting Congress to accept much of an agenda.

Influencing Public Opinion We have seen in Chapter 10 how presidents attempt to generate public opinion supportive of their policies. The president has tremendous advantages over Congress in access to the media and ability to communicate directly to the public. Congress, of course, is not without means of its own in influencing public opinion. Congressional debates are widely publicized; and individual members of Congress spend long hours in their districts explaining to one group after another their activities in Washington and seeking to build public support. Yet it is a simple fact that hundreds of these individual efforts cannot match the impact of a single, well-executed presidential address on national television.

Using the Power of Persuasion Perhaps the presidential resource most often overlooked in popular accounts of Washington politics is the power of persuading Congress directly of the merits of presidential proposals. This persuasion takes place in several ways. Earlier in this chapter we saw how President Johnson tried to influence important members of Congress through extensive White House briefings. And occasionally Johnson, like other presidents, would meet or telephone members of Congress privately to argue the merits of pending legislation. Most persuasion by the executive branch, however, occurs not at the White House but through formal congressional hearings in the House and Senate when high-ranking executive officials make the administration's case for or against a legislative proposal. Through the congressional hearing process the expertise and the vast information resources of the executive branch—from the White House staff down to the most obscure bureaucrat—can be marshaled to support the president's programs. Former Senator Walter F. Mondale once described the effectiveness of such selective use of resources:

I have been in many debates, for example on the Education Committee, that dealt with complicated formulas and distributions. And I have found that whenever I am on the side of the administration, I am surfeited with computer print-outs and data that comes within seconds, whenever I need it to prove how right I am. But if I am opposed to the administration, computer print-outs always come late,

prove the opposite point, or always are on some other topic. So I think one of the rules is that he who controls the computers controls the Congress . . . (Keefe, 1980:111).

If, as is often said, "information is power," then some part of the president's influence in the system of separation of powers must be attributed to the use of facts and arguments to persuade others.

Cutting Deals It would, of course, be naive to suggest that in direct dealings with members of Congress administration officials limit their endeavors to reasoned persuasion through facts and arguments. Often this is simply not enough; a representative or senator may hold out for a more tangible or immediate benefit for his or her constituents—for example, a new federal project, high price supports or subsidies for agricultural products, or the postponement of a planned closing of a military base. Sometimes presidents are in a position to act directly; at other times they may be asked simply to support or oppose measures before Congress. There were widespread reports, for example, during the contest over the budget in the spring and summer of 1981 that President Reagan cut numerous deals with critical members of the House to help build majority support for his tax and spending cuts.

One of the more common types of deals arranged between the executive and legislative branches has little to do with the well-being of individual districts or states and much to do with the personal interests of the representatives and senators themselves. This occurs when members of Congress seek to benefit politically from an incumbent president's popularity. Members of Congress who are of the same party as the president may seek a firm commitment that the president will actively campaign in their behalf in the next election. Members who are of a different party from the president may make their support for the president's policies contingent on a promise that the president will not actively campaign against them. In the spring of 1981, President Reagan took the initiative in suggesting this kind of arrangement when he let it be known that he would find it very difficult to campaign against any Democrat in 1982 who supported him on his key budget proposals.

This appeal was directed specifically to conservative southern Democrats who were generally more inclined toward Reagan's policies than most other Democrats and in whose districts Reagan was quite popular.

It would not be accurate, however, to give the impression that presidents enter into explicit deals with members of Congress on a regular basis. Some presidents find this kind of bargaining quite distasteful. As Jimmy Carter said in an interview in 1978: "Horse-trading and compromising and so forth have always been very difficult for me to do. I just don't feel at ease with it, and it is a very rare occasion when any member of Congress or anyone else even brings up a subject that could be interpreted by the most severe cynic as a horse-trade" (Edwards, 1980:175). But even presidents less squeamish about bargaining for votes must be quite cautious. A former aide to President Johnson explained why. "If it ever got around the Hill that a President was trading patronage for votes, then everyone would want to trade and all other efforts at persuasion would automatically fail. Each member would tell his neighbor what he got for his votes and soon everyone would be holding out, refusing to decide until the President called" (Kearns, 1976:236). Thus, presidential favor is usually bestowed in reward for a broad pattern of support, rather than for a single supportive vote, and most bargains are based on implicit, not explicit, understandings.

Exercising the Veto As important as the above resources are, there are many times when they are not sufficient. A president may discover that taking the initiative does not control subsequent actions, that public opinion resists efforts to move it (as President Carter discovered on the energy issue), that a majority of the House and Senate cannot be persuaded to go along, and that not enough deals can be struck to carry the day. When all else fails, however, and Congress persists in going its own way, there remains the *veto,* perhaps the most powerful instrument the president possesses next to the position of commander in chief.

The veto, of course, is not absolute. It may be overridden by two-thirds of the House and Senate. As we have seen, however, in the vast majority of cases presidential vetoes are upheld. Moreover, the

mere *threat* of a veto can sometimes serve to keep Congress in line.

The major limitation of the veto is not that it can be overridden, but that it operates negatively. The veto—or the threat of one—can be used to prevent Congress from acting, but not to make it act.

The Resources of Congress

As formidable as the president's resources are, they have not created a permanent imbalance in the system of separation of powers. Congress, after all, is not without its own resources to draw upon in a conflict with the executive. The most important of these are formal lawmaking authority, congressional staff, investigations of the executive branch, the Senate's authority over confirmations of presidential appointments, the legislative veto, and the impeachment power.

Formal Lawmaking Authority As every schoolchild knows, Congress possesses the formal authority to pass legislation for the national government. Yet as obvious and well known as this simple fact is, its full implications are often overlooked by the American public. This is demonstrated by the way we hold the president to account for the successes and failures of the governmental system, even though the president can do little, especially in the domestic arena, without positive legislation. A Congress reluctant to amend or revoke old laws and to pass new ones can thwart the best efforts of a dynamic or activist president. To create (or abolish) social programs, to determine agricultural price supports, to set national transportation policy, to promote (or retard) the civil rights of American citizens, to establish the number of people in the armed forces and endorse new weapons systems, and to determine taxing and spending policy are all powers that fall under the Constitutional purview of the legislative branch. The president may recommend policies in these areas and may influence how congressional statutes are interpreted and carried out, but Congress retains the decisive authority.

Nor has Congress hesitated to wield that authority in an active way, even in periods of supposed presidential dominance. For example, one study of ninety major laws enacted from 1880 to 1945 found that while presidents could take most of the credit for influencing final passage of 20 percent of the laws, Congress could take credit for 40 percent; joint presidential-congressional efforts accounted for 30 percent; and external pressure groups were responsible for the remaining 10 percent. Moreover, seventy-seven of the bills were originally introduced without presidential backing; some of these languished for years in congressional committees, only to be adopted later by presidents who revived them and pushed them through Congress (Chamberlain, 1969). Other studies have shown that Congress continues to take important policy initiatives, with or without presidential backing, in science, consumer and environmental protection, antipoverty programs, transportation, civil rights, labor policy, taxation, and even foreign affairs (Johannes, 1972; Moe and Teel, 1970).

There are several types of congressional initiative. In some cases, Congress may see a need for legislation, draft a bill, hold hearings and mark-up sessions, and enact a law, even over presidential opposition. The Labor-Management Relations (Taft-Hartley) Act of 1947, passed by a Republican-controlled Congress over President Truman's veto, is an important example of such start-to-finish legislation. In other cases, a president may "steal" legislation after Congress has laid the groundwork for it. Lyndon Johnson, for instance, preempted antipollution measures, and John Kennedy proposed his own version of drug safety legislation that had stalled in a Senate committee. In both instances members of Congress had pinpointed a problem, publicized it, conducted extensive investigations, and developed solutions before the White House showed interest in the matter. Occasionally, however, the reverse of this process occurs: Congress preempts proposals developed by the executive branch. In 1946, for example, after President Roosevelt had failed to press for passage of the Employment Act during World War II, interested legislators adopted and maneuvered it through Congress. Again, after President Eisenhower rejected a civil rights bill prepared by the Justice Department, liberals in Congress made it their own; the result was the Civil Rights Act of 1957. Finally, Congress sometimes takes the policy initiative indirectly. After the successful launching of the Soviet satellite Sputnik in 1957, for instance, Congress examined American space and defense policy and threatened to develop on its own a program for space exploration. The Eisenhower administration took the hint and came up with an alternative program (Johannes, 1972).

Thus, although no one can question the importance and perhaps preeminence of the executive branch in making policy, Congress plays a considerable and often innovative part in the process. Indeed, its decentralized structure undoubtedly enhances its ability to develop the most diverse and complex legislation. Subcommittee assignments permit members of Congress to specialize and to acquire expertise rivaling that of executive branch officials. In short, those who suggest that the "president proposes and Congress disposes" have underrated Congress as the country's supreme lawmaking power.

Congressional Staff The 535 members of Congress could hardly hope to master their modern responsibilities and maintain a position of strength without some assistance. Consequently, as noted in Chapter 9, Congress now employs some 23,000 people in supportive staff roles. This number marks a tremendous increase since the 1970s and reflects in part a desire of Congress to be more assertive in dealing with the executive branch.

Control of information in Washington is a major source of power. It has often been argued, for example, that the executive was able to dominate Congress in certain areas during the 1960s because of a lack of congressional expertise. Today, by contrast, congressional staffs supply a potential counterweight to executive branch information in almost every area. Usually the executive agencies still enjoy a distinct advantage over Congress, but they seldom possess the monopoly of information that, in some areas, they once possessed. In budgeting, for example, Congress now has the Congressional Budgeting Office (CBO) to prepare alternative budgets to match those prepared by the Office of Management and Budget (OMB) in the executive branch. Similarly, in foreign affairs, the increase in the last decade in the number of foreign affairs and intelligence experts as staff assistants has greatly facilitated Congress's willingness and ability to involve itself in what would previously have been considered the details of foreign policy-making (see Chapter 18).

The existence of greater staff capacity seems on first impression to allow members of Congress to assume more effectively the role that they want—and should play—in a system of separation of powers. But first impressions can sometimes be deceiving. To the extent that the growing assertiveness of Congress has been a result of the increase in staff, it may represent less a conscious decision on the part of present members of Congress to challenge the executive than merely a way of doing business that they have now come to accept without questioning. Although the original impetus of increasing the size of the staffs came from members of Congress, once in place, staff assistants began to generate work of their own and to provide encouragement for members of Congress to become more active in different areas. In addition, the size of staffs has in certain cases led to a situation in which the members of Congress are merely overseeing a decision-making process in the hands of staff members (Malbin, 1981).

Investigations   One of the most far-reaching and important powers of Congress is the power to conduct formal investigations into the operation of the executive branch. Although this power is not specifically mentioned in the Constitution, it is understood to be implied in the grant of other powers—that is, it is "necessary and proper" for carrying out the specifically enumerated powers. Congress may initiate investigations for several different purposes: to seek evidence of illegality or wrongdoing in executive departments or agencies, to discover whether government officials have subtly undermined the original intention of congressional statutes, to determine whether problems exist within the functioning of the executive branch which should be made public, or simply to harass or embarrass the administration for partisan reasons.

One of the most controversial congressional investigations during the past several decades was the series of hearings conducted by Senator Joseph McCarthy in the early 1950s into allegations that numerous members of the Communist party or its

Senator Joseph McCarthy used Senate hearings to make wild charges of communism in government; he destroyed many careers before his fellow senators finally censured him in 1954.   *(Eve Arnold/Magnum)*

sympathizers had infiltrated important policy-level positions within the State Department. McCarthy used the hearings to appeal to widespread public fears regarding the communist menace in America. Most political historians regard McCarthy's high-handed tactics—misuse of evidence, guilt by association, innuendo—as an abuse of the congressional investigatory power.

In more recent years, the most widely publicized congressional investigation was that conducted by a specially appointed Senate committee, chaired by Sam Ervin, to investigate various allegations of wrongdoing within the executive branch arising out of the Watergate affair. The revelations that came to light before Ervin's committee subsequently led to impeachment proceedings in the House of Representatives and ultimately to the resignation of Richard Nixon from the presidency. A few years later, special committees in both the House and the Senate conducted controversial investigations into charges that the Central Intelligence Agency (CIA) had abused its powers in the domestic and the international arenas. The evidence unearthed at these hearings led directly to new procedures of congressional oversight to monitor the operation of the CIA.

As these examples indicate, a congressional investigation can have more than just symbolic effects. When properly used, it is a formidable weapon for preserving the balance of powers between the two political branches.

Confirmations   One of the best known of the checks and balances explicitly written into the original Constitution is the Senate's veto power over high presidential appointments. Nominations to ambassadorships, the federal judiciary, and the Cabinet, as well as other important positions, must be approved by a majority of the Senate. Traditionally, the Senate has granted chief executives great leeway in making executive branch appointments. Seldom does partisan politics play a role. On those few occasions when the Senate balks at a presidential nomination—as in Reagan's selection of Ernest Lefevre for assistant secretary of state for human rights—it is because substantial questions have been raised about the candidate's qualifications or fitness for the job.

The same pattern holds for nominations to the Supreme Court—although Richard Nixon charged that the Democratic Senate's refusal to confirm his nominations of Clement Haynesworth and Harold Carswell to the Supreme Court was the result of the antisouthern and liberal biases of his political opponents. For appointments to the lower federal courts, however, the usual order of nomination by the president and confirmation by the Senate is virtually reversed. This is a result of the principle of "senatorial courtesy." According to this norm, members of the Senate will not confirm the nomination of a federal district judge who is opposed by the senior senator of the president's party representing the state in which the judge would serve. The norm also applies to other executive nominations affecting only one state. It gives individual senators so much clout that it virtually forces the president to request the names of acceptable candidates at the very beginning of the appointment process. By selecting one of these, the president in effect "confirms" the person "nominated" by the senator.

The overriding importance of the Senate's confirmation power, however, is not that it allows senators to promote their own candidates, but rather that it induces presidents to select candidates of substantial merit, fitness, and presumed integrity for positions of high public trust. The Senate's power is a beneficial check on the damage that could result from the actions of a misguided or corrupt chief executive.

Legislative Veto   Until recently, one device Congress employed to maintain its influence over decisions made by the executive branch was the so-called "legislative veto." In the typical case, the legislative veto provision authorized the president (or an executive agency) to undertake certain kinds of actions, but reserved for Congress the right to overturn the president's (or the agency's) actions within a specified period of time—usually sixty to ninety days. Depending upon how the provision was written, the "veto" could be exercised by a majority in one house or both houses, or occasionally simply by a committee. Presidential actions that were subject to this kind of control included reorganization of the executive branch, introduction of armed forces into combat, and the sale of large amounts of weapons to foreign nations. In total, over 200 statutes enacted between 1932 and 1983 included some form of legislative veto.

Several recent presidents vigorously opposed the growing use of the legislative veto on both policy and constitutional grounds. Jimmy Carter, in particular, complained that "the Legislative veto injects the Congress into the details of administrating substantive programs and laws. . . . Such intrusive devices infringe on the Executive's constitutional duty to faithfully execute the laws" (presidential message to Congress, June 21, 1978). Congress, on the other hand, maintained that the veto was the only effective way to control the vast delegations of authority it made to the executive branch. As with so many other vital questions in American society, however, the final word on the use of the device has fallen to the federal courts. A ruling handed down by the Supreme Court in June 1983 has called into question the constitutionality of this mingling of executive and legislative powers.

In *Immigration and Naturalization Service v. Chadha,* the Supreme Court held that legislation allowing either house of Congress to veto certain executive branch decisions was in violation of the constitutional doctrine of separation of powers. While acknowledging that legislative veto provisions have been "appearing with increasing frequency in statutes which delegate authority to executive and independent agencies," the Court held that this practice violates the explicit provisions of the Constitution which require that legislative powers be exercised through action by both houses of Congress and presentation to the president for signature or veto. Drawing on sources including the records of the Constitutional Convention and the *Federalist Papers,* Chief Justice Burger stated: "With all the obvious flaws of delay, untidiness, and potential for abuse, we have not yet found a better way to preserve freedom than by making the exercise of power subject to the carefully crafted restraints spelled out in the Constitution" (*New York Times,* 1983:B5). The ultimate consequences of this important decision for the exercise of powers delegated to the executive along with legislative veto provisions may not be clear for some time; but this action by the Supreme Court shows once again that the ongoing need for adaption and change must take into account the basic purposes which underlie our institutional arrangements. Now that

the legislative veto has been declared unconstitutional, some see this as releasing the executive branch from the close control which has been exercised by recent Congresses. Others, however, believe that Congress will be less willing to delegate authority to the executive or will carefully limit those powers it does delegate. Only time will tell.

Impeachment   As important as all these resources are to Congress for upholding its proper Constitutional role in the American system of separation of powers, they pale in comparison with the power of impeachment. Impeachment and removal of a president from office is the ultimate check available to the legislative branch on an aggrandizing chief executive.

Under the Constitution, a president, a vice president, a high executive branch official, or a federal judge may be removed from office if accused by a majority of the House and convicted by two-thirds of the Senate of "treason, bribery, or other high crimes and misdemeanors." The procedure is the same for the president as for other officers of the government, with the single exception that the chief justice of the Supreme Court presides at the trial of a president in the Senate.

Before Richard Nixon's presidency and the Watergate scandal, the only president who had come close to this type of involuntary retirement was Andrew Johnson, who acceded to the presidency upon Abraham Lincoln's death. Johnson was bitterly opposed by large majorities in both branches of Congress for his moderate Reconstruction policies, and his vetoes of numerous congressional statutes designed to undermine his control of the executive branch and the Army were regularly overturned by Congress. Yet even Johnson was able to survive the impeachment process (by one slim vote in the Senate). The failure of this one serious impeachment effort, combined with the judgment of later generations that the Congress of 1868 had dangerously abused its authority in a highly partisan fashion, made subsequent impeachment efforts much less likely. By the middle of the twentieth century, many Constitutional scholars had come to judge the impeachment provisions of the document of 1787 as very much a dead letter, too drastic a penalty to contribute to the subtle dynamics of the American system of separation of powers.

With a strangely inappropriate gesture of victory, Richard Nixon left Washington after resigning from the presidency on August 9, 1974, rather than face impeachment. *(Dennis Cook/UPI)*

The presidency of Richard Nixon managed to change all this. Revelations that some of his subordinates had helped to plan a break-in at the Democratic national headquarters (in the Watergate office building in Washington, D.C.) in June 1972, and that others obstructed the FBI investigation into the break-in, led in 1974 to the initiation of formal impeachment hearings before the Judiciary Committee of the House of Representatives. After several months of hearing testimony and collecting evidence, the committee voted out three articles of impeachment against the president. Before these could be taken up by the full House, however, the Supreme Court ruled unanimously in *United States v. Nixon* that the president had to turn over to the special prosecutor tape re-

cordings of conversations that had taken place in the Oval Office between Nixon and his top aides. Nixon, who repeatedly denied any involvement in the break-in or its cover-up, had been withholding these tapes on grounds of executive privilege and separation of powers. Because the tapes contained the clearest evidence to date that Nixon had been personally involved in the cover-up from the beginning, the little support he still had in Congress rapidly dissolved. Nixon resigned from office before the impeachment process had been completed (see Box 11-3).

The Nixon episode demonstrated the great vitality of the American checks-and-balances system. Only a few short years after many serious scholars had argued that the presidency had achieved "imperial" dimensions under Nixon, Congress was able to force the incumbent from office for violating his Constitutional obligations to "take care that the laws are faithfully executed" and to "preserve, protect, and defend the Constitution."

BASES FOR COOPERATION

It is common in accounts of the American separation-of-powers system to emphasize the conflict that occurs between the legislative and executive branches of government. This is hardly surprising, since, as we saw earlier in this chapter, institutional jealousies and structural and representational differences all contribute to clashes between the branches. The story, however, is not complete if we leave it at that, for there must also be some degree of cooperation between the presidency and Congress if anything useful or important is to be accomplished. Indeed, as we saw in the discussion of Lyndon Johnson, that cooperation can at times be quite close and fruitful.

What are the forces, then, that encourage cooperation? What inclines these two distinct institutions to work together constructively to promote the national well-being?

Political Party

The one political institution in American national politics that makes a significant contribution to bridging the gap between the presidency and Con-

---

BOX 11-3

A WATERGATE CHRONOLOGY: HIGHLIGHTS OF THE WATERGATE CRISIS

1972

June 17 — Arrest of five men for breaking into Democratic national headquarters

1973

March 5 — Disclosure, in Senate Judiciary Committee hearings, that officials of the Nixon reelection committee tried to obstruct FBI investigation of break-in

July 16 — Disclosure, in Senate Select Committee on Presidential Campaign Activities, that President Nixon's White House and Executive Office conversations had been regularly tape-recorded since 1971

July 26 — Rejection by Nixon of subpoenas of White House tapes and documents by Senate Select Committee and Watergate special prosecutor Archibald Cox

October 20 — "Saturday night massacre": Nixon orders Attorney General Elliot Richardson to dismiss special prosecutor Cox; Richardson and Deputy Attorney General William Ruckelshaus resign rather than comply

1973

November 1 — Appointment of Leon Jaworski as new special prosecutor

1974

May 9 — Beginning of formal impeachment hearings by House Judiciary Committee

July 24 — 8–0 Supreme Court ruling that Nixon must relinquish tapes to special prosecutor Jaworski

July 27, 29, 30 — Approval by House Judiciary Committee of three articles of impeachment charging Nixon with obstruction of justice, abuse of presidential powers, and contempt of Congress

August 5 — Release of transcripts by Nixon showing clearly his early involvement in cover-up attempt

August 8 — Resignation of Nixon

September 8 — Unconditional pardon of Nixon by President Ford

---

gress is the political party. Although the Democratic and Republican parties have no Constitutional basis or status, they have a very real (if declining) influence in generating cooperation between the two political branches. The president, after all, is the effective leader of one of the two major parties; and both parties, as we have seen, play an important role in the structure and organization of the House and Senate. The leaders of the president's party in Congress have been his natural allies and have usually worked closely with the president in promoting his programs. This was certainly true during the Reagan administration, when House Minority Leader Robert Michel and Senate spokesmen for administration policy within Congress.

To some degree, this duty to support the president has been felt by nearly all the members of his party in Congress. Nonetheless, it is nearly always true that at least some party members will break with the president, even on key issues. Rarely has a president held every member of his party in the House or Senate on a controversial matter. President Reagan, however, managed this in the House on several key votes on his budget proposals in the spring and summer of 1981. This shows that as weak as political parties may have become in the twentieth century, they are not without some influence in shaping political events and decisions.

The Coattail Effect

One way in which a political party may encourage cooperation between the two branches is through the electoral process. In some national elections, an especially popular presidential candidate has helped to sweep members of his own party into office on his "coattails." This was particularly true when straight-party voting was more common than it is now. If a presidential candidate generated real enthusiasm among the electorate, thousands of people might vote who would otherwise stay home. And if some of these pulled the party lever in the voting booth, numerous other candidates for national, state, or local office would benefit.

In the past few decades, the rise of split-ticket voting and the decline in the number of those who identify strongly with one of the two major parties have weakened the coattail effect. The classic example was the election of 1972. In the contest for the presidency, Richard Nixon, the Republican, scored a landslide victory over the Democrat, George McGovern, by winning 61 percent of the national vote. Yet in this same election the public returned large Democratic majorities to control in the House and Senate. Democrats won 243 of the 435 House seats and 16 of the 33 open Senate seats, maintaining a 57-43 margin in the Senate. As one Nixon aide lamented later: "We had tremendous public and electoral support. But that and a dime couldn't buy a cup of coffee. It was still a question of what we didn't have: what we didn't have was enough Republican congressmen" (Light, 1982:29).

It would, however, be an exaggeration to say that the coattail effect is dead. The elections of 1964 and 1980 suggest otherwise. In the first of these, when Lyndon Johnson overwhelmingly defeated Barry Goldwater for the presidency, 39 Democratic challengers ousted Republican incumbents from the House of Representatives. Two years later, most of these Democrats were themselves removed from office. Most of the evidence suggests that they owed their original election to the Johnson landslide. Similarly, Reagan's solid victory over Carter and John Anderson in 1980 was accompanied by dramatic Republican advances in Congress: twenty-seven Republican challengers ousted Democratic incumbents from the House, and nine Republican challengers did the same in the Senate, giving Republicans their first majority in that body since 1954.

The existence and strength of the coattail effect are always subject to interpretation. It is impossible to determine precisely whether the success of congressional candidates of the same party as the presidential winner is a spillover of the popularity of the head of the ticket or broad-based national endorsement of one party over the other. But whatever the true explanation, what matters most is whether many members of Congress *believe* that they owe their election at least in part to the president. If they think this, true or not, then the combination of gratitude and their desire to repeat their earlier success will incline them to support the president's programs while they serve in Congress.

Crisis

Perhaps the most powerful, if shortest-lived, stimulus for interbranch cooperation is the existence of a national crisis. The economic collapse of the 1930s, for example, did more than any other single factor to foster a close cooperation between the presidency and Congress in Franklin Roosevelt's first term. The bombing of Pearl Harbor in 1941 did the same in the military and foreign policy areas. More recently, the classic case is the hurried passage by Congress of the Gulf of Tonkin Resolution in 1964, giving President Johnson virtually unlimited authority to act militarily in southeast Asia. In response to administration reports that North Vietnamese torpedo boats had attacked an American destroyer in international waters, the members of Congress voted 414-0 in the House and 88-2 in the Senate to support the president's request for additional military authority. Eventually, the spirit of cooperation between the two political branches dissolved in the face of growing opposition within Congress to presidential policy on Vietnam. Nonetheless, there is no denying how powerful a sense of crisis or urgency can be in counterbalancing, at least for a time, the many forces that make for conflict between the separate branches of American government.

Common Purpose

The final factor that generates cooperation between the presidency and Congress is the most difficult to identify and classify. Its pervasiveness in the political process is overshadowed by the more obvious forces that draw together or drive apart the executive and legislature. This is the simple fact that amidst all the political squabbles, the institutional jealousies, and the clashes of interest and perspective, those who serve in the two political branches often share a genuine desire to work together to achieve common goals—goals, for example, like a sound national defense, a healthy economy, and the protection of the rights and liberties of the American citizenry. Agreement on certain basic ends may cut across partisan as well as institutional barriers and thereby foster cooperative efforts among members of both parties and both branches.

This is not to say that conflict will be absent from the political arena (is it ever?), but only to point out that conflict need not necessarily divide the institutions from one another. For example, when the great battles were waged over national civil rights legislation in the early and middle 1960s, the conflicts did not divide one branch of government from the other or even one political party from the other, but rather one region of the country—the south—and its congressional representatives from the rest. Throughout the conflict a majority of those in the House and Senate worked closely with the Johnson administration to bring about fundamental political and social change.

In this respect, the sense of common purpose is like the reaction to a national crisis: the members of the two branches work together to meet a recognized national need. It is different, however, in that it is usually less forceful, less urgent, and of a longer duration than the reaction to a crisis. Although this force for cooperation is often ignored in accounts of presidential-congressional interaction, its consequences are quite real.

CONCLUSION

There is no denying that the sources of conflict between Congress and the presidency are powerful and deep. This conflict was quite intentionally built into the system by its architects, and it has effectively achieved its principal purpose: to keep any one branch from concentrating all powers within its hands and tyrannizing over the others. Indeed,

it is rare in American history that one branch of government has been truly dominant (perhaps Congress after the Civil War and the presidency in Franklin Roosevelt's first term). As was discussed in Chapter 10, the pendulum tends to swing back and forth between the branches. Whenever one seems to overstep its proper Constitutional bounds, the other is able to employ a variety of weapons to resist these excesses. This promotes both adherence to the constitutional framework and stability in the governmental system.

Critics like Lloyd Cutler, on the other hand, complain that this conflict does more harm than good: that it makes coherent policymaking almost impossible, that it drastically slows down the response of government to pressing national problems, that it hinders public accountability, and that it results finally in a "stalemate" between the branches of government. But would structural reforms designed to introduce a smooth-running majoritarian democracy—as opposed to the present system that includes many pluralistic elements—really improve the character of popular government? If there are conflict and stalemate in government, most likely they reflect divisions and uncertainty in American society itself. In that case, perhaps prolonged discussion and debate are better than rushing to "do something" about the nation's problems. If so, the system of separation of powers encourages the building of consensus, the gradual working out of the "cool and deliberate sense of the community." The would-be constitution maker must ask whether a parliamentary-style system could foster such moderation.

We have seen, after all, that there is more to the relationship between Congress and the presidency than just conflict. The forces that encourage or promote cooperation can have quite lasting and desirable effects. These should not be discounted in any assessment of the American system of separation of powers.

SOURCES

Chamberlain, Lawrence H.: "The President, Congress, and Legislation," in Aaron Wildavsky (ed.), *The President*, Little, Brown, Boston, 1969, pp. 440–453.

Cutler, Lloyd: "To Form a Government," *Foreign Affairs,* fall 1980, pp. 126–143.

Edwards, George C., III: *Presidential Influence in Congress,* Freeman, San Francisco, 1980.

Jefferson, Thomas: *The Portable Thomas Jefferson,* Merrill Peterson (ed.), Viking, New York, 1975.

Johannes, John R.: "Congress and the Initiation of Legislation," *Public Policy,* spring 1972, pp. 281–309.

Kearns, Doris: *Lyndon Johnson and the American Dream,* Harper and Row, New York, 1976.

Keefe, William J.: *Congress and the American People,* Prentice-Hall, Englewood Cliffs, N.J., 1980.

Light, Paul: *The President's Agenda,* Johns Hopkins Press, Baltimore and London, 1982.

Malbin, Michael J.: "Delegation, Deliberation, and the New Role of Congressional Staff," in Thomas E. Mann and Norman J. Ornstein (eds.), *The New Congress,* American Enterprise Institute, Washington, D.C., 1981, pp. 134–177.

McPherson, Harry: *A Political Education,* Little, Brown, Boston, 1972.

Moe, Ronald C., and Steven C. Teel: "Congress as Policy-Maker: A Necessary Reappraisal," *Political Science Quarterly,* September 1970, pp. 443–470.

New York Times, June 24, 1983.

Polsby, Nelson W.: *Congress and the Presidency,* 3d ed., Prentice-Hall, Englewood Cliffs, N.J., 1976.

Schmitt, Gary: *Executive Agreements and Separation of Powers,* Ph.D. dissertation, University of Chicago, 1980.

Sundquist, James L.: *The Decline and Resurgence of Congress,* Brookings Institution, Washington, D.C., 1981.

Wilson, James Q.: "In Defense of Separation of Powers," in Thomas E. Cronin (ed.), *Rethinking the Presidency,* Little, Brown, Boston, 1982, pp. 179–182.

RECOMMENDED READINGS

Fisher, Louis: *The Politics of Shared Power: Congress, and the Executive,* Congressional Quarterly Press, Washington, D.C., 1981. Analyzes the complex interrelationship between the presidency, the bureaucracy, and the Congress, emphasizing legal and Constitutional elements.

Light, Paul: *The President's Agenda,* Johns Hopkins Press, Baltimore and London, 1982. An account of how the agenda of public policy has been formed in recent administrations.

Sundquist, James L.: *The Decline and Resurgence of Congress,* Brookings Institution, Washington, D.C., 1981. An examination of the role of Congress in the policymaking process in recent decades.

Wayne, Stephen J.: *The Legislative Presidency,* Harper and Row, New York, 1978. An examination of the role of the presidency in the legislative process.

Chapter 12

The Judiciary

CHAPTER CONTENTS

"The power of the Supreme Court is indeed great, but it does not extend to everything; it is not great enough to *change* the Constitution. . . ." These words have a contemporary ring, for in recent years the courts—and particularly the United States Supreme Court—have often been accused of reading their own policy preferences into the law. Yet the voice is that of Spencer Roane, chief justice of the Virginia Supreme Court, registering his indignation at the decision of *McCulloch v. Maryland* (1819), one of the early landmark cases of the United States Supreme Court (Gunther, 1969:11).

As Roane's words suggest, controversy about the role of the courts in American politics is nothing new. Thomas Jefferson, who at first had defended judicial power, later railed against many of the decisions of the Supreme Court, warning that the nation was in danger of falling under a "judicial despotism." In the mid-nineteenth century, the Court entered into the midst of the slavery controversy in the decision of *Dred Scott v. Sanford* (1857), striking down the Missouri Compromise and ruling that black people could not be citizens of the United States in the full sense. In the 1930s, the Supreme Court declared major parts of President Franklin Roosevelt's New Deal program unconstitutional, leading to the president's famous confrontation with the judiciary over his plan to "pack" the Court in 1937. During the 1950s, the Supreme Court's decision in *Brown v. Board of Education* (1954) outlawing school segregation provoked widespread resistance in the south and helped set in motion the entire civil rights movement of the next decade. In the 1960s and 1970s, decisions outlawing prayer in the public schools, extending the rights of defendants, requiring the reapportionment of state legislatures, granting women a right to abortion, and limiting the states' ability to combat obscenity placed the role of the Supreme Court at the center of political controversy, sometimes as a major issue in presidential campaigns. In the past decade, congressional legislation or Constitutional amendments have been introduced to overturn the Court's decisions on abortion, school prayer, and busing.

For better or worse, the courts in the United States have been deeply involved in political issues. As Tocqueville remarked in the 1830s, when the role of the courts was clearly more modest than it is today, "There is hardly a political question in the United States which does not sooner or later turn into a judicial question" (1968:270). There is surely no more distinctive feature of American politics, when compared with the politics of other western democracies, than the extraordinary power and influence of the courts. In some sixty nations, the law proclaims the power of judicial review, and in a few cases—India, Australia, and France—the judiciary will occasionally exercise it. But in no nation does the level of judicial involvement in key decisions approach that played by the courts in the United States. Decisions in other democratic nations that would be considered entirely "political" and would be made by elected officials are routinely made or influenced in the United States by appointed judges on the basis of purportedly legal grounds.

Yet, while conflict over judicial decisions is nothing new, some observers maintain that the courts' involvement in ordinary policymaking in recent years is unprecedented, in both its scope and its character. The courts in this view have become virtually a second legislature, intervening in a variety of policy areas—for example, prison administration, welfare administration, and environmental policy—which were formerly the exclusive preserve of the political branches. And rather than merely deciding conflicts between litigants, the courts have used individual cases to announce broad policy requirements. These decisions have sometimes required political authorities not merely to desist from conduct deemed illegal or unconstitutional (which was the nature of most judicial remedies in the past), but to establish specific, positive programs, like the busing of schoolchildren, to change existing circumstances. Such a role for the courts, critics maintain, goes far beyond what was ever intended by the founders and has created a guardian institution that is remaking American society according to its own standards and undermining popular government in the process (Elliott, 1974; Nisbet, 1982).

Not all commentators, however, endorse this negative assessment of recent judicial activity. Some deny that the courts' decisions mark a radical departure from the past. The courts, they argue, are merely enforcing legal and Constitutional norms in new fields of governmental activity.

To the surprise and displeasure of many, Chief Justice Earl Warren led the Supreme Court's broad and active intervention in behalf of racial desegregation in the 1950s. *(Karsh, Ottowa / Woodfin Camp)*

As Congress and federal administrative agencies have ventured into new policy fields, creating additional legal requirements, they have prompted litigation and thereby involved the courts more deeply in governing. Other commentators, while acknowledging that the courts have sought out unprecedented responsibilities, argue that this represents a positive development, since it increases government's responsiveness to certain public needs, especially those of underprivileged groups said to be inadequately represented in the ordinary political process (Ely, 1980; Neely, 1981).

This debate raises a controversy of major importance. Have the courts in recent years taken on a new role in governing? If so, what accounts for this phenomenon? Does it represent a positive or a negative development? These modern questions, however, cannot be intelligently discussed until an even more basic one has been asked: What role should the courts play in governing in the United States? Coming to grips with this question will re-

quire us to analyze the nature of the judicial power, the special place of judicial review, and the organization and operation of the federal court system. We can then return to the issues of the judiciary's place in American politics and analyze the contemporary debate over its expanded role.

THE ROLE OF THE COURTS

"It is emphatically the province and duty of the judicial department," Chief Justice John Marshall proclaimed in *Marbury v. Madison,* "to say what the law is." The courts do this in the course of deciding disputes (cases) which require the interpretation of law and its application. Federal law comes primarily from three sources: the United States Constitution, Congress, and federal administrative agencies. The Constitution specifies the powers of the national government, divides those powers among the various branches, and places limitations on both the national and the state governments. Federal statutes, enacted by Congress, either impose legal requirements or outlaw certain kinds of behavior. Federal regulations, established by administrative agencies, both give further specificity to acts of Congress and prescribe rules which agencies must follow in carrying out their responsibilities. (In addition, because of the federal character of our system, the law also includes the state constitutions and all state and local laws and administrative rulings; where relevant, federal judges may apply these as well.)

Judicial interpretation of all types of law involves the courts in deciding questions that vitally affect government policy. However, an important distinction must be drawn between judicial interpretation of statutes and regulations on the one hand and judicial interpretation of the Constitution on the other. In the case of interpretation of statutes and regulations, court decisions—important as they may be—represent an attempt to define what Congress or the administrative agency intended and to fill in the gaps in their laws or rules. If Congress or the administrative agency disagrees with a court interpretation, it can overturn or correct the interpretation by simply passing another law or writing another regulation. By contrast, when the courts interpret the Constitution, their

---

BOX 12-1

A GLOSSARY OF LEGAL TERMS

Affirm   To uphold the decision of a lower court.

Amicus curiae brief   "Friend of the court" brief. A brief submitted with Supreme Court permission by an interested group which is not a party in a case.

Appeal   A petition to a higher court for review of a lower court decision.

Appellate jurisdiction   The power of a court to hear appeals.

Brief   A document prepared by legal counsel which presents legal arguments, facts, and other considerations which support his or her client's position in a case.

Certiorari   "To make certain." A petition for Supreme Court review of a lower court decision, which the Court has complete discretion to grant or refuse.

Civil law   The division of law dealing with the definition and enforcement of legal rights. These rights may result from either private action (for example, contracts between parties) or governmental action.

Conference   The closed meeting of Supreme Court justices, in which they vote on whether to hear cases and both discuss and vote on cases in which they have heard oral argument.

Constitutional law   The division of law dealing with the interpretation of the Constitution and with determining the validity of laws and official actions taken under its authority.

Criminal law   The division of law dealing with crimes and punishments.

General-jurisdiction courts   Courts authorized to hear cases involving all subjects within federal jurisdiction.

Jurisdiction   The power of a court to hear a case. This power may be limited to specific geographical areas, subject matters, or persons.

Limited-jurisdiction courts   Courts limited to hearing only cases involving certain specific subjects.

Magistrate   A judicial officer authorized to hear minor cases and act for district court judges in certain court functions, such as setting bail.

Original jurisdiction   The power of a court to hear and decide cases before their consideration by any other court.

Per curiam   "By the court." An unsigned opinion issued by the court collectively.

Precedent   A decision on a point of law which provides guidance for the decision of subsequent cases.

Reverse   To overrule the decision of a lower court.

Stare decisis   "Let the decision stand." The doctrine that principles of law enunciated in judicial decisions should not be overruled in subsequent decisions.

---

power is much greater. Here the courts speak for the Constitution, which is the fundamental law of the land. This leaves the other political agencies with no ordinary recourse, since they are bound to respect the Constitution. It is this power of the courts to interpret the Constitution that is the core of the doctrine of *judicial review.*

The Meaning of Judicial Review

"Judicial review" is the power of courts to rule on whether government actions conflict with the Constitution (or any higher law) and are therefore null and void.* The government actions that may be declared invalid are of almost every conceivable kind—laws passed by Congress, regulations written by agencies, laws and regulations enacted by state or local authorities, or actions taken by any government official, from the president of the United States down to the local police officer. All

---

*The higher law in question may be a federal law in relation to a state or local law or a state constitutional provision in relation to a state law. Our focus on judicial review in this chapter will be exclusively on the interpretation of the Constitution.

courts in the United States theoretically possess the power of judicial review. In practice, however, when state courts or lower federal courts pronounce an important statute unconstitutional, their rulings are invariably appealed to higher courts and ultimately to the Supreme Court. During this period of appeal, the rulings of the lower courts generally hold only for the particular cases that have been tried and only for courts within the jurisdiction of the highest court that has ruled. Everyone awaits a more definite decision from the higher court and ultimately from the Supreme Court.

It should not be assumed that the power of judicial review operates only where courts actually hold certain actions unconstitutional. As in the case of the president's veto power, the power of judicial review "works" by the anticipation that it might be used as well as by its actual use. It is the "restraining power of its presence" rather than the frequency of its application that makes judicial review so important in the governmental process of the United States (Abraham, 1975:319). The fact that judicial review exists serves to make most legislators aware that their actions must take Constitutional considerations into account when they make their decisions.

The most dramatic decisions involve those instances in which the courts judge a federal law or an action taken by the president, for in these instances the power of the judicial branch is posed against institutions chosen by the people of the entire nation. Consider the following examples.

In 1974 Congress passed a landmark piece of legislation regulating the financing of all campaigns for public office. In 1976, in the midst of the primary campaign for the presidency, the Supreme Court in the decision of *Buckley v. Valeo* declared numerous provisions of this law to be unconstitutional, including a limitation on spending for congressional campaigns, a limitation on what individuals could spend on their own to support a candidate, and limitations on what candidates could spend on their own behalf.

In 1973, President Nixon had in his possession a series of tape recordings that included several private discussions on the subject of the break-in at the Watergate Hotel. Citing the doctrine of "executive privilege," the president refused to divulge the contents of these tapes either to Congress or to the courts. In the celebrated case of *United States v. Nixon* (1974), the Court required the president to turn over the tapes to a lower court for use in a criminal prosecution. This led to the disclosure of an incriminating discussion that forced the president's resignation.

Insofar as federal laws are concerned, the Supreme Court since the beginning has declared some 105 provisions of federal law unconstitutional, excluding the large number voided by the 1983 decision which struck down the use of the legislativive veto (see Table 12–1). Only two such provisions were struck down before 1860; and most of the activity has been in this century, in the 1920s and

TABLE 12-1
JUDICIAL REVIEW *
Provisions of Federal Law Held Unconstitutional by the Supreme Court

Period	Number of provisions held unconstitutional
1790–1839	1
1840–1889	17
1890–1919	19
1920–1929	15
1930–1939	13
1940–1949	2
1950–1959	4
1960–1969	18
1970–1978	16
Total	105

Provisions of State Laws and Local Ordinances Held Unconstitutional by the Supreme Court

Period	Number of provisions held unconstitutional
1790–1839	19
1840–1889	121
1890–1919	192
1920–1929	140
1930–1939	91
1940–1949	58
1950–1959	69
1960–1969	140
1970–1979	177
Total	1007

* Through end of 1977 term.
Source: Congressional Research Service, 1973, 1978.

1930s and again after the 1950s. However, *Dred Scott v. Sanford* in 1857 and the series of cases against economic welfare legislation in the 1920s and especially from 1933 to 1936 were far more significant in their immediate impact than the decisions made since 1960. Most of the provisions of federal law declared unconstitutional have been relatively minor, with the exception of parts of the campaign finance legislation voided by *Buckley v. Valeo* and a bill that sought to lower the voting age to 18 for all elections, state as well as federal. The Court denied that Congress had the power to lower the voting age for state elections in *Oregon v. Mitchell* (1970), but the decision was overturned by the Twenty-Sixth Amendment.

The Court's power of Constitutional interpretation involves not only the substance of public policy but also the important task of helping to define the respective powers of the institutions of the national government. Although the Court has generally been reluctant to insert itself into ordinary struggles between the president and Congress, it has on occasion stepped in to establish the nature and boundaries of the executive, legislative, and judicial powers. For example, in *Immigration and Naturalization Service v. Chadha* (1983), the Court enforced a strict interpretation of the Constitutional doctrine of separation of powers in voiding the legislative veto, which had become a common device used to allocate authority between Congress and the executive branch.

Less dramatic, but equally important for understanding the power of the courts, is judicial review of state and local laws and of the activities of state and local officials. Under the power of judicial review, the courts have acted to desegregate public schools, to limit state power, and to adjust the powers and behavior of police officers, prosecutors, and local judges and juries. In the last area mentioned, there have been literally thousands of cases in which the courts have ruled on whether police interrogations and searches for evidence have violated the Constitutional rights of suspects.

The Supreme Court and federal courts more generally have been much less reluctant to strike down state laws as unconstitutional. According to one count, the Supreme Court has invalidated over 1,000 state laws and constitutional provisions (see Table 12–1), and other federal courts have voided many times that number. Several considerations, apart from the obvious fact that there are more state laws passed, account for the judiciary's more frequent invalidation of state enactments.

First, the Constitutional basis for judicial review of state legislation is considerably clearer than for federal legislation. In establishing a national government to take the place of the weak Confederation, the founders were especially careful to include in the Constitution a clause stipulating the supremacy of the Constitution, federal laws, and treaties over state constitutions and laws (Article VI). The Supreme Court under Chief Justice Marshall was quick to seize on this supremacy clause and use it as a basis of authority for federal courts over the actions of state officials. Second, the Court has recognized that the Constitutional judgment of a local political majority is entitled to less deference than the judgment of a national political majority as expressed in legislation by a coequal branch of government. The Court, therefore, approaches state legislation with a much greater willingness to question its validity and to impose its own judgments. (Frequently, however, the state laws struck down do have the support of national majorities, as evidenced by the fact that many or all states may have similar kinds of laws.) Third, the courts since the 1920s have dramatically increased the areas of state activity potentially subject to Constitutional invalidation by extending the Bill of Rights to apply to most actions of the states. Before the 1920s, the Bill of Rights applied only to relations of the individual to the national government. But since the 1920s, the federal courts have gradually incorporated most of these rights into the due process clause of the Fourteenth Amendment, which is directed against state governments. Finally, state legislatures are perhaps more likely than Congress to adopt unconstitutional legislation.

This last point is not surprising. Although most of the founders in the end supported the idea of federalism (some reluctantly), they were generally quite wary of the danger posed by local majorities. Recall James Madison's famous argument in *Federalist* 10. The most serious problem facing democratic governments, Madison pointed out, is majority faction, that is, the combination of a majority of citizens to pursue ends "adverse to the rights of other citizens, or to the permanent and aggregate interests of the community." To lessen this danger, the founders withdrew policy control in certain do-

---

BOX 12-2

HUNT v. WASHINGTON APPLE ADVERTISING COMMISSION (1977):
THE SUPREME COURT RULES A STATE LAW UNCONSTITUTIONAL

The parties

The Washington Apple Advertising Commission, acting on behalf of the state's apple growers and distributors; James B. Hunt, governor of North Carolina.

The issue

The Washington commission claimed that North Carolina's apple-container legislation, by discriminating in favor of local producers and impeding the free flow of interstate commerce, violated the commerce clause (Article I, Section 8) of the United States Constitution.

The background of the case

In 1973, the North Carolina legislature, responding to the lobbying efforts of state producers, passed legislation which prohibited sale in the state of closed containers of apples bearing inspection grades other than those developed by the U.S. Department of Agriculture (USDA). The statute had no effect on North Carolina producers, since the state had no inspection system. However, it did affect Washington's apple business, the largest in the nation, since the state had a mandatory inspection system even stricter

than the USDA's. After inspection, apples were packed in containers premarked with their state inspection grades, until their destination was determined. Compliance with North Carolina's law thus required either transferring the apples to unmarked boxes or obliterating the state grade from boxes going to the state. Either procedure would involve considerable additional expense.

The legal confrontation

The Washington commission argued that the act constituted an attempt to protect state producers by deterring the importation of Washington apples. North Carolina replied that the measure set a uniform requirement to protect consumers from fraud and confusion resulting from a multiplicity of labeling schemes.

The Court's decision

The Supreme Court, affirming the decision of a federal district court, unanimously ruled that the law unconstitutionally discriminated against the interstate shipment of Washington apples.

---

mains from the states and placed it in the hands of the federal government. National majorities, they reasoned, would tend to be more moderate than state majorities, for they would include a greater variety of groups and lessen the probability that any single group would constitute a majority. This approach lessens the danger of majority faction and of oppressive legislation within the states. (For example, in many southern states before the 1970s, black citizens were denied voting rights and forced to attend segregated schools.) Alternatively, the factional legislation may be designed to protect groups within the state at the expense of out-of-state groups—for example, laws protecting local producers against out-of-state competition. Such laws, interfering with the free flow of interstate commerce, violate the Constitution.

Given the greater tendency of the states to pass unconstitutional legislation, some have considered

the power to review state laws as even more important than the corresponding power over federal laws. Justice Oliver Wendell Holmes observed more than half a century ago:

> I do not think that the United States would come to an end if we lost our power to declare an Act of Congress void. I do think that the Union would be imperiled if we could not make that declaration as to the laws of several states (Holmes, 1921:295–6).

Statutory Interpretation

Although judicial review may represent the most dramatic instance of judicial participation in governing, it is by no means the only way in which the courts exercise power. Typically, only about two-thirds of Supreme Court cases—and less than 5 percent of lower federal court cases—involve Constitutional questions. Many of the remaining cases involve the interpretation of federal statutes (laws). In interpreting the meaning of the statutes, the courts often must resolve major policy disputes.

The need for judicial interpretation of statutes is inescapable in any legal system, for statutes are rarely "self-interpreting." In part, the necessity of interpretation stems from the difficulty inherent in attempting to control future events. As Justice Felix Frankfurter noted: "The intrinsic difficulties of language and the emergence after enactment of situations not anticipated by the most gifted legislative imagination reveal doubts and ambiguities in statutes that compel judicial construction" (Murphy and Pritchett, 1974:414). Frequently the need for interpretation results from intentional ambiguity in statutes. Since it is easier to forge agreement on broad goals (for example, equality of educational opportunity) than on specific means of achieving those goals, members of Congress— eager to secure passage of legislation—often word statutes vaguely in order to secure maximum support. In doing so, legislators open the door not only to broad discretion on the part of those in the bureaucracy who administer the law but also to the courts, since broad and vague statutes are almost certain to be challenged by citizens who are unhappy with administrative decisions.

Griggs v. Duke Power Company (1971) illustrates how statutory interpretation can involve the courts in the exercise of significant policymaking authority. Title VII of the 1964 Civil Rights Act prohibited job discrimination on the basis of "race, color, religion, sex, or national origin." An amendment to the legislation specified that employers could continue to use employment tests which were "not designed, intended, or used to discriminate." In *Griggs,* several black employees challenged the Duke Power Company's practice of requiring a high school diploma and success on standardized tests as conditions of employment, noting that this operated to disqualify substantially more black than white applicants. Did this employment requirement violate the Civil Rights Act? Given the widespread use of standardized tests, the Court could not avoid making an important policy decision, for to rule in favor of either party would have broad consequences for society. The Court ruled that in order to use tests which disadvantaged a racial minority, an employer must demonstrate that the tests are related to job performance. This decision precipitated a flood of suits challenging other employment requirements and has had a major impact on hiring practices throughout the nation.

As observed earlier, when the courts interpret statutes, Congress retains the authority to "overturn" such interpretations by passing another law specifying what it wants. This occurs in many instances. Yet statutory interpretation nonetheless gives the courts a great deal of authority because, as we saw in the study of the legislative process, it is not easy to pass a law in the United States. Groups that profit from court interpretations can mobilize to prevent the passage of a new law. Moreover, when the courts interpret federal statutes, they are often dealing with statutes that were passed many years ago, and the members of Congress who enacted the statute have long since departed. Unless the current Congress is interested in and highly dissatisfied with a court decision, the courts will normally have the last word.

Review of Administrative Activity

The actions and regulations of federal administrative agencies also come under judicial scrutiny when litigants charge that they violate or do not properly fulfill the purpose of federal laws. It is often in this seemingly detailed and technical arena of administrative law that important interests in society do battle to promote their viewpoints.

A case in point is *Calvert Cliffs' Coordinating Committee v. AEC* (1971). In this case the coordinating committee, an antinuclear group, challenged the legality of the Atomic Energy Commission's (AEC) action in issuing a license for construction of a nuclear power plant on the Chesapeake Bay. A federal court of appeals agreed, ruling that the AEC violated the National Environmental Protection Act by not requiring submission of an environmental impact statement. The effects of the decision were substantial. Nuclear plants which had not filed environmental impact statements could not operate until Congress authorized the commission to issue interim licenses. Even more important, the decision dramatically increased both the difficulty and the cost of obtaining a license for the construction of such plants (Cook, 1980).

JUDICIAL REVIEW AND THE LIMITS OF JUDICIAL AUTHORITY

"Judicial review," to repeat, is the power of the courts to pronounce the laws or actions of any government in the United States, or any officials of those governments, contrary to any higher law and therefore null and void. When the courts interpret the Constitution, they seem to possess an awesome power from which there is little recourse except the difficult process of amendment. What is the basis of this power? What problems does it pose in a representative democracy? And what kinds of checks exist against it? These are the questions we shall explore in this section.

The Historical Foundation

Marbury v. Madison (1803) ranks as the Supreme Court's most important decision because it authoritatively established the power of federal courts to review the constitutionality of federal laws. Marshall's classic argument began with the assertion that the Constitution established a government of limited powers. What happens, he then asked, if Congress exceeds its constitutional bounds and enacts laws "repugnant to the Constitution"? Marshall's answer was disarmingly simple: Since the Constitution is the fundamental law and superior to ordinary legislative enactments, laws which conflict with it are necessarily void. When deciding cases which involve a conflict between the Constitution and a legislative enactment, the courts must apply the Constitution and refuse to apply the law. The duty to say what the law is entails the power to say what it is not—and therefore includes the power to strike down laws as unconstitutional.

Impressive as Marshall's argument is, it has encountered a great deal of criticism from scholars who argue that the founders never intended that the courts should exercise so formidable a power. Nowhere in the Constitution, they note, is the power of judicial review explicitly granted. Nor do the records of the Constitutional Convention show that the delegates ever explicitly debated granting this power to the judiciary. Marshall's opinion in *Marbury,* in this view, represents one of history's great thefts—the stealing of a power that rightfully belonged to or was shared by Congress and the president (Thayer, 1981).

Yet, when all the evidence is taken into account, it seems fairly certain that most public officials at the time the Constitution was proposed regarded judicial review, *in some form,* as implied by the nature of the government being adopted (Black, 1960). Although the delegates at the Convention did not debate the issue, their remarks nonetheless suggest that they assumed or contemplated the existence of judicial review. And certainly the leading treatise on the Constitution, *The Federalist,* explicitly argued that the courts would exercise this power. As Hamilton wrote in *Federalist* 78, foreshadowing Marshall's argument in *Marbury,* "whenever a particular statute contravenes the Constitution, it will be the duty of the judicial tribunals to adhere to the latter and disregard the former."

Judicial Review: The Fundamental Problem

The doctrine of judicial review clearly poses a fundamental problem in a political system based on the principle of self-government. That problem has been simply stated by John Hart Ely: "A body that is not elected or otherwise politically responsible in any significant way [is] telling the people's elected representatives that they cannot govern as they'd like" (1980:4–5). This countermajoritarian aspect of judicial review is most evident when the Supreme Court strikes down the actions of a coequal branch of government, Congress or the president, for these branches are responsible through elections to national majorities. But it may apply no less forcefully to certain state laws that have the backing not only of local majorities but of a majority of the American people as a whole.

It might, of course, be argued that the problem posed by this extraordinary power of the Court is more imaginary than real. This argument would run as follows: Because the founders created a Constitutional system of limited powers, not a system that allowed an unbridled majority to work its will, the Court in striking down unconstitutional acts merely protects the Constitution. Furthermore, since the Constitution (along with its amendments) represents the expression of the public's most solemn will, the Court in protecting the Constitution actually protects the will of the people! As Hamilton argued in *Federalist* 78, the doctrine of

---

BOX 12-3

MARBURY v. MADISON: ESTABLISHING THE POWER OF JUDICIAL REVIEW

The parties

William Marbury and other persons appointed as justices of the peace in Washington, D.C.; James Madison, secretary of state under President Thomas Jefferson.

The issue

Marbury and the plaintiffs were asking the Supreme Court to issue a *writ of mandamus* ordering Madison to deliver the commissions entitling them to take office as justices of the peace.

The political context

The case arose during the waning days of President John Adams's administration. Adams and his Federalist party had been soundly defeated in the election of 1800 by Thomas Jefferson and his forces. Adams sought to safeguard his party's interests by appointing as many Federalist judges as possible before leaving office; the lame-duck Congress, which the Federalists dominated, cooperated by creating fifty-eight new judgeships. William Marbury was appointed to one of those positions, but John Marshall—who was still serving as secretary of state despite his recent appointment as chief justice of the Supreme Court—failed to deliver Marbury's commission before Jefferson's inauguration. President Jefferson was furious at Adams's attempt to pack the judiciary and, although Marbury and others had been appointed and confirmed by the Senate, ordered Madison not to deliver their commissions.

Chief Justice Marshall had little love for Jefferson, his cousin and longtime political adversary. However, he recognized the political peril posed by Marbury's petition. Congress, which was dominated by Jefferson

partisans, had already postponed the Supreme Court's term and abolished some courts created during Adams's administration. If Marshall ruled in favor of Marbury, Jefferson would certainly refuse to deliver the commissions and thus demonstrate the political impotence of the Court. Indeed, a ruling in favor of Marbury might well trigger impeachment proceedings against the justices. On the other hand, Marshall did not wish to endorse Jefferson's refusal to deliver the commissions.

The Court's opinion

Marshall initially made clear that Marbury had a right to the commission and that Madison was duty-bound to deliver it. He also noted that mandamus was the proper remedy in the case. He held, however, that the Supreme Court could not issue the writ. The Constitution specified the Court's original jurisdiction, and Congress could not add to it by ordinary legislation. In sum, the Court could not issue the writ because the legislation granting it that power was unconstitutional.

The effects of the decision

The immediate effect of the decision was that Marbury and the other petitioners did not receive their commissions. Marbury never did receive his and eventually became a bank president. In a sense, therefore, Jefferson had won, although he complained about "twistifications" in Marshall's opinion, particularly his gratuitous criticisms of the failure to deliver the commissions. But in denying that it had the power to issue the writ, the Court secured a much more important power, the power to declare acts of Congress unconstitutional.

---

judicial review does not, in reality, set the judges over the legislature. It "only" supposes that "where the will of the legislature, declared in its statutes, stands in opposition to that of the people, declared in the Constitution, the judges ought to be governed by the latter rather than the former." There is in fact much to the argument, and it has served as one of the principal justifications for judicial re-

view. Yet one can also see that its simple elegance slides over some of the thorny problems that emerge in the real world, where the "people," expressing their will through their legislators, have a view in conflict with the Constitution or with the judges' interpretation of it. Consider the following three difficulties.

First, the exercise of the power of judicial review

frequently involves the Supreme Court in ruling on important government programs. Historically, the Court's agenda has reflected the most pressing issues that have faced the nation. Before the Civil War, the main political controversy involved the distribution of power between the national and state governments, and the Court's Constitutional decisions generally involved it in defining the respective spheres of those governments. Following the Civil War, the nation experienced rapid industrial development and the growth of huge economic enterprises. When the government attempted to cope with these developments, the scope of governmental regulatory authority became the main issue on the Court's agenda. In the wake of the New Deal, which led to a major expansion in federal regulatory activity, the occasions for conflict between government and business temporarily multiplied. Since the 1930s, the Court has extended the application of the Bill of Rights to the states, making the reconciliation of individual liberties and governmental power into one of the chief areas of focus of Court activity. In addition, the Court has interpreted the Fourteenth Amendment's equal protection clause in such a way as to involve itself in large numbers of general cases on the distribution of political resources. Judicial review, accordingly, has not been limited to issues of marginal concern to the public, but often has involved key issues of the day.

Second, not only does the Supreme Court rule on the validity of important governmental policies, but its rulings are also generally the final, and thus the decisive, determination. Unless the Court reverses itself in a later case, its ruling that a law or official action is unconstitutional can be reversed only by Constitutional amendment. Despite popular dissatisfaction with numerous Court decisions, only five amendments overruling Court decisions have been ratified. In other words, when the Court stands its interpretation of the Constitution against that of a coequal branch, the Court usually prevails.

Finally, and perhaps most important, the task of Constitutional interpretation, even when undertaken in good faith, is not a technical or mechanical one. In most cases that reach the Supreme Court, the questions to be decided are complex and ambiguous. The Constitution, while a law in some sense, is not an ordinary law with hundreds of qualifications and definitions. Often, its words are very general, and it is therefore impossible to lay a statute down next to the Constitutional provision in question and determine easily whether the statute is valid or invalid. Consider, for example, the broad language of the Eighth Amendment, which bans "cruel and unusual punishments." Does this outlaw automatic life imprisonment for persons convicted of three felonies, as the Court ruled in *Rummel v. Estelle* (1980)? Or consider the First Amendment which prevents Congress from passing any law that abridges the freedom of speech. Does this ban any attempt by Congress to limit what a candidate for federal office can spend on his or her own behalf, as the Court ruled in *Buckley v. Valeo* (1976)? Obviously, the text of the Constitution, taken by itself, does not supply automatic answers.

The fact that the language of the Constitution is often general does not necessarily mean that it is without content or can provide no guidance. But it does mean that the Constitution must be interpreted and that the act of interpretation is not an automatic or simple process. It involves the difficult task of trying to say what the Constitution means; and judges, as fallible human beings, can make mistakes or even exceed what could reasonably be considered a valid effort at interpretation.

In sum, the problem of judicial review centers on two issues that sometimes overlap. First, a majority of Americans may have a view different from that in the Constitution; and, second, the exact meaning of the Constitution is not always clear, but must be interpreted. Given the respect Americans have for the Constitution, there is every reason to believe that most Americans have no difficulty accepting the general premise that current majorities ought to yield to what is truly in the Constitution. But, as its meaning is sometimes admittedly difficult to interpret, many have not been willing to accept the Court as the final interpreter without any checks or balances.

Stated in the most bald form, the problem of judicial review seems threatening: The Supreme Court says what the Constitution means, and the Constitution is the final and highest law of the land; therefore, the Court rules as it wants. In fact, there is much that reduces the seriousness of this problem in practice. Looking at the matter from the view of the judges, it cannot be supposed that most judges want to "govern" beyond the mandate of the Constitution; and the method of selecting judges by the president and Senate usually ensures some degree of conformity between public officials and the judiciary. On the other side, it is *not* the case that the other institutions simply accept what the Court says and offer no resistance. In fact, there is often a struggle between the institutions when they are in conflict, with each calling on certain of its resources. Let us look first at the potential checks that can be called on by others against the Court and then at the ways in which the Court itself has behaved in the system of separation of powers.

External Checks on the Power of the Courts

Are the other branches obliged to recognize the Supreme Court's Constitutional rulings as authoritative? If they disagree with those rulings, what steps may they legitimately undertake to change them? The answers given to these questions throughout our history suggest that the Constitutional authority of the Supreme Court is limited. Yet, unlike the checks and balances between the president and the Congress, most of which have a clear foundation in the Constitution, the limitations on the power of the Supreme Court are in practice often rather ambiguous doctrines, the use of which many have called into question. These doctrines have undergone important changes that reflect different conceptions of the role of the courts in American politics.

The Doctrine of Concurrent Responsibility Although judges may "say what the law is" in cases coming before them, this does not necessarily determine the binding force of those pronouncements. The doctrine of concurrent responsibility, espoused by some presidents in the nineteenth century, held that *each* branch had a responsibility to determine the constitutionality of a matter on its own and to act accordingly within its own sphere. In short, the Court might say what the law is, but so could the president and Congress.

The first to state this view was Jefferson, who as president declared that the "branch which is to act ultimately, and without appeal, on any law, is the rightful expositor to the validity of the law, uncontrolled by the opinions of the other co-ordinate branches." Usually, this doctrine poses no serious problem, for there is no direct power conflict if, for example, a president vetoes a bill in the belief that it is unconstitutional, even if the Court and earlier presidents and Congresses had considered similar legislation to be Constitutional. The president in this case, as Andrew Jackson argued when he vetoed the national bank, must be "guided by [his] own opinion of the Constitution—and support it as he understands it, and not as it is understood by others" (Richardson, 1896:II, 582). No harm follows when presidents employ their own power in this way. However, in those instances in which the Court seeks to prevent the president or Congress from doing what either believes to be constitutional, or in those instances in which the Court requires executive assistance to enforce a ruling of unconstitutionality with which the president disagrees, there is a direct conflict. Here the doctrine that each branch should be "guided by its own opinion of the Constitution" can result in a kind of chaos. Jefferson, of course, was aware of these difficulties, but thought that putting up with this ambiguity was less dangerous than vesting an unaccountable branch of government with ultimate authority over all Constitutional questions.

In this open and unabashed form, the doctrine of concurrent responsibility seems almost to have lost support as a respectable Constitutional doctrine. Both President Truman in the steel seizure case (*Youngstown Sheet and Tube Co. v. Sawyer,* 1952) and President Nixon in the Watergate tapes case left the issue publicly in doubt for a time about whether they would comply with an unfavorable judicial ruling. In the end, both gave in and submitted to the Court, although another president under different circumstances might possibly act differently. By and large, however, both Congress and the president in this century have come closer and closer to recognizing a judicial monopoly over Constitutional interpretation.

Limited Applicability of Court Decisions The *Dred Scott* decision rested on an interpretation of the Constitution that was directly at odds with the central plank of the Republican party. In dealing with this problem Abraham Lincoln, then a candidate for the state senate in Illinois, sought to clarify further the possible limits on the authority of Supreme Court rulings. The Court's rulings, he noted, do two things simultaneously: they decide the case before the Court, and they create precedents that may serve as the basis of further decisions. According to Lincoln, a Court decision is always authoritative with regard to a particular case, but its value for determining future cases varies. Some decisions, by virtue of their consistency with established legal principles, fully settle Constitutional questions and should be overturned only by Constitutional amendment. But decisions that lack Constitutional foundation, like *Dred Scott,* are without value as precedents. They can be a legitimate subject of debate in the political arena by political parties and candidates for public office. Victory by a party opposing a Supreme Court decision can be taken as a sign that the Court's decision should be reversed. (Indeed, following his election Lincoln appointed to the Supreme Court men who shared his opposition to the *Dred Scott* decision.) In Lincoln's view, then, the pronouncement of a Constitutional interpretation need not end the debate and leave people with the sole—and difficult—remedy of a Constitutional amendment. Rather, where widespread public opposition exists, the discussion of Constitutional questions in the political arena can reopen a question.

This position, repeated by President Nixon in his campaign in 1968 in regard to some of the decisions of the Warren Court on rights of criminal defendants, involves a difficult distinction between respect for the Court's rulings in particular cases and opposition to a general policy enunciated by the Court. Lincoln clearly did not want to argue that Court decisions should regularly be subject to the returns of the ballot box. But neither was he willing to concede that the Court could decide a fundamental Constitutional issue without the possibility of a check from the political process. Knowledge that this check was possible might limit the Court's willingness to embark on dubious Constitutional interpretations.

What this view indicates is that the other institutions must send signals to the Court about their view of what the Constitution means. Since the 1970s, some members of Congress have employed certain techniques to express their "dissatisfaction"

with the Court by introducing laws that assume different interpretations from those that have been employed by the Court. Thus in the 1970s, numerous bills were introduced to limit the use of busing as a remedy for school segregation. In 1981, Senator Jesse Helms introduced legislation to overturn the Court's ruling on abortion. (The legislation asserted that human life begins at conception.) These proposed laws, which run directly counter to the thrust of the Court's Constitutional interpretations, were intended to register public sentiment and thereby perhaps to "encourage" the Court to shift ground.

"Disciplining" the Court In the Constitution, there are several potential weapons that the political branches have at their disposal to curb the power of the Court. One is impeachment, which Jefferson once contemplated using to win control of the judiciary from the Federalists (Baum, 1981). However, very early on, in 1805, the Senate's acquittal of Justice Samuel Chase in an impeachment trial seemed to establish the precedent that judicial impeachment was not a tool to discipline the opinions of the judges, but only something to be used in cases of corruption or dubious ethical behavior.

A second device is to change the size of the Court. The number of judges on the Court is set *not* by the Constitution but by law. Congress therefore could increase or diminish the number of judges in order to influence its rulings. In fact, it did so three times during the 1860s. In the 1930s, President Roosevelt followed in the same tradition, seeking to "pack" the Court by expanding its membership, at least temporarily, to fifteen. The attempt was widely seen as an illegitimate attack on judicial independence, and it failed to pass Congress. It did nonetheless convince one judge of the seriousness of the threat to the Court and led him to change his mind on several key decisions that came before the Court in the next term. Some have called this the "switch in time that saved nine." In any case, since President Roosevelt's partial failure with the Court-packing plan, the present size of the Supreme Court (nine judges) has become virtually an accepted part of the unwritten constitution.

A third device, based on what seems to be a technical legality, is perhaps potentially the most

After the Supreme Court outlawed racially segregated education in 1954, segregationists called for the impeachment of Chief Justice Earl Warren, but their demands failed to sway the Congress or intimidate the Court. *(Danny Lyon/Magnum)*

threatening to the Court. The Constitution, as we shall see, gives the Supreme Court original (or automatic) jurisdiction over cases in only a few areas. Most of the cases that reach the Court come to it under its *appellate* authority, which is based on federal statute and which could possibly, therefore, be revoked, either in its entirety or in part. In one instance, following the Civil War, Congress used this power to curtail the Court's authority over one aspect of the power of habeas corpus, and the Court quickly recognized Congress's right to define its appellate jurisdiction (*McCardle, ex parte,* 1869). In the 1970s and 1980s, many bills have been introduced in Congress to remove the jurisdictional authority of the federal courts in large areas of policy, such as school desegregation and abortion. No such law, however, has cleared Congress; and many legislators who have opposed Court decisions have nevertheless voted against reducing its jurisdiction, on the grounds that it would compromise the independence of the judicial system and that it might in many instances be unconstitutional. While the matter is far from settled, the present view in Congress seems to be that a reduction of appellate jurisdiction is not in keeping with the spirit of the Constitution.

The Amending Process Congress can initiate and the states can ratify Constitutional amendments to overturn Court decisions. This has occurred in the past on at least four occasions; and in the early 1980s a number of different amendments were pushed, unsuccessfully, to overturn Court decisions in the areas of school prayer and abortion.* But reliance on the amending process, which in any case is a difficult hurdle to clear, can only with much hesitation be spoken of as a "check" on the Court. When others disagree with the Court's Constitutional interpretations and resort to the amendment process to make changes, they in effect concede that the Court is the ultimate arbiter of the meaning of the Constitution.

---

*The clear instances of amendments that overturned Court decisions were the Eleventh Amendment, broadening state immunity from lawsuits, which overturned *Chisholm v. Georgia* (1793); the Fourteenth Amendment, guaranteeing citizenship for blacks, which overruled *Dred Scott v. Sanford;* the Sixteenth Amendment, permitting a federal income tax, which overruled *Pollock v. Farmer's Loan and Trust* (1895); and the Twenty-Sixth Amendment, establishing 18 years as the legal voting age, which overturned part of the decision of *Oregon v. Mitchell* (1970).

Internal Checks on the Power of the Court

Judges in the past have sometimes sought ways to limit their own involvement in major policies, both as a matter of prudence and as a matter of judicial philosophy. Although justices act to "say what the law is," they are usually not oblivious to their political situation in respect to the other branches and the public. Experience has shown, from what occurred after the Civil War and what nearly occurred after the New Deal, that the political branches can "wage war" against the judiciary. The Court's authority, to be sure, rests on the public perception that it is a nonpolitical body exercising a judicial function. Yet to maintain the power of the Court, which will ordinarily be one of the justices' objectives, they must be aware of the possibility that the other political institutions will act to limit its authority.

Part of the Court's restraint, in other words, may come from the justices' perception that other political institutions might use their authority and weight to curtail judicial power or independence if the Court becomes too actively engaged in political affairs (McCloskey, 1960). Indeed, because the judicial power lacks the inherent claim of majority backing possessed by the president and Congress, it might be thought that the Court would be wary of too direct a challenge of the other branches. Yet the Court also possesses its own resources of authority, and the judges, frequently, are willing to run bold risks. In the future, moreover, the willingness of judges to show restraint will be based in part on their estimation of the likelihood that the other branches will use the "weapons" of reprisal against the Court that they have at their disposal.

The Nature of the Judicial Power Part of the restraint of the courts derives from the very nature of the judicial power. The courts themselves do not initiate judgment. Rather, they make judgments in response to specific cases or controversies brought to them in the course of trying criminal cases or hearing civil suits. The courts, in other words, are "passive"; it is not for them to step in where they please and enter general rulings on matters of Constitutional significance. By the very nature of the legal process, the courts' role as policymakers—supposing that policymaking is what they wanted to do—is limited. These limitations, however, are

not insuperable obstacles to an active judicial role. As we shall see later, our entire society has become more given to suits and litigation, a change that the courts have facilitated by easing the definition of what constitutes a "case" and "controversy." The sample of policy questions that arrives before the courts, therefore, is much larger than ever before, and this enables the courts to become involved in many more areas.

Traditional Techniques of Restraint Supreme Court justices have devised certain judicial doctrines to prevent excessive control over policy and to sidestep certain issues that are too touchy or that might not admit easily of any judicial remedy. The most important of these is the *political-question doctrine,* under which the Court refuses to rule when the challenged government action involves matters which the Constitution leaves directly to the discretion of one of the two political branches. What constitutes a "political question" is of course something that the Court itself decides; and issues that have been judged political questions in one area—for example, the problem of malapportionment of legislatures—have subsequently been declared proper subjects of judicial remedy and intervention. In general, however, the political-question doctrine provides the Court with a reason for not taking action in certain difficult areas, frequently those involving the discretion of the president in the conduct of foreign affairs. The usefulness of this doctrine in avoiding interbranch conflict is illustrated by *Goldwater v. Carter* (1980), in which the Court refused to decide whether President Carter could terminate a treaty with Taiwan without congressional authorization.

A second doctrine the Court has employed in the past to limit its role is that of according the actions of Congress or the president a "presumption of Constitutionality." As noted, no more than 105 federal laws have been struck down, most of them of minor importance. In part, this deference reflects, in the words of Justice Harlan Fiske Stone, a recognition that "courts are not the only agency of government that must be assumed to have the capacity to govern" (*United States v. Butler,* 1936). In part, since congressional or presidential action indicates a belief that the action is constitutional, it is an acknowledgment that the Constitutional judgment of coequal branches is entitled to great weight. As in the case of the political-question doctrine, the success of the "presumption of constitutionality" in avoiding excessive judicial intervention depends on the Court's willingness to adhere to it. At times the Court has been extremely deferential, while at other moments it has seemingly tried to settle by itself the most "political" questions facing the nation. Finally, it should be observed that both the doctrines noted here apply only to the Court's relationship to the other branches of the federal government and not to its relations to the states.

Judicial Philosophies: Activism and Restraint

Like "liberalism" and "conservatism," the terms "activism" and "restraint" can be overused and inappropriately applied. In using these terms, many people confuse the involvement of the Court (the number of laws, for example, that it finds to be unconstitutional) with the Court's intentions (the extent to which the Court does or does not want to make policy). In fact, the degree to which the Court becomes involved may be much less dependent on its intentions than on the activities of Congress and the states. If Congress or the states happen to pass a great deal of clearly unconstitutional legislation, then the Court, in saying "what the law is," would necessarily appear active in striking down these laws. To do less in such circumstances would be not so much to show restraint as to abdicate. By the same token, if the other branches or the states are careful and pass no clearly unconstitutional legislation, but the Court nonetheless imposes its own will on a few occasions, its level of activity might seem restrained, but its intentions would be activist. From this discussion, it is obvious that what one sees as activism or restraint will depend greatly how one interprets the Constitution in particular instances.

Recognizing the problematic character of these terms, we can nevertheless apply them to refer to a certain mood or disposition on the part of the judges. As such, the terms reflect judicial intentions about their role. Restraint in this sense would refer to a judicial disposition that accords a "presumption of constitutionality" to the actions of the other branches and the states. Where a tenuous interpretation is involved, those advocating restraint would say that it should be the views of the political

branches, and not those of the courts, that should prevail. Activism, by contrast, refers to a judicial disposition which is much less deferential to the judgment of the political branches and which holds that the courts can and should involve themselves in broadly interpreting the law according to how they see it. Indeed, a particularly active form of activism holds that the courts should "use" the law with some license to make "good" policy.

Obviously, few judges readily admit to an *extreme* form of activism, as it conflicts with the accepted role of the courts as interpreters rather than legislators. Yet certain scholars have been willing to discuss these matters more bluntly; and for those who entertain an activist position, the key question becomes not simply whether the Court is activist, but for what and for whom. Most defenders of activism today deplore the type of activism of the Court during the late nineteenth and early twentieth centuries, when the decisions were made on behalf of property rights; instead, they favor an activism that protects rights of free expression or helps to secure the interests of those said to be inadequately represented in the political process (see Box 12-4).

The Institutional Resources of the Courts

The emphasis in this section has been on the problem of judicial review and hence on the extreme instances of potential conflict between the courts and the other institutions. In fact, much of the time there is little or no serious conflict. Judges, appointed by the president and confirmed by the Senate, are not usually "out of step" with the majority. Nor do they—usually—have a desire to involve the Court in conflict. For their part, the other branches and the public both respect and support an independent judiciary having a legitimate claim to judicial review (though perhaps not to an uncontested role in interpreting the Constitution).

Still, there is the possibility of conflict. The majority of judges are often appointed well before the current majority coalition governing the country has come into being, and they may tend to see matters in a quite different light. Moreover, judges in doing their duty of interpreting the law sometimes run into conflict with the other national institutions or with majorities as these bodies express their will

---

BOX 12-4

JUDICIAL ACTIVISM AND RESTRAINT

One advocate of judicial activism is Abram Chayes, professor of law at Harvard University:

> . . . The growth of judicial power has been, in large part, a function of the failure of other agencies to respond to groups that have been able to mobilize considerable resources and energy. . . . In my view, judicial action only achieves . . . legitimacy by responding to, indeed by stirring, the deep and durable command for justice in our society. . . . In practice, if not in words, the American legal tradition has always acknowledged the importance of substantive results for the legitimacy and accountability of judicial action (Murphy and Pritchett, 1974:60–61).

In his dissenting opinion in *West Virginia State Board of Education v. Barnette* (1943), Supreme Court

Justice Felix Frankfurter argues for judicial restraint in assessing the constitutionality of a West Virginia statute compelling students to salute the flag in classrooms:

> In can never be emphasized too much that one's own opinion about the wisdom or evil of a law should be excluded altogether when one is doing one's duty on the bench. The only opinion of our own even looking in that direction that is material is our opinion whether legislators could in reason have enacted such a law. In the light of all the circumstances, including the history of this question in this Court, it would require more daring than I possess to deny that reasonable legislators could have taken the action which is before us for review . . . (Murphy and Pritchett, 1974:729).

---

through state law. These conflicts can be more frequent and severe as judges interpret their role in an active sense and commit themselves to expansive interpretations of the law. The Court has accordingly known periods of tremendous opposition, most notably under the early years of Chief Justice Marshall's tenure, at the time of the *Dred Scott* decision, during the stormy decade of the depression, and, most recently, in the later years of Chief Justice Warren's term.

In the test of will that ensues between the courts and the other bodies, the courts have many resources to call on. They have, of course, the political support of the groups that benefit from their decisions; they have the general support of lawyers, who constitute a powerful element in society that tends to respect the principle of judicial determination on policies; and finally, they have the general support of the American public, who accept the idea of Constitutional rights and the role of the courts as interpreters of the Constitution.

On the other hand, of course, the courts lack the direct popular backing of the public that the executive or legislature possesses. Being unelected officials, justices cannot claim to represent the public's immediate will. The president and Congress (if not

the state governments) also possess certain weapons, as we have seen, that they *could* conceivably bring to bear against the courts, although in recent times these have perhaps appeared more as distant threats than immediate possibilities. It is true, of course, that popular dissatisfaction with some court decisions has been great, and the courts may have changed or adjusted somewhat to meet that dissatisfaction in certain areas; yet it is still probably safe to claim that the courts are in a stronger position today than at any point in our history. The other branches have seemingly accepted judicial supremacy in Constitutional interpretation and have avoided any direct assaults on judicial authority. Therefore, the extent to which judges will continue to involve themselves in policy will depend, relative to the past, less on *external* restraints and more on who are appointed judges and what the prevailing judicial philosophies are.

THE COURT SYSTEM

Judicial power in the United States is divided between the federal courts and fifty state court systems. The state courts handle most adjudication in the nation for the simple reason that most laws in the nation are enacted by state and local authorities. The state courts initially handle all matters that arise exclusively under state law as well as some matters wherein federal law is involved.

State courts vary in structure from state to state, but in general there are three levels: the trial court, the appellate court, and the state supreme court. Litigants may appeal cases within the state systems up to the supreme court of each state, which gives the most authoritative interpretation of the law in that state and binds all the lower state courts. The rulings of the state supreme courts are final unless the case comes to involve a "substantial federal question," as determined by the United States Supreme Court. When the Supreme Court determines that a substantial federal question is involved, the case may then enter the federal courts from the state courts and be heard by the Supreme Court or, where the law stipulates, by a lower federal court.

Much of the federal litigation in the area of rights of the accused and on criminal procedures illustrates how a case can move from the state to the federal courts. Persons convicted of violating a state criminal statute are tried in state courts and, after exhausting all appeals within the state system, make appeals to the Supreme Court on the grounds that a substantial federal question, such as a violation of a Constitutional right, is involved. In *Furman v. Georgia* (1972), for example, Furman, who was convicted of murder under state law and sentenced to death, appealed his case on the grounds that the death sentence violated the Constitutional ban in the Eighth Amendment on cruel and unusual punishments. A sufficient number of judges on the Supreme Court, having determined that this issue was ripe for consideration, agreed to hear the case on the grounds that a substantial federal question was involved. The Court voided Furman's death sentence in a complicated decision that touched off a decade-long struggle on the limits of capital punishment (see Chapter 17). This case illustrates how the Supreme Court can use its power of review over state court decisions to move into "new" areas of litigation. It should also be clear, however, that the power is essential to ensure the uniform interpretation of federal law. Without this power, the state courts would be able to interpret or ignore federal law as they pleased.

The scope of the federal judicial power is defined by the Constitution, although Congress plays a decisive role in establishing the federal judicial structure and determining the jurisdiction of the courts. There seem to have been two basic considerations that informed the founders' definition of the scope of the judicial power. First, the power enables courts to decide matters of national concern. This includes, most obviously, the application and interpretation of Constitutional law, federal laws, and treaties. It also includes cases in which the national government itself is a party or in which a foreign government is involved, as decisions in such cases could affect the nation's foreign relations. The federal judicial power, in short, potentially extends to all areas that lie within the jurisdiction of Congress or that involve the essential sovereignty of the nation. The founders did not intend to grant powers to the federal government that could not be adjudicated in federal courts.

Second, the judicial power extends to cases in which the neutrality of the state courts might be suspect. This forms the basis for the federal judiciary's *diversity jurisdiction.* Because state courts could conceivably favor the citizens or government of their own state, the Constitution permits out-of-state parties to have their suits tried in federal courts. This provision was obviously designed to prevent the disintegration of the union by the device of using state courts to pursue interstate rivalries. Overall then, the federal judicial power is defined in terms of subject matter (such as cases under federal law) or the parties involved in the case (such as the United States government, a foreign government, or citizens of different states).

With the exception of the Supreme Court, whose existence is specifically mentioned in the Constitution and whose original jurisdiction is defined, Congress creates all federal courts and assigns them their respective jurisdictions. Congress, in fact, determines whether to confer the full potential range of judicial power to the federal courts. For example, although the federal judicial power extends to cases between citizens of different states, Congress has limited the federal courts' diversity jurisdiction to cases involving more than $10,000. (With the tremendous growth in the work load of the federal courts, many have questioned whether this jurisdiction should be further curtailed or perhaps eliminated altogether.) Congress also deter-mines whether the federal courts shall have exclu-sive jurisdiction over a category of cases or whether, as more often occurs, state courts can ex-ercise concurrent jurisdiction over the same type of cases. For example, under the diversity jurisdiction, Congress allows cases of *more* than $10,000 to be heard in a state court if both parties agree.

The Lower Federal Courts

The Constitution, as just noted, authorizes Con-gress to create federal courts below the Supreme Court and to define their respective jurisdictions. In the Judiciary Act of 1789, the First Congress established two sets of general jurisdiction courts, the district courts and the circuit courts of appeals. Remarkably, the basic structure of the federal gen-eral-jurisdiction courts has remained unchanged to the present day. Since then, Congress has also cre-ated various limited-jurisdiction courts, such as the United States Court of Claims and the United States Tax Court. These courts, listed in Box 12-5, have very significant powers within their designated ju-risdictions, but we shall limit ourselves in this chap-ter to the more important general-jurisdiction courts.

The District Courts The district courts serve as the major original-jurisdiction (trial) courts of

---

BOX 12-5

THE FEDERAL COURT SYSTEM (1983)

The Supreme Court of the United States
- 9 justices

United States courts of appeals
- 12 circuit courts (plus 1 special court of appeals)
- 132 judges

United States district courts
- 94 courts
- 516 judges

United States magistrates
- Created by the Federal Magistrates Act (1968)
- 488 full- and part-time magistrates
- Assist in processing of cases

Specialized courts

United States Court of Claims*
- Created in 1855
- Primarily concerned with claims arising out of public contracts
- 7 judges

United States Customs Court (also known as "Court of International Trade")
- Created in 1956
- Primarily concerned with disputes about customs duties and the value of imported goods
- 9 judges

United States Court of Customs and Patent Appeals
- Created in 1909
- Reviews the decisions of the U.S. Customs Court and U.S. Patent Office
- 5 judges

United States Tax Court*
- Created in 1924
- Considers citizen challenges to Internal Revenue Service tax decisions
- 16 judges

United States Court of Military Appeals*
- Created in 1950
- Reviews appeals from courts-martial
- 3 judges with fifteen-year terms

*A court created under Article I of the Constitution. The decisions of these courts are not directly reviewable by other federal courts.

the federal court system, handling both criminal and civil cases. Altogether, there are 94 district courts staffed (in 1982) by 516 judges, with at least 1 court located in each state. A single judge—sitting with a jury unless all parties and the judge agree to waive it—hears a tremendous variety of cases, major and minor, that arise under federal law. These include cases involving personal bankruptcies, kidnappings (an automatic federal offense), suits over certain civil rights, and mail fraud. Since less than 15 percent of the decisions of district courts are appealed, these courts make the final rulings in the vast majority of federal cases.

The district courts have experienced a massive increase in case filings during recent years. Although during the 1970s federal criminal cases actually declined, 168,797 civil cases were commenced in district courts in 1980, almost double the cases filed a decade earlier. At the same time, district court judges have become more heavily involved in the ongoing supervision of governmental activity. For example, Judge Arthur Garrity, who ordered the desegregation of Boston public schools in the mid-1970s, responded to noncompliance with his orders by placing a Boston high school in "receivership" and taking over the administration of the school (Buell, 1982). The increasing case loads and responsibilities have resulted in long delays in the processing of cases. In 1980, for example, the median time for disposing of cases in the district courts was 8 months for civil cases and 3.2 months for criminal cases.

To relieve case load pressures, Congress in 1978 enacted the Omnibus Judgeship Act, which increased the number of district court judgeships from 399 to 516. It also expanded the number and duties of the federal magistrates, who are assigned to assist the district court judges. Under the Federal Magistrate Act of 1979, these magistrates are authorized not only to relieve the judges of routine tasks, such as setting bail, but also to try some civil cases and all federal misdemeanor cases. Yet these measures have provided only temporary relief, and other methods of relieving court congestion are currently under consideration, such as narrowing the jurisdiction of federal courts and eliminating jury trials in complex civil suits.

Courts of Appeals Litigants dissatisfied with district court decisions have a right of appeal to the federal court of appeals serving their region. There are today thirteen courts of appeals, eleven of them based on geographical districts among the states and territories, plus one for Washington, D.C., and one that oversees some of the specialized courts. The courts of appeals are also still frequently referred to as "circuit courts" because they were originally staffed by justices of the Supreme Court who spent much of their time on horseback "riding circuit" and hearing appeals from district court decisions. Although the practice of riding circuit has long since been abandoned, Supreme Court justices are still assigned to the various appeals courts. Virtually all the work on these courts, however, is now done by the permanent appeals court judges. Several judges serve on each court of appeals, with the number varying from circuit to circuit because of differences in population and work load.

The courts of appeals exercise an exclusively appellate jurisdiction, receiving appeals not only from the district courts but also from federal independent regulatory commissions (such as the Federal Communications Commission) and certain administrative agencies (for example, the Environmental Protection Agency). Thousands of appeals are filed each year; but many of these cases are dropped, settled by the parties before a hearing, or summarily disposed of after screening by the judges. Only in about half the cases filed do the courts of appeals actually consider arguments, which are presented either in oral hearings or in legal briefs. To decide most cases, the courts divide into three-judge panels, with the judges rotating the panels on which they serve. Only in cases of national importance—for example, the Watergate tapes cases—do the judges sit as a unit (en banc).

Like the district courts, the appeals courts have been plagued by case load pressures. From 1970 to 1980, the number of appeals that were filed more than doubled. Although the Omnibus Judgeship Act of 1978 increased the number of appeals court judgeships from 97 to 132, this has not speeded the flow of cases through the federal courts. Currently, the median time from filing in a district court to decision in a court of appeals is over two years.

The district courts and courts of appeals, as Fig-

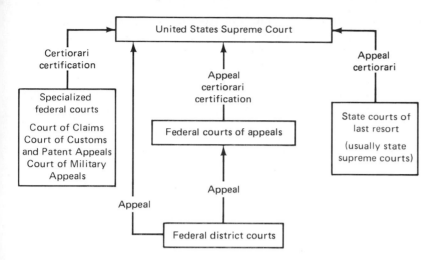

FIGURE 12-1
How cases reach the Supreme Court.

ure 12 1 shows, are subordinate to the Supreme Court, which stands at the apex of the judicial system and has the power to review decisions of lower courts. Nevertheless, the lower federal courts play an important independent role in administering federal justice. First, the Constitutional and statutory interpretations they make in deciding cases frequently influence the Supreme Court's ultimate resolution of the issues. By their opinions or decisions they help to frame the issues. Second, the lower courts—especially the district courts—play a crucial role in ensuring the implementation of Supreme Court decisions. Supreme Court decisions are often worded in general terms; and frequently only the general principles are decided, with the cases being remanded (turned back) to lower courts to implement the decision in the particular cases and others like them. The district courts carry much of the burden for this implementation, which often involves a great deal of discretion. Finally, the lower courts make the final decision in the vast majority of cases that enter the federal courts. As noted, less than 15 percent of district court decisions are appealed, and less than 4 percent of the appeals court decisions are reviewed by the Supreme Court. Moreover, this is not merely a sifting process whereby all important cases make their way to the Supreme Court. What is involved more closely resembles a division of labor. Since the Supreme Court is primarily concerned with Constitutional issues, nonconstitutional issues of great practical importance are routinely decided by the courts of appeals. A president of the American Bar Association recognized this when he termed the second circuit's court of appeals, which includes New York, Connecticut, and Vermont, the "court of last resort for the most important commercial and financial problems of one of the great financial centers of the world" (Abraham, 1975).

The Supreme Court

The Supreme Court serves as the final arbiter in cases coming from the federal and state court systems. Its decisions are final for the litigants—there is no court to which they can appeal the Supreme Court's decisions. They are final as well for the lower courts, establishing precedents which guide their decisions in subsequent cases. Most important, they are final in most instances for the entire political system. This power to say ultimately what the law is has made the Supreme Court the most powerful court in the world.

In practice, of course, the finality of Supreme Court interpretations is slightly less decisive than its legal authority might suggest. We have observed already how the other branches may challenge or thwart the Court in some measure. Moreover, within the judicial system itself, compliance is not absolute. The lower federal courts and the state courts are "under" the Supreme Court, but they have a range of latitude in interpreting its general orders and may sometimes resist—by omission or subversion—the Supreme Court's policies. The Court, unlike an executive, is not in a simple "command" relationship with its subordinates, but must instead proceed by hearing cases or issuing legal orders. The state courts on occasion have been particularly slow in interpreting cases in the exact spirit intended by the Supreme Court (Baum, 1981). Beyond the court system itself, administrators and other officials may not always comply with Court rulings. The Court system is not a national police system, and in some areas—where suits have not been brought in every jurisdiction—compliance with interpretations of the Court is limited. In a large number of public school classrooms, for example, illegal prayers are routinely recited each day.

The Business of the Supreme Court The statutes regulating the Supreme Court's appellate jurisdiction supply two primary modes of access to the Court: appeal and *certiorari*. Litigants may appeal a case under specific circumstances determined by federal law; when doing so, they theoretically have a right to have their case heard. Under *certiorari*, litigants ask for the privilege of having their case reviewed; the Court determines whether it wants to hear the case as a matter of discretion. In practice, the Court is hardly ever *obliged* to hear a case under appeal, and for all intents and purposes exercises virtually unlimited discretion in determining what cases it will decide. In part, this has resulted from congressional legislation—most notably the Judiciary Act of 1925—narrowing the categories of cases in which parties have a right of appeal to the Court. Over 90 percent of petitions for review are on writ of *certiorari*. In addition, the Court can dismiss appeals which fail to raise a "substantial federal question." It has used this power to maintain control over its docket. This control makes the Court no ordinary tribunal doing justice on the demand of litigants, but rather a kind of legal policy tribunal that sifts through a mass of potential cases, considering the particulars of the

cases involved, but more frequently weighing the significance of the issues that are raised.

Since the justices receive far more petitions for review than they can possibly grant, they have established a process for screening incoming petitions. First, the individual justices and their law clerks review all incoming petitions. These petitions range from the polished products of prestigious law firms to the handwritten pleas submitted by prisoners and indigents. Unless at least one justice favors hearing a case, it is "dead-listed" and review is automatically denied. Since many of the petitions lack sufficient merit, roughly 75 percent of all petitions are eliminated in this fashion. Petitions which survive this stage are then acted upon collectively by the justices during conference. A case is accepted if four justices vote to hear it (the so-called "rule of four"). About 80 percent of the petitions considered in conference are rejected. In sum, the Court hears only about 5 percent of all cases in which review is sought.

In deciding which cases to hear, the Court is not primarily concerned with righting individual wrongs. As a former chief justice, Fred Vinson, once noted, "Everyone who comes here has had one trial and one appeal already" (Vinson, 1949:551). Rather, the Court seeks to hear cases which raise issues of major legal or practical importance. Often these include the most pressing political issues in the nation.

The Decision-Making Process In making its decisions, the Court relies heavily on four sources of information: decisions of lower courts, the legal briefs of the parties in a case, legal briefs of interested parties (*amicus curiae* briefs), and oral argument before the Court. Once the Court decides to hear a case, counsel for both parties submit briefs. These briefs are essentially "partisan" documents, that is, attempts to persuade the Court. By providing interpretation of relevant legal materials (precedents, statutes, and Constitutional provisions) and factual information favorable to their case, lawyers attempt to convince the Court to rule in favor of their clients or position. The Court at its discretion may permit *amicus* briefs by parties declaring their desire to help and perhaps having a tangible interest in the outcome of the case. Thus in *Branzburg v. Hayes* (1972), a celebrated case concerning whether reporters could refuse to disclose the identity of confidential sources, several newspapers and press organizations filed briefs, along with the American Civil Liberties Union, an association committed to a broad interpretation of First Amendment freedoms. *Amicus* briefs may provide additional perspectives on the issues confronting the Court and alert the justices to the broader implications of their decisions. Briefs for the modern judicial process are based in part on legal reasoning (precedents, law review articles, and the like) and in part on attempts to show that a favorable decision would be good policy and fair to the parties. The discussion of policy concerns, though certainly not a twentieth-century innovation, is clearly done today with much greater openness and less attempt to integrate the arguments with pure law. Parts of judicial briefs today hardly differ at all from the types of information supplied to legislators or administrators (Shapiro, 1978).

The final opportunity to influence the justices comes during oral argument. During the early nineteenth century, oral arguments were often great occasions in Washington, as the Court would be packed with spectators anxious to hear the long and often eloquent discourses of famous lawyers such as Daniel Webster. Although today the Court generally limits oral presentations to a half hour for each party, these sessions are frequently lively. The justices often bombard counsel with questions and requests for clarification, seeking to gauge the strengths and weaknesses of their arguments. For the unprepared or inexperienced lawyer, it can be a harrowing experience. Through these inquiries the justices can explore issues on which they are undecided, and an effective response to the justices' questions can affect the outcome of a case. As Justice John Marshall Harlan once acknowledged, oral argument "may in many cases make the difference between winning and losing, no matter how good the briefs are" (Lewis, 1964:162).

On each Friday during its term, the justices meet in closed conference to discuss the cases heard during the preceding week. Disagreement is common—clear-cut cases are seldom accepted for review—and debate can be heated. At the conclusion of their deliberations, the justices vote on each case. A chief justice who has voted with the Court majority in a case determines who will write the opinion of the Court (majority opinion). If the chief justice has not voted with the majority, the senior justice in the majority decides who will write the majority opinion. The other justices remain free to express their views in concurring or dissenting opinions. In its 1980 term, dissents were filed in over 75 percent of the Court's decisions.

The vote in conference is not binding. During the extended period between the vote and announcement of the Court's decision, the opinion of the Court and dissenting opinions are prepared and circulated among the justices. These draft opinions are carefully reviewed. A persuasive opinion may convince justices to switch votes, and a draft dissent might in this way even become the opinion of the Court. But even if no votes change, this phase of the process is vitally important. Justices may request changes in the language or argument of an opinion of the Court as a condition for endorsing it. Negotiation over the content of opinions at times reflects a concern with the soundness of the legal justification for the Court's decision. Even more, these negotiations reflect the individual justices' concern about the implications of the Court's arguments, since Court decisions serve as precedents that will influence the course of future cases. An example of such negotiations occurred in *United States v. Nixon* (1974), which involved the president's refusal to surrender tapes of White House conversations. Although the Court unanimously rejected the president's claim of executive privilege as a basis for retaining the tapes, announcement of the decision was delayed until Chief Justice Warren Burger accommodated several justices by modifying the view of presidential power outlined in his opinion (Woodward and Armstrong, 1979).

Once the justices have reached their final positions, the Court announces its decision in open court. The authors of opinions in the case briefly summarize their arguments, and copies of the opinions are published in *United States Reports*. By the conclusion of the Court's term in late June, the process will have repeated itself more than 150 times, and the justices will have written opinions filling four or five volumes of *United States Reports,* totaling over 4,000 pages.

THE JUDGES

When Justice William Douglas retired in 1975, he had served on the Supreme Court for over 35 years. His judicial career stretched from the New Deal to Watergate and spanned the inauguration of seven presidents. Yet remarkable as Douglas's tenure is, it is so only in degree. In order to safeguard judicial independence, the Constitution specifies that judges "shall hold their offices during good behavior" and receive a salary "which shall not be diminished" while in office. Although judges remain susceptible to impeachment, it has not, as noted, been used as an instrument against the opinions of the judges. Only a handful of federal judges, and no Supreme Court judges, have been removed in this manner.* Long—usually life—tenure in offices typifies the federal judiciary, and prolonged life expectancy may have increased the average tenure served now by federal judges. This long tenure allows judges to participate in deciding thousands of cases and thereby provides the opportunity for individual judges to exercise a considerable influence over the development of American law. It is important, therefore, to take a close look at who the judges are and how they are selected.

The Politics of Judicial Selection

Article II of the Constitution provides that the president shall appoint federal judges with the advice and consent of the Senate. The simplicity of the Constitutional language masks a more complex reality. Different actors play decisive roles in the selection of lower court judges versus Supreme Court justices; and this difference affects the types of persons elevated to these respective positions.

Lower Court Judges An assistant attorney general in President John Kennedy's administration aptly characterized the process for selecting district court judges when he remarked, "The Constitution is backwards. Article II, Section 2 should read: 'The senators shall nominate, and by and

---

*In 1969 Judge Fortas resigned from the Supreme Court, almost certainly because of the fear that impeachment proceedings would be brought against him. The reason had to do with a possible conflict of interest, and not directly with his judicial opinons.

with the consent of the president, shall appoint.'" Although Constitutional responsibility for nominating judges is lodged with the president, the primary power in selecting district court judges in fact resides in the Senate—and more particularly with the senators from the state in which the judge is to serve.

The mechanism by which the Senate dominates selection of district court judges is the unwritten policy of *senatorial courtesy*. Under this informal rule, the Senate, under its power to confirm presidential nominees, rejects any nominee who is opposed by senators from the president's party representing the state in which the vacancy occurs. Therefore, the president's staff, which plays a much more active role than the president in the nomination process, must negotiate with the state's senators to ensure confirmation. If the senators favor a particular candidate (and ordinarily they will, since district court judgeships represent major patronage positions), then that candidate ordinarily will receive the nomination.

Traditionally, the nomination of judges for the courts of appeals has followed a somewhat similar pattern. Because of the importance of these positions, the attorney general and other high officials of the Justice Department typically play a much more active role in determining prospective nominees for the appeals courts. Nevertheless, a modified form of senatorial courtesy has operated here as well. Although the appeals court encompasses more than a single state, senatorial courtesy has been extended to specific seats informally allocated to each state in the circuit. Thus, agreement between the executive branch and the appropriate senators has remained a necessity for confirmation.

President Jimmy Carter introduced major changes in these selection processes. Under his direction, thirteen merit selection panels were established to assist in filling vacancies on the courts of appeals. (Most Democratic senators, under administration urging, established similar commissions for district court nominations.) When a vacancy on an appeals court occurred, the appropriate panel was instructed to propose five candidates for the judgeship. By guaranteeing representation on the panels for women, minority group members, and nonlawyers, Carter hoped to tap a wider range of views on suitable candidates and foster the nomination of more minority members and women to these positions. Passage of the Omnibus Judgeship Bill, which created 35 new appeals judgeships and 117 district court judgeships, gave the panels an opportunity to have a major impact on court staffing (Goldman, 1980). President Carter ended up appointing a higher percentage of blacks, hispanics, and women to the branch than any previous president, although he did not depart from the traditional practice of selecting party activists for judgeships. With the election of President Ronald Reagan, these special panels were dissolved; but Attorney General Smith encouraged Republican senators to institute advisory panels for district court nominations and indicated that the administration would have its own appeals court panels.

The selection process for lower court judges results in the appointment of particular sorts of people. First, the judges have usually been politically active members of the president's party. Judge Joseph Perry, recounting how he was appointed to the federal bench, recalled his realization that "if I wanted that appointment, I had better get back into politics—which I did" (Murphy and Pritchett, 1974:169). Second, since state party contacts are particularly important in securing support, the judges have typically been active in state or local, rather than national, politics. They therefore tend to share the political perspectives dominant in the state. This can prove a problem, as illustrated by the reluctance of some southern district court judges to enforce the Supreme Court's school desegregation decisions (Peltason, 1961). Finally, members of multijudge courts are selected in part to provide representation for ethnic and religious groups served by the court. President Carter's merit selection panels in part served this very function by attempting to create a more diverse and demographically representative judiciary.

Supreme Court Justices The appointment of Supreme Court justices is among the president's most important responsibilities, and presidents take an active part in the selection process. Historically, four qualities in particular have characterized presidential nominees for the high court: (1) they have been high in national stature and distinguished service; (2) most (85 percent) have shared the same party affiliation as the president; (3) many have been members of groups whose presence on the Court has been sought to "balance" its composition (geography, race, religion, and now gender have

In 1981, President Reagan appointed Sandra Day O'Connor as the first female Supreme Court justice. *(Owen/Black Star)*

been considerations); and (4) they have generally shown compatibility with the president's views on major Constitutional issues.

The Senate has the power to confirm or reject presidential nominees and has not been reluctant to reject proposed candidates. As of 1982, the Senate had refused to confirm 26 out of a total of 127 Supreme Court nominees, although only 4 of the rejections have been in this century. The Senate has rejected nominees because of its own opposition to the president, a frequent practice in the nineteenth century. President John Tyler, for example, who had alienated the Senate membership of his party, named six nominees before the Senate finally accepted his choice. In this century, political considerations may linger in the background, but the explicit reasons for rejection have involved some "objective," nonpartisan standard. Thus, it was apparent breaches of judicial ethics that doomed President Nixon's nomination of Clement Haynesworth and President Johnson's attempt to promote Justice Abe Fortas to chief justice. Statements opposing black suffrage and labor unions led to the rejection of John J. Parker, nominated by President Hoover. And the undeniably undistinguished judicial service of Harold Carswell, also nominated by President Nixon, prevented his elevation to the Court.

Since a vacancy on the Court occurs, as observed, an average of every two years, the appointment power offers presidents substantial influence over the direction of Supreme Court decisions. Numerous presidents, however, have watched in disbelief as their appointees made decisions very different from what they had expected. President Dwight Eisenhower, asked if he had made any mistakes during his administration, replied: "Yes, two, and they are both sitting on the Supreme Court." This presidential disappointment, however, is not completely surprising. Many of the issues the justices confront arise after appointment, and presidents therefore may have given no attention to their nominees' views in these areas. The controversial decision on abortion, for example, was decided by the Court at the beginning of President Nixon's second term, with two of the justices whom the president had appointed voting for the decision; the president himself strongly opposed it and even supported a Constitutional amendment to reverse it. More important, once justices are appointed, they are no longer dependent on the president. They are now justices of the Supreme Court with a life tenure, and they naturally come to consider the interests of the Court to be more important than those of the president. One scholar of the judiciary, Alexander Bickel, summed up the limits of the appointment process for determining Court decisions: "You shoot an arrow into a far-distant future when you appoint a Justice and not even the man himself can tell you what he will think about some of the problems he will face" (Abraham, 1975:75). Or, as Harry Truman put it, "Packing the Supreme Court simply can't be done.... I've tried it and it won't work" (Abraham, 1975:75).

TABLE 12-2

OCCUPATIONS OF SUPREME COURT DESIGNEES
AT TIME OF APPOINTMENT

Federal officeholder in executive branch	22
Judge of inferior federal court	22
Judge of state court	22
Private practice of law	18
U.S. senator	8
U.S. representative	4
State governor	3
Professor of law	3
Associate justice of U.S. Supreme Court*	2
Justice of Court of International Justice	1

*Justices White and Stone, who were promoted to the chief justiceship in 1910 and 1930, respectively.
Source: Abraham, 1980:65, table III, updated to September 1983.

The Personal Factor in Judging

Justice Owen Roberts once suggested that in ruling on Constitutional questions

> the judicial branch of the Government has only one duty—to lay the article of the Constitution which is invoked beside the statute which is challenged and to decide whether the latter squares with the former (*United States v. Butler,* 1936).

Yet this description of judicial decision making is clearly too simple. Broad Constitutional mandates, such as "due process of law" and "equal protection of the laws" provide general directions but not precise instructions. Precedents cannot altogether relieve the judges of the necessity of choice, since contending parties will either urge the applicability of different precedents or (less frequently) suggest why earlier decisions should be overruled. And even in the area of statutory interpretation, as Justice Frankfurter noted, the "area of free judicial choice is considerable." Thus judicial interpretation, as we have seen, is far from being an automatic process; and it is precisely because it is not automatic that the judicial philosophies, political opinions, and personalities and experience of the justices influence the Court's decisions.

Judges bring to bear their own concerns and viewpoints and, like all human beings, are occasionally "driven" by petty concerns in their relations with others, including, of course, their long-term colleagues on the Court. Judges also have their own experience in affairs, which can inform (or color) their opinion. For example, Justice George Sutherland's opinion in an important case involving the president's power in foreign affairs, *United States v. Curtiss Wright* (1936), borrowed heavily from a book on the same subject that he had written while a senator. Finally, like anyone else, justices are susceptible to the impact of historical events, which can change their views. As Justice Benjamin Cardozo remarked, "The great tides and currents which engulf the rest of men do not turn aside in their course, and pass the judges idly by" (Cardozo, 1921:168).

Does all this mean, however, that justices simply read their own views into the law? Undoubtedly, this can and does occur to some extent, but there are powerful constraints that limit the justices' inclination and ability to make their simple personal opinions on issues the basis of their legal interpretations. The judges operate under institutional restraints that considerably affect their purely personal discretion. Ultimately, of course, the judges may have to come back to some kind of personal view, but this view may be limited and informed by a complex set of considerations that emerges from their activity as judges.

First, since judicial authority derives from the idea that judges are interpreting the law, they are obliged to seek direction from the law in deciding cases. In doing so, they are at least partly constrained by the informal principle of *stare decisis,* according to which past precedents normally bind current decisions. The justices, in other words, feel some responsibility to adhere to the Court's previous rulings; if they did not, every decision would be challenged and the entire notion of interpreting the law would become a mockery. From time to time, however, the Court will ignore past precedents where the rulings are ambiguous; and on certain occasions, it will openly overturn a decision, admitting that an earlier argument was false or is now somehow inapplicable. One famous instance of such a reversal is *Brown v. Board of Education* (1954), which overturned *Plessy v. Ferguson* (1896). The "separate but equal" standard established by *Plessy v. Ferguson* had endorsed racial segregation. Another famous instance is *Baker v. Carr* (1962), which reversed the decision of *Colgrove v. Green* (1946) that federal courts would not hear reapportionment cases.

Second, judges must write opinions that publicly justify their decisions in terms of the law. This serves as a major limitation on judicial discretion. On a multijudge court, judges who wish to influence their colleagues must do so by persuasive legal arguments. Studies of the inner workings of the Supreme Court, for example, have consistently portrayed the justices as concerned with and responsive to legal arguments. This is reinforced by the possibility of dissenting opinions, which can expose the weaknesses of decisions not rooted in the law. Although district court judges need not convince colleagues, the possibility of appeal and reversal serves as a constraint on their decisions.

Finally, and most important, judges are constrained by their own conception of the office. As Justice Frankfurter once observed:

> There is a good deal of shallow talk that the judicial robe does not change the man within it. It does. The fact is that on the whole judges do lay aside private views in discharging their judicial functions. This is achieved through training, professional habits, self-discipline, and that fortunate alchemy by which men are loyal to the obligation with which they are entrusted (*Public Utilities Commission v. Pollack,* 1959).

Yet it is important to point out that the "distance" from personal opinions spoken of by Frankfurter does not always work to reduce conflict among the judges. Justices may work under judicial philosophies that vary so greatly that their disagreements are sharpened rather than diminished. In particular, there may be the attitudes of restraint and activism, spoken of earlier, that lead justices further apart.

In sum, while judges cannot escape exercising personal judgment in deciding cases, there are numerous constraints that operate to channel that judgment and to transform it, much of the time, into something other than the more personal opinions that judges might express as citizens. These limitations may reduce somewhat the concern many have about judicial policymaking. But they certainly do not altogether resolve the problems that are at the basis of that concern. Conscientious judges can—and do—disagree among themselves; and judges can operate with very different conceptions of the meaning of their judicial role.

THE EXPANDING ROLE OF THE COURTS

As case load figures document, the federal courts are deciding more cases than ever before. This increase far exceeds what would be expected from population growth or any other specific demographic or economic factor. Moreover, the cases the courts are deciding often concern particularly contentious policy issues, such as busing, abortion, and affirmative action, or involve them in entirely new branches of law, such as environmental law. Finally, the courts have increasingly become involved not only in resolving disputes but also in supervising the details of administration of various governmental programs. What accounts for the increased level of judicial activity? Does it represent a usurpation of power by the courts, or is it caused by factors outside their control? Does it involve merely an expansion in scope, or does it represent a change in the character, as well as the level, of judicial activity?

Why the Judicial Role in Governing Has Grown

Three interrelated factors are primarily responsible for the judiciary's broader role in governing: (1) changes in the scope and character of governmental activity, (2) the lowering of barriers limiting access to the courts, and (3) the increased willingness of groups to use the courts to pursue political ob-

jectives. The last two factors may in turn have been encouraged by the growth of an activist judicial philosophy among judges, especially in the 1960s and 1970s, and the increased confidence by the courts in their institutional power.

The Growth of Government As noted in previous chapters, government at all levels has grown immensely over the past few decades. This growth is the primary factor that accounts for the increase in judicial activity. Expanding the scope of governmental responsibility inevitably increases the level of legal regulation; and when government increases the body of law, it provides new opportunities for litigation. When Congress passes a law, it creates both legal obligations and rights and thereby promotes litigation designed to enforce those requirements and vindicate those rights. For example, the passage of the Black Lung Benefits Act of 1972, by permitting coal miners to collect damages if they contracted black lung disease, ensured an increase in court cases. As Figure 12-2 indicates, there is almost certainly a direct relationship between congressional legislation and the growth in the business of the courts.

However, it is not merely the growth of government but also the changing character of governmental regulation which has prompted an expanding judicial role in governing. Whereas the volume of public bills passed annually by Congress has not increased since 1946–1948, the volume of administrative regulations has increased substantially. Taking the most general measurement, the size of the *Federal Register,* in which administrative regulations are published, has grown from 2,619 pages in 1936 to more than 65,000 pages at present. This expansion of administrative regulation is particularly important in promoting litigation, for litigants often challenge administrative regulations as being inconsistent with congressional legislation. Business, for example, may take cases to court where administrative agencies require large capital expenditures to meet certain requirements; and environmental groups are frequently in the courts attempting to pressure agencies to enforce standards claimed to be in the laws.

Access to the Courts The judiciary has also increased its role in governing by lowering proce-

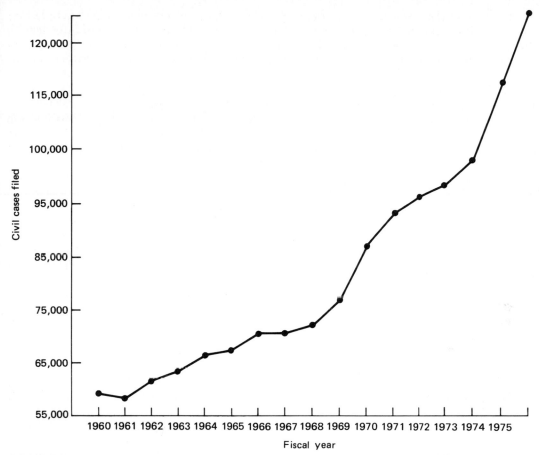

FIGURE 12-2
Civil cases filed in United States district courts, fiscal years 1960–1976. (*Source: Report of the Administrative Office of the Courts of the United States*, 1977:120.)

dural barriers that prevented some politically charged issues from coming to the courts. Under Article III of the Constitution, the federal courts' jurisdiction extends to "cases" and "controversies." In the past, the courts have interpreted this as a limitation on judicial power by refusing, for example, to decide cases in which the party instituting the suit lacked "standing," that is, a personal stake in the outcome of the case. Since the 1960s, however, the courts have greatly reduced this limitation and have expanded the parties who can challenge governmental actions in court. The range of issues that the courts now confront has increased

dramatically over the last twenty years. A particularly important development in this area has been the Court's decision to open the judicial system to more class-action suits. In a class-action suit, one or more persons bring suit for themselves and for "all others similarly situated" who claim a common legal right. These suits can relieve the courts of the burden of deciding a succession of cases involving the same legal right. Even more important, they increase the use of the courts by greatly reducing the costs of litigation for litigants and by increasing the potential rewards. (Attorneys' fees in such suits are contingent on winning and are deducted from the award in the case.) A great many consumer groups have sued businesses on this basis, and the class-action suit has been widely used in the area of litigation of discrimination in employment.

Litigation as a Political Strategy Increased access to the courts would mean little if groups were reluctant to bring issues to them. However, in recent years a myriad of groups—civil rights groups, consumer groups, and environmental groups, to name a few—have chosen to pursue their objectives through litigation. They have done so in part because they perceived that the court would be more receptive to their claims. In addition, they recognized that even without winning favorable rulings, a litigation strategy may offer considerable benefits.

There are several reasons why groups whose claims are rejected by the legislative and executive branches (the "political" branches) can expect to fare better in the courts. First, the criteria for success in the courts differ from those in other forums. As Hamilton argued in *Federalist* 78, "The judiciary ... may truly be said to have neither FORCE nor WILL but merely judgment." Whereas success in the political arena may depend upon the number and influence of those supporting a position, in the courts the primary criterion is legality. Thus even politically powerless groups—aliens, for example—can win major victories by convincing the judges that federal law or the Constitution supports their claims.

Second, the courts in recent years have indicated an unusual receptivity to attempts to overturn government policies. This is reflected in the increasing number of federal and state laws declared unconstitutional. It is also evident from the invalidation of long-standing state policies in such areas as pornography, legislative districting, abortion, and criminal justice. This apparent willingness to overturn government policy, in turn, encourages groups to bring their claims to the courts, thereby expanding the range of policies subject to judicial review.

Third, the success of some groups, most notably the NAACP's Legal Defense Fund, has demonstrated the potentialities of a litigation strategy. During the 1930s and 1940s, the NAACP sponsored a series of cases in which litigants sued to require states to provide equal facilities for blacks, supposedly guaranteed by the Court's "separate but equal" ruling in *Plessy v. Ferguson* (1896). Victories in these cases increased awareness of the effects of segregation and prepared the way for *Brown v. Board of Education* (1954), in which the Supreme Court outlawed racial segregation in education. In succeeding years, the NAACP sponsored further litigation designed to ensure full compliance with the *Brown* decision.

The NAACP's campaign has provided a model for other groups—for example, the environmental and consumer movements—and their success has promoted wider adoption of this strategy. Even where the prospect of a favorable ruling is slight, litigation can prove to be an effective strategy, as illustrated by the case of *Consumers Power Company v. Aeschliman* (1978). In this case, antinuclear groups appealed a decision of the Nuclear Regulatory Commission granting a construction permit for a nuclear power plant in Midland, Michigan. The antinuclear groups did not really expect a favorable decision, and in the end did not obtain one. But the unsuccessful appeal process served their purposes nonetheless. It delayed the start of construction and increased construction costs; it demonstrated to other power companies that they would encounter delays and additional costs if they decided to build nuclear plants; and finally it provided a forum for the antinuclear groups to focus public attention on the issue of nuclear power and its dangers (Cook, 1980). It was, in a sense, a political power play conducted on judicial turf.

The Contemporary Role of the Courts

In 1972, patients involuntarily confined in Bryce Hospital, Alabama's largest state mental health facility, filed a class-action suit, arguing that the state had not provided minimum standards of care and treatment as mandated by the Constitution (*Wyatt v. Stickney*, 1971). The federal district court judge agreed and ordered the Alabama Department of Mental Health to remedy the situation. When state officials did not make acceptable progress, the judge intervened once more and established detailed standards for care, treatment, and rehabilitative programs at the hospital. In prescribing a judicial remedy, the judge assumed the tasks normally performed by the legislators and state administrative officials. Largely as a result of *Wyatt v. Stickney,* Alabama's expenditures for mental health institutions jumped from $14 million in 1971 to $58 million in 1973.

Although the *Wyatt* case represents an extreme example of judicial intervention, it is hardly unique in contemporary American politics. A survey of administrative agencies in eight states found that nearly half of their largest agencies were operating under judicially mandated programs of some sort (Hale, 1979). This "positive" type of intervention, in which the courts prescribe broad remedies, dates from the decision of *Brown v. Board of Education* (1955) that authorized district court judges, if necessary, to impose their own desegregation plans. The success of the federal courts in supervising this effort, along with the support for the philosophy of judicial activism on the part of many influential commentators, probably convinced many judges that the courts can undertake such responsibilities. Moreover, the demands on the courts have changed with the shifting nature of modern law and the modern state. Many recent cases have involved complaints not of illegal actions in the classic sense but of governmental failure to meet its affirmative responsibilities to achieve certain results. In such circumstances, where judges also conclude that they cannot rely on administrative officials to remedy the situation, they have chosen active judicial participation in the formulation and implementation of remedial programs. As Judge Frank Johnson, who decided *Wyatt v. Stickney,* observed:

> Desegregation is not the only area of state responsibility in which Alabama officials have forfeited their decisionmaking powers by such a dereliction of duty as to require judicial intervention. . . . State officers by their inaction have also handed over to the courts property tax assessment plans; standards for the care and treatment of mentally ill and mentally retarded persons committed to the State's custody; and the procedures by which such persons are committed (Johnson, 1976:906).

With increasing frequency, courts make decisive determinations on important public issues. When they require specific remedial measures, they establish public policy; and in supervising the implementation of their directives, they administer it. Moreover, in directing governmental attention and funds to the solution of a particular problem, the courts inevitably influence the entire public policy process, for by requiring that government address one problem, they necessarily divert funds and personnel, which are limited, from other programs.

A number of court decisions—for example, on abortion, busing, and prayer in public schools—have been widely criticized. But even apart from the defensibility of particular decisions, the level of court involvement in governing is itself a source of controversy. Should the courts play such an important role? Can they do so successfully? Such questions might, of course, seem inappropriate. If the courts are simply "saying what the law is," then the obvious answers would seem to be that the courts should be involved exactly as they are. But from what we have seen, opponents as well as certain proponents of an active role for the courts seem to agree that the courts have gone further than a strict or modest interpretation of what the law requires. (Opponents deplore this, while proponents applaud it.) The courts in some measure have voluntarily expanded their policymaking role—though their behavior is not without past precedent. Given that the courts have chosen to make more policy than they might, and given that many believe that they can make policy well, it is important to ask about their effectiveness and the consequences of their interventions.

Commentators have identified a variety of considerations that affect the success of governmental policies. These have never been applied systematically to all the institutions, but many have raised questions about the courts' effectiveness according to these criteria. The following points, brought mainly by critics of an active role for the courts, should be read as the initial round of a debate that is certain to continue.

Timeliness of Addressing Problems Timing plays an important part in successful policymaking, for problems addressed too early may only aggravate a situation while those addressed too late may admit of no solution. The courts, in contrast to the other branches, have very little control over when they will take on problems. Since their jurisdiction is limited to cases and controversies, they must await litigants' decisions to bring problems to the courts. Moreover, since most courts—the Supreme Court is the notable exception—cannot refuse to decide cases, they cannot postpone considering problems even when that would be desirable. Thus it is in part a matter of chance whether courts will address a problem at the most appropriate time.

Adequacy of Information Effective policymaking depends upon obtaining and using the information relevant to an issue. Yet when the courts gather information, it is in terms of a particular case. This poses no difficulty if the case is representative of all situations that the court's decision will affect. But this is not always, or even usually, what happens. As Donald Horowitz has observed, "Because courts respond only to the cases that come their way, they make general law from what may be very special situations" (Horowitz, 1977:44). Insofar as the courts affect situations on which they lack information, they are not likely to deal with them adequately.

There is also the problem of the capacity of judges to digest all the relevant information. The judges themselves tend to be very busy and lack the staff resources of many legislators or executives. Judges in general-jurisdiction courts decide cases in a variety of fields. Thus, in considering cases which involve complex issues of public policy, they approach the issues as generalists, rather than as experts. This may mean that they bring a fresh perspective to problems, but it can also mean that they lack the background which concentration on a particular field brings. Moreover, when confronted with expert testimony, they often lack the skills necessary for evaluating experts' claims or, if the experts disagree, for knowledgeable choice among conflicting views.

Finally, in gathering information, the adversarial system in the litigation process means that there are usually only two parties to the conflict, with possible supporters. This means that information relevant to these parties alone is given or emphasized. As a result many concerns never arise in litigation that would emerge in a legislative setting. Of necessity, also, the information-gathering process focuses on legal factors as much as the desirability or consequences of a particular result. To the extent that law is the guiding force in the decision, this makes sense. But sometimes, as noted, the primary objective is general policymaking, and the adequacy of the information the judges receive may be suspect.

Flexibility of Response The more flexibility policymakers have in dealing with a problem, the more likely they are to deal with it successfully. Yet courts have considerably less flexibility than the other branches. Since courts must decide on the basis of law, policymaking in the judicial arena inevitably focuses on solutions cast in terms of the rights and duties of the parties in a dispute. This permits little consideration of compromise solutions, however desirable. It also limits the balancing of costs and benefits: if persons possess a right, they possess it regardless of cost. Thus in *Wyatt v. Stickney,* for example, the effect on Alabama's budget could not be a consideration in the court's decision.

Once it is discovered that an illegal condition exists, courts have fewer alternative means than the other branches for remedying it. Courts can forbid, permit, or require actions. However, they can neither tax nor spend (although, of course, their orders may require expenditures by the other branches). They cannot create new agencies to administer their directives or appoint officials to oversee their implementation. In sum, the courts have less range of choice in devising adequate remedies.

Monitoring the Effects of Decisions Once a policy is established, effective governing requires monitoring its implementation to ensure that the policy has been complied with, that it has had the desired effect, and that adjustments can be made. Except in a few areas, the courts have difficulties in meeting these objectives. Once they announce decisions, courts typically turn to other cases rather than continue their involvement in a particular field. Furthermore, they do not usually receive systematic reports on the effects of decisions, nor do they have the staff available to study the full impact of their decisions. Moreover, the courts have a special problem in making adjustments in any particular policy. Their decisions are frequently based on rights which cannot be compromised; and under a system that gives such great weight to precedent,

Court-ordered busing to achieve racial balance in school districts is a highly controversial example of modern judicial intervention. *(Eugene Richards / Magnum)*

courts cannot easily admit the failure of a previous directive and backtrack from it. These attributes of the legal process are precisely those that ought to be involved in matters where Constitutional rights or duties are at stake; but when (or if) the legal process is extended into the policymaking area, these same attributes can become inflexible impediments to the resolution of problems.

The Impact of Judicial Intervention

Whether the courts have become more involved in policymaking because of a larger government or because of an activist disposition on the part of judges is a question that can be resolved only by studying specific cases of law. Almost certainly, however, the greater activity of courts has led some in society to alter their method of pursuing political objectives, abandoning their struggle in the political arena and turning instead to a strategy of litigation. According to critics of an activist judiciary, groups rely more on specialized lawyers to plead their cases in a judicial setting than on mobilizing constituencies in a legislative setting.

By the same token, the political branches, aware that the courts are involved in more and more

areas, may sidestep difficult political issues and allow the courts to "take the heat" (McCormack, 1975). Both by encouraging reliance on the courts and by underwriting political irresponsibility, the expansion in court activity, according to certain critics, has undermined the vigor of popular government. Of course, if valid Constitutional rights have been abridged, it is clearly the role of the Courts to intervene; but a result-oriented activism, while it might achieve certain policies, could weaken the ability of democratic institutions to operate effectively in the long run.

CONCLUSION

In a system in which popular influences on the government predominate, the judiciary stands out as a striking exception. By the method of choice (appointment), the length of tenure (life), and the mode of deliberation (secrecy), the federal judicial system embodies attributes that are clearly different from the normal practices of democratic institutions. The founders intended the judiciary to have such characteristics precisely because the protection of the rule of law would be enhanced by an independent and nondemocratic institution. Although the founders clearly wanted this institution to be powerful, they did not seek to establish judicial supremacy over the other branches. The power balance among the institutions, rooted in their competing claims of authority as established by the Constitution and by tradition, was not fully resolved by the founders and remains a question that faces each generation. Today, as at a few other moments in history, the power and role of the courts stand as major questions of controversy.

SOURCES

Abraham, Henry: *The Judicial Process,* 3d and 4th eds., Oxford University Press, New York, 1975, 1980.

Baum, Lawrence: *The Supreme Court,* Congressional Quarterly Press, Washington, D.C., 1981.

Black, Charles L., Jr.: *The People and the Court,* Macmillan, New York, 1960.

Buell, Emmett, Jr.: *School Desegregation and Defended Neighborhoods,* Lexington Books, Lexington, Mass., 1982.

Cardozo, Benjamin N.: *The Nature of the Judicial Process,* Yale University Press, New Haven, Conn., 1921.

Congressional Research Service: *The Constitution of the United States of America: Analysis and Interpretation,* U.S. Government Printing Office, Washington, D.C., 1973, 1978.

Cook, Constance Ewing: *Nuclear Power and Legal Advocacy,* Lexington Books, Lexington, Mass., 1980.

Elliott, Ward: *The Rise of Guardian Democracy,* Harvard University Press, Cambridge, Mass., 1974.

Ely, John Hart: *Democracy and Distrust,* Harvard University Press, Cambridge, Mass., 1980.

Goldman, Jerry: *Ineffective Justice: Evaluating the Preappeal Conference,* Sage, Beverly Hills, Calif., 1980.

Gunther, Gerald (ed.): *John Marshall's Defense of McCulloch v. Maryland,* Stanford University Press, Stanford, Calif., 1969.

Hale, George E.: "Federal Courts and the State Budgetary Process," *Administration and Society,* November 1979.

Holmes, Oliver Wendell: *Collected Legal Papers,* Harcourt, Brace, New York, 1921.

Horowitz, Donald L.: *The Courts and Social Policy,* Brookings Institution, Washington, D.C., 1977.

Johnson, Frank M.: "The Constitution and the Federal District Judge," *Texas Law Review,* June 1976, pp. 903–916.

Lewis, Anthony: *Gideon's Trumpet,* Vintage, New York, 1964.

McCloskey, Robert G.: *The American Supreme Court,* University of Chicago Press, Chicago, 1960.

McCormack, Wayne: "The Expansion of Federal Question Jurisdiction and the Prisoner Complaint Caseload," *Wisconsin Law Review,* no. 2, Summer 1975, pp. 523–551.

Murphy, Walter F., and C. Herman Pritchett: *Courts, Judges, and Politics,* 2d ed., Random House, New York, 1974.

Neely, Richard: *How Courts Govern America,* Yale University Press, New Haven, Conn., 1981.

Nisbet, Robert: *Prejudices: A Philosophical Dictionary,* Harvard University Press, Cambridge, Mass., 1982.

Peltason, Jack: *Fifty-Eight Lonely Men,* Harcourt, Brace and World, New York, 1961.

Report of the Administrative Office of the Courts of the United States, U.S. Government Printing Office, Washington, D.C., 1977.

Richardson, James D. (ed.): *Messages and Papers on the Presidents,* vols. 1–10, U.S. Government Printing Office, Washington, D.C., 1896–1899.

Shapiro, Martin: "The Supreme Court: From Warren to Burger," in Anthony King (ed.), *The New American Political System,* American Enterprise Institute, Washington, D.C., 1978.

Thayer, James B.: "The Origin and Scope of the American Doctrine of Constitutional Law," reprinted in Gary L. McDowell (ed.), *Taking the Constitution Seriously,* Kenall Hunt, Dubuque, Iowa, 1981; originally published in 1873.

Tocqueville, Alexis de: *Democracy in America,* J. P. Mayer (ed.), Doubleday, Garden City, N.Y., 1968.

Vinson, Fred: "Work of the U.S. Supreme Court," *Texas Bar Journal,* December 1949, pp. 551–552.

Woodward, Bob, and Scott Armstrong: *The Brethren,* Simon and Schuster, New York, 1979.

Cases

Baker v. Carr, 369 U.S. 186 (1962).

Branzburg v. Hayes, 408 U.S. 665 (1972).

Brown v. Board of Education of Topeka, 347 U.S. 483 (1954); and 349 U.S. 294 (1955).

Buckley v. Valeo, 421 U.S. 1 (1976).

Calvert Cliffs' Coordinating Committee v. AEC, 449 F. 2d 1109 (1971).

Chisholm v. Georgia, 2 Dallas 419 (1793).

Colegrove v. Green, 328 U.S. 549 (1946).

Consumers Power Company v. Aeschliman, 435 U.S. 519 (1977).

Dred Scott v. Sanford, 19 Howard 393 (1857).

Furman v. Georgia, 408 U.S. 238 (1972).

Goldwater v. Carter, 444 U.S. (1979).

Griggs v. Duke Power Company, 401 U.S. 424 (1971).

Hunt v. Washington Apple Advertising Commission, 432 U.S. 333 (1977).

McCardle, ex parte, 7 Wallace 506 (1869).

McCulloch v. Maryland, 4 Wheaton 316 (1819).

Marbury v. Madison, 1 Cranch 137 (1803).

Oregon v. Mitchell, 400 U.S. 112 (1970).

Plessy v. Ferguson, 163 U.S. 537 (1896).

Pollack v. Farmer's Loan and Trust, 157 U.S. 429 (1895).

Public Utilities Commission v. Pollack, 343 U.S. 451 (1951).

Rummel v. Estelle, 445 U.S. 263 (1980).

United States v. Butler, 297 U.S. 1 (1936).

United States v. Curtiss Wright, 299 U.S. 304 (1936).

United States v. Nixon, 417 U.S. 683 (1974).

West Virginia State Board of Education v. Barnette (1943).

Wyatt v. Stickney, 344 F. Supp. 373 (1971).

Youngstown Sheet and Tube Co. v. Sawyer, 343 U.S. 579 (1952).

RECOMMENDED READINGS

Abraham, Henry J.: *The Judicial Process,* 4th ed., Oxford University Press, New York, 1980. Discusses the operation of the judicial branch in the United States and compares the American judicial process with that of other democratic nations.

Baum, Lawrence: *The Supreme Court,* American Enterprise Institute, Washington, D.C., 1981. An overview of the operation of the Supreme Court, with careful attention given to the Court's role as a national policymaking institution.

Cardozo, Benjamin N.: *The Nature of the Judicial Process,* Yale University Press, New Haven, Conn., 1921. A former justice of the Supreme Court discusses the factors that weigh in a judicial decision.

Corwin, Edward S.: *The Constitution and What It Means Today,* 14th ed., rev. by Harold W. Chase and Craig R. Ducat, Princeton University Press, Princeton, N.J., 1978. A line-by-line gloss on the Constitution as it has been interpreted by Court decisions.

Lewis, Anthony: *Gideon's Trumpet,* Random House, New York, 1964. A highly readable account of the story of one of the Court's most famous decisions, *Gideon v. Wainright* (1963), in which the Court ruled for a poor person's right to free counsel.

McDowell, Gary L. (ed.): *Taking the Constitution Seriously,* Kenall Hunt, Dubuque, Iowa, 1981. A collection of essays on the Constitution and the role of the courts in the United States political system.

Chapter 13

The Bureaucracy

CHAPTER CONTENTS

Lately, it seems, presidential candidates spend much of their time campaigning against a common opponent. Richard Nixon attacked the "mess" in Washington in 1968. Alabama's George Wallace railed against "pointy-headed" bureaucrats during his several tries for the office of chief executive. George McGovern, perceived by many voters as a liberal when he ran under the Democratic party banner in 1972, also heavily criticized the Washington establishment. Jimmy Carter attracted support four years later when he touted his virtues as an outsider who would pare the federal behemoth down to size and streamline its operations. In 1980, President Carter could no longer score political points as an outsider, but Ronald Reagan was quick to adopt the theme: federal civil servants were wasting the taxpayers' money, frustrating the public will, and inhibiting the innovative potential of American individuals and businesses. It was time to "get the government off the backs of the people," said Reagan, and this theme helped to carry him to victory.

It is rare indeed to find politicians of virtually every stripe in agreement about an issue. The American bureaucracy seems unloved. And yet despite the attacks mounted so frequently against the "permanent government," it persists. In fact, the federal government now employs about as many people as it did a generation ago, administers more programs, and spends much more money. One encounters, then, an ironic fact: the bureaucracy receives the blame for many important problems of American political life, yet it seems to be thriving nonetheless.

This phenomenon worries many citizens who are concerned about preserving representative government (Peters, 1981; Yates, 1982). They wonder whether American government has become a headless monster—huge, ponderous, unresponsive, and undirected—a force unto itself. They reason: if the bureaucracy is so influential, and if elected officials attack the bureaucracy and yet have not been able to solve its problems or get rid of it, can the people really rule? Or, putting this question into the terms mentioned in Chapter 1, we can say that the issue is really whether the bureaucratic model of governance most accurately describes the American situation today.

The whole subject of government bureaucracy often seems shrouded in mystery and confusion. For example, people use the term "bureaucracy" in diverse fashions. Many employ it to signify complicated, wasteful, and dehumanizing governmental activity. Few Americans would feel complimented if they were labeled bureaucrats. Although, as we shall see, the bureaucracy of the United States government often exhibits undesirable characteristics such as these, we shall utilize the term in a more neutral and descriptive sense. Employing the term in this less pejorative fashion was popularized through the work of a German sociologist named Max Weber, who used it to refer to large organizations that possessed the following characteristics: a hierarchy of superior-subordinate relations, official positions with fixed jurisdictions, personnel appointed on the basis of their ability to perform their jobs, rule-governed behavior, and written records of the organization's business (Weber, 1946).

Anyone who has had many dealings with the executive branch of the national government can probably recognize these characteristics there. It is a hierarchical arrangement of offices with positions, and people are usually appointed to these positions on the basis of merit rather than on the basis of, say, skin color or social connections (although certainly some federal bureaucrats are *not* good at their jobs and some received their appointments for reasons other than merit). The executive branch is governed by rules and inundated with paperwork and massive computerized records. It is, in short, a bureaucracy, as are most large organizations in and out of government in today's developed world (Jacoby, 1973). Examples of bureaucracies in the American government include the Urban Mass Transportation Administration, the Postal Service, the Small Business Administration, and the Army.

There is another respect in which bureaucracy is mysterious. For most Americans, the bureaucracy is the part of their government with which they are most likely to have contact. It is difficult for many people to go very long without having personal dealings with one federal bureaucrat or another: postal workers, veterans' affairs counselors, tax collectors (employees of the Internal Revenue Service), agents of the Federal Bureau of Investigation, or military personnel, to mention just a few examples. In addition, millions of bureaucrats

This vast office in the Social Security Administration, filled with workers impersonally applying complex rules that affect the lives of millions of Americans, typifies the modern governmental bureaucracy.   *(Dennis Brack / Black Star)*

working for state or local government are paid wholly or in part from federal funds, and much federal policy is executed by or influences the activities of these state and local personnel. These people include teachers, police officers, social workers, highway crews, and public health officials. Yet for many private individuals, the bureaucracy seems the most difficult part of their government to understand. The president, the Congress, and the court system are well known and closely studied. Their actions are usually comprehensible, even when one may not agree with them. But the bureaucracy employs obscure people who speak unintelligible jargon and use complicated technologies. The result is that Americans may not even feel capable of judging whether their administrative agencies act in the public interest.

In certain respects modern American government is bureaucratic government, although the bureaucracy is subject to a number of important constraints. How has it come to be that the bureaucracy as an institution occupies such a significant role in American public life? How can the bureaucracy be at the same time necessary and yet exceedingly controversial? How does the bureaucracy operate, and what, if any, are its virtues as

well as vices? Can a bureaucratic state be a democratic one? These questions are very complex and have been a focus for study and debate among political analysts for a considerable period, so we cannot hope to provide definitive answers here. However, we can touch upon these questions and in so doing suggest the tremendous significance of the bureaucracy to American government. We turn first, briefly, to the past for an explanation of how and why this seemingly unpopular but necessary institution emerged.

THE BUREAUCRACY: THE FIRST 200 YEARS

We have seen that the earliest American constitution makers devoted considerable attention to many of the most important institutions of American government. The delegates at the Constitutional Convention thought, wrote, and debated about the presidency, Congress, and the judiciary. But despite their wisdom and foresight, almost all the founders paid little mind to the possibility that this nation's administrative agencies might be significant centers of public decision.

The Constitution itself contains not a word about the bureaucracy. In fact, the term was not even a part of the common language yet. Even in *The Federalist,* not a great deal of attention was devoted to the potential opportunities and problems that might be created for American government by large administrative agencies. The framers were most interested in establishing a basic structure of government which, they believed, would further republican ideals. When they addressed the details of administration, they tended to do so in rather ambiguous fashion.

For instance, the Constitution refers to "departments" and "executive departments" (for example in Article II, Section 2) but nowhere stipulates what such departments should do or who should supervise them. This lack of clarity led to considerable political debate in the succeeding years about the proper roles of the president and the Congress in supervising administrative agencies. The founders generally seemed to believe that their constitutional framework would permit administrative units to be established when necessary in the future. As one student of administrative history has observed, "It appears that those who wrote our constitution assumed that there was no problem to worry about, that any question about the constitutional status of administrative agencies could be answered readily and easily enough if only an adequate basic framework of government was brought into existence" (Millett, 1976:361).

Yet while the founders as a whole ignored the issue, one of them did not. Alexander Hamilton clearly envisioned an efficient and stable civil service under the superintendence of the chief executive (*Federalist* 72). He thought that organizing administration in this fashion would enable the president to exercise leadership and energy in the tasks of governing. In his concern for efficiency and stability, as well as in his idea about presidential control over administration, he raised issues that were left basically unresolved by the founders. But the themes he developed were to become important later on.

It is really not so surprising that the subject of government bureaucracy received so little attention at the time of the founding. The framers had plenty of other more pressing issues to handle. In the struggle to establish a basic structure of government, to resolve such essential matters as federalism, civil liberties, and representation, they had little time or reason to expend energy on administrative activity. In fact, for most of the nation's existence the "problem" of bureaucracy remained in the background. From the founding through most of the nineteenth century, the American bureaucracy was small and relatively insignificant (Nelson, 1982). Before we examine the growth of government during the current century and the consequences of this expansion, therefore, it might be useful to survey briefly the bureaucracy of those earlier, placid times.

The Bureaucracy through the Nineteenth Century

A Small Bureaucracy During the first century of this nation's existence, the American bureaucracy seemed to pose few political issues or problems. Although the government handled important tasks, most of these required no large or expensive administrative apparatus. American society was relatively simple and agrarian, and the complex patterns of interdependence so common to modern society—intricate transportation systems, congested population centers, mass production and distribution enterprises—were absent. Most of the government's large-scale problems were deemed matters of necessity and were based on considerable popular support. American civil servants through the nation's first century busied themselves in the execution of a relatively few tasks: delivering mail, fighting wars, and administering programs designed to build the nation's basic facilities—for example, constructing roads and canals or encouraging the development of western lands.

Compared with the size of today's American government, the early bureaucracy was tiny (see Figure 13-1). At the outset of the nineteenth century, the whole civil service system included only about 2,000 full-time employees (Van Riper, 1958). Several departments and agencies, some of which today employ hundreds of thousands of people, were cozy units in which most people knew each other. As the years wore on, the bureaucracy grew as the boundaries of the nation pushed farther apart and the population increased. However, throughout most of the previous century bureau-

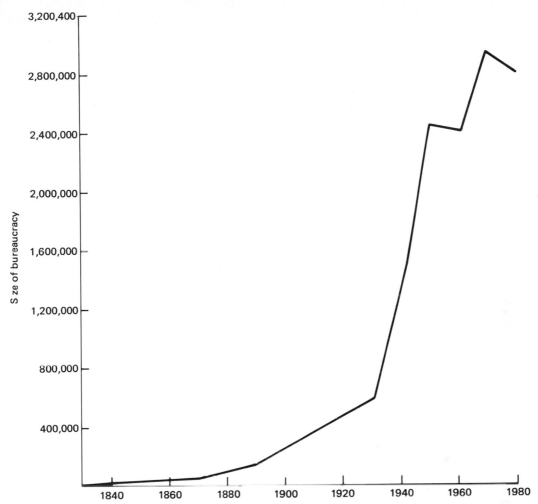

FIGURE 13-1
Paid civilian employment, federal executive branch, 1830–1980. (*Source: Historical Statistics of the United States: Colonial Times to 1970,* 1975:1102.)

cratic activity was characterized by two important features. First, the simplicity of most government programs meant that, if they so desired, ordinary citizens could fathom what their officials were doing. Second, few programs were controversial.

There were occasional exceptions, the most important of which was the major dispute in the 1830s about the national bank. The Second Bank of the United States was not, strictly speaking, a public bureaucracy; it was a corporation chartered by Congress and charged with some public duties. This unit became an object of controversy between President Jackson and the Congress, partially because of the way it handled some of its tasks (for instance, there were charges of political favoritism in its policies on loans) and partially because of its unique structure, which insulated it somewhat from public control (White, 1954). The bank's official responsibilities were ended in 1836.

It is important to realize, however, that this example was a rarity. In almost every other instance, the federal government's agencies were widely supported or at least tolerated. Operations of the Treasury, the War Department, and such bureaus as the Patent Office were not always routine, but units like these hardly stimulated the controversy that we associate these days with modern federal energy programs or welfare or environmental regulation. Americans did not much worry that their bureaucracy would make important policy decisions or develop significant independence from elected political officials.

In fact, through much of that century a major complaint was just the reverse: the American bureaucracy, after a fashion, was *too* closely linked to the country's political leadership. Given the fact of today's attacks by politicians on the bureaucracy, such a criticism may seem quite puzzling. However, this earlier problem and the reform that it engendered have had permanent impacts on today's American bureaucracy. Thus it is important that we examine the character of this earlier civil service and see how reactions to it have affected modern government.

Political Connections We have seen in previous chapters that the issue of who had the right to appoint and remove federal officials was a bone of contention between the presidency and Congress for much of early American political history. However, from the first years of the republic—thanks partially to legislation passed in 1789—presidents exercised formal authority to use broad appointment power (Van Riper, 1958). The first American bureaucrats were offered positions with no guarantee of job protection. If clerks in some federal office had been appointed through the grace of one president, there was no assurance that they would be able to maintain their jobs under a new chief executive, no matter how heroically they had been performing their tasks.

As a matter of fact, however, the earliest presidents did not exercise this authority in a crude fashion. Although Washington and Adams, for instance, tended to staff their offices with civil servants who were sympathetic to their own political inclinations, they also tried to ensure that the fledgling bureaucracy was competent and respectable. This was partially a matter of socioeconomic status (Mosher, 1982). Public servants during the first several decades of the nineteenth century were markedly different from most of their fellow citizens. The bureaucrats had more prestigious backgrounds (see Table 13-1), more money, and more education than other Americans. Thus early American bureaucracy was unrepresentative of the people in social and economic terms, but it had some potential links with the president and was for the

TABLE 13-1
FAMILY BACKGROUND OF EARLY HIGHER-RANKING BUREAUCRATS
(Primary Occupations of Fathers of Higher-Ranking Bureaucrats)

	Percent of all occupations under various presidents		
	Adams, $n = 100$	Jefferson, $n = 104$	Jackson, $n = 129$
High-ranking occupations			
Landed gentry	22	29	21
Merchants	22	13	17
Professionals	26	18	15
Total	70	60	53
Middle-ranking occupations*	23	25	39
Unknown	7	15	8
Total	100	100	100

*Middle-ranking category includes artisans, proprietors, farmers, teachers, sea captains, and shop- or tavern keepers.
Source: Mosher, 1982:61; Aronson, 1964:61.

most part reasonably competent. Furthermore, wholesale removals at the change of administrations did not occur. A fair number of civil servants were allowed to keep their positions. Even when the presidency passed from the hands of one party to the other, shifts in the bureaucracy were moderate.

However, this pattern did not remain constant. During the tenure of President Andrew Jackson, appointment practices differed only slightly from those under his predecessors, but he argued for a dramatically different conception of the public service. In a speech to Congress in 1829, Jackson developed a theme that was to become a potent political issue under later administrations: "The duties of all public officers are, or at least admit of being made, so plain and simple that men of intelligence may readily qualify themselves for their performance; and I can not but believe that more is lost by the long continuance of men in office than is generally to be gained by their experience" (Van Riper, 1958:36). The president proposed that all administrative appointments be limited to a four-year maximum tenure.

This idea that government tasks can be performed by common people and that positions in the bureaucracy can be used as rewards by executives to political loyalists became the heart of the *spoils system*. Under succeeding presidents and until the civil service reform late in the century, the spoils system dominated federal appointments. Federal agencies were no longer the preserve of the upper class, but they were also no longer always sources of efficiency and stability. Horror stories circulated, and many of them were true. Illiterates, crooks, and other incompetents occupied government positions.

Customs agents and inspectors, for instance, were often unqualified and dishonest. Some of them never even bothered to go to work except to collect their pay. Others demanded bribes and drank heavily on the job. Those in New York were labeled "parasites" by the government's own commissioner of customs. The bureaucrats in the Office of Indian Affairs defrauded the Indians as a matter of course. In the navy yards, thousands of positions were filled at the behest of various members of Congress, and many more people were hired temporarily during presidential campaigns (White, 1958). Bureaucratic work became a reward for partisan efforts on behalf of candidates at election

time. Changes in administration meant dramatic shake-ups in many a federal office, and presidents-elect were besieged with requests from insistent job seekers. President Garfield, for example, complained to his wife that he "had hardly arrived [in Washington] before the doorbell began to ring and the old stream of office-seekers began to pour in. They had scented my coming and were lying in wait for me like vultures for a wounded bison" (White, 1958:6). Abuses became so widespread that suggestions for reform were heard more and more insistently after the Civil War. With the assassination of Garfield by one of those whom he had not hired, civil service reform became a popular issue. Many Americans had come to believe that the salvation of their government lay in the installation of a neutral and competent bureaucracy that would be protected from manipulation by politicians (see Box 13-1).

Who Was to Control the Bureaucracy? One other development of importance occurred in the latter part of the century. Increasingly, the "boss" of the bureaucracy became the Congress, not the president. The chief executives did little to manage the government's growing apparatus, and department heads often worked directly with legislators on major policy matters as well as day-to-day operations. Congress participated in patronage bargaining, as suggested above; examined the details of agency spending plans; scrutinized bureaucratic operations; and overturned certain agency decisions. This method of oversight often did not work very well, but a succession of presidents seemed to have neither the means nor the inclination to direct the bureaucracy. Thus the issue of control, which had been left unresolved by the founders, began to stimulate controversy. Some reformers echoed the thoughts of Hamilton a century earlier. The civil service should be not only neutral and competent, they said, but also directed by the executive, who would be the government's principal manager. Both these themes were soon to become important.

The Rise of the Administrative State

Civil Service Reform The rudiments of civil service reform became reality in 1883 with the passage of the Pendleton Act. This new law made it

---

BOX 13-1

SPOILS AND MERIT: CONTRASTING PERSPECTIVES

A century ago, at the time of civil service reform, the spoils system seemed to many to be one of the major problems with American government. The reformers argued that a merit system was necessary for true representative government. As one put it:

> The villages, the cities, the army posts, the special agencies, the custom-houses, the mayors, the governors, the consulates, the revenue officers, the president—in short, public affairs of every nature and officers of every class—are involved in distrust and are degraded in popular estimation, by reason of the opportunities afforded by a partisan-spoils system of office and the use that is made, or is believed to be made, of these opportunities. . . . Can anyone undertake to estimate how much it has done to impair confidence in institutions, to cast suspicion over all official life, to disgust the people with the very name of politics, to drive good men from the polls, to bring republicanism into disrepute both at home and abroad? (Eaton, 1880:444)

Yet in modern times a number of people criticize civil service because such systems, by protecting bureaucrats from political interference, also shield public employees from the people or their elected officials. One observer of the federal establishment has argued:

> Anyone who has had a reasonable amount of contact with the federal government has encountered people who should be fired. . . . Yet fewer than one per cent are fired each year. . . .
> . . . I would urge cutting [the civil service] by 50 per cent, and filling the remaining half with political appointees who can be fired at any time. . . .
> . . . If the government is to work, policy implementation is just as important as policy making. No matter how wise the chief, he has to have the right Indians to transform his ideas into action, to get the job done (Peters, 1979:263–267).

---

possible for the federal government gradually to institute a merit system throughout virtually the entire bureaucracy. Today almost all federal employees are hired through competitive examinations that rate candidates on their ability to perform the specialized tasks required of the jobholders, whether these skills involve accounting or engineering or typing or managing the work of other bureaucrats (see Table 13-2). Those employed under the federal merit system are also provided with considerable job security as a protection against intrusion by politicians into the supposedly technical matters that occupy administrative agencies. However, the civil service reform near the end of the nineteenth century marked the beginning of the period during which the problems of bureaucracy—how to organize, administer, and control the agencies of government—first really came to the fore.

Social Change and Governmental Response
Throughout the first century of United States government, as we have seen, the bureaucracy was a

rather insignificant force. However, at the end of the nineteenth century and the beginning of the twentieth, this situation altered significantly. American society was becoming more complex and more highly organized, and the government responded in kind (Skowronek, 1982; Waldo, 1948).

At the turn of the century, the United States was a society in transition. Goods and services were, as before, being produced mostly through a private market economy, but that economy was no longer composed primarily of small entrepreneurs. The growth of the modern corporation and the arrival of mass production brought great changes. Considerable power gathered in the hands of the managers of these enterprises rather than the owners. For the first time, the skills of organizing people and resources became paramount. The earlier and simpler American society was disappearing under the onslaught of urbanization, waves of immigrants, and large-scale organization.

Many were concerned about government's ability to cope with these developments, to maintain a tranquil and free society in the face of the complex

TABLE 13-2
PERCENTAGE OF FEDERAL BUREAUCRACY INCLUDED
UNDER MERIT SYSTEM PROTECTION

Year	Percent included
Before Pendleton Act of 1883	0.0
1891	22.5
1901	46.0
1911	58.7
1921	81.5
1931	78.4*
1941	69.9
1951	87.3
1961	87.1
1970	83.3
1979	92.0†

*Temporary decreases in the proportion of the federal bureaucracy subject to merit protection have occasionally resulted from expansions in the size and scope of federal activity, for example during the New Deal years. Typically, new agencies and programs have come under merit protection shortly after creation.

†In recent years the positions *not* included here have included federal attorneys, faculty in the service academies, undercover narcotics agents, certain employees without full-time status, positions in Navy or Air Force communications intelligence, bank examiners, certain key high-level positions, positions overseas filled by noncitizens, and a few other categories.

Source: *Historical Statistics of the United States*, 1975:1102; *Federal Personnel Guide, 1979.*

developments occurring nationwide. Could the American constitutional order withstand the forces of modernization? The response of many government reformers at this time was that it could, but only if government assumed new duties and restructured itself for the task.

New Policies The national government began to enact new types of policies (Lowi, 1979). For instance, regulatory legislation first appeared on the books in the 1880s as the Interstate Commerce Commission was established to control prices charged and routes utilized for transporting people and goods between states. Other regulatory policy has followed, so that today the national government is charged with overseeing such diverse activities as the allocation of radio and television franchises, the effectiveness and purity of food and drugs, the operations of the stock exchanges, corporate advertising practices, air transportation, the

safety of nuclear power plants, working conditions in factories and office buildings, and equal employment opportunity practices. In the twentieth century, and especially following the great depression, the national government also came to assume some responsibility for the well-being of many groups of citizens. Mere mention of social security, welfare, health research and assistance, and public housing construction indicates the diverse sorts of programs over which the United States has established some jurisdiction. The important point here is that this active government posture began near the turn of the century, although many of today's most important policies were not initiated until later.

Professional Public Administration The reformers who were seeking to adapt American government to the new age were not content merely to push for new policies. They argued that if the new policies that were needed to cope with industrializing America were to be executed successfully, well-managed administrative agencies would be necessary—units staffed by experts and organized to operate efficiently. Thus developed a political argument that was to have a profound effect on the operations of modern American government.

Perhaps the clearest version of this important idea was written by the young Woodrow Wilson, who was a political scientist long before he became president. In Wilson's 1887 essay "The Study of Administration," he captured much of the spirit of the modern age that was to follow. In words that future generations of public administrators were to take very seriously, he suggested that Americans had built a workable constitutional framework, but that it was now time to devote attention to the administrative agencies that would be the key institutions of government in the emerging complex society:

> The weightier debates of constitutional principle are even yet by no means concluded; but they are no longer of more immediate practical moment than questions of administration. It is getting to be harder to *run* a constitution than to frame one (Wilson, 1887:200).

Centralizing Control Wilson and plenty of other turn-of-the-century reformers during the progressive era criticized Americans for being excessively devoted to the limited and fragmented government that they had inherited from the era of the founding. The progressives sought some of the same goals as had many of the framers of the Constitution a century earlier, but the responses of the two groups differed markedly. James Madison, for instance, had written eloquently of the need for American government to be structured so as to combat "instability, injustice, and confusion" (*Federalist* 10). We have seen the constitutional product of this concern, a structure built to limit the likelihood of any faction's being able to rule. Wilson and the progressives also hoped to reduce the chances that their increasingly organized, specialized, and technological society would be subject to instability, injustice, and confusion. But they saw salvation in a governmental apparatus that would be strong, active, well-organized itself, and fairly *centralized*. In a sense, these administrative reformers took their advice not from Madison and his allies but from Hamilton and his idea of presidential control over the bureaucracy.

Wilson suggested that when governmental power is fragmented, no one can get much done. Thus administration is likely to be irresponsible and out of touch with the public's needs—in other words, overly pluralistic government can reduce majoritarian influences. In essence, the administrative reformers argued that the new age required a more active government that would engage in planning and executing complex new programs. These programs would in turn demand large bureaucracies that would be administered by experts who understood the numbing details and puzzling technologies of, say, transportation regulation. One had to ensure that government would remain responsible to popular will in this era of big bureaucracy. Authority should be centralized in relatively few hands. Then these top-level executives—especially the president—should be provided with sufficient staff help and formal power to effect their will. The bureaucracy should be converted into a fine-tuned machine that would execute with economy and efficiency the policy decisions made at the top. Finally, the highest policymakers should be held to account through periodic popular election.

Providing dollar bills seems like a simple, mechanical function for the federal bureaucracy; but printed money makes up only a part of the nation's money supply, and politicians and economists argue endlessly over the amount of money that should be circulated. *(Bob Adelman/Magnum)*

Separating Policy and Administration But if so much importance was to be attached to administrative agencies in the bureaucracy, how could Americans be certain that these units would not become political forces in their own right and thus challenge democratic government? Would bureaucratic growth mean that the bureaucratic model of governance (Chapter 1) would begin to dominate? The administrative reformers had an answer to this important question, although—as we shall discuss—this answer turned out to be fundamentally inadequate. Their argument was really very simple. Government does two things: it makes decisions and it executes them. Making decisions—policy— is the task of politicians; carrying them out is the job of public administration. The government's large bureaucracies are the organizations that are charged with this latter task, which is itself a largely technical question of efficiency. Once again, Wilson put the point clearly:

> The field of administration is a field of business. It is removed from the hurry and strife of politics; it at most points stands apart even from the debatable ground of constitutional study. It is a part of political life only as . . . machinery is part of the manufactured product (1887:209–210).

Thus, said the reformers, the rise of bureaucratic government would not threaten popular rule, because bureaucracies, when organized and staffed correctly, are nonpolitical instruments of implementation. In fact, they actually *strengthen* democratic government by increasing the ability of the executive to effect the popular will. Civil service reform fit neatly with this idea, since the essence of such a reform was to install politically neutral technocrats in government service, insulate them from partisan meddling, but require them to carry out the goals of popular government as expressed by elected leaders. It is not too much of an exaggeration to say that the American administrative reformers, who helped organize and staff the national bureaucracy as it began to grow at the start of this century, thought of the government's administrative agencies almost as vending machines: policy would be inserted at the top, wend its way through the bureaucratic mechanism, and emerge at the bottom—carried out by experts but essentially undamaged and unchanged (Weber, 1946).

Other complementary ideas also became popular in succeeding years. Reformers sought to make the growing and professionalizing bureaucracies more businesslike by such devices as reorganizing offices, instituting a variety of suggestions concerning economy and efficiency, establishing (in 1921) a formal federal budget to keep track of proposed expenditures, and strengthening the president's role as general manager of the vast array of offices in the executive establishment.

Presidential Management This last idea of the reformers became prominent later, especially during the New Deal years of President Franklin D. Roosevelt. The perspective of the president as the head of federal administration contrasted sharply with the practice of congressional supervision in the late nineteenth century. But under crisis conditions such as those of the great depression, this Hamiltonian notion acquired a certain persuasiveness. In 1937, for instance, Roosevelt appointed a high-level Committee on Administrative Management, chaired by a public administration expert, Louis Brownlow, to propose improvements in the operations of government. This group made a number of suggestions, all based on the idea that the president should be the person responsible for running the bureaucracy, much like the chief executive officer in a business firm. One important proposal of theirs was that there ought to be an Executive Office of the President to help the chief executive manage the federal establishment. This unit was created in 1939, during Franklin Roosevelt's second term.

Thus, the notion of the president as head of the bureaucracy, while unpopular with many of the founders, became widely accepted as the years went by. It was a premise not simply of New Dealers or Democrats, either. Former President Herbert Hoover, a conservative Republican, headed governmental study commissions in the 1940s and 1950s; these groups utilized the idea, as did the Ash Council, a group of advisers to President Nixon (Arnold, 1976).

Yet even though the principle of presidential leadership was accepted by many, it was never fully adopted by Congress or the public. The question remains incompletely resolved even today, with the president often perceived as the manager of the bureaucracy while the Congress in reality exercises a good deal of detailed oversight. This tension helps to explain the considerable amount of name-calling still directed these days at the bureaucracy, an institution often caught between executive and legislature.

The Impact of Bureaucratization The notion that the bureaucracy should be reformed and strengthened obviously has had a dramatic effect on American government. This section has documented some of the changes at the national level. In addition, many of our state and local governments today also bear the impact of the administrative reform movement. For instance, the city manager form of government, now the most widely used structure for the governance of American municipalities, was first tried in 1908 in Staunton, Virginia, as a method of bringing to the local level many of the ideas we have been discussing here.

Nevertheless, the idea that the public administrative structure needed to be professionalized, consolidated, strengthened, and perhaps enlarged has never met with anything like unanimous approval by citizens or political leaders. Throughout the course of the twentieth century, nearly every proposal for an expanded bureaucracy or an increased jurisdiction for it has stimulated rebuttal by those worried about the size of government or the role of the bureaucracy in the constitutional order. As we have seen, many efforts by presidents to bolster their authority to direct the bureaucracy have been resisted by members of Congress who have believed that they also should have a legitimate role in overseeing the operations of administrative agencies. Today's federal bureaucracy is no monolith. In fact, it is important to note that American administration is probably more diversified, fragmented, and open to contact from legislators and citizens than any of its counterparts in western Europe. The significant changes in the size and shape of the federal establishment have not eliminated the influence of our political leaders or our system of separation of powers; thus, pluralistic and majoritarian influences continue to function even within our bureaucratic institutions.

Despite this last point, however, it is clear that the past century has brought a significant bureaucratization of the federal structure. One hundred years after the country was founded, federal agencies were still small, relatively few in number, and staffed through the use of political patronage. As American society has modernized, as the nation has become more complex and its parts more interdependent, as the private economy, from General Motors to General Electric to General Dynamics, has itself become more highly organized and filled with bureaucracies, the federal government has responded in kind. The end of the country's first 200 years finds the nation's capital filled with huge agencies—complex beyond comprehension, touching in some fashion nearly every aspect of private life, full of all sorts of experts, highly controversial, but also frequently indispensable.

TODAY'S BUREAUCRACY: ITS STRUCTURE AND ITS PEOPLE

The bureaucracy is the home of almost all federal employees, approximately 2.8 million in recent years. It is through the bureaucracy that most federal money is spent and most national policy is carried out. It is useful, therefore, to take a closer look at just what the bureaucracy is and also how it operates.

Perhaps the first point that should be noted is this: despite the fact that the federal bureaucracy may sound mammoth when one hears how many people inhabit its corridors and cubicles, even this measure of its extent actually understates its proportions. The nearly 3 million employees mentioned here exclude those in the military as well as part-time or seasonal federal workers. Furthermore, the influence of the federal establishment extends to state and local government, whose bureaucracies are not included in this total but which have mushroomed in size during recent decades. State and local public servants now outnumber their federal counterparts fourfold, and in many cases they are heavily influenced by federal agencies that help to fund their efforts and to direct, supervise, and audit their activities. (See Chapter 14 for a discussion of the intergovernmental grant system through which these operations take place.)

Finally, considerable federal business is contracted out to private consultants and enterprises. These units are often used by federal bureaus to handle nonroutine tasks or to circumvent adminis-

BOX 13-2

CONSULTANTS AND THE BUREAUCRACY

The use of private consultants, or contractors, to perform part of the public's business has been widespread and controversial in recent years. Estimates vary widely on just how much work the federal bureaucracy actually delegates to these outside firms, but among the agencies using consultants most frequently are the departments of Energy and Defense.

Some of the largest contractors in the defense field perform research and development tasks and build much of the nation's weaponry. Others, in energy, defense, and elsewhere, perform management studies, do auditing work, study various policy problems, and sometimes even provide typing services. Certain companies, such as the Rand Corporation, have become famous for performing almost all their work for the government. (Rand was started to handle certain research and development tasks for the Air Force, hence its name.)

The use of some consulting is inevitable in today's governmental system. These firms often have more flexibility than federal agencies do and can sometimes produce results more quickly and efficiently. They also often pay better salaries, so the quality of their expertise may be impressively high. Outside contractors can provide fresh approaches to troublesome problems, and they also can be a real boon to agencies faced with a frequently recurring conflict: being required to carry out certain tasks but being forbidden by federal restrictions to hire the necessary staff. Some agencies—the Energy Department is one—are increasingly becoming repositories of managers or overseers, with most of their actual detailed work (e.g., auditing Mobil Oil) being handled by outsiders.

The heavy use of consultants by the federal bureaucracy has been challenged for a number of reasons. Legislators are concerned about potential conflicts of interest: a contractor may tailor its advice or analysis for the government to benefit some of its other clients. Because of their higher salaries, consulting firms can also lure bureaucrats from federal agencies to the companies; using consultants may thus sometimes be a way of paying more money for the same product. Critics are also concerned that outside firms are less visible to the public and less closely controlled by government officials, so it is more difficult to tell whether the public interest is being served. And there are a number of examples of federal agencies paying handsomely for nearly worthless products from consultants. Such was the case when the Department of Energy hired the Cabot Consulting Group, a small firm, to analyze the effects of the 1979 gasoline shortage, the company documented in detail the not-so-startling fact that the shortage had caused Americans to drive less. More recently, it was learned that members of the nonsalaried board of the federal Legal Services Corporation appointed by President Reagan had hired themselves out as consultants to their own agency, to the tune of nearly $200,000 in 1982.

The Office of Management and Budget has placed some restrictions on the use by agencies of consultants, and legislation is proposed from time to time to deal with the problem. In 1981, the Omnibus Reconciliation Act included a provision for reducing federal spending on outside experts by $500 million for fiscal year 1982. Yet agencies and consultants caution against regulating the activity too tightly, and it is certain that private firms will continue to be employed, as federal agencies seek to carry out their tasks.

---

trative constraints. The Energy Department is one unit that has made extensive use of consultants. In 1980, nearly 80 percent of the agency's budget of $12 billion was spent on contracts. A considerable part of this money went to run government-owned laboratories. Other activities included audits of oil companies, engineering studies on coal conversion, and a great deal of data collection and analysis.

There have been criticisms recently of the use of so many consultants by the bureaucracy, and the last few years have seen a reduction. Nevertheless, outside firms continue to perform a great deal of work (Brewer, 1973; Guttman and Wilner, 1976). Thus the size of the national government's budget and its change over time may be a more accurate indicator of the reach of the federal bureaucracy, although

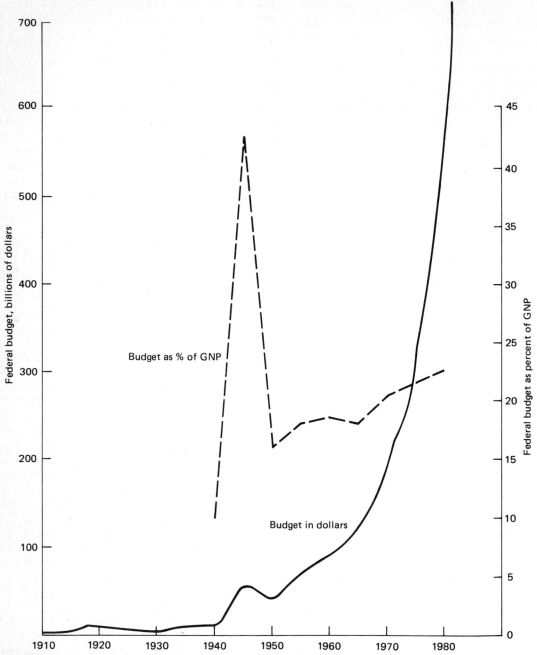

FIGURE 13-2
Growth of the federal budget. (*Source: Historical Statistics of the United States: Colonial Times to 1970*, 1975:1114; *Statistical Abstract of the United States*, 1981:245.)

even this measure is not without misleading features (see Figure 13-2).

Perhaps, however, it would be more accurate or more useful to recognize that the executive branch, aside from the president, actually consists of *many* bureaucracies, each with different tasks to perform. The enforcement of laws prohibiting the trafficking in illegal drugs is the province of the Drug Enforcement Administration. The regulation of the airwaves is handled by the Federal Communications Commission. The Bureau of the Census counts people every decade and tabulates other items like governments and industrial firms in intervening years. The formal structure of the executive branch shows all these units, which are often called "agencies" or "bureaus," reporting in one fashion or another to the president, the chief executive. However, as we shall see, there is considerable variation in the degree to which federal bureaus are actually directed by the president.

The president presides over a mind-boggling array of agencies that carry out an even larger number of public programs. Figure 13-3 gives some idea of the complexity that faces one who is seeking to become familiar with the federal bureaucracy, but even this picture is oversimplified. For instance, each Cabinet-level federal department—there are currently thirteen of these—is itself composed of multiple bureaus pursuing multiple goals. The Department of Agriculture, for instance, has more than a score of major subunits involved in tasks such as education, regulation, subsidization, rural development, and foreign aid (see Figure 13-4).

What sorts of units compose the bureaucracy, and who inhabits them? These are the questions to which we now turn.

The Shape of the Federal Bureaucracy

Federal agencies do not just happen: they are the conscious creations of the nation's elected officials, the president, and Congress (Rourke, 1978). Each is established to carry out some purpose that has been authorized by law. All the actions they undertake and all the dollars they spend are supposed to be directed at these authorized goals. This does not mean that the federal bureaus exercise no judg-ment on their own, as will be discussed later. But it does mean that bureaucrats do not do just anything they want to do.

Several types of public agencies compose the nation's executive branch (see Table 13-3, page 438). A brief comment about each is in order.

The Executive Office of the President This important unit was discussed in Chapter 10, on the presidency. Its general purpose is to assist the chief executive in the performance of presidential duties. Many of its most significant subunits, other than the Office of Management and Budget, are composed primarily of presidential appointees, not career bureaucrats.

The Executive Departments While the Executive Office of the President is a creation of the twentieth century, the nation has utilized executive departments ever since President Washington served as the country's first chief executive. Departments are established (or abolished) by law, and the actual number of them has varied widely during American history. There is no Constitutional or other directive on this matter. When certain policy problems ascend or descend in importance, or at least when president and Congress perceive that this is the case, they promote new departments or demote old ones. In 1970, the Post Office was removed from the president's Cabinet and lost its departmental status, since the nation's political leaders decided that the task of delivering the mail—important though that may be—was not significant enough to be placed on a par with defense or commerce or the federal treasury. On the other hand, during President Carter's term in office, two new departments were created, Energy and Education. As one can see from Table 13-3, departments may vary significantly in size and spending. Some that are relatively tiny are nonetheless important because of their mission. The State Department, for instance, is smaller than most but handles American diplomacy all over the globe. And some larger ones are less single-purpose units than combinations of numerous diverse and divergent activities. The Department of Health and Human Services is perhaps the best example. Its tasks include providing assistance to poor families, regulating drugs,

The government of the United States

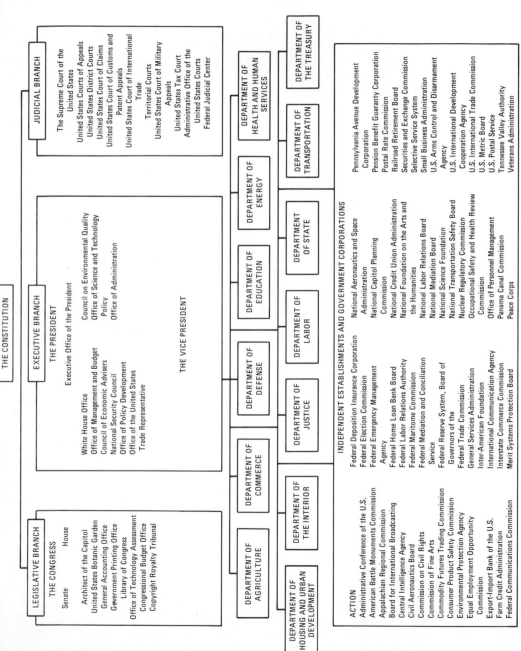

This chart seeks to show only the more important agencies of the government. See text for other agencies.

FIGURE 13-3

Organizational chart of the United States government. Note that only the more important agencies are shown. (*Source: The United States Government Manual 1982/83, 1982.*)

Department of Agriculture

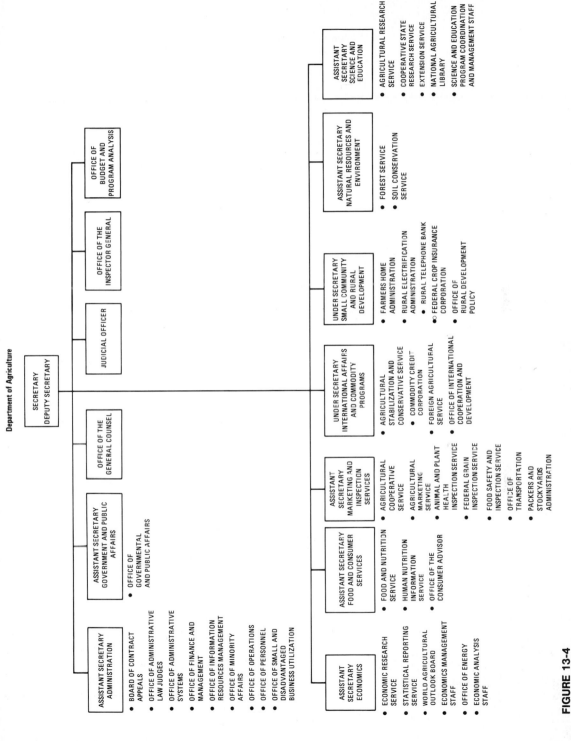

FIGURE 13-4
Organizational chart of the U.S. Department of Agriculture. (*Source: The United States Government Manual 1982/83,* 1982.)

TABLE 13-3
SIZE OF SOME FEDERAL AGENCIES AND BUREAUS

Agency	Civilian employment, 1981	1982 budget outlay, $ millions
White House Office	435	18.9
Department of Defense	974,281	185,790.9
Environmental Protection Agency	14,511	5,434.3
Department of Agriculture	121,585	29,442.4
Federal Trade Commission	1,852	68.0
Postal Service	659,889	*
Veterans Administration	232,802	24,134.1

*The Postal Service is a government corporation, and part of its funding is "off-budget." This unit also raises a substantial portion of its own revenue.
Source: Budget of the United States Government, Fiscal Year 1983, 1982; Statistical Abstract, 1981:268–269.

funding medical care for the elderly, distributing social security, and alleviating illnesses like Legionnaires' disease, herpes, and hepatitis.

When a federal unit is made an executive department, it acquires Cabinet-level status. Its head, such as the secretary of labor, is a member of the president's Cabinet and may, but does not necessarily, have a direct line of communication to the chief executive. All department heads are chosen by the president, although their appointments must also be confirmed by the Senate. They serve in office only as long as the president decides to keep them; they have no job protection. Presidents may ignore some of their department heads and may defer to the wishes of others in the bureaucracy. The Federal Bureau of Investigation (FBI) is an agency within the Department of Justice; but when J. Edgar Hoover, who used to head the FBI, wanted the ear of the president, he often got it much more quickly than did the attorney general, who was his nominal superior. Formal structure is by no means the only determinant of bureaucratic power in any political system. Although federal departments have no additional powers or duties resulting from their being of departmental rank, the status of the Cabinet, with its potential for more direct contact with the key policymakers, has been enough to encourage many interests to lobby for the promotion of their favorite federal agencies to the level of "department." Organized education interests pushed successfully in this fashion for the

Office of Education's elevation—from a subunit within the now-defunct Department of Health, Education and Welfare to a department in its own right.

As mentioned earlier, departments themselves may be composed of many agencies handling tasks related to the overall mission of the department. The Soil Conservation Service (in the Department of Agriculture), the Small Business Administration (in the Department of Commerce), and the Federal Highway Administration (in the Department of Transportation) are examples. Except for the fact that the top bureaucrats in such units report to a Cabinet-level official rather than directly to the president, these agencies are much like many other federal bureaus located outside the departments altogether.

Other Federal Agencies Headed by Single Executives Much important national policy is implemented through other federal agencies. The National Aeronautics and Space Administration (NASA) provides a good illustration. NASA carries out the space exploration activities of the United States and reports directly to the president. Some agencies in this category, such as the Veterans Administration, actually dwarf many of the executive departments. Normally, the chief administrators of these bureaus are presidential choices, and, like the department heads, they serve only at the pleasure of the chief executive.

Independent Regulatory Commissions One set of federal agencies differs in several ways from those so far discussed. These are the independent regulatory commissions. When government regulates, it uses its coercive authority through the application of general rules to limit the discretion of persons, including legal entities such as corporations, in what would otherwise be private economic activity (O'Toole and Montjoy, 1984). Nearly 100 years ago federal policymakers established the first regulatory commission in the national government, the Interstate Commerce Commission, to control the prices charged by companies for transporting people and goods across state lines.

Several times since then, laws have been passed that authorized the federal government to regulate some portion of the private economy in the public interest. The stock market, the airwaves, the airlines, advertising, the nuclear power industry—all these segments of the marketplace are partially controlled by independent commissions. Although not all regulatory activity in Washington is conducted in such units (for instance, the Environmental Protection Agency helps to control pollution but is organized as a single-headed agency), much of it is.

One of the most important independent bodies that affects the entire economy, not just a single industrial group, is the Federal Reserve Board (Beck, 1982). It supervises and regulates banks in the United States, and it also performs the very significant task of determining the nation's money supply—that is, it sets monetary policy. This function can have a major effect on the rate of inflation in the country. The American arrangement is unusual; most other nations place these decisions under more direct political control. An independent Federal Reserve Board (the "Fed") is one reason why neither the Congress nor the president is always able to carry out a unified, consistent idea for influencing the economy.

A good example of a single economic sector that has been heavily affected by the more typical regulatory commissions is the television industry. In the United States, most television programs are produced in private hands (such as the networks), broadcast by privately owned stations, and supported by business through commercial advertis-

ing. Yet the Federal Communications Commission (FCC) determines who gets to run stations, which have to be licensed before operating. The FCC also allocates frequencies on the broadcast spectrum; regulates obscenity, slander, and political views expressed over the airwaves; and influences the spread of technological innovations such as cable television. Furthermore, another unit, the Federal Trade Commission, sets rules to restrict false and deceptive advertising on commercials. There are still significant decisions outside government hands (for instance, most choices about program content and scheduling), but independent regulatory commissions do have a large effect.

What makes regulatory commissions different, besides the fact that they all help to direct parts of the private sector's activity? These organizations are structured so as to insulate them from the usual channels of political influence—the president and Congress. Agencies like the Securities and Exchange Commission or the Federal Trade Commission are headed by a multimember, odd-numbered (for example, three- or five-member) board, not a single top administrator. Typically, the terms of the board members, or commissioners, are longer than that of the president and staggered so that they cannot all be appointed at the same time. Thus, a single president has not often had a chance to alter the entire composition of a commission during his term of office. Also, regulatory commissioners serve for fixed terms (for example, six years), not at the pleasure of the president. Chief executives who appoint commissioners, but are displeased with the decisions they make as they carry out federal regulatory policy, have no direct recourse. Presidents can, of course, use their influence with the media and public opinion. Also, they can make their own preferences known to a commission. But aside from these indirect means of persuasion they can only wait for another opportunity to fill an opening on the commission. Furthermore, commissioners are usually required to be chosen so that members of a single political party can command only a slight majority of the positions on the regulatory body. The result of all these stipulations should be clear. Independent regulatory commissions are designed so that elected leaders, in the short run at least, will not be able to direct their activity. Their multiple membership and the requirement that one political party cannot control all the top slots increase the chance that more than one viewpoint will be brought to bear on the most important regulatory policy matters which come before the commissions. The commissioners' fixed and staggered terms of office reinforce their insulation from the nation's elected leaders.

In short, the commissions have been designed to separate their activities from politics, or at least from politics as conventionally conceived, and to buffer regulatory decisions against drastic shifts in policy following elections. (The fact that their top membership changes slowly creates this tendency toward conservatism.) The structure of regulatory commissions illustrates well a partial contradiction in the thought of the progressive reformers. Some of them sought to remove administration from politics, while others attempted to give the chief executive more control. Commissions are an example of implementation of the former idea at the expense of the latter. Some observers and some regulated businesses approve of such an arrangement, since they feel that regulatory decisions can so significantly affect a segment of the nation's industry that they should be reached in an independent, insulated, fairly impartial tribunal that is unlikely to reverse itself very often. But it should be noted that the structural features of regulatory commissions do not really remove these bodies from politics at all, if by "politics" we mean the search for public support and influence (Welborn, 1977; Gormley, 1979; Quirk, 1981).

Later in this chapter we shall suggest some reasons why virtually all federal agencies engage in politics and seek to generate support for themselves. Independent regulatory commissions are no different. To survive, they need to be able to demonstrate that they serve a constituency or are backed by higher political officials. Because of their insulation from much of the government, however, they must often look for support from those who are most intensely interested in their decisions. Since the constituency of many regulatory commissions is the regulated industry itself, this type of federal agency runs the danger of becoming especially—some would say excessively—dependent upon keeping in the good graces of the regulated

businesses. Critics of some federal regulatory commissions charge that the units have become "captured" by the industries they are supposed to regulate. Such indictments are difficult to demonstrate conclusively. There are counterexamples, such as the proconsumer Federal Trade Commission during the late 1970s (Clarkson and Muris, 1981). And in any event one does not need to impute stupidity or malevolence to commission members to understand why they may often defer to the wishes of their constituency. The most important point to remember, nevertheless, is that independence does not remove commissions from politics altogether; it only changes the type of political environment in which the agency is located.

Government Corporations Some activities that the federal government performs are very much like activities in which private businesses engage. The production of goods and the provision of many sorts of services are "normal" business enterprises, but occasionally the nation's public agencies are charged with similar responsibilities. For example, the Constitution itself gives Congress the authority to establish post offices, although the existence of the private United Parcel Service provides evidence that handling the mail is a task technically similar to running a business. The United States government has not nationalized many businesses to run them in the public interest, but this country has created a number of government corporations to handle certain important public jobs. The Tennessee Valley Authority, for example, generates electric power, builds recreational facilities, and otherwise helps to develop the economy of a multistate region in the southeast. The Postal Service is also a government corporation; it was created in 1970 to take the place of the Post Office. The Federal Deposit Insurance Corporation handles a responsibility much like those taken on by private insurance companies. It was created after the collapse of the banking system during the great depression and insures the bank deposits of virtually all Americans.

The government corporation is a type of agency that looks and operates much like any other sort of corporation. It is chartered by Congress, given a mandate and a set of powers, and freed from many of the restrictions placed upon regular government agencies. These units may be able to circumvent the usual regulations regarding the hiring of personnel, the assigning of tasks to them, and the determination of salary levels. Furthermore, government corporations may be allowed to use revenue they might generate, rather than returning such funds to the treasury. In this fashion, these units may find that their degree of dependence upon the regular appropriations process—and thus political leaders—may be reduced. (Many of these agencies do receive federal funds to supplement the revenue that they generate on their own.) Government corporations are not totally independent of the president and Congress. Nevertheless, this type of agency does have substantially freer rein than the others. These units can often be more innovative and meet pressing deadlines with greater ease than those that labor under the usual amount of red tape (Tierny, 1981). This freedom may bring a price, however. If government corporations are less restricted, they are also less directly accountable then regular agencies (Smith, 1975; Walsh, 1978). Nevertheless, when crisis conditions confront the nation and quick solutions are needed, the government corporation is frequently chosen as the vehicle to be used for finding and implementing the nation's response. During the years of the depression, for example, the federal government contained approximately 100 such units, whereas only a fraction of that number are active today.

The Nation's Bureaucrats

If the preceding section demonstrated anything, it showed that there really is no such thing as a typical federal agency. These units vary greatly in structure, power, size, and function. Similarly, there is no such thing as a typical federal bureaucrat. The nation's millions of public servants are a diverse—perhaps surprisingly diverse—collection.

One important point to know about federal bureaucrats is that, despite popular impressions to the contrary, most of them do not lurk in hallways or loaf in offices in Washington. In fact, most of them are located nowhere near the nation's capital at all. The nation's employees work mostly "in the field," as the bureaucratic jargon puts it—away from the agency's headquarters. Approximately 87 percent of federal civil servants live in the cities and towns across the United States—or, in the case of some units like the Department of State, around the world. They carry the mission of their bureau to the people: guarding the nation's borders to help prevent the smuggling of contraband, assisting farmers who seek low-interest loans, dealing with state and local officials to help construct a mass transportation network, dredging a harbor in one of the nation's port cities. In a geographical sense, at least, the bureaucracy is indeed a part of the government that is "close to the people." The regulatory commissions are the one principal exception. Some of these have only a small proportion of their staff located around the country.

Washington is the nerve center for much of the nation's bureaucracy. Most, though not all, federal agencies have their central office and their top officials in or near the District of Columbia, and it is these headquarters offices that occupy block after block of office space of official Washington. Many of these buildings are several times the size of the White House and Capitol located nearby. In the thousands of offices of these hundreds of buildings, and in the smaller units all across the country, American bureaucrats make so many decisions that affect millions.

Who are these bureaucrats? What are they like? To a considerable extent, they look very much like the rest of us. Some are heroic, some lazy and venal; but most occupy that vast middle ground—they often work long hours, take pride in their tasks, feel frustrated with bureaucracy and red tape, hope to make a real contributon to their nation, frequently feel that they are underappreciated, enjoy the protection that the civil service system gives them, but may believe that some of their colleagues have become too secure in their own niches (Office of Personnel Management, 1979). The bureaucracy contains experts in nearly every imaginable field—diplomats, physicians, agronomists, economists, social workers, mathematicians, law enforcement officers, computer experts, and on and on (see Box 13-3). Perhaps the only profession unrepresented in the bureaucracy is the one often euphemistically referred to as the "world's oldest."

Demographic Representativeness One fashion in which the federal work force is somewhat unrep-

---

BOX 13-3

SOME BUREAUCRATIC CELEBRITIES

By the very nature of their calling—working quietly in huge public organizations—the nation's bureaucrats seldom acquire celebrity status. In fact, as one analyst put it, bureaucrats should have a "passion for anonymity." Yet sometimes, because of their work or even accidental circumstances that may be unrelated to the job they perform, American civil servants have become widely known to the general public or have acquired celebrity status within a group of their peers. Here are a few examples:

Peter Buxtun was hired as a venereal disease investigator by the U.S. Public Health Service. In the course of his work he learned of the Tuskegee syphilis study, an experiment that involved keeping medical treatment for this serious disease away from certain black males. Buxtun persistently raised questions of ethics and legality with superiors, and he finally told the story to a news reporter and testified before a Senate committee. Buxtun is generally credited with bringing the scandalous experiment to a halt.

Dr. Marshall W. Niremberg had spent his scientific career as a federal employee in the National Institutes of Health (NIH). In 1968, when he was serving as chief of the Laboratory of Biochemical Genetics of NIH's Heart Institute, he was awarded a Nobel prize in physiology/medicine for his pioneer research into the question of how genes determine the functions of cells. Niremberg was the first federal civil servant to receive the Nobel prize while under the employ of the government, but several others have followed since then.

Neil Armstrong, the first human to set foot on the moon, did so in his capacity as a GS-16 permanent merit system employee of the National Aeronautics and Space Administration.

A. Ernest Fitzgerald was deputy for management systems in the office of the assistant secretary for financial management of the Air Force. In 1968 he disclosed to a congressional committee that the Air Force's C-5A aircraft then under construction had a cost overrun of $2 billion. He had earlier reported this disturbing news to his superiors, but they sought to conceal it. Because he went public, Fitzgerald was removed from his position and even was immortalized as a target of President Nixon, as revealed in the White House tapes released during the Watergate crisis. Fitzgerald appealed the actions taken against him and ultimately was reinstated in his position and given back pay.

Thomas Ahern was a twenty-year veteran of the State Department bureaucracy; **Colonel Leland James Holland** was a specialist in military intelligence; and **Kathryn L. Koob** was a cultural officer in the International Communications Agency. These three plus forty-nine other Americans were held hostage for 444 days by Iranian captors in the American embassy in Teheran. Their ordeal became one of the major national events of 1980, and their release on the day Ronald Reagan was inaugurated (January 20, 1981) was said by Jimmy Carter to be the happiest moment of his presidency.

---

resentative is in its degree of professionalism and education. Especially at the middle and upper levels, bureaucrats have impressive credentials. And the nation's agencies also expend considerable resources on training their employees even further—in seminars, workshops, universities, and elsewhere. But in most other respects—family background, regional origin, age, and so forth—federal employees look much like employees in the private sector. The bureaucracy is somewhat more white and much more male, especially in its upper reaches, than the American population at large.

But under recent administrations, especially during the Carter years, the government made a more concerted effort to recruit qualified women and minorities for posts with its agencies. As one looks at the *highest* ranks in the nation's permanent bureaucracy (that is, the civil servants hired through the merit system and provided with some job protection), one finds, not surprisingly, that these people appear as an elite group—they are less representative of the general population than is the bureaucracy as a whole. These people, who wield particularly strong influence in determining how national policy is administered, tend to be very ambitious, highly educated, and mostly from somewhat higher-status backgrounds than the average citizen. (Of course, who would not want very well-trained bureaucrats in the positions of most significance? Would one choose someone unschooled in military strategy for a high-level Army appointment? Or an amateur to direct the nation's Center for Disease Control?) Yet even here, some evidence indicates that the elite civil service corps in the United States is probably more representative, socioeconomically, of the public than are many of the top groups of civil servants in other nations—or the legislators in Congress (Meier, 1975; Krislov and Rosenbloom, 1981).

Responsiveness to the Public When one tries to understand what federal bureaucrats are like, however, it may be less important to consider whether they *look* like the American population and more important to examine whether they are in touch with the *views* of the people. Why? If it is true, as we shall see shortly, that the nation's bureaucrats can never be completely controlled in their activities and will always have to have some independence in making important public decisions, then their actions will be guided partially by their beliefs and opinions about what should be done. If the federal bureaucracy were totally divorced from the citizenry, and if it were to think along completely different channels, the danger would increase that this portion of the government

might be unresponsive to the people's wishes. Of course, this is not to say that the bureaucrats should simply obey opinion polls. The whole point of having permanent experts to help make important decisions is so that they can use their detailed knowledge, which most people simply do not have, to solve problems and reach sound conclusions. In fact, one characteristic of the nation's large group of permanent civil servants—and this could be considered either a virtue or a vice, depending upon one's perspective—is that it exerts a stabilizing influence on the actions of the government. Politicians may come and go, public opinion may fluctuate, but the bureaucracy quietly continues.

Nonetheless, the representativeness of bureaucrats' attitudes can be a significant question, for the reasons noted. Evidence on this question is not completely clear, but it does appear that American bureaucrats have political views that are quite close to those of the people. A few years ago, when a sample of public employees at all levels of government were asked their views on a variety of questions, most of their responses were quite similar to the responses of a sample of the population at large (see Table 13-4). In another study, senior civil service officers were quizzed on their own ideological leanings. Their responses, too, were quite close to those of the citizenry (see Table 13-5). Other data support such conclusions, and in some cases suggest that the bureaucracy may be more in harmony with the general public than are the elected leaders themselves (Meier, 1975; 1979; Romzek and Hen-

TABLE 13-4
PUBLIC EMPLOYEES' POSITIONS ON ISSUES

Issue	Public employees responding favorably, %	Members of population responding favorably, %
Vote for Nixon in 1972	61.0	64.6
Republican party identification	32.3	34.6
Withdrawal from Vietnam	47.6	43.7
Trade with communists	83.3	64.1
Increase in taxes on high incomes	60.0	52.8
Legalization of marijuana	31.9	23.7
Protection of the rights of the accused	50.7	43.1
Government help for minorities	51.4	44.1

Source: Meier, 1975:541.

TABLE 13-5
IDEOLOGY OF FEDERAL HIGHER CIVIL SERVICE EMPLOYEES
COMPARED WITH GENERAL POPULATION*
(Figures in Percent)

	Very liberal	Liberal	Middle	Conservative	Very conservative
Higher civil service†	30	27	14	22	10
Population	23	29	17	15	9

*Responses indicate respondents' characterizations of themselves. Survey was conducted in 1974.
†These employees represented the "supergrades," or top few levels, in the federal service.
Source: Meier, 1979:173.

dricks, 1982). The irony here is interesting. We began the chapter by noting that the bureaucracy is perhaps the most common scapegoat for popular frustration with federal activity, and yet here we note that the same institution may have more in common with the people than the people's elected leaders do.

Bureaucrats as Advocates There may be many reasons why the attitudes of the bureaucracy as a whole are fairly close to those of the public. But one more piece of information about the bureaucracy's representativeness may contribute to an explanation. Even if the nation's civil servants, when viewed as a group, have opinions similar to those of the populace, that does not mean that the bureaucrats in each individual agency do. This matter can be put simply. Individually unrepresentative units when lumped together may make the whole group appear representative. In fact, to some extent, this seems to be the case. Bureaucrats in the Department of Interior tend to think that conservation programs are more important than the rest of us do. Public servants in some of the nation's social service bureaus are more likely to believe that *they* handle the top-priority items. And Defense Department personnel rank defense close to the top of *their* list. That is, this country's bureaucrats tend to believe in what they are doing (Meier and Nigro, 1976). Many people are attracted to work in a field they consider to be important or, once there, begin to believe in its significance—that is, bureaucrats tend to be advocates of their own programs. This pattern is reinforced by two facts of life in the federal bureaucracy: (1) training and ca-

reer patterns and (2) the political environment surrounding most agencies.

Training and Career Patterns Typically, federal bureaucrats in the United States join an agency and spend their careers inside it. Assignments and promotions tend to take place within the bureau. As one bureaucrat put it:

> The ordinary civil servant comes into government being hired by a particular person in a bureau and right away he's got a sponsor. Then he'll probably have a training program and a set of promotion possibilities laid out in the bureau and pretty soon he's walking down the hall almost as if he had a badge out in front of him saying, "I'm a Bureau X man," or "I'm a Bureau Y man" (Heclo, 1977:116).

The usual result is that upper-level management consists primarily of people who were trained as technical experts in the fields they now supervise. The U.S. Forest Service provides an illustration. This is the government agency that manages the national forests and warns the public (e.g., through Smokey the Bear) about the danger of forest fires. The Forest Service promotes primarily from within, and most of its new recruits are recent graduates of the schools of forestry throughout the country. The agency works with the schools to ensure that their curricula reflect the skills and, to some extent, the values of the Forest Service itself (Kaufman, 1960). As a consequence, from top to bottom the agency has a coherent sense of mission and view of the world. Thus the training and career patterns in the American bureaucracy elevate good technical specialists to public managers and reinforce the tendency for bureaucrats to view their own unit as most important (Kanter, 1977). In some other nations, for example Great Britain, upper-level management positions are more likely to be filled by "generalists," that is, people who are well-educated in a classical sense but not necessarily skilled in the technical specialty of the agency. British higher civil servants can be moved from unit to unit as the need arises. Therefore, they frequently lack training in the bureau's expertise but are also less likely to develop a narrow viewpoint than their American counterparts are.

To reduce the tendency toward extreme specialization among senior American public administrators, President Carter proposed the creation of a Senior Executive Service (SES). This system, enacted into law in 1978, was intended to move the United States slightly in the direction of the British system. A cadre of the government's top few thousand permanent bureaucrats was to become more available for flexible assignments. Outstanding service was to be rewarded with cash bonuses, but demotions would also be possible. As of the early 1980s, however, the SES had little impact on the career patterns in federal agencies. Most agencies continued to promote from within. Furthermore, congressionally imposed pay ceilings and budget cutting in the Reagan White House limited the financial inducements to administrators who wished to depart from this pattern. Whether the SES will eventually alter the character of the upper-level civil service is still an open question.

Political Environment A second factor encouraging bureaucrats to emphasize the importance of their own agency and its programs is the American political system. This subject is discussed below. Suffice it to say here only that agencies are often compelled to defend their turf against challenges from other units, hostile interest groups, or unfriendly political leaders. Outside forces thus impel bureaucrats to be their own best advocates.

To put the matter in perspective, however, it is not at all obvious that most people would really prefer bureaucrats *not* to be strong backers of their own programs. Would one feel comfortable if the public servants charged with responsibility for the federal government's role in, say, drug enforcement did not really think that this task was so impor-

tant? Still, the fact that the federal bureaucracy may appear to the citizenry as a collection of special pleaders may reduce their stature somewhat. It is also true that the nation's top elected officials have often expressed frustration with the bureaucracy's defense of its terrain, even in the face of overt pressure to change, and have made their feelings public. Richard Nixon, for instance, was suspicious of the bureaucracy's resistance to his initiatives, particularly in the field of social service policy (Aberbach and Rockman, 1976). He sought through a series of administrative maneuvers, such as personnel appointments, reorganizations, shifts in the intergovernmental system (see Chapter 14), and careful use of the White House Office, to circumvent the established agencies (Nathan, 1975). But Nixon's general concerns were the same as those of virtually every recent president. Bureaucratic resistance, it should be noted, does not mean that chief executives cannot ever successfully pursue changes unpopular with the bureaucracy; it means rather that success may require some effort. Nixon himself wound up exerting important influence, even on programs in which there was much conflict between the president and the bureaucracy (Randall, 1979; Cole and Caputo, 1979).

We should not make too much of the question of bureaucratic representativeness and advocacy. As one can see, the whole notion of representativeness is complex, as the framers themselves recognized when debating the institutions of Congress and the presidency. A representative bureaucracy is no guarantee of wisdom, and an unrepresentative one is no sure sign that the government is out of control. Nevertheless, the data we have examined provide quite a bit of information on what American public servants are like and how closely they are attuned to popular thought.

The attitudes of the bureaucracy surely affect the way they make decisions on the job; but federal law restricts a civil servant's ability to express certain political attitudes overtly, either at work or after hours. The job protection granted to federal bureaucrats and their relative freedom from political interference in their jobs are provided in exchange for their abstinence from active participation in partisan political campaigns at the national level. These restrictions, placed upon the bureau-

BOX 13-4

INFLUENCES ON AGENCY "PERSONALITY"

Just as with individuals, no two federal agencies are alike. Each has its own distinctive organizational personality. The character of a bureau today may be shaped by a number of factors, including past decisions and events, the nature of the unit's dominant professions and sense of mission, and the political executives appointed to head the unit.

The **Federal Bureau of Investigation (FBI),** for instance, cannot be understood without recognizing the importance of such factors. J. Edgar Hoover, who directed the agency for decades, left his permanent mark on the FBI. He reformed its procedures and organization, established its personnel system, and built respect and support in the organization's political environment. Even the tight supervisory practices, the "clean-cut" image, and the distrust of political dissidence characteristic of the Bureau's operations are extensions of Hoover's personality. The dominant professions of law and accounting are the recruiting pool for agency positions, and these groups reinforce the agency's self-perception as an elite law enforcement outfit. In the past decade, the FBI has suffered from criticism of its belated efforts at controlling white-collar crime and its illegal tactics employed in earlier years to gather intelligence and monitor protesters. Recent political appointees have sought to refurbish the FBI's professionalism and sense of mission.

The **Foreign Service** officer corps of the U.S. State Department constitutes the elite professional group in that agency. These are the nation's diplomats. For years the department recruited liberal arts graduates from the country's most prestigious universities. Selection criteria deemphasized technical specialists and favored the hiring of those who tended to dislike conflict. The promotion system established in the unit further discouraged open, frank communication within the bureaucracy; and political attacks from outside the department (e.g., allegations in the 1950s that the State Department contained many communists) encouraged the organization to be very cautious in its operations. A series of reforms during the past decade has been aimed at stimulating more innovation, expertise, and productive debate within the Foreign Service. Yet the American diplomatic community remains a target of criticism for many.

The **U.S. Department of Agriculture (USDA)** is one of the best examples of a long-standing federal agency operating to benefit a particular clientele group. The department is composed of a number of bureaus, each handling a separate portion of the unit's task, such as inspecting grain or compiling agricultural statistics. Mostly, the bureaucrats performing these duties think of their job primarily as one of helping the agricultural community in this country. The USDA attracts professional staff disproportionately from rural areas, the personnel tend to feel protective and supportive of the farmer, and this pattern is reinforced by the political environment of the department. The Extension Service provides an intricate field network of contact with the agricultural interests on a county-by-county basis throughout the country and via the land-grant college system state by state. Secretaries of agriculture are recruited from the same fold.

The **Environmental Protection Agency (EPA)** was created during a time when the nation perceived itself in the midst of an environmental crisis in 1970. Federal activities on this front were consolidated in a new agency for a coordinated attack on the problem. The agency attracted a highly motivated young group of professional lawyers and environmental specialists who often saw their task as protecting the nation's resources for the long term against "special interests," especially economic ones. The first several EPA directors also had favorable reputations among conservationists. During the Reagan administration, however, the president sought a change in the direction of EPA. Staff and budgets were reduced, and greater consideration was given in some areas to economic development. Temporarily, these changes created turmoil in the agency and angered environmental groups. The agency in 1982 was embroiled in controversy and scandal, and a major shake-up occurred in 1983.

cracy by the Hatch Act of 1939, have been challenged by some employees in recent years but upheld in federal court. In any event, whether or not the bureaucracy could act as a political force, flexing its muscle during election campaigns, may be less significant than the attitudes its members quietly hold as they go about their normal duties day after day (see Box 13-4).

Professional Associations and Unions One other characteristic of today's federal bureaucracy needs to be mentioned. A large number, in fact a majority, of American civil servants now belong to professional associations or public employee unions. These memberships may be productive and useful. For example, the fact that the federal government's scientists join in associations with their colleagues in university and business research units means that they stay apprised of developments in their specialty and are more likely to feel bound by the ethical standards of their profession. Other federal employees, both white- and blue-collar, participate in public employee unions that represent their interests before the government's managers. Federal bureaucratic unionism grew particularly rapidly following the increased status and rights granted to such employee organizations under presidents Kennedy and Nixon. As a result of these developments, communication channels within the bureaucracy have been strengthened and civil servants' grievances may often be resolved easily.

However, the increased levels of professional and union membership evident in recent years also suggest a reason for concern (Rosenbloom, 1971; Martin, 1980). Professionals—doctors, lawyers, social workers, or whoever—are notoriously resistant to direction or commands from superiors. They are trained to obey the norms of their profession and seek approval from their colleagues, not politicians, for the actions they undertake. Active professionals in the bureaucracy may thus sometimes confront a conflict between their desire to be left alone to do their job and perceived interference on the part of their bosses. The result may be bureaucratic resistance, which poses at least a potential threat to the democratic order (McGregor, 1974; Wollan, 1977; Mosher, 1982). A similar case may be made regarding unionization. Bureaucrats who are union members may find themselves torn

between their desire to bargain for special advantage with their employer and their duty to be servants of the public through its agency. This choice faced the nation's air traffic controllers in the summer of 1981. Their union reached an impasse with their agency, the Federal Aviation Administration. The controllers struck and were promptly fired by President Reagan (see Box 13-5). The example illustrates the turbulence generated by the unionization issue.

Thus, federal bureaucrats today may feel split between loyalty to associates and loyalty to political superiors. Such conflicts may reduce the ability of an agency to act as a coordinated whole on many issues. On some significant matters, a bureau is less a unified implementer of policy and more a set of contending coalitions.

Between the Experts and the Politicians: The Political Executives

We have provided considerable descriptive information about how the permanent bureaucracy is arranged and what the nation's bureaucrats are like. Now we turn to the political appointees at the top of the federal establishment, who serve as the link between the president and the civil service.

If presidents had to try to direct the federal bureaucracy and yet had no allies to help them manage things, their job would be next to impossible. Presidents do, however, have a chance to effect some policy because approximately 3,000 of the top federal positions are not protected by the civil service system. These are subject to political appointment. A president, with the assistance of others, gets to select individuals to fill these slots and is not restricted by conventional merit criteria. For most of these appointments, moreover, presidents can remove individuals for their own reasons at any time. (Of course, as we noted earlier, presidential control over regulatory commissions is somewhat more restricted.)

At the peak of most federal agencies sits a rather small group of political executives. For instance, the secretary of an executive department, the undersecretary, most assistant secretaries, and often other positions of a high policy-determining character are included in this collection. Presidents

In 1981, members of the Professional Air Traffic Controllers Association walked out on their jobs despite a provision in their contract forbidding strikes. They were stunned when President Reagan subsequently fired them. *(Adam Scull/Black Star)*

BOX 13-5

BUREAUCRATS ON STRIKE

In 1981 the Professional Air Traffic Controllers Organization (PATCO) began to bargain with the Federal Aviation Administration (FAA) on behalf of its membership. PATCO, headed by Robert Poli, represented the 13,000 FAA public employees who directed the nation's civilian air transportation system. The bureaucrats wanted salary increases and better working conditions; the agency rejected most of the union's demands. In August, after numerous bargaining sessions over a period of months, the PATCO membership overwhelmingly rejected the government's final offer. More than 90 percent of the bureaucrats struck the agency, and the American air transportation system temporarily collapsed.

President Reagan dismissed the striking workers, fined the union, rehired some retired workers, and let the FAA borrow military controllers on an emergency basis. The strike was not broken, and the government was forced to begin the slow process of recruiting thousands of new personnel and training them over a period of years. By the end of 1982 some officials, e.g., the National Transportation Safety Board, continued to voice concern about the level of training being provided to the replacements.

The striking workers had violated the agreement they made upon their employment with the FAA: ''I am not participating in any strike against the government of the United States or any agency thereof, and I will not so participate while an employee of the government of the United States or any agency thereof.''

This was not the first strike by federal employees since their right to union membership had been clarified in 1962, but it was the first that had provoked such a strong response on the part of a president.

usually fill these offices with people they know well or have reason to believe are loyal. President Reagan chose his own personal attorney, William French Smith, as attorney general; and he hired another longtime California associate, William Clark, as secretary of the interior. Once located in the most influential spots in federal agencies, these people may administer their units in conscious coordination with the objectives of the chief executive. Through political executives, a president thus has a fighting chance to translate an electoral mandate into the processes and products of governmental action. Presidents have even been known, occasionally, to appoint as agency heads persons who do not believe in the activities of their units. President Nixon did so when he was trying to dismantle the Office of Economic Opportunity. More recently, President Reagan chose as his first secretary of energy James Edwards, a former governor who had already gone on record as favoring the abolition of the Department of Energy.

Three thousand patronage jobs may sound like a great deal, but it is really only about one-tenth of 1 percent of the entire bureaucracy. Furthermore, chief executives rarely have detailed plans for how to fill all these positions. Only the top few hundred slots usually receive close presidential attention. President Reagan himself deliberated over his choice of Jeane Kirkpatrick as ambassador to the United Nations, but he spent no time at all on his several appointments in the U.S. Patent Office. With the decline of party strength and political patronage, presidents-elect have utilized panels of nonpartisan outside evaluators, plus a rather small staff hired during the transition period between election and inauguration, to sort through the applicants and seek out promising ones. President-elect Reagan's advisers were flooded with thousands of candidates, and the task of appointment was so complex that many of the positions remained unfilled when he took office. Presidents also share some appointment power with Congress, interest groups (organized labor has more than a casual interest in Labor Department selections, as do financiers in the top choices for Treasury), and others. And they make appointments for a variety of reasons aside from political loyalty—appointees' ability to work well with their units, geographical and ethnic representation, and competence in their

assigned tasks. The result is that the nation's political executives themselves are not unanimously in the camp of their superior.

Even when they do feel close ties to the president, political executives are also under some pressure to defend the activities and intentions of their own unit. Otherwise, the permanent bureaucrats may try to resist or sabotage any initiatives. For this and other reasons, presidential appointees usually do not last long in office. Sometimes chief executives try to get rid of certain appointees, as did President Carter with Secretary of Health, Education and Welfare Joseph Califano and President Reagan with National Security Adviser Richard Allen. But more often, political executives resign of their own accord. In recent administrations, the average appointee has remained in office less than two years. The political executives are thus a crucial link between the president and the bureaucracy; but they are not a homogeneous group, and their job is not an easy one (Heclo, 1977; Greenberg, 1980).

WHAT DOES THE BUREAUCRACY DO?

Executing Policy

For each complex job that the government has decided to undertake, there is a bureaucratic unit assigned the responsibility of carrying it out. This activity is the task of *implementation,* discussed further in Chapter 15, on the policymaking process (Montjoy and O'Toole, 1979; Ripley and Franklin, 1982). Every day federal bureaucrats manage the nation's defenses, construct huge public works projects, enforce drug laws, care for vast tracts of federal land, and direct airplane pilots to safe landings. Furthermore, a sizable number of units spend most of their time and resources administering grants-in-aid, transfers of funds to be used by state and local governments for some public purpose such as pollution control. (Until the last couple of years, an increasing proportion of bureaucratic effort had been going in this direction.)

The Veterans Administration (VA), created in 1930, is a prime example of a federal bureaucracy that directly executes important policy. A series of laws enacted during this century have given the VA a remarkably broad and complicated range of policies to administer. The agency's general task is to provide help to former military personnel who have sacrificed for the nation's welfare.

For instance, the VA operates a series of loan programs to assist veterans as they try to buy houses or mobile homes. The bureaucracy guarantees or insures the loans so that veterans can borrow the money more cheaply than other people can. Permanently disabled veterans are sometimes eligible for grants from the VA to purchase houses equipped to meet their special needs. To execute this policy, the VA bureaucrats spend a great deal of effort appraising properties, making sure that new homes are being constructed properly, and checking the decisions of lending institutions like savings and loan companies. The agency also carries out policies designed to improve educational opportunities for veterans. It distributes funds to them for the completion of high school, college, and vocational, professional, or other types of education. To reduce the chance that this money might be wasted, VA employees work with states to ensure that the various schools measure up to a certain level of quality. Furthermore, the VA is charged with distributing various compensation and pension benefits, for example, life insurance, vocational rehabilitation for disabled veterans, and disability compensation and pensions—these include such items as specially designed clothing and equipment for those who need them. The VA even operates the National Cemetery System, through which some veterans may be buried free of charge in national cemeteries.

Perhaps the greatest portion of the agency's work load, however, consists of medical care for veterans. Almost everyone has seen or heard of huge VA hospitals, VA clinics providing assistance to those with psychiatric or drug problems, and VA nursing homes in which thousands of old and disabled veterans reside. In these facilities, tens of thousands of federal bureaucrats quietly and often conscientiously tend to the less than glamorous details of the nation's policy commitment to those who have served in the armed forces (*Federal Regulatory Directory,* 1981–82:517).

Sometimes, doing away with the bureaucracy, or at least with most of it, may sound like an attractive idea in the abstract. But when one looks at all the specific programs being handled by specific agencies like the VA, one often sees a different story. While many people would like to see these units operate more efficiently, few would suggest a total dismantling of the VA, or the agencies handling social security, contributing to health research, administering the nation's energy policy, and so forth. It is true that there is lively debate on just *which* activities the federal government should handle through its many agencies. For instance, how much of what sort of aid should the government provide to its neediest citizens? (See Chapter 16, on social welfare policy.) Does Washington need to continue such an expensive arsenal of agricultural subsidy programs? But most American political discussion revolves around the exact size and direction of federal involvement, not the real necessity of bureaucracy. After the accident at Three Mile Island, one heard many complaints about the performance of the Nuclear Regulatory Commission. But hardly anyone, least of all the private utility companies, suggested that the government did not need a bureaucracy to regulate nuclear power plants. The plain fact is that all civilized nations employ large bureaucracies to cope with the heavy responsibilities of modern government.

An illustration that suggests the permanence of the federal bureaucracy in our modern civilization is the performance of President Reagan. He was elected after an antibureaucratic campaign, and his administration seemed more distrustful than that of any recent president toward the activities of federal agencies. However, for all the controversy generated by his proposals to cut back the federal establishment, Reagan's suggestions really amounted to only a small trimming of the government's total size. In fiscal year 1981, for instance, the national government's work force of 2.8 million was reduced by only 15,000 employees. Some agencies were more severely affected, of course. Yet a decrease of more than 10 percent in Washington's social service agencies was more than countered by a growth of 24,000 in the Defense Department (*Public Administration Times,* 1982). No responsible president could seriously suggest that doing away with the federal bureaucracy could be accomplished without major catastrophe.

Tasks as complex as the ones performed by the bureaucracy require the coordinated efforts of many public servants working to fulfill their assigned responsibilities. Success is no foregone conclusion. Administrators in bureaus like the VA spend their time hiring appropriate people, organizing them to work together, supervising their actions, and trying to develop rules to guide their behavior. These efforts often require considerable attention. This is particularly true because public administrators in the United States must try to maximize the advantages of bureaucratic behavior—efficiency, predictability, and resistance to favoritism—while minimizing the problems and frustrations that can also be hallmarks of agency activity. Public offices that are efficient may also be prone to treating citizens as numbers rather than individuals. Bureaus that operate through predictable routines may be difficult to redirect toward new national goals. And units that take care to resist favoritism may find themselves bogged down in cumbersome procedural safeguards. What seems like red tape to one frustrated American may seem like essential protection against bureaucratic abuse to another (Kaufman, 1977). There are certainly numerous examples of bureaucratic "pathologies"—wasteful, ineffective, or even malicious bureaucrats, agencies, and programs. But federal agencies have performed many complicated tasks impressively well (Sapolsky, 1972; Mazmanian and Nienaber, 1979; Bragaw, 1980). The same government that sometimes takes a week to deliver a piece of mail across town also has placed men on the moon, had its bureaucrats receive major prizes for scientific achievements, and enforced dramatic civil rights reforms. (See Box 13-6.)

Exercising Discretion and Making Policy

Yet important and difficult as these tasks may be, it would be a mistake to assume that the nation's bureaucracies are *merely* involved in the systematic execution of policy made by elected political leaders. Our administrative agencies do not simply carry out decisions—they *make* decisions, e.g., ordering the recall of certain consumer products or determining which cities will receive federal aid. Why is the bureaucracy a force in its own right instead of an arm of government that simply executes policy established by president and Congress? In other words, why does the bureaucracy not operate

as the neutral machine envisioned by earlier reformers such as those who helped establish the civil service system? A few moments' reflection can suggest numerous reasons why American administrative agencies, though they can be subject to important controls by political leaders, will never be merely instruments that make no significant decisions on their own.

For one thing, bureaucrats are compelled to make major decisions because elected political officials have neither the time nor the ability to do so. Each day thousands of such decisions are made, and there is no way all these issues could be debated and decided by Congress or the president (Weaver, 1977; Regens and Rycroft, 1981). One example should illustrate this point clearly. Federal law protects Americans by requiring that dangerous foodstuffs be kept from supermarket shelves. But which foods are really dangerous? How can we tell? How much evidence is needed? Members of Congress may be bright and energetic, but they are hardly in a position to make a reasoned judgment about the thousands of products that could be marketed. Nor can they rely on the manufacturers of such products for an accurate analysis. Instead, bureaucrats at the Food and Drug Administration combine their skills with administrative guidelines to draw conclusions and make decisions. If elected officials occupied their time with these matters, they would have no chance to think about many issues of even more importance. Besides, a certain amount of technical knowledge is required for decisions like these, and bureaucrats are in position to use their expertise when the evidence is complex. The truth is that experts are influential.

Many of these major bureaucratic decisions of policymaking significance appear as official regulations. The *Federal Register,* a government publication printed five times a week, is composed almost entirely of proposed and newly established regulations produced by various agencies (see Box 13-7). Every year thousands of such pages appear, and these do not even include a multitude of additional guidelines of less importance produced for the internal use of agencies as they do their work. All bureaus have such guidelines. The military, for instance, is engulfed in standard operating procedures. More and more rules can always be written and, once produced, can constrain bureaucratic in-

BOX 13-6

BUREAUCRATIC SUCCESSES AND FAILURES

Successes

Among the most obvious bureaucratic success stories are these:

The Fleet Ballistic Missile (FBM) program This activity developed, procured, and deployed the Polaris missile on nuclear-powered submarines for the United States. The program was administered by the Special Projects Office of the Department of the Navy, and its success played a major role in the nation's strategic defense system from the 1960s into the 1980s. The program produced a technically superior product several years ahead of schedule and within budget.

The implementation of the Voting Rights Act of 1965 The execution of this policy stimulated major changes in electoral politics. As of 1965 racial prejudice kept blacks from voting in many locations in the south. In Alabama, for instance, several counties with tens of thousands of black citizens had no blacks who had been able to register to vote. The passage of this act enabled federal marshals from the Justice Department to enforce the right to vote in locations throughout the south. Black voting increased dramatically within a few years.

The Apollo space program President John Kennedy announced in 1961 the goal of placing an American on the moon by 1970. The Apollo program in the National Aeronautics and Space Administration was established, the technological and administrative developments necessary to achieve this result were accomplished (albeit at a cost of tens of billions of dollars), and the goal was achieved in 1969.

Failures

These are some of the programs that the bureaucracy seldom mentions:

The Mohole project In the 1960s the National Science Foundation sought to manage the drilling of a hole in the ground, a hole deeper than any ever before. The goal was the development of scientific knowledge about the earth's crust and mantle. ''The results were cost-overruns, slippages in schedule, and fights among scientists, engineers, and contractors for control and direction of the program'' (Lambright, 1976:144–145). The project was abandoned after millions were expended.

The Tuskegee syphilis experiment The project began as an effort of the Public Health Service (PHS) in the 1930s to treat this venereal disease in six rural black populations in the south. Funding problems, bureaucratic decisions, and the influence of the medical community contributed to a change in program from one of treatment to one in which medical assistance for syphilis was systematically denied to a group of 400 men—even after penicillin was shown to be an effective cure. The subjects of the experiment were monitored for forty years, until publicity forced an end in 1972. Many untreated victims had died from the disease or suffered permanent damage; but the program was fostered and protected by many PHS bureaucrats, including a number of physicians, to the end (Jones, 1981).

The swine flu fiasco Federal officials were concerned as the winter of 1976–1977 approached that there might be an outbreak of a swine flu epidemic like the one that killed millions in 1918–1919. A $135 million crash program of mass inoculations was established. The expected flu never developed. The results of the program were large expenditures; confusing implementation; 120 deaths and numerous other injuries from side effects, especially Guillain-Barre syndrome; and liability claims against the government of approximately $1.2 billion. Although the bureaucratic agency involved, the Department of Health, Education and Welfare (HEW), was not entirely to blame for the program—it was endorsed by President Ford and passed by Congress—HEW did have responsibility for testing the vaccine, supervising inoculations, and developing warnings. The agency had also pushed hard for rapid mass inoculations, rather than a more limited program aimed at particularly vulnerable populations (*CQ Almanac,* 1978:72).

BOX 13-7

THE FEDERAL REGISTER

A excerpt from the government's daily record of regulations, announcements, and proposed decisions.

§ 203.24 Distribution and dispensing of patient package inserts.

*   *   *   *   *

  (a) * * *
  (2) For a drug product in a unit-of-use container, the manufacturer and distributor shall provide a patient package insert (i) in or with each package of the drug product that the manufacturer or distributor intends to be dispensed to a patient or; (ii) in accordance with paragraph (a)(1) of this section.

*   *   *   *   *

PART 431—CERTIFICATION OF ANTIBIOTIC DRUGS

  2. In Part 431, § 431.16 is revised by redesignating existing paragraph (b) as new paragraph (c) and by adding a new paragraph (b) to read as follows:

§ 431.16 Changes in facilities or controls; changes in mailing or promotional pieces.

*   *   *   *   *

  (b) Advance approval is not required to implement labeling changes under a patient package insert requirement under Part 203 of this chapter. However, the applicant shall submit specimens of the labeling when first used.

*   *   *   *   *

  These amendments involve reconsideration of issues which were the subject of recent rulemaking, and implement conforming changes consistent with previously expressed agency intentions. Moreover, they do not impose additional duties or burdens on any person but instead relieve requirements and facilitate compliance with regulations requiring patient package inserts. Accordingly, the Food and Drug Administration finds that notice and public procedure and delayed effective date are unnecessary and not in the public interest, and that the amendments may become effective upon the date of publication in the **Federal Register.** However, interested persons may, on or before March 3, 1981, submit to the Dockets Management Branch (HFA-305), Food and Drug Administration, Rm. 4-62, 5600 Fishers Lane, Rockville, MD 20857, written comments on this final rule. Four copies of any comments are to be submitted, except that individuals may submit one copy. Comments are to be identified with the docket number found in brackets in the heading of this document. Received comments may be seen in the office above between 9 a.m. and 4 p.m., Monday through Friday.
  Any person who will be adversely affected by the amendment of § 431.16 may file objections to it, request a hearing, and show reasonable grounds

for the hearing. Any person who decides to seek a hearing must file (1) on or before February 2, 1981, a written notice of participation and request for hearing, and (2) on or before March 3, 1981, the data, information, and analyses on which the person relies to justify a hearing, as specified in 21 CFR 430.20. A request for a hearing may not rest upon mere allegations or denials, but must set forth specific facts showing that there is a genuine and substantial issue of fact that requires a hearing. If it conclusively appears from the face of the data, information, and factual analyses in the request for a hearing that no genuine and substantial issue of fact precludes the action taken by this order, or if a request for hearing is not made in the required format or with the required analyses, the Commissioner of Food and Drugs will enter summary judgment against the person(s) who request(s) the hearing, making findings and conclusions and denying a hearing.
  The procedures and requirements governing the amendment of § 431.16, a notice participation and request for hearing, a submission of data, information, and analyses to justify a hearing, other comments, and grant or denial of a hearing are contained in 21 CFR 430.20.
  All submissions under this amendment must be filed in four copies, identified with the docket number appearing in the heading of this order and filed with the Dockets Management Branch (formerly the Hearing Clerk's office) (HFA-305), Food and Drug Administration, Rm. 4-62, 5600 Fishers Lane, Rockville, MD 20857.

  Effective date. This regulation shall be effective January 2, 1981.
(Secs. 201, 502, 503, 505, 507, 701, 52 Stat. 1041 as amended, 1050–1053 as amended, 1055–1056 as amended, 55 Stat. 851, 59 Stat. 463 as amended (21 U.S.C. 321, 352, 353, 355, 357, 371); (sec. 351, 58 Stat. 702 as amended (42 U.S.C. 262)))
  Dated: December 22, 1980.
Mark Novitch,
Acting Commissioner of Food and Drugs.
[FR Doc. 80–40583 Filed 12–31–80; 8:45 am]
BILLING CODE 4110–03–M

---

21 CFR Part 522

Implantation or Injectable Dosage Form New Animal Drugs Not Subject to Certification; Oxytetracycline Hydrochloride Injection

AGENCY: Food and Drug Administration.
ACTION: Final rule.

SUMMARY: The Food and Drug Administration (FDA) amends the

animal drug regulations to reflect approval of a supplemental new animal drug application (NADA) filed by Diamond Shamrock Corp. providing for safe and effective use of a 100-milligram-per-milliliter (mg/ml) oxytetracycline (as oxytetracycline hydrochloride or OTC HCl) injection for treating certain infections of swine.

EFFECTIVE DATE: January 2, 1981.

FOR FURTHER INFORMATION CONTACT:
Richard A. Carnevale, Bureau of Veterinary Medicine (HFV-125), Food and Drug Administration, 5600 Fishers Lane, Rockville, MD 20857, 301–443–1788.

SUPPLEMENTARY INFORMATION: Diamond Shamrock Corp., 1100 Superior Ave., Cleveland, OH 44114, filed a supplemental NADA (97–452) providing for use of a 100 mg/ml OTC HCl injection in swine for treating bacterial enteritis, pneumonia, and leptospirosis. The firm currently holds approval for use of this product in sows as an aid in controlling infectious enteritis in suckling pigs and in cattle for treating pneumonia and shipping fever complex.
  Several OTC HCl injectable preparations manufactured by Pfizer, Inc., were subjects of a review by a National Academy of Sciences/National Research Council (NAS/NRC), Drug Efficacy Study Group. The evaluation was published in the **Federal Register** of July 21, 1970 (35 FR 11646). In that document, the NAS/NRC and FDA concluded that the preparations were probably effective for treating infections in cattle, sheep, swine, horses, cats, dogs, chickens, and turkeys caused by pathogens sensitive to OTC HCl. Holders of NADA's were provided 6 months to submit revised labeling that reflected the NAS/NRC evaluation or adequate documentation in support of the labeling used.
  Pfizer responded to the evaluation notice by submitting a supplemental NADA (8–769) that revised the labeling for safe and effective use of injections containing 50 mg/ml of OTC HCl for treating cattle, swine, and poultry. The supplemental application was approved by a regulation published in the **Federal Register** of September 18, 1974 (39 FR 33509). The regulation reflecting this approval amended 21 CFR 135b.65 (recodified as 21 CFR 135.1662a) by adding new paragraph (d). This regulation contains provisions for intramuscular use of the drug in swine at 3 to 5 milligrams per pound (mg/lb) of body weight per day for treating bacterial enteritis (scours, colibacillosis) caused by *Escherichia coli*, pneumonia caused by *Pasteurella multocida*, and

dependence in the future. But rules and regulations can also slow down the operations of government, increase the cost of public business, and tie the bureaucracy in knots of red tape. Past a certain point, further restrictions are not an unmixed blessing.

Second, sometimes when a particularly controversial issue arises, the president and Congress may feel compelled to establish an administrative agency and ask it to search for a solution. Such a move is particularly likely when political leaders know that the people desire government action but are unsure or divided on what to do. The Department of Education is an example of a federal unit created to help solve the educational problems of the nation, despite the fact that many experts disagree with each other about what the problems and solutions might be. One can hardly expect the bureaucracies to follow orders from elected officials if there are no clear instructions. Many agencies, therefore, spend a considerable amount of their time and resources developing policy precisely because they are expected to do so. Sometimes, the policy ideas developed in the bureaucracy are then utilized by other political actors as they push for clearer legislation. For instance, in 1977 President Carter attempted to enact important welfare reform laws. These were actually drafted by bureaucrats in two executive departments (Meier, 1979). In fact, many of the new policy ideas considered by the government and much of the actual legislative language debated by lawmakers have their origins in the various agencies. The policymaking activity of federal units is so important that the bureaucracy is sometimes referred to as the "fourth branch of government" (Ripley and Franklin, 1975). The role of the bureaucracy in the policymaking process is discussed further in Chapter 15.

Third, one cannot realistically expect any federal agency to carry out policy in a purely mechanical fashion. Bureaucracies are composed of people, not cogs. As any large federal organization goes about its business, the people who do its work will be imperfectly and unevenly attuned to their tasks. Different officials will interpret similar laws or regulations differently (Kaufman and Couzens, 1973; Simon, 1976). The structure of an agency—the arrangement of its offices and positions—will affect how it does its job, as will the personalities of its employees. As we have seen, training and career patterns can produce bureaus with a highly developed sense of mission. In such units, thoughtful and conscientious public servants will sometimes have reservations about the orders given to them by their political superiors—especially when the orders conflict with previous policy. They may try to change a superior's mind or perhaps silently alter or disobey the directive. In 1981, bureaucrats in the Interior Department openly revolted against shifts in policy initiated by their top administrator, Secretary James Watt. Some of them believed he was attempting to weaken their initiatives. Even high-level appointees of the chief executive can often safely resist the intentions of the president. As one ex-bureaucrat put it:

> Half of a President's suggestions, which theoretically carry the weight of orders, can be safely forgotten by a Cabinet member. And if the President asks about a suggestion a second time, he can be told that it is being investigated. If he asks a third time, a wise Cabinet officer will give him at least part of what he suggests. But only occasionally, except about the most important matters, do Presidents ever get around to asking three times (Daniels 1974:247).

Within the permanent bureaucracy public officials may be able to exercise even more independence, which is aided by their relative obscurity and their civil service status. While this point may rightly worry citizens who hope that their government is answerable to them, such possibilities are inevitable whenever many people are organized to perform complex tasks.

Thus, if it is true, as we saw earlier, that presidents or Congresses can make their mark on federal agencies, it is also true that not all presidential or congressional initiatives are converted into action. There are even some occasions when agencies exercise an independent influence on public actions when they would rather just obey their superiors. Large bureaucracies often respond sluggishly to innovation because they consist of so many people tied together through complex patterns and routines; that is, federal agencies are imperfectly adaptable. This was a lesson President Kennedy learned in Ocober 1962, when he was faced with the decision about how to respond to the presence of Soviet nuclear missiles in Cuba. Kennedy established a policy: the missiles should be eliminated by a neat surgical air strike that would harm no Cuban civilians but would eliminate the threat. Yet the policy was never executed. The bureaucracy—the Air Force in this case—told the president it did not have a standard procedure available that would produce this result. Ultimately, Kennedy had to settle for a Naval blockade, a complicated routine the Navy already had in its repertoire (Allison, 1971).

Finally, bureaucratic independence is sometimes a valuable commodity. Many of the attorneys in the Justice Department's Civil Rights Division resisted President Nixon's attempt, shortly after his inauguration, to slow the speed of school desegregation. They believed that their duty was to uphold their interpretation of the law, even over the orders of their superiors. A number of them were ultimately fired or reprimanded for their intransigence. More than a decade later 200 attorneys in the same department protested President Reagan's brief attempt to give tax breaks to segregationist religious schools. Popular culture, as indicated by television series such as *Quincy,* highlights bureaucrats (albeit a local bureaucrat in this case) who ignore or evade the wishes of their bosses, usually for some presumed higher good. The point is not that bureaucrats should have free rein, for much evil could come of that alternative as well. But citizens do derive benefits from the fact that our nation's bureaucracy is staffed with many who are not total captives of the organizations that they serve. The alternative would be a bureaucracy made up of people like Adolf Eichmann, the Nazi bureaucrat who suspended his own judgment and patiently helped to administer the holocaust of European Jews, and many non-German Christians as well, a generation ago.

Of course, there are many ways in which the bureaucracy is limited and directed as it pursues its goals, and these limitations allow for the influence of majoritarian and pluralistic pressures. Federal agencies receive attention and guidance from outside their own halls, and a number of these sources of influence will be discussed later.

Engaging in Bureaucratic Politics

Perhaps the agency behavior that bothers many citizens the most is *bureaucratic politics:* the process by which administrative units actively seek support for what they are doing, try to acquire more business, and vigorously protect their own turf. The government's agencies are often their own best advocates. They express their advocacy in many ways.

They jealously defend their own budgets and programs from other agencies and from political cutbacks by politicians. The bureaucratic competition is often especially intense among units that perform similar functions (Wilson, 1978). For instance, the Bureau of Reclamation (in the Interior Department), the Corps of Engineers (of the Army), and the Soil Conservation Service (in Agriculture) battle each other for water projects and geographical jurisdiction. The competition may help keep bureaucrats on their toes, but it also generates seemingly wasted motion. When asked to justify their existence, agencies often take great care to show Congress and others just how essential they are to the nation's welfare. For years, the Federal Bureau of Investigation (FBI) was sure to report at budget-making time that the value of stolen cars it had recovered or reported as recovered far exceeded the agency's request for funding—as if that fact alone somehow documented the Bureau's efficiency and indispensability.

When new policy initiatives are likely to generate significant political support or substantial new resources, various bureaus may well squabble with each other for a piece of the action (Seidman, 1980). In the 1970s, for example, when Congress began to consider a major new program for the development of solar energy, each of several existing agencies and bureaus argued that this responsibility properly belonged under its respective roof. These included the National Science Foundation, Department of Housing and Urban Development, Federal Power Commission, National Aeronautics and Space Administration, Energy Research and Development Administration, and Atomic Energy Commission. (Ultimately, in 1977 the matter was settled by the creation of a new Department of Energy.) Many of the claimants were sincere. But, as one wise old hand from the bureaucracy, Rufus Miles, puts it, on issues like this one, "where you stand depends upon where you sit" (Miles, 1978).

As they defend their jurisdiction or launch efforts to expand it, agencies actively seek the support of the public, especially interest groups. Much of the activity of the Department of Agriculture is conducted in tandem with the private American Farm Bureau Federation and many similar organizations. The Federal Highway Administration has more than casual ties with road-building associations and groups of state highway officials. Federal agencies cultivate their clientele and use the support they can generate to further the causes they have been charged with defending or new causes they hope to acquire. When federal agencies, their interest groups, and the appropriate congressional committee become united on a course of action, they can be very influential. This sort of triad of political actors appears on many different policy issues and is usually dubbed a "triple alliance" or "iron triangle." These recurring patterns of influence create a sort of pluralism in American government, since there are different centers of influence on different issues. Yet critics of the arrangement point out that the competition among interests on any single issue is quite limited—the agency, the legislative committee, and the organized clientele tend to see eye to eye quite often. This issue is treated in more detail in Chapter 15, on the American policymaking process.

One of the best illustrations of this relationship is the activities of the Army Corps of Engineers. This agency carefully cultivates its relations with oversight committees in Congress and with various lobbyists, especially the National Rivers and Harbors Congress. In fact, members of the United States Congress itself are enrolled as members of the interest group. As a result of this relationship, the Corps of Engineers has made plenty of friends in the legislature and the lobbying groups (Maass, 1951; but see Mazmanian and Nienaber, 1979).

Some agencies are much more successful than others in developing support for themselves and their actions. Many factors can account for these differences. Among the most important are the size and strength of a bureau's constituency and the nature of the unit's jurisdiction (Rourke, 1976).

Certain agencies like the Veterans Administration have a huge, diversified, well-organized constituency in the millions. Organizations of officers retired from the armed forces, the American Legion, the Veterans of Foreign Wars, the Disabled American Veterans, and others populate nearly every hamlet in the country. They have lodges, magazines, rallies, and other mechanisms of mobilization on behalf of the VA and its programs. Other agencies are not so lucky. The Agency for International Development (AID), the United States' foreign aid agency, may participate in worthy activities; but its beneficiaries live thousands of miles away, and no elected American political leader needs to worry about their votes. AID usually has a very tough time surviving the annual budget process.

Exciting, attractive, or important mandates help agencies acquire support as well. This fact explains why federal bureaus are on the lookout for ways to add, selectively, to their jurisdiction. The solar energy example, above, illustrates this point. For years, the National Institutes of Health (NIH), a federal agency that does research on various diseases, was able to portray its job as extremely important, at least to many influential members of Congress—especially elderly legislators who understandably had developed an interest in cures for various illnesses. The NIH was often given a larger budget than it had requested!

This sort of "bureaucratic imperialism" (Holden, 1966) is sometimes frustrating to people who wish federal agencies would work on behalf of the overall public interest instead of their own special interests. However, we have seen that from the outset the American government was designed so that no one, least of all bureaucrats, could impose one overall view of the public interest on the process of public decision making. The American political system, even including the bureaucracy, is pluralistic; and bureaucrats know that if *they* do not become active in defense of their agency in the process of national politics, few others will do so (Bergerson, 1980; and Lewis, 1980). As one political scientist put the issue:

It is clear that the American system of politics does not generate enough power at any focal point of leadership to provide the conditions for an even par-

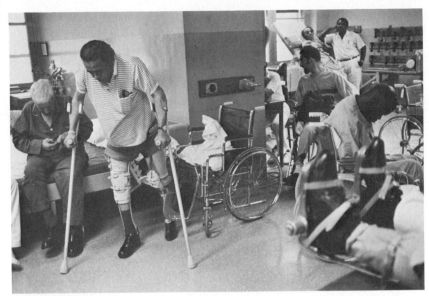

Because tens of thousands of Veterans Administration workers provide services for veterans, (such as physical therapy for the disabled), and because millions of well-organized veterans support the VA, Congress rarely threatens its budget.   *(Sepp Seitz/Woodfin Camp)*

tially successful divorce of politics from administration. Subordinates cannot depend upon the formal chain of command to deliver enough political power to permit them to do their jobs. Accordingly they must supplement the resources available through the hierarchy with those they can muster on their own, or accept the consequences in frustration—a course itself not without danger (Long, 1978:9).

This conclusion means, however, that the more active the bureaucracy becomes in the political process, the more modern American democracy may be threatened by the permanent unelected government.

BUREAUCRACY AND DEMOCRACY: THE RECURRING PROBLEM OF CONTROL

It is perhaps ironic that over the past century the United States has moved from a period during which the federal bureaucracy seemed too closely tied to political leaders to one in which so many citizens worry about a lack of accountability on the part of the government's administrative agencies. If the bureaucracy cannot realistically be eliminated and if the nation cannot remove discretion from these organizations, must one conclude that the nation's public agencies are uncontrolled? Not necessarily. We said earlier that the question of control over the bureaucracy was one left unresolved by the founders; it remains so today. Yet the founders did institute formal mechanisms of outside influence. The nature of the American system of separation of powers makes it difficult to conclude who does or should run the bureaucracy. But that is a far cry from concluding that it is completely independent.

The primary oversight role has been shared by the president and Congress throughout the nation's history. Today, chief executives are able to have an impact on bureaucratic activity by appointing key executives and by managing the budget process in the executive branch. They can also affect the shape of the bureaucratic structure by enacting modest reorganizations on their own and proposing major ones to the legislature. In addition to formal powers like these, certain presidents have found ways to gain footholds in the bureaucracy. For instance, Franklin Roosevelt used to give overlapping jurisdictions to some of his subunits and encourage them to compete with each other for presidential favor. He also established redundant communications networks to decrease the chance of being misled by any office. By working hard at the task, then, chief executives can make a real difference in what the bureaucracy does, even if they cannot actually control it. All these channels provide possibilities for the exercise of diffuse majoritarian influence.

Yet even if this century has seen a shift in oversight toward presidential control, the Congress plays a potent role and has not been reluctant to exercise it in recent years. The Senate confirms top-level administrative appointments of the president. The legislature exercises its power of the purse as it makes its budgetary decisions that matter so much to the various bureaus. Congressional committees, in a sometimes bewilderingly pluralistic process, check and recommend the legislation that is the original source of bureaucratic activity. And the lawmakers are also charged with examining and investigating the conduct of federal agencies. Many a television evening news broadcast features a spirited conflict between a congressional committee and an administrative unit over something the latter has done or would like to do. Bureaucrats frequently chafe under this scrutiny, often believing that the legislature should give the agency experts more leeway. The views of one civil servant on this subject are fairly typical:

> The real hard fact about life on the hill [i.e., in Congress] is that very few times does Congress, acting together and well-informed, pass the laws. . . . You [an administrative official] go up there and explain to the subject-matter committee how these things work and why. . . . We [administrators] draw up good legislation in the national interest with all the parts fitting into the whole properly, and what happens to it when it hits the hill is like a Christian among the heathen (Burnham, 1976:133).

Still, the discomfort of this bureaucrat illustrates that the control has some effect (Ogul, 1976; Dodd and Schott, 1979).

Legislators also use a congressional agency, the General Accounting Office, to check on the propriety and effectiveness of various programs being executed by the bureaucracy (Mosher, 1979; Pois, 1979). Furthermore, members of Congress and their staffs maintain frequent contact with bureaus as the lawmakers do casework for their constituents—investigating a complaint about administrative abuse, expediting a loan application, and so on. For their part, agencies are keenly aware of the importance of the legislature for their own continued existence, and they often treat the concerns of these elected officials very seriously—even when they would prefer the lawmakers to leave them alone (Arnold, 1979).

Yet president and Congress are not the only sources of control over the bureaucracy. The federal courts can also be important. If a citizen feels wronged by some agency's action, an appeal can force the decision to be reviewed. Under certain circumstances judges can change administrative decisions that do not conform to the evidence, and they also may force the reconsideration of an issue if bureaucrats have violated established procedures (Fesler, 1980). These possibilities often encourage the nation's bureaucrats, especially those making regulatory decisions, to behave correctly and decide judiciously. While safeguards like these may slow down the operations of agencies, many observers argue that the trade-off is worth it.

Other less formal checks on bureaucratic action also exist and can be very significant. Competition from other agencies may provide a type of pluralistic control, as we have seen. Also, interest groups and their lobbyists may pay close attention even to the tiny details of executive branch behavior because they know that many seemingly mundane decisions there have important consequences for them. In a number of instances, these interests even have formal channels of participation in agency action. Committees of farmers, for example, have formal input into normal Agriculture Department decisions about price supports and acreage allotments for various crops. Many critics suggest that such detailed supervision and participation by interest groups is not always a good idea, because in such a system the most highly organized and intensely interested are better represented than the rest of the public (Ripley and Franklin, 1975; Aberbach and Rockman, 1978). But no one can argue that interest groups do not provide yet another source of direction and advice for the nation's bureaucracy. Thus the process of bureaucratic politics described in the last section, an activity that sometimes seems like such a challenge to democratic government, may also serve to limit bureaucratic excess. Even the press, which relies heavily on federal agencies for many of its sources and much of its information, not infrequently "blows the whistle" on various recalcitrant units. And the bureaucracy even has its own internal checks to encourage responsible behavior: its rules, its representativeness, its patterns of training and professionalization.

The founders left the question of bureaucratic control unresolved, and they reinforced the ambiguity through the enactment of separation of powers. Therefore, it is not surprising that today the pattern of controls is so complicated and controversial. Thus this most contemporary political issue finds its roots in Constitutional matters—some decided long ago, some debated to the present. Yet it is not really accurate to paint the American bureaucracy as unresponsive or uncontrollable. If federal agencies exercise some independence, they are also constrained by a variety of forces. Some though not all of these encourage republican government.

SUMMARY AND CONCLUSION

The bureaucracy, a frequent target of attack by politicians in recent years, is a necessary and important part of modern American government, but it was a subject not much discussed by the founders. They left the question unresolved as to what might be the proper place of administrative agencies in the new government. The Constitutional principle of separation of powers has meant that the bureaucracy in practice has not been a protected institution with a single superior and a clear, widely accepted role to play in American politics.

During the first part of the nation's existence, the bureaucracy was not the focus of much controversy. But during the last century, major social and political changes stimulated a growth in the federal establishment and a set of important reforms. Agencies proliferated, they came to represent merit and neutrality more than political loyalty, and—

especially since the New Deal—the presidency has increasingly become considered the leader in the task of bureaucratic management.

Today's bureaucracy is huge, staggering in its expenditures, and widely dispersed geographically. The bureaucracy actually consists of *many* bureaus organized in a variety of ways, some (like several executive departments) tied closely to the chief executive, some (like government corporations) designed for speed and flexibility, and some (like independent commissions) structured to maximize deliberation and neutrality.

At the peak of the bureaucracy are the political executives, charged with the difficult task of translating political mandates into agency routine. Below this level are the permanent bureaucrats themselves, who are highly educated and possess many skills. The federal establishment as a whole displays attitudes surprisingly representative of the population; but to some extent this fact masks the degree to which agencies, by virtue of recruitment, training, and socialization, develop staffs who are advocates for their own programs.

The actions of the bureaucracy are diverse and complicated. Virtually all agencies, however, implement policy as well as develop it, and engage in a struggle for resources and territory. This politics of bureaucracy derives not so much from the peculiarities of agency leaders as from the decentralized, competitive nature of the American political system.

That same system provides multiple checks on bureaucratic excess and thus allows for influence by one or another portion of the public. Yet fundamentally, the combination of Constitutional design (i.e., separation of powers) and the demands of modern society guarantee that the problem of bureaucratic power will remain unsolved. For if public servants in the United States are provided with so *many* directives on how to act, their discretion may actually be greater. If the law and regulations seem to say one thing, the president another, Congress a third, and one's professional training still a different thing altogether, even the most loyal bureaucrats may sometimes be left to their own devices. And today's bureaucracy may play one of its institutional bosses off against another, to gain a bit more leeway. This, then, is the paradox: bureaucracy is necessary if American government is to handle the most important contemporary public problems with dispatch; but the existence of bureaucratic government itself raises potential challenges to the democratic order. Can the American bureaucratic state be a democratic one? This question, we have seen, was not addressed clearly at the outset of this republic, and partially as a result of this fact it has become a central question in American political life.

Many of the specific issues raised about the bureaucracy in recent years thus really touch upon this fundamental constitutional one; therefore, they are likely to remain important over the next several years as well. Efforts to trim the bureaucracy or to impose additional controls on it from other governmental institutions like Congress; controversy over the power of unionized civil servants; frustrations with the insulation afforded experts by the merit system; legal and political battles over the recruitment of minorities and women into the public service; attempts to restrict the role of consultants to federal agencies; reformers' efforts to disrupt the iron triangle; tension between bureaucratic incentives for self-advocacy and efforts to create an elite senior civil service—all these concrete subjects are likely to recur as topics of concern in the future. All are specific manifestations of a general question that will occupy Americans well into the nation's third century: How can we reap the advantages of bureaucracy while guarding against the possibility that the bureaucratic model of governance will come to dominate public life?

It is no wonder, then, that the problem of the bureaucracy is such an oft-repeated refrain by presidential candidates and others. The issue, then, is not really a question of how to eliminate or "straighten out" the bureaucracy. It is the more serious and difficult question of how to combine popular opinion and expert knowledge to produce the public interest. It is unlikely that this issue—which is really another way of asking the question "Who should rule?"—will fade in the years ahead.

SOURCES

Aberbach, Joel D., and Bert A. Rockman: "Clashing Beliefs within the Executive Branch: The Nixon Administration," *American Political Science Review*, vol. 70, no. 2, 1976, pp. 456–468.

——— and ———: "Bureaucrats and Clientele Groups: A View from Capitol Hill," *American Journal of Political Science*, vol. 22, no. 4, 1978, pp. 818–832.

Allison, Graham: *Essence of Decision*, Little, Brown, Boston, 1971.

Arnold, Peri E.: "The First Hoover Commission and the Managerial Presidency," *Journal of Politics*, vol. 38, no. 1, 1976, pp. 46–70.

Arnold, R. Douglas: *Congress and the Bureaucracy*, Yale University Press, New Haven, Connecticut, 1979.

Aronson, Sidney H.: *Status and Kinship in the Higher Civil Service*, Harvard University Press, Cambridge, Mass., 1964.

Beck, Nathaniel: "Presidential Influence on the Federal Reserve in the 1970s," *American Journal of Political Science*, vol. 26, no. 3, 1982, pp. 415–445.

Bergerson, Frederick A.: *The Army Gets an Air Force: Tactics of Insurgent Bureaucratic Politics*, Johns Hopkins Press, Baltimore, 1980.

Bragaw, Louis K.: *Managing a Federal Agency*, Johns Hopkins Press, Baltimore, 1980.

Brewer, Garry D.: *Politicians, Bureaucrats, and the Consultant*, Basic Books, New York, 1973.

Budget of the United States Government, Fiscal Year 1983, Office of Management and Budget, Washington, D.C., 1982.

Burnham, James: "Some Administrators Unkindly View Congress," in Robert T. Golembiewski et al. (eds.), *Public Administration*, 3d ed., Rand McNally, Chicago, 1976.

Clarkson, Kenneth W., and Timothy J. Muris (eds.): *The Federal Trade Commission since 1970: Economic Regulation and Bureaucratic Behavior*, Cambridge University Press, New York, 1981.

Cole, Richard L., and David A. Caputo: "Presidential Control of the Senior Civil Service: Assessing the Strategies of the Nixon Years," *American Political Science Review*, vol. 73, no. 2, 1979, pp. 399–413.

CQ Almanac, Congressional Quarterly, Inc., Washington, D.C., 1978.

Daniels, Jonathan, as quoted in Morton H. Halperin: *Bureaucratic Politics and Foreign Policy*, Brookings Institution, Washington, D.C., 1974.

Dodd, Lawrence C., and Richard L. Schott: *Congress and the Administrative State*, Wiley, New York, 1979.

Eaton, Dorman B.: *Civil Service in Great Britain*, Harper, New York, 1880.

Federal Personnel Guide, 1979, Federal Personnel Publications, Washington, D.C., 1979.

Federal Regulatory Directory, 1981–82, Congressional Quarterly Press, Washington, D.C., 1981.

Fesler, James W.: *Public Administration: Theory and Practice,* Prentice-Hall, Englewood Cliffs, N.J., 1980.

Gormley, William T.: "A Test of the Revolving Door Hypothesis at the FCC," *American Journal of Political Science,* vol. 23, no. 4, 1979, pp. 665–683.

Greenberg, George D.: "Constraints on Management and Secretarial Behavior at HEW," *Polity,* vol. 13, no. 1, 1980, pp. 57–79.

Guttman, Daniel, and Barry Wilner: *The Shadow Government,* Pantheon, New York, 1976.

Heclo, Hugh: *A Government of Strangers,* Brookings Institution, Washington, D.C., 1977.

Historical Statistics of the United States: Colonial Times to 1970, U.S. Bureau of the Census, Washington, D.C., 1975.

Holden, Matthew, Jr.: " 'Imperialism' in Bureaucracy," *American Political Science Review,* vol. 60, no. 4, 1966, pp. 943–951.

Jacoby, Henry: *The Bureaucratization of the World,* University of California Press, Berkeley, Calif., 1973.

Jones, James H.: *Bad Blood: The Tuskegee Syphilis Experiment,* Basic Books, New York, 1981.

Kanter, Arnold: "The Career Patterns of Air Force Generals," *American Journal of Political Science,* vol. 21, no. 2, 1977, pp. 353–379.

Kaufman, Herbert: *The Forest Ranger,* Johns Hopkins Press, Baltimore, 1960.

———: *Red Tape: Its Origins, Uses, and Abuses,* Brookings Institution, Washington, D.C., 1977.

———, with the collaboration of Michael Couzens: *Administrative Feedback: Monitoring Subordinates' Behavior,* Brookings Institution, Washington, D.C., 1973.

Krislov, Samuel, and David Rosenbloom: *Representative Bureaucracy and the American Political System,* Praeger, New York, 1981.

Lambright, W. Henry: *Governing Science and Technology,* Oxford University Press, New York, 1976.

Lewis, Eugene: *Public Entrepreneurship: Toward a Theory of Bureaucratic Political Power,* Indiana University Press, Bloomington, 1980.

Long, Norton: "Power and Administration," in Francis E. Rourke (ed.), *Bureaucratic Power in National Politics,* 3d ed., Little, Brown, Boston, 1978.

Lowi, Theodore J.: *The End of Liberalism,* 2d ed., Norton, New York, 1979.

Maass, Arthur: *Muddy Waters: The Army Engineers and the Nation's Rivers,* Harvard University Press, Cambridge, Mass., 1951.

Martin, James E.: "Federal Union-Management Relations: A Longitudinal Study," *Public Administration Review,* vol. 40, no. 5, 1980, pp. 434–442.

Mazmanian, Daniel A., and Jeanne Nienaber: *Can Organizations Change?* Brookings Institution, Washington, D.C., 1979.

McGregor, Eugene B., Jr.: "Politics and the Career Mobility of Bureaucrats," *American Political Science Review,* vol. 68, no. 1, 1974, pp. 18–26.

Meier, Kenneth J.: "Representative Bureaucracy: An Empirical Analysis," *American Political Science Review,* vol. 69, no. 2, 1975, pp. 526–542.

———: *Politics and the Bureaucracy,* Duxbury, North Scituate, Mass., 1979.

——— and Lloyd G. Nigro: "Representative Bureaucracy and Policy Preferences: A Study in the Attitudes of Federal Executives," *Public Administration Review,* vol. 36, no. 4, 1976, pp. 458–469.

Miles, Rufus C., Jr.: "The Origin and Meaning of Miles' Law," *Public Administration Review,* vol. 38, no. 5, 1978, pp. 399–403.

Millett, John D.: "The Constitution and Public Administration," in Robert T. Golembiewski, Frank Gibson, and Geoffrey Y. Cornog (eds.), *Public Administration,* 3d ed., Rand McNally, Chicago, 1976.

Montjoy, Robert S., and Laurence J. O'Toole, Jr.: "Toward a Theory of Policy Implementation: An Organizational Perspective," *Public Administration Review,* vol. 39, no. 5, 1979, pp. 465–476.

Mosher, Frederick C.: *The GAO: The Quest for Accountability in American Government,* Westview, Boulder, Colo., 1979.

———: *Democracy and the Public Service,* 2d ed., Oxford University Press, New York, 1982.

Nathan, Richard P.: *The Plot That Failed: Nixon and the Administrative Presidency,* Wiley, New York, 1975.

Nelson, Michael: "A Short, Ironic History of American National Bureaucracy," *Journal of Politics,* vol. 44, no. 3, 1982, pp. 747–778.

Office of Personnel Management: *Federal Employee Attitude Survey Scales,* Washington, D.C., 1979.

Ogul, Morris S.: *Congress Oversees the Bureaucracy,* University of Pittsburgh Press, Pittsburgh, 1976.

O'Toole, Laurence J., Jr., and Robert S. Montjoy: *Regulatory Decision Making: The Virginia State Corporation Commission,* University Press of Virginia, Charlottesville, Va., 1984.

Peters, B. Guy: "The Problem of Bureaucratic Government," *Journal of Politics,* vol. 43, no. 1, 1981, pp. 56–82.

Peters, Charles: "A Kind Word for the Spoils System," in Charles Peters and Michael Nelson (eds.), *The Culture of Bureaucracy,* Holt, New York, 1979.

Pois, Joseph: *Watchdog on the Potomac: A Study of the Comptroller General of the United States,* University Press of America, Washington, D.C., 1979.

Public Administration Times, Jan. 15, 1982.

Quirk, Paul J.: *Industry Influences in Federal Regulatory Agencies,* Princeton University Press, Princeton, N.J., 1981.

Randall, Ronald: "Presidential Power versus Bureaucratic Intransigence: The Influence of the Nixon Administration on Welfare Policy," *American Political Science Review,* vol. 73, no. 3, 1979, pp. 795–810.

Regens, James L., and Robert W. Rycroft: "Administrative Discretion in Energy Policy-Making: The Exceptions and Appeals Program of the Federal Energy Administration," *Journal of Politics,* vol. 43, no. 3, 1981, pp. 875–888.

Ripley, Randall B., and Grace A. Franklin: *Policy-Making in the Federal Executive Branch,* Free Press, New York, 1975.

——— and ———: *Bureaucracy and Policy Implementation,* Dorsey, Homewood, Ill., 1982.

Romzek, Barbara S., and J. Stephen Hendricks: "Organizational Involvement and Representative Bureaucracy: Can We Have It Both Ways?" *American Political Science Review,* vol. 76, no. 1, 1982, pp. 75–82.

Rosenbloom, David H.: *Federal Service and the Constitution,* Cornell University Press, Ithaca, N.Y., 1971.

Rourke, Francis E.: *Bureaucracy, Politics, and Public Policy,* 2d ed., Little, Brown, Boston, 1976.

——— (ed.): *Bureaucratic Power in National Politics,* 3d ed., Little, Brown, Boston, 1978.

Sapolsky, Harvey M.: *The Polaris System Development,* Harvard University Press, Cambridge, Mass., 1972.

Seidman, Harold: *Politics, Position, and Power: The Dynamics of Federal Organization,* 3d ed., Oxford University Press, New York, 1980.

Simon, Herbert A.: *Administrative Behavior,* 3d ed., Free Press, New York, 1976.

Skowronek, Stephen: *Building a New American State: The Expansion of National Administrative Capacities, 1877–1920,* Cambridge University Press, New York, 1982.

Smith, Bruce L. R. (ed.): *The New Political Economy: The Public Use of the Private Sector,* Wiley, New York, 1975.

Statistical Abstract of the United States, 1981, U.S. Bureau of the Census, Washington, D.C., 1981.

Tierny, John T.: *Postal Reorganization: Managing the Public's Business,* Auburn House, Boston, 1981.

The United States Government Manual 1982/83, National Archives and Records Services, Washington, D.C., 1982.

Van Riper, Paul P.: *History of the United States Civil Service,* Row, Peterson, Evanston, Ill., 1958.

Waldo, Dwight: *The Administrative State,* Ronald, New York, 1948.

Walsh, Annmarie Hauck: *The Public's Business: The Politics and Practices of Government Corporations,* M.I.T. Press, Cambridge, Mass., 1978.

Weaver, Suzanne: *Decision to Prosecute: Organization and Public Policy in the Antitrust Division,* M.I.T. Press, Cambridge, Mass., 1977.

Weber, Max: "Essay on Bureaucracy," in H. H. Gerth and C. Wright Mills (eds.), *From Max Weber,* Oxford University Press, New York, 1946.

Welborn, David M.: *Governance of Federal Regulatory Agencies,* University of Tennessee Press, Knoxville, Tenn., 1977.

White, Leonard D.: *The Jacksonians,* Macmillan, New York, 1954.

———: *The Republican Era,* Macmillan, New York, 1958.

Wilson, James Q.: *The Investigators: Managing F.B.I. and Narcotics Agents,* Basic Books, New York, 1978.

Wilson, Woodrow: "The Study of Administration," *Political Science Quarterly,* vol. 2, no. 2, 1887, pp. 197–222.

Wollan, Laurin A., Jr.: "Lawyers in Government—'The Most Serviceable Instruments of Authority,'" *Public Administration Review,* vol. 37, no. 6, 1977, pp. 105–112.

Yates, Douglas: *Bureaucratic Democracy: The Search for Democracy and Efficiency,* Harvard University Press, Cambridge, Mass., 1982.

RECOMMENDED READINGS

Dodd, Lawrence C., and Richard L. Schott: *Congress and the Administrative State,* Wiley, New York, 1979. An analysis of how the national legislature attempts to cope with the influential bureaucracy.

Heclo, Hugh: *A Government of Strangers,* Brookings Institution, Washington, D.C., 1977. A study of the role of political appointees in the executive establishment and the tensions in their relationship with the permanent bureaucracy.

Kaufman, Herbert: *Red Tape: Its Origins, Uses, and Abuses,* Brookings Institution, Washington, D.C., 1977. A brief overview of the causes of seemingly excessive administrative requirements and reasons for their intractability.

Meier, Kenneth J.: *Politics and the Bureaucracy,* Duxbury, North Scituate, Mass., 1979. An examination of the role of the bureaucracy in the policy process.

Rourke, Francis E.: *Bureaucracy, Politics, and Public Policy,* 2d ed., Little, Brown, Boston, 1976. A survey of the sources and uses of agency power in the American system.

Seidman, Harold: *Politics, Position, and Power: The Dynamics of Federal Organization,* 3d ed., Oxford University Press, New York, 1980. A perceptive account of the political implications of federal bureaucratic structure.

Waldo, Dwight: *The Administrative State,* Ronald, New York, 1948. A study of the political theory of the American public administration reform movement.

Yates, Douglas: *Bureaucratic Democracy: The Search for Democracy and Efficiency,* Harvard University Press, Cambridge, Mass., 1982. A recent analysis of the democracy-bureaucracy conflict.

Chapter 14

Intergovernmental Relations

January 14, 1981, was a mild, sunny day in southern California. Ronald Reagan prepared to board the U.S. Air Force jet that would take him to Washington for his inauguration as president. As he was about to leave Los Angeles for the nation's capital, reporters and friends gathered around to listen to the former governor's last words before departing. Reagan spoke forcefully, as he discussed what he believed to be the primary responsibility of his administration. He talked not of defense or inflation or crime or civil rights. He addressed, instead, the issue of *intergovernmental relations.*

It was time, he told his fellow Californians, for the national government to return power to the state and local levels. Americans, he said, had been trying to do too much from Washington. The results were, on the one hand, that the national government had failed to achieve its goals and, on the other, that the state and local governments of the nation had become weaker. They had not been allowed to exercise their creative energies because of hundreds of narrow restrictions placed upon them by federal authorities. Reagan promised that his term in office would see a rebirth of authentic decentralization, a restoration of balance among American governments, and a new chance for citizens to influence the public decision makers closest to them.

Reagan's words were debatable. Some observers might have disagreed with his contention that the involvement of the federal government in state and local affairs was too great or largely ineffective. (In fact, as of mid-1982 a higher proportion of the American public believed they get more for their taxes from the federal government than from state or local levels, and a majority supported federal aid to state and local governments in all major categories of current expenditures [Advisory Commission on Intergovernmental Relations (ACIR), 1982:3, 8; see also Reeves and Glendening, 1976]. Others might have argued that state and local power had not been lost. Some, with a knowledge of American politics from years past, might have questioned whether there *ever* had been a time when policies now involving action at the national level were handled entirely by the states themselves—thus, to suggest "returning" responsibilities might be to distort history for political purposes.

But if Reagan's comments were contentious, they were hardly new. In fact, his concerns echoed those of many others from earlier days. For instance, fully a generation before, a high-level commission had reported to President Eisenhower the following suggestion:

> Leave to private initiative all the functions that citizens can perform privately; use the level of government closest to the community for all public functions it can handle; reserve national action for residual participation where state and local governments are not fully adequate (Commission on Intergovernmental Relations, 1955:6).

However, under Eisenhower and all succeeding presidents until Reagan there was a growth rather than a shrinkage of the national government's role in public decision making.

Yet President Reagan followed up his preinaugural rhetoric with action. More than any chief executive in modern times, he worked to produce a real shift in responsibilities away from Washington. In 1981, his efforts produced changes in the federal government's grant system toward greater state influence. In 1982, he announced a much more ambitious and dramatic program to redistribute power. Reagan's initiatives, quickly dubbed the "new federalism" (just as were the less radical ideas of several of his predecessors), seemed to strike a responsive chord with many people, for the growth of the national government's role had increasingly become a matter of political controversy.

Nevertheless, before long, Reagan's attempts to produce results had themselves generated disagreements. Most of his major proposals had been stalled, not only by Congress and other national policymakers but also through the opposition of governors, mayors, and other apparent beneficiaries of the plan.

It would seem that this prime issue raised during the Reagan presidency—what are, or should be, the relations between the national government and other American governments?—was not so simple. The topic seems to lack the inherent excitement of a debate over nuclear arms or affirmative action. But the fact of the matter is that questions of intergovernmental relations—how our governments deal with each other, which ones have responsibilities and jurisdiction over which sorts of problems, how conflicts among them are resolved —frame and directly affect many of the more specific policy concerns that interest all of us. From the Civil War to civil rights, from public education to pollution control to the development of energy resources, intergovernmental relations have been highly significant.

Furthermore, debates about intergovernmental relations really address some of the most important *constitutional* questions that have endured for centuries, such as the appropriate mix of liberty and equality, the scope of government's role in the society, and the proper arrangement of governmental institutions and distribution of power. How and why this is so, how our governments relate to each other today, and what some of the implications are of this American pattern of intergovernmental relations—these are the topics of this chapter.

Of course, in the early chapters of this book, especially in our discussion of the founding and constitutional development, we touched upon the issue of the relative roles of the national and state governments in the federal system of the United States. It should be noted here that the term "federal" can be used in two senses. One is as a synonym for "national." The other, as in this paragraph, designates the form of government that constitutionally divides responsibilities between independent central and regional units—in this country, the nation and the states (Davis, 1978). In this chapter the meaning should be clear from the context. Certainly, the subject of federalism concerned the founders as they sought to establish the republic. But we have not analyzed intergovernmental relations directly in the last several chapters.

We have discussed American government and politics at length as if the national level were a fully independent entity, and as if it were responsible for most if not all public activity. Nothing could be further from the truth. While a few matters such as national defense and foreign policy are handled almost entirely by the central government, virtually all others require the actions of state and local governments in some fashion.

A moment's reflection will suggest the importance of these other levels of government. State governments are deeply involved in such tasks as handling highway networks, providing social services to citizens, running park systems, encouraging industrial development, and setting the rates we pay for insurance, telephone, and electrical service. Local government officials are perhaps the most familiar of all to us. Police officers walking the beat, school board members deciding which textbooks to authorize for use in social studies classes, zoning officials allowing the creation of a suburban housing development, sanitation workers clearing city streets of refuse, and public health experts checking patients for venereal disease—these people represent some of the varied responsibilities and activities of American local governments.

In Chapter 13, we pointed out that the national government had increased the scope of its actions during the past century, but that the size of the federal bureaucracy had remained relatively constant over the most recent decades. State and local governments have also gotten involved in many new activities during the same period, but unlike the national government they have grown tremendously in size. Figure 14-1 suggests the phenomenal expansion that has occurred. By the measure of either dollars expended or people employed, at least, state and local governments are nowhere near dead or outmoded.

A large portion of the growth in American state and local government has been a direct result of policies at the national level. Many of the programs currently carried out by lower levels of government are substantially financed and directly controlled by the federal government. State universities, for instance, are subject to an impressive list of requirements from a variety of national agencies on matters such as equal employment opportunity and research on humans. State welfare systems are not without some flexibility but operate within a lengthy set of regulations which emanate from Washington. In almost all areas of domestic policy—housing, transportation, education, environment, energy, human services, health, law enforcement—*all* levels of American government now play some part.

The relations between these governments are often so complex, even confusing, that they sometimes almost defy description. The system is now tremendously interdependent. This arrangement often serves the pragmatic and immediate needs of

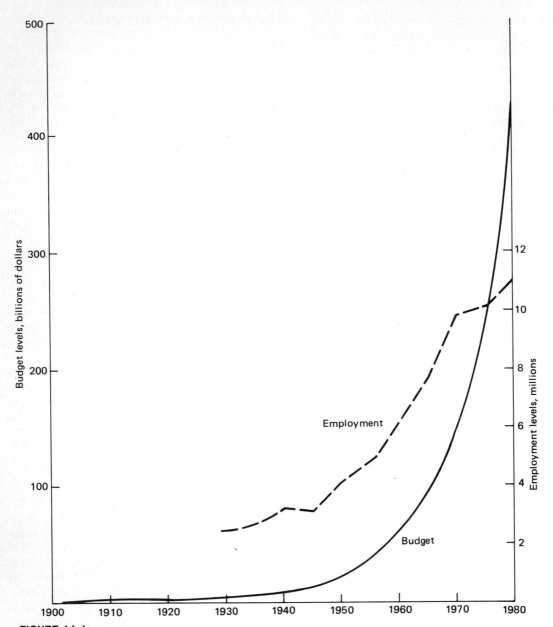

FIGURE 14-1
Levels of employment and of budgets of state and local governments over time.
(*Source:* U.S. Bureau of the Census, 1975; *Statistical Abstract of the United States,* 1981.)

the American people but sometimes seems to make government less accountable overall. Thus, if the American Constitution is to survive and accommodate itself to the demands of the nation's third century, the pattern of governments created by it must be studied for its characteristics and likely consequences.

This subject of intergovernmental relations is as complex as it is immense, and in a book devoted primarily to the American national government we must inevitably limit ourselves somewhat in what we discuss here. For example, while judicial aspects of intergovernmental relations are important, these were covered briefly in Chapter 12. Here we shall concentrate on topics not developed previously. To be sure, certain decisions in the federal courts on topics such as racial discrimination and school desegregation, educational finance, and legislative reapportionment have initiated (or settled) major intergovernmental controversies. Increasingly, federal judges have become active even in the day-to-day administration of some intergovernmental issues, such as school busing and prison reform. Yet other aspects of intergovernmental relations, such as the politics of federal aid, are those that will receive special attention here.

As we focus on intergovernmental relations, it is helpful at the outset to recognize a paradox. In the introductory chapter we mentioned that the Constitution seemed to suggest a fairly clearly delineated division of powers between the national government and the states. Yet in the present chapter we have already observed that *all* levels of government are now involved in most spheres of American policy. How did this apparent shift occur? Is it consistent with the Constitution? Does it, as President Reagan suggested, imply a dangerous redistribution of power in the country and pose a threat to the vitality of state and local government—indeed to the freedom of American citizens?

A genuine understanding of current and future political issues, such as these constitutional questions, depends first upon an adequate grounding in at least two subjects: basic facts of American government structure and some knowledge of the most significant events from the past. We discuss each in turn, before we turn to the current politics of intergovernmental relations and their significance.

A MULTITUDE OF GOVERNMENTS

The States

The Constitution, as the fundamental law of the land, created two separate, independent—though at least partially interdependent—levels of government: the national, or federal level, on the one hand, and the regional governments—the states—on the other. Although not the nearly autonomous entities they were under the Articles of Confederation, the states were to be, by intent of the framers at least, governments of substantial strength. This form of federal structure was a completely new style of government at the time of the founding, but in the years since then many other nations have adopted a similar one: Canada, West Germany, and Australia, for instance. American federalism has been one of the major contributions this country has made to the structure of governance in the modern world.

All fifty states have organized themselves via a tripartite separation of powers—executive, legislative, and judicial—much like the national government. Nevertheless, the formal structures of the states vary significantly. Some, like New York, have chief executives (governors) with great formal authority; others, like Mississippi, give the legislature much more control than the governor. One state, Nebraska, has even organized its legislature into a "unicameral," or one-house, body. The politics and interests of the states are impressively varied as well (Elazar, 1972): one-party Democratic strongholds like Alabama, where conservative interests and agricultural organizations are frequently in control; two-party competitive states with labor union influence, like Michigan; traditional Republican, religious polities like Utah, a bastion of the Mormons; and the diverse, fragmented, weak-party politics of California. All states, however, have created a great many *other* governments—local governments. In fact, there are about 79,000 of them inhabiting the American political landscape. There are so many, and they exist in such variety and complexity, that the U.S. Census Bureau periodically counts and classifies them—just as it does people, businesses, and houses with indoor plumbing! What are these other governments?

Counties

First are the *counties,* known as "parishes" in Louisiana and "boroughs" in Alaska. These units, numbering more than 3,000, serve most of the land area and population of the United States (U.S. Bureau of Census, 1977). A couple of New England states, the District of Columbia, and selected portions of a few other states (such as the "independent cities" of Virginia) have no county government. But for most Americans, counties are governments of some significance.

Originally, counties were created as little more than arms of state authority at the local level. Until modern times, counties rarely represented local interests in any systematic fashion (Torrence, 1974:6–7). Even today, most states rather tightly control their county governments on such matters as financial affairs. However, especially in urbanized areas, counties have acquired substantially more authority. Many of them now provide a full range of local services such as public health, libraries, sanitation, recreation, in addition to more traditional county duties of highway maintenance, law enforcement, and the like. Especially in these larger jurisdictions, but also elsewhere, counties are now full-fledged local governments representing and servicing local interests. In some states, especially in the more heavily populated regions, a few counties have actually been given a "home rule" charter—that is, these counties are able to pass their own local laws and raise their own local revenue without traveling back to the state capital to seek approval.

For a number of reasons, counties are on the rise as a form of local government. Counties are often the local base for politically powerful suburban populations and are the one government capable of serving the entire metropolitan area for many of the nation's smaller urban centers. As a result, there has been some shifting of responsibilities to the counties in recent decades, despite the fact that counties, like all other local governments, are creatures of the states.

It is important to emphasize, however, the fundamental difference in legal status between the levels of government. States and the national government both have Constitutional status. Neither can eliminate the other or ignore totally the interests the other was created to represent. However, local governments, no matter how important, are derivative of the states. Although, as we shall see, some local governments have increasingly looked to Washington for support and for a certain amount of freedom from this lesser status, the dependent nature of American local governments vis-à-vis the states has affected state and local politics markedly.

Municipalities

Municipalities are the cities and villages of the United States—from the giant megalopolises like Los Angeles and New York to small villages like Gambier, Ohio. These are the political subdivisions incorporated by the state to "provide general local government for a specific population concentration in a defined area" (U.S. Bureau of Census, 1977:2). Whereas counties were originally meant to serve state interests, muncipalities have been "created mainly for the interest, advantage, and convenience of the locality and its people" (Ohio Supreme Court, 1857, quoted in Torrence, 1974:6). While most of the nation's municipal corporations (there are more than 18,000 of them) are tiny villages or very large cities, most American residents of municipalities live in the largest ones.

Traditionally, municipalities have been the most independent of local governments. Nevertheless, the independence even of this group has been strictly limited by state legislative action and judicial interpretation for most of American history. The major principle restricting municipal autonomy was "Dillon's rule," named after the pronouncement of a judge in the state of Iowa. Dillon's rule states that municipalities have only the powers expressly delegated to them by the states. American courts have basically relied upon this notion up to the present. Although many states now provide the opportunity for their largest cities to acquire a measure of self-sufficiency through home rule, the relations between states and municipalities, especially large cities, have been stormy throughout American history. Traditionally, states have tended to keep a fairly close watch on their major cities, while urban political leaders have sought to make decisions on their own.

New England town meetings still provide the classic image of democratic self-government, even though many decisions that affect the townspeople are made at the state or national level. (*George Bellerose/Stock*)

Townships

To complicate the picture even more, many states have created *townships*. Most of these, numbering about 17,000 in all, are subdivisions of rural counties and for the most part perform few functions. In the nation's midwest, for instance, townships are rather plentiful, but it is almost stretching the point to call them separate governments at all. They do little besides maintain country roads, and they might have died out by now were it not for an infusion of money they received during the past dec-

ade from the national government through revenue sharing.

In a few places, especially in New England and certain other states of the northeast, townships (or "towns," as they are called in some locations) do serve important functions. In the New England towns, there is the venerable tradition of American local self-government. There, town meetings antedated the states themselves and are good examples of early American efforts at democracy. New England towns are actually the most important units of local government in that region and have assumed the role played by municipalities throughout the rest of the country.

School Districts

Everywhere in the United States except five states, the District of Columbia, and certain cities, another form of local government plays an important role. *School districts,* numbering approximately 15,000, are unique governments. Their sole purpose is to run public educational systems, usually at least through the high school level. American school districts are evidence of the long-held importance of education as a duty of local government and of the strength of educational interests and professionals, who have long sought to keep schools out of politics—or at least away from the conflicts and uncertainties that involve much of the rest of local government.

Of course, one should recognize that creating school districts does not really remove education from politics altogether. And these days, school administrators fully recognize how much they themselves must become involved in intergovernmental relations—for example when obtaining funds from the state and federal governments and when adhering to regulations established by them.

Special Districts

Finally, there are the *special districts,* consisting of a hodgepodge of limited-purpose units, some partly resembling general-purpose local governments (i.e., units that deal with most types of local issues and needs, whether public safety or public roads) and some hardly distinguishable from agencies of other governments (a local bridge or tunnel authority, for example).

Many of these governments are called "districts," "commissions," or "authorities." They perform all sorts of tasks and range widely in size; they exist in both rural and metropolitan areas. Special districts have been created to handle such duties as managing natural resources (e.g., drainage, irrigation, and flood control districts), ensuring fire protection in rural regions, supplying water in cities, building and maintaining housing, running park systems and hospitals, and even operating cemeteries and controlling mosquitoes. If you live in or near a large city, your mass transit system may be governed by a special district. If you live in a rural area, a water conservation district may be making decisions that affect you.

Creating special districts allows people to match the jurisdiction of a local government to the problem that needs to be solved, like pollution in a river basin (Ostrom, 1976). These units often possess a political advantage as well, since they may provide a service for which users can be charged directly, such as fees for sewage collection. Since no one pays who does not benefit, the activities of these special districts may thus be less controversial. More than other governmental forms, the 25,000 special districts probably typify Americans' pragmatic adaptation of their public institutions to the needs of different people at different times.

Yet critics of these governments raise some of the same sorts of constitutional questions often at the core of American political debate. For example, many complaints center on whether the independence of these governments and their officials from traditional electoral and administrative constraints encourages irresponsible behavior (Caro, 1974). Others argue that the crazy-quilt pattern of many duplicating and overlapping jurisdictions in the same region impairs efficiency, a value governments should pursue. How many police departments does a single urban area need? they ask. Nevertheless, American special districts have displayed impressive persistence and will have a significant impact on intergovernmental relations in the future. These and the other varieties of government are today constantly dealing with each other to get things done.

If the Constitution seemed to prescribe neatly divided spheres of authority for the states and the national government, how is it that today virtually all American governments must deal with each other so frequently and on so many matters? To answer this most important political issue of the present, we must cast our glance briefly toward an earlier era.

AMERICAN INTERGOVERNMENTAL RELATIONS: DEVELOPMENT TOWARD INTERDEPENDENCE

The earliest supporters of the Constitution found much to praise in the American experiment of federalism. The union of states into a "compound republic," as James Madison phrased it in *The Fed-*

eralist papers, was designed to safeguard freedom and prevent the tyranny of any faction. Few if any of the founders, however, could have imagined how compound and complex the republic would become over two centuries. Surely Madison himself would scarcely recognize the patterns that have evolved. Yet today's American intergovernmental relations were framed in significant respects by that Constitution. That document established a nation composed of participants—institutions and individuals—representing different interests, guaranteed a degree of independence, but also fundamentally interdependent. This basic fact has remained a constant. Over time, an increased recognition of this interdependence and recurrent efforts on the part of citizens and their governments to deal with it have altered American politics in significant respects.

Early Years: A Dual Federalism?

The Constitution of 1787 established a set of governments, national and state. But how were they to deal with each other? The Constitutional document itself provided contrary signals. The new framework seemed to divide responsibilities—some expressly given to the national government (e.g., coining money, regulating commerce with other nations, declaring war), some to the states (e.g., selecting electors to help choose the president). The

states seemed to have received the benefit of the doubt as regards jurisdiction since the Tenth Amendment, added as part of the Bill of Rights in 1791, declared, the "powers not delegated to the United States by the Constitution, nor prohibited by it to the States, are reserved to the States respectively, or to the people." Yet the national government was not, by any means, prevented from exercising significant powers. Thus, in addition to the specific grants of power given to the federal government, such as coining money, Congress was empowered to "provide for the . . . general Welfare of the United States" and to "make all Laws which shall be necessary and proper" for carrying out this duty (Article I, Section 8). With such carefully chosen ambiguous phrases, it is no wonder that reasonable people have differed over the years on just what the national government or the state governments are allowed to do (see Box 14-1).

Yet for all the ambiguity, it is quite clear that most of the founders pictured the system as one of *dual federalism:* the two levels of government operating side by side, but in different spheres—the national government handling certain issues, the states taking care of others. While there would be some occasions for overlap, thereby inviting cooperation or conflict, the image was more like a "layer cake" (Grodzins, 1966; the analogy was first made by McLean, 1952:5).

Did the governments actually practice dual fed-

BOX 14-1

POWERS IN THE FEDERAL SYSTEM

Express powers are those explicitly granted to the national government by the Constitution. The power to declare war is an express power of Congress.

Implied powers are those not explicitly granted to the national government but reasonably suggested from the express powers. Regulating television is nowhere mentioned in the Constitution but is implied by the express power of Congress to regulate interstate commerce.

Concurrent powers are those shared at both national and state levels, such as the power to tax.

Reserved powers are those left to the states to exercise. The Constitution does not list the reserved powers, but leaves the states all powers granted neither to the national government nor directly to the people themselves. An example is the power to set policy to promote public safety.

Denied powers are those prohibited to one or both levels of government. The power to establish an official religion is denied to the national government.

eralism? It is difficult to answer this question briefly and accurately. If one examines American intergovernmental relations in the nineteenth century, there are many clear examples of the doctrine of dual federalism. While the Supreme Court during the Taney years (1835–1863) developed the idea of *concurrent powers*—powers possessed simultaneously by state and national authorities—most of its decisions reinforced at least the judicial foundations of dual federalism (Walker, 1981:50). In terms of decisions outside the courtroom, also, public officials often seemed to act on the premise that national and state spheres were separate. One of the clearest statements of this principle was made by Madison himself, when he was president, as he vetoed a piece of legislation that would have established federal financing of certain public works construction projects.

> I am not unaware of the great importance of roads and canals and the improved navigation of water courses, and that a power in the National Legislature to provide them might be exercised with signal advantage to the general prosperity. But seeing that such a power is not expressly given by the Constitution, and believing that it cannot be deduced from any part of it without an inadmissible latitude of construction and a reliance on insufficient precedents; believing also that the permanent success of the Constitution depends on *a definite partition of powers between the Federal and State Governments* . . . , I have no option but to [veto the bill] . . . (quoted in Elazar, 1962:15; italics added).

Public works projects were not the only example of dual federalism in practice. On economic development, education, and other social policies, the states acted, and the national government abstained. The institution of slavery is perhaps the most prominent example from the previous century of a major state policy defended through reference to dual federalism on the basis of states' rights.

Nevertheless, state-national relations were not without interdependence for most of the nineteenth century. First, the two levels of government often clashed over jurisdiction. The Civil War is the most dramatic illustration, although some other national-state disagreements were also intense. The most frequent disputes focused upon how much independence the states should be permitted to exercise on

matters of commerce, labor, and social welfare (Walker, 1981:55–56). Later, both governmental levels sought preeminence in such matters as economic regulation. Even in the early years of this nation, therefore, American governments did not simply go their own way (Scheiber, 1966).

In fact, they cooperated with each other more often than has usually been recognized. Some observers of intergovernmental relations even claim that American federal-state relations can basically be summarized as a long history of "cooperative federalism" (Elazar, 1962). While this description seems to exaggerate the degree of cooperation in the nineteenth century, it is certain that all levels of American government have enjoyed partnerships with each other, at least on certain issues. For example, joint stock companies, part public and part private, were a fairly popular device in the early nineteenth century. A corporation would be established to handle a specific matter such as the creation of a bank or the construction of a canal or railroad system. Then, the stock of the corporation would be purchased by the federal government, one or more states, sometimes various localities, and even, quite often, private individuals. Control was placed in a board of directors appointed by the stockholders. This mechanism, used to circumvent what seemed to be the possible Constitutional obstacles to intergovernmental cooperation, has a surprisingly contemporary ring. The early American joint stock company was not unlike current bodies such as Washington, D.C.'s, Metropolitan Area Transportation Authority (WMATA), which runs the mass transit in and around the nation's capital. WMATA was created as the result of a compact between the District of Columbia (and thus the federal government), the states of Maryland and Virginia, and the cities of Falls Church and Alexandria, Virginia. All these governments have contributed monetary support for this venture.

Intergovernmental cooperation took place during the last century on a wide variety of construction, finance, education, and related projects. And technical assistance, particularly by the federal government on behalf of the states, was commonplace. In the latter part of the century, a most important cooperative intergovernmental development took place. The first significant federal grants, *land grants,* were established. States had

---

BOX 14-2

A LAND GRANT FOR HIGHWAYS

The financing and construction of the National Road through Ohio, Indiana, Illinois, and Missouri were the first major uses of revenues received from the sale of [federal] public lands for improvements in the field of transportation. The federal government arranged to do this by the device of advancing money to those four states from the Three Per Cent Fund. (This fund was a federal distribution to the public-land states from the annual proceeds of the sale of public lands within their boundaries to be used for internal improvements, particularly roads. . . .) Initially, only two per cent of the proceeds from land sales were granted. When it became apparent that this amount was not sufficient to maintain the needed rate of construction, Congress speeded the process by increasing the grant to 3 per cent and then "loaning" the money to the states until the loan could be repaid from future land sale revenues. This system was maintained until the road was turned over to the states. . . .

The first of these co-operative arrangements involving land grants passed the Congress in 1823. A grant of land was made to the state of Ohio to aid in the construction of a road to the border of the Michigan Territory. This grant was justified on the grounds of national security, under the war powers of Congress. . . . Actually, its greatest value was as a means of connecting the then isolated settlements of the Michigan Territory with the settled parts of the country. In the debate in the House of Representatives, it was openly opposed by only one person, Cooke of Tennessee, who argued that if the Michigan settlers thought such a road was necessary, they should build it themselves. When the vote was taken, all those voting nay were from the states without public lands, who opposed the measure as discriminatory rather than unconstitutional.

This grant set the pattern for many subsequent ones. It consisted of a right of way 120 feet wide plus a mile-wide strip of land on each side that was to be sold to raise money for actual construction of the road. Although the grant contained no provisions for revocation, the federal government included a provision that the land could not be sold for less than the minimum price of other lands in the public domain ($1.25 per acre) and that the road had to be completed in four years.

Source: Elazar, 1962:134–136.

---

long been providing support for their local governments, but this early federal aid marked the onset of an arrangement that currently ties American governments together in complicated and consequential ways. Land grants were gifts of land by the national government, which in those days had much land and little money. The federal government owned huge tracts in the states carved out by westward expansion; even today, the national government is the principal landowner in the western states. Land grants were designed to help the states construct roads, develop educational systems, and set up small-scale welfare programs. Typically, the states were to sell the land and use the proceeds to carry out these tasks (see Box 14-2).

Some land grants had a major, permanent impact on the nation. The Morrill Act of 1862, for instance, provided federal aid as national policy for establishing colleges of agriculture and the mechanical arts. Today's land grant colleges and universities—Purdue, Michigan State, North Carolina State, and parts of Cornell, to mention a few—were built from this intergovernmental program. These early grants, unlike most of those operating today, required little extra attention on the part of the states that received aid; administrative requirements were few. There were even some small cash grants from the federal government during these years. However, as was explained in Chapter 13, on the bureaucracy, the size and activity of American government remained fairly modest until the twentieth century.

Despite such impressive examples of federal-state and federal-state-local partnership, the dominant theme of intergovernmental relations throughout the first half or more of the nation's existence was the "layer cake," dual federal model, in which the national government and the states each performed separate functions without hindrance. But the turn of the century saw undeniable shifts.

An increased federal role and the shift toward interdependence were occasioned by multiple factors: changing views by Americans about what governmental arrangements were likely to achieve the goals they valued, an acceptance of a broader role for government in the society, a recognition of the complexity of modern problems, and altered financial circumstances. The terms of the constitutional bargain were altered.

The Twentieth Century: The Rise of Interdependence

While the linkages forged by intergovernmental cooperation did not really begin to multiply dramatically until the New Deal era of the 1930s, some of the early events of the twentieth century signaled the decline of dual federalism. Those people advocating political equality for all Americans including blacks were distressed with the maintenance of a segregated society via Jim Crow laws in the south. Civil rights activists throughout the century have viewed the national government as more congenial to their cause. Even today, nonwhite citizens are much more likely to feel that the national government has their interests at heart (ACIR, 1982). During the progressive period, political forces pressed for national government activity in policy fields previously either left to the states or avoided by government altogether, such as highway construction, economic regulation, and conservation. Arguments for intergovernmental cooperation came from interest groups that hoped to benefit, for instance, from large expenditures or involvement by the national government. These interests were joined by the rapidly professionalizing federal and state bureaucracies that also saw advantages to more intergovernmental involvement. Political pressures quite similar to these help to account for more recent intergovernmental programs as well.

Yet, for all this activity, the federal government would not have been able to extend its role in domestic policymaking nearly as much as it did were it not for certain other developments. In 1913, after

As this 1913 cartoon suggests, many supporters of the federal income tax amendment saw it as basically a tax on the rich, who were few in number and little admired. (*Ding Darling/Culver*)

years of political controversy, a Constitutional amendment authorizing a federal income tax was passed. It is difficult to overestimate the importance of this event for the later development of intergovernmental relations. A national income tax, especially a "progressive" and "elastic" income tax—that is, one that taxes higher incomes at a greater rate than lower ones and that more than keeps pace with economic growth—eventually gave the federal government the means to generate funds and to increase its revenue without continually having to enact tax increases.

The Role of Grants First gradually, then dramatically, the national government increased the quantity and the proportion of its budget devoted to *grants-in-aid* to states, and eventually to local governments, too. Figure 14-2 clearly indicates this development. In fact, grants-in-aid have become perhaps the primary "glue" of American intergovernmental relations. Grants now provide the principal mechanism through which our governments deal interdependently and continually with each other and assist state and local governments in a variety of policy areas (see Table 14-1).

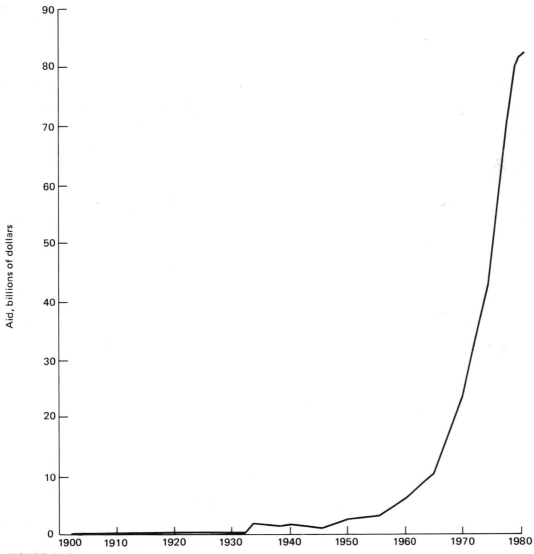

FIGURE 14-2
Federal aid to state and local governments over time. (*Source:* U.S. Bureau of the Census, 1975; *Statistical Abstract of the United States,* 1981; *ACIR,* 1980a.)

TABLE 14-1
PERCENTAGE DISTRIBUTION OF FEDERAL GRANT-IN-AID OUTLAYS, BY FUNCTION,
FOR SELECTED YEARS FROM 1958 TO 1978

Function	1958	1963	1968	1973	1978
Natural resources and environment	1	2	2	3	5
Agriculture	5	5	3	1	1
Transportation	32	36	23	13	11
Community and regional development	1	3	7	8	9
Education, training, employment, and social services	7	8	25	28	26
Health	4	5	15	14	16
Income security	46	38	23	21	18
General-purpose fiscal assistance	2	2	2	17	12
Other	1	1	1	2	1
Total	100	100	100	100	100

Source: ACIR, 1980a:134.

But was the grant-in-aid, which really ended the dominance of dual federalism, a Constitutionally permissible tool to effect intergovernmental partnership? To answer this question it would be useful to understand what a grant involves. Grants (and for practical purposes this means, these days, grants of cash) are transfers of resources from one government to another, for a specific purpose. The purpose may be broad (for instance, to help cope with the general matter of social services), in which case the transfer is a *block grant*. Or the purpose may be narrow (for instance, to eliminate rats in urban sewer systems), in which case the transfer is a *categorical grant*. Of course, there may be all sorts of gradations in between.

The shift of funds is made by using some rule or principle to determine which recipient governments should receive how much money. Grants that allocate funds to governments on the basis of some calculable formula are, not surprisingly, *formula grants*. (For example, states might receive federal aid to combat unemployment based on the population of the state and the unemployment statistics.) President Reagan's proposed block grants are all formula grants as well. On the other hand, if the donor government opts to retain some judgment about how much the potential recipient governments should receive, the transfer is a *project grant*. (Thus, states might receive aid for the unemployment problem on the basis of how strong and innovative an argument they can make.)

One example may help to clarify how grants work in practice. The interstate highway system is a program originally authorized by federal law in 1956. The goal, as backed by President Eisenhower, was to build a first-class transportation system linking the entire nation. The original rationale was for national defense, but anyone who travels on the interstate system these days recognizes that the military has not been the major user of the network. Highway construction was traditionally regarded as, first and foremost, a state responsibility. Thus, to achieve the goal of a national highway system while not usurping the states' prerogative, the federal government established a grant program to encourage but not coerce states to cooperate. The mechanism was a categorical formula grant from the national government to the states. Usually grants require some form of matching on the part of the recipient government; for instance, states may need to commit $1 of their own money for every $2 supplied by the federal government. In the case of the interstate highway grant, the states typically contribute $1 for every $9 paid by the federal government. The recipient government itself carries out the activity for which the grant was set up. Thus, for example, it is the states that contract to build the interstate highways.

Grants have another characteristic. They come with strings attached. The donor government specifies certain conditions that must be met before funds are given. Interstate highways must be constructed to a certain thickness from approved materials, and the exit and entrance ramps must meet detailed standards. Regulations have even covered the use of billboards near the roadway. States may have to agree to financial controls, audits, and other conditions as well. Recipients may have to complete reports on how the funded activity is progressing. States might be required to establish special agencies to execute the job. Even with some of the earliest federal land grants, there were a few strings. Such conditions are a way for the donor to make sure that some of its own preferences or policies are included. The usual situation is for each level of government to engage in some bargaining with the other; each tries to increase its own influence over the activity and reduce the number of unpredictable restrictions placed upon it from the other level.

Expanded Federal Influence   Are grants legitimate? Or are they really a national intrusion on states' independence within their own sphere? This subject acquired a renewed currency when President Reagan announced his desire to "demand recognition of the distinction between the powers granted to the federal government and those reserved to the states or to the people" (*Weekly Compilation of Presidential Documents,* 1981). Yet the question was even more controversial in the earliest years of the development of the federal grant system. Then, the pressure of circumstance and politics, and the availability of federal funds, helped stimulate the creation of eleven cash grant programs by 1920 (Walker, 1981:61). The issue finally reached the judiciary, and in 1923 the Supreme Court ruled. Two related cases, *Massachusetts v. Mellon* and *Frothingham v. Mellon* (262 U.S. 447) cleared the way for a near revolution in intergovernmental relations. In the former case, the Court decided that grants did not constitute an unconstitutional extension of the national government's role, since states (or, ultimately, local governments) were free to reject federal aid and thus federal strings. In the latter decision, the Court determined that individuals who were not pleased with the use of federal funds to support programs with which they disagreed had no legal standing to stop allocations.

The result of both cases, in essence, was to val-idate the grant as a major tool of federal influence, for despite the Court's assessment that states could withhold participation in any grant program that seemed unpalatable, the political truth was much different. Understandably, officials representing governments that are offered federal grants have great difficulty resisting support tendered for purposes that are laudable or to solve problems that are pressing. Potential recipients have usually felt compelled to accept the aid, and thus the accompanying strings. The validation both in law and in practice of the grant system, when coupled with the other factors mentioned earlier, made it possible for a great deal of federal-state, federal-local, and federal-state-local activity to occur over the years in various policy fields when political conditions became ripe.

The first major expansion of this type of intergovernmental activity occurred during Franklin Roosevelt's administration, with the New Deal. The nation's serious economic problems stimulated national policymakers, such as President Roosevelt, to start large-scale federal programs. By the late 1930s, the Supreme Court too had begun to interpret federal authority more broadly, and the national government committed itself deeply and permanently to intergovernmental programs. During a two-year period (1933–1935), federal decisions created new grants for such programs as the distribution of surplus farm products to the poor, free school lunches, child welfare, maternal and children's health and crippled children's services, old-age assistance, aid to dependent children, aid to the blind, general health services, emergency highway expenditures, and emergency work relief (Elazar, 1962).

All these programs were established by *national* decisions, but they were carried out and significantly influenced by the *states.* Dual federalism had clearly been replaced by something else, as federal dollars increased by tenfold for intergovernmental programs within a decade. Various phrases have been used to characterize this altered state of affairs. Perhaps the easiest way to think of it, however, is in terms of a shift from the layer cake of dual federalism to the "rainbow or marble cake, characterized by an inseparable mingling of differently colored ingredients, the colors appearing in vertical and diagonal strands and unexpected whirls" (Grodzins, 1960:265). During the last few decades nearly every governmental task has been spread across governmental levels in intricate, complex patterns. Government programs now typically involve two or more levels, each working on parts of a detailed whole.

Periodically, since the end of the New Deal, there have been some efforts to extricate the federal government from its intergovernmental role as granter, regulator, and overseer. President Eisenhower announced this intention, but the 1950s nonetheless witnessed a growth in federal involvement. President Nixon, too, foretold a "new American revolution" for the 1970s and a shift in decision making to state and local governments. Some important changes did occur during those years, but the national government remained as heavily committed as before. By the time President Reagan took the oath of office, the federal establishment was providing one-quarter of state and local revenues, more than $80 billion, and was involved in literally hundreds of intergovernmental programs. By this time, however, the many strengths and weaknesses of American intergovernmental relations had become clear to most public officials and many citizens. To gain the most intelligent perspective on the current intergovernmental system, we must first look briefly at some fairly recent developments; in the fifteen years or so preceding the Reagan period, the interdependence among American governments skyrocketed.

Recent Developments: The Intergovernmental Web

Grant Programs A major step in the development of intergovernmental relations was initiated during the administration of Lyndon Johnson. The "Great Society" led to an explosion in federal intergovernmental grant programs equal in significance to that of the New Deal. Federal efforts to combat rural poverty; to solve the urban crisis; and to accommodate the demands being voiced by the politically, socially, and economically disadvan-

taged resulted in many new activities. The innovations were usually appealing to social activists (despite limited funding) and were sometimes threatening to parts of the state and local establishment. Some grant programs actually had the effect of attacking existing local or state political systems. One of the best known of such grant programs from this period, the Community Action Program (CAP), distributed financial support to local organizations of poor people, and sometimes even challenged the activities of their local governments if these seemed to be working contrary to the group's interests (Moynihan, 1969). CAP stimulated a storm of controversy, was revised, and ultimately was terminated.

In 1964, there were 51 different grants-in-aid, which may seem like a rather healthy number; but by 1967, there were 379. The number continued to climb after Johnson left office—to 550 in 1974, for instance—but the acceleration was at its peak in the late 1960s (ACIR, 1980a). Today, no one, including federal, state, and local officials, really has a clear count on the number and size of all these federal programs! President Johnson called his era a time of "creative federalism," and it certainly was a period during which there were major intergovernmental experiments. Almost all the new programs were categorical ones, and most were project-funded rather than formula-funded. This arrangement made it relatively easy for the federal government to be sure that its money was being used for nationally approved purposes; but it also meant that recipient governments felt increasingly tied to a long list of federal priorities, and that state and local political leaders had less control over their own governments' actions. At the same time, many of the new programs provided a very high donor-to-recipient matching ratio—that is, the federal government offered to pay most of the money—so it became even more difficult for recipients to decline participation. But the "strings" became increasingly detailed. Federal aid accounted for a larger and larger share of state budgets (see Figure 14-3).

FIGURE 14-3
Opposite page: Some signs of intergovernmental interdependence in recent years.
(*Source: ACIR,* 1980a:120–121.)

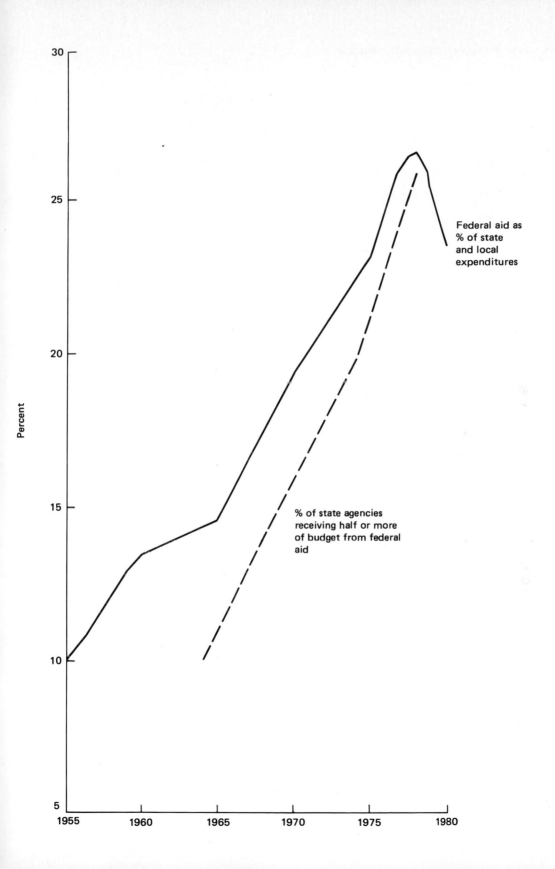

Percent

Federal aid as
% of state
and local
expenditures

% of state agencies
receiving half or more
of budget from federal
aid

Devastated inner-city areas like the South Bronx have received both direct and intergovernmental federal aid, ranging from block grants to specific programs for improving early education and rehabilitating housing.   *(Sepp Seitz / Woodfin Camp)*

One other result was very important. Federal assistance directly to local governments, especially cities, became sizable, particularly because urban leaders turned to Washington for a more sympathetic hearing than they had previously received from their states. As one might imagine, state governments came to view the direct federal-local interdependence with mixed feelings. On the one hand, they could hardly complain about federal help for their own citizens. But, on the other, these governments would have preferred that *they* be allowed to have a hand in decisions about how the money would be spent and the programs run. State officials sometimes saw these developments as threatening, with the feds and the locals (state creations) teaming up to combat the priorities of the states.

In response to these concerns, and as part of a political backlash against the antipoverty social activism that the Johnson years represented, Presi-dent Nixon announced a policy of "new federalism." The aims were to shift some power to the state and local levels and to increase the strength of the general-purpose political leaders—mayors, governors, county commissioners, etc.—relative to the functional specialists such as welfare administrators, highway bureaucrats, and state education officials. In fact, there were policy changes at the national level during the 1970s that were directed toward these ends, although sometimes the actual consequences did not square with these expectations. Some categorical grants were combined into block grants, so that recipient governments would have more ability to make their own decisions. One example is the community development block grant, established in 1974, which gives money to localities for housing, park restoration, sewer repair, and a variety of other purposes. It replaced several narrower programs (Bunce, 1979; see also Frieden and Kaplan, 1975).

Block grants provided by formula have indeed altered the intergovernmental picture by creating the assumption that, for certain broad fields of policy at least, state and local governments are entitled to aid (Stenberg and Walker, 1977). Yet most grants were left unchanged, and the block grants themselves often proved to be politically vulnerable (Robins, 1976). As time went by, Congress tended to tighten requirements for them to ensure that the money was spent wisely, at least from the perspective of national authorities. This inclination sometimes is humorously referred to as "hardening of the categories." Moreover, more new grants were born than old ones were killed. These trends are understandable, since all grants have supporters, most of whom can make powerful cases about the need for national involvement in a particular area, such as law enforcement or urban poverty, for the general welfare of all. Furthermore, many intergovernmental programs do provide impressive relief for severe problems.

Revenue Sharing   Another major intergovernmental change of the past decade, an innovation reflecting some of the same themes as did the establishment of block grants, has been the creation of the federal program of *general revenue sharing*. In 1972, with the support of President Nixon, Congress enacted a historic piece of legislation. The State and Local Fiscal Assistance Act of that year obligated the federal government to transfer approximately $30 billion over five years to all the nation's general-purpose governments, that is, all units aside from school districts and special districts. Thus, approximately half of American local governments were included under the program. The funds were allocated on a formula basis, and almost no restrictions were placed upon their use (Beer, 1976). In 1976, general revenue sharing was renewed for several more years with some minor adjustments. And in 1980, it was renewed once again for local governments, although the states were omitted from the program this time. This was because some states had developed budget surpluses (these mostly turned out to be transitory) and some had reduced state taxes (in most cases only to increase them again a couple of years later). Ironically, perhaps, one of the causes for the temporarily improved fiscal position of the states was

federal pressure on states to modify their tax structures in certain ways. Eventually, when federal budgets became very tight, it became difficult for national politicians to support revenue sharing for states that did not seem to need it.

The aim of the general revenue sharing program is clear enough. It is to use the taxing power of the federal government to supply funds to state and local governments, without directing how the money should be used. In this fashion, political leaders in recipient governments might be more able to assert their own priorities and serve the needs of their own constituencies, instead of merely using their governments to carry out federal policies. To a certain extent, revenue sharing accomplished this goal. Different communities have used the funds for widely varying activities: increasing police forces, building civic centers, paying off state or local debt, cutting taxes (Caputo and Cole, 1974, 1976; Nathan et al., 1975, 1977). However, revenue sharing is really only a small part of the budget in many important recipient governments; it is only a relatively minor part of the federal aid many governments receive. Thus, it does not alter the political interdependence of American governments in any fundamental way; it does not emancipate the recipients from federal oversight.

In addition, those governments, especially small local ones, which had not been receiving much support from the national government before the onset of revenue sharing are now *more* rather than *less* reliant on the feds for what they do. Some cynics draw an analogy to drug addiction: in this case, the governments are hooked on federal dollars. The comparison is not really appropriate, since the funds usually go to support worthwhile activities and the "addiction" is thus really a political incentive to benefit citizens. However, there is no question that governments heavily reliant on revenue sharing have become more dependent on the national government for their own viability.

During the Nixon administration, and in fact during the succeeding period into the Reagan years as well, many efforts were made to reduce some of the administrative complexity of the intergovernmental system, especially for state and local governments. While there have been some real improvements (for instance, it now takes less time for state or local government to find out whether a request for aid has been approved or not), many of the most troubling complaints continue to be raised by officials at all levels. In large part, these derive from the fact that American federal, state, and local governments are tied together so tightly and in so many, many ways that the pattern looks much like an impenetrable web which cannot be controlled or directed from *any*place in the system.

The result today is an intergovernmental system that retains certain important and controversial characteristics, despite recent reform efforts. We now turn to the operations of the system today and the important issues that concern those who would improve it.

THE INTERGOVERNMENTAL SYSTEM TODAY

Most of the important characteristics of today's system of intergovernmental arrangements can be derived from what has been said so far. The collection of American governments is very large, and all levels are linked to each other in complicated ways. The level of interdependence is high, as measured in nearly any fashion, but especially when considered from the perspective of the many channels of grants-in-aid that flow from unit to unit. In addition to the massive amounts of *federal* money transmitted, *state* aid to local governments approaches 60 percent of the general revenue they collect from their own sources (ACIR, 1980a:128). American governments simply cannot afford, financially or politically, *not* to deal with each other regularly to solve the problems they confront. And yet these American governments jealously guard their own autonomy: each has its own constituency, priorities, and constraints; each seeks to have its wishes carried out when it deals with other units. The result tends to be a complicated pattern of nearly endless bargaining between governments over what policy should be and how it should be implemented (Doolittle, 1981). The results may often be messy, but they may also be necessary in a pluralistic federal system that is designed simultaneously to preserve independence and foster interdependence—to balance liberty with the pursuit of equity (Glendening and Reeves, 1977; Hale and Palley, 1981).

What are some of the consequences of such a system for governments, and ultimately for citizens

themselves? Some have already been alluded to; some have yet to be mentioned.

Major Policy Achievements

The increased activism of the national government in domestic policy matters has contributed to numerous initiatives by other American governments in recent years. Because for most of this century the states lacked both the financial resources and the political will to address certain sorts of concerns, federal intergovernmental programs were decisive in getting states heavily involved in health care, mass transportation, pollution control, welfare, civil rights, and scores of other activities. While people frequently debate which of these are necessary and which are not, it cannot be denied that many of these intergovernmental programs have been striking successes.

Shifted Priorities

Another consequence is more controversial. Intergovernmental programs established by the national government shift, or "skew," the policy choices that states and localities are likely to make. If you were the mayor of a large city, how you would spend your budget, and therefore what your priorities would be, would depend partly on the costs of different options. Federal aid has the effect of lowering the costs of certain choices (e.g., building a new city sewer system), thus making it more likely that local choices will move into line with the preferences of national political leaders (Welch and Thompson, 1980). Of course, that is usually the whole point behind an intergovernmental program, but it sometimes causes concern among state or local officials. This is particularly the case under conditions such as those of recent years, when hundreds of programs offered by the national government change the costs (and therefore the priority rankings) of hundreds of policy options.

Plural Decision Making

The founders made a constitutional choice to disperse power among and within American governments so that no one would be able to carry too much weight. To a considerable extent, their intentions are still being fulfilled. Now federal, state, and local governments are tied together ever more tightly, but none can act unilaterally. The federal bureaucracy, for instance, cannot run local school systems, and certain federal goals (e.g., school desegregation) require local support for execution. However, local educational systems are dependent upon federal support for school lunches, aid for poor children, programs for the handicapped and gifted students. Nor are the states excluded; they regulate the structure of curricula, certify teachers, provide budgetary assistance, and so on. Thus, the American system of intergovernmental relations distributes influence among different governments and constituencies. Since so many units have to deal with each other for anything to happen, chances are that numerous points of view will be taken into account. This structure of plural decision making thus may sometimes enhance the liberty of individuals or groups, provide for flexibility, and create opportunities for accommodation. This is particularly true for those who seek to resist or veto an intergovernmental activity. Because many units must often agree before there is any action, many points of access are available for those who want to delay the action. This may be reassuring to those who wish to ensure that government does not trample their rights underfoot, but it may also be troubling to those who push for public action on a specific problem.

National Leadership

While it is true that the American intergovernmental network retains a plural character, it is also true that the national government is the prime mover in the system. Its actions have fostered interdependence among American governments and have sometimes encouraged equity as well. Federal aid can induce at least some minimal action in a policy field, such as welfare, across all the states. And the grant system provides an opportunity for redistributing wealth toward those places that really need it.

While it cannot force state or local governments to act in certain ways, Washington does have some advantages that make it relatively more powerful. One of the advantages possessed by the feds has already been discussed: the ability to raise revenue.

The federal government's reliance on a progressive and elastic income tax, and its ability to enact deficit spending when it so chooses, have given the national government more flexibility than state and local entities have. National policymakers, until recently at least, have had fewer political constraints on them when they desired new, sometimes costly, programs. Most states have had to enact tax increases fairly regularly to pay for the programs (between 1980 and 1982, all but ten states raised taxes to cover spiraling costs); and they have operated under constitutional restrictions on debt (*National Journal,* 1982). Many older governments, especially cities, have had even more severe financial problems. Thus for years the feds have had the one relatively ready source of easy money to direct at urgent problems. This superior revenue position of the national government has given that level more bargaining power. It remains to be seen whether the improved financial positions of a few states—especially those with natural resources like oil and coal, which are currently in demand—and the worsened situation in Washington will mean that some states will begin to act more independently of federal direction on certain issues.

Furthermore, there is only one national government—albeit a complicated and multifaceted one—while there are fifty states and thousands of localities. This fact sometimes means that the potential recipients of federal support must vie with each other for advantage. States and local governments seldom speak with one voice on an issue; and thus it is rare for, say, states to act as a unified, equal force in bargaining with the federal establishment. While states and local governments have recently tried to coordinate themselves in their dealings with national officials, any such coalition of multiple governments is precarious, as was obvious in 1980 when representatives of these units split on the issue of how revenue sharing should be extended.

Federal power is particularly evident on project grants. In these programs, competition between potential recipient governments is overt and often intense. The winners are those who can put together a spending proposal that most clearly meets the preferences of the federal officials, often permanent bureaucrats (Saltzstein, 1977; Stein, 1979, 1981). Those state and local governments best able to

BOX 14-3

THE GRANT SYSTEM: VIEWS OF SOME PARTICIPANTS

While intergovernmental aid seems indispensable to many federal, state, and local officials, they are quick to express frustration with their counterparts, with how the system affects them, and with the sorts of stratagems they feel required to employ as they deal with each other.

Federal bureaucrats frequently believe that they should have a firm hand in directing and controlling how national dollars are spent by state and local governments and that recipient governments are often greedy and irresponsible. As one fed puts it, "Every city official I've ever talked to is concerned with money—the more the better." Another comments, "As a rule, I don't think that city managers and *certainly* city councils are interested in problem solving. But they want money and they don't want to take the heat of raising it themselves."

Yet from the perspective of recipient governments, it is the feds who are unreasonable and inefficient. One governor sums up the situation this way:

Some of the worst features of bureaucratic control are manifest in the Federal-aid program. Some administrative forms are so complex that they make administration unnecessarily unwieldy. States frequently experience troublesome delays in obtaining needed decisions from regional and national offices. Sometimes authority to act in behalf of Federal agencies will be too indecisive, at other times too arbitrary.

The many federal aid programs are conceived, established, and managed independently of each other.

A former chief executive from another state described an incident from his experience to make a similar point.

The next to the last year I was in office, I sent the executive director of our State board of health to Washington on a year's leave of absence, badly as we needed him, just so he could learn how to operate with Federal people. He has been a great help to us since that time. But you ought not to have to do that kind of thing to learn just how to get along and through this morass.

One local official from Syracuse, New York, is quite candid on the task of her agency.

Our first function is to manipulate the system to get as much of the money as we can into the City of Syracuse, in the first instance, at least, to be used to meet city priority needs. That includes grant negotiations, most heavily in the categorical grants and block grant systems; it includes the preparation of our applications, some of them more intelligible than others. It also includes the development of a state legislative program and the follow-up lobbying effort, which has become a much more important aspect of our activities than it used to be and takes a great deal of my time.

And the mayor of Omaha, Nebraska, speaks for many other local representatives when he expresses concern about the financial dependence of his government on state and federal support.

Are we going to wake up some morning and find that only 25 per cent of city employees are working on city business?

Source: Pressman, 1975:88; Carroll and Campbell, 1976:241; Wright, 1982:56, 59, 271.

draft such proposals may receive much more aid than others. The importance attached to this task of "grantsmanship," as it is called, is demonstrated by the fact that most states and sizable local governments now hire specialists whose job it is to stay in touch with federal funding sources and to develop skills in writing grant proposals (see Box 14-3). Obviously, under these circumstances the national government has the upper hand. The po-

tential recipients are each seeking to please the feds so that their own government will receive support.

Intergovernmental Lobbying in Washington

Since the national government has become so important in the system, a good deal of intergovernmental politics now takes place among participants in the nation's capital. Of course, interest groups, officials, and politicians who care chiefly about one specific program or policy area have an important impact on intergovernmental relations, and their role will be discussed in the next section. However, it is also important to realize that organizations of governments *themselves* have been created and play a part in American intergovernmental relations.

These groups, which often refer to themselves as "*public interest groups*," or "PIGs" (believe it or not), handle some important functions for American state and local governments (Farkas, 1971; Haider, 1974). At present, there are seven such important umbrella groups: the National Governors' Association, the National Conference of State Legislatures, the Council of State Governments, the U.S. Conference of Mayors, the National League of Cities, the International City Management Association, and the National Association of County Officials. (Certain more specialized groups, like the Rural Governments Coalition, are somewhat less influential.) As the names imply, these organizations represent general-purpose governments. All have Washington offices and permanent staffs. These units help to keep their membership informed about what the national government is doing—or planning to do—that might affect them. For example, during the period when President Reagan proposed establishing new block grants, the PIGs served as vital information sources for state and local officials seeking knowledge about what was happening. These groups also provide information *to* the federal government on behalf of their membership. And, as one might expect, when a group of state or local officials is united in its stand on some intergovernmental issue, the appropriate PIG makes this position known and lobbies in Washington on its behalf. As was mentioned earlier, a large group of mayors or county officials rarely agree on much; but when they do, their point of view may be influential. The PIGs were quite active in dealing with the Reagan administration on the "new federalism" proposals. Several have even banded together occasionally into the State and Local Coalition in an attempt to present a single perspective.

Most states and numerous local governments do not rely solely on the PIGs to represent their interests in Washington. During the past decade, many governments have established their own offices near the centers of decision making in Washington. For example, approximately 100 cities had employed representation in the nation's capital by 1980 (*National Journal,* Sept. 6, 1981:1485–1487). This trend is very understandable, given what we have said so far about the increased interdependence among American governments. These offices are almost like miniature versions of embassies, containing emissaries from other governments who gather information and bargain in a type of intergovernmental diplomacy.

Interest Groups, Administrative Agencies, and Legislative Committees

It should be clear that today's American intergovernmental system is one of plural decision making with national eminence, one presenting opportunities for continually raising the question of how to mix the values of liberty and equality across the nation. Among those plural decision makers, however, some are more influential than others. For a particular intergovernmental program like building highways, the relevant interest groups, administrative agencies, and legislative committees at one or more levels of government are among the most important.

Few people will be as intensely interested or well-informed about a program as this trio. For an intergovernmental program on highway construction, the Federal Highway Administration, the relevant House and Senate committees, the asphalt manufacturers and road building associations, the tire companies, the organization of state highway officials, and some state transportation departments and legislative committees will deal with each other extensively, over a considerable period of time. Often, groups of specialists like these develop similar points of view, especially on the desirability of sustained support for the program.

The triple alliance of bureau, legislative committee, and interest group is often decisive in American policymaking, as was mentioned in Chapter 13 and will be discussed in more detail in Chapter 15. Intergovernmental programs are no different, although the triple alliance—when extended across two or three governments—may be especially impenetrable to those (like governors, mayors, other general-purpose executives, or average citizens) outside it. Why? Collections of these policy specialists who bargain and reach agreements intergovernmentally are interdependent with each other. General political leaders at any level of government often have great difficulty directing or controlling their own specialists. A governor might want to initiate a change in the way his or her state handles its Medicaid program, for example. But the state agency that carries out the program receives much of its own budget from the federal government's Department of Health and Human Services. The federal specialists in the area have established standards that may conflict with the governor's ideas, and the state unit cannot afford to ignore federal requirements. The federal agency even has some control over the way the state unit is organized and the sorts of people it hires. It may be difficult to tell *what* level of government has added a particular requirement to a program in one state or another. And sometimes, especially when a program involves all three levels of government, it is difficult to figure out whether certain parts of a program are requirements at all or simply suggestions that one level makes to another.

There are several important consequences of these facts of intergovernmental life. First, the strength of specialists in intergovernmental politics has helped stimulate the professionalization of state and local bureaucracies. As federal experts have developed program requirements for the grants they administer, they have often made sure that the bureaucracies of the recipient governments are staffed with technically qualified, often highly educated people (Derthick, 1970, 1976). In fact, during the course of this century the intergovernmental system has been one of the main factors behind the decline of political machines at the state and local levels.

Second, now that decisions are diffused across specialists among several governments, it is more difficult to tell who is responsible for the decisions made in policy areas like transportation, economic development, and environmental affairs. When something goes wrong (or right), it is hard to figure out who should be held accountable. Decisions about intergovernmental programs may be parceled out in so many specialized offices of several governments that nearly everyone involved can blame someone else for any difficulties that arise. To put it simply, it may be more difficult to ensure responsible conduct on the part of public officials when complicated programs cross intergovernmental lines. Thus these days, when suggestions for reform of the system are so frequently voiced, people are really reopening the constitutional question of how to structure our governmental institutions to ensure accountability (Thompson, 1980).

Third, to the extent that intergovernmental program specialists *do* pay attention to the concerns of others, they may be more responsive to their counterparts at *other* levels of government than to the generalist political leaders in their own jurisdiction. Partly this is a matter of experts' being more inclined to trust other experts than to defer to politicians. And partly, it is a case of state or local specialists' paying close attention to federal specialists who control grants that support the recipients' programs. In one survey of state agency heads, for example, nearly half of those who were asked answered yes to the question "In practice, is your department/agency less subject to supervision by the governor and legislature in federally-financed activities than in activities financed solely by the state?" (Wright, 1978:273, and 1982:314–326).

The overall conclusion is that specialists frequently outweigh generalists in intergovernmental policies. For this reason, governors, mayors, county executives, and similar officials have generally supported revenue sharing and other measures that might increase their control over various parts of their own governments. For this reason, too, political leaders at the state and local levels have frequently supported block over categorical grants. However, it is precisely because of the shift in power that revenue sharing and block grants signify that program specialists at *all* levels often oppose these changes. It should not be surprising, for example, that senior citizens groups that benefit from—and public service professionals who handle—various federal aid programs for the elderly would resist a move that would end their categorical programs and lump them in with assistance for lots of other people. A change like this one reduces the certainty of support. The groups that have been successful at getting narrow categorical grants established—and these are numerous, as one can tell from surveying the hundreds of programs now on the books—can be expected to resist strongly any attempts to weaken their programs. Thus, the generalists work to protect the integrity of and support for their own government, while the specialists try to ensure the same for their own program (see Box 14-4). This helps to explain the political significance of President Reagan's current efforts to shift from categorical to block grants (see below). And it also helps to explain why similar efforts by earlier presidents did not radically transform the system. The strength of narrowly defined, intensely felt interest groups in American politics can be seen clearly in the intergovernmental system (Beer, 1978:17–18).

Difficulties of Interdependence

We have already discussed some of the problems generated by the fact that American governments are now tied so closely together. It may be useful to examine this issue a bit more carefully.

Some of the difficulties of interdependence stem from the simple truth that our governments must work together but do not always see eye to eye—that is, there are overt *political differences*. The skewing effect of federal aid is one of the most important manifestations of these political differences. Another political difficulty is the so-called "*mandate* issue." When the federal government makes its aid conditional on certain actions of the recipient unit, these conditions are called "mandates." There are many, many kinds of mandates that may be imposed (requirements that federally supported transportation facilities be accessible to the handicapped, that construction projects not damage the environment, that state and local hiring practices meet federal guidelines, etc.), but of course all are efforts by the feds to have their own goals achieved through other governments. A few mandates may be an expected part of an intergovernmental bargain. But when the national government tries to impose a large number of mandates, political controversy is to be expected. Between 1956 and 1960, the federal government set up only four new mandates. Yet between 1976 and 1978, 413 were created (Lovell, 1979:72; Lovell and Tobin, 1981). As more and more state and local activities are constrained by more and more man-

dates, many state and local officials have become frustrated and angered; and this problem too received some attention from the Reagan administration. Some of the recipient governments have even turned down federal aid because of their distaste at implementing so many externally imposed policies. Political conflicts like these are the inevitable consequence when different governments have to deal with each other so extensively, as is demonstrated by the fact that states themselves impose as many mandates on their local governments as the feds do, or more.

Yet some of the difficulties created by interdependence do *not* stem from failures of American governments to see eye to eye. These matters are what might be considered *coordination problems*. What are they? An analogy may be helpful. You may recall playing a game called a "three-legged race" in which you tied one of your legs to one of your partner's legs and the two of you raced to the finish line against similarly bound couples. The game was funny because each member of a pair of racers was only imperfectly coordinated with the other. Despite the fact that you and your partner shared the same goal (racing to the finish line), you may have slipped, staggered, and otherwise appeared pretty silly. A similar, although more significant, version of this behavior happens in intergovernmental relations. If you think of each person as a government, and people being tied together as intergovernmental interdependence, you can see the point—except that in the real world things are more complicated than a simple *three-legged race*. Often, *several* governments are bound to each other, sometimes in complex, crisscross patterns. The point is that the interdependence among governments can make matters cumbersome, even if all participants (national, state, and local governments) are more or less agreed about what to do (see Box 14-5).

An example may illustrate this point. President Reagan proposed a shift from categorical grants to certain block grants. Many state officials liked the idea, but at the same time it created some major problems for them. Because state spending decisions are very dependent on federal funding decisions, Reagan's proposal meant that state officials might have to redraft their own priorities almost overnight. In many states during 1981, for in-

BOX 14-4

THE ELEMENTARY AND SECONDARY EDUCATION ACT (ESEA): NATIONALIZING PART OF PUBLIC EDUCATION

The development and implementation of ESEA, passed in 1965 and amended many times since then, illustrate in one policy area some of the forces that increased the national government's role over the years in various phases of domestic activity.

Although the federal government had provided some types of assistance for education to state and local governments in the years preceding the mid-1960s, most of these programs were very small and uncontroversial. Educating children has always been primarily a local activity in the United States, but starting in the 1940s various groups began to push for federal aid on a much broader scale. The two political parties endorsed the general concept (Democrats in 1944, Republicans four years later), and public opinion was favorable; but the issue was complicated by: (1) the politically controversial nature of national involvement in an area traditionally so decentralized; (2) the race issue, since federal aid to schools raised the question of how the national government would deal with segregated and discriminatory school systems; and (3) church-state relations, since any general assistance to education stimulated argument about how to treat parochial (church-affiliated) schools.

Many interest groups were generally in favor of federal aid. The most important of these included organized labor, as represented by the American Federation of Labor–Congress of Industrial Organizations (AFL-CIO); professional educators, especially through the National Education Association (NEA) and American Federation of Teachers; and Catholic religious leadership, via the U.S. Catholic Conference (USCC). In Congress, there was also significant support for federal assistance by the late 1950s, and a series of limited federal programs (e.g., help for school construction) was passed during this period. Yet by the early 1960s no large-scale package had been approved. Conflicts between the major interests, stimulated by the issues mentioned above plus the type of formula that might be used to dispense money, stymied proponents. For example, in 1961 a bill backed by the Kennedy administration and many of the groups was strongly opposed by the USCC because it denied aid to parochial schools. The Congress, acting through various committees, reflected this division of opinion. The House Education and Labor Committee pushed for a bill, while the Rules Committee, containing some southern Democrats concerned about protecting segregated schools, did not.

Several years of delay and failure chastened nearly all the participants and encouraged them to mute their differences in the interest of getting some sort of solution. In 1965, Lyndon Johnson was fresh from an overwhelming electoral victory and had the support of a liberal, predominantly Democratic Congress.

Furthermore, the passage of the 1964 Civil Rights Act seemed to have settled the race issue. Accordingly, Johnson's commissioner of education, Francis Keppel, conducted a series of negotiating sessions with the major private, state, and local interest groups involved, particularly the NEA and USCC. Agreement was reached on the idea that federal assistance would be considered as aid to disadvantaged children, not to schools, even though the schools would receive the dollars. This option simultaneously cleared the religious barrier and tied educational dollars to Johnson's then-popular "war on poverty." With strong backing from the executive branch, the act was approved by Congress in short order. Its major component was "Title I," which distributes aid to school districts on the basis of a formula taking into account state expenditures on education and the number of economically disadvantaged children in the district.

Because of their repeated disagreements on previous attempts, the major interest groups were not as active as they might have been in pushing the legislation; but once it was enacted, educational professionals along with the congressional authorizing committees sought to protect the program from cutbacks or elimination.

In the years since then, the ESEA has stimulated considerable additional conflict: the funding formula has been altered, and the law has involved the national government's education bureaucracy more directly than had been anticipated—in school desegregation, for instance. Yet additional titles (and thus new categorical grants and federal regulations) were added over the years. These too were initiated by educational professionals and interest groups (e.g., those concerned about aid to handicapped children) and once enacted have been protected by bureaucratic, congressional, and recipient groups.

President Nixon tried without success to weaken the grip of these specialists over federal involvement in education by proposing a broad educational block grant in place of the large collection of categorical ones, especially those funded by ESEA. President Reagan tried to do something quite similar, and at the peak of his popularity did create a modest block grant for education. Yet the most important pieces of federal aid, e.g., those under Title I, remain in place—zealously protected by the educational establishment.

The case of ESEA illustrates (1) the process of gradual adoption of a sizable federal role in a policy area, (2) the importance of state and local professionals and interest groups in the process, (3) the impact of regional differences, (4) the sometimes significant role played by national political leaders, and (5) the autonomy often exercised by intergovernmental networks once in place.

Source: Bailey and Mosher, 1968; Murphy, 1973; Bresnick, 1979; ACIR, 1981a; *National Journal,* various issues, 1981–1982.

BOX 14-5

INTERGOVERNMENTAL COMPLEXITY: FIFTY-TWO PROGRAMS FOR FIREFIGHTERS

The sometimes bewildering complexity of the intergovernmental system is illustrated by the example of federal aid available to state and local governments for fire prevention and control. Despite the fact that fighting fires would seem to be a preeminently local activity—one with which the national government would not be involved—as of 1980 there were fifty-two federal grant programs in operation to assist other American governments in some phase of this activity. All federal departments but two (Defense and State), plus more than ten other agencies, are somehow involved in this network. It is no wonder that state and local officials find the pattern unwieldy and difficult to understand.

The U.S. Forest Service in the Department of Agriculture, for instance, supervises aid for cooperative federal-state forest fire control, research on the subject, and protection of rural communities from fires. Another bureau in the same department (the Science and Education Administration) helps states perform research on a similar subject. A third unit in Agriculture, the Soil Conservation Service, gives grants to help indirectly through a program aimed at resource conservation. The Public Health Service in the Department of Health and Human Services, meanwhile, administers a number of intergovernmental programs designed to educate people about safety, perform research on eliminating safety hazards, train workers in on-the-job fire prevention, educate emergency personnel, and improve medical services for fire victims. The Department of Housing and Urban Development works with local governments to upgrade building safety. The Bureau of Mines in the Interior Department aims at preventing coal mine fires—and so does the Mine Safety and Health Administration in the Department of Labor, with a different program. There is even a special federal agency, the U.S. Fire Administration, to handle additional grants and to coordinate all the others, although it really has no means to encourage other units to go along. Furthermore:

> Eight agencies make loans of money or equipment that can be used to improve fire protection. Five collect data related to fire incidence, injuries, and losses, and many provide some kind of technical assistance and information available to those who request it (ACIR, 1980b:7).

These programs have different standards for eligibility, different strings attached, and different matching and administrative requirements.

Source: ACIR, 1980b.

---

stance, the state budget process was delayed for a long time while everyone waited to see what would happen in Washington. This sort of interdependence makes it quite difficult for any one government to plan its own decisions quietly and rationally (Doherty, 1978).

It is very important to remember, however, that American government was not designed only for efficiency. If the founders had wanted a Constitutional framework to encourage quick, decisive action without any messiness at all, they never would have settled on a federal system. The collection of American governments was built to accommodate multiple, even partially contradictory values: speed and decisiveness are moderated by—some might say sacrificed to—flexibility, pluralism, and experimentation (Light, 1978b).

Some of the most significant policy innovations in this nation, such as food and drug control, transportation regulation, and child labor laws, occurred first at the state level. The federal system thus provides many centers from which ideas can be generated and tested (Landau, 1973). Today, variations abound in many policy areas. In some parts of the country (e.g., New Orleans) alcoholic beverages can be consumed in bars at any hour of the day or night; other jurisdictions prohibit such drinking altogether. States differ significantly in their policies about education, criminal justice, drug abuse control, taxation, and a multitude of other subjects. The founders' framework, therefore, provides numerous opportunities for local liberties to be exercised. The American intergovernmental system helps to sustain vitality and diversity across the landscape of the nation's political communities.

Perhaps the key question is whether the nation is adaptable to the demands for decisiveness and the real interdependence that are likely to be part of its next century. Can and should American governments maintain independence and integrity as they are bound ever more closely together by need and circumstance? Or alternatively, have the advantages of federalism been lost as the national government has acquired more power? Once again, it should be obvious that this important issue about the future of the nation reflects an enduring concern raised by the framers. We cannot hope to answer the question here. However, the timeliness of these topics can be demonstrated through brief analyses of three specific intergovernmental policy difficulties: Reagan's "new federalism," the nation's urban problem, and the rise of new regional tension in this country.

POLICY DILEMMAS

Reagan's "New Federalism"

Ronald Reagan's proposed changes in the American intergovernmental system would, if approved, involve extraordinary changes. The Reagan package of ideas, produced during the early years of his presidency, was complex in its details but can be understood as consisting of three major interrelated suggestions:

1 *Block grants.* Reagan proposed combining many of the national government's categorical programs into block grants provided by formula with very few regulations attached and no matching required. The number of grants Reagan proposed consolidating has varied but ranges to more than 100. Most of the categorical grants nominated for elimination have been small programs.

2 *A "swap."* Reagan suggested a major trade, or swap, of program responsibilities between national and state governments. In his first version of this idea, he offered to have the feds assume full financial and program authority for Medicaid, an expensive intergovernmental program to benefit the country's medically needy (see Chapter 16, on social welfare policy), if the states would in turn take complete control over the nation's food stamp

and Aid to Families with Dependent Children programs, two of the most important American welfare activities. Later, he changed the terms of his idea to make it more palatable to state officials— e.g., by offering to have Washington continue to handle food stamps.

3 *A "turnback."* The president linked to his trade proposal the idea that sixty-one other intergovernmental programs, including most of the remaining expensive ones, would be turned back to the states. The feds would withdraw completely from participating in these activities. A federal fund of $28 billion per year would be used for several years to help states pay the cost for their increased responsibilities, but by 1991 the national government would turn these tax sources over to the states and eliminate aid or involvement of any sort from Washington.

Reagan added other suggestions, such as reductions in federal administrative requirements for existing programs, but the above ideas were his most sweeping. In effect, they reopened the debate on at least three constitutional questions we discussed in the opening chapter. He argued that the role of government generally in society should be reduced; that the institutions of state and local government could, more appropriately than the feds, handle much of the public's business (thus addressing the question of who should rule); and that the intergovernmental system had shifted too much toward interdependence and redressing disparities (e.g., overemphasizing equality across the states) and should be changed to revitalize diversity and local liberty (Williamson, 1982).

Despite the widely recognized problems with the current system, however, Reagan's proposals stimulated considerable opposition. In 1981, seventy-seven categorical programs were, at the president's urging, combined into block grants. But this change was not so dramatic—the amalgamations were mostly small ones, and the new legislation contained many of the old federal controls. A new set of block grants suggested by him the following year went nowhere; and his swap and turnback offers faced strong attack from many local officials, who worried about their role under a state-centered intergovernmental system. Even state leaders, including many Republicans as well as Democrats, were reluctant to endorse the detailed plan. They

A rather bewildered-looking gaggle of governors attempt to answer reporters' questions after discussing possible shifts in federal and state responsibilities with President Reagan in 1981.   (*Charles Steiner/Sygma*)

worried about whether they would lose financially and whether such revolutionary shifts in the constitutional bargain would be best for the United States. The National Governors' Association, for instance, proposed reopening the idea that the federal government should assume primary responsibility for the income security of the American people; if so, all welfare programs should perhaps be transferred to the national level.

Many state and local officials were also concerned about the nation's poorest and weakest states and citizens, who might be disadvantaged still further without federal help. On this issue, they were joined by bureaucrats involved in intergovernmental programs, many congressional leaders, and interest groups traditionally supportive of categorical programs—the Children's Defense

Fund, the National Association of Community Health Centers, the Coalition on Block Grants and Human Needs, and so on.

Reagan's ambitious package was derailed, reconsidered, revised, and scaled down. Part of the opposition was directly self-interested. Big-city mayors become concerned these days when, as they try to find a way of balancing their budgets, someone suggests policy changes likely to make their fiscal condition even more perilous (but see Dye and Hurley, 1978). This problem was made more severe by the fact that Reagan accompanied his proposals with cutbacks overall. But part of the opposition was generated by concern and disagreement over the deeper constitutional matters.

Some such alterations in the American intergovernmental system may eventually be made as a result of the proposals debated now. Yet any renegotiation of the federal bargain will have to confront the massive extent of intergovernmental interdependence in the 1980s. Constitutional changes of such magnitude are not made lightly. In any event, the "new federalism" controversy illustrates clearly how exciting, contemporary, and practical are the constitutional questions of American government.

The Urban Problem

American cities, especially the larger and older cities of the northeast and midwest, face serious problems in the coming years. It is not possible to explain these difficulties or their causes in any systematic fashion here, but some ways in which the intergovernmental system affects the nation's urban areas can be highlighted.

The larger, older metropolitan areas of the country share certain common characteristics. The "central cities"—the main governmental centers—have a stable or declining population. Those who leave the central cities for the surrounding governmental jurisdictions—the suburbs—tend to be wealthier; those who stay tend to be poorer members of racial and ethnic minority groups. Furthermore, most of the new jobs and industry in metropolitan areas are being established in the suburbs. The result is that many of the nation's cities have become poor, relative to the surrounding local units, and yet the central city population must be provided with more services (welfare, police protection, etc.) than the communities around it (see Box 14-6).

There are many reasons for these developments. One has been intergovernmental policies. In the past, at least, state policies have tended to encourage the development of suburban enclaves—which house middle-class commuters—instead of a single government serving the whole metropolitan region (Colman, 1975:70–79). And a variety of policies established by the federal government in years past have contributed to the problems of the cities. Several examples should illustrate the point. National transportation policy emphasized the building of highways for most of the post-World War II years. The interstate system, established through federal grants, made it easy for those who could afford cars and suburban homes to move out of the central city

and yet commute to work without difficulty; those who remained tended to be those who could not afford to take advantage of this federal transportation subsidy. Federally financed home mortgage programs (such as Federal Housing Administration and Veterans Administration loans) were used by millions of young, middle-class Americans to escape to the suburbs, where federally insured mortgages were more likely to be approved. For years, federal policy on housing explicitly encouraged the segregation of "inharmonious racial groups"—in the phrase of an FHA manual. Even in more recent years, when national policy did not overtly favor such developments (see Rich, 1982), programs like public housing, urban renewal, and even federal aid for water and sewer facilities tended to reinforce the segregation of urban populations by race and income level (Wood, 1975).

Meanwhile, political leaders in the central cities, faced with declining tax bases and rising demands for services, became increasingly dependent on intergovernmental aid from the state or national government. By 1981, for instance, federal aid alone accounted for large portions of the budget in many cities—22 percent in Detroit, 26 percent in Chicago, 36 percent in New Orleans (*National Journal,* Jan. 4, 1981:4; ACIR, 1980c; 1981b; Perry and Watkins, 1977). Some of this assistance was generated at the national level by a real concern for the problems that the state and federal governments had already helped to create for cities (Long, 1978). Yet now that these local units have become so tied to the national government, it may be difficult for either level to function as a separate entity. For better or worse, therefore, the national government has been and will remain a part of the American urban problem. Likewise, the cities are now part of the national government's difficulties.

Nowhere is this interdependence more obvious and its effect more telling than in the case of New York City, whose government has had severe budgetary and political problems in recent years. Once again, the causes have been multiple. One problem has been the operations of the intergovernmental system. A combination of local decisions and intergovernmental opportunities tied New York's finances closely to federal (and state) policies. In 1975, when the city became virtually bankrupt, local officials blamed other levels of government for the problem, while federal officials claimed that

---

BOX 14-6

IS THE UNITED STATES A NATION OF CITIES?

By most measures, the United States is indeed a nation of cities. The country has become steadily more urban with the passage of time:

Year	Urban population as percent of total
1790	5.1
1800	6.1
1810	7.3
1820	7.2
1830	8.7
1840	10.8
1850	15.2
1860	19.7
1870	24.8
1880	28.1
1890	35.1
1900	39.6
1910	45.5
1920	50.9
1930	56.0
1940	56.4
1950	63.8
1960	69.6
1970	73.3
1980	73.7

Yet this general trend glosses over some important facts. First, in the decade between 1970 and 1980, the increasing urbanization characteristic of the previous several decades leveled off significantly.

Second, many of the people counted as "urban" live not in, but rather near, the country's cities, e.g., in suburbs. Third, many people live in small cities in the United States. Thus, growth in the 1970s was 6.7 percent with the nation's older cities, but 17.4 percent in suburbs and smaller metropolitan areas, and 16 percent in nonmetropolitan places. (Yet the nation's farm population continued its decline: 30.1 percent of the population in 1920, 15.3 percent in 1950, only 2.7 percent in 1980.) Fourth, sun belt cities like Houston, Los Angeles, San Antonio, Phoenix, and Tampa grew rapidly while frost belt ones—Buffalo, Detroit, Cleveland, Newark—declined. In 1970, seven of America's ten largest cities were located in the frost belt. In 1981, only four were. The west is now, surprisingly, the most urban region in the country (83.9 percent). Fifth, central cities were much more likely to be habitats for black and hispanic Americans than for the white middle class. And sixth, most of the new manufacturing jobs created in this country in recent years have been generated outside metropolitan areas. These last two bits of data suggest that many of the jobs most likely to be open to the nation's poorest citizens in the upcoming years will be generated far from where they live.

In general, the trend is for continued residential segregation on racial and economic lines—and thus for intergovernmental tension within urban areas—as well as disparities between sun belt and frost belt cities.

Source: U. S. Bureau of the Census, 1975:9–10; *Statistical Abstract of the United States,* 1981; *National Journal,* Nov. 14, 1981:2022.

New York's problems were of its own making. Yet none could really afford to ignore the others. The federal government helped the city over its short-term problems by guaranteeing loans, while also insisting upon strings in the form of city financial reforms and service cutbacks. Thus, the result once again has been increased interdependence.

If the New York case is similar to those in other cities—and there is some evidence to indicate that this is so—it may be that the nation's urban areas face a dilemma in the future. The intergovernmental system has helped to generate an urban prob-

lem, and the American central cities may now have trouble surviving as independent political entities. The solution is by no means clear-cut, and the problem may threaten the vitality of the American intergovernmental system.

Sun Belt and Frost Belt: The New Regionalism

When this land was first settled by the Europeans, they heavily populated what is now the northeastern area. That section of the United States became the center for the population and dominant economic activity in the new nation. New England, the middle Atlantic states, and the heavy manufacturing states of the midwest were the locations into which immigrants moved, where cities grew, and where the nation's voters were concentrated.

Now, it is difficult to remember how very much the country's activities until recently seemed to center on the so-called "frost belt" region. One nonpolitical indicator may be worth mentioning: until 1955, there was not a single major league baseball team whose home was either south or west of St. Louis, Missouri. Now there are ten.

Certainly there have been political tensions between American regions earlier in the nation's existence. The disputes between large states and small over representational guarantees in the Constitution are one example. And the American Civil War remains the bloodiest and most obvious reminder of the intensity of the nation's sectional disputes. However, the political and economic balance of power remained with the frost belt until quite recently. Yet for the past several decades, the geographical center of the nation's population has moved steadily to the south and west.

In the recent past, that movement has accelerated. States constituting the "sun belt" (the old Confederacy through the arid southwest to California) have grown rapidly in population, and much of the increase is due to an influx from the older regions. A greater than proportionate share of new industry (both domestic companies and branches of foreign-owned companies) has located in the sun belt. And of special importance is the fact that a significant segment of the frost belt's industrial base is relocating to the new regions of growth. In a turnabout from former years, the south is the land of growth and opportunity, while the north is becoming a region of economic decline. The example of New York City is again instructive. That city has lost hundreds of thousands of people and jobs from within its borders during the past decade. Hundreds of headquarters of major international corporations have moved elsewhere (Berry and Kasarda, 1977). As the previous section suggested, many of these relocated to the suburbs in New York, New Jersey, and Connecticut. Yet others have left the frost belt altogether.

Why the shift? The reasons are many, and few could have been decisively controlled by any sort of national policy. The south had long been an underdeveloped, undersettled region. Once the nation's transportation system reduced the time and expense of movement, these areas were bound to advance. In addition, the climate and lifestyle have been major attractions. Also, state and local governments in the sun belt have become aggressive in encouraging these political and economic changes. Many states of the sun belt have attracted business and young professionals by offering low tax rates (and, thus, not-as-generous social welfare policies), financial concessions to new enterprises (through devices such as the so-called "industrial development bonds"), and a more antiunion political environment. Some officials of the frost belt have resented these inducements used to weaken their own economy, and a few have tried to compete along similar lines. However, the frost belt cannot compete with one of the major recent advantages of the sun belt: its relative abundance of energy resources (Light, 1978a). While the northeast is heavily reliant on foreign oil or energy produced elsewhere in this country, the sun belt has more ready access to cheaper energy and, in any event, reaps the economic profit from its own resources (see Box 14-7). The energy industry has been largely responsible for the recent prosperity of states like Texas, Louisiana, and Oklahoma, while even places like Alabama find the financial problems of government eased by receipts from offshore oil leases.

Thus sectional competition is once again prominent. Yet there are some significant differences from the conflicts of previous years. As has just been indicated, for instance, the economic roles of the nation's regions are being reversed. In addition, the sun belt is gaining political weight, as wealth and population grow there. For instance, the sun belt gained a substantial number of seats in Congress for the 1980s (Florida added four, while New York lost five), and presidential candidates can afford to focus on the concerns of the growing region.

Perhaps most significantly, the new sectionalism between sun belt and frost belt is gaining ground now in an era of great intergovernmental interdependence, as this chapter has demonstrated. Governments in all regions are now tied by purse strings and policy to Washington. To add to the controversy, the nation may be facing a future of

---

BOX 14-7

REGIONAL COMPETITION ON ENERGY: THE CASE OF THE SEVERANCE TAX

One of the policy topics creating tension across regions of the country is energy. The 1980s are lean times for most American governments. The energy-rich states, located mostly in the south or west, are using this important resource to help raise revenue for their treasuries. In so doing, however, they are creating strained relationships with the rest of the country, particularly the frost belt.

One example of how this regional conflict has developed is the case of the severance tax. A "severance tax" is one placed upon some natural resource extracted ("severed") from a locale. Most states use some severance taxes to generate funds; but by far the most significant severance taxes are those levied on energy resources—coal, gas, and especially oil—in the energy-rich states.

Montana, for instance, imposes a steep 30 percent tax on its coal, and the receipts cover approximately 12 percent of the state's total revenue requirements. The most heavily severance-taxing governments in dollar terms, however, are eight other energy-rich states, all in the south or west: Texas, Louisiana, Alaska, Oklahoma, New Mexico, Kentucky, Florida, and Wyoming. Louisiana uses its taxing power, especially on gas and oil, to cover 23 percent of its budget. Texas raised an enormous $1.5 billion in 1980 from similar sources. And Alaska has benefited from its oil to such an extent that the state has distributed surpluses to its citizens.

The reason these taxes generate such regional conflict is that they are, in effect, imposed by energy-producing states upon consumers or corporations located elsewhere. A calculation of the impact of Alaska's oil severance tax shows that approximately 85 percent of the tax is exported (Northeast-Midwest

Institute, 1981:18). Just *who* pays the tax on energy resources depends upon a number of factors—in some cases, energy-producing firms (like oil companies) pay part; in other cases, consumers (like the residents of the frigid northeast and midwest) subsidize the more advantaged states.

In 1981, the U.S. Supreme Court upheld the constitutionality of state severance taxes, so the political conflict on this intergovernmental issue has shifted to Congress and the president.

Representatives of energy-consuming states are trying to enact legislation imposing a ceiling on such taxes; they threaten retaliatory taxes on goods they produce, should they not be successful. A group of frost belt legislators, the Northeast-Midwest Congressional Coalition, has labeled the energy-producing states the "United American Emirates" in a direct comparison to the middle eastern nations that have taken advantage of American dependence on foreign oil. Even President Reagan's advisers have considered taking energy wealth into account in their plans for reform of the grant system.

However, the energy-rich states have organized themselves in defense of their policies and have used the Western Governors' Policy Office to build support and coordinate among themselves. Representatives from this region argue that they are obligated to tax these resources to help pay the costs of development and to provide help for the future, when the states' bounty is depleted. Montana, for instance, has set up a special fund from severance tax receipts to be used in future years.

Projections are for revenues in the energy-rich states to increase dramatically in the next few years, and the issue is likely to become even more explosive.

Source: New York Times, 1981; Northeast-Midwest Institute, 1981; *National Journal,* Aug. 29, 1981.

---

relatively limited economic growth; the "pie" may not grow as rapidly as in the past, and thus certain governments or regions may benefit only at the expense of others.

This last problem has thrown the national government squarely into the middle of this new sectionalism. Politicians and interest groups all over the country are scrutinizing the federal grant sys-

tem ever more closely. Do the formulas for urban aid favor the frost belt? Do the grants for energy development subsidize the sun belt? Does indirect federal support (e.g., the location of military bases) provide a boon to one region when others need assistance more desperately?

The truth of the matter is difficult to discover. It does appear that federal aid tends to favor—albeit slightly—the sun belt (*National Journal,* Feb. 7, 1981:233–235; Markusen et al., 1981), but *each* region is suspicious of the other and protective of its own interests. In Congress, regional representatives have begun to form coalitions on intergovernmental and regional questions. For instance, those from the frost belt have formed the Northeast-Midwest Congressional Coalition. Groups of legislators now try to redraft funding formulas to benefit their region. State officials do likewise in their own lobbying efforts with Washington. The Coalition of Northeast Governors works for a larger portion of the intergovernmental package, while the Southern Growth Policies Board does the same. And with the federal government's own budget problems having become severe in recent years, the competition between regions is certain to increase.

In fact, the nation's regions and governments have grown so interdependent that the federal government cannot avoid playing some sort of role in the new sectionalism. A decision about deregulating the price of natural gas is perceived by nearly everyone as a pro-sun belt choice, since the resource is located there. A policy to support public mass transportation systems on the basis of how dense a local population center is would be seen as a pro-frost belt option, since the nation's most crowded locales are there. There are even some analysts who now propose that the national government adopt an explicit policy of aiding the shift toward the sun belt (President's Commission, 1980). Once again, then, interdependence is a crucial factor. The national government and the states are now embroiled in a situation such that the fates and political fortunes of each are bound up with the actions of the others. The American intergovernmental system did not create sectional controversy, but the system may make that conflict more intense.

SUMMARY AND CONCLUSION

Since the time of the founders, when the Constitution established a federal system of national and state governments, Americans have struggled with the issues of intergovernmental relations: how our governments deal with each other, which ones have responsibilities and jurisdiction over which sorts of problems, and how conflicts between them are resolved. This general topic bears importantly on almost every contemporary domestic policy problem.

In the earliest years of the republic, the notion of dual federalism dominated national discussion of intergovernmental relations. While there were some instances of federal-state or federal-state-local cooperation, for instance via land grants, the more usual situation was for central and regional authorities to seek independence within their own spheres. The national government's role, especially, was quite limited.

However, the twentieth century has seen the rise of intergovernmental interdependence on a grand scale. The growth of this network was stimulated and nourished by an expanding national government influence following the establishment of an income tax, by the development of a grant-in-aid system and its validation as a legitimate policy tool, and by political pressures—some for national assistance and others for the retention of significant local liberty and regional diversity. The links between levels of American government have been forged over decades, with interdependence particularly accelerated during periods of crisis or unusual policy initiatives such as the New Deal and Great Society years.

Now, in the decade of the 1980s, there are 79,000 American governments. These units are impressively varied. Among local governments, for instance, some, such as the nation's cities and (increasingly) the counties, perform important functions; others, like townships, are generally weak and much less significant. Certain others, like school districts, illustrate the success professionals have sometimes had in removing their activities from more turbulent environments. Finally, the example of special districts demonstrates that seemingly esoteric issues of government structure have real, practical consequences. Now, these governments have become tied together by fiscal, political, and administrative forces made possible, but no less controversial, by the founders' Constitutional framework.

Today, the American intergovernmental system does continue to preserve areas of regional independence. And on issues from education to law enforcement, the pattern of plural decision making among the levels does provide substantial opportunities for access to public decision making. Yet the current network of interdependence has not developed without tensions. The national government possesses certain bargaining advantages because of its centrality in terms of revenue and structure. Washington can and does influence greatly the choices of other levels of government—to the extent that these have even joined in the process of lobbying in the nation's capital. The contemporary intergovernmental system also gives some cause for unease, since it helps to diffuse responsibility about public decisions and sometimes fosters great administrative complexity. The concrete problems now facing the United States, such as which responsibilities to locate at various levels of the federal system, what to do about the urban crisis, and how to deal with the new regionalism, demonstrate that the issues of intergovernmental relations are likely to be difficult and enduring.

In this chapter we have described a considerable amount of political controversy, and it is perhaps easy to lose sight of the noteworthy strengths of the American intergovernmental system. Through it, a remarkable number and variety of governments have devised pragmatic approaches to vexing problems. Flexibility, pluralism, and experimentation have sometimes been clearly in evidence, yet the national government has not been powerless to act when politics has so dictated.

Yet there is no denying that the system is currently under challenge. President Reagan and many conservative political activists have sought to remove the national government from the preeminent role it has assumed at the center of the intergovernmental web. The idea of states and localities making their decisions freely, without the "intrusion" of Washington, may be attractive to some. Yet such a move would be no cure-all. States are capable of making poor decisions too—as is obvious from the issue of civil rights. The nonnational governments *do* find advice and support from Washington useful—all those intergovernmental programs were created because there was real political demand at other levels for them. And, as the preceding section has demonstrated, the national government cannot choose to avoid interdependence with the other units. The feds will inevitably be part of the problem or part of the solution. It is far from clear how to extricate the national government from its current responsibilities, or which

tasks should be turned over to other governments. In fact, some are suggesting today that allocating tasks to their "proper" level of government might mean *increased* responsibilities on the national scene in fields like welfare or medical care.

This is not to say that all change is impossible or undesirable. Nor is it to make light of the considerable problems faced by *all* American governments as they deal with each other. It is to say that the challenge of how to run a compound republic in an era of interdependence will be a major constitutional issue occupying citizens and political leaders in the years ahead.

SOURCES

Advisory Commission on Intergovernmental Relations (ACIR): *The Federal Role in the Federal System: The Dynamics of Growth—A Crisis of Confidence and Competence,* Report A-77, July 1980a.

————: *The Federal Role in the Federal System: The Dynamics of Growth—The Federal Role in Local Fire Protection,* Report A-85, October 1980b.

————: *Central City–Suburban Fiscal Disparity and City Distress, 1977,* Report M-119, December 1980c.

————: *The Federal Role in the Federal System: The Dynamics of Growth—Intergovernmentalizing the Classroom: Federal Involvement in Elementary and Secondary Education,* Report A-81, March 1981a.

————: *Significant Features of Fiscal Federalism, 1980–81 Edition,* Report M-132, December 1981b.

————: *Changing Public Attitudes on Governments and Taxes,* Report S-11, 1982.

Bailey, Stephen K., and Edith K. Mosher: *ESEA: The Office of Education Administers a Law,* Syracuse University Press, Syracuse, N.Y., 1968.

Beer, Samuel H.: "The Adoption of General Revenue Sharing," *Public Policy,* vol. 24, no. 2, 1976, pp. 127–195.

————: "Federalism, Nationalism and Democracy in America," *American Political Science Review,* vol. 72, no. 1, 1978, pp. 9–21.

Berry, Brian J. L., and John D. Kasarda: *Contemporary Urban Ecology,* Macmillan, New York, 1977.

Bresnick, David: "The Federal Educational Policy System: Enacting and Revising Title I," *Western Political Quarterly,* vol. 32, no. 2, 1979, pp. 189–202.

Bunce, Harold L.: "The Community Development

Block Grant Formula: An Evaluation," *Urban Affairs Quarterly*, vol. 14, no. 4, 1979, pp. 443–464.

Caputo, David A., and Richard L. Cole: *Urban Politics and Decentralization: The Case of General Revenue Sharing*, Heath, Lexington, Mass., 1974.

———: *Revenue Sharing*, Heath, Lexington, Mass., 1976.

Caro, Robert A.: *The Power Broker*, Knopf, New York, 1974.

Carroll, James D., and Richard W. Campbell (eds.): *Intergovernmental Administration*, Maxwell School of Citizenship and Public Affairs, Syracuse University, Syracuse, N.Y., 1976.

Colman, William G.: *Cities, Suburbs, and States*, Free Press, New York, 1975.

Commission on Intergovernmental Relations (Kestenbaum Commission): The *Final Report of the Commission on Intergovernmental Relations*, 84th Cong., 1st Sess., House doc. 198, U.S. Government Printing Office, Washington, D.C., 1955.

Davis, S. Rufus: *The Federal Principle: A Journey through Time in Quest of Meaning*, University of California Press, Berkeley, 1978.

Derthick, Martha: *The Influence of Federal Grants*, Harvard University Press, Cambridge, Mass., 1970.

———: "Professional Fiefdoms Appraised: The Case of Social Services," *Publius*, vol. 6, no. 2, 1976, pp. 121–134.

Doherty, J. C.: "Problems with 'The Feds': An Overview," *Small Town*, July 1978, pp. 4–9.

Doolittle, Fred: "Auditing Disputes in Federal Grant Programs: The Case of AFDC," *Public Administration Review*, vol. 41, no. 4, 1981, pp. 430–436.

Dye, Thomas R., and Thomas L. Hurley: "The Responsiveness of Federal and State Governments to Urban Problems," *Journal of Politics*, vol. 40, no. 1, 1978, pp. 196–207.

Elazar, Daniel J.: *The American Partnership: Intergovernmental Cooperation in the Nineteenth Century*, University of Chicago Press, Chicago, 1962.

———: *American Federalism: A View from the States*, 2d ed., Thomas Y. Crowell, New York, 1972.

Farkas, Suzanne: *Urban Lobbying: Mayors in the Federal Arena*, New York University Press, New York, 1971.

Frieden, Bernard J., and Marshall Kaplan: *The Politics of Neglect: Urban Aid from Model Cities to Revenue Sharing*, M.I.T. Press, Cambridge, Mass., 1975.

Glendening, Parris, and Mavis Mann Reeves: *Pragmatic Federalism*, Palisades, Pacific Palisades, Calif., 1977.

Grodzins, Morton: "The Federal System," in *Goals for Americans: Report of the President's Commission on National Goals and Chapters Submitted for the Consideration of the Commission*, Prentice-Hall, Englewood Cliffs, N.J., 1960.

———: *The American System: A New View of Governments in the United States*, Daniel J. Elazar (ed.), Rand McNally, Chicago, 1966.

Haider, Donald H.: *When Governments Go to Washington*, Free Press, New York, 1974.

Hale, George E., and Marian Lief Palley: *The Politics of Federal Grants*, Congressional Quarterly Press, Washington, D.C., 1981.

Landau, Martin: "Federalism, Redundancy and System Reliability," *Publius*, vol. 3, no. 2, 1973, pp. 173–196.

Light, Alfred R.: "Drawing the Wagons into a Circle: Sectionalism and Energy Politics," *Publius*, vol. 8, no. 1, 1978a, pp. 21–37.

———: "Intergovernmental Sources of Innovation in State Administration," *American Politics Quarterly*, vol. 6, no. 2, 1978b, pp. 147–166.

Long, Norton E.: "Federalism and Reverse Incentives: What Is Needed for a Workable Theory or Reorganization for Cities?" *Publius*, vol. 8, no. 2, 1978, pp. 77–98.

Lovell, Catherine H.: *Federal and State Mandating on Local Governments: Exploration of Issues and Impacts*, final report to the National Science Foundation, June 20, 1979.

——— and Charles Tobin: "The Mandate Issue," *Public Administration Review*, vol. 41, no. 3, 1981, pp. 318–331.

Markusen, Ann R., Annalee Saxenian, and Marc A. Weiss: "Who Benefits from Intergovernmental Transfers?" *Publius*, vol. 11, no. 1, 1981, pp. 5–36.

McLean, Joseph E.: "Politics Is What You Make It," *Public Affairs Pamphlet No. 181*, Public Affairs Press, Washington, D.C., 1952.

Moynihan, Daniel P.: *Maximum Feasible Misunderstanding: Community Action and the War on Poverty*, Basic Books, New York, 1969.

Murphy, Jerome T.: "The Education Bureaucracies Implement Novel Policy: The Politics of Title I of ESEA, 1965–1972," in Allan P. Sindler (ed.), *Policy and Politics in America*, Little, Brown, Boston, 1973.

Nathan, Richard P., et al.: *Monitoring Revenue Sharing,* Brookings Institution, Washington, D.C., 1975.

————: *Revenue Sharing: The Second Round,* Brookings Institution, Washington, D.C., 1977.

National Journal, Jan. 4, 1981.

————, Feb. 7, 1981.

————, Aug. 29, 1981.

————, Sept. 6, 1981.

————, Nov. 14, 1981.

————, Aug. 7, 1982.

New York Times, Oct. 15, 1981.

Northeast-Midwest Institute: *The United American Emirates: State Revenues from Non-Renewable Energy Resources,* Washington, D.C., June 1981.

Ostrom, Eleanor: "Size and Performance in a Federal System," *Publius,* vol. 6, no. 2, 1976, pp. 33–73.

Perry, David C., and Alfred J. Watkins (eds.): *The Rise of the Sunbelt Cities,* Sage, Beverly Hills, Calif., 1977.

President's Commission for a National Agenda for the Eighties: *Urban America in the Eighties: Perspectives and Prospects,* Washington, D.C., 1980.

Pressman, Jeffrey L.: *Federal Programs and City Politics,* University of California Press, Berkeley, 1975.

Reeves, Mavis Mann, and Parris N. Glendening: "Areal Federalism and Public Opinion," *Publius,* vol. 6, no. 2, 1976, pp. 135–167.

Rich, Michael J.: "Hitting the Target: The Distributional Impacts of the Urban Development Action Grant Program," *Urban Affairs Quarterly,* vol. 17, no. 3, 1982, pp. 285–301.

Robins, Leonard: "The Impact of Converting Categorical into Block Grants: The Lessons from the 314(d) Block Grant in the Partnership for Health Act," *Publius,* vol. 6, no. 1, 1976, pp. 49–70.

Saltzstein, Alan L.: "Federal Categorical Aid to Cities: Who Needs It versus Who Wants It," *Western Political Quarterly,* vol. 30, no. 3, 1977, pp. 377–383.

Scheiber, Harry N.: *The Condition of American Federalism: An Historian's View,* submitted by the Committee on Government Operations, Subcommittee on Intergovernmental Relations, U.S. Senate, 89th Cong., 2d Sess., Oct. 15, 1966.

Statistical Abstract of the United States, 1981, U.S. Bureau of the Census, Washington, D.C., 1981.

Stein, Robert M.: "Federal Categorical Aid: Equalization and the Application Process," *Western Political Quarterly,* vol. 32, no. 4, 1979, pp. 396–408.

————: "The Allocation of Federal Aid Monies: The Synthesis of Demand-Side and Supply-Side Explanations," *American Political Science Review,* vol. 75, no. 2, 1981, pp. 334–343.

Stenberg, Carl W., and David B. Walker: "The Block Grant: Lessons from Two Early Experiments," *Publius,* vol. 7, no. 2, 1977, pp. 31–60.

Thompson, Dennis F.: "Moral Responsibility of Public Officials: The Problem of Many Hands," *American Political Science Review,* vol. 74, no. 4, 1980, pp. 905–916.

Torrence, Susan W.: *Grass Roots Government,* Luce, Washington, D.C., 1974.

U.S. Bureau of the Census: *Historical Statistics of the United States: Historical Times to 1970,* vols. 1, 2, U.S. Government Printing Office, Washington, D.C., 1975.

————: *1977 Census of Governments,* U.S. Government Printing Office, Washington, D.C., 1977.

Walker, David B.: *Toward a Functioning Federalism,* Winthrop, Cambridge, Mass., 1981.

Weekly Compilation of Presidential Documents, Jan. 26, 1981.

Welch, Susan, and Kay Thompson: "The Impact of Federal Incentives on State Policy Innovation," *American Journal of Political Science,* vol. 24, no. 4, 1980, pp. 715–729.

Williamson, Richard S.: *Federalism in Perspective: A Republican Monograph,* Washington, D.C., June 1982.

Wood, Robert: "Suburban Politics and Policies: Retrospect and Prospect," *Polity,* vol. 51, no. 1, 1975, pp. 45–52.

Wright, Deil S.: *Understanding Intergovernmental Relations,* Wadsworth, Belmont, Calif., 1978.

————: *Understanding Intergovernmental Relations,* 2d ed., Brooks/Cole, Monterey, Calif., 1982.

RECOMMENDED READINGS

Advisory Commission on Intergovernmental Relations: *The Federal Role in the Federal System: The Dynamics of Growth—A Crisis of Confidence and Competence,* Report A-77, July 1980. Provides considerable commentary and much data on the contemporary intergovernmental system and its development.

Derthick, Martha: *The Influence of Federal Grants,*

Harvard University Press, Cambridge, Mass., 1970. One of the best case studies of intergovernmental negotiation, especially between bureaucracies.

Elazar, Daniel J.: *The American Partnership: Intergovernmental Cooperation in the Nineteenth Century,* University of Chicago Press, Chicago, 1962. Excellent historical examination of intergovernmental cooperation in the federal system.

Hale, George E., and Marian Lief Palley: *The Politics of Federal Grants,* Congressional Quarterly Press, Washington, D.C., 1981. A competent discussion of the political dimension of today's grant system.

National Journal. Articles in this periodical contain some of the best reportorial coverage of current developments.

Walker, David B.: *Toward a Functioning Federalism,* Winthrop, Cambridge, Mass., 1981. A well-argued, well-documented book on the ways in which the American system is "overloaded" with interdependence.

Wright, Deil S.: *Understanding Intergovernmental Relations,* 2d ed., Brooks/Cole, Monterey, Calif., 1982. Perhaps the most complete text on the varied aspects of intergovernmental relations.

Part Four

The Policy Process

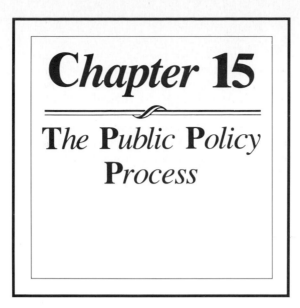

Chapter 15
The Public Policy Process

CHAPTER CONTENTS

Washington, D.C., it is said, is a one-industry town. It often seems as though virtually everyone in the nation's capital is always engaged in politics. Of course, this is not really the case. Thousands of Washingtonians expend their energies on the sorts of pursuits that occupy most other Americans. Yet it would be a mistake to think that so many are so deeply involved in political activity merely because it is fun, or merely because they feel an insatiable lust for power or a detached sense of duty. Rather, it is *policy* that stimulates their interests. People in Washington care about what the government does, or doesn't do.

But almost all of us share these concerns. Whereas few Americans care about all policies, almost all are interested in some policies. Should the price of gasoline be fixed by government regulation or allowed to fluctuate in the market? Should the nation require registration of the handguns owned by its citizens? Should abortions be treated by the state as a deplorable crime or an acceptable medical practice? What should be the nation's responsibility toward the children of the poorest families in the United States? Should 18- and 19-year-olds be required to make themselves available for drafting by the United States armed forces? What should the nation do about the fact that millions of aliens have obtained illegal entry into this country in recent years? These questions, and a multitude of others, constitute the stuff of policy.

Officials in the nation's capital may seem especially influential because they are more deeply involved in the *policymaking process* than most other individuals. Yet if democratic government is to be more than an empty symbol, the views, preferences, even demands of ordinary citizens must somehow be made a part of that process. What is the government's policymaking process, and how closely does it approach the democratic ideal?

In this chapter, we shall investigate these crucial questions about the process by which American policy is made. The focus will be on *how* policy is created, rather than on a survey of what the substance of American policy actually *is*. In Chapters 16, 17, and 18, we shall examine the contents of three varieties of American public policy: social welfare policy, policy on civil rights and civil liberties, and foreign policy. Of course, this neat division of labor is somewhat artificial. First, one

cannot discuss how a policy is made without explaining something of what the policy is all about. Thus, this chapter is full of concrete illustrations. And second, to some degree at least, the process of policymaking is shaped by what kind of policy is being considered. Therefore, here it will be useful to devote some thought to a few of the different kinds of policies enacted in this country. Nevertheless, it is worth remembering that the emphasis is on the policymaking *process,* with special attention to how that process rates if one judges it by the standard of democracy.

THE IMPORTANCE OF THE POLICYMAKING PROCESS

Concern about the American policymaking process is pressing today, when so many worry whether the government can meet the severe challenges it faces in the years ahead. Can the nation resolve its energy crisis? What role should United States foreign policy play in the interdependent world of tomorrow? Can the United States do anything to reduce the chances of nuclear annihilation? How can the country deal with its growing number of needy elderly citizens when economic considerations limit the total wealth available to all Americans? These are very timely and practical issues. Yet concerns about the policymaking process were also important to the nation's founders 200 years ago. They were faced with the problem of designing a new government capable of making policy about a host of matters that were, for that era, also timely and practical.

A glance at the Constitution reveals little of the founders' interests in specific policy issues, for that document was designed to provide some general structure to the process—the founders, that is, addressed the constitutional question of who governs. Yet a look at the Declaration of Independence, written eleven years earlier, suggests that numerous policy disputes provided a backdrop during the period. The revolutionaries affixing their signatures to the Declaration complained there about several policies imposed upon them by King George III of Great Britain—policies on taxation and international trade, for instance. They even charged that the king had stimulated attacks by the "merciless Indian Savages, whose known rule of warfare is an undistinguished destruction of all ages, sexes, and conditions"! One need not agree with the signers of the Declaration on this issue to recognize that policy problems were no less a matter of concern 200 years ago than they are now.

The Constitution established a framework that directly affects how policy matters are handled in the United States. In our discussions of government institutions, such as the judiciary, and their interaction (relations between Congress and the presidency), we have dealt with important elements of the policymaking process. Yet the institutions constructed through the Constitution are not the only participants in the process. Political parties, interest groups, the media, and others play important roles. In nearly every section of this book, we have discussed and referred to specific policies and the policymaking process. However, examination of the parts in isolation from each other is not enough to gain an understanding of how the whole operation works. Studying *only* the institutions and the segments of the policymaking process can convey a sense of unreality about the dynamics of American government. For example, the strategies, tactics, and behavior of policymakers like the president are linked inextricably to the actions of other people and institutions in the process.

The point is analogous to learning about football. One can absorb the rules and the characteristics of each position, but until one sees how all the players function together, one is unlikely to understand much about the real game. The comparison should not be taken too far. There are important differences between making policy and playing football, of course—for instance, policymakers (say, the president and the bureaucracy) may not even agree on where they should be going; football players on the same team usually have the same goal in mind.

Since we have said so much about the importance of the policymaking process, and discussed much of this topic earlier in this book, it may seem unnecessary to explain what public policy is. Doesn't everyone understand what constitutes public policy? Policies are decisions about what to do. Yet the nature of public policy is not always so obvious. A series of examples should demonstrate the real complexity of this issue and provide a useful

way to begin thinking about the policymaking process.

WHAT IS PUBLIC POLICY?

If policies are decisions about what to do, what are *public* policies? One is tempted to think that these are decisions that affect the people at large, for example, a choice to wage war. Yet in the United States there are numerous important decisions that affect many people but that we might not want to consider public policy. If General Electric decides to close a manufacturing plant in a small town, that choice has a dramatic effect on the citizens of the community, but the choice is in private hands. In recent years, options selected by major oil companies in this country about how to invest their money, where to drill for new oil, and how much heating oil to produce have touched everyone's lives—probably more directly than the policies of many government agencies. But are these public policies (Nadel, 1975; Dye, 1978)?

In this book and in most other places, the notion of public policy refers to decisions of the government. Therefore, choices by oil companies are not included. It is important to notice that private decisions like oil companies' investment options are partially defined and directed by public policy. (The government could give tax breaks to Arco and Mobil on condition that they invest their profits in energy exploration and production.) Yet even so, in this country a significant proportion of the decisions that affect the public are private decisions, not public policy. This is so by design of the founders, who sought to protect freedom by limiting the scope of government involvement in the lives of the people. Thus, a constitutional choice has been made that the government does not exercise all the power in this nation, and we do not seek here to explain all exercise of power in the country.

Of course, there are many who argue for an expanded role for the government in influencing decisions now in private hands, and thus seek to reopen one of the important constitutional questions we mentioned in Chapter 1. Following the energy crisis that was initiated, at least symbolically, by the Arab oil embargo in 1973, critics of the industry argued that the United States should nationalize the oil companies so that energy production and

The sudden shortages of gasoline in 1973 and 1978 stirred many Americans to demand government action—but while some people clamored for more government control of the oil industry, others urged the government to free the industry from price controls. *(Jim Pozarlik/Liaison/Gamma)*

related decisions would be made by the government, not by greedy corporations. Meanwhile, economic conservatives suggested that one major cause of the nation's energy mess was too much government involvement—for example, by helping to keep the price of gasoline artificially low. They proposed turning more of these decisions over to the private hands of the industry. No one ever argued that these matters did not *affect* the public, but the debate was whether energy decisions should be in public (that is, government) hands.

Critics of American society or the American form of government sometimes claim that public decisions on important matters are controlled by big business or some other elite group, so that public policy is really made in private locations—corporate boardrooms, country clubs, and such—with the public officials then carrying out the bidding of the private elite. The general criticism, then, is that

public policy is directed by private hands and inaccessible to influence by the whole citizenry. We return to this issue later, when we consider various interpretations of the policymaking process.

Intentions versus Practice

Sometimes the government enacts a policy, and everything proceeds smoothly: the bureaucracy carries out the decision with little muss or fuss, and the outcome is just about what had been anticipated. If we simplify somewhat, the Voting Rights Act of 1965 is such a case. The federal government enacted a law the intent of which was to make sure citizens could exercise their basic right to vote. The policy was aimed primarily at eliminating discrimination against black voters, who had been intimidated and challenged by a variety of methods—including literacy tests, fraud, and gerrymandered election districts—when they sought to vote in many locations in the south (see Chapter 17, on American civil rights policy). In certain areas, federal marshals were to be used to enforce the provisions of the new law. After passage of the statute, the Justice Department began to execute its provisions, and by virtually any measure the results soon met the expectations of those who framed the act. Black registration and voting dramatically increased by hundreds of thousands within months. In some deep south states the change was even clearer. Mississippi went from having 7 percent of its blacks registered before the act to 61 percent by 1967. Today, blacks register and vote at a rate somewhat lower than that of white citizens (Rodgers and Bullock, 1972; Verba and Nie, 1972). Yet participation of blacks is much closer to that of whites than it was previously, and this change is one factor responsible for a dramatic increase in the number of black elected officials, especially in the south. The law worked.

Symbolic Policies Often, however, *formal* policies like laws differ from the actual operations of government *in practice*. Occasionally, even those who produce the formal policy have no intention that it be taken seriously or have any really direct effect on the world. The Humphrey-Hawkins bill, passed by Congress and signed by President Carter in 1978, is a good example. The law, which is still in force, proclaimed that it was the government's intention to reduce unemployment in this country to a level at or below 4 percent of the work force by 1983 and to lower the inflation rate to 3 percent in 1983 and to zero by 1988. Yet in its final version the law provided no real mechanism by which these goals could actually be accomplished, partially because there was no agreement on what would work. Furthermore, it is clear from the process by which the law was enacted that, once the president's signature made the policy "official," virtually no one expected much to happen. Policies of this sort may be considered *symbolic policies* (Edelman, 1964).

Implementation Yet even when policymakers really intend to accomplish what their policies state, problems may arise. One can identify at least two general types of reasons why. The first is a problem of *implementation*. Sometimes a policy

says one thing, but those who are charged with carrying it out—the task of implementation—do something else. The bureaucracy is usually given the responsibility for implementing policy, as Chapter 13 demonstrated, but for a variety of reasons it might do nothing, or delay, or do something entirely different from the intentions of the original policymakers.

In the early 1970s, a couple of federal policies—Executive Order 11598, signed by President Nixon on June 16, 1971, and the Vietnam Veterans' Readjustment Assistance Act of 1972—established a program in the Department of Labor, the Vietnam-Era Veterans' Employment Services Program. The idea behind the policy was to help veterans of that time acquire jobs after they were discharged from military service. Employment service agencies of state and local governments, which received funding from the federal government, were supposed to comply with the details of the new mandate. Specifically, for instance, these agencies were directed to reassign staff to specialize in problems of veterans' employment and to give qualified veterans the edge in any job openings of which the offices were informed. Yet the results were much different. Full compliance with the policy would have necessitated major changes in office procedures and costly overhaul of record-keeping systems. As a result, few staff members were reassigned, and nonveterans often were told of job opportunities when veterans were not (U.S. Government Accounting Office, 1974; Montjoy and O'Toole, 1979). There had been a problem of implementation.

Impact A second type of problem could occur, however. Sometimes a policy is established and is implemented as directed, yet the results are not at all what anyone anticipated. In this case, the policy is executed, but it simply does not work. Earlier in this century the first freeways were built in and around the nation's cities. Many policymakers who were responsible for the decision to build had expected that these roadways would reduce traffic congestion. The expressways were completed (that is, the policy was implemented), but the result often seemed to be an *increase* in traffic congestion and pollution. New roads meant that more people bought cars and more car owners drove more often.

When a well-implemented policy does not have the expected result, there is a problem of *impact*.

Some critics of the nation's urban renewal policy of the 1950s and 1960s charge that it too suffered from an impact problem. The policy was designed to improve housing opportunities for the poorest city residents. Yet there is at least some evidence that in practice urban renewal may have *reduced* the number of decent dwellings in the centers of urban areas (Anderson, 1964).

The fact that policies may not meet with success because of either or both of these problems, implementation and impact, should suggest to people some of the complexities of the policy process. Since implementation does not always proceed without a hitch, implementation itself may actually be a key component of the policymaking process. Thus, those who implement policy must be included in the group of policymakers who actually determine what government does. Accordingly, implementation is treated here as one important part of the process of policymaking. If policymakers such as members of Congress, who are chosen by popular election, often have their intentions thwarted when policies are implemented, the policymaking process poses a potential challenge to democratic government.

Furthermore, when policies do not produce the expected impact, this result is evidence that even democratically selected policies could be more carefully designed. In recent decades, the American national government has made some efforts to reduce the likelihood of unanticipated consequences—that is, problems of impact—by incorporating more rational analysis in the process by which public policy is designed. If urban renewal does not improve housing for poor people, are there other policies that might? What are they? These efforts to do *policy analysis* have not always been striking successes, and in any event they frequently pose certain sorts of difficulties for public decision makers. Because of the importance of rationality to the successful achievement of the government's policy goals, the topic of policy analysis receives some attention later in the chapter.

At this point, it is important to understand that the creation of a public policy by no means guarantees the conversion of governmental intention into action. The process of policymaking does not stop with the passage of a law or the announcement of a judicial decision. For government to serve the people, not only must appropriate policies be selected, but they must be implemented properly and achieve the desired results.

Inconsistent Policies

We have just explained that formal policy is sometimes inconsistent with policy in practice. A related problem can be illustrated by the matter of federal policy about tobacco. Tobacco is a crop produced almost solely for use in smoking. One federal policy, the law and appropriations dealing with agricultural subsidies, in effect pays farmers to grow this commodity. Yet another policy of the same government—regulations of the Federal Trade Commission and the Federal Communications Commission, plus some portions of federal law—seeks to discourage the consumption of this product by prohibiting cigarette commercials on radio and television and by requiring that ominous messages ("Warning: The Surgeon General Has Determined That Cigarette Smoking Is Dangerous to Your Health") be prominently displayed on cigarette packages and print advertisements. In both cases the formal policy is consistent with the policy in practice; the problem is that the formal policies themselves are inconsistent. (That is, they are inconsistent unless the real intention of the government is to kill some of its citizens with their full knowledge, which is hardly likely. And even here, there are surely more efficient mechanisms!)

What is public policy on tobacco? It is simply inconsistent, and this is not the only example of inconsistency in public policies. Laws sometimes conflict with each other or with other policies like administrative decisions. Sometimes different actors in the government disagree with each other, and one may try to ignore the other. Presidential impoundment, discussed in Chapter 11, is one illustration of what can happen when the president disagrees with Congress on budgetary decisions. The Supreme Court sometimes concludes that certain public policies (for instance, laws) conflict with the primary policy document, the Constitution (see Chapter 12, on the judiciary). For Constitutional issues, the ability to take the matter to court is a mechanism to enforce consistency. But there remain many policies inconsistent, not with the Constitution, but with each other. To some degree, this fact is a result of the founders' intentional fragmentation of the government via separation of powers. (Checks and balances, such as the Court's ability to rule on Constitutionality, provide a partial remedy.) Yet aside from separation of powers, other features of the American policymaking process encourage disjointed policymaking (Lindblom, 1980). Some of these have been discussed in earlier chapters. For instance, the congressional practice of writing legislation in scores of subcommittees provides ample opportunity for inconsistent policies to be approved even by the most hardworking, but overloaded, lawmakers.

Issues outside the Policy Process: "Nondecisions"

The range of distribution of income for individuals in the United States is very wide, although not so much as in some other nations. The top 20 percent of the population receives seven or eight times as much income as the bottom 20 percent (Lineberry, 1977:212). This basic distribution has remained essentially unchanged for decades. It would be technically possible for the government to enact public policies to reduce dramatically the income disparity. The government has established some programs such as welfare, Medicaid, and food stamps to help the poorest citizens. But it has also set up policies to benefit the most affluent; these include a complicated system of tax breaks and subsidies. Although some radical policy shifts could stimulate a change—dramatic alterations in inheritance law, nationalization of some key industries, sweeping revisions in the income tax code, major new income transfer programs—ideas like these virtually never arise in the nation's policymaking process. Public decision makers, and even many of the poorest citizens in the United States, believe strongly in such ideas as property rights and an individual's freedom to use income however he or she chooses.

Thus some of the most far-reaching options are never even considered in the policy process. Yet the fact that policies are debated only within a relatively narrow range of alternatives without challenging certain basic beliefs about how a society

should operate is very important. This conclusion means that one of the most significant policy choices is the determination of which issues are actually legitimate ones to consider, debate, and decide—and therefore, by implication, which others are so fundamental (such as the sanctity of private property) that they never even make it onto the policy agenda. But these issues may affect policy greatly by limiting the number of alternatives actually considered in the course of decision making. As we saw in Chapter 1, such limitations may give an advantage to those, like the economically privileged, who can exercise power in the private sphere (see the later discussion of the power elite). Thus, the issues that are *not* considered—some political scientists have called them the "nondecisions"— may be as important as, or more important than, the choices a government actually reaches during policymaking (Bachrach and Baratz, 1963). We return to this matter later.

Policies as Guidelines

So far, we have referred to public policies as decisions by the government about what to do. However, it may be useful to identify two kinds of governmental decisions, since not every decision by the government involves the making of policy. When an agent of the federal Drug Enforcement Administration decides to investigate and arrest a suspected narcotics dealer, we do not normally think of that decision as the establishment of a policy; instead, we consider it a decision to apply a policy, already established, to a specific case. Governmental decisions that establish goals, rules, standards, or practices to apply over time to a *series* of actions or cases are public policies. That is, policies are intended to have some general effect and some stability (Jones, 1978).

Once this point has been made, however, it should be qualified a bit. For one thing, it is not always easy to distinguish the making of a policy from a decision to apply it in a specific case. The last section made clear that creating and implementing public policy are closely related.

Also, decisions about certain kinds of cases help to establish far-reaching policy. The courts are the most important example. When the Supreme Court ruled on abortion cases in 1971, policy was

Safety became a public policy when the federal government made automobile manufacturers install seat belts; but only state and local laws and enforcement efforts can persuade people to buckle up.   *(Ford Motor Company)*

set that applied to every woman (and every embryo, at least for the first three months following conception) in all fifty states (Jaffee et al., 1981). The federal courts are prime participants in the policymaking process because as they try to apply the principles of government policy, e.g., the Constitution or a statute, to the facts of a case, they elaborate, clarify, and interpret the principles themselves (Casper, 1976).

Finally, although policies are decisions intended to apply over time to a series of events or cases, this is not to suggest that policies are immutable. Shortly, we shall consider some reasons why a great deal of American public policy changes only slowly and *incrementally,* that is, just a bit at a time. Yet policies do change, sometimes even quickly and abruptly. Just because policies are designed for stability does not mean they must be considered engraved permanently in stone.

The example of policy on abortion is again instructive. The Supreme Court's decision in *Roe v. Wade* was a clear, if controversial, interpretation of

the Constitution. The result squared with the views of many millions of Americans who had been in favor of allowing the practice of abortion under at least some circumstances. Yet there were also a large number of citizens who were unhappy with the Court's decision, and they were able to prevent the use of public funds for abortions in certain instances. This example illustrates that even an authoritative decision by the branch of American government that is least politically responsive can be narrowed or attenuated under the onslaught of an active and sizable political coalition. Public policies may be designed for stability, but they are often susceptible to change.

So far, we have raised, by way of examples, a number of questions about what public policy really is. By thinking about what constitutes policy, we are alerted to several important facts of life about government. First, public policymaking is important, but so are many private decisions. Second, there is often much more—or less—to policy than the formal documents and statements produced by government leaders: the process of policymaking begins long before votes are taken or the flowery language of legislative debate or judicial opinion is drafted, and that process continues far past the signing of laws or the publishing of regulations. American public policy is not a neat, consistent set of rules, but, rather, a complex, shifting, partially contradictory amalgam of choices. Furthermore, knowledge of the policymaking process can help people determine whether government decision making comports with the standard of democracy.

Another important conclusion, moreover, can be drawn. We have seen that there is not simply *one* process by which policy is made in American government; there are *many* policymaking processes. Indeed, this lesson emerges from nearly every chapter of this book. Therefore, it is not possible here to provide a neat description or explanation of how every single policy is set by the government. One must be content with a general outline of the different steps, or stages, which tend to occur when government makes policy. In this chapter, we shall outline such a description and illustrate the policymaking process with numerous examples. Before we focus systematically on the step-by-step business of policymaking, however, another issue should be addressed. What is the best sort of explanation for how policy is made?

DIFFERENT VIEWS OF POLICYMAKING

Sometimes people believe that what government decides to do is not very important, that public policy makes little or no difference in the everyday lives of individuals. The policies used already to illustrate various points—for instance, public decisions about abortion—clearly demonstrate, however, the importance of policy for average citizens. In fact, policies have effects on people in countless ways. The very definition of what people can treat as their own property—whether a plot of land, an automobile, or even a slave—is a matter of public policy. Government influences the level and type of economic activity in the society; plays a part in determining how secure citizens are from threats to the public safety or threats from abroad; affects the distribution of opportunities to individuals and organizations through directives, sanctions, and rewards; and allocates some of the burden of these tasks through the tax system.

Thus, it is very important that we come to grips with how policy is established. Chapter 1 in this book raises this issue by mentioning four models that have been used to try to explain who governs in this country. In the earlier chapters we have covered the various institutions and participants in the policy process. It is now time to return to the question of who governs.

The preceding chapters show conclusively that public policy emerges from American governmental *institutions*. These exercise some independence, but they are also affected by other influences. Who or what affects the decisions of the institutions? That is, who is really in charge?

One model, the bureaucratic model of governance, asserts that it is really the administrative apparatus that is in control. The evidence discussed in this book, especially in Chapter 13, on the bureaucracy, does show that for certain decisions the bureaucracy seems to direct policy. Yet that institution, we have seen, is not completely autonomous and is subject to a variety of outside influences. The bureaucratic model tells only a small part of the story.

The other models—elitism, majoritarianism,

and pluralism—do not claim that a single governmental institution holds the reins of power. They are thus a little more difficult to summarize and evaluate. All three help to make sense of the American public policy process, although none is completely satisfactory.

A Power Elite?

What can we conclude about the elitist perspective? The first comment that should be made is that political scientists still disagree vigorously among themselves about how convincing the elitist model is, or the majoritarian or the pluralist model, for that matter (Zuckerman, 1977). Even those who spend their professional lives studying this question are often not certain of the answer. The most we can do here is make you aware of some of the factors and evidence to be considered in analyzing this important issue.

The less significant version of the elitist model (Chapter 1) is the milder one. This view holds that there is a core of highly educated, well-positioned people who have the right credentials and get to make the important decisions. This book has shown that in this sense, at least, there *is* an elite of policymakers. In some policy arenas, this group is unusually well-defined. For instance, Chapter 18, on American foreign policy, discusses the foreign policy "establishment."

If there are policymaking elites, the more significant questions relate to whether these elites are cohesive, whether they are subject to influences by others, and whether they make decisions in the public interest or not. The stricter version of the elitist model raises these concerns.

Karl Marx, the famous German philosopher of the nineteenth century whose ideas about power and politics have proved so influential, argued that in places like the United States, economic power determines political power. Those who own the capital, the money and businesses necessary for production, make sure that on important matters their interests are served.

Marx's analysis was powerful, and Marx was not alone in his belief. An American sociologist of the twentieth century, C. Wright Mills, studied the exercise of influence in this country's public life and concluded that a *power elite,* as he put it, controlled things (Mills, 1956). Mills's claim was that the members of this group, a relatively small number of high-level military leaders, politicians, and business executives, had similar backgrounds and made all the key decisions similarly—they were cohesive and functioned as a single elite even if they did not actually sit down together and develop a "party line." Furthermore, said Mills, this power elite in the United States made decisions in their own interests, not the public's. Many other analysts find this stricter version of the elitist perspective persuasive (Domhoff, 1967; Miliband, 1969; Prewitt and Stone, 1973). And several bits of evidence help to make it so.

For one thing, the "nondecisions" of American policy, discussed earlier, do assist the nation's powerful economic interests in maintaining their influence—since many important subjects are excluded from public deliberation.

Also, social scientists *have* been able to demonstrate that there seems to be a significant concentration of power in the hands of a fairly small group of people. One study concluded that just a few thousand people control about half of the nation's resources (Dye, 1979).

Furthermore, the economy and economic power are important influences on the policymaking process itself. Economic factors are significant in policymaking for various reasons (Dawson and Robinson, 1963; Sharkansky and Hofferbert, 1972; Hofferbert, 1974; Lewis-Beck, 1977; Salamon and Siegfried, 1977; Mazmanian and Sabatier, 1980). First, in the most general sense, the level of economic activity helps to determine the size of government and the sorts of policy problems requiring resolution. Only in a United States so affluent that there is a television in nearly every home, for instance, does the matter of cable TV become a public issue. Second, as a body of interest groups, the economically strong have significant advantages. This observation was made even as long ago as the time of the founders. As Chapter 8, on interest groups, indicated, Madison himself took note of the special strength of economic forces. The most prominent leaders of the American business community possess impressive resources which help them be heard in the policymaking process. They are invariably well-organized, and their wealth allows them to lobby and stay abreast of decision

making in Washington with an effectiveness that most other interests, such as organized labor, envy. The funding devoted by the business sector to representing its interests in the nation's capital (see Box 15-1) dwarfs that spent by any other portion of the society (Adamany and Agree, 1975). Third, as one political scientist has noted, businesses occupy a special position which gives them leverage over policymaking (Lindblom, 1977). A productive economy is absolutely essential for American society, but in a capitalist system the government cannot order that private businesses be established and manufacture their products. Instead, government is put in the position of creating a climate congenial enough (and potentially profitable enough) that people or corporations will risk their capital toward the generation of some good or service. If Washington does not make life reasonably comfortable for the business sector, the economy dies. This fact, the indispensability of business to the society, gives the economically privileged political clout as well. Of course, business leaders exaggerate their hardships and frequently "cry wolf" about the anticipated effects of certain policies considered by government. And government officials, on the other hand, may often discount the dire projections of business executives, who are hardly the most impartial evaluators of their own circumstances. Nevertheless, when all is said and done, government and the society cannot do without business; the economic rewards must be sufficiently great to induce participation.

Reaching this conclusion helps one to make sense of the government's policies regarding the treatment of the American automobile industry in recent years. In 1980, after much consideration, federal policy provided loan guarantees at the level of $1.5 billion to the financially troubled Chrysler Corporation. Policymakers decided that without assistance Chrysler was likely to collapse, and the thought of this alternative and its effect on the nation's economic and social well-being was too drastic to contemplate. By 1982, the nation was in a recession, and all the American auto companies experienced declining sales, millions of dollars in losses, and massive layoffs at their manufacturing plants. The federal government, which had already limited Japanese imports, began to consider seriously policy shifts which would wipe out or delay

---

BOX 15-1

LOBBYING AND SPENDING BY INTEREST GROUPS

There are thousands of organized groups pushing various causes in Washington. While labor, the poor, and single-issue groups like the religious right, the environmentalists, and the gun lobby have units backing their interests, these are overwhelmed in expenditures, organization, and staff by business.

One way to see this point is by looking at the political action committees, or PACs, set up by interests to assist various candidates for election. By 1981, organized labor had established 303 PACs, while there were 1,251 corporate PACs. Some labor PACs, like those created by the auto workers, the steelworkers, and the machinists, were very large and well-financed; but spending by realtors, insurers, and other business groups surpassed that by any other interest. Dow Chemical Company alone had eight PACS and spent several hundred thousand dollars in the 1980 elections.

Even groups of small businesses are fairly well represented in the policy process, by organizations like the National Federation of Independent Business, which has spent approximately $500,000 in recent years on its lobbying activities. The group maintains an office staff of twenty in Washington.

The financial industry is a good example of a very well organized and supported industrial group. Large lobbying outfits like the American Bankers Association, the U.S. League of Savings Associations, the Credit Union National Association, Inc., and the Mortgage Bankers Association of America are supplemented with many smaller groups plus lobbyists for the largest institutions like Citicorp. This industry alone set up more than 280 PACs in 1980.

Yet any official count or total is an understatement. As one economist observes:

> Corporate funds go to political campaigns and to parties, to lobbying and other forms of corporate communication with government officials, to entertainment and other factors for government officials, to political and institutional advertising in the mass media, to educational materials for the public schools, and to litigation designed to influence governmental policy or its enforcement.

We have no adequate figures on how much of their funds they allocate for these political activities, all of which overwhelm those of ordinary citizens. But there are a million corporations in the United States, 40,000 with at least 100 employees. Each of the largest of them takes in more receipts than most national governments. We also know that American businesses allocate roughly $60 billion per year to sales promotion, a large part of which is institutional advertising with a political content, like Exxon's "Energy for a Strong America." On top of that are additional amounts available explicitly for politics. Hence the scale of corporate spending dwarfs political spending by all other groups.

Source: *Congressional Quarterly*, 1982:42, 114, 127; Weinberger and Greevy, 1982:VII-6; Lindblom, 1977:194–195.

---

regulations about mileage, pollution control, and safety features on American cars. Washington hoped to breathe some life into Detroit.

Finally, it is worth remembering that, even aside from its influence in the public policymaking process, business, as was discussed earlier, is bound to be influential in American society because of its control over so many important *private* decisions, such as creating jobs or establishing patterns of technological development.

Yet it is essential to recognize that there is a big difference between saying that a power elite (such as a group of business executives, perhaps in con-

cert with certain others) controls the policy process (see Box 15-2) and saying that in this process certain interests (such as business) possess significant advantages. In fact, it would be very difficult to support a generalization that any single interest wins on every policy issue, or even on every policy issue it cares greatly about (Dahl, 1961). There are many policies which clearly benefit big business, from tax policy, to various subsidies, to tariff protection. But there are also other policies which work against businesses. If the federal government's relaxation of mileage standards for American cars represents a victory for the industry, the

---

BOX 15-2

AN ELITIST PERSPECTIVE ON POLICYMAKING

Most American leftists argue that policymaking can at present best be understood from the elitist perspective. They say that policy is often made to benefit those who hold concentrated wealth in this capitalist system. Socialists advocate a shift away from this system to weaken control by the economic elite. This perspective is clear in the following excerpt from an editorial in an American socialist newspaper:

We do not see "socialism" as the issue in American politics, but as a set of principles with

which we attempt to understand the issues of the day. We counterpose these principles to the underlying principle of conservative and corporate liberal politicians, which is the protection and promotion of corporate profit. To us, the overriding issue in American public life is . . . corporate capitalism and what its domination of American life means.

A politics that is centered on this issue is socialist if it can counterpose democratic control of investment to the joint conservative and liberal principle, and we see no reason why it can't. . . .

Source: *In These Times*, 1982.

1970 policy requiring pollution control devices on those same vehicles was achieved over the determined opposition of the automobile makers.

Proponents of the elitist model might claim, in response, that these policy shifts were actually controlled by another, more well hidden, elite. Yet this point illustrates one difficulty sometimes encountered when one pushes the elite perspective too far: it becomes too attenuated to disprove (Lineberry, 1977:51).

It is difficult to explain other policies from the power elite perspective. Many chapters of this text contain good examples. Two discussed in detail in later chapters of Part Four are federal civil rights policy (Chapter 17) and the establishment of an American social welfare state (Chapter 16). One further example will suffice here. In 1970, the U.S. Occupational Safety and Health Administration (OSHA) began operations. This agency was created by a new federal policy intended to ensure that there be proper working conditions for those employed in the nation's factories, offices, and farms. The issue was backed by organized labor and opposed by business lobbyists. Once established, OSHA began to do its job with gusto. The unit developed regulations concerning even the most miniscule details of on-the-job safety and health, such as rules about portable toilets at construction sites. Businesses complained bitterly to

Washington, especially through their congressional representatives. Some of the most controversial OSHA regulations were relaxed, but the basic structure and thrust of agency operations continued as before, at least until the years of the Reagan administration, when there were policy shifts. One day, the regulated businesses may succeed in killing OSHA, and the power elite perspective could explain that decision. But it cannot adequately account for the establishment of the policy in the first place, or the vigor with which it was pursued, without resorting to tortured logic. The elitist model thus may help to explain American policymaking, but it does not provide a complete explanation.

Majoritarianism?

If we mean by "pure democracy" a system in which the people determine, directly, the content of public policy, the United States is obviously a far cry from it. This whole book has documented such a conclusion. The framers of the Constitution designed a republic, one in which the views of citizens would at least be filtered through political representatives and complex institutional arrangements, such as those in Congress. Some parts of the nation's policymaking apparatus, like the court system, are intentionally insulated from popular opinion, even through representational channels. It is clear, too, from the discussion of public opinion and political participation in earlier chapters that political activism is quite limited in this country; a huge segment of "the people" do not even vote, and fewer still ever make known their preferences on policy issues to their representatives. Those Americans who participate in the political process are not fully representative of the entire populace. And finally, as was indicated in the preceding section and in Chapter 8, on interest groups, not all who participate carry equal weight.

No one seriously argues that the United States is a pure democracy. But is the model of strict majoritarianism—a system in which the majority of citizens get to control policy—a convincing explanation for policymaking in this country? No. The preceding paragraph, which summarizes many points made in earlier chapters, bolsters this conclusion as well. Yet in some ways the notion of strict majoritarianism often looks like an attractive ideal, especially when one realizes that the current system seems to provide so many ways for a citizen's preferences to go unnoticed. The "linkage" between citizens and policies is so indirect (Luttbeg, 1981) that it might seem preferable to establish some sort of participatory democracy. However, even if we as constitution makers could start from scratch, ignoring the designs of the founders and creating our own system through which policy would be decided, we would not be able to set up a purely majoritarian arrangement. Why not?

First, upon reflection, we might very well not want to. We might, for instance, conclude that certain policy topics (such as freedom of religion, speech, the press, and assembly—the guarantees in the First Amendment to the Constitution) are so deserving of protection that we would not allow a popular majority to tinker with them. But even if we had definitely decided to establish a perfect public opinion democracy, we would not be successful in doing so. Even in a setting in which all citizens are interested in politics and anxious to participate in the establishment of policy, there would always be serious barriers. Two of these are worth brief attention.

For one thing, the number and complexity of policy issues would overwhelm all citizens, even the brightest and most interested ones. Nowadays, even those who labor full time over a few policy matters—the president, members of Congress, lobbyists, bureaucrats, justices—struggle to keep up with their work load. Strict majoritarianism involving widespread participation would mean that people would have time for little but policymaking.

Second, there is no neutral or unbiased way of putting together, or aggregating, individuals' preferences on anything—including policy issues or candidates for office—to decide a collective outcome. Part of the attractiveness sometimes felt for a strict majoritarian system comes from the illusion that if we count everyone's view, we thereby remove bias, since there are then no back-room deals between special interests or bargaining between those who are insiders in the policymaking process. But *all* ways of deciding policies—including voting, with majority rule determining the winner— are biased, not in the sense of being dishonest but rather in the sense that they make some outcomes more likely than others. This concept may be a difficult one to grasp, but Box 15-3 provides a simple illustration of how a seemingly fair and unambiguous voting rule is not neutral toward the policies being decided.

One especially important example of bias in a majoritarian system is the matter of intense minorities versus less intense majorities. A seemingly essential part of the democratic ideal is that a majority should be able to have its way. Another, however, is that those who care the most about a policy (or are the most directly affected by it) should have more of a say than those who hardly care at all. Yet if we set policy by simply allowing people to indicate their preference—through polling, voting, or whatever—and select as policy the most popular option, we shall have counted an intensely held opinion only as much as one expressed by the least interested citizen. An apathetic majority of 51 percent may outweigh a passionate minority of 49 percent. The system is thus biased against taking into account how strongly people feel about things.

It is important to notice here that this sort of problem would occur with any system that we were to establish, since there can be no neutral ones. No democratic system can ever be so pure that it is free from all traces of biases like this one. The whole purpose of constitutions, including the voting rules they establish and the institutions they construct to

---

BOX 15-3

ONE PROBLEM WITH PURE DEMOCRACY

Even if citizens were well-informed and had the time and inclination to make important public decisions directly, there would be no neat, simple way to translate their views into policy. The rules used for collecting their preferences and converting them into a decision can never be neutral. *Any* rules will influence the result.

To illustrate this point, we pose a hypothetical situation. Let us assume that current estimates are that next year's federal budget as presently projected will be in deficit by $100 billion, and the citizens are going to get to decide directly what to do about this fact. Let us further assume, for simplicity's sake, that only three options are being seriously considered by anybody: (1) across-the-board spending cuts to balance the budget; (2) an income tax increase to cover the deficit; or (3) allowing the deficit as projected.

To continue the example, suppose all Americans of voting age had clear opinions on the matter. Their views were as follows:

30% liked option (1) best, and option (2) second-best

30% liked option (2) best, and option (3) second-best

40% liked option (3) best, and option (1) second-best

Thus no alternative would have a majority. To decide policy, suppose we arranged one vote between two of the options, with the winner against the third alternative.

Notice the results. If option (1) were first tested against option (2), the first would win 70% to 30%. In the run-off between (1) and (3), (3) would win 70% to 30%. Thus, it would seem, pure democracy would require enactment of the deficit.

But suppose we had started the contest with (1) versus (3). The latter would have entered the run-off against (2), and *lost*—60% to 40%! Increasing income taxes would seem to be the people's choice.

If the first race had been (2) against (3), with the winner to battle (1), the outcome would be spending cuts, by a 70-to-30 margin. (Can you see why?)

Notice that the outcome changed, despite the fact that people did not change their minds and despite the apparent fairness and neutrality of the rules.

What the public prefers is often not such an easy thing to identify.

Source: Arrow, 1963.

---

take part in the policymaking process, is to structure choices and therefore affect policy outcomes. We have seen in earlier chapters that the United States Constitution does so in many fashions. The president and the Congress not infrequently conflict with each other, for instance, partly because the former was designed to be especially sensitive to crisis situations and problems affecting the whole nation, while the latter was meant to pay closer attention to the concerns of particular regions and interests. This is not to argue, of course, that any given system of policymaking, such as the current American one, could not be made considerably more responsive to the people by various alterations, if they were deemed desirable. The point is rather that it is not mere perversity, ill will, or

ignorance which keeps this country from making public policy through a pure majoritarian arrangement.

Yet this is not to say that majoritarian influences are absent from American policymaking. As the franchise has expanded and elections of president and senators have become more closely tied to the people, majoritarian influence actually has grown. Studies of the correspondence between majority views and public policy produce mixed and complicated findings. Policies at the national and state levels are by no means always in line with public opinion—but majority opinion surely does exert some leverage on policymakers and institutions (Sullivan and O'Connor, 1972; Weber and Schaffer, 1972; Erikson, 1976; Ginsberg, 1976; Edwards and Sharkansky, 1978:20–22). Especially on the most important issues that capture the attention of the citizenry, majoritarian influence can be seen.

The example of the Vietnamese war is sometimes used to support this assertion. For all the controversy about American military involvement in southeast Asia from the 1950s until 1975, and for all of the efforts on the part of American political leaders to direct public opinion on the issue, shifts in majority view seemed to have significantly influenced the options chosen by policymakers (Gelb and Betts, 1979).

Nevertheless, majoritarianism is not entirely satisfactory as an interpretation of American policymaking. There are many decisions of the government that it, too, cannot explain. Although the views of the people are directed in multiple ways to the policymakers, the translation is, at most, indirect. The pluralist perspective helps to account for some of these differences.

Pluralism

A *pluralist system* is one in which power is dispersed among a number of groups in such a fashion that nobody can consistently control the outcomes. In a pluralist arrangement, that is, power is shared, and policymaking is somehow the product of competition, bargaining, and accommodation among those who participate.

As we have seen, one version of a pluralist policymaking process is what many of the founders intended when they designed the American Constitution. As Madison explained it, the idea was to construct this republic so that any "faction," even one to which a *majority* of the people belonged, would have a tough time enacting a policy that worked against the real interests of the public as a whole. The Constitutional provisions for separation of powers (segmenting influence across Congress, the president, and the courts) and for a federal structure (separating national from state power) were conscious attempts to instill pluralism into the policy process.

Public Opinion Yet these institutional arrangements do not wholly encompass the participants in American pluralist policymaking. Public opinion, of course, plays a role, both by selecting representatives and by influencing some of their actions while in office. The importance of public opinion has shifted since the Constitution was first established, so the framers' version of pluralism has been adapted to redistribute the pattern of influence: women and blacks, formerly excluded even from the act of voting, now may participate; and selection of senators and the president is now tied more directly to popular control than the founders had desired. It is useful to notice that both the original framework and the version now in operation are pluralist designs, but today's system includes more participants in the arrangement of shared power—i.e., is a more majoritarian pluralism. Therefore, when one says a system or a policy process is a "pluralist" one, that means that power is shared, not necessarily that *everybody* has a share or that all shares are of equal weight. We return to this point a bit later.

Interest Groups Your study of American government has also included a look at a number of other institutions and groups, unmentioned in the Constitution, that also play some part in the process of policymaking. Some of these were expected by the founders to be active participants. The framers recognized the importance, for instance, of special interests. The "causes of faction," said Madison, "are . . . sown in the nature of man." Interest groups, as Chapter 8 demonstrated, are among the prime actors in the policymaking process. Business organizations may be quite influential, as we have seen. Yet others cannot be discounted when we try to understand how American policy is made. Labor leaders, civic associations, religious and ethnic organizations, and other groups that are coalesced around various causes help to determine the direction of government policy from time to time at least.

The Media The media also play a role by affecting the policy agenda (see below), informing citizens about public issues and events, and shaping opinions in and out of Washington. The founders recognized that a free press could contribute to pluralism by serving as an external check on the use or abuse of official power—they even enhanced its influence by safeguarding its position through the

Bill of Rights. The precise function and importance of the media to the policymaking process may have shifted during the nation's first two centuries, as has been shown earlier. But today's government leaders view the press's influence on policymaking in terms remarkably like those of the earliest leaders. President Reagan, respected and knowledgeable legislators on Capitol Hill, and other officials are sometimes frustrated and angered when the media do not simply serve as conduits for their own interests and perspectives. Yet the Constitutionally established policymakers often recognize that a watchful, even activist, press can help to check the possibility of tyranny. This healthy ambivalence of the government toward the media is just what the framers intended and, in fact, felt themselves. Thomas Jefferson, for example, expressed his distress over the influence exerted by the press in the most extreme terms. "Nothing can now be believed," he said, "which is seen in a newspaper. Truth itself becomes suspicious by being put into that polluted vehicle. . . . The man who never looks into a newspaper is better informed than he who reads them; inasmuch as he who knows nothing is

nearer to truth than he whose mind is filled with falsehoods and errors." Yet in his more tranquil moments, Jefferson was also a forceful defender of the press's position. "Were it left to me to decide whether we should have a government without newspapers, or newspapers without a government," he even asserted, "I should not hesitate a moment to prefer the latter" (Jefferson to John Norvell, June 11, 1827; and to Colonel Edward Carrington, Jan. 16, 1787).

Parties Political parties are one group that a number of the founders had hoped would *not* become a participant in the American political process, as was documented earlier in this book. For a considerable period of time, however, parties exerted important influences over policymaking in this nation, especially by selecting candidates for office. The two major parties were the most important, yet even third parties sometimes served as vehicles for getting public attention focused upon new and controversial policy options. The Socialist party, led by Eugene V. Debs during its most active phase in the early part of this century, was respon-

In the early 1900s, the perennial Socialist party candidate Eugene V. Debs used his campaign speeches to mobilize labor and sway public opinion in favor of such ideas as a minimum wage and a graduated income tax. *(Brown Brothers)*

sible for national discussion and debate about a series of then-novel ideas that have since been enacted into policy: a graduated income tax and a minimum wage, for example. Today, the role of parties in the tasks of policymaking is relatively small. However, Democratic party activists do as a group differ significantly from Republican leaders on many of the issues—considerably more so than do the average party members themselves (see McClosky et al., 1960; Montjoy et al., 1980). To the extent, therefore, that party leaders retain *some* leeway in tasks such as selecting candidates, it is likely that parties too will be a participant, albeit a less important one, in the shaping of public policy.

The Bureaucracy Finally, some key participants in the pluralist process were by and large unanticipated by the founders. The bureaucracy is the most important actor of this type. In the earliest years of American government there was little bureaucracy at all and only slight influence exerted by the few small agencies that did exist. Yet today, bureaucrats outnumber all other principal policymakers combined. And, what is more important, the agencies of the federal government exert especially significant direction over the shape of public policy at many stages of the process.

Pluralism and Democratic Government Policymaking in American government is complex enough and involves such a number of participants that it can often be fairly and accurately explained as a process of pluralism at work. In fact, this has often been the implicit model of policymaking used as a framework throughout this book. How democratic are pluralist systems? How quickly, accurately, and frequently do they translate citizens' preferences into public policies? This important question is not an easy one to answer satisfactorily. A pluralist system is certainly no *guarantee* of democratic government. Pluralism may prevent a single tyrant from monopolizing power. In fact, the founders were more interested in setting up a framework that would prevent tyranny than they were in translating popular opinion into policy. But political systems could disperse power across several participants in a policy process while still excluding significant segments of the public. If the

"big three" automobile manufacturers were to sit down with labor representatives from the United Auto Workers, an adviser to the president, and a few key members of Congress to work out a policy restricting the importation of foreign cars into the country, these actors would not all have the same interests at heart. There would probably be much bargaining and disagreement before any policy achieved consensus. But it would be quite possible for all these participants to reach agreement on a policy which neglected certain interests or conflicted with the views of most citizens (Lowi, 1979). Thus, the pluralist model may still mean that on some issues the bargaining among groups is restricted to a narrow range of options. The competition, that is, may be among elites themselves and may neglect the viewpoint of larger publics (Bachrach, 1967; Walker, 1966).

To put the point more generally, just because a policymaking process is a pluralist one does not necessarily mean that the participants who decide are fully representative of the views or interests of the nation at large.

One of the best actual examples of this point is federal policy on gun control. For years now, virtually every respected opinion poll in the United States has documented an overwhelming majority in favor of stricter control of firearms, especially handguns, possessed by the citizenry. Some people favor banning handguns altogether; others suggest making it more difficult to purchase such weapons quickly, stopping the importation of parts used to make "Saturday night specials," and requiring mandatory jail sentences for those using handguns when committing a crime. The majority favoring controls grows even larger following assassinations or assassination attempts directed against prominent persons, such as President Kennedy, Martin Luther King, Jr., President Ford, John Lennon, and President Reagan. However, federal policy on gun control has not been tightened in years. In fact, among the possible changes in legislation considered by lawmakers in recent years, the ones attracting most legislative support would actually *weaken* existing controls. (One reason is the strength of the American gun lobby, a group discussed again later.) For instance, by 1981 a Proposed Federal Firearms Law Reform Act, which would have reduced federal regulation of firearms, had been backed by President Reagan and cosponsored in Congress by 54 senators and 152 representatives.

Nevertheless, this example and the discussion that preceded it should not be taken to mean that a pluralist policymaking process *necessarily* neglects or ignores the wishes of the general public. The earlier parts of this book document in detail the operations of a pluralist system in which majoritarian influences are in evidence. Yet the elitist model also adds an important perspective missing or underemphasized by the others. The brief analysis in this chapter suggests that no single, simple answer to the question of who governs can cover the entire range of American policymaking.

THE STAGES OF POLICYMAKING

Since there is not just one American policy process but many of them, and since different issues stimulate different actors to involve themselves in diverse ways as public decisions are reached, the task of summarizing just what happens is not straightforward. Nevertheless, despite this complexity, policymaking can be understood as a process which involves a series of distinguishable stages (Anderson, 1979; Dye, 1981; Peters, 1982). We describe them briefly here, in logical order, but you should not forget that the real world is never as neat and orderly as a textbook presentation. As some policies are being executed, others are but gleams in the eyes of policymakers. Certain public decisions are even being undone almost before they are put into place. In American government, policy is made not once and for all but in an unending series of steps.

Setting the Agenda

Policymakers simply cannot consider every issue, or every possible solution to every public problem. In fact, the same set of public problems does not magically appear simultaneously in the minds of all those involved in the policy process. Those issues that actually do get considered and discussed as government sets policy constitute the *agenda* for decision (Cobb and Elder, 1972).

Government sets policy about so many different topics that it is hard sometimes to believe that the government is not making policy about everything at once. Within an average day a typical senator might find it necessary to devote attention to policies about endangered species, an embargo on the sale of arms to Turkey, a torts bill, an authorization for the Department of Housing and Urban Development, a Strategic Arms Limitation Treaty, the complexities of environmental pollution, possible solutions to the problem of juvenile delinquency, the purchase of military hardware, and ideas about how the government might improve the economy. (This list is a partial enumeration of the items on the schedule of Senator John C. Culver during one twenty-four-hour period in the summer of 1978; see Drew, 1979.) Yet many matters are never seriously considered for any government action. What constitutes a public problem worthy of inclusion on the agenda of policymakers is not always clear-cut, so the process by which issues *become* public issues in the first place is an important one.

Government's Capacity to Act Some topics are not included on the agenda of government if there is a general belief that the government is incapable of doing anything, one way or the other, to affect the result. You never hear policymakers discussing whether the federal government should initiate a research program to eliminate the problem of death. Other items never reach the agenda because virtually all participants in the process of policymaking believe that these topics are outside the proper reach of government. These are the nondecisions mentioned early in the chapter. The boundary line identifying what issues might be included on the policy agenda is not a constant, however, and has tended to shift toward the inclusion of more and more issues over time.

There are some exceptions, and the attempts by presidents Carter and Reagan in recent years to deregulate certain issues (for instance, the price of oil) can be seen as an effort to take certain items *off* the public agenda. Also, a favorite strategy of presidents who wish to remove an item from divisive public discussion, at least for a while, is to establish a blue-ribbon presidential commission to study the matter. In the mid-1960s, when urban riots forced the difficult issue of race-related violence onto the agenda, President Lyndon Johnson established such a group, the Kerner Commission, to investigate quietly and thus, perhaps, defuse the issue. Reducing the agenda is almost always a very difficult task for any policymaker, since matters already being discussed or enacted into policy may have well-organized and well-supported backers. On the other hand, a number of factors encourage the inclusion of new items. What are some of these?

The Impact of Ideas Changed ideas can add items to the public agenda. In the nineteenth century, curing poverty was not a policy of the government, because many Americans—including those involved in the policymaking process—thought of poverty as a private hardship or evidence of moral weakness, not as a public problem. During the past couple of generations, however, the notion that government is responsible for ensuring the basic needs of all citizens has become much more widespread. This belief is the cornerstone of a social welfare state, a topic which is discussed in Chapter 16.

Ideas may change slowly, or some stimulus may trigger their alteration. In 1961, the newly elected president, John Kennedy, read a book entitled *The Other America,* by Michael Harrington. The topic of the volume was the great amount of relatively invisible poverty that still existed in the United States. Kennedy was so impressed with the book that he worked to get the poverty issue prominently on the agenda. Harrington's argument, and Kennedy's sponsorship of the issue, quickly stimulated considerable public discussion and, ultimately, some new policy. This example illustrates that ideas can be an extremely important source of items for inclusion on the agenda. Intellectuals, those who study and write about the world and generate creative thoughts, can sometimes have great influence over agenda setting. A book or article can create a receptive audience for an issue. Many ideas for the agenda are generated within the government's bureaucracy, where experts may be experienced at developing ideas and communicating them to others involved in policymaking. Intellectuals at universities and private research units—"think tanks"—have also identified issues and argued successfully for their inclusion on the agenda. Supply-side economics, the approach that formed the basis of President Reagan's major eco-nomic program, was the creation of thinkers such as Professor Arthur Laffer, now of the University of Southern California (see Box 15-4).

Science and Technology In less direct ways, as well, the generation of new knowledge can help set the public agenda. As scientific information grows, technology can develop. More technology means both more problems to deal with and also more capability on the part of government to act. In the late 1970s, when biologists developed the technical capacity to manipulate the genes of living organisms, the problem of whether and how to control this potentially dangerous tool virtually leapt onto the national policy agenda. And when physicists unlocked the secrets of the atom, the idea of nuclear weapons received the secret but immediate attention of the highest military and civilian government officials during World War II. Increased knowledge can also uncover information about unintended consequences of old policies, and thus help give some new items public attention (Wildavsky, 1979b). Policies established earlier this century allowed for the largely unregulated disposal of low-level nuclear waste materials. Yet because decision makers are now aware of some of the potential consequences of this earlier decision, the worrisome problem of long-term damage to the environment is now being considered by those who make policy.

Crises The occurrence of crises or prominent events can sometimes add issues to the agenda in a hurry (Schulman, 1975; 1980). The great depression helped stimulate a new set of policy discussions about the role of government in the economy; the huge oil spill off the coast of Santa Barbara, California, in 1969 gave widespread public attention to the environmental movement; the Arab oil embargo of 1973 was the event that triggered serious discussion of the nation's energy problem. Sometimes such events are utilized as resources by interest groups that have long been struggling to attract the attention of policymakers. Once again, the example of federal gun-control policy provides a useful illustration. In 1968, the assassinations of Martin Luther King and Senator Robert Kennedy within two months of each other shocked and outraged millions of Americans. Gun-control advo-

BOX 15-4

AGENDA SETTING: THE EXAMPLE OF SUPPLY-SIDE ECONOMICS

The field of economic policy is one in which intellectuals have often had influence. Some details of American policy for managing the economy are covered in Chapter 16, which also discusses supply-side economics. Here we will summarize briefly only how this idea arrived prominently on the nation's agenda.

The notion of supply-side economics is that government "ought to strive to influence . . . not demand but supply—not the amount of money that consumers have to spend on goods and services but, rather, the amount of incentive that producers are given to engage in productive enterprise." This idea conflicts with most of the orthodox economic theory taught in the United States, and until recently it was not very popular in government circles either.

In the early 1970s, however, the economies of the United States and other western nations began to face serious difficulties (see Chapter 16). Policymakers began to look for ways of improving economic performance. A few economists, the early supply-side theorists, meanwhile had sketched an alternative.

As early as 1971, at a conference in Bologna, Italy, the Columbia University economist Robert Mundell presented some of his supply-side ideas in preliminary form. Others there were skeptical, but some elsewhere were intrigued. Arthur Laffer, for instance, a young academic on leave from the University of Chicago to work as chief economist in the Office of Management and Budget, was a follower of Mundell and his ideas. Laffer was also in contact with economists such as Norman Ture of the Brookings Institution, who had been working along similar lines. And at the same time,

Jude Wanniski, a columnist for the *National Observer*, met Laffer, and the two developed close ties.

The group of intellectual believers in supply-side theory slowly expanded, and the economy continued to do poorly. In 1974, Laffer, Wanniski, and a White House official of the Ford administration met for cocktails at a Washington restaurant. In an attempt to explain how supply-side economics works, Laffer grabbed a napkin and drew a graph, one now known as the famous "Laffer curve." Wanniski began to publicize it, and the publicity increased as he went, as editor, to the *Wall Street Journal*. The *Journal* became a prime exponent of the theory.

The group noticed in 1977 that a tax-cut bill was being proposed in Congress by Representative Jack Kemp and Senator William Roth. The Kemp-Roth bill basically conformed to supply-side principles. The theory and the bill attracted serious attention. In 1978–1979, following the passage of the tax-cutting Proposition Thirteen in California, Ronald Reagan began to notice. He used supply-side rhetoric in his presidential campaign. Several of his key political appointments shortly after the election went to members of the group. (Ture became an undersecretary of the Treasury, as did Paul Craig Roberts, another core member of the group. David Stockman, a convert to the doctrine, was hired to direct OMB.) The administration backed the Kemp-Roth bill, a slightly modified version of which went into effect October 1, 1981.

Intellectuals, especially in union with attentive and sympathetic media representatives, had had an influence.

Source: Brooks, 1982:96.

cates made use of the tragedies to raise once again the issue of regulation and to push hard for a new law. A few months earlier, very few key policymakers in Congress gave the problem any attention, but the climate had been changed overnight. The Gun Control Act was swiftly approved by Congress. The new policy was not all the proponents had hoped for, but it did impose restrictions on access to handguns; no gun-control laws have been passed since. Gun-control opponents have also

attempted to use crises to influence the policy agenda. During the winter of 1981–1982, when martial law in Poland had captured the attention of Americans, the National Rifle Association (NRA), an anti-gun-control interest group, purchased full-page newspaper ads suggesting that the idea of gun control should stay off the public agenda; Poland, they declared, is a prime example of what could happen if citizens allowed government control over private firearms.

Interest-Group Activity: Multiple Channels
This last example is related to another way in which issues may be added to the policy agenda. Even when no major ideas or technological advances spur consideration of new policy issues, or no crises or prominent events take place, or no massive shifts in beliefs occur, a variety of individuals and interest groups may be trying to attract the attention of policymakers. They are sometimes successful. Depending upon the issue and the political makeup of the proponents, interests may use various routes—with varying degrees of success—to get national attention for their issue. Some of the advantages and disadvantages of several alternatives can be understood if you think about the institutions and processes of American government covered earlier.

The bureaucracy If somebody can interest the bureaucracy in an item, for instance, there are real advantages. Bureaucrats possess expertise and near permanence; they are in a strategic location to raise an issue coherently, impressively, and repeatedly. Even if the immediate political climate is not ripe, bureaucrats may eventually find ways to get attention directed to it. They are, after all, often the ones who help draft the speeches, provide the information, write the legislation, and frame the programs run from Washington. Potential policy ideas may gestate in agencies for years before attracting a wider public.

Congress Congress, particularly the Senate, is another potential channel. In the upper house, the terms are longer, and some members may be looking for issues to use for generating national attention—in recent years senators often have considered the prospect of running for national office. Thus, for example, the idea of national health insurance attracted attention to Senator Edward Kennedy through his chairmanship of the corresponding Senate committee. Because of the decentralized nature of Congress and the importance of committee work in the policy process, the legislature may seem like a particularly attractive route to some group seeking to add to the agenda. If you find a sympathetic committee or subcommittee leader, you may at least be able to initiate hearings on a subject. On the other hand, if an interest gets access to the agenda through a congressional sponsor or committee, there is no guarantee that Congress as a whole will seek resolution of the issue in the group's favor. In a decentralized legislature it is relatively easy to start, but also to halt, the progress of an idea toward policy.

The judicial system The courts may provide particularly attractive access to the policy agenda for some interests if conditions are just right. In general, one needs a strong case—although not necessarily strong political support—to get serious consideration of an issue. Not all issues receive attention by the courts, since the judiciary is reactive. It is basically in the business of validating, interpreting, and making consistent the policies established by the more political organs of government; the courts do not venture into entirely new fields. But the norms of procedural fairness increase the chances that a valid claim will get a careful hearing.

The president In many ways, the president has the most significant influence on the national agenda. As Chapter 10, on the presidency, demonstrated, the chief executive has become the nation's prime agenda setter, since even much of congressional business consists of reaction to or investigation of the proposals put forward by the occupant of the White House. The president is responsible annually for some of the most obvious and formal agenda-setting activities of the government, such as delivering a state of the union address, producing a detailed budget proposal and legislative program, and even providing an economic report. When an interest group has attracted the president's attention to a policy issue and it becomes a priority of the president, the issue gets noticed. The problem of civil rights appeared prominently on the policy agenda in the 1960s through several routes and for several reasons (via courts and school desegregation, via the media through dramatic scenes such as police dogs attacking defenseless blacks on national television, and so forth), but one of the most important channels was through the president (see the discussion of civil rights policy in Chapter 17). Civil rights groups like the National Association for the Advancement of Colored People (NAACP) and the Congress on Racial Equality (CORE) were able to convince Lyndon Johnson to elevate this issue to prime importance. The president not only did so but also used his political skill to help produce several new policies. Yet presidents usually do not add a multitude of issues to the agenda; they use their political influence cautiously by picking a few items to emphasize. Thus, many of those who seek access for their concerns must find another channel.

The media The media are an obvious route, which may be especially utilized by relatively less powerful groups. These may have trouble being taken seriously when they seek to reach the agenda through the more obviously political institutions, such as Congress. The paths available for many weak constituencies are limited, and thus when such interests seek attention for some problem or issue, they may resort to protests or other "media events" as a way of attracting a broader audience (Lipsky, 1968). The civil rights march from Selma to Montgomery, Alabama, in 1965 is an example of an effective protest. The activity was covered in detail by the national press and attracted even more attention when state police began to beat peaceful marchers. Civil rights activists used the demonstration as a political symbol of repression that was communicated by the media and ultimately had a direct impact on the passage of the Voting Rights Act. The media can thus be an institution which helps set the agenda and through which support can be built (Meadow, 1976).

This multiplicity of channels to the public agenda may make the policy process seem confusing, yet this discussion illustrates one of the most important characteristics of pluralistic decision making: many points of access increase the chances that government will give some attention to the needs, wants, and expectations of citizens. This conclusion does not necessarily mean that everybody can obtain for his or her favorite issue a serious hearing by policymakers. The agenda is limited, and all the institutions of government have at least some ability to influence which issues they actually have to face. Nor do all groups face the *same* difficulty getting attention for their causes from policymakers. The best-organized and most well financed groups, and those with the most cohesive and sizable constituency, have an obvious advantage. There is some truth to the statement made by one observer of the American political system of policymaking. "The flaw in the pluralist heaven," he observed, "is that the heavenly choir sings with a strong upper-class accent" (Schattschneider, 1960:35).

Still, it is not only the upper class which sets the agenda. The civil rights example makes this point. Nor is agenda setting performed solely by long-established, politically experienced interests. One recent illustration to the contrary is the success achieved by the Reverend Jerry Falwell, a fundamentalist preacher from Lynchburg, Virginia. He used the print, radio, and especially television media to organize, overnight and almost personally, thousands of supporters into a conservative group, the Moral Majority. Most members were not affluent and had had almost no experience in political affairs. Yet Falwell and his organization gained the ear of national legislators and the president for the group's causes (see Box 15-5). Falwell's efforts also illustrate the point that even *individuals,* especially energetic and talented ones, may have an impact on the policy agenda.

Defining the Problem

When the topic of energy appeared on the national agenda in the 1970s, the government was still a long way from setting clear policy on the matter. It is by no means obvious, for example, just what the energy problem *is.* Until one is able to define a problem, one is unlikely to be able to decide on an appropriate solution. Is the "energy crisis" really a problem of oil companies creating artificial shortages, misleading government and consumers, and reaping exorbitant profits? Is it an example of misguided government regulations draining capital from a critical sector of the economy that needs massive investment? Is it a matter of American consumers being so energy-inefficient in their use of power, for instance by purchasing gas-guzzling automobiles, that they have squandered a nonrenewable resource? Might it be a foreign policy problem: a few oil-rich nations exploiting a vulnerable United States? There are plenty of definitions of the problem, and, depending upon which is chosen, various options make more sense than others. To continue the example, if the problem with energy really were that Exxon, Conoco, and the others saw little financial incentive to explore for new oil, a tax on excess profits would make little sense.

Various participants in the process of policy-

BOX 15-5

THE MORAL MAJORITY

Until 1976, Jerry Falwell was just a preacher who led a large congregation at his Thomas Road Baptist Church in Lynchburg, Virginia. He had acquired a local reputation for his activism on behalf of conservative and right-wing causes. But in that year, when he criticized the presidential candidate, Jimmy Carter, for remarks Carter had made in an interview with *Playboy* magazine, the national media began to pay attention.

Falwell aired a nationally broadcast radio show and then a weekly television *Old Time Gospel Hour*. In 1978, some religious political activists paid Falwell's outfit $25,000 for the mailing list developed from the contributors and correspondence to the television show. The list was used to generate membership for a new organization, the Moral Majority. Falwell was named as president. There were semiautonomous chapters in all fifty states by 1982. Falwell claimed to be raising approximately $70 million by 1980, $7 million of which went directly to Moral Majority. (The remainder went toward a variety of activities, including

producing the show, building Liberty Baptist College, and others.)

Moral Majority established separate units for political lobbying and campaign work so that the tax-exempt status of the central organization would be preserved. All, however, are closely coordinated. Falwell's outfit now has a small office in Washington with a full-time staff of three.

Falwell utilizes the organization to push a list of legislative goals, such as passing constitutional amendments to ban abortion and allow prayer in schools, preventing national health insurance, attacking homosexuality, getting tougher penalties for crimes against "morality" like pornography and the illegal selling of drugs, and pushing for stronger national defense. In 1980 and 1982, the Moral Majority's state organizations targeted for defeat certain legislators who were viewed by them as antimorality. Falwell and the organization had become controversial national political figures.

Source: Congressional Quarterly, 1982:107–110; Fitzgerald, 1981.

---

making compete for influence as the problem is defined. All or any of the contestants mentioned in the previous section may play a role. In the case of energy policy, four recent presidents, chairs of congressional committees, interest groups such as Ralph Nader's consumer organization, an industry association (the American Petroleum Institute), coal producers, environmentalists, advocacy groups for low-income citizens, and many others have offered several partially competing definitions of the issue. The energy problem is in truth a complicated issue with many ramifications, so many of these individuals and groups seek to have *their* portion of the "truth" used to frame any policy debate. Some of the oil companies have even taken to establishing seminars and inviting professors, media representatives, leaders from consumer and labor groups, legislators, and others to discuss energy questions in hopes that the companies' point of view will at least be communicated to opinion leaders and potential participants in the policy process.

Developing Options and Building Support

The task of defining a policy problem, however, rarely takes place independently of certain other activities: developing policy options and building support for various alternatives. One can separate these features of the process for analytical purposes, but they often occur simultaneously. Presidents, for instance, make use of television to define problems, propose solutions, and stimulate popular enthusiasm, all within the time it takes to make a brief address. Lyndon Johnson did so on the issue of civil rights, and he was followed by Richard Nixon, Gerald Ford, and Jimmy Carter on energy, and more recently by Ronald Reagan on the economy.

Interest-group representatives draft legislative proposals, find friendly sponsors to introduce them, and seek to build coalitions in support of their alternatives. One way is by bargaining with other interest groups, with members of Congress, or with the president. Party ties do provide a coordinative link in helping to create support for alternative proposals among legislators and between the president and Congress. Coalition building on behalf of various alternatives often takes place in an atmosphere of compromise. Many of the participants know that they must deal with each other on many other decisions over a long period of time, so for the central actors there is considerable incentive to seem "reasonable." This bargaining stage is therefore often marked by a limitation on the intensity of conflict, a frequently observed characteristic of the American policymaking process.

Another way interest groups build support is for an organization to demonstrate that it really represents the strong views of a large number of citizens. Officers and staff members of interest groups contact their membership across the country to inform them of various policy proposals and to encourage them to contact legislators. One of the main reasons why the NRA has, over the years, been so effective in limiting gun control is that the organization is able to generate hundreds of thousands of letters to Congress within a couple of days. Legislators know that NRA members are extremely interested in gun-control issues whereas many citizens who support tighter regulation do not care nearly so much. Many of the former group may ultimately vote for or against their representative on the basis of his or her stand on this one issue. Often, then, the policy process works to benefit the intense minorities at the expense of the less intense majority. Yet this, too, is a product of pluralism at work.

The bureaucracy also often plays a role at this stage of the policy process. Many of the bills considered and approved in Washington are actually drafted in the agencies that will eventually implement them. And these units are not neutral or idle as support shifts among various options being considered for handling a policy problem. They work with friendly members of Congress and interest groups. In fact, agencies have even been known to aid in the *creation* of interest groups that will support the proposals of the agency. The Agriculture Department successfully did so years ago when it helped to organize the Farm Bureau.

The courts are not very active in formulating options and generating popular interest in them, yet they are used as policy paths by those who may have difficulty building strength for their issues in other arenas. The NAACP won on the school desegregation issue in 1954, despite the lack of support for its position with President Eisenhower and the Congress (see Chapter 17).

The amount of conflict generated as policy problems are defined, options are developed, and support is built varies considerably from issue to issue. Foreign policy issues are distinctive, for instance, and the process by which they are handled is a bit different, as discussed in Chapter 18. Since there are so many policy issues with which government must deal and since policymakers and citizens find some problems more important than others, there are many policies established far out of the limelight (see below). Besides the particular interests of policymakers and citizens, however, one very important factor in determining whether a policy option seems benign or controversial is the way the option is framed. Take the issue of overpopulation. If the size of the American population were to become viewed as a major problem in future years, and if all policymakers and even all citizens were to agree that there should be a national policy to address this problem, several alternatives would be possible. But these would undoubtedly vary tremendously in their palatability. Public education on birth control, tax breaks for small rather than large families, and mandatory sterilization of welfare clients are some examples of alternatives which would certainly *not* be viewed as interchangeable. The lesson here is that the type of policy proposal affects the kind of politics which result. (For two efforts to distinguish types of policies and suggest the kinds of politics that result see Lowi, 1964, and Wilson, 1973.) In general, the more clearly and directly an option tends to favor or disfavor a particular group, the more likely that group will become active in support or opposition.

Making Decisions

Policy options can get sidetracked or vetoed, may be compromised or incorporated into newer options, or might be approved—that is, adopted as public policy. A typical situation in the process is for some participants to be pushing anxiously for a decision, while others find their interests served by delay. The pluralist process is likely to have an effect on the sorts of decisions eventually reached.

Veto Points We saw earlier that multiple access points help get issues onto the agenda. Yet on major issues it is difficult for any single group's policy option to make it all the way through unscathed. There are a remarkable number of veto points, steps at which a policy proposal may be stopped. Some are obvious, such as the president's Constitutionally established ability to veto bills. Others derive from the complicated twists and turns of the legislative process. Before any major proposal arrives on the president's desk, it must surmount at least twelve different formal chances to kill the idea—in the two houses, various committees and subcommittees, and so forth. Accommodation to diverse points of view, therefore, is especially likely if policy on a major issue is to be enacted. Even if an interest group, for instance, is not able to generate support for its own proposals at every stage of the decision-making process, it may well be able to find some way to stymie others' alternatives. One veto point, be it a House subcommittee or a successful court challenge, is enough. This point is illustrated in Chapter 16, where we discuss efforts to reform federal welfare policy. Be-

cause of these realities, major policies which emerge from the process often either reflect only incremental changes from existing policy or are short on specifics.

Incrementalism Incrementalism means making decisions that are only slightly different from previous ones. Major policy changes have on occasion occurred quickly, but modest alterations are more typical. A good example is decision making about the federal budget (see Box 15-6). Recent presidents have campaigned on the idea of a balanced budget and sought to make massive shifts in funding. Yet they have found it very difficult to enforce their will at all stages of the budget process. President Reagan had this item very high on his personal agenda and spent a considerable portion of his term working on the budget problem. There were, as a result, changes in the way the federal government spent its revenues, but the budget was never actually cut; Reagan achieved, instead, a reduction in the rate of increase. The effect of all his efforts was a difference of a few percent in the total budget picture. As Reagan's chief budget adviser, David Stockman, commented, "The budget isn't something you reconstruct each year. The budget is a sort of rolling history of decisions. All kinds of

---

BOX 15-6

INCREMENTALISM AT WORK

Members of Congress and agency officials recognize that the federal budget is usually produced in an incremental policymaking process. One congressman testifying before the House Rules Committee put it this way: "If you will read the hearings of the subcommittees you will find that most of our time is spent talking about the changes in the bill which we will have next year from the one we had this year, the reductions made, and the increases made. That which is not changed has little, if anything, said about it."

Agency leaders defend their budgets especially strongly against any cutbacks that are more than token—they protect their "base" from one year to the next. An official of the Fish and Wildlife Service told the Senate Appropriations Committee, for instance, "It so happens that our budget is so tight that we have no provisions at all for any leeway in this amount."

If agencies ask for no major changes, they have an easier time in the budget process. A senator on the Appropriations Committee commented in one case that the committee members "do not think it is necessary to go into details of the estimate, as the committee has had this appropriation before it for many years."

On complicated matters like budgets, incrementalism is attractive to policymakers as a way of simplifying their decisions.

Source: Wildavsky, 1979a:15, 104.

decisions, made five, ten, fifteen years ago, are coming back to bite us unexpectedly" (*Atlantic,* 1981:51).

Imprecise Policies The process of policymaking also may produce fairly vague decisions, especially on legislation. As participants bargain and jockey for support, options may have to become somewhat more general in order to attract a sufficiently large coalition to ensure passage. This outcome is especially likely when policymakers are agreed about a problem but do not know, exactly, what to do about it. For instance, federal law on solving the problem of juvenile delinquency identifies no real solution but in effect directs the appropriate agency to look for one. Often, participants in the process—such as bureaus or interest groups—who see their preferred options disappear in favor of a vague policy in the legislature seek to enact their preferences again later, during implementation. In fact, when the laws are *very* general, the real task of policymaking is devolved to the bureaucracy; sometimes, also, to the courts for interpretation; and, in certain cases, to state and local governments that may wind up making the most important decisions.

The "Triple Alliance" Yet not all policies attract so many participants that decision makers have to consider many diverse points of view. If an issue is framed in such a way that it does not attract a large audience, it may be decided without so much of the skeptical scrutiny afforded more prominent items. In American policymaking, there are a number of issues like this—matters that may even affect everyone, but in such a way that only a very few would find it seemingly worth their while to pay attention. Subsidies for agricultural crops illustrate this situation. Federal policy supports the price of soybeans above that which would be established by the market. Everyone pays the cost, but not many people write letters to Congress or decide their presidential choice on the basis of a few pennies, more or less, in a household budget. Who really cares about soybean prices? The answer is (1) soybean growers, who have an organization to monitor issues like this; (2) the Agriculture Department, whose clientele consists mostly of farmers; and (3) the House and Senate Agriculture committees. Federal policy on soybeans is pro-

duced largely by these relatively few participants, who think pretty much alike on the subject. These three policy actors—interest groups, agencies, and congressional oversight committees—constitute a most significant decision center for the less prominent but still important issues like this one. There are many such centers throughout the government dealing with all kinds of substantive policy topics. They are often referred to by various labels, such as "subgovernments," or the "triple alliance," or the "iron triangle." Whatever the label, however, the result is the same: intense minorities, or special interests, exert weight greatly in excess of their numbers. Depending on the type of issue being decided, therefore, including how it is framed and how many participants are attracted during the stage that options are developed and supporters are mobilized, many or few perspectives can be brought to bear at the point of decision (Price, 1978). The fact that some issues are decided by small groups that can thus be relatively powerful on certain issues, coupled with the fact that there are a number of such groups, helps to explain how policy inconsistencies arise. The example of tobacco policy, mentioned earlier in the chapter, is an excellent one. Tobacco subsidies are primarily controlled by an agricultural group, while the issue of regulated cigarette advertising attracts a much broader set of participants.

Therefore, one can see that policymaking in the United States varies greatly in the degree to which it is responsive to the public. Some decisions, like presidential executive orders, are especially sensitive to a national majority; others, as in the soybean illustration, are most heavily influenced in settings favorable to intense minorities; and still others, for instance court decisions, may be quite insulated from popular opinion, regardless of what it is.

Implementation and Impact

As we observed earlier, the policymaking process does not stop with the passage of laws or the giving of orders. These decisions must be executed, and in that process of implementation, policy may also be created (Pressman and Wildavsky, 1980; Edwards, 1980; Larson, 1980). Vague statutes obviously require the bureaucracy to make decisions during implementation, but these are not the only instances in which implementers create policy. Even carefully crafted laws or seemingly unambiguous directives require the continual exercise of judgment by agencies.

One day in August 1971 President Nixon announced a policy initiated by executive order. It was just about the clearest statement one could hope to see from a major public official. Nixon imposed an immediate freeze on all wages and prices for almost everyone in the country. A few items, such as raw agricultural products, were to be exempted, and the policy was to remain in effect for a strictly limited period. The Office of Emergency Preparedness and the Cost of Living Council began to implement the decision and found that even in this case the policy had left hundreds of questions unanswered. Were interest rates to be considered prices and therefore frozen? Was fish an agricultural product and thus able to be sold at a higher amount? Were labor union members who had already signed an agreement with their employers for wage hikes to be denied the increase in violation of their contract? The agency found itself swamped with such sticky policy decisions (Kagan, 1978).

Every year, thousands of pages of the *Federal Register,* the newspaper printed by the government, are filled with important policy enacted by administrative units during implementation. As we saw in Chapter 13, on the bureaucracy, other policymakers such as Congress and the president may exercise some oversight during the implementation stage, but there is simply no denying the bureaucracy a significant, often decisive, role.

Sometimes policies have the intended impact, and sometimes they do not. As American government has moved from handling relatively simple tasks to solving more complex problems, the likelihood of successful impact has become more problematic. A few years after President Johnson's "war on poverty" in the 1960s, there was widespread debate about whether the programs had had any effect; if so, how much; and, in any case, whether the policies were worth the expenditures or could have been achieved better through other options.

Questions like these are a standard part of the policymaking debate these days. It hardly makes sense to continue ineffective policies in force, and since there are always so many other claimants for a place on the federal agenda and a share of the budgetary pie, the task of evaluating policies for their impact has become a popular one in recent years. Policy analysts examine established programs and also sort through options at earlier stages in the policy process.

Policy analysis is an effort to interject a rational consideration of policies and potential policies into the government's process of decision (Rivlin, 1971; Weiss, 1977). The government itself employs thousands of such analysts in various agencies of the bureaucracy, as well as on the staffs of congressional committees and legislative units like the Congressional Budget Office. Many more work in and around Washington, for instance in think tanks like the Brookings Institution.

Policy analysts employ, by and large, the perspective of economists. They seek a systematic, usually quantitative, evaluation of the costs and benefits of policies. The idea sometimes seems to be to temper the influence of purely political factors in the policy process, so that mere power, political muscle, does not solely determine what government does. There is no question but that policy analysis can raise the level of thought given to policy problems by comparing alternatives and encouraging explicit consideration of the connection between intentions and actions. Yet there is no way that policy analysis can replace the politics of policymaking. Evaluating policies is a tricky business, for instance, and one can seldom be confident of what might have happened had a policy not been in effect. Many of the costs of policy alternatives are difficult to measure with precision. And many of the benefits cannot be effectively compared with each other. Is it worth spending an additional several billion dollars on nuclear power plant safety to reduce somewhat the chances of a major accident with 10,000 lives lost? No analysis can answer this question without facing such deeply political questions as how much a human life is worth. Yet the strengths of policy analysis are such that many participants in the process employ it as a tool to inform themselves, convince others, and improve actual outcomes.

SUMMARY AND CONCLUSION

The task of this chapter has been to explain how American government makes policy and to answer the Constitutional question of how closely that pro-

The Nuclear Regulatory Commission sets safety standards for the nuclear power industry—but many citizens do not want NRC's policy analysts to decide how many safeguards are enough when the consequences may be measured in billions of dollars and thousands of lives. *(John Lazenby/Black Star)*

cess approaches the standard of popular rule. In carrying out these tasks we have actually integrated much of the material presented in earlier parts of this book.

Public policy is what attracts many to the activities of government, and yet it is not always clear just what policy encompasses. Some important decisions lie outside government hands and thus are excluded from consideration. Governmental intentions frequently meet with failure for various reasons, and sometimes inconsistent decisions make it difficult to decipher whether there *is* a governmental intention and what it might be. Furthermore, some of the most important issues are the ones which never arise. Yet there are a great many public policies, if one means to include governmental

decisions which establish goals, rules, standards, or practices to apply over time to a series of actions or cases. These policies do make a difference, and therefore it is important to consider how government arrives at them.

Trying to explain American policymaking through reference to a model of who rules is a task that has occupied numerous analysts. The existence of a power elite is a plausible explanation because a good deal of economic wealth is concentrated in relatively few hands and because the economically powerful do reap impressive benefits through policy. Yet this model cannot accommodate the full range of American policies. A strict majoritarian model has weaknesses in explaining many policies and is also impossible to achieve in practice. Pluralism, the dispersion of power among a number of centers, provides an explanation which is consistent, at least in broad outline, with the framers' designs. And the pluralist perspective helps one understand a good deal of the contemporary American policymaking process. Yet all these models contribute to an explanation of American policymaking.

There are numerous participants in the process—some Constitutionally designated, some less official but no less important, some unanticipated in the original scheme. Pluralism can be seen at work in the several stages of the policy process: as the public agenda is established; while various parties take part in defining policy problems, developing options, and building support; as decisions are reached; and even, to some extent, when the policy is implemented. The precise nature of the process in a particular case is affected by many factors, including who participates, what institutional channels are used at various stages, the nature of the problem, the way the options are framed, and even the degree to which policy analysis is used as a tool.

On issues receiving broad consideration, policies are more likely to develop through a process of compromise toward an incremental result. Sometimes tough decision making is delayed or handed over to bureaucrats and others. Less visible items, however, may be handled by few participants (such as the triple alliance), with less debate, and with greater weight going to those who feel the effects of the policy most immediately.

How closely does American policymaking actually approach popular government? There is no answer to this constitutional question that is both simple and accurate. Different stages and channels vary greatly in their accessibility to the people. Some parts are more in tune with the depth of public opinion than with its breadth, whereas in other segments the converse is true. No single group or interest seems to control policymaking, yet some interests clearly have more weight than others. The policy agenda is finite, yet growing. Access to it, while not always easy, is also not strictly limited to the wealthy and established. In short, one can derive only an ambivalent evaluation when scoring the process for its success on this criterion. Yet it is worth remembering that the system was designed primarily to protect against tyranny, not to implement democracy. The founders hoped that the public will would be an *important* determinant of policy, not the *sole* one. In an analysis of contemporary policymaking in the United States, one finds the founders' general intentions on this topic put into practice. It remains for today's Americans, a newer generation of constitution makers, to decide upon the appropriateness of that system.

SOURCES

Adamany, David W., and George E. Agree: *Political Money,* Johns Hopkins Press, Baltimore, 1975.

Anderson, James E.: *Public Policy Making,* 2d ed., Praeger, New York, 1979.

Anderson, Martin: *The Federal Bulldozer,* M.I.T. Press, Cambridge, Mass., 1964.

Arrow, Kenneth: *Social Choice and Individual Values,* 2d ed., Wiley, New York, 1963.

Atlantic, December 1981.

Bachrach, Peter: *The Theory of Democratic Elitism; a Critique,* Little, Brown, Boston, 1967.

———and Morton Baratz: "Decisions and Nondecisions: An Analytical Framework," *American Political Science Review,* vol. 57, no. 3, 1963, pp. 632–642.

Brooks, John: "The Supply Side," *New Yorker,* Apr. 19, 1982, pp. 96–150.

Casper, Jonathan D.: "The Supreme Court and National Policy-Making," *American Political Science Review,* vol. 70, no. 1, 1976, pp. 50–63.

Cobb, Roger W., and Charles D. Elder: *Participation in American Politics: The Dynamics of Agenda-Building,* Johns Hopkins Press, Baltimore, 1972.

Congressional Quarterly, Inc.: *The Washington Lobby,* 4th ed., Congressional Quarterly Press, Washington, D.C., 1982.

Dahl, Robert: *Who Governs?* Yale University Press, New Haven, Conn., 1961.

Dawson, Richard, and James Robinson: "The Relation between Public Policy and Some Structural and Environmental Variables in the American States," *Journal of Politics,* vol. 25, no. 2, 1963, pp. 265–289.

Domhoff, G. William: *Who Rules America?* Prentice-Hall, Englewood Cliffs, N.J., 1967.

Drew, Elizabeth: *Senator,* Simon and Schuster, New York, 1979.

Dye, Thomas R.: "Oligarchic Tendencies in National Policy-Making: The Role of the Private Policy-Planning Organizations," *Journal of Politics,* vol. 40, no. 2, 1978, pp. 309–331.

————: *Who's Running America?* 2d ed., Prentice-Hall, Englewood Cliffs, N.J., 1979.

————: *Understanding Public Policy,* 4th ed., Prentice-Hall, Englewood Cliffs, N.J., 1981.

Edelman, Murray: *The Symbolic Uses of Politics,* University of Illinois, Urbana, 1964.

Edwards, George C., III: *Implementing Public Policy,* Congressional Quarterly Press, Washington, D.C., 1980.

————and Ira Sharkansky: *The Policy Predicament,* Freeman, San Francisco, 1978.

Erikson, Robert S.: "The Relationship between Public Opinion and State Policy: A New Look Based on Some Forgotten Data," *American Journal of Political Science,* vol. 20, no. 1, 1976, pp. 25–36.

Fitzgerald, Frances: "A Disciplined Charging Army," *New Yorker,* May 18, 1981, pp. 53–141.

Gelb, Leslie H., with Richard K. Betts: *The Irony of Vietnam: The System Worked,* Brookings Institution, Washington, D.C., 1979.

Ginsberg, Benjamin: "Elections and Public Policy," *American Political Science Review,* vol. 70, no. 1, 1976, pp. 41–49.

Hofferbert, Richard: *The Study of Public Policy,* Bobbs-Merrill, Indianapolis, 1974.

In These Times, Sept. 22–28, 1982.

Jaffe, Frederick S., Barbara L. Lindheim, and Philip R. Lee: *Abortion Politics: Private Morality and Public Policy,* McGraw-Hill, New York, 1981.

Jones, Charles O.: *An Introduction to the Study of Public Policy,* Duxbury, Boston, 1978.

Kagan, Robert A.: *Regulatory Justice: Implementing a Wage-Price Freeze,* Russell Sage, New York, 1978.

Larson, James S.: *Why Government Programs Fail: Improving Policy Implementation,* Praeger, New York, 1980.

Lewis-Beck, Michael S.: "The Relative Importance of Socioeconomic and Political Variables for Public Policy," *American Political Science Review,* vol. 71, no. 2, 1977, pp. 559–566.

Lindblom, Charles E.: *Politics and Markets,* Basic Books, New York, 1977.

————: *The Policy-Making Process,* 2d ed., Prentice-Hall, Englewood Cliffs, N.J., 1980.

Lineberry, Robert L.: *American Public Policy: What Government Does and What Difference It Makes,* Harper and Row, New York, 1977.

Lipsky, Michael: "Protest as a Political Resource," *American Political Science Review,* vol. 62, no. 4, 1968, pp. 1144–1158.

Lowi, Theodore J.: "American Business, Public Policy, Case Studies and Political Theory," *World Politics,* vol. 16, no. 4, 1964, pp. 672–715.

————: *The End of Liberalism,* 2d ed., Norton, New York, 1979.

Luttbeg, Norman R. (ed.): *Public Opinion and Public Policy,* 3d ed., Peacock, Itasca, Ill., 1981.

Mazmanian, Daniel A., and Paul A. Sabatier: "A Multivariate Model of Public Policy-Making," *American Journal of Political Science,* vol. 24, no. 3, 1980, pp. 439–468.

McClosky, Herbert, Paul J. Hoffmann, and Rosemary O'Hara: "Issue Conflict and Consensus among Party Leaders and Followers," *American Political Science Review,* vol. 54, no. 2, 1960, pp. 406–427.

Meadow, Robert G.: "Issue Emphasis and Public Opinion: The Media during the 1972 Presidential Campaign," *American Politics Quarterly,* vol. 4, no. 2, 1976, pp. 177–192.

Miliband, Ralph: *The State in Capitalist Society,* Weidenfeld and Nicholson, London, 1969.

Mills, C. Wright: *The Power Elite,* Oxford University Press, New York, 1956.

Montjoy, Robert S., and Laurence J. O'Toole, Jr.: "Toward a Theory of Policy Implementation: An Organizational Perspective," *Public Administration Review,* vol. 39, no. 5, 1979, pp. 465–476.

————, William R. Schaffer, and Ronald E. Weber: "Policy Preferences of Party Elites and Masses: Conflict or Consensus?" *American Politics Quarterly,* vol. 8, no. 3, 1980, pp. 319–343.

Nadel, Mark V.: "The Hidden Dimension of Public Policy: Private Governments and the Policy-Making Process," *Journal of Politics,* vol. 37, no. 1, 1975, pp. 2–34.

Peters, B. Guy: *American Public Policy: Process and Performance,* F. Watts, New York, 1982.

Pressman, Jeffrey L., and Aaron Wildavsky: *Implementation,* 2d ed., University of California Press, Berkeley, 1980.

Prewitt, Kenneth, and Alan Stone: *The Ruling Elites,* Harper and Row, New York, 1973.

Price, David E.: "Policy Making in Congressional Committees: The Impact of 'Environmental' Factors," *American Political Science Review,* vol. 72, no. 2, 1978, pp. 548–574.

Rivlin, Alice: *Systematic Thinking for Social Action,* Brookings Institution, Washington, D.C., 1971.

Rodgers, Harrell R., Jr., and Charles S. Bullock, III: *Law and Social Change: Civil Rights Laws and Their Consequences,* McGraw-Hill, New York, 1972.

Salamon, Lester M., and John J. Siegfried: "Economic Power and Political Influence: The Impact of Industry Structure on Public Policy," *American Political Science Review,* vol. 71, no. 3, 1977, pp. 1026–1043.

Schattschneider, E. E.: *The Semi-Sovereign People,* Holt, New York, 1960.

Schulman, Paul R.: "Nonincremental Policy Making: Notes toward an Alternative Paradigm," *American Political Science Review,* vol. 69, no. 4, 1975, pp. 1354–1370.

————: *Large-Scale Policy Making,* Elsevier, New York, 1980.

Sharkansky, Ira, and Richard I. Hofferbert: "Dimensions of State Policy," in Herbert Jacob and Kenneth N. Vines (eds.), *Politics in the American States,* 2d ed., Little, Brown, Boston, 1972.

Sullivan, John L., and Robert E. O'Connor: "Electoral Choice and Popular Control of Public Policy: The Case of the 1966 House Elections," *American Political Science Review,* vol. 66, no. 4, 1972, pp. 1256–1268.

U.S. General Accounting Office: "Employment Services for Vietnam-Era Veterans Could Be Improved," B-178741, Nov. 29, 1974.

Verba, Sidney, and Norman H. Nie: *Participation in America: Political Democracy and Social Equality,* Harper and Row, New York, 1972.

Walker, Jack: "A Critique of the Elitist Theory of Democracy," *American Political Science Review,* vol. 60, no. 2, 1966, pp. 285–295.

Weber, Ronald E., and William R. Schaffer: "Public Opinion and American State Policy Making," *Midwest Journal of Political Science,* vol. 16, no. 4, 1972, pp. 683–699.

Weinberger, Marvin, and David U. Greevy (comps.): *The PAC Directory,* Ballinger, Cambridge, Mass., 1982.

Weiss, Carol H.: *Using Social Research in Public Policy Making,* Heath, Lexington, Mass., 1977.

Wildavsky, Aaron: *The Politics of the Budgetary Process,* 3d ed., Little, Brown, Boston, 1979a.

————: "Policy as Its Own Cause," in *Speaking Truth to Power: The Art and Craft of Policy Analysis,* Little, Brown, Boston, 1979b.

Wilson, James Q.: *Political Organizations,* Basic Books, New York, 1973.

Zuckerman, Alan: "The Concept of 'Political Elite': Lessons from Mosca and Pareto," *Journal of Politics,* vol. 39, no. 2, 1977, pp. 324–344.

RECOMMENDED READINGS

Dahl, Robert: *Who Governs?* Yale University Press, New Haven, Conn., 1961. A case study of governance in New Haven, Connecticut; a pluralist interpretation.

Jones, Charles O.: *An Introduction to the Study of Public Policy,* Duxbury, Boston, 1978. One of the best introductory, book length treatments of the policy process.

Lindblom, Charles E.: *The Policy-Making Process,* 2d ed., Prentice-Hall, Englewood Cliffs, N.J., 1980. Another examination of the policy process, with a focus on some of the most influential participants.

Lowi, Theodore J.: *The End of Liberalism,* Norton, New York, 1979. A critique of policy and politics in the United States, with special attention to the impediments to majoritarian influence.

Luttbeg, Norman R. (ed.): *Public Opinion and Public Policy,* 3d ed., Peacock, Itasca, Ill., 1981. A set of essays on the linkages and barriers between public opinion and American policy.

Mills, C. Wright: *The Power Elite,* Oxford University Press, New York, 1956. A classic exposition of the elitist interpretation of American policymaking.

Pressman, Jeffrey L., and Aaron Wildavsky: *Implementation,* 2d ed., University of California Press, Berkeley, 1980. A case study of the multiple problems that can occur during an attempt to convert policy into action.

Rivlin, Alice: *Systematic Thinking for Social Action,* Brookings Institution, Washington, D.C., 1971. A brief argument for the use of policy analysis to improve government programs.

Chapter 16

The Social Welfare State

CHAPTER CONTENTS

In American politics, there are probably few ideas that inspire as much controversy as the notion of *welfare*. These days, the national government faces the prospect of huge budget deficits (during the early 1980s, deficit projections were routinely running at $100 to $200 billion per year); and several states, such as California and Massachusetts, have encountered "taxpayers' revolts"—organized efforts on the part of citizens' groups to lower taxes and cut back on government spending. It is no wonder, then, that a policy of social "welfare," which often seems to suggest that people can or should get something for nothing, leaves an unpleasant taste with many. President Reagan thus often struck a responsive chord when he went on the attack against "free spenders," "government giveaways," and "welfare cheats."

Yet matters are not so simple. While welfare has not been popular lately, the American social welfare state has continued to grow in absolute terms—even, by some measures, throughout the Reagan years! This development has occurred partially as a result of certain characteristics of the American policymaking process (including its incrementalism and its fragmentation), as will be discussed shortly. But the prominence of the American social welfare state cannot be explained entirely as a product either of accident or of various features of the system by which policy is made in the United States.

For one thing, whereas most Americans are *against* supporting freeloaders, most of those same Americans are *for* supporting those who really do require aid. That is to say, many citizens are ambivalent about their social welfare state. Few would dismantle it entirely. In fact, some of the most significant features of American social welfare policy were the items around which Franklin Roosevelt built his New Deal coalition, as discussed in earlier chapters, and a number of the policies have become part of our twentieth-century American constitutional heritage. Republican presidents as well as Democratic ones have accepted or expanded large parts of the social welfare state in this country during the years since Roosevelt. And even President Reagan has suggested to the American people that the nation should commit itself to a "social safety net" for the "truly needy." Second, the truly needy and the shiftless welfare cheats are not the only people who receive one or another form of government aid, or welfare assistance, in the United States of the 1980s. Many middle- and upper-income citizens—including, it is likely, most of the readers of this book—receive some form of support from the American welfare state: grants, loans, insurance, veterans' benefits, tax subsidies, and so forth. American business also benefits from governmental largess. The welfare state has grown, therefore, in part because it supports so many of us. And third, some of the values upon which the American social welfare state is based are quite congenial to some of the most powerful ideas in American politics, as will be illustrated. The welfare state in the United States finds its supporters among those who believe in equality, in fairness, and even in liberty—hardly un-American values.

Yet the current challenges to the social welfare state in this country are not simply wrongheaded—the result of misunderstandings, perhaps, or selfishness on the part of some citizens who are unwilling to help others. These factors may explain some but not all the unpopularity of the idea of welfare. The more important criticisms of contemporary American social welfare policy raise serious issues which it would be foolish or dishonest to avoid. First of all, social welfare policy attempts to achieve visible, complicated goals (e.g., eliminating poverty or providing accessible, humane, affordable health care), often by restricting or eliminating the rights or privileges available to a substantial portion of the citizenry (e.g., by regulating more directly or taxing more heavily). Naturally, then, such trade-offs provoke serious and sustained disagreements. Second, any sober assessment of the results of the policies of the social welfare state in the United States must identify not only benefits produced—and these have often been considerable—but also failures and problems generated. Some important and expensive policies have simply not achieved or approached their goals. Furthermore, some social welfare policies have resulted in substantial benefits but also unanticipated and negative consequences. Those who say, for instance, that American policy treats some people paternalistically, or discourages the incentive to work, or contributes to the disintegration of the family are not entirely without foundation. Third, even if social welfare policy in the United States *derives* from some strongly held political values in this country, portions of the American social welfare state also *challenge* or contradict some of these same values.

Obviously, therefore, those who want to understand politics and government in the United States need to devote careful attention to the social welfare state in this country. That subject, then, is the focus of this chapter.

First, perhaps, we should define just what we are talking about. We have already referred to the social welfare *state*. By "state," here, we do not mean one of the fifty constituent units of the United States (Montana, Louisiana, etc.); instead, the term refers to a government—in this case, the national government. A *social welfare state* is a government that, as a matter of formal policy, has assumed responsibility for guaranteeing the security (especially income security) of its citizens (Furniss and Tilton, 1977). In the strictest sense, no government on the earth has been completely successful in enacting the social welfare state, if "success" means having made all its citizens free from economic worry. Yet a number of nations, mostly western industrial ones like the United States, have in various ways assumed this responsibility—entirely or partially, through broad policy decisions or via a series of smaller step-by-step enactments.

It is worth noting that this idea of the social welfare state goes considerably beyond the everyday use of the concept of welfare to designate monthly checks distributed by a social work bureaucracy. Any measures that have as their intent increasing the economic security of Americans are part of this country's social welfare policies (Dahl and Lindblom, 1953). As we shall indicate shortly, there are a large number of these policies, and they affect us all in multiple and significant ways. In fact, because there are so many policies forming the social welfare state in the United States and because several of these policies are so complicated and farreaching, this chapter really provides the barest of introductions. We shall discuss only the most important features of a few of the major policies, and we shall ignore all else.

The goal of the chapter, in short, is to acquaint you with the development and significance of some of the main components of the American social welfare state and to place today's policy debates in the United States into some perspective. Chapter 15 provided an analysis of the American policymaking process, that is, *how* policies are produced here. The present chapter is designed to explain *what* some of the most important policies actually are, how they have changed, how they relate to some of the constitutional questions raised in earlier chapters, and what some of the options for the future might be. Yet just as in Chapter 15, on the policy process, where we found it impossible to consider the process without referring to the substance of actual policies, in this chapter we shall not be able to ignore completely the process of policymaking (Starling, 1979; Dye, 1981; Paul and Russo, 1982). In fact, at the conclusion of the chapter we shall point out some of the ways in which the substance of policy for the social welfare state in the United States reflects the process by which it has been made. For now, however, it is necessary that we try to see what the American social welfare state is actually like.

THE DEVELOPMENT OF THE AMERICAN SOCIAL WELFARE STATE

The American social welfare state, which has been so controversial lately, is not really or simply a creation of the last few years (Trattner, 1974). A brief survey of the development of social welfare policies in this country is thus helpful, for it illustrates three important themes. First, these policies have been in gestation or in the process of enactment for many years. Second, while the recent growth of the social welfare state in the United States has been substantial, this fact obscures the point that this country was considerably later in the enactment of many of its policies than were most other western industrialized nations. Finally, despite the extent of economic support and security now provided by the government to American citizens, the social welfare state here is smaller in relative terms and provides less comprehensive protection to those in the United States than several other social welfare states.

This section provides a broad sketch of the American social welfare state in historical and comparative terms. Later sections of the chapter focus in more detail on the specifics of policy development in three areas: managing the economy, providing income security, and regulating social and economic behavior.

The Early Years

The founders of the United States, or at least most of the founders, had no intention whatsoever of creating a social welfare state. It is true that the authors of the Constitution listed as one of their main intentions to "promote the general Welfare" (Preamble), and they gave Congress the power to "provide for the . . . general Welfare" (Article I, Section 8). But it was far from their goal to have the national government involved in the care of poor people, the search for a solution to the problem of poverty, any direct management of economic forces, or any extensive regulation of economic or social activity.

The existence of poor people and the problems implied by their existence—hunger and malnourishment, poor housing, crime, suffering—were not in fact much on the minds of the founders, who were more interested in creating and making palatable to the citizenry a limited government than in placing the social welfare of the needy on the policy agenda. Their view of the role of government was much more restricted. Most of the founders clearly considered economic distress (at least as indicated by poverty) to be an inevitable fact of human life for many—and one, in any event, that was not the proper province of the federal government. The ideas of Thomas Jefferson on this subject are fairly representative. He viewed the problem of poverty with equanimity: poor people could usually be taken care of by family, friends, the religious community, or perhaps local government. In any event, he did not perceive the matter to be a severe one, as the following demonstrates:

> From Savannah to Portsmouth you will seldom meet a beggar. In the large towns, indeed, they sometimes present themselves. These are usually foreigners. . . . I never yet saw a native American begging in the streets or highways. A subsistence is easily gained here . . . (Koch and Peden, 1944:250–251).

Yet even Jefferson discovered that he himself was not fully insulated from the effects of economic hardship. Late in life he found himself strapped for

resources and felt compelled to conduct a lottery of some of his belongings to raise cash.

There was a bit more of a difference of opinion among the founders on whether and how the new government should become involved in influencing economic forces. The year 1776 was not only the time of American independence; it was also the date of publication in the United Kingdom of *The Wealth of Nations* by Adam Smith. Smith's argument, which was to be popular in this country, was that a free market economy would in fact generate results favorable to the general welfare: efficient production and distribution of the goods and services constituting a nation's economy. Most of the founders here believed that the new government's role in economic policy should be restricted to a minimum: enforcing contracts, protecting property, establishing a stable currency, eliminating ruinous competition in commerce between states, and perhaps a few other actions. It was not for another 100 years that the first federal regulatory agency was created.

It is true that there were disagreements, as we have seen, between the Federalists and Antifederalists on how much the United States government should do to further the nation's "commercial prosperity," to use Hamilton's phrase (*Federalist* 12). Hamilton himself favored the use of government to aid the urban industrial structure. And the national bank dispute during Jackson's years as president illustrates this point clearly as well (see Chapter 13, on the bureaucracy). Yet the idea of laissez-faire (free market) capitalism, based on nearly unrestrained private enterprise for profit with only a slight role for government, was the prevailing national economic public policy in the United States for the first century of the nation's existence.

There were occasional efforts to move early welfare state policies onto the national agenda during that period. Reformers, for example, were successful in getting Congress in 1854 to approve a land grant to the states for the construction of mental hospitals. But President Franklin Pierce vetoed the idea, partially on the grounds that this program would be the opening wedge of federal intrusion into the welfare field. "It cannot be questioned," he claimed, "that if Congress have the power to make provision for the indigent insane . . . , it has the same power to make provision for the indigent who are not insane; and thus to transfer to the Federal Government the charge of all the poor in the States" (Tropman, 1977:37). By and large, the only significant national developments that directly affected American economic security (that is, leaving aside indirect activities such as the enactment of tariffs, the conduct of war and peace, etc.) until late in the nineteenth century were land grants for the development of the nation's economic infrastructure—roadways, railroad expansion to the west, canal systems, and so forth. Even these, as was explained in Chapter 14, on American intergovernmental relations, were controversial measures which frequently encountered presidential vetoes. And the problem of the poor themselves would remain a private or a state and local concern in the United States until the New Deal era.

The Progressive Period

Other issues of the social welfare state did not gestate quite so long as did federal policy on the poor. In particular, in the latter part of the nineteenth century and early years of the twentieth—that is, around the time of the progressive era—some Americans began to express concern about whether the effects of laissez-faire capitalism upon the general welfare were all to the good. The increasing concentration of several American industries (e.g., steel, sugar, oil) brought criticism that trusts and collusion were replacing free market competition. The development of certain unscrupulous practices in various mass production enterprises, such as the use of child labor and the persistence of unsafe working conditions, stimulated widespread complaint. And the claim was more insistently heard that the public interest required governmental supervision of certain commercial transactions (e.g., transportation across state lines) and products (e.g., unwholesome food and drugs). The first significant policies of the American welfare state—national regulatory policies—were the result (as discussed later). Several such important policies, designed in part to provide security by reducing undesired side effects of free enterprise, were enacted between 1887 and 1914.

The progressive era brought with it an awareness that unrestrained laissez-faire capitalism had led to many unfair and unsafe practices, including the use of child labor in such hard and dangerous work as coal mining. *(Culver Pictures)*

The New Deal

Despite some early welfare reform, the major enactments of the American social welfare state awaited the great depression and constituted the essentials of the New Deal response. In the 1930s when Roosevelt took office, the issue of economic security was uppermost in most Americans' minds. One-quarter of all Americans were out of work, wages had sunk dismally, life savings—invested in the stock market or deposited in bank accounts—had disappeared. Roosevelt's answer included major new policies to tackle the issues of income security, economic management, and—to some extent—business regulation. Of permanent impact on the American social welfare state were the Social Security Act of 1935 (income security); the first conscious use of fiscal policy by the national government (economic management); and the establishment of a system for stabilizing American savings and investments by regulating the exchange of stocks and bonds, plus regulation and insuring of the operations of banks and savings and loan companies (business regulation). The multiple welfare state enactments of the New Deal era, some of which are examined later in this chapter, do not provide the only example of American policymaking to ensure economic security, but that period did mark a clear commitment in the United States to a continuing governmental presence in this field. Until the 1980s, at least, most major policymakers at the national level have felt bound to retain or expand that commitment.

Post-New Deal Expansion

Expansion of the American welfare state has in fact taken place numerous times since the 1930s. Most of the significant additions, at least in terms of monetary commitments, were made during the 1960s and 1970s, but some occurred before that time (Sundquist, 1968; Grønbjerg, 1977). Table 16-1 lists some of the major enactments of social welfare policy in the United States between the New Deal and President Reagan's term in office. There are simply too many to discuss here, although once again the most significant will receive some treatment later. At this point we can simply observe that in all three major sectors of welfare state activity—managing the economy, providing income security, and regulating private behavior—the federal government's commitments increased quite steadily over the years. Until the 1980s, there were few successful attempts to decrease the national government's role as a social welfare state. (One slight exception was the deregulation efforts under the Ford and Carter administrations during the latter part of the 1970s.) By and large, expansions in the United States welfare state have occurred under the aegis of, or as a result of prodding by, Democratic political leaders. But this generalization does not always hold. During his time in office, for instance, President Nixon, a Republican, became known as one of the nation's most active presidents ever on social welfare issues. He instituted a wage-price freeze when he thought the economy required it, he helped to federalize some

TABLE 16-1
SOME MAJOR SOCIAL WELFARE POLICIES ENACTED
BETWEEN THE NEW DEAL AND THE REAGAN YEARS

Managing the economy		Providing income security		Regulating behavior	
Date	Policy	Date	Policy	Date	Policy
1946	Unemployment Act of 1946	1949	Public housing	1933–38	Banks, securities; agriculture; communications; labor relations; air transportation
1962	Kennedy's stimulative tax cut	1962	Employment training		
		1964	War on poverty		
1971	Nixon's wage-price freeze	1965	Medicaid, Medicare	1946	Nuclear power
1981–	Reagan's supply-side policy; tax cuts	1970	Food stamps	1964–65	Civil rights; voting rights
		1972	Expansion of social security payments and indexing to cost of living; Supplemental Security Income program	1968	Open housing
				1970	Occupational safety and health; clean air amendments
		1975	Earned income credit	1972	Equal employment opportunity; consumer product safety; water pollution control amendments
		1977	Increased social security taxes		
		1981–	Reagan program cuts	1974	Hazardous materials; pension reform; privacy act
				1974–	Deregulation (e.g., airlines, oil, trucking)

income-support programs, he sought (unsuccessfully) the enactment of a negative income tax so that all Americans would be guaranteed a certain minimum (Moynihan, 1973; Burke and Burke, 1974), and he at least acquiesced in numerous other policy expansions.

A list of programs and their dates of enactment is helpful in getting a quick overview of the development of the American social welfare state, but it glosses over some useful information. For example, some of the most controversial programs included in the table are by no means among the most expensive welfare state policies in this country (at least in direct monetary terms); and, conversely, some of the most expensive programs have few severe critics. Thus the current turbulence about the American social welfare state, while *related* to the high costs of producing economic security, is not completely *explained* by the size of Washington's expenditures on welfare programs. This point will be addressed later.

Furthermore, indicating dates of enactment obscures, and thus to some extent deemphasizes, the incremental nature of the adoption of social welfare programs in this country. While a few programs (e.g., Lyndon Johnson's "war on poverty") moved from idea to reality in a few months, many more took years. Thus large-scale federal support for medical care, initiated in 1965, had been an issue on the nation's policy agenda since the second decade of this century and had even been a major priority of President Truman in 1949. The process of policy formulation on this issue alone took generations and, in fact, is not over yet. Some policy activists in the 1970s and 1980s have been arguing the case for national health insurance.

Other major expansions of the American welfare state occurred as amendments to already existing policies (e.g., clean air and clean water regulation in the 1970s and an increase in the social security system in 1972). These sorts of policy changes also suggest incrementalism in action. Of course *many* incremental policy enactments can, over time, form a major policy change. This point is made by some of today's critics of the social welfare state in the United States. They argue that most of the nation's individual programs make sense or are not outrageously extravagant, but now that so many policies and programs have been cumulated, the result is a haphazard and increasingly expensive mess. This issue, too, will be addressed later.

A Brief Comparison

Today's controversy about the American social welfare state takes on a somewhat different aspect when we compare social welfare policy in the United States with the sorts of policies that have been enacted in other industrial nations. In general, American commitments to specific social welfare programs have occurred later and been somewhat less comprehensive than in many other comparable nations. Japan, Canada, and the western European nations (e.g., Great Britain, France, West Germany, Sweden, Italy, Denmark, the Netherlands) are all countries with reasonably democratic governments, substantial free enterprise, and commitments to social welfare. Yet a fair generalization is that all but Japan have moved toward the enactment of social welfare policy more quickly and more definitively than has the United States. (Japan is unique in that Japanese business takes on a much larger responsibility for the social welfare of employees than do companies in western nations.)

Figure 16-1 and Tables 16-2 and 16-3 provide some evidence on these points. From Figure 16-1, you can see that by comparison with most other developed social welfare states in the western world, the United States has been last or near last to enact many of the most important economic security policies, including such programs as unemployment compensation, assistance for the elderly, and health care (Shonfield, 1966; Wilensky, 1975; Heclo, 1975; Ashford, 1978). All these nations except this one now provide at least a modest level of automatic income support to their very poorest families.

Only the world's richest countries can much afford to commit themselves seriously to the social welfare state. But among these countries, the level of commitment varies considerably. Table 16-2 demonstrates this point by comparing the proportions of various nations' economies devoted to social insurance. (The spending of money, alone, of course, is no certain indicator that a government is actually providing any economic security to anybody. But by comparing allocations in this one area

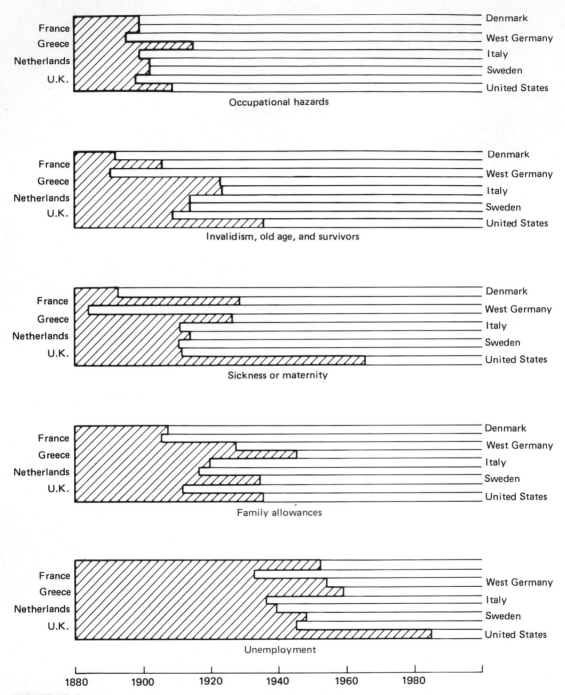

FIGURE 16-1
Dates of enactment of various social welfare programs, selected countries. Bars indicate period before enactment. (*Source:* Heidenheimer et al., 1975:189.)

TABLE 16-2

SOCIAL INSURANCE IN VARIOUS COUNTRIES AS
PERCENT OF GROSS DOMESTIC PRODUCT, 1976–1977

Country	% devoted to social insurance
Canada	16.4
United States	14.8
Japan	12.5
Denmark	24.5
France	26.0
West Germany	23.0
Italy	20.8
Norway	20.7
Sweden	33.9
United Kingdom	18.8

Source: International Labor Organization, 1981:58–61.

we can get at least a rough idea of how committed various nations are to this goal.) Once again, the United States trails the other nations in how much of the country's economy is devoted directly to this social welfare end.

To some degree our government's lower level of spending is explained by the larger proportion of our budget allocated to defense. In fact, one might argue that the United States supports the social welfare states of western Europe. By our providing,

TABLE 16-3

TAX BURDENS AND MARGINAL TAX RATES IN VARIOUS COUNTRIES, 1976

Country	Percent of gross earnings*	Marginal rate†
Denmark	33	55
West Germany	27	34
Netherlands	31	42
Norway	27	42
Sweden	35	63
Britain	26	41
United States	17	32

*The percentages of gross earnings paid by the average production worker in national, state, and local income taxes and social security taxes combined.

†The combined tax rates that would be applied to the next 10 percent of gross earnings by the same worker.

Source: Dolbeare, 1982:88.

directly or indirectly, for a considerable portion of their defense, they can thus devote their resources more to economic security. Yet this point does not entirely clarify matters, as Table 16-3 demonstrates. The United States government not only *spends* less, proportionately, on social welfare; it also taxes its citizens less heavily *overall*. In short, and for whatever reasons, the American government has chosen to place less of the nation's resources in public hands for public spending than have most other western industrial democracies. Some of today's critics of the social welfare state in the United States argue that taxation is too high for some of the most important or potentially productive members of American society—or even that the *effective* tax rate is higher in some cases in this country than in many European nations (Gilder, 1981). But by most measures, Americans seem to be a less heavily taxed people.

Why? Why has the United States committed itself less wholeheartedly than other countries to the policies of a social welfare state? Many reasons have been suggested.

No Social Democratic Party or Tradition Most other developed countries in the western world have had during the twentieth century an active political party or movement that has been committed to a socialist, but democratic, vision. These parties have been largely based in the working class and have generally pushed for comprehensive welfare state programs. No such American political party has seriously stood a chance of controlling Congress or the presidency. In any event, as we saw in Chapter 5, American parties are relatively unprogrammatic and have been growing weaker.

The careful reader of Chapter 15, on the policy process, may be able to identify some other reasons. Here are a few.

Incrementalism Policies, we have seen, tend to alter bit by bit over the years. Thus nations that were among the first to enact social welfare policies have had more time to tinker with them (but see Collier and Messick, 1975). The incremental changes in all nations have tended gradually to include more people under established programs and to grant them more benefits.

Because many American social welfare policies are intergovernmental, state regulations can have a major influence on the benefits that people like these unemployed workers may receive.   *(J. P. Laffont/Sygma)*

The Structure of American Government We know of two ways by which the founders sought to fragment or decentralize our government so that tyranny could be prevented: by separating powers and by establishing a federal (national-state) system. Both of these features of American government probably slow the enactment of welfare state policy.

The separation of powers among the institutions of the national government, and in fact the generally pluralized nature of the policy process in Washington, mean that various veto points can halt the enactment of a new policy, as the preceding chapter demonstrated. In the case of social welfare policy, which is often controversial, frequently somewhere in the policy process there is a decision maker who finds a proposal unpalatable or unwise. Richard Nixon encountered this problem in 1969 when he proposed his Family Assistance Plan for welfare reform. He convinced the House of Representatives to support the idea, but the program was buried in the Senate. More recently, Jimmy

Carter could not build a coalition large enough in the Congress to support "catastrophe" health insurance. Often it is difficult to pass social welfare policy at the national level because nearly any specific proposal is attacked by some policymakers as too generous and by others as too stingy.

The division of authority between national and state governments has also meant that the American welfare state is smaller than it might have been otherwise. Despite the growth in national activity on domestic policy matters, the states retain significant jurisdiction over many policies that affect social welfare. In fact, many social welfare policies in the United States, especially those aimed at income security—for example, Aid to Families with Dependent Children, Medicaid, school lunches, public housing, unemployment compensation, etc.—are intergovernmental, with substantial discretion exercised away from Washington. This decentralization probably reduces the ability of the national government to establish and enforce major policy changes, either increases or decreases. As we have seen, the concept of a "new federalism" as proposed by President Reagan provides the states with even more control over social welfare policy.

The Role of Ideas Perhaps a factor that is just as important—and that may actually explain some of the other ones we have mentioned—is the role of ideas in American politics. Visitors from abroad to the United States seldom fail to be struck by the distinctive notions which frame debate and decisions about social welfare in this country. Many bits of evidence, from opinion polls to Fourth of July speeches, confirm the importance to most Americans of such values as individualism, limited government, the right to property, free market capitalism, and the work ethic. Commentators from Tocqueville to Ronald Reagan have noted, too, the important role of voluntary associations—churches, community groups, and so forth—in this society and in its approaches to the problem of social welfare. The strength of this set of ideas, perhaps more than anything else, constrains the efforts of those who seek a larger, more active welfare state in this country (King, 1973).

In any event, the present-day social welfare state here is one that often satisfies few. To some, who look to an earlier era and to some important concerns expressed by the first American constitution makers, it seems overgrown, dangerous, and overburdened (Friedman, 1962; Nozick, 1974). To others, who compare it with the commitments made by other nations and who are concerned by the very real economic insecurities faced by many of this country's citizens, it seems woefully inadequate to the task. The existence of so many American programs for social welfare would seem to be strong evidence that the elitist model of policymaking is seriously flawed. Yet the limited benefits available convince some analysts that the policies serve the interests of the economically privileged by giving the poor just enough to be pacified but not enough to acquire real power (Piven and Cloward, 1971; O'Connor, 1973; Mandell, 1975; Ryan, 1976). The American social welfare state today comprises, to a considerable extent, the legacy of the founders as adapted to the constraints and opportunities of today's complicated world. It is thus appropriate that we now examine the policies of the

contemporary American social welfare state in more detail.

THE AMERICAN SOCIAL WELFARE STATE IN ACTION

Managing the Economy

Under the model of a perfect free market, it would be not only unnecessary for a government to manage the economy but also folly for it to attempt to do so. This was the argument of the exponents of *laissez-faire capitalism*. The public interest would result, they said, only if buyers and sellers in the United States worried solely about their own immediate goals—a good price, on the one hand, and a healthy profit, on the other. In this fashion, the economy would take care of itself, productivity would be encouraged, growth would benefit all, and unemployment would be reduced to a minimum. The government, went the idea, should do only what is absolutely necessary to allow private commerce to proceed expeditiously. This image of the proper role of American government in the nation's economy typified the prevailing sentiment for most of the nation's existence. While American government protected business through tariffs and supported private development via public subsidy of construction projects, federal policy until the twentieth century called for virtually no role by Washington in the overall management or direction of economic forces in this country.

Government regulation to correct some of the perceived imperfections in the market began in the 1880s (discussed later), but it was not until the depression years that the nation took its first steps toward a considerably expanded governmental role in national economic management. In 1932 Franklin D. Roosevelt campaigned on a platform that stressed a cut in government spending and a balanced federal budget as two keys to a successful economic recovery for the United States. But once in office, he acted otherwise. Roosevelt and his advisers recognized that federal expenditures had assumed amounts large enough to mean that spending decisions the government decided to make could have a significant effect on the entire economic picture in the country. The government therefore embarked on a policy of large increases in spending to stimulate the American economy.

Such a strategy was, of course, popular in the United States at the time, since the widespread belief was that the New Deal expenditures were improving the situation and putting people back to work. This idea for an expanded federal role in economic activity was then given a further boost by the theory of an influential economist from England, John Maynard Keynes. Keynes suggested that, left to its own devices, a free market economy would *not* necessarily be self-correcting. Governments, he sought to demonstrate, can "balance" their nations' economies by stimulating investment and "aggregate demand," that is, how much a nation's people and businesses are willing to commit themselves to spend at a given time (Keynes, 1936). A simple summary of some of Keynes's major suggestions for governments would be that they can "fine-tune" their economies by spending beyond their revenues and perhaps cutting taxes when the economy is slack, while enacting budget surpluses and possibly tax increases when the economy is "overheated" (e.g., experiencing excess demand and inflation). In this fashion, he said, nations can reduce economic insecurity by dampening erratic swings between boom and bust and by ensuring a low level of unemployment.

The theory of *Keynesian economics* was very persuasive to many American economists. Within a short time, the notion that the federal government should be required, as a matter of policy, to concern itself with economic stability, growth, and employment appeared prominently on the agenda. The Employment Act of 1946 enacted the idea of government as economic manager into law, created a Council of Economic Advisers (CEA) to help the president in this task, and required an annual report from the president on the state of the nation's economy and economic policy. The laissez-faire model had disappeared, at least from formal policy. From that time to the present, the federal government has often been actively involved in helping to direct American economic forces; decisions have frequently been made in the Keynesian mold. For example, President Kennedy pushed for a major income tax cut in 1962 on the advice of his Keynesian chairman of the CEA. The economy thrived. Some of these ideas for economic management had

become palatable even to Republican leaders like President Nixon, who said—in defense of his 1972 budget proposal that included a projected deficit—"I am now a Keynesian in economics" (Reichley, 1981:220).

Types of Policies for Economic Management What tools has the government at its disposal to help manage the economy? What types of policy decisions influence the larger economy? Several major kinds can be sketched briefly.

Fiscal policy Fiscal policy comprises a set of decisions about *how much revenue* the government will collect from the economy and *how much* in turn will be *spent*. The issue of *who* should pay for what proportion of the revenue can be considered part of fiscal policy, but we will discuss that issue separately, as tax policy. The question of *what* the government does with its spending is often thought of as fiscal policy too, but for simplicity we designate that subject, later, as "budgetary policy." Fiscal policy can be very important. With expenditures as large as the federal government makes (more than $750 billion in 1983, roughly 22 percent of the GNP), changing the level of revenue collection or of spending can have dramatic repercussions throughout the entire economy. Spending more than is raised stimulates the economy; raising more than is spent quiets it. Thus when policymakers try to decide whether to enact a budget deficit—and, if so, how much—they are considering an issue of fiscal policy. Fiscal policy is one of the major tools employed by Keynesians. The president, with advice from the CEA and the Office of Management and Budget, plays a major role in fiscal decisions; but presidents cannot enact such decisions unilaterally. Raising revenue requires the action of the House Ways and Means Committee, the Senate Finance Committee, and Congress in general. Deciding on levels of spending involves the Budget and Appropriations committees in Congress and, eventually, action by the whole legislature.

Furthermore, many of the programs the federal government has enacted over the years obligate the nation to pay for certain expenditures in the future. The most prominent among these are the so-called "entitlement programs," like veterans' benefits and social security. The total amount to be spent on

TABLE 16-4
REVENUE AND SPENDING BY THE FEDERAL GOVERNMENT, 1945–1983

Year	Receipts, $ billions	Outlays, $ billions	Surplus or deficit, $ billions
1945	45.2	92.7	−47.5
1950	39.5	42.6	−3.1
1955	65.5	68.3	−3.0
1960	92.5	92.2	0.3
1961	94.4	97.8	−3.4
1962	99.7	106.8	−7.1
1963	106.6	111.3	−4.8
1964	112.7	118.6	−5.9
1965	116.8	118.4	−1.6
1966	130.9	134.7	−3.8
1967	149.6	158.3	−8.7
1968	153.7	178.8	−25.2
1969	187.8	184.5	3.2
1970	193.7	196.6	−2.8
1971	188.4	211.4	−23.0
1972	208.6	232.0	−23.4
1973	232.2	247.1	−14.8
1974	264.9	269.6	−4.7
1975	281.0	326.2	−45.2
1976*	381.7	461.1	−79.4
1977	357.8	402.7	−44.9
1978	402.0	450.8	−48.8
1979	465.9	493.6	−27.1
1980	520.1	579.6	−59.6
1981	600.3	655.2	−54.9
1982†	626.8	725.3	−98.6
1983†	666.1	757.6	−91.5

*This fiscal year contained five quarters.
†Estimates.
Source: Statistical Abstract, 1981, 1981:245; U.S. Office of Management and Budget, 1982.

such activities in an upcoming year is partially de- termined by how many "entitled" recipients there are. The government cannot directly control, say, how many elderly Americans there will be three years from now or what portion of people eligible for food stamps will actually apply for them during the next spending cycle. A growing proportion of federal social welfare spending has been going for entitlements in recent years (a discussion of some of these programs follows later). One important re- sult has been that policymakers now have more dif- ficulty controlling expenditures directly and thus making fiscal policy.

The revenue and spending decisions of the United States government from 1946 to the present are displayed in Table 16-4. Note that in the last few decades virtually every year has seen a deficit. Some conservative critics of the nation's economic management during this time point to these persis- tent deficits as a sign that policy has been irrespon- sible. The idea for a Constitutional amendment to require a balanced budget has received support from Ronald Reagan, a number of legislators, and a substantial segment of the American people (see Box 16-1). Defenders of the decisions enacted over the past years note that while the deficit has in-

BOX 16-1

A BALANCED-BUDGET AMENDMENT?

In 1975, the National Taxpayers Union (NTU), an interest group that presses for lower taxes and reduced government spending, began organizing a drive to amend the Constitution of the United States in support of their cause. The federal government had been in deficit for several years, and as the national debt increased significantly (see Table 16-4), the drive gathered momentum.

The general idea was to add a Constitutional requirement to force national policymakers to cover expenditures with revenues every year. Other allied interest groups such as the National Tax Limitation Committee, which claimed 600,000 members by the early 1980s, joined the cause.

The strategy of the NTU was to achieve its goal by the usual route chosen in the past to amend the Constitution: a two-thirds vote of each house of Congress and subsequent ratification by the legislatures of three-quarters of the states. Yet other enthusiasts chose to emphasize a different tack, one also allowed by the fundamental law of the land: having two-thirds (i.e., thirty-four) of the states require Congress to call for a national constitutional convention.

The effort to call such a convention spread quickly among several states in the late 1970s, slowed in 1980, but then picked up steam again as President Reagan—long a proponent of limited spending—endorsed budgets that would enact massive deficits. By 1983, thirty-one states had petitioned for a constitutional convention.

Meanwhile, in 1982 the Senate approved 69-31 one version of a balanced-budget amendment; it would limit both taxing and spending but would allow deficits if approved by three-fifths of Congress and would waive controls in wartime. Reagan backed the proposal, but it did not pass in the House during that Congress.

Many legislators found the problem a difficult one to address. Requiring a balanced budget is a politically popular notion. (A September 1981 survey, for instance, found public support by a margin of 67 to 19.) But critics point out several difficulties. They question whether technical decisions on revenue and spending ought to be made in the Constitution itself. (Some members of Congress support a law but not a Constitutional change toward this end.) They point out that amending the Constitution is a slow process, and such a change would do nothing about federal spending for at least eight years. Some disagree with the economic theory avowed by the budget balancers and also claim that the amendment proposals receiving consideration are vague.

Perhaps the most serious concerns have to do with calling a constitutional convention. None has been held since the founders' effort two centuries ago. No one knows what the procedures would be, and it is quite possible that, once convened, such a group could try to rewrite many parts of the Constitution on matters entirely apart from budget balancing.

Nevertheless, current budget proposals and projections for future years show no signs that the federal treasury will soon be headed out of the red. The issue may be explosive.

Source: National Journal, Oct. 9, 1982; Gallup Report, 1982:9; CQ Weekly Report, Mar. 27, 1982, Aug. 7, 1982; Washington Post, 1982.

creased, the total national debt until very recently has declined as a proportion of the entire economy. Many also argue that a Constitutional amendment on the subject is unwise and may reduce rather than increase the rationality of the nation's fiscal decisions.

Monetary policy The federal government not only collects revenue and spends it; it also determines the amount of money in circulation and the supply of credit available. "Loose money" (an ex-panded money and credit supply) makes it easier to get and borrow money and thus helps to encourage companies to go into debt to finance expansion and encourages potential homeowners to acquire mortgages. A "tight money" policy can be used to slow down inflation. (One can think of inflation as one economist described it: too much money chasing too few goods.) Typically, monetary policy aims at increasing the money supply at a rate commensurate with the rate of real economic growth in the country, so as to find a way between inflation and recession.

In one way or another, the national government has used monetary policy for a long time. Even early in the eighteenth century, the United States had to make decisions about money and credit. Thus controversy about the Bank of the United States was really a monetary dispute. Monetary decisions seem less direct and obtrusive in the economy than do fiscal actions, and so for a good part of American political history the government made monetary decisions without really taking responsibility for the economy's performance.

In 1914, the Federal Reserve System (the "Fed") was created to set the government's monetary policies. The Fed is a system composed of a central policy board, a set of twelve regional banks, and thousands of private member banks. (This last group encompasses most of the banks in this country.) The Fed determines the amount of money in circulation by buying and selling government securities, by setting the rate of interest to be charged member banks when they borrow, and by regulating what proportion of its deposits a member bank must keep on hand (and thus how much the bank can use for loans). The members of the board are presidential appointees, but they serve for long (fourteen-year) terms. Thus, individual presidents are unlikely to be able to exercise much direct control over monetary policy, and Congress is even less influential. Therefore, in this nation monetary policy is made and executed for the most part outside of the usual political process.

Monetarists, or people who believe that monetary policy should be the government's prime tool in economic management, often find themselves at odds with Keynesians, who tend to be more liberal and to believe more in the efficacy of decisions about taxing and spending for controlling the economy. Milton Friedman is one prominent conservative economist who considers himself a monetarist. Friedman—who taught at the University of Chicago, writes a column for *Newsweek* magazine, and frequently advises policymakers—argues that the federal government should pursue a prudent monetary policy and do very little else to the economy; in this fashion, he says, many of our current economic troubles would be lessened.

It is thus easy to see that the division of power among president, Congress, and Fed, coupled with the division of doctrine among economists, often means that policymaking in the councils of government is confused or contradictory. It is not altogether unusual to see a president seeking to stimulate the economy through fiscal policy while the Fed withdraws money from circulation to control inflation. Matters may become even more heated or more complicated because monetary policies can have different impacts on different people: tight money may slow inflation and thus help the elderly living on fixed incomes, but the same policy makes it more difficult for savings and loan companies to lend money to young families seeking new homes.

Tax policy Deciding how much revenue the government needs to raise at a given time stimulates some related policy issues. What methods should the United States use to collect its money? And who should pay what portion of the tab? Needless to say, these questions are of concern to all Americans. In addition, federal tax policy is an instrument to assist the government in its efforts to manage the economy. Some types of taxes, for instance, are "regressive"; that is, they tax people with low incomes at a higher rate than those who earn more. Such policies might reduce the economic security of the former group and also lower overall demand for consumer goods. On the other hand, very heavy taxes on the wealthy might cut the level of investment in the country and thus dampen economic expansion. So policymakers cannot avoid paying attention to tax policy when they try to manage the nation's economic forces.

The major sources of federal revenues are shown in Table 16-5. (The table omits state and local taxes.) It will come as no surprise to most taxpaying Americans that the two largest sources of money for the national treasury are individual income taxes and payroll taxes (that is, social security taxes and, mainly from employers, unemployment compensation). Together, these two account for three-quarters of the total. Taxes on corporations, especially the corporate income tax, make up another sizable chunk.

Social security taxes have been increasing fairly rapidly in recent times as a result of legislation, enacted in 1977, which has been taking effect over a period of years (Derthick, 1979). Yet funding for social security remains inadequate to cover benefits

TABLE 16-5
MAJOR SOURCES OF FEDERAL REVENUE, 1981

Source	Amount, $ billions	Percent of total revenue
Individual income taxes	284.0	46.7
Social insurance taxes and contributions	184.8	30.4
Corporation income taxes	66.0	10.9
Excise taxes	44.4	7.3
Estate and gift taxes, customs duties	14.3	2.4
Miscellaneous receipts	13.9	2.3

Source: Statistical Abstract, 1981, 1981:247.

(discussed later). A proposal backed by President Reagan and passed into law in 1981 reduces the levels at which individual and corporate incomes would be taxed. Nevertheless, the hope (thus far unrealized) was that the total amount of revenue collected via income taxes would increase because the entire economy would be more productive and would generate more tax revenues.

A short discussion of the income tax illustrates some of the issues raised for the American social welfare state by tax policy. Who pays how much of the income tax? This question is, perhaps, a surprisingly complicated one to answer. The basic structure of the income tax system in the United States is progressive: the greater your earnings, the greater *proportion* of your income you are asked to pay in taxes. Those making $10,000 are taxed at the nominal rate of approximately 10 percent, while the few souls earning $100,000 pay 50 percent (down from 70 percent as of 1982). One rationale for a progressive income tax system like this is that it serves the ends of social welfare: the more people make, the more they can afford to be taxed.

However, almost all wealthy people—and, in fact, most of those who earn only moderate incomes—avoid paying the basic rate. They do so not by cheating (breaking the law), but by employing deductions (special advantages, or "loopholes," written into the law). A huge number of deductions are available, and they benefit both businesses (e.g., for some business expenses) and individuals. They make up the income tax code, probably the

lengthiest and most complicated policy in American government. Those who earn the most have more ability to take advantage of tax loopholes since they have more discretion as to how they can use and save their money and since some tax breaks (e.g., tax-free municipal bonds) become profitable only when one reaches the upper tax brackets.

But most of the dollars saved by citizens through tax avoidance, and thus not available to the government, are in the form of deductions by the middle class. Many of these Americans, who sometimes criticize welfare recipients for receiving handouts from the government, forget that they too are the indirect beneficiaries of federal support through "tax expenditures" (as these loopholes are often labeled). One of the best examples is the deduction for mortgage interest on homes. A wage earner making $30,000 per year who buys a $60,000 home with a thirty-year mortgage at today's interest rates is able to deduct perhaps $7,000 or $8,000 from his or her income for tax purposes during the first few years. The deduction will save the taxpayer thousands of dollars in income tax. In effect, this one loophole amounts to a federal subsidy to homeowners and the housing industry of several billion dollars per year.

Of course, there are hundreds of other special provisions of the tax code. Some reflect the political clout or perceived importance of certain groups or businesses. (An example is the deduction for royalty owners of oil lands.) Many are aimed at achieving one or another social purpose. (These include helping old people, through the deduction for social security income and a special exemption for the elderly; stimulating economic growth, through the investment tax credit; and supporting health care, through the deductions for medical expenses and insurance premiums.) And some are aimed at assisting the poorest citizens. (The earned income credit works this way for the working poor.)

In short, federal income tax policy has no single goal but, rather, a multitude of goals. Some fit with and contribute to the goals of a social welfare state, and some do not. The result is a confusing system that is not very progressive in its effect except at the very lowest levels (see Figure 16-2 for an illustration of the effects of the system before the latest tax reductions), and that is really comprehensible

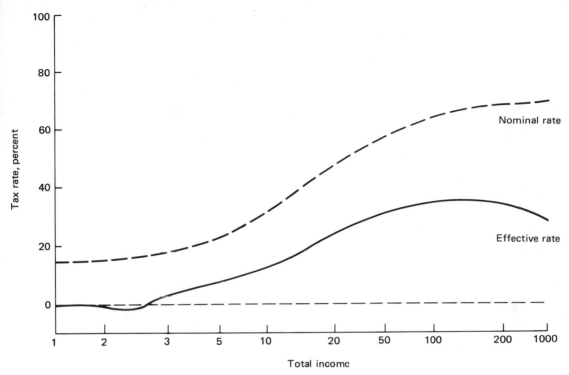

FIGURE 16-2
Individual income tax rates before tax reductions enacted 1981–1984. (*Source:* Pechman, 1977:72, 349–350; Council of Economic Advisors, 1982:119.)

only to a few accountants and attorneys. The policy as a whole has few ardent defenders, although individual provisions are often zealously protected. Thus candidates for national office frequently promise "tax reform" but find comprehensive change difficult. A variety of alternatives have been proposed and debated in recent years. These include simply eliminating loopholes (a difficult to impossible task), changing to another type of tax for most federal revenue (e.g., a value-added tax, which is something like a sales tax), or shifting the system to a flat rate instead of a progressive one but eliminating all deductions (an option backed by some corporations such as United Technologies). Every alternative invites criticism because the stakes are so high.

Budget policy   Each year the government makes thousands of decisions about what federal revenues should be spent for. Collectively these ac-

tions amount to the expenditure level that is a prime component of fiscal policy. Many of the specific budget items also directly affect the nation's social welfare either by contributing to the income support of individuals (discussed later) or by assisting various sectors of the economy. Examples of the latter type of program include special aid for small businesses and federal assistance to those parts of the country that experience substantial unemployment. During the years from the late 1960s to the beginning of the Reagan administration, the part of the budget devoted to purposes of the social welfare state increased significantly, while the relative weight given to defense declined. President Reagan started a reversal of that trend (see Figure 16-3).

Not all specific decisions by the government to establish a program or to provide financial support to some group actually appear as expenditures in

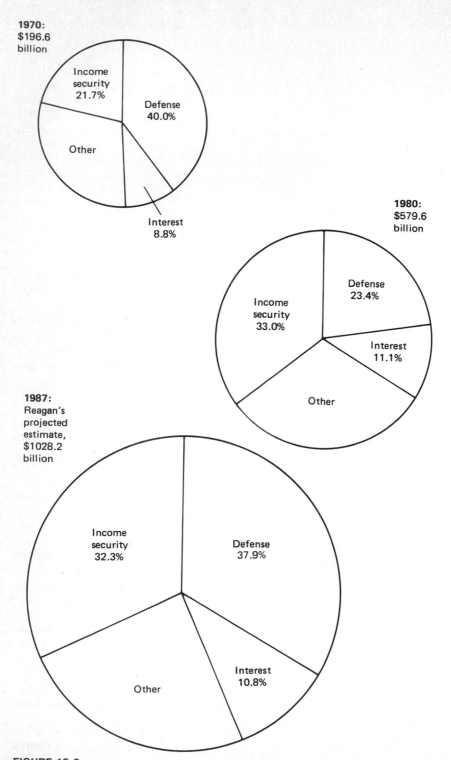

FIGURE 16-3
Budget outlays by function, selected years. (*Source: Statistical Abstract, 1981*, 1981:248;
U.S. Office of Management and Budget, 1982:3–33.)

the federal budget. Some are so-called "off-budget" items, such as payments from the Social Security Trust Fund. In a variety of even less obvious ways the government provides financial support for different sectors of the economy. One very important example is the set of federal decisions to guarantee loans made to certain governments (for instance, New York City) or firms (such as Chrysler Corporation). In these cases Washington spends no money if the debtors repay the loan, but without federal guarantees the loans never would have been risked by bankers in the first place. Another not-so-obvious policy which in effect budgets resources to support the economy is federal insurance, e.g., for the nation's banks and savings and loan companies. The hundreds of billions of dollars Americans have deposited with these financial institutions are protected by the government's coverage, a fact that increases confidence in the system and thus helps stabilize the economy.

As earlier chapters suggested, budget decisions in American government are made with the participation of numerous policy actors including, in formal terms, the president, the OMB, the CEA, the Congressional Budget Office, and Congress itself, especially through the Budget and Appropriations Committee of both the House and the Senate.

Wage and price controls   Sometimes governments participate more directly in guiding or managing the economy. Wage and price controls, often referred to as "incomes policy," can be employed to regulate the amounts that private parties can charge or pay for goods or services. Wage and price controls have been used only rarely in the United States, the most recent time being in 1971. Then, President Nixon, acting under congressional authority, imposed a freeze on almost all wages, salaries, prices, and rents for a ninety-day period, and imposed a somewhat less severe set of controls for an additional time. Incomes policy directly supplants the operations of the market and thus is viewed by Americans and American policymakers as an extreme measure.

"Moral suasion"   A less severe version of economic management than direct controls consists of a policymaker, usually the president in this country, exhorting citizens and businesses to alter their economic behavior in accord with the national interest, as expressed by the policymaker. Moral suasion (see Peters, 1982) often consists of appeals to moderate wage demands or price hikes. Lyndon Johnson when chief executive used his technique of "jawboning" (personal discussion and persuasion) to reduce inflationary increases in some industries, and Gerald Ford appeared on national television to suggest that Americans wear "WIN" buttons (Whip Inflation Now) to combat the inflationary psychology of the mid-1970s. Moral suasion, being reliant on voluntary cooperation in a marketplace rewarding self-interest, is often less than effective.

Government ownership   Perhaps the most extreme form by which a government can manage a nation's economy is by nationalizing it, or parts of it, that is, taking over ownership (Harrington, 1972, 1976; Lindblom, 1982). The option of direct public enterprise is not a popular one in the United States. There are a few sectors of the economy that technically might be handled by private business but are not, such as electric power produced and sold by the Tennessee Valley Authority. But more of the economy is in private hands in this country than anywhere else in the western industrialized world.

The American Economy in Recent Years
With all the policy tools at the government's disposal and all the economic expertise available to policymakers, one might think that the nation's economy should be well-managed. Yet most American economic decisions are not publicly determined but, rather, remain private. More important, perhaps, economics remains far from an exact science, and political conflicts about economic options are inevitable.

There may be more controversy than ever these days about the government's management of the economy. This is because the economy has performed rather poorly for most of the last decade. From the Second World War to the early 1970s, the United States and most other developed nations in the west experienced low inflation, fairly low unemployment, and an expanding economy—though the expansion was not so great in the United States as in a number of other countries. Yet since 1973 or so, things have not gone very well. Unemployment has reached levels not seen since the depression of the 1930s, while the inflation rate remained persistently high for most of this period. This combination of maladies, unanticipated by most Keynesian analysis, has been dubbed "stagflation" and has been complicated by the absence of much growth during recent administrations. By 1982 the United States had slipped to ninth place in GNP per person among the industrial nations. No combination of fiscal, monetary, incomes, or other policies seemed to produce dramatic results. Stagflation violated the conventional wisdom that the economy could experience inflation or recession, but not both simultaneously. Part of the problem could be attributed to American dependence on foreign oil controlled by the Organization of Petroleum Exporting Countries (OPEC). Part might be explained by pressure on the economy generated by the Vietnamese war. But whatever the causes, economists and policymakers have been groping for new and better approaches to economic management. The policies of the Reagan administration on this important social welfare topic are discussed later, but it is important to remember that this policy subject is likely to remain a matter

of intense interest and concern for some time to come.

Securing Americans' Income

Like every other nation in the world, the United States has a considerable number of poor people and a significant number of others who are not poor but will at some time in their lives be threatened by economic insecurity—through death or injury to a breadwinner, loss of a job during difficult economic times or because of technological advance, catastrophic medical expenses, and so forth.

What is the extent of poverty in the United States? A reliable assessment is difficult to make. If we use the federal government's figures, which are based primarily upon an estimate of minimal living expenses, the number of poor people in this country today is over 25 million—that is, approximately 12 percent of the nation's population (*Social Security Bulletin,* 1982:60). This figure is only a rough guess, however. It does not take into

One direct form of federal help for Americans below the poverty line is the distribution of surplus federal food stocks to the needy; but state or local agencies generally administer such programs.   *(Bill Strode/Woodfin Camp)*

account "in-kind" payments by the government to the citizenry (for instance, food stamps); a large segment of the American poor are helped by anywhere from one to more than five in-kind programs (Storey et al., 1973; U.S. Bureau of the Census, 1982). Thus the estimate above may overstate, by at least a slight extent, the number of Americans falling below the poverty line. Yet the poverty population is defined very narrowly by the government. (In 1979, for example, poverty figures *excluded* those who, by Census Bureau estimates, would have been able to spend 57 cents or more per meal per person.) More than one-quarter of the population of the United States falls below the level of income called "austere" by the federal Bureau of Labor Statistics. In addition, of course, many other Americans are vulnerable to hardship should they experience, for instance, a long-term and expensive medical problem. Thus the problem or potential problem of income security is neither small nor confined to a few isolated groups of the population. The young, the old, families with fathers absent, and the nonwhite members of the society are more likely to experience the most severe distress, but none of these groups dominates the poverty picture (McCrone and Hardy, 1978).

The policy problem is this: Should government seek to reduce the possibility that Americans will not have income adequate to take care of their needs? Under which situations? For which citizens? How? Our earlier review of American policy for managing the economy suggested that the government seeks income security for its citizens at least indirectly, by working for reduced unemployment, lower inflation, and increased growth. It is also true that through a variety of specific programs of the social welfare state the United States government intends income security for at least some Americans. A brief discussion and analysis of a few of these programs is the aim of this section.

The number and diversity of social welfare programs operating under government auspices confuse even the experts. The programs generally are designed to assist different, but often overlapping, constituencies. Some programs have huge expenditures while others are relatively small; some are quite generous in the benefits they provide to recipients, while others give only modest help. The various policies have divergent criteria for determining

who is eligible to receive help. Some benefits go to only those citizens who contribute part of the cost when they receive their benefits; others go to those who have provided payments like insurance premiums during a preceding period; some go to all who apply and have a clearly demonstrated need; others grant assistance to all within certain age or other boundaries; while still others go to virtually all Americans within certain income categories, whether they apply or not. Some income security programs in this country are run entirely by the national government, but a substantial portion of the American social welfare state is intergovernmental. There are even some programs that are entirely state-operated. (We shall not discuss this last group further.)

Two distinctions in governmental assistance are particularly useful to make: *contributory* versus *noncontributory* programs and *cash* versus *in-kind* assistance (see Table 16-6). These distinctions suggest politically significant differences.

Contributory Programs Contributory (sometimes called "social insurance") programs are those for which the recipients have provided a direct contribution, usually throughout their working

TABLE 16-6
MAJOR SOCIAL WELFARE STATE PROGRAMS THAT SUPPORT INCOME SECURITY, 1981

Type and program	Expenditures, $ billions
Contributory, cash	
OASDI (social security)	140.0
Unemployment insurance	20.0
Veterans' disability and retirement	13.0
Contributory, in-kind	
Medicare	45.0
Noncontributory, cash	
AFDC	8.0
SSI	8.0
Noncontributory, in-kind	
Food stamps	11.0
Medicaid	18.0
Housing assistance	6.0
School lunches	3.5

Source: Dolbeare, 1982:217.

lives. These programs are not really "insurance" programs in the usual sense of that term; the level of a recipient's benefits may not be limited by the size of his or her contribution, for instance. Social insurance programs make up the great bulk of the American social welfare state's payments for income security; approximately three-quarters of the total dollars expended directly by the federal government for programs of the social welfare state go toward contributory programs. These are also the programs that account for most of the growth in recent years of social welfare expenditures and thus explain much of the pressure on the federal budget. Accordingly, they are stirring political controversy.

Yet contributory programs are more acceptable to Americans than noncontributory ones since the former have less the appearance of a handout or giveaway. Furthermore, the great bulk of the money paid out by today's contributory programs goes to the elderly. This group commands respect and compassion from most Americans and is perceived as especially vulnerable to economic misfortune. Thus it is difficult for policymakers to trim the American social welfare state at its most expensive spot. This problem reflects the complexity and ambivalence of public opinion in the United States on welfare issues, as shown in Box 16-2 (Prysby, 1979).

BOX 16-2

AMERICAN PUBLIC OPINION ON WELFARE ISSUES

Here are some questions asked, and the responses received, by public opinion pollsters:

• Do you favor a balanced budget, but not if it means cutting out funds for those who are poor and on welfare (asked in August 1980)? 65 percent yes, 31 percent no, 4 percent not sure.

• Do you favor or oppose a cut in federal government spending for:

	Favor cut	Oppose cut	Not sure
Welfare payment grants	72 percent	24 percent	4 percent
Subsidized housing	66	28	6
Federal jobs programs	62	31	7
Food stamp program for people with low incomes	54	41	5
Grants for Medicaid	39	57	4
School lunch and other nutrition programs	35	63	2
Social security	20	77	3
Medicare for elderly	15	83	2

(Questions asked in January 1981, before Reagan's cutbacks.)

• In November 1981, after the first round of Reagan's cuts in social programs had been implemented and a second round had been proposed, the following question was asked: "The additional cuts for social purposes come to about $11 billion. Do you feel that this amount is too high, too low or about right?" Too high: 43 percent; too low: 8 percent; about right: 35 percent; don't know: 14 percent.

The last results were gathered in a Gallup poll; all others were obtained in Harris polls.

Source: Hastings and Hastings, 1982:366; and *Gallup Report*, 1982:7.

Noncontributory Programs Noncontributory (or public assistance) programs are those that provide support for people who have not contributed payments. Both contributory and noncontributory programs are redistributive because they provide help to recipients at least in part from others who do not benefit. But noncontributory programs are the ones typically considered "welfare" and typically the focus of antagonism because here the redistributive aspect is more obvious: people receive benefits without paying anything in return.

Noncontributory programs are designed to pay on the basis of need, but need is defined differently for different programs. Because of the necessity to determine whether potential recipients meet the need criteria, many noncontributory programs also have heavier administrative expenses. They employ bureaucrats to determine eligibility, prevent fraud, and otherwise limit the extent of improper payments. This aspect of noncontributory programs, too, adds to their difficulty in obtaining strong political support. Some of the programs, even if necessary, are perceived as wasteful and also as demeaning to those who must demonstrate their limited economic assets. The American public assistance programs are by and large smaller in budget but larger in number than the nation's social insurance programs.

Cash versus In-Kind Support Some programs support people by providing them with money; others in effect bolster people's income by providing them with a free or partially subsidized good or service, such as food or health care. These are cash and in-kind programs, respectively. Supporters of cash transfer payments to those who need help suggest that such programs are preferable because they leave the decisions about how people's incomes should be spent in their own hands, thus emphasizing liberty as a value. This option avoids governmental intrusion and also allows flexibility— people can then be their own judge of their most urgent needs at any time. Supporters of in-kind payments desire to target the government's assistance to alleviate particular problems. An advantage for some of the in-kind programs is that there is thus less chance that assistance for helpless people (e.g., little children) will be wasted on frivolous items by those who receive the payments (e.g., irresponsible parents). Neither employment training nor public housing, for example, is easily exchanged for a color television set or a vacation to Acapulco.

Programs for Income Support Having described some of the major differences in the types of programs constituting American policy for income support, we are now in a position to take a cursory look at the programs themselves. Space does not permit more than a superficial mention of most of the important programs. We pay a bit more attention to one of the programs, Aid to Families with Dependent Children, for it illustrates, in effect, a constitutional debate over which values should be pursued by the social welfare state in this country.

Unemployment compensation This is an intergovernmental social insurance program that provides cash benefits to those who become involuntarily unemployed, as long as they continue to look for a job. Part of the cost is financed by payroll taxes paid mostly by employers, but for the past few years some of the funds have come from general federal revenues. Benefits are usually exhausted after six months of payments to unemployed workers. Sometimes, however, benefits have been extended by legislation. Obviously, this program is designed to provide temporary support to those between jobs.

Social security The major, or at least the costliest, component of the American social welfare state that aims at the provision of income security is the social security program (technically, Old Age, Survivors, and Disability Insurance, OASDI). This contributory cash program provides assistance to retired and disabled workers or their survivors. The social security system was initiated in 1935 and continues to be a major source of support for millions of Americans. The program is run by the national government and is funded through a trust fund to which employers and workers contribute through a tax on income up to a certain level. Benefit levels have been expanded numerous times through amendments to the act, and until the early 1980s, at least, payments increased automatically to keep pace with the rising cost of living. In recent years the social security tax has surged upward dramatically as Congress has sought to be generous to the elderly while also keeping the trust fund solvent. Nevertheless, costs have continued to outpace revenues, in part because there are relatively fewer workers now to support the growing number of retired people. Yet the popularity of the program is probably unmatched by any other American policy. The result is a political thicket. In 1981, the Senate voted unanimously for a resolution rejecting President Reagan's suggestion that cutbacks might be made in this program. Reagan then established a bipartisan commission to study the matter. In 1983 the group recommended a combination of benefit cutbacks and tax increases, hardly a popular suggestion. Thus policymakers and Americans generally are having to face some difficult questions about this segment of their social welfare state.

Supplemental security income The Social Security Act enacted in 1935 created programs in addition to OASDI. The other ones were noncontributory public assistance programs. Among these were Old Age Assistance (originally for those elderly who were not covered by provisions of "regular" social security), Aid to the Blind, and Aid to the Permanently and Totally Disabled. The intention obviously was to support the income of certain groups among the poor who were deemed particularly unfortunate and deserving of assistance. The states participated in these programs, and benefits as well as eligibility criteria varied considerably from place to place. In 1974, a major shift in the policy of the American social welfare state went into effect. A change in federal law that had been proposed by President Nixon merged these three programs into one and substantially federalized its operation. Nationwide criteria and minimums were established. The new programs, dubbed "Supplemental Security Income (SSI)," effectively created a guaranteed, even if low, annual income for those Americans who fit into one or more of these categories.

Health care The threat of costly medical problems poses a major concern to many Americans. Most citizens have some form of health insurance coverage. However, millions do not; and for many who do have some protection, the extent of coverage would be inadequate to pay for costly or long-term health difficulties. Medical problems are most severe for two groups: the elderly, who often need more care and yet frequently are tied to fixed incomes, and the poor, who have a higher incidence of health problems than the rest of the population and yet often avoid even routine medical care because of the expense involved. Americans' vulnerability to economic insecurity because of medical problems is made more likely by the changing costs of health care, which have been escalating more rapidly than inflation for a number of years (Sidel and Sidel, 1977).

Health care in the United States is mostly organized through a network of private providers, but the government is involved through a variety of programs. The two most significant—on the basis of expenditures and also impact on income security—are Medicare and Medicaid. Both programs were enacted in 1965, after years of debate among policymakers, interest groups, and citizens. Medicare is funded solely at the federal level, while Medicaid is funded and administered in a combined federal-state system. Both are in-kind programs, obviously, since they help only with medical care; the former is a contributory system, the latter noncontributory.

Medicare draws much more heavily upon federal funds (see Table 16-6), and it is larger than Medicaid even when state support is taken into account. The goal of Medicare is to provide some protection to elderly and disabled citizens, mostly those covered by social security. Hospital bills and charges for extended-care facilities (e.g., nursing homes) are paid from social security payroll taxes. For those who choose to contribute additional payments at the time they become eligible for Medicare, coverage for some doctors' services is added; this part of the program is also supported by the federal government's general revenue. Medicare does not provide unlimited health care. Federal regulations restrict the sorts of services that will be supported, charge deductibles, require that part of the recipients' bills be paid for from their own funds ("copayments"), and impose ceilings for maximum benefits.

Medicaid is a public assistance program for covering some of the medical expenses for millions of the nation's poor. In all states, coverage extends to those who qualify for public assistance under the other sections of the Social Security Act (Medicaid itself is an amendment to the act) for certain basic

---

BOX 16-3

THE PUBLIC ASSISTANCE MAZE: THE CASE OF MATTIE DUDLEY

In the summer of 1982, Mattie Dudley, an elderly, disabled citizen of Charlottesville, Virginia, was notified by a state social services bureaucrat that she would no longer be eligible for Medicaid benefits. This was so, despite the facts that she was wheelchair-ridden and had been making only a meager living by selling newspapers for $5 per week and receiving SSI from the federal government. What had happened?

Five years earlier, she had used her life savings to purchase a burial plot. Since then, the value of this small parcel of land had increased to $1,500—an amount greater than the maximum value of assets allowed for SSI recipients. A routine check of Ms. Dudley's situation triggered her removal from the SSI rolls. This was only the start of her troubles.

Virginia and fifteen other states set their own Medicaid eligibility standards. Mattie Dudley had qualified for Medicaid under the state's rules, but termination from SSI also meant the end of Medicaid benefits too. To become eligible to receive her SSI checks again, she gave away her burial plot to a longtime friend. But under the rules, a willful disposal of property like this made her ineligible for Medicaid for at least two years.

The uproar caused by this seeming injustice stimulated Health and Human Services Secretary Richard Schweiker to propose a change in federal rules to exempt the purchase of burial plots. Yet even this change would not help Ms. Dudley, because of Virginia's rules.

The case of Mattie Dudley is an illustration of the sorts of inequities that exist in the complex and decentralized American system for providing income security.

Source: Atlanta Constitution, 1982; personal interviews.

---

services. States may choose to supplement these with "optional coverages" and may use their discretion in rules governing copayments. Today's system thus has substantial variations from state to state, and in most parts of the country Medicaid constitutes a major segment of the states' budgets.

These two programs have grown rapidly since their inauguration a generation ago. They have unquestionably improved the level of health care provided to the elderly, the disabled, and the poor. Yet controversy is at least as acute now as at any time earlier. Some critics point to growth of the programs as a major problem, and there is some evidence that the structure of these programs helps to accelerate the increase in medical costs affecting all Americans. Medicaid as a public assistance program is particularly subject to challenge. States and the federal government have authored very complicated regulations in their attempts to balance compassion with frugality. But any such rules will inevitably create situations of perceived unfairness. One such case is that of Mattie Dudley, a woman who lost her medical coverage in 1982 because she had bought a burial plot for herself with her meager savings (see Box 16-3). Of course the free market also can produce wealth or poverty, including some results that would seem "unfair" to nearly any observer, but in that system the injustices seem to stem from impersonal market forces, rather than from a set of rules drafted by specific people. The administered unfairnesses, plus the fact that many poor people are left uncovered by Medicaid, attract the attention of other critics who argue that wider health care coverage should be provided by the American social welfare state.

In-kind public assistance Besides Medicaid, a number of other noncontributory, in-kind programs are available to some Americans of limited income. The most important is probably the food stamp program, which helps subsidize the food budgets of more than 17 million people. Stamps are given to or purchased by (depending upon income) qualified recipients. They are distributed by public assistance agencies around the country and can be used to exchange for food at many stores in the United States. The great majority of food stamps are used for their authorized purpose, but in recent years some abuses (e.g., black market trading of stamps for unapproved purposes) have stimulated efforts to trim or reform the program. Other in-kind programs have been established to provide for some basic needs of at least a portion of the poor in the United States. Public housing, employment training, and school lunches are examples. These have been the subject of significant cutbacks in recent years.

Aid to Families with Dependent Children   The most controversial welfare program in the United States consumes less than 3 percent of the federal government's social welfare budget. The nation's Aid to Families with Dependent Children (AFDC) program illustrates quite well some of the tensions and competing values at the heart of this nation's social welfare state.

AFDC was established, along with social security and other public assistance programs mentioned earlier, by the act of 1935. The goal was to provide cash to poor families with children younger than 18 years old. AFDC is an intergovernmental program (states and in some places local governments also play a part), and the states have considerable discretion over eligibility criteria and payment levels. Again, the results include substantial variation. In Mississippi the average qualifying family received $88 per month in 1980, while the average in California was nearly $400. An intact family (both parents living with the children) in Virginia (and twenty-one other states) would receive no AFDC money whatsoever, while the same family with an unemployed father would be eligible for the program in, say, Ohio.

AFDC is controversial for many reasons. It is the only federal program that provides cash directly to able-bodied people of working age who have not been involuntarily unemployed. (There are regulations that aim to restrict AFDC to those families with parents who *would* work if given the chance.) Thus the program's beneficiaries seem less "deserving" to many Americans. Cash grants give more discretion to recipients; some of the money is therefore bound to be spent for purposes others might deem inappropriate. The program's intended beneficiaries are primarily children, but the payments must of course be given to parents; it is thus virtually impossible to make sure that the children receive the support due them. In 1935, when the program was started, it was very small

and mostly benefited white women—often widows. During the 1960s and since, AFDC rolls have become much larger, as more people have become aware of the program and as more poor, single-parent households (usually headed by women) have been created. AFDC rolls are now more nonwhite and include many families headed by unmarried mothers, usually with very small children. Thus racial antagonisms and questions of morality render the program more vulnerable to political challenge. The result is a program that is administered by state and local government social work bureaucracies, which try to provide help but also try to police their welfare rolls strictly for cheaters and for changes in family status that would make people ineligible.

The difficulties involved in reforming this part of the American social welfare state are considerable and illustrate well the complex values that the system seeks to reconcile. In an effort to get able-bodied men to support their families, AFDC regulations in many states forbid payments to families headed by unemployed fathers. This restriction provides an incentive for poor fathers to leave their children so the children can get government help; thus a program intended to support families sometimes aids in their disintegration. Generous benefits protect poor citizens from income insecurity but also may be unfair to the working poor and may create an incentive to get on rather than off public assistance. Yet stingy benefits encourage recipients to avoid reporting income they earn and thus to violate the law.

One way to encourage AFDC recipients to get off welfare is by making it worthwhile to work. However, most AFDC recipients have few skills. Putting young mothers to work means giving them skills (which costs money), taking care of their children while they work (e.g., via federally subsidized day care, which also costs money), and thus as a by-product perhaps further reducing the contact between parent and child. For those who can work, if their earned income is taxed very much, their incentive to work is diminished. If the tax is only a gradual one, however, AFDC expenses to the government go way up.

Two presidents in recent years, Richard Nixon and Jimmy Carter, sought to solve at least some of these problems by welfare reform. Nixon's proposal, the Family Assistance Plan, would have meant a guaranteed income for all Americans. Some conservatives were unhappy with the guarantee, some liberals with the level of benefits and tax rate on earned income. The idea died in the Senate. Carter's proposed Program for Better Jobs and Income would have included a guaranteed income for all and public service jobs for many of the unemployed. The plan was to eliminate the food stamp program, and this idea drew the wrath of liberals; also, total costs would have increased (as benefit levels would have become more equalized), so conservatives were not pleased. The proposal did not pass either house of Congress (Leman, 1980).

The difficulties that have faced AFDC and welfare reform illustrate the complications of policy in this country. On the basis of a concern for equality, the United States has slowly adopted programs that constitute a social welfare state. Yet these increase the presence of government in a predominantly private economy. They challenge the work ethic with a commitment to income security. The policies suggest a clash between those who desire freedom from want and those who want freedom to spend their own income without having it redistributed to others. The policies provide multiple programs for multiple needs, but also ignore some among the poor who are left uncovered by any protection whatsoever. And they invite a choice between a vigorous intergovernmental system that seems to create inequities and a centralized, more equitable one that weakens the role of the states in the federal system. The different and partially contradictory values that have long been important in American politics are thus exhibited in the programs of today's social welfare state.

Regulating Economic and Social Activity

Regulation is the use of the government's authority through the application of general rules to limit the discretion of persons (including legal "persons" such as corporations) in what would otherwise be private economic or social activity (O'Toole and Montjoy, 1984). It is perhaps less obvious why regulatory policies are part of a social welfare state than it is for policies that are aimed at managing the economy or directly providing some form of income security. However, many American regulatory policies are designed to help the marketplace function, to "correct" aspects of free enterprise activity that would produce side effects contrary to the public interest, or to improve the information or protection provided in the market to consumers, workers, and others (Okun, 1975). In these respects, at least, regulation may be consistent with the social welfare state's aim of security, especially income security (Kelman, 1978).

Much American regulatory policy began in the states themselves, and even today the states engage in substantial regulatory decision making. This point is obvious when you consider that currently the states determine the prices charged by utility companies, regulate the insurance business, and license various occupations from barbers to attorneys to doctors. However, the major growth in regulatory policy during this century has been at the federal level.

"Old" Regulation and "New"   Much of the earliest regulation initiated at the national level (most of which continues to this day) aimed at a direct impact on some phase of economic behavior. American regulation of economic behavior began in 1887 with the Interstate Commerce Commission, which was established to bring some order to the interstate transportation of goods and people by rail—and ultimately, by truck, bus, etc.—and to prevent monopoly exploitation by transporters. Since then, a number of other regulatory policies have established more federal units to police different aspects of the nation's economic life, from new modes of transportation (Civil Aeronautics Board) to radio and television (Federal Communications Commission), from the stock market (Securities and Exchange Commission) and banks (Comptroller of the Currency) to anticompetitive business practices and consumer protection against deceptive advertising (Federal Trade Commission), to energy (Department of Energy).

American policy also includes other sorts of regulatory measures. These usually aim at protecting the public against various forms of insecurity arising from health and safety dangers or discriminatory or unfair practices. Much (but not all) of this regulation of social behavior is a product of the last fifteen or twenty years and has thus been dubbed the "new" regulation (Lilly and Miller, 1977). Examples include the safety features of nuclear power plants (handled by the Nuclear Regulatory Commission); air transportation (the Federal Aviation Administration); highways (the National Highway Administration); and consumer products like children's toys and clothing (the Consumer Products Safety Commission). Safety and health at the workplace is the province of the Occupational Safety and Health Administration (OSHA), while the Environmental Protection Agency (EPA) and the Food and Drug Administration (FDA) focus directly on health. (EPA also has some mandates to consider aesthetics such as scenic beauty.) A variety of policies and agencies have something to do with controlling discrimination. Perhaps the most well known bureau is the Equal Employment Opportunity Commission (EEOC), which seeks to protect minorities and women from bias in hiring, wages, and promotion. The National Labor Relations Board regulates management-labor dealings, for example through supervising votes by workers on whether to unionize.

Thus, while not all American regulatory policy is tied directly to income security, a great deal of it is designed to enhance at least the general goal of a social welfare state. The major economic and social regulatory units of the federal government are displayed in Table 16-7.

Regulation: Pros and Cons   Both economic and social regulation have been criticized heavily in recent years, and lately there have been some policy shifts toward *deregulation*. Why?

Economists, especially, have been among the chief antagonists of some of the older economic regulatory units. They have charged that American regulation of interstate commerce, of airline transportation, of energy production, and of other segments of industry has actually worked against the goal of economic security for the nation's citizens. Studies have suggested that certain federal regulatory policies, by authorizing restrictions on entry into various lines of business, through controlling trading routes and prices, and via other means, have actually imposed costs on consumers. The costs are hidden since the regulatory agencies themselves spend little money. But they show up in reduced competition, higher prices, and slower technological innovation than would otherwise be

TABLE 16-7
MAJOR AMERICAN REGULATORY AGENCIES

Regulator	Date created
Economic	
Comptroller of the Currency	1863
Interstate Commerce Commission	1887
Federal Reserve System	1913
Federal Trade Commission	1914
Packers and Stockyards Administration	1916
Federal Maritime Commission	1916
Federal Grain Inspection Service	1916
Agriculture Marketing Service	1916
Federal Power Commission (later the Federal Energy Regulatory Commission and the Department of Energy)	1920
Commodity Futures Trading Commission	1922
Federal Home Loan Bank Board	1932
Federal Deposit Insurance Corporation	1933
Commodity Credit Corporation	1933
Agricultural Stabilization and Conservation Service	1933
Securities and Exchange Commission	1934
Federal Communications Commission	1934
National Labor Relations Board	1935
Civil Aeronautics Board	1938
Council on Wage and Price Stability	1942
Cost Accounting Standards Board	1970
Social	
Animal and Plant Health Inspection Service	1883
Food Safety and Quality Service	1907
Food and Drug Administration	1907
Mining Enforcement and Safety Administration	1910
Coast Guard	1915
Employment Standards Division	1931
Federal Aviation Administration	1938
Nuclear Regulatory Administration	1946
Civil Rights Division	1964
Equal Employment Opportunity Commission	1964
National Highway Traffic Safety Administration	1966
Federal Railroad Administration	1966
Consumer Credit Protection	1968
Environmental Protection Agency	1970
Occupational Safety and Health Administration	1970
Consumer Product Safety Commission	1972
Drug Enforcement Administration	1973
Office of Human Development (for the handicapped)	1973
Energy Conservation	1974
Labor-Management Services Administration (pensions)	1974
Federal Election Commission	1974/76

Source: Advisory Commission on Intergovernmental Relations, 1980:78–79.

BOX 16-4

DEREGULATING THE AIRLINES

Since 1938, the federal government had regulated many economic aspects of the air transportation industry. The Civil Aeronautics Board (CAB) licensed airlines for business, allocated routes between cities, set rates to eliminate price competition, and in general structured the operations of this sector of the economy in great detail.

By the 1970s, a number of economists argued the case for deregulating the airlines. The companies, protected from the turbulence of the marketplace, had little incentive for efficient operations. Prices along interstate routes were often much higher than those for intrastate journeys of similar length in states like Texas and California. (Intrastate transportation companies are not subject to federal regulation.) Some air carriers favored deregulation too, since they hoped to move into new, more profitable markets (e.g., the New York–Miami, and Los Angeles–Honolulu runs) and discard other, marginal ones.

The election of Jimmy Carter brought a supporter of deregulation into the White House. Carter appointed the economist Alfred Kahn to head the CAB, and Kahn began to relax controls over the industry. Subsequently, the passage of the Airline Deregulation Act of 1978 established a policy requiring a gradual move to almost complete deregulation. By 1982, the CAB no longer controlled domestic routes, and in the following year, fares had also been totally deregulated. The agency itself was scheduled for abolition in 1985.

Regulation was originally intended to protect the stability of this important industry and to ensure widespread service. Thus the results of deregulation were quite predictable but were also controversial. Small- and medium-sized cities lost air service. Newport News, Virginia, for instance, was left in 1982 without any major carriers. Passengers along densely traveled routes enjoyed more flights and sometimes intense price competition. (It is frequently cheaper to travel from New York to San Francisco than to Omaha.) And some airlines suffered huge losses. Braniff Airways, for instance, became bankrupt in all but a technical sense. 1981 was the worst financial year in the industry's history to that point. (Air transportation netted a loss of $300 million.) Some companies and cities called for "reregulation."

The conflicts raised by this subject illustrate well the trade-offs involved in deciding between market and regulation.

Source: Federal Regulatory Directory, 1979–80, 1979:81–87; National Journal, Mar. 6, 1982:404–409.

---

the case. Depending upon the issue, then, both conservatives and liberals have been known to support deregulation—conservatives because deregulation increases the operation of market forces and reduces the action of government, liberals because certain forms of deregulation may seem likely to lower prices for consumers. For one reason or another, the extent of American economic regulation in some industries has been reduced in the past few years. The best examples are in trucking, energy prices, and domestic passenger air travel. (See Box 16-4 for a more detailed discussion of airline deregulation.) The Federal Trade Commission has also had its authority reduced by Congress in the 1980s and is now headed by James Miller, who used to serve as a watchdog over federal regulators from the Council on Wage and Price Stability.

Social regulation, too, has its critics. Some point out that the regulation of pollution or job discrimination or the packaging of consumer products requires detailed intervention by the government into the decisions and actions of business firms, consumers, and others. Thus, the claim is that these policies are a direct and offensive invasion of people's freedom. Furthermore, it is argued that social regulation may be even more costly in economic terms than direct economic regulation is. The costs include requirements for expensive equipment or procedures to protect health and safety, increased administrative and legal expenses for the paperwork and monitoring required by federal agencies, and so forth. By the late 1970s, the critics were estimating these costs in the scores of billions of dollars per year. Regulators singled out for harshest attack were the EPA, OSHA, and EEOC. Even universities began to protest the costs associated with federal oversight of hiring practices, building design and construction (e.g., for compliance with standards regarding energy efficiency and accessibility to the handicapped), scientific experiments, workers' safety, and numerous other activities.

Accordingly, the social regulators, too, have had their authority trimmed in recent years. The Carter administration, for example, successfully sought a cutback in the most controversial OSHA regulations. President Reagan has gone further, primarily by seeking to appoint regulators who are on record in favor of some deregulation. These included Anne Burford, a prodevelopment attorney, as head of the EPA, and various persons nominated to the EEOC. (Burford was forced to resign in 1983, and two nominees to EEOC ran into resistance from Congress during confirmation proceedings and ultimately were not appointed.) Each of the last three administrations in Washington has enacted restrictions on agencies in an attempt to reduce the likelihood that frivolous, expensive, or offensive regulations could easily go into effect.

But the nation's regulatory apparatus has by no means been dismantled (Wilson, 1980). One reason is that public opinion has remained perhaps surprisingly supportive of even the more controversial social regulation. The American people are in favor of stringent safety regulations for nuclear power plants, consumer protection, and safe workplaces, even when they know that these policies can be expensive (Nelkin, 1981). A July 1982 Harris poll showed strong backing for the current air and water pollution control policies (85 percent to 10 percent) and affirmative action programs in employment (69 percent to 21 percent) (*Birmingham Post-Herald*, 1982). Furthermore, some notable successes have been scored by the nation's regulatory agencies, for instance on improving water quality, reducing injuries and deaths at the workplace, and preventing harm to small children from accidental poisoning. Whereas the critics point to the apparently excessive costs of some "successes," proponents argue that benefits have been understated and that, anyway, even some of the costliest regulation can be justified on grounds of fairness (Kelman, 1978). This argument received a boost from the Supreme Court in 1981, when the Court ruled that regulatory policies (in this case it was

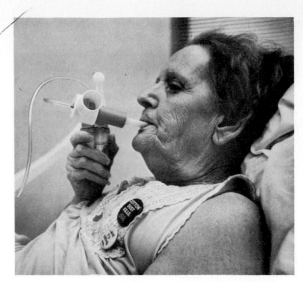

While Americans generally want to see social welfare costs cut, they believe that social welfare policy should be fair, especially to people like this textile worker hospitalized with brown lung disease.

one that protected textile workers from brown lung disease) do not necessarily have to be justified in terms of an economist's cost-benefit analysis (*American Textile Manufacturers Institute, Inc. v. Donovan*). Thus, today's debate about economic and social regulations, less obvious but still important components of American social welfare policy, is not an easy one to resolve neatly.

Having surveyed the main components of social welfare policy in the United States and some of the matters at issue, we now focus on the Reagan administration's approach to the subject since 1981.

THE REAGAN ADMINISTRATION AND AMERICAN SOCIAL WELFARE POLICY

The constitutional shift toward a social welfare state in this country has been prompted by some basic American values, such as equality, fairness, and freedom from want. As president, Ronald Reagan sought to trim this system, and his effort also has relied on some values of long-standing concern in American politics.

Reagan campaigned for the presidency with a stance against big government and against bureaucracy; he promised to get government out of people's lives, to lessen their "dependence" on the social welfare state. After his inauguration he continued to develop these themes, which are quite consistent with ideas stemming back to the Antifederalists of the eighteenth century. His attacks on the welfare state derived partially from a belief that government simply is not capable of fulfilling its promises. Reagan, throughout his political career, was also impressed by the incompatibility of even an effective social welfare state with liberty, free market principles, and the vitality of private associations. In his public statements, then, President Reagan claimed that big government challenges individual freedom and demeans individual responsibility (e.g., through the welfare system). He argued that Washington's efforts to ensure economic well-being reduces productive incentives in the economic system (e.g., through the tax system and regulations). And he asserted that the welfare state's tendency to seek a national response to social problems leaves untapped the American spirit of voluntarism and self-help (e.g., by antifamily policies allowing abortion, prohibiting school prayer, etc., and by underutilization of the charitable potential of individuals and business).

If you listened only to Ronald Reagan's rhetoric or that of his critics, you might easily have received the impression that he was engaged in a wholesale dismemberment of the American social welfare state. The reality is a bit more complicated: Reagan attempted some fundamental shifts in the nature of that system, but he did not embark on a crusade to destroy it entirely. A brief discussion of social welfare policy in the Reagan years can illuminate this point. (We omit here deregulation, which was discussed earlier and in any event began before the Reagan years.)

Supply-Side Economics and Budget Balancing

The weak performance of the American economy in recent years has meant serious challenges to the conventional wisdom about how to manage the economy. A different perspective from that of Keynes has been offered by some conservative economists and policy analysts in recent years. This idea, *supply-side economics,* suggests that the major problems of high inflation and slow growth (plus, ultimately, unemployment) can be resolved if the government embarks on a policy to encourage productive investment and entrepreneurial activity. The best way to do so, say the supply-siders, is to cut taxes, especially for businesses and investors. The immediate goal is not to stimulate demand, but to get the productive centers of the economy moving. More potential for profit will increase innovation and production, thus generating growth, jobs, and income for everybody. A simplified version of the argument would be that by helping the wealthy (those with money to invest), the whole economy ultimately benefits.

Various versions of this idea had been heard for years, especially among business leaders and Republican party candidates. But Reagan and some of his advisers (e.g., his budget director, David Stockman) were especially impressed with claims by supply-side economists like Arthur Laffer that cutting taxes significantly would actually *increase* the amount of revenue collected by the government. This would be so, it was claimed, because so much new economic activity would be generated. (Note that this notion, if shown to be true, might attract the support of those who urge an expanded social welfare state.) Conservative members of Congress, backed by Reagan, pushed for legislation (the Kemp-Roth bill) to turn the theory into reality, and in 1981 the largest income tax cut in American history was enacted.

Yet in the succeeding years, federal revenues did not meet projections. Deficits in fact increased, and Reagan announced his support for a controversial Constitutional amendment to require a balanced federal budget.

On the issue of managing the economy, then, the Reagan initiatives are not easy to categorize. The president tried to increase the relative size of private enterprise and to Constitutionally prohibit Keynesian economics. On the other hand, he never avoided the idea that federal policy has and should have a major impact on the nation's economy. In fact, fiscal and tax goals such as those espoused by Reagan, if achieved, could lead to federal growth.

Income Security: The "Social Safety Net" and the "New Federalism"

In line with the ideas of individual self-reliance and the importance of preserving a vital American intergovernmental system, President Reagan sought, and in some cases had enacted, significant changes in policy on income security.

First, Reagan attempted to stimulate significant cutbacks in several selected income-security programs. In some cases, the reductions would be not in absolute dollars but in the rate of increase the programs had been experiencing. The most drastic reductions were to occur in some of the most controversial programs, especially several public assistance ones. AFDC and some of the in-kind aid to the nation's poor were targeted for trimming, e.g., food stamps and Medicaid; or elimination, e.g., the government's job training program, initiated through the Comprehensive Employment Training Act, CETA (see Stockman, 1975). Yet several programs, including some of the largest, were designated by Reagan as the nation's "social safety net," to ensure that the "truly needy" would not suffer. This group included most of OASDI, Medicare, SSI, and others. In truth, of course, the cutbacks *would* have affected the poor, especially those not among the elderly. Reagan's expressed hope was that families and voluntary charity would help to take up the slack. Nevertheless, it is worth remembering that under Reagan's plan the total amount of public American social welfare expenditures would continue to grow, though at a reduced rate.

Most of the Reagan administration's ideas on income security were passed into law during the summer of 1981 in a very complicated package called the Omnibus Reconciliation Act. Shortly thereafter, however, policymakers in the White House and Congress were having to face up to the fact that pressures on the federal budget were continuing and that there were fewer and fewer programs to be cut without touching the "safety net." The fiscal year 1983 budget contained a cut in Medicare benefits of more than $10 billion, and policymakers began to eye social security as an-

other possible target. Easy answers had become scarce.

The second policy initiative suggested by Reagan on the subject was his idea for a "new federalism," by which he proposed that the national government withdraw from some of its major domestic policy programs—especially some of those dealing with income security. As was described in Chapter 14, on intergovernmental relations, "new federalism" was a suggestion that drew philosophical support from Reagan's belief in strong state governments, which would acquire major new responsibilities if Washington turned over programs to them. "New federalism" also seemed an attractive way to reduce the strain on the national budget in the 1980s. The proposal did not meet with an enthusiastic response from most of the states, however, and the difficulty of getting consensus on any such agreement delayed action.

Thus, the Reagan years are marked by policy shifts but certainly not by a clear, consistent effort to deny a governmental role in fostering income security.

The "Social Issue"

One other set of initiatives during the Reagan years is related to welfare state policy. This is the so-called "social issue" that has become an important element of the Republican party's political agenda.

The Reagan administration and conservative Republicans were active in pushing for policy changes that they believed would strengthen such essential institutions as family and organized religion (but see Kirschten, 1981). Believing, with Tocqueville, that these private associations are among the nation's strongest bulwarks against tyranny and the deadening influence of strong central authority, the Reagan administration—with the support of some in Congress—backed a variety of measures on the argument that they benefit the home or the church. Some proposals have been relatively insignificant (repealing the "marriage penalty" whereby working spouses pay more income tax than if they were single), some exceedingly controversial (opposition to abortion) or likely to become more so (opposition to equal rights for homosexuals). Others were strongly backed by Catholics (tax credits for parents who send their children to religious schools) and fundamentalist Christians (support for school prayer). A few of the proposals are ironic in that they place the conservatives on the side of greater government regulation—as with the abortion issue.

Directly, at least, the policy initiatives do not challenge the effort of the social welfare state to reduce economic insecurity. But indirectly, they do suggest a significant shift. Whereas social welfare policy has aimed at solving the *material* needs of people, proponents of the "social issue" suggest that government should help to secure certain institutions important to the social, moral, and political fabric of the nation. Major policy changes here, however, have been relatively slow, partially because public opinion is sharply divided, with the majority in many cases opposed to the suggested changes.

The Reagan years thus mark the most obvious shift in American social welfare policy at least since the New Deal. A clear effort was made to temper the growth of big government with a concern for other values that, some have argued, have been too long neglected in public policy. Yet Reagan's initiatives have hardly quieted the controversy. Conservatives complain about the welfare state that continues to expand, liberals decry the material harm done to the poor by the cutbacks of the 1980s. The contrasting views are, if anything, in sharper focus today than ever.

SUMMARY AND CONCLUSION

The American social welfare state, which seeks economic security for its citizens, has developed more slowly and less comprehensively than have those in other western industrial nations. Social welfare policy in this country has been enacted in fits and starts, some parts the product of lengthy policy debate, some enacted quickly at times of crisis.

The policy scheme is not a consistent whole. The United States has for decades now sought to manage indirectly its market economy to improve growth, provide jobs, and trim inflation. A variety of policy tools are used toward this end, though in the 1980s it is clear that these instruments, at least as applied in the past and present, have not been able to attain their goals consistently. The problem may derive from our limited knowledge of economics as well as from our political system itself—with the pluralistic policy process benefiting well-organized interest groups, for instance in tax policy, and with separation of powers providing the opportunity for divergent policies to be pursued by the president, Congress, and the Federal Reserve.

Policies for income security are no simpler to comprehend. They embrace a dizzying set of programs that provide the chance for some citizens (e.g., AFDC recipients in more generous states who qualify for various other types of in-kind assistance) to be fairly well-protected against misfortune, while others (e.g., the working poor, especially in less affluent or more miserly states) remain in desperate need. Much of the system operates intergovernmentally, thus increasing variety but often reducing perceived fairness. And even the most controversial features of the income-security system are difficult to reform since programs like AFDC touch upon so many conflicting values and since the veto points of the policy network make any controversial changes difficult to enact.

Government regulation, with its less direct effect on economic security, has also grown over time. Yet its effectiveness and efficiency have been challenged. Regulatory reforms may occur, but the volume of federal rule making will undoubtedly continue to increase, despite certain exceptions. Public opinion, plus scientific and technological developments, continues to keep regulatory issues on the agenda.

In the last few years, the Reagan administration and parts of the Republican party have mounted the most important constitutional challenge to the American social welfare state thus far. In all the policy areas just discussed, and on the subject of the "social issue," efforts have been made to reinforce the traditional value ascribed in this country to individual freedom and responsibility, the work ethic and the market, private association, and limited government. Yet all but the most conservative have sought to fix, not eliminate, the social welfare state. And some of the proposed changes have foundered without support from the public or within the policy system itself. If the American policymaking process, with its checks, multiple institutions, and intergovernmental system, renders it difficult to enact new programs in a hurry, it also makes it tough to eliminate old ones, as Reagan himself discovered when he tried to tinker with social security or enact a "new federalism."

Yet intractable as the policy system may sometimes seem, it can respond to the concerns of its citizens. These days, there may be no more important, if complicated, policy issues on the nation's agenda than those of the social welfare state. The social security system *is* running out of funds. There *are* deserving American poor who are sick and malnourished. The economy *does* face severe problems. Government regulators *do* impose costs but also provide benefits. Private associations *are* an important component of American society.

All these social welfare matters have impacts on values that the founders considered as they framed this government. They intended no social welfare state but established a system through which one could be established. Has the government now tried to do too much and thus weakened the traditional values on which the nation was established? Or does a proper understanding of the founders' concerns, when enlightened by present circumstances, suggest new commitments that the American social welfare state should undertake? These questions are as tangible as a hungry child or an income tax refund. But they are also lofty. They suggest constitutional issues for the nation's third century.

SOURCES

Advisory Commission on Intergovernmental Relations: *The Federal Role in the Federal System: The Dynamics of Growth—A Crisis of Confidence and Competence,* Report A-77, U.S. Government Printing Office, Washington, D.C., July 1980.

Ashford, Douglas E. (ed.): *Comparing Public Policies: New Concepts and Methods,* Sage, Beverly Hills, Calif., 1978.

Atlanta Constitution, Aug. 14, 1982.

Birmingham (Ala.) Post-Herald, Aug. 13, 1982.

Burke, Vincent, and Vee Burke: *Nixon's Good Deed: Welfare Reform,* Columbia University Press, New York, 1974.

Collier, David, and Richard E. Messick: "Prerequisites versus Diffusion: Testing Alternative Explanations

of Social Security Adoption," *American Political Science Review,* vol. 69, no. 4, 1975, pp. 1299–1315.

Council of Economic Advisers: *Economic Report of the President,* U.S. Government Printing Office, Washington, D.C., February 1982.

CQ Weekly Report, Mar. 27, Aug. 7, 1982.

Dahl, Robert, and Charles Lindblom: *Politics, Economics, and Welfare,* Harper, New York, 1953.

Derthick, Martha: *Policymaking for Social Security,* Brookings Institution, Washington, D.C., 1979.

Dolbeare, Kenneth M.: *American Public Policy: A Citizen's Guide,* McGraw-Hill, New York, 1982.

Dye, Thomas R.: *Understanding Public Policy,* 4th ed., Prentice-Hall, Englewood Cliffs, N.J., 1981.

Federal Regulatory Directory 1979–80, Congressional Quarterly Press, Washington, D.C., 1979.

Friedman, Milton: *Capitalism and Freedom,* University of Chicago Press, Chicago, 1962.

Furniss, Norman, and Timothy Tilton: *The Case for the Welfare State: From Social Security to Social Equality,* Indiana University Press, Bloomington, 1977.

Gallup Report, April 1982.

Gilder, George: *Wealth and Poverty,* Basic Books, New York, 1981.

Grønbjerg, Kirsten A.: *Mass Society and the Extension of Welfare, 1960–1970,* University of Chicago Press, Chicago, 1977.

Harrington, Michael: *Socialism,* Bantam, New York, 1972.

———: *The Twilight of Capitalism,* Simon and Schuster, New York, 1976.

Hastings, Elizabeth Hann, and Philip K. Hastings (eds.): *Index to International Public Opinion, 1980–1981,* Greenwood, Westport, Conn., 1982.

Heclo, Hugh: "Frontiers of Social Policy in Europe and America," *Policy Sciences,* vol. 6, no. 4, 1975, pp. 403–421.

Heidenheimer, Arnold J., Hugh Heclo, and Carolyn Teich Adams: *Comparative Public Policy: The Politics of Social Change in Europe and America,* St. Martin's, New York, 1975.

International Labor Organization: *The Cost of Social Security, Tenth International Inquiry, 1975–1977,* International Labor Organization, Geneva, Switz., 1981.

Kelman, Steven: "Regulation That Works," *New Republic,* Nov. 28, 1978.

Keynes, John Maynard: *The General Theory of Employment, Interest, and Money,* Harcourt, Brace, New York, 1936.

King, Anthony: "Ideas, Institutions, and the Policies of Governments: A Comparative Analysis," *British Journal of Political Science,* vol. 3, nos. 3, 4, 1973, pp. 291–313, 409–423.

Kirschten, Dick: "Putting the Social Issues on Hold: Can Reagan Get Away with It?" *National Journal,* Oct. 10, 1981, pp. 1810–1815.

Koch, Adrienne, and William Peden (eds.): *The Life and Selected Writings of Thomas Jefferson,* Random House (Modern Library), New York, 1944.

Leman, Christopher: *The Collapse of Welfare Reform,* M.I.T. Press, Cambridge, Mass., 1980.

Lilly, William, III, and James C. Miller, III: "The New 'Social Regulation,'" *The Public Interest,* no. 47, 1977, pp. 49–61.

Lindblom, Charles E.: "The Market as Prison," *Journal of Politics,* vol. 44, no. 2, 1982, pp. 324–336.

Mandell, Betty Reid (ed.): *Welfare in America: Controlling the Dangerous Classes,* Prentice-Hall, Englewood Cliffs, N.J., 1975.

McCrone, Donald J., and Richard J. Hardy: "Civil Rights Policies and the Achievement of Racial Economic Equality, 1948–1975," *American Journal of Political Science,* vol. 22, no. 1, 1978, pp. 1–17.

Moynihan, Daniel Patrick: *The Politics of a Guaranteed Income,* Random House, New York, 1973.

National Journal Mar. 6, 1982.

———, Oct. 9, 1982.

Nelkin, Dorothy: "Some Social and Political Dimensions of Nuclear Power: Examples from Three Mile Island," *American Political Science Review,* vol. 75, no. 1, 1981, pp. 132–142.

Nozick, Robert: *Anarchy, State, and Utopia,* Basic Books, New York, 1974.

O'Connor, James: *The Fiscal Crisis of the State,* St. Martin's, New York, 1973.

Okun, Arthur: *Equality and Efficiency: The Big Trade-off,* Brookings Institution, Washington, D.C., 1975.

O'Toole, Laurence J., Jr., and Robert S. Montjoy: *Regulatory Decision Making: The Virginia State Corporation Commission:* University Press of Virginia, Charlottesville, 1984.

Paul, Ellen F., and Philip A. Russo (eds.): *Public Policy: Issues, Analysis, and Ideology,* Chatham House, Chatham, N.J., 1982.

Pechman, Joseph A.: *Federal Tax Policy,* 3d ed., Brookings Institution, Washington, D.C., 1977.

Peters, B. Guy: *American Public Policy: Process and Performance,* F. Watts, New York, 1982.

Piven, Frances Fox, and Richard Cloward: *Regulating the Poor: The Functions of Public Welfare,* Pantheon, New York, 1971.

Prysby, Charles L.: "Mass Policy Orientations on Economic Issues in Post-Industrial America," *Journal of Politics,* vol. 41, no. 2, 1979, pp. 543–563.

Reichley, A. James: *Conservatives in an Age of Change: The Nixon and Ford Administrations,* Brookings Institution, Washington, D.C., 1981.

Ryan, William P.: *Blaming the Victim,* rev. ed., Vintage, New York, 1976.

Shonfield, Andrew: *Modern Capitalism,* Oxford University Press, London, 1966.

Sidel, Victor W., and Ruth Sidel: *A Healthy State: An International Perspective on the Crisis in United States Medical Care,* Pantheon, New York, 1977.

Social Security Bulletin, November 1982.

Starling, Grover: *The Politics and Economics of Public Policy,* Dorsey, Homewood, Ill., 1979.

Statistical Abstract, 1981, U.S. Bureau of the Census, Washington, D.C., December 1981.

Stockman, David: "The Social Pork Barrel," *The Public Interest,* no. 39, spring 1975, pp. 3–30.

Storey, James R., Alair A. Townsend, and Irene Cox: *How Public Welfare Benefits Are Distributed in Low-Income Areas,* Joint Economic Committee, 93d Cong., 1st Sess., Washington, D.C., March 1973.

Sundquist, James L.: *Politics and Policy: The Eisenhower, Kennedy, and Johnson Years,* Brookings Institution, Washington, D.C., 1968.

Trattner, Walter I.: *From Poor Law to Welfare State: A History of Social Welfare in America,* Free Press, New York, 1974.

Tropman, John E.: "American Welfare Strategies: Three Programs under the Social Security Act," *Policy Sciences,* vol. 8, no. 1, 1977, pp. 33–47.

U.S. Bureau of the Census: *Alternative Methods for Valuing Selected In-Kind Transfer Benefits and Measuring Their Effect on Poverty,* no. 50, U.S. Government Printing Office, Washington, D.C., March 1982.

U.S. Office of Management and Budget: *Budget of the United States Government 1983,* U.S. Government Printing Office, Washington, D.C., 1982.

Washington Post, Aug. 8, 1982.

Wilensky, Harold L.: *The Welfare State and Equality,* University of California Press, Berkeley, 1975.

Wilson, James Q. (ed.): *The Politics of Regulation,* Basic Books, New York, 1980.

RECOMMENDED READINGS

Derthick, Martha: *Policymaking for Social Security,* Brookings Institution, Washington, D.C., 1979. An analysis of one of the most important American social welfare policies before recent efforts to revise the program.

Dolbeare, Kenneth M.: *American Public Policy: A Citizen's Guide,* McGraw-Hill, New York, 1982. One of the best volumes available on an introductory survey of American social welfare policies; some comparative information.

Furniss, Norman, and Timothy Tilton: *The Case for the Welfare State: From Social Security to Social Equality,* Indiana University Press, Bloomington, 1977. An argument for the expansion of the American social welfare system along the lines of those in parts of western Europe.

Gilder, George: *Wealth and Poverty,* Basic Books, New York, 1981. A book that received attention for its popularity with prominent Reagan advisers; argues that free market capitalism is more efficient and more productive than welfare state systems, and morally superior as well.

Harrington, Michael: *Socialism,* Bantam Books, New York, 1972. Suggests that a radical expansion of public control would promote the social welfare.

Heidenheimer, Arnold J., Hugh Heclo, and Carolyn Teich Adams: *Comparative Public Policy: The Politics of Social Change in Europe and America,* St. Martin's, New York, 1975. Provides comparative perspectives, especially on social and economic policies.

Piven, Frances Fox, and Richard Cloward: *Regulating the Poor: The Functions of Public Welfare,* Pantheon, New York, 1971. A well-known critique of American welfare policy from the elitist perspective.

Reichley, A. James: *Conservatives in an Age of Change: The Nixon and Ford Administrations,* Brookings Institution, Washington, D.C., 1981. A study of welfare state policy during years when members of the GOP occupied the White House.

Sundquist, James L.: *Politics and Policy: The Eisenhower, Kennedy, and Johnson Years,* Brookings Institution, Washington, D.C., 1968. A volume similar in scope to Reichley's, but for the earlier years during which much important American domestic policy was developed.

Chapter 17

Civil Liberties and Civil Rights

Imagine that you had been born in South Africa. The schools you could attend, the job you could get, the place you could live, even your ability to move freely about the country would be determined by the color of your skin. Move in your imagination across the globe to the Soviet Union. You are Alexander Solzhenitsyn. Gifted with immense energy, keen intelligence, and a rare command of language, you find yourself at the age of 26 sentenced to eight years of forced labor for making derogatory remarks about Stalin in a private letter to a friend which the authorities intercepted and read. It is no wonder that when we Americans take pride in our country, it is most often because of our tradition of protecting civil rights and liberties. The very core of what most citizens believe to be good about the United States is found in our freedom to think, believe, and say what we want without fear.

Yet when we look at the record of the United States in protecting civil rights, we find cause for humility as well as pride. One whole race of people, the blacks, was held in slavery until the Civil War and then denied the elementary political rights of voting and serving on juries for nearly a century. Until the 1960s, the laws of many states prevented blacks from going to the same schools as whites, eating in the same restaurants, or riding in the same sections of trains and buses. Other groups and many individuals have also faced significant infringements of their rights. Japanese Americans on the west coast were forced into relocation camps during World War II, hispanics have often been denied their lawful rights to vote and work free from harassment, and women have been barred from certain jobs by arbitrary physical requirements of height and weight. Although the United States, by the Declaration of Independence and the Constitution, is dedicated to protecting the rights of its citizens, the political problem has been, and remains, to translate this dedication in principle into laws, customs, and attitudes that provide daily protection for these rights.

In this chapter we shall consider the American experiment in protecting civil rights. We shall begin by considering what a civil right is and why protection of civil rights is a leading principle of the American form of government. After seeing that civil liberties and rights are the constitutional expressions of the two basic principles of liberal democracy, liberty and equality, we shall examine how these two principles can sometimes conflict and why citizens can so greatly disagree over how to secure rights and liberties. A consideration of the Constitutional foundations for the protection of civil rights will lead us to a discussion of some of the most important rights and liberties. Finally we shall examine the successes or failures of contemporary civil rights movements to broaden the scope of liberty and equality.

WHAT ARE RIGHTS?

While Americans are accustomed to thinking of their civil rights as legal rights, it is important to realize that the term "rights" has a wider usage in our political vocabulary. Antiabortion advocates, for example, claim there is a "right to life" for an unborn fetus, which ought to receive legal recognition and protection but does not. A "right" is a just claim to the possession or use of something, be it a material object like a piece of property, one of our own faculties like our ability to speak, or some privilege or authority like voting. What rights people have and how they are protected involve issues touching all aspects of our political life: what our goals are, the purpose and limits of government, and how power is distributed.

Civil Rights and Human Rights

A "civil" right in the strict sense is a right that one has because one is a citizen of a particular country. However, such rights may also extend to noncitizens who live or work in a country. Noncitizens who live in the United States are sometimes granted certain civil rights, such as the basic rights that exist for Americans in the prosecution of individuals for a crime. But the status of rights for noncitizens is qualified and partial. Noncitizens, for example, cannot vote. In 1979 during the period in which American hostages were being held by the Iranian government, the United States government restricted the freedom of Iranians living in the United States to engage in demonstrations or move about the country. These people could not claim the full protection of the Constitution as their right.

Civil rights may be distinguished from "natural" rights or "human" rights. These are rights that people have simply because they are human, not because they are citizens of a particular country. All people, according to the Declaration of Independence, are "endowed by their Creator" with the rights to "life, liberty, and the pursuit of happiness." On the basis of these natural or human rights, many organizations—including, sometimes, the American government—condemn those nations that abridge the basic rights of their peoples. But civil rights in the United States are those that are granted to Americans by law. The basic rights derive their legitimacy in the United States from the conviction that they are in fact based on natural rights, but the specific elaboration of these rights derives from the law, and the full exercise of all rights is given only to American citizens.

Civil Liberties and Civil Rights

The term "civil liberty" is frequently used interchangeably with the term "civil right." One can speak of free speech as either a civil liberty or a civil right. But the term "civil liberty" emphasizes the freedom one has to do something, while the term "civil right" emphasizes one's just and equal claim to something. Freedom of speech in strict usage is a civil liberty; the entitlement to equal access to the courts is a civil right.

The distinction between civil liberties and civil rights reflects one of the most important issues underlying the American concern with civil rights and liberties. The United States is committed to the two great goals of liberal democratic government, equality and liberty, but these principles are not always in perfect harmony with each other. Liberty implies diversity and the possibility of inequality: if people are free to engage in business and commerce, as they are in the United States, some will become rich and others will not. Differences in native abilities, acquired business skills, family advantages, educational opportunities, and pure luck will lead to success for some and failure for others. Similarly, if people are allowed to speak freely, those skilled at speaking or writing who have access to public forums will gain advantages over those who cannot speak so well or have fewer opportunities to speak to important audiences. Freedom of speech gives much greater power to the

owners and writers of the *New York Times* than it does to the average American.

Equality, on the other hand, may threaten liberty. The owners of the *Times* and the average American could be made equal in their ability to influence public events only by destroying the *Times*'s freedom to print what it wants. In 1974, Congress passed a campaign finance law limiting what an individual could spend to support a candidate for public office. Under this law, people would have been restricted from buying space in newspapers to argue their position. The objective was to reduce inequalities of influence. The Supreme Court, however, struck down this provision of the law as a violation of freedom of speech (*Buckley v. Valeo*, 1976). These are only two examples of the tension between the pursuit of liberty and the desire for equality, which, as we shall see, underlies many contemporary disputes about civil rights and liberties.

The founders of the United States thought that the way to reconcile these two principles was to form a government dedicated to protecting the equal rights of all its citizens. Equality should mean, not equality in everything (such as everyone's having the same income), but equality in rights under the law. Unlike an aristocracy, in which the privileges and wealth of a particular group are guaranteed by the law, a liberal democracy grants no special privileges to any particular persons or groups. There would be inequalities in the United States, the founders thought, but they would not determine rights under the law or be guaranteed to particular persons by the law. Liberty, on the other hand, would mean not freedom to do whatever anyone wanted to do but freedom to exercise one's rights under the law. Both liberty and equality would properly be restricted for the sake of protecting the rights of other citizens and the security of the country, but they would not be restricted for the sake of directing people to a way of life thought good by the government. By saying that government should *protect* the equal rights of all citizens, but not force them to *exercise* those rights in a particular way, the founders thought they had discovered a distinction which would gain the advantages of both liberty and equality for the United States while avoiding their harmful excesses.

To decide that the aim of government is in securing the equal rights of all citizens is not, however, to bring an end to dispute about rights. Agreement on a broad goal does not dispose of all the difficulties in implementing it. Since the founding there has been a constitutional commitment to protecting civil rights, but there has been dispute, sometimes vociferous, about what these rights are and how they should be protected.

HOW ARE RIGHTS PROTECTED?

Protection of civil rights and liberties involves some of the most difficult kinds of judgments Americans are called upon to make. This is because protection of rights in particular circumstances often involves issues affecting fundamental constitutional questions. Will increased freedom for works thought obscene by some lead to a more robust and open society or to a sordid society without the self-restraint needed for a people who are to govern themselves? Where does privacy begin and the reach of government stop? Should competing views of the importance of various rights be resolved by the courts or by legislatures?

Issues in Determining Rights

In general, there are four important questions citizens and political leaders must face in trying to secure the equal rights of all citizens.

First: *Who has rights?* This is one of the most fundamental questions. Right-to-life advocates, for example, argue that an unborn child has the same right to life as a person who has been born. Freedom-of-choice proponents argue (and the Supreme Court agrees) that a fetus has no civil rights. The Supreme Court recently ruled that the state of California could discriminate against noncitizens in hiring peace officers (*Cabell v. Chavez-Salido,* 1982). Before the Civil War, some people argued that blacks possessed no rights under the Constitution. These kinds of disagreements have involved questions of the most profound kind: Who is human? What is a citizen? (Brant, 1965).

Second: *What is a right?* People sometimes disagree whether an alleged right is indeed a right. In *Griswold v. Connecticut* (1965) the Supreme Court held that there is a Constitutional right of privacy

which protects the right to use or to advise others in the use of contraceptives. This same right was later held to limit the state's power to regulate abortions (*Roe v. Wade,* 1973) and marriage (*Zoblocki v. Redhail,* 1978). The Court argued that this right, although not explicitly mentioned in the Constitution, was implied by various provisions of the Bill of Rights (*Griswold v. Connecticut,* 1965). Others have thought that the judges invented this right in order to achieve the policy result they desired.

Interpretation of particular rights frequently involves defining more exactly what the right in question is. When motion pictures were first invented, the question arose as to whether they were protected by the First Amendment, which safeguards freedom of the press but which makes no mention, of course, of freedom of motion pictures. At first the Court held that motion pictures were not protected because movies were not a medium for informing citizens as the press was, but instead were an entertainment medium akin to amusement parks or horse racing. As such, they could be regulated. Later the Court reversed itself, giving freedom of the press a broader meaning that accorded protection to movies.

Third: *How are rights reconciled with other rights and duties?* The protection of the rights of one person may conflict with the protection of the rights of another person or with the security of the country or orderly civil life. When Dr. Samuel Sheppard, a wealthy Cleveland doctor, was tried for murdering his wife, newspapers and radio covered the story and Dr. Sheppard's love life in lurid detail. Journalists flooded the courtroom, frequently disrupting the proceedings. The Supreme Court ruled that such freedom for the news media had undermined Dr. Sheppard's right to a fair trial (*Sheppard v. Maxwell,* 1966).

In time of war, unrestricted rights to publish whatever one wants may conflict with the government's duty to secure the lives of its citizens and the victory of its armies. When Charles Schenck mailed circulars to young men urging resistance to the draft during World War I, the Supreme Court ruled that the threat of disruption of the war effort was such an evil that Schenck's freedom to publish could be restricted (*Schenck v. United States,* 1919).

Fourth: *Who secures rights?* Just as people dis-

Individual rights sometimes fall victim to wartime hysteria; 100,000 American citizens were stripped of their property and sent to remote detention camps during World War II, because they were of Japanese descent.   (*National Archives*)

agree over what rights should be secured, or which rights are more important than others, they also disagree about who should make such decisions. In the complex system of government found in the United States there are often several choices. Should rights be protected by the national government or by state and local governments? Liberals generally have argued that national protection is needed to guard against local prejudices, while conservatives have argued that local and state officials understand better the particular problems of an area in attempting to reconcile the conflicting claims characteristic of civil rights enforcement.

Within the national government, where should protection originate? All the branches of government have assumed some responsibility in protecting rights. In recent years Congress has passed important civil rights acts, the president has supplemented these with executive orders and has used presidential powers to enforce laws and court orders, and the courts have made many landmark rulings. But where should the primary responsibility lie—with elected representatives who have their fingers on the pulse of the country or with judges protected from popular prejudices? Who should decide, if there are disagreements among the branches, how civil rights ought to be enforced? This issue has led to conflict among the three branches over such issues as school prayer, busing for the purpose of school integration, and protection of the rights of those accused or convicted of crimes.

Beyond the problem of the responsibilities of the three branches, there is the question of the role that administrative agencies play. Much civil rights legislation has been general in character, leaving it to administrative agencies to determine how the general commands of the law are to be interpreted in specific rules. Most of the specific goals and timetables the federal government has imposed in job hiring and promotion in recent years are the result, not of explicit orders of Congress (which has generally rejected specific quotas), but of administrative decisions. It can be argued, of course, that if there is to be effective legislation in this field, the details of enforcement must be left to administrative agencies in order to leave Congress free to look at the big picture. But many administrative interpretations impose substantial costs, make profound changes in the lives of citizens, and even alter the principles of the law. In such instances, elected representatives, either by their own desire to avoid difficult problems or by their unwillingness to discipline bureaucracies, allow fundamental public policy to be made by unelected officials.

Constitutional Protection—The Bill of Rights

Protection of civil rights in the United States rests upon explicit provisions of the Constitution. When an American thinks of civil rights, the Bill of Rights immediately comes to mind. The first ten amendments to the Constitution, passed by the First Congress and ratified by the states in 1791, contain specific substantive and procedural protections of civil rights and liberties. The First Amendment protects the core of republican liberty: freedom of religion, speech, press, and assembly. Amendments 2 through 8 guard the individual against the threat of arbitrary force by the state. Amendments 2 and 3 protect against abuses by the military forces. Amendments 4 through 8 protect against abuses by legislatures, police, prosecutors, judges, jailers, and others who are in a legal position to take away people's property (through fines or confiscations) or liberty (through jailing) or lives (through execution).

Important as the Bill of Rights is, however, it is not exhaustive in listing the Constitutional protection of the civil rights of American citizens. The original Constitution also contains many provisions that define and protect civil rights, such as prohibiting titles of nobility and religious tests for public offices (see Chapter 2). Some subsequent amendments have added important protections for civil liberties (see Box 17-1).

Court interpretations have also been a means of extending Constitutional protection of rights and even (as in the case of the "right of privacy") of developing new rights. The most significant extension of Constitutionally protected rights by means of court interpretation has occurred through the gradual "incorporation" of the Bill of Rights into the Fourteenth Amendment. Originally, as noted in Chapter 2, the Bill of Rights restricted actions only of the national government. Through the process of "incorporation" the core of the Bill of Rights now applies to the laws and actions of all political authorities in the United States.

In 1925, in the case of *Gitlow v. New York,* the Supreme Court began a process of interpreting the Fourteenth Amendment, which protects liberty

---

BOX 17-1

EXTENSION OF CIVIL RIGHTS AND LIBERTIES BY CONSTITUTIONAL AMENDMENT

Amendment 13 Prohibits slavery.
Amendment 14 Prohibits states from abridging the "privileges and immunities" of citizens, or denying persons the "due process" or the "equal protection" of the laws.
Amendment 15 Prohibits denial of the right to vote on account of "race, color, or previous conditions of servitude."
Amendment 19 Prohibits denial of the right to vote on account of sex.
Amendment 24 Prohibits poll taxes.
Amendment 26 Prohibits denial of the right to vote on account of age for those over 18 years old.

against the actions of states, to include various provisions of the Bill of Rights. At first the process moved slowly. In a series of cases from *Gitlow* (freedom of speech) in 1925 to *Everson v. Board of Education* (prohibition on establishing religion) in 1947, the Court incorporated all the First Amendment freedoms into the Fourteenth. However, the Court continued to maintain that most of the protections guarding criminal procedure in the Fourth through Eighth Amendments did not apply to the states. In *Palko v. Connecticut* (1937) the Court drew a distinction between those rights which were essential to a "scheme of ordered liberty" and those which were not. Only the essential or fundamental rights were protected against state action by the Fourteenth Amendment. However, under the leadership of Chief Justice Earl Warren (1953–1969), the Court moved rapidly to declare most of the remaining provisions of the Bill of Rights to be "fundamental" and thus protected by the Fourteenth Amendment. Only the Fifth Amendment requirement of grand jury indictments in criminal cases and the Seventh Amendment requirement of jury trials in civil cases remain as important provisions of the Bill of Rights not applied to the states (Abraham, 1977).

Protection by Government or from Government?

Underlying the disputes over how to protect rights is the question whether rights are secured primarily by a strong and effective government with the will to protect them, or primarily by placing restrictions upon government. In defending the omission of a bill of rights from the original Constitution, some argued that the Constitution itself was the best possible bill of rights. It provided a government which had the strength to protect people's rights from foreign and domestic dangers. At the same time the danger posed by a strong government could be lessened by means of separation of powers and checks and balances (see Chapter 2). The government would ultimately be controlled by the people's will through voting.

Others felt, however, that such safeguards as popular voting and separation of powers were insufficient to protect the rights of the people adequately. There needed to be an explicit statement

of what the government could not do. Such a statement became our Bill of Rights. It implies that the citizens ought to see themselves in something of an adversary role to the government—they ought to stand up and assert their rights against the government, not through the government.

The Constitution as amended by the Bill of Rights in effect incorporates both of these traditions. It provides two ways of protecting rights: first, it empowers a government designed to work effectively and strongly for protecting rights; second, it sets explicit limitations upon that government that can be enforced by the branch of government most removed from political pressures, the courts. But there is some tension between these two traditions. The different methods may lead to different results; but, more importantly, they also call upon and foster different attitudes and skills among Americans. Should people see themselves primarily as participants in or adversaries of government? Should people learn the art of forming political coalitions or that of arguing court cases? Although the easy answer is both, the attitudes and skills required for the two courses are sufficiently diverse that in practice one is likely to be employed at the expense of the other.

The ultimate protection for civil rights in a republican system rests with the character of its people and the opinions they hold. As observed in Chapter 4, without a constitutional level of public opinion that supports equal rights for all, the protections afforded by the Constitution, the courts, Congress, and the president are likely to be short-lived. All the discussion of rights and liberties, therefore, takes place within the context of a system dedicated fundamentally to the realization of Liberalism, although there have been different interpretations of the meaning of Liberalism and powerful motives at times for ignoring its precepts.

Rights, then, are secured in the United States by a complex mixture of actions by state and national governments, by courts, legislatures, and administrative agencies. Enshrined in the Constitution, they are protected both by the arts and forms of self-government and by explicit prohibitions on government. Ultimately they are protected by public opinion. Yet all these means have never perfectly guaranteed people's rights. In part this is because of the strength of opposing interests and

prejudices. It is also because of the difficulty of reconciling conflicts between the rights of some and
those of others, and between the rights of individuals and the security of all.

Let us turn, now, to look at some specific liberties and rights.

CIVIL LIBERTIES

In considering civil liberties, we shall be considering the freedom of individuals from governmental
control. These liberties are granted and protected
not only because they are considered to be good for
individuals, but also because they are thought to
advance the common good.

Because civil liberties are protected by a complex array of opinions and doctrines deriving from
the Constitution, laws, court decisions, and executive actions, it is impossible to discuss every aspect
of every liberty. In this section we shall discuss the
two most important liberties protected by the First

Amendment (freedom of speech and religion) and
the rights of the accused protected by the Fourth
through the Eighth Amendments. This will enable
us to see how the broad prohibitions of the Constitution can give rise to disputes about their meaning
and how these disputes come to be resolved in particular instances.

Freedom of Speech

"Congress shall make no law abridging the freedom of speech. . . . " Shortly after the end of World
War II, in which some 6 million Jews died in Nazi
concentration camps, a leader of the American
Nazi party by the name of Terminiello held a rally
in a Jewish neighborhood of Chicago. The advertisements for the gathering spoke disparagingly of
Jews and were filled with invective and hatred. The
night of the meeting, angry Jews with a clear memory of the holocaust gathered in protest outside the
building in which the meeting was held. Inside, the

Because the right to speak freely is vital to a democratic society, American courts
generally have not curbed even the most antidemocratic voices, except during
wartime. *(Tom Simon/Gamma-Liaison)*

BOX 17-2

TERMINIELLO v. CHICAGO (1949)

The facts

Terminiello, who refused to stop delivering an anti-Semitic and racist speech in an auditorium surrounded by an angry and turbulent crowd, was arrested and convicted for breach of the peace. He alleged that his freedom of speech had been violated.

The majority opinion of Justice Douglas

"A function of free speech under our system of government is to invite dispute. It may indeed best serve its high purpose when it induces a condition of unrest, creates dissatisfaction with conditions as they are, or even stirs people to anger. Speech is often provocative and challenging."

The dissenting opinion of Justice Jackson

"In the long run, maintenance of free speech will be more endangered if the population can have no protection from the abuses which lead to violence. There is danger that, if the Court does not temper its doctrinaire logic with a little practical wisdom, it will convert the constitutional Bill of Rights into a suicide pact."

The decision

The Court overturned Terminiello's conviction.

Nazi leader gave a fiery speech inciting his audience to hatred of Jews. He referred to his adversaries as "slimy scum," "snakes," and "bedbugs." Outside the crowd grew more angry, yelling "Fascists, Hitlers!" at those seeking to go inside. Rocks were thrown and windows broken. After asking Terminiello to desist, and not receiving cooperation, the police arrested him for "breach of the peace" and bore him off to the police station. Terminiello claimed that his Constitutional rights of free speech had been violated (a 5-4 Supreme Court agreed with him; see Box 17-2). The police mantained that the alternative to his arrest would have been riot, since they did not have the personnel to control the mob otherwise, and that Terminiello could reasonably be held responsible for the almost certain consequences of his speech (*Terminiello v. Chicago,* 1949).

Was the decision of the Court correct? What factors are relevant to determining the answer to this question? Does the issue turn on the likelihood of riot? Would it make a difference if the Nazi leader were instead a partisan of the Democratic party in a Republican stronghold? Should Terminiello have the right to say what he wanted regardless of the consequences?

Such cases show that the protection of free speech often involves not simply a contest between good guys and bad guys, but competing claims, both of which may have some merit. It is good that a person can say what he or she wants; it is also good to maintain peace so that no one gets hurt. How the balance is to be drawn between the competing goods requires sensitivity to the character of particular circumstances; it also requires an understanding of the character and place of free speech in republican government.

Speaking (or writing), unlike our unspoken thoughts, is not merely a private activity but also a means by which we reach out and communicate with others. The doctrine of free speech has been defended on the grounds of (1) its benefits for the development of culture (art, literature, philosophy, etc.) and (2) its benefits for the political order. We shall first speak of the political benefits of speech, then consider some of the wider implications of this freedom.

Traditionally free speech has been understood to have two great political benefits: (1) To the extent that people are able to voice their complaints and concert their actions with others, they can more effectively defend themselves against a despotic government. For this reason, totalitarian and authoritarian regimes have always tried to restrict speech. (2) If people are free to discuss possible policies, criticize existing ones, and examine both officials and institutions, their participation in government, through elections or other means, is enhanced. Free speech is thus essential to free, democratic government (Meiklejohn, 1975).

Yet reasonable people have also long recognized that free, democratic government also requires some restrictions on speech. Some speech can harm or destroy the rights of other persons. The classic example in American law is that of a person falsely shouting "Fire!" in a crowded theater and causing a panic (*Schenck v. United States,* 1919). Some speech can harm the country as a whole as well as individuals. Freedom to publish the names of CIA agents might jeopardize not only the life of an individual agent, but also the ability of the country to find out what potential enemies are doing.

The general presumption in the United States is that speech is free; the burden of proof is upon those who wish to restrict it. What restrictions are justified? From an understanding which stressed the first purpose of free political speech—defense against tyranny—at the time of the founding, Americans gradually came to appreciate its second purpose better as a fundamental requirement for those who participate in their own governing. It was not until after World War I, however, that the Supreme Court first interpreted the speech and press provisions of the First Amendment. Since then the Court has ruled on dozens of cases involving free speech. Perhaps the most important question raised by these cases for the understanding of the place of free speech in republican government is whether restrictions on speech can be used to protect the underlying political consensus on which liberal democracy rests or whether that consensus can be maintained only by free and open discussion.

Restrictions on Speech   There are four kinds of speech that governments have often tried to restrict: (1) speech which would tend to undermine officially supported religious opinions, (2) speech that tends to damage the reputation or property of other people, (3) speech that threatens to disrupt public order or undermine the government, and (4) speech considered obscene. In the first area, because the principles of American government stand in opposition to state-supported religious opinions, freedom of religious speech under the First

Amendment is virtually absolute. Americans have generally agreed with Thomas Jefferson that there is no public injury if their neighbors say there are twenty gods or no God. In the second area, laws that punish speech which endangers the safety or reputation of other individuals have been generally accepted. Personal libel laws have been controversial only when they have resembled restrictions on criticisms of the government—as in the case where the person libeled is a public official. But in the third and fourth areas—restricting criticism of the government and its policies and controlling speech thought obscene—we find the strongest disagreement among Americans. We shall look at each of these, spending the most time on the criticism of government to see how a doctrine of law has grown and developed over 200 years (see Murphy, 1972).

No "Prior Restraint"   The records of the First Congress, which wrote the Bill of Rights, do not show extensive discussion of the meaning of free speech. In a famous book, *Legacy of Suppression,* Leonard Levy showed that the authors of the First Amendment accepted the traditional view of English law regarding freedom of speech and press (Levy, 1960). According to this view, there could be no prior restraint upon publication—that is, the government could not require a license *before* works could be printed or prevent a work from being published. *After* publishing, the author could be held responsible and fined or thrown into jail if the publication undermined the security or welfare of the government, or the safety, character, or property of individuals.

Although we today would regard such an interpretation of free speech as a very narrow one, freedom from prior restraint is still the bedrock of freedom of speech. When the *New York Times* in 1971 began serial publication of the "Pentagon papers," a classified government document stolen by an anti-Vietnamese war activist, the Justice Department sought to prevent the newspaper from publishing any more of it. The Supreme Court held that the *Times* was free to publish the papers even though they might have been stolen and protected by a legitimate government classification. The Court reasoned that the attempt to stop the *Times* constituted an effort at prior restraint of publication, which could be justified only by the most compelling reasons. The Court left open the possibility that the *Times* might later be prosecuted for what was actually published (*New York Times Co. v. United States,* 1971). The Justice Department, however, did not press charges. The insistence that one can be punished for a writing only after publication is so important because it means that those who would restrict speech must prove to a court that a work is illegal before it can be suppressed; they cannot first suppress a work and then put the burden of proof upon the publisher to show that it should not be censored. All the safeguards of the judicial process—a public trial, a jury of one's peers, the right to present evidence, etc.—will be in effect *before* censorship can take place.

Truth as a Defense and Trial by Jury The traditional view of English common law was that freedom of speech meant no prior restraint of publication; it did not, however, forbid punishment for harmful speech *after* publication. This understanding of free speech formed the basis for the first national law that attempted to limit speech—the Sedition Act of 1798. In the charged atmosphere created by the French Revolution and the growing partisan struggle at home, the Federalist majorities in Congress made it a crime to write, utter, or publish "any false, scandalous, and malicious writing" against the president, the Congress, or the government "with the intent to defame" the government or to "excite against [the government] the hatred of the people." This law, along with its companion, the Alien Act, used with partisan zeal by Federalist judges, was bitterly opposed by the Republicans, led by Jefferson and Madison (Miller, 1951).

In defending this law (an example of a law of "seditious libel"), the Federalists argued that although the First Amendment prohibited prior censorship of the press, it did not prohibit punishing a newspaper for a false and malicious story. Just as an individual has a right to protect his or her reputation by suing someone for libel, so, they argued, does a government have a right to sue to protect its reputation. A government's reputation, after all, may be much more important for the common good than the reputation of any individual. (This argument slid over the problem that political officials may easily confuse damage to their own reputation or position with damage to the country.)

However, the issue thus raised was not met head on, for the Republicans did not in general believe that prosecutions for seditious libel ought not to be made, but only that they ought not to be made by the national government. They saw the issue as one of states' rights, rather than as one of freedom of speech. Both Republicans and Federalists believed that there were some opinions sufficiently dangerous or harmful that they could be properly punished, if only by state laws (Chafee, 1969; Berns, 1976).

The Alien and Sedition acts expired with the Republican victory of 1800, and Jefferson pardoned all who had been convicted under them. The courts never ruled on their constitutionality, but the Federalists were so damaged politically by these acts that there was no further attempt by the national government to prosecute its critics by means of a federal seditious libel statute until World War I. The electoral defeat of the Federalists thus led to an advance in the protection of free speech.

The controversy aroused by the Alien and Sedition acts led to reform in state laws. Two aspects of the traditional doctrines of English common law in particular were rejected as not in keeping with American democratic principles. First, under English law a person could not defend himself or herself against a charge of seditious speech by arguing that the words spoken were true. Respect for the government and the monarch's reputation, it was believed, were more important than the public's right to know. But this line of reasoning, which may have had some logic in protecting a monarch who could not be deposed, was inapplicable in a democracy. If people are to control their government, they must be free to speak the truth about it, even if it brings it into disrepute. American laws were accordingly changed to allow truth as a defense in libel actions. Second, juries, rather than judges, were given the right in the reformed laws to determine whether the words spoken were actually libelous. The average person on a jury, it was thought, would be less likely than a governmental official (the judge) to see libel in criticism of the government (Berns, 1976). Thus, under the guidance of state legislatures and courts, in response to a national political controversy, the law protecting free speech was extended and strengthened in accordance with the principles of democratic government.

The Development of National Protection Jefferson's Republicans in the controversy over the Alien and Sedition acts had maintained that the states, rather then the national government, were the ones who could Constitutionally make laws restricting speech and that they would be unlikely to abuse this power because of their closeness to the people. Experience did not bear out this view. The Republican position was taken up by some southern states before the Civil War to assert their control over the spread of abolitionist publications. Many southerners saw very clearly that speech was not impotent, that abolitionist writings could work to undermine the institution of slavery. Yet the south was caught in a bind with regard to its principles, for it also wished the national government to prevent abolitionist publications from being sent through the mail. Many southerners wanted both to deny national jurisdiction over free speech and to enlist the aid of the national government in restricting speech. In any event, experience clearly showed that liberty could not be protected simply by relying on the the discretion of the states, as the Republicans had maintained.

In the aftermath of World War I, the Supreme Court finally interpreted the free speech provision of the First Amendment. An antidraft agitator, Charles Schenck, published a pamphlet denouncing conscription and circulated it to young men about to be called to military service. He was charged with obstructing the draft. Justice Oliver Wendell Holmes, Jr., speaking for a unanimous court, laid down a test for determining what kind of speech could be constitutionally punished. He distinguished between language that merely critized the government and that which incited people to illegal acts. "The question in every case," he said, "is whether the words used are used in such circumstances and are of such a nature as to create a clear and present danger that they will bring about the substantive evils that Congress has a right to prevent" (*Schenck v. United States,* 1919). Although the Court ruled that Schenck's pamphlet fell within this test and hence could be punished, in subsequent cases Justice Holmes joined by Justice Brandeis developed this "clear and present danger"

test into a greater protection for free speech. They stressed that to meet the test the danger must be imminent and serious and that the speech must actually incite people to action, not merely advocate a dangerous course. Although the Court has not always used the test of clear and present danger in free speech cases, the test remains as one important way by which the Court has tried to reconcile the competing claims in such cases.

A second step in developing national protection of free speech occurred in the case of *Gitlow v. New York* in 1925. The Supreme Court ruled for the first time that the freedom of speech provided by the First Amendment was among the "fundamental personal rights" protected against state action by the due process clause of the Fourteenth Amendment.

Since the *Schenck* and *Gitlow* cases, the Supreme Court has dealt with cases ranging from someone shouting obscenities on a street corner, to religious groups refusing to salute the flag, to organized conspiracies trying to overthrow the government. The great variety of contexts in which issues of free speech arise provides occasion for many disputes and disagreements. People have also disagreed as to the Constitutional standards which should guide judges in approaching these contexts. Various constitutional tests have been devised, most of which are variants of either a "balancing" test or an "absolutist" interpretation of the First Amendment (Krislov, 1968). The "clear and present danger" test is an example of a balancing test. In such tests, freedom of speech is weighed against other goods, such as national security. Such tests seek to provide a means by which weight can be assigned to various goods to answer the question "What is the value of free speech in relation to the value of national security, of civil peace, of orderly administration?" People may disagree as to whether the test assigns too great a weight to free speech or too little. Some have argued that these tests really leave it to the discretion of judges to determine the weight assigned various goods and hence that they may not be an effective means of guaranteeing free speech when it comes under attack (Anastaplo, 1971).

To meet this objective, some have argued for an "absolutist" interpretation of the First Amendment (Meiklejohn, 1975). The leading exponent of this view on the Supreme Court was Justice Hugo Black, whose career on the bench spanned more than thirty years (1937–1971). This view holds that whatever is meant by "speech" in the Constitution is fully protected by the Constitution regardless of the other goods that might come in competition with it. One might debate, in Black's view, whether burning one's draft card is a form of speech. If it is, however, then it is protected conduct whether done in wartime or peacetime, whether it threatens to disrupt the draft or not. The key to this test is to determine what is meant by "freedom of speech." Does it refer primarily to political speech or to all forms of speech? No matter how one answers this question, some believe that an absolutist interpretation leads to a dogmatic preference for free speech in competition with other rights and goods.

Communist Prosecutions   In 1940, Congress, worried by the threat of both Nazi and communist subversion, passed a sedition law known as the "Smith Act." Unlike the Sedition Act of the eighteenth century, it did not seek to punish those critical of the government, but rather sought to punish those who willfully advocated the overthrow of the government by force and violence. Not the content of the speech but its intended effect was the standard by which speech was to be judged. The Smith Act also made it illegal to organize, or be a member of, a group that advocated the forceful overthrow of the government. After the war, the act was used to prosecute leading figures of the Communist party in the United States.

In bringing leading members of the Communist party to trial, the government alleged that these men and women were teaching and advocating the violent overthrow of the government, or that they were members of an organization they knew to be advocating its overthrow. In the first case to reach the Supreme Court, *Dennis v. United States* (1951), the Court ruled 6-2 that the conviction of leading communists under the act was constitutional. Interpreting the "clear and present danger" test to mean that the danger of an attempt to overthrow the government did not need to be imminent, or have any likelihood of success, the Court said the government did not have to wait "until the *putsch* is about to be executed, the plans have been laid and the signal is awaited." The evil of such an attempt to overthrow the government was so great, the Court argued, that the government had a right to prevent it, even though the attempt or its success was very unlikely. (see Box 17-3.)

Although many were subsequently successfully prosecuted under the Smith Act, the act gradually became a dead letter. The climate of opinion in which the Court ruled changed. During the early

---

BOX 17-3

DENNIS v. UNITED STATES (1951)

The facts

Dennis and ten other leaders of the Communist party were charged and convicted under the Smith Act of conspiring to advocate and teach the violent overthrow of the United States government and to organize the Communist party for the same purpose.

The majority opinion of Chief Justice Vinson

"Overthrow of the Government by force and violence is certainly a substantial enough interest for the Government to limit speech. Indeed, this is the ultimate value of any society, for if a society cannot protect its very structure from armed internal attack, it must follow that no subordinate value can be protected."

The dissenting opinion of Justice Douglas

"The political censor has no place in our public debates. Unless and until extreme and necessitous circumstances are shown, our aim should be to keep speech unfettered and to allow the process of law to be invoked only when the provocateurs among us move from speech to action."

The decision

The Court upheld the convictions.

1950s there had been widespread fear of communist subversion. This fear was fanned by Senator Joseph McCarthy of Wisconsin, who made unsubstantiated charges as to the extent of communist infiltration in the government and elsewhere. Many patriotic Americans found their reputations tarnished, and some had their careers damaged or ruined. However, in 1954 McCarthy was censured by the United States Senate, and the cause he represented was thereby greatly discredited. Without declaring the Smith Act unconstitutional, the Court moved in the direction of interpreting the requirements needed to prosecute someone successfully under the act in such a way that convictions became increasingly difficult and finally impossible. The major step in this process was the *Yates* case in which the Court distinguished between the expression of a philosophical belief and the advocacy of an illegal act (*Yates v. United States,* 1957). Thereafter the government had to prove that a person actually intended to overthrow the government and that the words spoken were actually calculated to incite overthrow, not merely that the individual favored overthrowing the government. This test was virtually impossible to satisfy.

The provisions of the Smith Act and of varying state laws making it a crime to belong to organizations advocating the overthrow of the government were also gradually eroded. In 1967, the Court ruled that Communist party membership as such did not disqualify one from teaching in public schools, and in 1974 it held that the Communist party of Indiana could not be kept off the ballot because its officers refused to file an affidavit that the party did not advocate the violent overthrow of the government (*Keyishian v. Board of Regents,* 1967; *Communist Party of Indiana v. Whitcomb,* 1974). Today, one can advocate any political opinion, or join organizations advocating such opinions, so long as one's words or actions do not imminently incite people actually to go out and attempt to overthrow the government.

Thus we see that the limits of free speech have been affected by the climate of opinion in the country at large. Sometimes changes in these limits have been the result of the actions of the states, sometimes of those of Congress or the executive, and often of decisions by the federal courts.

Obscene Speech While the founders clearly meant the First Amendment to protect religious and political speech, it is much less clear what other kinds of speech, if any, they meant to protect. Courts have interpreted the amendment to cover many other kinds of speech, including speech in the realm of literature, philosophy, and art.

But does the freedom to speak in this sense cover any kind of publication regardless of its character or quality? In fact, American law has never supported such a position. Speech that is deemed obscene has not been protected by the First Amendment. However, the definition of obscenity has been narrowed in recent years so that this exception is but a ghost of what it used to be. The current standard for judging obscenity, established largely in the case of *Miller v. California* in 1973, says that a work may be judged obscene if it appeals to "purient interests" as judged by the "average person using contemporary community standards" or if it portrays specifically defined sexual conduct in a patently offensive way and if the work taken as a whole lacks "literary, artistic, political, or scientific value." This standard is somewhat more strict than the one which had previously been developed by the Court in that it allows the community standards to be local standards rather than standards which might apply everywhere in the country, and allows an otherwise obscene work to be protected by its literary, artistic, political, or scientific value only if the work *as a whole* has such value. Previously the Court had held that if the work could be said to contain any literary, artistic, political, or scientific value at all, it could not be declared obscene (*Roth v. United States,* 1957; Lewis, 1976).

The issue of censorship of obscenity has not died away completely, however. Not only do traditionalists argue sometimes for greater censorship, but some in the feminist movement have argued that the degrading portrayals of women in pornography ought to be more strictly limited. Whether a republican government which depends upon the character of its citizens can be completely indifferent to works which many think degrade and corrupt that character is an issue likely to recur (Clor, 1969).

Other Forms of Expression Some activities other than speaking or writing seem to share the

Many people who reject all political censorship would like to see pornography banned; feminists, for example, argue that pornography degrades women and undermines the respect for others which is vital to a democratic society.   *(Jim Anderson / Black Star)*

qualities that make speech protected under the First Amendment. This may be particularly true if the good protected by the First Amendment is understood to be the individual good of expressing oneself, rather than the public goods of defending against tyranny, discussing public affairs, or encouraging arts and sciences. When children in a Des Moines school wore armbands to school to protest the Vietnamese war despite school regulations, the Court held that they were exercising a Constitutionally protected form of expression (*Tinker v. Des Moines School District,* 1969). However, expressive actions have generally received less protection from the Court than has speech itself. In *United States v. O'Brien* (1968) the Court held that burning one's draft card could be punished even though it might be a means of protesting governmental policies. The majority argued that the gov-

ernment's interest in an efficient system of selective service outweighed any infringement of the right of expression.

Freedom of Religion

"Congress shall make no law respecting an establishment of religion, or prohibiting the free exercise thereof. . . ." Freedom of religion both protects religious belief and worship from dictation by government and prevents religion from dictating to the government. It stems from the fundamental premise that the government of the United States does not derive its powers from divine authority and that the government's purpose is to protect people's rights, not to tell them how they should save their souls.

While there is widespread agreement in the

United States in favor of religious freedom, there have been many matters of controversy. First, does the Constitution protect the right of a person to disobey an otherwise valid law because of religious conviction? The traditional answer to this question was no. In *Reynolds v. United States* (1878), the Supreme Court held that a Mormon who claimed polygamy as his religious duty was not exempt from the federal law making bigamy a crime. The Court said that people were free to *believe* whatever they wanted, but the *actions* of religious people could be subject to the same constraints as the actions of anyone else. In recent years, however, the Court has held that in some cases people may be exempt from laws because of their religious convictions. In *Sherbert v. Verner* (1963), the Court held that a Seventh-Day Adventist who could not find employment because she would not work on Saturday was entitled to unemployment compensation in spite of a law barring benefits if a worker failed to accept "suitable work when offered." The Court held that the law was generally valid and could be used to compel others to work on Saturday, but interfered with the free exercise of Ms. Sherbert's religion. In another case, *Wisconsin v. Yoder* (1972), the Court ruled that the Amish need not obey a compulsory school attendance law of Wisconsin—a law valid for other citizens of the state.

Has the Court, in seeking to protect the free exercise of religion, violated the First Amendment prohibition against establishing religion? The issue shows that it is not always easy to reconcile the two provisions of the First Amendment respecting religious liberty: the free exercise clause which suggests that religions cannot be interfered with, and the establishment clause which suggests that religions cannot be given special privileges.

The second question in dispute concerns the establishment clause. Everyone agrees that the clause prevents Congress from establishing a state church (a particular church supported by state funds and given special privileges). Controversy has arisen, however, as to whether the government may give aid to religion or religious groups provided the aid is given to achieve nonreligious ends. Can religion be aided or accommodated by government as a means to the secular ends of society?

The most important cases which have raised this question have involved education and tax exemption for churches. May public schools have prayers or Bible reading as part of their program or release children from school time in order to receive religious instruction? May government give aid to church-related schools? The Supreme Court has developed a three-pronged test for dealing with these questions. First, the aid or religious practice must have a secular purpose to be constitutional. Second, its "principle or primary effect [must] neither advance nor inhibit religion." Finally, it must not foster an "excessive government entanglement with religion" (*Committee for Public Education v. Regan,* 1980).

The difficulty of defining rights in concrete circumstances is nowhere better illustrated than in this area of church-state relations. In *Everson v. Board of Education* (1947) the Court ruled that a New Jersey law authorizing school districts to reimburse bus fares paid by children traveling to and from schools, including church-related schools, had the secular purpose of getting children safely to school and was neutral between religious believers and nonbelievers. Therefore, the law was constitutional. In *Walz v. Tax Commission* (1970) Chief Justice Burger, speaking for the Court, held that tax exemption for religious property was constitutional, although it indirectly aided religion because it required less government involvement with religion than would taxing it. On the other hand in *Abington School District v. Schempp* (1963), the Court held that a Pennsylvania law requiring Bible reading in the public schools was unconstitutional because the Bible reading was a religious exercise violating the required neutrality between religious believers and nonbelievers. Many forms of aid to religious schools, but not all, have been held unconstitutional because of the difficulty of distinguishing the secular purpose of such aid from the pervasive religious character of parochial schools (Morgan, 1975).

The line separating Constitutionally permitted aid to religion from forbidden aid is not drawn with any certainty at the present time. It is sometimes difficult to see consistency in the Court's opinions. Why should tax exemption for churches, a very substantial and seemingly direct aid to religion, be constitutional while state payments to church-sponsored schools to cover the costs of tests and reports mandated by the state, an indirect aid serving a required state purpose, be unconstitutional (*Levitt v. Committee for Public Education,* 1973)? The Court is sharply divided on the meaning of the three tests mentioned, and some members do not think the tests are the proper ones. Some think the Constitution permits more aid to religion than the tests seem to allow, others less.

Many Americans have disagreed with recent Court rulings in the area of religious freedom. There have been persistent attempts in Congress to pass a Constitutional amendment permitting prayer in the public schools. President Reagan endorsed such an amendment. It is also likely that important issues involving aid to religion may come before the Court in the years ahead. In the past several sessions of Congress there have been proposals put forward for federal income tax credit for tuition payments to schools including religious schools. In trying to decide whether such a law would be constitutional, it is necessary to consider the tests developed by the Court. It is also necessary, particularly in an area where the Court has been as uncertain as it has in this one, for democratic citizens to ask for themselves what the proper Constitutional standard is. Tuition tax credits might have profound effects for good or ill on the character and quality of American education, and possibly on efforts to achieve integration in American society. The Constitutional dimensions of such an issue cannot be left solely to the reflections of the Court without greatly diminishing the self-government of the American people.

Rights of Those Accused of Crimes

In our federal system the administration of criminal justice is principally a function of the states. As explained at the beginning of this chapter, and shown in Box 17-4, most of the protections in the Fourth through the Eighth Amendments for those accused of crimes have been held to apply to the

---

BOX 17-4

APPLICATION OF CRIMINAL PROCEDURAL RIGHTS TO THE STATES

Right	Case and year
Fourth Amendment	
Unreasonable search and seizure	*Mapp v. Ohio* (1961)
Fifth Amendment	
Grand jury clause	Not incorporated
Double jeopardy clause	*Benton v. Maryland* (1969)
Self-incrimination clause	*Malloy v. Hogan* (1964)
Sixth Amendment	
Speedy trial clause	*Klopfer v. North Carolina* (1967)
Public trial clause	*In re Oliver* (1948)
Jury trial clause	*Duncan v. Louisiana* (1968)
Notice clause	*Cole v. Arkansas* (1948)
Confrontation clause	*Pointer v. Texas* (1965)
Compulsory process clause	*Washington v. Texas* (1967)
Right-to-counsel clause	*Gideon v. Wainwright* (1963)
	Argersinger v. Hamlin (1972)
Eighth Amendment	
Excessive fines and bails clause	Not incorporated
"Cruel and unusual punishments" clause	*Robinson v. California* (1962)

Source: Rossum, 1978:125.

states through the process of "incorporation" into the Fourteenth Amendment. As a result, since the 1960s the Court has increased requirements related to the right to counsel (Sixth Amendment) and protections against unreasonable searches and seizures (Fourth Amendment) and against self-incrimination (Fifth Amendment). It has also used the Eighth Amendment's prohibition of cruel and unusual punishments to place restrictions upon capital punishment. Other lesser protections have also been extended.

The increased protection of rights in criminal cases extended by the Warren Court during the 1960s created great controversy. Richard Nixon promised during the 1968 presidential campaign that if elected he would appoint judges that would favor crime prevention over procedural rights. Congress has acted to try to overturn or modify several of the Court's decisions. In the wake of the decision limiting the death penalty, most states enacted new death penalty statutes in attempts to get around the apparent objections of the Court.

All this opposition has had some effect upon the Court. Although the Burger Court, with four Nixon appointees, plus one by Ford and one by Reagan, has not retreated from the basic protections extended by the Warren Court, it has interpreted them more narrowly. It has been particularly reluctant to overrule state court decisions in the area of unreasonable searches and seizures. And it has upheld some death penalty statutes. However, it has also extended some protections beyond the position of the Warren Court, such as in the area of prison administration. Let us look at the four main areas in which the rights of the accused have been extended.

Searches and Seizures   The Fourth Amendment prohibits "unreasonable searches and seizures." The central meaning of this prohibition is that the police may not search a person or premises without a warrant issued by a magistrate upon demonstration that there is a probable cause to believe that there is something illegal or incriminating to be found. However, there are several circumstances in which police may make searches without a warrant. The most important of these is a search incident to a lawful arrest. An arresting officer may search the person being arrested and the immedi-

ate vicinity without a search warrant in order both to make certain that the arrested person does not have a concealed weapon which might endanger the officer and to keep evidence from being destroyed.

While there has been disagreement about how much discretion the police should be given to perform their job, the chief controversy surrounding searches and seizures has involved the "exclusionary rule." This rule states that evidence unconstitutionally or illegally obtained cannot be used in a trial. It is a means which courts have used to enforce due process protections. If the police gain evidence without a search warrant or extract a confession without the accused having been given the right to counsel, the evidence or confession cannot be used in a trial. Although the Court held that the prohibition against "unreasonable searches and seizures" applied to the states in the case of *Wolf v. Colorado* in 1949, it was not until the case of *Mapp v. Ohio* in 1961 that the Court ruled that this prohibition must be enforced by means of the exclusionary rule.

The alternative (as practiced in many other countries) would be to admit illegal evidence at a trial, but then to make the offending officers subject to penalties for their illegal activities. The proponents of this alternative argue that it does not make sense to let a known criminal go free, even if the evidence has been illegally obtained. The proper penalty should be applied to the offending officer, not to society as a whole. On the other hand, the proponents of the exclusionary rule argue that it is difficult to punish law enforcement officials when they have succeeded in catching criminals, even if they have acted illegally. Police may be reluctant to collect evidence against their fellow officers, prosecutors to bring cases, and juries to convict. Besides, they argue, it is demeaning to the law to enforce it by illegal means.

Self-Incrimination   One of the most important of several provisions contained in the Fifth Amendment is that "no person . . . shall be compelled in any criminal case to be witness against himself." This privilege may be invoked before any official body with the power to compel testimony under oath. It thus applies to legislative committees and grand juries as well as to criminal trials.

BOX 17-5

THE EXCLUSIONARY RULE AND THE CORRUPTION OF JUSTICE

The "exclusionary rule" prohibits the use of illegally obtained evidence as proof of guilt in a trial. One of the arguments concerning this rule is whether it encourages or discourages illegal actions by police. Those who favor the rule argue that it discourages illegal actions by police to obtain evidence. Those opposed argue that it merely encourages police officers to give false testimony about how they obtained evidence. A group of students at Columbia University Law School analyzed the places where police alleged that evidence was found in misdemeanor narcotics cases in New York City before and after the *Mapp v. Ohio* (1961) decision, which had extended protection against searches of persons. They found the following:

New York City Police Officers' Allegations
Regarding Discovery of Evidence in Misdemeanor Narcotics Offenses, 1960–1962

How evidence was found	Percent of arrests during six-month period		Percent change
	Before Mapp	After Mapp	
Narcotics bureau			
Hidden on person	35	3	−32
Dropped or thrown to ground	17	43	+26
Uniform			
Hidden on person	31	9	−22
Dropped or thrown to ground	14	21	+7
Plainclothes			
Hidden on person	24	4	−20
Dropped or thrown to ground	11	17	+6

Source: Oaks, 1970:698.

Major controversy in the last two decades has centered on the question of the admissibility of confessions at trials. The Court had long held that coerced confessions were not admissible on the grounds that they might be unreliable, but that voluntary confessions could be. Torture was not a good way to the truth. However, the Court gradually came to see this exclusion as a means of regulating the police as well as preventing false confessions, blurring the distinction between voluntary and coerced confessions. Instead of looking for evidence of physical torture, the Court looked at evidence that psychological pressure had been applied. Because all police inquiries involve some psychological pressure, the issue became how much pressure there must be before the confession cannot be admitted in court.

In the case of *Malloy v. Hogan* in 1964, the Court held that the protection against self-incrimination is included within the due process protections of the Fourteenth Amendment. This led to decisions in the cases of *Escobedo v. Illinois* (1964) and *Miranda v. Arizona* (1966) establishing the rule that a confession would not be admissible in Court unless the accused had been advised both of the right to remain silent and of the right to counsel. (The privilege against self-incrimination and the right to counsel are intimately connected because lawyers will immediately advise clients not to incriminate themselves.) While the Burger Court has not reversed this basic position, it has ruled that a confession obtained in violation of the *Miranda* rule might be introduced in court for the purpose of proving that a defendant is lying although not for the purpose of proving he or she is guilty of the crime (*Harris v. New York*, 1971).

Right to Counsel Because the law is frequently complex, as are the procedures implementing it, it has been recognized that a fair trial may require the assistance of legal counsel. Before 1963 the Court had held that a state was obliged to provide counsel for a defendant who could not afford one in a capital case but not in less serious crimes. However, in that year the Court held in *Gideon v. Wainwright* that free legal counsel must be provided an indigent defendant in noncapital cases. In the cases of *Escobedo* and *Miranda* it held that counsel must be provided in the pretrial stage if confessions are to be admitted in court. The general rule is that counsel must be available at every "critical stage of the prosecution."

Cruel and Unusual Punishment In 1972 the Supreme Court ruled that the death penalty statute of Georgia violated the Eighth Amendment's prohibition against "cruel and unusual punishments" (*Furman v. Georgia*, 1972). However, only two of the justices argued that all capital punishment was unconstitutional. The others in the 5-4 majority argued that the statute allowed too wide discretion to judges and juries, was too infrequently used, or was applied in a discriminatory manner. Many states enacted new death penalty laws to meet these objections. In *Gregg v. Georgia* (1976) the Court upheld a new Georgia death penalty law which contained procedures directing the jury to the particular circumstances of the crime involved and provided general rules to guide the jury as to when the death penalty should be invoked.

The Court has refined its criteria governing the procedures required in meeting Constitutional standards since *Gregg*. In *Coker v. George* (1977) the Court forbade the use of the death penalty to punish rape. It seems that the death penalty will pass Constitutional scruples only when it is used in murder cases, and then only if careful procedural requirements are met. The majority of states now have death penalty statutes, and the number of people sentenced to death is large, but the number actually executed remains small.

The opposition aroused by these decisions in the area of criminal procedures has achieved only mod-

est results. The attempt to change these rulings by appointing new members to the Court has resulted in some modifications but not a basic reversal of direction. Legislatures have succeeded in writing constitutional death penalty statutes, but these are confined to a narrow class of cases and have not resulted in large numbers of executions.

CIVIL RIGHTS

In the issues we have looked at thus far in this chapter, the question of individual liberty has been uppermost. In the ones we will now turn to—those we are calling "civil rights"—the issue is primarily one of equality. These include the protection of the rights of blacks, hispanics, other minorities, and women who have been denied full participation in the country's political life or have been treated as second-class citizens under the law.

There are two related aspects to fulfilling the promise of the equality of all persons within our constitutional system. One is guaranteeing equal participation in voting and other aspects of the governing process. The other is protecting the individual's right to be treated equally under the laws. As we have discussed voting and other political rights in other chapters, we shall concentrate here on the issue of treating people equally under the law.

The Fourteenth Amendment guarantees all persons the equal protection of the laws, and the courts have held that the due process clause of the Fifth Amendment has a similar "equal protection" component. This does not mean that the laws cannot make distinctions between individuals or groups. The tax laws require people with high incomes to pay taxes at a higher rate than those with low incomes. This is not a violation of the equal protection of the laws, because the distinction made by the law is a reasonable one—it is not arbitrary and is related to legitimate policy goals, such as raising revenues. However, some distinctions between individuals or groups do violate their civil rights. Nearly everyone would agree that a law which permitted only whites to vote would violate the rights of nonwhites. Other cases are more difficult. May the law extend special benefits to blacks or women in order to help remedy the effects of past discrimination?

As this photograph from the early 1960s makes clear, segregated public facilities in the old south, justified under the motto ''separate but equal,'' were far from equal. *(Elliott Erwitt / Magnum)*

Racial Equality

Before 1954 the Court's understanding of what equality under the law meant with regard to race had been established in the case of *Plessy v. Ferguson* (1896). The majority in the case had held that legally mandated segregation in Louisiana trains was constitutional as long as the separate facilities were equal. No one was injured so long as the separate facilities were equal, required separation did not imply the inferiority of either race, and the purposes of ensuring public order and providing for the convenience and comfort of passengers were sufficient to justify the segregation.

Through the efforts of the National Association for the Advancement of Colored People (NAACP) and others, the courts were gradually induced to move away from the entrenched segregationist position established in the wake of *Plessy*. The great change came in 1954. In the years preceding 1954

various instances of educational discrimination had been ruled unconstitutional because the education offered to blacks was not equal to that offered to whites. In the early 1950s, Oliver Brown tried to enroll his daughter in an all-white public school in Topeka, Kansas. When the NAACP took the case to court, the lower federal court ruled that the black and white schools of Topeka were equal in quality and therefore constitutional under the *Plessy* doctrine. Accepting the judgment that the schools were equal in most exterior ways, the Supreme Court faced the question: Were separate but equal schools constitutional? In an atmosphere of great drama, the Supreme Court, on May 17, 1954, announced its unanimous decision: segregated schools are inherently unequal and therefore in violation of the equal protection clause of the Fourteenth Amendment (*Brown v. Board of Education of Topeka,* 1954). Although the decision involved only public education, it signaled the end of legalized segregation everywhere. In subsequent decisions, the Court began to condemn legally supported segregation wherever it was found.

The *Brown* decision marked a great advance for racial equality in the United States. Although resistance was initially massive and progress toward desegregation slow, by 1970 the dual school systems of the nation were destroyed. At the same time it helped to spur new *political* efforts to increase legal protection for civil rights. The civil rights movement of the 1950s and 1960s, begun with the nonviolent movement of Martin Luther King, continued through a variety of organizations and helped to dramatize the issue and form public opinion. The cause of segregation was discredited by brutal murders and beatings of civil rights workers, and moderate whites and blacks joined to form a broad coalition in favor of new protection for civil rights.

President Johnson seized the emotional moment of the assassination of President Kennedy to galvanize opinion in favor of legislative action. The result was the Civil Rights Act of 1964. Although some civil rights legislation had been passed in 1957 and 1960 (covering aspects of voting rights), the law of 1964 was sweeping in its coverage, adding protections for the right to vote and the right to access to public accommodations, and for desegregation of public facilities and education, and increasing the powers of the Commission on Civil Rights (charged with enforcing important aspects of civil rights legislation). It also contained provisions guaranteeing nondiscrimination in federally assisted programs and equal employment opportunities. Racial distinctions were to be eradicated from American law and practice.

The Civil Rights Act was followed by the Voting Rights Act of 1965, which was meant to assure blacks and others of the right to vote. Subsequently, additional legislation was passed, but the acts of 1964 and 1965 were the most sweeping and important, and provided the key breakthroughs.

The *Brown* decision and its aftermath, both legally and politically, thus resulted in a great advance for equality under the law. However, the meaning of the Constitutional guarantee of equal protection of the laws has not been fully clarified and is a source of renewed controversy in contemporary politics. Justice Harlan, in the *Plessy* case,

had issued a ringing dissent in which he said, "In view of the Constitution, in the eye of the law, there is in this country no superior, dominant, ruling class of citizens. There is no caste here. Our Constitution is color-blind and neither knows nor tolerates classes among citizens." But the Court in the *Brown* case did not make a blanket declaration that all racial discrimination in the law was illegal. It rather argued that segregated schools could not be equal because of the stigma they placed upon black children—because of the psychological harm done to black children. This left open the possibility that racial discrimination which did not stigmatize might be constitutional.

The Court subsequently developed a view of the equal protection clause which held that most classifications and distinctions made by law would be constitutional provided they were reasonably related to some valid governmental objective. But in some cases the standards were stricter, and the laws would have to meet *strict judicial scrutiny*. This meant the burden of proof would be upon the government in these cases to show that there was a compelling governmental interest which required the classification—a standard difficult to meet. This more difficult standard is required if burdens are put upon a class of persons who have been harmed by governmental and societal actions in the past (a "suspect" class) or if the classifications affect *fundamental rights*—particularly those rights the denial of which prevents the political process from working effectively, such as freedom of speech and the right to vote.

This interpretation of the equal protection clause seems to suggest the possibility that one can constitutionally put burdens on the majority white population (a nonsuspect class) which one could not put on racial minorities (suspect classes). The record of the Court is ambiguous on this possibility. When Allan Bakke, a white applicant, was twice denied admission to the medical school of the University of California at Davis, he brought suit arguing that the university had denied him his Constitutional rights by setting aside sixteen places in the entering class for minority students and admitting students whose qualifications were substantially below his own. The California Supreme Court agreed that Bakke's rights had been violated.

A sharply divided Supreme Court went on to say that the explicit racial quota of the school violated either the equal protection clause of the Fourteenth Amendment or the Civil Rights Act of 1964 (the majority was divided in its opinion). But another majority made up of a different combination of justices agreed that race could be used as a criterion for admission provided it was only one of several factors taken into account. Thus the case condemned explicit quotas, but seemed to uphold more subtle preferences (*Regents of the University of California v. Bakke,* 1978).

Another case, decided a year after *Bakke,* lent additional support to preferences for minorities ("affirmative action" programs) when they are the result of private agreements and not governmental mandates. In *United Steelworkers of America v. Weber* (1979) the Court ruled that the Civil Rights Act of 1964 did not prohibit "all private, voluntary race-conscious affirmative action plans." As a result of an agreement between his union and the Kaiser Company, Weber, a white, had been passed over for a training program in preference for a black with less seniority. The Court argued that the literal reading of the Civil Rights Act which pro-

hibited such preferences had to give way to the spirit of the act, which the Court thought was to advance the position of blacks in American society.

Finally, in the case of *Fullilove v. Klutznick* (1980) the Court seemed to uphold the constitutionality of racial classifications in order to achieve broad social goals. The Public Works Employment Act of 1977 required that at least 10 percent of all the money granted for projects under the act be expended for minority business enterprises. This was the first time in American history that Congress had passed a law creating a broad legislative classification for entitlement to benefits based solely upon racial characteristics. By a 6-3 vote the Court held this classification constitutional, arguing that the harm done the whites excluded from the benefits was minor and did not stigmatize them. (See Box 17-6.)

But these Court cases have not resolved the issue of affirmative action, both because the Court remains sharply divided (the majority in *Fullilove* could not agree on the reasons for its decision) and because the country as a whole remains divided. Proponents of affirmative action argue that past discrimination has created a situation which can be

---

BOX 17-6

FULLILOVE v. KLUTZNICK, 1980

The facts

The Public Works Employment Act of 1977 required that 10 percent of all funds granted for public works projects be expended on minority business enterprise (comprising citizens who are Negroes, Spanish-speaking persons, Asians, Indians, Eskimos, and Aleuts).

The Court's opinion by Chief Justic Burger

" . . . We reject the contention that in the remedial context the Congress must act in a wholly 'color-blind' fashion. . . . When effectuating a limited and properly tailored remedy to cure the effects of prior discrimination, such a 'sharing of the burden' by innocent parties is not impermissible. . . . In the past some nonminority businesses may have reaped

competitive benefit over the years from the virtual exclusion of minority firms from these contracting opportunities.''

The dissenting opinion of Justice Stewart

'''Our Constitution is color-blind, and neither knows nor tolerates classes among citizens. . . .' Today, the Court upholds a statute that accords a preference to citizens who are 'Negroes, Spanish-speaking, Orientals, Indians, Eskimos, and Aleuts . . .' I think today's decision is wrong for the same reason that *Plessy v. Ferguson* was wrong. The rule cannot be any different when the persons injured by a racially biased law are not members of a racial minority.''

The decision

The Court upheld the constitutionality of the act.

remedied only by using racial classifications. Temporary racial preference is justified as the only way to achieve racial equality. The alternative is to perpetuate a situation created by the unjust treatment of minorities. Opponents argue that affirmative action violates the basic principle of American law that individuals are responsible for their own actions and are not to be blamed or penalized because of the group to which they belong. They further suggest that the temporary acceptance of racial quotas will pit one racial group against another and will in the long run create vested interests in favor of the perpetuation of racial distinctions in order to gain racial benefits.

The end of overt, *legal* discrimination against blacks in the United States has not resolved the issue of racial equality. Blacks remain disproportionately at the bottom of the socioeconomic ladder. How this situation should be dealt with poses one of thorniest and most controversial questions in contemporary politics. The meaning of equality under the law as a principle to guide the handling of the issue remains a controversial and profound question for the future of American democracy.

Rights of Hispanics

The protection of the rights of hispanic Americans, who have become an increasingly large segment of the American population, raises many of the same problems that have faced other racial and ethnic groups in the past. It also raises some new problems. One major issue is illegal immigration, particularly from Mexico. It is difficult to calculate the number of illegal immigrants in the United States, as those who have entered illegally are not usually eager to make themselves known. In 1981 the attorney general estimated that there were 3 million to 6 million illegal aliens in the United States. Such people may be particularly open to manipulation and exploitation. Recent sessions of Congress have seen various proposals to deal with this situation, usually involving some combination of granting legal status to those who have been here for some time and trying to find more effective methods of controlling illegal immigration (such as making it illegal to hire illegal aliens, thus reducing the motive for people to cross the border unlawfully). However, these proposals have been very controversial, and Congress has yet to pass a comprehensive measure. The Court has also concerned itself with the problem. In 1982 it held unconstitutional a Texas law which denied state funds for education of illegal alien children. The majority ruled that no sufficiently important state purpose was served to justify distinguishing between citizens and illegal aliens in determining who was entitled to free public education, and hence that the statute violated the equal protection of the laws (*Pyler v. Doe,* 1982).

Equal Rights for Women

Women, like blacks, hispanics, and others, have found themselves the objects of discrimination in securing jobs, status, and equal treatment under the law. As in the other areas, the import of the nation's dedication to equality for the relationship between the sexes has been a matter of considerable debate. At the time of the founding and throughout the nineteenth century, women were generally denied full civil and political rights. Although there was nothing in the Constitution that restricted the right to vote to men, the state legislatures, which determined voting qualifications, universally denied the right to women. This denial generally rested on the argument that the political order was composed of families, not individuals, and that the differences between men and women made fathers and husbands the proper representatives of women.

Beginning in the 1840s women began to organize to achieve the right to vote. The movement for women's equality, like that of the blacks', could appeal to basic American principles to gain support. The Seneca Falls Convention of 1848, a crucial milestone in the national coordination of the women's movement, adopted as its statement of principles the Declaration of Independence (with, of course, the clear understanding that it meant that "all men *and women* are created equal"). The goal of women's suffrage was finally realized in the nation as a whole by the ratification of the Nineteenth Amendment prohibiting denial of the vote on account of sex in 1920. (Some individual states had previously granted women the vote.)

Even after gaining the right to vote, however, many inequalities continued to exist both in law and in practice. Some of these were based on the supposition that women required special protection, such as laws which limited the hours women could work but did not limit men. Others recognized what was thought to be women's special role in society, such as laws which preferred the mother when establishing custody in divorce cases. Many simply gave preferences to men, particularly in economic and business matters. Beginning in the 1950s, the women's movement gained new strength in its battle against inequality. At the same time, women were entering the work force in increasing numbers. This led to new laws requiring equal pay for equal work, prohibiting sex discrimination in employment and between students in schools receiving federal funds, and forbidding discrimination against pregnant women in the workplace (Flexner, 1975).

A major effort was undertaken by feminist groups to secure passage of the Equal Rights Amendment to the Constitution. This amendment would have prohibited denying equality of rights under the law on account of sex. Although the proposed amendment initially received the overwhelming endorsement of Congress and swept through many state legislatures, the movement for its passage stalled and it was eventually defeated, despite an extension of the time limit for ratification by Congress.

While the defeat of the Equal Rights Amendment was a setback for the feminist movement, it did not necessarily show a widespread lack of support for equal rights for women in the United States. Not only did 35 states ratify the proposed amendment, but most people seemed to agree that women should have equal rights. There was much disagreement, however, about what those equal rights were, and many opponents of the amendment feared the answer that might be given by the courts. Particularly effective in the campaign against the amendment were the arguments that it might be read to require drafting women for combat duty or that it might undermine laws that protected women on the job (Boles, 1979). Opposition to the proposal was itself led and organized by women, and the Equal Rights Amendment became an issue that symbolized a struggle over a wide range of cultural issues.

It may be that an attempt to secure an equal rights amendment will be renewed. It also seems likely that many of the goals desired by supporters of the Equal Rights Amendment will be achieved by legislative or court actions. The Supreme Court has not regarded sex classifications as inherently suspect, as they have racial classifications (discussed earlier), but they have moved in the direction of requiring a demonstration that some important governmental purpose be served in order for such classifications to be held valid. The Court has upheld the all-male draft with the argument that restriction of combat duties to men creates a reasonable distinction serving an important governmental interest that allows Congress to draft men but not women (*Rosteker v. Goldberg,* 1981). But it has barred many differences based on sex, such as state laws establishing different ages at which men and women become legal adults (*Stanton v. Stanton,* 1975).

CONCLUSION

Civil rights and liberties define limits on governmental action, specifying certain areas that lie beyond the reach of government and certain methods that government may or may not employ in acting on matters within its control. These limits help serve not only to define the character of liberty, but also to elaborate the meaning of equality. Other policies of government, as we have seen, also affect the nature of liberty and equality, but the concrete designation of rights and liberties is the most important foundation of these fundamental values of American society.

Although there is a wide area of consensus on rights and liberties, disagreements arise over certain claims to rights, over who possesses them, and over how they can be reconciled with other rights and duties. There have also been many conflicts over who should decide these questions. Rooted in important provisions of the Constitution, civil rights and liberties receive much of their definition and support from decisions of the courts. To this extent, the policymaking *process* for rights and liberties is decidedly and peculiarly nonmajoritarian; one hesitates, however, to call it elitist in any traditional sense, for while the decisions are made by a small number of persons, they have for some time now usually been made not to aid a minority of the wealthy, but more often to aid individuals and groups that have suffered historical injustices. The protection of rights and liberties, however, is not exclusively the province of the judicial branch. Legislatures and executive officials and agencies have played important roles in determining civil rights policy, and organized citizens' groups have been instrumental in bringing about important changes. Thus one finds elements of majoritarian, pluralist, and bureaucratic decision making in the elaboration of rights and liberties. In a deeper sense, moreover, the security of rights and liberties rests ultimately on the majoritarian base of their support in public opinion as a fundamental constitutional element of the American system articulated in the Declaration of Independence.

SOURCES

Abraham, Henry J.: *Freedom and the Courts: Civil Rights and Liberties in the United States,* 3d ed., Oxford University Press, New York, 1977.

Anastaplo, George: *The Constitutionalist: Notes on the First Amendment,* Southern Methodist University Press, Dallas, 1971.

Berns, Walter: *The First Amendment and the Future of American Democracy,* Basic Books, New York, 1976.

Boles, Janet: *The Politics of the Equal Rights Amendment,* Longman, New York, 1979.

Brant, Irving: *The Bill of Rights,* Bobbs-Merrill, Indianapolis, Kansas City, New York, 1965.

Chafee, Zechariah, Jr.: *Free Speech in the United States,* Atheneum, New York, 1969.

Clor, Harry M.: *Obscenity and Public Morality : Censorship in a Liberal Society,* University of Chicago Press, Chicago, 1969.

Flexner, Eleanor: *Century of Struggle: The Women's Rights Movement in the United States,* rev. ed., Harvard University Press, Cambridge, Mass., 1975.

Krislov, Samuel: *The Supreme Court and Political Freedom,* Free Press, New York, 1968.

Levy Leonard: *Legacy of Suppression,* Belknap Press, Cambridge, Mass., 1960.

Lewis, Felice Flanery: *Literature, Obscenity and the Law,* Southern Illinois University Press, Carbondale and Edwardsville, 1976.

Meiklejohn, Alexander: "The First Amendment Is An Absolute," in Philip B. Kurland (ed.), *Free Speech and Association: The Supreme Court and the First Amendment,* University of Chicago Press, Chicago, 1975, 1–22.

Miller, John C.: *Crisis in Freedom: The Alien & Sedition Acts,* Little, Brown, Boston, 1951.

Morgan, Richard E.: "The Establishment Clause and Sectarian Schools: A Final Installment?" in Philip B. Kurland (ed.), *Church and State: The Supreme Court and the First Amendment,* University of Chicago Press, Chicago, 1975.

Murphy, Paul: *The Meaning of Freedom of Speech,* Greenwood Press, Westport, Conn., 1972.

Oaks, Dallin H.: "Studying the Exclusionary Rule in Search and Seizure," *University of Chicago Law Review,* vol. 37, 1970.

Rossum, Ralph A.: *The Politics of the Criminal Justice System: An Organizational Analysis,* Dekker, New York, 1978.

Cases

Abington School District v. Schempp, 374 U.S. 203 (1963).

Argersinger v. Hamlin, 407 U.S. 25 (1972).

Brown v. Board of Education of Topeka, 347 U.S. 483 (1954).

Buckley v. Valeo, 424 U.S. 1 (1976).

Cabell v. Chavez-Salido (1982).

Civil Rights Cases, 109 U.S. 3 (1883).

Coker v. Georgia, 433 U.S. 584 (1977).

Cole v. Arkansas, 338 U.S. 345 (1948).

Committee for Public Education and Religious Liberty v. Regan, 444 U.S. 646 (1980).

Communist Party of Indiana v. Whitcomb, 414 U.S. 441 (1974).

Dennis v. United States, 431 U.S. 494 (1951).

Duncan v. Louisiana, 391 U.S. 145 (1968).

Escobedo v. Illinois, 378 U.S. 478 (1964).

Everson v. Board of Education, 330 U.S. 1 (1947).

Fullilove v. Klutznick, 100 S. Ct. 2758 (1980).

Furman v. Georgia, 408 U.S. 238 (1972).

Gideon v. Wainwright, 372 U.S. 335 (1963).

Gitlow v. New York, 268 U.S. 652 (1925).

Gregg v. Georgia, 428 U.S. 153 (1976).

Griswold v. Connecticut, 381 U.S. 479 (1965).

Hammer v. Dagenhart, 247 U.S. 251 (1910).

Harris v. New York, 401 U.S. 222 (1971).

In re Oliver, 333 U.S. 257 (1948).

Joseph Burstyn, Inc. v. Wilson, 343 U.S. 684 (1952).

Keyishian v. Board of Regents, 385 U.S. 589 (1967).

Klopfer v. North Carolina, 386 U.S. 213 (1967).

Levitt v. Committee for Public Education, 413 U.S. 479 (1973).

Luchner v. New York, 198 U.S. 45 (1905).

Molloy v. Hogan, 378 U.S. 1 (1964).

Mapp v. Ohio, 367 U.S. 643 (1961).

Miller v. California, 413 U.S. 15 (1973).

Milliken v. Bradley, 418 U.S. 717 (1974).

Miranda v. Arizona, 384 U.S. 436 (1966).

Mutual Film Corp v. Industrial Commission of Ohio, 236 U.S. 230 (1915).

Nebbia v. New York, 291 U.S. 502 (1934).

New York Times Co. v. United States, 403 U.S. 713 (1971).

Palko v. Connecticut, 302 U.S. 319 (1937).

Plessy v. Ferguson, 163 U.S. 537 (1896).

Pointer v. Texas, 380 U.S. 400 (1965).

Pyler v. Doe, 102 S. Ct. 2382 (1982).

Regents of the University of California v. Bakke, 438 U.S. 269 (1978).

Reynolds v. United States, 98 U.S. 145 (1878).

Robinson v. California, 370 U.S. 660 (1962).

Roe v. Wade, 410 U.S. 113 (1973).

Rosteker v. Goldberg, 453 U.S. 57 (1981).

Roth v. United States, 354 U.S. 478 (1957).

Schenck v. United States, 249 U.S. 47 (1919).

Sheppard v. Maxwell, 384 U.S. 333 (1966).

Sherbert v. Verner, 374 U.S. 398 (1963).

Slaughterhouse Cases, 16 Wall. 36 (1873).

Stanton v. Stanton, 421 U.S. 7 (1975).

Swann v. Charlotte Mecklenburg, 403 U.S. 1 (1971).

Terminiello v. Chicago, 337 U.S. 1 (1949).

Tinker v. Des Moines School District, 393 U.S. 503 (1969).

United States v. E. C. Knight, 156 U.S. 1 (1895).

United States v. O'Brien, 391 U.S. 367 (1968).

United Steelworkers of America v. Weber, 443 U.S. 193 (1979).

Walz v. Tax Commission, 397 U.S. 664 (1970).

Washington v. Texas, 338 U.S. 14 (1967).

West Coast Hotel v. Parrish, 300 U.S. 379 (1937).

Wickard v. Filburn, 317 U.S. 111 (1942).

Wisconsin v. Yoder, 406 U.S. 205 (1972).

Wolf v. Colorado, 338 U.S. 25 (1949).

Yates v. United States, 354 U.S. 298 (1957).

Zablocki v. Redhail, 434 U.S. 374 (1978).

RECOMMENDED READINGS

Abraham, Henry J.: *Freedom and the Court: Civil Rights and Civil Liberties in the United States*, 3d ed., Oxford University Press, New York, 1977. Analyses of the most important cases on civil rights and liberties.

Berns, Walter: *The First Amendment and the Future of American Democracy*, Basic Books, New York, 1976. An examination of the meaning of the First Amendment's protections of speech, press, and religious freedom which takes issue with recent Supreme Court interpretations.

Flexner, Eleanor: *Century of Struggle: The Women's Rights Movement in the United States*, rev. ed., Harvard University Press, Cambridge, Mass., 1975. An account of the strategy and goals of the feminist movement from its beginnings to the 1970s.

Levy, Leonard W.: *Legacy of Suppression: Freedom of Speech and Press in Early American History*, Harvard University Press, Cambridge, Mass., 1960. Ground-breaking study of the founders' understanding of freedom of speech and press.

Mill, John Stuart: *On Liberty*, Prentice-Hall, Englewood Cliffs, N.J., 1947. The classic defense of freedom of speech and press.

Myrdal, Gunnar: *An American Dilemma: The Negro Problem and Modern Democracy*, Harper and Row, New York, 1962. An account of race relations in the United States which examines the problem in the light of American political principles.

Sindler, Allan P.: *Bakke, DeFunis, and Minority Admissions*, Longmans, New York, 1978. Analysis of the Supreme Court's first case on affirmative action.

Wilson, James Q.: *Thinking about Crime*, Basic Books, 1975. Fresh approach to the problem of crime in the United States.

Chapter 18

Foreign Policy

CHAPTER CONTENTS

Every morning millions of Americans awake to perform their daily ritual at breakfast of spreading melting butter over their toast or warm biscuits. This seems an improbable place to begin a discussion of American foreign policy, but its very improbability serves to underline the complex nature of conducting modern international relations. The story begins in 1981. Under a long-standing policy of agricultural price supports, the federal government purchases all butter not sold above an established minimum price. In the spring of 1981, farmers produced more butter than the public would buy, forcing the government to purchase tons of it and place it in storage. Faced with the prospect of spoilage and the loss of its investment, the government began looking quickly for foreign purchasers.

The most promising buyer was the Soviet Union, a country whose failing agricultural production has regularly forced it to purchase staples like grain and dairy products from capitalist countries. But selling butter to the Soviets posed a problem for the Reagan administration, which had come to power taking a tougher line against the Soviets. After President Reagan had lifted the grain embargo imposed by his predecessor, the United States was supplying the Soviet Union with bread; would sending butter as well not lead the Soviets and some of our allies to doubt the Reagan administration's commitment to halting Soviet expansion? Still, there were the tons of butter and the administration's desire to reduce future price supports, both of which created pressure to make a sale. Not surprisingly, the Agriculture Department, backed by dairy producers, was urging a deal. But the State Department advised otherwise. Reports of a split were leaked to the press, creating the impression of an administration in disarray. Meanwhile, it became known that the world's other major exporters of dairy products would be certain to oppose any sale of butter at prices subsidized by the United States government. Their protests could not be taken lightly.

The decision that the administration finally made—to sell the butter at the subsidized price to New Zealand, allowing that nation to dispose of it on the world market—was by itself hardly a memorable occasion in the history of American foreign policy. But the decision speaks volumes about the difficulties of conducting contemporary international politics. It illustrates (1) how a seemingly isolated economic decision (selling butter) can today also quickly become a diplomatic question of considerable significance; (2) how our relations with the Soviet Union are not themselves isolated, but, rather, are conditioned by our relations with our allies; and finally (3) how so many different actors, ranging from traditional domestic interest groups to various government bureaucracies, now typically play a role in foreign policy decision making.

THE STUDY OF FOREIGN POLICY

Foreign affairs is the realm of politics that deals with a nation's relations to the world outside its own borders—with other governments, with worldwide agencies, and with groups in or publics of other nations. In practice, of course, it is impossible to neatly separate foreign and domestic affairs. The strength of a nation, for example, will inevitably have much to do with its internal cohesion and consensus, matters that on first analysis might seem predominantly "domestic." Nevertheless, the difference between the two realms makes intuitive sense, even when one is referring to something belonging predominantly to one realm. For example, viewed from the perspective of domestic policymaking, internal consensus is something desirable in its own right, for the peace of mind and continuity that it provides the citizenry. Viewed from the perspective of foreign policymaking, consensus is an element of strength that prevents an enemy from playing on internal divisions. Domestic policy thinking, then, considers what is best for ourselves; foreign policy thinking considers how our decisions and actions affect other nations and the world in general.

There are certain classic objectives that the United States, along with most other nations, pursues in foreign affairs. Foremost among these is the protection of our security, for without security and independence we would be unable to pursue any other goals. In practice today, we have linked our security to that of a number of our closer allies, who rely on American military might for their defense and with whom we have negotiated pacts for mutual protection. The pursuit of security today calls for attention to the balance of military power between the United States and its allies on the one hand and the Soviet Union and other states allied with it on the other. But military power is not the only "weapon" in the battle for security. A wide range of other measures, such as intelligence-gathering capabilities, propaganda efforts, and skillful diplomacy, contribute to the ongoing search for security.

A second objective is the promotion of our interests. These include not only conventional economic matters, such as protecting our markets in foreign countries, but also certain long-term global issues, such as the protection of the world's environment and the alleviation of worldwide poverty. Thus American foreign policy today extends to questions of world hunger and overpopulation and to the proper management of the earth's resources in a way that will assure the United States of needed materials and at the same time preserve the world from harmful exploitation.

Finally, as a third objective, a nation may seek to promote certain values within the world, not only for security reasons but because of its belief that these values are universally valid or (as in the case of the Soviet Union's belief in Marxism) destined by immutable laws of history to prevail. Not all nations, of course, have been concerned with promoting values throughout the world. It has long been part of the political culture of the United States, however, to feel some obligation to spread the "light" of republicanism to absolute monarchies and totalitarian regimes. How this should be done—and how much it should be done—have been questions that have divided Americans, sometimes bitterly, throughout our history. And today, with the United States assuming the major burden of protecting other nations' security against the Soviet Union, it is obvious that the objective of spreading republican values must often be weighed and balanced against the demands of security and the claims of interest. Nations that are important to us for security reasons may have less than enviable human rights records, and if the United States were allied with none but republican regimes it would have only a handful of friends.

The pursuit of these objectives—security, inter-

est and republican values—takes place in the context of the world situation over which we have only a certain degree of influence. It is almost meaningless to speak of objectives in the abstract, as the methods required to promote them inevitably change with shifts in the world balance of forces and relations between nations. In the nineteenth century, when our security was protected by our geographic position and the British navy, our diplomacy could be quite different from what it has been since World War II, when intercontinental missiles have eliminated many geographical advantages and when we have had to assume military leadership of the noncommunist world. Inevitably, the situation of power within the world greatly influences how we pursue our objectives; and a nation is often forced to undertake burdensome tasks like supporting large armaments, far-flung alliances, and secret intelligence agencies in order to adjust to the demands of the prevailing international order.

Because foreign affairs are different from domestic affairs, involving different tasks and requiring different capacities, it is not surprising that our policymaking process for foreign affairs is not the same as that in domestic affairs. The Constitution gives the president and the Senate certain powers in the one which they do not possess in the other; and the laws have created special departments and agencies, such as the State Department, the Central Intelligence Agency, and the National Security Council, to deal with the task of conducting our foreign policy. Part of understanding foreign policy, therefore, involves a study of its special institutional arrangements and policymaking machinery.

The three elements of foreign affairs just discussed—objectives, the world situation, and the machinery for decision making—form the core of any analysis of foreign policy. These elements are interdependent: that is, no one of them can be understood without taking into account the effects of the other two. In this chapter, after discussing a few of the classic observations on these three elements, we shall observe their interaction in a historical context, beginning with the thought of the founders and ending with challenges and circumstances facing policymakers in this decade.

DEMOCRACY AND FOREIGN POLICY:
AN INHERENT TENSION?

Is the United States equipped to act in its new role of a major power in world affairs? European intellectuals have traditionally charged American diplomacy with being naive, ignoring balance-of-power and security considerations, and bending to powerful currents of domestic moral opinion, whether for crusades to make the world safe for democracy or for an isolationism that turns its back in revulsion from great-power politics. The charges may or may not be just, but one thing certainly is clear: the American public and its political system have only recently been faced with the importance of foreign affairs as an ongoing concern. For most of our history, we were physically isolated from the main arenas of diplomacy and were concerned chiefly with settling, civilizing, and industrializing a new continent. Foreign affairs were of importance only episodically. This began to change with World War II, when the United States was thrust into a position of world leadership; and events since World War II have shown how deeply we are affected, politically and economically, by events beyond our borders.

It is not just that Americans are new to the responsibilities of foreign affairs; it is also that for any democratic people, and especially a nation that has known the relative harmony of the United States, understanding the nature of foreign affairs is extremely difficult. Consider how different international politics and American domestic politics have been. The United States has in its laws, ordinances, and regulations a comprehensive set of rules designed to govern the relations of its citizens with one another. It has a government endowed with sovereignty and the right to enforce these rules against those who violate them. Its citizens share a broad consensus on the basic values of the society, including that of adherence to the government. In the international setting, however, all these elements either are entirely absent or are present only in a very modest form.

The meeting of these two very different realms of policy, the foreign and the domestic, produces a profound problem in American politics. Foreign policy is meant to protect and promote the security interests and values of the United States; yet, it must operate in a world which is bound by few of the laws and norms of our political system. If the United States is to compete on equal terms with other nations, it must consider using methods which, if they were applied domestically, would be regarded by most Americans as inappropriate and even abhorrent. This tension is clear in the case of our military capabilities. They exist because the United States may become embroiled in disputes which can be settled to its satisfaction only by the threat of armed force. Yet a resort to force to settle disputes stands in sharp contrast to the beliefs that govern American domestic politics, where an entire system has been devised to avoid the resolution of conflict by force, which is regarded as illegitimate. And, to complete the contrast, those instances in which the use of force in domestic politics is regarded as legitimate—when it is used by legal authority to enforce the law—cannot be reproduced on the international level, where there is no binding law and no authority universally recognized as having the right to employ force against lawbreaking states. A basic tenet of our domestic political system is thus inapplicable to our relations with other peoples; we must depart from our principles in order to protect them.

Here we find the difficult task posed by foreign policy for the United States or any other democracy. The nation must cope with a world in which the competition for power is much less softened by institutional safeguards and ethical norms than it is in domestic politics. Republican principles, if applied too strictly to the means of conducting diplomacy, would place the United States at a serious disadvantage. But if the United States feels bound by no restrictions in its struggle with a threatening international environment, its foreign policy might repudiate the deepest principles for which the country stands. How frequently and how seriously can the United States compromise its principles in international politics before they begin to break down in domestic politics as well? While American foreign policy must be conducted to preserve national ideals, policymakers may sometimes be compelled to employ means which do not seem to square with American values.

Alexis de Tocqueville expressed this problem of a tension between democracy and the conduct of foreign policy, extending it to the difficulties democracies encounter in devising and implementing prudent policies. "For my part," he said, "I have no hesitation in saying that in the control of society's foreign affairs democratic governments appear decidedly inferior to others" (Tocqueville, 1969:228). The common sense of the people might successfully cope with questions of domestic policy; it was not equal to the demands of a hostile international environment. Foreign policy and democracy were simply not suited for each other.

Tocqueville cited three main problems in democratic control of foreign policy: democracies are apt to project their own trusting nature on a world that is governed by a Machiavellian struggle for power and advantage; democracies tend to conduct an unstable foreign policy, changing their positions to accommodate the shifting sentiments of public opinion; and democracies find it difficult to maintain important secrets, because the very openness of democratic politics makes total secrecy next to impossible. Democratic systems could, of course, develop institutions to counteract these tendencies; and experience with foreign affairs could, over time, teach a democratic political system of the need for special care in the conduct of foreign affairs. But the weaknesses Tocqueville listed are al-ways just beneath the surface, and learning from experience is a luxury that sometimes cannot be afforded: "Many nations may perish for lack of the time to discover their mistakes" (1969:225). For example, the pacifist tendencies in Great Britain and France before World War II left those nations woefully unprepared to face Nazi Germany in 1939 and almost cost them their freedom.

The opposite side of this equation is that nondemocratic regimes tend to be strong on the very points where democracies are weak. When Tocqueville wrote, he drew a contrast between aristocratic and democratic regimes; much the same contrast, even more to the disadvantage of democratic regimes, could be drawn between democracies and totalitarian regimes. As closed societies, totalitarian systems are able to maintain secrets in a way that no democracy can; more important, totalitarian regimes can ignore public opinion—which scarcely exists—and extract from society for military purposes a quantity of resources that seems almost impossible in a democratic system. Thus in 1979, when the leaders of the Soviet Union decided to invade Afghanistan, they had to worry very little

When the Soviets invaded Afghanistan in 1979, President Carter cut off sales of grain to the Soviet Union—but American farmers' complaints persuaded President Reagan to renew grain sales in 1983 despite continuing Soviet aggression. *(Francois Lochon/Gamma)*

about popular opposition. And the Soviet Union, with an economy only one-quarter as wealthy as that of the United States, manages nonetheless to spend one-third more on defense. (However, this comparison does not reach the question of the efficiency with which these resources are spent in the two countries.)

Of course, democratic nations are not without certain strengths. Once a policy is adopted and agreed on, democracies, having the support of the public, can often produce amazing results. The war efforts by Great Britain and the United States during World War II were striking examples of the power and energy of a democratic people, once mobilized and committed to a task. Moreover, democratic systems need not fall prey completely to their own dangerous tendencies. Sound institutions and prudent diplomacy can minimize the risks, and Tocqueville no doubt offered his grave assessment of democratic capabilities in foreign affairs to awaken democracies to the dangers they faced and to encourage them to take steps to avoid these dangers.

THE FOUNDERS AND FOREIGN POLICY

As we observed in Chapter 2, one of the most important reasons for establishing a national government in the United States in 1787 was the inadequacy of the government of the Articles of Confederation in conducting foreign policy. The founders feared that even with the great oceans as protective shields, a weak and divided confederacy would invite intervention by European powers, perhaps with the support of state governments seeking the assistance of these powers to gain advantages against other states. The Constitution was created in large part to meet the requirements of conducting international affairs in a world of potentially hostile states.

On one point the founders were in substantial agreement: the conduct of foreign policy should be the province of the federal government and not the states. The states were explicitly banned by the Constitution from making treaties or agreements with foreign nations or levying taxes on imports or exports. The federal government was given the power to raise armed forces as well as to assume control over the militias of the states when required to execute the law or protect the nation. In short, the federal government was given full sovereignty in conducting diplomacy, in regulating foreign commerce, and in providing for the national defense.

Having decided to make the conduct of foreign affairs the province of the federal government, the founders then had to face the difficult problem of trying to fit the powers and institutions most likely to preserve republican government at home with those best-suited to the execution of an effective foreign policy.

Ultimately, of course, these two objectives were related, since, as Hamilton wrote, "no government could give us tranquillity and happiness at home, which did not possess sufficient stability and strength to make us respectable abroad" (Farrand, 1937). Still, this generality left open the question of just how much weight should be given to foreign policy concerns when these conflicted with certain republican ideals.

The Power of National Defense

One group of delegates at the Constitutional Convention wanted to place Constitutional limitations on the federal government in the area of defense policy. In the name of protecting republican principles, they argued that a limitation on the size of the army in peacetime should be written into the Constitution. One delegate proposed a ceiling of 3,000 men! This proposal—and others like it—reflected the powerful sentiments of a people attached to a popular government and suspicious of organizations that had been used in the past to subvert those values. But the majority of the delegates at the Convention, while sharing these sentiments, voted against such proposals. What they might *wish* to do in a better world was different from what they *had* to do in the world as it existed—a world in which "nations in general will make war whenever they have a prospect of getting anything by it" (*Federalist* 41). James Madison best expressed the views of those who, however reluctantly, saw the need for compromise of a pure republican sentiment in order to defend the nation in a system of rival states:

> It is vain to oppose constitutional barriers to the impulse of self-preservation. . . . If one nation maintains constantly a disciplined army ready for the service of ambition or revenge, it obliges the most pacific nations who may be within reach of its enterprise to take corresponding precautions (*Federalist* 41).

The founders rejected any extraordinary Constitutional limitations on what the government could do to provide for the national defense, leaving defense decisions instead to the discretion of those exercising power. Yet even this solution, broad as it was, has not resolved the potential for conflict between the claims of the need for defense and the principles of republicanism. At moments of crisis or perceived crisis, the government has sometimes asserted authority to limit the usual rights of citizens. How far government should be able to go under circumstances of crisis has been a problem that has vexed Americans throughout our history. In practice, in times of war—the Civil War, World War I, and World War II—the federal government has assumed powers that would clearly be of dubious constitutionality in peacetime, including the limitation and suppression of certain rights, such as *habeas corpus* and freedom of speech. The courts have taken an ambivalent view of these actions, unwilling on the one hand to deny the government the means of self-defense, but reluctant on the other hand to admit that fundamental Constitutional rights can be abrogated in times of necessity. During alleged crises, as we shall see in the case of the Alien and Sedition acts and the program of domestic surveillance ordered by President Nixon, the resistance to governmental limitations of rights has been very great.

The Institutional Machinery for Foreign Policymaking

Having defined the basic scope of the national security power, the founders then had to determine the institutional mechanisms for conducting foreign policy. Both the executive and the legislative branches had certain advantages and disadvantages. As for the executive, the founders believed that only a unified energetic presidency would be able to play the intricate game of statecraft on equal terms with the courts of Europe. Hamilton praised the "decision, activity, secrecy, and despatch" which allowed this branch of government to take advantage of fleeting opportunities, adhere to bold plans, and maintain confidentiality when necessary (*Federalist* 70). At the same time, however, many in the nation feared that these very qualities made the executive branch too similar in its powers to the monarchs of the old world. Too often, these monarchs, for their own enrichment, power, glory, or amusement, had disregarded the natural inclinations of their peoples toward peace and instead had forced them to become unwilling participants in war, the "sport of kings." The founders viewed such an assertive foreign policy, with its burdensome taxes and suppression of "treasonous" activities, as a danger to liberty.

Legislative control over foreign affairs posed a different set of problems. Congress, as the more popular and open branch, inspired less fear among the populace. Because the legislature had many members and required time to deliberate, the people would have more opportunity to make their wishes known to their representatives before a decision was taken. Moreover, with biennial elections, the public might be able to halt unwise foreign adventures before they went too far by replacing offending members. On the other hand, the legislators' concern with constituency interests meant that they could be narrow-minded, too easily changed, and unwilling to take necessary but unpopular measures. Their openness meant that confidential information necessary to the nation's defense might be made available to foreign foes. And most important, as a plural institution divided between two separate legislative bodies, the Congress lacked the essential capacity to act with vigor and energy.

Fearing tyranny if the executive were given full control of foreign policy and ineffectiveness if this function were conferred upon the legislature, the founders sought to escape their dilemma by taking advantage of the strengths of both institutions.

They divided control over defense and foreign policymaking between the legislature and the executive, assigning to each the functions for which it was best suited. With an eye to the respective strengths and weaknesses of each, they devised an institutional arrangement under which some powers were to be exercised by the president, some by the Congress, some shared by the president and Congress, and some by the president and the Senate.

Congress was given the general power to lay taxes in order to "provide for the common Defence and general Welfare of the United States." To enable Congress to exercise this authority wisely, it was granted specific powers most suited to its openness, representativeness, and deliberation: the power to regulate commerce with foreign nations, the power to raise armed forces (to protect and defend national interests), and the power to declare war. The Senate, having fewer members, who served longer terms, was entrusted with additional powers that were in some ways more executive in nature. The advice and consent of two-thirds of its members were required for the making of treaties with other nations, and a simple majority was required for the appointment of ambassadors, other ministers, and consuls. The continuity and familiarity with the nation's long-term interests provided by staggered elections made senators peculiarly well-suited to participate in the first task, while their acquaintance with the prominent citizens of their home states gave them information useful in the second.

Congress, then, was given broad powers to influence the outlines of American foreign policy and to provide the means by which policy was carried out. Presidents were limited in the extent to which they could commit the nation to a course of action abroad without the concurrence of the legislature; nor did the presidents have control over the instruments of foreign policy—troops, money, and materiel—which would enable them to defy the people's representatives and threaten civil liberties.

Consistent with what they saw as the particular genius of the executive branch, the founders required of the president duties that needed quick action, confidentiality, and less reliance on short-term trends in public opinion. In the event of an armed conflict, the framers provided that Congress should "declare" war and that the president should be commander in chief of American forces. The president was to "receive Ambassadors and other public ministers"; this grant of power has been interpreted as including the authority to decide whether a foreign government should be accorded formal diplomatic recognition, a decision which has sometimes had great importance in American foreign policy. Although the president's power in foreign affairs is tightly circumscribed by Constitutional provisions, it is clear nevertheless that the president possesses much greater authority and discretion in the realm of foreign policy than in domestic policy. It is therefore only natural that as foreign policy has become more important to the nation as a whole in the last half century, the presidency has become a much more powerful institution.

The founders thus regarded foreign affairs as both too important and too dangerous to be given entirely to either the executive or the legislative branch. But this division of powers has created problems. The Constitution has been aptly described as an "invitation to struggle for the privilege of directing American foreign policy" (Corwin, 1957:171). This struggle, moreover, has included not only the areas specifically mentioned in the Constitution, but others as well, since the listing of specific grants of power in the Constitution is not exhaustive. For example, shortly after ratification, President Washington decided to issue a proclamation of neutrality in the war then beginning between France and Great Britain. Was it within the president's prerogatives to commit the nation publicly to such a position, or did his initiative have to be ratified as a kind of treaty by the Senate?

In dealing with this controversy and with the many others that have followed, some have argued that in the realm of foreign affairs any power not specifically granted to other branches of government should be left within the purview of the executive branch. Others have suggested that a careful examination of the founders' intentions will disclose, case by case, whether a particular power should be considered executive or legislative. And still others have maintained that it is a continuous process of political confrontation, compromise, and bargaining between the two branches that should determine their powers in foreign affairs. All three methods have been utilized at one time or another, and there has been no lack of opportunity for trying them. Important issues of foreign policy have produced many conflicts between the branches and between their principles and the demands of expediency.

The division of powers in foreign policymaking between the president and the Congress—and even the courts in some instances—represented a reasonable decision by the founders. Viewed from a domestic context, this division possesses many of the virtues associated with our political system: checks, balances, and possibilities for readjustment from multiple sources. Viewed from the outside, however, and especially by foreign nations, the American system possesses many inconveniences. The president negotiates American foreign policy, but frequently the product of these negotiations can be modified or even turned down. After World War I, President Wilson committed the United States to the League of Nations, only to have this initiative rejected. In the 1970s President Carter negotiated an arms limitation agreement (SALT II) with the Soviets, which was withdrawn early in 1980 when it became apparent that the Senate would refuse its consent. In numerous other areas, from arms sales to tariffs, foreign nations find that they must deal not only with the president but with the United States Congress as well. The nation, in short, lacks the unity in foreign policymaking that most other nations possess, but this is one of the prices Americans pay for their conception of republican liberty.

The Founders' Conception of International Politics

The Constitution settled—or attempted to settle—the questions of the federal government's powers in foreign policy and the nature of the distribution of authority in the foreign policymaking process. But it did not—indeed a constitution cannot—define the nation's conception of international politics. This question had to be left to the realm of politics, and it was not long before two very different conceptions or impulses of international politics were articulated. These conceptions were expressed by two figures who clashed over many other issues in the nation's formative years—Thomas Jefferson

and Alexander Hamilton. They were based on different views about the extent to which the nation's domestic republican philosophy could or should be applied to relations with the outside world and on different assumptions about the possibilities of peace and harmony between the nations of the world (see Box 18-1).

Jefferson stood for the proposition that nations and individuals were—or, rather, could be—governed by the same ethical code. Traditional diplomatic practice, it was true, had fallen short of this rule: nations behaved much worse toward one another than did individuals. But this was the result of unrepresentative governments ruled by aggressive monarchs and selfish nobles who were used to practicing fraud and deceit. Honest, open, and responsible republican government could, by its deeds and by its example, introduce a new standard of conduct into diplomacy higher than that of traditional conceptions of national interest. Jefferson believed it would be possible to overcome the conflict between what republican principles demanded and what expediency in the conduct of a successful foreign policy required. Hamilton, by contrast, was convinced that the rules governing behavior between nations were greatly different from those guiding the conduct of individuals in everyday life. Self-interest was the motive force behind the foreign policy of all nations. The concern for the good of a greater society which restrained the goals and tactics of participants in American politics could only slightly improve the conduct of international relations. Far from seeking to overturn the diplomatic system which rested on these harsh realities (a goal which, in any case, was unrealizable), Hamilton believed that the United States, if it wished to survive and prosper, would have to make itself proficient in all the diplomatic arts, including those for which its domestic experience with republicanism had left it unprepared.

While conflict between the Hamiltonian and Jeffersonian philosophies was largely avoided during the first Washington administration, it quickly broke into the open in the 1790s in the debate over whether to honor the Franco-American Treaty of 1778 by supporting revolutionary France in its war against Great Britain. Was the United States, like an individual, bound by a debt of gratitude to a nation which had aided it in the past? Jeffer-

BOX 18-1

THE ONGOING DEBATE OVER FOREIGN POLICY AND ETHICS

"I know but one code of morality for man whether acting singly or collectively. He who says I will be a rogue when I act in company with a hundred others but an honest man when I act alone, will be believed in the former assertion, but not in the latter. . . . Let us hope that our new government will take some . . . occasion to show that they mean to proscribe no virtue from the canons of their conduct with other nations."
—**Thomas Jefferson, 1789**

"It may be affirmed as a general principle, that the predominant motive of go[od] offices from one nation to another is the interest or advantage of the Nations, which performs them. . . . The rule of morality is [in] this respect not exactly the same between Natio[ns] as between individuals. The duty of making [its] own welfare the guide of its action is much stronger upon the former than upon the latter. . . ."
—**Alexander Hamilton, 1793**

"We have an inevitable role of leadership to play. . . . But our foreign policy ought not be based on military might nor political power nor economic pressures. It ought to be based on the fact that we are right and decent and honest and truthful and predictable and respectful; in other words, that our foreign policy itself accurately represents the character and ideals of the American people. But it doesn't. We have set a different standard of ethics and morality as a nation than we have in our own private lives as individuals who comprise the nation. And that ought to be changed."—**Jimmy Carter, 1975**

"It is part of American folklore that, while other nations have interests, we have responsibilities; while other nations are concerned with equilibrium, we are concerned with the legal requirements of peace. We have a tendency to offer our altruism as a guarantee of our reliability. . . . Such an attitude makes it difficult to develop a conception of our role in the world. It inhibits other nations from gearing their policy to ours in a confident way—a 'disinterested' policy is likely to be considered 'unreliable'. . . . Principle, however lofty, must at some point be related to practice. . . . Interest is not necessarily amoral; moral consequences can spring from interested acts."—**Henry Kissinger, 1968**

Source: Boyd, 1958:XV, 367; Syrett, 1969:XV, 85–86; Carter, 1977b:71–72; Kissinger, 1969:91–93.

son's Democratic-Republicans generally said yes. Moreover, as a general matter of policy, they seemed to believe that by following the noble sentiments of republicanism in the conduct of world affairs, they could remake the world of international politics in the image of American principles. Hamilton's Federalists generally said no to support for France, believing it was not in the interest of the United States to ally itself with Britain's enemy when Britain ruled the seas. As a general matter of policy, the Federalists tended to believe that the conduct of international politics, while it might be marginally influenced by the new methods of republican diplomacy, could not be fundamentally changed. As a result, the country would have to accommodate itself to the harsh realities of the outside world.

Either one of these general attitudes toward international affairs, if pursued dogmatically, could lead to failure or disaster, as events during the dan-

gerous era of the Napoleonic wars (1793–1815) demonstrated. On the one hand, Federalist beliefs that the needs of foreign policy had to override domestic scruples lay behind the Alien and Sedition acts of 1798. In their attempt to halt domestic criticism of the Adams administration's foreign policy, these acts threatened fundamental liberties and deepened divisions at a time of national danger. On the other hand, after 1800, Republican attempts to conduct foreign affairs on the basis of Jeffersonian republican principles led first to a serious weakening of American military preparedness and then to Jefferson's famous "experiment" in international affairs—an embargo of trade with Britain and France in 1807. This policy, designed as a substitute for military action that would compel others to recognize American interests, failed to sway either of these warring nations. It severely disrupted the American economy and eventually helped to bring on what it had been designed to avoid—a war in 1812 with one of the contending powers, Great Britain, for which the United States was unprepared.

Never were the alternatives more starkly posed. If the United States assumed that the methods used in its domestic politics could be easily transferred to its foreign relations, it could be taken advantage of and blunder into situations where war or surrender was the only escape. But if the United States concluded that the "primacy of foreign policy" and the seriousness of outside threats demanded compromises of its principles, it could lose those liberties in areas of domestic life where foreign policy impinged upon them. It was a sobering choice.

A BRIEF HISTORY OF AMERICAN FOREIGN POLICY

The Nineteenth Century

Fortunately for the nation, it was spared the necessity of making a choice immediately in its approach to foreign affairs. The end of the Napoleonic wars brought a much more favorable set of circumstances. These included a naval supremacy held by Great Britain, whose interests often coincided with those of the United States; a sufficiency of American unity and power to deter direct threats to our security (except during the Civil War, when the division of the United States almost engendered the alliance of the Confederacy with European powers); and a preoccupation of the great powers of Europe with imperial expansion in Africa and Asia and with the European balance of power.

This situation left the United States relatively free to pursue its own moral and political consensus without fearing interference by outside forces. Guided by what it called its God-given "manifest destiny" of occupying North America from the Atlantic to the Pacific, the United States expanded across a vast continent which, because it was largely uninhabited, could be subdued without the harsher military and diplomatic methods that Americans criticized in other nations. (In fact, however, although Americans seldom admitted it to themselves, continental expansion was made possible by a war against Mexico and by constant fraud and force exercised against the Indian nations.) Sheltered by the British Navy, the United States could issue the Monroe Doctrine in 1823, opposing further European colonization in the Americas, assert the rights of neutrals in wartime, and proclaim its principles concerning freedom of the seas with relative safety. Because the United States was not called on to back up its pronouncements with military force, it seemed plausible that American efforts to bring world politics under the rule of law were succeeding without resort to those practices of old world diplomacy, such as spheres of influence or the balance of power, which were thought to be so dangerous.

This belief came all the easier because on those few occasions when the country had the clear opportunity to advance American ideas at the cost of sacrificing its isolationist, domestically oriented political practices, it declined to do so. In 1821, when presented with demands that the nation do something to aid Latin Americans struggling to overthrow Spanish colonialism, Secretary of State John Quincy Adams replied:

> Wherever the standard of freedom and independence has been or shall be unfurled, there will be America's heart, her benedictions, and her prayers. But she goes not abroad in search of monsters to destroy. She is the well-wisher to the freedom and independence of all. She is the champion and vindicator only of her own (LaFeber, 1965:45).

And when discontent broke out in uprisings across Europe in 1848, the American government, despite its sympathy for some of the revolutionaries, refused to undertake any action.

Because it saw the liberalizing, democratizing trend of history moving in its direction in any event, the United States saw no reason to interfere with the building of the good society for its citizens at home in order to hurry the process abroad. The example of American republicanism's success and the unsupported warnings of American representatives abroad were sufficient to lead those in other countries to see things as Americans saw them. Nothing more was expected of a nation in the fortunate position which the United States occupied. As James Bryce observed in 1889, "America lives in a world of her own. . . . Safe from attack, safe even from menace, she hears from afar the warring cries of European races and faiths." Like a fortunate vessel in good weather, Bryce remarked, the United States "sails upon a summer sea" (Bryce, 1889).

For most of the nineteenth century, then, the United States lived in a unique and protected set of circumstances. This situation allowed Americans to speak in noble terms reminiscent of Jefferson, all the while living sheltered from the harsh realities of international politics. At the same time, Americans could believe that by their isolation they were still promoting republican values throughout the world. And to some extent they were. But it was the happy set of circumstances more than the validity of their assumptions that allowed them to enjoy their successes. What the United States would have to do in less favorable circumstances was a question seldom posed, let alone answered. For nearly a century, the American people did not have to ponder the possible conflict between an effective diplomacy and the preservation of their own liberties, because they did not find it necessary to conduct much of a diplomacy at all.

The Early Twentieth Century

The early twentieth century brought the United States into greater contact with the world, but the encounters were generally short-lived. An American flirtation with imperialism went on from about 1895 to 1905. It gained the country a handful of colonies—including the Philippines and Puerto Rico—as the result of a short and relatively painless war against Spain, but ended before the neo-Hamiltonian ideas of leaders such as Theodore Roosevelt and Admiral Alfred Thayer Mahan could become accepted American beliefs.

Woodrow Wilson eventually proved as willing as Roosevelt to employ the power of the United States abroad, though at the service of different ends. Whereas Roosevelt had sought to join the traditional game of diplomacy in order to secure and protect hard, often materialistic, national interests, Wilson went to war in order to promote American ideals and to punish those who flagrantly violated them, in either their domestic political institutions or their international conduct. Wilson adopted a world view reminiscent of Jefferson's, although for Wilson the use of force in one great crusade was necessary to change the face of the world and make possible a new kind of diplomacy. In fighting a war to "make the world safe for democracy," Wilson planned a peace afterwards in which the United States would play an ongoing role in the context of a new world organization, the League of Nations. Jeffersonian ends were realizable, in Wilson's view, but only if the United States was prepared to commit its noble impulses to a continuous involvement on the world scene.

Woodrow Wilson's effort to involve the United States in a new world order ended in failure. The Senate rejected Wilson's peace treaty because of opposition to the proposed form of the League of Nations. In part, this rejection was the result of an unwillingness on Wilson's part to compromise with the Senate. For their part, leading senators like Henry Cabot Lodge were dubious of Wilson's great dreams and wary of the possibility that the United States would have to sacrifice part of its sovereignty to a new international body. It could be said that the Senate, in choosing a kind of isolationism, adopted the Jeffersonian idea of refusing to accept the primacy of international affairs, even for supposedly Hamiltonian ends.

The Senate's rejection of the League was in effect ratified in the election of 1920, when Warren G. Harding was elected after opposing the League during the campaign. The actions of the United States were guided for the next twenty years by a policy of isolationism. The United States wished to have economic but not long-term political ties to other countries. To the extent that these other countries imitated American domestic arrangements, they would be favorably regarded; if they chose not to do so, the United States might criticize them, but would not attempt to persuade or force them to change their ways. In essence, American conduct was Jeffersonian in its determination not to let the demands of foreign policy interfere with its domestic concerns, but it lacked the buoyant confidence in pressing its example on the rest of the world that some of the followers of Jefferson had displayed.

The Twentieth Century Since World War II

All this changed in the cataclysm of the Second World War, a global upheaval that required a complete rethinking of American diplomacy. The

United States, against its will and normal inclinations, was thrust onto the center stage of international affairs. From now on, the United States had to deal not with weak Indian tribes or a collapsing Spanish empire, but with powerful nations resolute in defending their rights and their interests. The United States could no longer avoid the "corrupt" diplomacy of the old world, and in fact was forced to deal with new challenges more difficult and "corrupt" than anything known in the nineteenth century (Aron, 1974). The postwar years have tested American diplomacy with dramatic new challenges and drawn attention to geographical areas and subject matters never before considered proper objects of American foreign policy (see Box 18-2).

Containment and the Cold War (1948–1968)
Faced with these new problems, the United States nevertheless managed after World War II to reach a consensus on the basic outlines of the conduct of foreign policy. This period of consensus can be dated from the presidential election of 1948, in which the two major candidates (Harry S. Truman for the Democrats and Thomas E. Dewey for the Republicans) adopted very similar policies of "toughness" toward the Soviet Union. Its end can be dated to President Lyndon Johnson's announcement in 1968 that he was withdrawing as a candidate for renomination and reelection, at a time when his conduct of the country's foreign policy, especially in the war in Vietnam, was under severe attack. During the intervening years, American public opinion was generally united in support of containment as the proper course to follow in the cold war.

The term "cold war" denotes a relationship of hostility between the United States and the Soviet Union deep enough to keep the world in a state of tension and even fear, but never so immediately threatening and irreconcilable that the two antagonists engaged in direct armed conflict. From the American perspective, the cold war emerged out of a double threat posed at the end of World War II: the dictatorial ideology of communism and the increased power of the Soviet state. Communist ideology attacked Americans' most deeply held political, social, economic, and religious beliefs; Soviet power threatened the freedom of other nations and ultimately even that of the United States itself. American policy was therefore directed at "con-

taining" both—that is, at ensuring that neither expanded to control nations other than those in which it had been imposed in the chaos following the war's end. Essentially defensive in its strategy, containment nonetheless held out the hope that once the Soviet Union saw that prospects for expansion were futile, it might lose confidence in its ideology, resulting in a modification of its system (Kennan, 1951).

The fact that containment could be justified as a defense of both American principles and American interests, and that it seemed defensive rather than aggressive in character, helps to explain why it received broad popular support and did not become the subject of intense party competition. Bipartisanship united Democrats and Republicans in opposition to Soviet expansionism. The effects of bipartisanship have been disputed: some say that this unity gave the nation strength, confidence, and wisdom; others charge that it demanded conformity of thought and stifled debate that might have prevented foreign policy errors (Acheson, 1969; Halberstam, 1969). In either case, bipartisanship was much in evidence during these twenty years of containment, in striking contrast to the periods before and since.

This consensus was most notably reflected in the emergence and durability of the "foreign policy establishment." This was a small group of people who acted as opinion leaders, helping to sustain the containment consensus, and who staffed many of the government's foreign and defense posts in administrations of both parties, thus maintaining continuity of policy across administrations. The establishment was centered on the eastern seaboard, and its critics on both the right and the left long identified it as an economic elite composed of "Wall Street bankers." Yet it was always more diverse than that, containing not only financiers, but also representatives of the great Washington and New York law firms, universities and policy research centers, private foundations, journalism, industry and commerce, and labor unions. More important than their economic status were their interest in and knowledge of foreign affairs, a subject which was of only secondary concern to most Americans. The establishment was highly successful in promoting some initiatives, such as the Marshall Plan, and in opposing others, such as proposals to cut American troop strength in Europe. It is important

BOX 18-2

MAJOR EVENTS IN AMERICAN DIPLOMACY IN THE POSTWAR ERA

1945 Establishment of the *United Nations.* Founding of the *International Monetary Fund* and the *International Bank for Reconstruction and Development,* two financial institutions designed to set the rules for an open world financial and commercial economy, based on the United States dollar as its principal reserve currency.

1947 Announcement of the *Truman Doctrine,* pledging American help to free peoples threatened by subversion or external aggression.

1948 Occurrence of the first and most serious crisis over West Berlin, in which Soviet and East German forces blockaded that city and in which United States, Great Britain, and France broke the blockade with the *Berlin airlift.*

1948–1951 Operation of the *Marshall Plan,* which provided American assistance to restart the economies of western Europe.

1949 Negotiation of the *North Atlantic Treaty Organization,* a defensive alliance between sixteen nations of North America and western Europe.

1949 Establishment of a communist government in China, as a result of that country's civil war.

1949 Explosion by the Soviet Union of its first atomic weapon.

1950–1953 Fighting of the *Korean war,* between South Korea, supported by the United Nations (principally the United States and its allies), and North Korea, supported by China and the Soviet Union, ending in an armistice.

1953 *Enunciation of the doctrine of ''massive retaliation,''* under which the United States threatened to respond to aggression elsewhere in the world supported by the Soviet Union by attacking the Soviet Union itself; accompanied by the *''new look''* in defense spending, which increased the portion of the defense budget going to nuclear arms and decreased that for conventional forces.

1961 Redirection of American defense policy toward *''flexible response,''* which increased spending for conventional arms to enable the United States to respond to local wars locally in the field.

1962 The *Cuban missile crisis,* in which the United States and the Soviet Union went to the brink of nuclear war over the Russians' secret introduction of nuclear missiles into Cuba and the Americans' (ultimately successful) demand that they be withdrawn.

1964 Explosion by China of its first atomic weapon.

1964–1973 Large-scale United States involvement in the *Vietnamese war,* to aid South Vietnam in its struggle against North Vietnam, supported by the two great communist powers.

1970 Development of the *Nixon Doctrine,* under which the United States increased its security assistance to allies, but announced that it would no longer send troops itself.

1971 Collapse of the international monetary system established in 1945, as the United States, burdened by its own economic difficulties, announced that it would no longer redeem dollars in gold, thus shaking the dollar's position as the world's reserve currency.

1972 Ratification of the *SALT I* agreement, limiting the strategic arsenals of the United States and the Soviet Union.

1972 Visit by President Nixon to China and reestablishment of more normal relations with that country.

1973–1974 Embargo of oil shipments to the United States by Arab members of the Organization of Petroleum Exporting Countries, demonstrating American dependence on foreign supplies.

1975 Conquest of South Vietnam by North Vietnam, negating the years of American effort in the war.

1979 Invasion of *Afghanistan* by Russian forces, chilling even further American-Soviet relations, which were already deteriorating.

1979–1981 Holding of American hostages in the United States embassy in Tehran by the new revolutionary government of Iran.

1980 Withdrawal by President Carter of the *SALT II* arms agreement from Senate consideration, on the grounds that the state of American-Soviet relations made ratification impossible.

1981 Crackdown in *Poland* by the government on democratic forces there, adding anew to east-west tensions.

1982–1983 Extensive American involvement in Central America through open military assistance to the government of El Salvador and covert CIA support for rebels opposing the Nicaraguan regime.

to note, however, that, while it helped to lead public opinion, the establishment was not independent of the popular mood. When the country as a whole began to divide once more over questions of foreign policy in the 1960s, consensus ended among members of the establishment as well, and no one view can be said to characterize them today.

The containment era is notable also because it was during this time that American military strength reached its highest point relative to that of the Soviet Union (Spanier, 1977). Military might, however, was only one of the tools employed by the United States in this period. Alliance systems like the North Atlantic Treaty Organization (NATO), the Southeast Asia Treaty Organization (SEATO), and the Japanese-American Mutual Security Treaty were created in order to deter war. International organizations such as the International Monetary Fund (IMF), the International Bank for Reconstruction and Development (IBRD), and the General Agreement on Tariffs and Trade (GATT) were set up so that world economic relations could be carried on in a more productive, cooperative manner. Openly, through agencies like the Voice of America, and covertly, through ones like Radio Free Europe, the United States undertook to direct propaganda messages at friend and foe.

Yet, despite all these instruments of diplomacy, there were instances when the United States went to the brink of, or entered, warfare. In 1950, when the Soviet-sponsored regime in North Korea attacked its American-supported counterpart in South Korea, the United States organized an international response through the United Nations and threw its own forces into the battle. We suffered heavy casualties, especially when China entered the war to save North Korea, and fought through three more painful years until an armistice could be arranged that restored the situation to what it had been before the war. In Lebanon in 1958 and again in the Dominican Republic in 1965, Washington dispatched troops to small countries thought to be in immediate danger of takeover by communist or communist-backed forces. In 1962, the world came as close as it ever has come to nuclear destruction in the Cuban missile crisis, in which, for several days, the prospect of a nuclear exchange between the superpowers appeared very

real, until the Soviet Union acceded to the United States's demand to remove the intermediate-range missiles it had installed in Cuba.

The longest and most difficult of these experiences with the use of armed force came in Vietnam. A gradually increasing series of commitments under presidents Truman, Eisenhower, and Kennedy to South Vietnam culminated in full-fledged involvement in that country's war with North Vietnam under presidents Johnson and Nixon. American participation ended with the negotiated withdrawal of American forces in early 1973, but the war continued, and in the spring of 1975 the Saigon government fell to the North Vietnamese. The United States had lost more than 50,000 lives and spent billions of dollars in what eventually was a losing venture. It was a defeat of major proportions.

The Postcontainment Years   Vietnam destroyed the foundation of support for American foreign policy as it had been conducted in the cold war years. Consensus on the rightness of an active role for the United States in opposing Soviet moves was replaced by a determination not to act as the "world's policeman" and by uncertainty over whether the cold war had actually been the responsibility of Moscow or Washington. Bipartisanship in foreign policy matters dissolved into mutual recriminations over the conduct of the war. American military superiority over the Soviet Union disappeared, first as defense resources were diverted into the war, and then as disillusionment over its costs and despair over eventual defeat produced a reaction against all military spending, even as Moscow continued a steady increase of its own forces. No longer could the world as it had been defined by containment be taken for granted; a search for alternative policies began.

The incoming Nixon administration in 1969 put forth the first attempted substitute for cold war containment: détente. Its objective was to move "from an era of confrontation to an era of negotiation" through an emphasis on forces for cooperation between the superpowers (Nixon, 1969:9). Arms control and scientific collaboration on such matters as health care and space exploration were to be particularly important. The United States would maintain its alliances, but it would normally

President Nixon's decision to establish relations with China in 1971 ended two decades of hostile confrontation, yet many Americans decried the move as amoral power politics that betrayed our Asian allies.   *(Ollie Atkins/Contact)*

aid its friends through monetary and material assistance, and only in the most extreme cases with intervention by its own forces; and it would not assume that every outbreak of conflict around the world was fomented by Moscow and thus required an American response. This policy was based on (1) a calculation of the new equilibrium of power between the United States and the Soviet Union in which the United States was no longer superior and (2) the belief that Russian foreign policy was no longer strictly dictated by the demands of Marxist-Leninist ideology. While superpower relations would still be competitive, the Soviet Union could be dealt with pragmatically on the basis of its interests. The assumption of the "deideologization" of Soviet policy meant that American policy could be less concerned with questions of ideology as well: thus the establishment of links to China, a dictatorship which rejected American democratic values but could serve as a useful counterweight to the greater power of the Soviet Union; thus also the new American willingness to be more aggres-

sive in pursuing American interests in economic differences with west European and Japanese allies, differences that had previously been downplayed in order to preserve harmony among the democratic nations of the west.

Nixon and his chief adviser Henry Kissinger intended our own deemphasis on ideology as a way of preventing moralistic crusades in foreign policy that might drag the country into conflicts where its true interests were not at stake. As such, détente as practiced from 1969 to 1977 received widespread applause for being sober, judicious, and realistic. But, increasingly as the years passed, many criticized the policy as mistaken or amoral. By refusing to be outspoken in condemning the tyranny of the Soviet regime, by treating the democratic nations of western Europe and Japan simply as competing players in the balance-of-power game with little public recognition of the values they shared with the United States, by ignoring widespread human rights abuses in certain third world states that were deemed strategically vital, the Nixon and Ford administrations, some charged, were sapping the country's greatest strength—its moral position. Conservatives tended to argue that, in abandoning anticommunism, the deemphasis on ideology robbed American policy of its most potent weapon against the Soviet Union by depriving it of a clear rallying cry. Liberals more often said that, in abstaining from criticism of human rights practices by our (mostly rightist) allies, the United States was alienating the progressive majority in the less-developed world. Both felt that treating foreign policy simply as a matter of interests was not enough.

It was when these criticisms reached their height in 1977 that the new Carter administration arrived in Washington determined to disassociate itself from the policy of its predecessors. Détente would be continued; and the search for cooperation, particularly in the Strategic Arms Limitation Treaty (SALT) talks, would be intensified. But a moral quality would be added. In making itself the champion of human rights, the United States would attain three objectives. It would regain the high ground of world public opinion and place the Soviet Union on the defensive. It would revitalize the links binding the United States to the world's other major democratic nations, who were also its most important security and economic partners. And it would place itself on the right side of what was seen as the inevitable move of the third world toward liberty and equality. Presented with these favorable trends, the country would regain its confidence in itself without returning to an outdated cold war mentality characterized by President Carter as "that inordinate fear of communism" (Carter, 1976:I, 956).

Yet this second conception of détente, too, came under criticism. Opponents of the administration—including the conservatives as well as many of the original architects of détente, such as Nixon and Kissinger—charged that Carter's emphasis on morality was both naive and self-righteous. According to their indictment, the administration was unable or unwilling to see that there were occasions when a morally correct stance could not substitute for the exercise of American power; it failed to recognize that some elements of its policy—such as the simultaneous castigation of the Soviet government for human rights violations and the ardent

pursuit of an arms control agreement with that government—could conflict; and it appeared incapable of dispelling the impression that the United States was intent merely on demonstrating its own rectitude by preaching to the rest of the world. These signs of dissatisfaction combined with an undercurrent of concern—present since the early 1970s and steadily growing in intensity—over continued Soviet military advances that threatened to outstrip those of the west, and with disillusionment brought on by Moscow's attempts to take advantage of turmoil in places such as Angola, Mozambique, Ethiopia, and Afghanistan. Foreign policy thereby became a potent issue in the 1980 campaign and an important factor in the defeat of President Carter.

Some observers saw in this ongoing debate a repetition of the early struggle between Hamiltonians and Jeffersonians over the direction of American foreign policy. The Nixon-Ford-Kissinger approach, like that of the Federalists of the 1790s, was to take national interests as the guide for American diplomacy and to look with suspicion on calls for morality in international politics. Members of the Carter administration, like the Democratic-Republicans of the 1800s, felt that the United States as a collectivity was just as much bound by standards of personal morality as any private person. In the 1980 election, the voters questioned both courses by selecting the Reagan administration, which entered office pledged to "rearm America"; to negotiate on arms control, but only from a position of strength; to stand by friendly nations in the less-developed world, even when they did not meet American democratic standards; and to be more vigorous in pressing the ideological battle against the many tyrannical aspects of the Soviet Union. But this new course, like the two versions of détente, had difficulties in balancing the country's diplomatic capabilities and its national interests with its republican tradition and the public self-confidence that depended on adherence to that tradition. President Reagan successfully pushed for an increased defense budget (though he obtained much less than he requested) and showed himself to be less hesitant than President Carter about supporting nondemocratic but militarily important partners. On the other hand, he was more reluctant to allow the demands of foreign policy to interfere with the commercial and personal liberties of Americans, as he demonstrated when he ended the grain embargo against the Soviet Union instituted by President Carter and when he only unwillingly continued draft registration (Rosenfeld, 1982).

DEFINING CHARACTERISTICS OF THE MODERN ERA

Four fundamental conditions have defined the environment in which the United States has found itself in the post-World War II world: (1) an increase in the concern for military security and the difficulty of obtaining it; (2) a breakdown in the minimal consensus on international norms that had existed over most of the world during much of American history; (3) a perception of mutual and common threats and problems shared by the world's major adversarial powers; and (4) an increasing economic and political interdependence between the United States and foreign nations that makes it ever more difficult to separate foreign and domestic issues neatly. Individually, each of these problems would have required a considerable restructuring of the previous approach of the United States to the outside world; together, they have almost completely transformed it.

Military Security

During the past generation, security concerns have required more attention and demanded more resources than ever before. World War II marked the final collapse of a European balance of power that had protected American security since the days of Napoleon. The destruction or diminution of the traditional European great powers—France, Germany, and Italy—meant that no effective force remained to oppose the expansion of the one remaining continental power, the Soviet Union. The decline of Great Britain meant that no foreign navy remained to police the oceans. If any nation was to counterbalance the Soviet Union effectively in the immediate postwar period, it could only be the United States. The possession by both superpowers of nuclear weapons and the lack of any equal competitors made them both global powers, with a greater reach and more widespread interests than those held by dominant nations in previous eras.

Yet this situation in which the United States is one of the world's two great "superpowers" has not brought us a greater sense of security. The very nature of the worldwide system of conflict and of modern weaponry makes security, in the sense in which that term was used before World War II, all but impossible. The United States has met part of its security needs by establishing far-flung alliances, with all their attendant difficulties in accommodating the various interests of their members and in protecting these nations against possible aggression. The threat of immediate nuclear destruction has deprived the United States of the margin of security that in the past gave it time to arm and prepare in moments of danger. Mobilization, far from being a wartime expedient, has become continuous, and thus vastly more expensive. The great size of the nation's postwar military outlays, both in absolute dollars and as a percentage of the federal budget and the gross national product, indicates the increased efforts for security made necessary by events of the past forty years (U.S. Department of Defense, 1980).

Ideological Confrontation

Conflicts born of clashing interests have been sharpened by ideological differences between the United States and the Soviet Union. The gulf in ideology which separates the United States from its primary rival has made the international environment seem all the more threatening to American principles of republicanism because any setback for Washington and its allies can be interpreted as a defeat not just for its power interest but for its most basic values. The successes of avowedly communist nations have called into question the traditional American belief—fundamental to the country's nineteenth-century optimism and exemplified in Woodrow Wilson—that liberal democracy was the eventual destiny of all people. This sense that its basic values are under attack heightens any nation's sense of insecurity.

Moreover, disagreement between the world's two major powers on first principles has weakened the world's institutional means for settling disputes. In the nineteenth century following the Congress of Vienna, a time in which there was a minimal international consensus on what constituted governmental legitimacy and acceptable diplomatic behavior, there was tremendous growth in international law and other norms. By contrast, the lack of any such consensus since the Second World War has weakened the United Nations. Even as it has complicated disputes over interests, then, ideological diversity has hindered their possible solution.

Disagreements on rules of proper diplomatic behavior have come not only from the east-west split, however. Another significant factor is to be found in the rise of the third world to unprecedented importance in world affairs. The dissolution of the great European colonial empires and their replacement by a multitude of newly independent states have transformed the international arena. Norms of conduct today must be made acceptable not to the approximately 50 sovereign nations of the world of 1945 but to nearly 160 states, of widely varying sizes and interests. Moreover, these newer nations are founded in cultures vastly different from the western political heritage which shaped the outlines of traditional international law; and many of them are suspicious of this tradition, believing it to be a front for continued western attempts at control over their destinies. "World opinion" is not a monolith; it is sometimes difficult to say that it exists at all.

Forces for Cooperation

Ironically, despite these grave differences, the two superpowers also have much in common. Both see their status as founding members of the nuclear "club" threatened by continuing nuclear proliferation. (Since the 1950s, four other nations—Great Britain, France, China, and India—have definitely joined the nuclear club; and several others, including Pakistan, Israel, and South Africa, either have developed or are believed to be on the verge of developing an independent nuclear capacity.) And each superpower can feel a twinge of sympathy for the other as it struggles to meet the demands of dissatisfied allies. But the greatest danger they face is the threat of nuclear war between themselves. The extent of destruction that would be suffered by both victor and vanquished in a nuclear exchange

gives the two the most potent common interest in avoiding such a catastrophe. The existence of nuclear weapons has revolutionized international relations by placing new limits on how far major powers can go in expressing their hostility; it helps explain why, in a period of tremendous tension and suspicion, there has been no hot war between Washington and Moscow. Repelled by their clashing interests and ideological enmity, the superpowers are simultaneously attracted by their knowledge of the perils both face if their struggle should get out of hand.

Yet the "balance of terror" that has existed since World War II may be only temporary. New and more sophisticated weapons might make missile technology obsolete. Should the Soviets gain a decisive advantage in any new and revolutionary weapon system, the threat once again to our security would be genuine. The brutal reality of this possibility means that the current phase of security based on the potential of mutual destruction cannot be taken for granted. For all its *seeming* absurdity, both superpowers find themselves compelled to continue the race for new weapons, pushing the search into new and more sophisticated systems that increasingly resemble those of science fiction films. Only by a political decision in which both sides agreed to renounce such research, permit outside verification of their actions, and take other steps to build confidence in the process of arms control could this race be halted. Thus far, this goal has escaped American policymakers, and the dangers attendant upon an arms race continue to threaten the world.

The Decline of the Foreign-Domestic Distinction

A final characteristic of the postwar situation is the increasing difficulty of separating foreign and domestic issues. No longer is the line dividing the two areas as clear as it may once have seemed. During the nineteenth century, diplomacy was primarily concerned with questions of "high politics"—the drawing of national boundaries, the extension of sovereignty over other countries or areas, issues of war and peace. The economic and social matters that make up "low politics" were in the United States uncontrolled by government. Domestically, they were left to the operation of a free market;

As this flood of Japanese cars on a New Jersey dock attests, many industries now depend on worldwide markets, making economic policy an increasingly important influence on many American foreign policy decisions. *(Jean-Pierre Laffont/Sygma)*

internationally, they were governed by a world financial and commercial system that also apparently worked free of the control of any government. Only in one economic policy area—tariffs—was the United States government continually involved. Here, the American solution was to ignore the foreign implications of the tariff and treat it solely as a matter of domestic welfare. As late as 1932, Secretary of the Treasury Ogden Mills could declare, "The rates in our tariff laws are a purely domestic question to be determined by the Congress of the United States without consultation with foreign governments" (Beard, 1934:331).

All this was altered by the New Deal and World War II. The United States government committed itself to economic cooperation with its friends and allies abroad and assumed responsibility for economic stability at home. These two tasks sometimes conflict with each other, as when adherence to the rules of an open international economic system increases domestic unemployment or inflation. Their combination has placed the government in the position of regulating many more fields of activity than it did in the past and, as part of its reg-

ulatory responsibility, weighing competing foreign and domestic demands.

Moreover, economic concerns have assumed greater importance in world politics over the last decade. The economies of the world's nations have become increasingly dependent on each other, and the partial thawing of the cold war under the influence of détente made many states less willing to sacrifice economic interests in order to protect security concerns. Economic difficulties are also to some extent the problems of success; American partners in western Europe and Japan—shattered recipients of American aid after World War II—have become keen economic competitors. It is the task of the United States to manage a relationship with its allies that is now more equal, while at the same time protecting the welfare of its own economy against their competition. This has greatly increased the importance to American foreign policy of issues such as foreign assistance and international trade.

Along with the increasing importance of economic questions on the policymaking agenda, other new issues have been added—those of human rights, the environment, energy, population, and food. None of these problems can be handled by diplomacy alone; all touch important domestic interests. Yet neither can they be managed completely by any individual state through its domestic political process. They require both careful negotiations with other countries in bilateral and multilateral settings and continuous domestic political bargaining. A satisfactory American response to the world's shortage of food, for example, must consider the needs of countries with a food deficit, such as India, as well as the interests of other major food-exporting nations, the Food and Agriculture Organization of the United Nations, and American farmers and exporters. Policies developed in response to the increasing American dependence on petroleum and other raw materials imported from abroad involve similarly complex considerations. With problems such as these on the new agenda of world politics, domestic and foreign concerns become ever more tightly linked with each other.

THE FOREIGN POLICYMAKING PROCESS IN THE MODERN WORLD

The Constitution, as we have seen, divided the power to conduct foreign relations in a complex way between the president and the Congress. Even without the difficulties associated with the separation of powers, the creation of such new functions as a large intelligence-gathering effort would have posed major problems for any republican government; with the complexities of a separation of powers, these problems have been all the more difficult to resolve. The new role of the United States in world affairs has placed great strains on our political system, and the government today is still experiencing the frustrations of attempting to adapt its foreign policymaking machinery to a new situation.

In this section we shall analyze the growth of the nation's foreign policymaking machinery within the executive branch, the relations between the president and the Congress, and the general nature of policymaking in the foreign policy area. The postwar period, as we shall see, has been characterized by three developments: (1) the increasing difficulty experienced by the executive branch in maintaining some of the very qualities it was de-

signed to promote, such as unity and secrecy; (2) a shifting power relation between the Congress and the president, from a period in which Congress accorded great discretion to the president to one in which it has become extensively involved in the foreign policymaking process; and (3) an increased involvement of interest groups and public opinion in the making of foreign policy decisions, as foreign policy generally has become much more important to American citizens.

The Growth of the Foreign Policymaking Machinery in the Executive Branch

Beginning during World War II and continuing throughout the cold war to the present, the executive branch has been continuously enlarged by additions of new agencies, a vastly expanded work force, and tremendously increased budgets. Much of this growth has occurred in the nation's armed forces and, as such, has been an expansion of a traditional governmental function. But some of it has come through the assumption of tasks previously performed only fitfully or not at all, such as the gathering and analysis of intelligence and the leadership of an extensive system of alliances.

All agencies concerned with foreign policy have shared in the growth. Gone are the days when Secretary of State Jefferson presided over a department staffed by 8 persons in Washington; in the 1980s, the State Department has a staff of nearly 25,000 scattered around the world. Today, in addition to a large staff in Washington, the State Department manages diplomatic missions in almost all the countries of the world. These missions are headed by an ambassador, or, in a few cases, a chargé d'affaires. They are assisted by foreign service officers with responsibilities for political, economic, consular, administrative, and scientific and technological affairs, and also frequently by defense attachés, intelligence officers, and representatives of the Drug Enforcement Administration, all of whom, while they are presumably under the final authority of the ambassador, report also to their own agencies in Washington. (See Figure 18-1.)

This complexity in jurisdiction reflects the extension of the scope of governmental activity and the blurring of the line between foreign and do-

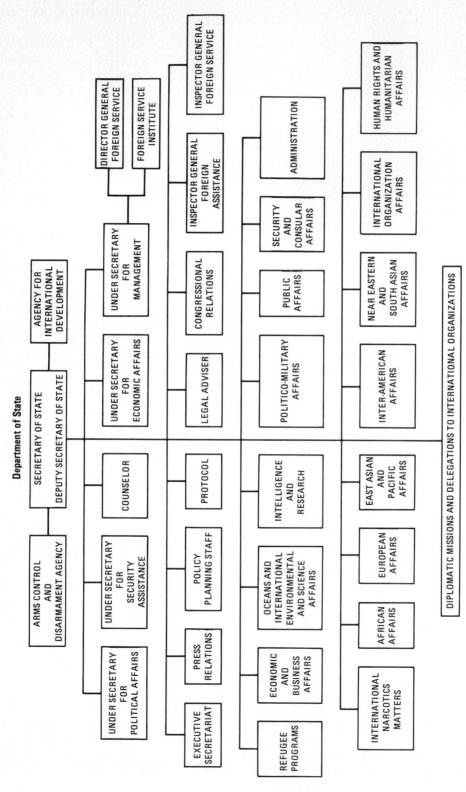

FIGURE 18-1

Organizational chart of the Department of State, 1983. Note that the Arms Control and Disarmament Agency is a separate agency, with the director reporting directly to the secretary of state and serving as the principal adviser to the secretary and the president on arms control and disarmament. (*Source:* Adapted from Kissinger, 1982; and Washington Monitor, *Federal Yellow Book, 1982*)

mestic policy. The result has been to bring into the foreign policymaking process many agencies previously unconcerned with it. The Commerce Department is deeply involved in the promotion of American trade abroad. The departments of Labor and Agriculture are pressed into the international arena when the interests of domestic groups associated with them demand it. The Treasury, the departments of Interior and Energy, the National Aeronautics and Space Administration, the Nuclear Regulatory Commission, the Arms Control and Disarmament Agency, and scores of other organizations are mandated or feel compelled to intervene in some facet of the dealings of the United States with other countries or organizations overseas.

The Problem of Unity An important consequence of this buildup in the administrative structure is that it impairs the unity, vigor, and expedition which the founders felt were necessary to successful executive leadership in foreign affairs. These qualities are difficult to achieve in instances where policy is bargained to the lowest common denominator among a host of contending executive actors. The process can be extremely time-consuming and can result in decisions which, while unobjectionable to all the parties concerned, are ineffective (Kissinger, 1982). "A plurality in the Executive," Hamilton warned, "tends to conceal faults and destroy responsibility" (*Federalist* 70). While the country has but one president at a time, the proliferation of agencies supposedly under presidential direction, but actually often pursuing goals of their own, has become the functional equivalent in many cases of a plural executive. Mistakes can be lost in the vastnesses of the State Department or the Pentagon. And responsibility for decisions is frequently so easy to avoid that the best that can be done is to cope with the situation by establishing new interdepartmental coordinating committees. Foreign policy must be negotiated within the United States government before it can be discussed with other nations.

One particularly vigorous attempt to bring some order to the foreign relations machinery came with the National Security Act of 1947. This act created a National Security Council (NSC) as a forum for exchanges among the agencies of American government most immediately concerned with foreign affairs (most prominently the State and Defense departments). The NSC was intended to promote consultation among the most significant executive branch officials on the advice they should present to the president, and to help coordinate the implementation of presidential decisions. These innovations, like the amendments to the National Security Act during the 1950s which strengthened the control of the president's secretary of defense over the services, constituted a determined effort to restore unity to the executive.

But the success of these changes has been limited. Struggles among agencies and organizations over the direction of American foreign policy— usually termed "bureaucratic politics"—have not abated. One reason is that bureaucratic agencies with a claim to be consulted on foreign affairs have proliferated faster than the responses designed to restore some centralized control over them. The intelligence "community," for example, has not remained a CIA monopoly; other members of the community include the National Security Agency, the Defense Intelligence Agency, the Bureau of Intelligence and Research of the Department of State, Army Intelligence, Navy Intelligence, Air Force Intelligence, the Federal Bureau of Investigation, the Department of the Treasury, the Department of Energy, and the Drug Enforcement Administration. Aside from these principal members, there are more than thirty other agencies and bureaus that exercise some intelligence functions within the American government (Crabb and Holt, 1980). Second, the coordinating bodies, instead of providing opportunities for consultation and coordination among the departments, have at times become rivals of the departments. The National Security Council has acted as a "little State Department" in the White House, and the national security adviser has sometimes threatened to supplant the secretary of state. The growth of NSC staff which permits this rivalry began slowly in the 1960s and exploded in the early 1970s; the size of the staff has diminished somewhat since then, but remains far above what it was during the Truman and Eisenhower administrations. Under these circumstances, neither the State Department nor the NSC can fully speak for the president, and infighting between the two has often been the result. This lack of executive unity may be found in almost all areas of American foreign policy, especially since efforts to coordinate policy in the newly important economic realm are only beginning.

The plurality within the executive in foreign policymaking has certain advantages. Struggles among the various bureaucratic agencies ensure that certain interests, which might otherwise be overlooked, are strongly represented and that important differences among the various agencies can come to the attention of the president. The complexity of many modern decisions is often such that no central planner can initially take into account all the necessary factors; the resistance of various bureaucratic agencies provides a mechanism by which the benefits and costs of any policy can be more accurately weighed. Thus a secretary of state, concerned perhaps with a diplomatic goal, might give less weight to security matters than would a secretary of defense, charged with overseeing the nation's military. The conflict among these policymakers, sometimes barely concealed, forces attention on more aspects of any decision. Obviously, however, there comes a point at which the struggles become more harmful than helpful and prevent the effective implementation of policies.

This picture of bureaucratic politics, while accurate in the main, should not be exaggerated. Effective presidents, in areas where they have a clear policy, can often impose a unity of will on the squabbling agencies under their authority. President Nixon, for example, was able to devise and implement a general strategy of diplomacy during his administration that involved a great many actions in different areas. Yet even here, in pursuing this complicated strategy the president sometimes had to work around certain agencies, excluding them from the decision-making process and presenting them with surprise decisions taken at a higher level. A president, in short, needs to be able to exercise a careful kind of diplomacy within the executive branch.

The Problem of Secrecy What of another quality expected of the executive by the founders—secrecy? This question is related to that of the size of the American foreign policymaking machinery, since the larger the number of people who know a secret, the more likely it is that the secret will be exposed, inadvertently or by design. The likelihood that secrets will be leaked is also increased by the lack of unity on policy preferences displayed by various segments of the foreign policy bureaucracy.

This problem can grow extremely serious when sensitive questions of national security are under discussion. During the debate over SALT II in 1978–1979, supporters and opponents of the proposed treaty within the executive branch seemed to be engaged in competitive leaking of confidential information concerning American negotiating positions and strategic capabilities, each side with the aim of bolstering its case before the public. During the summer of 1980, Americans were treated to revelations that President Carter, incensed by leaks on a split within the administration over proposed military aid to Morocco, had demanded that the secretary of state, national security adviser, director of the CIA, and dozens of other top-level officials sign written affidavits denying that they were responsible. Generalizations on the subject of leaks are hazardous, since one never knows of those secrets that *are* kept, but secrecy does not appear to be the hallmark of the contemporary executive branch.

Despite lapses, however, the executive remains capable and desirous of keeping some secrets. This secrecy generates controversy. Many charge that too many executive branch officials have authority to classify documents and that too many documents are classified. Critics cite the example of the "Pentagon papers," relating to the history of the Vietnamese war, which were published over the objections of the Nixon administration in 1971. The refusal of the administration to agree to the publication of even that material that had appeared in American newspapers a decade before demonstrated the excessive lengths to which officials sometimes go in classifying materials of even the most harmless nature (Sheehan, 1971). The motto of policymakers is said to be, "When in doubt, classify"; and this practice, opponents warn, elevates the country's interest in protecting its security over its interest in maintaining a free, popular government open to public scrutiny.

During the 1970s, a number of executive orders and amendments to the Freedom of Information Act reduced the number of officials who can classify documents and tightened the regulations gov-

The space shuttle illustrates the conflict between an open society and the need for military secrecy; the astronauts' activities are shown on nationwide television, except when they are launching top-secret spy satellites. *(NASA)*

erning the type of classifications that can be applied. These steps satisfied some of the objections to excessive secrecy, but they have not dealt with the opposite problem—protecting legitimate secrets. Currently, any government employee who leaks agricultural price support figures before their official release is subject to criminal penalties, but an employee who does the same with documents relating to national security is not. Is the government, many ask, too lax in protecting vital secrets of state?

The problem of secrecy is posed in its starkest terms, however, not in the exposing of negotiating positions, but in revelations of intelligence-gathering activities. Is the government's classification scheme abused, as its critics state, in order to conceal from the American people acts committed by intelligence services which, if the people ever knew of them, they would properly disavow as repugnant

to American practices and ideals? Or is it, as its defenders say, an unpleasant but necessary response to threats from a world outside that is not governed by American notions of fair play? These questions cannot readily be answered by reverting to the quieter diplomatic practices of earlier years, when Secretary of State Henry L. Stimson could sniff, "Gentlemen don't read other people's mail." It would seem either that the code of gentlemen and gentlewomen must change, or that there is no place for these people in the modern intelligence community.

The Intelligence Community The existence of modern intelligence services like the CIA raises the perennial conflict between the values of secrecy and national security on the one hand and openness and democracy on the other. Critics of the intelligence services wonder whether activities beyond the simple collection and analysis of information should be allowed at all. They cite such controversial policies as the CIA's support under the Reagan administration for a war by Nicaraguan rebels against their government; and they point to a series of proven or alleged CIA abuses: plots to assassinate foreign leaders; attempts to overthrow the governments of other countries such as Iran, Guatemala, and Chile; the use of journalists, members of the clergy, and other American citizens abroad as agents; the opening of mail from American citizens to selected foreign nations; and collaboration with the FBI in spying on American citizens by means such as the infiltration of protest groups. They point out that the "White House plumbers" unit which carried out the Watergate burglary had originally been set up to trace leaks of information on matters of national security coming from the staff of the NSC. These activities, which have created a pattern of abuses dangerous to domestic liberty, have their origin in practices infringing on individual rights by those acting for the United States government overseas. This disrespect for law and for the rights of others outside the United States, it is said, inevitably seeps back into this country, undermining the very constitutional system which the intelligence community is sworn to protect (Schlesinger, 1973).

Defenders of the intelligence community admit that some problems and abuses have occurred, but add that the solution cannot be to destroy the nation's intelligence-gathering capacity. The intelligence community, if it is to be effective in protecting the United States and its Constitution from adversaries, must be free to take actions abroad which would be unacceptable if they were undertaken at home. If certain rules and norms of conduct are honored by other nations only in the breach, is the United States alone to be bound to honor them in the observance? Defenders say that secrecy to protect such actions is essential, and they point to the assassination in 1976 of a CIA agent in Greece after his name had been revealed publicly by those opposed to the CIA's activities. In short, domestic and foreign practices must be differentiated, because the nation can be secure only if it is free to do abroad what it is rightly prohibited from doing at home (Kissinger, 1979).

The debate on the American intelligence community has, as a practical matter, been narrowed in the Congress not to questioning the existence of these services, but to scrutinizing the terms under which they operate. All agree on the need for a new charter to govern the conduct of the CIA and other intelligence agencies; but some would virtually remove the activities of covert agencies, while others insist that the charter must not be too specific or restrictive in order to leave some discretion to accomplish necessary, if unpleasant, goals.

With legislators as of 1983 unable to agree on the terms of a new CIA charter, the issue has become one of the extent of congressional oversight. Until the mid-1970s, this function was left to a few members of the Armed Services committees of the two houses, who were told little, and frequently wanted to know less, about CIA operations. With the revelations of CIA misconduct, this attitude changed dramatically. Members of Congress demanded more control, which led to the decision of both houses to establish new intelligence oversight committees with rotating memberships and to require executive agencies to make full, and in some cases prior, reports of their activities to them.

The operation of this more stringent congressional oversight has in some cases confirmed the fears of its opponents as to the ability of representatives, who pride themselves on their close ties with the people, to keep national security secrets from the people. For example, in 1974, Congressman Michael Harrington, unable to persuade either the House Foreign Affairs Committee or the Senate Foreign Relations Committee to investigate CIA activities in Chile, simply released to the press secret testimony on the subject by William Colby, the director of the CIA. (Harrington's unauthorized disclosures brought about his removal from the House Select Committee on Intelligence in 1975.) Proposals to restrict the number of members given sensitive intelligence reports are under consideration as part of the new charter, but defenders of the intelligence community continue to worry that members and their vastly augmented staffs may release with little fear of punishment confidential information damaging to the foreign relations of the United States. Like the founders, they have not yet found a problem-free way of balancing diplomacy's need for secrecy and democracy's need for open discussion.

The Role of Congress and the Separation of Powers in Today's Diplomacy

During the period of bipartisanship over containment that followed World War II, Congress effectively ceded to the president great discretion over the control of foreign policy. But with the diplomatic reversals of the 1960s, Congress reasserted its claim to a larger role. In doing so, it has made its special virtues and concerns—open debate, free discussion, the rule of fixed law—more nearly equal competitors with the rival claims posed by the demands of diplomacy and executive action. The main outlines of the debate on the responsibility that the Congress should assume today in making foreign policy differ hardly at all from the debates at the Constitutional Convention in 1787. The classic arguments over the separation of powers in this area again become topics of current discussion.

The debate between the critics and defenders of the more assertive role of Congress has centered on two different critiques of congressional influence on the foreign policymaking process: its volatility and its rigidity. Opponents of greater congressional authority over foreign policy insist that the legislative branch is too likely to change its collective mind, to respond to every shift in the popular mood, and to denounce as unacceptable what it only recently recommended as wise. Members of the executive branch have been especially likely to make this charge and to hold Congress responsible for vacillation in American foreign policy from near hysteria one day to neoisolationism and unconcern for events abroad the next. This vacillation is said to produce an unreliability that severely hampers American relationships with both allies and adversaries, neither of whom ever knows quite what to expect from Washington. President Johnson often contrasted the near unanimity with which Congress passed the Gulf of Tonkin Resolution in 1964 with the crescendo of congressional criticism of the war in Vietnam that confronted him three to four years later; he was enraged by what he saw as evidence of Capitol Hill's fickleness and lack of resolve. His two successors, presidents Nixon and Ford, also criticized Congress for its failure to uphold an American commitment by refusing to appropriate the sums they requested for aid to South Vietnam and Cambodia.

But chief executives have not been alone in deploring congressional unreliability. During the early 1970s, when sentiment in both houses seemed to be shifting in favor of Senator Mansfield's move to require large reductions in American forces stationed in western Europe, major segments of the American foreign policy establishment, both in and out of government, joined President Nixon in denouncing the plan. Criticism has come from a similarly broad range of sources on Congress's steadfast refusal over the years to make multiyear financial commitments to American bilateral and multilateral foreign assistance programs. The insistance on appropriating sums for one year only, it is said, makes it impossible for agencies providing foreign financial assistance to plan with confidence for agricultural or construction projects covering a more extended period of time.

To all this, Congress has responded with a vigorous defense of its role in the American constitutional system. Members of the House and Senate, it is true, were not intended by the founders to bend with every passing breeze of public opinion, but they *were* intended to respond eventually to the "deliberate sense of the community" (*Federalist* 63). Congressional elections are frequent, and members of Congress are more like their constituents than are appointive executive officials, who need never face election at all. Proponents of a strong role for Congress in the making of foreign policy argue that Congress, as the representative of the people, must have the freedom to alter or terminate policies in which it has lost faith. This includes the right to end ill-conceived wars and to reduce large-scale troop commitments. It certainly includes the use of the power of the purse to decide annually, in the light of events abroad and economic conditions at home, how much the United States can afford to spend elsewhere. In short, the right of Congress to make decisions about the broad outlines of American foreign policy, even if the executive controls the operational details, includes the right to change basic decisions.

Legislators may also feel they are fighting a two-front war. While they are being attacked as timid and unwilling to stand firm in support of a policy even when it proves difficult and unpopular, they are also accused of rigidity in the requirements they place on executive officials. "Tying the president's hands" and "placing the president in a straitjacket" are two of the phrases most often used to decry the attempts of Congress to regulate American foreign relations by law instead of leaving them to the discretion of diplomatic personnel in a better position to take advantage of opportunities that arise in the fluid world of international politics. Again, critics of the legislative branch point to Vietnam. When Congress in 1973 prohibited the spending of any funds to support further American combat activities in Indochina, it removed any threat that American forces would respond to violations of the Paris Peace Accords of that year and thus relieved the North Vietnamese of the fear of any risk from that quarter if they should (as they did) reopen the war and conquer the south (Franck and Weisband, 1979).

Given congressional dissatisfaction with over a decade of frustrating fighting in a distant corner of the world whose importance to the true interests of the United States was never satisfactorily explained, members may well have intended this result. But if taken literally, the legislation would also have prohibited the use of American forces to evacuate Americans and their local allies from Saigon and Phnom Penh when those two cities fell to enemy forces, or to rescue American citizens held by the Khmer Rouge after their seizure of the American freighter *Mayaguez*. When President Ford took these actions in 1975, he was making a conscious decision to defend American lives and interests at the cost of violating the law.

Congressional actions of this type do not restrict only military actions. Experts concerned with foreign aid, for example, have complained for years of Congress's tendency to write prohibitions, restrictions, and requirements directed against particular countries into international assistance bills. For example, prohibitions of direct or indirect aid to "Marxist" Angola and Mozambique have become almost routine. Such provisions, it is said, often simply provoke target nations to defiance, without allowing American officials to respond to partial progress. This is the consequence, they argue, of taking procedures appropriate to the political consensus of a stable society and applying them to a world environment which forms only a very partial society, has very little consensus, and is anything but stable.

Members of Congress and their supporters say that all this misses the point. Granted that law is a blunt instrument for dealing with the complexities of international relations, the need for it would not arise if American diplomatic representatives were more responsive to congressional preferences. When executive officials continue a purposeless war long after the people whom they are supposed to represent have lost patience with it, or when American tax monies are spent with little regard for American values on projects with no discernible results, Congress has a duty to step in. When it does so, it necessarily acts through legislation. And it must do so, because the intertwining of foreign and domestic policy means that if the rule of law is to be preserved in the one sphere, it cannot be excluded from the other. Executive officials, having shown by their past abuses that they cannot be trusted, must be made accountable to the law.

Strengthened Congressional Tools If Vietnam provided the motive for a new combativeness on the part of Congress, two other congressional prerogatives supplied the means by which it might succeed. An active foreign policy is a costly foreign policy. Control over the appropriations necessary to foreign policy has given Congress a much greater voice in international affairs, and it has particularly increased the role of the House of Representatives, which has no part in the treaty ratification process. Second, Congress has provided itself with much better staff support. The decade of the 1970s witnessed an explosive growth in congressional staff, which has freed members from their previous dependence on information and analysis supplied by professionals in executive bureaucracies. Congress now has its own foreign policy experts, a fact which enables it to challenge the policies of executive agencies and, if it is not satisfied with their responses, to rewrite their budgets and force them to change. Increases in staff, of course, make the members independent not only of the expertise supplied by executive agencies but also of the guidance supplied by party leaders and by knowledgeable fellow members who have specialized in a particular area of public policy. If the executive lacks unity, therefore, Congress cannot be expected to supply it.

This lack of unity does not appear to have inhibited Congress from new initiatives, however. Its renewed boldness can be seen in many of its actions. It has employed with new vigor its old power of utilizing public investigations to put the administration on the defensive and to influence mass opinion. The hearings conducted by Senator J. William Fulbright looking into the conduct of the Vietnamese war in the late 1960s, those held by Senator Frank Church on abuses of civil liberties by the CIA in the mid-1970s, and those conducted by Congressman Clarence Long on American involvement in El Salvador in 1981 are three examples. As we saw earlier, Congress has become considerably more strict in its oversight of the intelligence community. Moreover, before being ruled unconstitutional, the legislative veto was attached to numerous pieces of legislation dealing with foreign affairs, the most significant perhaps being that governing sales of military equipment to other countries. Although no arms sales were vetoed, several offers were withdrawn or modified when the president saw that he could not win a legislative veto fight.

Checks on Executive Agreements Congress's recent willingness to oppose its judgment to that of the president is most evident in its attempt to undo what it saw as generations of presidential usurpation of the power to put the country at war. Although Congress always retained its Constitutionally granted authority to "declare" war, presidents—from James K. Polk, who sent American troops into territory disputed by the United States and Mexico, to Franklin Roosevelt, who was carrying on an undeclared naval war against German submarines before Pearl Harbor—have managed to place American forces in situations where they were likely to become engaged in hostilities, thus forcing legislators to support a conflict already in progress. Members of Congress have seen the *executive agreement* as one instrument of this presidential aggrandizement at their expense. Executive agreements between the United States and another nation are of two types: those which are approved by a simple majority of both houses of Congress by resolution or by statute, and those (the so-called "pure" executive agreements) which are concluded on the authority of the president alone and receive no legislative ratification. Both bypass the Constitutional hurdle confronted by treaties, the need for approval by two-thirds of the Senate; legislators particularly oppose the second type because it may commit the United States to certain actions abroad without their consent or even their knowledge. In 1972, therefore, Congress mandated that executive agreements, of all types, be transmitted to it within sixty days after they enter into force. Legislators would at least no longer be taken by surprise.

The War Powers Act But the fear still existed that presidents could drag the country into war without congressional consultation, or even over congressional opposition. To meet this fear, the following year Congress passed, over President Nixon's veto, the War Powers Act. The president was to consult with Congress "in every possible instance" before introducing military forces into hostilities or into situations where hostilities seemed likely. Once such an introduction had taken place, the president was to report it to Congress within forty-eight hours. The use of such forces could continue no longer than sixty days—plus thirty more for an evacuation—without explicit congressional approval. And Congress could, at any time, pass a concurrent resolution, not subject to presidential veto, terminating the involvement.

Never again, proponents of the act believed, would a president be able to slip the nation surreptitiously into war. No longer could presidents use congressional appropriations to support troops already engaged on the battlefield as evidence that the legislators were authorizing the war. Clearly, the prevalent opinion was that in passing the War Powers Act Congress was returning the nation to the original Constitutional scheme, although not all Constitutional scholars have concurred (Bessette and Tulis, 1981:115–153).

The War Powers Act gave Congress a new weapon for its struggle with the executive. Although Congress has never used it to stop any presidential initiative in international affairs, the War Powers Act has highlighted an era of increased congressional interest in, and control over, American foreign policy. One decade after its enactment, however, an important element of Congress's authority under this law was called into question by a landmark Supreme Court decision (*Immigration and Naturalization Service v. Chadha,* 1983) which nullified the "legislative veto"—the scheme by which Congress, without the president's consent, could block executive action. How Congress will attempt to redefine its power in the wake of this decision remains to be seen.

Interest-Group Activity Another reason for the growing influence of Congress in foreign policymaking has been the decline in the distinction between foreign and domestic politics. Because of greater economic interdependency between the United States and other nations, economic interest groups that formerly dealt primarily with domestic concerns now are often equally concerned about foreign affairs. They may want to adjust tariff barriers, protect an area's security to ensure the safety of their investments, or promote friendly relations with a nation to enhance the possibilities of long-term trade. Such activities by economic interest groups, of course, are not new, but their scope seems to have increased. The same can be said of many ideological and cultural groups, which, because of the more extensive role of the United States in the world, are constantly prodded to exercise a say in American foreign policy. Thus the Americans for Democratic Action and the American Conservative Union regularly take stands on issues of foreign policy and rate members of Congress on their agreement with those propositions. Other groups, motivated by cultural, religious, ethnic, and racial ties to nations abroad, also are active. These include Jewish groups concerned about American policy toward Israel, black groups that take stands on American policy toward South Africa and the nations of black Africa, and groups of hispanics that have formed to deal with American policy toward Latin America.

The activity of these groups is not limited, of course, to lobbying in Congress. Like all interest groups, they seek to exercise pressure wherever decisions are made, whether in the White House, in the departments, or even in the courts. But interest-group activity in foreign affairs has both been stimulated by and stimulated congressional resurgence in the foreign policymaking process, since Congress generally is the institution best suited to the representation of particular interests. The watchword on Capitol Hill is not "neutral competence" but "democratic responsiveness." Representatives of interest groups bring valuable information, and members of Congress are generally willing to listen.

How far interest groups' influence may properly extend, however, remains a classic conflict. The founders praised American pluralism and described the balancing of interests as a means of defending liberty. But they also sought to demonstrate the advantages of unity in dealing with other nations, criticized disagreements in America's diplomatic councils, and warned of foreign influences pressing themselves into discussions of foreign policy. One of the best-known responses to interest-group pressures in recent years, the 1975 cutoff by Congress of military assistance to Turkey because of its invasion of Cyprus, is widely regarded as a notorious example of foreign policy failure (Franck and Weisband, 1979). The friends of Greece, with almost no group pressure in favor of Turkey to oppose them, carried the day against the administration and the leadership of both parties. One set of interest groups made American policy, and competing concerns were ignored. But neither is there any assurance that in other instances, where pressure is not all one way, decisions will be wisely made. The battle over American policy in the middle east pits two adversaries—American oil companies and American Zionist organizations—against each other. The pressures are much more evenly balanced than in the Turkish aid dispute. Yet, can one be certain that the point at which these forces reach an equilibrium is inevitably most desirable for the government and the people of the United States as well? When do governmental actors, in the executive and in Congress, become automatons, programmed by the interest group dominant on a particular issue, or by the compromise reached by conflicting groups? Is the national interest no more than the sum of the nation's special interests, especially in foreign affairs?

Policymaking in Foreign Affairs

According to the analysis of Alexis de Tocqueville, popular governments inevitably suffer from certain disadvantages in the conduct of foreign policy when compared with governments that are free from the constraints of republican principles. Republican governments find it difficult to keep secrets, and they are frequently forced into actions that are designed to satisfy temporary popular desires but that conflict with long-term security interests. The founders, aware of these shortcomings inherent in a republican form of government, sought to adopt certain institutional solutions that would protect the foreign policymaking process from the worst dangers of democratic politics. They did so by creating a slightly different decision-making system in foreign affairs that, in comparison with domestic affairs, sought to give more discretion to those government officials who could act quickly and without quite as much direct pressure from immediate sanction by public opinion. The president was given greater authority in foreign affairs than in domestic politics, and much of the authority granted to the legislature was given *only* to the Senate.

In practice today, the foreign policymaking process is somewhat different from that in domestic policymaking. The president and the Senate play a larger role in making foreign policy, and the direct influence of interest groups and democratic politics is slightly less. But these differences between foreign and domestic politics are *relative,* not absolute. The differences today appear somewhat less than the founders had hoped for or that some had come to expect during the years immediately following World War II. The reasons, already discussed, relate to the changing character of our national institutions (the presidency and the Senate are both more democratic bodies than in 1787), the growing interdependence of foreign and domestic issues, and the greater absolute importance of foreign affairs for the American public. The impor-

tant point to stress, however, is that the conduct of foreign affairs, while it was to be conducted under a slightly different process from domestic affairs, was never intended to be outside the reach of domestic conflict and controversy. In fact, whenever foreign affairs have deeply affected and divided the American people, as in the 1790s in the conflict over the Jay Treaty, as in 1900 in the conflict over "imperialism," or as in 1920 in the debates over the League of Nations, the political parties have tended to express these divisions as much as in domestic affairs, and the outcomes of these elections have heavily influenced national policies. In recent years, since the 1950s, foreign affairs and security issues have played an important role in nearly every presidential election. The fact that foreign policy was not emphasized by political parties in many elections before World War II was a result of its relative unimportance to most Americans and not of any institutional process that prevented public opinion and democratic politics from exercising influence.

Who, then, exercises the decisive "say" on foreign policymaking? The answer is not radically different from the answer we have given for domestic policymaking. As a general rule, governing authorities and certain bureaucracies, most notably the State Department, act on most issues with more freedom from constraint by public opinion and pressure groups than is the case in domestic politics. Secrecy is somewhat more a part of the process. The president and to some extent the Senate have much greater authority over the making of policy than they do in domestic politics. The foreign policy establishment has exercised a guiding influence not often found outside foreign affairs, although its opinions were never unchallenged. For all this, however, the great issues of foreign affairs are not isolated from the democratic political process. Whenever matters of foreign affairs have occupied the attention of the American public, which has frequently been the case since World War II and is likely to remain so, the great issues are debated in the political arena and are often of central importance to the outcome of presidential elections. The mandates of these elections, whether real or fictive, influence policy in foreign affairs in much the way they do in domestic affairs.

A CASE STUDY:
THE DEBATE OVER HUMAN RIGHTS

The issue of human rights serves as a classic study of the uneasy meeting of foreign policy and domestic principles, and of the problems this may pose for American diplomacy. Institutional rivalries have played a part in the debate as well, for human rights is one of the questions on which Congress has most vigorously attempted to combat executive supremacy in foreign affairs. The intensity of the "great debate" over human rights in the 1970s and 1980s has rivaled that of the most far-reaching reexaminations of American foreign policy in the past.

Of course, the United States has long stood for a large measure of humanitarianism in international affairs. But demands for stronger action on behalf of the ideals of human rights increased during the 1970s, largely for two reasons. First, despite a relative decline from its abnormally favored position immediately following World War II, the United States remains the most powerful nation on earth. Its predominance during the past generation has endowed it with many levers of influence on other nations. Therefore, it is not easy to dismiss calls for taking a stand in favor of morality in foreign policy on the ground that such appeals would be ineffective. The second reason, ironically, is to be found in a diminution of the force of the first. Despite its great power, the United States no longer retains the edge it once held, in terms either of military or of economic capabilities; and in the agonizing experience of Vietnam, it failed in a test of those capabilities. Containment of the Soviet Union, the doctrine used by successive administrations to justify American involvement in Vietnam, was a clear application of a traditional maxim of international politics, the preservation of the balance of power. Frustrated by the exercise of power in Vietnam in pursuit of a traditional end like containment, many Americans turned to new national goals, seemingly less tainted by obsolete notions of power politics, and in particular to the protection of human rights. (See Box 18-3.)

Yet though the immediate issues may have been unprecedented, the choices which they present to policymakers are very old indeed. Those wary of emphasizing human rights acknowledge the necessity, utility, and wisdom of providing the utmost protection for human dignity in all places subject to American legal jurisdiction. But when confronted with the plea to make American practices binding on other governments as well, they are likely to echo the exasperated protest of James Wilson to the convention of 1787: "To pretend to *define* the law of nations which depended on the authority of all the civilized nations of the world, would have a look of arrogance, that would make us ridiculous" (Farrand, 1937:II, 615). American values are not shared everywhere, and attempts to press them on others may well provoke resistance and create diplomatic tensions where there were none before. In such cases, the pursuit of human rights in foreign affairs, if not tempered by a concern for the national interest, may interfere with other equally necessary policies. What an undiscriminating anticommunism was to another era, an imprudent human rights policy could become today—an attempt to transplant American preferences abroad, which succeeds neither in having those principles accepted elsewhere nor in serving American diplomatic interests. Moreover, the "quiet diplomacy" favored before the Carter administration by Secretary of State Henry Kissinger and after it by President Reagan and Secretary of State Alexander Haig may, because it is not viewed by other countries as a public intrusion into their domestic affairs, be more effective in combating injustice and oppression.

Advocates of a more assertive policy respond that this formulation stands the problem on its head. The United States does not exist so that it may engage in diplomacy; it engages in diplomacy to ensure its continued existence and that of its basic values. If these values are to remain prized in American society, they must be promoted abroad; to say that they are for domestic consumption only, and not for export, is to cheapen them. Unconcern for human rights overseas can lead to their betrayal at home, the argument runs, as the excesses of the Nixon administration demonstrated. Finally, human rights activists say, Tocqueville was correct when he declared that the United States was great because it was good, and that if it ever ceased to be good, it would cease to be great. Diplomatic success—greatness—can be gained only when a nation espouses morally right policies which the pub-

---

BOX 18-3

IMPORTANT EVENTS IN THE DEBATE OVER HUMAN RIGHTS

1974   The public safety program of the Agency for International Development is abolished because of charges its funds were used by Latin American recipients for torture and other forms of police brutality.

1974   Congress denies the Soviet Union most-favored-nation trade status because of its restrictions on free emigration.

1974–1976   Congress curtails aid to the authoritarian government of Chile in a series of laws passed after the military takeover of that country in 1973.

1975   State Department establishes an "Office of Co-ordinator for Humanitarian Affairs."

1976   Congress requires the executive branch to report annually on the human rights practices of all nations for which American assistance is being proposed, and to terminate or restrict aid to all that violate human rights, unless extraordinary circumstances make continued aid in the national interest.

1977   United States representatives to all multilateral agencies except the International Monetary Fund are required to use their "voice and vote" to channel assistance away from countries with poor human rights records.

1977   Congress, with the approval of the new Carter administration, upgrades the Office of Co-ordinator to a Bureau of Human Rights in the State Department and provides for an assistant secretary of state whose sole responsibility is to oversee human rights.

1977   President Carter meets in the White House with one Soviet dissident, Vladimir Bukovsky, and sends a personal letter of support to another, Andrei Sakharov, still in the Soviet Union.

1981   In his farewell address, President Carter identifies human rights as one of three issues of overriding importance to the world and says that "America did not invent human rights. . . . Human rights invented America."

1981   Speaking for the new Reagan administration, Secretary of State Haig asserts that international terrorism and Soviet expansionism are the two greatest threats to human rights today.

---

lic will support and for which it will sacrifice; support for human rights is one such policy. Unmitigated *realpolitik* will not receive the public backing necessary to success.

Thus the two contending sides in the contemporary American debate over human rights tend to start from different premises—the supporters, from the necessity of proclaiming the important truths of republicanism against the threats posed by hostile ideologies; the skeptics, from the necessity of maintaining the nation's power and foreign interests and ameliorating international tensions as far as possible. The one begins with democracy, the other with diplomacy. While each admits that there is some worth in the position of the other, their dispute often cannot be settled simply by "splitting the difference"; the conflict is too fundamental to admit of such an easy solution. It will confront statesmen and stateswomen of the 1980s, just as it did those of the 1970s and the 1780s.

CONCLUSION

The experience of the United States has in general demonstrated that Hamilton was more correct than Jefferson: the relations among the great collectivities that make up the world's state system cannot be governed merely by the same maxims which Americans follow, either in their private lives or in their domestic politics. Foreign affairs as a subject matter differs from other areas of public policy in that it must deal with problems not wholly under the control of the Constitution of the United States, its laws, or its customary political practices. Yet Jefferson was in a way also right: foreign policy, because it affects our lives so deeply, cannot be considered wholly outside the American political system and its tenets of republicanism, either. Diplomacy is no longer something confined to far-off embassies in exotic settings; it affects our lives every day. And it is entrusted to officials who are responsible to the American people and subject to their laws and norms.

The uneasy meeting of these two realms gives rise to some of the most perplexing problems facing policymakers today. The founders recognized these problems and sought to provide a framework for dealing with them. Since World War II, when the protective isolation that the United States had enjoyed since the early nineteenth century ended, Americans have been relearning the lessons the founders taught. Today, those lessons must be applied in a foreign policy setting characterized by a continuing need for military security, an ideological split that exacerbates world tensions, countervailing forces for cooperation, and a decline in the usefulness of the distinction between foreign and domestic policies. Whatever balance is struck between diplomacy and democracy must take into account the great growth in the size of government, the continuing controversy over secrecy in foreign policy matters, and the newly strengthened role of Congress in foreign affairs. Contemporary discussions of the place of human rights in American diplomacy and the part interest groups should play in the policy process illustrate the difficulty of arriving at a generally acceptable answer.

At times one solution has seemed more appropriate to Americans, at times another. Policy after 1945 emphasized executive leadership and the freedom to meet foreign dangers. Policy during the 1970s was affected by a new emphasis on congressional authority and domestic constitutional restraints.

Despite the importance of choices made during these times, the necessity for deciding wisely on the balance to be struck between effective diplomacy and democratic values will be even greater in the 1980s, when the United States will face tremendous world problems while having lost much of the margin for error which its postwar political, military, and economic superiority had given it. In such a situation, skillful diplomacy becomes even more vital, as the difficulty of reconciling our search for security with an adherence to traditional American republican values becomes more acute.

SOURCES

Aron, Raymond: *The Imperial Republic: The United States and the World, 1945–1973,* Frank Jellinek (trans.), Prentice-Hall, Englewood Cliffs, N.J., 1974.

Acheson, Dean: *Present at the Creation: My Years in the State Department,* Norton, New York, 1969.

Beard, Charles A.: *The Idea of National Interest: An Analytical Study in American Foreign Policy.* Macmillan, New York, 1934.

Bessette, Joseph M., and Jeffrey Tulis (eds.): *The Presidency in the Constitutional Order,* Louisiana State University Press, Baton Rouge, 1981.

Boyd, Julian P. (ed.): *The Papers of Thomas Jefferson,* vols. 1–60, Princeton University Press, Princeton, N.J., 1958.

Bryce, James: *The American Commonwealth,* vols. 1, 2, Macmillan, New York, 1889.

Carter, Jimmy: *A Government as Good as Its People,* Simon and Shuster, New York, 1977a.

————: *Public Papers of the Presidents of the United States,* Jimmy Carter, 1977, vol. 1, Office of the Federal Register, National Archives and Records Service, Washington, D.C., 1977b.

Corwin, Edward S.: *The President's Control of Foreign Relations,* Princeton University Press, Princeton, N.J., 1957.

Crabb, Cecil V., Jr., and Pat M. Holt: *Invitation to Struggle: Congress, the President and Foreign Policy,* Congressional Quarterly Press, Washington, D.C., 1980.

Farrand, Max (ed.): *The Records of the Federal Convention of 1787,* vols. 1–4, Yale University Press, New Haven, Conn., 1937.

Franck, Thomas M., and Edward Weisband: *Foreign Policy by Congress.* Oxford University Press, New York, 1979.

Halberstam, David: *The Best and the Brightest,* Random House, New York, 1969.

Kennan, George F.: *American Diplomacy, 1900–1950,* New American Library, New York, 1951.

Kissinger, Henry A.: *American Foreign Policy,* Norton, New York, 1969.

————: *White House Years,* Little, Brown, Boston, 1979.

————: *Years of Upheaval,* Little, Brown, Boston, 1982.

LaFeber, Walter (ed.): *John Quincy Adams and the American Continental Empire,* Quadrangle Books, Chicago, 1965.

Nixon, Richard M.: *Public Papers of the Presidents of the United States,* Richard Nixon, 1970, Office of the Federal Register, National Archives and Records Service, Washington, D.C., 1969.

Rosenfeld, Stephen S.: "Mixed Signals," *Washington Post,* Jan. 22, 1982, p. A15.

Schlesinger, Arthur M., Jr.: *Imperial Presidency,* Houghton Mifflin, Boston, 1973.

Sheehan, Neil (ed.): *The Pentagon Papers,* Bantam, New York, 1971.

Spanier, John: *American Foreign Policy Since World War II,* 7th ed., Praeger, New York, 1977.

Syrett, Harold C. (ed.): *The Papers of Alexander Hamilton,* vols. 1–26, Columbia University Press, New York, 1969.

Tocqueville, Alexis de: *Democracy in America,* George Lawrence (trans.), Doubleday, Garden City, N.Y., 1969.

U.S. Department of Defense: *Annual Report, Fiscal Year 1981,* U.S. Government Printing Office, Washington, D.C., 1980.

Washington Monitor: *Federal Yellow Book, 1982.*

RECOMMENDED READINGS

Aron, Raymond: *The Imperial Republic: The United States and the World, 1945–1973,* Frank Jellinek (trans.), Prentice-Hall, Englewood Cliffs, N.J., 1974. The period of greatest predominance in world affairs for the United States as analyzed by a sympathetic European observer.

Crabb, Cecil V., Jr.: *American Foreign Policy in the Nuclear Age,* 4th ed., Harper and Row, New York, 1982. Comprehensive description of both the policies of American diplomacy and the institutions which formulate and execute it.

Franck, Thomas M., and Edward Weisband: *Foreign Policy by Congress,* Oxford University Press, New York, 1979. Traces the resurgence of congressional interest in and control over foreign policy during the 1970s.

Gilbert, Felix: *To the Farewell Address: Ideas of Early American Foreign Policy,* Princeton University Press, Princeton, N.J., 1961. Investigates the thinking of the founders on matters of international relations.

Graebner, Norman A. (ed): *Ideas and Diplomacy: Readings in the Intellectual Tradition of American Foreign Policy,* Oxford University Press, New York, 1964. Graebner uses the speeches and writings of American leaders to trace the ideas lying behind American foreign policy through the country's history.

Kennan, George F.: *The Nuclear Delusion: Soviet-American Relations in the Atomic Age,* Pantheon, New York, 1982. A collection of essays by one of the foremost American diplomats on contemporary problems in foreign affairs.

Kissinger, Henry A.: *White House Years,* Little, Brown, Boston, 1979; and *Years of Upheaval,* Little, Brown, Boston, 1982. A history and series of reflections on American diplomacy from 1969 to 1974, told by a man who served as both secretary of state and national security adviser to the president.

Spanier, John: *American Foreign Policy since World War II,* 7th ed., Praeger, New York, 1977. Concise survey of continuity and change in postwar American foreign policy.

Appendixes

Appendix 1

The Declaration of Independence

In Congress, July 4, 1776
The Unanimous Declaration of the
Thirteen United States of America

When, in the course of human events, it becomes necessary for one people to dissolve the political bands which have connected them with another, and to assume, among the powers of the earth, the separate and equal station to which the laws of nature and of nature's God entitle them, a decent respect to the opinions of mankind requires that they should declare the causes which impel them to the separation.

We hold these truths to be self-evident: That all men are created equal; that they are endowed by their Creator with certain unalienable rights; that among these are life, liberty, and the pursuit of happiness; that, to secure these rights, governments are instituted among men, deriving their just powers from the consent of the governed; that whenever any form of government becomes destructive of these ends, it is the right of the people to alter or to abolish it, and to institute new government, laying its foundation on such principles, and organizing its powers in such form, as to them shall seem most likely to effect their safety and happiness. Prudence, indeed, will dictate that governments long established should not be changed for light and transient causes; and accordingly all experience hath shown that mankind are more disposed to suffer, while evils are sufferable, than to right themselves by abolishing the forms to which they are accustomed. But when a long train of abuses and usurpations, pursuing invariably the same object, evinces a design to reduce them under absolute despotism, it is their right, it is their duty, to throw off such government, and to provide new guards for their future security. Such has been the patient sufferance of these colonies; and such is now the necessity which constrains them to alter their former systems of government. The history of the present King of Great Britain is a history of repeated injuries and usurpations, all having in direct object the establishment of an absolute tyranny over these states. To prove this, let facts be submitted to a candid world.

He has refused to assent to laws, the most wholesome and necessary for the public good.

He has forbidden his governors to pass laws of immediate and pressing importance, unless suspended in their operation till his assent should be obtained; and, when so suspended, he has utterly neglected to attend to them.

He has refused to pass other laws for the accommodation of large districts of people, unless those people would relinquish the right of representation in the legislature, a right inestimable to them, and formidable to tyrants only.

He has called together legislative bodies at places unusual, uncomfortable, and distant from the depository of their public records, for the sole purpose of fatiguing them into compliance with his measures.

He has dissolved representative houses repeatedly, for opposing, with manly firmness, his invasions on the rights of the people.

He has refused for a long time, after such dissolutions, to cause others to be elected; whereby the legislative powers, incapable of annihilation, have returned to the people at large for their exercise; the state remaining, in the mean time, exposed to all the dangers of invasions from without and convulsions within.

He has endeavored to prevent the population of these states; for that purpose obstructing the laws for naturalization of foreigners; refusing to pass others to encourage their migration hither, and raising the conditions of new appropriations of lands.

He has obstructed the administration of justice, by refusing his assent to laws for establishing judiciary powers.

He has made judges dependent on his will alone, for the tenure of their offices, and the amount and payment of their salaries.

He has erected a multitude of new offices, and sent hither swarms of officers to harass our people and eat out their substance.

He has kept among us, in times of peace, standing armies, without the consent of our legislatures.

He has affected to render the military independent of, and superior to, the civil power.

He has combined with others to subject us to a jurisdiction foreign to our constitution and unacknowledged by our laws, giving his assent to their acts of pretended legislation:

For quartering large bodies of armed troops among us;

For protecting them, by a mock trial, from punishment for any murders which they should commit on the inhabitants of these states;

For cutting off our trade with all parts of the world;

For imposing taxes on us without our consent;

For depriving us, in many cases, of the benefits of trial by jury;

For transporting us beyond seas, to be tried for pretended offenses;

For abolishing the free system of English laws in a neighboring province, establishing therein an arbitrary government, and enlarging its boundaries, so as to render it at once an example and fit instrument for introducing the same absolute rule into these colonies;

For taking away our charters, abolishing our most valuable laws, and altering fundamentally the forms of our governments;

For suspending our own legislatures, and declaring themselves invested with power to legislate for us in all cases whatsoever.

He has abdicated government here, by declaring us out of his protection and waging war against us.

He has plundered our seas, ravaged our coasts, burned our towns, and destroyed the lives of our people.

He is at this time transporting large armies of foreign mercenaries to complete the works of death, desolation, and tyranny already begun with circumstances of cruelty and perfidy scarcely paralleled in the most barbarous ages, and totally unworthy the head of a civilized nation.

He has constrained our fellow-citizens, taken captive on the high seas, to bear arms against their country, to become the executioners of their friends and brethren, or to fall themselves by their hands.

He has excited domestic insurrections among us, and has endeavored to bring on the inhabitants of our frontiers the merciless Indian savages, whose known rule of warfare is an undistinguished destruction of all ages, sexes, and conditions.

In every stage of these oppressions we have petitioned for redress in the most humble terms; our repeated petitions have been answered only by repeated injury. A prince, whose character is thus marked by every act which may define a tyrant, is unfit to be the ruler of a free people.

Nor have we been wanting in our attentions to our British brethren. We have warned them, from time to time, of attempts by their legislature to extend an unwarrantable jurisdiction over us. We have reminded them of the circumstances of our emigration and settlement here. We have appealed to their native justice and magnanimity; and we have conjured them, by the ties of our common kindred, to disavow these usurpations, which would inevitably interrupt our connections and correspondence. They, too, have been deaf to the voice of justice and of consanguinity. We must, therefore, acquiesce in the necessity which denounces our separation, and hold them, as we hold the rest of mankind, enemies in war, in peace friends.

We, therefore, the representatives of the United States of America, in General Congress assembled, appealing to the Supreme Judge of the world for the rectitude of our intentions, do, in the name and by the authority of the good people of these colonies, solemnly publish and declare, that these United Colonies are, and of right ought to be, FREE AND INDEPENDENT STATES; that they are absolved from all allegiance to the British crown, and that all political connection between them and the state of Great Britain is, and ought to be, totally dissolved; and that, as free and independent states, they have full power to levy war, conclude peace, contract alliances, establish commerce, and do all other acts and things which independent states may of right do. And for the support of this declaration, with a firm reliance on the protection of Divine Providence, we mutually pledge to each other our lives, our fortunes, and our sacred honor.

John Hancock [*President*]
[*and fifty-five others*]

Appendix 2

The Constitution of the United States of America

Preamble

We the People of the United States, in Order to form a more perfect Union, establish Justice, insure domestic Tranquility, provide for the common defence, promote the general Welfare, and secure the Blessings of Liberty to ourselves and our Posterity, do ordain and establish this Constitution for the United States of America.

The legislature

ARTICLE I

Division into Senate and House

Section 1 All legislative Powers herein granted shall be vested in a Congress of the United States, which shall consist of a Senate and House of Representatives.

House membership

Section 2 The House of Representatives shall be composed of Members chosen every second Year by the People of the several States, and the Electors in each State shall have the Qualifications requisite for Electors of the most numerous Branch of the State Legislature.

No Person shall be a Representative who shall not have attained to the age of twenty five Years, and been seven Years a Citizen of the United States, and who shall not, when elected, be an Inhabitant of that State in which he shall be chosen.

Representatives and direct Taxes shall be apportioned among the several States which may be included within this Union, according to their respective Numbers, which shall be determined by adding to the whole Number of free Persons, including those bound to Service for a Term of Years, and excluding Indians not taxed, three

Note: The marginal notes provided are not part of the Constitution; they are included to help the reader locate different sections. Portions of the Constitution printed in *italic* have been superseded or changed by later amendments, as indicated in the footnotes. The attestation and signatures of the delegates at the Constitutional Convention have been omitted.

fifths of all other Persons.[1] The actual Enumeration shall be made within three Years after the first Meeting of the Congress of the United States, and within every subsequent Term of ten Years, in such Manner as they shall by Law direct. The Number of Representatives shall not exceed one for every thirty Thousand, but each State shall have at Least one Representative; and until such enumeration shall be made, the State of New Hampshire shall be entitled to chuse three, Massachusetts eight, Rhode-Island and Providence Plantations one, Connecticut five, New-York six, New Jersey four, Pennsylvania eight, Delaware one, Maryland six, Virginia ten, North Carolina five, South Carolina five, and Georgia three.

When vacancies happen in the Representation from any State, the Executive Authority thereof shall issue Writs of Election to fill such Vacancies.

House's power to impeach

The House of Representatives shall chuse their Speaker and other Officers; and shall have the sole Power of Impeachment.

Senate membership

Section 3 The Senate of the United States shall be composed of two Senators from each State, *chosen by the Legislature thereof,*[2] for six Years; and each Senator shall have one Vote.

Immediately after they shall be assembled in Consequence of the first Election, they shall be divided as equally as may be into three Classes. The Seats of the Senators of the first Class shall be vacated at the Expiration of the second Year, of the second Class at the Expiration of the fourth Year, and of the third Class at the Expiration of the sixth Year, so that one third may be chosen every second Year; *and if Vacancies happen by Resignation, or otherwise, during the Recess of the Legislature of any State, the Executive thereof may make temporary Appointments until the next Meeting of the Legislature, which shall then fill such Vacancies.*[3]

No Person shall be a Senator who shall not have attained to the Age of thirty Years, and been nine Years a Citizen of the United States, and who shall not, when elected, be an Inhabitant of that State for which he shall be chosen.

Vice president's role in the Senate

The Vice President of the United States shall be President of the Senate, but shall have no Vote, unless they be equally divided.

The Senate shall chuse their other Officers, and also a President pro tempore, in the Absence of the Vice President, or when he shall exercise the Office of President of the United States.

Senate's power to try impeachments

The Senate shall have the sole Power to try all Impeachments. When sitting for that Purpose, they shall be on Oath or Affirmation. When the President of the United States is tried the Chief Justice shall preside: And no Person shall be convicted without the Concurrence of two thirds of the Members present.

Judgment in Cases of Impeachment shall not extend further than to removal from Office, and disqualification to hold and enjoy any Office of honor, Trust or Profit under the United States: but the Party convicted shall nevertheless be liable and subject to Indictment, Trial, Judgment and Punishment, according to Law.

Laws governing election of members of Congress

Section 4 The Times, Places and Manner of holding Elections for Senators and Representatives, shall be prescribed in each State by the Legislature thereof; but

---

[1]Modified by the Fourteenth Amendment, Section 2, and by the Sixteenth Amendment.
[2]Superseded by the Seventeenth Amendment.
[3]Modified by the Seventeenth Amendment.

the Congress may at any time by Law make or alter such Regulations, except as to the Places of chusing Senators.

The Congress shall assemble at least once in every Year, and such Meeting shall be on the *first Monday in December, unless they shall by Law appoint a different Day.*[4]

Internal rules of Congress

Section 5   Each House shall be the Judge of the Elections, Returns and Qualifications of its own Members, and a Majority of each shall constitute a Quorum to do Business; but a smaller Number may adjourn from day to day, and may be authorized to compel the Attendance of absent Members, in such Manner, and under such Penalties as each House may provide.

Each House may determine the Rules of its Proceedings, punish its Members for disorderly Behavior, and, with the Concurrence of two thirds, expel a Member.

Each House shall keep a Journal of its Proceedings, and from time to time publish the same, excepting such Parts as may in their Judgment require Secrecy; and the Yeas and Nays of the Members of either House on any question shall, at the Desire of one fifth of those Present, be entered on the Journal.

Neither House, during the Session of Congress, shall, without the Consent of the other, adjourn for more than three days, nor to any other Place than that in which the two Houses shall be sitting.

Privileges and immunities of members

Section 6   The Senators and Representatives shall receive a Compensation for their Services, to be ascertained by Law, and paid out of the Treasury of the United States. They shall in all Cases, except Treason, Felony and Breach of the Peace, be privileged from Arrest during their Attendance at the Session of their respective Houses, and in going to and returning from the same; and for any Speech or Debate in either House, they shall not be questioned in any other Place.

Disabilities of members; ban on holding federal appointive offices

No Senator or Representative shall, during the Time for which he was elected, be appointed to any civil Office under the Authority of the United States, which shall have been created, or the Emoluments whereof shall have been encreased during such time; and no Person holding any Office under the United States, shall be a Member of either House during his Continuance in Office.

Section 7   All Bills for raising Revenue shall originate in the House of Representatives; but the Senate may propose or concur with Amendments as on other Bills.

Procedure for enacting laws; president's veto power and method of overriding

Every Bill which shall have passed the House of Representatives and the Senate, shall, before it become a Law, be presented to the President of the United States; If he approve he shall sign it, but if not he shall return it, with his Objections to that House in which it shall have originated, who shall enter the Objections at large on their Journal, and proceed to reconsider it. If after such Reconsideration two thirds of that House shall agree to pass the Bill, it shall be sent, together with the Objections, to the other House, by which it shall likewise be reconsidered, and if approved by two thirds of that House, it shall become a Law. But in all such Cases the Votes of both Houses shall be determined by yeas and Nays, and the Names of the Persons voting for and against the Bill shall be entered on the Journal of each House respectively. If any Bill shall not be returned by the President within ten Days (Sundays excepted) after it shall have been presented to him, the Same

---

[4]Superseded by the Twentieth Amendment, Section 2.

shall be a Law, in like Manner as if he had signed it, unless the Congress by their Adjournment prevent its Return, in which Case it shall not be a Law.

Every Order, Resolution, or Vote to which the Concurrence of the Senate and House of Representatives may be necessary (except on a question of Adjournment) shall be presented to the President of the United States; and before the Same shall take Effect, shall be approved by him, or being disapproved by him, shall be re-passed by two thirds of the Senate and House of Representatives, according to the Rules and Limitations prescribed in the Case of a Bill.

Enumeration of the powers of Congress

Taxes and spending; the "general welfare" clause

Section 8 The Congress shall have Power To lay and collect Taxes, Duties, Imposts and Excises, to pay the Debts and provide for the common Defence and general Welfare of the United States; but all Duties, Imposts and Excises shall be uniform throughout the United States;

Borrowing

To borrow Money on the credit of the United States;

Commerce

To regulate Commerce with foreign Nations, and among the several States, and with the Indian Tribes;

Naturalization and bankruptcy

To establish an uniform Rule of Naturalization, and uniform Laws on the subject of Bankruptcies throughout the United States;

Money

To coin Money, regulate the Value thereof, and of foreign Coin, and fix the Standard of Weights and Measures;

To provide for the Punishment of counterfeiting the Securities and current Coin of the United States;

Post office

To establish Post Offices and post Roads;

Patents and copyrights

To promote the Progress of Science and useful Arts, by securing for limited Times to Authors and Inventors the exclusive Right to their respective Writings and Discoveries;

Establish courts

To constitute Tribunals inferior to the supreme Court;

To define and punish Piracies and Felonies committed on the high Seas, and Offences against the Law of Nations;

Declare war

To declare War, grant Letters of Marque and Reprisal, and make Rules concerning Captures on Land and Water;

Raise army and navy

To raise and support Armies, but no Appropriation of Money to that Use shall be for a longer Term than two Years;

To provide and maintain a Navy;

To make Rules for the Government and Regulation of the land and naval Forces;

Call the militia

To provide for calling forth the Militia to execute the Laws of the Union, suppress Insurrections and repel Invasions;

To provide for organizing, arming, and disciplining, the Militia, and for governing such Part of them as may be employed in the Service of the United States, reserving to the States respectively, the Appointment of the Officers, and the Authority of training the Militia according to the discipline prescribed by Congress;

Authority over the District of Columbia

To exercise exclusive Legislation in all Cases whatsoever, over such District (not exceeding ten Miles square) as may, by Cession of Particular States, and the Acceptance of Congress, become the Seat of the Government of the United States, and to exercise like Authority over all Places purchased by the Consent of the Legislature of the State in which the Same shall be, for the Erection of Forts, Magazines, Arsenals, dock-Yards, and other needful Buildings;—And

"Necessary and proper" clause

To make all Laws which shall be necessary and proper for carrying into Execution the foregoing Powers, and all other Powers vested by this Constitution in the Government of the United States, or in any Department or Officer thereof.

Enumeration of restraints of powers of Congress

Slave trade

Section 9 The Migration or Importation of such Persons as any of the States now existing shall think proper to admit, shall not be prohibited by the Congress prior to the Year one thousand eight hundred and eight, but a Tax or duty may be imposed on such Importation, not exceeding ten dollars for each Person.

Habeas corpus

The Privilege of the Writ of Habeas Corpus shall not be suspended, unless when in Cases of Rebellion or Invasion the public Safety may require it.

No bill of attainder or ex post facto law

No Bill of Attainder or ex post facto Law shall be passed.

No Capitation, or other direct, Tax shall be laid, *unless in Proportion to the Census or Enumeration herein before directed to be taken.*[5]

No Tax or Duty shall be laid on Articles exported from any State.

No Preference shall be given by any Regulation of Commerce or Revenue to the Ports of one State over those of another; nor shall Vessels bound to, or from, one State, be obliged to enter, clear or pay Duties in another.

Appropriations and expenditures

No Money shall be drawn from the Treasury, but in Consequence of Appropriations made by Law; and a regular Statement and Account of the Receipts and Expenditures of all public Money shall be published from time to time.

No titles of nobility

No Title of Nobility shall be granted by the United States: And no Person holding any Office of Profit or Trust under them, shall, without the Consent of the Congress, accept of any present, Emolument, Office, or Title, of any kind whatever, from any King, Prince, or foreign State.

Enumeration of restraints on the states

Section 10 No State shall enter into any Treaty, Alliance, or Confederation; grant Letters of Marque and Reprisal; coin Money; emit Bills of Credit; make any Thing but gold and silver Coin a Tender in Payment of Debts; pass any Bill of Attainder, ex post facto Law, or Law impairing the Obligation of Contracts, or grant any Title of Nobility.

No State shall, without the Consent of the Congress, lay any Imposts or Duties on Imports or Exports, except what may be absolutely necessary for executing its inspection Laws: and the net Produce of all Duties and Imposts, laid by any State on Imports or Exports, shall be for the Use of the Treasury of the United States; and all such Laws shall be subject to the Revision and Controul of the Congress.

No State shall, without the Consent of Congress, lay any Duty of Tonnage, keep Troops, or Ships of War in time of Peace, enter into any Agreement or Compact with another State, or with a foreign Power, or engage in War, unless actually invaded, or in such imminent Danger as will not admit of delay.

The executive

ARTICLE II

"Executive power" and term of office

Section 1 The executive Power shall be vested in a President of the United States of America. He shall hold his Office during the Term of four Years, and, together with the Vice President, chosen for the same Term, be elected, as follows:

Method of election

Each State shall appoint, in such Manner as the Legislature thereof may direct, a Number of Electors, equal to the whole Number of Senators and Representatives to which the State may be entitled in the Congress: but no Senator or Represen-

[5]Modified by the Sixteenth Amendment.

tative, or Person holding an Office of Trust or Profit under the United States, shall be appointed an Elector.

The Electors shall meet in their respective States, and vote by Ballot for two Persons, of whom one at least shall not be an Inhabitant of the same State with themselves. And they shall make a List of all the Persons voted for, and of the Number of Votes for each; which List they shall sign and certify, and transmit sealed to the Seat of the Government of the United States, directed to the President of the Senate. The President of the Senate shall, in the Presence of the Senate and House of Representatives, open all the Certificates, and the Votes shall then be counted. The Person having the greatest Number of Votes shall be the President, if such Number be a Majority of the whole Number of Electors appointed; and if there be more than one who have such Majority, and have an equal Number of Votes, then the House of Representatives shall immediately chuse by Ballot one of them for President; and if no Person have a Majority, then from the five highest on the List the said House shall in like Manner chuse the President. But in chusing the President, the Votes shall be taken by States, the Representation from each State having one Vote; a quorum for this Purpose shall consist of a Member or Members from two thirds of the States, and a Majority of all the States shall be necessary to a Choice. In every Case, after the Choice of the President, the Person having the greatest Number of Votes of the Electors shall be the Vice President. But if there should remain two or more who have equal Votes, the Senate shall chuse from them by Ballot the Vice President.[6]

The Congress may determine the Time of chusing the Electors, and the Day on which they shall give their Votes; which Day shall be the same throughout the United States.

Qualifications for office

No Person except a natural born Citizen, or a Citizen of the United States, at the time of the Adoption of this Constitution, shall be eligible to the Office of President; neither shall any person be eligible to that Office who shall not have attained to the Age of thirty five Years, and been fourteen Years a Resident within the United States.

In Case of the Removal of the President from Office, or of his Death, Resignation, or Inability to discharge the Powers and Duties of the said Office, the Same shall devolve on the Vice President, and the Congress may by Law provide for the Case of Removal, Death, Resignation or Inability, both of the President and Vice President, declaring what Officer shall then act as President, and such Officer shall act accordingly, until the Disability be removed, or a President shall be elected.[7]

Presidential salary

The President shall, at stated Times, receive for his Services, a Compensation, which shall neither be encreased nor diminished during the Period for which he shall have been elected, and he shall not receive within that Period any other Emolument from the United States, or any of them.

Oath of office

Before he enter on the Execution of his Office, he shall take the following Oath or Affirmation:—"I do solemnly swear (or affirm) that I will faithfully execute the Office of President of the United States, and will to the best of my Ability, preserve, protect and defend the Constitution of the United States."

[6]Superseded by the Twelfth Amendment.
[7]Modified by the Twenty-Fifth Amendment.

Presidential powers
Commander in chief

Section 2 The President shall be Commander in Chief of the Army and Navy of the United States, and of the Militia of the several States, when called into the actual Service of the United States; he may require the Opinion, in writing, of the principal Officer in each of the executive Departments, upon any Subject relating to the Duties of their respective Offices, and he shall have Power to grant Reprieves and Pardons for Offences against the United States, except in Cases of Impeachment.

Pardons

Treaties and appointments

He shall have Power, by and with the Advice and Consent of the Senate, to make Treaties, provided two thirds of the Senators present concur; and he shall nominate, and by and with the Advice and Consent of the Senate, shall appoint Ambassadors, other public Ministers and Consuls, Judges of the supreme Court, and all other Officers of the United States, whose Appointments are not herein otherwise provided for, and which shall be established by Law: but the Congress may by Law vest the Appointment of such inferior Officers, as they think proper, in the President alone, in the Courts of Law, or in the Heads of Departments.

The President shall have Power to fill up all Vacancies that may happen during the Recess of the Senate, by granting Commissions which shall expire at the End of their next Session.

State of the union

Section 3 He shall from time to time give to the Congress Information of the State of the Union, and recommend to their Consideration such Measures as he shall judge necessary and expedient; he may, on extraordinary Occasions, convene both Houses, or either of them, and in Case of Disagreement between them, with Respect to the Time of Adjournment, he may adjourn them to such Time as he shall think proper; he shall receive Ambassadors and other public Ministers; he shall take Care that the Laws be faithfully executed, and shall Commission all the Officers of the United States.

Convening Congress

Receiving ambassadors
"Take care" clause

Grounds for impeachment

Section 4 The President, Vice President and all civil Officers of the United States, shall be removed from Office on Impeachment for, and Conviction of, Treason, Bribery, or other high Crimes and Misdemeanors.

The judiciary

ARTICLE III

Federal courts; judicial tenure and salary

Section 1 The judicial Power of the United States, shall be vested in one supreme Court, and in such inferior Courts as the Congress may from time to time ordain and establish. The Judges, both of the supreme and inferior Courts, shall hold their Offices during good Behavior, and shall, at stated Times, receive for their Services, a Compensation, which shall not be diminished during their Continuance in Office.

Jurisdiction of federal courts

Section 2 The judicial Power shall extend to all Cases, in Law and Equity, arising under this Constitution, the Laws of the United States, and Treaties made, or which shall be made, under their Authority;—to all Cases affecting Ambassadors, other public Ministers and Consuls;—to all Cases of admiralty and maritime Jurisdiction;—to Controversies to which the United States shall be a Party;—to Controversies between two or more States;—*between a State and Citizens of another State,*[8]—between Citizens of different States;—between Citizens of the same State

[8]Modified by the Eleventh Amendment.

claiming Lands under Grants of different States, and between Citizens of the same State claiming Lands under Grants of different States, and between a State, or the Citizens thereof, and foreign States, Citizens or Subjects.

In all Cases affecting Ambassadors, other public Ministers and Consuls, and those in which a State shall be Part, the supreme Court shall have original Jurisdiction. In all the other Cases before mentioned, the supreme Court shall have appellate Jurisdiction, both as to Law and Fact, with such Exceptions, and under such Regulations as the Congress shall make.

Trial by jury

The Trial of all Crimes, except in Cases of Impeachment, shall be by Jury; and such Trial shall be held in the State where the said Crimes shall have been committed; but when not committed within any State, the Trial shall be at such Place or Places as the Congress may by Law have directed.

Definition of treason and procedures for punishment

Section 3 Treason against the United States, shall consist only in levying War against them, or in adhering to their Enemies, giving them Aid and Comfort. No Person shall be convicted of Treason unless on the Testimony of two Witnesses to the same overt Act, or on Confession in open Court.

The Congress shall have Power to declare the Punishment of Treason, but no Attainder of Treason shall work Corruption of Blood, or Forfeiture except during the Life of the Person attainted.

Interstate relations

ARTICLE IV

Full faith and credit

Section 1 Full Faith and Credit shall be given in each State to the public Acts, Records, and judicial Proceedings of every other State. And the Congress may by general Laws prescribe the Manner in which such Acts, Records and Proceedings shall be proved, and the Effect thereof.

Privileges and immunities

Section 2 The Citizens of each State shall be entitled to all Privileges and Immunities of Citizens in the several States.

Extradition

A person charged in any State with Treason, Felony, or other Crime, who shall flee from Justice, and be found in another State, shall on Demand of the executive Authority of the State from which he fled, be delivered up, to be removed to the State having Jurisdiction of the Crime.

No Person held to Service or Labour in one State, under the Laws thereof, escaping into another, shall, in Consequence of any Law or Regulation therein, be discharged from such Service or Labour, but shall be delivered up on Claim of the Party to whom such Service or Labour may be due.[9]

Creation and admission of new states

Section 3 New States may be admitted by the Congress into this Union; but no new State shall be formed or erected within the Jurisdiction of any other State; nor any State be formed by the Junction of two or more States, or Parts of States, without the Consent of the Legislatures of the States concerned as well as of the Congress.

Control of national territories and property

The Congress shall have Power to dispose of and make all needful Rules and Regulations respecting the Territory or other Property belonging to the United States; and nothing in this Constitution shall be so construed as to Prejudice any Claims of the United States, or of any particular State.

---

[9]Superseded by the Thirteenth Amendment.

Guarantees to states

Section 4 The United States shall guarantee to every State in this Union a Republican Form of Government, and shall protect each of them against Invasion; and on Application of the Legislature, or of the Executive (when the Legislature cannot be convened) against domestic Violence.

Method of amending the Constitution

ARTICLE V

The Congress, whenever two thirds of both Houses shall deem it necessary, shall propose Amendments to this Constitution, or, on the Application of the Legislatures of two thirds of the several States, shall call a Convention for proposing Amendments, which, in either Case, shall be valid to all Intents and Purposes, as Part of this Constitution, when ratified by the Legislatures of three fourths of the several States, or by Conventions in three fourths thereof, as the one or the other Mode of Ratification may be proposed by the Congress; Provided that no Amendment which may be made prior to the Year One thousand eight hundred and eight shall in any Manner affect the first and fourth Clauses in the Ninth Section of the first Article; and that no State, without its Consent, shall be deprived of its equal Suffrage in the Senate.

Debts, supremacy, oaths

Assumption of Confederation debts

Supremacy of federal laws and treaties

ARTICLE VI

All Debts contracted and Engagements entered into, before the Adoption of this Constitution, shall be as valid against the United States under this Constitution, as under the Confederation.

This Constitution, and the Laws of the United States which shall be made in Pursuance thereof; and all Treaties made, or which shall be made, under the Authority of the United States, shall be the supreme Law of the Land; and the Judges in every State shall be bound thereby, any Thing in the Constitution or Laws of any State to the Contrary notwithstanding.

The Senators and Representatives before mentioned, and the Members of the several State Legislatures, and all executive and judicial Officers, both of the United States and of the several States, shall be bound by Oath or Affirmation, to support this constitution; but no religious Test shall ever be required as a Qualification to any Office or public Trust under the United States.

No religious test for office

Method of ratification of the Constitution

ARTICLE VII

The Ratification of the Conventions of nine States, shall be sufficient for the Establishment of this Constitution between the States so ratifying the Same.

Amendments I–X, known as the "Bill of Rights," ratified in 1791

Freedom of religion, speech, press, assembly

AMENDMENT I

Congress shall make no law respecting an establishment of religion, or prohibiting the free exercise thereof; or abridging the freedom of speech, or of the press; or the right of the people peaceably to assemble, and to petition the Government for a redress of grievances.

AMENDMENT II

Right to bear arms

A well regulated Militia, being necessary to the security of a free State, the right of the people to keep and bear Arms, shall not be infringed.

AMENDMENT III

Restrictions on quartering of troops

No soldier shall, in time of peace be quartered in any house, without the consent of the Owner, nor in time of war, but in a manner to be prescribed by law.

AMENDMENT IV

Prohibition on unreasonable searches and seizures

The right of the people to be secure in their persons, houses, papers, and effects, against unreasonable searches and seizures, shall not be violated, and no Warrants shall issue, but upon probable cause, supported by Oath or affirmation, and particularly describing the place to be searched, and the persons or things to be seized.

AMENDMENT V

Rights of the accused; grand juries; double jeopardy; self-incrimination; due process; eminent domain

No person shall be held to answer for a capital, or otherwise infamous crime, unless on a presentment or indictment of a Grand Jury, except in cases arising in the land or naval forces, or in the Militia, when in actual service in time of War or public danger; nor shall any person be subject for the same offence to be twice put in jeopardy of life or limb; nor shall be compelled in any criminal case to be a witness against himself, nor be deprived of life, liberty, or property, without due process of law; nor shall private property be taken for public use, without just compensation.

AMENDMENT VI

Rights when on trial

In all criminal prosecutions, the accused shall enjoy the right to a speedy and public trial, by an impartial jury of the State and district wherein the crime shall have been committed, which district shall have been previously ascertained by law, and to be informed of the nature and cause of the accusation; to be confronted with the witnesses against him; to have compulsory process for obtaining witnesses in his favor, and to have Assistance of Counsel for his defence.

AMENDMENT VII

Trial by jury in common-law suits

In Suits at common law, where the value in controversy shall exceed twenty dollars, the right of trial by jury shall be preserved, and no fact tried by a jury, shall be otherwise reexamined in any Court of the United States, than according to the rules of the common law.

AMENDMENT VIII

Bails, fines, and punishments

Excessive bail shall not be required, nor excessive fines imposed, nor cruel and unusual punishments inflicted.

AMENDMENT IX

Rights retained by the people

The enumeration in the Constitution, of certain rights, shall not be construed to deny or disparage others retained by the people.

AMENDMENT X

Powers reserved to the states

The powers not delegated to the United States by the Constitution, nor prohibited by it to the States, are reserved to the States respectively, or to the people.

Ratified in 1795

Suits against the states

AMENDMENT XI

The Judicial power of the United States shall not be construed to extend to any suit in law or equity, commenced or prosecuted against one of the United States by Citizens of another State, or by Citizens or Subjects of any Foreign State.

Ratified in 1804

Election of the president and vice president

AMENDMENT XII

The Electors shall meet in their respective states and vote by ballot for President and Vice President, one of whom, at least, shall not be an inhabitant of the same state with themselves; they shall name in their ballots the person voted for as President, and in distinct ballots the person voted for as Vice President, and they shall make distinct lists of all persons voted for as President, and of all persons voted for as Vice President, and of the number of votes for each, which lists they shall sign and certify, and transmit sealed to the seat of the government of the United States, directed to the President of the Senate;—The President of the Senate shall, in the presence of the Senate and House of Representatives, open all the certificates and the votes shall then be counted;—The person having the greatest number of votes for President, shall be the President, if such number be a majority of the whole number of Electors appointed; and if no person have such majority, then from the persons having the highest numbers not exceeding three on the list of those voted for as President, the House of Representatives shall choose immediately, by ballot, the President. But in choosing the President, the votes shall be taken by states, the representation from each state having one vote; a quorum for this purpose shall consist of a member or members from two-thirds of the states, and a majority of all the states shall be necessary to a choice. *And if the House of Representatives shall not choose a President whenever the right of choice shall devolve upon them, before the fourth day of March next following, then the Vice President shall act as President, as in the case of the death or other constitutional disability of the President.*—[10] The person having the greatest number of votes as Vice President, shall be the Vice President, if such number be a majority of the whole number of Electors appointed, and if no person have a majority, then from the two highest numbers on the list, the Senate shall choose the Vice President; a quorum for the purpose shall consist of two-thirds of the whole number of Senators, and a majority of the whole number shall be necessary to a choice. But no person constitutionally ineligible to the office of President shall be eligible to that of Vice President of the United States.

Ratified in 1865

Prohibition of slavery

AMENDMENT XIII

Section 1   Neither slavery nor involuntary servitude, except as a punishment for crime whereof the party shall have been duly convicted, shall exist within the United States, or any place subject to their jurisdiction.

Section 2   Congress shall have power to enforce this article by appropriate legislation.

---

[10]Superseded by the Twentieth Amendment, Section 3.

Citizenship; requirement of "due process" and "equal protection of the laws" by the states

AMENDMENT XIV

Section 1   All persons born or naturalized in the United States and subject to the jurisdiction thereof, are citizens of the United States and of the State wherein they reside. No State shall make or enforce any law which shall abridge the privileges or immunities of citizens of the United States; nor shall any State deprive any person of life, liberty, or property, without due process of law; nor deny to any person within its jurisdiction the equal protection of the laws.

Section 2   Representatives shall be apportioned among the several States according to their respective numbers, counting the whole number of persons in each State, excluding Indians not taxed. But when the right to vote at any election for the choice of electors for President and Vice President of the United States, Representatives in Congress, the Executive and Judicial officers of a State, or the members of the Legislature thereof, is denied to any of the male inhabitants of such State, being *twenty-one*[11] years of age, and citizens of the United States, or in any way abridged except for participation in rebellion, or other crime, the basis of representation therein shall be reduced in the proportion which the number of such male citizens shall bear to the whole number of male citizens twenty-one years in such State.

Section 3   No person shall be a Senator or Representative in Congress, or elector of President and Vice President, or hold any office, civil or military, under the United States, or under any State, who, having previously taken an oath as a member of Congress, or as an officer of the United States, or as a member of any State legislature, or as an executive or judicial officer of any State, to support the Constitution of the United States, shall have engaged in insurrection or rebellion against the same, or given aid or comfort to the enemies thereof. But Congress may by a vote of two-thirds of each House, remove such disability.

Section 4   The validity of the public debt of the United States, authorized by law, including debts incurred for payment of pensions and bounties for services in suppressing insurrection or rebellion, shall not be questioned. But neither the United States nor any State shall assume or pay any debt or obligation incurred in aid of insurrection or rebellion against the United States, or any claim for the loss or emancipation of any slave; but all such debts, obligations and claims shall be held illegal and void.

Section 5   The Congress shall have power to enforce, by appropriate legislation, the provisions of this article.

Ratified in 1870

Right to vote cannot be abridged on racial grounds

AMENDMENT XV

Section 1   The right of citizens of the United States to vote shall not be denied or abridged by the United States or by any State on account of race, color, or previous condition of servitude.

Section 2   The Congress shall have power to enforce this article by appropriate legislation.

[11]Changed by the Twenty-Sixth Amendment.

Ratified in 1913

Permits federal income tax

AMENDMENT XVI

The Congress shall have power to lay and collect taxes on incomes, from whatever source derived, without apportionment among the several States, and without regard to any census or enumeration.

Ratified in 1913

Popular election of senators

AMENDMENT XVII

The Senate of the United States shall be composed of two Senators from each State, elected by the people thereof, for six years; and each Senator shall have one vote. The electors in each State shall have the qualifications requisite for electors of the most numerous branch of the State legislatures.

When vacancies happen in the representation of any State in the Senate, the executive authority of such State shall issue writs of election to fill such vacancies: *Provided,* That the legislature of any State may empower the executive thereof to make temporary appointments until the people fill the vacancies by election as the legislature may direct.

This amendment shall not be so construed as to affect the election or term of any Senator chosen before it becomes valid as part of the Constitution.

Ratified in 1919

Prohibition of manufacture and sale of liquor

AMENDMENT XVIII

Section 1 *After one year from the ratification of this article the manufacture, sale, or transportation of intoxicating liquors within, the importation thereof into, or the exportation thereof from the United States and all territory subject to the jurisdiction thereof for beverage purposes is hereby prohibited.*

Section 2 *The Congress and the several States shall have concurrent power to enforce this article by appropriate legislation.*

Section 3 *This article shall be inoperative unless it shall have been ratified as an amendment to the Constitution by the legislatures of the several States, as provided in the Constitution, within seven years from the date of the submission hereof to the States by the Congress.*[12]

Ratified in 1920

Right to vote cannot be abridged on grounds of sex

AMENDMENT XIX

The right of citizens of the United States to vote shall not be denied or abridged by the United States or by any State on account of sex.

Congress shall have power to enforce this article by appropriate legislation.

Ratified in 1933

Terms of office

AMENDMENT XX

Section 1 The terms of the President and Vice President shall end at noon on the 20th day of January, and the terms of Senators and Representatives at noon on the 3d day of January, of the years in which such terms would have ended if this article had not been ratified; and the terms of their successors shall then begin.

---

[12]Repealed by the Twenty-First Amendment.

Convening of Congress

Section 2 The Congress shall assemble at least once in every year, and such meeting shall begin at noon on the 3d day of January, unless they shall by law appoint a different day.

Presidential succession

Section 3 If, at the time fixed for the beginning of the term of the President, the President elect shall have died, the Vice President elect shall become President. If a President shall not have been chosen before the time fixed for the beginning of his term, or if the President elect shall have failed to qualify, then the Vice President elect shall act as President until a President shall have qualified; and the Congress may by law provide for the case wherein neither a President elect nor a Vice President elect shall have qualified, declaring who shall then act as President, or the manner in which one who is to act shall be selected, and such person shall act accordingly until a President or Vice President shall have qualified.

Section 4 The Congress may by law provide for the case of the death of any of the persons from whom the House of Representatives may choose a President whenever the right of choice shall have devolved upon them, and for the case of the death of any of the persons from whom the Senate may choose a Vice President whenever the right of choice shall have devolved upon them.

Section 5 Sections 1 and 2 shall take effect on the 15th day of October following the ratification of this article.

Section 6 This article shall be inoperative unless it shall have been ratified as an amendment to the Constitution by the legislatures of three-fourths of the several States within seven years from the date of its submission.

Ratified in 1933

AMENDMENT XXI

Prohibition repealed

Section 1 The eighteenth article of amendment to the Constitution of the United States is hereby repealed.

Section 2 The transportation or importation into any State, Territory, or possession of the United States for delivery or use therein of intoxicating liquors, in violation of the laws thereof, is hereby prohibited.

Section 3 This article shall be inoperative unless it shall have been ratified as an amendment to the Constitution by conventions in the several States, as provided in the Constitution, within seven years from the date of the submission hereof to the States by the Congress.

Ratified in 1951

AMENDMENT XXII

Limitations on president's term of office

Section 1 No person shall be elected to the office of the President more than twice, and no person who has held the office of President, or acted as President, for more than two years of a term to which some other person was elected President shall be elected to the office of the President more than once. But this Article shall not apply to any person holding the office of President when this Article was proposed by the Congress, and shall not prevent any person who may be holding the office of President, or acting as President, during the term within which this Article becomes operative from holding the office of President or acting as President during the remainder of such term.

Section 2 This Article shall be inoperative unless it shall have been ratified as an amendment to the Constitution by the legislatures of three-fourths of the several States within seven years from the date of its submission to the States by the Congress.

Ratified in 1961

Presidential electors for the District of Columbia

AMENDMENT XXIII

Section 1 The District constituting the seat of Government of the United States shall appoint in such manner as the Congress may direct:

A number of electors of President and Vice President equal to the whole number of Senators and Representatives in Congress to which the District would be entitled if it were a State, but in no event more than the least populous State; they shall be in addition to those appointed by the States, but they shall be considered, for the purposes of the election of President and Vice President, to be electors appointed by a State; and they shall meet in the District and perform such duties as provided by the twelfth article of amendment.

Section 2 The Congress shall have power to enforce this article by appropriate legislation.

Ratified in 1964

Poll taxes banned for federal elections

AMENDMENT XXIV

Section 1 The right of citizens of the United States to vote in any primary or other election for President or Vice President, for electors for President or Vice President, or for Senator or Representative in Congress, shall not be denied or abridged by the United States or any State by reason of failure to pay any poll tax or other tax.

Section 2 The Congress shall have power to enforce this article by appropriate legislation.

Ratified in 1967

Presidential disability

Method of filling vice presidential vacancies

AMENDMENT XXV

Section 1 In case of the removal of the President from office or of his death or resignation, the Vice President shall become President.

Section 2 Whenever there is a vacancy in the office of the Vice President, the President shall nominate a Vice President who shall take office upon confirmation by a majority vote of both Houses of Congress.

Section 3 Whenever the President transmits to the President pro tempore of the Senate and the Speaker of the House of Representatives his written declaration that he is unable to discharge the powers and duties of his office, and until he transmits to them a written declaration to the contrary, such powers and duties shall be discharged by the Vice President as Acting President.

Section 4 Whenever the Vice President and a majority of either the principal officers of the executive departments or of such other body as Congress may by law provide, transmit to the President pro tempore of the Senate and the Speaker of the House of Representatives their written declaration that the President is unable to discharge the powers and duties of his office, the Vice President shall immediately assume the powers and duties of the office as Acting President.

Thereafter, when the President transmits to the President pro tempore of the Senate and the Speaker of the House of Representatives his written declaration that no inability exists, he shall resume the powers and duties of his office unless the Vice President and a majority of either the principal officers of the executive department or of such other body as Congress may by law provide, transmit within four days to the President pro tempore of the Senate and the Speaker of the House of Representatives their written declaration that the President is unable to discharge the powers and duties of his office. Thereupon Congress shall decide the issue, assembling within forty-eight hours for that purpose if not in session. If the Congress, within twenty-one days after receipt of the latter written declaration, or, if Congress is not in session, within twenty-one days after Congress is required to assemble, determines by two-thirds vote of both Houses that the President is unable to discharge the powers and duties of his office, the Vice President shall continue to discharge the same as Acting President; otherwise, the President shall resume the powers and duties of his office.

Ratified in 1971

Voting age set at 18 years old

AMENDMENT XXVI

Section 1 The right of citizens of the United States, who are eighteen years of age or older, to vote shall not be denied or abridged by the United States or by any State on account of age.

Section 2 The Congress shall have power to enforce this article by appropriate legislation.

Appendix 3

The Federalist: Number 10 and Number 51

Note: *The Federalist* was a series of eighty-five essays published during the ratification debate (1787–1788) in support of the Constitution. The essays bore the pen name "Publius"; they were written by James Madison, Alexander Hamilton, and John Jay. *Federalist* 10 and *Federalist* 51, written by James Madison, are widely considered to be two of the most important papers in the series.

NUMBER 10

Among the numerous advantages promised by a well-constructed Union, none deserves to be more accurately developed than its tendency to break and control the violence of faction. The friend of popular governments never finds himself so much alarmed for their character and fate as when he contemplates their propensity to this dangerous vice. He will not fail, therefore, to set a due value on any plan which, without violating the principles to which he is attached, provides a proper cure for it. The instability, injustice, and confusion introduced into the public councils have, in truth, been the mortal diseases under which popular governments have everywhere perished, as they continue to be the favorite and fruitful topics from which the adversaries to liberty derive their most specious declamations. The valuable improvements made by the American constitutions on the popular models, both ancient and modern, cannot certainly be too much admired; but it would be an unwarrantable partiality to contend that they have as effectually obviated the danger on this side, as was wished and expected. Complaints are everywhere heard from our most considerate and virtuous citizens, equally the friends of public and private faith and of public and personal liberty, that our governments are too unstable, that the public good is disregarded in the conflicts of rival parties, and that measures are too often decided, not according to the rules of justice and the rights of the minor party, but by the superior force of an interested and overbearing majority. However anxiously we may wish that these complaints had no foundation, the evidence of known facts will not permit us to deny that they are in some degree true. It will be found, indeed, on a candid review of our situation, that some of the distresses under which we labor have been erroneously charged on the operation of our governments; but it will be found, at the same time, that other causes will not alone account for many of our heaviest misfortunes; and, particularly, for that prevailing and increasing distrust of public engagements and alarm for private rights which are echoed from one end of the continent to the other. These must be chiefly, if not wholly, effects of the unsteadiness and injustice with which a factious spirit has tainted our public administration.

659

By a faction I understand a number of citizens, whether amounting to a majority or minority of the whole, who are united and actuated by some common impulse of passion, or of interest, adverse to the rights of other citizens, or to the permanent and aggregate interests of the community.

There are two methods of curing the mischiefs of faction: the one, by removing its causes; the other, by controlling its effects.

There are again two methods of removing the causes of faction: the one, by destroying the liberty which is essential to its existence; the other, by giving to every citizen the same opinions, the same passions, and the same interests.

It could never be more truly said than of the first remedy that it was worse than the disease. Liberty is to faction what air is to fire, an ailment without which it instantly expires. But it could not be a less folly to abolish liberty, which is essential to political life, because it nourishes faction than it would be to wish the annihilation of air, which is essential to animal life, because it imparts to fire its destructive agency.

The second expedient is as impracticable as the first would be unwise. As long as the reason of man continues fallible, and he is at liberty to exercise it, different opinions will be formed. As long as the connection subsists between his reason and his self-love, his opinions and his passions will have a reciprocal influence on each other; and the former will be objects to which the latter will attach themselves. The diversity in the faculties of men, from which the rights of property originate, is not less an insuperable obstacle to a uniformity of interests. The protection of these faculties is the first object of government. From the protection of different and unequal faculties of acquiring property, the possession of different degrees and kinds of property immediately results; and from the influence of these on the sentiments and views of the respective proprietors ensues a division of the society into different interests and parties.

The latent causes of faction are thus sown in the nature of man; and we see them everywhere brought into different degrees of activity, according to the different circumstances of civil society. A zeal for different opinions concerning religion, concerning government, and many other points, as well of speculation as of practice; an attachment to different leaders ambitiously contending for pre-eminence and power; or to persons of other descriptions whose fortunes have been interesting to the human passions, have, in turn, divided mankind into

parties, inflamed them with mutual animosity, and rendered them much more disposed to vex and oppress each other than to co-operate for their common good. So strong is this propensity of mankind to fall into mutual animosities that where no substantial occasion presents itself the most frivolous and fanciful distinctions have been sufficient to kindle their unfriendly passions and excite their most violent conflicts. But the most common and durable source of factions has been the verious and unequal distribution of property. Those who hold and those who are without property have ever formed distinct interests in society. Those who are creditors, and those who are debtors, fall under a like discrimination. A landed interest, a manufacturing interest, a mercantile interest, a moneyed interest, with many lesser interests, grow up of necessity in civilized nations, and divide them into different classes, actuated by different sentiments and views. The regulation of these various and interfering interests forms the principal task of modern legislation and involves the spirit of party and faction in the necessary and ordinary operations of government.

No man is allowed to be a judge in his own cause, because his interest would certainly bias his judgment, and, not improbably, corrupt his integrity. With equal, nay with greater reason, a body of men are unfit to be both judges and parties at the same time; yet what are many of the most important acts of legislation but so many judicial determinations, not indeed concerning the rights of single persons, but concerning the rights of large bodies of citizens? And what are the different classes of legislators but advocates and parties to the causes which they determine? Is a law proposed concerning private debts? It is a question to which the creditors are parties on one side and the debtors on the other. Justice ought to hold the balance between them. Yet the parties are, and must be, themselves the judges; and the most numerous party, or in other words, the most powerful faction must be expected to prevail. Shall domestic manufacturers be encouraged, and in what degree, by restrictions on foreign manufacturers? are questions which would be differently decided by the landed and the manufacturing classes, and probably by neither with a sole regard to justice and the public good. The apportionment of taxes on the various descriptions of property is an act which seems to require the most exact impartiality; yet there is, perhaps, no legislative act in which greater opportunity and temptation are given to a predominant party to trample on the rules of justice. Every shilling with which they overburden the inferior number is a shilling saved to their own pockets.

It is in vain to say that enlightened statesmen will be able to adjust these clashing interests and render them all subservient to the public good. Enlightened statesmen will not always be at the helm. Nor, in many cases, can such an adjustment be made at all without taking into view indirect and remote considerations, which will rarely prevail over the immediate interest which one party may find in disregarding the rights of another or the good of the whole.

The inference to which we are brought is that the *causes* of faction cannot be removed and that relief is only to be sought in the means of controlling its *effects*.

If a faction consists of less than a majority, relief is supplied by the republican principle, which enables the majority to defeat its sinister views by regular vote. It may clog the administration, it may convulse the society; but it will be unable to execute and mask its violence under the forms of the Constitution. When a majority is included in a faction, the form of popular government, on the other hand, enables it to sacrifice to its ruling passion or interest both the public good and the rights of other citizens. To secure the public good and private rights against the danger of such a faction, and at the same time to preserve the spirit and the form of popular government, is then the great object to which our inquiries are directed. Let me add that it is the great desideratum by which alone this form of government can be rescued from the opprobrium under which it has so long labored and be recommended to the esteem and adoption of mankind.

By what means is this object attainable? Evidently by one of two only. Either the existence of the same passion or interest in a majority at the same time must be prevented, or the majority, having such coexistent passion or interest, must be rendered, by their number and local situation, unable to concert and carry into effect schemes of oppression. If the impulse and the opportunity be suffered to coincide, we well know that neither moral nor religious motives can be relied on as an adequate control. They are not found to be such on the injustice and violence of individuals, and lose their efficacy in proportion to the number combined together, that is, in proportion as their efficacy becomes needful.

From this view of the subject it may be concluded that a pure democracy, by which I mean a society consisting of a small number of citizens, who assemble and administer the government in person, can admit of no cure for the mischiefs of faction. A common passion or interest will, in almost every case, be felt by a majority of the whole; a communication and concert results from the form of government itself; and there is nothing to check the inducements to sacrifice the weaker party or an obnoxious individual. Hence it is that such democracies have ever been spectacles of turbulence and contention; have ever been found incompatible with personal security or the rights of property; and have in general been as short in their lives as they have been violent in their deaths. Theoretic politicians, who have patronized this species of government, have erroneously supposed that by reducing mankind to a perfect equality in their political rights, they would at the same time be perfectly equalized and assimilated in their possessions, their opinions, and their passions.

A republic, by which I mean a government in which the scheme of representation takes place, opens a different prospect and promises the cure for which we are seeking. Let us examine the points in which it varies from pure democracy, and we shall comprehend both the nature of the cure and the efficacy which it must derive from the Union.

The two great points of difference between a democracy and a republic are: first, the delegation of the government, in the latter, to a small number of citizens elected by the rest; secondly, the greater number of citizens and greater sphere of country over which the latter may be extended.

The effect of the first difference is, on the one hand, to refine and enlarge the public views by passing them through the medium of a chosen body of citizens, whose wisdom may best discern the true interest of their country and whose patriotism and love of justice will be least likely to sacrifice it to temporary or partial considerations. Under such a regulation it may well happen that the public voice, pronounced by the representatives of the people, will be more consonant to the public good than if pronounced by the people themselves, convened for the purpose. On the other hand, the effect may be inverted. Men of factious tempers, of local prejudices, or of sinister designs, may, by intrigue, by corruption, or by other means, first obtain the suffrages, and then betray the interests of the people. The question resulting is, whether small or extensive republics are most favorable to the election of proper guardians of the public weal; and it is clearly decided in favor of the latter by two obvious considerations.

In the first place it is to be remarked that however

small the republic may be the representatives must be raised to a certain number in order to guard against the cabals of a few; and that however large it may be they must be limited to a certain number in order to guard against the confusion of a multitude. Hence, the number of representatives in the two cases not being in proportion to that of the constituents, and being proportionally greatest in the small republic, it follows that if the proportion of fit characters be not less in the large than in the small republic, the former will present a greater option, and consequently a greater probability of a fit choice.

In the next place, as each representative will be chosen by a greater number of citizens in the large than in the small republic, it will be more difficult for unworthy candidates to practise with success the vicious arts by which elections are too often carried; and the suffrages of the people being more free, will be more likely to center on men who possess the most attractive merit and the most diffusive and established characters.

It must be confessed that in this, as in most other cases, there is a mean, on both sides of which inconveniencies will be found to lie. By enlarging too much the number of electors, you render the representative too little acquainted with all their local circumstances and lesser interests; as by reducing it too much, you render him unduly attached to these, and too little fit to comprehend and pursue great and national objects. The federal Constitution forms a happy combination in this respect; the great and aggregate interests being referred to the national, the local and particular to the State legislatures.

The other point of difference is the greater number of citizens and extent of territory which may be brought within the compass of republican than of democratic government; and it is this circumstance principally which renders factious combinations less to be dreaded in the former than in the latter. The smaller the society, the fewer probably will be the distinct parties and interests composing it; the fewer the distinct parties and interests, the more frequently will a majority be found of the same party; and the smaller the number of individuals composing a majority, and the smaller the compass within which they are placed, the more easily will they concert and execute their plans of oppression. Extend the sphere and you take in a greater variety of parties and interests; you make it less probable that a majority of the whole will have a common motive to invade the rights of other citizens; or if such a common motive exists, it will be more difficult for all who feel it to discover their own strength and to act in unison with each other. Besides other impediments, it may be remarked that, where there is a consciousness of unjust or dishonorable purposes, communication is always checked by distrust in proportion to the number whose concurrence is necessary.

Hence, it clearly appears that the same advantage which a republic has over a democracy in controlling the effects of faction is enjoyed by a large over a small republic—is enjoyed by the Union over the States composing it. Does this advantage consist in the substitution of representatives whose enlightened views and virtuous sentiments render them superior to local prejudices and to schemes of injustice? It will not be denied that the representation of the Union will be most likely to possess these requisite endowments. Does it consist in the greater security afforded by a greater variety of parties, against the event of any one party being able to outnumber and oppress the rest? In an equal degree does the increased variety of parties comprised within the Union increase this security. Does it, in fine, consist in the greater obstacles opposed to the concert and accomplishment of the secret wishes of an unjust and interested majority? Here again the extent of the Union gives it the most palpable advantage.

The influence of factious leaders may kindle a flame within their particular States but will be unable to spread a general conflagration through the other States. A religious sect may degenerate into a political faction in a part of the Confederacy; but the variety of sects dispersed over the entire face of it must secure the national councils against any danger from that source. A rage for paper money, for an abolition of debts, for an equal division of property, or for any other improper or wicked project, will be less apt to pervade the whole body of the Union than a particular member of it, in the same proportion as such a malady is more likely to taint a particular county or district than an entire State.

In the extent and proper structure of the Union, therefore, we behold a republican remedy for the diseases most incident to republican government. And according to the degree of pleasure and pride we feel in being republicans ought to be our zeal in cherishing the spirit and supporting the character of federalists.

PUBLIUS

NUMBER 51

To what expedient, then, shall we finally resort, for maintaining in practice the necessary partition of power among the several departments as laid down in the Constitution? The only answer that can be given is that as all these exterior provisions are found to be inadequate the defect must be supplied, by so contriving the interior structure of the government as that its several constituent parts may, by their mutual relations, be the means of keeping each other in their proper places. Without presuming to undertake a full development of this important idea I will hazard a few general observations which may perhaps place it in a clearer light, and enable us to form a more correct judgment of the principles and structure of the government planned by the convention.

In order to lay a due foundation for that separate and distinct exercise of the different powers of government, which to a certain extent is admitted on all hands to be essential to the preservation of liberty, it is evident that each department should have a will of its own; and consequently should be so constituted that the members of each should have as little agency as possible in the appointment of the members of the others. Were this principle rigorously adhered to, it would require that all the appointments for the supreme executive, legislative, and judiciary magistracies should be drawn from the same fountain of authority, the people, through channels having no communication whatever with one another. Perhaps such a plan of constructing the several departments would be less difficult in practice than it may in contemplation appear. Some difficulties, however, and some additional expense would attend the execution of it. Some deviations, therefore, from the principle must be admitted. In the constitution of the judiciary department in particular, it might be inexpedient to insist rigorously on the principle: first, because peculiar qualifications being essential in the members, the primary consideration ought to be to select that mode of choice which best secures these qualifications; second, because the permanent tenure by which the appointments are held in that department must soon destroy all sense of dependence on the authority conferring them.

It is equally evident that the members of each department should be as little dependent as possible on those of the others for the emoluments annexed to their offices. Were the executive magistrate, or the judges, not independent of the legislature in this particular, their independence in every other would be merely nominal.

But the great security against a gradual concentration of the several powers in the same department consists in giving to those who administer each department the necessary constitutional means and personal motives to resist encroachments of the others. The provision for defense must in this, as in all other cases, be made commensurate to the danger of attack. Ambition must be made to counteract ambition. The interest of the man must be connected with the constitutional rights of the place. It may be a reflection on human nature that such devices should be necessary to control the abuses of government. But what is government itself but the greatest of all reflections on human nature? If men were angels, no government would be necessary. If angels were to govern men, neither external nor internal controls on government would be necessary. In framing a government which is to be administered by men over men, the great difficulty lies in this: you must first enable the government to control the governed; and in the next place oblige it to control itself. A dependence on the people is, no doubt, the primary control on the government; but experience has taught mankind the necessity of auxiliary precautions.

This policy of supplying, by opposite and rival interests, the defect of better motives, might be traced through the whole system of human affairs, private as well as public. We see it particularly displayed in all the subordinate distributions of power, where the constant aim is to divide and arrange the several offices in such a manner as that each may be a check on the other—that the private interest of every individual may be a sentinel over the public rights. These inventions of prudence cannot be less requisite in the distribution of the supreme powers of the State.

But it is not possible to give to each department an equal power of self-defense. In republican government, the legislative authority necessarily predominates. The remedy for this inconveniency is to divide the legislature into different branches; and to render them, by different modes of election and different principles of action, as little connected with each other as the nature of their common functions and their common dependence on the society will admit. It may even be necessary to guard against dangerous encroachments by still further precautions. As the weight of the legislative authority requires that it should be thus divided, the weakness of the executive may require, on the other hand, that it should be fortified. An absolute negative on the legislature appears, at first view, to be the natural defense with which the executive magistrate should be armed. But perhaps it would be neither altogether safe nor alone sufficient. On ordinary occasions it might not be exerted with the requisite firmness, and on extraordinary occasions it might be perfidiously abused. May not this defect of an absolute negative be supplied by some qualified connection between this weaker department and the weaker branch of the stronger department, by which the latter may be led to support the constitutional rights of the former, without being too much detached from the rights of its own department?

If the principles on which these observations are founded be just, as I persuade myself they are, and they be applied as a criterion to the several State constitutions, and to the federal Constitution, it will be found that if the latter does not perfectly correspond with them, the former are infinitely less able to bear such a test.

There are, moreover, two considerations particularly applicable to the federal system of America, which place that system in a very interesting point of view.

First. In a single republic, all the power surrendered by the people is submitted to the administration of a single government; and the usurpations are guarded against by a division of the government into distinct and separate departments. In the compound republic of America, the power surrendered by the people is first divided between two distinct governments, and then the portion allotted to each subdivided among distinct and separate departments. Hence a double security arises to the rights of the people. The different governments will control each other, at the same time that each will be controlled by itself.

Second. It is of great importance in a republic not only to guard the society against the oppression of its rulers, but to guard one part of the society against the injustice of the other part. Different interests necessarily exist in different classes of citizens. If a majority be united by a common interest, the rights of the minority will be insecure. There are but two methods of providing against this evil: the one by creating a will in the community independent of the majority—that is, of the society itself; the other, by comprehending in the society so many separate descriptions of citizens as will render an unjust combination of a majority of the whole very improbable, if not impracticable. The first method prevails in all governments possessing an hereditary or self-appointed authority. This, at best, is but a precarious security; because a power independent of the society may as well espouse the unjust views of the major as the rightful interests of the minor party, and may possibly be turned against both parties. The second method will be exemplified in the federal republic of the United States. Whilst all authority in it will be derived from and dependent on the society, the society itself will be broken into so many parts, interests and classes of citizens, that the rights of individuals, or of the minority, will be in little danger from interested combinations of the majority. In a free government the security for civil rights must be the same as that for religious rights. It consists in the one case in the multiplicity of interests, and in the other in the multiplicity of sects. The degree of security in both cases will depend on the number of interests and sects; and this may be presumed to depend on the extent of country and number of people comprehended under the same government. This view of the subject must particularly recommend a proper federal system to all the sincere and considerate friends of republican government, since it shows that in exact proportion as the territory of the Union may be formed into more circumscribed Confederacies, or States, oppressive combinations of a majority will be facilitated; the best security, under the republican forms, for the rights of every class of citizen, will be diminished; and consequently the stability and independence of some member of the government, the only other security, must be proportionally increased. Justice is the end of government. It is the end of civil society. It ever has been and ever will be pursued until it be obtained, or until liberty be lost in the pursuit. In a society under the forms of which the stronger faction can readily unite and oppress the weaker, anarchy may as truly be said to reign as in a state of nature, where the weaker individual is not secured against the violence of the stronger; and as, in the latter state, even the stronger individuals are prompted, by the uncertainty of their condition, to submit to a government which may protect the weak as well as themselves; so, in the former state, will the more powerful factions or parties be gradually induced, by a like motive, to wish for a government which will protect all parties, the weaker as well as the more powerful. It can be little doubted that if the State of Rhode Island was separated from the Confederacy and left to itself, the insecurity of rights under the popular form of government within such narrow limits would be displayed by such reiterated oppressions of factious majorities that some power altogether independent of the people would soon be called for by the voice of the very factions whose misrule had proved the necessity of it. In the extended republic of the United States, and among the great variety of interests, parties, and sects which it embraces, a coalition of a majority of the whole society could seldom take place on any other principles than those of justice and the general good; whilst there being thus less danger to a minor from the will of a major party, there must be less pretext, also, to provide for the security of the former, by introducing into the government a will not dependent on the latter, or, in other words, a will independent of the society itself. It is no less certain than it is important, notwithstanding the contrary opinions which have been entertained, that the larger the society, provided it lie within a practicable sphere, the more duly capable it will be of self-government. And happily for the *republican cause,* the practicable sphere may be carried to a very great extent by a judicious modification and mixture of the *federal principle.*

PUBLIUS

Acknowledgments

"American public opinion on welfare issues." Table adapted from Hastings, Elizabeth Hann, and Philip K. Hastings, eds. 1982. INDEX TO INTERNATIONAL PUBLIC OPINION, 1980–1981. Westport, Connecticut: Greenwood Press. P. 366. Reprinted by permission of Louis Harris and Associates, Inc.; Gallup Report (April 1982:7), American Public Opinion on Welfare Issues.

"Application of criminal procedural rights to the states." Box reprinted from Rossum, Ralph A. THE POLITICS OF THE CRIMINAL JUSTICE SYSTEM. AN ORGANIZATIONAL ANALYSIS. New York: Marcel Dekker, 1978. Reprinted from p. 125 by courtesy of Marcel Dekker, Inc.

"Apportionment of Congressional seats by region, 1910 and 1984." Figure 9-1 reprinted from Norman J. Ornstein, Thomas E. Mann, Michael J. Malbin, and John F. Bibby, VITAL STATISTICS ON CONGRESS, 1982. Washington, D.C.: American Enterprise Institute, 1982, p. 52, updated by present authors.

"Attitudes on equality of the races." Figure 4-4. Sources: National Opinion Research Center, General Social Surveys, 1958–1970, 1972, 1976, 1977, 1980; and survey by the Gallup Organization, latest that of July 21–24, 1973. Reprinted with permission.

"Attitudes on political economy." Figure 4-3. Sources: Cambridge Reports, March 12–22, 1976, and May 21–June 13, 1979; Civic Service, Inc., March 5–18, 1981; Louis Harris and Associates survey conducted for Atlantic Richfield Company, October 15–26, 1982. Reprinted with permission.

"Attitudes of selected groups on the three dimensions of liberalism and conservatism." Table reprinted from Garry Owen and E. J. Dionne, "The Next New Deal," *Working Papers,* May, June 1981. Copyright Trusteeship Institute 1981.

"Attitudes on support for the political system and on political culture." Figure 4-5. Sources: Gabriel A. Almond and Sidney Verba. THE CIVIC CULTURE: POLITICAL ATTITUDES AND DEMOCRACY IN FIVE NATIONS. P. 102. Copyright 1963 by Princeton University Press, Little, Brown and Co., Inc., Copyright 1965; Roper Organization (Roper Reports, 77-3), February 12–26, 1977; National Election Studies, Center for Political Studies, University of Michigan; American Enterprise Institute, Public Opinion Magazine, January–February 1979. Reprinted with permission.

"Average yearly presidential approval rating, 1953–1980." Figure 10-1. Gallup Opinion Index. Reprinted with permission.

"Blacks and women in Congress, 1947–1982." Table reprinted from *Guide to Congress,* 2d ed., Congressional Quarterly, Inc., Washington, D.C., 1976, pp. 526–528. *Congressional Almanacs,* 1977–1982,

Congressional Quarterly, Inc.. Reprinted with permission.

Carter, Jimmy. Portrayal. Excerpts from James Fallows, "The Passionless Presidency," June 1979. Copyright 1979 by the Atlantic Monthly Company, Boston, Massachusetts. Reprinted with permission.

"Characteristics of political activists." Figure 7-4. Reprinted from Raymond Wolfinger, Martin Shapiro, and Fred Greenstein, DYNAMICS OF AMERICAN POLITICS, 2d ed., 1980, p. 220. Reprinted by permission of Prentice-Hall, Inc., Englewood Cliffs, N.J.

"A contemporary looks at his fellow delegates." Box. Excerpts from Farrand, Max, ed. THE RECORDS OF THE FEDERAL CONVENTION OF 1787. Four Volumes. Revised Edition. New Haven, Connecticut: Yale University Press, 1966. Volume III, 87–97.

"Dates of enactment of various social welfare programs, selected countries." Figure 16-1. Adapted from COMPARATIVE PUBLIC POLICY by Heidenheimer, Heclo, and Adams. Copyright 1975 by St. Martin's Press and reprinted by permission of the publisher.

"Department of State in 1983." Chart. Adapted from Henry Kissinger, YEARS OF UPHEAVAL. P. 98. Boston: Little, Brown and Company. Copyright 1982 by Henry A. Kissinger. Also adapted from the Washington Monitor, FEDERAL YELLOW BOOK, 1982. Reprinted with permission.

"The Elections of 1800, 1828, 1860, 1896, 1932." *The Congressional Quarterly Guide to U.S. Elections.* Reprinted by permission of the Congressional Quarterly, Inc.

"The election of 1980." Congressional Quarterly Weekly Reports, April 25, 1981, America Votes, 1981: 19–20; and Congressional Quarterly, 1981, America Votes, ed. Richard Scammon and Alice McGillivray, Washington D.C., Congressional Quarterly, Inc. 1981; American Enterprise Institute, Public Opinion Magazine, February/March 1980, December/January 1982, August/September 1982: Gallup Organization Surveys, the latest that of June 25–28, 1982. Reprinted by permission.

"The exclusionary rule and the corruption of justice." Box. From Oaks, Dallin H., "Studying the Exclusionary Rule in Search and Seizure," copyright 1970 by the University of Chicago. Reprinted by permission from 37 U. Chi. L. Rev. 698 (1970).

"The expansion of the role of the federal government." Quotation from Herbert Kaufman, RED TAPE (Washington, D.C.: Brookings Institution), 1977. Reprinted with permission.

"Family background of early higher-ranking bureaucrats." Table adapted from Aronson, Sidney H. 1964. STATUS AND KINSHIP IN THE HIGHER CIVIL SERVICE. Cambridge: Harvard University Press, p. 61. Reprinted with permission.

"Ideology of federal higher civil service compared with general population." Table reprinted from Meier, Kenneth J. POLITICS AND THE BUREAUCRACY. 1979. North Scituate, MA: Duxbury Press. P. 173. (From Ph.D dissertation, Syracuse University, 1975.)

"Ideological orientation of the American populace." Figure 4-6. American Enterprise Institute, Public Opinion Magazine, October/November 1982; National Opinion Research Center, General Social Surveys, Feburary to April, 1982; surveys by Gallup Opinion Index. Reprinted with permission.

"Incumbency in the House and Senate, 1946–1982, Advantage of." Table reprinted from Congressional Quarterly Weekly Report, April 5, 1980, p. 908; and November 9, 1980, pp. 3302, 3320–3321. Congressional Quarterly, Inc.

"Individual income tax rates before tax reductions enacted 1981–1984." Table from Pechman, Joseph A. 1977. FEDERAL TAX POLICY, 3d ed. Brookings Institution, Washington, D.C., 1977:72, 349–350.

"The Influence of Group Membership on Opinions." Reprinted from American Enterprises Institute, Public Opinion Magazine, April/May 1981 and April/May 1982; CBS, New York Times Poll: Grankovick, 1982:445

Lyndon B. Johnson. Portrayal. Abridged excerpts from pages 176, 178, 239–240 in LYNDON JOHNSON AND THE AMERICAN DREAM by Doris Kearns. Copyright 1976 by Doris Kearns. Reprinted by permission of Harper & Row, Publishers, Inc.

"Judicial activism and restraint." Box. Abridged excerpt from Walter F. Murphy and C. Herman Pritchett: COURTS, JUDGES AND POLITICS. New York: Random House, 1979 pp. 60–61 and p. 729.

"Major parties." Figure 5-1. Reprinted from the *Congressional Quarterly Guide to U.S. Elections,* Congressional Quarterly, Inc. Reprinted with permission.

"Membership in various types of organizations, by nation." Table reprinted from Gabriel A. Almond and Sidney Verba, THE CIVIC CULTURE: POLITICAL ATTITUDES AND DEMOCRACY IN FIVE NATIONS. Copyright 1963 by Princeton University Press; Little, Brown and Company, Inc., © 1965. Table, p. 302, reprinted by permission of Princeton University Press.

"Growth of nonparty political action committees, 1974–1980." Figure 8-2 reprinted from Ornstein, Norman J., Thomas E. Mann, Michael J. Malbin, and John F. Bibby, VITAL STATISTICS ON CONGRESS, 1982, Washington, D.C.: American Enterprise Institute, 1982, p. 75.

"Occupations of Supreme Court designees at time of appointment." Table reprinted from THE JUDICIAL PROCESS: AN INTRODUCTORY ANALYSIS OF THE COURTS OF THE UNITED STATES, ENGLAND, AND FRANCE, 4th ed., by Henry J. Abraham. Copyright 1962, 1968, 1975, 1980 by Oxford University Press, Inc. Reprinted with permission.

"Participation in presidential elections (1860–1980) and House elections (1930–1982)." Figure 7-2. Reprinted from *Historical Statistics of the United States, Colonial Times to 1970, 1975*:1071–1072; *Statistical Abstract of the United States 1980*, 1980:517; *Congressional Quarterly Weekly Report*, November 13, 1982.2050, Ornstein, Norman J., Thomas E. Mann, Michael L. Malbin, and John F. Bibby, VITAL STATISTICS ON CONGRESS, 1982, Washington, D.C.: American Enterprise Institute, 1982:37, 75, and 52.

"Party competition and party coalitions." Quotation from Leon D. Epstein, "Presidential Parties and the Nominating Process" (a paper prepared for a Wilson Center Colloquium, May 13, 1980).

"Party Identification of the American Electorate." Figure 7-3. Reprinted from Kristi Anderson. THE CREATION OF A DEMOCRATIC MAJORITY, 1928–1936 (Chicago University Press, 1979). Davis, Jane A., and Smith, Tom W. *General Social Surveys 1972–1982: Cumulative Code Book* (Chicago, National Opinion Research Center, 1982) p. 70.

"Type of political participation." Table reprinted from PARTICIPATION IN AMERICA: POLITICAL DEMOCRACY AND SOCIAL EQUALITY by Sidney Verba and Norman H. Nie. Copyright 1972 by Sidney Verba and Norman H. Nie. Reprinted by permission of Harper & Row, Publishers, Inc. Page 31, Table 2.1.

"Presidential primaries, 1912–1980." Table adapted from Arteron, Chris. "The Media Politics of Presidential Campaigns." In James David Barber, ed. RACE FOR THE PRESIDENCY. Englewood Cliffs, N.J.: Prentice-Hall, 1978:7. Reprinted by permission of The American Assembly, Columbia University, New York.

"Public employees' positions on issues." Table reprinted from Meier, Kenneth J. 1975. "Representative Bureaucracy: An Empirical Analysis." *American Political Science Review*, 69, 2 (June), p. 541.

"Public opinion and public policy." Figure 4-1. Reprinted from the American Enterprise Institute, Public Opinion Magazine, December/January 1980 and February/March 1981.

"Relationships of social characteristics to presidential voting, 1944–1980." Table reprinted from Abramson, Paul R., John Aldrich, and David Rhode. CHANGE AND CONTINUITY IN THE 1980 ELECTIONS. Washington D.C.: Congressional Quarterly Press, 1982. Reprinted by permission, Congressional Quarterly, Inc.

Ronald Reagan. Portrayal. Reprinted from *U.S. News & World Report* of July 6, 1981: "9 Hours Inside the Oval Office," pp. 13–15.

"Senators who campaigned for president, 1960–1980." Box reprinted from *Presidential Elections Since 1789*, Congressional Quarterly, Inc., Washington, D.C., *Elections, 1980*, Congressional Quarterly, Inc.

"On Separation of Powers." Boxes excerpted from James Q. Wilson, "In Defense of Separation of Powers II. From an AEI Forum (1980) PRESIDENT VS. CONGRESS: DOES THE SEPARATION OF POWERS STILL WORK? Reprinted by permission, American Enterprise Institute. Excerpted also from Lloyd Cutler, "To Form a Government—On the Defects of Separation of Powers." Excerpted by permission of *Foreign Affairs*, Fall 1980. Copyright 1980 by the Council on Foreign Relations, Inc..

"Shifting concerns of the American public." Figure 4-7. Reprinted from American Enterprise Institute, Public Opinion Magazine, December/January, 1980; Gallup Opinion Index, Gallup Report of March 1982, September 1982. Reprinted with permission.

"Social welfare state programs that support income security." Table reprinted from Delbeare, Kenneth M. AMERICAN PUBLIC POLICY: A CITIZEN'S GUIDE. New York: McGraw-Hill, 1982, p. 217. Reprinted with permission.

"Sources of campaign contributions to House and Senate candidates, 1972–1980." Table reprinted from Gary C. Jacobson, THE POLITICS OF CONGRESSIONAL ELECTIONS, p. 53. Copyright by Gary C. Jacobson. Reprinted by permission of Little, Brown and Company.

"Growth of subcommittees, 1945–1979." Table reprinted from Samuel Patterson, "The Semi-Sovereign Congress," in *The New American Political Sys-*

tem, ed., Anthony King (Washington, D.C.: American Enterprise Institute, 1979), p. 160; and John F. Bibby, Thomas E. Mann, and Norman J. Ornstein, eds., *Vital Statistics on Congress, 1980* (Washington, D.C.: American Enterprise Institute, 1980), pp. 58–59. Reprinted with permission.

"Tax burdens and marginal tax rates, various countries, 1976." Table reprinted from Dolbeare, Kenneth M. AMERICAN PUBLIC POLICY: A CITIZEN'S GUIDE. New York: McGraw-Hill, 1982, p. 88. Reprinted with permission.

"Time of presidential vote choice, 1952–1980." Table reprinted from SRC/CPS election studies and Herbert Asher, PRESIDENTIAL ELECTIONS AND AMERICAN POLITICS, Revised Edition. Homewood, Illinois: Dorsey Press, 1980, p. 316. Reprinted with permission.

"Tolerance on civil liberties." Figure 4-2. Reprinted from COMMUNISM, CONFORMITY AND CIVIL LIBERTIES by Samuel A. Stouffer. Copyright 1955 by Samuel A. Stouffer. Reprinted by permission of Doubleday and Company, Inc. National Opinion Research Center, General Social Surveys, 1977; American Enterprise Institute, Public Opinion Magazine, December/January, 1980. Reprinted with permission.

"Views of a machine politician." Box excerpted from William L. Riordan, PLUNKITT OF TAMMANY HALL (New York: E. P. Dutton, 1963). Reprinted with permission.

"Voluntary retirements from Congress." Table reprinted from the American Enterprise Institute: John F. Bibby, Thomas E. Mann, Norman J. Ornstein, VITAL STATISTICS ON CONGRESS, 1980. (Washington, D.C.: American Enterprises Institute, 1982, pp. 14–15). Reprinted with permission.

"Voting patterns of partisan identifiers, 1952–1980." Table reprinted from Gallup Opinion Index, Gallup Poll, published November 1968, December 1968, December 1972, and December 1976.

"Voter turnout in major national elections in western nations, 1960–1978." Figure 7-1. Reprinted from G. Bingham Powell, Jr., "Voting Turnout in Thirty Democracies," in Richard Rose, ed., ELECTORAL PARTICIPATION: A COMPARATIVE ANALYSIS (London and Beverly Hills, Sage Publications, 1980). P. 6. Reprinted with permission.

"Who likes the Democrats?" Table reprinted from Gallup Poll data as tabulated in Jeane J. Kirkpatrick, "Changing Patterns of Electoral Competition," in Anthony King, ed., THE NEW AMERICAN POLITICAL SYSTEM (Washington, D.C.: American Enterprise Institute, 1978), pp. 264–265. Copyright 1978 by the American Enterprise Institute. Reprinted with permission. 1980 data from CBS News/New York Times survey.

Woodrow Wilson. Portrayal. From Wilson, Woodrow. CONSTITUTIONAL GOVERNMENT IN THE UNITED STATES. New York: Columbia Paperback Edition, 1961. Reprinted with permission.

Name Index

Subject Index